WITHDRAWN

the
$\mathcal{P}$*sychology*

of $\mathcal{M}$*usic*

SECOND EDITION

This is a volume in
Academic Press
Series in Cognition and Perception
A Series of Monographs and Treatises

the Psychology of Music

SECOND EDITION

Edited by
Diana Deutsch
Department of Psychology
University of California, San Diego
La Jolla, California

Academic Press
An Imprint of Elsevier

Amsterdam Boston Heidelberg London New York Oxford Paris San Diego
San Francisco Singapore Sydney Tokyo

Academic Press
An Imprint of Elsevier
525 B Street, Suite 1900, San Diego, California 92101-4495, USA
http://www.academicpress.com

Academic Press
Harcourt Place, 32 Jamestown Road, London NW1 7BY, UK
http://www.academicpress.com

Library of Congress Catalog Card Number: 98-58210

ISBN-13: 978-0-12-213565-1
ISBN-10: 0-12-213565-2

PRINTED IN THE UNITED STATES OF AMERICA
07 08 09 10 11 MM 15 14 13 12 11 10

CONTENTS

CONTRIBUTORS   XIII
PREFACE   XV

1

THE NATURE OF MUSICAL SOUND

JOHN R. PIERCE

 I. Musical Sound   1
 II. From Classical Times   2
 III. Vibration and Tone: Mersenne and Galileo   3
 IV. Time Resolution of the Ear   3
 V. Time Resolution and Musical Sounds   5
 VI. Externalization   6
 VII. Spectra   7
 VIII. Linearity   7
 IX. Spectra and Sound   8
 X. Resonance and Musical Instruments   10
 XI. Complexity of Periodic Sounds   11
 XII. Helmholtz, Plomp, and Dissonance   12
 XIII. Pitch   13
 XIV. Quasi-Musical and Unmusical Sounds   16
 XV. Descriptions of Musical Sounds   17
      Acknowledgments   20
      References   20

2

CONCERT HALLS: FROM MAGIC TO NUMBER THEORY

MANFRED R. SCHROEDER

I. The Three Problems of Concert Hall Acoustics   25
II. The Physical Problem   26
III. The Subjective Problem   33
IV. Multipurpose Halls   44
V. Conclusion   45
   Appendix   45
   References   46

3

MUSIC AND THE AUDITORY SYSTEM

NORMAN M. WEINBERGER

I. Introduction   47
II. A Brief Overview of the Auditory Pathway   48
III. Experimental Approaches in the Neurobiology of Music   60
IV. The Auditory System and Elements of Music   61
V. Pitch   61
VI. Harmony, Consonance   67
VII. Contour, Melody   68
VIII. Rhythm, Temporal Coding   75
IX. Future Directions   80
   Acknowledgments   82
   References   83

4

THE PERCEPTION OF MUSICAL TONES

RUDOLF RASCH AND REINIER PLOMP

I. The Psychoacoustics of Music   89
II. Perceptual Attributes of Single Tones   93
II. Perceptual Attributes of Simultaneous Tones   102
IV. Conclusion   108
   References   109

5

EXPLORATION OF TIMBRE BY ANALYSIS AND SYNTHESIS

JEAN-CLAUDE RISSET AND DAVID L. WESSEL

I. Timbre   113
II. Timbre and the Fourier Spectrum: The Classical View   114
III. The Shortcomings of the Classical Conception   116
IV. Attack Transients   117
V. Complexity of Sounds: Importance of Characteristic Features   118
VI. Instrumental and Vocal Timbres: Additive Synthesis   118
VII. Additive Synthesis: Percussion Instruments   124
VIII. Cross-Synthesis and Voice Synthesis   126
IX. Subtractive Synthesis   128
X. Global (or Nonlinear) Synthesis   130
XI. Physical Modeling as a Synthesis Technique   131
XII. Sampling   134
XIII. The Importance of Context: Musical Prosody, Fusion, and Segregation   135
XIV. Analysis-Synthesis as Fitting Physical and Perceptual Models to Data   138
XV. The Use of Analysis-Synthesis Models of Timbre   141
XVI. Timbral Space   146
XVII. Conclusion   149
Appendices   151
References   158

6

THE PERCEPTION OF SINGING

JOHAN SUNDBERG

I. Introduction   171
II. Function of the Voice   172
III. Resonatory Aspects   174
IV. Phonation   188
V. Aspects of Voice Timbre   194
VI. Vibrato   195
VII. Pitch in Practice   203
VIII. Expression   207
IX. Concluding Remarks   209
References   210

7

INTERVALS, SCALES, AND TUNING

EDWARD M. BURNS

  I. Introduction   215
 II. Why Are Scales Necessary?   215
III. Musical Interval Perception   219
 IV. Natural Intervals and Scales   240
  V. Conclusions and Caveats   257
     Acknowledgments   258
     References   258

8

ABSOLUTE PITCH

W. DIXON WARD

   I. Introduction   265
  II. Genesis of AP   268
 III. Measurement of AP   270
  IV. Stability of the Interval Standard   280
   V. Neurological Correlates of AP   282
  VI. Learning AP   283
 VII. Colored Hearing   286
VIII. Absolute Tonality   286
  IX. Spontaneous and Elicited Auralization   288
   X. The Value of AP   289
      References   294

9

GROUPING MECHANISMS IN MUSIC

DIANA DEUTSCH

  I. Introduction   299
 II. Fusion and Separation of Spectral Components   301
III. Larger Scale Groupings   313
 IV. Grouping of Rapid Sequences of Single Tones   313
  V. Grouping of Multiple Tone Sequences in Space   321

VI. Equal-Interval Tone Complexes   336
VII. Conclusion: Relationships to Music Theory and Practice   340
References   342

10

THE PROCESSING OF PITCH COMBINATIONS

DIANA DEUTSCH

I. Introduction   349
II. Feature Abstraction   350
III. Higher Order Abstractions   359
IV. Paradoxes Based on Pitch Class   376
V. The Pitch Memory System   390
VI. Conclusion   403
References   404

11

NEURAL NETS, TEMPORAL COMPOSITES, AND TONALITY

JAMSHED J. BHARUCHA

I. Neural Representation   413
II. Neural Association and Learning   424
III. Discussion   435
Acknowledgments   436
Appendices   436
References   437

12

HIERARCHICAL EXPECTATION AND MUSICAL STYLE

EUGENE NARMOUR

I. The Invocation of Extraopus Style   442
II. Empirical and Rationalistic Levels of Style   443
III. Learned Stylistic Levels as "Theme" and "Variation"   444
IV. Defining Levels   445
V. Representing Hierarchical Levels   446

VI. Problems with Level Displays   448
VII. The Parametric Nature of Hierarchical Style Structures   451
VIII. Style Structures as Composite Cognitive Paths   456
IX. Refining Further Hierarchical Displays   457
X. Neuronal Representation: A Speculation   460
XI. The Musical Reality of Style-Structural Hierarchies   464
XII. Archetypes   466
XIII. Style Change: Toward Greater Complexity   466
XIV. Conclusion: The Limits of Style   468
References   471

13

RHYTHM AND TIMING IN MUSIC

ERIC F. CLARKE

I. Introduction   473
II. The Work of Paul Fraisse   473
III. Form Perception   476
IV. Rhythm Perception   478
V. Timing in Music   489
VI. Rhythm, Timing, and Movement   494
VII. Summary   496
Acknowledgments   497
References   497

14

THE PERFORMANCE OF MUSIC

ALF GABRIELSSON

I. Introduction   501
II. Performance Planning   502
III. Sight-Reading   509
IV. Improvisation   513
V. Feedback in Performance   515
VI. Motor Processes in Performance   516
VII. Measurements of Performance   523
VIII. Models of Music Performance   550
IX. Physical Factors in Performance   557
X. Psychological and Social Factors   561

XI. Performance Evaluation   577
     Acknowledgments   579
     References   579

15

THE DEVELOPMENT OF MUSIC PERCEPTION AND COGNITION

W. JAY DOWLING

I. Introduction   603
II. Development   604
III. Summary   620
     Acknowledgment   621
     References   621

16

MUSICAL ABILITY

ROSAMUND SHUTER-DYSON

I. Concepts of Musical Ability   627
II. Studies of Musical Abilities   629
III. Music Ability and Other Abilities   643
IV. Conclusions   645
     References   645

17

NEUROLOGICAL ASPECTS OF MUSIC PERCEPTION AND PERFORMANCE

OSCAR S. M. MARIN AND DAVID W. PERRY

I. Introduction   653
II. Amusias   655
III. Auditory Agnosias and Verbal Deafness   667
IV. Progress in the Classification of Auditory Disorders   673
V. Cerebral Hemisphere Asymmetry in Music Perception and Production   679
VI. Progress in the Neuropsychology of Human Music Perception   699

VII. Music Perception as a Skill 704
VIII. Perspectives for the Neuropsychological Study of Music 708
Acknowledgments 712
References 712

18

COMPARATIVE MUSIC PERCEPTION AND COGNITION

EDWARD C. CARTERETTE AND ROGER A. KENDALL

I. Introduction and Overview 725
II. Pitch 730
III. Pitch Systems 736
IV. Tonality 743
V. Melody 751
VI. Rhythm 758
VII. Timbre and Spectra 762
VIII. Creativity, Communication, Meaning, and Affect 765
IX. Verbal Attributes and Semantics 766
X. Species Differences: Animal Speech and Music 770
XI. Perception of Tonality by the Monkey 776
XII. Notes on the Neurophysiology of Music Perception 776
XIII. Cognitive Musical Universals 780
XIV. Coda 780
References 782

INDEX 793

CONTRIBUTORS

Numbers in parentheses indicate the pages on which the authors' contributions begin.

Jamshed J. Bharucha (413) Department of Psychology, Dartmouth College, Hanover, New Hampshire 03755

Edward M. Burns (215) Department of Speech and Hearing Sciences, University of Washington, Seattle, Washington 98105

Edward C. Carterette (725) Department of Psychology and Department of Ethnomusicology & Program in Systematic Musicology, University of California, Los Angeles, Los Angeles, California 90095

Eric F. Clarke (473) Department of Music, University of Sheffield, Sheffield S10 5BR, United Kingdom

Diana Deutsch (299, 349) Department of Psychology, University of California, San Diego, La Jolla, California 92093

W. Jay Dowling (603) Program in Cognitive Science, University of Texas at Dallas, Richardson, Texas 75083

Alf Gabrielsson (501) Department of Psychology, Uppsala University, S-75142 Uppsala, Sweden

Roger A. Kendall (725) Department of Psychology and Department of Ethnomusicology & Program in Systematic Musicology, University of California, Los Angeles, Los Angeles, California 90095

Oscar S. M. Marin[1] (653) Department of Neurology, Good Samaritan Hospital, Portland, Oregon 97210

Eugene Narmour (442) Department of Music, University of Pennsylvania, Philadelphia, Pennsylvania 19104

[1]Present address: 222 Hudson Place, Cliffside Park, NJ 07010.

David W. Perry   (653)   Department of Neurology and Neurosurgery, Montreal Neurological Institute, McGill University, Montreal, Quebec, Canada H3A 2B4

John R. Pierce   (1)   Department of Music, Stanford University, Stanford, California 94305

Reinier Plomp   (89)   Faculty of Medicine, Free University, Amsterdam, The Netherlands

Rudolf Rasch   (89)   University of Utrecht, Utrecht, The Netherlands

Jean-Claude Risset   (113)   Laboratoire de Mécanique et d'Acoustique, Marseille, France

Manfred R. Schroeder   (25)   Drittes Physikalisches Institut, Universität Göttingen, D-37073 Göttingen, Germany and AT&T Bell Laboratories, Murray Hill, New Jersey 07974

Rosamund Shuter-Dyson   (627)   8 St. Swithuns Close, East Grinstead, RH 19 3BB, England

Johan Sundberg   (171)   Department of Speech, Music, and Hearing, Royal Institute of Technology, SE-100 44 Stockholm, Sweden

W. Dixon Ward*   (265)   Hearing Research Laboratory, University of Minnesota, Minneapolis, Minnesota 55455

Norman M. Weinberger   (47)   Department of Psychobiology and Center for the Neurobiology of Learning and Memory, University of California, Irvine, Irvine, California 92625

David L. Wessel   (113)   Center for New Music and Audio Technologies, Department of Music, University of California, Berkeley, Berkeley, California 94709

*Deceased.

PREFACE

The aim of this book is to interpret musical phenomena in terms of mental function—to characterize the ways in which we perceive, remember, create, and perform music. At the time the first edition was written, the field as we know it was just emerging. In particular, increasing numbers of psychologists were recognizing the value of musical materials in exploring mechanisms of attention, memory, shape recognition, and so on. In parallel, musicians were becoming increasingly interested in the experimental testing of theoretical ideas, as well as the practical application of experimental findings to musical composition and performance.

The field has progressed considerably in the 16 years since the first edition was published. Several factors in particular have contributed to this development. The opportunity to generate, analyze, and transform sounds by computer is no longer limited to a few researchers with access to large multiuser facilities, but rather is available to individual investigators on a widespread basis. In addition, advances in the field of neuroscience have profoundly influenced our thinking about the way that music is processed in the brain. Third, collaborations between psychologists and musicians, which were evolving at the time the first edition was written, are now quite common; to a large extent we speak a common language and agree on basic philosophical issues.

The present volume is intended as a comprehensive reference source for musicians, in particular for those who are interested in the way that music is perceived, apprehended, and performed. It is also intended as a reference source for perceptual and cognitive psychologists. In addition, this volume is designed for use as a textbook for advanced courses in the psychology of music.

An interdisciplinary book such as this one requires much interaction between researchers in different fields, and can only be considered a group endeavor. My thanks go to all the authors, who have given so generously of their time in bringing the work to fruition. It is with great sadness that I note the recent death of W. Dixon Ward, whose important contributions are so evident in this book. Dix was loved and admired by numerous friends and colleagues all over the globe, and he will be sorely missed. Finally, I am much indebted to Katie Spiller, whose skill and professionalism in producing the book have contributed substantially to its success.

Diana Deutsch

1

THE NATURE OF MUSICAL SOUND

JOHN R. PIERCE

Department of Music
Stanford University
Stanford, California

I. MUSICAL SOUND

A. WHAT IS MUSICAL SOUND?

Imagine that you are standing with your eyes closed. Off to the left is the faint sound of water rushing along a stony streambed. Near your feet you hear a tiny creature rustling among dry leaves. A cawing bird flies into the tree above you; you hear it lighting on a branch, followed by the faint sounds of restless movement. There are other sounds. Among these is a man singing as he walks slowly toward you.

Is the man's voice the only musical sound you hear? It may be that if you open your eyes you will find yourself indoors, listening to a soundscape in stereo, of which the singing is one part. Perhaps *all* of the sounds were intended as music.

But if, with your eyes still closed, you were able to wander about, you could tell music concrete from a real auditory scene. In a real scene, compact sound sources remain compact and fixed in position. Today, for a listener who doesn't move about, we can concoct sounds that seem near or far and sounds that move around (Chowning, 1971; Kendall, Martens, & Decker, 1989; Moore, 1989). We can characterize such sounds as musical. But it is either impractical or impossible to reproduce within a room the exact auditory effect of a number of discrete sources that are firmly fixed in space, be they sounds of nature or sounds of musicians playing or singing.

We have gone willingly beyond the world of unnatural sounds as we hear them out there. We have also gone beyond the sounds of instrumentalists and singers in a salon or concert hall. We can accept natural sounds, processed natural sounds, and electronically concocted sounds as music. In listening to traditional music, we judge recordings as recordings, whether they were recorded in a concert hall or a studio. In popular music, recorded music is typically produced by processing and mixing together many sound tracks. The sound of the final recording does not exist in "real time" until that recording is played.

In addressing the nature of musical sound, we must stray somewhat beyond the traditional sounds of music. But, whatever our view, we must address traditional aspects of musical sound, including rhythm, pitch, and timbre.

An understanding of such matters must involve some understanding of the physical properties of musical sounds and of the instruments that produce them. It must involve vibrations of solid bodies and waves reaching our ears through the air.

Understanding must also involve the capabilities of human hearing, our ability in listening to sounds to make judgments, say, of pitch or loudness, that are consistent with physical differences in sound waves. But, differences that the ear can't detect don't matter musically.

What really matters musically is the percept, the musical quality of a sound. In addressing the percept, we must describe the sound wave in some sort of analytical term and try to relate this description to musical perception.

We must give primacy to what our ears tell us. But, our listening must be guided by and checked against a lore of music that has evolved over centuries. And, we must take into account such experiments as truly cast light on various aspects of musical sound. I have not hesitated to make informal experiments in seeking light on dubious points.

It isn't easy to get started, for we must use terms before they are explained or commented on. And, matters will be raised that will be treated in more detail in later chapters. Readers should consider this chapter as an introduction to the understanding of the nature of musical sound.

II. FROM CLASSICAL TIMES

Our approach will be to begin with some musical ideas that originated in classical times and have persisted ever since.

We associate ratios of small integers with consonant musical intervals, and our musical scales have a numerical basis. These ideas are found in other cultures, as, the Chinese, but the Western world inherited them from the Greeks.

The association of ratios of integers with musical intervals could not have arisen from any contemplation of or insight into singing. It came from observations relating the musical sound of a plucked string of constant tension to its length. Consonant intervals were found to correspond to lengths having the ratios of small integers, as: 1:2, octave; 2:3, fifth; 3:4, fourth; 4:5, major third; and so on.

It is plausible that the Greeks made use of beats in actually tuning instruments, but the idea of relating pitch to rate of vibration came much later. A sort of mysticism about numbers pervaded classical science and philosophy. The association of integers with musical intervals was regarded as sufficient in itself, rather than as a spur to further explication.

Along with the association of musical intervals with the ratios of integers went a numerical basis for the construction of a musical scale, the Pythagorean scale, through successive perfect fifths and their octaves. The discrepancy between Pythagorean intervals (other than the fifth and fourth) and the ratios of small integers was a matter of concern.

The association of consonant intervals with ratios of integers is still with us; it is present in a musical scale described by Mathews and Pierce (1988), in which the ratios 3:5:7:9 form the basis of the scale. Beyond this, it is known further that Maureen Chowning, a coloratura soprano, has learned to sing in the scale, and Richard Boulanger has composed a considerable piece using the scale.

Numerologies of the tuning of keyboard instruments have persisted. It is plausible that compromise tunings such as mean-tone tuning were actually arrived at by ear, but they, along with equal temperament and just intonation with special keyboards are argued on mathematical or numerological as well as acoustical and psychological grounds.

III. VIBRATION AND TONE: MERSENNE AND GALILEO

The relation of musical pitch to rate of vibration was discovered, apparently independently, by Mersenne and Galileo in the 17th century. Mersenne, a natural philosopher and mathematician, was the first to measure the velocity of sound. He was also the first to hear pitches higher than the pitch frequency in the sounds of strings—we would recognize this as hearing out the first five partials of the tone (Plomp, 1966). Mersenne wrote a long treatise, *Harmonie Universelle,* published in 1636–1637. Galileo's ideas can be found in *Dialogues Concerning Two New Sciences,* published in 1637 and available in translation through Dover.

Besides giving engaging arguments for the association of rate of vibration with pitch, Galileo put forward an ingenious explanation of consonance. The periodic puffs of air that constitute a musical tone beat on the drum of the ear. He says:

> Agreeable consonances are pairs of tones which strike the ear with a certain regularity— The first and most pleasing consonance is, therefor, the octave, for every pulse given to the tympanum by the lower string, the sharp string delivers two—

Thus, Galileo proposed an essentially rhythmic theory of consonance. Consonant tones beat in a regular, repeating pattern on the drum of the ear.

IV. TIME RESOLUTION OF THE EAR

It may be of some interest to ask, *could* Galileo's theory explain, or be a part of an explanation of, musical consonance? Certainly, rhythm plays an important part in music, but we usually think of the rhythm of slow, countable or almost-countable patterns of notes. Is the time resolution of the ear acute enough to support a rhythmical explanation of consonance?

Experiments intended to give data on the time resolution of the ear are somewhat varied in nature. In some, the subject listens to stimuli with headphones, either because this is essential, or because reflections of loudspeaker sounds from the walls in an ordinary room could change the results.

One way to measure time resolution is to sound two tones of different pitch, the second beginning T seconds after the first. How great must we make T in order to tell reliably which tone commenced first? The answer appears to be around 20 msec for tones a half second long (Hirsh, 1959).

Tones only a hundredth of a second long behave differently: for them T may be as small as 1.5 msec (Patterson & Green, 1970). But, are such tones "musical"? It seems likely that they are clicky.

Another approach is to use two stimuli that commence at different times but are essentially the same. Say, two very short pulses, one more intense than the other. If these are separated by the interval T, how great must T be if the pattern strong-weak is to sound different from weak-strong? The answer appears to be around 2 msec or less (Resnick & Feth, 1975; Ronken, 1970). Related reversed-time waveform experiments confirm this (Patterson & Green, 1970).

There are other approaches to the time resolution of the ear. A classical approach is binaural lateralization of sinusoidal tones. The sine wave presented to one ear is delayed a little with respect to that presented to the other ear. The tone is heard "inside the head," centered for no delay, or away from the side with delay. This works only up to frequencies of 1300–1400 Hz (Mills, 1958; Zwislocki & Feldman, 1956).

It may be noted that in some animals nerve firings are statistically correlated with peaks of sine waves up to several thousand hertz. But, there is no perceptual evidence of frequency tracking in humans above 1400 Hz.

One can produce periodic sequences of short positive or negative pulses (Flanagan & Guttman, 1960) or of band-pass-filtered pulses or tone bursts (Guttman & Flanagan, 1964; Pierce, 1990) for which the pulse or tone-burst rate is different from the fundamental frequency. The pulse pattern + + + − is an example; the fundamental frequency is 1/4 of the pulse rate, while for the sequence + + + + the fundamental frequency is equal to the pulse rate. At low rates, these two sequences sound the same when the pulse rates are the same; at high rates, they sound the same when the fundamental frequencies are the same. Match can be on tone-burst rate up to 350 tone bursts a second or higher, corresponding to a time resolution of 3 msec or better.

Another approach to estimating time resolution is to listen to pulses produced randomly in time but with an adjustable rate. Consider a signal in which there is a probability P of producing a pulse of amplitude A every forty-thousandth of a second—and a probability $(1 - P)$ that no pulse will be produced. The average number of pulses per second is 40,000 x P, but the time of occurrence of pulses is unpredictable. I have listened to the sound of such randomly occurring pulses and have compared it with the sound of white noise.

At low rates (very small P) individual pulses are heard, occurring randomly and sounding like a Geiger counter. As the rate is increased, at around 1000 pulses a second the sound is a good deal like that of white (flat-spectrum) noise, but with a rougher, erratic sound. Although for 1000 pulses a second the average time between pulses is 1 msec, the time between some successive pulses will be several times this. It appears that the ear can detect such gaps, and so differentiate the random pulses' sound from white noise. As P is increased and the average pulse rate becomes higher, gaps of detectable length become more infrequent. Above 3000 pulses per second, it is hard to differentiate the random pulse stream from white noise of the same power level.

The experiment with random pulses indicates a time resolution of the ear around a millisecond. So do the experiments with periodic patterns of pulses and patterns of tone bursts. Perception of the order of a weaker and a stronger pulse indicates a time resolution of around 2 msec. Binaural lateralization indicates a useful time resolution of less than a millisecond, but in this case, there is no phenomenon competing with time resolution. Order of onset of half-second tones indicates a time resolution of 20 sec. It appears that time resolution is far better for very short waveforms than for tones of moderate length and different pitches.

At this point it seems clear that Galileo's theory of consonance cannot be correct. Consonance is observed over the whole range of the piano keyboard, which extends from the leftmost key, A_0 with a pitch frequency of 27.5 Hz, to the rightmost key, C_8 with a pitch frequency of 4186 Hz. The time resolution of the ear would not allow the resolution of rhythmical patterns produced by consonant dyads or triads in the upper range of musical pitches.

V. TIME RESOLUTION AND MUSICAL SOUNDS

We came to consider the time resolution of the ear through Galileo's theory of consonance and concluded that it was insufficient to support such a theory. Is the human's acute time resolution of any use in music?

What about sensing and ordering the onset of musical tones? We have seen that the time resolution for this is considerably greater than a millisecond. Experiments by Rasch (1979) indicate that synchronization of tones in performed small-ensemble music is accurate to only 30 to 50 msec. Work by Gordon (1987) indicates that in setting onset times for simultaneity of perceived attack of musical tones, there are not only differences for different instruments, but differences among observers and among observations. For the same instrument, onset times may be set over a range of around 20 msec.

In Gordon's work, all sounds came from the same loudspeaker, whereas Rasch's work involved physically separated instruments. The velocity of sound is 1087 feet per second, and a time difference of 10 msec corresponds to a distance of travel of 11 feet. In realistic musical situations, synchronization may involve both direct sound and reflected sound. It may be governed more by the travel time of sound, or by other considerations, than by lack of temporal resolution of the ear.

Western music is most commonly performed indoors. Besides the sound energy that reaches the ear directly, much, and often the major part, arrives later, reflected by the walls. Gardner, in a paper published in 1968, gives an excellent review of perception of such reflected sound.

If a strong reflection is present within 60 to 70 msec after the direct sound, we hear no echo. Joseph Henry noted this around 1851, and you can verify it by clapping as you walk slowly away from a large plane wall.

Echoes are disastrous to the quality of musical sound, but we are saved from hearing early echoes by what is called the precedence effect, or sometimes, the Haas effect (Gardner, 1968). And, when there are strong reflections within less that 60–70 msec, all of the sound seems to come from the direction of first arrival, the direction of the performer.

If we think this over, we find it very puzzling. It seems unreasonable that the waveform of the sound on its first arrival could be stored in the nervous system in much detail. Somehow, the precedence effect must depend on waveform "events" of which the ear takes note.

A host of smaller, later multiple reflections are not heard of as echoes but as reverberation, which gives a pleasant quality to musical sound. The optimal duration of reverberation is larger for large halls than small, and for orchestral or organ music than for song.

Reverberation not only improves sound quality; the amount of reverberation gives us a clue to the remoteness of the sound source. In an enclosure, we judge a sound with little reverberation as originating nearby, and a sound with more reverberation as coming from farther away. Thus, Chowning (1971) has used a larger reverberation, together with a spectrum with less high-frequency energy, to give the sense of a remote as compared with a nearby source of sound.

VI. EXTERNALIZATION

As we noted at the very beginning of this chapter, in standing among sound sources, we have a very vivid sense of a world outside of ourselves. What we hear is *out there,* not inside of our heads. In listening over headphones, it is hard to get the sound outside of the head.

In principle, if we recorded with tiny microphones in the canals of our ears and played the recordings suitably into headphones, we *should* get such an externalization (Blauert, 1983). To a degree, we can. The degree of externalization appears to vary among subjects.

VII. SPECTRA

We cannot go further in considering the nature of musical sounds without some discussion of the representation of waveforms as sums of sinusoidal components called *partials*.

The idea that any periodic waveform can be represented exactly as a sum of sine waves can be traced back to the work of Jean-Baptiste-Joseph Fourier, 1768–1830. Such a representation of periodic waveforms by their spectrum (sum of sine waves, each with a particular frequency) became a vital part of all considerations of musical instruments and the perception of their sounds through the work of Helmholtz (1821–1894). By an extension of Fourier's analysis, nonperiodic sounds can be represented by a continuous distribution of sine waves, in which amplitude and phase are a function of frequency.

The representation of a sound wave in terms of its spectrum is just another way of describing the sound wave. If we are given the component frequencies and their amplitudes and phases, the sound wave, the variation of amplitude with time, can be reconstructed.

The very fact that it is useful to represent musical sounds by a spectrum, a sum of sine waves, tells us a good deal about musical instruments, musical sounds, and about the mechanism of hearing.

Mathematically, a sine wave is a solution of a linear differential or partial-differential equation. Sine waves and spectra are useful in connection with linear (or nearly linear) systems.

That sine waves are useful in describing the physical behavior of musical instruments indicates that the oscillations of such instruments must be very nearly linear.

The fact that representation of waveforms as a sum of sine waves is useful in the elucidation of human hearing indicates that something involved in hearing is linear or nearly linear.

VIII. LINEARITY

What do we mean by *linear*? If we put a sine wave into an amplifier or loudspeaker and get out a sine wave of the same frequency, and nothing else, and if the amplitude of the output sine wave is proportional to the amplitude of the input sine wave, the amplifier or loudspeaker is linear.

Suppose that a system is linear and that we represent the input as a sum of sine waves. We can calculate the output due to each input sine wave as if the others were not there. We can then add these outputs and get the overall output due to all of the input sine waves together.

The strings of a musical instrument, and its sounding board, and the column of air in a wind instrument are very nearly linear systems. So are the eardrum, the little bones in the middle ear, and the cochlea, with its round and oval windows and its basilar membrane that vibrates in accord with the sound wave reaching the ear. Such is not the case for the nervous system and its function in human hearing.

Both musical instruments and the parts of the auditory system that vibrate in accord with the sounds they produce have nonlinearities that are important to their function.

Nonlinearities are crucial in the production of sound in many musical instruments, and in noisy and erratic details of the sound waves produced. Thus, in the vocal tract, turbulence can produce not only the noise essential in fricative sounds, but frequencies not present of the vibration of the vocal folds (Teager & Teager, 1983, 1990). In singing very loudly, through nonlinearities, the peaks of the spectrum can depart from those implied by the shape of the vocal tract and its resonances (Kaiser, 1983). Nonlinearities are important in the bowed string, accounting for the triangular shape of the waveform and pitch flattening, and for the shape of flute and clarinet waveforms (Mcintyre, Schumacher, & Woodhouse, 1983). Nonlinearities also account for pulsed noise and unstable waveform in the clarinet and violin (Chafe, 1990a, 1990b).

In listening to collections of sinusoids, we hear frequencies (as faint pitches) that are not present in the sound we are listening to (Goldstein, 1967; Plomp, 1965).

Still, the vibrating strings and air columns of musical instruments and the early mechanical stages of the human auditory system are linear enough to make sine waves and the representation of sound waveforms by spectra (by collections of sine waves, or partials) useful in studies of musical sound.

IX. SPECTRA AND SOUND

A sine wave as a mathematical function lasts forever, but musical sounds do not. In discussing musical sound waves, it is most profitable to think of them as made up of a number of roughly sinusoidal components or partials that rise, persistently oscillate, and fall in amplitude, and that waver a little in frequency and/or amplitude.

Vibrato can tie frequency components together, can make them into one sound rather than a diversity of separate sounds (Chowning, 1980; McAdams, 1984). A shared rise, fall, and wavering are essential to musical sounds. In traditional instruments, they cannot be avoided. They are easily avoided in electronic instruments. Such a lack of wavering is one cause of the unnatural, electronic sound quality of some synthesized tones.

The human voice and the sounds of most musical instruments are made up of many nearly harmonically related frequency components, or partials. The general distribution of sound energy among partials of different frequencies is important to the timbre or quality of musical sounds.

This is most easily appreciated in the sounds of vowels, spoken or sung. Such sounds are characterized by various peaks in their spectra that correspond to the resonances of the vocal tract. It is the locations of such peaks or *formants* that give the vowels their distinctive quality. Thus, the vowel sound in *who'd* has peaks or formants at 300, 870, and 2240 Hz, whereas the vowel in *heed* has formants at 270, 2290, and 3010 Hz. The generally higher frequencies in the formants of *heed* than in the formants of *who'd* give the sound a "higher" sound. Should one describe such differences among vowel sounds in terms of pitch, and say that the pitch of the vowel in *heed* is higher than the pitch of the vowel in *who'd*? The quality is present in whispered vowels, in which the excitation of the vocal tract is a noise that has no pitch. Further, we can recognize vowels when the vocal tract is excited by a single glottal pulse. Such a sound can sometimes be uttered with difficulty. In work at Stanford toward his thesis on speech synthesis, Perry Cook has isolated a single glottal pulse and used it to excite a computer-modeled vocal tract.

The vowels that are least easily recognized are vowels sung by sopranos at high pitches. For pitches much above 500 Hz (C_5), there is no spectral component to depict the lowest formant, and a couple of spectral lines must depict the whole resonant pattern of the second and third formants. In a high-pitched voice, the small amounts of noise inherent in the process of producing sound are spectrally modified by the resonances of the vocal tract, and this noise spectrum may help the ear to hear the characteristic vowel spectrum.

The recognition of characteristic sounds can depend on changes or transitions in spectra. The words *we* and *you* are made by sliding from one spectrum to another, and in one word the time order is the reverse of the other. We don't recognize any similarity in the sounds of the words.

Although some musical sounds, such as sung vowels, have spectra characterized by peaks or formants whose locations are roughly independent of pitch, for some instrumental sounds, such as the woodwinds, the general shape of the waveform is roughly constant with frequency. In the clarinet, odd harmonics are strong and even harmonics very weak. The tones of a piano have no clear formants, but the number and amplitude of the spectral components are very different for low and high notes.

The importance of transitions in musical sounds is exemplified in work of Risset and Mathews (1969), Risset (1978), and Risset and Wessel (1982). Perhaps the most accessible illustrations of the effects of transitions are to be found among the text and recorded sounds that are a part of Pierce's *The Science of Musical Sound* (1983), and especially, the examples cited next.

Example 3.6 shows that in synthesizing a natural bell sound it is important that the higher frequency components decay more rapidly than components of lower frequency. Also, because actual bells are not perfectly symmetric, various degenerate modes of oscillation (two patterns with the same frequency) are broken up to give pairs of closely spaced frequency components. These beat together to give a wavering that is important to the bell-like quality of the sound.

Example 3.7 demonstrates the effect of making the spectral components of a bell sound rise and fall successively in time. This gives what Risset calls "fluid textures," which are musically attractive but don't sound at all like bells.

In his studies of brasslike sounds (Example 3.3) Risset found that the higher harmonics rise in amplitude later than the lower harmonics. Mathews succeeded in producing a bowed sound with a trumpet-like quality by delaying the rise of higher partials (Example 3.9).

The general spectral shape is crucial to timbral quality. We can appreciate this by filtering out the higher frequencies, which makes musical sounds dull or low, or by filtering out low frequencies, which makes musical sounds bright, or tinny. Strangely, such filtering tends not to render musical instruments unrecognizable. Changes in the sound with time are of crucial importance to the character and to the identification of sounds. And so are noisy sounds, particularly those associated with attack.

X. RESONANCE AND MUSICAL INSTRUMENTS

The vibration of physical systems can be described in terms of *modes*, or different spatial patterns of excitation with different frequencies of oscillation. If a string is plucked or a bell struck, the ensuing sound wave is a collection of exponentially decaying sine waves.

The various frequency components of an oscillating string are very nearly some fundamental frequency f_0 and frequencies $2f_0$, $3f_0$, $4f_0$, and so on. Such frequencies are called harmonics of f_0. All of these frequency components, including f_0, are *harmonic partials* of the tone. Small departures from perfect harmonicity are important to the warm, wavering tone of the piano (Fletcher, 1964; Fletcher, Blackham, & Stratton, 1962).

The partials of orchestra chimes are not harmonics of a fundamental frequency, but the fourth, fifth, sixth, and seventh partials are approximately the second, third, fourth, and seventh harmonics of one (missing) frequency, which corresponds to the perceived pitch of the chimes (Rossing, 1990).

Traditional tuned bells (Hemony bells) are designed to have roughly harmonically related partials, but these are in the nature of a minor chord. Brilliant work by Schoofs, Van Asperen, Maas, and Lehr (1987), by Houtsma and Tholen (1987), and by Lehr (1987) has resulted in carillons in which the minor third is replaced by a major third. This appears to be more pleasing to most listeners than the Hemony tuning.

The spectra of the sounds of pianos, bells, and other percussive instruments are determined directly by the natural modes of vibration of their structures. In violins and wind instruments, the relationship between resonance and the pitch and spectrum of the sounds produced is not so direct. The forced vibration of the string or air column in such an instrument is always at or very near a resonant frequency, but which resonant frequency determines the pitch can be controlled by the player. Thus the violinist can bow to produce a harmonic. In woodwinds, there are distinct ranges of pitch that correspond to different resonant harmonics. In the brasses, the pitch is that of a comparatively high harmonic; a particular one of these can be selected through strength of blowing, so that one of a number of notes can be solicited.

In instruments in which the vibration is forced, the partials are nearly harmonic, and the chief components of the spectrum must be at least approximately harmonics of the fundamental frequency. But, as has been noted, details of waveform, variations of frequency and amplitude of various spectral components with time, and noisy or erratic spectral components can be important in musical sound.

XI. COMPLEXITY OF PERIODIC SOUNDS

We can learn something about the possible spectral complexity of musical sounds that are nearly periodic from things that are true of periodic sounds.

Periodic sounds are made up of frequency components $f_0, 2f_0, 3f_0$, and so on. It takes just two numbers to describe the amplitude and phase of a sine wave. Hence, if the line spectrum of a periodic sound has N frequency components, it takes $2N$ numbers to specify the spectrum and, hence, the waveform.

Let us make the rough assumption that most of the quality of a musical sound depends on frequencies below 11,000 Hz. If the fundamental frequency of a periodic wave is f_0 Hz, the number N of frequency components is approximately $11,000/f_0$, and the number of numbers required to describe the periodic waveform is approximately $2N = 22,000/f_0$. We may note that, according to the sampling theorem, this is just the number of samples necessary to represent the duration of one period if the bandwidth is 11,000 Hz. For various reasons, including the limited time resolution of the ear, this number overestimates the capability of the ear to make distinctions among waveforms.

Let us consider the potential variety or complexity of waveforms corresponding to various pitches by means of Table I.

We see that the variety of waveforms available goes down as the pitch of the fundamental goes up. Low-pitched notes can have a wide variety of distinct vow-

TABLE I

Note	Frequency (Hz)	$2N$
A_0	27.5	800
A_1	55	400
A_2	10	200
A_3	220	100
A_4	440	50
A_5	880	25
A_6	1760	12
A_7	3520	6

els and vowel-like sounds. Further, they can sound much like repeated noise, or a buzzy sequence of clicks, or periodic chirps (changes in frequency). It is principally the relative phases of the spectral components that are different in the spectra representing noiselike, buzzy, and chirpy waveforms.

It is very noticeable that around A_3 the range of variety of sounds due to different spectra becomes much diminished. Above A_4, the variety is very limited. This is notable in work by Henckel (1990) on the detection of complex harmonic signals at various frequencies.

Spectrum is crucial to the quality of and distinction among vowel sounds, but, as we have noted, envelope, changes in spectrum during the tone, and sounds associated with attack are also crucial in sound quality.

XII. HELMHOLTZ, PLOMP, AND DISSONANCE

Our earlier consideration of Galileo's theory of consonance was more a ruling-out of an ingenious conjecture than a serious investigation. It was useful in leading us into a consideration of time discrimination in hearing.

Today it is generally believed that dissonance arises when frequency components of simultaneously sounding pure tones are close together in frequency. Helmholtz (1877/1954) proposed that (presumably audible) beats of nearby frequency components are the source of dissonance. In 1966, R. Plomp, in his short book, *Experiments on Tone Perception,* somewhat extended this idea. The experiments underlying his work showed that a dissonant sound is heard when two sine waves are sounded close together in frequency even when no distinct beats can be heard. He presented data and generalized curves for calculating the total amount of dissonance in a complex of closely spaced sinusoidal tones.

Whatever the quantitative degree of such dissonance may be, it can be clearly heard as a roughness accompanying the sound of two sine waves as their frequencies approach one another. This roughness is particularly noticeable at most frequencies when the separation of the sine waves is less than a minor third (a quarter of an octave). Such dissonance can be explored on a DX7 or other digital keyboard voiced to produce sine waves.

This sort of dissonance seems related closely to the idea of musical dissonance. When tones with successive harmonic partials are sounded together, for the octave, the least dissonant interval, the partials of the upper tone all fall on partials of the lower tone, and hence cannot add roughness or dissonance.

If the number of partials is modest (six to nine), a number of partials will coincide for the next most consonant interval, the fifth, and the separation of the partials that do not coincide will be fairly wide. To a lesser degree, this is true for other consonant intervals, such as the fourth, the major third, and the minor third.

The association of dissonance with interaction of sine waves close in frequency is thus a plausible explanation of musical consonance. Can we see this at work in musical harmony? There is an ingenious demonstration on the 1987 Houtsma,

Rossing, and Wagenaars IPO-NIU-ASA compact disk *Auditory Demonstrations*. The demonstration is based on the fact that if both the intervals of the scale and the spacings of initially harmonic partials are stretched to the same degree in a logarithmic fashion, partials of simultaneously sounding tones that coincided before stretching will coincide after stretching. Thus, the basis for the sort of consonance and dissonance that Helmholtz and Plomp proposed will be preserved. The demonstration on the disk makes use of an unstretched scale and a scale stretched so that the "octave" ratio is 2.1 instead of 2. Two sorts of tones with nine partials are used: tones with harmonic partials, and tones in which the partial spacing is stretched in accord with a 2.1 "octave."

In the demonstration, a four-part Bach chorale is played in four ways: (a) both scale and partial spacing unstretched, (b) both scale and partial spacing stretched to 2.1 "octave," (c) only the scale stretched, and (d) only the partial spacing stretched. Option (a) of course sounds harmonious; (b) sounds harmonious but just slightly odd; (c) and (d) sound awful—because the separation of partials of various tones has been completely upset. This is a striking vindication of the Helmholtz-Plomp explanation of consonance and dissonance.

We should note that we can apply Plomp's ideas to the consonance or pleasingness of the timbre of a single musical tone. If a tone has many strong successive partials, it is bound to have a harsh, buzzy, "electronic" sound because of the small spacing of the higher partials. Indeed, a lot of high partials with a common phase is in essence a periodic sequence of filtered clicks that sound more buzzy than pitchy.

In traditional instruments, the intensity of partials falls off with increasing frequency. In the violin, dips in the resonance of the body punch holes in the spectrum. In the human voice, successive partials have appreciable intensities only near the resonant frequencies of the vocal tract, the formant frequencies.

In connection with electronic synthesis, in 1977, R. A. Moog proposed that the higher partials be separated by an appreciable fraction of an octave in order to avoid an unpleasant tone quality.

XIII. PITCH

Chavez composed a toccata for percussion. Rhythm and timbre are more central to Varese's *Ionization* than is pitch. Yet pitch is the primary quality of sound in Western music. Up to this point, pitch has been mentioned but not discussed.

When do we hear a clear musical pitch? In an informal experiment, I listened with earphones to short sinusoidal tone bursts or wavelets—waveforms in which a sine wave rises and falls smoothly in amplitude. I had a few colleagues listen also. What do tone bursts of various length sound like?

If the tone burst is several tens of cycles long, it sounds like a clear, though short, musical tone. If the tone burst is only 2 to 4 cycles long, it sounds like a click. It has a spectral quality of dull (for a low frequency) or bright (for a high frequency) but no clear sense of the pitch of a musical tone. This appears to be roughly true regardless of the frequency of the sinusoid. Below 1000 Hz, perhaps 16 cycles are required if there is to be no click; above 1000 Hz, perhaps up to 32.

For tone bursts of intermediate lengths, one hears both a click and a pitch. As the number of cycles per tone burst is increased, the click fades away and the sensation of a tone with pitch increases. Of course, if a sine wave of considerable duration is turned on abruptly, we hear a click followed by a sensation of a steady tone.

It seems plausible that it takes time for the auditory system to produce a clear sensation of pitch. This may be reflected in studies (Liang & Chistovich, 1960; B. C. J. Moore, 1973) that show that the JND (just-noticeable difference) of pitch falls as the length of a sinusoidal stimulus is increased, at first rapidly, and then leveling off completely at around a second.

The number of cycles taken in producing a clear sensation of pitch could be the number of cycles necessary to establish a steady pattern of vibration along the basilar membrane. If we turn a sine wave on abruptly, there will initially be a broad and rapidly changing pattern of excitation on both sides of the "place" (of vibration) associated with the frequency of the sinusoid. As the sine wave persists, the pattern of vibration stabilizes to a smooth, asymmetric peak around that place, falling off more rapidly on the low-frequency (apical) side of the peak than on the basal side.

The assimilation of various harmonic frequency components into one sense of a pitched tone is an amazing aspect of pitch. We have noted that, before the days of sine waves, Mersenne heard the pitches of the first five harmonics in string sounds. Helmholtz found it possible to "hear out" individual harmonic frequency components through calling attention to them by listening through a resonator that filtered them out, or through calling attention to them by beats with a tone of nearby frequency. In periodic synthetic sounds, giving one harmonic component a vibrato will cause the component to be heard with a separate pitch.

The ability to hear out harmonics improves with training. The trained ability to hear harmonics out varies among subjects, but most can learn to hear out harmonics up to around the sixth. The surprising thing is not the ability to hear harmonics out, but the tendency to fuse them into a single tone with a single pitch. This can be demonstrated with such a synthesizer as the Yamaha DX7 by making the tones sinusoidal with a common amplitude and, preferably, using just intonation. As one adds harmonically related sinusoids 1 through 6—for instance, C, C', G', C'', E'', G''—one hears each added harmonic briefly, but each is soon absorbed into a tone with a pitch corresponding to that of the fundamental. Yet, if one turns a particular harmonic off and on by repeatedly lifting and depressing a key, one hears the harmonic come and go.

That is, one hears the harmonic come and go, unless one is toward the bottom of the piano keyboard. If at a moderate level, the successively added sinusoidal tones are C_0, C_1, G_1, C_2, E_2, and G_2, one hears the first three tones faintly as the keys are depressed. But, releasing C_0 produces no, or almost no, audible effect in this frequency range. The same is true for C_1. Removing and adding G_2 produces a slight effect. For comparable intensities, the lowest two or three sinusoidal tones sound very faint and have no effect on either the timbre or pitch of the overall tone. Yet, that tone has a definite timbre and pitch.

This is in accord with an observation reported by Fletcher in 1924. He found that filtering out the lowest few sinusoidal components of musical tones had no effect on pitch and only a minor effect on timbre.

Fletcher felt that the fundamental frequency must be present in order to give a sense of pitch and that it was reintroduced by nonlinearities in the ear. This reflects the "winning side" of a controversy that could not be settled with the technology of the nineteenth century. Plomp (1966) gives an excellent historical account.

In 1938, Schouten showed decisively that the fundamental need not be present among harmonic partials in order to hear a pitch corresponding to its frequency. He canceled the fundamental out; you could hear it come and go, but the pitch did not change. In his 1938 publication, Schouten refers to "a tacit assumption that the perception of pitch is determined by the lowest harmonic actually present in the ear."

What we can actually observe, as, by means of the DX7, is that pitch is determined by salient harmonic components.

Toward the top of the piano keyboard, the fundamental is essential to the pitch; if we omit it, the pitch goes up to that of the next harmonic component. In this frequency range, for harmonics of equal intensity, the higher the harmonic, the less its loudness and salience.

Toward the bottom of the piano keyboard, the situation is different. In this frequency range, for sinusoidal frequency components of equal intensity, the higher the frequency, the louder the component sounds, the more salient it is. Hence it is the higher frequency components, the fourth, fifth and sixth harmonics in the observation cited earlier, that determine both the pitch and the timbre. The lower harmonics can come and go with no effect on the pitch and little on the timbre.

The behavior of tones with odd harmonic components only is peculiar. With the DX7, tones with the first six odd harmonic partials (the 1st, 3rd, 5th, 7th, 9th, and 11th) in equal amplitudes can be generated and compared with tones with the first successive six harmonic partials (the 1st, 2nd, 3rd, 4th, 5th, and 6th).

For tones with odd harmonics only, toward the top and even the middle part of the piano keyboard, the component of fundamental frequency is essential to a musical pitch associated with the frequency of the fundamental.

Toward the bottom of the keyboard, the sensation of pitch is peculiar. D_1 with odd partials sounds much like C_2 with successive partials. For these two tones, the top three frequency components nearly coincide. This is in agreement with the observation in de Boer's excellent summary paper on residue pitch (1976) that the presence of odd harmonics does not result in a residue pitch corresponding to the frequency of the missing fundamental.

What is residue pitch? It is just a musical pitch corresponding to the frequency of the fundamental in the absence of a component of the fundamental frequency.

There has been a great deal of work on residue pitch, mostly involving musically strange combinations of frequency components. Through the work of Terhardt (1974), what had been called *residue pitch* came to be called *virtual pitch.* Virtual pitch is opposed to *analytic* listening (in which harmonics are heard out), contrasted with *synthetic listening,* in which they are fused into one tone and one pitch.

For traditional musical tones, the pitch, while in accord with experiments on virtual pitch, seems comparatively straightforward. There are sometimes octave confusions. There appear to be no other pitch confusions. The pitch is determined by salient harmonics. The saliency of harmonics depends on frequency range, on position on the keyboard. This has been investigated by Moore, Glasberg, and Peters (1985). Changing the frequency of a selected harmonic changes the pitch of the overall tone. The harmonic that has the greatest effect on pitch is different for different pitches. It is a higher harmonic at the lower pitches and a lower harmonic at the higher pitches. In general, it lies among the lowest six harmonics.

XIV. QUASI-MUSICAL AND UNMUSICAL SOUNDS

The sorts of sounds that have been used in trying to untangle aspects of auditory perception are various. Many of these sounds are not musical sounds, or, at best, are only quasi-musical sounds.

It seems natural to classify sine waves as quasi-musical sounds. Unlike musical sounds, sine waves change pitch appreciably with intensity (Morgan & Garner, 1951), whereas musical tones do not (Lewis & Cowan, 1936). At the bottom of the piano keyboard, a sine wave of moderate intensity is a low, scarcely audible hum without a strong sensation of pitch; the pitch of low piano tones is conveyed by salient harmonics.

Other quasi-musical or unmusical tones include sequences of short pulses and the sequences of short bursts of tone that were mentioned in connection with the time resolution of hearing. Such sequences, although they can be matched to a degree to a musical tone whose pitch frequency is the same as the same number of pulses or tone bursts per second, sound buzzy and unmusical (Davis, Silverman, & McAuliffe, 1951). So do all tones made up of sequences of successive high harmonics only (say, harmonics above the 20th—Houtsma & Smurzynski, 1990).

The range of rate or periodicity below which such waveforms do not elicit a clear musical pitch is designated as not having pitch or musical pitch (Guttman & Pruzansky, 1963) , or as having infrapitch (Warren, 1982).

Musical tones have many harmonic partials. They owe their pitch chiefly to salient harmonics from the first through the sixth. And, complexes of the first sixth harmonics exhibit pitch from the top to the bottom of the piano keyboard (27.5 Hz), where many waveforms, including sine waves, give little sense of pitch.

The lowest key on the piano keyboard and the adjacent higher keys give definite sensations of pitch. What *is* distinctive of the tones toward the left end of the keyboard is harmonic effect: chords in the root position do not sound chordlike, and only open chords are harmonically effective.

Shepard tones (Shepard, 1964), which seem to rise or fall endlessly in pitch, should be thought of as quasi-musical tones. They demonstrate admirably the distinction between pitch class (which note in the scale) and pitch height, or brightness. But, because they are made up of octave partials, Shepard tones do not exhibit the strong harmonic effects of musical tones.

Matters vitally important to the perception of musical sound can be studied through the use of quasi-musical and unmusical sounds. Yet it is important to understand that in listening to musical sounds, or at least, to traditional musical sounds, we do not encounter and are not puzzled by strange perceptual features that can be demonstrated by using quasi-musical or unmusical sounds.

XV. DESCRIPTIONS OF MUSICAL SOUNDS

We may wish to describe a musical sound in order to gain insight into the perception of musical sounds, in order to reproduce musically sounds exactly, in order to transform musical sounds in some way, or perhaps for other purposes.

In work published in 1977, J. M. Grey discussed his multidimensional scaling of the sounds of a number of musical instruments. He represented various instrumental sounds by points in a three-dimensional space. The distance between two points was a measure of the rated dissimilarity of two instrumental sounds represented. This representation, and his discussion of it, pointed out various qualities of musical sounds.

A means for representing musical sounds may give little or no insight into their qualities. The Yamaha and Boesendorf recording pianos can make a precise recording on a compact disc of the details of each keystroke and use of the pedals. The piano can then replay a performance with very high fidelity. The total number of bits needed so to recreate the performance is abut a thousandth of the number required for a stereo sound recording on a compact disc, yet the quality of the reproduction by means of the recording piano is higher. Thus, in the case of the piano, a record of keystrokes and pedaling is more economical than a recording of sound waveform. And, we may note that a recording of keystrokes could be used in transposing the piano performance into another key, or in speeding up or slowing down the performance. A recording of waveform does not allow such transformations.

The waveform of a musical sound is a safe way of reproducing *any* sound, but staring at the waveform doesn't even give us a measure of how complicated it is or can be. Something called the sampling theorem does.

If a waveform has no frequency components outside of a bandwidth B, it can be represented accurately by $2B$ numbers a second. These numbers represent or sample the amplitudes of the waveform at *any* successive sampling times spaced $1/2B$ seconds apart. Sampling is important in that, as in the case of a Fourier series or transform, the waveform can be recovered *exactly* from exact samples.

Sampling plays an important part in all digital representations and analyses of waveforms, which currently means, in all analyses of waveforms. An efficient analysis can describe the waveform by means of 2B numbers a second. Or, in the case of an inefficient analysis, by more numbers a second.

One useful but somewhat limited means for analyzing and representing the waveform of a sound is called linear prediction (see Schaefer & Markel, 1979). The output of a linear predictor consists of 10 or so prediction coefficients, and a *residual* waveform, which is essentially the error in predicting the waveform the next time it is sampled. If we have both the prediction coefficients and the residual, we can reconstruct the waveform exactly.

Linear prediction was first used in describing and reproducing the human voice. The prediction coefficients are associated with the shape of the vocal tract, and the residual chiefly with the excitation (glottal wave and/or noise).

In the reconstruction of a sound from prediction coefficients and residual, we can change the pitch by changing the periodicity of the residual. Or, we can slow the sound down or speed it up without changing its residual by slowing down or speeding up the rate at which the prediction coefficients change with time.

Or, we can change the sound by leaving the prediction coefficients alone but changing the residual to one characteristic of some other sound, such as a chuffing train.

Linear prediction has been used in a great deal of early transformations and combinations of sounds.

Fourier transforms of some sort are now more common in describing and processing sound. We have noted that *in principle* we can describe the waveform of any sound by means of a Fourier integral and recover the original waveform by means of an inverse transform. Musically, this would be a useless exercise if we could carry it out, because the spectrum so obtained is characteristic of the whole combination and sequence of musical tones. And, we cannot actually make such an exact description of a long musical passage.

What we can do is to represent the spectrum of a signal, the amplitude and phase of frequency components, as a function of both frequency and time. Such a representation is sometimes characterized as a *phase vocoder* (again, see Schafer & Markel, 1979). In any such representation, both frequency and time are necessarily smeared. A single sine wave appears as a narrow band of frequencies. A very short pulse is spread out in time. The finer the representation in frequency, the coarser that in time.

Whether the resolution is high in frequency and low in time, or low in frequency and high in time, there is an economical way of smearing such that the successive spectra can be described completely by 2B numbers a second, where B is the total bandwidth of the signal. This is just the number of numbers per second we get from the sampling theorem. And, as in the case of sampling, the original waveform can be reconstructed exactly from the 2B numbers a second that describe completely the successive spectra (Schaefer & Markel, 1979).

The representation of a waveform by means of successive spectra does not give us a more economical representation of a musical tone, but it does enable us to sort out the spectral peaks representing a tone of slowly varying amplitude and pitch from a random welter of noise. With such information, we can resynthesize a signal with a transposition in pitch, or a slowing or speeding in time. Such tamperings with pitch and tempo involve arbitrary choices as to just what is done.

Recently what is called a wavelet transform has found favor (Combes, Grossman, & Tchamitchian, 1989). In the wavelet transform, the frequency resolution is constant in octaves rather than in hertz, and the time resolution is inversely proportional to frequency. This is in accord with the way pitch frequency varies with pitch. It is also in accord with the fact that to be perceived as a tone, a tone burst or wavelet must have a certain minimum number of periods, or a minimum duration that is inversely proportional to frequency. The original waveform can be accurately recovered from the wavelet representation.

The most economical wavelet representation of a signal again requires $2B$ numbers a second, just the number of numbers a second required to represent the waveform by means of samples.

In principle, there are just as many different waveforms in the frequency range from 10,000 Hz to 20,000 Hz as there are in the frequency range between 0 Hz and 10,000 Hz. But, in musical sounds, the frequency components lying between 0 Hz and 10,000 Hz are much more important than those lying between 10,000 Hz and 20,000 Hz. Can we somehow take this into account in representing musical sounds?

Two sections of noise waveform of the same bandwidth and power differ wildly in the details of their waveform. Yet, they sound alike. Can we not somehow take this into account in representing musical sounds?

We can make our representations of musical sounds more economical and pertinent only if we take into account the limitations of the ear. Our sense of hearing is such that the wildly different waveforms of noise do not result in any perceptual difference. Our sense of hearing is such that what lies between 10,000 Hz and 20,000 Hz does not have as much perceptual complexity as what lies between 0 Hz and 10,000 Hz.

In a thesis written in 1989, Xavier Serra took a huge step forward in the representation of musical sounds by separating the representation of the tonal or *deterministic* part of an instrumental waveform from a noisy or *stochastic* part. Serra started out with spectra in which the amplitude and phase as a function of frequency were evaluated about every 20 msec. The time interval between successive spectra was somewhat different in different cases. Knowing that the frequency components in the tonal part of the musical sound do not change much in amplitude or phase in 20 msec or so, Serra identified spectral peaks that occurred at about the same frequency in successive spectra as spectral components of the tonal or deterministic part of the musical sound. In resynthesizing the original sound, Serra used slowly varying sine waves to represent this part of the waveform.

Serra subtracted the spectrum of this deterministic part of the waveform from the total spectrum. This left a residual stochastic spectrum. In resynthesizing the waveform, Serra provided a time-varying noise with roughly the same spectrum as the residual noise spectrum.

The details of this overall process are more complicated than one might guess from this brief outline. In some cases, Serra took the phase of the sinusoidal components into account. This gave a reconstruction of the musical tone that it was hard to tell from the original tone. When the phase was not taken into account, the reconstructed sound was convincingly a high-quality piano, or flute, or vocal, or guitar, or drum sound, but one might be able to tell the difference from the original if they were heard in quick succession.

The representations of instrumental sounds that Serra recreated required somewhat less than $2B$ numbers a second. But, it was quality, not economy, that Serra sought, and he attained it amazingly. For example, for a piano tone, the deterministic or tonal component alone sounded musical but not like a piano. The addition of the stochastic or noise component, present most prominently during the attack when the hammer is in contact with the string, resulted in a completely convincing piano tone.

Serra's primary interest in his novel description of musical tones lay in its potential use in modifying and synthesizing musical sounds. Surely, a simple description of a musical sound that is convincing to the ear should be of use in such modification and synthesis. But, such a description has a value in itself. It tells us what is important to the ear. In Serra's description, the details of the noise waveform are not important; a roughly correct noise spectrum is sufficient. It should be valuable to know what distinctions the *ear* makes among musical sounds. It appears that Serra has shown us where and how to look.

ACKNOWLEDGMENTS

I thank Professor Earl D. Schubert for reading and commenting on the manuscript and for supplying many essential references to the literature. Schubert's book, *Psychological Acoustics* (1979), has been a great deal of help. I am also grateful to Chris Chafe and Perry Cook for providing information and references concerning the effects of nonlinearities in sound production.

REFERENCES

Blauert, J. (1983). *Spatial hearing.* Cambridge, MA: MIT Press.
de Boer, E. (1976). On the "residue" and auditory pitch perception. In W. Keidel & W. D. Neff (Eds.), *Handbook of sensory physiology, Vol. V. Auditory system, Part 3. Clinical and special topics* (pp. 479–583). New York: Springer-Verlag.
Chafe, C. (1990a). Pulsed noise in self-sustained oscillations of musical instruments. *Proceedings of the IEEE International Conference on Acoustics, Speech, and Signal Processing, Albuquerque, NM* (1157–1160).

Chafe, C. (1990b). *Pulsed noise and microtransients in physical models of musical instruments* (Stanford University Department of Music [CCRMA] Technical Report STAN-M-64). Stanford, CA: Stanford University, Department of Music.

Chowning, J. M. (1971). The simulation of moving sound sources. *Journal of Audio Engineering Society, 19,* 2–6.

Chowning, J. M. (1980). Computer synthesis of the singing voice. In J. Sundberg (Ed.), *Sound generation in winds strings and computers* (pp. 4–13). Stockholm: Royal Swedish Academy of Music.

Combes, J. M., Grossman, A., & Tchamitchian, P. (Eds.). (1989). Wavelets, time-frequency methods and phase space. *Proceedings of the International Conference, Marseille, France, December 14–18, 1987.* New York: Springer-Verlag.

Davis, H., Silverman, S. R., and McAuliffe, D. R. (1951). Some observations on pitch and frequency. *Journal of the Acoustical Society of America, 23,* 40–42.

Flanagan, J. L., & Guttman, N. (1960). On the pitch of periodic pulses. *Journal of the Acoustical Society of America, 32,* 1308–1319.

Fletcher, H. (1924). The physical criterion for determining the pitch of a musical tone. *Physical Review, 23,* 427–437.

Fletcher, H. (1964). Normal vibration frequencies of a stiff piano string. *Journal of the Acoustical Society of America, 36,* 203–209.

Fletcher, H., Blackham, E. D., & Stratton, R. (1962). Quality of piano tones. *Journal of the Acoustical Society of America, 34,* 749–761.

Galileo Galilei. (1954). *Dialogues concerning two new sciences* (H. Crew & A. de Salvio, Trans.). New York: Dover Publications. (Original work published 1637)

Gardner, M. B. (1968). Historical background of the Haas and/or precedence effect. *Journal of the Acoustical Society of America, 43,* 1243–1248.

Goldstein, J. L. (1967). Auditory nonlinearity. *Journal of the Acoustical Society of America, 41,* 676–689.

Gordon, J. W. (1987). The perceptual attack time of musical tones. *Journal of the Acoustical Society of America, 82,* 88–105.

Grey, J. M. (1977). Multidimension perceptual scaling of musical timbres. *Journal of the Acoustical Society of America, 61,* 1270–1277.

Guttman, N., & Flanagan, J. L. (1964). Pitch of high-pass-filtered pulse trains. *Journal of the Acoustical Society of America, 36,* 757–765.

Guttman, N., & Pruzansky, S. (1963). Lower limits of pitch and musical pitch. *Journal of Speech and Hearing Research, 5,* 207–214.

Helmholtz, H. L. F. (1954). *On the sensations of tone as a physiological basis for the theory of music* (A. J. Ellis, Trans.). New York: Dover. (Original work published 1877)

Henckel, P. (1990). *Detection of complex harmonic signals with phase derived envelopes.* Unpublished thesis, Stanford University, Stanford, CA.

Hirsh, I. (1959). Auditory perception of temporal order. *Journal of the Acoustical Society of America, 31,* 759–767.

Houtsma, A. J. M., Rossing, T. D., & Wagenaars, W. M. (1987). *Auditory demonstrations* [CD]. Philips 1126-061, tracks 68–61.

Houtsma, A. J. M., & Smurzynski, J. (1990). Pitch identification and discrimination for complex tones with many harmonics. *Journal of the Acoustical Society of America, 87,* 304–310.

Houtsma, A. J. M., & Tholen, H. J. G. M. (1987). A carillon of major-third bells: II. A perceptual evaluation. *Music Perception, 4,* 255–266.

Kaiser, J. F. (1983). Some observations on vocal tract operation from a fluid flow point of view. In I. R. Titze & R. C. Scherer (Eds.), *Vocal fold physiology* (pp. 358–386). Denver, CO: Denver Center for Performing Arts.

Kendall, G. S., Martens, W. L., & Decker, S. L. (1989). Spatial reverberation; discussion and demonstration. In M.. V. Mathews & J. R. Pierce (Eds.), *Current directions in computer music research* (pp. 65–87). Cambridge, MA: MIT Press.

Lehr, A. (1987). A carillon of major-third bells: III. From theory to practice. *Music Perception, 4,* 267–280.

Lewis, D., & Cowan, M. (1936). The influence of intensity on the pitch of violin and 'cello tones. *Journal of the Acoustical Society of America, 8,* 20–22.

Liang, C., & Chistovich, L. A. (1960). Difference limens as a function of tonal duration. *Soviet Physics Acoustics, 6,* 75–80.

Mathews, M. V., Pierce, J. R., Reeves, A., & Roberts, L. A. (1988). Theoretical and experimental explorations of the Bohlen-Pierce scale. *Journal of the Acoustical Society of America , 84,* 1214–1222.

McAdams, S. (1984). *Spectral fusion, spectral parsing, and the formation of auditory images* (Stanford University Department of Music (CCRMA) Technical Report STAN-M-22). Stanford, CA: Stanford University.

Mcintyre, M. E., Schumacher, R. T., & Woodhouse, J. (1983). On the oscillations of musical instruments. *Journal of the Acoustical Society of America, 74,* 1325–1345.

Mills, A. W. (1958). On the minimum audible angle. *Journal of the Acoustical Society of America, 30,* 237–246.

Moog, R. A. (1987). *Amplifier with multiplier.* U. S. Patent number 4,117,413.

Moore, B. C. J. (1973). Frequency difference for limens for short-duration tones. *Journal of the Acoustical Society of America, 54,* 610–619.

Moore, C. J., Glasberg, B. R., & Peters, R. (1985). Relative dominance of individual partials in determining the pitch of complex tones. *Journal of the Acoustical Society of America, 77,* 1853–1860.

Moore, F. R. (1989). Spatialization of sounds over loudspeakers. In M. V. Mathews & J. R. Pierce (Eds.), *Current directions in computer music research* (pp. 89–103). Cambridge, MA: MIT Press.

Morgan, C. T., & Garner, W. R. (1951). Pitch and intensity. *Journal of the Acoustical Society of America, 23,* 658–663.

Patterson, J. H., & Green, D. M. (1970). Discrimination of transient signals having identical energy spectra. *Journal of the Acoustical Society of America, 48,* 894–905.

Pierce, J. R. (1983). *The science of musical sound.* New York: Scientific American Books.

Pierce, J. R. (1990). Rate, place, and pitch with tonebursts. *Music Perception, 7,* 205–212.

Plomp, R. (1965). Detectability threshold for combination tones. *Journal of the Acoustical Society of America, 37,* 1110–1123.

Plomp, R. (1966). *Experiments on tone perception.* Soesterberg, The Netherlands: Institute for Perception RVO-TNO, National Defense Research Organization TNO.

Rasch, R. A. (1979). Synchronization in performed ensemble music. *Acustica, 43,* 121–131.

Resnick, S. B., & Feth, L. L. (1975). Discriminability of time-reversed clicks pairs. *Journal of the Acoustical Society of America, 57,* 1493–1499.

Risset, J. C., & Mathews, M. V. (1969). Analysis of instrument tones. *Physics Today, 22,* 23–30.

Risset, J. C. (1978). Musical acoustics. In E. C. Carterette & M. P. Friedman (Eds.), *Handbook of perception: Vol. IV. Hearing* (pp. 521–564). New York: Academic Press.

Risset, J. C., & Wessel, D. A. (1982). Exploration of timbre by analysis and synthesis. In D. Deutsch (Ed.), *The psychology of music* (pp. 25–58). San Diego: Academic Press.

Ronken, D. A. (1970). Monaural detection of a phase difference between clicks. *Journal of the Acoustical Society of America, 47,* 1091–1099.

Rossing, T. D. (1990). *The science of sound,* 2nd ed. Reading, MA: Addison Wesley.

Schafer, R. W., & Markel, J. D. (Eds.). (1979). *Speech analysis.* Piscataway, NJ: IEEE Press.

Schouten, J. F. (1938). The perception of subjective tones. *De Koninklijke Nederlandse Akademie voor Wetenschappen Proceedings, 41,* 1086–1093.

Schoofs, A., van Asperen, F., Maas, P., & Lehr, A. (1987). A carillon of major-third bells: I. Computation of bell profiles using structural optimization. *Music Perception, 4,* 245–254.

Schubert, E. D. (Ed.). (1979). *Psychological acoustics.* Stroudsburg, PA: Dowden, Hutchinson, & Ross.

Serra, X. (1989). *A system for sound analysis/transformation/synthesis based on a deterministic plus stochastic decomposition* (Center for Computer Research in Music and Acoustics, Department of Music Report No. STAN-M-56). Stanford, CA: Stanford University.

Shepard, R. N. (1964). Circularity in judgments of relative pitch. *Journal of the Acoustical Society of America, 36,* 2345–2353.

Teager, H. M., & Teager, S. M. (1983). The effects of separated air flow in vocalizations. In D. M. Bless & J. Abbs (Eds.), *Vocal fold physiology* (pp. 124–145). San Diego, CA: College Hill Press.

Teager, H. M., & Teager, S. M. (1990). Evidence for nonlinear production mechanisms in the vocal tract. in W. V. Hardcastle & A. Marchal (Eds.), *Speech production and speech modelling.* Dordrecht, The Netherlands: Kluwer Academic Publishers.

Terhardt, E. (1974). Pitch, consonance, and harmony. *Journal of the Acoustical Society of America, 55,* 1061–1069.

Warren, R. M. (1982). Auditory perception, a new synthesis. In *Pitch and infrapitch* (pp. 80–85). Elmsford, NY: Pergamon Press.

Zwislocki, J. J., & Feldman, R. S. (1956). Just noticeable differences in dichotic phase. *Journal of the Acoustical Society of America, 28,* 860–864.

2

CONCERT HALLS: FROM MAGIC TO NUMBER THEORY

MANFRED R. SCHROEDER

Drittes Physikalisches Institut
Universität Göttingen
Göttingen, Germany
and
AT&T Bell Laboratories
Murray Hill, New Jersey (ret.)

I. THE THREE PROBLEMS OF CONCERT HALL ACOUSTICS

Sound transmission in enclosures is an old art to which the ancient Greeks had already made notable contributions. One has only to think of the large amphitheaters of antiquity that even today astound us by the excellent speech intelligibility possible within them. How did the Greeks do it? Equally surprising, many concert halls constructed during the past century, such as the Vienna Musikvereinssaal, are renowned for their superb acoustics. Were these early acoustic successes based on some unrecoverable magic?

On the other hand, many a modern auditorium is deficient in acoustic quality for both speech and music, and some well-known halls had to undergo extensive (and expensive) alterations. Whence this descent into an acoustic abyss? Why, precisely, is concert hall acoustics such a difficult subject? The reason, simply stated, is that concert hall acoustics is governed by three sets of *interacting* problems, all three of them exceedingly complex in themselves:

1. The physical problem of wave propagation and attenuation in irregularly shaped enclosures;
2. The psychological problem of how we, the human listeners, perceive the sound waves impinging on our ears; and, finally,
3. The problem of subjective preference: What do people really prefer to hear, do tastes change, and so on?

II. THE PHYSICAL PROBLEM

If concert halls were bare rectangular boxes with no chairs, human performers, or listeners inside, the physical problem would be easy. The wave equation for sound in air (at levels below the threshold of pain) is linear and simple enough, and for rectangular shapes, the independent variables (the three spatial coordinates and time) are separable. Thus, the wave equation for the sound pressure (a second-order partial differential equation) can be integrated explicitly, leading to the well-known sinusoidal solutions in space and time. These solutions are called resonances or *normal modes*—much talked about by expert and layman alike, but *audible* as such only in small, tiled bathrooms and similar enclosures with highly reflective walls.

Normal modes are, of course, not the prerogative of bare, rectangular chambers but prevail in more complicated shapes too—with one important difference: They can no longer be calculated and specified explicitly. The magnitude of the problem is further aggravated by the fact that a large hall, such as Boston Symphony Hall, has a total of more than 10 *billion* normal modes in the audio frequency range (20–20,000 Hz, for young listeners), not one of which we know or can ever hope to know.

At this stage of comprehension of the magnitude of the problem, it would seem to be quite reasonable to give up any attempt to shed light on concert hall acoustics by physical *theory*. But that is not in human nature. The very complexity of the problem suggests other viewpoints and, in fact, implies different solutions. The enormous number of normal modes means that the wavelengths of audible sounds are small compared with the overall dimensions of the hall. Thus, at least for smooth inner surfaces, one can, as an approximation, assume the wavelength to be zero, thereby neglecting all effects of wave diffraction. As a result, sound propagation is described in terms of *rays*—just as the light rays emerge from electromagnetic wave theory by letting the wavelength go to zero.

A. GEOMETRICAL ACOUSTICS

The discipline based on ray *approximation* is commonly called *geometrical acoustics* in analogy to geometrical optics. Geometrical acoustics has been, and continues to be, one of the mainstays of concert hall design. Because of the close analogy to light rays, the propagation of sound in an enclosure is often studied by means of optical scale models lined with mirrors (and sometimes filled with smoke to enhance the visibility of the light rays).

In recent times, ray tracing has been taken over by computers, thereby giving further impetus to geometrical acoustics. In fact, one of the oldest but still unresolved problems of architectural acoustics is presently being successfully attacked by computer ray studies: the relationship between the reverberation time of an enclosure and the sound absorption of the materials covering its surfaces. (The absorption of sound in the air *inside* the enclosure is in general negligible, except at high frequencies. In any case, it presents no theoretical difficulties because the air, and therefore its absorptive effect, is spread *evenly* throughout the entire three-dimensional space as opposed to the wall absorption, which is distributed highly nonuniformly, being confined to a two-dimensional subspace—the surface of the enclosure.)

The requirements for high acoustic quality of a concert hall include freedom from noise and echoes, good spectral balance, and a reverberation time appropriate to the musical repertoire (about 2 sec for classical music). Reverberation time (usually designated by the letter T) is defined as the time in which the sound energy density at a given point decays to one millionth of its starting value after all sound sources have been turned off (Kuttruff, 1979). The statistical uncertainties inherent in the original method based on decay measurements can be avoided by a method in which the squared impulse response is integrated over time (Schroeder, 1965). Experience teaches us that reverberation time, in most halls, is not a strong function of location, and in this sense we can speak of *the* reverberation time of the hall. However, reverberation time may depend on frequency and on whether the hall is empty or occupied by people. If no frequency value is stated, quoted values usually refer to mid-audio frequencies (500–1000 Hz). For example, the value of T for the Vienna Musikvereinssaal is 2.0 sec.

Modern concert halls are designed so that the unoccupied seats have very nearly the same absorption as that of an adult person sitting in that seat (Kuttruff, 1979). Thus, reverberation time becomes nearly independent of attendance. In older halls, with wooden seats and little upholstery, reverberation time of the empty hall may be much higher than in the fully occupied hall, making orchestra rehearsals extremely unpleasant. As a remedy, "rehearsal curtains" are used to shut out excessive reverberation from the empty hall.

At frequencies below 250 Hz, one often finds an increase in reverberation time by 20% or more (a significant increase, because a 5% difference can be perceived by an attentive listener). Most experts agree that such an increase in reverberation time at low frequencies is desirable for music (but not for speech).

The relation between sound absorption and reverberation time was studied extensively by Wallace Clement Sabine at Harvard University around the turn of the century. He derived a formula (named after him) for reverberation time (Kuttruff, 1979).

$$T = 55.2 \ V/cS\alpha, \tag{1}$$

where V is the total volume of the enclosure, S is its surface area, c is the velocity of sound, and α is the (average) absorption coefficient of the walls. Its derivation proceeds roughly as follows. The energy, as a function of time, of one wave packet of sound energy traveling as a ray is given by

$$E(t) = E(0) \times (1 - \alpha)^{n(t)} \tag{2}$$

where $n(t)$ is the number of "collisions" of the ray during the time interval $(0, t)$ with the absorbing walls, assumed here to have a uniform absorption coefficient α. By the definition of α, the energy of the ray is reduced by a factor $(1 - \alpha)$ after each wall reflection. Thus, Equation 2 follows immediately.

Different sound rays, however, have different fates. Thus, $n(t)$ depends on the particular sound ray considered. The average energy of many sound rays is given by an *ensemble* average, indicated by acute brackets $\langle \ \rangle$.

$$\langle E(t) \rangle = E(0) \times \langle (1 - \alpha)^{n(t)} \rangle. \tag{3}$$

Unfortunately, the average on the right-hand side of Equation 3 is unknown in all but the most trivial cases. What is known is the average number of collisions for a spatially uniform ensemble of rays:

$$\langle n(t) \rangle = cSt/4V. \tag{4}$$

An abbreviated proof of Equation 4 is given in the Appendix. Equation 4 is a most interesting result: It asserts that $\langle n(t) \rangle$ is independent of the shape of the enclosure; it is a function only of its volume V and the surface area S.

Given the insolubility of Equation 3 and the neat result of Equation 4, physicists, throwing mathematical rigor to the wind, gave in to the temptation of transferring the ensemble average in Equation 3 to the exponent, resulting in

$$\langle E(t) \rangle = E(0) \times (1 - \alpha)^{cSt/4V} \tag{5}$$

Now with $\langle E(t) \rangle = E(0) \times 10^{-6}$, one easily obtains

$$T = -55.2 \ V/sC \ln(1 - \alpha). \tag{6}$$

This is the Eyring-Schuster-Waetzmann reverberation time formula (Kuttruff, 1979), which, as $\alpha \rightarrow 0$, goes over into Sabine's formula (Equation 1). For enclosures with surfaces having nonuniform absorption coefficients, the α in Equation 6 or Equation 1 is replaced by an average absorption coefficient:

$$\alpha = \sum_i \alpha_i S_i / S,$$

where α_i is the absorption coefficient of a subsurface and S_i is its area.

These formulas, simple and easy to apply, are unfortunately incorrect. They do not allow for wave diffraction effects, which are of course not included in the ray theory on which these formulas are based. More seriously, the standard formulas do not take absorber *location* into account. The importance of absorber position is illustrated in Figures 1 and 2. These figures show the incident sound energy fluxes (the small numbers) on 12 different "wall" segments of two-dimensional rectangular enclosures and the resulting reverberation times T obtained by solving appropriate integral equations (Schroeder & Hackmann, 1980). By moving just one absorbing "panel" to a different location, the reverberation is increased by 45%! The reason is that in the configuration shown in Figure 2 the absorber panels can "see" each other. As a consequence, the energy incident on them is smaller than in Figure 1, which of course results in a high value of T.

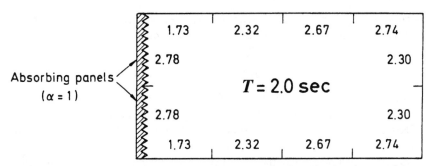

FIGURE 1   Calculated incident sound energy fluxes in a two-dimensional enclosure and the resulting reverberation time $T = 2.0$ sec.

In concert halls, the main sound absorption stems from the audience area (e.g., clothes, hair, carpets) and is thus concentrated as in Figure 1. It is therefore not surprising that in applying Equations 1 or 6 to concert hall design, the resulting reverberation time usually turns out to be smaller than predicted—giving a noticeably "dry" sound. Many modern concert halls are mute witnesses to this acoustical deficiency.

Another important application of the reverberation time formulas is the deter-.aination of the sound absorption coefficient α of new acoustical materials by measuring the reverberation time T in a so-called reverberation chamber. In this method, reverberation times of the bare chamber and the chamber *partially* lined with absorbing material are measured. Values for α determined in this manner are

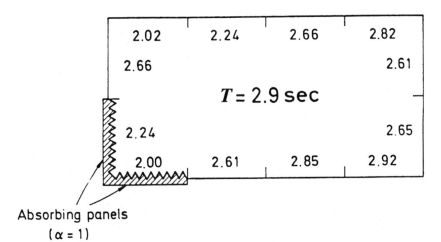

FIGURE 2   The same enclosure as shown in Figure 1 with one "absorbing panel" moved to a different location. The reduced energy fluxes on the absorbing panels lead to a 45% increase in the reverberation time to $T = 2.9$ sec.

usually too large. In fact, calculated values of the absorption coefficient often exceed 100%—a physical impossibility for a passive material!

B. COMPUTER RAY STUDIES

Ray studies on the computer have shed considerable light on this perplexing situation. They have shown again that reverberation time depends not only on volume, surface area, and average absorption coefficient, but also on the *shape* of the enclosure and the spatial distribution of the absorbing materials.

Figure 3 illustrates one of the many two-dimensional configurations studied by ray simulations (Schroeder, 1973). The "enclosure" is a quadrangle (Figure 3) with one "surface" highly absorbing ($\alpha = 0.8$) while the others have no absorption ($\alpha = 0$). A sound source near the lower right-hand corner emits 300 rays of equal initial energy at angles 1.2° apart. The computer follows these 300 rays through many reflections until their energy has decayed to less than one millionth of the initial value. The reflection can either be specular (as shown for one ray in Figure 3) or random ("diffuse") following, for example, Lambert's cosine law, as would be expected in the case of highly irregular walls (as found in many older concert halls).

Absorption coefficients for most materials depend, of course, on the angle of incidence. Presently available reverberation theories work with an average absorp-

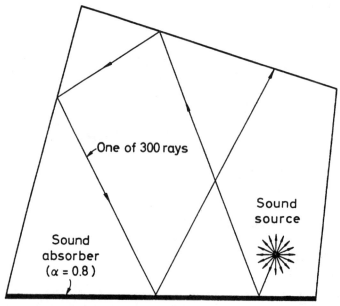

FIGURE 3   Sound ray tracing on a digital computer.

tion coefficient for *random* incidence, that is, for angles of incidence uniformly distributed over the solid angle. Naturally, any deviation from this angular uniformity can lead to errors.

The total energy as a function of time is shown in Figure 4 (the "wiggly" curve). Energy is plotted in decibels (dB), a logarithmic unit for energy ratios, with 10 dB corresponding to an energy ratio of 10. The reverberation time can be easily determined by a straight-line fit to the computed decay curve. The result obtained for the configuration shown in Figure 3 is $T_{simulated} = 0.38$ sec. The corresponding theoretical formulas for two-dimensional enclosures give considerably higher values: $T_{Sabine} = 0.63$ sec and $T_{Eyring} = 0.56$ sec. These discrepancies have, indeed, been traced to the "sloppy" averaging in the derivation of the theoretical formulas.

What are the potential benefits of these simulation studies for the acoustical consultant? For one, instead of relying on imperfect formulas, the consultant could work out a specific reverberation time formula for a hall by ray simulation on the computer before construction starts. Naturally, for complicated hall shapes, the programming will not be easy. But there are no principal obstacles, and the extra expense ought to be less than the costly mistakes revealed by the finished hall.

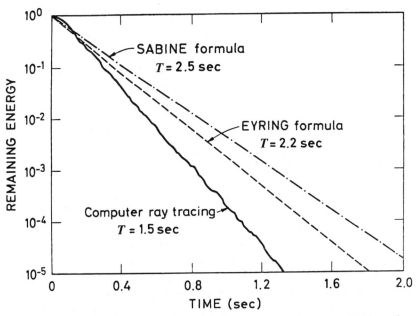

FIGURE 4   Sound energy decay calculated by computer ray tracing compared with two theoretical predictions that overestimate the reverberation time by as much as 67%.

In addition to digital ray tracing, continued theoretical work should lead to new reverberation time formulas that take dependence on hall shape and absorber distribution into account—perhaps in the form of two or three additional parameters related to the geometry of the hall.

C. COMPUTER WAVE STUDIES?

If we can trace sound rays on the computer, why cannot we simulate sound waves by digital machines? A simple calculation shows how utterly impossible that would be. The sampling theorem tells us that we must know the sound pressure at points closer than $\lambda/2$ apart, where λ is the shortest wavelength of interest. In the time domain, we must know the sound pressure at least every $1/2f$ seconds apart, where $f = c/\lambda$. Thus, for a space with volume V, we must perform at least 16 cV/λ^4 "calculations" per second, with each calculation comprising several basic computer operations. For a volume of 10^4 m^3, a shortest wavelength of $\lambda = 2$ x 10^{-2} m and with $c = 340$ m/sec, the computing time divided by real time may exceed 100 million! Although this figure may not impress the astronomer or particle physicist as excessively large, it does mean years of computing time for every second of sound—not counting core storage, reliability, and other problems. (This estimate also shows how fabulously fast an analog computer the real world is.— But is a concert hall really an analog computer? Sound in an enclosure is mediated by quantized motions of a finite number of discrete molecules. However, the "finite" number is very large indeed (order of magnitude 10^{30}). With that many "components" at her disposal, nature, in transmitting music through the air, can even afford to run her "analog" computer with the perturbations caused by *random* thermal motions rather than a deterministic program.)

However, the digital computer is not completely out of place at the "wave front." The exceedingly large number of normal modes, even within the bandwidth of a single mode, permits the successful application of statistical methods to the ensemble of modes. In any auditorium, the turning on of a single frequency in the audio frequency range (radiated, e.g., from a loudspeaker) will excite a large number of normal modes that, at some distance from the source, will add up with random amplitudes and phases. As the frequency is slowly increased, the complex transmission function between loudspeaker position and point of observation changes likewise in a random manner. For practical purposes, the transmission function between two points in an enclosure can be considered a complex Gaussian process with a one-sided exponential spectrum (Schroeder, 1954/1987). (Note that the spectrum of a function of frequency is itself a function of a variable with the dimension of time.) The Gaussian behavior follows directly from the central limit theorem of probability theory applied to the case of a large number of independent normal modes. The spectrum of the transmission function is, of course, nothing but the squared impulse response between source and receiver positions.

Thus, although we know almost nothing about the normal modes of an irregularly shaped enclosure, we know everything that can be known about its sound transmission function if the shape details of the enclosure are not specified. The situation is analogous to statistical mechanics, where without knowing the exact motions of the individual molecules, we can still make very precise statements about average quantities such as pressure and temperature. Some of the average quantities in the case of the acoustics of large halls are the average level difference between maxima and minima of the sound transmission function (roughly 10 dB) and the average distance between response maxima $(4/T)$ (Schroeder, 1973).

In 1935, E. C. Wente of Bell Laboratories first reported the wild fluctuations of room response curves and, as a telephone engineer, was understandably worried by them. He wondered how people could hear as well as they did in reverberant enclosures in the face of response irregularities exceeding 40 dB. The question was not settled until 25 years later, when it was shown that the human ear, in listening to speech or music, has a time resolution of about 1/50 sec and a correspondingly poor frequency-resolving power that "irons out" most of the spectral irregularities of a room. However, in the intervening decades, a large number of frequency-response curves were measured in auditoriums around the world in a vain effort to distill criteria for acoustic excellence from what must be considered essentially *noise* (albeit in the frequency domain).

Nevertheless, room response curves are relevant for electroacoustic systems (e.g., public address systems). Application of Nyquist's criterion for stability (freedom from "howling") of such systems led to a problem in extremal statistics for which only approximate analytic solutions exist. Here the digital computer has closed a significant gap by its ability to generate, Monte Carlo fashion, complex transmission functions *en gros* and using a simple threshold logic to implement the Nyquist criterion. The result of such Monte Carlo computation on the digital computer shows that public address systems become unstable for an open-loop gain of about –12 dB relative to the average power gain. Some of this loss in stability can be recovered by inserting an electronic "frequency shifter" (single-side-band modulator) with a 5-Hz shift into the acoustic feedback loop somewhere between microphone and loudspeaker (Schroeder, 1964).

Several other problems in wave acoustics have been solved by a proper statistical formulation of the situation and a Monte Carlo simulation on a digital computer.

III. THE SUBJECTIVE PROBLEM

A. DIGITAL SIMULATION OF SOUND TRANSMISSION

So far we have mentioned the simulation by digital computer of sound rays and random wave fields. The purpose of these simulations is to elucidate some of the physical problems in room acoustics. What about the subjective questions of sound quality and individual preference? Can they be attacked in a systematic manner also?

If we could describe human hearing and the functioning of our brains by mathematical formulas—as we describe sound transmission outside the ear by the wave equation—there would at least be hope to tackle the subjective problems in the accustomed rational manner. It is a truism that we cannot do this. There is, at present, only one "measuring process" that can determine the subtleties of acoustic quality relevant to the enjoyment of music—and that measuring process is a human being listening to music.

How we satisfy this requirement for actual listening is determined by economic and other factors. Thus, we could build a concert hall, based on what we believe to be the best available information, and have people listen in it for a few months. Then we tear it down and build a new hall , and so on. If the economic constraints should be unreasonably stringent, one could perhaps compromise occasionally and only rip out the interior of the hall. At any rate, practical experience with attempts along these lines have proved to be rather unprofitable.

A more sensible approach is the building of scale models of proposed halls (Kuttruff, 1979). In such models, sound, translated in frequency by the scale factor, can be radiated from small loudspeakers and recorded on high-speed tape recorders. On playback, the tape speed is slowed down by the appropriate factor and the result can be listened to and evaluated subjectively. This method, as one might expect, has a number of difficulties. Although frequencies scale easily, in a manner reciprocal to geometrical dimensions, absorption factors are more cumbersome to translate. In modeling the audience area, for instance, one needs acoustic materials that have the proper absorptive properties between 2000 Hz and 400,000 Hz (assuming the scale factor to be 20). Obviously, compromises must be made.

In another approach, one records, on an oscilloscope, acoustic impulse responses from small electrical sparks located, for example, on the "stage" of the scale model. These impulse responses, lengthened by the scale factor, are then simulated by electrical networks to be used as filters for the selected program material. In still another possible variant of this method, the impulse response is simulated *digitally,* that is, as a digital filter on a general-purpose computer, thereby allowing greater precision and flexibility. In fact, the microphone output from the model could be fed directly into the computer, without prior recording, and converted automatically into a digital filter response sample by sample. This is an attractive hybrid (part analog, part digital) possibility for model studies.

A refinement of this method has been applied to a study of the acoustic qualities of existing concert halls at the University of Göttingen (Schroeder, Gottlob, & Siebrasse, 1974). Impulse responses from a powerful spark gap have been recorded in 20 major European concert halls, including Royal Festival Hall (London), the Berlin Philharmonie, Amsterdam's Concertgebouw, and the Musikvereinssaal in Vienna. The recordings were made with a carefully designed dummy head that was "seated" in various locations in these halls. Two high-quality microphones form the dummy's eardrums, and their outputs are recorded on a two-track tape machine.

After these stereo-impulse responses have been transferred into the computer's memory, digital tape recordings of reverberation-free music (recorded by the London Chamber Orchestra in a "dead" room) are convolved (i.e., filtered) with these impulse responses resulting in a pair of signals corresponding precisely to the acoustic signals at the dummy's eardrums had the orchestra in fact produced the same sound in one of the halls under study.

The remaining problem is to transfer these two signals to the eardrums of a human listener for subjective evaluation. Simply converting these digital signals into analog form and applying them to stereo earphones will not suffice because the auditory impression when listening over earphones is generally not the same as listening in a free sound field. One shortcoming of the earphone presentation is fairly obvious: in turning one's head, the acoustic image (and therefore the entire hall) would turn with the head. Also, in listening over earphones, one has difficulty in "externalizing" the sound. It is as if the music originated in one's head. Such an unnatural acoustic condition would, of course, interfere seriously with any subtle quality judgments.

How then do we get the proper acoustic signals to the listener's eardrums in a *free-field* listening condition? The answer lies in sophisticated signal processing (Schroeder, 1970). Implementation of the method requires the prior measurement of the complex transmission function $S(f)$ and $A(f)$ (i.e., amplitude and phase as functions of frequency) between a loudspeaker in an anechoic chamber and the right and left eardrums of a human listener (or a dummy). In the original experiment, the loudspeaker was located in front of the listener at a distance of about 3 m and 22.5° to the right. If there was no cross talk from the loudspeaker on the right to the left ear, the task would be simple: filtering the loudspeaker signal by the inverse of the transmission function to the right ear, $S^{-1}(f)$, would be all that is necessary.

However, there is cross talk, due to sound diffraction around the human head, and it must be canceled. This can be done by a second loudspeaker, 22.5° to the left, radiating an appropriately filtered signal.

A solution to this filtering and cancellation problem is illustrated in Figure 5, where $C(f) = -A(f)S^{-1}(f)$ is the cross-talk compensation filter. The overall transmission function from the right input (R) to the right ear (r) is then

$$R_r(f) = (1 - C^2)^{-1}S^{-1}S + C(1 - C^2)^{-1}S^{-1}A = 1 \qquad (7)$$

as required. The overall response from the right input (R) to the left ear (l) is

$$R_l(f) = (1 - C^2)^{-1}S^{-1}A + C(1 - C^2)^{-1}S^{-1}S, \qquad (8)$$

which, for $C = -AS^{-1}$, vanishes, also as required.

For the method to work, $A(f)S^{-1}(f)$ must be a realizable filter response, that is, its inverse Fourier transform must vanish for negative times. Measurements have shown that this is indeed the case within measurement accuracy. (One wonders under what general conditions this is true. In other words, what are the necessary

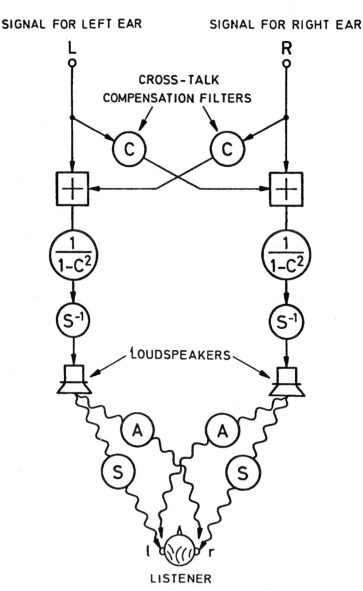

FIGURE 5   Sound reproduction system for concert hall studies.

conditions for the ratio of the transmission functions from a point in space containing diffracting surfaces to two other points to be a realizable filter response?)

In contrast, the filter $S^{-1}(f)$, which also appears in Figure 5, does not have to be realizable because it does not occur inside a feedback loop. In fact, $S^{-1}(f)$, containing a substantial *negative* delay, is never realizable. However, for a suitable large positive delay, τ, $S^{-1}(f)$ exp($-i2\pi f\tau$) is always realizable within arbitrarily small error bounds.

The practical experience with the schema of Figure 5 has been nothing less than amazing. Although the two loudspeakers are the only sound sources, virtual sound images can be created far off to the sides and even behind the listener. In fact, even the elevation angle of a sound source is properly perceived. Because the entire system is linear, many sound sources and their echoes can be reproduced simultaneously, without mutual interference, provided the listener is sitting in the proper position between the loudspeaker and does not turn his or her head away from the front direction by more than about $\pm 10°$. The spatial illusion is, indeed, so convincing that one is tempted to "look around" for the invisible sound sources. The moment one gives in to this temptation, however, the realistic illusion vanishes, frequently changing into an "inside-the-head" sensation because the crosstalk compensation filter now produce pressure waves at the eardrums that could not possibly have come from an external source.

The sound reproduction method illustrated in Figure 5 has opened up completely new possibilities in the study of concert hall acoustics. Before, in comparing two halls, one had to base one's judgment on listening to pieces of music, played at different times, often by different orchestras under different conductors (Beranek, 1962). Even if all other factors were equal, the fact that two musical experiences are separated by days, weeks, or even months makes any subtle quality assessments exceedingly unreliable if not impossible.

With the new reproduction method, instantaneous comparisons of identical program material has become possible. Listeners will rarely forget the moment they first switched themselves from a seat in the Berlin Philharmonie, say, to one in Vienna Musikvereinssaal listening to Mozart's *Jupiter* Symphony. All that they believed about the differences between these two halls on the basis of previous visits (but were not too sure about) suddenly became a matter of easy distinction.

In the first study that used this method, paired comparisons tests for individual preference and triadic comparisons for subjective similarity were used. The resulting psychological preference and similarity spaces, obtained by multidimensional scaling, are highly correlated, showing that common factors underlie these judgments of acoustical quality. Figure 6 shows the first two dimensions (denoted by x and y) of a three-dimensional solution of paired-comparison preference data obtained from 10 subjects listening to recordings from a total of 10 locations in four different halls. The 10 arrows are unit vectors representing the 10 different listeners. (The fact that vector 6 seems relatively short means that it has a substantial component in the third dimension, which is not shown in Figure 6.) The letters designate different halls and the numbers refer to particular seats in these halls. The normal projection of the hall/seat points onto a given listener's vector reflect that listener's preference score (with 85% of the total variance accounted for by dimensions x and y).

As can be seen in Figure 6, all listeners' vectors (except for Listener 4) point into the right half plane, that is, they have a positive component in the x direction.

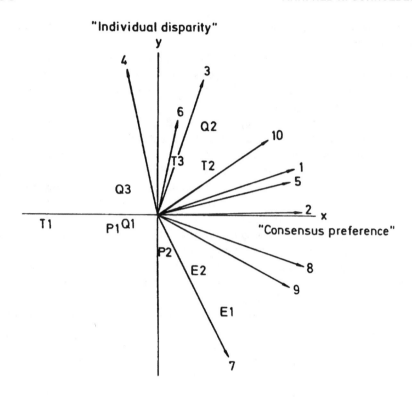

E1 - T3 : 10 seats (4 halls)

1 - 10 : 10 different listeners

FIGURE 6   Preference space obtained from paired comparison tests of 10 hall/seat combinations by 10 listeners.

The *x*-axis has therefore been labeled "Consensus preference" because, if a given hall/seat point lies to the right of some other hall/seat point, all listeners (except Listener 4) have higher preference scores for the given hall/seat.

Because some listeners point into the upper half-plane and some into the lower, the *y*-axis has been labeled "Individual disparity" because it reflects differences in the preferences of the individual listeners.

An important aspect of this psychometric method based on multidimensional scaling of preference and similarity is its avoidance of any undefined subjective descriptors such as "warmth," "brilliance," "clarity," "fullness," immersion," and so on (several dozen of these more or less picturesque terms are known in the art), which may mean different things to different people (assuming the terms mean anything).

The next step in the analysis is correlating the coordinates along dimensions *x* and *y* of the preference space shown in Figure 6 with the physical attributes of the hall, such as its width, and with the acoustic parameters of the particular locations, such as reverberation time and interaural coherence (i.e., the short time correlation between the two ear signals). The result of one such correlation analysis is shown in Figure 7 for halls with reverberation times less than 2 sec. As is to be expected, reverberation time correlates positively with the consensus preference (x) dimensions and has almost zero correlation with the individual disparity (y) dimension. In other words, for halls with short reverberation times (<2 sec), most listeners prefer longer reverberation times, irrespective of individual musical tastes.

By contrast, Figure 7 also shows that most listeners dislike a large interaural coherence, that is, a monophonic effect; they want to be "bathed" in sound fields with small interaural coherence (Ando, 1985). This is not surprising because it is well known that people prefer stereophonic over monophonic sound on their home hifi-systems.

The negative correlation with the width of the hall (*average* width for fan-shaped halls) can be explained in the same manner. People don't dislike wide halls per se, but wide halls have weak lateral reflections compared with the sound energy arriving at their heads in the median plane from the front (the stage) and above (the ceiling). Such an energy flux distribution around the human head leads to a high degree of interaural coherence, that is, low preference (Barrow & Marshall, 1981). Thus, the main reason for the relatively poor performance of many modern concert halls appears to be their excessive width aggravated by relatively

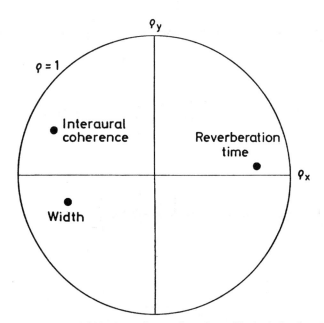

FIGURE 7 Correlation of subjective preference dimensions with physical and acoustic data of the 10 hall/seats shown in Figure 6.

low ceilings compared with most older "shoe box" type halls. (Note that high ceilings are no longer required for providing air to breathe, a function now accomplished by air conditioning.)

The importance of strong lateral reflections is further confirmed by the method of *digital modification,* in which lateral reflections are added on to the two impulse responses at the two ears (Figure 8). These artificial lateral reflections lead indeed to higher preference scores.

How can we live, acoustically speaking, with the modern low-and-wide halls, dictated, as they are, by low budgets and wider audiences? The main monophonic component at the listeners' positions could be eliminated by redirecting the reflective pattern from the ceiling into a broad lateral pattern. This can be achieved by structuring the ceiling as a reflection phase-grating based on certain number-theoretic principles (Schroeder, 1986), such as quadratic residues (Figure 9). Such ceilings reflect an incident sound wave not like a mirror but scatter the wave into many different directions. Figure 10 shows quadratic-residue diffusion, based on the prime number 17, which effectively scatters frequencies over five musical octaves. Such reflection phase-gratings have been successfully installed not only in

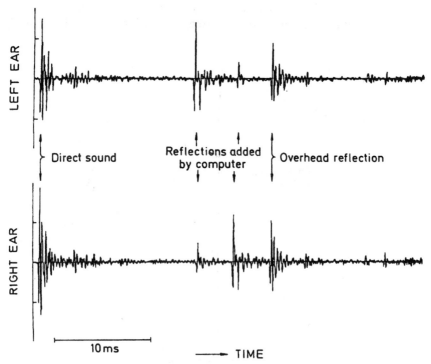

FIGURE 8   Binaural impulses responses, digitally modified by adding lateral reflections to enhance subjective preference.

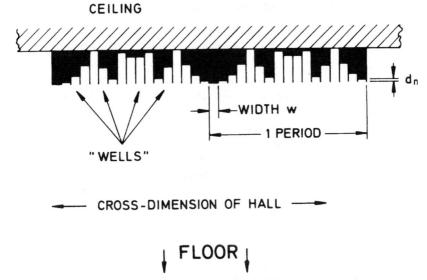

FIGURE 9 Number-theoretic diffusor design based on quadratic residues of the prime number 17. The shown diffusor covers a frequency ratio of 1:32 (five musical octaves).

concert halls but also in churches, lecture halls and even private homes and, especially, recording studios, wherever strong specular reflections from a hard wall are considered acoustically harmful.

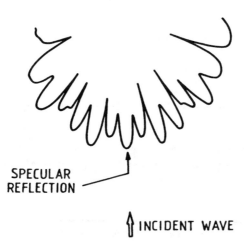

FIGURE 10 Broad lateral scattering of single incident sound wave by the number theoretic diffusor (reflection phase-grating) shown in Figure 9.

B. DIGITAL SIMULATION OF NONEXISTENT HALLS

Although the study of existing concert halls (as described in the preceding section) is a valuable tool for design of future concert halls, it does not satisfy all the needs of the acoustic engineer faced with a new design, in particular a design that departs from past practice—a trend dear to many modern architects. For this situation, a new simulation method is suggested: On the basis of the architectural plans and the building materials to be used, it should be possible to determine a fairly accurate "echo" response, including directions of arrival, at a given seat in the audience. Only prominent echoes, that is, echoes whose presence can be individually detected, must be individually represented in the response. The remaining reflections are represented by a reverberation process with the proper echo density, directional distribution, and decay characteristics as a function of frequency. Such specified reverberation processes can be simulated digitally in a manner indistinguishable from natural reverberation. The two main requirements for artificial reverberation to be indistinguishable from natural reverberation are:

1. The reverberation must be "colorless," so that reverberated white noise sounds white (and not like rain on a tin roof).
2. The reverberation must be free of unwanted flutter (so that a pistol shot sounds like a single, decaying shot and not like a burst from a machine gun).

A crucial element in the solution of both problems is an all-pass filter with an exponentially decaying impulse response (Schroeder, 1962). Such a filter is shown in block diagram form in Figure 11. The impulse response between input and output of this filter is shown in Figure 12. The corresponding power transfer function is independent of frequency! Yet it has an exponentially decaying impulse response (see Figure 12).

These so-called all-pass reverberators (because they pass all frequencies equally well) have played a decisive role in the digital simulation of natural sound-

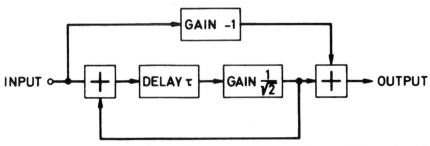

FIGURE 11   All-pass reverberator that does not alter the spectral balance of the reverberated sound.

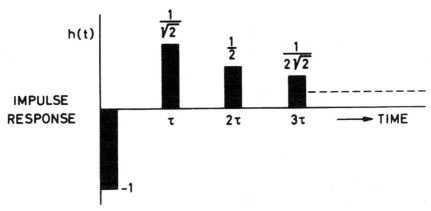

FIGURE 12   Exponentially decaying impulse response of all-pass reverberator shown in Figure 11.

ing reverberation and have found wide commercial application. In order to obtain the required echo density, several all-pass reverberators are connected in tandem (which preserves the all-pass characteristic) choosing "incommensurate" delays τ to avoid periodic flutter echoes. As a first test of this method of simulating halls before construction, an existing auditorium (Arnold Auditorium at Bell Laboratories in Murray Hill, NJ) has been simulated by using only information from architectural plans. Comparison with the actual hall demonstrated the feasibility of this simulation method: the actual hall and the simulated hall sounded alike (Schroeder, 1973).

B. DIGITAL SIMULATION OF PROPOSED ALTERATIONS

A variant of the digital simulation of concert halls has already been used to troubleshoot Philharmonic Hall in New York. One of the more apparent problems was a rather pronounced echo from the rear of the hall. The source of the echo was located in a certain region of the rear wall. The physical remedy was, of course, obvious: to cover those wall sections with absorbing material. But what would the perceptual consequences be? How much absorption was necessary to "kill" the echo without reducing the already short reverberation time even further?

This question was studied by digital simulation. The troublesome echo was identified in the impulse response of the hall and successively reduced in strength on the computer until it could no longer be heard when "dry" music was played through the computer with the reduced echo. Thus, the digital simulation method is useful also for studying proposed alterations in an existing concert hall.

After the installation of the absorbing material on the rear wall, the leading music critic of the *New York Times* (Harold Schoenberg) reported another, persistent echo. Subsequent measurements at his seat revealed that there was, indeed, another echo coming from the balcony faces. (This echo, which affected only a few seats, could have been eliminated by tilting the balcony faces or covering them with sound-absorbing material.)

Another problem studied by "digital alterations" was that of weak lateral reflections. By adding lateral reflections to the hall's impulse responses, listener preference could substantially improve (see Figure 8).

IV. MULTIPURPOSE HALLS

Many modern halls for music are required to serve other acoustic purposes as well, including drama theater, congresses, and lectures. For any but very small enclosures with fewer than 600 seats, it is difficult to accommodate such disparate uses with a fixed architectural design. In the Salle de Projection at the Institut de Recherche et Communication Acoustique/Musique (Centre Pompidou, Paris), the walls consist of triangular pyramids that can be rotated to expose surfaces with different reflective properties, as proposed by V. Peutz. But such changeable acoustics are expensive even for small spaces. In the 6000-seat Palace of Congresses in the Moscow Kremlin, a fixed high degree of absorption optimizes the acoustics for speech. For musical performances, the necessary reverberation is applied electroacoustically by means of loudspeakers that radiate artificially reverberated sound from reverberation chambers in the palace's basement.

Some such electroacoustic means are pressed into service for corrective purposes, as in London's 3000-seat Royal Festival Hall, which lacked in low-frequency reverberation ("warmth"). Unbeknown to the public, the owners installed an "assisted resonance" system consisting of hundreds of microphones, amplifiers, filters, and loudspeakers acting as an active feedback for frequencies in the range from 58 to 700 Hz (Parkin & Morgan, 1970). As a result, the reverberation time was raised from about 1.4 sec to around 2 sec below 300 Hz. Another successful multichannel electroacoustic system for raising reverberation that comprised 54 microphones and 104 loudspeakers was installed in the 2000-seat Concert House at Stockholm (Dahlstadt, 1974).

Conversely, in halls with sufficient reverberation for music but too much for speech, public-address systems have been widely installed, especially in large lecture halls and churches. The amplified speech sound, with its high-frequency components emphasized and its low frequencies (<300 Hz) suppressed, should be focused by vertical loudspeaker columns into the audience area, where it is quickly absorbed (by clothes and hair) without being allowed to bounce around in the enclosure to interfere with good speech intelligibility. To preserve the illusion that the speech is emerging from the speakers' lips, the loudspeakers should be fed by speech that is delayed by about 10 msec relative to the direct sound (Kuttruff, 1979). Such a public-address system exploiting the Haas effect, which allows sounds to be reinforced by delayed sounds without interfering with the perceived direction, was first installed in St. Paul's Cathedral, London, in the early 1950s.

In all, it appears that electroacoustical systems to modify and improve prevailing acoustic conditions will play an increasingly important role in modern spaces for listening. The fast-advancing art of digital signal processing will further enlarge the scope of artificial ("virtual") sound environments.

V. CONCLUSION

Designing concert halls and opera houses to satisfy different musical tastes is difficult. The physics is very complex, and the subjective questions cannot be solved by mathematical formulas. An important tool for the proper design of halls for music is modeling—either by analog scale models or by digital computer models simulating the propagation of sound rays or stage-to-listeners transmission functions. Given the great accuracy, reproducibility, and flexibility of computers and their ever-increasing availability, digital simulation of concert hall acoustics can be expected to play an important role in future designs. For the subjective aspects, careful psychometric analysis, based on multidimensional scaling of listener preference, is required. Sound-diffusing surfaces based on number theory have proven of great value in redirecting sound into preferred lateral ("stereophonic") patterns.

APPENDIX

The probability that a given wave packet will hit a surface element dS with an angle of incidence between α and $\alpha + d\alpha$ in time t is given by

$$dn = (ct \cos \alpha d\alpha \, dS)/V \qquad (9)$$

where $ct \cos \alpha d\alpha \, dS/V$ is the volume of the (oblique) column above dS containing all the wave packets that will hit dS within a time interval of length t with an angle of incidence between α and $\alpha + d\alpha$. In order to get the desired probability we have to divide this volume by the total volume of the enclosed space—assuming, as we do, that the probability of finding a wave packet without prior knowledge is uniform throughout the entire space.

If, in addition, angles of incidence are uniformly distributed over the half sphere, averaging over α yields

$$\langle dn(t) \rangle = ct \, dS/4V. \qquad (10)$$

For the expected number of collisions with any of the surface elements, we have to integrate over the entire surface area. If the assumption of a directionally uniform distribution of the wave packets is fulfilled everywhere, then integration becomes trivial and the total expected number of surface collisions becomes

$$\langle n(t) \rangle = ct \, S/4V, \qquad (11)$$

which is the desired Equation 4.

REFERENCES

Ando, Y. (1985). *Concert hall acoustics.* Berlin: Springer.

Barrow, A., & Marshall, A. H. (1981). Spatial impression due to early lateral reflections in concert halls: The derivation of a physical measure. *Journal of the Acoustical Society of America, 77,* 211-232.

Beranek, L. L. (1962). *Music, acoustics and architecture.* New York: John Wiley.

Dahlstadt, S. (1974). Electronic reverberation equipment in the Stockholm concert hall. *Journal of the Audio Engineering Society, 22,* 627.

Kuttruff, H. (1979). *Room acoustics* (2nd ed.). London: Applied Science Publishers.

Parkin, P. H., & Morgan, K. (1970). "Assisted resonance" in the Royal Festival Hall, London: 1965–1969. *Journal of the Acoustical Society of America, 48,* 1025–1035.

Schroeder, M. R. (1962). Natural sounding artificial reverberation. *Journal of the Audio Engineering Society, 10,* 219–223 .

Schroeder, M. R. (1964). Improvement of acoustic feedback stability by frequency shifting. *Journal of the Acoustical Society of America, 36,* 1718–1724.

Schroeder, M. R. (1965). New method for measuring reverberation time. *Journal of the Acoustical Society of America, 37,* 409–412.

Schroeder, M. R. (1970). Digital simulation of sound transmission in reverberant spaces. *Journal of the Acoustical Society of America, 47,* 424–431.

Schroeder, M. R. (1973). Computer models of concert hall acoustics. *American Journal of Physics, 41,* 461–471.

Schroeder, M. R. (1986). *Number theory in science and communication* (2nd enlarged ed.). Berlin: Springer.

Schroeder, M. R. (1987). Statistical parameters of the frequency response curves of large rooms. *Journal of the Audio Engineering Society, 35,* 299–306 . (Original work published 1954)

Schroeder, M. R., Gottlob, D., & Siebrasse, K. F. (1974). Comparative study of European concert halls: Correlation of subjective preference with geometric and acoustic parameters. *Journal of the Acoustical Society of America, 56,* 1195–1201.

Schroeder, M. R., & Hackmann, D. (1980). Iterative calculation of reverberation time. *Acustica, 45,* 269–273

3

MUSIC AND THE AUDITORY SYSTEM

NORMAN M. WEINBERGER

Department of Psychobiology and
Center for the Neurobiology of Learning and Memory
University of California, Irvine
Irvine, California

I. INTRODUCTION

The goal of this chapter is to provide an introduction to and overview of the physiology of the auditory system as it relates to music. The dividing line between sensory processes and music is not fixed. To a large extent, this is because of the difficulty of providing definitions of sound that distinguish clearly between musical sounds and nonmusical sounds. Indeed, such a distinction may not be possible.

At present, no field of the neurophysiology of music really exists. This is in contrast to the well-developed field of the neuropsychology of music (see Chapter 17, this volume). Virtually all neurophysiological studies of the auditory system have been conducted in animal subjects and have been concerned with issues in sensory physiology, not explicitly with stimuli that are particularly relevant for the neural substrates of the perception of music. This is understandable on several grounds.

First, the development of auditory physiology was based on the use of simple sensory stimuli (e.g., isolated pure tones), based both on conceptual grounds and on the limitations of equipment that generated acoustic stimuli. Second, the neurosciences, like other biological sciences, have used mainly nonhuman subjects. Third, and related to the second point, the relevance of music and music behavior to nonhuman animals has been considered dubious at best (but see the final section of this article). Also, sensory physiology has traditionally used anesthetized subjects, largely for appropriate technical and ethical reasons. Thus, although one would like to know how musical stimuli are processed in the auditory system of waking, behaving humans, auditory physiology provides data mainly for the responses of neurons to nonmusical stimuli in anesthetized, nonhumans.[1]

---

[1]Hereafter, the term *animal(s)* will be used to refer to nonhuman animals.

47

However, since the first edition of *The Psychology of Music* was published in 1982, there have been several developments that provide some rationale for this chapter. First, the use of complex stimuli, including those that have direct relevance for music, has increased. This increase seems to be due to the ready availability of laboratory computers, which both permitted the investigation of longstanding issues best addressed with complex stimuli and motivated thinking about how the new technology could be exploited. Second, use of unanesthetized, behaving animal subjects has increased substantially. This development seems also to have benefited from some technical developments but more likely was motivated largely by a more dynamic view of brain function in which the full, or perhaps even the normal, aspects of brain physiology could not be studied in anesthetized subjects. Third, technological advances have made it possible to remotely record localized activity within the human auditory cortex in waking, behaving humans. The human auditory cortex has been studied intensively with magnetoencephalography (MEG), which will be explained in a later section.

The rest of this chapter consists of four parts: (a) a brief overview of the auditory pathway itself, (b) consideration of methodological aspects of neurobiological studies of music perception, (c) a selected review mainly of neurophysiological studies of relevance to the following elements of music—pitch, harmony/consonance, contour/melody, and rhythm/temporal processing, and (d) a concluding section concerning future directions.[2]

II. A BRIEF OVERVIEW OF THE AUDITORY PATHWAY

Numerous excellent reviews of the auditory pathway, for neuroanatomy, neurophysiology, and behavior have been published (e.g., Brugge & Reale, 1985; Helfert, Snead & Altschuler, 1991; Phillips, Reale & Brugge, 1991; Pickles, 1988; Whitfield, 1985). The present brief review is provided only for the convenience of readers and is not a substitute for detailed and authoritative sources.

A. ANATOMY OF THE AUDITORY PATHWAY

The auditory pathway consists of the outer, middle, and inner (i.e., cochlea) ears, the auditory nerve, nuclei at each level of the brain stem, and the several fields of the auditory cortex. The major brain-stem structures are as follows, starting with the termination of the auditory (VIIIth) nerve: cochlear nucleus, trap-

---

[2]Areas that concern the neurobiology of complex acoustic stimuli but are outside the scope of this chapter, and suggested readings, include the following: birdsong (Clayton & Bischof, 1990; Konishi, 1989; Nottebohm, 1991), species-specific acoustic communication (Gerhardt, 1988; Huber, 1983), primate vocalization (Kirzinger & Jurgens, 1991; Pelleg-Toiba & Wollberg, 1991; Yeshurun, Wollberg, & Dyn, 1989), and combination ("two-tone") neurons (Olsen, 1992). For an interesting and entertaining, but not necessarily highly relevant, account of W. A. Mozart and bird vocalization, see West and King (1990).

ezoid body, superior olivary nucleus, nuclei of the lateral lemniscus, the inferior colliculus, and the medial geniculate body. Each of these is further subdivided into constituent nuclei. The auditory cortex consist of several fields, including so-called primary and secondary fields.

Neural processing is both centripetal and centrifugal, that is, there is both an ascending and a descending auditory system; the latter is not discussed here (for review see Spangler & Warr, 1991). The vast majority of knowledge concerns the ascending system (Figure 1).

B. FUNCTIONAL ORGANIZATION OF THE AUDITORY PATHWAY

1. Single Neurons and Receptive Fields

Neurophysiological studies provide the basis for determining the functional organization of a neural system. Several types of neurophysiological phenomena could be used in the analysis of sensory systems. The electroencephalogram (EEG), while widely used in clinical applications, has limited utility because of its lack of a high degree of spatial and temporal resolution. Thus, the exact sites and times of responses to stimuli cannot easily be pinpointed. Evoked potentials are transient aspects of the EEG and have been used effectively to determine responses of auditory structures to sound. Averages of evoked potentials to many stimuli provide reliable measures of response. However, they also have limited spatial resolution. The responses of single neurons or groups of neurons that are recorded from the same microelectrode form the basis of most sensory physiological study. This approach has revealed the detailed and specific response properties of neurons while providing for accurate determination of the site of response within a given neural structure. Some workers hold that the responses of single neurons are necessary and sufficient to understand perceptual phenomena whereas others believe that the coordinated responses of groups ("networks," "assemblies," etc.) subserve perception. In the latter case, it is recognized that analysis of single neurons is of major importance, although it may not provide a comprehensive account of perception. Technologies for recording simultaneously from many neurons over a designated area of the brain are under development but are not yet in routine use.

Given the fact that the discharges of neurons form the basis of functional analysis, we must first consider a fundamental concept, that of the "receptive field" of a neuron. For present purposes, the receptive field (RF) of a neuron is defined by the set of peripheral sensory stimuli that modifies the discharges of the neuron under examination. Cells can have both excitatory and inhibitory RFs. For example, a neuron in the auditory cortex that responds best to a frequency of 10.0 kHz may be inhibited by adjacent higher or lower frequencies.

The "frequency tuning" of an auditory neuron is given by its response across frequency and also across intensity. The frequency that excites a cell at threshold is called the characteristic frequency (CF). At higher intensities, the CF is still

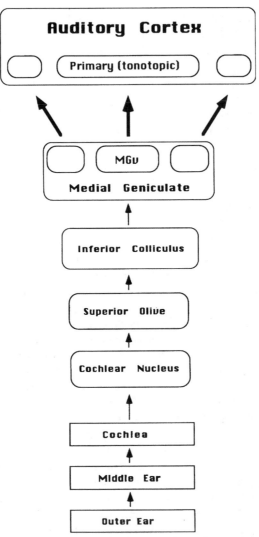

FIGURE 1   A highly simplified schematic of the ascending auditory pathway, emphasizing relationships between the auditory thalamus (medial geniculate body) and the auditory cortex. The auditory pathway is largely crossed above the cochlear nucleus (not shown). Throughout the auditory pathway, a "lemniscal" tonotopic representation of the acoustic frequency organization of the cochlea is "projected" to successive levels along the auditory neuraxis. At the thalamus, this tonotopic frequency map is found within the ventral medial geniculate nucleus (MGv), which is afferent to several similarly organized "primary auditory cortical fields. For example, the cortical field "A1" receives topographic projections from the MGv and exhibits a frequency map of low to high frequency along a caudal to rostral axis. Although this organization seems to exist in all cases, the amount of representation for behaviorally important frequencies in this primary field can be increased by learning (reviewed in Weinberger, 1995). The medial geniculate body and auditory cortex also contain acoustic processing regions that do not have simple frequency organizations (indicated by blank icons), and at the thalamic level, at least some of these are affected by learning.

effective but adjacent lower and higher frequencies also become effective. Thus, the range of frequency tuning generally becomes wider as intensity increases. The area outlined by the threshold at each intensity is called the "response area" or the frequency threshold curve (Figure 2). The frequency that produces the greatest response of a cell at a given level of stimulus intensity is referred to as the "best frequency" (BF); thus, at threshold, the CF and BF are identical. Figure 3 shows

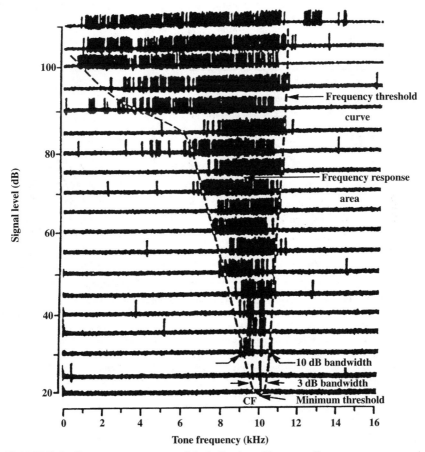

FIGURE 2   Frequency response area of single fiber in cochlear nerve. Frequency response area is mapped out by sweeping a continuous tone successively upward and downward in frequency, increasing the tone level by 5 dB at the end of each sweep. At the lowest intensities, the fiber responds to a narrow band of frequencies at 10 kHz. This is its *characteristic frequency* . At higher levels, the excitatory frequency band becomes progressively wider. For fibers of this high characteristic frequency, the response area is asymmetrical, extending on the low-frequency side to form a low-frequency "tail" above about 80 dB SPL. The boundary of the frequency response area is called the frequency threshold curve. (Guinea-pig: from Evans, 1972, p. 263. Reprinted by permission of The Physiological Society.)

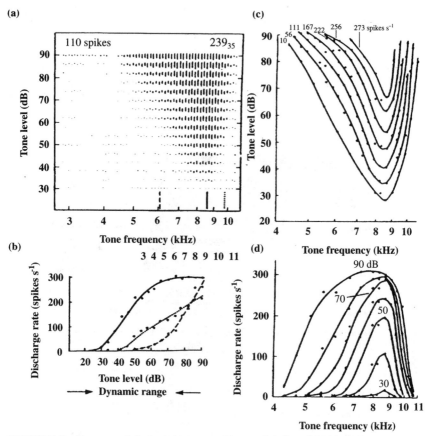

FIGURE 3 Response of single cochlear nerve fiber as a function of frequency and intensity. (a) Frequency "map" of fiber. The length of each vertical line indicates the average number of spikes evoked by a 50-msec stimulus at the frequency and intensity indicated by the center of the line. (b) Vertical "sections" through (a) at frequencies indicated by dashed, continuous, and dotted lines, respectively. These are known as rate-intensity or rate-level functions. Note restricted *dynamic range* over which the fiber can signal intensity at its characteristic frequency and *saturation* of discharge rate at high levels. (c) Isorate contours. Each contour indicates the tone frequencies and intensities evoking a given discharge rate. These are obtained by taking horizontal "sections" through a family of rate-level functions as in (b). (d) Isointensity contours, that is, horizontal "sections" through (a). Note flattening of the contours at the highest levels, because of saturation of the response, and a shift in frequency of maximum response. (Cat: From Evans, 1978, p. 369.)

different representations of the response of a single VIIIth nerve fiber. Cells can also have nonmonotonic intensity functions, so that they respond best to a small range of frequencies within a small range of intensities. In general, when experimenters refer to the "frequency tuning" of a neuron in the auditory system, they are designating the CF, that is, response at threshold. It is well to keep in mind that at stimulus levels within the usual range of perception and behavior, there is considerable overlap in the responses of neurons that are tuned to the same range of frequencies at perhaps 20–50 dB above threshold.

Individual neurons are also sensitive to variation in frequency. One such variation is frequency modulation (FM), consisting of increases or decreases in the frequency of a continual stimulus, that is, a "frequency glide." Some cells in the auditory cortex respond best to FM stimuli, and may even show "directional specificity," that is, response to an ascending but not to a descending FM stimulus (for review, see Whitfield, 1985). Another type of variation is amplitude modulation (AM), which is discussed in Section VIII,A.

2. "Mappings" of Parameters of Sound

Given that many cells in the auditory system exhibit frequency tuning, the question arises as to whether frequency tuning is represented in a systematic manner. Indeed, the ascending auditory pathway has a "tonotopic" organization from the cochlea through the primary and some other fields of the auditory cortex. That is, the physical stimulus attribute of frequency (for pure tones) activates neighboring regions of the cochlea and neighboring neurons within the brain stem nuclei and parts of the auditory cortex. Thus, the attribute of "frequency" is said to be "mapped" in the auditory system. For example, within the primary auditory cortex (AI) of the cat, which is the most extensively studied subject, the frequency representation is from low to high frequencies along the posterior to anterior axis. In its adjacent anterior auditory field (AAF), the frequency representation is a mirror image (Figure 1). Maps of frequency are more complex topographically within the brain stem nuclei but the same principle holds: a systematic organization of frequencies is present in each part of the classical or so-called "lemniscal" ascending auditory system. This is in distinction to the "lemniscal-adjunct" parts of the system, to which reference will be made later.

One factor that is not generally appreciated is that the frequency map is best seen at threshold. As pointed out earlier, as stimulus intensity increases, the frequency bandwidth of response of a cell increases. Thus, at a stimulus level of 90 dB, a neuron tuned to 10.0 kHz might respond over a range of at least two octaves (e.g., 5–20 kHz). Maximal discharge may still be at or near the CF of 10.0 kHz across intensity, but the amount of cortical tissue that is activated by a suprathreshold pure tone can be quite large (Taniguchi, Horikawa, Moriyama, & Nasu, 1992).

Why the frequency of vibrations of air should be mapped in the auditory system in a systematic and easily discernible manner is unclear. However, such mappings are found for other acoustic parameters (e.g., binaural processes) and in other sensory modalities, most notably in the visual and somatosensory systems. Therefore, one or more fundamental principles are probably responsible. However, consideration of this issue lies beyond the scope of this chapter.

The auditory pathway also exhibits functional organization for other attributes of acoustic stimulation. Chief among these attributes is the location of sound sources. Input from the two ears converges first at the level of the superior olivary complex. At this and higher levels of the pathway, neurons are sensitive to cues that are used to locate sound sources. These cues include differences in the time of arrival of acoustic stimulation at the two ears, differences in intensity, and differences in phase (studied by the use of pure tones). Maps of sound sources in space have been sought, and there is excellent evidence for such maps in the inferior and superior colliculi (the latter being an important midbrain region in which auditory and visual inputs converge; Knudsen, 1991). The presence of "sound in space" maps at the level of the auditory cortex is more controversial.

Current research also concerns the extent to which there are mappings of features such as frequency modulation, the amplitude (sound level) of stimuli (so-called ampliotopic organization), and sharpness of frequency tuning (for review see Schreiner, 1992). Within bats that use biosonar, highly specialized regions have been identified for stimulus parameters concerned with the location of prey (for a review, see Suga, 1990).

A potentially important distinction is that between maps that reflect actual stimulus parameters and maps that use stimulus parameters to construct representations of acoustically important features. For example, tonotopic maps reflect the stimulus parameter of frequency, which is represented at the level of the sensory receptor itself, that is, at the cochlea. In this sense, tonotopic maps within the auditory system can be thought to represent a parameter of the energy that impinges on the auditory receptive apparatus. In contrast, maps of sound location in space do not map parameters such as intensity of sound at the ear but rather compare these parameters at the two ears to construct ("compute") a map of sound in space. The existence of such computational maps (Knudsen, 1991) greatly increases the possibilities of many yet undiscovered mappings. Moreover, it suggests that even higher order representations may be constructed within the auditory system. Some of these higher order mappings could be important for music, for example, maps involved in the analysis of periodic changes in signal amplitude, as discussed in Section VIII,A.

3. Attention and Learning in the Auditory System

Sensory systems, including the auditory system, are involved in attention and learning, particularly as studied in sensory cortex. Thus, even a brief review of the auditory pathway cannot be confined to sensory physiological studies.

C. ATTENTION

Systematic studies of selective attention in monkeys have revealed a considerable dependence of neuronal discharge in the auditory cortex on task variables. That is, responses to the same physical acoustic stimulus (usually pure tones) is a function not only of the physical parameters of the stimulus but also of whether or not the subject is selectively attending, preparing to make a specified behavioral response, and so on. For example, the discharge to an attended stimulus can greatly exceed the response to that identical stimulus when it is not attended. The effects of attention extend to all major characteristics of neuronal response: probability of response, rate of evoked discharge, latency of discharge, and pattern of discharge. Although some effects may be attributed to the overall level of arousal, selective attention itself is definitely a major factor in neuronal response to acoustic stimuli. Reviews of two extensive research programs have been provided by Goldstein, Benson, and Hienz (1982) and Miller, Pfingst, and Ryan (1982).

D. LEARNING

Early studies of learning, using mainly Pavlovian (classical) conditioning and also instrumental tasks in animals, revealed that responses in the auditory cortex to an initially neutral sound developed systematic changes (e.g., increased responses) as the sound was associated with a reward or punishment and acquired the ability to elicit a conditioned behavior (reviewed in Weinberger & Diamond, 1987). Such findings present a challenge to views of sensory systems as detectors of particular stimulus features because the response of a cell is governed not only by the physical parameters of a stimulus but also by its acquired meaning. However, learning effects might be important for understanding the neural bases of perception.

The actual tuning (frequency-receptive fields) of cells in the primary auditory cortex is altered by learning. Specifically, responses to the frequency of the training stimulus (conditioned stimulus, CS, in classical conditioning) are increased while responses to other frequencies are generally decreased (Figure 4). This CS-specific RF plasticity is associative (Figure 5), develops rapidly, is discriminative, and lasts for weeks (Figure 6; reviewed in Weinberger et al., 1990a; Weinberger, Ashe & Edeline, 1994; see also Edeline & Weinberger, 1993; Edeline, Pham, & Weinberger 1993; Weinberger, Javid, & Lepan, 1993). These findings suggested that the actual frequency map on the auditory cortex would be changed by learning, with important frequencies receiving greater representation than unimportant frequencies (Weinberger et al., 1990a). Evidence in support of this prediction has been reported in a study of discrimination training in the monkey (Recanzone, Schreiner, & Merzenich, 1993).

In a complementary manner, habituation due to repeated presentation of the same tone frequency produces a highly frequency specific decrement in response at the repeated frequency with side-band enhancement at adjacent nonrepeated frequencies (Condon & Weinberger, 1991).

Although studies of neuronal discharges provide fine-grain temporal information about neuronal activity, they provide little information about the spatial distribution of effects of experience. The use of metabolic markers of neuronal activity, however, can be applied to the entire brain. The gain in spatial information is at the expense of temporal resolution. Ultimately, a combination of both techniques is likely to prove most enlightening.

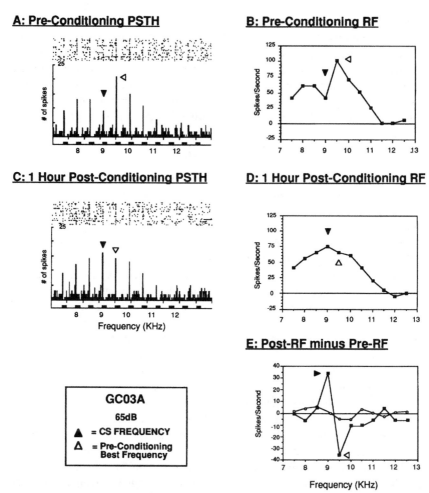

A: Pre-Conditioning PSTH

B: Pre-Conditioning RF

C: 1 Hour Post-Conditioning PSTH

D: 1 Hour Post-Conditioning RF

E: Post-RF minus Pre-RF

GC03A

65dB

▲ = CS FREQUENCY

△ = Pre-Conditioning
Best Frequency

FIGURE 4   Classical conditioning can result in the conditioned stimulus (CS) frequency becoming the best frequency. Preconditioning (A) and 1-hr postconditioning (C) poststimulus time histograms (PSTHs) and raster show that conditioning caused the CS frequency (9.0 kHz, filled arrowhead) to become the best frequency. Receptive fields (RFs) are quantified in (B) and (D). Receptive field difference function (E) reveals a maximal increase at the CS frequency and maximal decrease at the pretraining best frequency (9.5 kHz, open arrowhead). (Reprinted from *Brain Research, 536,* Bakin, J. S. & Weinberger, N. M., Classical conditioning induces CS-specific receptive field plasticity in the auditory cortex of the guinea pig, p. 276, Copyright 1990, with permission from Elsevier Science.)

Metabolic studies of the involvement of the auditory system in learning have been performed by the laboratories of Gonzalez-Lima and Scheich.[3] They have found CS-specific increases in metabolic activity due to classical conditioning using tonal stimuli in the auditory cortex (Gonzalez-Lima & Scheich, 1986) and at

[3]For studies of neural mechanisms in acoustic imprinting in birds, see Scheich (1987).

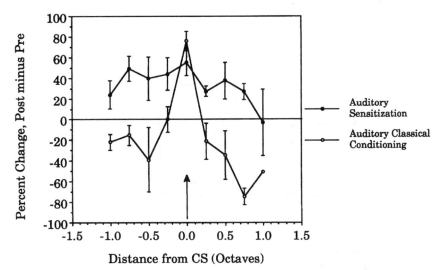

FIGURE 5 Comparison of the effects of conditioning and sensitization on auditory cortex receptive fields in the guinea pig. Group receptive field difference functions for classical conditioning (n = 7;
open circles) and auditory sensitization (n = 7; filled circles) reveal that although both treatments increase responses at the frequency of the conditioned stimulus (CS, arrow), they differ in the overall
effect on the receptive field. Conditioning produces a highly specific increase in the receptive field such
that only the frequency of the CS is increased whereas the responses to almost all other frequencies are
decreased. In contrast, sensitization training with an auditory CS produces a broad-band increase in
response magnitude across a large frequency range. (Reprinted from *Brain Research, 577*, Bakin, J. S.,
Lepan, B., & Weinberger, N. M., Sensitization induced receptive field plasticity in the auditory cortex
is independent of CS-modality, p. 230, Copyright 1992, with permission from Elsevier Science.)

all other levels of the auditory system with the possible exception of the medial
geniculate nucleus (Gonzalez-Lima & Agudo, 1990; Gonzalez-Lima & Scheich,
1984a, 1984b) . Selective decreases in the thalamocortical auditory system were
found in studies of long-term habituation (Gonzalez-Lima, Finkenstadt & Ewert,
1989a, 1989b).

Differences in both training conditions and types of neural data have not yet
permitted complete reconciliation of the neurophysiological and the metabolic
studies. Nonetheless, that learning greatly modifies the processing of sound in the
auditory system seems well established.

In providing a background for the review of music and auditory neurophysiology, it is important to keep in mind the distinction, made above, between "lemniscal" and "lemniscal adjunct" regions of the auditory pathway. In contrast to the
lemniscal pathway, lemniscal-adjunct regions do not contain tonotopic maps, although they could contain maps of acoustic features that have not yet been studied,
perhaps of a high level of complexity.

This distinction has been explored mainly in the thalamocortical part of the
pathway, that is, for parts of the medial geniculate nucleus and certain auditory
cortical fields. Briefly, the medial geniculate consists of three major subdivisions,

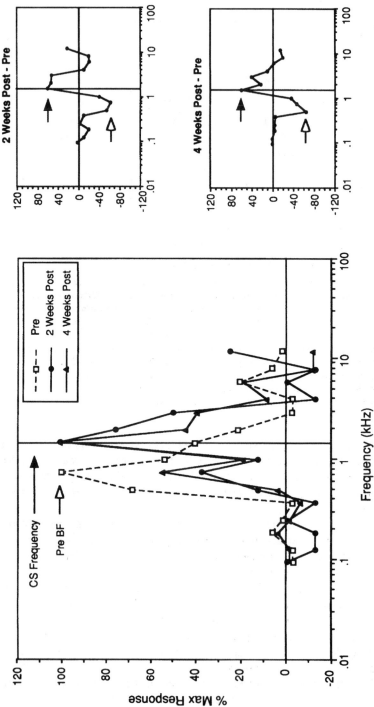

FIGURE 6 Frequency receptive fields (60 dB) illustrating very long term retention of more than 4 weeks and complete shift of tuning. In this experiment, animals were trained while awake, but receptive fields were obtained while they were anesthetized. Pretraining best frequency (BF) = 0.75 kHz, conditioned stimulus (CS) frequency = 1.5 kHz. Note the shift of tuning so that the CS frequency became the new BF, shown here at 14 and 32 days posttraining, the last recording available for this subject. Ordinate is

the ventral (MGv), the dorsal (MGd), and the medial/magnocellular (MGm) (Figure 1). The MGv is the lemniscal component, being tonotopically organized and projecting in a point-to-point manner to fields of the auditory cortex that also possess a tonotopic organization. The MGd projects to so-called secondary (nontonotopic) auditory cortical fields. The MGm projects to all fields of the auditory cortex, both tonotopic and nontonotopic. Neither the MGd nor the MGm has a tonotopic map, and cells in the MGm are very broadly tuned and have complex frequency-receptive fields. Moreover, MGm cells are labile.

A further distinction between the MGv and the MGm may prove instructive. First, although both project to the primary auditory cortex and another tonotopic field, the AAF, their laminar targets differ. The MGv provides precise topographically organized frequency information to Layer IV of the AI and the AAF. In contrast, the MGm provides diffuse input to Layer I of the AI and the AAF (as well as to all other auditory cortical fields). Second, they are differentially plastic when studied in animal learning experiments. The MGv exhibits little or no change in discharges to a CS during learning; in contrast, the MGm *rapidly develops physiological plasticity* during conditioning (Gabriel, Miller & Saltwick, 1976; Ryugo & Weinberger, 1978; Weinberger, 1982). Thus, learning alters processing of the CS in the nonlemniscal MGm nucleus but *not* in the lemniscal MGv. Neurophysiological studies of the medial geniculate nucleus suggest that receptive field plasticity in the auditory cortex is not simply "projected" to the cortex from the medial geniculate because (a) there is only transient and very limited learning-induced RF plasticity in the MGv (Edeline & Weinberger, 1991) and (b) although enduring RF plasticity is found in the MGm, its neurons are much more broadly tuned than are cells in the auditory cortex (Edeline & Weinberger, 1992). A model of how MGm plasticity could contribute more specific changes in the frequency tuning of cortical cells has been proposed (Weinberger et al., 1990 a, 1990b; see also Edeline & Weinberger, 1991, 1992).

E. SUMMARY

In summary, the auditory system is dynamic. The processing of acoustic stimulation, particularly in the auditory cortex, is not limited to the passive detection of acoustic features. Rather, the responses of neurons are also affected by attention and by learning. Moreover, the effects of these processes can be quite prominent. Therefore, the processing of music in the auditory system may well engage attentive or learning processes or both. Additionally, memory for music is likely to

---

percentage of maximal response, normalized within session by expressing response rate to each frequency as a percentage of response to the frequency that elicited the maximum response; therefore 100% indicates the best frequency for each session. Normalization was done because absolute rate of discharge could vary over sessions as absolute depth of anesthesia may not have been constant. (Reprinted with permission from Weinberger, N. M., Javid, R., & Lepan, B, *Proceedings of the National Academy of Sciences,* 90. Copyright 1993, National Academy of Sciences, U.S.A.)

involve the auditory system in ways that transcend the physical analysis of musical sounds.

III. EXPERIMENTAL APPROACHES IN THE NEUROBIOLOGY OF MUSIC

In general, one would like to understand the brain mechanisms that underlie the perception of music. One way of approaching this problem is to locate neurons, if any, that respond selectively to the basic elements of music. This will be the main focus of this article. However, the larger experimental context should be made explicit because it reveals that no single type of approach or finding can provide a full account of the brain mechanisms underlying the perception of music.

The type of research program and findings that might be able to help provide a comprehensive understanding of brain mechanisms in music perception would be faced with the same problems that confront all lines of inquiry concerning the brain mechanisms underlying a behavioral or psychological phenomenon. Although a full discussion of relevant issues cannot be provided here, it is important to note that neither lesions nor neurophysiological findings alone can provide a truly satisfactory account.

A comprehensive line of inquiry would probably have to include the following components: (a) Behavioral characterization of the phenomenon under study. (b) Neurophysiological determination of the relationships between the responses of specified brain regions and the various stimuli and conditions that produce the musical entity under examination. Ideally, these two steps would be accomplished concurrently, within the same subjects. The results would be a set of relationships that would reveal the extent to which behavioral and neural responses to the musical entity were *correlated*. (c) If significant correlations were found, a further step would be to determine if there were a *causal* relationship between neural responses and behavior. For example, if the latency of the neural responses were shorter than the latency of the behavioral/psychological responses, then one could determine if the neural responses were predictive of behavior on a trial by trial basis. (d) Further efforts should then be made to *disrupt* any close relationships to determine the extent to which the neurons in question are *both necessary and sufficient for the perception*. Standard methods include lesions, ablations, or reversible inactivation of the brain region under examination. Such interventions would have to be extremely limited in the case of human subjects. Thus, only reversible inactivations would be acceptable and it might not be possible to attain detailed localization. If the neural substrates of the perception are distributed rather than highly localized, the difficulty of achieving success would be significantly increased.

Of course, the initial observations could as appropriately begin with findings from brain damage, as is the case in neuropsychological investigations. But the major point is that lesions/brain damage data alone can only locate necessary and sufficient brain structures. They cannot provide an account of how the structures and their constituent neurons accomplish perception. Similarly, neurophysiological studies alone are not adequate to determine the necessity and sufficiency of the brain regions under study.

Although this type of research program is formidable, it is feasible. For example, Suga and his colleagues have been concerned with the brain mechanisms underlying prey catching in bats that use biosonar. Suga and colleagues have achieved considerable success using this type of experimental approach (e.g., Riquimaroux, Gaioni, & Suga, 1991).

IV. THE AUDITORY SYSTEM AND ELEMENTS OF MUSIC

We turn now to the following elements of music—pitch, harmony/consonance, contour/melody, and rhythm/temporal processing. However, before we consider the neurophysiological literature, several caveats should be kept in mind.

first, most of the findings reviewed here are from animal subjects, and most of these were studied while they were under general anesthesia. Second, most neurophysiological data were obtained from recordings of the discharges of single neurons or neuron clusters. However, musically relevant phenomena might be organized at a higher level, for example, in local or distributed networks of cells. Third, very few auditory physiology studies have been concerned directly with music or musical attributes. Therefore, the findings summarized in this section have been gleaned from publications that have come to the writer's attention by one means or another. These limitations render the following discussion idiosyncratic rather than systematic. Fourth, the findings are not necessarily limited to music but may also apply to the processing of other complex stimuli, including vocalizations and language. Fifth, the literature review was completed in 1993.

V. PITCH

Of all acoustic stimulus parameters, frequency has been studied far more extensively than any other stimulus parameter. As pointed out earlier, there is a systematic organization with respect to acoustic frequency in the cochlea; the basal portions of the basilar membrane respond best to high frequencies and the apical parts of this membrane respond to low frequencies. There is a point-to-point projection from the basilar membrane to the cochlear nucleus and because the pattern of termination of VIIIth nerve fibers within this nucleus maintains the frequency organization of the basilar membrane, frequency is "mapped" in the cochlear nucleus. Moreover, frequency is mapped at all higher levels of the auditory system, including the auditory cortex.

Strictly speaking, this type of organization is "cochleotopic." In fact, electrical stimulation of different parts of the basilar membrane was one of the first means by which this systematic mapping was discovered (Walzl & Woolsey, 1943). Nevertheless, the term "tonotopic," that is, "frequency-topic," has been applied almost universally. It has been argued that, in a strict sense, this term is an interpretation rather than a definition because this organization has been explored and revealed by the use of pure-tone stimuli alone. In contrast, the map might be one of *pitch* rather than *frequency*, but without the use of complex stimuli, such as harmonic series lacking the fundamental frequency, it is unwarranted to conclude that frequency rather than pitch is the mapped parameter (Pantev, Hoke, Lutkenhoner, & Lehnertz, 1989; Schwarz & Tomlinson, 1990).

In this section, we address the following questions about the auditory system and pitch, confining the discussion largely to the auditory cortex, for which both human and animal data exist.

1. Do animals perceive pitch rather than only frequency?
2. Is the auditory cortex necessary for, or at least implicated in, the perception of pitch? (This question is addressed for humans in Chapter 17, this volume.)
3. Is "tonotopic" organization based on frequency or based on pitch?
4. Do single neurons encode pitch?

A. DO ANIMALS PERCEIVE PITCH?

This question has been addressed by investigating periodicity ("virtual") pitch, as illustrated in the following example. Cats were first trained to discriminate between two stimuli consisting of different harmonic series, each lacking their fundamental frequencies, in a shock-avoidance task. A specified response to one stimulus series was rewarded (shock avoidance), while responses to the other series were punished. (The harmonic series used give rise to periodicity pitch in humans.) Later, the subjects were tested for transfer by being presented on different trials with the fundamental frequency of each harmonic series. The animals showed a high degree of transfer to the fundamental frequencies, that is, discriminative behavior to the fundamental frequencies that was similar to behavior for their respective harmonic series. This was taken as evidence for periodicity pitch. Additional controls showed that behavior was governed by the pitch relationships rather than, for example, by responding to novel stimuli (Chung & Colavita, 1976).

Periodicity pitch has been demonstrated in the cat (Chung & Colavita, 1976; Heffner & Whitfield, 1976), birds (Cynx & Shapiro, 1986), and monkeys (Schwarz & Tomlinson, 1990). Interested readers are referred to the original publications for details. That animals have the capacity to make discriminations based on pitch provides a basis for neurobiological studies in which the effects of lesions and the exploration of cellular responses to pitch can be studied.

B. IS THE AUDITORY CORTEX NECESSARY FOR THE PERCEPTION OF PITCH?

There are positive answers to this question. In humans, for example, Zatorre (1988) found that pitch perception was impaired for right temporal lesions in non-musicians; left temporal lesions did not impair pitch judgments (see Chapter 17, this volume, for an authoritative review of this issue).

The only animal study that appears to have addressed this question is attributable to Whitfield (1980). In a very clever study, subjects were first trained to discriminate harmonic series without the fundamental frequency and also to discriminate various pure tones. As pointed out earlier, they were able to demonstrate perception of the missing fundamental (Heffner & Whitfield, 1976). The animals then received bilateral lesions of the auditory cortex. Thereafter, they were unable to perceive the missing fundamental. However, basic sensory, motor, motivational, and mnenomic capabilities were intact because the could still respond correctly to the pure-tone stimuli. In short, they could perceive and accurately respond to absolute frequencies but not to pitch as indexed by the missing fundamental.

C. IS TONOTOPIC ORGANIZATION BASED ON FREQUENCY OR ON PITCH?

No animal studies have been done of this issue. However, there are several electrophysiological studies of the human auditory cortex, and among these, the issue of tonotopic organization based on frequency vs. pitch has been the subject of explicit investigation. Before we review these findings, it will be helpful to have some background information on the investigation of the physiology of the human auditory cortex.

MEG is now widely used to record the responses of the auditory cortex to sound stimuli. This technique is based on the fact that changes in neuronal potentials across cell membranes are accompanied by the flow of currents, and current flows induce magnetic fields. A major advantage of MEG over EEG is that, unlike changes in voltage, changes in magnetic dipoles are relatively unaffected by the intervening tissue, including bone and scalp. MEG provides better localization of the source(s) of activity. However, because of the very small magnetic fields induced by neuronal activity and because of ambient magnetic fields, special techniques must be used. Supercooled magnetometers ("superconducting quantum interference device," or SQUID) of one to several channels have been used successfully. The SQUID is placed near the head, often in a magnetically shielded room. Readers are referred to Hari (1990) for an excellent and comprehensive review of the use of MEG in studies of the human auditory cortex.

MEG provides both good temporal and spatial resolution. An important advantage of MEG is that it can localize sites of activity at various depths below the surface of the skull. This is of particular importance in the case of humans because the primary auditory cortex lies in Heschel's gyrus, which is within the Sylvian fissure. The surface of primary auditory cortex thus extends more or less perpendicular to the surface of the temporal bone, in depth within the fissure.

The evoked MEG response to sound has several components. A voltage change with a latency of approximately 100 msec (termed the N100m) appears to have a tonotopic distribution, as first reported by Romani, Williamson, Kaufman, and Brenner (1982). Several other laboratories also reported a systematic spatial distribution of the N100m as a function of stimulus frequency (Arlinger et al., 1982; Eberling, Bak, Kofoed, Lebech, & Saermark, 1982; Hari & Makela, 1986; Kaukoranta, Hari, & Lounasmsmaa, 1987; Makela, Hari, & Linnankivi, 1987; Pantev et al., 1988; Yamamoto, Uemura, & Llinas, 1992). A study of cerebral blood flow using positron emission tomography also supports a tonotopic organization (Lauter, Herscovitch, Formby, & Raichle, 1985). Unfortunately, there is not yet universal agreement on the detailed location of the various frequency responses in the auditory cortex. Failure to find a tonotopic organization has also been reported (Pelizzone, Williamson, & Kaufman, 1985). It seems likely that differences in stimulus parameters and other technical details using the still-developing MEG technology may be responsible for the current lack of agreement (Hari, 1990). At this point, it seems likely that the human auditory cortex, particularly its primary field on Heschel's gyrus, has a tonotopic organization, the details of which need to be worked out.

In any event, Pantev and associates (Pantev et al., 1989, 1991) have moved on to a question of critical interest for this chapter, that is, whether or not the tonotopic organization reflects an organization for frequency or for pitch. They presented three types of stimuli: a complex stimulus consisting of the fourth through seventh harmonics of a fundamental of 250 Hz, a pure tone of 250 Hz, and a pure tone of 1000 Hz. To make certain that the harmonic series did not also stimulate the basilar membrane at the 250-Hz locus, they used continuous narrowband masking noise centered on 250 Hz.

Pantev and associates reported that the locus of response to the harmonic series was at the same point as the locus for responses to the fundamental frequency of 250 Hz. However, the locus for responses to 1000 Hz was at a different site. The authors concluded that the tonotopic organization of the human auditory cortex is actually an organization based on pitch rather than frequency. The different loci were confirmed by magnetic resonance imaging recordings to lie in the primary auditory cortex on Heschel's gyrus (Pantev et al., 1991).

A case report of electrical stimulation of the brain is taken as support for pitch organization in the human. Bhatnagar, Andy, and Linville (1989) found that stimulation of the supratemporal gyrus (not primary auditory cortex but auditory "association" cortex) in a patient undergoing neurosurgical procedures resulted in verbal reports of percepts of higher or lower sounds ("vowel-like") at two different loci along the supratemporal gyrus. However, the perceptions could not be replicated at both loci.

In summary, few direct data concerning pitch organization in the auditory cortex are available, and those data are from studies of humans. The MEG study of

Pantev and associates is certainly intriguing and provides stronger evidence of electrical stimulation than does the case report. Clearly, confirmation and additional data are needed. In particular, it will be important to investigate the possible organization for pitch using more frequencies over a wider range.

D. DO SINGLE NEURONS ENCODE PITCH?

Animal studies provide a potential answer to the question of whether single neurons respond to pitch, rather than merely to absolute frequency. However, there appear to be few directly relevant studies.

An enduring question, beyond the scope of this chapter, is the extent to which the auditory system uses spatial information ("place" on the basilar membrane) vs. temporal information (temporal pattern of auditory nerve discharges) to construct the acoustic environment. Recent findings, in distinction to traditional views, provide evidence that the pitch of complex sounds is fully coded in the distribution of spike intervals across the fibers of the auditory nerve (Cariani, Delgutte, & Kiang 1992; see details as later published in Cariani & Delgutte, 1996a, 1996b). The interpretation in terms of pitch rather than frequency is based on the use of various complex stimuli that produce the same pitch judgments in humans. Cariani et al. reported that different stimuli that give rise to the same perception of pitch produce the same pattern of discharge across the auditory nerve. The issue of whether single nerve fibers code pitch does not arise for the VIIIth nerve because the frequency spectrum of complex stimuli that give rise to a certain pitch generally exceeds the tuning bandwidth of a single fiber. However, within the central auditory system, particularly for broadly tuned cells, the question can be posed to single neurons.

Schreiner's laboratory has reported that many cells in the dorsal part of the AI of the cat are "multipeaked" (Schreiner & Sutter, 1992; Sutter & Schreiner, 1991). That is, they exhibit frequency-selective responses at threshold to more than one frequency, most often two but sometimes three frequencies. According to our prior review of the auditory system, such cells are said to have more than one CF at threshold. Another way to view the responses of cells is to determine their rate of discharge across frequency, at a single stimulus intensity level. As pointed out previously, this constitutes the frequency receptive field at that level. Schreiner and Sutter found that, in contrast to cells in the middle of the AI, which have a single peak (inverted V-shaped receptive field), neurons in the dorsal part of this field have more than one peak (e.g., "M-shaped" receptive fields if tuned best to two frequencies).

That many cells are tuned to more than one frequency raises the question of whether, for a given cell, these frequencies are related harmonically. The answer seems to be "yes." For all multipeaked neurons, the median ratio of CFs (higher frequency to lower frequency) was 1.56 (Sutter & Schreiner, 1991). This is very close to a ratio of 1.50. which corresponds to the ratio of the third to the second harmonic. This finding suggests that multipeaked cells would respond particularly well, perhaps maximally, to the simultaneous presentation of the second and third harmonic. Unfortunately, harmonic stimuli were not used in these studies.

A direct search for neurons that respond to pitch has been reported by Schwarz and Tomlinson (1990), using waking monkeys that had exhibited pitch perception in a previous behavioral study of the missing fundamental (Tomlinson & Schwarz, 1988). They used a variety of stimuli, including fundamental frequencies alone and harmonic series that consisted of, for example, the third through eighth harmonics. These stimuli differed across neurons, depending on each cell's CF and range of frequency response. The CFs of cells ranged from 100 Hz to 18.0 kHz, thus covering most of the audible spectrum, and the sample size was large, consisting of well-characterized responses of 251 single neurons.

The authors failed to find a single neuron that responded to a harmonic series in a manner closely similar to the way it responded to the fundamental frequency of the harmonic series used. They concluded that pitch is not likely to be represented in the primary auditory cortex and other adjacent fields that they studied.

Schwarz and Tomlinson criticized the findings of Pantev et al. (1989) on several grounds, which are of sufficient interest to warrant consideration. First, the authors believed that Pantev et al. did not adequately demonstrate that their MEG responses were generated in the AI. Second, they suggested that responses to the harmonic series were caused by the narrowband noise that was used to mask the missing fundamental because "noise was almost certainly changed when the test tone was switched on and off...." Third, given the reasonable assumption that the primary auditory cortex of the monkey and the human are very similar in functional organization, and given their negative findings with more direct methods than MEG, Schwarz and Tomlinson believe that their findings are more definitive than those of Pantev et al.

Regarding the first issue of locus, Schwarz and Tomlinson did not have the benefit of the magnetic resonance imaging data that were published after their article appeared. With reference to the possible response to the noise masker, the article by Pantev et al. clearly states that the noise was on continuously, so it seems unlikely that the responses to the harmonic complex included responses to the onset of the masker. Concerning the more direct measures of neurons from the cortex vs. MEG, there appears to be no dispute. However, the failure to find single neurons that respond to pitch does not necessarily imply that there is no pitch organization in the AI. Although it is true that the MEG response reflects the synchronous discharge of many neurons, it may be that pitch is a property of a group or network of cells, which may respond together, but none of which alone codes for pitch.

In summary, the scant cellular data on single neurons and pitch, although suggestive (Sutter & Schreiner, 1991), more strongly indicate that single neurons in the auditory cortex do not respond to pitch (Schwarz & Tomlinson, 1990). In contrast, evidence suggests that the human primary auditory cortex is organized according to pitch rather than frequency (Pantev et al., 1989, 1991). At this point, no definitive conclusions can be drawn. It may be more important that direct questions concerning pitch are finally being addressed. With additional research both with humans and animals, the answers are likely to become more consistent.

VI. HARMONY, CONSONANCE

Neurophysiological studies of pitch, although scant, can be discerned by the use of two or more types of stimuli that give rise to the same pitch, as defined behaviorally. However, in the case of harmony, the guidance is not so straightforward. Strictly speaking, harmony involves processes that are produced by three or more simultaneous tones. For relevance to music, presumably these tones ought to have interval relationships that are recognized in Western music. There appear to be no such relevant neurophysiological studies. Several studies in which harmonic series were used were discussed in the Section V. Instead, in this section, we will consider the only study known to us that specifically concerns musical consonance and dissonance neurophysiologically, which we take to be related to issues in the study of harmony.

Tramo, Cariani, and Delgutte (1992) studied the discharges of single fibers in the auditory nerve of the anesthetized cat, in response to musical intervals composed of pure tones vs. harmonic complex tones. Their framework was the attribution of tonal dissonance to changes in amplitude of components of a complex signal that may produce the sensation of roughness and beats. Suprathreshold stimuli (60 dB SPL) were presented as (a) two simultaneous pure tones whose components comprised a major fifth (ratio of 1:2), a major fourth (2:3), a minor second (15:16), and the tritone (32:45) or (b) two simultaneous complex tones having fundamental frequencies at the same ratios, each composed of six harmonics. A beating pattern[4] of nerve discharge was produced by the pure-tone minor second, which was the most dissonant of the pure-tone intervals, but not for other pure-tone intervals. Beating patterns for harmonic complex intervals were produced when the fiber's CF was near two closely spaced component frequencies. For the complex minor second, beating patterns were found over the full frequency range of the nerve. The most consonant harmonic complex intervals (the fourth and fifth), produced only weak beating patterns, and these were limited to fibers whose CFs were near the most closely spaced component frequencies. The complex tritone showed beating patterns over an intermediate number of CFs. Complementary findings were reported by Delgutte and Cariani (1992).

Overall, the findings indicate that there is a high correlation between tonal dissonance of musical intervals and the total number of auditory nerve fibers that show beating patterns. The authors concluded that the findings support the view

---

[4]Beating patterns could be determined by analysis of the poststimulus time histogram, which provides the number of discharges across time during stimulus presentation and also the autocorrelogram, in which all the intervals between discharges in a spike train are correlated with each other. Interested readers are referred to the original paper and to standard references on auditory neurophysiology, such as Pickles (1988).

that "the dissonance of complex tones reflects the sum of the dissonances of adjacent partials."

This study (see also Cariani & Delgutte, 1996a, 1996b) is distinctive in having a direct musical rationale and framework in the field of auditory neurophysiology. It reflects a welcome, and one hopes increasing, trend. It also provides a rare case in which perception and neurophysiology in music are very closely related. If these findings are substantiated, it would appear that at least one aspect of consonance/dissonance is determined at the most peripheral level of the central auditory system.

VII. CONTOUR, MELODY

Contour refers to the overall pattern of frequency change in a melody. Contour is conserved even when the sizes of successive intervals are changed, if the order of successive increases and decreases in frequency is maintained. For a melody to be the same, of course, contour must be conserved and so must the original intervals.

Neurophysiological studies of melody might entail manipulations such as determining the responses of the auditory system to a melody before and after its transposition to another key. For single unit studies, such transposition would presumably have to maintain the frequency spectrum of the melody within the frequency-receptive field of the cell. In any event, no such studies have been found. Appropriate studies of contour might maintain contour while altering intervals, to determine if the overall direction of frequency change is "detected" by neurons. Although such studies have not been found, two experiments have used tonal sequences containing the same tones in permuted orders and determined the responses of single neurons to the same frequencies within the sequences as a function of this manipulation. These studies, reviewed later, seem most closely to related to the musical element of contour but may also be relevant to melody. Their complicated experimental designs require some detailed presentation.

Weinberger and McKenna (1988) and McKenna, Weinberger, and Diamond (1989) determined the responses of single neurons in the primary and secondary auditory cortex of the waking cat.[5] Stimuli were five-tone sequences (pentads) consisting of pure-tone stimuli (40–80 dB, 300 msec). Intertone intervals were of 300, 600, or 900 msec; intersequence intervals were 900, 1500, or 1800 msec, for the respective intertone intervals. These parameters were kept constant within permutations of the pentad studied for each neuron. The following contours were used: ascending (frequencies), descending, "mixed" in which the contour had dif-

---

[5]These two papers include many common data plus some findings that are unique to each article. This unusual duplication of publication resulted from the fact that the original manuscript included the discussion of issues both in music perception and in auditory physiology. The editorial policies of relevant physiology journals eschewed the dual contexts, and therefore the findings and discussion relevant to music perception were published in an invited chapter (Weinberger & McKenna, 1988).

ferent portions that incremented and decremented in frequency, and "horizontal," that is, all frequencies the same ("monotone" series). In all pentads, the frequency of the third tone was the same. In some cases, the third tone was deleted. Single isolated tones were also used on occasion (Figure 7). All frequencies were within the excitatory receptive fields of the cell under study. The response of each cell to each frequency in the pentad was determined for all contours. All pentads were repeated 25 times to obtain sufficient data for statistical analysis. Responses for a given pentad were stable, with no adaptation, fatigue, or habituation across the repetitions. The first stimulus condition used with a cell was often repeated at the end of recording for that neuron and revealed no difference from the initial responses, ruling out possible changes in cellular excitability over time.

The first question addressed was whether neurons in the auditory cortex can respond to all tones in a sequence with subjects in the state of general anesthesia. This is an important issue because the vast majority of auditory neurophysiology studies (indeed of all sensory neurophysiology experiments) have been conducted with subjects under general anesthesia. Foundational data have been obtained under this state, and knowledge of brain physiology would be enormously impoverished without data from anesthetized subjects, in part because anesthesia does allow for the highest degree of stimulus control of the tympanic membrane. Nonetheless, one cannot assume that the anesthetized brain will reveal all of the operations of the waking brain.

Monotone pentads presented to cats under general anesthesia yielded strong responses to the first stimulus in the pentad and considerably fewer discharges to succeeding stimuli in the pentad. Intersequence intervals of 900–1800 msec were sufficient to produce "recovery," so that the first tone in each succeeding pentad produced strong responses (Figure 8A). Nonetheless, it proved impossible to fully investigate the effects of contour because strong responses were not elicited by the last four stimuli within a pentad (Weinberger & McKenna, 1988).

Full experiments were therefore conducted in waking subjects in which responses to all tones in a sequence were obtained (Figure 8B–D). The responses to each frequency were determined for that frequency in each of the different contours of the pentads. In the vast majority of cases, the responses to the same puretone stimulus was different for different pentads. Of a total of 70 neurons fully studied, 65 (93%) were so affected (AI = 42/47; secondary auditory cortex, AII = 23/23). An example is given in Figures 9 and 10. The response to a given tone when that frequency was in a pentad consisting of all different frequencies (ascending, descending, or mixed) could not be predicted from its response to a series of five identical tones (monotone).

Permutations of contour changed the serial position of a frequency within a pentad. For example, in an ascending series of 1, 2, 3, 4, and 5 kHz, vs the same frequencies in a descending series, 1 kHz is in the first and fifth positions, respectively, and so on. Indeed, some of the contour effects could be attributed to serial position in the pentad. However, effects were also found for the third frequency, which did not change serial position. In addition to serial position, contour effects

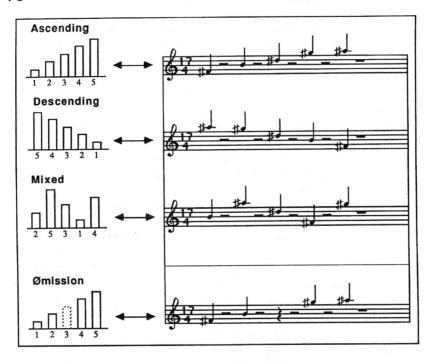

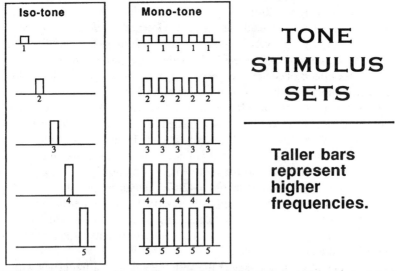

FIGURE 7   Summary of types of acoustic stimuli and sequences used. The musical notation is for general illustrative purposes only and does not necessarily depict any actual sequence. Frequencies used were not necessarily related (e.g., as thirds, fifths), but rather were selected to cover the range of frequencies to which individual neurons were responsive. Tone duration is 300 msec and intertone interval is 300 msec in this figure. (Reprinted with permission from Weinberger & McKenna, 1988. ©1988 by The Regents of the University of California.)

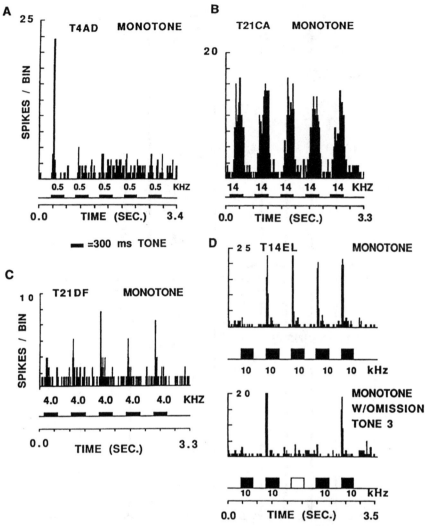

FIGURE 8 Poststimulus histograms of responses of four neurons to pentads consisting of identical tones (i.e., "monotones"). T4AD (A1, 70 dB) in anesthetized cat responds only to the first stimulus in the pentad. (B) T21CA (A1, 70 dB) in waking cat shows strong responses to all tones. (C) Data from T21DF (A1, 70 dB) in waking cat had a small response to the first stimulus of the sequence, followed by larger responses to subsequent tones. (D) T14EL (A1, 60 dB) in waking cat; this neuron failed to respond to the first tone of the sequence but thereafter responded very strongly (top). Omission of the third tone revealed that this neuron required two consecutive tones in order to respond (bottom).(Reprinted with permission from Weinberger & McKenna, 1988. ©1988 by The Regents of the University of California.)

could also be attributed to interval distance between two consecutive tones. Also, responses to tones within pentads consisting of different frequencies was often greater than responses to the same frequency when it was presented in a monotone

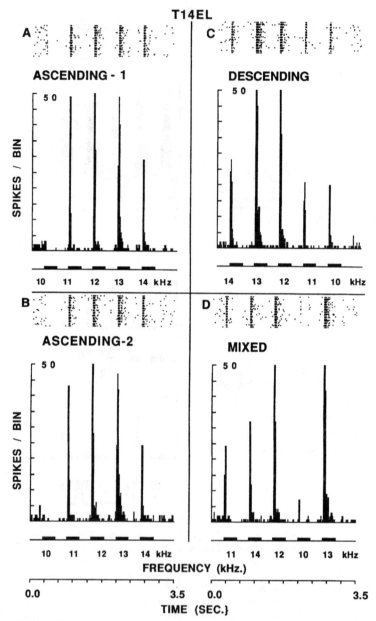

FIGURE 9   Effects of contour on discharges of Neuron T14EL (A1, 60 dB). Rasters and post-stimulus histograms show responses to ascending (A, B), descending (C), and mixed (D) sequences. The two ascending sequences were presented 45 min apart, the other sequences were presented during that period. Rasters above each histogram denote discharges for each repetition of the sequence, read from top to bottom. Number of sequences = 25; bin size = 10 msec. Note the reliability of discharges within each sequence, as denoted by similar raster patterns for each presentation of the same sequence within a contour type (ascending, descending, mixed). Note also the reliability between repetitions of

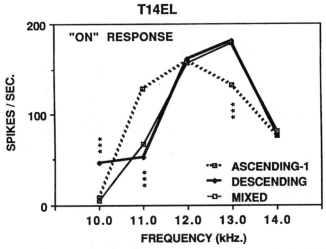

FIGURE 10 Statistical summary of responses (mean peak response) to each of the five tones in the pentads for the three contour types for the data shown in Figure 9. Stars indicate statistical differences (all $p < .002$, t test). The best frequency (peak of frequency function) was 13.0 kHz for the descending and mixed sequences and 12.0 kHz for the ascending sequence. This graph also shows that some frequencies (12.0 and 14.0 kHz) elicited the same magnitude for all three contour types. (Reprinted with permission from Weinberger & McKenna, 1988. ©1988 by The Regents of the University of California.)

series, that is, all frequencies identical (Figure 11). Finally, omission of the third tone produced significant modifications of response to other tones in the vast majority of cells (87%), with effects extending up to 3 sec after the gap. Neurons in both AI and AII displayed all effects; the only significant difference was that cells in AII were more likely to show gap effects than were those in AI.

The intertone intervals used and the intervals over which effects were found could not be attributed to neural refractoriness, adaptation, or fatigue. Most likely, complex patterns of excitation and inhibition were responsible. However, the locus of responsible mechanisms is unknown and could involve subcortical levels of the auditory system. Unfortunately, the studies failed to use frequencies within a pentad that were based on important scale intervals (e.g., fifth). The findings do demonstrate (a) the importance of using waking subjects to study the responses of cortical cells to extended sequences of tones, (b) the very high degree of neuronal sensitivity to contour of a tone series, and (c) the facilitating effects of different vs. the same tonal frequency in a sequence.

The foregoing experiments were incomplete in that they did not use all possible permutations of five-tone sequences. This would have required testing each cell

---

the ascending sequences. Discharges to the same tone varied significantly between different contour types for some frequencies (see Figure 10). (Reprinted with permission from Weinberger & McKenna, 1988. ©1988 by The Regents of the University of California.)

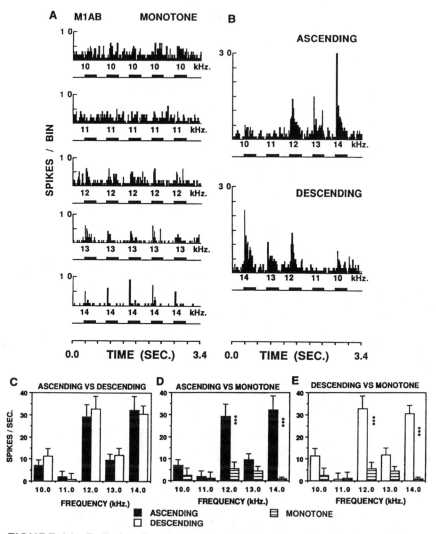

FIGURE 11 Facilitating effect of presenting pentads of different rather than the same frequencies. Data for Cell M1AB (A1, 80 dB). (A) Monotone sequences, (B) ascending and descending sequences; (C–E) statistical summaries, as labeled. Although this particular neuron was not sensitive to *different* contours, that is, no significant differences between ascending and descending sequences (C), responses to 12.0 and 14.0 kHz were significantly greater ($p < .002$) when presented in ascending (D) and descending (E) types of contour than in monotone ("no contour"). (Reprinted with permission from Weinberger & McKenna, 1988. ©1988 by The Regents of the University of California.)

with 2^5 sequences. However, Espinosa and Gerstein (1988) recorded from the AI of the cat using sequences in which three tones were given in all permutations of three different tones, requiring only six sequences per recording. In this seminal study, the authors recorded the discharges of 8–24 neurons simultaneously from many of microelectrodes, thus enabling them to determine how a local network of neurons processes tone sequences.

Subjects were tested while under very light anesthesia. Stimuli consisted of permutations of three different pure tones (63-msec duration) with intertone intervals of 140 msec and intersequence intervals of 975 msec. Typically, one of the three tones was the best frequency, at a stimulus level 30 dB above threshold, and the other two tones were generally 500 Hz above and below this frequency. The range of best frequencies tested was 7 to 15 kHz. Functional connectivity between all pairs of neurons recorded for a given set of three-tone sequences was determined by cross-correlograms of spikes trains for each frequency in each triad. It was possible to distinguish between cellular responses in neuron pairs to shared input from another source and direct relationships in which the discharges of one cell were followed by discharges in other cells at an appropriate latency. (For additional details, the original publication should be consulted). The connectivity patterns involved as many as 24 neurons from which simultaneous spike trains were obtained. This is remarkable and perhaps unprecedented. Even the connectivity patterns for eight neurons that were more usual go far beyond most such studies in which the interactions between or among two or three cells are described.

The authors discovered that the connectivity patterns for direct influence of one neuron on other neurons were specific for a given sequence of three tones but usually differed for different sequences. More specifically, the direct functional connectivity pattern of a group of neurons in response to the same tone changed when that tone (e.g., "C") was preceded by a different tone (e.g., "ABC" vs. "BAC"; Figure 12). The findings reveal that stimuli are processed dynamically and at the level of networks.

The findings are of major importance because they reveal, for the first time, that the functional connections among cells are not fixed but rather depend on the pattern of tone sequences. This implies that contour or melody or both are coded at the level of neuronal groups or networks.

VIII. RHYTHM, TEMPORAL CODING

In this section, we consider the following aspects of temporal coding and rhythm: amplitude modulation, temporal pattern, and gap detection.

A. AMPLITUDE MODULATION

Music, as other complex stimuli such as species-specific vocalizations and human speech, involves the temporal patterning of stimulus features in addition to the well-known spectral aspects of stimuli. Schreiner and Langner (1988a) and Langner (1992) have provided excellent reviews.

Langner (1992) has emphasized that animal communication sounds, human speech, many natural nonliving sound sources of biological importance, and music all contain periodic fluctuations in amplitude, that is, envelopes of AM. Such

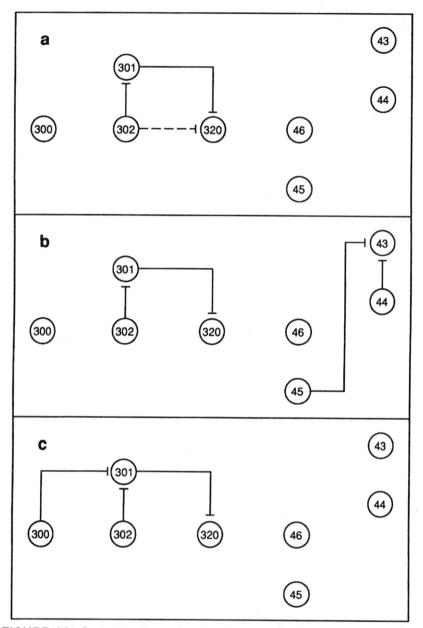

FIGURE 12   Connectivity diagrams for stimulated conditions. Session 5683. Only direct connections are shown. (a) Stimulus was tone A preceded by tone sequence CB. (b) Stimulus was tone A
preceded by tone sequence BC. (c) Stimulus was tone B preceded by tone sequence AC. Circles represent neurons and numbers are cell identifications. Direct excitatory connections are shown by lines
terminating in short cross bar (solid lines = high statistical confidence, broken lines = lower confidence). Note particularly that functional connectivity differed for responses to the same stimulus A
when it was preceded by two tones (B and C) that differed in order; compare (a) and (b). Note also that

AM information can be used to "bind" sounds in various frequency channels, as separated by the cochlea, into a common sound source. Langner further points out that to make use of this type of information, the central auditory system must perform a periodicity analysis.

Many investigators have studied the responses of auditory neurons to AM stimuli, with important results. Although the details of this field cannot be covered in this chapter, we will review the ability of neurons at different levels of the auditory system to respond reliably to different rates of AM sounds.

A common measure of response to AM stimuli is the "modulation transfer function." This provides an index of the ability of a neuron to respond synchronously to AM envelopes of pure tones. The rate of AM to which a cell responds maximally is called the "best modulation frequency" (BMF). A fundamental question is the extent to which neurons at various levels of the auditory system respond to AM signals, that is, to what extent are BMFs the same or different within the auditory system? Langner has reviewed a large number of studies in which BMFs have been obtained from a variety of animals (rat, gerbil, cat, bat, as well as various birds and monkeys). Across this spectrum of animals, a general principle has emerged—BMFs decrease as the auditory system is ascended. For example, the mean BMF of the gerbil auditory nerve is 370 Hz. For the inferior colliculus of many animals, BMFs range from 20 to 120 Hz. At the auditory cortex, the mean BMFs are considerably lower, 4–28 Hz.

Creutzfeldt, Hellweg, and Schreiner (1980) have provided dramatic direct evidence of the difference between the ability of the medial geniculate nucleus and the auditory cortex to process temporal information. In a tour de force, they recorded simultaneously from pairs of neurons that were directly connected functionally, one in the MGm, the other in the auditory cortex, in the waking guinea pig. Thus, they were able to determine the responses of the two cells to the same stimuli simultaneously. In response to unmodulated pure tones, MGm cells responded more tonically than cortical cells; that is, they could respond throughout the duration of tones of as much as 600 msec duration, whereas cortical cells responded mainly at tone onset. In response to AM stimuli, geniculate cells could follow modulations of approximately 100 Hz whereas cortical cells were limited to AM rates of 20 Hz, often lower. The same range of BMFs were found for AM components of species-specific vocalizations.

As pointed out previously, the auditory cortex actually consists of several fields. In the cat, there are two tonotopically organized fields: the AI and the AAF. Other fields include the AII, the posterior auditory field, and the ventroposterior auditory field. Currently, little is known about why there are multiple fields or what, if any, particular stimulus parameters might be specially processed within

---

the number of cells engaged by a stimulus differed for the three different stimulus conditions. (Reprinted from *Brain Research, 450,* Espinosa & Gerstein, Cortical auditory neuron interactions during presentation of three-tone sequences: Effective connectivity, pp. 39–50, Copyright 1988, with permission from Elsevier Science.)

the various fields. Schreiner and Urbas (1986, 1988) found that the various fields do respond differently to AM stimuli. The AAF has the highest BMF (31 Hz), AI has a moderately high BMF (14 Hz) but all of the other fields have significantly less ability to respond consistently to AM stimuli: AII, posterior auditory field, and ventroposterior auditory field had mean BMFs of 5–7 Hz. Therefore, one important difference among auditory cortical fields is their temporal response characteristics.

In addition to the well-known mapping of frequency in the auditory system, a mapping of stimulus periodicity has recently been found. Langner and Schreiner (1988) and Schreiner and Langner (1988b) found that there is a systematic topographic distribution of BMFs within the inferior colliculus of the cat. A map of periodicities also has been found in the auditory cortex of the bird. Hose, Langner, and Scheich (1987) recorded the responses of single neurons in field L of the myna bird (*Gracula religiosa intermedia*) to AM stimuli. BMFs ranged mainly between 0.3 and 20 Hz and were arranged systematically across the depth (layers) of field L. The authors concluded that field L is the "dominant site for rhythm analysis."

Noteworthy is the fact that these maps do not simply reflect the projection of the sensory epithelium from the basilar membrane into the central auditory system, as appears to be the case for frequency mapping. Rather, maps of "periodicity coding" are "computed," that is, arise from presumably complex excitatory and inhibitory interactions within the central auditory system itself.

The range of AM envelope fluctuations found in music would be of great interest, but I know of no systematic studies. Such information would make it possible to determine the extent to which some of the temporal features of music might be processed at different levels of the auditory system and in different fields within the auditory cortex.

B. TEMPORAL PATTERN

The perception of music involves the perceptual organization of patterns in time. Behavioral studies have revealed that listeners organize or group streams of sounds and silence (for review, see Bregman, 1990; Deutsch, 1982). Recently, Robin, Abbas, and Hug (1990) have sought the neurophysiological basis for perceptual temporal organization by recording evoked potentials in the auditory nerve, brain stem, and auditory cortex in the cat. Previous behavioral studies in humans suggested that grouping is done on the "run and gap" principle, namely, that patterns are organized to begin with the longest run of like elements and end with the longest gap (Garner, 1974). For this neurophysiological study, two patterns were used; one pattern was perceptually unambiguous and the other was ambiguous. These can be represented as a series of X's and o's where "X" denotes the presentation of a noise burst followed immediately by silence of an equal duration and "o" symbolizes a period of silence equal to the total duration of an "X." The unambiguous pattern was XXXooXooo, and the ambiguous pattern was XXoXoXXoo. Note that the former starts with the longest run of elements containing sound and ends with the longest run of silence, whereas the latter could begin and end at more than one place, based on the gap-run principle. Recordings were obtained for responses to various temporal parameters (element durations = 40, 80, 160 or 300 msec, yielding pattern repetition rates of 3.13, 1.56, 0.78, or 0.42 Hz) at 50, 70 and 90 dB SPL. However, the overall findings were similar across these parameters.

For the unambiguous pattern, the largest evoked potential was elicited by the first element in the pattern, with smaller responses to other elements at the auditory nerve, auditory brain stem, and particularly at the auditory cortex. In contrast, the ambiguous pattern elicited responses with no such clear outcome. These findings support the view that perceptual grouping of temporal sequences is based on the stimulus element that elicits the largest response in the auditory system. The authors attribute the amplitude of responses to neural adaptation; the longest silent period, which perceptually completes a sequence, allows for the longest time for recovery, which would produce the largest response to the first element of the next pattern presented.

The findings suggest that the auditory nerve is an important locus for neural mechanisms underlying the perception of temporal patterns used, although the effect might be exacerbated at the level of the auditory cortex. The close correspondence between perception and neurophysiology is noteworthy. It would be interesting to know if cats exhibit the same perceptual grouping with these patterns as do humans. Also, it should be possible to record evoked potentials to these same patterns in humans.

C. GAP DETECTION

The detection of brief gaps in noise has been used as a measure of temporal resolution in the auditory system and indexes the ability of the auditory system to process transient amplitude shifts. Such gaps may be likened to rests in a musical composition. Two types of studies have been done in the auditory system to investigate the mechanisms underlying gap detection, neurophysiological and functional ablation.

Buchfellner, Leppelsack, Klump, and Hausler (1989) recorded the responses of single neurons in field L (auditory cortex of birds) of the starling to stimuli that included gaps of various durations. They compared the sensitivity of neurons to behavioral data obtained previously (Klump & Maier, 1989). The authors found that neuronal detection of gaps was almost the same as behavioral detection, suggesting that neurons in field L might mediate behavioral gap detection.

Ison, O'Connor, Bowen, and Bocirnea (1991) used functional decortication to determine the role of the auditory cortex of the rat in gap detection. Gaps in white noise (70 dB) ranged from 2 to15 msec, and gap detection was measured as gap inhibition of an acoustic startle reflex that was elicited by a loud sound 100 msec after the end of the gap. Normal animals detect gaps on the order of 2–4 msec. Cortical function was temporarily eliminated in the experimental condition by the use of reversible spreading depression induced by application of potassium chloride to the cortex. Under this condition, subjects failed to detect gaps of any duration, up to and including the maximum of 15 msec.

The authors conclude that gap detection requires a functional cortex. Because spreading depression affects all of the cortex, and could have some subcortical involvement, the auditory cortex alone cannot yet be identified as the critical site. These findings are complementary both to the results reported by Buchfellner et al. (1989) and to studies that show that the auditory cortex is particularly responsive to transients (e.g., Creutzfeldt et al., 1980).

IX. FUTURE DIRECTIONS

In this concluding section, we briefly discuss two issues related to future directions in research on music and the auditory system: changing views of the auditory system and the relevance of animal research to music.

A. CHANGING VIEWS OF AUDITORY SYSTEM FUNCTIONS

The possibility of understanding the brain mechanisms underlying music, particularly music perception, logically begins with the auditory system but by no means ends with this system. Although this chapter concerns the auditory system, the spectrum of sensory, perceptual, emotional, cognitive, mnemonic, aesthetic, and performance processes involved in music strongly indicates that the brain's substrates transcends the auditory system. Even so, an emerging broader view of the auditory system includes functions such as perception, attention, learning, and memory that heretofore have been largely excluded.

Traditionally, the auditory system and other sensory systems have been viewed largely as, admittedly highly complex but nonetheless, basically filters in which networks of excitatory and inhibitory processes yield more or less specific feature detectors in the form of neurons that are tuned specifically to the physical parameters of sound, light, touch, and so on. A more dynamic view is emerging at both the behavioral and the neurobiological levels. Comments here are restricted to the auditory system.

It is becoming increasingly evident that the auditory system as a whole is not limited to what is classically understood as "sensory" processes. Moreover, as will be mentioned later, functions within the auditory system, particularly at cortical levels, appear to transcend perceptual processes, so that the distinction between perceptual and cognitive processes is less clear than in the past.

Regarding behavioral studies, Yost (1992) has pointed out that a long held view is that "the auditory system processes sound by monitoring the output of (frequency) channels." This so-called "critical band" model has been successful in dealing with a large number of problems in auditory psychophysics. However,

Yost argues that this model cannot account for three fairly recently discovered phenomena: profile analysis, comodulation masking release, and modulation detection interference. (For details, consult Yost and appropriate references cited therein.) All three of these cases indicate that "robust perceptual interactions occur across a wide frequency range" (Yost, 1992).

Additional evidence of a changing view of the auditory system in perception is evident in the increased concern with auditory objects rather than the individual frequency components of a sound source (Bregman, 1990; Moore, 1991; Yost, 1991).

Within neurobiology, several types of findings point to a view of the auditory system as more dynamic than previously recognized, as reviewed in previous sections of this chapter. First, evidence shows that the auditory cortex is involved with, and may be organized according to, pitch rather than to frequency. Second, both the responses to the same physical stimulus at the level of single cortical cells and at the level of their functional connectivity depend on the acoustic "context" within which the stimulus is presented. Third, attention to a sound produces a different response than when the same stimulus is presented in a control condition. Fourth, learning specifically alters the frequency tuning of cells; it favors responses to the reinforced frequency while decreasing responsiveness to other frequencies (classical conditioning) or attenuates responses to a repeated frequency while increasing responses to adjacent frequencies (habituation). Such retuning apparently extends to the entire tonotopic organization of the primary auditory cortex, increasing the number of cells that respond to the training frequency and increasing the amount of cortex that is tuned to the training frequency. Fifth, and not previously mentioned, selective cochlear damage in the adult animal does not leave the denervated part of the auditory cortex silent, but rather produces an expansion of the frequency representations for immediately higher and lower frequencies into the deafferented zone (Robertson & Irvine, 1989). All of these findings demonstrate that the adult auditory cortex is dynamic.

One implication for music perception is the possibility that the analysis, perception, and storage of information concerning a musical entity may all involve the same region of the auditory system, perhaps even the same neurons. That auditory cortex has been most intensively studied tends to bias attention to this level of the system. The need is clearly for additional investigation of both the auditory cortex and of subcortical auditory structures.

B. ANIMAL BRAINS AND HUMAN MUSIC

A review of comparative psychoacoustics reveals that animals and humans have the same basic psychoacoustic functions (Fay, 1988). Also, some of the findings reviewed in this chapter indicate close relationships between human and animal behavior and animal neurobiology. But these type of findings may be insufficient to force the conclusion that animal research on music must be pursued. One could easily argue that because music is largely, if not entirely, a human endeavor, the study of brain mechanisms of music in animals is largely irrelevant and ultimately fruitless. Exactly the same arguments have been advanced concerning the neurobiology of language. Perhaps consideration of the relevance of animal research to music perception can benefit from some of the conceptual insights and experimental findings in the field of speech perception.

Briefly, the fact that animals do not exhibit language does not necessarily imply that nothing about human language can be learned from animal behavior and animal neurobiology. Processes and capabilities that evolved in animals, based on selective pressures for nonlinguistic situations, might nonetheless be used in humans for language. For example, categorical perception in language, based upon voiced-onset times for distinctions between speech elements such as /ba/ and /pa/ was thought to require mechanisms that had evolved specially in humans. However, animals demonstrate categorical perception of such voicing elements (see Kuhl, 1986 for a review of the issue). More recently Sinex, McDonald, and Mott (1991) have studied the responses of the auditory nerve to variations in voiced-onset times based on similarities in the behavior of human and chinchilla listeners. They found a close relationship between the latency and rate of discharge in the VIIIth nerve and voiced-onset times; moreover, these were sufficient to explain the categorical perceptual boundary in relevant speech sound discrimination. Sinex (1992) has devised a mathematical model based on these findings that produces computer-simulated VIIIth nerve responses to voiced-onset times parameters that accurately match the physiological data. Further, the data from the simulation closely match human performance.

In summary, it would be premature to dismiss animal studies of music on either conceptual or empirical grounds. Given the emergence of the cognitive sciences and their increasing involvement with the neural sciences, a logical and appropriate next step would be for the explicit development of a cognitive neurobiology of music perception that builds on the strong foundation of auditory neurophysiology and animal behavior.

Fortunately, technologies are now available to study the human auditory cortex more thoroughly. Virtually any auditory perception experiment could be conducted with simultaneous recording from many sites in the auditory cortical fields of humans by using multichannel SQUID devices, which are now available. At the same time, animal studies should be conducted more or less in parallel, with the advantages offered by the opportunity to seek the mechanisms of music processing in the auditory system and elsewhere in the brain.

ACKNOWLEDGMENTS

Preparation of this chapter was supported in part by ONIR 00014-914-1193 and an unrestricted grant from the Monsanto Corporation. This review was completed at the end of 1992 and thus includes literature up to that year. Bibliographic searches were aided by the Music Brain Information Center (MBIC), University of California Irvine; I wish to thank Lorna Shaw for her assistance on the MBIC.

Thanks are due to Jacquie Weinberger for preparation of the manuscript and to Jon Won for redrawing a figure. I also thank Dr. Thomas McKenna, who was instrumental in undertaking and completing work that reported the effects of contour on cortical cells and for innumerable stimulating dialogues over the years.

REFERENCES

Arlinger, S., Elberling, C., Bak, C., Kofoed, B., Lebech, J., & Saermark, K. (1982). Cortical magnetic fields evoked by frequency glides of a continuous tone. *EEG & Clinical Neurophysiology, 54*, 642–653.

Barlow, H. B., & Mollon, J. D. (Eds.) (1982). *The senses.* New York: Cambridge University Press.

Bhatnagar, S. C., Andy, O. J., & Linville, S. (1989). Tonotypic cortical representation in man (case report). *Pavlovian Journal Biological Science, 24*(2), 50–53.

Bregman, A. S. (1990). *Auditory scene analysis.* Cambridge, MA: MIT Press.

Brugge, J. F., & Reale, R. A. (1985). Auditory cortex. In A. Peters & E. G. Jones (Eds.), *Cerebral cortex : Association and auditory cortices* (pp. 229–271). New York: Plenum Press.

Buchfellner, E., Leppelsack, H.-J., Klump, G. M., & Hausler, U. (1989). Gap detection in the starling (*Sturnus vulgaris*): II. Coding of gaps by forebrain neurons. *Journal of Comparative Physiology, 164*, 539–549.

Cariani, P. A., & Delgutte, B. (1996a). Neural correlates of the pitch of complex tones: I. Pitch and pitch salience. *Journal of Neurophysiology, 76*, 698–716.

Cariani, P. A., & Delgutte, B. (1996b). Neural correlates of the pitch of complex tones: II. Pitch shift, pitch ambiguity, phase invariance, pitch circularity, rate pitch, and the dominance region for pitch. *Journal of Neurophysiology, 76*, 1717–1734.

Cariani, P. A., Delgutte, B., & Kiang, N. Y. S. (1992). The pitch of complex sounds is simply coded in interspike interval distributions of auditory nerve fibers. *Society for Neuroscience Abstracts, 18*, 383.

Chung, D. Y., & Colavita, F. B. (1976). Periodicity pitch perception and its upper frequency limit in cats. *Perception & Psychophysics, 20*, 433–437.

Clayton, N., & Bischof, H. J. (1990). Neurophysiology and behavioral development in birds: song learning as a model system. *Naturwissenschaften, 77*, 123–127.

Condon, C. D., & Weinberger, N. M. (1991). Habituation produces frequency-specific plasticity of receptive fields in the auditory cortex. *Behavorial Neuroscience, 105*, 416–430.

Creutzfeldt, O., Hellweg, F. C., & Schreiner, C. (1980). Thalamocortical transformation of responses to complex auditory stimuli. *Experimental Brain Research, 39*, 87–104.

Cynx, J., & Shapiro, M. (1986). Perception of missing fundamental by a species of songbird (*Sturnus vulgaris*). *Journal of Comparative Psychology, 100*, 356–360.

Delgutte, B., & Cariani, P. (1992). Coding of the pitch of harmonic and inharmonic complex tones in the interspike intervals of auditory nerve fibers. In M. E. H. Schouten (Ed.), *The processing of speech* Berlin: Mouton-De Gruyer.

Deutsch, D. (1982). Grouping mechanisms in music. In D. Deutsch (Ed.), *The psychology of music* (pp. 99–134). New York: Academic Press.

Edeline, J.-M., Pham, P., & Weinberger, N. M. (1993). Rapid development of learning-induced receptive field plasticity in the auditory cortex. *Behavioral Neuroscience, 107*, 539–551.

Edeline, J.-M., & Weinberger, N. M. (1991). Thalamic short term plasticity in the auditory system: Associative retuning of receptive fields in the ventral medial geniculate body. *Behavorial Neuroscience, 105*, 618–639.

Edeline, J.-M., & Weinberger, N. M. (1992). Associative retuning in the thalamic source of input to the amygdala and auditory cortex: Receptive field plasticity in the medial division of the medial geniculate body. *Behavorial Neuroscience, 106*, 81–105.

Edeline, J.-M., & Weinberger, N. M. (1993). Receptive field plasticity in the auditory cortex during frequency discrimination training: Selective retuning independent of task difficulty. *Behavioral Neuroscience, 107*, 82–103.

Elberling, C., Bak, C., Kofoed, B., Lebech, J., & Saermark, K. (1982). Auditory magnetic fields: Source location and 'tonotopic organization' in the right hemisphere of the human brain. *Scandinavian Audiology, 11*, 61–65.

Espinosa, I. E., & Gerstein, G. L. (1988). Cortical auditory neuron interactions during presentation of 3-tone sequences: Effective connectivity. *Brain Research, 450*, 39–50.

Evans, E. F. (1972). The frequency response and other properties of single fibres in the guinea-pig cochlear nerve. *Journal of Physiology, 226*, 263–287.

Evans, E. F. (1978). Place and time coding of frequency in the peripheral auditory system: Some physiological pros and cons. *Audiology, 17*, 369–420.

Fay, R. R. (1988). Comparative psychoacoustics. *Hearing Research, 34*, 295–305.

Gabriel, M., Miller, J. D., & Saltwick, S. E. (1976). Multiple-unit activity of the rabbit medial geniculate nucleus in conditioning, extinction and reversal. *Physiological Psychology, 4*, 124–134.

Garner, W. R. (1974). *The processing of information and structure*. Hillsdale, NJ: Erlbaum.

Gerhardt, H. C. (1988). Acoustic properties used in call recognition by frogs and toads. In B. Fritzsch (Ed.), *The evolution of the amphibian auditory system* (pp. 455–483). New York: John Wiley and Sons.

Goldstein, M. H., Benson, D. A., & Hienz, R. D. (1982). Studies of auditory cortex in behaviorally trained monkeys. In C. D. Woody (Ed.), *Conditioning representation of involved neural functions* (pp. 307–317). New York: Plenum Press.

Gonzalez-Lima, F., & Agudo, J. (1990). Functional reorganization of neural auditory maps by differential learning. *Neuroreport, 1*(2), 161–164.

Gonzalez-Lima, F., Finkenstadt, T., & Ewert, J. P. (1989a). Learning-related activation in the auditory system of the rat produced by long-term habituation: A 2-deoxyglucose study. *Brain Research, 489*, 67–79.

Gonzalez-Lima, F., Finkenstadt, T., & Ewert, J. P. (1989b). Neural substrates for long-term habituation of the acoustic startle reflex in rats: A 2-deoxyglucose study. *Neuroscience Letters, 96*(2), 151–156.

Gonzalez-Lima, F., & Scheich, H. (1984a). Classical conditioning enhances auditory 2-deoxyglucose patterns in the inferior colliculus. *Neuroscience Letters, 51*, 79–85.

Gonzalez-Lima, F., & Scheich, H. (1984b). Neural substrates for tone-conditioned bradycardia demonstrated with 2-deoxyglucose: I. Activation of auditory nuclei. *Behavioral Brain Research, 14*(3), 213–33.

Gonzalez-Lima, F., & Scheich, H. (1986). Neural substrates for tone-conditioned bradycardia demonstrated with 2-deoxyglucose. II. Auditory cortex plasticity. *Behavioral Brain Research, 20*(3), 281–293.

Hari, R. (1990). The neuromagnetic method in the study of the human auditory cortex. In F. Grandori, M. Hoke, & G. L. Romani (Eds.), *Auditory evoked magnetic fields and electric potentials* (pp. 222–282). Basel: S. Karger.

Hari, R., & Makela, J. P. (1986). Neuromagnetic responses to frequency modulation of a continuous tone. *Acta Otolarngolia Suppl, 432*, 26–32.

Heffner, H. E., & Whitfield, I. C. (1976). Perception of the missing fundamental by cats. *Journal of the Acoustical Society of America, 59*, 915–919.

Helfert, R. H., Snead, C. R., & Altschuler, R. A. (1991). The ascending auditory pathways. In R. A. Altschuler, R. P. Bobbin, B. M. Clopton, & D. W. Hoffman (Eds.), *Neurobiology of hearing: The central auditory system* (pp. 1–26). New York: Raven Press.

Hose, B., Langner, G., & Scheich, H. (1987). Topographic representation of periodicities in the forebrain of the mynah bird: One map for pitch and rhythm? *Brain Research, 422*, 367–373.

Huber, F. (1983). Neural correlates of orthopteran and cicada phonotaxis. In F. Huber & H. Mark (Eds.), *Neuroethology and behavioral physiology* (pp. 108–135). Berlin: Springer-Verlag.

Ison, J. R., O'Connor, K., Bowen, G. P., & Bocirnea, A. (1991). Temporal resolution of gaps in noise by the rat is lost with functional decortication. *Behavioral Neuroscience, 105*, 33–40.

Kaukoranta, E., Hari, R., & Lounasmsmaa, O. V. (1987). Responses of the human auditory cortex to vowel onset after fricative consonants. *Experimental Brain Research, 69*, 19–23.

Kirzinger, A., & Jurgens, U. (1991). Vocalization–correlated single-unit activity in the brain stem of the squirrel monkey. *Experimental Brain Research, 84*, 545–560.

Klump, G. M., & Maier, E. H. (1989). Gap detection in the starling (*Sturnus vulgaris*): I. Psychophysical thresholds. *Journal of Comparative Physiology, 164*, 531–538.

Knudsen, E. I. (1991). Dynamic space codes in the superior colliculus. *Current Opinion Neurobiology, 1*, 628–632.

Konishi, M. (1989). Birdsong for neurobiologists. *Neuron, 3*, 541–549.

Kuhl, P. K. (1986). Theoretical contributions of tests on animals to the special-mechanisms debate in speech. *Experimental Biology, 45*, 233–265.

Langner, G. (1992). Periodicity coding in the auditory system. *Hearing Research, 60*(2), 115–142.

Langner, G., & Schreiner, C. E. (1988). Periodicity coding in the inferior colliculus of the cat: I. Neuronal mechanisms. *Journal Neurophysiology, 60*, 1799–1822.

Lauter, J. L., Herscovitch, P., Formby, C., & Raichle, M. E. (1985). Tonotopic organization in human auditory cortex revealed by positron emission tomography. *Hearing Research, 20*, 199–205.

Makela, J. P., Hari, R., & Linnankivi, A. (1987). Different analysis of frequency and amplitude modulations of a continuous tone in the human auditory cortex: A neuromagnetic study. *Hearing Research, 27*, 257–264.

McKenna, T. M., Weinberger, N. M., & Diamond, D. M. (1989). Responses of single auditory cortical neurons to tone sequences. *Brain Research, 481*, 142–153.

Miller, J. M., Pfingst, B. E., & Ryan, A. F. (1982). Behavioral modification of response characteristics of cells in the auditory system. In C. D. Woody (Ed.), *Conditioning representation of involved neural functions* (pp. 345–361). New York: Plenum Press.

Moore, B. C. J. (1991). *An introduction to the psychology of hearing*. London: Academic Press.

Nottebohm, F. (1991). Reassessing the mechanisms and origins of vocal learning in birds. *Trends in Neurosciences, 14*, 206–211.

Olsen, J. F. (1992). High-order auditory filters. *Current Opinion in Neurobiology, 2*, 489–497.

Pantev, C., Hoke, M., Lehnertz, K., Lutkenhomer, B., Anogianakis, G., & Wittkowski, W. (1988). Tonotopic organization of the human auditory cortex revealed by transient auditory-evoked magnetic fields. *EEG and Clinical Neurophysiology, 69*, 160–170.

Pantev, C., Hoke, M., Lutkenhoner, B., & Lehnertz, K. (1989). Tonotopic organization of the auditory cortex: pitch versus frequency representation. *Science, 246*(4929), 486–488.

Pantev, C., Hoke, M., Lutkenhoner, B., & Lehnertz, K. (1991). Neuromagnetic evidence of functional organization of the auditory cortex in humans. *Acta Otolaryngology Suppl., 491*, 106–115.

Pellizzone, M., Williamson, S. J., & Kaufman, L. (1985). Evidence for multiple areas in the human auditory cortex. In H. Weinberg, G. Stroink, & T. Katila (Eds.), *Biomagnetism: Applications and theory* (pp. 326–330). New York: Pergamon Press.

Pelleg-Toiba, R., & Wollberg, Z. (1991). Discrimination of communication cells in the squirrel monkey: "Call detectors " or "cell ensembles"? *Journal of Basic and Clinical Physiology and Pharmacology, 2*, 257–272.

Phillips, D. P., Reale, R. A., & Brugge, J. F. (1991). Stimulus processing in the auditory cortex. In R. A. Altschuler, R. P. Bobbin, B. M. Clopton, & D. W. Hoffman (Eds.), *Neurobiology of hearing: The central auditory system* (pp. 335–366). New York: Raven Press.

Pickles, J. O. (1988). *An introduction to the physiology of hearing*. 2nd ed. San Diego, CA: Academic Press.

Recanzone, G. H., Schreiner, C. E., & Merzenich, M. M. (1993). Plasticity in the frequency representation of primary auditory cortex following discrimination training in adult owl monkeys. *Journal of Neuroscience, 13*, 87–103.

Riquimaroux, H., Gaioni, S. J., & Suga, N. (1991). Cortical computational maps control auditory perception. *Science, 251*(4993), 565–568.

Robertson, D., & Irvine, D. R. (1989). Plasticity of frequency organization in auditory cortex of guinea pigs with partial unilateral deafness. *Journal of Comparative Neurology, 282*(3), 456–71.

Robin, D. A., Abbas, P. J., & Hug, L. N. (1990). Neural responses to auditory temporal patterns. *Journal of the Acoustical Society of America, 87*, 1673–1682.

Romani, G. L., Williamson, S. J., Kaufman, L., & Brenner, D. (1982). Tonotopic organization of the human auditory cortex. *Science, 216*, 1339–1340.

Ryugo, D. K., & Weinberger, N. M. (1978). Differential plasticity of morphologically distinct neuron populations in the medial geniculate body of the cat during classical conditioning. *Behavioral Biology, 22*, 275–301.

Scheich, H. (1987). Neural correlates of auditory filial imprinting. *Journal of Comparative Physiology, 161*, 605–19.

Schreiner, C. E. (1992). Functional organization of the auditory cortex: maps and mechanisms. *Current Opinion in Neurobiology, 2*, 516–521.

Schreiner, C. E., & Langner, G. (1988a). Coding of temporal patterns in the central auditory nervous system. In G. M. Edelman, W. E. Gall, & W. M. Cowan (Eds.), *Auditory function* (pp. 337–361). New York: Wiley & Sons, Inc.

Schreiner, C. E., & Langner, G. (1988b). Periodicity coding in the inferior colliculus of the cat: II. Topographical organization. *Journal of Neurophysiology, 60*, 1823–1840.

Schreiner, C. E., & Sutter, M. L. (1992). Topography of excitatory bandwidth in cat primary auditory cortex: Single-neuron versus multiple-neuron recordings. *Journal of Neurophysiology, 68*, 1487–1502.

Schreiner, C. E., & Urbas, J. V. (1986). Representation of amplitude modulation in the auditory cortex of the cat. I. The anterior auditory field (AAF). *Hearing Research, 21*, 227–241.

Schreiner, C. E., & Urbas, J. V. (1988). Representation of amplitude modulation in the auditory cortex of the cat: II. Comparison between cortical fields. *Hearing Research, 32*(1), 49–64.

Schwarz, D. W., & Tomlinson, R. W. (1990). Spectral response patterns of auditory cortex neurons to harmonic complex tones in alert monkey (*Macaca mulatta*). *Journal of Neurophysiology, 64*(1), 282–298.

Sinex, D. G. (1992). Simulation of neural responses that underlie speech discrimination. In F. Eeckman (Eds.), *Analysis and modeling of neural systems II* . Norwell, MA: Kluwer.

Sinex, D. G., McDonald, L. P., & Mott, J. B. (1991). Neural correlates of nonmonotonic temporal acuity for voice onset time. *Journal Acoustical Society of America, 90*, 2441–2449.

Spangler, K. M., & Warr, W. B. (1991). The descending auditory system. In R. A. Altschuler, R. P. Bobbin, B. M. Clopton, & D. W. Hoffman (Eds.), *Neurobiology of hearing: The central auditory system* (pp. 27–46). New York: Raven Press.

Suga, N. (1990). Biosonar and neural computation in bats. *Science, 262*, 60–68.

Sutter, M. L., & Schreiner, C. E. (1991). Physiology and topography of neurons with multipeaked tuning curves in cat primary auditory cortex. *Journal of Neurophysiology, 65*, 1207–1226.

Taniguchi, I., Horikawa, J., Moriyama, T., & Nasu, M. (1992). Spatio-temporal pattern of frequency representation in the auditory cortex of guinea pigs. *Neuroscience Letters, 146*, 37–40.

Tomlinson, R. W., & Schwarz, D. W. (1988). Perception of the missing fundamental in nonhuman primates. *Journal Acoustical Society of America, 84*, 560–565.

Tramo, M. J., Cariani, P. A., & Delgutte, B. (1992). Representation of tonal consonance and dissonance in the temporal firing patterns of auditory nerve fibers: Responses to musical intervals composed of pure tones vs. harmonic complex tones. *Society for Neuroscience Abstracts, 18*, 382.

Walzl, E. M., & Woolsey, C. N. (1943). Cortical auditory areas of the monkey as determined by electrical excitation of nerve fibers in the osseous spiral lamina and by click stimulation. *Federation Proceedings, 2*, 52.

Weinberger, N. M. (1982). Sensory plasticity and learning: The magnocellular medial geniculate nucleus of the auditory system. In C. D. Woody (Ed.), *Conditioning: Representation of involved neural function* (pp. 697–710). New York: Plenum Publishing.

Weinberger, N. M. (1995). Dynamic regulation of receptive fields and maps in the adult sensory cortex. *Annual Review of Neuroscience, 18,* 129–158.

Weinberger, N. M., Ashe, J. H., & Edeline, J.-M. (1994). Learning-induced receptive field plasticity in the auditory cortex: Specificity of information storage. In J. Delacour (Ed.), *Neural bases of learning and memory* (pp. 590–635). Singapore: World Scientific Publishing.

Weinberger, N. M., Ashe, J. H., Metherate, R., McKenna, T. M., Diamond, D. M., & Bakin, J. S. (1990a). Retuning auditory cortex by learning: A preliminary model of receptive field plasticity. *Concepts in Neuroscience, 1*(1), 91–131.

Weinberger, N. M., Ashe, J. H., Metherate, R., McKenna, T. M., Diamond, D. M., Bakin, J. S., Lennartz, R. C., & Cassady, J. M. (1990b). Neural adaptive information processing: A preliminary model of receptive field plasticity in auditory cortex during Pavlovian conditioning. In M. Gabriel & J. Moore (Eds.), *Neurocomputation and learning: Foundations of adaptive networks* (pp. 91–138). Cambridge, MA: Bradford Books/MIT Press.

Weinberger, N. M., & Diamond, D. M. (1987). Physiological plasticity in auditory cortex: Rapid induction by learning. *Progress in Neurobiology, 29,* 1–55.

Weinberger, N. M., Javid, R., & Lepan, B. (1993). Long-term retention of learning-induced receptive field plasticity in the auditory cortex. *Proceedings of the National Academy of Science U. S. A., 90,* 2394–2398.

Weinberger, N. M., & McKenna, T. M. (1988). Sensitivity of single neurons in auditory cortex to contour: Toward a neurophysiology of music perception. *Music Perception, 5,* 355–390.

West, M. I., & King, A. P. (1990). Mozart's starling. *American Scientist, 78,* 106–114.

Whitfield, I. C. (1980). Auditory cortex and the pitch of complex tones. *Journal of the Acoustical Society of America, 67*(2), 644–647.

Whitfield, I. C. (1985). *The role of auditory cortex in behavior.* New York: Plenum Press.

Yamamoto, T., Uemura, T., & Llinas, R. (1992). Tonotopic organization of human auditory cortex revealed by multi-channel SQUID system. *Acta Otolaryngology, 112,* 201–204.

Yeshurun, Y., Wollberg, Z., & Dyn, N. (1989). Prediction of linear and non-linear responses of MGB neurons by system identification methods. *Bulletin of Mathematical Biology, 51,* 337–346.

Yost, W. A. (1991). Auditory image perception and analysis: The basis of hearing. *Hearing Research, 56,* 8–19.

Yost, W. A. (1992). Auditory perception and sound source determination. *Current Directions in Psychological Science, 1*(6), 179–184.

Zatorre, R. J. (1988). Pitch perception of complex tones and human temporal-lobe function. *Journal of the Acoustical Society of America, 84,* 566–572.

4

THE PERCEPTION OF MUSICAL TONES

RUDOLF RASCH

Utrecht University
Utrecht, Netherlands

REINIER PLOMP

Faculty of Medicine, Free University
Amsterdam, Netherlands

I. THE PSYCHOACOUSTICS OF MUSIC

A. INTRODUCTION

The aim of research in music perception is to explain how we respond subjectively to musical sound signals. In this respect, music perception is a part of psychophysics, the general denomination for scientific fields concerned with the relationship between the objective, physical properties of sensory stimuli in our environment and the sensations evoked by them. If the stimuli are of an acoustic nature, we speak of *psychoacoustics*. Psychoacoustics can be of a general, theoretical nature, it can also be applied to a certain class of auditory stimuli, such as music and speech. This chapter is devoted to *musical psychoacoustics*.

In this chapter, we focus our discussion on some basic perceptual properties of musical tones (pitch, loudness, timbre) and the phenomena that occur when several tones are presented simultaneously, which is what usually happens in music (beats and roughness, combination tones, consonance and dissonance). However, before we deal more extensively with them, some attention must be given to the methodology of psychoacoustics and to the frequency-analyzing power of the ear, a capacity that is fundamental to its perceptual functioning.

B. METHODOLOGY

Psychoacoustics is an empirical or, rather, experimental science. Observations from daily life and informal tryouts may be starting points for psychoacoustical

---

knowledge, but the core of the scientific content is the result of laboratory investigations. In this respect, psychoacoustics is an interdisciplinary field of research. Contributions have been made both by experimental psychologists and by physicists and acousticians.

A psychoacoustical experiment can be described most simply in a stimulus-response scheme. The *stimulus* is the sound presented to the subject. The experiment requires the subject to give a *response*. The experimenter tries to discover the relationship between the stimulus and response characteristics. Both stimulus and response are observable events. The subject is considered a "black box" that cannot be entered by the experimenter. Psychoacoustical research is often carried out without an attempt to explain the experimental results functionally in terms of sensory processes. Such attempts are made in research that is labeled *physiological acoustics*, a part of sensory physiology and neurophysiology.

Our ears are very sensitive organs. Because of this, very accurate control of the stimulus variables is required in psychoacoustical experiments. Sound pressure level differences of less than 1 dB, time differences of a few milliseconds, and frequency differences of less than 1 Hz can have a profound effect on the subjective response to a stimulus. It is impossible to obtain well-controlled psychoacoustic stimuli by manual means, such as playing tones or chords on a musical instrument. The precision of the ear in distinguishing fine nuances is much greater than our ability to produce these nuances. As a rule, psychoacoustics makes use of electronic audio equipment (usually computer-controlled) that can produce sound stimuli according to any specification. The computer can also be used for storage and analysis of stimuli and response data. Most of the problems concerning the production of the stimuli in psychoacoustical experiments may be considered solved. After the sound stimulus has been produced, it must reach the subject's eardrum with the least possible distortion. Usually high-quality headphones are used unless the spatial effect of the listening environment is involved. Background noises should be reduced, if not eliminated.

It is possible to have the subject describe his perception verbally. However, this response is often insufficient because our sensations allow much finer distinctions than our vocabulary does. Moreover, the use of words may differ from subject to subject. Because of this, in psychoacoustics most results are derived from responses made on the basis of a certain perception without direct reference to the perception itself. For example, if we have to indicate in which of two time intervals a sound has occurred, the response is a time indication based on an auditory sensation. A great deal of inventiveness is often required from the experimenter in designing his experimental paradigms.

The procedures used most often in psychoacoustical experiments are choice methods and adjustment methods. A single presentation of a sound event (one or more stimuli) to which a response must be made is called a *trial*. Using *choice methods*, the subject has to make, for each trial, a choice from a limited set of well-defined alternatives. The simplest case is the one with two alternatives, the *two-*

alternative forced choice. The insertion of the word forced is essential: The subject is obliged to choose. Subjects must guess when they are incapable of making a meaningful choice.

For example, let us assume that the investigator is studying under what conditions a probe tone can be heard simultaneously with another sound, or a masking sound. Each trial contains two successive time periods marked by visual signals. The masking sound is continuously present; the probe tone occurs in one of two time periods, randomly determined. If the probe tone is clearly detectable, the subject indicates whether it was presented in the first or in the second period. If the tone is not perceived at all, the subject must guess, resulting in approximately 50% correct responses. The transition from clearly detectable to not detectable tones is gradual. It is reflected by a gradual slope of the so-called *psychometric curve* that represents the percentage of correct responses plotted as a function of the sound pressure level of the target tone. The sound pressure level that corresponds to a score of 75% correct responses is usually adopted as the threshold for detection.

In order to arrive at an accurate estimate of the threshold, the experimenter varies the sound pressure level of the tone for the successive trials. In the *constant stimuli* method, the experimenter presents the tones according to a fixed procedure. The method of constant stimuli is time consuming because a number of trials are definitely suprathreshold or infrathreshold and, therefore, do not give much information. Another class of choice methods, called *adaptive methods*, makes a more efficient use of trials. The experimental series is started with a certain initial value of the stimulus variable. One or more correct responses, depending upon the experimental strategy adopted, result in a change in the stimulus variable that makes it harder for the subject to make a correct choice. If the subject makes one or more false responses, the experimental task is facilitated. In this way, the value of the stimulus variable fluctuates around a certain value, which can be defined to be the threshold for perception.

Other than choice methods, there is the *adjustment method.* The subject controls the stimulus variable himself and uses this control to find an optimal value. This method is not always feasible. The adjustment method is suitable for stimulus variables that allow an optimal quality in perception: the best pitch for a tone in a musical interval, the most comfortable loudness, the greatest similarity or dissimilarity, and so on. The optimal adjustment behaves like a stable equilibrium between lower and higher, both suboptimal, adjustments. Adjustment methods have the advantage that the results can be derived directly from the adjusted value and do not have to be derived indirectly from the psychometric curve.

C. THE EAR AS A FREQUENCY ANALYZER

Only by the ear's capacity to analyze complex sounds are we able to discriminate simultaneous tones in music. *Frequency analysis* may be considered the most characteristic property of the peripheral ear (Plomp, 1964). The cochlea is divided over its entire length into two parts by the basilar membrane. In 1942, Von Békésy was the first to observe, with ingenious experimentation, that at every point along its length, this membrane vibrates with maximum amplitude for a specific frequency. This finding confirmed the hypothesis, launched 80 years earlier by Helmholtz, that the cochlea performs a frequency analysis. Sound components with high frequencies are represented close to the base; components with low frequencies are represented near the apex of the cochlea. The frequency scale of the sound is converted into a spatial scale along the basilar membrane.

This capacity of the ear means that any periodic sound wave or *complex tone* is resolved into its frequency components, also called *partials* or *harmonics* (see Figure 1). In mathematics, the analogous procedure of determining the sinusoidal components of a periodic function is called *Fourier analysis*. In contrast with the theoretically perfect Fourier analysis, the frequency-analyzing power of the ear is limited: only the lower harmonics can be analyzed individually.

The extent to which the ear can separate simultaneous tones can be studied in many ways. Only two approaches are considered here. The first method investigates how many harmonics (with frequencies nf, $n = 1, 2, 3, 4$, etc.) can be distinguished in a complex tone. This can be done by using the two-alternative forced choice procedure: The listener has to decide which of two simple (sinusoidal) tones—one with frequency nf, the other with frequency $(n \pm \frac{1}{2})f$—is also present in the complex tone. The percentage of correct responses varies from 100 for low values of n to about 50 for high values of n. Experiments along these lines have shown (Plomp, 1964) that, on the average, listeners are able to distinguish the first five to seven harmonics.

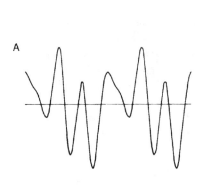

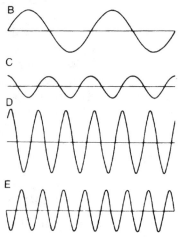

FIGURE 1   The waveform A, a complex tone, is in fact the sum of the simple tones B–E. This is an illustration of Fourier's theorem that every vibration of frequency f, $2f$, $3f$, and so on. These sinusoidal vibrations are called the harmonics.

A quite different approach involves measuring the minimum sound pressure level necessary for a probe tone to be audible when presented simultaneously with a complex tone. This is the so-called masked threshold; by varying the probe-tone frequency, we obtain the *masking pattern* of the complex tone. Such a pattern is reproduced in Figure 2. The masking pattern of a complex tone of 500 Hz reveals individual peaks corresponding to the first five harmonics, nicely demonstrating the limited frequency-analyzing power of the ear.

The usual measure indicating how well a system is able to analyze complex signals is its bandwidth. The finding that the fifth harmonic can be distinguished from the fourth and the sixth harmonics means that the mutual distance should be a minor third or more. This distance constitutes a rough, general estimate of the bandwidth of the hearing mechanism, known in the psychophysical literature as the *critical bandwidth* (Figure 3). A detailed review (Plomp, 1976) revealed that the bandwidth found experimentally is dependent on the experimental conditions. The values may differ by a factor of two.

In the lower frequency region (below 500 Hz), critical bandwidth is more or less constant if expressed in hertz. That means that musical intervals (frequency ratios) larger than the critical bandwidth at high frequencies may fall within the critical bandwidth at lower frequencies.

II. PERCEPTUAL ATTRIBUTES OF SINGLE TONES

A. PITCH

Pitch is the most characteristic property of tones, both simple (sinusoidal) and complex. Pitch systems (like the diatonic-chromatic and the 12-tone systems) are among the most elaborate and intricate ever developed in Western and non-West-

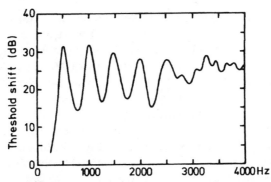

FIGURE 2   Masking pattern of a complex tone consisting of the first 12 harmonics of 500 Hz. Only the first five harmonics are analyzed by the ear. (Based on Plomp, 1964.)

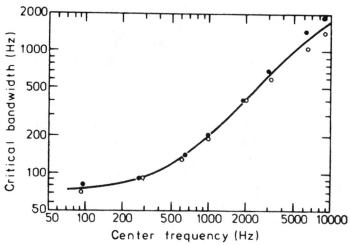

FIGURE 3 Critical bandwidth as a function of frequency. Curve is a rough approximation only.

ern music. Pitch is related to the frequency of a simple tone and to the fundamental frequency of a complex tone. The frequency of a tone is a property that can usually be controlled in production and is well preserved during its propagation to the listener's ears.

For our purposes, pitch may be characterized as a *one-dimensional* attribute, that is, all tones can be ordered along a single scale with respect to pitch (but see Chapters 8, 9 and 11, this volume). The extremes of this scale are *low* (tones with low frequencies) and *high* (tones with high frequencies). Sometimes tones with different spectral compositions (timbres) are not easily comparable as to pitch. It is possible that the clearness of pitch varies, for example, as result of important noise components or inharmonic partials, or that the subjective character of the pitch varies, for example when comparing the pitch of simple and complex tones. There are a number of subjective pitch scales:

1. The mel scale (see Stevens, Volkmann, & Newman, 1937). A simple tone of 1000 Hz has by definition a pitch of 1000 mel. The pitch in mels of other tones with another frequency must be determined by comparative scaling experiments. A sound with a pitch subjectively twice that of a 1000 Hz tone is 2000 mel; "half pitch" is 500 mel, and so on. Because phrases such as "a pitch half as high" or "a pitch twice as high" have no unambiguous subjective meaning, the mel scale is a rather unreliable scale. It is not used very often.

2. The musical pitch scale (i.e., the ordinary indications C_1, D_1, ..., C_4, ..., A_4, ...). These indications are usable only in musical situations.

3. The physical frequency scale in hertz. In psychoacoustical literature, the pitch of a tone is often indicated by its frequency or, in the case of complex tones, by its fundamental frequency. Because the correspondence between frequency

and pitch is monotonic, frequency is a rough indication of our pitch sensation. It must be realized, however, that our perception operates more or less on the basis of a logarithmic frequency scale.

Pitch in its musical sense has a range of about 20–5000 Hz, which is roughly the range of the fundamental frequencies of piano strings and organ pipes. Tones that have higher frequencies are audible but without definite pitch sensation. Low tones in the range of 10–50 Hz can have the character of a rattling sound. The transition from the perception of single pulses to a real pitch sensation is gradual. Pitch can be perceived after very few periods of the sound wave have been presented to the ear.

Simple tones have unambiguous pitches that can be indicated by means of their frequencies. These frequencies may serve as reference frequencies for the pitches of complex tones. The pitch sensation of complex tones is much more difficult to understand than the pitch of simple tones. As was discussed, the first five to seven harmonics of a complex tone can be distinguished individually if the listener's attentions is drawn to their possible presence. However, a complex tone, as heard in practice, is characterized by a single pitch, the pitch of the fundamental component. This pitch will be referred to as *low* pitch here. In psychoacoustical literature, this pitch is known under a variety of other terms, such a *periodicity pitch*, *repetition pitch*, *residue pitch*, and *virtual pitch* (De Boer, 1976, 1977). Experiments (Terhardt, 1971) have shown that the pitch of a complex tone with fundamental frequency f is somewhat lower than that of a sinusoidal tone with frequency f. The existence of low pitch of a complex tone raises two questions. First, why are all components of the complex tones perceived as a perceptual unit; that is, why do all partials fuse into one percept? Second, why is the pitch of this perceptual tone the pitch of the fundamental component?

The first question can be answered with reference to the Gestalt explanation of human perception. This may be formulated as follows. The various components of a complex tone are always present simultaneously. We become familiar with the complex tones of speech signals (both of our own speech and of other speakers) from an early age. It would not be efficient to perceive them all separately. All components point to a single source and meaning, so that perception of them as a unit gives a simpler view of the environment than separate perception. This mode of perception must be seen as a perceptual learning process. Gestalt psychology has formulated a number of laws that describe the perception of complex sensory stimuli. The perception of low pitch of complex tones can be classified under the heading of the *law of common fate*. The harmonics of a complex tone exhibit *common fate*.

The second question can also be answered with the help of a learning process directed toward perceptual efficiency. The periodicity of a complex tone is the most constant feature in its composition. The amplitudes of the partials are subjected to much variation, caused by selective reflection, absorption, passing of objects, and so on. Masking can also obscure certain partials. The periodicity, however, is a very stable and constant factor in a complex tone. This is reflected in the waveform built up from harmonics. The periodicity of a complex tone is at the same time the periodicity of the fundamental component of the tone. The perception of complex tones can be seen as a pattern-recognition process. The presence of a complete series of harmonics is not a necessary condition for the pitch recognition process to succeed. It is sufficient that at least a few pairs of adjacent harmonics are present so that the periodicity can be determined. It is conceivable that a perceptual learning process exists that makes possible the recognition of fundamental periodicity from a limited number of harmonic partials. This learning process is based on the same experiences as those that led to singular pitch perception. Pattern recognition theories of the perception of low pitch are of relatively recent origin. They have been worked out in detailed mathematical models that simulate the perception of complex tones (Gerson & Goldstein, 1978; Goldstein, 1973; Houtsma, 1979; Piszczalski & Galler, 1979).

The classical literature on tone perception abounds with theories based on von Helmholtz's (1863/1954) idea that the low pitch of a complex tone is derived from the fundamental component. The higher harmonics are thought only to influence the timbre of the tones but not to be strong enough to affect pitch. However, low pitch perception also occurs when the fundamental component is not present in the sound stimulus. This was already observed by Seebeck (1841) and brought to the attention of the modern psychoacousticians by Schouten (1938). These observations led Schouten to the formulation of a *periodicity pitch theory*. In this theory, pitch is derived from the waveform periodicity of the unresolved higher harmonics of the stimulus, the *residue*. This periodicity does not change if a component (e.g., the fundamental one) is removed. With this theory, the observations of Seebeck and Schouten concerning tones without fundamental components could be explained. An attempt has also been made to explain the low pitch of a tone without fundamental (the missing fundamental) as the result of the occurrence of combination tones, which provide a fundamental component in the inner ear. However, when these combination tones are effectively masked by low-pass noise, the sensation of low pitch remains (Licklider, 1954).

In musical practice, complex tones with weak or absent fundamentals are very common. Moreover, musical tones are often partially masked by other tones. These tones can, however, possess very clear low pitches. Effective musical sound stimuli are often incomplete when compared with the sound produced by the sources (instrument, voice).

Experiments in tone perception have pointed to a *dominance region* for pitch perception, roughly from 500 to 2000 Hz (Plomp, 1967; Ritsma, 1967). Partials falling in this dominance region are most influential with regard to pitch. One way of showing this is to work with tones with inharmonic partials. Assume a tone with partials of 204, 408, 612, 800, 1000, and 1200 Hz. The first three partials in isolation would give a pitch of 204 Hz. All six together give a pitch of 200 Hz because of the relative weight of the higher partials, which lie in the dominance region. The low pitch of complex tones with low fundamental frequencies (under 500 Hz) depends on the higher partials. The low pitch of tones with high fundamental frequencies is determined by the fundamental because they are in the dominance region. This dominance of the low frequencies shows that the low pitch of complex tones is the result of a kind of pattern-recognition process of the frequencies of harmonics separated by the ear's frequency-analyzing power, rather than based on the periodicity of the higher harmonics.

Tones with inharmonic components have been used quite frequently in tone perception research. An approximation of the pitch evoked by them is the fundamental of the least-deviating harmonic series. Assume a tone with components of 850, 1050, 1250, 1450, and 1650 Hz. The least-deviating harmonic series is 833, 1042, 1250, 1458, and 1667 Hz, which contains the fourth, fifth, sixth, seventh, and eighth harmonics of a complex tone with a fundamental of 208.3 Hz. This fundamental can be used as an approximation of the pitch sensation of the inharmonic complex (Figure 4). Let us consider an inharmonic tone with frequency components of 900, 1100, 1300, 1500, and 1700 Hz. This tone has an ambiguous pitch, because two approximations by harmonic series are possible, namely one with a fundamental of 216.6 Hz (the component of 1300 Hz being the sixth harmonic in this case) and one with a fundamental of 185.9 Hz (1300 Hz being the seventh harmonic).

If not all partials of a complex tone are necessary for low pitch perception, how few of them are sufficient? The following series of experimental investigations

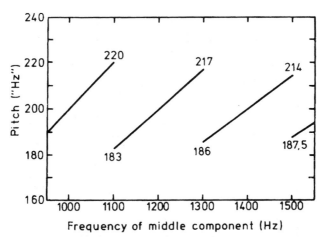

FIGURE 4   Schematic diagram of the low pitch of a complex tone consisting of five (inharmonic) components 200 Hz apart. The horizontal axis represents the frequency of the middle component. This component is taken as the fifth, sixth, seventh, or eighth pseudo-harmonic partial of a complex tone with low pitch, which is indicated along the vertical axis. The figure in the graph indicate the "pitches" of the stimuli with ambiguous pitch.

show a progressively decreasing number (see Figure 5). De Boer (1956) worked with five harmonics in the dominant region; Schouten, Ritsma, and Cardozo (1962), with three; Smoorenburg (1970), with two; and Houtsma and Goldstein (1972), with one plus one—that is, one partial presented to each ear.

In the latter case it is also possible to elicit low pitch perception. The authors concluded that low pitch is a central neural process not brought about by the peripheral sense organ (the ears). The last step in the series should be a low pitch perception evoked by one partial. That this is also possible has been shown by Houtgast (1976). The following conditions have to be fulfilled: The frequency region of the low pitch has to be filled with noise, the single partial must have a low signal-to-noise ratio, and attention has to be directed to the fundamental frequency region by prior stimuli. These conditions create a perceptual situation in which it is not certain that the fundamental is not there, so that inference from earlier stimuli suggest to the auditory system that the fundamental should be there.

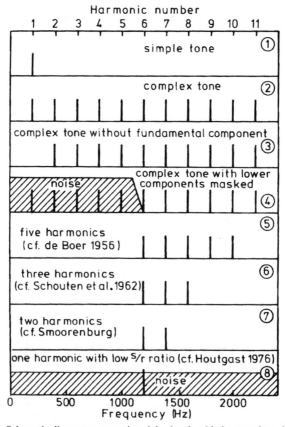

FIGURE 5   Schematic diagram representing eight signals with the same low pitch.

B. LOUDNESS

The physical correlate that underlies the *loudness* of a tone is intensity, usually expressed as sound pressure level in decibels. Sound pressure level is a relative measure, expressed either relative to a zero level defined in the experimental situation or relative to a general reference sound pressure of 2×10^{-5} N/m². Sound pressure levels of performed music vary roughly from 40 dB for a pianissimo to about 90 dB for a full orchestral forte-tutti (Winckel, 1962). By means of electronic amplification, higher levels are reached in pop concerts. These levels, sometimes beyond 100 dB, are potentially damaging to the ear in case of prolonged presentation (Fearn, 1975a, 1975b; Flugrath, 1969; Rintelman, Lindberg, & Smitley, 1972; Wood & Limpscomb, 1972).

The subjective assessment of loudness is more complicated than the physical measurement of the sound pressure level. Several *loudness scales* have been proposed in the past. None of them, however, can be applied fully satisfactorily in all conditions. We give the following summary review:

1. The *sone* scale is a purely psychophysical loudness scale (Stevens, 1936). The loudness of a simple (sinusoidal) tone of 1000 Hz with a sound pressure level of 40 dB is defined to be 1 sone; a tone with double loudness is assigned the loudness of 2 sones, and so on. In general, a sound of X sones is n times louder than a sound of X/n sones. The experimental determination of the relationship between the physical sound level and the psychophysical loudness is not very reliable because of the uncertainty of what is actually meant by "X times louder."

2. The *phone* scale is a mixed physical-psychophysical loudness scale with scale values expressed in decibels and, therefore, termed *loudness level*. The loudness level of a sound in phones is equal to the sound pressure level of a 1000-Hz tone with the same loudness. For tones of 1000 Hz, sound pressure level equals loudness level. The loudness level of simple tones of other frequencies and of complex tones or other sounds (noises, etc.) is found by comparison experiments, which can be done with acceptable reliability. These comparisons may be used to draw contours of equal loudness as a function of frequency.

3. The *sensation-level* scale is also a mixed scale. Sensation level is defined as the sound pressure level relative to threshold level and, as such, is also expressed in decibels. It may differ as a function of frequency or other characteristics of a sound but also from subject to subject.

4. In many papers on psychoacoustics, no loudness indications are given. Instead, physical levels are mentioned. For the researcher, physical levels are the most precise reference and at the same time a rough indication of subjective loudness.

In the description of the relationship between sound pressure level and loudness, a clear distinction must be made between sounds with all spectral energy within one critical band and sounds with spectral energy spread over more than one critical band. If all sound energy is limited to one critical band, the loudness L

in sones increases monotonically with intensity I. The relation is often approached by the equation

$$L = k\,I^n,$$

in which k and n are empirically chosen constants. A consequence of this relation is the rule that equal intensity ratios result in equal loudness ratios. Now, an intensity ratio is a fixed level difference (in decibels) so that the rule can also be formulated as follows: A certain loudness ratio corresponds to a certain level difference. Psychophysicists have been much interested in the level difference that results in double or half loudness, and many experiments have been done to establish this difference. The outcomes of these experiments are disappointingly inconsistent. Stevens (1955) summarized all experiments known to him with the median value of 10 dB for doubling loudness, later (Stevens, 1972) modified to 9 dB. These values correspond to values of $n = 0.3$ and $n = 0.33$, respectively, for the exponent in the formula. It is also possible to interpret the subjective loudness judgment as an imaginary judgment of the distance to the sound source. In this theory (Warren, 1977), half loudness must correspond to double distance, which gives, in free field conditions, a decrease of 6 dB in sound pressure level. Warren conducted experiments in which this value was indeed found.

The assessment of loudness is a complicated matter if sound energy is present in more than one critical band. This situation is the common one for musical tones, especially for chords, and music played by ensembles, choirs, and orchestras. Total loudness is greater than when the same amount of sound energy is concentrated within one critical band. A number of models have been proposed that intend to be simulations of the perceptual processes involved and the parameters of which have been assigned values in accordance with psychophysical experiments. The models by Stevens (1955), Zwicker, Flottorp, and Stevens (1957), Zwicker and Scharf (1965) and Stevens (1972) are well known. These models have also been applied to musical sounds, especially to organ tones (Churcher, 1962; Pollard, 1978a, 1978b).

Although loudness variations play an important role in music, they are less important than pitch variations. The number of assignable loudness degrees in music is limited to about five, coded musically from soft to loud as pianissimo, piano, mezzo forte, forte and fortissimo. The definition of these loudness degrees is rater imprecise (Clark & Luce, 1965; Clark & Milner, 1964; Patterson, 1974). Judgment of musical loudness cannot have the degree of reliability and preciseness that is possible with the judgments of (relative) pitch, duration, tempo, and so on. This is a consequence of the fact that the underlying physical dimension, intensity, is hard to control precisely. Sources of variation are encountered in sound production, in the fixed acoustic conditions of a room (absorption and thus attenuation by walls, floor, ceiling, etc.), in variable acoustic conditions (e.g., the presence or the absence of an audience, the relative positions of sound source and listener, disturbing external noises), and in the hearing thresholds of the listeners.

In all the stages on the road from sound production to sound perception, sound pressure level is liable to be altered whereas frequency is not.

C. TIMBRE

Timbre is, after pitch and loudness, the third attribute of the subjective experience of musical tones. Subjectively, timbre is often coded as the function of the sound source or of the meaning of the sound. We talk about the timbre of certain musical instruments, of vowels, and of sounds that signify certain events in our environment (e.g., apparatus, sound from nature, footsteps, a door slamming).

What are the physical parameters that contribute to the perception of a certain timbre? In a restricted sense, timbre may be considered the subjective counterpart of the spectral composition of tones. Especially important is the relative amplitude of the harmonics. This view was first stated by Helmholtz over a century ago and is reflected by the definition of timbre according to the American Standards Association (Acoust. Terminology S1.1., 1960): "Timbre is that attribute of auditory sensation in terms of which a listener can judge that two steady-state complex tones having the same loudness and pitch are dissimilar." Research has shown that temporal characteristics of the tones may have a profound influence on timbre as well, which has led to a broadening of the concept of timbre (Schouten, 1968). Both onset effects (e.g., rise time, presence of noise or inharmonic partials during onset, unequal rise of partials, characteristic shape of rise curve) and steady-state effects (e.g., vibrato, amplitude modulation, gradual swelling, pitch instability) are important factors in the recognition and, therefore, in the timbre of tones.

Experiments (e.g., Berger, 1964; Clark, Robertson, & Luce, 1964; Saldanha & Corso, 1964) have shown that the identification of instrumental sounds is impaired when temporally characteristic parts of tones (especially the onsets) are removed.

Sounds cannot be ordered on a single scale with respect to timbre. Timbre is a *multidimensional attribute* of the perception of sounds. Dimensional research is highly time-consuming and is therefore always done with a restricted set of sound stimuli. The dimensions found in such an investigation are of course determined by the stimulus set.

Dimensional research of timbre leads to the ordering of sound stimuli on the dimensions of a timbre space. An example of such research is that by Von Bismarck (1974a, 1974b). His stimulus set contained a large number (35) of tone and noise stimuli. The most important factors found by him can be characterized as follows: (a) *sharpness*, determined by a distribution of spectral energy that has its gravity point in the higher frequency region and (b) *compactness*, a factor that distinguishes between tonal (compact) and noise (not compact) aspects of sound.

In some studies, sound stimuli have been submitted to multidimensional scaling, both perceptual and physical. The physical scaling can be based on the spectral composition of the sounds, as was done in Plomp's (1979) experiments with tones from a number of organ stops. Figure 6 gives the two-dimensional represen-

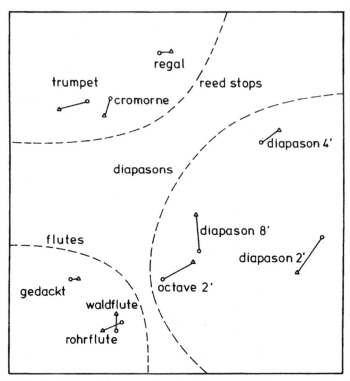

FIGURE 6   Result of matching a two-dimensional perceptual timbre representation (circles) of organ stops with the corresponding physical (spectral) representation (triangles) of the same sounds. The timbre scaling is the result of multidimensional scaling applied to triadic comparison data. The physical scaling is based on a factor analysis of the spectral composition of the tones. The vertical dimension can be labeled as few versus many higher harmonics. (Based on Plomp, 1979.)

tation of 10 sounds, both perceptual and physical. The configurations correspond rather well, leading to the conclusion that in this set of stimuli the sound spectrum is the most important factor in the perception of timbre.

Other examples of dimensional research on timbre are the investigations by Plomp (1970), Wedin and Goude (1972), Plomp and Steeneken (1973), Miller and Carterette (1975), Grey (1977), and De Bruijn (1978).

III. PERCEPTUAL ATTRIBUTES OF SIMULTANEOUS TONES

A. BEATS AND ROUGHNESS

In this and the following sections, we discuss perceptual phenomena that occur as the result of two simultaneous tones. We call the simultaneously sounding tones the *primary tones*.

We consider first the case of two simultaneous simple tones. Several conditions can be distinguished, depending on frequency difference (Figure 7). If the two primary tones have equal frequencies, they fuse into one tone, in which the intensity depends on the phase relation between the two tones. If the tones differ somewhat in frequency, the result is a signal with periodic amplitude and frequency variations with a rate equal to the frequency difference. The frequency variations are only slight and are not considered here. The amplitude variations, however, can be considerable and result in a fluctuating intensity and perceived loudness.

These loudness fluctuations are called *beats*, if they can be discerned individually by the ear, which occurs if their rate is less than about 20 Hz (Terhardt, 1968a, 1968b, 1974b; Zwicker, 1952). A stimulus equal to the sum of two simple tones with equal amplitudes and frequencies f and g:

$$p(t) = \sin 2\pi f t + \sin 2\pi g t,$$

can be described as:

$$p(t) = (2\cos 2\pi \tfrac{1}{2} [g - f]t) \times (\sin 2\pi \tfrac{1}{2} [f + g]t)$$

This is a signal with a frequency that is the average of the original primary frequencies and an amplitude that fluctuates slowly with a *beat frequency* of $g - f$ Hz (Figure 8). Amplitude variation is less strong if the two primary tones have different amplitudes.

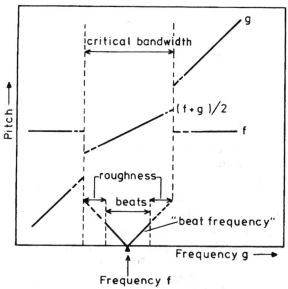

FIGURE 7 Schematic diagram representing perceptual phenomena that may occur when two simple tones with a small frequency difference sound simultaneously. The frequency of one tone is set constant (f); the frequency of the other tone (g) varies along the horizontal axis. (Based on Roederer, 1975.)

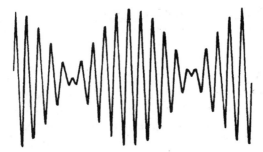

FIGURE 8   Waveform arising from the superposition of two simple tones with a small frequency difference.

When the frequency difference is larger than about 20 Hz, the ear is no longer able to follow the rapid amplitude fluctuations individually. Instead of the sensation of fluctuating loudness, there is a rattle-like sensation called *roughness* (Terhardt, 1974a). Beats and roughness can only occur if the two primary tones are not resolved by the ear (that means, not processed separately but combined). If the frequency difference is larger than the critical band, the tones are perceived individually with no interference phenomena.

In musical sounds, beats can occur with just noncoinciding harmonies of mistuned consonant intervals of complex tones. If the fundamental frequencies of the tones of an octave (theoretically 1:2) or fifth (2:3) differ a little from the theoretical ratio, there will be harmonics that differ slightly in frequency and will cause beats. These beats play an important role when tuning musical instruments. Experiments by Vos (1984) have shown that the beats perceived most dominantly in the fifth and the major third originate from the lowest pair of adjacent harmonics.

B. COMBINATION TONES

Two simple tones at a relatively high sound pressure level and with a frequency difference that is not too large can give rise to the perception of so-called combination tones. These combination tones arise in the ear as a product of nonlinear transmission characteristics. The combination tones are not present in the acoustic signal. However, those tones are perceived as if they were present. The ear cannot distinguish between perceived components that are "real" (in the stimulus) and those that are not. The combination tones are simple tones that may be canceled effectively by adding a real simple tone with the same frequency and amplitude but opposite phase. This cancellation tone can be used to study combination tones.

Psychoacoustical research on combination tones has shown that the pitches of the combination tones agree with the frequencies predicted by nonlinear transmission (Hall, 1975; Plomp, 1965; Schroeder, 1975b; Smoorenburg, 1972a, 1972b; Weber & Mellert, 1975; Zurek & Leskowitz, 1976). However, the correspondence between the relative amplitude predicted and the subjective loudness measured is far from perfect. Clearly the phenomenon of combination tones is more complicated that can be described in a simple formula. Moreover, there are individual differences, which should be expected because this is a distortion process. Experiments have shown that the following combination tone frequencies are the most important: the so-called *difference tone* with frequency $g - f$ Hz, the *second-order difference tone* with frequency $2f - g$ Hz, and the *third-order difference tone* with frequency $3f - 2g$ Hz (Figure 9).

The diagram illustrates that the combination tones are stronger for small frequency differences of the primary tones than for large differences; this indicates that the origin of combination tones is tightly connected with the frequency-analyzing process in the inner ear. It should be noted that the importance of *summation tones* (with frequency $f + g$) and the so-called *aural harmonics* (with frequencies $2f$, $3f$, etc. and $2g$, $3g$, etc.) is questionable.

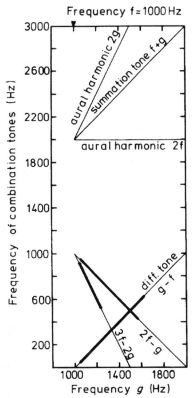

FIGURE 9 Frequency ranges over which particular combination tones can occur. The frequency f of the lower primary tone is 1000 Hz. The frequency of the higher primary tone (g) varies from 1000 Hz up to 2000 Hz. The thin lines correspond to the various theoretically possible combination-tone frequencies; the solid lines represent the combination tones found most often.

Although combination tones were discovered by musicians in musical contexts (Tartini and Sorge in the 18th century), their significance for music is not very high. Combination tones can be easily evoked by playing loud tones in the high register on two flutes or recorders or double stops on the violin. In a normal listening situation, however, their levels are usually too low to attract attention. Moreover, they will be masked by the tones of other (lower) instruments. Some violin teachers (following Tartini) advise the use of combination tones as a tool for controlling the intonation of double-stop intervals. Because audible combination tones behave more as simple tones in lower frequency regions than the complex tones to be intonated, a pitch comparison of comparison tones and played tones should not be given too much weight.

C. CONSONANCE AND DISSONANCE

The simultaneous sounding of several tones may be pleasant or euphonious to various degrees. The pleasant sound is called *consonant*; the unpleasant or rough one, *dissonant*. The terms consonance and dissonance have been used here in a perceptual or sensory sense. This aspect has been labeled *tonal consonance* (Plomp & Levelt, 1965) or *sensory consonance* (Terhardt, 1976), to be distinguished from consonance in a musical situation. Musical consonance has its root in perceptual consonance, of course, but is dependent on the rules of music theory, which, to a certain extent, can operate independently from perception.

The perceptual consonance of an interval consisting of two simple tones depends directly on the frequency difference between the tones, not on the frequency ratio (or musical interval). If the frequency separation is very small (less than a semitone) or larger than critical bandwidth, the two tones together sound consonant. In the first case, the tones fuse to a single one, in the second case, the tones do not interfere with each other. Dissonance occurs if the frequency separation is less than a critical bandwidth (see Figure 10). The most dissonant interval arises with a

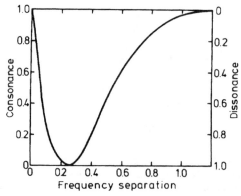

FIGURE 10   Consonance of an interval consisting of two simple tones as a function of frequency separation, measured relative to critical bandwidth. (Based on Plomp & Levelt, 1965.)

separation of about a quarter of the critical bandwidth: about 20 Hz in low-frequency regions, about 4% (a little less than a semitone) in the higher regions (Figure 11). The frequency separation of the minor third (20%), major third (25%), fourth (33%), fifth (50%), and so on, is usually enough to give consonant combination of simple tones. However, if the frequencies are low, the frequency separation of thirds (and eventually also fifths) is less than critical bandwidth so that even these intervals cause a dissonant beating. For this reason, these consonant intervals are not used in the bass register in musical compositions.

The consonance of intervals of complex tones can be derived from the consonances of the simple-tone combinations the complex tones comprise. In this case, the dissonance is the additive element. The dissonance of all combinations of neighboring partials can be determined and added to give the total dissonance and, inversely, the total consonance of the sound. Sounds with widely spaced partials, such as clarinet tones (with only the odd harmonics), are more consonant than sounds with narrowly spaced partials. The composition of the plenum of an organ is such that the partials are widely spaced throughout the spectrum. Some mathematical models have been worked out that describe the dissonance of a pair of simple tones and the way in which the dissonances of partial pairs in tone complexes have to be added (Hutchinson & Knopoff, 1978; Kameoka & Kuriyagawa, 1969a, 1969b; Plomp & Levelt, 1965; Terhardt, 1974a, 1976, 1978). As far as can be decided, these models give a good picture of consonance perception. Recent experiments by Vos (1988), in which various 12-tone tuning systems were compared, have shown that their perceptual acceptability to musically trained listeners could be accurately predicted from a linear combination of the purity ratings of the isolated harmonic fifths and major thirds of the tuning systems involved.

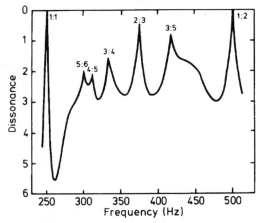

FIGURE 11   Consonance of an interval consisting of two complex tones (with six harmonics). The lower tone (f) has a fundamental frequency of 250 Hz; the fundamental frequency of the higher tone is the variable along the horizontal axis. The consonance/dissonance values are predictions from the model of Plomp and Levelt (1965).

The consonance of a musical interval, defined as the sum of two complex tones with a certain ratio in fundamental frequency, is highly dependent on the simplicity of the frequency ratio. Intervals with frequency ratios that can be expressed in small integer numbers (say, less than 6) are relatively consonant because the lower, most important components of the two tones are either widely apart or coincide. If the frequency ratio is less simple, a number of partials from the two tones will differ only a little in frequency, and these partial pairs give rise to dissonance. It seems that intervals with the number 7 in their frequency proportions (7/4, 7/5, ...) are about on the borderline between consonance and dissonance.

Experiments with inharmonic partials (Pierce, 1966; Slaymaker, 1970) have shown that consonance or dissonance is indeed dependent on the coincidence of partials and not necessarily on the simple frequency ratio between the fundamental frequencies (which is usually the cause of the coincidence).

If the number of partials in a complex tone increases or if the strengths of the higher harmonics (with narrow spacing) increase, the tone is perceived as more dissonant (compare the trumpet with the flute, for instance). However, the nth partial is required in order to make an interval with frequency ratio $n:m$ or $m:n$ relatively consonant. For example, if the fifth harmonic is absent, the usual beating (dissonance) of a mistuned major third (4:5) will be absent (see also Figure 11).

Musical consonance in Western polyphonic and harmonic music is clearly based on perceptual consonance of complex (harmonic) tones. Intervals with simple frequency ratios are consonant. Intervals with nonsimple frequency ratios are dissonant. The way in which consonance and dissonance are used in music theory and composition varies considerably from one historical period to another.

IV. CONCLUSION

More than a century ago, Helmholtz published his classic volume *On the Sensations of Tone* (1863). The subtitle specifically indicates the intention of this study: *As a Physiological Basis for the Theory of Music.* For Helmholtz, the theory of music (as a compendium of rules that control composition and as such the musical sound stimulus) could only be understood fully if it could be shown that its elements had their origin in the perceptual characteristics of our hearing organ. Helmholtz's working hypothesis has been put aside by later investigators, both those who worked in music and those who worked in psychoacoustics. Several reasons for this can be given. First, before the introduction of electroacoustic means of tone production and control in the 1920s, it was not possible to carry out the necessary psychoacoustical experiments, while Helmholtz's observations proved to be insufficient in many ways. Second, it turned out that music theory has its own rules apart from the perceptual relevance of the characteristics of the sounds that it creates. Therefore, it is not clear, either for the music theorist or for the psychoacoustician, which aspects of music theory should be subjected to psychoacoustical research and which should not. Fortunately, in recent years much research has been initiated to determine the relationship between musical-theoretical and perceptual entities. For the time being, no complete view can be given, but it may be expected that Helmholtz's fundamental thesis on the relation between the properties of the human auditory perceptual system and the elements of musical composition will be a permanent inspiration to researchers in the field of musical psychoacoustics for quite a long time to come.

REFERENCES

Békésy, G. von (1942). Über die Schwingungen der Schneckentrennwand beim Präparat und Ohrenmodell. *Akustische Zeitschrift, 7,* 173–186.

Berger, K. W. (1964). Some factors in the recognition of timbre. *Journal of the Acoustical Society of America,36,* 1888–1891.

Bismarck, G. von. (1974a). Timbre of steady sounds: A factorial investigation of its verbal attributes. *Acustica, 30,* 146–159.

Bismarck, G. von. (1974b). Sharpness as an attribute of the timbre of steady sounds. *Acustica, 30,* 159–172.

Boer, E. de. (1956). On the *"residue"* in hearing. Unpublished doctoral dissertation, University of Amsterdam, Amsterdam.

Boer, E. de. (1976). On the "residue" and auditory pitch perception. In W. D. Keidel & W. D. Neff (Eds.), *Handbook of sensory physiology: Vol. V. Auditory system: Part 3. Clinical and special topics* (pp. 479–583). Berlin: Springer-Verlag.

Boer, E. de. (1977). Pitch theories unified. In F. F. Evans & J. P. Wilson (Eds.), *Psychophysics and physiology of hearing* (pp. 323–335). New York: Academic Press.

Bruijn, A. de. (1978). Timbre-classification of complex tones. *Acustica, 40,* 108–114.

Churcher, B. G. (1962). Calculation of loudness levels for musical sounds. *Journal of the Acoustical Society of America, 34,* 1634–1642.

Clark, M., Jr., & Luce, D. (1965). Intensities of orchestral instrument scales played at prescribed dynamic markings. *Journal of the Audio Engineering Society, 13,* 151–157.

Clark, M., Jr., & Milner, P. (1964). Dependence of timbre on the tonal loudness produced by musical instruments. *Journal of the Audio Engineering Society, 12,* 28–31.

Clark, M. Jr., Robertson, P., & Luce, D. (1964). A preliminary experiment on the perceptual basis for musical instrument families, *Journal of the Audio Engineering Society, 12,* 199–203.

Fearn, R. W. (1975a). Level limits on pop music. *Journal of Sound and Vibration, 38,* 591–592.

Fearn, R. W. (1975b). Level measurements of music. *Journal of Sound and Vibration, 43,* 588–591.

Flugrath, J. M. (1969). Modern-day rock-and-roll music and damage-risk criteria. *Journal of the Acoustical Society of America, 45,* 704–711.

Gerson, A., & Goldstein, J. L. (1978). Evidence for a general template in central optimal processing for pitch of complex tones. *Journal of the Acoustical Society of America, 63,* 498–510.

Goldstein, J. L. (1973). An optimum processor theory for the central formation of the pitch of complex tones. *Journal of the Acoustical Society of America, 54,* 1496–1516.

Grey, J. M. (1977). Multidimensional perceptual scaling of musical timbres. *Journal of the Acoustical Society of America, 61,* 1270–1277.

Hall, J. L. (1975). Nonmonotonic behavior of distortion product. 2f1–f2: Psychophysical observations. *Journal of the Acoustical Society of America, 58,* 1046–1050.

Helmholtz, H. von. (1954). *On the sensations of tone as a physiological basis for the theory of music* (A. J. Ellis, Trans.). New York: Dover. (Original work published 1863)

Houtgast, T. (1976). Subharmonic pitches of a pure tone at low S/N ratio. *Journal of the Acoustical Society of America, 60,* 405–409.

Houtsma, A. J. M. (1979). Musical pitch of two tone complexes and predictions by modern pitch theories. *Journal of the Acoustical Society of America, 66,* 87–99.

Houtsma, A. J. M., & Goldstein, J. L. (1972). The central origin of the pitch of complex tones: Evidence from musical interval recognition. *Journal of the Acoustical Society of America, 51,* 520–529.

Hutchinson, W., & Knopoff, L. (1978). The acoustic component of Western consonance. *Interface, 7,* 1–29.

Kameoka, A., & Kuriyagawa, M. (1969a). Consonance theory: Part I. Consonance of dyads. *Journal of the Acoustical Society of America, 45,* 1451–1459.

Kameoka, A., & Kuriyagawa, M. (1969b). Consonance theory: Part II. Consonance of complex tones and its calculation method. *Journal of the Acoustical Society of America, 45,* 1460–1469.

Licklider, J. C. R. (1954). "Periodicity" pitch and "place" pitch. *Journal of the Acoustical Society of America, 26,* 945.

Miller, J. R., & Carterette, E. C. (1975). Perceptual space for musical structures. *Journal of the Acoustical Society of America, 58,* 711–720.

Patterson, B. (1974). Musical dynamics, *Scientific American, 31,* 78–95.

Pierce, J. R. (1966). Attaining consonance in arbitrary scales. *Journal of the Acoustical Society of America, 40,* 249.

Piszczalski, M., & Galler, B. A. (1979). Predicting musical pitch from component frequency ratios. *Journal of the Acoustical Society of America, 66,* 710–720.

Plomp, R. (1964). The ear as a frequency analyzer. *Journal of the Acoustical Society of America, 36,* 1628–1636.

Plomp, R. (1965). Delectability threshold for combination tones. *Journal of the Acoustical Society of America, 37,* 1110–1123.

Plomp, R. (1967). Pitch of complex tones. *Journal of the Acoustical Society of America, 41,* 1526–1533.

Plomp, R. (1970). Timbre as a multidimensional attribute of complex tones. In R. Plomp, & G. F. Smoorenburg (Eds.), *Frequency analysis and periodicity detection in hearing* (pp. 397–414). Leiden: Sijthoff.

Plomp, R. (1976). *Aspects of tone sensation.* New York: Academic Press.

Plomp, R. (1979). Fysikaliska motsvarigheter till klanfärg hos stationära ljud. In *Vår hörsel och musiken* (pp. 16–29). Stockholm: Kungl Musikaliska Akademien.

Plomp, R., & Levelt, W. J. M. (1965). Tonal consonances and critical bandwidth. *Journal of the Acoustical Society of America, 38,* 548–560.

Plomp, R., & Steeneken, H. J. M. (1973). Place dependence of timbre in reverberant sound fields. *Acustica, 28,* 49–59.

Pollard, H. F. (1978a). Loudness of pipe organ sounds: I. Plenum combinations. *Acustica, 41,* 65–74.

Pollard, H. F. (1978b). Loudness of pipe organ sounds: II. Single notes. *Acustica, 41,* 75–85.

Rintelmann, W. F., Lindberg, R. F., & Smitley, F. K. (1972). Temporary threshold shift and recovery patterns from two types of rock-and-roll music presentation. *Journal of the Acoustical Society of America, 1,* 1249–1255.

Ritsma, R. J. (1967). Frequencies dominant in the perception of the pitch of complex sounds. *Journal of the Acoustical Society of America, 42,* 191–198.

Roederer, J. G. (1975). *Introduction to the physics and psychophysics of music* (2nd ed.). New York and Berlin: Springer.

Saldanha, F. I., & Corso, J. F. (1964). Timbre cues and the identification of musical instruments. *Journal of the Acoustical Society of America, 36,* 2021–2026.

Schouten, J. F. (1938). The perception of subjective tones. *Proceedings of the Koninklijke Nederlandse Akademie van Wetenschappen, 34,* 1418–1424.

Schouten, J. F. (1968). The perception of timbre. In *Report of the Sixth International Congress on Acoustics, Tokyo,* Paper GP-6-2.

Schouten, J. R., Ritsma, R. J., & Cardozo. B. I. (1962). Pitch of the residue. *Journal of the Acoustical Society of America, 34,* 1418–1424.

Schroeder, M. R. (1975a). Models of hearing. *Proceedings of the IEEE, 63,* 1332–1350.

Schroeder, M. R. (1975b). Amplitude behavior of the cubic difference tone. *Journal of the Acoustical Society of America, 58,* 728–732.

Seebeck, A. (1841). Beobachtungen über einige Bedingungen der Entschung von Tönen. *Annalen der Physik und Chemic, 53,* 417–436.

Slaymaker, F. H. (1970). Chords from tones having stretched partials. *Journal of the Acoustical Society of America, 47,* 1569–1571.

Smoorenburg, G. F. (1970). Pitch perception of two-frequency stimuli. *Journal of the Acoustical Society of America, 48,* 924–942.

Smoorenburg, G. F. (1972a). Audibility region of combination tones. *Journal of the Acoustical Society of America, 52,* 603–614.

Smoorenburg, G. F. (1972b). Combination tones and their origin. *Journal of the Acoustical Society of America, 52,* 615–632.

Stevens, S. S. (1936). A scale for the measurement of a psychological magnitude: Loudness. *Psychological Review, 43,* 405–416.

Stevens, S. S. (1955). The measurement of loudness. *Journal of the Acoustical Society of America, 27,* 815–829.

Stevens, S. S. (1972). Perceived level of noise by Mark VII and decibels (E). *Journal of the Acoustical Society of America, 51,* 575–601.

Stevens, S. S., Volkmann, J., & Newman, E. B. (1937). A scale for measurement of the psychological magnitude pitch. *Journal of the Acoustical Society of America, 8,* 185–190.

Terhardt, E. (1968a). Über die durch amplitedenmodulierte Sinustöne hervorgerufenen Hörenempfindung. *Acustica, 20,* 210–214.

Terhardt, E. (1968b). Über akustische Rauhigkeit und Schwankungsstärke. *Acustica, 20,* 215–224.

Terhardt, E. (1971). Die Tonhöhe harmonischer Klänge und das Oktavinterval. *Acustica, 24,* 126–136.

Terhardt, E. (1974a). Pitch, consonance and harmony. *Journal of the Acoustical Society of America, 55,* 1061–1069.

Terhardt, E. (1974b). On the perception of periodic sound fluctuations (roughness) *Acustica, 30,* 201–203.

Terhardt, E. (1976). Psychoakustisch begründetes Konzept der musikalischen Konsonanz. *Acustica, 36,* 121–137.

Terhardt, E. (1978). Psychoacoustic evaluation of musical sounds. *Perception & Psychophysics, 23,* 483–492.

Vos, J. (1984). Spectral effects in the perception of pure and tempered intervals: Discrimination and beats. *Perception &Psychophysics, 35,* 173–185.

Vos, J. (1988). Subjective acceptability of various regular twelve-tone tuning systems in two-part musical fragments. *Journal of the Acoustical Society of America, 83,* 2383–2392.

Warren, R. M. (1977). Subjective loudness and its physical correlate. *Acustica, 37,* 334–346.

Weber, R., & Mellert, C. (1975). On the nonmonotonic behavior of cubic distortion products in the human ear. *Journal of the Acoustical Society of America, 57,* 207–214.

Wedin, I., & Goude, G. (1972). Dimensional analysis of the perception of instrumental timbre. *Scandinavian Journal of Psychology, 13,* 228–240.

Wightman, F. L. (1973). The pattern-transformation model of pitch. *Journal of the Acoustical Society of America, 54,* 407–416.

Winckel, F. W. (1962). Optimum acoustic criteria of concert halls for the performance of classical music. *Journal of the Acoustical Society of America, 34,* 81–86.

Wood, W. S. III, & Limpscomb, D. M. (1972). Maximum available sound-pressure levels from stereo components. *Journal of the Acoustical Society of America, 52,* 484–487.

Zurek, P. M., & Leskowitz, B. (1976). Measurements of the combination tones f2 - f1 and 2f1 - f2. *Journal of the Acoustical Society of America, 60,* 155–168.

Zwicker, E. (1952). Die Grenzen der Hörbarkeit der Amplitudenmodualtion und der Frequenzmodulation eines Tones. *Acustica, 2,* Beihefte 125–135.

Zwicker, E., Flottorp, C., & Stevens, S. S. (1957). Critical bandwidth in loudness summations. *Journal of the Acoustical Society of America, 29,* 548–557.

Zwicker, E., & Scharf, B. (1965). A model of loudness summation. *Psychological Review, 72,* 3–26.

5

EXPLORATION OF TIMBRE BY

ANALYSIS AND SYNTHESIS

JEAN-CLAUDE RISSET

Directeur de Recherche au CNRS
Laboratoire de Mécanique et d'Acoustique
Marseille, France

DAVID L. WESSEL

Center for New Music and Audio Technologies
Department of Music
University of California, Berkeley
Berkeley, California

I. TIMBRE

Timbre refers to the quality of sound. It is the perceptual attribute that enables us to distinguish among orchestral instruments that are playing the same pitch and are equally loud. But, unlike loudness and pitch, timbre is not a well-defined perceptual attribute. Definitions tend to indicate what timbre is not rather than what it is. Take as an example the following enigmatic definition provided by the American National Standards Institute (1960, p. 45): "Timbre is that attribute of auditory sensation in terms of which a listener can judge that two sounds similarly presented and having the same loudness and pitch are dissimilar."

The notion of timbral constancy or invariance is even vaguer than that suggested in the definitions of timbre as a basis for discrimination. It would seem that a form of timbral constancy is implied by the common observation that a sound source can be reliably identified over a wide variety of circumstances. For example, a saxophone is readily identified as such regardless of the pitch or dynamic it is playing. Furthermore, the saxophone remains a saxophone whether it is heard over a distortion-ridden pocket-sized transistor radio or directly in a concert hall. Thus, the question arises as to the physical correlates of this constancy. Is there a physical invariant or a characteristic feature mediating a given timbre?

The issue is not only academic: it has musical relevance, because electronic and computer technology promises access to an unlimited world of timbres. One

---

must, however, know how to evoke a given timbre; that is, how to describe it in terms of the physical structure of sound.

II. TIMBRE AND THE FOURIER SPECTRUM: THE CLASSICAL VIEW

Physicists have been analyzing musical instrument tones for some time. The goal of many of these acoustical analyses is to determine the physical correlates of tone quality.

Many results of such analyses have been published (Culver, 1956; Meyer & Buchmann, 1931; Miller, 1926; Olson, 1967; Richardson, 1954). The general conclusion of such studies was that musical sounds are periodic and that the tone quality is associated solely with the waveshape, more precisely with the Fourier spectrum of the waveshape. These early analyses were strongly motivated by the theorem of Fourier, which states that a periodic waveshape is completely defined by the amplitudes and phases of a harmonic series of frequency components (see Feynman, Leighton, & Sands, 1963, chapters 21–25; Jenkins & Watts, 1968). But the claim, often known as Ohm's acoustical law, is that the ear is phase deaf. Put more precisely, Ohm's acoustical law states that if the Fourier representations of two sounds have the same pattern of harmonic amplitudes but have different patterns of phase relationships, a listener will be unable to perceive a difference between the two sounds, even though the sounds may have very different waveforms (see Figure 1).

It has been argued that the ear is not actually phase deaf. It is indeed true that under certain conditions, changing the phase relationship between the harmonics of a periodic tone can alter the timbre (Mathes & Miller, 1947; Plomp & Steeneken, 1969); however, this effect is quite weak, and it is generally inaudible in a normally reverberant room where phase relations are smeared (Cabot, Mino, Dorans, Tackel, & Breed, 1976; Schroeder, 1975). One must remember, though, that this remarkable insensitivity to phase, illustrated by Figure 1, holds only for the phase relationship between the harmonics of periodic tones.[1]

Thus, it would appear that timbre depends solely on the Fourier spectrum of the sound wave. The most authoritative proponent of this conception has been Helmholtz (Helmholtz, 1877/1954). Helmholtz was aware that "certain characteristic particularities of the tones of several instruments depend on the mode in which they begin and end," yet he studied only "the peculiarities of the musical tones which continue uniformly," considering that they determined the "musical quality of the tone." The temporal characteristics of the instruments were averaged out by

---

[1]A varying phase can be interpreted as a varying frequency. Also, dispersive media (for which the speed of propagation is frequency dependent) cause inaudible phase distortion for periodic tones and objectionable delay distortion for nonperiodic signals (e.g., the high frequencies can be shifted by several sounds with respect to the low ones in a long telephone cable: this makes speech quite incomprehensible).

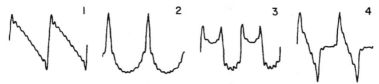

FIGURE 1   The waves 1 to 4 correspond to tones generated with the same spectrum but with different phase relations between the components: these tones with quite different waveforms sound very similar (Plomp, 1976).

the early analyses (Hall, 1937); but because different instruments had different average spectra, it was believed that this difference in average spectrum was utterly responsible for timbre differences. This view is still widely accepted: a reputed and recent treatise like the *Feynmann Lectures on Physics* gives no hint that there may be factors of tone quality other than "the relative amount of the various harmonics."

Actually, even a sine wave changes quality from the low to the high end of the musical range (Köhler, 1915, Stumpf, 1926). In order to keep the timbre of a periodic tone approximately invariant when the frequency is changed, should the spectrum be transposed so as to keep the same amplitude relationship between the harmonics or should the absolute position of the spectral envelope be kept invariant? This question produced a debate between Helmholtz and Herman (cf. Winckel, 1967, p. 13). In speech, a vowel corresponds approximately to a spectrum with a given formant structure. A formant is a peak in the spectral envelope that occurs at a certain frequency and is often associated with a resonance in the sound source. This is the case for voice sounds, and the formants can be related to resonances in the vocal tract.

Indeed, in many cases, a fixed formant structure (Figure 2) gives a timbre that varies less with frequency than a fixed spectrum—a better invariance for "sound color," as Slawson (1985) calls timbre for nonchanging sounds (Plomp, 1976, pp. 107–110; Plomp & Steeneken, 1971; Slawson, 1968).

Certain characteristics of the spectrum induce certain timbral qualities. This can easily be demonstrated by modifying the spectrum with filters. Brightness (or sharpness) relates to the position of the spectral envelope along the frequency axis (see Section XVI). Presence appears to relate to strong components around 2000 Hz.

The concept of critical bandwidth,[2] linked to the spectral resolution of the ear (Plomp, 1966), may permit a better understanding of the correlation between spectrum and timbre. In particular, if many high-order harmonics lie close together, that is, within the same critical bandwidth, the sound becomes very harsh.

[2]The critical bandwidth around a certain frequency roughly measures the range within which this frequency interacts with others. The width of a critical band is about one third of an octave above 500 Hz and approximately 100 Hz below 500 Hz (cf. Scharf, 1970). This important parameter of hearing relates to spectral resolution (Plomp, 1964, 1976).

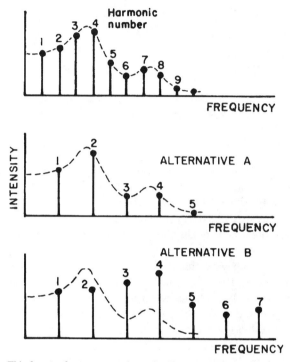

FIGURE 2   This figure refers to an experiment by Slawson (1968) comparing alternative predictions of invariance in timbre under octave increases in fundamental frequency. The experiment rules out alternative B, that of the relative pitch or overtone theory, in favor of alternative A, that of the fixed-frequency or formant theory.

Hence, for instance, antiresonances in the frequency response of string instruments play an important part in diminishing the roughness of the tones. It may be more significant to display spectra modified so as to take critical bands into account. This was done in some studies: the frequency axis is converted into so-called Bark units: 1 Bark corresponds to the width of one critical band over the whole frequency range (cf. Grey & Gordon, 1978; Moore & Glasberg, 1981; Scharf, 1970; Zwicker, 1961).

III. THE SHORTCOMINGS OF THE CLASSICAL CONCEPTION

So, for periodic tones, timbre depends upon spectrum. It has long been thought that musical tones are periodic, at least for most of their duration. Musical tones are often thought of as comprising three sections: attack, steady state, and decay. Helmholtz and his followers considered timbre to be determined by the spectrum of the steady state. However, this conception suffers from serious difficulties. As we noted at the beginning of this chapter, musical instruments can be recognized even from a very poor recording, despite the fact that their spectra are radically changed by such distortion (Eagleson & Eagleson, 1947).

In fact, a normally reverberant room has an incredibly jagged frequency response, with fluctuations up to 20 dB, and this frequency response is different at every point in the room (Wente, 1935). Hence, spectra are completely changed in ways that depend on the specific location. However, when one moves in the room, the corresponding timbres are not completely upset as one would expect them to be if they depended only on the precise structure of the frequency spectrum.

Also, various methods of sound manipulation show that temporal changes bear strongly on tone quality. Removing the initial segment of notes played by various instruments impairs the recognition of these instruments, as noted by Stumpf as early as 1910 (Stumpf, 1926). Subsequently, tape-recorder manipulation (George, 1954; Schaeffer, 1966) has made it easy to demonstrate the influence of time factors on tone quality. For instance, playing a piano tone backwards gives a non-piano-like quality, although the original and the reversed sound have the same spectra. However, temporal factors were not taken into account in most early analyses (cf. Hall, 1937): the analysis process could not follow fast temporal evolutions.

Recently, computer sound synthesis (Mathews, 1963, 1969) has made it possible to synthesize virtually any sound from a physical description of that sound. Efforts have been made to use the results of analyses of musical instrument tones that are to be found in treatises on musical acoustics as input data for computer sound synthesis. In most cases, the sounds thus obtained bear little resemblance to the actual tones produced by the instrument chosen; the tones thus produced are dull, lacking identity and liveliness (Risset & Mathews, 1969). Hence, the available descriptions of musical instrument tones must be considered inadequate, because they fail to pass the foolproof synthesis test. This failure points to the need for more detailed, relevant analyses and for a more valid conception of the physical correlates of timbre. Clearly, one must perform some kind of "running" analysis that follows the temporal evolution of the tones.

IV. ATTACK TRANSIENTS

A few attempts have been made since 1930 to analyze the attack transients of instrument tones (Backhaus, 1932; Richardson, 1954). These transients constitute an important part of the tones—in fact, many tones like those from the piano or percussion instruments have no steady state—yet their analysis has not produced much progress. The transients are intrinsically complex, and they are not reproducible from one tone to another, even for tones that sound very similar (Schaeffer, 1966). Most analyses have been restricted to a limited set of tones, and the researchers have tended to make generalizations that may be inappropriate even for different samples collected from the same instruments. These shortcomings have produced many discrepancies in the literature and cast doubt on the entire body of acoustic data.

V. COMPLEXITY OF SOUNDS: IMPORTANCE OF CHARACTERISTIC FEATURES

Sounds are often intrinsically complex. Musical instruments have a complex physical behavior (Benade, 1976); often the damping is low, and transients are long compared with note duration. Also, the tones are not generated by a standardized mechanical player, but by human musicians who introduce intricacies both intentionally and unintentionally. Even if a human player wanted to, a human being could not repeat a note as rigorously as a machine does. If the musician has good control of the instrument, he or she should be able to play two tones sounding nearly identical, but these tones can differ substantially in their physical structure. More often the performer will not want to play all notes the same way, and the performer's interpretation of some markings depends on the performer's sense of style and technique. All these considerations, which involve different disciplines—physics, physiology, psychology, esthetics—certainly make it difficult to isolate characteristic invariants in musical instrument sounds.

This points out the need to extract significant features from a complex physical structure. Also, one must be able to control through synthesis the aural relevance of the features extracted in the analysis—to perform *analysis by synthesis*. Only recently has this been possible, thanks to the precision and flexibility of the digital computer.

We shall now review pioneering work on the exploration of timbre by computer analysis and synthesis.

VI. INSTRUMENTAL AND VOCAL TIMBRES: ADDITIVE SYNTHESIS

The study of trumpet tones performed in the mid-1960s by one of the authors (Risset, 1966; Risset & Mathews, 1969) illustrates some of the points just made. We chose trumpet tones because we were experiencing difficulties in synthesizing brasslike sounds with the computer. The tones synthesized with fixed spectra derived from the analysis of trumpet tones did not evoke brass instruments.

To obtain more data, we recorded musical fragments played by a professional trumpet player in an anechoic chamber. Sound spectrograms suggested that, for a given intensity, the spectrum has a formant structure; that is, the spectrum varies with frequency so as to keep a roughly invariant spectral envelope. The spectrograms gave useful information, although it was not precise enough. Thus, selected tones were converted to digital form and analyzed by computer, using a pitch-synchronous analysis (PISA program, Mathews, Miller, & David, 1961). Pitch-synchronous analysis assumes that the sound is quasi-periodic; it yields displays of the amplitude of each harmonic as a function of time (one point per fundamental pitch period). The curved functions resulting from the analysis program were approximated with linear segments (Figure 3). These functions were then supplied to the MUSIC IV sound-synthesis program, and the resulting synthetic tones were indistinguishable from the originals, even when compared by musically skilled listeners. Hence, the additive synthesis model, with harmonic components controlled by piecewise linear functions, captures the aurally important features of the sound.

Conceptually, the model is simple. The pitch-synchronous analysis yields a string of snapshot-like spectra, hence a kind of time-variant harmonic analysis that is further reduced by fitting the linear segments to the amplitude envelope of each component. Computationally, however, this model is not very economical. Figure 3 shows that the functions can be quite complex, and the parameters must be estimated for every tone. So further simplifications of the model were sought. By systematic variation of the various parameters— one at a time—the relative importance of the parameters was evaluated. Whereas some parameters were dismissed as aurally irrelevant—for example, short-term amplitude fluctuations—a few physical features were found to be of utmost importance. These include the following: the attack time, with faster buildup of the low-order harmonics than the

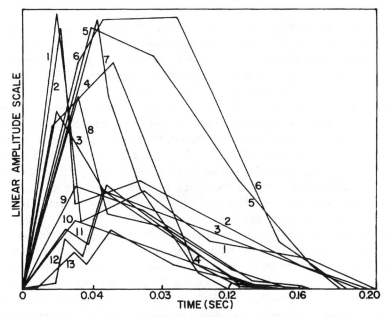

FIGURE 3   Line-segment functions that approximate the evolution in time of 13 harmonics of a D_4 trumpet tone lasting 0. 2 sec. Functions like these, obtained by analysis of real tones, have been used to control the harmonic amplitudes of synthetic tones (Risset & Mathews, 1969).

high-order ones; for certain tones, a quasi-random frequency fluctuation; and, most importantly, a peak in the frequency spectrum between 1000 and 1500 Hz and an increase in the proportion of high-order harmonics with intensity.

In fact, the latter property permitted us to abstract a simplified model of brasslike tones. Here only the amplitude function for the first harmonic was provided, and the amplitude functions for the other harmonics were deduced as fixed functions of this first harmonic amplitude, such that they increased at a faster rate (Risset, 1969). The specification was much more economical than the previous one and did not need to be precisely adjusted to yield the brasslike quality. Hence this property of an increase in spectral width with amplitude seems to be the most salient physical correlate of brasstone quality. This shows that, in addition to the way spectra vary over the pitch range, the variation in time of the spectrum can be critical to determine timbre. In the case of the brass, it can be described in terms of a nonlinear characteristic that enriches the spectrum when the amplitude increases. During the short attack of a brass tone, lasting less than 50 msec, the ear interprets the increase of spectral width as a brassy onset, even though it cannot describe what happens.

Beauchamp (1975) studied nonlinear interharmonic relationships in cornet tones and ascribed the brasslike character to the type of nonlinear relationship between the different harmonics, which are all functions of the first one regardless of the general level. This relationship has been found to have an acoustical basis (Backus & Hundley, 1971; Benade, 1976, pp. 439–447). This nonlinear property was used in the late sixties by Moog to produce brasslike sounds with his analog synthesizers: the cutoff frequency of a low-pass filter was made to go up with the amplitude, which was easy to achieve through voltage control. This characteristic has also been implemented in a very simple, satisfying way, using Chowning's powerful technique of spectral generation by frequency modulation described later (see Section X; Chowning, 1973; Morrill, 1977).

It was found in the trumpet-tone study that some factors may be important in some conditions and inaudible in others. For instance, details of the attack were more audible in long sustained tones than in brief tones. Also, it appeared that some listeners, when comparing real and synthetic tones, made their decision about whether a tone was real or synthetic on the basis of some particular property. For instance, they often assumed that the real tones should be rougher, more complex than the synthetic ones. This suggests that by emphasizing roughness in a synthetic tone, one could cause the listeners to believe it was a real tone. In his striking syntheses of brassy tones, Morrill (1977) has simulated intonation slips that greatly enhance the realistic human character of the tones. Similarly, in their study of string tones, Mathews, Miller, Pierce, and Tenney (1965, 1966) had included an initial random-frequency component, which simulates the erratic vibration that takes place when the string is first set in motion by the bow. When exaggerated, this gives a scratchy sound strikingly characteristic of a beginning string player. Such idiomatic details, imperfections, or accidents (Schaeffer, 1966) are characteristic of the sound source, and the hearing sense seems to be quite sensitive to them. Taking this into account might help to give stronger identity and interest to synthetic sounds. Indeed, a frequency skew imposed on even a simple synthetic tone can help strongly endow it with subjective naturalness and identity. The pattern of pitch at the onset of each note is often a characteristic feature of a given instrument: the subtle differences between such patterns (e.g., a violin, a trombone, a singing voice) act for the ear as signatures of the source of sound.

The paradigm for the exploration of timbre by analysis and synthesis followed in the latter study has been much more thoroughly pursued by Grey and Moorer (1977) in their perceptual evaluation of synthesized musical instrument tones. Grey and Moorer selected 16 instrumental notes of short duration played near E♭ above middle C. This pitch was selected because it was within the range of many instruments (e.g., bass clarinet, oboe, flute, saxophone, cello, violin); thus, the tones represented a variety of timbres taken from the brass, string, and woodwind families of instruments. The tones were digitally analyzed with a heterodyne filter technique, providing a set of time-varying amplitude and frequency functions for each partial of the instrumental tone. Digital additive synthesis was used to produce a synthetic tone consisting of the superposition of partials, each controlled in amplitude and frequency by functions sampled in time. Each of the 16 instrumental notes could appear in at least four of the five following conditions: (a) original tone; (b) complex resynthesized tone, using the functions abstracted from the analysis; (c) tone resynthesized with a line-segment approximation to the functions (4 to 8 line segments); (d) cut-attack approximation for some of the sounds; and (e) constant-frequencies approximation. In order to evaluate the audibility of these types of data reduction, systematic listening tests were performed with musically sophisticated listeners. The tones were first equalized in duration, pitch, and loudness. An AA AB discrimination paradigm was used. On each trial four tones were played, three of them identical and the fourth one different; the listeners had to detect whether one note was different from the others, to tell in which pair it was located, and to estimate the subjective difference between this note and the others. The judgments were processed by multidimensional scaling techniques.

The results demonstrated the perceptual closeness of the original and directly resynthesized tones. The major cue helping the listeners to make a better than chance discrimination was the tape hiss accompanying the recording of the original tones and not the synthetic ones. The results also showed that the line-segment approximation to the time-varying amplitude and frequency functions for the partials constituted a successful simplification, leading to a considerable information reduction while retaining most of the characteristic subjectivity (see Figure 4). This suggests that the highly complex microstructure in the time-varying amplitude and frequency functions is not essential to the timbre and that drastic data reduction can be performed with little harm to the timbre. The constant-frequencies approximation (for tones without vibrato) was good for some tones but dramatically altered other ones. The importance of the onset pattern of the tones was confirmed by the cut-attack case.

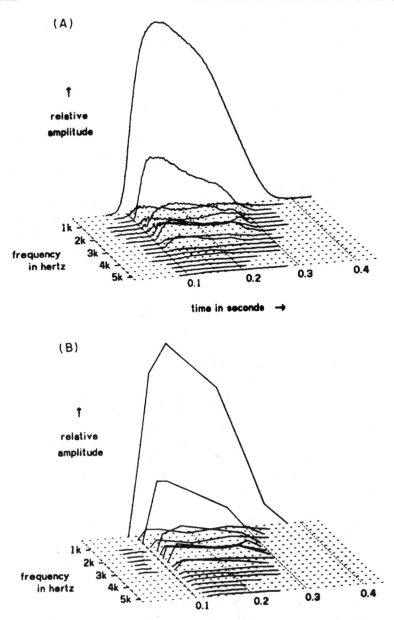

FIGURE 4 (A) Time-varying amplitude functions derived from heterodyne analysis from a bass clarinet tone, shown in a three-dimensional perspective plot. (B) Line-segment approximation to the function plotted in A. Both of these functions have been used to resynthesize the tone. Form B gives a considerable information reduction (Grey & Moorer, 1977).

A later study by Charbonneau (1979) has demonstrated that the simplification can go even further for most of the tones studied by Moorer and Grey (i.e., short tones of nonpercussive instruments). The various envelopes controlling each harmonic are replaced by a single averaged envelope; for each harmonic, this curve is weighted in order to preserve the maximum amplitude for this harmonic; it is also warped in time in order to preserve the times of appearance and extinction of the various harmonics. Although this is not a proper model for flute tones, it permits a good imitation for most of the other instruments. We shall mention other examples of simplified resynthesis in the following paragraphs.

Fletcher and his collaborators (Fletcher & Bassett, 1978; Fletcher, Blackham, & Christensen, 1963; Fletcher, Blackham, & Stratton, 1962; Fletcher & Sanders, 1967) studied the timbre of several instruments by analysis and synthesis, using an additive synthesis model. (The earlier of these studies did not use a computer but ad hoc analysis and synthesis devices). A study of the quality of piano tones (Fletcher et al., 1962) indicated that the attack time must be less than 0.01 sec, whereas the decay time can vary from 20 sec for the lowest notes to less than 1 sec for the very high ones. The variation of partial level versus time during the decay was highly complex and not always monotonic—the partials at times increase in intensity rather than decrease. However, the complexities of the decay pattern did not appear to be very relevant to the ear because the much simplified syntheses could sound similar to the original sounds—although it appeared in later studies that the dissimilarity between the behavior of different partials is often linked to liveliness. The piano study provided a major insight. It ascribed subjective warmth to the inharmonicity of the partials. The frequencies of the successive partials of a low piano tone are close to, but higher than, the frequencies of the harmonic series, to the extent that the 15th partial frequency can be 16 times that of the lowest one (Young, 1952). Now this slightly inharmonic pattern gives rise to a complex pattern of beats that induces a peculiar lively and warm quality. This is an important feature for low piano tones (and also for organ tones; cf. Fletcher et al., 1963).

Many analyses have been performed on piano sounds (Martin, 1947). They have been used to devise electronic pianos (Dijksterhuis & Verhey, 1969) whose tone quality (although not fully satisfying) depends on the simplified model abstracted from the analyses. Acoustic piano tones are extremely complex: low notes may comprise 100 or more significant spectral components, and the spectra fluctuate considerably. The quality of the acoustic piano may be hard to approach by synthesis. The issue is of practical significance, however, because digital pianos can be made much cheaper than acoustic ones, and, even more important, they are much easier to insulate acoustically. Current digital pianos obtained by sampling—that is, by recording of actual pianos tones—are not satisfactory: they fail to emulate the extremely responsive character of the acoustic piano, where the spectrum changes drastically with loudness, and also the interaction between strings occurring thanks to the soundboard.

In a study of violin tones, Fletcher and Sanders (1967) investigated the slow frequency modulation (around 6 Hz) known as vibrato, showing that it also modulates the spectrum of the tone. They also pointed to two features that enhance naturalness if they are simulated in the synthetic tones: the bowing noise at the onset of the tone and the sympathetic vibrations coming from the open strings (the latter occur substantially only when certain frequencies are played).

Clark, Luce, and Strong have also performed significant research on wind instrument tones by analysis and synthesis. In a first study (Strong & Clark, 1967a) wind instrument tones were synthesized as the sum of harmonics controlled by one spectral envelope (invariant with note frequency) and three temporal envelopes. (A more specific model was also sought for brass instruments, cf. Luce & Clark, 1967). Listeners were tested for their capacity to identify the source of the tones. Their identification was nearly as good as for real instrument tones, which indicates that this model grasps the elements responsible for the difference between the sounds of the different instruments. Incidentally, the probability of confusion between the tones of two instruments gives an indication of the subjective similarity between these tones; it has been used to ascertain the perceptual basis of the conventional instrument families (cf. Clark, Robertson, & Luce, 1964). The results suggest that some conventional families represent fairly well the subjective differentiations, especially the string and the brass family. A double reed family also emerged, comprising a tight subfamily (oboe and English horn) and a more remote member (the bassoon).

VII. ADDITIVE SYNTHESIS: PERCUSSION INSTRUMENTS

The aforementioned studies of timbre resorted to models of additive synthesis, whereby the sound was reconstituted as the superposition of a number of frequency components, each of which can be controlled separately in amplitude and frequency. Such models require much information specifying in detail the way each component varies in time: hence, they are not very economical in terms of the amount of specification or the quantity of computations they require. However, as was stated, the information on the temporal behavior of the components can often be simplified. In addition, the development of the digital technology has made it possible to build special processors with considerable processing power, for instance, digital synthesizers that can yield in real time dozens of separate voices with different envelopes (Alles & Di Giugno, 1977); so additive synthesis is a process of practical interest, considering its power and generality. It is not restricted to quasi-periodic tones; in fact, it can be used to simulate the piano and percussion instruments (Fletcher & Bassett, 1978; Risset, 1969).

In percussion instruments, the partials are no longer harmonics: their frequencies, found from the analysis, are those of the modes of vibration excited by the percussion and can sometimes be predicted from consideration of theoretical acoustics. The synthesis can correspond to a considerably simplified model and still be realistic, provided it takes into account the aurally salient features. Fletcher and Bassett (1978) have simulated bass drum tones by summing the contribution of the most important components detected in the analysis—these were sine waves decaying exponentially, with a frequency shift downward throughout the tone. The simulation was as realistic as the recorded bass drum tones. The authors noted, however, that the loudspeakers could not render the bass drum tones in a completely satisfactory way.

Timbre can often be evoked by a synthesis that crudely takes into account some salient properties of the sound. Bell-like tones can be synthesized by adding together a few sine waves of properly chosen frequencies that decay exponentially at different rates—in general, the higher the frequency, the shorter the decay time. The frequency tuning of the first components is often critical, as it is in church bells, for instance: the frequencies of the first components approximate frequencies falling on a harmonic series, so that a distinct pitch (the strike tone) can be heard, even though there is no component at the corresponding frequency. The lowest component, which rings longer, is called the hum tone (cf. Rossing, 1990). Chinese bells have modes that tend to occur in pairs; these bells can emit two distinct notes depending on where they are struck (Rossing, Hampton, Richardson, Satoff, & Lehr, 1988). The Chinese gong has a very rich sound, which can strongly vary in the course of the sound, owing to a nonlinearity that is strengthened by the hammering of the metal during construction. This nonlinearity induces a chaotic behavior (Legge & Fletcher, 1989).

Realism is increased by introducing slow amplitude modulation for certain components of the spectrum. Such modulations exist for real bells; they can be ascribed to beats between closely spaced modes because the bell does not have perfectly cylindrical symmetry. Beats in bell-like and gong-like sounds can produce an effect of warmth. Snare drums can also be imitated with additive synthesis: the decays are much faster than for bells, and the effect of the snares can be evoked by adding a high-pitched noise band (Risset, 1969). Bell-like or drum-like sounds synthesized this way can also be transformed morphologically by changing the envelopes controlling the temporal evolution of the components. Thus, for instance, bells can be changed into fluid textures with the same harmonic (or rather inharmonic)[3] content yet with a quite different tone quality (Figure 5).

Additive synthesis can be performed with components less elementary than sine waves—for instance, groups of sinusoidal components (Kleczkowski, 1989). This can simplify synthesis, and in many cases it will not affect the aural result much. Percussive sounds often contain a great number of modes of vibration: it is easier to simulate the resulting signal as a noiselike component than by using many sinusoids (Risset, 1969). X. Serra and Smith (1990) have implemented a very effective technique to emulate percussive sounds: the idea is to separate a "deterministic" part—which can rendered through additive synthesis, as the sum

[3]cf. *Inharmonique*, on CD INA C1003.

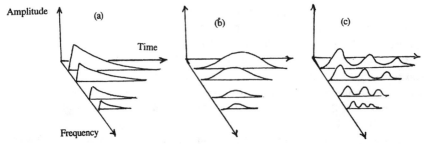

FIGURE 5 Perspective plots of synthetic *inharmonic* tones (i.e., with unequally spaced frequency components). Time runs from left to right, frequency increases from back to front, and amplitude increases from bottom to top. In (a), the sharp attack followed by a decay yields a bell-like tone. In (b), the time-varying amplitude function yields a fluid nonpercussive tones; because of differences in duration, the components are skewed in time, and they can be heard out much better than in the fused bell-like tone. In (c), the amplitude function has bounces: the components wax and wane, which causes a kind of timbral scintillation.

of a few sine-wave components controlled by amplitude and frequency envelopes—and a "stochastic" part, which is irregular but can be imitated by a proper time-varying noise component. In addition to this synthesis model, X. Serra and Smith developed an almost automatic analysis scheme, which extracts from a given sound the parameters to emulate this sound with the model. This approach has also been implemented by Depalle and Rodet in their fast Fourier transform (FFT) method (Cf. Section XIII). Rodet (1994) explores the possibility of controlling the proportion of chaos in sound synthesis: it can be low, for sounds perceived as harmonic, or high, for very noisy sounds. This applies to other instruments: for instance, flute sounds can be more or less breathy, and the shakuhachi flute sounds contain noise. It may also permit the synthesis of novel timbres.

VIII. CROSS-SYNTHESIS AND VOICE SYNTHESIS

In order to evaluate the relative significance of spectral and temporal envelopes, Strong and Clark (1967b) resorted to an interesting process: they exchanged the spectral and temporal envelopes among the wind instruments and asked listeners to attempt to identify these hybrid tones. The results indicated that the spectral envelope was dominant if it existed in a unique way for the instrument (as in the oboe, clarinet, bassoon, tuba, and trumpet); otherwise (as in the flute, trombone, and French horn), the temporal envelope was at least as important.

It should be noted that the above conclusions apply to wind instruments, which can have different temporal characteristics, although not very drastic ones. On the other hand, it is easy to verify by synthesis that a sharp attack followed by an exponential decay gives a plucked or percussive quality to any waveform. In this case, temporal cues tend to dominate over spectral ones.

One often speaks of cross synthesis to characterize the production of a sound that compounds certain aspects of a sound A and other aspects of a sound B. Instruments such as the Australian aboriginal didgeridoo and the Jews' harp function through a kind of cross-synthesis between the instrument alone and the human vocal tract. There are interesting possibilities for cross-synthesis when sound production can be modeled as the combination of two relatively independent processes. In particular, a sound source can often be thought of as comprising an excitation that is transformed in ways that can be characterized in terms of a stable response (Huggins, 1952)—think of someone hitting a gong or blowing into a tube. The temporal properties of the sound are often largely attributable to the excitation insofar as the response depends on the structural properties of a relatively stable physical system; the spectral aspects result from a combination of those of the excitation and those of the response. (Huggins suggests that the hearing mechanism is well equipped to separate the structural and temporal factors of a sound wave). A good instance is that of voice production (cf. Fant, 1960): the quasi-periodic excitation by the vocal cords is fairly independent of the vocal tract response, which is varied through articulation. Thus, the speech waveform can be characterized by the *formant* frequencies (i.e., the frequencies of the vocal tract resonances) and by the *fundamental* frequency (*pitch*) of the excitation— except when the excitation is noiselike (in unvoiced sounds like *s* or *f*).

A considerable amount of research on speech synthesis has demonstrated the validity of this physical model. It is possible to synthesize speech that sounds very natural. It remains difficult, however, to mimic with enough accuracy and suppleness the transitions in spectrum and frequency that occur in speech. In fact, although one can faithfully imitate a given utterance by analysis and synthesis, it is still difficult to achieve a satisfactory "synthesis by rule," whereby the phonetic elements (phonemes or dyads) would be stored in terms of their physical description and concatenated as needed to form any sentence, with the proper adjustments in the physical parameters performed automatically according to a set of generative rules. We cannot dwell at length here on this important problem; we can notice that the correlates of a speaker's identity are multiple: the spectral quality of the voice as well as the rhythmic and intonation patterns are significant. At this time, one cannot reliably identify speakers from their voiceprints as one can from their fingerprints (cf. Bolt, Cooper, David, Denes, Pickett, & Stevens, 1969, 1978), but recent research shows that a careful investigation of the prosodic parameters (cf. Section XIII) can provide good cues for identification.

The notion of independence between the vocal tract and the vocal cords is supported by an experiment by Plomp and Steeneken (1971); however, it has to be qualified for the singing voice. For high notes, sopranos raise the first formant frequency to match that of the fundamental in order to increase the amplitude (Sundberg, 1977, 1987): hence certain vowels (for instance i, as in *deed*) are so distorted that they cannot be recognized when sung on high pitches. Specific features detected in the singing voice have been confirmed by synthesis in the work of Sundberg, Chowning, Rodet, and Bennett (1981). Through certain processes of analysis (like inverse filtering or linear predictive coding; cf. Flanagan, 1972), one can decompose a speech signal to separate out the contributions of the vocal cords and the vocal tract. These processes made it possible for Joan Miller to synthesize a voice as though it were produced with the glottis of one person and the vocal tract of another one (cf. Mathews et al., 1961).[4] Actually, the source signal (because of the vocal cords) can be replaced by a different signal, provided this signal has enough frequency components to excite the vocal tract resonances (between, say, 500 and 3000 Hz). It is thus possible to give the impression of a talking (or singing?) cello or organ. Composers are often interested in less conspicuous effects, for instance in producing timbres from the combination of two specific tone qualities, using processes other than mere mixing or blending. This can be achieved through processes of analysis and synthesis, like the phase vocoder or the predictive coding process, or also through the reconstitution of the sounds through a certain model, like frequency modulation or additive synthesis. By physically interpolating the envelopes of the harmonics, Grey and Moorer (1977) have been able to gradually transform one instrumental tone into another one (e.g., a violin into an oboe) through monodic intermediary stages that do not sound like the superposition of a violin and a oboe.

IX. SUBTRACTIVE SYNTHESIS

Most of the work quoted in the preceding section on cross-synthesis and voice synthesis uses some form of subtractive synthesis. This method consists of submitting a spectrally rich wave to a specific type of filtering, thus arriving at the desired tone by eliminating unwanted elements rather than by assembling wanted ones. Subtractive synthesis is better adapted to certain types of sounds. As was mentioned, the process of speech articulation consists of shaping the vocal tract so that it filters in a specific way the spectrally rich source signal produced by the vocal cords. In fact, linear prediction coding consists of adjusting the parameters of a time-variant recursive filter so as to minimize the difference between the original speech signal and the signal obtained by filtering a single, quasi-periodic pulse wave by this recursive filter (see later).

Another instance in which subtractive synthesis has proven most useful is the case of violin tones, as demonstrated by Mathews' electronic violin. Mathews and Kohut (1973) have studied the aural effect of the resonances of the violin box

[4]Impressive examples of voice synthesis and processing for musical uses have been demonstrated in particular by Bennett, Chowning, Decoust, Dodge, Harvey, Lansky, Moorer, Olive, Petersen, Wishart, and others (Cf. records New Directions in Music, Tulsa studios; CRI SD 348; and CDs Wergo 2012-50, 2013-50, 2024-50, 2025-2, 2027-2, 2031-2, Elektra 9 60303-2, Neuma 450-73, New Albion Records NA 043, GMEM EI-06, Computer Music Journal Sound Anthology: 15-19, 1991-1995, and 20, 1996).

through electronic simulation. They have approximated the complex frequency response of a violin (which exhibits many peaks and minima—as many as 20 or more in the audible frequency range) with a set of electrical resonant filters (between 17 and 37). In this experiment, the vibration of the violin string near the bridge was converted into an electric signal by a magnetic pickup. This signal was approximately a triangular wave, as predicted by Helmholtz (Kohut & Mathews, 1971); hence, it consisted of a number of significant harmonic components whose amplitudes decay regularly with the rank. This signal was then subjected to the complex filtering approximating the response of the box. It was possible to change the characteristics of that filtering by changing both the damping of the resonances and their distribution along the frequency axis. It was found that a violin-like tone could be achieved with 20 or 30 resonances distributed in the frequency range of 200–5000 Hz, either randomly or at equal musical intervals (Figure 6). The best tone was obtained with intermediate values of damping, corresponding to a peak-

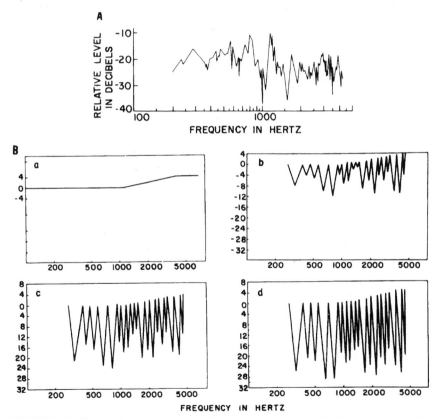

FIGURE 6   Relative frequency response: (A) as measured in a real violin from sine-wave excitation; (B) as simulated in the electronic replication of the violin tone: from (a) to (d), the Q of the simulated resonances increases from a value that is too low to a value that is too high (Mathews & Kohut, 1973).

to-valley ratio of about 10 dB in the response curve of the resonant filter. With too small a damping, the sound was even but dull; with too great a damping, the sound was hollow and uneven in intensity for various pitches.

The experimental equipment constitutes an electronic violin, which has been used musically to obtain either violin-like tones (e.g., in a quartet by M. Sahl) or sounds of very different qualities, by changing the filter settings (e.g., in pieces by V. Globokar, M. Urbaniak, or R. Boulanger).

This experiment has suggested to us that the specific quality of violin vibrato could be due to the interaction of the frequency modulation with the resonant peaks, producing a complex pattern of spectral modulation. Different harmonics are modulated in different ways, depending on the slope of the frequency response at the position of these harmonics. This can be verified by synthesis: the effect is not very sensitive to the parameters of a jagged frequency response. Imitative synthesis of violin tones (Schottstaedt, 1977) indicates that a good vibrato quality may be obtained in apparently simpler ways, not ensuring a truly fixed spectral envelope, but modulating the spectrum in a complex way. Actually the latter imitation was not obtained by subtractive synthesis, but through a variant of Chowning's audio frequency modulation, a powerful nonlinear technique evoked in the next section.

X. GLOBAL (OR NONLINEAR) SYNTHESIS

The additive synthesis method has been compared to the building a house by piling bricks, and subtractive synthesis has been likened to the sculpture of a block of stone by removing the unwanted material. There are ways to perform synthesis in a global way, by taking sound material and altering its shape, distorting it as when modeling clay. Such methods are nonlinear and hence difficult to understand and control. Global synthesis is more complex and less intuitive than additive or subtractive synthesis: but it is powerful and important.

Changing the shape of a sine wave while keeping the wave periodic will produce a new wave; in the Fourier analysis of this wave, one will find other components than the fundamental: hence this distortion has enriched the spectrum. This process is called nonlinear distortion or waveshaping. It can be implemented by taking a prescribed nonlinear function of a sine wave. When the amplitude of the sine wave increases, the amount of distortion also increases, so the spectrum gets richer. It is possible to determine a function that yields a desired spectrum through the distortion of a sine wave of a specific amplitude (cf. Arfib, 1979; Le Brun, 1979; Roads, 1996).

Another process uses frequency modulation (FM). FM is commonly used to emit radio waves. In the domain of musical sounds, FM is known as vibrato: for instance, the violin player modulates the audio frequency he plays (the carrier frequency) by slow periodic motions of his left hand, at a modulating frequency of about 6 Hz. This is heard as a specific tone quality rather than a frequency change.

Chowning had the idea to frequency modulate a sine tone by another sine tone, both tones being in the audio range. This results in a complex spectrum that is harmonic if the frequencies of the two tones are the same or in simple harmonic relation. The width of the produced spectrum—a quite salient parameter for the ear—depends on the amount of modulation—the so-called modulation index. By carefully controlling such parameters and their evolution in the course of the sound, Chowning (1973) has been able to produce a huge variety of timbres with dynamic spectra, including convincing simulation of many musical instruments and of the singing voice. Frequency modulation (FM) makes it possible to produce rich dynamic spectra including as many as 50 components with only three or four oscillators, whereas additive synthesis would require at least 100 oscillators. The string simulation mentioned earlier (Schottstaedt, 1977) used an elaboration of this technique, called multiple-carrier frequency modulation: this permits independent control of several formant regions.

Thus FM permits easy specification of certain aspects that are important for specifying timbre, particularly the global control of dynamic spectra. It is often said that FM sounds have an unmistakable sound of their own, like a trademark; but this is not necessarily so. Most users apply FM in a crude and lazy way, often with a high modulation index and very simple controls, which does result in stereotyped effects. But FM can be used with subtlety to achieve extremely fine results, as Chowning demonstrated with his imitations of the human voice (1980), or his interpolations between different timbres—*morphings* (Tellman, Haken, & Holloway, 1995) similar to the gradual metamorphosis, often performed today in image processing, of a shape into another shape.

The FM synthesis technique was implemented in the Yamaha DX-7 commercial digital synthesizers, which appeared in 1983: they met considerable success because they were affordable, Musical Instrument Digital Interface (MIDI)- compatible—this was the beginning of the MIDI standard (Loy, 1985)—and above all, because they provided a variety and quality of timbres unprecedented for commercial synthesizers. In addition to a host of ready-made "factory voices" imitating acoustic instruments or providing other timbres, users could do their own "voicing," that is, develop their own personal timbres by using the programming capabilities of the synthesizers (Chowning & Bristow, 1987). The control of the parameters has to be performed through MIDI. It is important to recall that the variety and quality of the timbres were not due simply to technological advances, but primarily to the know-how developed in the research of Chowning on timbre: technology enabled this know-how to be implemented at low cost.

XI. PHYSICAL MODELING AS A SYNTHESIS TECHNIQUE

Synthesis techniques described so far attempt to imitate the sound of the instrument: but the processes involved in the sound generation have little or no similarity with the working of the instrument. Hence it is often difficult to go from a signal produced physically to a set of synthesis parameters. When one alters these parameters, the heard changes are related in a complex way to the alterations performed: thus the auditory result is hard to control. On the other hand, instead of approximating the final result (the wave), one can try to emulate the physical processes at work in the instrument that physically produced this result. It is indeed possible to mathematically model the motions of the vibrating parts in a musical instrument.

This ambitious approach was first implemented by Hiller and Ruiz (1971) in their work on the use of physical models for string sounds. The analytical study of the acoustic behavior of an instrument can lead to differential equations governing the motion of the vibrating elements. One can try to synthesize the sound by solving these differential equations. This approach is in a way the reciprocal of the approach used in analog computers, in which one assembles a physical system with parameters governed by the equations to be solved. In the latter case, the measurement of these parameters gives solutions to these equations. In the study of Hiller and Ruiz, the resolution of the differential equations gives an approximation to the sound of the instrument. This approximation may be a good one if the differential equations embody a good physical model. Actually time represented on a digital computer is quantized: the differential equations of motion are approximated by finite difference equations. Ruiz could produce convincing demonstrations of the behavior of the violin strings. He also demonstrated the intriguing possibility of choosing completely unrealistic values for the physical parameters, for instance, negative stiffness. The numerical approximations, however, produced some spurious effects. Also, the considerable amount of computation required seemed prohibitive at the time.

Despite these difficulties, physical modeling has great virtues. The model is controlled through physical parameters, for instance length, tension, and stiffness of a string, which tend to be much more basic and intuitive than signal processing parameters such as component envelopes or modulation index. In fact, the early experience of sound synthesis has shown that timbres tend to have stronger identity for sounds that the listener can plausibly ascribe to a specific acoustic generation process—hitting, scraping or blowing—even though nothing hits, scrapes, or blows within a computer program (Freed,1990; Freed & Martens, 1986; also see Section XV,A). Physical modeling synthesis provides parameters that are closely related to physical features of the sound source, and so, by controlling them, one is likely to produce salient effects on the ear. This is indeed confirmed by experimenting with physical sonic models.

Thus physical modeling synthesis has gained popularity, especially with computers getting faster and faster. The basic technique used by Hiller and Ruiz was considerably developed by Cadoz, Luciani, and Florens (1984, 1993). To implement synthesis via physical modeling, they have written a modular compiler called Cordis, similar to synthesis programs such as MusicV (Mathews, 1969), except that the modules, instead of being signal synthesis or processing elements, emulate material elements (masses) and link elements (springs and dampers). These modules can be assembled into a network, and driving forces can be applied at various places. This permits simulation of vibrating strings or other mechanical objets, from a bouncing ball to a piano's double action. The simulation restores the sensory aspects of the objects (acoustic, but also visual, gestural, and tactile) by using specially devised transducers. The simulation can be done in real time, so that the user can operate in an "instrumental situation" (cf. footnote 5, later)—one would now speak of virtual reality. This requires a powerful dedicated computer installation with a specific architecture and house-built gestural-tactile interfaces: thus it has only recently begun to be used by musicians.

Morrison and Adrian (1993) have developed physical modeling synthesis using a modal approach, well known in mechanics: vibrating objects are represented as a collection of resonant structures that vibrate and interact together. Each structure is characterized by a set of natural modes of vibration. In the modal approach, the control parameters bear some similarity to those of additive and subtractive synthesis—a mode is similar to a resonant filter.

Smith (1992, 1996) has proposed simplified and powerful physical models. His method uses so-called waveguide filters—digital filters emulating propagation in a vibrating medium (e.g., along a string or within a pipe). Vibrating media, divided into sections of constant impedance, can be represented by pairs of delay lines. Several sections are coupled: waves propagate forward and backward through each section, which causes time delays. At interfaces between sections, absorption, transmission, and reflection occur. The method was first efficiently implemented for plucked strings by Jaffe and Smith (1983), from a modification of the so-called Karplus-Strong technique (Karplus & Strong, 1983). The imposed perturbation propagates back and forth along the string: here the model is very close to physical reality. Jaffe produced in his piece *Silicon Valley Breakdown* a tone sounding like a huge plucked string, bigger than the cables of the Golden Gate Bridge. Later, waveguide synthesis was adapted to wind instruments (cf. Cook, 1992; Smith,1992), to the vocal tract (cf. Cook, 1993), to the piano (Smith & Van Duyne, 1995) and to two-dimensional structures such as plates, drums, and gongs (cf. Van Duyne & Smith, 1993). The control of synthesis applies to parameters that have physical significance. Based on the digital waveguide technique, a "virtual acoustics" commercial synthesizer, the VL1, was introduced by Yamaha in 1993. Although its polyphonic resources are limited, the user can interactively act upon quasi-physical parameters and achieve robust and lively timbres.

Besides synthesis, physical modeling provides insight on the working of acoustic instruments. For instance, Weinreich (1977, 1979) has shown the contribution to the tone of the piano of the coupling between strings that are not exactly tuned to the same frequencies (this ensures the prolongation of the tone as well as a specific quality): he is currently applying this model successfully to the synthesis of piano-like tones. McIntyre, Schumacher, and Woodhouse (1983) have given a general formulation of oscillations in musical instruments, stressing the importance of nonlinear interaction between the exciter and the resonator. Keefe (1992) has applied this model to the synthesis of wind instruments. A recorder flute model has been developed by using advanced notions of fluid dynamics (Verge, Caussé, & Hirschberg, 1995). One should mention the growing attention given to nonlinearities in physical models (cf. Smith, 1996).

Physical modeling is clearly not limited to known acoustic sounds, because one can give unrealistic values to the physical parameters, vary them in ways that are not feasible in actual acoustic devices, and even program arbitrary physical laws. However, physical modeling is unlikely to make other methods obsolete. It is very complex and very demanding in terms of computational power. The necessary approximations can introduce artifacts of their own. It is quite difficult to find the proper physical model to emulate a given sound. Physical modeling has problems producing certain variants or metamorphoses of the original sound (cf. Section XV,C), because the implemented physical model implies some robust timbral characteristics. Physical modeling may not be able to produce certain sounds that can be obtained otherwise. For instance, one does not at this point know how to produce with physical models the auditory illusions or paradoxes demonstrated by Shepard (1964) and Risset (1971, 1989) using additive synthesis. This, however, might be feasible through physical models relying on different laws of physics: perception could be puzzled by sounds from a separate, different reality.

XII. SAMPLING

Given their overwhelming popularity, it seems appropriate to discuss "samplers." In the mid-1980s, a number of firms introduced musical instruments that stored sounds in memory and played them back on demand at different transpositions. Ironically, some of these devices are called sampling synthesizers. Actually, no synthesis and certainly no analysis is involved at all. The desired sounds are simply recorded into memory and played back in performance with little modification other than a typically small transposition, a bit of filtering, and some waveform segment looping to prolong the duration. Modern samplers are sophisticated sound playback devices and can be used to layer a large mixture of sounds.

More than just a popular means of producing electronic musical sound, samplers have come to dominate the electronic musical instrument industry. By the mid-1990s, the synthesis techniques described in the previous sections actually lay claim to only a tiny percentage of the commercial electronic musical instrument market. The FM synthesis technique has been all but abandoned by Yamaha, and their efforts to introduce a synthesizer based on the waveguide acoustic modeling technique has not been particularly successful commercially so far.

Why this present decline in the commercial interest in synthesis and the domination of sampling? We believe that there are several central reasons. Samplers provide a simple means of reproducing sounds accurately no matter how complex the sounds may be. By contrast, parameter settings for global and acoustic modeling synthesis methods are difficult to make and it turns out that only a small number of persons have mastered these synthesis voicing techniques. As we pointed out earlier, these global and acoustic modeling synthesis methods are limited to certain types of sound material and lack the generality or "take-on-all-sounds" character of the sampling approach. One cannot ignore familiarity as a factor. Many musicians like to reproduce familiar sounds such as those of the traditional instruments, be they acoustic instruments or vintage electronic, and it seems apparent that the demand for acoustic accuracy is higher for such familiar sounds.

Another important factor is impoverished control. Acoustic instruments are controlled by carefully learned gestures. For synthesizers, the MIDI keyboard is by far the most dominant controller (Loy, 1985; McConkey, 1984). These keyboard controllers start sounds, stop them, and control at the start of the sound the intensity at which the sound will be played. With few exceptions, like globally applied pitch bend and modulation, keyboards provide little in the way of control over the evolution of sounds once they have been initiated. Keyboards do not seem well adapted to the production of the expressive phrasing and articulation one hears in a vocal line or in that produced by a solo wind or bowed-sting instrument. Because almost no commercially available alternatives to the trigger-oriented keyboards and percussion controllers exist, there has been little demand for synthesizers that accommodate alternative forms of musically expressive control. It would seem then that because of the lack of alternatives to the trigger-oriented controller, the sampler may continue in its role as a satisfactory means of producing sound. However this could change with the commercial implementation of analysis-based synthesis methods (cf. Sections XIV and XV,D).

XIII. THE IMPORTANCE OF CONTEXT: MUSICAL PROSODY, FUSION, AND SEGREGATION

The importance of a given cue depends on context. For instance, details of the attack of trumpet-like tones (especially the rate at which various partials rise) are more significant in long sustained tones than in brief or evolving tones (Risset, 1965, 1966). In the case of a very short rise time (as in the piano), the subjective impression of the attack is actually more determined by the shape of the beginning of the amplitude decay (Schaeffer, 1966). The acoustics of the room may also play an important role (Benade, 1976; Leipp, 1971; Schroeder, 1966). The sound of an organ, for instance, depends considerably upon the hall or church in which it is located.

Most of the exploration of timbre by analysis and synthesis has focused on isolated tones, but music usually involves musical phrases. Throughout these phrases, the physical parameters of the tones evolve, and this evolution can obscure the importance of certain parameters that are essential for the imitation of isolated tones. Similarly, in the case of speech, the parameters of isolated acoustic elements (e.g., phonemes) undergo a considerable rearrangement when the elements are concatenated to form sentences. The specification of simple and valid models of this rearrangement is the problem of speech synthesis by rule. The importance of prosodic variations throughout the sentence is obvious in speech; pitch bends and glides—even subtle ones—are also essential in music. In a musical context, the evolution of various parameters throughout a musical phrase can be significant. The prosodic variation of one parameter may subjectively dominate other parameters. The difficulty in controlling phrasing is a major limitation of keyboard sampling synthesizers (cf. Section XII), which perform mere frequency transposition of the recorded sounds but do not make it easy to perform changes from one sound to the next. So it is essential to study musical prosody by analysis and synthesis. Actually, this appears to be the new frontier for exploration of analysis and synthesis. Of course, one had to first understand the parameters of isolated tones to be able to describe how they evolve in a musical phrase. The attempts made by Strawn (1987) to characterize note-to-note transitions show their variability, depending on performance techniques, and the importance of the context.

Currently, musical prosody studies appear difficult because the phrasing is likely to depend on the musical style. Its importance seems greater, for instance, in Japanese shakuhachi flute playing than in Western instrumental playing. In the latter, the music is built from fairly well defined and relatively stable notes from which the composer can make up timbres by blending, whereas in the former, the state of the instrument is constantly disrupted. Hence, a prosodic study on the shakuhachi is interesting, even necessary, because the sound can be described properly only at the level of the phrase. As initially suggested by Bennett (1981), Depalle has performed analysis and synthesis of musical phrases played by Gutzwiller, a shakuhachi master. Rodet, Depalle, and Poirot (1987) have been able to achieve proper resynthesis by concatenating elements similar to spoken diphones (in speech diphone synthesis, the word *Paris* is obtained by chaining together the diphones *Pa*, *ar*, *ris*) (cf. Rodet, Depalle, & Poirot, 1987): thus data on transitions are stored as well as data on sustained notes.

Mathews has used the GROOVE hybrid synthesis system (Mathews & Moore, 1970), which permits the introduction of performance nuances in real time, to explore certain correlates of phrasing, for instance, the role of overlap and frequency transition between notes in achieving a slurred, legato effect. Using his algorithms for trumpet synthesis, Morrill has looked for correlates of phrasing in the trumpet. Grey (1978) has studied the capacity of listeners to distinguish between recorded instrumental tones and simplified synthetic copies when the tones were presented either in isolation or in a musical context (single or multivoiced). He found that whereas multivoice patterns made discrimination more difficult, single-voice patterns seemed to enhance spectral differences between timbres, and isolated presentation made temporal details more apparent. This finding may relate to the phenomenon of *stream segregation* (Bregman, 1990; Bregman & Campbell, 1971; McAdams & Bregman, 1979); see also Chapter 9, this volume), an important perceptual effect that can be described as follows: if a melodic line is made up of rapidly alternating tones belonging to two sets that are sufficiently separated, the single stream of sensory input splits perceptually into segregated lines. (Baroque composers, such as Bach, resorted to this interleaving of lines to write polyphonic structures for instruments capable of playing only one note at a time.) This segregation is helped by increasing the frequency separation between the lines. Studies by van Noorden (1975) and by Wessel (1979) indicate that the influence of frequency separation on melodic fission has more to do with brightness—that is, with spectral differences—than with musical pitch per se, which appears to be linked with Grey's finding on single-voice patterns. Note that timbre differences without much brightness disparity (for instance, trumpet and oboe, or bombard and harpsichord) do not induce stream segregation in rapidly alternating tones.

Chowning (1980) has performed syntheses of sung musical phrases that sound supple and musical. In addition to carefully tuning the tone parameters for each note, specifically a vibrato (frequency-modulation) partly quasi-periodic and partly random, he has given due care to the change of musical parameters throughout the phrase. He has found that the parameters had to vary in ways that are to some extent systematic and to some extent unpredictable. These changes seem to be essential cues for naturalness. In fact, as in keyboard samplers, the musical ear may be "turned off" by a lack of variability in the parameters, which points to an unnatural sound for which even complex details may be aurally dismissed.

In musical performance, phrasing and expressivity are taken care of by the performer, who makes slight deviations with respect to a mathematically accurate rendering of the musical score. Performance practice has been studied by analysis (Sloboda, 1988; Sundberg, 1983), but also by synthesis: rules have been proposed to change parameters throughout the phrase, according to the musical context, so as to make the synthesis less machine-like and more musical (Friberg, 1991, Friberg, Frydén, Bodin, & Sundberg, 1991; Sundberg & Frydén, 1989). Some of these rules depend on the style of music—for instance, the notion of "harmonic charge" is mostly significant in tonal music—but many seem universal. Basically, they aim at making the musical articulation clearer to the listener. Timbral aspects intervene in leading the phrases. One hopes that such performance rules will be used to expressive ends in electroacoustic and computer music.

In his study of the singing voice, Chowning has given strong evidence that the addition of the same vibrato and jitter to several tones enhances the fusion of these tones, a fact that was investigated by Michael McNabb and Stephen McAdams (1982). Chowning's syntheses strongly suggest that the ear relies on such micromodulations to isolate voices among a complex aural mixture such as an orchestral sound. By controlling the pattern of micromodulations, the musician using the computer can make an aggregate of many frequency components sound either as a huge sonic mass or as the superposition of several voices. As Bregman indicates, the more two voices are fused, the more dissonant they can sound: preparation of a dissonance attenuates it by separating the dissonant voice from the rest of the chord. Fusion or segregation of two voices depends on their timbres and at the same time influences the perceived timbre(s).

Simultaneous fusion or fission and stream segregation are examples of perceptual organization, whereby hearing analyses the auditory scene and parses it into voices assigned to different sources (Bregman, 1990). Another aspect of perception is worth mentioning here: in a complex auditory situation, it often appears that one dominant feature can eradicate more subtle differences. The most striking aspect according to which the stimuli differ will be taken into consideration rather than the accumulation of various differences between a number of cues. Lashley (1942) has proposed a model of such behavior in which the dominant feature masks the less prominent features. This often seems to hold for perception in a complex environment. Certainly, in the case of musical timbre, which can depend on many different cues, context plays an essential role in assessing whether or not a given cue is significant.

XIV. ANALYSIS-SYNTHESIS AS FITTING PHYSICAL AND PERCEPTUAL MODELS TO DATA

Having described a number of significant studies of timbre by analysis and synthesis, we shall pause here to put these studies in a conceptual framework that will help us to understand possible applications of the analysis-synthesis approach.

A general scheme that we have found useful is shown in Figure 7. The analysis-synthesis process begins with a sound that is to be modeled. In these general terms, the analysis of a sound involves estimating the parameters of a model (e.g., in the Fourier analysis model the frequencies, amplitudes, and phases of a set of sine-wave components must be estimated). Once the parameters of the model have been estimated, the model can be driven with them to generate a synthetic version of the original sound. For our purposes, the appropriate goodness-of-fit evaluation technique is to make auditory comparisons between the original sound and its synthetic replica. If the analysis-synthesis model captures the essential perceptual features of the sound in a thorough way, then the listener should be unable to distinguish the difference between the original and the synthetic version.

The above criterion of validity characterizes what we call a *perceptual model*, as opposed to a *physical model*: the latter would mimic the physical mechanisms that give rise to the sound whereas the former simulates the sound through processes that may well not reflect the way the sound is really produced, provided the aural result comes close enough to the original. As we have seen, a good acoustic model can also be a good perceptual model; but the physical behavior of the sound-emitting bodies is very complex, and acoustic simulations require simplifications such that they can rarely sound faithful to the ear. Although hearing is very

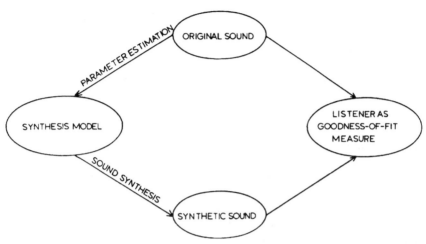

FIGURE 7   Conceptual framework of the analysis-synthesis process.

demanding in some respects, it is also very tolerant in other respects: perceptual models can concentrate on those features to which the ear is most sensitive. Recently, the expression *signal model* has been introduced to designate a model that mainly attempts to approximate the sound signal. Hence a signal model is in principle not a physical model. Is it a perceptual model? In general, a signal model calls for sophisticated signal processing techniques chosen so as to represent sounds in a way that can satisfy the listener: the auditory judgment is the final justification of the model. Yet the goodness-of-fit criteria used in the process of analysis are usually objective, especially when parameter estimation is programmed as an automatic procedure.

Physical and perceptual models often represent waveshapes in terms of certain mathematical functions. In the appendix, readers will find some general notions about representations of signals and their utility. A workable and reasonably general perceptual model is also described.

A lot of effort is devoted to the development of analysis procedures capable of automatically estimating parameters for a given synthesis model. This is a difficult problem, but one that is worth tackling. If this problem were solved, it would bypass the need for psychoacoustic know-how to recreate an existing timbre or to combine several timbres by cross-synthesis or morphing. It would turn synthesis techniques into powerful means of sound transformation. It would provide an easy way to inject the richness of arbitrarily recorded sounds, including acoustic sounds, into synthesizers based on the given synthesis model: such synthesizers have much more potential than samplers for sound transformation (see Section XV,D).

The need for parameter estimation was discussed by Tenney (1965), who called it demodulation. Justice (1979) was among the first to try to find an automatic procedure to approximate a given spectrum using FM. This is still a research problem, although partial solutions are under way (Delprat, Guillemain, & Kronland-Martinet, 1990; Horner, 1996a; Kronland-Martinet & Guillemain, 1993; Tan, Gam, Lim, & Tang, 1994).

The problem of parameter estimation is quite difficult for physical modeling— it is compounded by the need to construct the model capable of producing a given sound, a difficult task. When one has chosen a physical model, procedures to extract the parameters have been developed for certain situations—they can apply only to sounds that are within the possibilities of the selected model. This research, however, is still quite preliminary (cf. Smith, 1996).

It is generally easier to predict the potential of various perceptual or signal models. For instance, additive synthesis is well adapted to the simulation of quasi-periodic tones, or of sounds consisting of a limited number of frequency components (spectral lines), and it has trouble with noisy sounds: it takes a lot of randomly spaced sine waves to give the ear the impression of white noise (about 15 per critical bandwidth, according to unpublished tests by Andrew Gerszo). A number of procedures for analysis-synthesis have been developed: they often attempt a rather crude approximation to the signal to be reproduced, yet, insofar as certain aurally salient features are properly emulated, the resynthesis may be acceptable to the ear. The most crucial feature seems to be the profile of spectral evolution— the *spectromorphological gait*. Thus the evolution of spectra should be approximated. There are various methods to do that. In the technique of analysis and synthesis of tones by spectral interpolation (M.-H. Serra, Rubine, & Dannenberg, 1990), a substantial amount of information is dropped, yet this method can produce faithful reproductions of the original timbres.

Various methods have been used to solve the identification problem necessary to extract the parameters automatically: classical least square methods, multidimensional scaling (Kramer & Mathews, 1956; Laughlin, Truax & Funt, 1990; Sandell & Martens, 1995; Stapleton & Bass, 1988; Zahorian & Rothenberg, 1981), neural networks (Lee, Freed, & Wessel, 1991, 1992; Lee & Wessel, 1992), genetic algorithms (Cheung & Horner, 1996; Horner, Beauchamp, & Haken, 1993). The latter techniques are recent and advanced, yet they are quickly becoming widely available.

Various processes of analysis-synthesis are available. Models of resonance (Barrière, Potard, & Baisnée, 1985) extract parameters of the instrument response to feed Rodet's CHANT synthesis program (Rodet, Potard, & Barrière, 1984); they work very well for percussive sounds such as bells and marimbas. This is also true of the Prony method, which analyses the signal in terms of a sum of decaying sine waves (Dolansky, 1960; Huggins, 1957; Laroche, 1989). For additive synthesis, variants of the phase vocoder have been developed that track the evolution of the signal (Dolson, 1986; McAulay & Quatieri, 1986). The wavelet transform has been elaborated to extract precisely the amplitude and frequency of spectral lines (Guillemain & Kronland-Martinet, 1992). X. Serra and Smith have developed an analysis/synthesis program for nonharmonic sounds; they later improved it by separating the "deterministic" part, which can be emulated by a few additive synthesis components, and the "stochastic part," better evoked by using controlled random signals.

FFT^{-1} (Depalle & Rodet, 1992), as its name indicates, uses inverse fast Fourier transform for resynthesis: it could be said that it uses spectral frames, much like movie frames. It also implements the separation between deterministic and stochastic contributions to the sound. Implementation of FFT^{-1} has been specially optimized. This is a powerful method: its limitation may be spectral resolution and emulation of noise.

Spectral interpolation (M.-H. Serra et al., 1990) and wavetable interpolation (Cheung & Horner, 1996; Horner et al., 1993) are akin to cross-fading between fixed images: these are cruder techniques that can nonetheless be useful. To determine the optimal spectra or waveforms between which the synthesis process will interpolate, two techniques were used: principal component analysis and genetic algorithms.

We also mention below (cf. Section XVI) a fairly special technique implemented on pitched sounds using multidimensional scaling: it permits reconstitution of sounds, to perform morphings (interpolations between two sounds), to modify their duration, to alter them by keeping fewer dimensions from the representation (Hourdin, 1995).

XV. THE USE OF ANALYSIS-SYNTHESIS MODELS OF TIMBRE

The models drawn from analysis-synthesis of timbre can be useful for several purposes: (a) to provide insight and understanding, (b) for information reduction, (c) potentially to produce variants or modifications, and (d) in particular, to control musical prosody in real-time synthesis.

A. INSIGHT

Analysis-synthesis provides insight into the perception of timbre, which displays highly specific features. Many of these features can perhaps be better understood from an evolutionary perspective, considering the ways in which hearing has adapted to provide useful information about the environment. For instance, hearing is very sensitive to changes: it is well equipped to be on the alert, which makes sense because sounds propagate far and around obstacles. Perhaps this is why the musical ear tends to reject steady sounds as dull and uninteresting. Hearing is very sensitive to frequency aspects, which are only rarely modified between the sound source and the listener. Conversely, the ear is quite insensitive to the phase relations between the components of a complex sound, which is fortunate because these relations are smeared in a reverberant environment. Timbre is related to rather elaborate patterns that resist distortion (e.g., the relationship between spectrum and intensity in the brass). From these elaborate patterns, hearing has intricate ways of extracting information about loudness and distance (cf. Chowning, 1971, 1989): the listener can recognize that a sound has been emitted far away and loudly or close-by and softly. To do so, the listener resorts to fine cues: the ratio of direct to reverberated sound to appreciate the distance of the source, and also timbral cues to evaluate the energy of emission (e.g., for brassy tones, the spectral width, which increases with loudness). Segregation and fusion, mentioned in Section XIII, play an important role in helping the listener to disentangle a complex sonic mixture into components he or she can assign to different simultaneous sources of sound. Such extraordinary capacities have probably developed during the long evolution of animal hearing in the physical world: hearing plays an essential role for survival, because it provides warning and information about external events, even if they happen far away and out of view.

It appears that the listener tends to make an unconscious inquiry on the way the sound could have been produced in the physical world[5]: he or she tends to make a gross categorization of sounds in terms of their assumed origin. Schaeffer recommended hiding the origin of recorded sounds used in *musique concrète,* to prevent listeners from attaching labels to sounds, a reductionist trend that Smalley (1986, 1993) calls "source bonding." Hearing is adapted to performing "scene analysis" (Bregman, 1990): it can make fine identifications and discriminations with acoustic sounds, whereas it has more trouble differentiating sounds produced using straightforward electroacoustic or digital techniques—unless these latter sounds can be interpreted in terms of physical generation.

When such fine mechanisms are not called for, something may be lacking in perception. If electroacoustic or computer music plays only with amplification, it does not necessarily convey the feeling of sounds produced with energy. If the ear is deprived of fine cues for distance, the auditory scene seems to come from the plane of the loudspeakers, it sounds flat and lacks depth. On the contrary, by taking advantage of the specific mechanisms of hearing, one can produce a wide range of robust effects and vivid simulacra.

Models of timbre shed light on our capacity to assign different sounds to the same source, for instance, recognition of a note as such regardless of the register in which it is playing. The models help us to understand what properties form the basis of such categorization.[6] This understanding can be important in the fields of experimental music: a composer may want to confer some distinctive identity to certain artificial sounds.

---

[5]For instance, presented with recordings of metal objects struck with percussion mallets, the listener evaluates the hardness of the mallet (Freed, 1990). Such features make sense within the so-called ecological point of view on perception (Gibson, 1966; Neisser, 1976; Warren & Verbrugge, 1984).

[6]It seems clear that the identity of the timbre of an instrument such as the clarinet, whose high notes and low notes are physically very different, must be acquired through a learning process. It has been proposed that this learning process involves senses other than hearing. The experiments of Cadoz et al. (1984, 1993) aim at better understanding "motor" aspects of timbre perception, in particular how the gestural experience of producing a sound in a physical world interacts with its perception.

B. INFORMATION REDUCTION

Usually, we require that there should be many fewer parameters in the analysis-synthesis model than there are degrees of freedom in the data of the original signal. This is a form of data reduction. For example, consider a digitally sampled sound of 1-sec duration. If the sampling rate is 40,000 samples per second and if we wish to account for all these sample values in our model, then we could trivially simulate this signal with a model containing 40,000 parameters; however, a model with a reduced amount of information would be more practical.

In fact, much research on speech analysis-synthesis (e.g., the channel vocoders) has been performed to try to find a coding of speech that would reduce the bandwidth necessary to transmit the speech signal (Flanagan, 1972). Such a coding would in fact be an analysis-synthesis model because the speech would be analyzed before transmission and resynthesized at the other end (see Appendix). Such systems have only occasionally been put into practical use because it is difficult to preserve good speech quality and because the price of the transmission bandwidth has gone down substantially, so that the devices implementing analysis and synthesis at the ends of the transmission line would be more costly than the economized bandwidth. However, information reduction can work very well for certain types of sound, as we have already seen (Grey & Moorer, 1977): linear predictive coding is an economical way to store speech and is now used in portable speaking machines. In certain techniques for information reduction, specific properties of hearing are being taken advantage of, especially masking: it is useless to carefully transmit portions of the signal that are masked to the ear by the signal itself (cf. Colomes, Lever, Rault, Dehery, & Faucon, 1995; Schroeder, Atal, & Hall, 1979). This calls for sophisticated signal processing, as do a number of recent methods that can perform information reduction: simplified additive synthesis (Freedman, 1967; Grey & Moorer, 1977; Sasaki & Smith, 1980), multidimensional techniques (Kramer & Mathews, 1956; Sandell & Martens, 1995; Stapleton & Bass, 1988; Zahorian & Rothenberg, 1981), spectral interpolation (M.-H. Serra et al., 1990), multiple wavetable synthesis (Horner et al., 1993), and adaptive wavelet packets (Coifman, Meyer, & Wickerhauser, 1992).

The availability of powerful worldwide networks opens new possibilities in the domain of audio and music. Digital networks not only permit information about sounds to be conveyed but can transmit the sounds themselves. Digital networks even enable sound processing to be done on remote computers. This may give a new impetus to timbral manipulation in musical practice. However, sound uses a lot of bits compared with text, which can saturate the networks. Hence the growing success of networking gives a new motivation to research on information reduction. With the ever-increasing power of general-purpose computers, one can hope to use even complex coding techniques to transmit digital sound without needing special hardware to perform coding and decoding.

One should be aware that coding that permits substantial information reduction often takes advantage of specific properties of the signal to be compressed: hence it will not work for all types of signals. In addition, such coding tends to be highly nonlinear, which makes it difficult or even impossible to perform even simple transformations such as amplification or mixing on the coded version of the sounds.

C. POSSIBILITY OF PRODUCING VARIANTS

If one manipulates the parameters before resynthesis, one will obtain modifications of the original sound; such modifications can be very useful. For instance, starting with a recording of a spoken sentence, one can change the speed by playing it on a variable-speed tape recorder; however, the pitch and the formant frequencies will also be changed, completely distorting the original speech. Now if one analyzes this sentence according to an analysis-synthesis process, which separates glottal excitation and vocal tract response (e.g., channel vocoder, phase vocoder, linear predictive coding [Arfib, 1991; Dolson, 1986; Flanagan, 1972; Moorer, 1978]), the resynthesis can be performed so as to alter the tempo of articulation independently of pitch. Using the Gabor transform, Arfib has been able to slow down speech or music excerpts by a factor of 100 or more without losing quality or intelligibility. Rodet, Depalle, and Garcia (1995) took advantage of analysis-synthesis to recreate a castrato's voice for the soundtrack of the widely distributed movie *Farinelli*. Through processing with their FFT^{-1} method, they achieved smooth timbral interpolations—*morphings*—between the recorded voices from a countertenor at the low end and a coloratura soprano at the high end. These examples show the usefulness of analysis-synthesis in obtaining variants of the original sounds.

We shall distinguish between two uses of sound modification: classical musical processing and expanding timbral resources. In classical musical processing, the goal is to transform the sound so as to maintain timbral identity while changing pitch and/or duration (also possibly articulation and loudness). For instance, as mentioned in Section VIII, linear predictive coding or phase vocoder analysis-synthesis permits the changing of pitch and speed independently. Also, as was discussed at the beginning of this chapter (see Figure 2), it is often improper to keep the same spectrum as one changes pitch. It may also be necessary to change the spectrum as one changes loudness. Such changes are essential if one wants to use digitally processed real sounds (e.g., instrumental sounds) for music. Without resorting to analysis-synthesis processes, one can perform only rather superficial and often unsatisfying modifications of the sound. On the other hand, one should be aware that these processes are complex and difficult to implement, especially in real time. Even a fast digital processor can have difficulty in coping with the demands of real time if it has to perform analysis-synthesis processes. The analysis part is especially difficult, whereas processors or even fast general-purpose computers can now cope with real-time resynthesis. However analysis can be performed in advance for a corpus of sounds: then one can work live to perform intimate transformations on those sounds. Such a process was put to work using the FFT^{-1} method, implemented in an especially efficient way: powerful intimate transformations could be controlled interactively.

In expanding timbral resources, the goal is different: to change certain aspects of the tone so as to modify the timbre while preserving the richness of the original model. Here again, analysis-synthesis processes are essential for allowing interesting timbral transformations (like cross-synthesis), interpolation between timbres (Grey & Moorer, 1977), extrapolation beyond an instrument register, "perversion" of additive synthesis to produce sound paradoxes and illusions (Deutsch, 1975, 1995; Risset, 1971, 1978a, 1978b, 1978c, 1986, 1989; Shepard, 1964; Wessel & Risset, 1979), transformation of percussive sounds into fluid textures while preserving their frequency content, imposing a given harmony on sounds while preserving their dynamic characteristics[7] (see Figure 5). The extension of models can thus lead to the synthesis of interesting unconventional timbres, which is a fascinating area open to musicians.

D. CONTROLLING MUSICAL PROSODY IN REAL-TIME SYNTHESIS

As described earlier, analysis-synthesis permits transformation of the timbre and interpolation between different timbres. The intimate variations allowed by analysis-based synthesis permit the production of sound to be controlled so as to allow satisfactory prosodic control, even in real time.

As was mentioned in the discussion of samplers (Section XII), trigger-oriented control is not satisfactory to introduce prosodic specifications. It is often necessary to control the evolution of the sound once it has been initiated. Although MIDI keyboards are not adequate for this, the evolution of parameters could be controlled by means of other controllers (e.g., pressure-sensitive keys, breath controllers, bowlike sensors) or by functions of time. These functions could either be stored ahead of time and simply edited in real time or they could be generated by rule in real time. In any case, the synthesizing device should be able to perform the appropriate sonic changes. It is thus conceivable to design an "algorithmic sampler" (cf. Arfib, Guillemain, & Kronland-Martinet, 1992) by using analysis-based synthesis.

To date, no commercially available instrument has been introduced that applies the analysis-synthesis method to user-provided sound material. Although completely automatic "take-on-all" sound-analysis methods have yet to be fully developed, it would seem that they are within reach. Analysis-synthesis methodology

---

[7]Boyer has used a chromatic wavelet analysis to impose chords onto a signal (cf. Risset, 1991, p. 34). The musical transformations mentioned earlier can be heard in pieces like Morrill's *Studies for Trumpet and Computer*, Chowning's *Sabelith, Turenas* and *Phoné*, Risset's *Songes, Sud, Echo, Invisible*, Harvey's *Mortuos Plango*, Truax's *Pacific*, Reynold's *Archipelago* and *Transfigured Wind*, in many of Lansky or Dodge's pieces, on CDs quoted in footnotes 3 and 4, and on CDs Chenango CD1, CCRMA, Cambridge Street Records CSR-CD 9101, IRCAM CD0002, ICMA PRCD1300, Bridge Records BCD 9035, Neuma 450-74.

could become a core technology for electronic musical instruments. With just a little more engineering innovation, analysis-synthesis technology should accomplish for virtually all sounds the acoustic accuracy of recording playback as used in samplers. Thus research in analysis-synthesis is perhaps now more important than ever.

The advantages of decomposing musical sounds into controllable elements are significant. True, the traditional MIDI keyboard may not be able to use all potential for control but the users of sequencers and other composing and control software will be provided with many new expressive possibilities. In Figure 8, the relationships among sampling and synthesis techniques are presented to show the potentially important role for the analysis-synthesis methodologies. These methods should provide for both the acoustic accuracy of sampling and the musically expressive control as afforded by synthesis and yet be generally applied to a broad class of sounds.

Although Figure 8 indicates the value of analysis-based additive synthesis, in order to ensure musical expressivity, the analysis methodology should be informed by the musical controls that will be applied to the analysis-produced data.

XVI. TIMBRAL SPACE

We have discussed perceptual models; we have also said that analysis-synthesis is useful in modifying timbres. In this respect, it would be useful to have a good

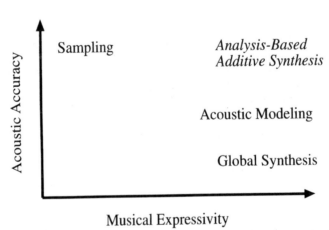

FIGURE 8 This figure displays the characteristics of various synthesis methods with regard to both acoustic accuracy and musical expressivity. Acoustic accuracy refers to the extent the electronically produced sound resembles the original sound, particularly with respect to the details. Musical expressivity refers to the extent to which the sound can be shaped and linked to other sounds. Here musical expressivity embodies the idea of control of phrasing and articulation as, for example, in vocal, wind, or bowed-string lines. (This diagram was first presented to us by Dana Massie, 1998.)

notion of the structure of the perceptual relationship between different timbres. This can be greatly eased by geometrical models provided by multidimensional techniques, which in effect provide displays of this structure. As was stated earlier by one of the authors: "A timbre space that adequately represented the perceptual dissimilarities could conceivably serve as a kind of map that would provide navigational advice to the composer interested in structuring aspects of timbre" (Wessel, 1973).

One can indeed propose geometric models of subjective timbral space such that individual sounds are represented as points in this space: sounds judged very dissimilar are distant, and sounds judged similar are close. The models are not constructed arbitrarily, but by asking subjects to rate for many pairs of sounds the dissimilarities between the sounds of each pair and by submitting the dissimilarity data to multidimensional scaling programs. These programs—strictly devoid of preconceptions about the data—provide a geometrical model that best fits these data. The dimensions of the model can then be interpreted (e.g., by investigating the stimuli that are least, or most, differentiated along these dimensions).[8] Wessel (1973, 1978) and Grey (1975) have thus already provided models of timbral space for string and wind instrument tones. These models unveil two dimensions—one that differs within the instruments of a same family (e.g., cello, viola, violin) and appears to relate to the spectral distribution of energy in the sound (cf. von Bismarck, 1974a, 1974b) and one that is the same within a family of instruments and seems to be linked to temporal features like the details of the attack (Grey, 1977; Wessel, 1973).

The corresponding representations of timbral space tempt one to fill the space, to draw trajectories through it, like the timbral interpolations mentioned earlier. According to Grey (1975), "The scaling for sets of naturalistic tones suggest a hybrid space, where some dimensions are based on low-level perceptual distinctions made with respect to obvious physical properties of tones, while other dimensions can be explained only on the basis of a higher level distinction, like musical instrument families." The intervention of cognitive facets, such as familiarity and recognition, indicates that a fully continuous timbre space may not be obtainable. Nevertheless, subjective space models can propose new paths and new intriguing concepts, such as that of analogies between timbral transitions (Wessel, 1979), which may permit one to do with timbres something similar to melodic transposition with pitches. Resolving timbre, that "attribute" defined as neither pitch nor loudness, into dimensions may uncover new features or parameters susceptible to precise differentiation and appropriate for articulating musical structures.

For instance, multidimensional scaling of timbre often unveils a dimension correlated with the frequency of the centroid of the spectral energy distribution, hence with that aspect of timbre termed *brightness*. As Wessel (1979) has shown, this

---

[8]From only quantitative judgments of dissimilarities between sounds, multidimensional scaling in effect unveils in what ways these sounds differ. Schaeffer failed to realize this in his criticism of the process as described by Babbitt (1965) (cf. Music and Technology (1971), pp. 77–78).

dimension is the one that can best articulate stream segregation (McAdams & Bregman, 1979). Here, isolating dimensions of timbres permits one to make predictions about the behavior of these timbres in context.

The timbre-space representation suggests relatively straightforward schemes for controlling timbre. The basic idea is that by specifying coordinates in a particular timbre space, one could hear the timbre represented by those coordinates. If these coordinates should fall between existing tones in the space, we would want this interpolated timbre to relate to the other sounds in a manner consistent with the structure of the space. Evidence that such interpolated sounds are consistent with the geometry of the space has been provided by Grey (1975). Grey used selected pairs of sounds from his timbre space and formed sequences of interpolated sounds by modifying the envelope break points of the two sounds with a simple linear interpolation scheme. These interpolated sequences of sounds were perceptually smooth and did not exhibit abrupt changes in timbre. Members of the original set of sounds and the newly created interpolated timbres were then used in a dissimilarity judgment experiment to determine a new timbre space. This new space had essentially the same structure as the original space with the interpolated tones appropriately located between the sounds used to construct them. It would appear from these results that the regions between the existing sounds in the space can be filled out and that smooth, finely graded timbral transitions can be formed.

The most natural way to move about in timbral space would be to attach the handles of control directly to the dimensions of the space. One of the authors examined such a control scheme in a real-time context (Wessel, 1979). A two-dimensional timbre space was represented on the graphics terminal of the computer that controlled the Di Giugno oscillator bank at the Institut de Recherche et Communication Acoustique/Musique (IRCAM). One dimension of this space was used to manipulate the shape of the spectral energy distribution. This was accomplished by appropriately scaling the line-segment amplitude envelopes according to a shaping function. The other axis of the space was used to control either the attack rate or the extent of synchronicity among the various components. Overall, the timbral trajectories in these spaces were smooth and otherwise perceptually well behaved. To facilitate more complex forms of control, we need an efficient computer language for dealing with envelopes. The basic idea behind such a language is to provide a flexible control structure that permits specification, sequencing, and combination of various procedures that create and modify envelopes. These procedures would include operations like stretching or shortening duration, changing pitch, reshaping spectrum, synchronizing or desynchronizing spectral components, and so forth. With such a language, it will be possible to tie the operations on the envelope collections directly to the properties of the perceptual representations of the material.

As we have mentioned, multidimensional techniques have been used for information reduction. Hourdin, Charbonneau, and Moussa have used multidimensional scaling to provide representations of pitched sounds that permit resynthesis of those sounds by additive synthesis. This work seems quite promising (Hourdin,

1995). Data from the analysis of sounds are submitted to scaling to reduce their dimensionality. Each sound is represented by a closed curve in the resulting objective timbre space. The curve is similar to a timbral signature, because the perception of the timbre is associated with the shape of this curve. From the curve, one can go back to additive synthesis data. Operations on the curves permit the reconstitution of sounds, interpolation between sounds, modification of their duration, and alteration of the sounds by keeping fewer dimensions from the representation. Further work providing ad hoc graphic tools could permit us to realize other interesting timbral operations from these curves.

Another field that may yield interesting possibilities is the objective representation of musical sounds as trajectories in phase space (or state space), a representation used for dynamic systems (Gibiat, 1988). This field is specially informative for multiphonic sounds, which are an instance of chaotic behavior (Lauberhorn, 1996). In this spatial representation, time is not available; however, it appears to be possible to use this representation to reconstruct sounds with the same morphology but with different time and frequency characteristics.

Representations of timbral space are topographic. It has also been attempted to provide verbal descriptions of timbre (Bismarck, 1974a, 1974b; Kendall & Carterette, 1993a, 1993b) that could even be operational, in the sense that musical timbre synthesis or transformation could be based on descriptive terms rather than numerical data (Ethington & Punch, 1994). In the latter work, listening experiments were performed in order to map verbal descriptions to synthesis or processing operations, then the verbal descriptions were mapped to timbral features using a space with a fixed set of dimensions. Although this work is preliminary, early results indicate that musicians may be able to control effectively synthesis programs or computer-controlled synthesizers by describing in words desired timbral characteristics or transformations.

XVII. CONCLUSION

As we explained before, the exploration of timbre by analysis and synthesis can serve several purposes: it provides insight into the physical parameters of the sound and the relevance of these parameters to the resulting timbre; it leads to simplified models that permit data reduction in the synthetic replication of the sound; and it uses models to perform transformations on the original sound, either from the point of view of classical musical processing (e.g., by independently changing pitch, duration, articulation, and loudness) or by expanding timbral resources (rearranging at will the complex variations abstracted from the analysis to obtain new and rich sounds).

Exploration of timbre by analysis and synthesis is difficult but rewarding. Since the development of analysis and synthesis devices, in particular the digital computer and its descendants, understanding of the physical correlates of timbre has improved and recipes for new musical resources have been developed.

Although much remains to be done, these new possibilities available to musicians will probably increase the musical role of timbre. In classical Western music, timbres were used mostly to differentiate musical lines. Later, this linear organization was disrupted. Debussy often used chords for their timbral effect rather than for their harmonic function—he was followed by Messiaen, who coined the expression "accord-timbre" ("timbre-chord"). Varèse (1983) longed for novel sonic materials that would lend themselves to novel architectures. In one of his *Five Orchestra Pieces* Op. 16 composed in 1909 and subtitled "Farben" ("Colors"), Schoenberg kept pitch constant and varied only the instruments—according to his instructions, only the changes in tone color should be heard by the listener (cf. Erickson, 1975, p. 37). Schoenberg wrote in 1911: "the sound becomes noticeable through its timbre and one of its dimensions is pitch ... The pitch is nothing but timbre measured in one direction. If it is possible to make compositional structures from timbres which differ according to height (pitch), structures which we call melodies, ... then it must be also possible to create such sequences from the other dimension of the timbres, from what we normally and simply call timbre." In the 1950s, Boulez submitted successions of timbre to serial organization. With the control of timbre now made possible through analysis and synthesis, composers can compose not only with timbres, but they can also compose timbres: they can articulate musical compositions on the basis of timbral rather than pitch variations. It has been argued that timbre perception is too vague to form the basis of elaborate musical communication; however, as Mathews has remarked, there already exists an instance of a sophisticated communication system based on timbral differentiation, namely human speech.[9]

Indeed, the exploration of timbre by analysis and synthesis has become an important musical tool. It requires the acute ear and judgment of the musician, some psychoacoustic know-how, and a good interactive environment helping him or her to achieve fine tunings and manipulations. The functional role of timbre in musical composition was already a central point in computer-synthesized pieces such as Risset's *Little Boy* (1968), *Mutations* (1969), *Inharmonique* (1977), Chowning's *Turenas* (1972), *Stria* (1977) and *Phone* (1981), Erickson's *Loops* (1976), Branchi's *Intero* (1980), Murail's *Désintégrations* (1983), Barrière's *Chréode* (1984), and Saariaho's *Jardin Secret I* (1985). The use of timbre in contemporary musical composition is discussed at length in the references by Erickson (1975), McAdams and Saariaho (1985), Emmerson (1986), Barrière (1991), and Risset (1994). The timbral innovations of electroacoustic and computer music have influenced the instrumental music of Varèse, Ligeti, Penderecki, Xenakis, Scelsi, Crumb, Dufourt, Grisey, Murail.

Hence the 20th century is that of the "eternal return of timbre" (Charles, 1980): from an ancillary function of labeling or differentiating, the role of timbre has extended to that of central subject of the music. Then, paradoxically, the very no-

---

[9]As Moorer demonstrated by analysis and synthesis, speech can remain intelligible under certain conditions after removal of pitch and rhythmic information.

tion of timbre, this catchall, multidimensional attribute with a poorly defined identity, gets blurred, diffuse, and vanishes into the music itself.

APPENDICES

A. SIGNAL REPRESENTATIONS AND ANALYSIS-SYNTHESIS PROCESSES

Analysis-synthesis according to a given process implies estimating the parameters of a model of the sound. This model may or may not be adequate; it may or may not lend itself to a good imitation of the sound. For instance, Fourier series expansion is a useful tool for periodic tones, and Fourier synthesis, using the data of Fourier analysis, indeed permits one to synthesize a faithful copy of a periodic sound. However, as was explained earlier, most sounds of interest are not periodic; hence, Fourier series expansion is inadequate to replicate, for instance, a sound whose spectrum varies with time.

A sound can be mathematically described by the waveshape function $p(t)$, giving the acoustic pressure as a function of time. Mathematics tells us that reasonably regular functions can be analyzed in a number of ways, that is, in terms of one or another set of basic functions. This set is said to be complete if an arbitrary function can indeed be obtained as the proper linear combination of these basic functions. (This proper combination is unveiled by the analysis process that consists of estimating the parameters of the corresponding model.) For instance, Fourier's theorem states that any periodic function (of frequency f) can be expanded as a linear combination of the sine and cosine functions of frequencies f, $2f$, $3f$, ..., so that this linear combination can be arbitrarily close to the periodic function. Hence, the set of sine and cosine functions of frequencies f, $2f$, $3f$, and so on is "complete" over the space of periodic functions of frequency f (cf. Panter, 1965; Rosenblatt, 1963).

Actually, the representation of nonperiodic signals in terms of basic functions usually requires an infinite number of basic functions so that the series expansion turns into a transformation. For instance, nonperiodic signals can be represented in terms of the so-called Fourier transform or Fourier integral, in which the discrete spectral components are replaced by a continuous amplitude spectrum; the discrete phases are also replaced by a phase spectrum. There are other transformations used for analysis-synthesis (e.g., the Walsh-Hadamard, the Karhunen-Loève, the Gabor, and the wavelet transforms). Such linear expansion in terms of a basic set of signals is similar to the expansion of a vector in terms of a set of basic vectors; it is practical (although not necessary for all purposes) to use orthogonal transforms—that is, to use functions that form an orthonormal (and complete) set (cf. Harmuth, 1972). For instance, using orthogonal wavelets as basic functions is a strong limitation, because it imposes an interval of 1 octave between two adjacent wavelets—whereas choosing an interval of a semitone can be musically useful (cf. footnote 6). In addition, this choice does not allow an easy evaluation of energy (Guillemain & Kronland-Martinet, 1996).

The application of a given transform to a sound signal provides a representation of the signal that may be revealing and should make it possible to restore the signal by means of the inverse transform. Hence, the representation of signals is closely linked to analysis-synthesis processes. Actually, the representation of signals purports both to characterize the information (bearing elements in the signal) and to describe in a simple way the effect of modifications of the signals (like those introduced by an imperfect transmission system or by a deliberate simplification of the signal).

Although we cannot go into much detail here, we would like to make several points:

1. Certain analysis-synthesis processes and the corresponding representation are intrinsically limited to certain classes of signals. Others can be transparent if they are complete in the above sense—for instance, the Fourier, the Walsh-Hadamard, the Gabor and the wavelet transforms, the phase vocoder, and the linear predictive coding scheme. However, the two latter schemes allow reproduction of the original signal only at the expense of a considerably detailed analysis, an information explosion instead of an information reduction. This can be substantially simplified only for certain classes of signals (quasi-periodic signals with relatively independent excitation and response mechanisms, such as speech; for instance, linear predictive coding is efficient in simulating oboe sounds but poor for low clarinet sounds because eliminating the even harmonics is taxing for the filter). Indeed, much work on analysis-synthesis and signal transformation was originally directed toward efficient coding of speech information for economical transmission over technical channels (Campanella & Robinson, 1971; Flanagan, 1972; Schafer & Rabiner, 1975). It is also for certain types of signals that the representation of the signal will be most enlightening (but, for instance, phase vocoders' programs implemented by Moorer, 1978, have permitted Castellengo to obtain useful information on nonharmonic "multiphonic" tones). Certain sounds, especially percussive sounds, can often be modeled efficiently as a sum of decaying exponentials (Dolansky, 1960 ; Huggins, 1957; Laroche, 1989).

Similarly, Gabor's expansion of a signal into gaussian elementary signals—"sonic grains" (sine waves with a gaussian amplitude envelope; see Figure 9)—has been proven to be complete (Bacry, Grossman, & Zak, 1975; Bastiaans, 1980), and so has the wavelet transform (Grossman & Morlet, 1984). Hence, these methods can in principle produce exactly what Fourier or other types of synthesis can produce (cf. Gabor, 1947; Roads, 1978 ; Xenakis, 1971). The idiosyncrasies of different complete analysis-synthesis methods appear only in the modifications they permit—or suggest—in a simplified, archetypal use. There are strong differences, however, between the representations and the transformations they allow by altering the analysis data before resynthesis. For instance, Gabor's grains are the sonic elements for the so-called granular synthesis, explored by Xenakis, Roads, and Truax to create novel textures *ex nihilo* without performing any analysis to extract parameters, but they have also been used by Arfib as the elementary signals for implementing the analysis-synthesis of existing sounds and for stretching them in time without altering the frequency content (cf. Arfib, 1991; Roads, 1996).

2. The Walsh-Hadamard transform seems promising because it leads to operations that are easy to implement with digital circuits. However, from a psychoacoustical standpoint, this transform is quite inappropriate. The basic functions do not sound elemental to the ear; they are spectrally very rich, and an approximated representation in those terms would lead to aurally unsatisfying results. The analysis-synthesis process does not deteriorate gracefully for the ear, and it has great difficulty in producing timbres that are not rich and harsh (for instance, it has trouble approaching a sine wave).

3. Fourier-type analysis (and synthesis) has been much criticized, often in a poorly documented way. Whereas Fourier series expansion is indeed inadequate for nonperiodic sounds, more elaborate variants of Fourier analysis have great utility. The Fourier transform provides complete information of an amplitude spectrum and a phase spectrum; however, the latter characterizes the evolution of the signal in time in a way that is unintuitive and very hard to use. Because this evolution in time is very significant to the ear, one needs some kind of running analysis to provide so-called sonagrams, that is, diagrams in the time-frequency plane showing the evolution of the frequency components as a function of time— the amplitude of the components being indicated by the blackness and thickness of the lines. This is obtained by calculating, as a function of time, the spectrum of the signal viewed through a specified *time window* (also called *weighting function*), which at any time only shows the most recent part of the past values of the signal. Such representations are very useful: they have been used in several of the studies previously described. The sound spectrograph (Koenig, Dunn, & Lacey, 1946) implements this type of running analysis: its windows are appropriate for a useful portrayal of speech sounds, but it often displays significant features of music as well (Leipp, 1971), even though the analysis is often too crude to provide data for a proper synthesis. Sonagrams give revealing and useful "photographs" of the sound (Cogan, 1984). They can now be produced by computer programs. If these programs preserve the phase information, the sound can be reconstituted: the short-term Fourier transform is also complete—it bears strong similarity to the Gabor transform.

The significance of Fourier analysis has a multiple basis. Clear evidence exists that the peripheral stages of hearing, through the mechanical filtering action of the basilar membrane, perform a crude frequency analysis with a resolution linked to the critical bandwidth (Flanagan, 1972; Plomp, 1964). The distribution of activity along the basilar membrane relates simply to the Fourier spectrum. Thus features salient in frequency analysis are of importance to perception. Sonagrams reveal much more about sounds than oscillograms do: Figure 1 shows that the inspection of waveforms is not very informative and can be misleading, even though the waveform of course contains all the information about the sound. Also, when the sound is quasi-periodic, the phase deafness of the ear (Figure 1) permits a substantial reduction of information. One can also in this case take advantage of the concentration of energy at the harmonic frequencies to describe the sounds by the evolution in time of the amplitude of few harmonics. We have seen that such additive synthesis was a very useful model (cf. Grey & Moorer, 1977; Guillemain & Kronland-Martinet, 1996; Keeler, 1972; Risset & Mathews, 1969).

Yet it may seem bizarre to try to represent a finite signal, such as a tone of a musical instrument, as a sum of sine waves, which never begin or end: this is only possible if the sum is infinite. Thus the Fourier transform of an unlimited sine wave consists of a single spectral line; but if this "sine wave" has a beginning and an end, its Fourier transform includes a continuous frequency-band, which is not easy to deal with. The time windows used for the so-called short-time Fourier transform deal with this problem through a kind of ad hoc mathematical treatment. As Gabor initially proposed, it may be more logical to try to represent a finite signal as a sum of basic functions that are limited in time—as well as in frequency. The basic functions proposed by Gabor are sine waves multiplied by a Gaussian time window of fixed length: the center frequency of such a function corresponds to the frequency of the sine wave. Both the time and the frequency resolution are determined by the time and spectral extension of the Gaussian window (see Figure 9). Theoretically this function is not limited in time, because the Gaussian function goes to zero only at infinity, however, this function is limited in practice, because sounds are represented with a finite number of bits. The expansion into Gabor's gaussian functions has been implemented; it permits faithful reconstitutions and useful transformations (Arfib, 1991).

A new representation, initially derived from Gabor's ideas by Morlet, is based on the "wavelet," an elementary function of constant shape rather than with a constant envelope: to vary the frequency, this function is shrunk or stretched in time (Figure 9). Thus the frequency resolution does not correspond to a constant frequency amount, but rather to a constant interval (e.g., one octave); conversely, the time resolution is finer at higher frequencies—a so-called constant Q or multiresolution process. Grossman generalized this representation by showing that one can expand well-behaved functions in terms of more general wavelets of constant shape, the requirements for a function to qualify as a wavelet being the following: the function must be limited in time, it must oscillate, and its average must be zero. This provides a quite general *time-scale* representation, rather than time-frequency, because the successive frequencies of the basic wavelets are scaled by the same factor. Thus the wavelet representation is well adapted to the investigation of fractal phenomena. It has already found applications in various domains, including sound and music (cf. Combes, Grossman, & Tchamitchian, 1989; Grossman & Morlet, 1984; Guillemain & Kronland-Martinet, 1992; Kronland-Martinet, 1989; Kronland-Martinet, Morlet, & Grossman, 1987). Such a universal method of representation cannot work miracles in itself, it has to be adapted to the specific problem at hand; however, it has some computational and practical virtues, including making it possible to choose specific basic wavelets. The wavelet representation

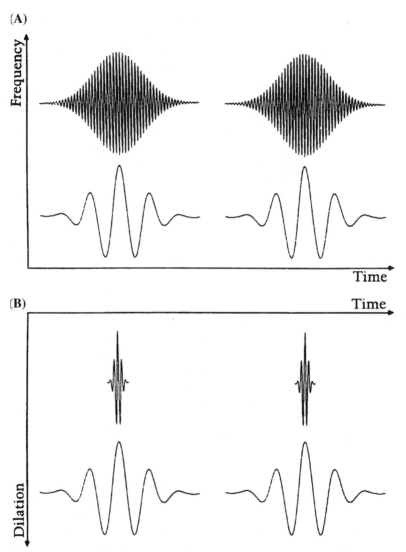

FIGURE 9   (A) Elementary grains used for the Gabor expansion in the time-frequency domain. (B) Elementary Morlet wavelets used for the wavelet expansion in the time-dilation domain.

has already be shown to permit faithful reconstitutions and to offer intriguing possibilities.

4. Auditory models have been exploited in the analysis-synthesis process, and their application shows promise. Auditory periphery models or "ear" models have been implemented in the form of computer programs and are able to reproduce via simulation a significant body of psychoacoustical phenomena. The goal is to simulate the various stages in the auditory periphery and supply as output a neural

code similar to that of the auditory nerve (Flanagan, 1962; Schroeder, 1975). Both physiologically inspired models (Duda, Lyon & Slaney, 1992; Slaney & Lyon, 1993) and more psychoacoustically inspired models (Licklider, 1951; Moore & Glasberg, 1981; Patterson, 1976) involve a filter bank at an early stage, followed by processing modules that implement a form of autocorrelation or periodicity analysis in each of the frequency bands. Thus they can track pitch, but also spectral variations, which often play an important role in the recognition of timbre.

These models have been shown to be useful as preprocessors to speech recognizers as well as in the determination of the pitch of complex time-variant tones. There is also a significant body of work in the newly emerging field called computational auditory scene analysis (Brown & Cooke, 1994a, 1994b), a follow-up to auditory scene analysis (Bregman, 1990); cf. Sections XIII and XV). The scheme for auditory organization proposed incorporates the lower level auditory or ear models into more elaborate models of auditory cognition. These models are being applied for the most part to the problem of auditory source separation, also known as the "cocktail party effect" in reference to the practice of selective listening in a din of conversation.

In a theoretical paper, Yang, Wang and Shamma (1992) demonstrated that a physiologically plausible model of the auditory periphery can be inverted and used to regenerate the original input completely. This is in an interesting result in that it suggests that the auditory system does not lose information about the acoustic signal in its early stages of processing. Slaney has inverted the Slaney and Lyon ear model and synthesized signals using data coming from the analysis of the signal by the ear model. He has applied aspects of this inversion method to sound morphing or timbral interpolation (Slaney, 1996; Slaney, Covell, & Lassitier, 1996).

5. Global methods like frequency modulation and nonlinear distortion, described in Section X, are appealing because they provide powerful control over salient features of the spectrum in terms of few parameters: the amount of specification and processing is much reduced as compared with additive synthesis. However, strength is at the expense of generality. Certain specific results are hard to achieve with the global methods, unless one uses them in refined ways that can quickly become quite complex (cf. Schottstaedt, 1977). It is difficult to develop analysis techniques extracting the parameters for resynthesis using a global model (see Section XIV).

B. A SYNTHESIS MODEL BASED ON PERCEPTUAL PRINCIPLES

We now give a brief account of how synthesis procedures can provide for direct control over some essential perceptual attributes of timbre. The essential principle underlying these synthesis schemes is the decomposition of a musical signal into perceptual attributes that are, for the most part, perceptually independent of each other. The motivation is to provide a reasonably general but simple control scheme for additive synthesis as this form of synthesis is becoming more and more practical with advances in the development of high-speed digital-synthesis hardware.

1. Pitch Versus the Global Impression of the Spectral Envelope

Several studies (Plomp & Steeneken, 1971; Risset, 1978b, 1978c) suggest that musical pitch and the global spectral energy distribution as perceptual attributes are reasonably independent of each other. This is true to a large extent for harmonic tones that tend to produce clear pitch percepts, but it is not true for inharmonic spectra whose ambiguous and otherwise multiple-pitch content depends on the spectral balance of the components. What we mean by independence is that it is possible to manipulate, for example, the placement and shape of formants without influencing the perceived pitch, and conversely, it is possible to manipulate the pitch while keeping the perceived shape of the spectrum constant. The voice provides an example of such an independent control scheme that operates over a reasonably wide range of pitches and spectral shapes. A singer can sing the same pitch with a large variety of vowel qualities and can likewise maintain a constant vowel quality over a substantial range of pitches.

2. Roughness and Other Spectral Line-Widening Effects

Terhardt (1978) has provided evidence that our impression of roughness in sounds depends on an additive combination of independent spectrally distributed amplitude fluctuations. Consider the following example using a tone consisting of the three components: 400, 800, and 1600 Hz. Here the components are widely distributed (i.e., more than a critical bandwidth between them) and amplitude fluctuations of say 10% of the component amplitude at frequencies between 10 and 35 Hz contribute independently to the overall impression of roughness. The implication for synthesis is to provide for independent control of the amplitude fluctuations in different regions of the spectrum.

By *spectral line widening,* we mean the spreading or smearing of energy around a spectral line. Such spectral line widening can be obtained by amplitude or frequency modulation of a sinusoid. Many instrumental timbres have noiselike effects in their attack transients and most often their spectral placement is essential to the timbre. For example, in the synthesis of stringlike attacks, the middle to upper spectral regions require more noise than the lower regions. It is to the synthesis model's advantage to allow for the independent placement of noiselike effects in separate spectral regions, which can be accomplished by widening the spectral lines in those regions.

3. Vibrato and Frequency Glides

Our impression of timbre is often strongly dependent on the presence of a vibrato or frequency glide, and the synthesis procedure should provide for an easy application of these effects without disrupting the global spectral energy distribution. A frequency glide of an oscillator with a fixed spectrum results as well in a glide of the spectral energy distribution and thus violates the desired independence. Such independence has been accomplished in the glissando version of Shepard's illusion (Shepard, 1964) produced by Risset (1969, 1978b, 1978c, 1986, 1989; cf. Braus, 1995).

In our additive synthesis procedure, we should be able to provide an overall spectral envelope that remains constant in spite of changes in the specific frequencies of the components. In addition, the model should provide for the independent placement of roughness and noiselike effects in separate regions of the spectrum again without violating the overall spectral envelope. These kinds of control can be accomplished fairly easily in most sound synthesis languages by the use of table-look-up generators, such as the VFMULT of the MUSIC V language. These generators allow one to store a spectral envelope function that is used to determine the sample-by-sample amplitude of a given component that could be executing a frequency glide. This technique works similarly for control of the spectral distribution of roughness or other line-widening effects. To obtain time-variant effects with these attributes, the spectral envelopes and roughness distributions are defined at successive and often closely spaced points in time, and interpolation is carried out between successive pairs of these functions.

REFERENCES

Allen, J. B., & Rabiner, L. R. (1977). A unified approach to short-time Fourier analysis and synthesis. *Proceedings of the IEEE, 65,* 1558–1564.

Alles, H. G., & Di Giugno, P. (1977). A one-card 64-channel digital synthesizer. *Computer Music Journal, 1*(4), 7–9.

American National Standards Institute. (1960). *USA standard acoustical terminology.* New York: American National Standards Institute.

Appleton, J. H., & Perera, R. C. (Eds.). (1975). *The development and practice of electronic music.* Englewood Cliffs, NJ: Prentice Hall.

Arfib, D. (1979). Digital synthesis of complex spectra by means of multiplication of non-linear distorted sine waves. *Journal of the Audio Engineering Society, 27,* 757–768.

Arfib, D. (1991). Analysis, transformation, and resynthesis of musical sounds with the help of a time-frequency representation. In G. De Poli, A. Picciali, & C. Roads (Eds.), *The representation of musical signals* (pp. 87–118). Cambridge, MA: MIT Press.

Arfib, D., & Delprat, N. (1993). Musical transformations using the modifications of time-frequency images. *Computer Music Journal, 17*(2), 66–72.

Arfib, D., Guillemain, P., & Kronland-Martinet, R. (1992). The algorithmic sampler: An analysis problem? *Journal of the Acoustical Society of America, 92,* 2451.

Babbitt, M. (1965). The use of computers in musicological research. *Perspectives of New Music, 3*(2).

Backhaus, W. (1932). Einschwingvorgänge. *Zeitschrift für Technische Physik, 13,* 31.

Backus, J. (1969). *The acoustical foundations of music.* New York: Norton.

Backus, J., & Hundley, J. C. (1971). Harmonic generation in the trumpet. *Journal of the Acoustical Society of America, 49,* 509–519.

Bacry, A., Grossman, A., & Zak, J. (1975). Proof of the completeness of lattice states in the kq-representation. *Physical Review, B12,* 1118.

Balzano, G. J. (1986). What are musical pitch and timbre? *Music Perception, 3*(3), 297–314.

Barrière, J. B. (Ed.). (1991). *Le timbre: Une métaphore pour la composition.* Paris: C. Bourgois & IRCAM.

Barrière, J. B., Potard, Y., & Baisnée, P. R. (1985). Models of continuity between synthesis and processing for the elaboration and control of timbre structure. *Proceedings of the 1985 International Music Conference* (pp. 193–198). San Francisco: Computer Music Association.

Bastiaans, M. J. (1980). Gabor's expansion of a signal into Gaussian elementary signals. *Proceedings of the IEEE, 68,* 538–539.

Beauchamp, J. W. (1975). Analysis and synthesis of cornet tones using non linear interharmonic relationships. *Journal of the Audio Engineering Society, 23,* 778–795.

Benade, A. H. (1976). *Fundamentals of musical acoustics.* London and New York: Oxford University Press.

Bennett, G. (1981). Singing synthesis in electronic music. In *Research aspects of singing* (pp. 34–40). Stockholm: Royal Academy of Music, Publication 33.

Berger, J., Coifman, R., & Goldberg, M. J. (1994). A method of denoising and reconstructing audio signals. *Proceedings of the 1994 International Music Conference* (pp. 344–347). San Francisco: Computer Music Association.

Berger, K. W. (1964). Some factors in the recognition of timbre. *Journal of the Acoustical Society of America, 36,* 1888–1891.

Bismarck, G. von. (1974a). Sharpness as an attribute of the timbre of steady sounds *Acustica, 30,* 159–172.

Bismarck, G. von. (1974b). Timbre of steady sounds: a factorial investigation of its verbal attributes. *Acustica, 30,* 146–158.

Blackman, R. B., & Tukey, J. W. (1958). *The measurement of power spectra from the point of view of communications engineering.* New York: Dover.

Bolt, R. H., Cooper, F. S., David, E. E., Jr., Denes, P. B., Pickett, J. M., & Stevens, K. N. (1969). Identification of a speaker by speech spectrogram. *Science, 166,* 338–343.

Bolt, R. H., Cooper, F. S., David, E. E., Jr., Denes, P. B., Pickett, J. M., & Stevens, K. N. (1978). *On the theory and practice of voice identification.* Washington, DC: National Research Council.

Boomsliter, P. C., & Creel, W. (1970). Hearing with ears instead of instruments. *Journal of the Audio Engineering Society, 18,* 407–412.

Braus, I. (1995). Retracing one's steps: an overview of pith circularity and Shepard tones in European music:1550–1990. *Music Perception, 12*(3), 323–351.

Bregman, A. S. (1990). *Auditory scene analysis: The perceptual organization of sound.* Cambridge, MA: MIT Press.

Bregman, A. S., & Campbell, J. (1971). Primary auditory stream segregation and perception of order in rapid sequences of tones. *Journal of Experimental Psychology, 89,* 244–249.

Bregman, A. S., & Pinker, S. (1978). Auditory streaming and the building of timbre. *Canadian Journal of Psychology, 32,* 19–31.

Brown, G. J., & Cooke, M. (1994). Computational auditory scene analysis. *Computers Speech Language (UK), 8*(4), 297–336.

Brown, G.J., & Cooke, M. (1994). Perceptual grouping of musical sounds: a computational model. *Journal of New Music Research (Netherlands), 23*(2), 107–132.

Cabot, R. C., Mino, M. G., Dorans, D. A., Tackel, I. S., & Breed, H. B. (1976). Detection of phase shifts in harmonically related tones. *Journal of the Audio Engineering Society, 24,* 568–571.

Cadoz, C., Luciani, A., & Florens, J. L. (1984). Responsive input devices and sound synthesis by simulation of instrumental mechanisms. *Computer Music Journal, 14*(2), 47–51.

Cadoz, C., Luciani, A., & Florens, J. L. (1993). CORDIS-ANIMA: a modeling and simulation system for sound and image synthesis—the general formalism. *Computer Music Journal, 17*(1), 19–29.

Campanella, S. J., & Robinson, G. S. (1971). A comparison of orthogonal transformations for digital speech processing. *IEEE Transactions on Communication Technology, COM-19,* 1045–1050.

Charbonneau, G. (1981). Timbre and the perceptual effect of three types of data reduction. *Computer Music Journal, 5* (2), 10–19.

Charles, D. (1980). L'eterno ritorno del timbro. In *Musica e Elaboratore* (pp. 94–99). Venice: Biennale.

Cheung, N. M., & Horner, A. (1996). Group synthesis with genetic algorithms. *Journal of the Audio Engineering Society, 44,* 130–147.

Chowning, J. (1971). The simulation of moving sound sources. *Journal of the Audio Engineering Society, 19,* 2–6.

Chowning, J. (1980). Computer synthesis of the singing voice. In *Sound generation in winds, strings, computers* (pp. 4–13). Stockholm: Royal Swedish Academy of Music.

Chowning, J. (1973). The synthesis of complex audio spectra by means of frequency modulation. *Journal of the Audio Engineering Society, 21,* 526–534.

Chowning, J. (1989). Frequency modulation synthesis of the singing voice. In M. V. Mathews & J. R. Pierce (Eds.), *Current directions in computer music research* (with a compact disk of sound examples) (pp. 57–63). Cambridge, MA: MIT Press.

Chowning, J., & Bristow, D. (1987). *FM theory and applications: By musicians for musicians.* Tokyo: Yamaha Foundation.

Clark, M., Robertson, P., & Luce, D. (1964). A preliminary experiment on the perceptual basis for musical instrument families. *Journal of the Audio Engineering Society, 12,* 194–203.

Cogan, R. (1984). *New images of musical sound.* Cambridge, MA: Harvard University Press.

Coifman, R, Meyer, Y., & Wickerhauser, V. (1992). Wavelet analysis and signal processing. In M. B. Ruskai, G. Beylkin, R. Coifman, I. Daubechies, S. Mallat, Y. Meyer, & L. Raphael (Eds.), *Wavelets and their applications* (pp. 153–178). Boston: Jones and Bartlett.

Colomes, C, Lever, M., Rault, J. B., Dehery, Y. F., & Faucon G. A.. (1995). Perceptual model applied to audio bit-rate reduction. *Journal of the Audio Engineering Society, 43,* 233–239.

Combes, J. M., Grossman, A., & Tchamitchian, P. (Eds.) (1989). *Wavelets.* Berlin: Springer-Verlag.

Cook, P. R. (1992). A meta-wind-instrument physical model controller, and a meta-controller for real-time performance control. *Proceedings of the 1992 International Music Conference* (pp. 273–276). San Francisco: Computer Music Association.

Cook, P. R. (1993). SPASM, a real-time vocal tract physical model controller; and Singer, the companion software synthesis system. *Computer Music Journal, 17*(1), 30–44.

Cook, P. R. (1996). Singing voice synthesis: history, current work, and future directions. *Computer Music Journal, 20*(3), 38–46.

Cosi, P., de Poli, G., & Lauzzana, G. (1994). Auditory modeling and self-organizing neural networks for timbre classification. *Journal of New Music Research (Netherlands), 23*(1), 71–98.

Culver, C. A. (1956). *Musical acoustics.* New York: McGraw Hill.

De Poli, G. (1983). A tutorial on sound synthesis techniques. *Computer Music Journal, 7*(4), 8–26.

Delprat, N., Guillemain, P., & Kronland-Martinet, R. (1990). Parameter estimation for non-linear resynthesis methods with the help of a time-frequency analysis of natural sounds. *Proceedings of the 1990 International Music Conference* (pp. 88–90). San Francisco: Computer Music Association.

Depalle, P., & Poirot, G. (1991). SVP: a modular system for analysis, processing, and synthesis of the sound signal. *Proceedings of the 1991 International Music Conference* (pp. 161–164). San Francisco: Computer Music Association.

Depalle, P., & Rodet, X. (1992). A new additive synthesis method using inverse Fourier transform and spectral envelopes. *Proceedings of the 1992 International Music Conference* (pp. 161–164). San Francisco: Computer Music Association.

Desain, P., & Honing, H. (1992). *Music, mind and machine.* Amsterdam: Thesis Publishers.

Deutsch, D. (1975). Musical illusions. *Scientific American, 233,* 92–104.

Deutsch, D. (1995). *Musical illusions and paradoxes* [CD]. La Jolla, CA: Philomel.

Dijksterhuis, P. R., & Verhey, T. (1969). An electronic piano. *Journal of the Audio Engineering Society, 17,* 266–271.

Dodge, C., & Terse, T. A. (1985). *Computer music: synthesis, composition and performance.* New York: Schirmer Books, McMillan.

Dolansky, L. O. (1960). Choice of base signals in speech signal analysis. *IRE Transactions on Audio, 8,* 221–229.

Dolson, M. (1986). The phase vocoder: A tutorial. *Computer Music Journal, 10*(4), 14–27.

Dowling, J., & Harwood, D. (1986). *Music cognition.* New York: Academic Press.

Duda, R. O., Lyon, R. F., & Slaney, M. (1990). Correlograms and the separation of sounds. *24th Asilomar Conference on Signals, Systems and Computers* (pp. 457–461), Pacific Grove, CA.

Eagleson, H. W., & Eagleson, O. W. (1947). Identification of musical instruments when heard directly and over a public address system. *Journal of the Acoustical Society of America, 19,* 338–342.

Emmerson, S. (Ed.) (1986). *The language of electroacoustic music.* London: McMillan Press.

Erickson, R. (1975). *Sound structure in music.* Berkeley, CA: University of California Press.

Ethington, R., & Punch, B. (1994). Seawave: a system for musical timbre description. *Computer Music Journal, 18*(1),30–39.

Fant, G. (1960). *Acoustic theory of speech production.* Gravenhage: Mouton.

Feynman, R. B., Leighton, R. B., & Sands, M. (1963). *The Feynman lectures on physics.* Reading, MA: Addison-Wesley.

Flanagan, J. L. (1962). Models for approximating basilar-membrane displacement. *Bell System Technical Journal, 41,* 959–1009.

Flanagan, J. L. (1972). *Speech analysis, synthesis and perception.* New York: Academic Press.

Fletcher, H., & Bassett, I. G. (1978). Some experiments with the bass drum. *Journal of the Acoustical Society of America, 64,* 1570–1576.

Fletcher, H., & Sanders, L. C. (1967). Quality of violin vibrato tones. *Journal of the Acoustical Society of America, 41,* 1534–1544.

Fletcher, H., Blackham, B. D., & Christensen, D. A. (1963). Quality of organ tones. *Journal of the Acoustical Society of America, 3S,* 314–325.

Fletcher, H., Blackham, B. D., & Stratton, R. (1962). Quality of piano tones. *Journal of the Acoustical Society of America, 34,* 749–761.

Fletcher, N. H., & Rossing, T. D. (1991). *The physics of musical instruments.* New York: Springer-Verlag.

François, J. C. (1995). Fixed timbre, dynamic timbre. *Perspectives of New Music, 13*(1), 112–118.

Freed, A., Rodet, X., Depalle, P. (1993). Synthesis and control of hundreds of sinusoidal partials on a desktop computer without custom hardware. In *Proceedings of the 1993 International Computer Music Conference* (pp. 98–101) San Francisco: Computer Music Association.

Freed, D. J, & Martens, W. L. (1986). Deriving psychoacoustic relations for timbre. In *Proceedings of the 1986 International Music Conference* (pp. 393–405). San Francisco: Computer Music Association.

Freed, D. J. (1990). Auditory correlates of perceived mallet hardness for a set of recorded percussive sound events. *Journal of the Acoustical Society of America, 87,* 311–322.

Freedman, M. D. (1967). Analysis of musical instrument tones. *Journal of the Acoustical Society of America, 41,* 793–806.

Friberg, A. (1991). Generative rules for music performance: a formal description of a rule system. *Computer Music Journal, 15*(2), 56–71.

Friberg, A., Frydén, L., Bodin, L. G., & Sundberg, J. (1991). Performance rules for computer-controlled contemporary keyboard music. *Computer Music Journal, 15* (2), 49–55.

Gabor, D. (1947). Acoustical quanta and the nature of hearing. *Nature, 159*(4).

George, E. B., & Smith, M. J. T. (1992). Analysis-by-synthesis: Overlap-add sinusoidal modeling applied to the analysis and synthesis of musical tones. *Journal of the Audio Engineering Society, 40,* 497–516.

George, W. H. (1954). A sound reversal technique applied to the study of tone quality. *Acustica, 4,* 224–225.

Gibiat, V. (1988). Phase space representations of acoustic musical signals. *Journal of Sound and Vibration, 123,* 529–536.

Gibson, J. J. (1966). *The senses considered as perceptual systems.* Boston: Houghton Mifflin.

Goad, P., & Keefe, D. H. (1992). Timbre discrimination of musical instruments in a concert hall. *Music Perception, 10*(1), 43–62.

Gregory, A. H. (1994). Timbre and auditory streaming. *Music Perception, 12*(3), 161–174.

Grey, J. M. (1975). *An exploration of musical timbre*. Doctoral dissertation, Stanford University, Stanford, CA.

Grey, J. M. (1977). Multidimensional perceptual scaling of musical timbres. *Journal of the Acoustical Society of America, 61,* 1270–1277.

Grey, J. M. (1978). Timbre discrimination in musical patterns. *Journal of the Acoustical Society of America, 64,* 467–472.

Grey, J. M., & Gordon, J. W. (1978). Perceptual effect of spectral modifications in musical timbres. *Journal of the Acoustical Society of America, 63,* 1493–1500.

Grey, J. M., & Moorer, J. A. (1977). Perceptual evaluation of synthesized musical instrument tones. *Journal of the Acoustical Society of America, 62,* 454–462.

Grossman, A., & Morlet, J. (1984). Decomposition of Hardy functions into square integrable wavelets of constant shape. *SIAM Journal of Mathematical Analysis, 15,* 723–736.

Guillemain, P., & Kronland-Martinet, R. (1992). Additive resynthesis of sounds using continuous time-frequency analysis techniques. *Proceedings of the 1992 International Music Conference* (pp. 10–13). San Francisco: Computer Music Association.

Guillemain, P., & Kronland-Martinet, R. (1996). Characterization of acoustic signals through continuous linear time-frequency representations. *Proceedings of the IEEE, 84,* 561-585.

Hall, H. H. (1937). Sound analysis. *Journal of the Acoustical Society of America, 8,* 257–262.

Handel, S. (1990). *Listening: An introduction to the perception of auditory events*. Cambridge, MA: MIT Press.

Harmuth, H. (1972). *Transmission of information by orthogonal functions*. New York: Springer.

Helmholtz, H. von. (1954). *Sensations of tone* (E. J. Ellis, Trans.). New York: Dover. (Original work published 1877)

Hiller, L. & Ruiz, P. (1971). Synthesizing musical sounds by solving the wave equation for vibrating objects: Part I. *Journal of the Audio Engineering Society, 19,* 463–470.

Horner, A. (1996a). Double-modulator FM matching of instrument tones. *Journal of the Audio Engineering Society, 44,* 130–147.

Horner, A. (1996b). Computation and memory tradeoffs with multiple wavetable interpolation. *Journal of the Audio Engineering Society, 44,* 481–496.

Horner, A., & Beauchamp, J. (1996). Piecewise-linear approximation of additive synthesis envelopes: a comparison of various methods. *Computer Music Journal, 20*(2), 72–95.

Horner, A., Beauchamp, J. , & Haken, L. (1993). Methods for multiple wavetable synthesis of musical instrument tones. *Journal of the Audio Engineering Society, 41,* 336–356.

Hourdin, C. (1995). *Etude psychophysique du timbre: Application au codage et à la synthèse des sons en musique*. Dissertation, l'Université Paris XI, Orsay.

Huggins, W. H. (1952). A phase principle for complex frequency analysis and its implication in auditory theory. *Journal of the Acoustical Society of America, 24,* 582–589.

Huggins, W. H. (1957). *Representation and analysis of signals: Part I. The use of orthogonalized exponentials*. Baltimore, MD: Johns Hopkins University, Report AF 19 (604)-1941, ASTIA n) AD133741.

Huron, D., & Sellmer, P. (1992). Critical bands and the spelling of vertical sonorities. *Music Perception, 10,* 129–150.

Iverson, P., & Krumhansl, C. K. (1993). Isolating the dynamic attributes of timbre. *Journal of the Acoustical Society of America, 94,* 2595–2603.

Jaffe, D. A., & Smith, J. O. (1983). Extensions of the Karplus-Strong Plucked String Algorithm. *Computer Music Journal, 7*(2), 56–69.

Jansson, L., & Sundberg, J. (1975/1976). Long-term average spectra applied to analysis of music. *Acustica, 34,* 15–19, 269–274.

Jenkins, G. M ., & Watts, D. G. (1968). *Spectral analysis and its applications*. San Francisco: Holden-Day.

Justice, J. (1979). Analytic signal processing in music computation. *IEEE Transactions on Speech, Acoustics and Signal Processing, ASSP-27,* 670–684.

Karplus, K., & Strong, A. (1983). Digital synthesis of plucked string and drum timbres. *Computer Music Journal, 7*(2), 43–55.

Keefe, D. H. (1992). Physical modeling of wind instruments. *Computer Music Journal, 16*(4), 57–73.

Keeler, J. S. (1972). Piecewise-periodic analysis of almost-periodic sounds and musical transients. *IEEE Transactions on Audio & Electroacoustics, AU-1O,* 338–344.

Kendall, R., & Carterette, E. C. (1993). Identification and blend of timbres as basis for orchestration. *Contemporary Music Review, 9,* 51–67.

Kendall, R., & Carterette, E. C. (1993a). Verbal attributes of simultaneous instrument timbres: I von Bismarck adjectives. *Music Perception, 10*(4), 445–467.

Kendall, R., & Carterette, E. C. (1993b). Verbal attributes of simultaneous instrument timbres: II. Adjectives induced from Piston's orchestration. *Music Perception, 10*(4), 469–502.

Kleczkowski, P. (1989). Group additive synthesis. *Computer Music Journal, 13*(1), 12–20.

Koenig, W., Dunn, H. K., & Lacy, L. Y. (1946). The sound spectrograph. *Journal of the Acoustical Society of America, 18,* 1949.

Köhler, W. (1915). Akustische Untersuchungen. *Zeitschrift fur Psychologie, 72,* 159.

Kohut, J., & Mathews, M. V. (1971). Study of motion of a bowed string. *Journal of the Acoustical Society of America, 49,* 532–537.

Kramer, H. P., & Mathews, M. V. (1956). A linear coding for transmitting a set of correlated signals. *IRE Transactions on Information Theory, IT2,* 41–46.

Kronland-Martinet, R. (1989). The use of the wavelet transform for the analysis, synthesis and processing of speech and music sounds. *Computer Music Journal, 12*(4), 11–20 (with sound examples on disk).

Kronland-Martinet, R., & Guillemain, P. (1993). Towards non-linear resynthesis of instrumental sounds. *Proceedings of the 1993 International Music Conference* (pp. 86–93). San Francisco: Computer Music Association.

Kronland-Martinet, R., Morlet, J., & Grossman, A. (1987). Analysis of sound patterns through wavelet transforms. *International Journal of Pattern Recognition and Artificial Intelligence, 11*(2), 97–126.

Laroche, J. (1989). A new analysis/synthesis system of musical signals using Prony's method. Application to heavily damped percussive sounds. *Proc. IEEE ICASSP-89,* 2053–2056.

Laroche, J. (1993). The use of the matrix pencil method for the spectrum analysis of musical signals. *Journal of the Acoustical Society of America, 94,* 1958–1965.

Lashley, K. S. (1942). An examination of the "continuity theory" as applied to discriminative learning. *Journal of General Psychology, 26,* 241–265.

La synthèse sonore [Special issue]. (1993). *Cahiers de l'IRCAM, 2.*

Lauberhorn, W. (1996). Nonlinear dynamics in acoustics. *Acustica (Acta Acustica), 82,* S46–S55.

Laughlin, R. G., Truax, B. D., & Funt, B. V. (1990). Synthesis of acoustic timbres using principal component analysis. *Proceedings of the 1990 International Music Conference* (pp. 95–99). San Francisco: Computer Music Association.

Le Brun, M. (1979). Digital waveshaping synthesis. *Journal of the Audio Engineering Society, 27,* 250–266.

Lee, M., & Wessel, D. (1992). Connectionist models for real-time control of synthesis and compositional algorithms. In *Proceedings of the 1992 International Music Conference* (pp. 277–280). San Francisco: Computer Music Association.

Lee, M., & Wessel, D. (1993). Real-time neuro-fuzzy systems for adaptive control of musical processes. In *Proceedings of the 1993 International Music Conference* (pp. 172–175). San Francisco: Computer Music Association.

Lee, M., Freed, A., & Wessel, D. (1992). Neural networks for classification and parameter estimation in musical instrument control. In *Proceedings of the SPIE Conference on Robotics and Intelligent Systems,* Orlando, FL.

Lee, M., Freed, A., Wessel, D. (1991). Real-time neural network processing of gestural and acoustic signals. In *Proceedings of the 1991 International Music Conference.* San Francisco: Computer Music Association.

Legge, K. A., & Fletcher, N. H. (1989). Non-linearity, chaos, and the sound of shallow gongs. *Journal of the Acoustical Society of America, 86*, 2439–2443.

Leipp, E. (1971). *Acoustique et musique.* Paris: Masson.

Licklider, J. C. R. (1951). A duplex theory of pitch perception. *Experientia, Suisse, 7*, 128–133.

Loy, G. (1985). Musicians make a standard: the MIDI phenomenon. *Computer Music Journal, 9*(4), 8–26.

Luce, D., & Clark, M., Jr. (1967). Physical correlates of brass-instrument tones. *Journal of the Acoustical Society of America, 42*, 1232–1243.

Maganza, C., Caussé, R., & Laloë, F. (1986). Bifurcations, period doublings and chaos in clarinet-like systems. *Europhysics Letters, 1*, 295–302.

Martin, D. W. (1947). Decay rates of piano tones. *Journal of the Acoustical Society of America, 19*, 535.

Massie, D. C. (1998). Wavetable sampling synthesis. In M. Kahrs & K. Brandenberg (Eds.), *Applications of digital signal processing to audio and acoustics.* Norwell, MA: Kluwer Academic Publishers.

Mathes, R. C., & Miller, R. L. (1947). Phase effects in monaural perception. *Journal of the Acoustical Society of America, 19*, 780–797.

Mathews, M. V. (1963). The digital computer as a musical instrument. *Science, 142*, 553–557.

Mathews, M. V. (1969). *The technology of computer music.* Cambridge, MA: MIT Press.

Mathews, M. V., & Kohut, J. (1973). Electronic simulation of violin resonances. *Journal of the Acoustical Society of America, 53*, 1620–1626.

Mathews, M. V., & Moore, F. R. (1970). Groove—a program to compose, store and edit functions of time. *Communications of the ACM, 13*, 715 –7 21.

Mathews, M. V., Miller, J. B., & David, B. B., Jr., (1961). Pitch synchronous analysis of voiced sounds. *Journal of the Acoustical Society of America, 33*, 179–186.

Mathews, M. V., Moore, F. R., & Risset, J. C. (1974). Computers and future music. *Science, 183*, 263–268.

Mathews, M. V. , Miller, J. B., Pierce, J. R., & Tenney, J. (1965). Computer study of violin tones. *Journal of the Acoustical Society of America, 38*, 912 (abstract only).

Mathews, M. V. , Miller, J. B., Pierce, J. R., & Tenney, J. (1966). *Computer study of violin tones.* Murray Hill, NJ: Bell Laboratories.

McAdams, S. (1982). Spectral fusion and the creation of auditory images. In M. Clynes (Ed.), *Music, mind and brain* (pp. 279–298). New York: Plenum Press.

McAdams, S., & Bigand, E. (Eds.) (1993). *Thinking in sound: The cognitive psychology of human audition.* Oxford: Clarendon Press.

McAdams, S., & Bregman, A. (1979). Hearing musical streams. *Computer Music Journal, 3*(4), 26–43.

McAdams, S., & Saariaho, K. (1985). Qualities and functions of musical timbre. In *Proceedings of the 1985 International Music Conference* (pp. 367–374). San Francisco: Computer Music Association.

McAulay, R., & Quatieri, T. (1986). Speech analysis-synthesis based on a sinusoidal representation. *IEEE Transactions on Speech, Acoustics and Signal Processing, ASSP-34*, 744–754.

McConkey, J. (1984). Report from the synthesizer explosion. *Computer Music Journal, 8*(2), 59–60.

McIntyre, M. E., Schumacher, R. T., & Woodhouse, J. (1983). On the oscillations of musical instruments. *Journal of the Acoustical Society of America, 74*, 1325–1345.

Melara, R. D., & Marks, L. E. (1990). Interaction among auditory dimensions: timbre, pitch and loudness. *Perception & Psychophysics, 48*, 169–178.

Meyer, B., & Buchmann, G. (1931). *Die Klangspektren der Musikinstrumente.* Berlin.

Miller, D. C. (1926). *The science of musical sounds.* New York: MacMillan.

Miskiewicz, A. (1992). Timbre solfege: a course in technical listening for sound engineers. *Journal of the Audio Engineering Society, 40*, 621–625.

Modèles physiques, création musicale et ordinateur. (1994). Actes du Colloque international de Grenoble. Paris: Editions de la Maison des Sciences de l'Homme.

Moore, B. C. J. (1982). *An introduction to the psychology of hearing.* London, Academic Press.

Moore, B. C. J., & Glasberg, B. R. (1981). Auditory filter shapes derived in simultaneous and forward masking. *Journal of the Acoustical Society of America, 69,* 1003–1014.

Moore, F. R. (1990). *Elements of computer music.* Englewood Cliffs, NJ: Prentice Hall.

Moorer, J. A. (1977). Signal processing aspects of computer music: a survey. *Proceedings of the IEEE, 6S,* I108–I137.

Moorer, J. A. (1978). The use of the phase vocoder in computer music applications. *Journal of the Audio Engineering Society, 26,* 42–45.

Moorer, J. A., & Grey, J. (1977a). Lexicon of analyzed tones: Part I: A violin tone. *Computer Music Journal, 1*(2), 3945.

Moorer, J. A., & Grey, J. (1977b). Part II: Clarinet and oboe tones. *Computer Music Journal, 1*(3), 1229.

Moorer, J. A., & Grey, J. (1978). Part III: The trumpet. *Computer Music Journal, 2*(2), 23–31.

Morrill, D. (1977). Trumpet algorithms for music composition. *Computer Music Journal, 1*(1), 46–52.

Morrison, J. D., & Adrien, J. M. (1993). MOSAIC, a framework for modal synthesis: a modeling and simulation system for sound and image synthesis—the general formalism. *Computer Music Journal, 17*(1), 45–56.

Moulines, E., & Laroche, J. (1995). Non-parametric techniques for pitch-scale and time-scale modification. *Speech Communication, 16*(2), 175–215.

Music and Technology. (1971). UNESCO and *Revue Musicale.* Paris: Ed. Richard Masse.

Neisser, U. (1976). *Cognition and reality.* San Francisco: Freeman.

Olson, H. F. (1967). *Music, physics and engineering.* New York: Dover.

Panter, P. F. (1965). *Modulation, noise and spectral analysis.* New York: McGraw Hill.

Patterson, R. D. (1976). Auditory filter shapes derived with noise stimuli. *Journal of the Acoustical Society of America, 59,* 640–654.

Pierce, J. R. (1983). *The science of musical sound* (with sound examples on disk). San Francisco: Freeman/Scientific American.

Plomp, R. (1964). The ear as a frequency analyzer. *Journal of the Acoustical Society of America, 36,* 1628–1636.

Plomp, R. (1966). Timbre as a multidimensional attribute of complex tones. In R. Plomp & F. G. Smoorenburg (Eds.), *Frequency analysis and periodicity detection in hearing.* Leiden: Suithoff.

Plomp, R. (1976). *Aspects of tone sensation.* New York: Academic Press.

Plomp, R., & Steeneken, J. M. (1969). Effect of phase on the timbre of complex tones. *Journal of the Acoustical Society of America, 46,* 409–421.

Plomp, R., & Steeneken, J. M. (1971). Pitch versus timbre. *Proceedings of the 7th International Congress of Acoustics, Budapest, 3,* 377–380.

Radvansky, G. A., Fleming, K. J., & Simmons, J. A. (1995). Timbre reliance in nonmusicians' and musicians' memory for melodies. *Music Perception, 13*(2), 127–140.

Richardson, E. G. (1954). The transient tones of wind instruments. *Journal of the Acoustical Society of America, 26,* 960–962.

Risset, J. C. (1965). Computer study of trumpet tones. *Journal of the Acoustical Society of America, 33,* 912.

Risset, J. C. (1966). *Computer study of trumpet tones.* Murray Hill, NJ: Bell Laboratories.

Risset, J. C. (1969). *An introductory catalog of computer-synthesized sounds.* Murray Hill, NJ: Bell Laboratories. Reissued as part of *The historical CD of digital sound synthesis,* Mainz, Germany: Wergo, 1995.

Risset, J. C. (1971). Paradoxes de hauteur. *Proceedings of the 7th International Congress of Acoustics, Budapest, 3,* 613–616.

Risset, J. C. (1978a). Musical acoustics. In E. C. Carterette & M. P. Friedman, *Handbook of perception: Vol. IV. Hearing* (pp. 521–564). New York: Academic Press.

Risset, J. C. (1978 b). *Paradoxes de hauteur* (with a cassette of sound examples). Paris: IRCAM Report No. 10.

Risset, J. C. (1978c). *Hauteur et timbre* (with a cassette of sound examples). Paris: IRCAM Rep. No. 11.

Risset, J. C. (1986). Pitch and rhythm paradoxes. *Journal of the Acoustical Society of America, 80,* 961–962.

Risset, J. C. (1989). Paradoxical sounds. In M. V. Mathews & J. R. Pierce (Eds.), *Current directions in computer music research* (with a compact disk of sound examples) (pp. 149–158). Cambridge, MA: MIT Press.

Risset, J. C. (1991). Timbre analysis by synthesis: representations, imitations and variants for musical composition. In De Poli, G., Picciali, A., & Roads, C., eds. *The representation of musical signals* (pp. 7–43). Cambridge, MA: MIT Press

Risset, J. C. (1994). Quelques aspects du timbre dans la musique contemporaine. In A. Zenatti (Ed.), *Psychologie de la musique* (pp. 87–114). Paris: Presses Universitaires de France.

Risset, J. C., & Mathews, M. V. (1969). Analysis of musical instrument tones. *Physics Today, 22*(2), 23–30.

Roads, C. (with Strawn, J., Abbott, C., Gordon, J., & Greenspun, P.). (1996). *The computer music tutorial.* Cambridge, MA: MIT Press.

Roads, C. (1978). Automated granular synthesis of sound. *Computer Music Journal, 2*(2), 61–62.

Roads, C. (Ed.). (1985). *Composers and the computer.* Cambridge, MA: MIT Press.

Roads, C. (Ed.). (1989). *The music machine.* Cambridge, MA: MIT Press.

Rodet, X, Potard, Y, & Barrière, J. B. (1984). The Chant project: From the synthesis of the sung voice to synthesis in general. *Computer Music Journal, 8*(3), 15–31

Rodet, X. (1994). Stability/instability of periodic solutions and chaos in physical models of musical instruments. In *Proceedings of the 1992 International Computer Music Conference* (pp. 386–393). San Francisco: International Computer Music Association.

Rodet, X. (1979, July). Time-domain formant-wave-function synthesis. *Proceedings of the NATO-ASI Meeting.* Bonas.

Rodet, X., & Bennett, G. (1980). Synthèse de la voix chantée par ordinateur. *Conférences des Journees d'Etudes du Festival du Son* (pp. 73–91). Paris: Ed. Chiron.

Rodet, X., & Depalle, P., & Poirot, G. (1987). Analyse et synthèse de la voix parlée et chantée par modélisation de l'enveloppe spectrale et de l'excitation. *Actes des 16èmes Journées d'Etude sur la Parole* (pp. 41–44). Paris: Société Française d'Acoustique.

Rodet, X., Depalle, P., & Garcia, G. (1995). New possibilities in sound analysis-synthesis. In *Proceedings of the International Symposium on Musical Acoustics* (pp. 421–432). Paris: Société Française d'Acoustique.

Roederer, J. G. (1974). *Introduction to the physics and psychophysics of music.* London: The English Universities Press.

Rosenblatt, M. (Ed.). (1963). *Time series analysis.* New York: Wiley.

Rossing, T. D.(1990). *The science of sound.* Reading, MA: Addison–Wesley.

Rossing, T. D. (Ed.). (1984). *The acoustics of bells.* New York: van Nostrand Reinhold.

Rossing, T. D., Hampton, D. C., Richardson, B. E., Sathoff, J., & Lehr, A. (1988). Vibrational modes of Chinese two-tone bells. *Journal of the Acoustical Society of America, 83,* 369–373.

Saldanha, E. L., & Corso, J. F. (1964). Timbre cues and the identification of musical instruments. *Journal of the Acoustical Society of America, 36,* 2021–2026.

Sandell, G. (1995). Roles for spectral centroid and other factors in determining "blended" instrument pairings in orchestration. *Music Perception, 13*(2), 209–246.

Sandell, G., & Martens, W. (1995). Perceptual evaluation of principal components-based synthesis of musical timbres. *Journal of the Audio Engineering Society, 43,* 1013–1028.

Sasaki, L. H., & Smith, K. C. (1980). A simple data reduction scheme for additive synthesis. *Computer Music Journal, 4*(1), 22–24.

Schaeffer, P. (1966). *Traité des objets musicaux* (with three records of sound examples). Paris: Ed. du Seuil.

Schafer, R. W., & Rabiner, L. R. (1975). Digital representations of speech signals. *Proceedings of the IEEE, 63,* 662–677.

Scharf, B. (). Critical bands. In J. V. Tobias (Ed.), *Foundations of modern auditory theory* (Vol. 1, pp. 157–202). New York: Academic Press.

Schoenberg, A. (1911). *Harmonielehre.* Leipzig and Vienna: Universal Edition.

Schottstaedt, W. (1977). The simulation of natural instrument tones using frequency modulation with a complex modulating wave. *Computer Music Journal, 1*(4), 46–50.

Schroeder, M. R. (1966). Complementarity of sound buildup and decay. *Journal of the Acoustical Society of America, 40,* 549–551.

Schroeder, M. R. (1975). Models of hearing. *Proceedings of the IEEE, 63,* 1332–1350.

Schroeder, M. R., Atal, B. S., & Hall, J. L. (1979). Optimising digital speech coders by exploiting masking properties of the human ear. *Journal of the Acoustical Society of America, 66,* 1647–1652.

Serra, M.-H., Rubine, D., & Dannenberg, R. (1990). Analysis and synthesis of tones by spectral interpolation. *Journal of the Audio Engineering Society, 38,* 111–128.

Serra, X., & Smith, J. (1990). Spectral modeling synthesis: a sound analysis/synthesis system based on a deterministic plus stochastic decomposition. *Computer Music Journal, 14*(4), 12–24.

Shepard, R. N. (1964). Circularity of relative pitch. *Journal of the Acoustical Society of America, 36,* 2346–2353.

Slaney, M. (1996). Correlograms and their inversion - the importance of periodicities in auditory perception. *Acustica, 82,* S91.

Slaney, M., Covell, M., & Lassitier, B. (1996). Automatic audio morphing. *Proceedings of 1996 ICASSP,* Atlanta.

Slaney, M., & Lyon, R. F. (1993). On the importance of time: A temporal representation of sound. In Cooke, M., Beet, S., & Crawford, J. (Eds.), *Visual representations of speech signals.* Sussex, England: J. Wiley.

Slaney, M., Lyon, R., & Naar, D. (1994). Auditory model inversion for sound separation. *Proceedings of 1994 ICASSP, Adelaide, Australia, 2,* 77–80.

Slawson, A. W. (1968). Vowel quality and musical timbre as functions of spectrum envelope and fundamental frequency. *Journal of the Acoustical Society of America, 43,* 97–101.

Slawson, W. (1985). *Sound color.* Berkeley: University of California Press.

Sloboda, J. (Ed.). (1988). *Generative processes in music performance.* Oxford: Oxford Science Publications.

Smalley, D. (1986). Spectromorphology and structuring processes. In S. Emmerson (Ed.), *The language of electroacoustic music* (pp. 61–93). New York: Harwood Academic Publishers.

Smalley, D. (1993). Defining transformations. *Interface, Netherlands, 22 ,* 279–300.

Smith, J. (1996). Physical modeling synthesis update. *Computer Music Journal, 20*(2), 44–56.

Smith, J. (1992). Physical modeling using digital waveguides. *Computer Music Journal, 16*(4), 74–91.

Smith, J., & Van Duyne, S. (1995). Recent results in piano synthesis via physical modeling. *Proceedings of the International Symposium on Musical Acoustics* (pp. 503–509). Paris: Société Française d'Acoustique.

Stapleton, J., & Bass, S. (1988). Synthesis of musical tones based on the Karhunen-Loève transform. *IEEE Transactions on Speech, Acoustics and Signal Processing, ASSP-36,* 305–319.

Strawn, J. (1987). Analysis and synthesis of musical transitions using the discrete short-time Fourier transform. *Journal of the Audio Engineering Society, 35,* 3–14.

Strong, W., & Clark, M., Jr., (1967a). Synthesis of wind-instrument tones. *Journal of the Acoustical Society of America, 41,* 39–52.

Strong, W., & Clark, M. Jr., (1967b). Perturbations of synthetic orchestral wind instrument tones. *Journal of the Acoustical Society of America, 41,* 277–285.

Stumpf, C. (1926). *Die sprachlaute.* Berlin and New York: Springer-Verlag.

Sundberg, J. (1977). The acoustics of the singing voice. *Scientific American, 236,* 82–91.

Sundberg, J. (Ed.) (1983). *Studies of music performance.* Stockholm: Royal Academy of Music, Publication 39.

Sundberg, J. (1987). *The science of the singing voice.* DeKalb, IL: Northern Illinois University Press.

Sundberg, J., & Frydén, L. (1989). Rules for automated performance of ensemble music. *Contemporary Music Review, 3,* 89–109.

Tan, B. T. G., Gan, S. L., Lim, S. M., & Tang, S. H. (1994). Real-time implementation of double frequency modulation (DFM) synthesis. *Journal of the Audio Engineering Society, 42,* 918–926.

Tellman, E., Haken, L., & Holloway, B. (1995). Timbre morphing of sounds with unequal numbers of features. *Journal of the Audio Engineering Society, 43,* 678–688.

Tenney, J. C. (1965). The physical correlates of timbre. *Gravesaner Blätter, 26,* 103–109.

Terhardt, E. (1974). Pitch, consonance, and harmony. *Journal of the Acoustical Society of America, 55,* 1061–1069.

Terhardt, E. (1978). Psychoacoustic evaluation of musical sounds. *Perception & Psychophysics, 23,* 483–492.

Toiviainen, M., Kaipainen, M., & Louhivuoiri, J. (1995). Musical timbre: similarity ratings correlate with computational feature space distances. *Journal of New Music Research (Netherlands), 24,* 282–298.

Valimaki, V., & Takala, T. (1996). Virtual musical instruments - natural sound using physical models. *Organised Sound (England), 1,* 75–86.

Van Duyne, S., & Smith, J. (1993). Physical-modeling with a 2-D digital waveguide mesh. In *Proceedings of the 1993 International Computer Music Conference* (pp. 30–37). San Francisco: International Computer Music Association.

van Noorden L. (1975). *Temporal coherence in the perception of tone sequences.* Eindhoven, Holland: Instituut voor Perceptie Onderzoek.

Varèse, E. (1983). *Ecrits* (L. Hirbour-Paquette, Ed.). Paris: C. Bourgois.

Verge, M. P., Caussé, R., & Hirschberg, A. (1995). A physical model of recorder-like instruments. *Proceedings of the 1995 International Computer Music Conference* (pp. 37–44). San Francisco: International Computer Music Association.

Wang, K., & Shamma, S. A. (1994). Self-normalization and noise-robustness in early auditory representations. *IEEE Transactions on Speech & Audio Processing, 2,* 421–435.

Wang, K., & Shamma, S. A. (1995). Spectral shape analysis in the central auditory system. *IEEE Transactions on Speech & Audio Processing, 3,* 382–395.

Warren, R. M. (1982). *Auditory perception.* Elmsford, NY: Pergamon Press.

Warren, W. H. Jr., & Verbrugge, R. R. (1984). Auditory perception of breaking and bouncing events: a case in ecological perception. *Journal of Experimental Psychology: Human Perception and Performance, 10,* 704–712.

Wedin, L., & Goude, G. (1972). Dimension analysis and the perception of instrumental timbre. *Scandinavian Journal of Psychology, 13*(3), 228–240.

Weinreich, G. (1977). Coupled piano strings. *Journal of the Acoustical Society of America, 62,* 1474–1484.

Weinreich, G. (1979). The coupled motions of piano strings. *Scientific American, 240*(1), 118–127.

Wente, E. C. (1935). Characteristics of sound transmission in rooms. *Journal of the Acoustical Society of America, 7,* 123.

Wessel D. L. (1978). *Low dimensional control of musical timbre.* Paris: IRCAM Report, No. 12 (with a cassette of sound examples).

Wessel, D. L. (1973). Psychoacoustics and music: A report from Michigan State University. *Bulletin of the Computer Arts Society, 30.*

Wessel, D. L. (1979). Timbre space as a musical control structure. *Computer Music Journal, 3*(2), 45–52. Reprinted in Roads, C., & Strawn, J. (Eds.), (1985). *Foundations of computer music.* Cambridge, MA: MIT Press.

Wessel, D. L., & Risset, J. C. (1979). *Les illusions auditives.* Universalia: Encyclopedia Universalis, 167–171.

Wessel, D. L. (1991). Instruments that learn, refined controllers, and source model loudspeakers. *Computer Music Journal, 15*(4), 82–86.

Wessel, D. L., Bristow, D., & Settel, Z. (1987). Control of phrasing and articulation in synthesis. *Proceedings of the 1987 International Computer Music Conference* (pp. 108–116). San Francisco: International Computer Music Association.

Winckel, F. (1967). *Music, sound and sensation.* New York: Dover.

Xenakis, I. (1971). *Formalized music.* Bloomington, IN: Indiana University Press.

Yang, X., Wang, K., & Shamma, S. (1992). Auditory representation of acoustic signals. *I.E.E.E. Trans. on Information Theory, 38,* 824–839.

Young, R. W. (1952). Modes, nodes and antinodes. *Journal of the Acoustical Society of America, 24,* 267–273.

Zahorian, S., & Rothenberg, M. (1981). Principal-component analysis for low-redundancy encoding of speech spectra. *Journal of the Acoustical Society of America, 69,* 823–845.

Zwicker, E. (1961). Subdivision of the audible frequency range into critical bands. *Journal of the Acoustical Society of America, 33,* 248.

Zwicker, E., & Scharf, B. (1965). A model of loudness summation. *Psychological Review, 72,* 3–26.

6

THE PERCEPTION OF SINGING

JOHAN SUNDBERG

Department of Speech, Music, and Hearing
Kungl Tekniska Högskolan
Stockholm, Sweden

I. INTRODUCTION

An understanding of the perception of singing may be developed from two different types of investigation. One type considers an acoustic property of singing, varies it systematically, and explores the perception of these variations. Such investigations are rare in singing research. Another type of investigation concerns the acoustic correlates of certain types of voices or phonations. The underlying typology of voices and phonations must be based mainly on aural perception. Consequently, even such studies have perceptual relevance. Most studies of singing have this type of perceptual relevance. However, research on the perception of singing is not as well developed as the closely related field of speech research. Therefore, readers will not find an exhaustive presentation in this chapter. Rather they will find a presentation of different studies only partly related to each other.

A confession on the part of the author of this chapter is in order here. Writing this chapter has been a bit embarrassing, because so many references to my own work seemed necessary. As readers may notice, it is difficult to be fully objective in the presentation of one's own investigations. However, as was just mentioned, relatively few studies on the perceptual aspects of singing have been published.

When we listen to a singer, a number of remarkable perceptual facts are apparent. For instance: How is it that we can hear the voice even when the orchestra is loud? How is it that we generally identify the singer's vowels correctly even though vowel quality in singing differs considerably from the vowel quality that we are used to in speech? How is it that we can identify the individual singer's sex, register, and voice timbre when the pitch of the vowel lies within a range common to all singers and several registers? How is it that we perceive singing as a sequence of discrete pitches even though the fundamental frequency events do not form a pattern of discrete fundamental frequencies? How is it that we hear a

.n a sequence of isolated tones? These are some of the main ques-
,scussed in this chapter. In order to understand the questions as well
.s, it is necessary to have a basic knowledge of the acoustics of sing-
ι therefore first briefly present what is known about this.

II. FUNCTION OF THE VOICE

The vocal organ consists of three basic components: (a) the respiratory system, which provides an excess pressure of air in the lungs; (b) the vocal folds, which chop the airstream from the lungs into a sequence of quasi-periodic air pulses; and (c) the vocal tract, which gives each sound its final characteristic spectral shape and thus its timbral identity. These three components are referred to as *respiration, phonation,* and resonance or *articulation,* respectively.

The chopped airstream (i.e., the *voice source*) is the raw material of all voiced sounds. It can be described as a complex tone composed of a number of harmonic partials. This implies that the frequency of the *n*th partial equals *n* times the frequency of the first partial, which is called the *fundamental.* The frequency of the fundamental (i.e., the *fundamental frequency*) is identical to the number of air pulses occurring in 1 sec or, in other words, to the frequency of vibration of the vocal folds. The fundamental frequency determines the pitch we perceive in the sense that the pitch would remain essentially the same even if the fundamental sounded alone. The amplitudes of the voice-source partials decrease monotonically with rising frequency. For medium vocal loudness, a given partial is 12 dB stronger than a partial located one octave higher; for softer phonation, this difference is greater. On the other hand, the slope of the voice-source spectrum is generally not dependent on which voiced sound is produced.

Spectral differences between various voiced sounds arise when the sound from the voice source is transferred through the vocal tract (i.e., from the vocal folds to the lip opening). The reason for this is that the ability of the vocal tract to transfer sound is highly dependent on the frequency of the sound being transferred. This ability culminates at certain frequencies, called the *formant frequencies.* In consequence, those voice-source partials that lie closest to the formant frequencies are radiated from the lip opening at greater amplitudes than are the other neighboring partials. Hence, the formant frequencies are manifest as peaks in the spectrum of the radiated sound.

The formant frequencies vary within rather wide limits in response to changing the position of the *articulators* (i.e., lips, tongue body, tongue tip, lower jaw, velum, pharyngeal sidewalls, and larynx). We can change the two lowest formant frequencies by two octaves or more by changing the position of the articulators. The frequencies of these two formants determine the identity of most vowels, that is, the *vowel quality.* The higher formant frequencies cannot be varied as much and do not contribute much to vowel quality. Rather, they are significant to the personal voice timbre, which henceforth will be referred to as *voice quality.*

Properties of vowel sounds that are of great importance to vowel quality can be described in a chart showing the frequencies of the two lowest formants, as in Figure 1. Note that each vowel is represented by a small area rather than by a point in the chart. In other words, these formant frequencies may vary within certain limits without changing the identity of the vowel. This reflects the fact that a given vowel normally possesses higher formant frequencies in a child or in a woman than in a male adult. The reason for these differences lies in differing vocal tract dimensions, as will be shown later.

In singing, more or less substantial deviations are observed from the vowel ranges shown in Figure 1. Indeed, a male opera singer may change the formant frequencies so much that they enter the area of a different vowel. For instance, in the vowel [i:][1] as sung by a male opera singer, the two lowest formant frequencies may be those of the vowel [y:] according to Figure 1. In female high-pitched opera singing, the formant frequencies may be totally different from those found in normal speech. Yet we tend to identify such vowels correctly. This shows that the frequencies of the two lowest formants do not determine vowel quality entirely. Next we will see how and why these deviations from normal speech are made in singing.

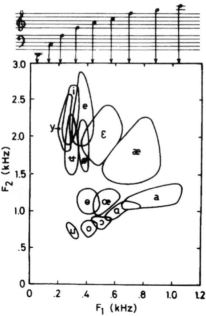

FIGURE 1   Ranges of the two lowest formant frequencies for different vowels represented by their symbols in the International Phonetic Alphabet (IPA). Above, the frequency scale of the first formant is given in musical notation.

---

[1]All letters appearing within [ ] are symbols in the International Phonetic Alphabet.

III. RESONATORY ASPECTS

A. SINGING AT HIGH PITCHES

1. Formant Frequencies

Most singers are required to sing at fundamental frequencies higher than those used in normal speech, where the voice fundamental frequencies of male and female adults center on approximately 110 Hz and 200 Hz, respectively, and generally do not exceed about 200 Hz and 350 Hz, respectively. The highest pitches for soprano, alto, tenor, baritone, and bass correspond to fundamental frequencies of about 1400 Hz (pitch C_6), 700 Hz (F_5), 523 Hz (C_5), 390 Hz (G_4), and 350 Hz (F_4), respectively. In speech the first formant is normally higher than the fundamental frequency, but in singing the normal value of the first formant frequency of many vowels is often much lower than these top fundamental frequencies, as shown in Figure 1. If the singer were to use the same articulation in singing a high-pitched tone as in normal speech, the situation illustrated in the upper part of Figure 2 would occur. The fundamental, that is, the lowest partial in the spectrum, would appear at a frequency far above that of the first formant. In other words, the capa-

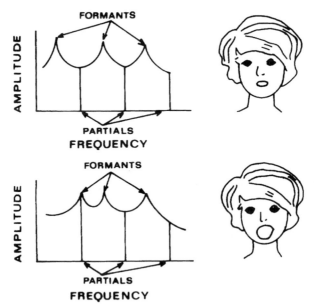

FIGURE 2   Schematic illustration of the formant strategy in high-pitched singing. In the upper case, the singer has a small jaw opening. The first formant appears at a frequency lower than that of the fundamental (i.e., the lowest partial of the spectrum). The result is a low amplitude of that partial. In the lower case, the jaw opening is widened so that the first formant is raised to a frequency near that of the fundamental. The result is a considerable gain in amplitude of that partial. (Reprinted from Sundberg, 1977b.)

bility of the vocal tract to transfer sound would be optimal at a frequency where there is no sound to transfer.

It seems that singers learn to avoid this situation. The strategy is to abandon the formant frequencies of normal speech and move the frequency of the first formant close to that of the fundamental. The main articulatory gesture used to achieve this tuning of the first formant is a widening of the jaw opening, which is particularly effective for increasing the first formant frequency (cf. Lindblom & Sundberg, 1971). This explains why singers tend to change their jaw opening in a pitch-dependent manner rather than in a vowel-dependent manner, as in normal speech.

The acoustic result of this strategy is illustrated in the lower part of Figure 2. The amplitude of the fundamental and hence the sound pressure level (SPL) of the vowel increases considerably. Note that this gain in SPL results from a resonatory phenomenon, obtained without increase of vocal effort.

Figure 3 shows formant frequencies measured in a soprano singing various vowels at varying pitches. As can be seen from the figure, the singer maintained the formant frequencies of normal speech up to that pitch where the fundamental comes close to the first formant. Above that frequency, the first formant is raised to a frequency in the vicinity of the fundamental.

Which singers use this pitch-dependent formant strategy? The strategy has been documented in soprano singers only, but it is probably adopted also in other cases where the singer sings at fundamental frequencies higher than the normal frequency of the first formant (Johansson, Sundberg, & Wilbrand, 1985; Sundberg, 1975). Consulting Figure 1 once again, we find that for bass and baritone voices most vowels have a first formant frequency that is higher than these top fundamental frequencies. For tenors and altos, the same applies to some vowels only. Thus, the pitch-dependent formant strategy can be assumed to be applied for some vowels at bass singers' top pitches, for some vowels in the upper range of tenors, for many vowels in the upper part of the alto range, and for most vowels in the upper part of the soprano range. A study of jaw opening in professional classical singers singing different vowels at different pitches seemed to confirm these assumptions (Sundberg & Skoog, 1997).

A widening of the jaw opening affects the first formant frequency, but higher formant frequencies also are affected. All formant frequencies are changed when the first formant is raised so as to remain above the fundamental frequency (Figure 3).

2. Sound Intensity and Masking

As was mentioned earlier, the amplitude of the fundamental increases when the first formant is tuned to that frequency. As the fundamental then becomes the strongest partial in the spectrum, this results in a gain in overall SPL. The magnitude of the gain can be seen in Figure 4, which shows the increase in SPL associated with the formant frequencies plotted in Figure 3. We can see that the pitch-dependent choice of formant frequencies results in a sound level gain of almost 30 dB in extreme cases. This corresponds to a thousandfold increase in sound power.

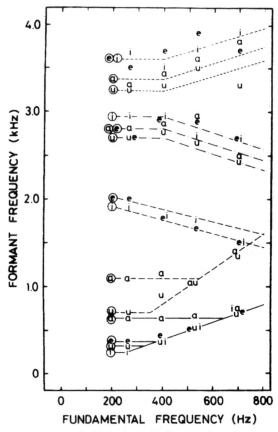

FIGURE 3 Formant frequencies of the vowels indicated (IPA symbols) measured in a professional soprano who sang different vowels at different pitches. The lines show schematically how she changed the formant frequencies with pitch. The values represented by circled symbols were observed when the subject sustained them in a speech mode.

A perceptually important conclusion is that the singer will gain in loudness to a corresponding extent without expending more vocal effort.

The singer's need for exceptionally high degrees of loudness is of course a consequence of the fact that opera singers are generally accompanied by an orchestra. The average SPL of an orchestra playing loudly in a concert hall is about 90–100 dB. This is much more than we can expect from a human speaker. The masking effect that an orchestral sound will exert on a singer's voice is determined by the distribution of sound energy along the frequency scale. A long-term-average spectrum of orchestral music shows the average of this distribution. Such a spectrum is shown in Figure 5. It was obtained from a phonogram recording of the "*Vorspiel*" of the first act of Wagner's opera *Die Meistersinger.* The frequency scale used in such spectra is significant to the graphs obtained. In this case it was

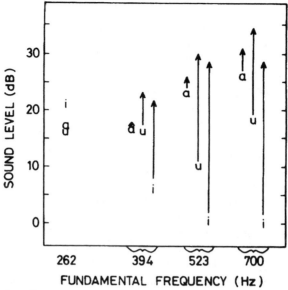

FIGURE 4 Overall sound level for the indicated vowels (IPA symbols) that would result at different fundamental frequencies if the formant frequencies were kept constant at the values observed at 260-Hz fundamental frequency in Figure 3. The lengths of the arrows show the gain in sound level resulting from using the pitch-dependent formant frequencies indicated by the lines in the same figure.

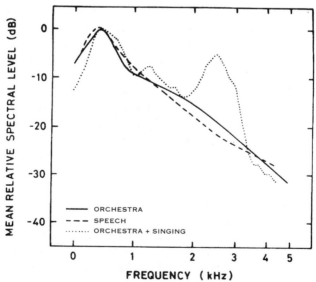

FIGURE 5 Idealized long-term-average spectra showing the mean distribution of sound energy in the *"Vorspiel"* of Act 1 of Wagner's *Die Meistersinger* opera (solid curve) and in normal speech (dashed curve). The dotted line shows the corresponding analysis for an opera singer singing with orchestra accompaniment. (From Sundberg, 1977b.)

nel unit, which is preferable in descriptions of masking and spectral cker & Feldtkeller, 1967). The graph shows that the strongest spec- nts are found in the region of 400–500 Hz. The average spectral level falls off steeply toward higher frequencies (Sundberg, 1972).

The masking effect of a noise with the spectrum shown in Figure 5 can be estimated from hearing theory (Zwicker & Feldtkeller, 1967). Avoiding details, we may say that the masking effect will be greatest at those frequencies where the masking sound is loudest and the masking effect will decrease as the amplitude of the masker decreases toward higher and lower frequencies. Thus, on the average, the masking effect of the sound of the orchestra will be greatest at 400–500 Hz and will decrease toward higher and lower frequencies.

What types of spectra does the human voice produce, then? From Figure 5, we can see that the long-term-average spectrum of normal speech is similar to that of the orchestra. This suggests that the combination of the sound of an orchestra with that of the human voice during normal speech is probably the most unfortunate one possible. If the sound level of the orchestra is considerably higher than that of the voice, the voice is likely to be completely masked. And, inversely, if the sound of the voice were much stronger (which is very unlikely), the orchestra may be masked. This implies that the acoustic characteristics of the human voice as observed in normal speech are not very useful for solo parts when combined with the sound of an orchestra. Therefore, these characteristics would need to be modified if both the singer's voice and the orchestral accompaniment are to be both loud and independently audible.

Let us now return to the case of high-pitched singing. The spectrum will be dominated by the fundamental if the first formant is tuned to the frequency of the fundamental, as mentioned. This can be expected to occur as soon as the fundamental frequency is higher than the normal frequency value of the first formant. This value is 300–800 Hz, depending on the vowel (see Figure 1). From what was said about masking, we see that all vowels are likely to be masked by the orchestra as long as their first formant is below 500 Hz, approximately. This will be the case for all vowels except [a:, a:, æ:] sung at fundamental frequencies lower than about 500 Hz, which is close to the pitch B_4. As soon as the fundamental frequency exceeds this value, the fundamental will be strong. Then, its frequency is also higher than that of the partial, which is likely to be the strongest in the accompaniment.

Summarizing, a female singer's voice can be expected to be masked by a strong orchestral accompaniment as soon as the vowel is not [a:, a:, æ:] and the pitch is below B_4. This seems to agree with the general experience with female voices in opera singing. Female opera singers are generally not difficult to hear when they sing at high pitches, even when the orchestral accompaniment is loud.

3. Vowel Intelligibility

We have seen that female singers gain considerably in loudness by abandoning the formant frequencies typical of normal speech when they sing at high pitches.

On the other hand, the formant frequencies are decisive to vowel intelligibility. This raises the question of how vowel intelligibility is affected by high pitches in female singing.

One of the first to study this problem was the phonetician Stumpf (1926). He used one professional opera singer and two amateur singers. Each singer sang various vowels at different pitches, with the singer's back turned to a group of listeners who tried to identify the vowels. The vowels sung by the professional singer were easier to identify (Figure 6A). The percentages of correct identifications dropped as low as 50% for several vowels sung at the pitch of G_5 (784 Hz). Identification was far better for most vowels when the vowel was preceded by a consonant, particularly [t]. This shows that vowels are much easier to identify when the acoustic signal contains some transitions. Incidentally, this seems to be a perceptual universal: changing stimuli are more easy to process than quasi-stationary stimuli.

Morozov (1965) studied intelligibility of syllables sung by professional singers (also males) as a function of fundamental frequency. According to his results, intelligibility drops below 80% correct identification above the pitch of E_4 (330 Hz) and B_4 (495 Hz) in male and female singers, respectively. At the pitches of C_5 (523 Hz) and C_6 (1046 Hz), intelligibility decreased to 50% and 10% correct identification for male and female singing, respectively. At the very highest pitches in female singing, all vowels tend to be perceived as an [a:] according to Howie and Delattre (1962). This appears to agree with results already mentioned on the formant frequencies in female high-pitched singing: The highest pitches would be sung with almost the same (i.e., maximum) jaw opening for all vowels; under such

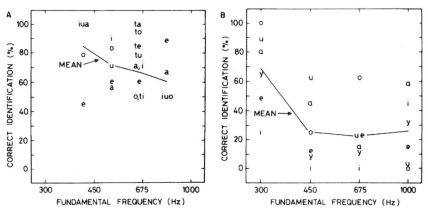

FIGURE 6   (A) Percentages of correct identification of vowels (IPA symbols) sung by a professional singer according to Stumpf (1926). The solid line represents the average. Note that the intelligibility increased at 675 Hz fundamental frequency when the vowels were preceded by the consonant [t]. (B) Corresponding values according to Sundberg (1977a) obtained in an experiment with synthesized vibrato vowels, each of which had the same formant frequencies regardless of fundamental frequency. The solid curve represents the average.

conditions, the formant frequency pattern would be similar regardless of which vowel is intended by the singer. Nelson and Tiffany (1968), Scotto di Carlo (1972), and Smith and Scott (1980) all found that vowel intelligibility was different for different vowels sung at the same pitch. For instance, Nelson and Tiffany found that open vowels were harder to interpret correctly than closed vowels and diphthongs. Scotto di Carlo and Germain (1985) and Gottfried and Chew (1986), who studied intelligibility of vowels sung by a soprano and by a countertenor, respectively, concluded that vocal register also is a factor of relevance.

All these results on intelligibility of vowels and syllables sung at high pitches seem to reflect two different effects. One is that singers systematically deviate from the formant frequency patterns of normal speech, as explained earlier. This deviation is likely to generate intelligibility problems, at least under certain conditions. The other effect is that in high-pitched vowels, few partials are distributed over the frequency band that normally contains the information we need to identify a sound as a specific vowel. Thus, spectral information about vowel quality is lacking at very high pitches. This effect will certainly add to the score of failing intelligibility in tests like those just mentioned. Vowel stimuli produced by living singers therefore contain two contributions to the difficulties in vowel identification.

The question of how the deviations from the formant frequencies of normal speech affect vowel intelligibility at high pitches can be studied in experiments with synthesized vowel stimuli (Sundberg, 1977a). A set of six vowels were synthesized (with vibrato) at different fundamental frequencies ranging from 300 to 1000 Hz. The formant frequencies were kept constant in each of the vowels. The sounds were presented to a group of phonetically trained listeners who tried to identify each of them as one of 12 given vowels. The results are shown in Figure 6b. It can be seen that, on the average, vowel intelligibility decreased monotonically as pitch increased, although there were exceptions and minor variations. More important, though, is that the percentages of correct identification were much lower than those reported by Stumpf, who used nonsynthetic vowels. A major difference between the synthetic vowels and the vowels used by Stumpf is that the first formant was presumably never lower than the fundamental in Stumpf's case. This being so, we may conclude that the pitch-dependent articulation in high-pitched singing actually improves vowel intelligibility when compared with the case in which the formant frequencies are kept constant regardless of the pitch.

Particularly in high-pitched vowel sounds, the amplitude of the lowest spectral component is influenced both by the distance to the first formant and by the phonatory characteristics. Thus, by varying the style of phonation, the amplitude of the fundamental can be varied by many decibels. One might ask, then, if the listener can tell if the partial was loud because of a particular style of phonation or because it was close to the first formant. This question was studied by Sundberg and Gauffin (1982). Synthesized sustained vowel sounds in the soprano range were used as stimuli, and subjects tried to identify the stimuli as vowels. The results showed that an increased amplitude of the fundamental was generally interpreted as a decrease in the first formant frequency. Thus, it seems that subjects could not separate the contributions from formants and voice source in sustained vowels. It is likely that the result would be different if the vowels are presented in a consonant context.

Smith and Scott (1980) studied the effect on vowel intelligibility of larynx height and consonantal environment as a function of pitch. Their results, which were based on material from a female singer, confirm that vowel identification is much simpler if the vowel is surrounded by consonants than if it is rendered in isolation. The results also showed that vowels sung with a raised larynx position are more intelligible than vowels sung with the lower larynx position, which their subject normally used in singing. A raised larynx shortens the vocal tract and, by consequence, raises the formant frequencies. Thus, their results suggest that high-pitched vowels are more intelligible if produced with somewhat higher formant frequencies than in normal singing. This assumption is in accordance with the findings of the Sundberg (1977a) study. The positive effect of transitions associated with consonant-vowel-consonant sequences offers formal evidence for Stumpf's observation of the decisive importance to perception of changes in stimuli.

Analyzing the formant frequencies in the spontaneous speech of one of the leading high sopranos at the Metropolitan Opera in New York, Sundberg (1990) found reasons to assume that this soprano had a particularly short vocal tract. This suggests that her short vocal tract might help her to produce intelligible vowels also at very high pitches.

An important point in this connection is the fact that a rise in pitch *must* be accompanied by a rise in formant frequencies if vowel quality is to be preserved. Slawson (1968) found that maximum similarity in vowel quality was obtained when the formant frequencies were increased by 10%, on the average, for each octave increase of fundamental frequency. Although Slawson used speechlike sounds with a fundamental that never exceeded 270 Hz, it seems likely that our hearing expects the formant frequencies to increase slightly when the fundamental frequency is increased.

The difference in the percentage of correct identifications between Stumpf's and Sundberg's studies may not depend solely on a difference in the formant frequencies. Other differences between synthetic and real vowels may very well have contributed. As was just mentioned, the beginning and ending of a sound are probably very revealing, and presumably the vowels in these two studies differed in this respect also; also in sustained vowels the onset may have contained formant changes when produced by a living singer. Therefore, a direct comparison using well-defined synthetic stimuli is needed before safe conclusions can be drawn as to whether or not the pitch-dependent choice of formant frequencies in high-pitched female singing really is a factor that contributes to vowel intelligibility.

B. BASS, BARITONE, AND ALTO SINGING

1. The "Singer's Formant"

The audibility problem is rather different for singers singing at lower and at higher pitches. At low pitches, singers do not seem to use pitch-dependent formant frequencies. This seemingly suggests that altos, tenors, baritones, and basses produce spectra that are rather similar to the average spectrum of the orchestral accompaniment (see Figure 5). Previously, we found that such a similarity in spectrum leads to maximum masking. Still, these voices can be heard readily even when the orchestral accompaniment is loud.

If vowel spectra of normal speech are compared with those produced by altos, tenors, baritones, and basses, at least one difference is almost invariably observed. The partials falling in the frequency region of 2.5–3.0 kHz, approximately, are much stronger in sung vowels than in spoken vowels. Thus, the spectral envelope exhibits a more or less prominent peak in the high-frequency region. This peak is generally referred to as the *singer's formant*.[2] It has been observed in most acoustic studies of altos, tenors, baritones, and basses (see, e.g., Bartholomew, 1934; Hollien, 1983; Rzhevkin, 1956; Seidner, Schutte, Wendler, & Rauhut, 1985; Sundberg, 1974; Winckel, 1953). On the other hand, it does not seem to exist to the same extent in sopranos. Figure 7 compares typical examples of a vowel produced with and without a singer's formant.

There are strong reasons for assuming that the singer's formant is an acoustic consequence of a clustering of the third, fourth, and fifth formant frequencies (Sundberg, 1974). If formants approach each other in frequency, the ability of the vocal tract to transfer sound increases in the corresponding frequency region. Hence, the spectral envelope peak called the singer's formant seems to be primarily a resonatory phenomenon. Its amplitude depends on how closely these formants are clustered and also, of course, on the characteristics of the source spectrum.

Formant frequencies are determined by the dimensions of the vocal tract, or, by articulation. An articulatory configuration that clusters the higher formants in such a way that a singer's formant is generated involves a wide pharynx (Sundberg, 1974). Mostly such a widening can probably be achieved by a lowering of the larynx, and a low larynx position is typically observed in male singers (Shipp & Izdebski, 1975). Thus, the singer's formant can be interpreted acoustically and articulatorily. It should be mentioned that other articulatory interpretations have also been suggested but not tested (Hollien, Keister, & Hollien, 1978).

2. Audibility

Another question is why opera singers add a singer's formant to their voiced sounds in singing. Probably the reason is perceptual. By means of a sound ex-

---

[2]In some earlier articles, the author referred to this phenomenon as the "singing formant" rather than the "singer's formant." Although not always realized (see e.g., Wang, 1986), these two terms are synonymous.

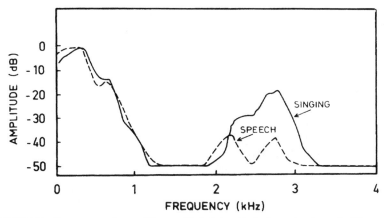

FIGURE 7   Spectrum envelopes of the vowel [u] spoken (dashed curve) and sung (solid curve) by a professional opera baritone singer. The amplitudes of the harmonics between 2 and 3 kHz, approximately, give a marked envelope peak in singing. This peak is called the singer's formant. It typically occurs in all voiced sounds produced by male singers and altos. (Adapted from Sundberg, 1978a.)

ample contained in Sundberg (1977b), it has been demonstrated that a singer's voice is much easier to discern against the background of a noise with the same average spectrum as the sound of an orchestra when the voice possesses a prominent "singer's formant". This effect is certainly associated with masking. The average spectrum of an orchestra culminates around 400–500 Hz and then decreases toward the higher frequencies (see Figure 5). The mean spectral level at 2.5-3.0 kHz is about 20 dB below the level at 400–500 Hz. It seems to be an extremely good idea to enhance the spectral partials in this frequency range. These partials are likely to be readily perceptible, because the competition from the orchestra's partials is moderate at these high frequencies.

Another perceptual advantage of producing vowels containing a singer's formant has been suggested by Winckel (1953, and personal communication). It relates to the sound-radiation characteristics of lip opening. Whereas low-frequency components scatter spherically from the lip opening, the radiation of the high-frequency components is more concentrated along the length axis of the mouth cavities (Flanagan, 1965; Marshal & Meyer, 1985). In other words, high spectral partials are radiated sagittally with greater efficiency than lower partials. For a singer facing the audience, the sound radiated behind and above his head is probably lost on an opera stage because of the high sound absorption in the backstage area. The high-frequency components contained in the singer's formant are lost to a lesser extent as their radiation is more limited to the sagittal direction. Hence, the relative amplitude of the singer's formant would be greater compared with the lower partials when the sound reaches the audience. This would help the audience to discern the singer's voice against the background of the orchestral accompaniment.

Many singers and singing teachers speak about "projecting" or "focusing" the voice as a requirement for the audibility of the voice in a large audience. These expressions appear to agree with the above reasoning that the singer's voice is radiated more efficiently in the sagittal direction if the voice contains a singer's formant.

Before we leave masking problems, one more fact should be mentioned. There are two exceptions to the principle that we cannot hear sounds that fall below the masked threshold resulting from a louder, simultaneous sound. One exception is when the softer sound starts some fraction of a second earlier than the masker sound (cf. Rasch, 1978). The other exception applies to the situation when the masker sound is time varying. Plomp (1977) has demonstrated that we can hear a sound below the masked threshold provided that the masker signal is interrupted regularly. Under these conditions, we can hear the signal continuously even in the presence of the masker. Both these cases might apply to the singer-orchestra combination. The orchestral sound, of course, varies in intensity. Given Plomp's results, it should not be necessary for the singer's formant to be heard all the time. It would be sufficient for it to be audible during the moments when the amplitude of the orchestral sound in this frequency region is low, provided that such moments are separated by sufficiently short time intervals.

As the singer's formant is a perceptually apparent characteristic of alto, tenor, baritone, and bass voices, it is not surprising that it is recognized as an important timbral attribute among singers and singing teachers. In general, we invent names for such attributes. The singer's formant seems to have a number of different names. Gibian (1972) synthesized vowels in which he varied the frequency of the fourth formant while the remaining formants were kept constant. An expert on singing found that the "placement in the head" of the tone was most "forward" when the fourth formant was 2.7 kHz, which was only 0.2 kHz above the third formant. Vennard, who was an eminent singing teacher and had a thorough knowledge of the acoustics of singing, simply speaks about "the 2800 Hz" that produces the "ring" of the voice (Vennard, 1967).

3. Modification of Vowel Quality

Just as in the case of high-pitched singing, singing with a singer's formant involves modifications of the vowel quality characteristics of normal speech. The main articulatory background of these modifications is probably the widening of the pharynx required for the generation of the singer's formant and the typically associated lowering of the larynx. These articulatory characteristics affect not only the third and higher formant frequencies but also the two lowest formant frequencies, which are critical to vowel quality, as mentioned. Sundberg (1970) measured formant frequencies in vowels sung by four singers and compared these frequencies with those reported by Fant (1973) for nonsingers. As shown in Figure 8, the differences are considerable. For instance, the second formant does not reach as high a frequency in sung vowels as in spoken vowels. This is the acoustic consequence of a wide pharynx and a low larynx. As a result, some vowels do in

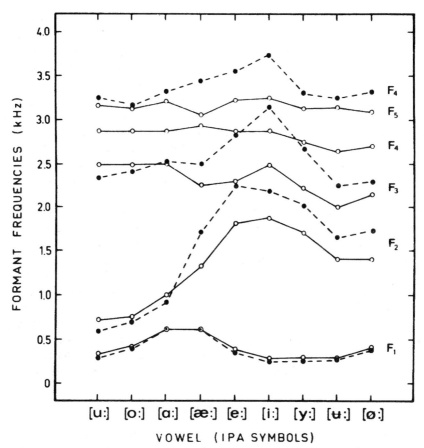

FIGURE 8 Average formant frequencies in different vowels as produced by nonsingers (dashed curves, according to Fant, 1973) and four bass/baritone singers (solid curves, according to Sundberg, 1970). Note that the fourth formant (F_4) in nonsingers is slightly higher in frequency than the fifth formant (F_5) for the singers. (From Sundberg, 1974.)

fact assume formant frequencies typical of a different vowel in singing. This poses the same question as was posed for high-pitched singing: Can we really identify the sung vowels correctly?

Unfortunately, no formal evidence is available to supply an answer to this question. (It will be recalled that the study by Morozov, 1965, concerned syllables, not isolated vowels.) On the other hand, the differences in quality between spoken and sung vowels are well known, at least to singers and singing teachers. Many singing teachers instruct their students to modify or "color" an [i:] toward a [y:], an [e:] toward an [oe], an [a:] toward an [a:] etc. (see e.g., Appelman, 1967). It is considered important that a vowel should not be *replaced by* but only *modified toward* another vowel. This would mean that the sung vowels should retain their vowel identify, although the two lowest formant frequencies are clearly "wrong."

These modifications seem to be the price for obtaining a singer's formant. It seems essential that the level of the singer's formant does not vary too much from one vowel to the other. For example, in neutral speech, the level of the third formant typically differs by approximately 28 dB between an [i] and an [u] because of the great difference in the second formant frequency. The second formant is much lower in a sung than in a spoken [i], and in a sung [u] the formants 3, 4, and 5 are densely clustered. As a consequence, the level of the singer's formant in [i] is much more similar to that of an [u] (Sundberg, 1990). The singer's formant seems to serve as something like a timbral uniform cap for sung vowels. It would represent an important tool for the singer to produce a legato in phrases containing different vowels and wide pitch jumps; timbral similarity seems to be required for creating a legato.

In summary, we can say that the departures from the formant frequencies typical of normal speech lead to modifications of vowel quality. This modification is kept small enough not to produce shifts of vowel quality. With front vowels, part of the reason for this might be that the singer's formant compensates for the effect of the too-low frequency of the second formant. It seems likely that transitions associated with consonants are the most important factors for vowel identification.

Before we leave this subject, reference should be made to a study by Simon, Lips, and Brock (1972). It concerns the spectra of a vowel sung with differing timbres by a professional singer. These measurements show how properties of the spectrum vary when the singer mimics different types of singing with labels such as *Knödel*. It seems that formant frequencies explain many of these differences.

C. VOICE CLASSIFICATION

As we all know, singing voices are classified in terms of soprano, mezzo-soprano, alto, tenor, baritone, and bass. The main criterion for such classification is the pitch range available to the singer. If a singer's range is C_3 to C_5 (131–523 Hz), his classification is tenor. Pitch ranges of different voice classifications overlap to some extent. In fact, the range C_4 to E_4 (262–330 Hz) is common to all voices, but even if we hear a voice singing in this narrow pitch range, we are rarely in doubt how to classify the voice. We can generally decide rather easily whether a tone in this range was sung by a male or a female singer, and often we can even judge the voice classification correctly.

Cleveland (1977) studied the acoustic background of this discrimination ability with regard to male singing. He presented five vowels sung at four pitches by eight singers classified as basses, baritones, or tenors to singing teachers who were asked to decide on the voice classification. The natural onsets and decays of the tones were eliminated. The results revealed that the major acoustic cue in voice classification is the fundamental frequency. Incidentally, the same result was found by Coleman (1976) in a study of maleness and femaleness in voice timbre. The result is not very surprising if we assume that we rely mainly on the most apparent acoustic characteristic in this classification task. By comparing vowels sung at the same pitches, however, Cleveland found that the formant frequencies serve as a secondary cue. The trend was that the lower the formant frequencies, the lower the pitch range the singer is assumed to possess. In other words, low formant frequencies seem to be associated with bass singers and high formant frequencies with tenors. In a subsequent listening test, Cleveland verified these results by presenting the same singing teachers with vowels synthesized with formant frequencies that were varied systematically in accordance with his results obtained from real vowel sounds.

Cleveland also speculated about the morphological background of these findings. As has been described, formant frequencies are determined by the dimensions of the vocal tract. These dimensions are smaller in children and females than in male adults, and the formant frequencies differ accordingly. As a longer tube resonator has lower resonance frequencies than a shorter tube, the formant frequencies of a given vowel produced by a male tend to be lower than those produced by a female. The female vocal tract is not simply a small-scale copy of the male vocal tract (Fant, 1973). The pharynx-to-mouth length ratio is smaller in females than in males. The acoustic consequence is that certain formant frequencies in certain vowels exhibit greater differences between sexes than others, as can be seen in Figure 9 (see also Nordström, 1977). The greatest variations are found in the two lowest formant frequencies. Figure 9 also shows the corresponding values that Cleveland found when he compared a tenor voice with a bass voice. There is a clear similarity suggesting a similar morphological background in the tenor/bass case as in the female/male case. It seems reasonable to hypothesize that tenors tend to have smaller pharynx-to-mouth ratios than basses do.

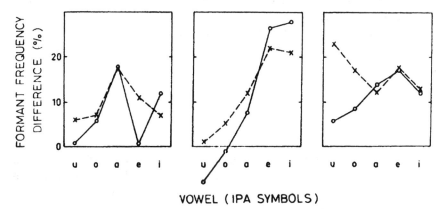

VOWEL (IPA SYMBOLS)

FIGURE 9   Percentage differences between various voice categories for the first (left panel), second (middle panel), and third (right panel) formant frequency for the vowels indicated (IPA symbols). Solid curves represent a comparison between a tenor and a bass singer (according to Cleveland, 1977). Dashed curves represent a comparison between male and female speakers in vowels from six languages. (From Fant, 1975.)

An investigation by Dmitriev and Kiselev (1979) supports this last-mentioned hypothesis. That study revealed a clear correlation between overall length of the vocal tract and the center frequencies of a peak in the long-term-average spectrum of voices of different classifications that corresponds to singer's formant in the cases of male singers and altos. Their subjects were basses, baritones, tenors, mezzo-sopranos and high sopranos. The correlation suggests that, with regard to male singers, the center frequency of the singer's formant is at least partly dependent on vocal tract length. It also suggests that sopranos have their higher formants at the highest frequencies of all singers.

Another important result of the same investigation was that the center frequency of singer's formant varied systematically with voice category: the higher this center frequency, the higher the voice category. For basses, the center frequency was 2.3 kHz, and for tenors, it was 2.8 kHz. The relevance of the center frequency of the singer's formant to voice quality was later supported in an investigation of sung vowels by Bloothooft and Plomp (1988)

In summary, the formant frequencies including the center frequency of the singer's formant typically differ between singers' voices, and these differences are significant to our possibility to classify them in terms of bass, baritone, and tenor. These differences probably reflect differences in vocal tract dimensions as well as in the pharynx-to mouth length ratios.

Why do not soprano voices possess a singer's formant? There may be several reasons for this, but one possible reason is purely perceptual. The basic principle for producing a singer's formant is that formants number 3, 4, and 5 are concentrated to a rather narrow frequency range. In high pitched singing, the frequency distance between the partials is obviously large (i. e., equal to the fundamental frequency). A soprano who clustered these higher formants would then produce vowels with a singer's formant only at those fundamental frequencies where there were a partial falling into the frequency range of the singer's formant; at some fundamental frequencies, no such partial exists. Such tones would sound very different from tones where a partial was in the singer's formant. Great differences in voice quality between adjacent tones in a phrase do not seem compatible with legato singing.

IV. PHONATION

Up to this point, we have focused primarily upon resonatory phenomena (i.e., on characteristics associated with formant frequencies). In the present section, some aspects on phonation will be presented (i.e., the behavior of the vibrating vocal folds and the acoustic properties of the resulting voice source).

A. LOUDNESS, PITCH, AND PHONATION TYPE

In the human voice, vocal loudness is varied by subglottal pressure; loud tones are produced with high subglottal pressure and soft tones with low subglottal pressures. Voice-source characteristics change with vocal loudness and with pitch as related to the pitch range of the individual voice. In the human voice as in most other music instruments, the amplitudes of the higher overtones increase at a faster rate than the amplitude of the lower overtones when vocal effort is increased. Thus, the spectral dominance of the higher overtones always increases with vocal loudness in both speech and singing.

In normal speech, the amplitude of the fundamental increases less than the overall sound level when vocal loudness is increased. The reverse applies when pitch is raised (cf., e.g., Fant, 1960); the fundamental becomes more dominant at high pitches than at low pitches. In both these respects, singing and neutral speech differ.

Gauffin and Sundberg (1989) measured both the waveform and spectrum of the voice source in singers by means of inverse filtering (Rothenberg, 1972). The results showed that in the low-frequency part of the source spectrum, up to about 1.5 kHz, the amplitude relationship between the fundamental and the overtones did not change greatly with vocal effort; when vocal effort was increased, the amplitude of the fundamental was found to increase at approximately the same rate as the SPL. SPL is mainly determined by the amplitude of the partial underlying the first formant. Except for high-pitched vowels, that partial is an overtone. Therefore, the amplitude of the fundamental increased at about the same rate as the amplitudes of the lower overtones in these singers.

Another finding of the same study was that the amplitude of the voice source fundamental depends mainly of the amplitudes of the airflow pulses that are created by the vibrations of the vocal folds. This amplitude can be varied by glottal adduction, that is, the force by which the folds are pressed against each other. When adduction is strong, "pressed" phonation results and the fundamental is weak. When it is reduced to a minimum for a nonbreathy type of phonation, "flow phonation" results, in which the fundamental is strong. Nonsingers tend to change phonation characteristics with pitch and loudness, so that high or loud tones are produced with a more pressed phonation than lower tones. Singers, on the other hand, seem to avoid such "automatic" changes of phonation.

The amplitudes of the transglottal airflow pulses are influenced by the glottal area. This means that they are dependent on vocal fold length, among other things; longer vocal folds open a greater glottal area than shorter folds. Therefore, at a given pitch, a singer with long vocal folds produces tones with a stronger voice-source fundamental than a singer with shorter vocal folds produces. As low voices have longer vocal folds than do higher voices, we may expect that also the amplitude of the fundamental belongs to the characteristics of different voice categories, along with the formant frequency effects discussed before. Likewise, this may help us hear if an individual phonates in the upper, middle, or lower part of his or her pitch range.

In summary, two main aspects of vowel sounds can be varied rather independently: the amplitude of the fundamental, which is controlled by glottal adduction, and the amplitude of the overtones, which is controlled by subglottal pressure. In nonsingers' voices glottal adduction is typically increased with pitch and vocal

loudness. Singers seem to avoid such automatic changes of the voice source induced by pitch or loudness changes. One might say that they orthogonalize glottal
phonatory dimensions.

B. REGISTER

1. Definition

One phonatory aspect of singing that has been subject to a considerable amount
of scientific effort is register (see Large, 1972). Still, register terminology is rather
chaotic, but there is a general agreement that a register is a series of adjacent tones
on the scale that (a) sound equal in timbre and (b) are thought to be produced in a
similar way. Also, it is generally agreed that register differences reflect differences
in the mode of vibration of the vocal folds (see Hollien, 1974).

Several objections can be raised against this definition because it relies so
heavily on subjective impressions. Nevertheless, lacking a definition based on
physiological facts, this definition must be accepted for the time being. To understand the significance of the term *register,* it is helpful to contrast two registers,
namely the modal (normal) and the falsetto register of the male voice. These are
two clear examples of different registers. For the female voice, singing voice experts often mention three registers: chest, middle, and head, which cover the lowest, the middle, and the top part of the pitch range, respectively. However, many
voice experts speak about two registers both in male and female voices: heavy and
light register, or modal and falsetto register.

2. Female Chest and Middle Register

Large, mostly with various co-authors, has published a series of studies about
the acoustic characteristics of different registers. With respect to the physiological
background of registers, Large, Iwata, and von Leden (1970) found that tones
sung in chest register consume more air than do tones sung in middle register.
They concluded that the conversion of airstream to sound is more efficient in the
chest registers.

Large and Shipp (1969) studied the influence of various parts of the spectrum
on discriminability of chest and middle registers. The material included the vowel
[a:] sung by 12 singers at the pitch E$_4$ (330 Hz). The quality of the vowel (but
obviously not its timbre) and its acoustic intensity were kept approximately constant by the singers. A test tape was made in which the onset and decay of each
tone were eliminated. The vowel sounds were presented with and without a 1400-
Hz low-pass filtering to a jury of voice experts who were asked to classify them
with respect to registers. The results revealed that generally the registers were
correctly identified when the vowels were unfiltered. When the vowels were low-
pass filtered, identification of register became more difficult, but the accuracy of
identification never dropped as far as the level of mere guessing. The authors concluded that the higher spectral partials merely contribute to register differences.

Large (1974) returned to this question in a later study. His results agreed with those of the previous study, but this time he studied the spectrum of the vowels more closely. The experiment showed typical differences between the registers in the amplitudes of the lower spectral partial. By and large, the chest-register vowels were found to possess stronger high partials than the middle-register vowels possessed. The differences, however, were all very small. Large found that the results support the assumption that register differences reflect differences in the vocal fold vibrations.

Sundberg (1977c) studied the voice-source and the formant frequency characteristics underlying timbre differences between the chest and middle register in one soprano singer. The subject sang a vowel in both registers at the same pitches. The intensity was left to the subject to decide. The results revealed a considerable source-spectrum difference in that the relative amplitude of the fundamental was more than 10 dB stronger in the middle register. This is much more than the small differences reported by Large (1974). Probably, the register difference was less pronounced in Large's subjects.

Sundberg (1977c) also found formant frequency differences between the registers, suggesting that the timbre differences between the registers may depend not only on voice source, but also on articulatory differences. In order to test this hypothesis, pairs of vowels were synthesized that differed in either formant frequencies or source spectrum. A group of singing teachers were asked to identify the registers in these pairs of vowel sounds. The results confirmed that both formant frequencies and source spectrum may contribute to register identification. Thus, some of the spectral differences reported in the previously mentioned studies may have been due to formant frequency differences. We will return to this question later.

3. Male Modal and Falsetto Registers

A number of studies of the differences between the modal and falsetto registers have been published. Although falsetto is rarely used in traditional Western singing—except, perhaps, in countertenor singing—the research in this field will be reviewed.

It has been shown that physiologically the vocal folds are longer, stiffer, and thinner in falsetto than in modal register. As a rule, the glottis is never completely closed in falsetto. This is in agreement with the finding of Large, Iwata, and von Leden (1972) that falsetto tones consume more air than comparable tones sung in the modal register. On the other hand, complete glottal closure may occur in falsetto (see Figure 35, frame F on page 71 in Vennard, 1967); and, inversely, incomplete glottal closure is sometimes observed in modal register phonation.

Part of the literature on falsetto and modal register focuses on the question of whether or not listeners can identify these registers in sustained, isolated vowel sounds. Even though difficulties sometimes arise, particularly when the vowels are sung by professional singers, the answer is generally found to be in the affirmative (see, e.g., Lerman & Duffy, 1970). A dependence on the subjects' voice training was also found, which is not surprising because singers are generally trained to blend registers (i.e., to reduce timbral differences between registers.) An experiment by Colton and Hollien (1973) allowed for more detailed conclusions. They found vocal registers to be a multidimensional phenomenon: "Under normal conditions it is the combination of pitch, loudness, and quality that an observer utilizes to distinguish two vocal registers. When pitch and loudness are equalized, register discrimination becomes more difficult."

The study by Large et al. (1972) used vowels recorded under conditions of equality in pitch and acoustic intensity. Under these conditions, the falsetto was found to produce weaker high overtones than the modal register produced. This agrees with the observation made by the same authors that more air is consumed in falsetto singing; the conversion of airstream into sound is less efficient in falsetto than in modal register.

Again equalizing pitch and acoustic intensity, Russo and Large (1978) compared the two registers perceptually and acoustically. Twelve expert listeners judged the similarity of pairs of tones sung in the different registers. The pairs that were perceived as most dissimilar in timbre differed mainly in (a) the amplitudes of the higher spectral overtones, which was lower in falsetto, and (b) the amplitude of the fundamental, which tended to be slightly greater in falsetto. Both these observations agreed with spectral data from singers and nonsingers (Colton, 1972).

These studies have dealt with the amplitudes of spectral partials. As we have seen, the amplitude of a spectral partial depends not only on the source spectrum but also on the frequency distance between the partial and the closest formant. Thus, the relationships between the amplitudes of individual partials and identification of registers are strongly influenced by the differences in formant frequency between the spectra compared. Against this background, it seems interesting to explore the properties of the voice source that characterize registers.

Monsen and Engebretson (1977) studied the voice source in various types of phonation. Their results with regard to voice-source spectral differences would represent reliable information. They found that the slope of the spectral envelope was much steeper in falsetto. In other words, the falsetto voice source was more dominated by the lower source-spectrum partials.

The data shown in Figure 10 have been selected from the study of Gauffin and Sundberg (1989) mentioned earlier. The waveform is smoother in the falsetto register than in the modal register, and the amplitude of the source-spectrum fundamental is much greater in falsetto. These results obviously agree qualitatively with those of Monsen and Engebretson.

On the other hand, Large and his co-authors mostly found very small differences with respect to the amplitude of the fundamental. There may be several reasons for this difference. One is the fact that all tones were sung with vibrato in the studies by Large et al. As will be shown, this implies that the frequency of each

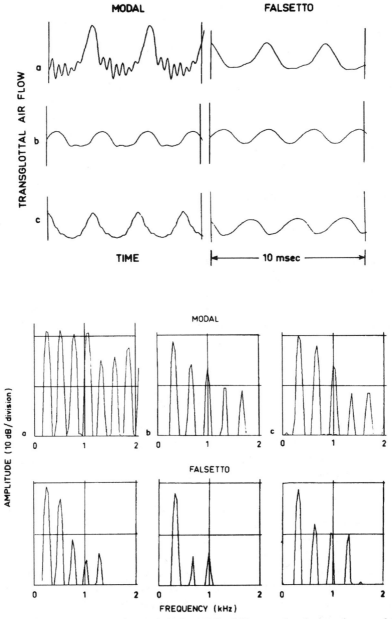

FIGURE 10 Voice source characteristics in modal and falsetto register in three singers as determined by inverse filtering (Rothenberg, 1972). The upper panels show the waveforms, and the lower panels show the corresponding spectra boosted by 6 dB per octave. The waveform ripple for modal register is an artifact due to incomplete cancellation of higher formants. Note that the fundamental is much more dominating in falsetto than in modal register.

partial varies, and a variation in the frequency of a partial leads to an amplitude variation. If spectra are compared that have not been sampled at identical vibrato phases, errors can be expected. Such errors will be greatest for partials with frequencies close to the formants. In most of the Large experiment, the vowel was [a:] and the fundamental frequency was 300 Hz. Then, the amplitudes of the four lowest partials will be rather dependent on the vibrato phase.

However, the main reason that the results differ between the spectral analyses of vowels and the analyses of the voice source probably is that acoustic intensity was not equated in the two types of studies. If the vowel is [a:] and the pitch is E_4, the second partial will be close to the first formant. The amplitude of the partial underlying this formant is normally quite decisive to the overall acoustic intensity of the vowel. Thus, if two vowels are produced in different registers at the same acoustic intensity, the amplitude of the second source-spectrum partial is presumably almost the same in both cases. How, then, should a singer phonate if he is required to produce an [a:] at this pitch at the same acoustic intensity in falsetto as in modal register? Probably by raising the amplitude of the second source-spectrum partial in the case of falsetto, that is, by increasing vocal effort. Thus, we arrive at the strange conclusion that equality in acoustic intensity may require a difference in vocal effort. If the above reasoning is correct, the difference in the results is a consequence of the fact that acoustic intensity was kept constant in one case while vocal effort was probably constant in the other case.

V. ASPECTS OF VOICE TIMBRE

A. LARYNX HEIGHT

The perception of voice seems to be very influenced by one's acquaintance with one's own voice. Thus, it seems reasonable that perceived vocal loudness is more correlated with subglottal pressure than with the sound level. Similarly, other perceptual dimensions of voice quality may be physiological rather than acoustic.

Vertical larynx positioning seems to be one perceptual dimension. The acoustic correlates of perceived changes in larynx height were investigated in a synthesis experiment (Sundberg & Askenfelt, 1983). The stimuli consisted of a series of ascending scales. Toward the end of the scale, acoustic signs of a raised larynx were introduced. Thus, voice-source properties, formant frequencies, and vibrato depth were varied. The stimulus characteristics were based on measurements on vowels that had been produced with deliberately changed larynx position. Thus, they could all be assumed to be realistic signs of a change in larynx height.

The stimuli were presented to a group of singing teachers. The teachers' task was to decide if the imagined singer was singing with a raised larynx or not. The results showed that the perception of a raised larynx was elicited most efficiently by an increase in the formant frequencies. However, also a voice-source effect, viz. a reduced amplitude of the fundamental, promoted the idea of a raised larynx.

#009 26-09-2016 9:42AM Item(s
) checked out to p10991670.

TITLE   AUTHOR
                  BARCODE DUE DATE
Envisioning information Tufte, Edward R (E
dward Rolf). 1942- 36010036 17-10-16

                        Please keep th
is receipt

#009 26-09-2016 9:42AM Item(s
) checked out to p10991670.

TITLE
  AUTHOR   BARCODE DUE DATE
An introduction to the psychology of
  Moore, Brian C. J. 01115956 17-10-16
hearing

                        Please keep th
is receipt

#009 26-09-2016 9:42AM Item(s
) checked out to p10991670.

TITLE   BARCODE DUE DATE
The psychology of music 36030659 17-10-16

                        Please keep th
is receipt

A reduced vibrato depth also contributed, provided that both forma[
and the amplitude of the fundamental were already suggesting a rai
   These results are not surprising and illustrate aspects of the str
ception. The strong dependence on formant frequencies is logical, as a raised larynx will necessarily induce an increase in the formant frequencies. Thus, an increase in formant frequencies is a reliable sign of a changed larynx position. The
reduced amplitude of the fundamental is a sign of a change toward a more pressed
phonation. Such a change does not necessarily accompany an elevation of the
larynx. Therefore it is logical that a reduced amplitude of the fundamental did not
work as a sufficient condition for evoking the perception of a raised larynx. The
same goes for a reduced depth of vibrato fluctuations.

B. NATURALNESS

Singing is primarily a perceptual phenomenon; it is tailored for human perception. In order to describe voice characteristics, physical descriptions are required.
It is then important to explore the relations between the physical description and
the perception of the same sound. Here synthesis seems an indispensable tool. All
signal properties constituting the physical description can be included in the stimuli and then assessed in listening tests. In this way, one can find to what extent the
description of a perceived quality is exhaustive or not.

In such experiments, the naturalness of the synthesized stimuli is essential. If
the stimuli do not sound natural, the relevance of the results of the listening test is
threatened. The naturalness may depend on quite unexpected characteristics of the
spectrum. Figure 11 offers a striking example showing two spectra of the same
vowel, one sounding natural, the other sounding unnatural. The spectra are almost
identical.

The difference, acoustically inconspicuous but perceptually important, consists
of a small detail in the shapes of the formant peaks in the spectrum. The version
that sounds unnatural had flanks that are too blunt. It is quite interesting that this
minute property of the spectrum is perceptually important. Again, however, perception strategy is quite logical. Such blunt spectral peaks can never be generated
by a human vocal tract and so can be safely used as a sign of naturalness.

VI. VIBRATO

A. BACKGROUND

Vibrato occurs in most Western opera and concert singing and often in popular
singing. Generally, vibrato develops more or less automatically during voice training (Bjørklund, 1961). Acoustically, vibrato corresponds to a fluctuation of the
fundamental frequency. As the spectra of voiced sounds are harmonic, the frequencies of all partials vary in synchrony with the fundamental. The amplitude of
a partial depends on how far it is from a formant, and the formant frequencies do

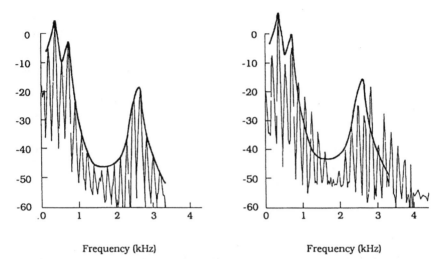

Frequency (kHz)   Frequency (kHz)

FIGURE 11   Spectra of the same vowel sounding clearly different with regard to naturalness. The envelope of the left spectrum has been superimposed also on the right spectrum. The right spectrum sounds unnatural mainly because the formant peaks have an unrealistic shape in that the flanks of the slopes are not concave enough. (After Sundberg, 1989.)

not seem to vary appreciably with the vibrato (Horii, 1989; Sundberg, 1984). Therefore, each partial varies in amplitude synchronously with the vibrato.

In popular music singing, another type of vibrato is sometimes used. It corresponds to a fluctuation of loudness rather than fundamental frequency. There are strong reasons to assume that this type of vibrato is generated by fluctuations of subglottal pressure. It sounds different from the opera singers' vibrato. Here we will consider the first mentioned type of vibrato only.

As vibrato is a rhythmic fluctuation (or modulation) of fundamental frequency, it can be described by two parameters. One is the rate of vibrato (i.e., the number of fluctuations occurring during 1 sec); the other is the extent of vibrato (the depth of the modulation expressed as a percentage of the average frequency). More often, however, the vibrato extent is given in number of cents. (One cent is the interval between two tones having the frequency ratio of $1:2^{1/1200}$.)

The physiological background of vibrato has been described by Hirano and coworkers (Hirano, Hibi, & Hagino, 1995). Electromyographic measurements on laryngeal muscles have revealed pulsations in synchrony with vibrato (Vennard, Hirano, Ohala, & Fritzell, 1970–1971). Probably, the pulsations that cause the pitch to fluctuate are those occurring in the pitch-raising cricothyroid muscle (Shipp, Doherty, & Haglund, 1990). Probably as secondary, induced effects, subglottic pressure and transglottal air flow sometimes fluctuate in synchrony with vibrato. Such pulsations can be observed in some recordings published by Rubin, LeCover, and Vennard (1967).

Several aspects of vibrato have been studied (for an overview, see Dejonkere, Hirano, & Sundberg, 1995). As early as the 1930s, Seashore (1938/1967) summarized, among other things, a series of studies that he and his co-workers had done on vibrato. He found the vibrato rate to vary slightly both within and between singers. The mean for 29 singers was 6.6 fluctuations per second (extremes, 7.8 and 5.9). The average extent was ±48 cents (extremes ±98 and ±31). Measuring vibrato rate and extent in 10 commercial recordings of a song, Prame (1994, 1997) found similar results. He also observed that the vibrato rate typically tended to increase toward the end of each tone.

B. PERCEPTUAL ASPECTS

1. Vowel Intelligibility

As mentioned before, the identification of vowels is assumed to be related to the detection of peaks in the spectral envelope. These peaks signal the frequencies of the formants, and the formant frequencies characterize the vowel. If the number of partials is lower than the number of formants (i.e., if the fundamental frequency is very high), the peaks in the spectral envelope signaling the formant frequencies would be impossible to detect because there may not be a partial in the neighborhood of every formant. It is not unreasonable to assume that vibrato plays a role here. If the frequency of a partial is slightly lower than that of a formant, an increase in fundamental frequency will raise the amplitude of that partial. If the partial is slightly higher in frequency than the formant, a decrease in the amplitude will result from the same situation, as is illustrated in Figure 12. Thus, the phase relationship between the fluctuations in frequency and amplitude in a vibrato tone actually informs about the frequency locations of the formants. The question,

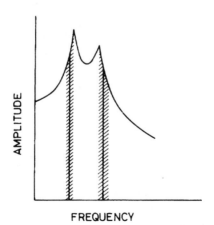

FIGURE 12   Illustration of the fact that, in a tone sung with a frequency vibrato, the amplitude and frequency of a spectrum partial vary in phase or in counterphase, depending on whether the partial is slightly lower or higher than the closest formant frequency. The hatched area represents the width of the frequency modulation, and the frequency scale is linear.

then, is whether the ear can detect and use this information. If so, vibrato would facilitate vowel identification for high-pitched vowels.

This question was studied in the experiment mentioned earlier concerning vowel identification in the soprano pitch range (Sundberg, 1977a). Each vowel in the test was presented both with and without vibrato. The interpretations made by phonetically trained subjects differed considerably.

The degree of agreement between the interpretations was measured in the following manner. Each response vowel was ascribed a set of three formant frequencies. Then all responses obtained for a given stimulus vowel could be regarded as a cloud of points in a three-dimensional space, in which each dimension corresponds to a formant. The center of this cloud was determined. The mean distance between the individual points and the center was next computed by using a formula for perceptual distance between vowels suggested by Plomp (1970). It was assumed that this average distance reflected the difficulty with which a vowel stimulus was identified as a specific vowel

The average distance, as defined earlier, between responses is shown in Figure 13. As can be seen in the figure, no consistent differences between the values pertaining to vibrato tones and those obtained for vibrato-free tones are apparent. Therefore, vibrato does not seem to facilitate vowel identification.

This conclusion may seem counterintuitive, and McAdams and Rodet (1988) did an experiment to test it. They presented tones with and without a vibrato to four subjects. The tones were equal when there was no vibrato and different when they were presented with a vibrato. Figure 14 shows the spectra and formant patterns McAdams and Rodet used to obtain this effect. The task of the subjects was to hear if two stimuli presented in succession were identical or not. The subjects were able to hear the difference in the vibrato stimulus, but the task appeared to be quite difficult. Some subjects needed no less than 35 training sessions to note an effect. On the other hand, once they had learned the effect, they could readily distinguish and also learn to identify the two different stimuli. This experiment shows that it is possible to recognize the effect but also that recognition of the effect is probably not used in vowel identification.

2. Singleness in Pitch

It is a well-established fact that fundamental frequency generally determines pitch. In the case of vibrato tones, however, this is not quite true. Although the fundamental frequency varies regularly in such tones, the pitch we perceive is perfectly constant as long as the vibrato rate and extent are kept within certain limits. What are these limits? Ramsdell studied this question at Harvard University in his thesis work that unfortunately was never published. Ramsdell varied the vibrato rate and extent systematically and had listeners decide when the resulting tone possessed an optimum "singleness in pitch." His results for a 500-Hz tone are shown in Figure 15.

Later Gibian (1972) studied vibrato in synthetic vowels. He varied the vibrato rate and extent and had subjects assess the similarity of this vibrato with human

EFFECT ON AGREEMENT OF INTERPRETATION

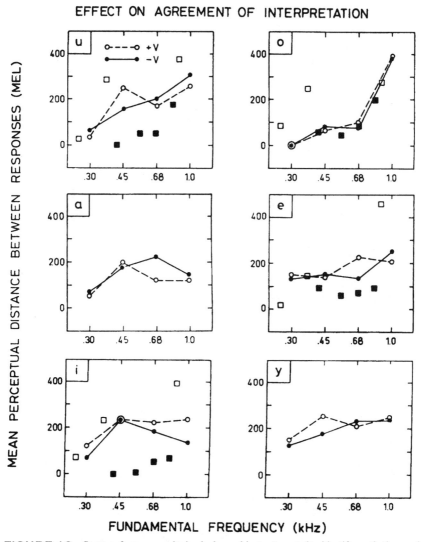

FIGURE 13 Scatter of responses obtained when subjects attempted to identify synthetic vowels with high fundamental frequencies. The formant frequencies were those of the vowels given in the top left corner of each panel. Dashed lines refer to vibrato vowels, and solid lines refer to nonvibrato vowels. The squares represent values reported by Stumpf (1926). They were observed when subjects identified vowels sung by two untrained sopranos (open squares) and one professional soprano (filled squares). The procedure used for deriving the measure of the scatter is described in the text. (From Sundberg, 1977a.)

voice vibrato. His results agree closely with Ramsdell's data, as can be seen in Figure 15. In addition to asking the listeners for the optimal singleness in pitch, Ramsdell also asked for an evaluation of the "richness" in the timbre. His data

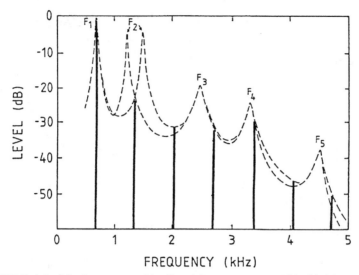

FIGURE 14 Stimulus spectra and implicated formant patterns used by McAdams and Rodet (1988) in an experiment testing the relevance of the vibrato to vowel identification; almost the same spectrum could be obtained by two different formant frequency patterns.

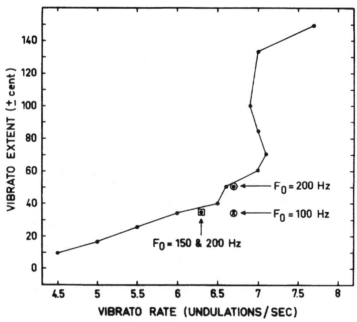

FIGURE 15 Values of the vibrato extent at different vibrato rates that give the impression of optimum "singleness in pitch" (filled circles, according to Ramsdell, see text). The other symbols show maximum values obtained by Gibian (1972) in a test where subjects judged the rate and extent that sounded most human-like. Ramsdell's data were obtained with a fundamental frequency of 500 Hz, whereas Gibian's data pertain to the fundamental frequency (F_0) values indicated on the graph.

showed that the optimum in regard to singleness in pitch as well as timbral richness corresponds to the values of rate and extent typically observed in singers.

It is interesting that Ramsdell's curve approaches a straight line in the neighborhood of seven fluctuations per second. This implies that the extent is not very critical for singleness in pitch at this rate. In contrast to this, there is a strong opinion among some singing teachers that not only slow but also fast vibrato rates are tolerable only if the extent is small. It should be interesting to repeat Ramsdell's experiment with modern equipment.

3. Pitch and Mean Fundamental Frequency

Another perceptual aspect of vibrato is perceived pitch. Provided that the rate and extent are kept within acceptable limits, what is the pitch we perceive? This question was studied independently by Shonle and Horan (1980) and Sundberg (1978a, 1978b).

Sundberg had musically trained subjects match the pitch of a vibrato tone by adjusting the fundamental frequency of a subsequent vibrato-free tone. The two tones, synthetic sung vowels, were identical except for the vibrato. The tones were presented repeatedly until the adjustment was completed. The vibrato rate was 6.5 fluctuations per second, and the extent was ±30 cents. Figure 16 shows the results. The ear seems to compute the average of the undulating frequency, and perceived pitch corresponds closely to this average.

Shonle and Horan used sine-wave stimuli and arrived at practically the same conclusion. However, they could also show that it is the geometric rather than the arithmetic mean that determines the pitch. The difference between these two means is very small in musically acceptable vibratos.

It is frequently assumed that the vibrato is useful in musical practice because it reduces the demands on accuracy of fundamental frequency (see, e.g., Stevens & Davis, 1938; Winckel, 1967). One possible interpretation of this assumption is

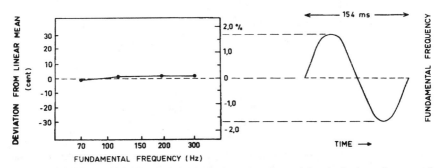

FIGURE 16 Left panel shows average fundamental frequency of a synthesized nonvibrato vowel that musically trained subjects tuned so that it appeared to possess the same pitch as the same vowel presented with vibrato. (After Sundberg, 1978b.) The right panel shows the waveform, rate, and extent used in the experiment. The pitch of the vibrato vowel corresponds almost exactly to the arithmetic mean of the undulating frequency.

that the pitch of a vibrato tone is less accurately perceived than the pitch in a vibrato-free tone. Another interpretation is that the pitch interval between two tones that sound simultaneously is perceived with less accuracy when the tones have a vibrato than when they are vibrato-free.

The first interpretation was tested by Sundberg (1978a; 1978b). The standard deviations obtained when subjects matched the pitch of a vibrato tone with the pitch of a vibrato-free tone were compared with the standard deviations obtained from similar matchings in which both tones lacked vibrato. As can be seen in Figure 17, the differences between the standard deviations were extremely small and decreased slightly with rising fundamental frequency. This implies that the vibrato reduces pitch-perception accuracy slightly for low frequencies. On the other hand, the effects are too small to explain any measurable effects in musical practice.

The second interpretation has not yet been tested, but it is tempting to speculate about it. If two simultaneous complex tones with harmonic spectra constitute a perfectly tuned consonant interval, some partials of one tone will coincide with some partials of the other tone. For instance, if two tones with fundamental frequencies of 200 and 300 Hz (i.e., producing a perfect fifth) sound simultaneously, every third partial of the lower tone will coincide with every second partial of the upper tone. Let us assume that this interval is mistuned by raising the frequency of the upper tone to 300.5 Hz, or by 2.9 cents, which is impossible for almost any listener to detect under any experimental conditions; the difference limen for frequency is at least 6 cents but may be considerably higher depending on the experimental method (see Rakowski, 1971). On the other hand, the partials from the two

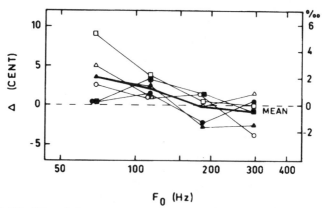

FIGURE 17 Effect of vibrato on accuracy of pitch perception at different fundamental frequencies (F_0). Musically trained subjects first matched the pitch of a nonvibrato stimulus vowel with a subsequent nonvibrato response vowel. Then, the experiment was repeated using a stimulus vowel with vibrato. The ordinate shows the differences in standard deviation obtained. Symbols refer to subjects and the bold curve represents the group mean. (From Sundberg, 1978b.)

tones will not coincide any longer. For instance, the fourth partial of the upper tone has a frequency of 4 x 300.5 = 1202 Hz. This partial will give two beats per second with the sixth partial of the lower tone, with a frequency of 1200 Hz. There are no difficulties in detecting such beats, provided that both partials have similar and sufficiently high amplitudes.

The point is that these beats will not occur if both tones have vibrato. Thus, if two voices sing perfectly "straight" (i.e., without vibrato), the demands on accuracy with respect to the fundamental frequency are higher than if they sing with vibrato. However, this advantage seems to be small. In an unpublished thesis work done at the Department of Speech Communication, Royal Institute of Technology in Stockholm, Ågren (1976) had musically trained subjects match different intervals formed by two simultaneous vibrato tones. The intervals were a major second, a major third, a pure fifth, and a pure octave. The tones were synthetic sung vowels. Some of the subjects obtained a standard deviation as low as 6 cents in repeated matchings of a given interval. If we may believe that mistunings of this small magnitude can be detected even in musical practice, it would seem that the demands on pitch accuracy are extremely high even when the singers use vibrato. It is likely that vibrato is accepted and used in singing for other reasons, as will be shown later.

Our conclusions are that the pitch of a vibrato tone is practically identical to the pitch of a vibrato-free tone with a fundamental frequency equal to the geometric mean of the fundamental frequency of the vibrato tone. Moreover, the accuracy with which the pitch of a vibrato tone is perceived is not affected to any appreciable extent by the vibrato.

VII. PITCH IN PRACTICE

A couple of studies on the perceived pitch of vibrato tones were mentioned earlier. These studies were done under well-controlled experimental conditions. Do the results thus obtained apply also to musical practice? A study of the accuracy of fundamental frequency in musical practice is likely to answer that question.

In a review of a number of investigations, Seashore (1938/1967) included a wealth of documentation of fundamental frequency recordings of professional performances of various songs. The trend was that long notes were sung with an average fundamental frequency that coincided with the theoretically correct value. This is in agreement with the experimental findings reported previously. On the other hand, long notes often "begin slightly flat (about 90 cent on the average) and are gradually corrected during the initial 200 msec of the tone." Moreover, a great many of the long tones were observed to change their average frequency in various ways during the course of the tone. Bjørklund (1961) found that such deviations were typical for professional singers as opposed to nonprofessional singers. One possible interpretation of this is that pitch is used as a means of musical expression.

With regard to short tones, the relationship between fundamental frequency and pitch seems to be considerably more complicated. The case is illustrated in Figure 18, which shows the fundamental frequency during a coloratura passage as sung by a male singer. The singer judged this performance to be acceptable. The registration reveals a careful coordination of amplitude, vibrato, and fundamental. Each note takes exactly one vibrato period, and most of the vibrato periods seem to center on the target frequency. However, if we try to apply what has been shown about pitch perception for vibrato tones, we run into trouble. The average fundamental frequency in a coloratura passage does not change stepwise between the target frequencies corresponding to the pitches we perceive; rather the average rises and falls monotonically at an approximately constant rate. Thus, we cannot explain why the passage is perceived as a rapid sequence of discrete pitches.

d'Alessandro and Castellengo (1991) studied the relations between fundamental frequency gestures of very short tones corresponding to half a vibrato period in duration, that is, tones of about 80-msec duration. Interestingly, they found that the rising half of a vibrato cycle, when presented alone, was perceived as 15 cents

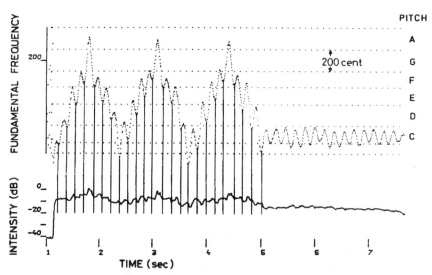

FIGURE 18 Simultaneous recording of fundamental frequency (upper graph) and overall intensity (lower graph) in a professional singer performing a coloratura passage (the pitches C_3, D_3, E_3, F_3, G_3, F_3, E_3, D_3, and C_3 repeated three times). The horizontal dotted lines represent the frequencies midway between the center frequencies of the scale tones as calculated according to equally tempered tuning from the mean frequency of the sustained final C_3. Each note is represented by a frequency gesture encircling the target frequency of the particular scale tone. Despite the sometimes failing accuracy, the pitch sequence was clearly perceived.

higher than the mean while the falling half was perceived as 11 cents below the mean. The authors conclude that the ending of such short pitch glides is more significant to pitch perception than is the beginning.

According to Seashore (1938/1967), the musical ear is extremely generous and operates in the interpretive mood when it listens to singing. On the other hand, this generosity certainly has limits. Also, what appears to be generosity may be sensitivity to small, deliberate, and meaningful deviations from what theoretically is correct.

Replicating a thesis work at the Department of Musicology, Stockholm University (Lindgren & Sundberg, 1972) Sundberg, Prame, and Iwarsson (1996) studied what mean fundamental frequencies were accepted as being "in tune" and "out of tune" in 10 commercial recordings of a song, presented to expert listeners on a iistening tape. A chart with the score of the excerpts was given to the listeners, who were asked to circle each note they perceived to be out of tune. The fundamental frequency was analyzed by measuring the frequencies of the high overtones in sound spectrograms (sonagrams) and averaging them for each tone. These mean frequencies were then related to equally tempered tuning, using the tuning of the accompaniment as the reference. The results showed a rather great variability in the judgments. Analysis of the clear cases, that is, tones that were accepted as in tune by all experts or deemed as out of tune by most listeners, revealed that for most tones accepted as in tune, the mean fundamental frequency varied within a band of about ±7 cents. Tones judged as out of tune were outside this rather narrow frequency band. Furthermore, the bands corresponding to tones perceived as in tune did not always agree with the fundamental frequencies of the equally tempered scale calculated from the tuning of the accompaniment. In some tones, however, the mean fundamental frequencies accepted as in tune were widely scattered. These tones seemed harmonically or melodically marked. Most of the singers seemed to adhere to certain principles in their deviations from the equally tempered tuning. One was to sing high tones sharp, that is, to add a fundamental frequency correction that was increased with pitch. The other was to sharpen and flatten scale tones situated on the dominant (right) and subdominant (left) side of the circle of fifths, where the root of the prevailing chord is the "12 o'clock" reference. Thus, the deviations from scale-tone frequencies according to equally tempered tuning seemed meaningful.

This idea is further supported by the data displayed in Figure 19, which shows the distribution of fundamental frequencies averaged over approximately the duration of one vibrato cycle. The data pertain to a part of a song performed by a first-rate opera singer. For comparison, a registration of the same song performed by a singing synthesizer is shown (Sundberg, 1978b). The vibrato rate and extent were approximately the same in the synthesis as in the real performance. The scale-tone frequencies are represented by peaks. These peaks are considerably wider in the case of the real singer than in the case of the synthesizer. This finding agrees with the assumption that deliberate deviations from theoretically correct pitches are used in singing.

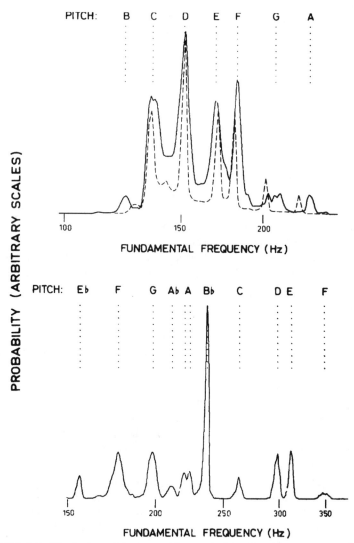

FIGURE 19 Distributions of fundamental frequencies in singing. The upper graphs were obtained from a professional singer (solid curve) and a singing synthesizer (dashed curve) performing the same song. In both cases, the fundamental frequency was averaged with a running time window corresponding to one vibrato cycle, approximately. Therefore, the distributions should be identical if the singer replicated the synthesizer's fundamental frequency contour. The lower graph was obtained from a distinguished barbershop quartet ("Happiness Emporium," Minneapolis) singing a chord progression. The widths of the scale-tone peaks are generally much narrower in the barbershop singers, who sing without vibrato, than in the opera singer, who sang with vibrato. This difference is not due to the vibrato per se, as it was practically eliminated by filtering, but reflects a greater variation in the tuning in the case of the opera singer. Note that pitch A corresponds to two peaks in the barbershop histogram, presumably because it appeared with different harmonic functions in the cadence.

Such meaningful deviations from the theoretically correct frequency values are used as expressive means in instrumental music (Sirker, 1973; Sundberg, Friberg, & Frydén, 1991). It would be astonishing if singing were exceptional in this regard. An important conclusion regarding the benefit of vibrato can be made. We have seen that vibrato-free representations of mistuned consonant intervals give rise to beats, and beats seem to be avoided in most types of music. By adding a vibrato, the singer escapes the beats.

The lower graph in Figure 19 shows the fundamental frequency distribution for the members of a distinguished barbershop quartet. Vibrato is not used in barbershop singing, so the chords must be perfectly tuned to avoid beats. In other words, the singers have very little freedom as regards fundamental frequency. The scale tones are seen to correspond to extremely narrow peaks. This means that the frequency value corresponding to a given scale tone varies very little in barbershop singing, probably because of the absence of vibrato. Although we need more measurements on vibrato-free singing, we may hypothesize that the vibrato offers the singer a freedom in the choice of fundamental frequencies that is used for musical expression.

VIII. EXPRESSION

Expressivity of singing poses four major questions: (a) How successfully is expressive information communicated? (b) What messages does expressivity convey? (c) What details in the performance contain these messages? and (d) What is the origin of the code?

It seems clear that, under certain conditions, expressive communication works pretty well in singing. About 60% to 80% correct identification has been observed in forced-choice listening tests about basic moods like anger, fear, and joy (Kotlyar & Morosov, 1976; Siegwarth & Scherer, 1995). In reality, however, musical experience seems more complex. For example, when listening to a song like Schumann's *Du bist wie eine Blume,* do we perceive anger, fear, or joy, or are we neutral? Indeed, most of what a singer expresses and most of what the listener perceives would lie beyond such simple basic emotions. On the other hand, it is often difficult to find verbal expressions for more complex emotional ambiences. This makes strict testing difficult. It seems fair to conclude, therefore, that the communication of emotions in singing is efficient, at least with respect to a few basic, well-defined emotions.

What messages are carried by expressivity? Marking of the musical structure seems to be an important principle in singing and in instrumental performances (Friberg, 1995a; Sundberg, Iwarsson, & Hagegård, 1995; Todd, 1985). Another principle that has been observed in instrumental performance is to enhance differences between different tone categories such as scale tones, musical intervals, and note values (Sundberg, 1993); obviously singers also must obey these principles.

Furthermore, it seems clear that lengthening beyond nominal duration can be used for the purpose of emphasizing semantically crucial syllables. By singing with expression, singers seem to aim at helping the listener with three mental tasks: (a) to realize which tones belong together and where the structural boundaries are, (b) to differentiate tone and interval categories, and (c) to sense the emotional landscape of the song. This seems to be the essence of the messages carried by expressivity in singing.

The details in the performance that contain the singer's messages about emotions were studied by Kotlyar and Morosov (1976). They had singers perform a set of examples so as to represent different moods. They noted important effects on tempo and overall loudness and also observed characteristic time patterns in pitch and amplitude, as well as micropauses between syllables. Siegwarth and Scherer (1995) found that the singer's tone production is also relevant, in particular the dominance of the fundamental and the amplitudes of the high partials. Deviations from nominal duration are used for the purpose of phrase marking. Sundberg and associates compared performances of a set of music excerpts (Sundberg et al., 1995). The excerpts were sung, without accompaniment, by a professional opera singer in two ways, as in a concert, and deliberately as void of musical expression as possible. In both versions, the singer systematically deviated from the nominal durations of the tones, initiating phrases with a slight accelerando and terminating them with a slight rallentando. Similar observations have been made in performances of instrumental music (Friberg, 1995b; Todd, 1985). The purpose of these deviations would be the marking of musical phrases.

The same study also revealed a number of characteristic fundamental frequency and sound-level patterns. In excerpts with an agitated ambiance, vibrato amplitude was mostly greater in the expressive than in the neutral version, and in excerpts with a calm ambience, the opposite difference was observed. In the expressive as opposed to the neutral versions, fundamental frequency sometimes approached its target value by a slow, ascending glide. According to Rapoport (1996), singers use an entire alphabet of such variations.

Regarding the origin of the code, speech is an obvious candidate. Indeed, it would seem most surprising if different codes were used for signaling emotions in speech and singing. Also, with regard to the communication of information on structure, identical codes seem to be used in speech and singing, although singing is more restricted because of the pitch and duration systems used (Sundberg, 1993). Yet it does not seem likely that singers simply import the code used in speech when they sing. As charmingly pointed out by Fónagy (1983), the actual origin of all changes in vocal sounds is the form of the vocal tract and the adjustment of the vocal fold apparatus. Fónagy argues that the expressiveness of speech derives from a pantomimic behavior of these organs. For example, in sadness, the tongue assumes a slow, depressed type of motion that stamps its own characteristics on the resulting sound sequences.

IX. CONCLUDING REMARKS

In this chapter, two types of facts about singing have been considered. One is the choice of acoustic characteristics of vowel sounds that singers learn to adopt and that represent typical deviations from normal speech. Three examples of such characteristics have been discussed: (a) pitch-dependent choice of formant frequencies in high-pitched singing, (b) the singer's formant, typically occurring in all voiced sounds in the male singing voice, and (c) the vibrato that occurs in both male and female singing.

We have strong reasons to assume that all three examples serve a specific purpose. The pitch-dependent formant frequencies and the singer's formant are both resonatory phenomena that increase the audibility of the singer's voice when the orchestral accompaniment is loud. As resonatory phenomena occur independently of vocal effort, the increase in audibility is gained without expense in terms of vocal effort; hence, a likely purpose in both these cases is vocal economy. The vibrato seems to serve the purpose of allowing the singer a greater freedom in the choice of fundamental frequency as it eliminates beats with the sound of the accompaniment. Thus, in these three cases, we see that singing differs from speech in a highly adequate manner. It is tempting to speculate that such characteristics have developed as a result of evolution; the singers who developed them became successful and hence their technique was copied by other singers.

A second kind of fact about singing discussed in this chapter is the acoustic correlates of various voice classifications that can be assumed to be based on perception. Such classifications are not only tenor, baritone, bass, and so on but also vocal effort (e.g., piano, mezzo piano), and register. We have seen that in most of these cases it was hard to find a common acoustic denominator, because the acoustic characteristics of the categories vary with vowel and fundamental frequency. Rather, the common denominator exists within the voice organ. In the case of the male voice classification—tenor, baritone, and bass—the characteristic differences in formant frequency could be assumed to result from morphological differences in the vocal tract and vocal fold length. The same is true for vocal effort and register, because they reflect differences in the control and operation of the vocal folds. Therefore, we may say that these examples of voice classification seem to rely on the function of the voice organ rather than on the acoustic properties of voice sounds. This is probably revealing as to the way in which we perceive singing voices. We seem to interpret the sounds in terms of how the voice organ was used in producing the sounds.

Artistic interpretation seems to contain at least three different components. One component is the differentiation of different note types, such as scale tones and note values. Another component is marking of boundaries between structural constituents such as motifs and phrases. These requirements of sung performance seems to apply to both speech and music. Probably they reflect properties of the human perceptual apparatus. The third component is the signaling of the emotional ambience of the text and the music. Also in this respect, perception of singing seems closely related to perception of speech. The coding of emotions in speech and singing would be similar and probably founded on a "body language" for communication of emotions. If this is true, our acquaintance with human emotional behavior and particularly speech serves as a reference in our decoding of the emotional information in the sounds of a singer's voice.

REFERENCES

Ågren, K. (1976). *Alt- och tenorröst och harmoniska intervall mellan dem.* Unpublished master's thesis, Department of Speech Communication & Music Acoustics, Kungl Tekniska Högskolan, Stockholm.

Appelman, D. R. (1967). *The science of vocal pedagogy.* London: Indiana University Press.

Bartholomew, W. T. (1934). A physical definition of "good voice quality" in the male voice. *Journal of the Acoustical Society of America, 6,* 25–33.

Bjørklund, A. (1961). Analysis of soprano voices. *Journal of the Acoustical Society of America, 33,* 575–582.

Bloothooft, G., & Plomp, R. (1988). The timbre of sung vowels. *Journal of the Acoustical Society of America, 84,* 847–860.

Cleveland, T. (1977). Acoustic properties of voice timbre types and their influence on voice classification. *Journal of the Acoustical Society of America, 61,* 1622–1629.

Coleman, R. O. (1976). A comparison of the contributions of two voice quality characteristics to the perception of maleness and femaleness in the voice. *Journal of Speech and Hearing Research, 19,* 168–180.

Colton, R. H. (1972). Spectral characteristics of the modal and falsetto registers. *Folia Phoniatrica, 24,* 337–344.

Colton, R. H., & Hollien, H. (1973). Perceptual differentiation of the modal and falsetto registers. *Folia Phoniatrica, 25,* 270–280.

d'Alessandro, C ., & Castellengo, M. (1991). *Etude, par la synthese, de la perception du vibrato vocal dans les transition de notes.* Paper presented at the International Voice Conference in Besançon, France.

Dejonkere P. H., Hirano M., & Sundberg J. (Eds.). (1995). *Vibrato.* San Diego: Singular Publishing Group.

Dmitriev, L., & Kiselev, A. (1979). Relationship between the formant structure of different types of singing voices and the dimension of supraglottal cavities. *Folia Phoniatrica, 31,* 238–241.

Fant, G. (1960). *Acoustic theory of speech production.* The Hague: Mouton.

Fant, G. (1973). *Speech sounds and features.* Cambridge, MA: MIT Press.

Flanagan, J. L. (1965). *Speech analysis, synthesis, and perception.* New York: Springer.

Fónagy I. (1983). *La vive voix.* Paris: Payot.

Friberg, A. (1995a). Matching the rule parameters of Phrase Arch to performances of "Träumerei": a preliminary study. In A. Friberg & J. Sundberg (Eds.), *Proceedings of the KTH Symposium on Grammars for Music Performance* (pp. 37–44). Stockholm: Department of Speech, Music, and Hearing, Kungl Tekniska Högskolan.

Friberg, A. (1995b). *A quantitative rule system for musical performance.* Unpublished doctoral dissertation, Kungl Tekniska Högskolan, Stockholm.

Gauffin, J., & Sundberg, J. (1989). Spectral correlates of glottal voice source waveform characteristics. *Journal of Speech and Hearing Research, 32,* 556–565.

Gibian, G. L. (1972). Synthesis of sung vowels. *Quarterly Progress Report, Massachusetts Institute of Technology, 104,* 243–247.

Gottfried, T., & Chew, S. (1986). Intelligibility of vowels sung by a countertenor. *Journal of the Acoustical Society of America, 79,* 124–130.

Hirano, M., Hibi, S., & Hagino, S. (1995). Physiological aspects of vibrato. In P. H. Dejonkere, M. Hirano, & J. Sundberg (Eds.), *Vibrato* (pp. 9–34). San Diego, CA: Singular Publishing Group.

Hollien, H. (1974). On vocal registers. *Journal of Phonetics, 2,* 125–143

Hollien, H. (1983). The puzzle of the singer's formant. In D. M. Bless & J. H. Abbs (Eds.), *Vocal fold physiology: Contemporary research and clinical issues* (pp. 368–378). San Diego, CA: College-Hill.

Hollien, H., Keister, E., & Hollien, P. A. (1978). Experimental data on "singer's formant" (Abstract). *Journal of the Acoustical Society of America, 64*(Suppl. 1), S171.

Horii, Y. (1989). Acoustic analysis of vocal vibrato: theoretical interpretation of data. *Journal of Voice, 3,* 36–43.

Howie, J., & Delattre, P. (1962). An experimental study of the effect of pitch on the intelligibility of vowels. *The National Association of Teachers of Singing Bulletin, 18*(4), 6–9.

Johansson, C., Sundberg, J., & Wilbrand, H. (1985). X-ray study of articulation and formant frequencies in two female singers. In A. Askenfelt, S. Felicetti, E. Jansson, & J. Sundberg (Eds.), *SMAC 83: Proceedings of the Stockholm International Music Acoustics Conference, Vol. 1* (pp. 203–218). Stockholm: The Royal Swedish Academy of Music, Publication No. 46(1).

Kotlyar, G. M., Morosov, V. P. (1976). Acoustical correlates of the emotional content of vocalized speech. *Soviet Physics Acoustics, 22,* 208–211.

Large, J. (1972, February-March). Towards an integrated physiologic-acoustic theory of vocal registers. *The National Association of Teachers of Singing Bulletin,* 18–36.

Large, J. (1974, October). Acoustic-perceptual evaluation of register equalization. *The National Association of Teachers of Singing Bulletin,* 20–41.

Large, J., Iwata, S., & von Leden, H. (1970). The primary register transition in singing. *Folia Phoniatrica, 22,* 385–396.

Large, J., Iwata, S., & von Leden, H. (1972). The male operatic head register versus falsetto. *Folia Phoniatrica, 24,* 19–29.

Large, J., & Shipp, T. (1969, October). The effect of certain parameters on the perception of vocal registers. *The National Association of Teachers of Singing Bulletin,* 12–15.

Lerman, J. W., & Duffy, R. J. (1970). Recognition of falsetto voice quality. *Folia Phoniatrica, 22,* 21–27.

Lindblom, B., & Sundberg, J. (1971). Acoustical consequences of lip, tongue, jaw, and larynx movements. *Journal of the Acoustical Society of America, 50,* 1166–1179.

Lindgren, H., & Sundberg, A. (1972). *Grundfrekvensförlopp och falsksång.* Unpublished master's thesis, Department of Musicology, Stockholm University.

Marshal, A. H., & Meyer, J. (1985). The directivity and auditory impressions of singers. *Acustica, 58,* 130–140.

McAdams, S., & Rodet, X. (1988). The role of FM-induced AM in dynamic spectral profile analysis. In H. Duifhuis, J. Horst, & H. Wit (Eds.), *Basic issues in hearing* (pp. 359–369). London: Academic Press.

Monsen, R. B., & Engebretson, A. M. (1977). Study of vibrations in the male and female glottal wave. *Journal of the Acoustical Society of America, 62,* 981–993.

Morozov, V. P. (1965). Intelligibility in singing as a function of fundamental voice pitch. *Soviet Physics Acoustics, 10,* 279–283.

Nelson H. D., & Tiffany, W. R. (1968, December). The intelligibility of song. *The National Association of Teachers of Singing Bulletin,* 22–33.

Nordström, P.-E. (1977). Female and infant vocal tracts simulated from male area functions. *Journal of Phonetics, 5,* 81–92.

Plomp, R. (1970). Timbre as a multidimensional attribute of complex tones. In R. Plomp & G. F. Smoorenburg (Eds.), *Frequency analysis and periodicity detection in hearing* (pp. 397–414). Leiden: Sijthoff.

Plomp, R. (1977, July). *Continuity effects in the perception of sounds with interfering noise bursts.* Paper given at the Symposium sur la Psychoacoustique Musicale, IRCAM, Paris.

Prame, E. (1994). Measurements of the vibrato rate of ten singers. *Journal of the Acoustical Society of America, 94,* 1979–1984.

Prame, E. (1997). Vibrato extent and intonation in professional Western lyric singers. *Journal of the Acoustical Society of America, 102,* 616–621.

Rakowski, A. (1971). Pitch discrimination at the threshold of hearing. *Proceedings of the 7th International Congress on Acoustics, Budapest, 3,* 373–376.

Rapoport, E. (1996). Expression code in opera and lied singing. *Journal of New Music Research, 25,* 109–149.

Rasch, R. A. (1978). The perception of simultaneous notes such as in polyphonic music. *Acustica, 40,* 21–33.

Rothenberg, M. (1972). The glottal volume velocity waveform during loose and tight voiced glottal adjustments. In A. Rigault & R. Charbonneau (Eds.), *Proceedings of the 7th International Congress of Phonetic Sciences, Montreal, 1971* (pp. 380–388). The Hague: Mouton.

Rubin, H. J., LeCover, M., & Vennard, W. (1967). Vocal intensity, subglottic pressure and airflow relationship in singers. *Folia Phoniatrica, 19,* 393–413.

Russo, V., & Large, J. (1978). Psychoacoustic study of the Bel Canto model for register equalization: male chest and falsetto. *Journal of Research in Singing, 1*(3), 1–25.

Rzhevkin, S. N. (1956). Certain results of the analysis of a singer's voice. *Soviet Physics Acoustics, 2,* 215–220.

Scotto di Carlo, N. (1972). Etude acoustique et auditive des facteurs d'intelligibilité de la voix chantée. In A. Rigault & R. Charbonneau (Eds.), *Proceedings of the 7th International Congress of Phonetic Sciences, Montreal, 1971* (pp. 1017–1023). The Hague: Mouton.

Scotto di Carlo, N., & Germain, A. (1985). A perceptual study of the influence of pitch on the intelligibility of sung vowels. *Phonetica, 42,* 188–197.

Seashore, C. E. (1967). *Psychology of music.* New York: Dover. (Original work published 1938)

Seidner, W., Schutte, H., Wendler, J., & Rauhut, A. (1985). Dependence of the high singing formant on pitch and vowel in different voice types. In A. Askenfelt, S. Felicetti, E. Jansson, & J. Sundberg (Eds.), *SMAC 83: Proceedings of the Stockholm International Music Acoustics Conference, Vol. 1* (pp. 261–268). Stockholm: The Royal Swedish Academy of Music, Publication No. 46(1).

Shipp, T., Doherty, T., & Haglund, S. (1990). Physiologic factors in vocal vibrato production. *Journal of Voice, 4,* 300–304.

Shipp, T., & Izdebski, C. (1975). Vocal frequency and vertical larynx positioning by singers and nonsingers. *Journal of the Acoustical Society of America, 58,* 1104–1106.

Shonle, J. I., & Horan, K. E. (1980). The pitch of vibrato tones. *Journal of the Acoustical Society of America, 67,* 246–252.

Siegwarth, H., & Scherer, K. (1995). Acoustic concomitants of emotional expression in operatic singing: the case of Lucia in Ardi gli incensi. *Journal of Voice, 9,* 249–260.

Simon, P., Lips, H., & Brock,. G. (1972). Etude sonagraphique et analyse acoustique en temps reel de la voix chantée a partir de differentes techniques vocales. *Travaux de l'Institut de Phonétique de Strasbourg, 4,* 219–276.

Sirker, U. (1973). Objektive Frequenzmessung und subjektive Tonhöhenempfindung bei Musikinstrumentklängen. *Swedish Journal of Musicology, 55,* 47–58.

Slawson, A. W. (1968). Vowel quality and musical timbre as functions of spectrum envelope and fundamental frequency. *Journal of the Acoustical Society of America, 43,* 87–101.

Smith, L. A., & Scott, B. L. (1980). Increasing the intelligibility of sung vowels. *Journal of the Acoustical Society of America, 67,* 1795–1797.

Stevens, S. S., & Davis, H. (1938). *Hearing, its psychology and physiology.* New York: Wiley.

Stumpf, C. (1926). *Die Sprachlaute*. Berlin and New York: Springer-Verlag.

Sundberg, J. (1970). Formant structure and articulation of spoken and sung vowels. *Folia Phoniatrica, 22,* 28–48.

Sundberg, J. (1972). Production and function of the "singing formant." In H. Glahn, S. Sorenson, & P. Ryom (Eds.), *Report of the 11th Congress of the International Musicological Society, II* (pp. 679–688). Copenhagen: Editor Wilhelm Hansen.

Sundberg, J. (1974). Articulatory interpretation of the "singing formant." *Journal of the Acoustical Society of America, 55,* 838–844

Sundberg, J. (1975). Formant technique in a professional female singer. *Acustica, 32,* 89–96.

Sundberg, J. (1977a). Vibrato and vowel identification. *Archives of Acoustics , 2,* 257–266.

Sundberg, J. (1977b). Singing and timbre. In *Music, room, acoustics* (pp. 57–81). Stockholm: Royal Swedish Academy of Music Publication No. 17.

Sundberg, J. (1977c). Studies of the soprano voice. *Journal of Research in Singing, 1*(1), 25–35.

Sundberg, J. (1978a). Effects of the vibrato and the singing formant on pitch. *Musicologica Slovaca, 6,* 51–69.

Sundberg, J. (1978b). Synthesis of singing. *Swedish Journal of Musicology, 60*(1), 107–112. (Sound example no. 7 on grammophone recording)

Sundberg, J. (1984). Using acoustic research for understanding aspects of the singing voice. *Transcripts of the 13th Symposium on Care of the Professional Voice* (pp. 90–104). New York: The Voice Foundation.

Sundberg, J. (1989). Aspects of structure. In S. Nielsén & O. Olsson (Eds.), *Structure and Perception of Electroacoustic Sound and Music: Proceedings of the Marcus Wallenberg Symposium in Lund, Sweden, August 1988* (pp. 33–42). Amsterdam: Excerpta Medica.

Sundberg, J. (1990). What's so special about singers? *Journal of Voice, 4,* 107–119.

Sundberg, J. (1993). How can music be expressive? *Speech Communication, 13,* 239–253.

Sundberg, J., & Askenfelt, A. (1983). Larynx height and voice source: a relationship? In J. Abbs & D. Bless (Eds.), *Voice physiology* (pp. 307–316). Houston, TX: Collegehill.

Sundberg, J., Friberg, A., & Frydén, L. (1991). Common secrets of musicians and listeners: An analysis-by-synthesis study of musical performance. In P. Howell, R. West, & I. Cross (Eds.), *Representing musical structure* (pp. 161–197). London: Academic Press.

Sundberg, J., & Gauffin, J. (1979). Waveform and spectrum of the glottal voice source. In B. Lindblom & S. Öhman (Eds.). *Frontiers of speech communication research, Festschrift for Gunnar Fant* (pp. 301–320). London: Academic Press.

Sundberg J., & Gauffin, J. (1982). Amplitude of the voice source fundamental and the intelligibility of super pitch vowels. In R. Carlson & B. Granström (Eds.), *The representation of speech in the peripheral auditory system: Proceedings of a symposium* (pp. 223–228). Amsterdam: Elsevier Biomedical Press.

Sundberg, J., Iwarsson, J., Hagegård, H. (1995). A singer's expression of emotions in sung performance (pp. 217–232). In O. Fujimura & M. Hirano (Eds.), *Vocal fold physiology: Voice quality and control*. San Diego, CA: Singular Publishing Group.

Sundberg, J., Prame, E., & Iwarsson, J. (1996). Replicability and accuracy of pitch patterns in professional singers. In P. J. Davis & N. H. Fletcher (Eds.), *Vocal fold physiology: Controlling complexity and chaos* (pp. 291–306). San Diego: Singular Publishing Group.

Sundberg, J., & Skoog, J. (1997). Dependence of jaw opening on pitch and vowel in singers. *Journal of Voice, 11,* 301–306.

Todd, N. (1985). A model of expressive timing in tonal music. *Music Perception, 3,* 33–58.

Vennard, W. (1967). *Singing, the mechanism and the technic* (2nd ed.). New York: Fischer.

Vennard, W., Hirano, M., Ohala, J., & Fritzell, B. (1970–1971). A series of four electromyographic studies. *The National Association of Teachers of Singing Bulletin,* October1970, 16–21; December 1970, 30–37; February-March 1971, 26–32; May–June 1971, 22–30.

Wang, S. (1986). Singer's high formant associated with different larynx position in styles of singing. *Journal of the Acoustical Society of Japan, 7,* 303–314.

Winckel, F. (1953). Physikalischen Kriterien ffür objektive Stimmbeurteilung. *Folia Phoniatrica (Separatum), 5,* 232–252.

Winckel, F. (1967). *Music, sound, and sensation: A modern exposition.* New York: Dover.

Zwicker, E., & Feldtkeller, R. (1967). *Das Ohr als Nachrichtenempfänger* (2nd ed.) Stuttgart: Hirzel Verlag.

7

INTERVALS, SCALES, AND

TUNING*

EDWARD M. BURNS

Department of Speech and Hearing Sciences
University of Washington
Seattle, Washington

I. INTRODUCTION

In the vast majority of musical cultures, collections of discrete pitch relationships—musical scales—are used as a framework for composition and improvisation. In this chapter, the possible origins and bases of scales are discussed, including those aspects of scales that may be universal across musical cultures. The perception of the basic unit of melodies and scales, the musical interval, is also addressed. The topic of tuning—the exact relationships of the frequencies of the tones composing the intervals and/or scales—is inherent in both discussions. In addition, musical interval perception is examined as to its compliance with some general "laws" of perception and in light of its relationship to the second most important aspect of auditory perception, speech perception.

II. WHY ARE SCALES NECESSARY?

The two right-most columns of Table I give the frequency ratios, and their values in the logarithmic "cent" metric, for the musical intervals that are contained in the scale that constitutes the standard tonal material on which virtually all Western music is based: the 12-tone chromatic scale of equal temperament. A number of assumptions are inherent in the structure of this scale. The first is that of octave equivalence, or pitch class. The scale is defined only over a region of one octave; tones separated by an octave are assumed to be in some respects musically equivalent and are given the same letter notation (Table I, column 3). The second is that pitch is scaled as a logarithmic function of frequency. The octave is divided into

*This chapter is dedicated to the memory of W. Dixon Ward.

TABLE I Interval Comparison in Different Mathematical Tuning Systems[a]

Interval name	Solfeggio	Letter notation	Pythagorean tuning			Just intonation			Equal temperament	
			Numerical origin	Frequency ratio	Cents	Numerical origin	Frequency ratio	Cents	Frequency ratio	Cents
Unison	DO	C	1:1	1.000	0.0	1:1	1.000	0.0	1.000	0
Minor second		Db	$2^8:3^5$	1.053	90.2	16:15	1.067	111.7	1.059	100
		C#	$3^7:2^{11}$	1.068	113.7	16:15	1.067	111.7	1.059	100
Major second	RE	D	$3^2:2^3$	1.125	203.9	10:9[b]	1.111	182.4	1.122	200
						9:8[c]	1.125	203.9		
Minor third		Eb	$2^5:3^3$	1.186	294.1	6:5	1.200	315.6	1.189	300
		D#	$3^9:2^{14}$	1.201	317.6	6:5	1.200	315.6	1.189	300
Major third	MI	E	$3^4:2^6$	1.265	407.8	5:4	1.250	386.3	1.260	400
Fourth	FA	F	$2^2:3$	1.333	498.1	4:3	1.333	498.1	1.335	500
Tritone		Gb	$2^{10}:3^6$	1.407	588.3	45:32	1.406	590.2	1.414	600
		F#	$3^6:2^9$	1.424	611.7	64:45	1.422	609.8	1.414	600
Fifth	SO	G	3:2	1.500	702.0	3:2	1.500	702.0	1.498	700
Minor sixth		Ab	$2^7:3^4$	1.580	792.2	8:5	1.600	813.7	1.587	800
		G#	$3^8:2^{12}$	1.602	815.6	8:5	1.600	813.7	1.587	800
Major sixth	LA	A	$3^3:2^4$	1.688	905.0	5:3	1.667	884.4	1.682	900
Minor seventh					7:4[d]	1.750	968.8			
		Bb	$2^4:3^2$	1.788	996.1	16:9[e]	1.777	996.1	1.782	1000
		A#	$3^{10}:2^{15}$	1.802	1019.1	9:5	1.800	1017.6	1.782	1000
Major seventh	TI	B	$3^5:2^7$	1.900	1109.8	15:8	1.875	1088.3	1.888	1180
Octave	DO	C	2:1	2.000	1200.0	2:1	2.000	1200.0	2.000	1200

[a] Adapted from Martin, 1962.
[b] Lesser.
[c] Greater.
[d] Harmonic.
[e] Grave.

12 logarithmically equal steps (semitones), the presumption being that all intervals that contain the same number of semitones are perceptually equivalent, regardless of the absolute frequencies of the tones composing the intervals. The names of the 13 intervals (including unison) that are contained in the 12-tone chromatic scale are given in column 1 of Table I.

Given that present Western music uses a relatively small set of discrete pitch relationships, an obvious question occurs: Is this use of discrete scale steps universal? That is, are there musical cultures that use continuously variable pitches? The evidence from ethnomusicological studies indicates that the use of discrete pitch relationships is essentially universal. The only exceptions appear to be certain primitive musical styles, for example, "tumbling strains" (Sachs & Kunst, 1962), or "indeterminate-pitch chants" (Malm, 1967), which are found in a few tribal cultures. Of course, pitch glides—glissandos, portamentos, trills, etc.—are used as embellishment and ornamentation in most musical cultures. However, these embellishments are distinct from the basic scale structure of these musics. The concept of octave equivalence, although far from universal in early and primitive music (e.g., Nettl, 1956; Sachs & Kunst, 1962), also seems to be common to more advanced musical systems.

A related question follows: does the 12-tone chromatic scale represent a norm or a limit to the number of usable pitch relationships per octave? A number of Western composers have proposed quarter-tone (i.e., 24 approximately equal intervals per octave) and other microtonal scales, but these scales have not gained wide acceptance. Numerous cultures have scales that contain fewer than 12 notes per octave. There are, however, apparently only two musical cultures that, in theory at least, use more than 12 intervals per octave: the Indian and the Arab-Persian. Both musical systems of India (Hindustani and Karnatic) are, according to tradition, based on 22 possible intervals per octave. They are not, however, equal, or even approximately equal intervals. The basic structure of the inclusive scale is essentially the same as that of the Western 12-interval chromatic scale, and the microtones (*shrutis*) are (theoretical) slight variations of certain intervals, the exact values of which are dependent on the individual melodic framework (*raga*) being played. There is evidence that in actual musical practice these microtonal variations of intervals are not played as discrete intervals but are denoted by a purposefully induced variability in intonation such as a slow vibrato (Callow & Shepherd, 1972; Jhairazbhoy & Stone, 1963).

The one system that may use true quarter tones (i.e., intervals that bisect the distance between the Western chromatic intervals) is the Arab-Persian system. In this system, there are various claims as to the number of possible intervals (ranging from 15 to 24) and some controversy as to whether they are true quarter tones or, as in the Indian system, merely microtonal variations of certain intervals (e.g., Zonis, 1973). The limited data on measured intonation in this system are ambiguous as to how accurately these quarter tones are actually produced (e.g., Caron & Safvate, 1966; Spector, 1966). It is clear, however, that neither the Indian nor

Arab-Persian scales are chromatically microtonal. That is, the quarter tones (or microtones) are never played contiguously but only as alternative versions of certain larger intervals.

Thus, the evidence indicates that no musical cultures exist wherein the smallest usable interval is smaller than the semitone. Although this, of course, does not prove that scales containing intervals smaller than semitones, or composed of more than 12 intervals, are not possible, it is certainly suggestive. What then is the probable basis for the use of a discrete number of tones in scales and for the apparent limitation on the number of tones per octave? In pairwise discrimination tasks, normal listeners can discriminate literally hundreds of different frequencies over the range of an octave, and well over a thousand over the range of frequencies used in music, so the discriminability of individual tones is clearly not a limitation. In keeping with Miller's (1956) "magical number 7 ± 2" limit for identification of stimuli along a unidimensional psychophysical continuum, most listeners are very poor at identifying individual tones varying only in frequency, that is, they can only place the tones over the entire frequency range of human hearing into about five categories with perfect consistency (e.g., Pollack, 1952). However, this limitation is irrelevant for melodic information in music. As is overwhelmingly evident from both everyday musical experience, from music theory, and as has been shown in formal experiments (e.g., Attneave & Olson, 1971; White, 1960), melodic information in music is mediated by the frequency ratio relationships among tones (i.e., the musical intervals) not by their absolute frequencies. Although it is true that the absolute frequencies of the tones composing the equitempered scale have been fixed (ranging from $C_0 = 16.4$ Hz to $B_8 = 7902.1$ Hz, with A_4, the designated tuning standard, at 440 Hz), this has been done primarily for the purpose of standardizing the manufacture of fixed-tuning instruments and has virtually no relevance for the perception of music (with the exception of the relatively few individuals who possess absolute pitch; see Chapter 8, this volume).

The most likely reason for the adoption of a relatively small number of discrete intervals as the tonal material for music is that discretization or categorization is a typical, if not universal, strategy used by animals in order to reduce information overload and facilitate processing when subjected to the high-information-content signals and/or high information rates from a highly developed sensory system (e.g., Estes, 1972; Terhardt, 1991). An obvious example is the processing of speech information by humans, wherein each language selects a relatively small portion of the available timbral differences that can be produced by the vocal tract as information-carrying units (phonemes) in the language. A related reason for discrete scales, and another obvious analogy with speech perception, lies in the social aspect of music. Music first developed as, and still largely remains, a social phenomenon associated with religious or other rituals that, like language, necessitated an easily remembered common framework.

Given this information-transfer-based speculation on the origin of discrete-tone musical scales, we might further speculate that the apparent limit of 12 semitones per octave is, in fact, related to the "channel capacity" for information transmission as delineated by the 7 ± 2 rule. According to this empirically based rule, subjects can place stimuli along a unidimensional psychophysical continuum into only five to nine categories with perfect consistency, which corresponds to about 2.3 bits ($\log_2 7$) of information. This phenomenon is remarkable for its robustness, having been observed for a wide variety on continuua, in all five sensory modalities (Miller, 1956). Although we shall see in Section III that musicians' channel capacity for musical interval identification clearly exceeds the predicted maximum of nine categories, the results also suggest that channel capacity may indeed be the factor limiting the number of tones per octave. It will also be shown that there are some intriguing similarities between musical scales and speech continuua in the relationship between identification and discrimination and in the separation of categories along their respective continuua.

III. MUSICAL INTERVAL PERCEPTION

With the exception of the small percentage of persons who possess absolute pitch, musicians are not able to label individual tones accurately (see, however, Chapter 8, this volume, regarding cross-cultural differences in the prevalence of absolute pitch). However, most trained musicians have developed what is termed relative pitch, the ability to identify musical intervals. For example, when presented with two tones whose frequency ratio corresponds to one of the intervals of the equal-tempered scale, either sequentially (melodic intervals) or simultaneously (harmonic intervals), possessors of relative pitch are able to identify the interval by using the appropriate verbal label (Table I, column 1). Equivalently, if told that one of the tones composing the interval is a particular note in the scale (e.g., "C"), they can give the letter name of the other note. Finally, if given a reference tone and the verbal label of an interval, they are able to produce the interval. Although this labeling ability is not essential to the ability to play music, it is necessary in certain situations (e.g., when a vocalist must sight-read a piece of music), and courses in "ear training," in which this ability is developed, are part of most music curricula. In this section, the limits and precision of relative pitch are explored, along with the limits of ability of relative pitch possessors to discriminate intervals in pairwise discrimination tasks. These results are discussed in relation to the concept of "categorical perception" and in relation to perception along other auditory continuua.

A. ADJUSTMENT OF ISOLATED MUSICAL INTERVALS

The method of adjustment is probably the oldest and most extensively used method for studying the perception of isolated musical intervals. It has been used primarily to study the octave (Burns, 1974b; Demany & Semal, 1990; Sundberg &

Lindquist, 1973; Terhardt, 1969; Walliser, 1969; Ward, 1954), but has also been used for other intervals (Burns & Campbell, 1994; Moran & Pratt, 1926; Rakowski, 1990; Rakowski & Miskiewicz, 1985). In the typical paradigm, the subject is presented with pairs of tones (either sequential or simultaneous), one of which is fixed in frequency and the other of which is under the control of the subject. The subject is instructed to adjust the frequency of the variable tone so that the pitch relationship of the two tones corresponds to a specific musical interval. It should be noted that this is a single-(temporal) interval procedure because the subject is adjusting to some internal standard. Thus, these adjustment experiments are akin to the single-interval identification experiments discussed later and not to the usual psychophysical adjustment experiment (where the subject adjusts the variable stimulus to equal some physically presented standard), which is essentially a two-(temporal) interval discrimination experiment.

Individual relative pitch possessors show very little variability for repeated adjustments of musical intervals relative to the variability typically obtained for adjusting ratios of stimulus magnitude or stimulus quality along a unidimensional psychophysical continuum. For example, when subjects adjust the intensity of a tone so that it is "twice as loud" as a reference stimulus, or set a frequency to be "twice as high" as a reference stimulus, intrasubject standard deviations are typically on the order of 25% and 12%, respectively (e.g., Stevens, 1976). By comparison, the average standard deviation of repeated adjustments by relative pitch possessors of sequential or simultaneous octaves composed of sinusoids is on the order of 10 cents (0.6%) (Terhardt, 1969; Ward, 1953, 1954). The average standard deviation is slightly less for octaves composed of complex tones (Sundberg & Lindquist, 1973; Terhardt, 1969; Walliser, 1969). A range of average deviations of from 14 to 22 cents for adjustments of the other intervals of the chromatic scale (simultaneous presentation of pure tones) has been reported by Moran and Pratt (1926). A particularly complete set of experiments was conducted by Rakowski and colleagues (Rakowski, 1990; Rakowski & Miskiewicz, 1985), who assessed variability for adjustments of the 12 intervals from the chromatic scale for both ascending and descending versions of melodic intervals, using both pure and complex tones, with reference frequencies ranging from 250 to 2000 Hz. Interquartile ranges of from 20 to 45 cents were reported. Burns and Campbell (1994) had three subjects adjust the 12 chromatic intervals by using pure tones with a reference frequency of 261.6 Hz (see inset at top of Figure 1). They also had the subjects adjust the intervals corresponding to the quarter tones between the chromatic intervals. The average standard deviation for the quarter-tone adjustments, 20.9 cents, was not significantly larger than that for the chromatic intervals, 18.2 cents (Burns & Campbell,1994). Other general trends evident from the results of adjustment experiments are (a) a small but significant day-to-day variability in intrasubject judgments; (b) significant intersubject variability; and (c) a tendency to "compress" (adjust narrower than equal-tempered intervals) smaller intervals (minor third or less) and "stretch" wider intervals (minor sixth or greater), especially the minor seventh, major seventh, and octave.

B. IDENTIFICATION OF ISOLATED MUSICAL INTERVALS

There are a number of variations on the one-(temporal) interval identification paradigm, depending on the number of response alternatives (R) relative to the number of stimuli (S): absolute identification, $S = R$; category scaling, $S > R$; and magnitude estimation, $S \ll R$ (e.g., R is any positive number).

1. Magnitude Estimation

Magnitude estimation procedures have been used to assess musical interval perception by Siegel and Siegel (1977b). Despite being given an unlimited number of categories, musicians produced magnitude estimation functions that were often steplike. That is, frequency ratios over a small range were estimated to have the same magnitude; then there was an abrupt transition to another estimate. The ranges over which the estimates were constant corresponded roughly to semitones. In addition, the function relating the standard deviation of repeated magnitude estimates to frequency ratio had a multimodal character, in which the modal peaks corresponded to the regions between the plateaus of the magnitude estimation function. These functions are unlike those associated with magnitude estimation of stimuli obeying the 7 ± 2 rule, which are typically smooth, monotonically increasing functions of stimulus magnitude, for both magnitude estimates and for standard deviations of repeated estimates (e.g., Stevens, 1976). The results do, however, resemble those found for certain speech stimuli (Vinegrad, 1972) and are further discussed in Section III,C.

2. Absolute Identification

One obvious exception to the 7 ± 2 rule for identification along a unidimensional psychophysical continuum is the performance of possessors of absolute pitch, that is, persons who have the ability to identify the pitch of a single tone—usually in terms of musical scale categories or keys on a piano. As discussed in Chapter 8 (this volume), the best possessors are able to identify perfectly about 75 categories (roughly 6.2 bits of information) over the entire auditory range, compared with about 5 categories (2.3 bits) for nonpossessors (Pollack, 1952).

It would appear that musicians with relative pitch are also exceptions to the 7 ± 2 rule. Clearly, the most competent possessors of relative pitch can recognize perfectly the 12 intervals of the chromatic scale in either harmonic or melodic modes (Killam, Lorton, & Schubert, 1975; Plomp, Wagenaar, & Mimpen, 1973). However, none of the absolute identification experiments have attempted to determine maximum interval identification ability, analogous, for example, to ascertaining the 75-category limit for absolute pitch. In order to assess identification resolution completely, the number of stimuli and/or the number of response categories in absolute identification or category-scaling experiments must be large enough that even the best subjects become inconsistent in their labeling. In informal experiments, we have found that although many musicians can identify the ascending and descending melodic intervals from unison to major tenth (32 categories) with near 100% accuracy, this still has not reached their identification limit. In addition, problems of interpretation arise from the fact that ascending and descending versions of the same interval may not be independent and from the fact that octave equivalence suggests that there may be more than one *perceptual* dimension involved despite the unidimensional physical continuum of frequency ratio. These problems will be further discussed in Section IV. However, evidence is presented in the next section suggesting that, even when labeling results are restricted to ascending melodic intervals within a one-octave range, identification resolution is much better than the 7 ± 2 rule predicts.

3. Category Scaling

A number of experimenters have obtained category-scaling identification functions for intervals spaced in increments of from 10 to 20 cents, over ranges of 2–5 semitones, where the labels are the relevant intervals from the chromatic scale. These functions have been obtained both for melodic intervals (Burns & Ward, 1978; Rakowski, 1990; Siegel & Siegel, 1977a, 1977b) and for harmonic intervals (Zatorre & Halpern, 1979). The identification functions are characterized by sharp category boundaries, high test-retest reliability, and a resistance to contextual effects such as shifts in the range of stimuli being identified. Such results are not typical of those obtained from category scaling of other unidimensional psychophysical continuua (i.e.,7 ± 2 continuua), or of results obtained from nonmusicians along the frequency-ratio continuum, both of which show inconsistent, often multimodal, identification functions with large category overlap and poor test-retest reliability (Siegel & Siegel, 1977a). This pattern is, however, consistent with the results of certain speech-token category-scaling experiments (e.g. Studdert-Kennedy, Liberman, Harris, & Cooper, 1970).

Two general findings are evident in the data from all of the category scaling experiments: (a) a tendency for identification categories for the narrower and wider intervals to be shifted relative to equal temperament; that is, for intervals less than a major third, relatively more flat versions of the intervals are included in the semitone categories (i.e., a compression of the scale relative to equal temperament), and for intervals greater than a major sixth, relatively more sharp versions of the intervals are included in the semitone categories (i.e., a stretch of the scale); and (b) small but reliable differences among observers in their perception of the relative width and placement of interval categories. These effects were noted for both ascending and descending intervals and are analogous to those seen in adjustment experiments.

Although the best possessors of relative pitch are able to identify chromatic semitones without error, they are not able to identify the quarter tones between chromatic semitones with perfect consistency (Burns & Ward, 1978) or to label stimuli consistently as "low," "pure," or "high" tokens of a single melodic (Burns, 1977; Miyazaki, 1992) or harmonic (Wapnick, Bourassa, & Sampson, 1982) interval. This is true even when the stimuli are limited to a very narrow range (Szende, 1977), or even, as is the case for Indian musicians, when the theoretical scales include microtonal variations of certain intervals (Burns, 1977). These types of experiments can be used, however, to estimate just how well possessors of relative pitch are able to identify frequency ratios and how their identification performance compares with the performance for observers for more typical psychophysical continuua. Figure 1 shows the results of four possessors of relative pitch in a category scaling task for melodic musical intervals, composed of complex tones, covering the range of frequency ratios from 25 to 1275 cents in 25-cent increments (Burns & Campbell, 1994). The response categories were the chromatic semitone categories, minor second through octave (solid lines) and the adjacent quarter tones (broken lines). In order to allow comparison between resolution in the category-scaling task and resolution in paired-comparison discrimination tasks, as well as to resolution along other psychophysical continuua (see below), the results shown in Figure 1 have been analyzed in terms of the bias-free metric, d' (e.g., Braida & Durlach, 1972).

The first entry in the "Identification" column in Table II shows the total resolution sensitivity in d' units across the octave range from 50 to 1250 cents; that is, the sensitivity in d' units between adjacent frequency ratios has been accumulated over the octave range and averaged across four subjects. Also shown are the results from a similar category-scaling task by two possessors of absolute pitch, who categorized pure tones over a one-octave range into the semitone categories from C_4 through C_5 and the adjacent quarter tones. Results for a typical 7 ± 2 continuum, absolute identification of pure tone intensity over a 54-dB range, are also shown for comparison. The total sensitivity over an octave range for identification of musical intervals by relative pitch possessors is similar to that for identification of pure-tone frequencies by possessors of absolute pitch, but is about three times greater than the total sensitivity for intensity resolution over essentially the entire dynamic range of human hearing The total sensitivity in d' units can be converted to information in bits (Braida & Durlach, 1972) for comparison with results of identification experiments that have been analyzed in terms of information transfer. Whereas the results for intensity identification correspond to about 2 bits of information (perfect identification of 4 categories), the results for relative pitch and absolute pitch correspond, on average, to roughly 3.5 bits of information (perfect identification of about 11 categories) over the one-octave range. In other words, both relative pitch and absolute pitch possessors are exceptions to the 7 ± 2 rule in terms of their ability to identify stimuli along a unidimensional continuum, even when the continuua for relative pitch and absolute pitch are restricted to the range of a single octave. This channel capacity of 3.5 bits per octave may indeed be a primary factor in the apparent limitation of 12 notes per octave in musical scales. It must also be stressed that this is an estimate of the limitation for *perfectly consistent* identification performance. Relative pitch possessors can categorize frequency ratios into more than 12 categories per octave at better than chance level performance, that is, they can judge "out of tune" intervals. For example, the subjects in Burns and Campbell (1994) showed average interval separations for a

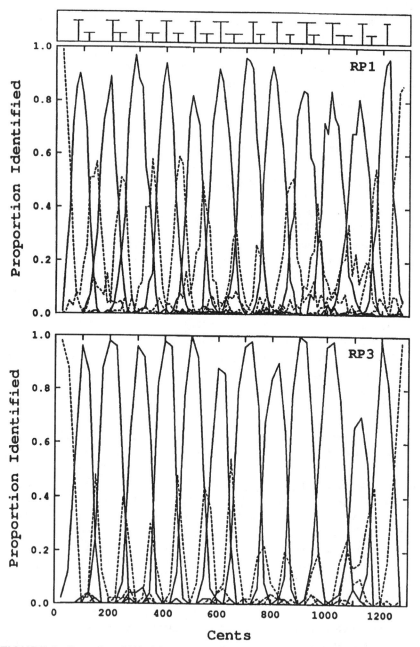

FIGURE 1   Proportion of 100 trials at each musical interval value that were placed in each of the 12 chromatic semitone (solid lines) or 13 quarter-tone (dashed lines) response categories by four possessors of relative pitch in a category scaling identification task. For purposes of clarity, the individual response categories are not labeled. However, the response consistency of the subjects is such that the plots are easily interpreted: the solid line peaking near 100 cents corresponds to the "minor second" category; the dashed line peaking between 100 and 200 cents to the "quarter tone between minor

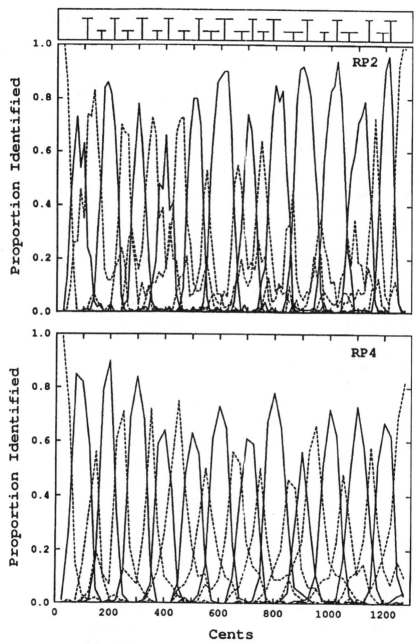

second and major second" category; the solid line peaking near 200 cents to the "major second" category, and so on. The small panels above the plots for subjects RP1 and RP2 show the mean (vertical lines) and ±1 standard deviation (horizontal lines) for a musical interval adjustment task. The taller lines are for adjustments to semitone categories, the shorter lines for adjustments to quarter-tone categories. (Reprinted with permission from E. M. Burns & S. L. Campbell, *Journal of the Acoustical Society of America, 96*(5) 2704–2719, November 1994. © 1994 Acoustical Society of America.)

resolution sensitivity of $d' = 1$ of about 30 cents, which means that they could, on average, differentially identify intervals separated by 30 cents with an accuracy of about 70% correct.

C. MUSICAL INTERVAL DISCRIMINATION AND CATEGORICAL PERCEPTION

The concept of categorical perception as it relates to the perception of musical intervals has been widely studied in the past 20 years (Burns & Campbell, 1994; Burns & Ward, 1978; Howard, Rosen, & Broad, 1992; Locke & Kellar, 1973; Siegel & Siegel, 1977a, 1977b; Zatorre, 1983; Zatorre & Halpern, 1979). Unfortunately, these studies have led to misunderstandings on the part of some musicians and musicologists, who have interpreted the studies (partially on the basis of rather unfortunate choices for the titles of some of the papers) as suggesting that musicians cannot detect any mistuning from chromatic interval categories, an interpretation that is clearly at odds with the everyday experience of musicians and, as noted in the preceding section, is also at odds with the experimental facts. In this section, a brief overview of the concept of categorical perception, and of a general perceptual model that provides an objective and quantitative basis for interpreting it, are provided. In addition, experiments that have directly addressed categorical perception of musical intervals are reviewed.

1. Categorical Perception

The term "categorical perception" was coined to describe the results of speech experiments that used synthetic speech tokens that varied along a single acoustic continuum. It was originally defined according to two criteria: (a) identification functions show sharp and reliable category boundaries when stimuli along the continuum are categorized in terms of phonetic labels; and (b) discrimination performance for stimuli equally spaced along the continuum can be well predicted from the identification functions if it is assumed that subjects can discriminate two stimuli only to the extent that they can differentially identify them (e.g., Studdert-Kennedy et al., 1970). Thus the discrimination function is nonmonotonic with a peak at the boundary between phonemic categories (the "category boundary effect.") This clearly contrasts with the usual situation in psychophysics, which is essentially a corollary of the 7 ± 2 rule: discrimination in paired-comparison discrimination tasks is much better than resolution in single-interval identification tasks and is typically a monotonic function of stimulus separation.

Ideal categorical perception as defined earlier was seldom actually seen: discrimination was almost always somewhat better than predicted from identification, and there have been many controversies over the degree to which the effect is influenced by such factors as training, inadequate identification paradigms, and differences in discrimination paradigms [for an extensive treatment of the many issues involved in categorical perception, see the book by Harnad (1987), and in particular, the chapters by Macmillan, Pastore, and Rosen & Howell]. Nonetheless, for certain continuua, the differences between discrimination and identification resolution are much smaller than for typical psychophysical continuua, and the category boundary effect is a persistent finding. Results meeting the criteria for categorical perception were initially obtained only with speech stimuli. These results formed a significant portion of the rationale for "speech is special" models of auditory processing (Studdert-Kennedy et al., 1970). Later, however, a number of experiments, including the experiments on musical interval perception discussed later, reported categorical perception for nonspeech stimuli (see Harnad, 1987). These results forced an extension of the concept of categorical perception to include continuua other than speech.

Macmillan and colleagues (Macmillan, 1987; Macmillan, Goldberg, & Braida, 1988) have studied categorical perception using the trace-context theory, originally developed as a model of auditory intensity perception (e.g. Braida & Durlach, 1988), as a framework. This theory was designed in part to explain paradigm-related differences in intensity resolution, including the classic discrepancy between resolution in discrimination and resolution in identification. The details of the theory are beyond the scope of this chapter, but briefly, the theory assumes that in all single-(temporal) interval tasks such as absolute identification, and in most multi-(temporal) interval discrimination tasks, performance is constrained by memory limitations. Only in the case of the two-interval, two-alternative forced choice (2AFC) discrimination task, where the same two (temporally) closely spaced stimuli are presented on every trial (fixed discrimination), is the listener's performance free from memory constraints and limited only by the efficiency of stimulus coding by the auditory system. Thus resolution of stimuli along a continuum is assumed to be optimal in a fixed discrimination task.

In the discrimination task that has been commonly used in categorical perception experiments (roving discrimination), where different pairs of stimuli drawn from the entire continuum range are presented in each trial, performance is constrained by the limitations of the two kinds of memory that the subject is assumed to be able to use: trace memory and context memory. Trace memory is the short-term iconic memory of the stimulus and fades rapidly with time. In context memory, the subject codes the stimulus as an imprecise verbal label relative to "perceptual anchors." These perceptual reference points are typically located at the ends of the stimulus continuum, but may also be located elsewhere (e.g., at points along a continuum corresponding to highly overlearned labels, or at boundaries between highly overlearned categories). In single-interval tasks, the subject can use only context memory, and therefore performance is constrained by the limitations of context memory. Subjects in roving-discrimination tasks are assumed to use the combination of trace and context memory that optimizes performance.

The trace-context theory thus predicts an ordering of performance across tasks for stimuli equally spaced along the physical continuum. Performance should be best in fixed discrimination, where there are no memory limitations, should be next best in roving discrimination, where subjects can use the optimum combination of trace and context memory, and will in general be poorest in single-interval tasks, where only context memory can be used. Only for conditions where context memory is much more efficient than trace memory will performance in the single-interval task be as good as in roving discrimination; and it can never be better. When the three different types of tasks are applied to simple psychophysical continua such as pure tones of different intensities, the above ordering obtains: resolution is much better for fixed discrimination than for roving discrimination, which is in turn much better than resolution for absolute identification. When Macmillan et al. (1988) applied the tasks to speech continua, they found non-monotonic roving-discrimination functions, and also found that, for certain stop-consonant continua, performance in identification was essentially equivalent to performance in roving discrimination. This result meets the criteria for categorical perception as originally defined and suggests that, for these continua, context memory is very efficient. However, even for these continua, performance is significantly better in fixed discrimination so that, according to this stricter criterion, even these speech tokens are not perceived categorically.

2. Musical Interval Discrimination

The first experiment that used a paired-comparison discrimination task to estimate just-noticeable differences (JNDs) in frequency ratio for musical intervals was that of Houtsma (1968). In a 2AFC task, subjects were asked to judge which of two pure-tone melodic intervals was larger. The first note of each of the intervals composing a trial was randomized to prevent the subjects from basing their judgments on a comparison of the frequencies of the second notes of the intervals. Points on the psychometric function were estimated using a fixed-discrimination paradigm, and the JND was defined as the 75% correct point. The average JND for three subjects at the physical octave was 16 cents, and JNDs for other ratios in the immediate vicinity of the octave were not significantly different. The JNDs at the ratios corresponding to the intervals of the chromatic scale were also determined for one subject, and ranged from 13 to 26 cents.

Burns and Ward (1978) used a similar 2AFC task, but the two stimuli to be discriminated on a given trial were adjacent intervals chosen at random from the set of melodic intervals separated by an equal step size (in cents) over the 300-cent range from 250 to 550 cents. That is, rather than a fixed-discrimination paradigm, it was a roving-discrimination paradigm such as that typically used in speech perception experiments. Identification functions were also obtained for the same set of intervals in a category-scaling task; the categories were the chromatic interval categories appropriate for that range (major second through tritone). The discrimination results, for step sizes of 25, 37.5, and 50 cents, were compared with discrimination functions predicted from identification functions. For some subjects, discrimination was somewhat better than predicted. In general, however, agreement between the obtained and predicted discrimination functions was as good or better than that shown by the most "categorically perceived" speech stimuli, stop consonants, in the various speech perception experiments. Thus, according to the accepted criteria at the time, melodic musical intervals were perceived categorically in this experiment.

Siegel and Siegel (1977b) interpreted the correlation between points along the frequency-ratio continuum where category boundaries in category-scaling identification functions occurred and points where the modal peaks were seen in the magnitude-estimation standard-deviation functions as indicative of categorical perception of melodic intervals. Although this correlation is consistent with the concept of categorical perception, it is not, strictly speaking, a test for categorical perception because these are both single-interval identification tasks.

Zatorre and Halpern (1979) and Zatorre (1983) investigated the identification and discrimination of harmonic musical intervals composed of pure tones, over a 100-cent range from minor third to major third. The 1979 study used a two-category (minor-major) identification task and a three-interval, roving-discrimination paradigm and compared discrimination to predicted discrimination as in Burns and Ward (1978). The 1983 study used a 2AFC, roving-discrimination paradigm and a rating-scale identification paradigm; in this case, d' was calculated for both paradigms and compared. In both studies, a strong category boundary effect was obtained, but discrimination was somewhat better than predicted discrimination. In the case of harmonic intervals, however, there are many possible cues other than interval width or interval quality that the subjects might use to discriminate two intervals. These include beats of mistuned consonances, distortion products, changes in (missing) fundamental pitch, and changes in the pitch of the upper tones (because the frequency of the lower tone of the intervals was not randomized).

The problem of possible extraneous discrimination cues is even more acute when the minor-major third continuum is investigated with pure-tone triads where only the middle tone is varied in frequency. This was the case in the study by Locke and Kellar (1973) and a replication by Howard et al. (1992). In both studies, most of the "musically experienced" listeners showed a strong category boundary effect, but there were often discrimination peaks at other points in the continuum as well. In the limiting case for harmonic intervals, where the intervals are composed of complex tones with many harmonics and the tones are of relatively long duration, subjects can easily distinguish very small deviations from small-integer frequency ratios on the basis of beating between nearly coincident harmonics (Vos, 1982, 1984; Vos & van Vianen, 1985a, 1985b).

In general, only musicians are able reliably to label musical intervals, and only musicians show evidence of categorical perception for musical intervals. Nonmusicians typically show much poorer discrimination performance than possessors of relative pitch and show no evidence of a category boundary effect (Burns & Ward, 1978; Howard et al., 1992; Locke & Kellar, 1973; Siegel & Siegel, 1977a; Zatorre & Halpern, 1983) . However, there are exceptions to these generalities, as discussed in Section III,D,4.

All of the aforementioned studies that specifically compared identification and discrimination of musical intervals used roving-discrimination paradigms. Although a quasi-fixed-discrimination task was also used in the Burns and Ward (1978) study, it was in the form of an adaptive 2AFC paradigm that was used to estimate JNDs for melodic interval discrimination at several points along the continuum, and the results could not be directly compared with the roving discrimination and identification data. Recently, Burns and Campbell (1994) used the methodology derived from trace-context theory to study the perception of melodic intervals composed of complex tones. Quarter-tone-identification functions (see Figure 1) and 2AFC discrimination functions from both fixed- and roving-discrimination paradigms were obtained for intervals separated by 25-cent increments over a one-octave range. The results are shown in Figure 2 in the form of resolution-sensitivity functions from data averaged across four subjects. All of the functions show the peak-trough form (category boundary effect) that typifies categorical perception, and more importantly, resolution sensitivity is, on average, actually better for identification than for either roving discrimination or fixed discrimination. This is also evident in the total resolution sensitivities shown in the first row of Table II.

This result is seemingly inconsistent with trace-context theory, which states that identification resolution can never be better than either roving- or fixed-discrimination resolution, and only in a trivial limiting case (where the continuum range is small, on the order of a JND) is identification resolution equal to fixed-discrimination resolution. The obvious explanation is that, for melodic intervals, fixed discrimination is not free from memory limitations. The process of determining the pitch distance or subjective frequency ratio between two sequential tones is apparently not a basic sensory process, that is, humans do not come equipped with frequency-ratio estimators, but instead involves learning and memory. This result does not therefore necessarily provide a contradiction to the trace-con-

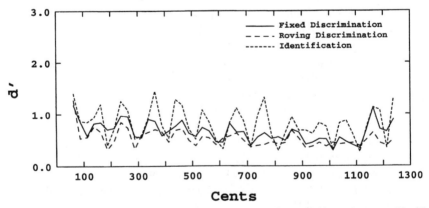

FIGURE 2   Resolution (in d' units) between adjacent melodic musical intervals separated by 25-cent increments for a category-scaling identification task and for fixed and roving discrimination tasks. Results are averaged across four possessors of relative pitch.

TABLE II   Total Sensitivity in d' Units for Resolution in Three Tasks: Identification, Fixed Discrimination, and Roving Discrimination

		Paradigm	
Continuum	Identification	Roving discrimination	Fixed discrimination
Relative pitch	38.7	25.5	32.9
Absolute pitch	33.6	118.3	136.8
Pure-tone intensity	13.0	50.0	98.0

Three continuua are compared: a one-octave range of melodic musical intervals by possessors of relative pitch, a one-octave range of pure-tone frequencies by possessors of absolute pitch, and à 54-dB range of pure-tone intensities. Intensity resolution data is from Braida and Durlach (1988).

text theory. However, the fact remains that it suggests melodic intervals meet the most rigid definition of categorical perception, a definition that is not met by even the most "categorically perceived" speech stimuli: melodic musical intervals apparently must be differentially identified in order to be discriminated.

It was noted earlier that possessors of relative pitch and possessors of absolute pitch have about the same resolution in identification, and both are exceptions to the channel capacity limitations of the 7 ± 2 rule. It is obvious from Table II, however, that absolute pitch is not an exception to the corollary of 7 ± 2, that is, it is not perceived categorically; as with intensity perception, resolution in roving discrimination and fixed discrimination is much better than in roving discrimination. It is also of interest that the average identification sensitivity between chromatic semitone categories (i.e., per 100 cents), on the order of 3 d' units for both relative and absolute pitch, is also roughly the same as the average identification sensitivity between phonemic categories in speech (Macmillan et al., 1988).

Whereas the identification of intervals is certainly a musical task, the discrimination of the "sizes" of two intervals is clearly a very artificial task of little musical relevance. Basically, categorical perception merely shows in a laboratory setting what many researchers in music perception have been aware of for a long time, a phenomenon Francès (1958/1988, pp. 28–30) called "note abstraction": namely, that there is a considerable latitude allowed in the tuning of intervals that will still be considered acceptable and will still carry the appropriate melodic information. In the next section, the perception of intervals in more musical contexts is examined to see if it varies greatly from perception in the sterile laboratory situation represented by the perception of isolated intervals.

D. MUSICAL INTERVAL PERCEPTION IN A MUSICAL CONTEXT

Thus far, only the 12-tone chromatic scale, which provides the tonal material for Western music, has been discussed. However, most Western music is composed and/or played in one of two seven-note subsets of this scale: the diatonic major and minor scales. In addition to specifying a fixed pattern of intervals, or a "tuning system" in the terminology of Dowling and Harwood (1986, chapter 4), these scales also specify hierarchical relationships among the tones composing the scale. The tonic ("C" in the example shown in Table I) is the most important. This combination of a tuning system and hierarchical relationships among the tones constitutes a "modal scale" (Dowling & Harwood, 1986). Although diatonic scales are discussed in Section IV in the context of the origination of scales, most of the consequences of the hierarchical relationships, such as "tonality" and "key," are beyond the scope of this chapter (see, e.g., Krumhansl, 1990; and Chapters 11· and 12, this volume). One aspect of diatonic scales that is relevant to this section, however, is that this hierarchical structure is recognized, even to a certain extent by nonmusicians (Krumhansl, 1990, pp. 22–25), and leads to certain harmonic and melodic expectations, as well as certain tendencies, such as "attractions" to certain notes, which have been shown to lead to the expansion or contraction of intervals containing these notes in played music (see Section IV,C). Among the obvious questions regarding perception of tuning in a musical context is whether this recognition of diatonic structure also affects the accuracy with which intervals are recognized and discriminated.

1. Adjustment of Melodic Intervals

Rakowski (1990) presented preliminary results for the adjustment of intervals in a melodic context. Subjects adjusted the interval that comprised the first two notes of one of six four-note melodies. The results suggested that the variability was slightly smaller than the variability for adjustments of isolated intervals (although these comparisons were between different groups of subjects), and that the mean values of the adjustments were slightly affected by "harmonic tension" and melodic contour.

2. Absolute Identification of Melodic Intervals

Several studies have compared error rates for melodic intervals in isolation and in musical context for groups of subjects whose relative-pitch skills were such that they were not able to recognize all of the chromatic intervals with perfect accuracy. Taylor (1971) measured error rates for identification of the 25 ascending and descending chromatic intervals (including unison) in isolation and in the context of four- or six-note melodies. Error rates were higher in context for all intervals and were not significantly correlated with the subjectively-judged tonal strength of the melodies. Shatzkin (1981) measured the accuracy of chromatic interval identification in isolation and in several contexts: one in which a preceding tone formed either a minor or a major third with the first note of the judged interval; and one in which a succeeding tone formed either a minor or major third with the second note of the judged interval. A later study (Shatzkin, 1984) used preceding and succeeding tones that formed either major second or a fourth with the first or second tone. As in the Taylor study, interval recognition was in general significantly poorer in context, but for specific intervals in specific contexts, for example, when the three tones formed a major or minor triad, or spanned an octave, recognition was sometimes slightly better in context.

One of the more intriguing cases of a context effect was reported by Keefe, Burns, and Nguyen (1991). In a category-scaling task (such as those described in Section III,B,3), a Vietnamese musician was unable reliably to categorize isolated intervals into modal-scale variants of intervals that he had previously tuned on a zither-like instrument. However, in a paradigm where the subject was asked to "contemplate the sentiment associated with a particular scale" and then asked to rate how well isolated intervals fit that scale, there was evidence that the subject was able to distinguish some of the interval variants among modal scales.

3. Detection of Mistuned Intervals in Melodies

Although several authors have stated that it is easier to detect the mistuning of an isolated interval than an interval in melodic context (e.g. Francès, 1958/1988, p. 41), the published experiments seem only to deal with detection of mistunings as a function of context manipulation, without a direct comparison to detection of mistunings in isolated intervals by the same subjects. For example, Francès (1958/ 1988, pp. 55–63) measured the detection of the mistuning (by either -12 or -22 cents) of particular notes in two short compositions. These compositions were constructed such that in the first composition the tendencies inherent in the musical structure for expansion or contraction of the intervals containing the mistuned notes were in the same direction as the mistunings, whereas in the second composition the mistunings were in the opposite direction. The subjects were significantly more accurate at detecting the mistunings in the second composition. In a much simpler version of this type of experiment, Umemoto (1990) showed that both musically experienced and musically inexperienced subjects were better at detecting a quarter-tone mistuning of one note in a six-note melody when the melody was tonal (i.e., involving only tones from one of the diatonic scales) than when it was atonal.

Using a 2AFC adaptive procedure, Lynch, Eilers, Oller, Urbano, and Wilson (1991) obtained estimates of JNDs for mistuning of one note of a seven-note melody. The melodies comprised notes from one of three scales: diatonic major, diatonic minor, and a Javanese scale. For experienced musicians, the JND values were quite small (on the order of 10 cents) compared with the values for isolated intervals obtained in other experiments (see Section III,C) and did not depend on the scale context. This was true both for the interval of a fifth, which was fixed serially in the melody, and apparently also for JNDs averaged over seconds, thirds, fourths and fifths (for the Western scales), where the serial position of the mistuned intervals was randomly varied. For less experienced musicians and nonmusicians, the JNDs were significantly worse in the context of the Javanese scale. However, because the absolute frequencies of the notes composing the melodies were not randomized (either within or between trials) for any of the conditions, the extent to which subjects were able to rely on frequency discrimination cues rather than interval discrimination cues is unclear.

4. Discrimination of Intervals and Categorical Perception

Wapnick et al. (1982) used the identification and roving discrimination paradigms typically associated with categorical perception experiments to examine the perception of the set of melodic intervals separated by 20-cent steps over the range from 480 to 720 cents. The intervals were presented both in isolation and as the 9th and 10th notes of a 10-note melody. The identification paradigm was a category-scaling task where the categories for each of the chromatic interval categories appropriate for the continuum (fourth, tritone, and fifth) could be further labeled as : "flat", "in tune," or "sharp." The authors asserted that the subjects were more accurate in the labeling task in the melodic context situation, but their measure of labeling accuracy was based on correct labeling relative to equal temperament rather than on consistency, and it is not clear that the difference was not primarily due to a propensity for the subjects to use different response categories in the two conditions. The discrimination paradigm used a variation of a same/different task ("same," "smaller," "larger") where subjects compared the intervals formed by the last two notes of two melodies. Rather than using an unbiased metric (such as d'), the authors compared performance in isolation and in context separately for "correct same" and "correct different" situations. Performance was better, although not significantly so, for the isolated intervals in the "same" situation and was significantly better for the in-context intervals in the "different" situation. Again, it is not clear whether this result simply represents a difference in subjects' response proclivities between the two situations rather than a true difference in discrimination performance. There was a strong category boundary effect for both the isolated and in-context intervals, so in that sense, the intervals were perceived categorically. However, the authors did not specifically compare discrimination and identification resolution.

Tsuzaki (1991) also used a same/larger/smaller discrimination task to assess the effects of context on melodic interval discrimination. In this case, the two melodic intervals to be discriminated were either isolated, or followed a tonal (a diatonic major scale from C_4 to C_5) or an atonal (chromatic scale from F_4 to C_5) context. The standard interval of the pair was either 100, 150, or 200 cents, and started on either B_4 or C_5. The comparison interval always started on the second note of the standard interval, and its size ranged from −80 cents below to +80 cents (in 20-cent steps) above the size of standard interval. Thus, depending on the size of the standard interval and its starting note, the various notes composing the intervals would in some cases belong to the preceding scales, but in other cases would not. Unfortunately, the metric used to measure discrimination in this experiment also does not separate sensitivity from response bias, so it is difficult to infer exactly what was changing as a result of the various contextual changes. It is clear, however that the context had a significant effect on both the "discriminability" (as measured by the author's "dispersion metric") and on the subjective sizes of the intervals (as measured by the points of subjective equality) and that these effects can be in either direction relative to discrimination of isolated intervals.

In a series of studies Fyk (1982a, 1982b) investigated the perception of mistunings from equal temperament in a melodic context and, for a few intervals, in isolation. The paradigm was similar to the discrimination paradigm used by Wapnick et al. (1982): subjects compared intervals that were composed of the last two notes of a short (two-bar) melody. In this case, however, the discrimination task was a true same/different task; the last interval in the second melody was either the same as, or mistuned from, the last interval in the first melody, and the subjects task was to indicate whether they detected a mistuning. Melodies were constructed such that the intervals were subjected to different harmonic and melodic tendencies, and groups of subjects with different levels of musical training were tested. The author did not use a bias-free discrimination metric, but attempted to correct the data for response bias by defining the JND for mistuning as the 50% point from the false-alarm value for no mistuning to the value where the "I can hear a difference" responses were 100%. The difference in cents between the JNDs for positive and negative mistuning was taken as the "tolerance zone" for mistuning. Not surprisingly, there were large differences in this tolerance zone as a function of different intervals, melodic contexts, and degree of musical training. A common finding was a large asymmetry (as denoted by the midpoint of the tolerance zone) for detecting positive versus negative mistuning as a function of melodic context. Unfortunately, only three intervals were measured both in isolation and in melodic context, and thus could be directly compared: unison, ascending minor second, and descending major second. Although the subjects with less musical training in most cases had wider tolerance zones for the isolated intervals, the results for intervals in isolation and in context were virtually identical for the highly trained subjects.

Overall, the results from experiments on the perception of intervals in a musical context, while sparse and somewhat messy, do not appear to warrant any major changes to the conclusions reached on the basis of results of experiments on the perception of intervals in isolation. Although context clearly can have an effect on the subjective size of intervals, intervals apparently still are perceived in a categorical manner in context, and the accuracy of identification and discrimination does not appear to be markedly different in context or in isolation. This interpretation of the data is also consistent with the results of measurements of intonation in performance (see Section IV,C).

Although these conclusions apply to experiments using trained musicians, context can have a profound effect on the performance of untrained listeners. Smith et al. (1994) showed that instructing musically naive listeners to associate intervals with the first two notes of well-known songs improves their performance in both identification and discrimination tasks, to an extent that a few individuals show performance comparable to that of trained musicians, including highly consistent labeling and a category-boundary effect in discrimination.

E. SOME OTHER ASPECTS OF MUSICAL INTERVAL
PERCEPTION

1. The Upper Frequency Limit for Relative and Absolute Pitch

One viewpoint in psychoacoustics is that the "musical pitch," operationally defined as the capacity for conveying melodic information, is coded in the auditory system by temporal information, that is, by the phase-locked firing of auditory neurons to the stimulus waveform (e.g., van Noorden, 1982; Moore, 1989, p. 165) This information is assumed to be distinct from the information coded by "place," that is, by the average firing rate of neurons tuned to specific frequencies by virtue of the mechanical tuning of the inner ear. It is assumed that, although the percept associated with this latter information can be ordinally scaled from "low to high," it does not carry melodic information. Evidence for this viewpoint comes from experiments that show that stimuli such as band-pass-filtered white noise, which would be expected to have minimal temporal cues, can be scaled from "low" to "high" but do not carry melodic information (e.g., Houtsma, 1984). Other evidence comes from alleged upper frequency limits for relative and absolute pitch and their correlation with the upper limit on phase locking by auditory neurons, which, based primarily on data from cats (e.g., Johnson, 1978), is on the order of 5 kHz. Attneave and Olson (1971), in their experiment on transposition of simple melodies, found an "abrupt" upper limit at about 5 kHz in their two subjects. Semal and Demany (1990), in an experiment in which 10 subjects adjusted the overall frequency of a melodic minor third interval until the upper tone was "just above the limit of musical pitch" found a "fuzzy" boundary in the region of 5 kHz. Upper limits for perception of absolute pitch are in rough agreement. Almost all possessors of absolute pitch report a "chroma fixation" above about 4 kHz, such that all tones appear to have the same pitch class, or the same relative position within an octave (e.g., Bachem, 1948; Ward, 1954).

However, there are exceptions to this 4–5 kHz upper limit both for relative pitch and for absolute pitch. For example, although seven of nine subjects in Ward's (1954) octave-adjustment task were unable to make consistent octave judgments when the lower tone was above 2700 Hz, two of the subjects "were able to make reliable settings even beyond 'octave above 5000 Hz.'" Burns and Feth (1983) showed that their three subjects consistently performed above chance in melody recognition and melodic dictation tasks for tones between 10 and 16 kHz. These subjects were also able to adjust melodic intervals from minor second through fifth for a reference frequency of 10 kHz, albeit with standard deviations from 3.5 to 5.5 times those obtained for adjustments with a reference frequency of 1 kHz. Similarly, Ohgushi and Hatoh (1992) showed that some absolute pitch possessors are able to identify some notes at better than chance level performance for frequencies up to 16 kHz. These results are not necessarily inconsistent with the hypothesis of temporal coding of musical pitch, however. Although the upper limit of phase locking is usually given as 5 kHz, more recent data (Teich, Khanna, & Guiney, 1993) suggest that there is some phase-locking information up to 18 kHz. Also, there are clear interspecies differences. The barn owl, for example, would be perpetually peckish if the upper limit of phase locking in his auditory nerve was 5 kHz, because his (dinner) localization ability depends on the use of temporal information at the brainstem level for frequencies up to at least 9 kHz (e.g., Moiseff & Konishi, 1981). Thus, although it appears that there is an indistinct upper limit to the ability to make relative pitch judgments, which may be based on the availability of temporal information, there is large individual variability in this limit, and this variability is based, at least in part, on the individual's experience with high-frequency tones (Ward, 1954). It should also be noted, however, that other psychophysical phenomena that are assumed to depend on temporal coding (e.g., Hartmann, McAdams, & Smith, 1990; Plomp, 1967) have upper frequency limits much lower than 4 kHz.

2. Effects of Absolute Pitch on Relative Pitch Judgments

As has been emphasized thus far, relative pitch is an ability that is closely connected to the processing of melodic information in music and is possessed by most trained musicians. Absolute pitch, on the other hand, is a relatively rare ability, and its utility for most musical situations is debatable. The question addressed in this section is whether absolute pitch overrides relative pitch in situations in which the task may be accomplished using either ability. Three studies have directly addressed this question. Benguerel and Westdal (1991) had 10 subjects with absolute pitch and 5 subjects with relative pitch categorize melodic intervals, where the interval sizes varied in 20-cent steps and the reference tones for the intervals were similarly mistuned relative to standard (A = 440 Hz) tuning. It was assumed that if subjects were using a relative pitch strategy, they would round the interval to the nearest category (this essentially assumed ideal categorical perception, with category boundaries at the equitempered quarter tones). If, on the other hand, absolute pitch subjects used a strategy in which they first identified separately the tones composing the interval, rounded to the nearest chromatic semitone category, and estimated the interval on this basis, they would sometimes make "rounding errors" and incorrectly identify certain mistuned intervals. Analyzed on the basis of these assumptions, the results indicated that only 1 of the 10 absolute pitch subjects appeared to use the absolute pitch strategy in making relative pitch judgments, and even he did not use the strategy consistently.

Miyazaki (1992, 1993, 1995), on the other hand, has presented evidence that suggests that in relative pitch tasks, many absolute pitch possessors do in fact use strategies based on absolute pitch. In the first study (Miyazaki, 1992), 11 subjects with absolute pitch and 4 subjects with relative pitch performed a category scaling task wherein they identified intervals (either in tune, or mistuned by ±16 or 30 cents re equal temperament) with "in tune," "sharp," or "flat" chromatic semitone categories. The reference tone was either C_4 or $C_4 + 50$ cents. The relative pitch subjects showed no difference in either identification accuracy (re equal temperament) or response time for the two reference conditions, whereas absolute pitch subjects showed longer response times and less accurate identification for the mistuned reference condition. Owing to the small number of subjects, it was not possible to compare the two subject groups directly.

In the second study (Miyazaki, 1993), three groups of absolute pitch possessors ("precise," "partial," and "imprecise," containing 15, 16, and 9 subjects, respectively) and one group of 15 relative pitch possessors performed a category-scaling task. Subjects identified melodic intervals, which varied over the range from 260 to 540 cents in 20-cent increments, using the categories minor third, major third, or fourth. There were three reference-tone conditions: C_4, $F\sharp_4$, and E_4 – 50 cents, preceded in each case by an appropriate chord cadence to set a key context. Identification accuracy was based on equitempered tuning with the category boundaries at the quarter tones, for example, the intervals from 360 to 440 cents were considered "correct" major thirds. Response time was also recorded. There was no significant difference in response accuracy among the groups for the "C" reference condition, although the relative pitch group did have significantly shorter response times. However, there was a significant decrease in identification accuracy for the other two reference conditions, and an increase in response times for all of the absolute pitch groups, but no decrease in accuracy, or increase in response times, for the relative pitch group. There were large intersubject differences in the absolute pitch group, with the identification performance for some subjects in the F♯ and E– conditions deteriorating to the extent where it resembled that of nonmusicians in the Siegel and Siegel (1977a) experiment.

The third study (Miyazaki, 1995) was essentially a replication of the previous experiment, but used a control subject group with good relative pitch, but without absolute pitch, in addition to an absolute pitch group. For the subjects with no absolute pitch, identification accuracy and response times did not differ significantly among the reference conditions. For the absolute pitch group, however, performance was similar to the that of the no-absolute-pitch group only for the C reference condition; for the E– and F♯ reference conditions, identification accuracy was significantly poorer, and response times were significantly longer. Thus, there is evidence that, for at least some possessors, absolute pitch overrides relative pitch, even in situations where its use is detrimental to performance.

3. Learning of Relative Pitch

Previous sections have pointed out similarities among relative pitch, absolute pitch, and speech phonemes, such as in accuracy of identification along a unidimensional continuum, and in separation of category prototypes along a continuum. One area where these percepts differ markedly, however, is in learning. Both absolute pitch and phonemes of a particular language must apparently be learned in childhood. It is virtually impossible for adults to learn absolute pitch (see Chapter 8, this volume) or to learn to discriminate and identify the phonemes of a foreign language that are not also present in their native language (e.g., Flege, 1988). Relative pitch, however, is learned fairly easily. As mentioned earlier, courses in ear training are required as part of most music curricula, and, given the number of music majors who graduate each year, the failure rate in these courses is presumably not inordinately high.

The probable reason for the relative ease with which relative pitch can be learned is the obvious fact that, as with the sounds of their native language, adults have been exposed to the intervallic content of the music of their culture. As noted earlier, adults from Western cultures are, in particular, familiar with the intervals and hierarchical structure of the diatonic scale. Developmental evidence suggests that this familiarity is acquired by fifth-grade level even in children who have not had explicit musical training (Speer & Meeks, 1985), and that by about 8 years of age Western children have acquired a sense of the correct intervals in their music (see Chapter 15, this volume). However, children typically are not reinforced with label names for the intervals.

At least two pieces of circumstantial evidence support this view. The first is that the ordering of intervals' "ease of learning" roughly follows a combination of the diatonic scale hierarchy and the frequency of occurrence of intervals in melodies (Jeffries, 1967, 1970; Vos & Troost, 1989). The second is that one of the common pedagogical techniques in ear training classes is to have the students relate the interval to the first two notes of a well-known song (thankfully, Leonard Bernstein finally provided an exemplar, "Maria" from *West Side Story*, for use of this technique with the dreaded tritone). More formal evidence for this view comes from the Smith et al. (1994) experiment discussed in Section III,D,4.

4. Confusions and Similarities Among Intervals

One possible consequence of the fact that musical listeners have acquired a knowledge of the diatonic scale structure is that judgments of interval similarity may not be based simply on a direct relationship between interval width and similarity. For example, on the basis of this knowledge it might be expected that [in the terminology of Balzano, 1982a)] scale-step equivalents (e.g., major and minor seconds) would be more similar than non-scale-step equivalents also a semitone difference in width (e.g., major second and minor third). Likewise, intervals with the same pitch class difference (i.e., equal distances from the tonic or octave, such as minor thirds and major sixths) would be more similar. These predictions have been tested by two methods. The first involves observing confusion errors in interval identification experiments, where performance was degraded by using relatively untrained musicians (Killam et al., 1975), by embedding the intervals in timbrally complex musical context (Balzano, 1982b), or by shortening the durations of the intervals (Plomp et al., 1973). The second method measures response times in interval-identification tasks (Balzano, 1982a, 1982b).

The primary identification confusions were in terms of interval width, but scale-step-equivalency confusions were more prevalent than other semitone-based confusions, both for pure- and complex-tone harmonic intervals (Killam et al., 1975; Plomp et al., 1973) and for complex-tone melodic intervals (Killam et al., 1975; Balzano, 1982b). There was also limited evidence for pitch class-distance confusions in the results for the harmonic intervals and in fourth/fifth confusions for the melodic intervals in the Killam et al. (1975) study. Balzano (1982a, 1982b) measured response times for a task where subjects were visually given the name of one interval, then heard a second interval played. Subjects were then asked to indicate whether the second interval was the same as, or different from, the visual foil. The assumption is that the response time is monotonically related to the "confusability" of the two intervals. Overall, response time was proportional to the distance between the two intervals, but the response time for scale-step-equivalent intervals was significantly longer than for nonscale-step intervals separated by a semitone, for both (pure-tone) melodic and harmonic intervals. In another version of this experiment, Balzano (1982a) compared response times for correct "same" judgments of intervals to response times for correct "same" judgments where the subjects had to indicate only if the played interval was a member of a scale-step-equivalent category (e.g., "either a minor or a major third"). Counterintuitively, but in keeping with the concept that the scale-step category is more basic than the semitone category, response times were actually faster for the two-category (i.e., scale-step) identification than for the semitone identification. Finally, there was also some evidence for pitch class-distance confusability in the "different" response time measurements for harmonic intervals, but not for melodic intervals.

IV. NATURAL INTERVALS AND SCALES

A. NATURAL INTERVALS AND THEIR POSSIBLE BASIS

Given the assumption that practical music is limited to a relatively small set of discrete pitch relationships, how are the specific values of these relationships chosen? That is, are there "natural" frequency ratios inherent in the manner in which the auditory system processes tonal stimuli that are perceptually salient or unique and, as such, define the intervals of the scale? According to traditional Western music theory, such natural intervals do exist. They are associated with the concept of consonance (and its inverse, dissonance) and are defined by small-integer frequency ratios. For example, the ratio 2:1 (octave) is the most consonant interval, the ratio 3:2 (fifth) is the next most consonant, and so on. Consonance, in general, decreases with increasing ratio complexity (large-integer ratios). The concept of consonance, however, is not precisely defined in music theory. Basically, it is associated with how well two or more simultaneously played tones fit together musically. The origin of the concept of consonance in terms of small-integer ratios is usually attributed to the Greek scholar Pythagoras, although the preference of the ancient Greeks for small-integer ratios was probably based as much on numerology as on psychophysics (see Hunt, 1992, pp. 10–18, for a complete discussion of this issue).

There are essentially three current explanations of the basis of consonance and of its association with small-integer frequency ratios, although these explanations are not totally independent. The first, and probably the most widely cited explanation, is based on the fact that most tones in music and in voiced speech are complex periodic tones whose partials are harmonically related (at least approximately) to the fundamental. For simultaneously presented harmonic complex tones whose fundamental frequencies are related by small-integer ratios, relatively more of the harmonics of the tones, as well as the nonlinear distortion products resulting from interaction between harmonics, will coincide in frequency. For example, with a ratio of 3:2, half of the harmonics of the upper tone will coincide exactly with those of the lower tone, and the others will lie halfway between. However, if the ratio is more complex, such as 10:9, or if it is slightly mistuned from a simple ratio, there will be many nearly coinciding harmonics that will interact to create a sensation of beating or roughness. This sensation is presumed to be related to dissonance, an explanation usually attributed to Helmholtz (1877/ 1954). Terhardt (e.g.,1984) calls the percept engendered by interfering partials "sensory dissonance," and distinguishes its inverse, "sensory consonance" from a second component of consonance that he calls "harmony" (see following paragraphs).

The second explanation for consonance is based on the manner in which the auditory system processes complex tones. The ear appears to "expect" complex tones to be harmonic. That is, complex tones whose partials are exact harmonics of a fundamental frequency in the range from roughly 50 to 600 Hz are generally heard as fused, unitary percepts with a single, albeit somewhat ambiguous, pitch. To the extent that partials are mistuned from exact harmonic ratios, they are heard out as separate entities (e.g., Hartmann et al., 1990), although other factors such as coherent frequency or amplitude modulation can, to a certain extent, fuse inharmonic complex tones (e.g., McAdams, 1983). Current models of complex-tone pitch perception are, in essence, pattern-matching models. These models assume that the auditory system first analyzes the complex tone into its component frequencies, then either matches these frequencies to a best-fit exact-harmonic template and assigns the pitch of the complex tone to approximately the fundamental frequency of the harmonic template (e.g., Gerson & Goldstein, 1978), or that it looks for matches among the subharmonics of the component frequencies (Terhardt, 1974). This predilection of the ear for tones with harmonically related partials is obviously suggestive relative to the use of small-integer frequency ratios in music.

The most extensive explanation of consonance based on the ear's preference for harmonically related tones is that of Terhardt (e.g., 1984). As distinguished from sensory consonance, "harmony" includes the affinity of tones related by an octave (2:1), fourth (4:3), and fifth (3:2), the so-called perfect consonances, and a resultant inherent appreciation of their interval qualities, for example, "fifthness" (Terhardt, 1988). This affinity is a consequence of the ambiguity of fundamental pitch estimates by the harmonic-template-matching procedure that produces, in addition to the primary estimate at the fundamental frequency of the tone, estimates at other frequencies, most of which are related by the ratios of octave, fourth, or fifth to the fundamental. Thus the overall pattern of pitch estimates will be similar for tones related by these frequency ratios. Harmony also includes an explanation of the "root" of chords whose component tones are in small-integer relationships, because the pattern-matching pitch processor also estimates the fundamental frequency of the overall complex tone composed of the complex tones constituting the chord. It should be emphasized, however, that although Terhardt's concept of harmony originates in the ear's predilection for exact harmonic relationships, it does not require exact small-integer relationships in musical practice, even for the octave, fourth, and fifth, because it relies on what are, to a certain extent, inexact and distorted templates of these intervals stored in subconscious memory.

The third explanation of consonance is based on the assumption that the brain prefers combinations of frequencies whose neural-firing patterns contain a common periodicity (e.g., Boomsliter & Creel, 1961; Meyer, 1898; Roederer, 1973, pp. 145-149). As noted earlier, one viewpoint holds that the pitch of pure tones is mediated by the temporal information in the phase-locked firing of auditory neurons. The time interval between firings corresponds to the period, or to multiples of the period, of the pure tone. Therefore, neural firing patterns for tones whose frequencies are related by small-integer frequency ratios will contain common periodicities; or equivalently, a mechanism looking at coincidences in firings across neurons will find more coincidences when the neurons are excited by frequencies related by small-integer ratios. Several of the pattern-matching complex-tone pitch models explicitly use such mechanisms (e.g., Moore, 1989, pp. 183–187; Srulovicz & Goldstein, 1983), and to this extent, this explanation is equivalent to some parts of Terhardt's harmony theory. The most detailed model of consonance and scale derivation based on periodicities in neural firings is that of Patterson (1986).

The explanations for small-integer-ratio consonance based on either sensory consonance or on common neural periodicities assume simultaneously presented tones. The argument is often made that because scales containing these natural intervals predate harmony and polyphony, explanations of scale development based on simultaneous presentation of tones are inappropriate. This argument is somewhat questionable because accompaniment in parallel octaves and fifths, as well as other intervals, is prevalent in many tribal music systems (see e.g., Nettl, 1956; Sachs & Kunst, 1962). In any case, both explanations have been extended to melodic intervals. The sensory-consonance explanation has been extended via the suggestion (and we are not making this up) that most early music was probably played in highly reverberant caves, thus providing pseudosimultaneous presentation of the complex tones (e.g., Wood, 1961, p. 181). Similarly, the neural-pattern explanation has been extended to melodic intervals by assuming some sort of "neural reverberation" (Boomsliter & Creel, 1971; Roederer, 1973, pp. 145–149). However, little hard evidence is available that can back up these primarily speculative extensions.

B. NATURAL SCALES AND TEMPERAMENT

Although numerous versions of the natural scale are based on these natural intervals, two general forms are usually distinguished. One is the scale of just intonation (JI), in which the scale elements within an octave are determined, in essence, by choosing the smallest possible whole-number frequency ratios relative to the tonic (i.e., the most consonant intervals, for example: 3:2 [fifth], 4:3 [fourth], 5:4 [major third], etc.). This process is fairly straightforward for choosing the notes of the diatonic major scale (do, re, me, fa, sol, la, ti, do; see Table I). However, attempts to fill in the remainder of the octave to give 12 approximately equally spaced steps result in fairly complex frequency ratios, and there are a number of alternative candidates for some of the intervals. Although JI is the scale most often cited as being *the* natural scale, it is but one version of the many "natural" scales originally proposed by Ptolemy (Hunt, 1992, p. 31) and its importance is probably to some extent a consequence of the development of harmony in Western music, especially the prominence of the major triad. One of the characteristics of JI is that the tonic, dominant, and subdominant triads (do, mi, sol; sol, ti, re; and fa, la, do—respectively) are all tuned in the exact ratios of 4:5:6.

The other prominent form of the natural scale, and the historically precedent one (allegedly devised by Pythagoras himself), is Pythagorean tuning (PT). PT is an attempt to construct a scale using only the so-called perfect consonances (2:1, octave; 3:2, fifth; and 4:3, fourth). This is accomplished by cyclic application of the fifth (and fourth) and the reduction of the resultant intervals to within an octave: for example, $(3/2 \times 3/2) = 9/4 = (2/1 \times 9/8)$ (major second), $(9/8 \times 3/2) = 27/16$ (major sixth), etc. If this process is repeated 12 times, the approximate original starting point is reached. However, because powers of three can never be an exact multiple of two, there is a discrepancy. For example, if the original starting note is C, the resultant is the enharmonic equivalent of C, B$\sharp$, which is sharp by a Pythagorean comma (24 cents). One may avoid this by proceeding downward in fifths (or equivalently, upward in fourths) for half of the intervals, thereby introducing the discrepancy at the tritone (F$\sharp$ = 612 cents or G$\flat$ = 588 cents). It can be seen in Table I that the main differences between JI and PT are in the major and minor thirds and major and minor sixths.

If the ratios between adjacent notes in the diatonic JI or PT scales are calculated (see Table I), it will be seen that there are three values for JI (two whole tones 10/9 and 9/8 and a semitone 16/15) and two values for PT (a whole tone of 9/8 and a semitone 256/242, which is not half the whole tone). This is one manifestation of the primary problem with either of the natural tuning systems: key modulations on fixed-tuning instruments require an inordinate number of tones per octave (at least 30 in the case of JI) because the same note will have a number of different values depending on the key in which it is derived. For example, if D in the diatonic just scale of C major is used as a keynote to derive a new diatonic major scale, the notes E and A in the new scale will have frequencies slightly different from the notes E and A in the old scale. In an effort to reduce these discrepancies, various temperament systems, that is, methods of adjusting the natural intervals, (e.g., "mean-tone tuning") were devised. Although some of these temperings still find limited use in organ and synthesizer tuning, systems other than equal temperament are primarily of historical interest and are not discussed here. (For a review of various temperings and tunings, see Barbour, 1951).

The scale of equal temperament, discussed in Section I, which divides the octave into 12 equal steps, was devised as a compromise that would permit modulation in any key but keep fifths, fourths, and thirds as close as possible to small-integer ratio values. Many musicians claim that equal temperament has destroyed the "inherent beauty" of the natural scales and that performers unencumbered by fixed tuning will tend to play in one of the natural scales. Some of the evidence regarding the perception and production of natural intervals and scales is reviewed in the next section.

C. EXPERIMENTAL EVIDENCE RELEVANT TO NATURAL INTERVALS AND SCALES

1. Sensory Consonance and Dissonance

Because the degree of consonance of musical intervals is defined by music theory in terms of the simplicity of frequency ratios, any attempt to rate consonance or dissonance of intervals by musicians who are able to identify the intervals is obviously subject to bias. Therefore, attempts to determine the physical parameters corresponding to the sensations of consonance and dissonance have often used musically naive observers. For example, van de Geer, Levelt, and Plomp (1962) used a semantic comparison task to show that naive observers use the term consonance synonymously with beautiful or euphonious, and conversely, the term dissonance synonymously with ugly or noneuphonious. Using such synonyms when necessary, Kameoka and Kuriyagawa (1969a, 1969b) and Plomp and Levelt (1965) asked musically naive observers to scale the consonance of simultaneous stimulus pairs composed of both pure and complex tones. Both groups of experimenters found that, for pure tones, consonance first decreases as a function of frequency-ratio magnitude, reaching a minimum at a value corresponding roughly to one quarter of a critical band (roughly one semitone for frequencies above 500 Hz) and then increases as a function of increasing frequency ratio. For complex tones, the consonance vs. frequency-ratio function shows, in addition, maxima at small-integer frequency ratios, that is, at those ratios dictated as consonant by music theory. The ordering of the absolute values of consonance at these maxima however, does not follow exactly the ordering of ratio simplicity. The results of a nonverbal triadic-comparison technique (Levelt, van de Geer & Plomp, 1966) also showed that subjects order both pure- and complex-tone ratios in terms of ratio magnitude, but that complex tones are additionally ordered along a dimension corresponding to simplicity of frequency ratio.

Other experimenters have shown that, for simultaneous pure tones, the term dissonance is essentially synonymous with perceived "roughness" (Plomp &

Steeneken, 1968; Terhardt, 1974, 1978), a quality that is highly correlated with the degree of amplitude modulation of the stimulus (Terhardt, 1978). The roughness of simultaneous pure-tone pairs as a function of frequency separation is limited at low frequencies by the frequency resolution of the ear and at high frequencies by the limits of the limits of the ear's ability to follow rapid amplitude modulations (Terhardt, 1978). Kameoka and Kuriyagawa (1969b) have formulated a dissonance perception model wherein the dissonance of a complex-tone interval can be predicted with fairly high accuracy by adding the "dissonance intensities" associated with the interaction of individual partials of the two tones, although Vos (1986) has suggested that some modifications to this model are necessary. Geary (1980), Pierce (1966), and Slaymaker (1970) have demonstrated that these considerations also predict the relative dissonance of inharmonic complex tones. These results are in essential agreement with Helmholtz's original hypothesis regarding the basis of consonance and dissonance.

Studies on the rating of intervals in terms of "purity," "acceptability," or "mistuning" (Hall & Hess, 1984; Vos, 1986) show that, for simultaneous intervals composed of two complex tones with many harmonics, subjects can easily distinguish on this basis intervals mistuned from exact small-integer ratios by as little as ±2 cents, and that the relevant cues result from interactions between nearly coinciding harmonics (Vos, 1986; see also Vos, 1982, 1984; Vos & van Vianen, 1985a, 1985b). However, when the intervals are composed of low-level simultaneous pure tones, or successive pure tones, deviations from just intonation of up to ±50 cents cannot be reliably distinguished. This result is consistent with the adjustment and category scaling data for melodic intervals cited in Section III.

The studies cited in this section clearly show that for harmonic intervals composed of complex tones with rich spectra, such as those produced by most musical instruments, subjects in a laboratory situation can use the beats and roughness associated with sensory dissonance to distinguish intervals that are mistuned from small-integer frequency ratios, that is, from just intonation.

2. Intonation in Performance

As noted earlier, proponents of natural scales claim that musicians unencumbered by fixed-tuning instruments will tend to play in one of the natural scales. Therefore measurements of intonation in performance are an obvious source for evidence regarding the natural-scale question. Interpretation of such measurements is not straightforward, however. A large number of factors are confounded with the desired measures, namely the values of the fundamental frequencies corresponding to the intervals that the musician is trying to produce and the consistency with which the musician is able to produce them. First, there is the problem of short-term variability. Some measurement techniques have sufficient time resolution to track the variations in fundamental frequency over the duration of the note; these include counting the individual periods in an oscillographic trace (e.g.,. Francès, 1958/1988, pp. 19–27), and computer-based pitch-tracking algorithms (e.g., Sundberg, 1982). Such measures show that significant short-term variability exists. Large variations are often seen at the beginning and the end of notes, due to transitions while the musician searches for the desired pitch, and/or to the physics of the pitch-control mechanism. However, even when the tones are truncated to a "steady state" portion, considerable variability remains. For example, Francès (1958/1988) reports a mean range of 104 cents and a mean interquartile range of 38 cents in the "instantaneous" frequencies of the 46 notes of a melody sung by three experienced singers whose intonation was judged to be "simple and in tune." A portion of this variability is of course due to the combination of variability in the musician's pitch percept and variability in the musician's motor-control mechanism. However, in Western music at least, a large amount is often due to purposefully induced variability, vibrato, which is an approximately periodic variation in frequency with an average extent of about 40 cents and an average period of about 6 Hz. Because of these short-term variations in frequency, studies of intonation in performance must use some average value of fundamental frequency to represent each note, and the manner in which this average is obtained is not always consistent across studies.

Another factor that must be considered in interpreting these studies is the musical setting. For example, is the musician is performing solo, with harmonic accompaniment where the accompaniment does not include the same notes the musician is playing, or in an ensemble situation where other musicians may be playing the same note? Finally, whereas some studies judge interval measurements relative to the keynote (for example, in a composition in the key of C, the fifth would be measured as the distance between any occurrence of the note G and the keynote C), other studies consider a fifth to be any interval of a fifth between two consecutive notes.

Ward (1970) summarized the results of four intonation studies: Greene (1937), who analyzed 11 solo violin performances by three violinists; Nickerson (1948), who analyzed both solo and ensemble performances by members of six string quartets; Mason (1960), who analyzed solo and ensemble performances of members of two woodwind quartets; and Shackford (1961, 1962a, 1962b), who analyzed ensemble performances of three string trios. Shackford analyzed both harmonic and melodic intervals, whereas the other studies analyzed only melodic intervals. In the Mason and Nickerson studies, the intervals were measured relative to the keynote, whereas in the Greene and Shackford studies they were measured between consecutive notes. Despite the differences in measurement techniques and context, the results were fairly consistent across studies. They show a fairly large variability for the tuning of a given interval in a given performance (ranges of up to 78 cents, interquartile values of up to 38 cents). There was no consistent propensity for either just or Pythagorean intervals; the general tendency was to play all intervals slightly sharp relative to equal temperament, with the exception of the minor second, which was substantially flattened. There does not appear to be a significant difference in variability, or in average interval sizes, between solo and ensemble situations in the studies that measured both. Two other studies are relevant to the question of intonation variability in ensemble and solo situations. Ternstrom and Sundberg (1988) measured the fundamental frequencies produced by six choir singers performing an eight-note cadence and found an average standard deviation across singers and notes of 13 cents, with individual deviations of ±45 cents. Loosen (1993) measured the intonation of eight solo violinists playing ascending and descending diatonic major scales over three octaves. Average standard deviations were on the order of 10 cents, and the interval sizes were fit equally well by JI and PT.

Although these studies involved only Western classical music and musicians, variability of the same order of magnitude, and the same tendency for playing slightly sharp relative to equal temperament, has also been found in measurements of intonation from a military band (Stauffer, 1954), from Swedish folk musicians (Fransson, Sundberg, & Tjernland, 1970), and from jazz saxophonists (Owens, 1974). Similarly, measurements of intonation in performance for Indian (Hindustani) classical music (Callow & Shepard, 1972; Jhairazbhoy & Stone, 1963) show variability of a magnitude similar to that found in Western music. There are even large variations in the intonation (ranges of up to 38 cents) of a given interval in the single performance of a composition by one musician. Callow and Shepard analyzed these variations in terms of melodic context and found no significant correlations. Large variability (±50 cents) was also found in the intonation of a Thai vocalist whose frame of reference was presumably an equally tempered seven-interval scale (Morton, 1974).

One major exception to the tendency to sharpen intonation relative to equal temperament was found in the measured intonation of barbershop quartets. Theoretically, barbershop singing should be the ideal venue for just intonation. The barbershop repertoire consists of songs with elaborate four-part harmonies sung in a slow tempo without vibrato. These conditions should maximize the ability to use sensory dissonance cues from nearly coinciding harmonics. Hagerman and Sundberg (1980) measured the intonation in two warm-up cadences sung by two barbershop quartets. The average standard deviation of the intervals produced was small (on the order of 10 cents). However, all of the intervals were narrower than equitempered intervals, even those for which the JI values are wider than the equal temperament values, such that deviations from JI of up to 40 cents were observed.

Shackford (1962a, 1962b) attempted to determine if there were systematic tuning differences related to musical context. Although the relatively high variability and relatively small number of examples of each interval in a particular context made this attempt difficult, some fairly clear context effects did emerge. For example, if the harmonic tritone was spelled as an augmented fourth (F♯ re C), its average size was 611 cents. If, however, it was spelled as a diminished fifth (G♭), its average size was 593 cents. Sundberg (1993) has attempted to quantify context effects ("melodic charge") as part of a generative rule system for music performance. Melodic charge represents a correction (re equal temperament) for the tuning of each interval based on its position in the circle of fifths relative to the root note of the prevailing chord. These corrections are primarily based on the intonation measurements of Garbuzov (1948).

The results of intonation studies appear to mirror somewhat the results of the adjustment and identification experiments using isolated intervals: there is a tendency to compress the scale for small intervals and stretch the scale for large intervals, in both ascending and descending modes of presentation. They are also broadly consistent with results for intervals in context, which showed some tuning deviations contingent on harmonic and melodic tendencies. The overall tendency to "play sharp" is compatible with the results of a perceptual study by Lindgren and Sundberg (1972, reported in Sundberg, 1982) in which recordings of samples of sung melodies were played to a panel of singing teachers and choir singers who were asked to judge which notes were out of tune. Although deviations from equal temperament of up to 70 cents were sometimes accepted as in tune, the vast majority of acceptable deviations were those sharper than equal temperament. Deviations flatter than equal temperament were almost always judged as out of tune. None of the studies, however, provides any convincing evidence that musicians tend to play in one or the other of the natural scales.

3. Non-Western Scales

Three of the major non-Western musical systems (Indian, Chinese, and Arab-Persian) have inclusive scales approximately equivalent to the Western chromatic scale and, hence, have the same propensity for the perfect consonances (octaves, fourths, and fifths). There are, however, a number of musical cultures that apparently use approximately equally tempered five- and seven-note scales (i.e., 240- and 171-cent step sizes, respectively) in which the fourths and fifths are significantly mistuned from their natural values. Seven-interval scales are usually associated with Southeast Asian cultures (Malm, 1967). For example, Morton (1974) reports measurements (with a Stroboconn) of the tuning of a Thai xylophone that "varied only ±5 cents" from an equally tempered seven-interval tuning. (In ethnomusicological studies, measurement variability, if reported at all, is generally reported without definition). Haddon (1952) reported another example of a xylophone (from the Chop tribe in Uganda) tuned in 171-cent steps. The scales with five notes and 240-cent step-sizes are typically associated with the gamelan (tuned gongs and xylophone-type instruments) orchestras of Java and Bali (e.g., Kunst, 1949). However, measurements of gamelan tuning by Hood (1966) and McPhee (1966) show extremely large variations, so much so that McPhee states: "Deviations in what is considered the same scale are so large that one might with reason state that there are as many scales as there are gamelans." Other examples of 5-interval, 240-cent-step-size tunings were reported by Wachsmann (1950) for a Ugandan harp (measured using a Stroboconn, with measurement "variations" of 15 cents), and by Bel (1991) for xylophones and for women singing without accompaniment ("5 cents accuracy"). Examples of equally tempered scales are sometimes reported for preinstrumental cultures (although in these cases, the concept of scales may be of doubtful validity). For example, Boiles (1969) reports measurements (with a Stroboconn, "±5 cents accuracy") of a South American Indian scale with equal steps of 175 cents, which results in a progressive octave stretch. Ellis (1965), in extensive measurements of melodies in Australian aboriginal preinstrumental cultures, reports pitch distributions that apparently follow arithmetic scales (i.e., equal separation in hertz). Finally, measurements of the tuning of the normal (i.e., unequal interval) pentatonic scales of a Vietnamese zither show two modal scales in which the interval corresponding to the Western fourth is significantly mistuned (up to 21 cents, with a standard error of ±3 cents) from JI (Keefe et al., 1991) .

In summary, there seems to be a strong propensity for perfect consonances (octaves, fourths and fifths) in the scales of most cultures, the main exceptions being in the ofttimes highly variable scales of cultures that either are preinstrumental, or whose main instruments are of the xylophone type.

4. Other Experimental Evidence

In a recent series of papers, Schellenberg and Trehub (1994, 1996a, 1996b) make a case for a "biological basis" for small-integer-ratio derived intervals. The three papers differ primarily in the subject groups used, musically untrained adults, 6-year-old children, and 9-month-old infants, respectively. The basic paradigm is the same in all cases, the subject's task is to detect a 1-semitone change in a repeating background sequence of intervals. The comparison is between when the background intervals are simple-ratio intervals (i.e., small-integer-ratio intervals, e.g., 3:2) and the change is to a complex-ratio interval (e.g., 45:32), and vice versa. The finding that allegedly supports simple ratios as natural intervals is that subjects' performance is asymmetric, they find it easier to detect a change from a background sequence of simple ratio intervals to complex, than from complex to simple. This is said to occur because the simple ratios are more "coherent" and are more easily processed. Of course, as the authors concede, for adults this asymmetry could simply reflect the influence of exposure to diatonic scale structure as noted by examples in Section III,D, (e.g., Umemoto, 1990), rather than a "biological basis" for simple-ratio intervals, which is their preferred conclusion. Thus the crucial experiment is that using infant subjects (Schellenberg & Trehub, 1996b), although given the body of speech-perception literature showing experience-based effects at ages as young as 6 months (e.g., Kuhl, Williams, Lacerda, Stevens, & Lindblom, 1992), even a robust demonstration of a preference for certain intervals at 9 months of age would not constitute conclusive proof of a biological basis for these intervals. As it turns out, the results of this experiment are far from robust. The performance of the infants in all conditions (d' values from 0.1 to 0.3) is far below what is considered threshold discrimination performance. In addition, there are methodological problems with the experiment: some of the procedures used in training and testing the infants are nonstandard. Finally, in none of the papers do the authors address the question of why equal-tempered versions of the simple intervals, which represent much more complex ratios than, for example, 45:32, are perceptually equivalent to the exact small-integer-ratio intervals in these types of experiments.

Elliot, Platt, and Racine (1987) compared the performance "musically experienced" and "musically inexperienced" subjects in adjusting musical intervals. Because the musically inexperienced subjects did not have verbally cued internal standards as referents, they were instructed to adjust the variable tone until it "harmonized best" with the fixed tone, and the range of adjustment was limited to ±1/2 semitone of the desired interval. For melodic intervals, the musically experienced subjects showed smaller variability in matches to small-integer-ratio derived intervals (i.e., octave, fifth, and fourth) than to other intervals, but the musically experienced subjects showed equal variability for all intervals.

5. Conclusions: Learned Versus Innate Categories and the Origins of Scales

Sensory dissonance information clearly allows subjects in a laboratory situation to distinguish harmonic intervals composed of complex tones tuned to small-integer frequency ratios. However, the evidence from measurements of intonation in performance strongly suggests that such information is little used in actual musical practice and that the standards for intonation are the learned categories of the intervals of the musical scale of the person's culture, with a considerable leeway in the intonation that remains acceptable. The Western music standard appears to be a version of the equal-tempered scale that is slightly compressed for the smaller intervals and slightly stretched for the wider intervals or, said another way, musicians prefer the narrower intervals played flat and the wider intervals played sharp. This conclusion is consistent with the conclusions from experiments on the perception of melodic musical intervals (and harmonic intervals composed of pure tones) reviewed in Section III; that is, subjects tend to perceive intervals categorically, based on learned chromatic semitone categories that show a similar compression/stretch relative to equal temperament. There was no evidence in these studies of any particular sensitivity to small-integer ratios in either the identification or the discrimination of melodic musical intervals. This leeway in intonation is understandable, both from the standpoint of the information transfer limitations discussed in Section III,B,3, and from the fact that the pitch of complex (or for that matter, pure) tones is itself not a one-to-one function of fundamental frequency. The pitch of a complex tone (as measured by matches to a constant-level pure tone) can vary over a range of up to 1 semitone around its nominal fundamental frequency value, depending on such factors as level, spectral content, and amplitude envelope (e.g. Terhardt, 1988).

Assuming, then, that the intonation of individual musicians is based on their ability to reproduce the learned interval categories of their musical culture, what is the origin of these categories? How were the intervals of the scales chosen? The idea that the intervals of a given culture originally were chosen at random seems untenable given the prevalence of perfect consonances in the scales of all of the world's major music cultures. The obvious candidates for the generation of the prototypes of interval categories, then, are the three explanations of consonance posited in Section IV,A: sensory consonance, harmony, and common neural periodicities. Clearly, it is impossible to differentiate among these possibilities with certainty because they all predict basically the same result, namely, the propensity for perfect consonances, and we have at best only circumstantial evidence. However, it is instructive to at least list some of this evidence.

The apparent propensity for an absence of "perfect" fourths and fifths and for highly variable intonation in cultures whose predominant instrumentation are gongs and xylophones suggests that sensory consonance may have played some role. Instruments of this type produce tones whose partials are largely inharmonic (e.g., Rossing, 1976). Minimal sensory dissonance for inharmonic complex tones depends on the exact spacing of partials for the particular instrument (e.g., Geary, 1980) and will not, in general, correspond to small-integer ratios of the "fundamental." In addition, the fundamental pitches of inharmonic tones are weaker and more ambiguous than those of harmonic complex tones (e.g., Terhardt, Stoll, & Seewann, 1982).

Terhardt's (1984) harmony hypothesis is intriguing in that it explains the predilection for perfect consonances. However, it assumes that humans have an inherent appreciation of "octaveness," "fifthness," and "fourthness," and an inherent appreciation for the affinity of tones related by these frequency ratios. In experiments using melodic intervals, there is, at best, only weak evidence for similarity among these tones as judged by nonmusicians (e.g., Terhardt, Stoll, Schermbach, & Parncutt, 1986). Also, as noted in Section III,E,4, there is only limited evidence for confusions among the perfect consonances in identification experiments; for example, scale-step equivalents are much more likely to be confused than are fourths and fifths. This theory also provides explanations for the apparently universal stretch of the scale for wider intervals (see Section D,3) and the tolerance for "impure" perfect consonances.

Patterson (1986) showed how a model based on common neural periodicities can generate the "primary" intervals of the diatonic scales (the perfect consonances plus thirds and sixths). Although cues based on common-temporal periodicities allow some subjects in laboratory situations to distinguish pure-tone harmonic intervals that are slightly mistuned from small-integer ratios (e.g., Feeney & Burns, 1993; Plomp, 1967), they are very weak cues that are limited to low frequencies and would not seem likely candidates for the generation of the prototype interval categories for a musical culture.

Finally, Balzano (1982c) has demonstrated that, given only the constraints of octave circularity and the existence of 12 (approximately) equispaced steps per octave, both the Western diatonic scales and the anhemitonic pentatonic scale, which together constitute the modal scales for a large portion of the world's music cultures, can be thought of as arising from the properties of the cyclic group structure of the 12 intervals. That is, the tuning system and hierarchical structure of these scales can be derived without any consideration of small-integer frequency ratios per se.

D. OCTAVE EQUIVALENCE AND PITCH CLASS

As was mentioned in Section I, octave equivalence (the assumption that tones separated by an octave are in many ways musically identical and that scales are uniquely defined by specifying the intervals within an octave) is common to all advanced musical cultures. Octave circularity of relative pitch is inherent in the conceptualizations of pitch as having two dimensions: (1) pitch height, which is correlated with absolute frequency; and (2) pitch class, which is correlated with relative position within an octave. This idea has often been graphically represented by a helix or torus (see Chapter 8, this volume). As we shall see, there are a number of reasons why, on an acoustical/physiological basis, the octave might be expected to have unique properties. However, given the ubiquity of the concept in music, the search for psychophysical correlates of octave equivalence has been particularly irksome. For example, if the results of some relevant experiments are accepted at face value, octave equivalence is shown by rats (Blackwell & Schlosberg, 1943), human infants (Demany & Armand, 1984), and musicians (Allen, 1967), but not by starlings (Cynx, 1993), 4- to 9-year-old children (Sergeant, 1983), or nonmusicians (Allen, 1967). Although some might claim to see commonalities among the respective groups that allegedly do or do not show octave equivalence, the underlying connection is not obvious. In this section, some of the studies on octave equivalence are reviewed and an attempt is made to reach some conclusions on its origin.

1. Possible Acoustical or Physiological Bases for Octave Equivalence

Not surprisingly, the acoustically based and physiologically based explanations for the uniqueness of the octave are connected with the various explanations for consonance previously delineated. For musical intervals composed of simultaneous complex tones whose partials are harmonically related, the exact octave is unique in that all of the partials of the higher frequency tone will coincide exactly with the even partials of the lower-frequency tone. Depending on the phase relationships, these will either add to or subtract from the amplitudes of the partials of the lower tone resulting in a composite tone that is simply a complex tone with a fundamental frequency equal to that of the original lower frequency tone, but with a different amplitude spectrum. Therefore, although it will have a somewhat different timbre, the octave interval will, in general, be no more dissonant than the lower-frequency complex tone alone.

Similarly, in a model of consonance based on detection of coincidences of phase-locked neural firings, octaves are also special in that, for octave-related pure tones, firings elicited by the lower frequency tone will always coincide with firings due to the higher frequency tone. Finally, the tonal affinity in Terhardt's (1984) concept of harmony is related to ambiguities in estimates of the fundamental pitch of complex tones predicted by pattern-matching models. The vast majority of ambiguous estimates are related by octaves (e.g., Terhardt et al., 1986).

There is also some "direct" evidence of a physiological basis for octave equivalence in the form of cortical neurons in animals that have multipeaked tuning curves sensitive to, for example, both first and second harmonic, or to the second and third harmonics without a response to the fundamental (e.g., Tsuzuki & Suga, 1988). These neurons are relatively rare, however, and are often located in specialized cortical regions such as the region associated with processing echolocation signals in bats and generalization to processing of octave-related frequencies by humans is probably unwarranted.

2. Psychophysical Evidence Regarding Octave Equivalence

The bidimensional representations of pitch imply that manifestations of octave equivalence should be found in experiments for which musical training is not a prerequisite. Moreover, if the bidimensional representation has a direct physiological basis, such as temporal coding for pitch class and tonotopic coding for pitch height, then octave equivalence should also be a characteristic of the hearing of nonhuman mammals and avians, whose peripheral auditory mechanisms are similar to those of humans. The classic, and apparently only, study that specifically looked for octave equivalence in mammals was that of Blackwell and Schlosberg (1943), who used a generalization paradigm with rats. They found evidence that rats trained on 10-kHz pure tones generalized to 5 kHz. However, this experiment has been repeatedly criticized, primarily because there may have been harmonic distortion in the stimuli, and the stimuli were, in any case, above the frequency region where humans show a pitch-class effect (see, however, Section III,E,1). This experiment has never been successfully replicated. In a recent study using a generalization paradigm with starlings, Cynx (1993) found no evidence for octave equivalence. However, a study in dolphins (Richards, Wolz, & Herman, 1984) did find evidence of spontaneous octave shifts in the *production* of sounds which the dolphins had been trained to produce.

Experiments that have required adult subjects to judge the similarity of isolated pairs of pure tones (Allen, 1967; Kallman, 1982; Terhardt et al., 1986; Thurlow & Erchul, 1977; Umemoto, 1989) have generally found that, for nonmusicians, similarity is strictly a function of frequency separation, with no evidence of any special similarity of the octave other than a very weak effect when the range of tones is restricted to the region near the octave (Kallman, 1982). On the other hand, most but not all musicians do show a strong octave-similarity effect in these experiments. Even when the similarity judgments were put in a more musical context, for example, judging the similarity of melodies distorted by mistuning one tone (Kallman, 1982), judging the "comfortableness" of a melodic interval preceded by a diatonic scale (Amano, 1989), or judging the "fit" of a tone preceded by a diatonic scale (Krumhansl & Shepard, 1979), the results were essentially the same, musicians tended to show significant octave effects, nonmusicians little or none. However, some "musically relevant" experiments have clearly shown evidence of octave equivalence that is not dependent on musical training. Although melody recognition is totally disrupted when the (correct pitch class) notes of the melody are chosen randomly from one of three octaves (Deutsch, 1972), nonmusicians perform at much better than chance level at recognizing well-known melodies when the component tones are distorted by octave transpositions with the restriction that melodic contour be preserved and unison intervals maintained (Kallman & Massaro, 1979).

Although octave similarity in adults seems to be in large measure a function of musical training, Demany and Armand (1984) have presented evidence indicating that 3-month-old infants did not notice the octave transposition of two notes of a three-note melody but did notice when the notes were instead transposed by a major seventh or a minor ninth. Strong evidence for octave equivalence in infants would provide support for a physiological basis for octave similarity, because the 3-month-old infants presumably would not have had sufficient exposure to music, or to harmonic complex tones in general, to acquire a learning-based sense of octave similarity. However, there are some methodological questions regarding this experiment and, like the Blackwell and Schlosberg (1943) experiment, it clearly begs for replication. Finally, Sergeant (1983) investigated octave similarity in a group of 54 children 4–9 years old. Using an array of chime bars, the children were asked to select the one that was "most like" a reference chime bar, or in another case, to complete an octave transposition. As with the nonmusician adults in the above-cited experiments, similarity was based primarily on frequency proximity, with no significant octave effect.

One psychophysical effect that appears to show clear evidence of the separability of pitch height from pitch class and of octave equivalence, and which does not depend heavily on musical training, is the so-called "Shepard illusion." Shepard (1964) used complex tones whose partials consist of only octaves of the fundamental. These complex tones were, in essence, passed through a band-pass filter that served to keep average tone height constant regardless of the fundamental frequency of the complex tone. When a set of tones of this type, whose fundamental frequencies cover the range of an octave in semitone steps, are played cyclically, or if the fundamental frequency is swept continuously over an octave range (see demonstration by Risset in Houtsma, Rossing, & Wagenaars, 1987), the impression is one of constantly rising or falling pitch. This illusion is often cited as evidence for circularity of relative pitch based on octave equivalence. The reasoning is that, whether a subject is following the pitch of an individual partial (Shepard, 1964), or is following the fundamental pitch (e.g., Terhardt et al, 1982), a sawtooth pattern of periods of increasing pitch, interspersed with sudden downward octave jumps, should be heard. Because the subjects do not, in general, hear the sudden downward jumps, it is assumed that this is a consequence of octave equivalence. Ueda and Ohgushi (1987) showed that multidimensional scaling techniques applied to these tones yielded the classic spiral representation of pitch class and pitch height. However, experiments by other researchers (Burns, 1981;

Nakajima, Tsumura, Matsuura, Minami, & Teranishi, 1988), using both inhar-monic and harmonic complex tones, have shown that octave separation of partials is not a prerequisite either for eliciting the illusion or for obtaining circular repre-sentations from multidimensional scaling techniques. Thus the experimental re-sults obtained using Shepard tones are not evidence for octave equivalence.

A series of psychoacoustical studies that provides some evidence for octave uniqueness ("harmonic octave templates") has been reported (Demany & Semal, 1988; 1990; Demany, Semal, & Carlyon, 1991). The results show that in low-uncertainty psychophysical tasks, for lower tone frequencies below about 1000 Hz, information exists that allows subjects to discriminate exact from mistuned octaves composed of simultaneous pure tones. Basically, the results are consistent with studies on the detection of mistuning of partials of complex tones from exact harmonic ratios (e.g., Hartmann et al., 1990) and on beats of mistuned conso-nances (e.g., Feeney & Burns, 1993), and with the idea that cross-channel tempo-ral information is used by the auditory system as part of the process by which the unitary percepts of complex tones are determined. However, it is unlikely that the low-level, low-frequency cues used by the subjects in these tasks are perceptible in "real-life" musical situations or that they are directly responsible for the unique status of the octave in music. Unfortunately, however, the results reviewed in this section do not suggest any other particularly strong candidates for this role.

3. The Octave Stretch Phenomenon

One of the most intriguing aspects of octave perception is the perceptual stretch of subjective octaves, in which exact octaves are perceived as being too small. This stretch was evident in all of the adjustment, category scaling, and measured intonation studies cited in Section III and has also been found in a forced-choice identification experiment (Dobbins & Cuddy, 1982). It also seems to be universal across musical cultures (Burns, 1974; and studies summarized by Dowling & Har-wood, 1986, p. 102), which rules out one of the early hypotheses: namely, that it is learned from the exposure to the stretched scales of pianos, which can in turn be explained by the inharmonicity of the partials in piano tones (Young, 1952). As noted in Section III, the octave stretch seems to reflect a general tendency to stretch all of the wider intervals. This has prompted some researchers (e.g., W. M. Hartmann, personal communication, May 1993) to propose that this stretch is a statistical artifact based on the fact that musicians find it acceptable to play some-what sharp, but unacceptable to play flat (see Section IV,C,2). This would lead to an asymmetric distribution in an adjustment experiment, where the modal value of the distribution is at the exact value of the octave, but where the mean is higher because of the skewed distribution. However, there is no evidence for this asym-metry in the category scaling results of individual listeners (see, e.g., Figure 1). The distributions are symmetric with, in many cases, "stretched" modal values.

In a forced-choice experiment where 91 subjects were presented with a se-quence of intervals ranging from 26 cents below to 60 cents above the true octave of 500 Hz and were asked to select the "best octave" (Hartmann, 1993a), there was some evidence for a bimodal distribution, with one mode at the exact octave (1200 cents) and another at about 1235 cents. Given that all of the previous experiments showing octave stretch have used trained musicians, it is surprising that, in this experiment, the subjects with more musical training tended to choose the true octave, and nonmusicians, the stretched octave.

Terhardt (1971, 1974) has provided an explanation for the octave stretch based on his pitch/consonance/harmony model. One facet of the model is that complex-tone pitch perception has an early learning component where pitches of individual harmonics are associated with the pitch of the fundamental. As part of this associative learning, individuals (unconsciously) learn the relationships between the pitches of the lower harmonics, which correspond to the intervals of octave, fifth, and so on. The pitches of the individual harmonics are, however, slightly altered by the presence of the other harmonics, resulting in a wider subjective interval between harmonics, and hence a stretched template (Terhardt, 1971). However, the octave stretch also obtains for simultaneous octaves (Ward, 1953, 1954; Demany & Semal, 1990), where these pitch shifts would presumably be accounted for. Although overall, across subjects and frequencies, the stretch is slightly but significantly smaller in the harmonic condition, for some frequencies in some subjects, the stretch is significantly greater in the harmonic condition. In addition, other researchers (e.g., Peters, Moore, & Glasberg, 1983) have not found these shifts in the pitches of individual harmonics.

Although the octave stretch would seem to rule out explanations based on neural synchrony, this is not necessarily the case. Ohgushi (1983) posited an explanation of the octave shift based on anomalies in the time intervals between phase-locked neural firings, which are due to refractory effects. Although Hartmann (1993b) has pointed out some inconsistencies in Ohgushi's model, he also proposes a modified version that in fact predicts the bimodal distribution found in Hartmann (1993a). In addition, Hartmann (1993b) showed that the octave stretch also obtains for a pitch that is created centrally (at the level of the brainstem or higher), because of the interaction of information from both ears, and that is not obtainable from the peripheral information from either ear alone. This result is clearly consistent with the existence of a learned template, such as that proposed by Terhardt (1971), but is not necessarily inconsistent with the Ohgushi/Hartmann model, because the temporal anomalies at the periphery might also influence this central pitch. It is notable that in some of the individual results in Demany and Semal (1988), which are presumably based on timing information, the minimum in the discrimination functions is not at the exact octave, but at a slightly "stretched" value.

As was the case in the preceding section, where a number of reasonable explanations for the unique position of the octave in music were presented, no compelling evidence favors any one of several reasonable explanations for the subjective stretch of the octave. It remains, however, an obvious candidate for further research.

V. CONCLUSIONS AND CAVEATS

A. CONCLUSIONS

On the basis of the evidence reviewed, the following conclusions regarding the perception of musical intervals and scales seem justified.

1. The use of a relatively small number of discrete pitch relationships in music is probably dictated by inherent limitations on the processing of high-information-load stimuli by human sensory systems. Quarter-tone music might be theoretically feasible given sufficient exposure, but the present 12-interval Western scale is probably a practical limit. Any division of the octave into intervals smaller than quarter tones is perceptually irrelevant for melodic information.

2. Natural intervals, defined as intervals that show maximum sensory consonance and/or harmony, may have influenced the evolution of the scales of many musical cultures, but the standards of intonation for a given culture are the learned interval categories of the scales of that culture. A corollary of this is that the intonation performance of a given musician is primarily determined by his or her ability to reproduce these learned categories and is little influenced, in most situations, by any of the psychophysical cues that may underlie sensory consonance or harmony.

3. Based on the results of musical interval adjustment and identification experiments, and on measurements of intonation in performance, the intonation standard for Western music appears to be a version of the equitempered scale that is slightly compressed for small intervals, and stretched for wide intervals, including the octave. However, there is a considerable latitude in the intonation that remains musically acceptable. This is manifested in the variability of intonation in (acceptable) performances, only a portion of which can be attributed to effects of musical context, and in the "categorical perception" of musical intervals in a laboratory situation.

4. From an experimental psychology perspective, the perception of musical intervals is unique in several respects. The variability of musicians in adjusting musical intervals along a frequency-ratio continuum is an order of magnitude smaller than the variability of subjects making magnitude production adjustments along other unidimensional psychophysical continuua. Also, possessors of relative pitch are, along with possessors of absolute pitch, the notable exceptions to the classic "magical number 7 ± 2" limit on information channel capacity along a unidimensional psychophysical continuum.

The perception of musical intervals shares a number of commonalities with the perception of phonemes in speech, most notably categorical-like perception, and an equivalence of spacing, in sensation units, of categories along the respective continuua. However, the perception of melodic musical intervals appears to be the only example of ideal categorical perception in which discrimination is totally dependent on identification. Thus, rather than speech being "special," as ofttimes proclaimed by experimental psychologists, it seems that it is music (or at least musicians) that is (are) truly special.

B. CAVEATS

Although the focus of this chapter on the perception of musical intervals naturally has the orientation of a "bottom up" approach to musical scales, readers should be aware that this is not the entire picture. That is, scales, and in particular melodies, are considerably more than just collections of intervals. Although some of the more cognitive "top-down" aspects of scales have been touched on, they are covered more fully in Chapters 10, 11, and 12 of this volume.

ACKNOWLEDGMENTS

I thank the following colleagues for commenting on a previous version of this manuscript: Shari L. Campbell, James C. Carlsen, William Morris Hartmann, Douglas H. Keefe, Johan Sundberg, Ernst Terhardt, and W. Dixon Ward. Support for preparation of this chapter came from the Virginia Merrill Bloedel Hearing Research Center at the University of Washington.

REFERENCES

Allen, D. (1967). Octave discriminability of musical and non-musical subjects. *Psychonomic Science, 7,* 421–422.

Amano, S. (1989). Perception of successive intervals in a musical context. In *Proceedings of The First International Conference on Music Perception and Cognition, Kyoto, 17–19 October* (pp. 155–158). Kyoto: ICMPC.

Attneave, F., & Olson, R. (1971). Pitch as a medium: A new approach to psychophysical scaling. *American Journal of Psychology, 84,* 147–166.

Balzano, G. J. (1982a). Musical vs. psychoacoustical variables and their influence on the perception of musical intervals. *Bulletin of the Council for Research in Music Education, 70,* 1–11.

Balzano, G. J. (1982b). The role of chroma and scalestep in the recognition of musical intervals in and out of context. *Psychomusicology, 2,* 3–32.

Balzano, G. J. (1982c). The pitch set as a level of description for studying musical pitch perception. In M. Clynes (Ed.), *Music, mind, and brain: The neuropsychology of music.* New York: Plenum Press.

Barbour, J. M. (1951). *Tuning and temperament.* East Lansing: Michigan State College.

Bel, B. (1991, 18 March). Equipentatonic tuning. *EthnoFORUM,* no. 38.

Benguerel, A., & Westdal, C. (1991). Absolute pitch and the perception of sequential musical intervals. *Music Perception, 9*(1), 105–119.

Blackwell, H. R., & Schlosberg, H. (1943). Octave generalization, pitch discrimination, and loudness thresholds in the white rat. *Journal of Experimental Psychology, 33,* 407–419.

Boiles, J. (1969). Terpehua thought-song. *Ethnomusicology, 13,* 42–47.

Boomsliter, P., & Creel, W. (1961). The long pattern hypothesis in harmony and hearing. *Journal of the Acoustical Society of America, 5,* 2–31.

Boomsliter, P., & Creel, W. (1971). *Toward a theory of melody.* Paper presented at the Symposium on Musical Perception, Convention of the AAS, December 28, Philadelphia, PA.

Braida, L. D., & Durlach, N. I. (1972). Intensity perception II: Resolution in one-interval paradigms. *Journal of the Acoustical Society of America, 51,* 483–502.

Braida, L. D., & Durlach, N. I. (1988). Peripheral and central factors in intensity perception. In G. Edelman, W. Gall, & W. Cowan (Eds.) *Auditory function.* New York: John Wiley and Sons.

Burns, E. M. (1974). Octave adjustment by non-Western musicians. *Journal of the Acoustical Society of America, Supplement, Fall, 56,* S25–26.

Burns, E. M. (1977). *The perception of musical intervals (frequency ratios).* Unpublished doctoral dissertation, University of Minnesota, Minneapolis.

Burns, E. M. (1981). Circularity in relative pitch judgments for inharmonic complex tones: The Shepard demonstration revisited, again. *Perception & Psychophysics, 30,* 467–472.

Burns, E. M., & Campbell, S. L. (1994). Frequency and frequency ratio resolution by possessors of relative and absolute pitch: Examples of categorical perception? *Journal of the Acoustical Society of America, 96,* 2704–2719.

Burns, E. M., & Feth, L. L. (1983). Pitch of sinusoids and complex tones above 10kHz. In R. Klinke & R. Hartmann (Eds.), *Hearing-Physiological Bases and Psychophysics.* Berlin: Springer-Verlag.

Burns, E. M., & Ward, W. D. (1978). Categorical perception-phenomenon or epiphenomenon: Evidence from experiments in the perception of melodic musical intervals. *Journal of the Acoustical Society of America, 63,* 456–468.

Callow, G., & Shepherd, E. (1972). Intonation in the performance of North Indian classical music. Paper presented at the 17th annual meeting of the Society of Ethnomusicology, November 30–December 3, Toronto, Canada.

Caron, N., & Safvate, D. (1966). *Les traditions musicales, Iran.* Correa, France: Buchet/Chastel.

Cynx, J. (1993). Auditory frequency generalization and a failure to find octave generalization in a songbird. *Journal of Comparative Psychology, 107,* 140–146.

Demany, L., & Armand, F. (1984). The perceptual reality of tone chroma in early infancy. *Journal of the Acoustical Society of America, 76,* 57–66.

Demany, L. & Semal, C. (1988). Dichotic fusion of two tones one octave apart: Evidence for internal octave templates. *Journal of the Acoustical Society of America, 83,* 687–695

Demany, L., & Semal, C. (1990). Harmonic and melodic octave templates. *Journal of the Acoustical Society of America, 88,* 2126–2135.

Demany, L., Semal, C., & Carlyon, R. (1991). On the perceptual limits of octave harmony and their origin. *Journal of the Acoustical Society of America, 90,* 3019–3027.

Deutsch, D. (1972). Octave generalization and tune recognition. *Perception & Psychophysics, 11,* 411–412.

Dobbins, P. A., & Cuddy, L. L. (1982). Octave discrimination: An experimental confirmation of the "stretched" subjective octave. *Journal of the Acoustical Society of America, 72,* 411–415.

Dowling, W. J., & Harwood, D. L. (1986). *Music cognition.* New York: Academic Press.

Elliot, J., Platt, J. R., & Racine, R. J. (1987). Adjustments of successive and simultaneous intervals by musically experienced and experienced subjects. *Perception & Psychophysics, 42,* 594–598.

Ellis, C. (1965). Pre-instrumental scales. *Journal of the Acoustical Society of America, 9,* 126–144.

Estes, W. K. (1972). An associative basis for coding and organization in memory. In A. W. Melton & E. Martin (Eds.), *Coding processes in human memory* (pp. 161–190). Washington, DC: Winston.

Feeney, M. P., & Burns, E. M. (1993). Dichotic beats of mistuned consonances [Abstract]. *Journal of the Acoustical Society of America, 93,* 2346–2347.

Flege, J. E. (1988). The production and perception of foreign language speech sounds. In H. Winitz (Ed.), *Human communication and its disorders* (pp. 224–401). Norwood, NJ: Ablex.

Francès, R. (1988). *La perception de la musique* (W. J. Dowling, Transl.). Hillsdale, NJ: Erlbaum. (Original work published 1958)

Fransson, F., Sundberg, J., & Tjernlund, P. (1970). *Statistical computer measurements of the tone-scale in played music* (STL-QPSR 2-3). Stockholm: Department of Speech Communication, Kungl Tekniska Högskolan.

Fyk, J. (1982a). Perception of mistuned intervals in melodic context. *Psychology of Music,* special edition, 36–41.

Fyk, J. (1982b). Tolerance of intonation deviation in melodic intervals in listeners of different musical training. *Archives of Acoustics, 7,* 13–28.

Garbuzov, N. (1948). *Zonnaja priroda zvukovysotnogo slucha*, Moscow, Akademija Nauk SSSR.

Geary, J. M. (1980). Consonance and dissonance of pairs of inharmonic sounds. *Journal of the Acoustical Society of America, 67,* 1785–1789.

van de Geer, J. P., Levelt, W., & Plomp, R. (1962). The connotation of musical consonance. *Acta Psychologica, 20,* 308–319.

Gerson, A., & Goldstein, J. L. (1978). Evidence for a general template in central optimal processing for pitch of complex tones. *Journal of the Acoustical Society of America, 63,* 498–510.

Greene, P. C. (1937). Violin intonation. *Journal of the Acoustical Society of America, 9,* 43–44.

Haddon, E. (1952). Possible origin of the Chopi Timbila xylophone. *African Music Society Newsletter, 1,* 61–67.

Hagerman, B., & Sundberg, J. (1980). Fundamental frequency adjustment in barbershop singing. *Journal of Research in Singing, 4,* 1–17.

Hall, D. E., & Hess, J. T. (1984). Perception of musical interval tuning. *Music Perception, 2*(2), 166–195.

Harnad, S. (Ed.) (1987). *Categorical perception.* Cambridge: Cambridge University Press.

Hartmann, W. M. (1993a). Auditory demonstrations on compact disk for large N. *Journal of the Acoustical Society of America, 93,* 1–16.

Hartmann, W. M. (1993b). On the origin of the enlarged melodic octave. *Journal of the Acoustical Society of America, 93,* 3400–3409.

Hartmann, W. M., McAdams, S., & Smith, B. K. (1990). Hearing a mistuned harmonic in an otherwise periodic complex tone. *Journal of the Acoustical Society of America, 88,* 1712–1724.

Helmholtz, H. von (1954). *The sensations of tone.* New York: Dover. (Original work published 1877)

Hood, M. (1966). Slendro and Pelog redefined. *Selected Reports in Ethnomusicology, Institute of Ethnomusicology, UCLA, 1,* 36–48.

Houtsma, A. J. M. (1968). Discrimination of frequency ratios [Abstract]. *Journal of the Acoustical Society of America, 44,* 383.

Houtsma, A. J. M. (1984). Pitch salience of various complex sounds. *Music Perception, 1*(3), 296–307.

Houtsma, A. J. M., Rossing, T. D., & Wagenaars, W. M. (1987). *Auditory demonstrations* (CD and booklet). Woodbury, NY: Acoustical Society of America.

Howard, D., Rosen, S., & Broad, V. (1992). Major/minor triad identification and discrimination by musically trained and untrained listeners. *Music Perception, 10*(2), 205–220.

Hunt, F. V. (1992). *Origins in acoustics.* Woodbury, NY: Acoustical Society of America.

Jeffries, T. B (1967). The effects of order of presentation and knowledge of the results on aural recognition of melodic intervals. *Journal of Research in Music Education, 15,* 179–190.

Jeffries, T. B. (1970). A further investigation of certain learning aspects in the aural recognition of melodic intervals. *Journal of Research in Music Education, 18,* 399–406.

Jhairazbhoy, N., & Stone, A. (1963). Intonation in present day North Indian classical music. *Bulletin of the School of Oriental and African Studies, University of London, 26,* 118–132.

Johnson, D. H. (1978). The relationship of post-stimulus time and interval histograms to the timing characteristics of spike trains. *Biophysics Journal, 22,* 413–430.

Kallman, H. J. (1982). Octave equivalence as measured by similarity ratings. *Perception & Psychophysics, 32,* 37–49.

Kallman, H. J., & Massaro, D. W. (1979). Tone chroma is functional in melody recognition. *Perception & Psychophysics, 26,* 32–36.

Kameoka, A., & Kuriyagawa, M. (1969a). Consonance theory part I: Consonance of dyads. *Journal of the Acoustical Society of America, 45,* 1451–1459.

Kameoka, A., & Kuriyagawa, M. (1969b). Consonance theory part II: Consonance of complex tones and its calculation method. *Journal of the Acoustical Society of America, 45,* 1460–1469.

Keefe, D. H., Burns, E. M., & Nguyen, P. (1991). Vietnamese modal scales of the dan tranh. *Music Perception, 8*(4), 449–468.

Killam, R. N., Lorton, P. V., & Schubert, E. D. (1975). Interval recognition: Identification of harmonic and melodic intervals. *Journal of Music Theory, 19*(2), 212–234.

Krumhansl, C. L. (1990). *Cognitive foundations of musical pitch.* New York: Oxford University Press.

Krumhansl, C. L., & Shepard, R. N. (1979). Quantification of the hierarchy of tonal function within a diatonic context. *Journal of Experimental Psychology: Human Perception and Performance, 5,* 579–594.

Kuhl, P., Williams, K., Lacerda, F., Stevens, K., & Lindblom, B. (1992). Linguistic experience alters phonetic perception in infants by 6 months of age. *Science, 255,* 606–608.

Kunst, J. (1949). *Music in Java* (Vol. II) The Hague: Martinus Nijhoff.

Levelt, W., van de Geer, J., & Plomp, R. (1966). Triadic comparisons of musical intervals. *British Journal of Mathematical and Statistical Psychology, 19,* 163–179.

Locke, S., & Kellar, I. (1973). Categorical perception in a non-linguistic mode. *Cortex, 9,* 355–368.

Loosen, F. (1993). Intonation of solo violin performance with reference to equally tempered, Pythagorean, and just intonations. *Journal of the Acoustical Society of America, 93,* 525–539.

Lynch, M., Eilers, R., Oller, K., Urbano, R., & Wilson, P. (1991). Influences of acculturation and musical sophistication on perception of musical interval patterns. *Journal of Experimental Psychology: Human perception and Performance, 17,* 967–975.

Macmillan, N. A. (1987). Beyond the categorical/continuous distinction: A psychophysical approach to processing modes. In S. Harnad (Ed.), *Categorical perception* (pp. 53–85). Cambridge: Cambridge University Press.

Macmillan, N. A., Goldberg, R. F., & Braida, L. D. (1988). Resolution for speech sounds: Basic sensitivity and context memory on vowel and consonant continua. *Journal of the Acoustical Society of America, 84,* 1262–1280.

Malm, W. P. (1967). *Music Cultures of the Pacific, the Near East, and Asia.* Englewood Cliffs, NJ: Prentice-Hall.

Martin, D. W. (1962). Musical scales since Pythagoras. *Sound, 1,* 22–24.

Mason, J. A. (1960). Comparison of solo and ensemble performances with reference to Pythagorean, just, and equi-tempered intonations. *Journal of Research of Music Education, 8,* 31–38.

McAdams, S. (1983). Acoustic cues contributing to spectral fusion. *Proceedings of the 11th International Congress on Acoustics* (pp. 127–129).

McPhee, C. (1966). *Music in Bali.* New Haven, CT: Yale University Press.

Meyer, M. (1898). Zur Theorie der Differenztone and der Gehorseempfindungen uberhaupt. *Beitr. Akust. Musikwiss. 2,* 25–65.

Miller, G. A. (1956). The magical number seven, plus or minus two: Some limits on our capacity for processing information. *Psychological Review, 63,* 81–96.

Miyazaki, K. (1992). Perception of musical intervals by absolute pitch possessors. *Music Perception, 9*(4), 413–426.

Miyazaki, K. (1993). Absolute pitch as an inability: Identification of musical intervals in a tonal context. *Music Perception, 11*(1), 55–71.

Miyazaki, K. (1995). Perception of relative pitch with different references: Some absolute-pitch listeners can't tell musical interval names. *Perception & Psychophysics, 57,* 962–970.

Moiseff, A., & Konishi, M. (1981). Neuronal and behavior sensitivity to binaural time differences in the owl. *The Journal of the Neurosciences, 1,* 40–48.

Moore, B. C. J. (1989). *An introduction to the psychology of hearing* (3rd ed.). London: Academic Press.

Moran, H., & Pratt, C. C. (1926). Variability of judgments of musical intervals. *Journal of Experimental Psychology, 9,* 492–500.

Morton, D. (1974). Vocal tones in traditional Thai music. *Selected reports in ethnomusicology* (Vol. 2, pp. 88–99). Los Angeles: Institute for Ethnomusicology, UCLA.

Nakajima, Y., Tsumura, T., Minami, H., & Teranishi, R. (1988). Dynamic pitch perception for complex tones derived from major triads. *Music Perception, 6*(1), 1–20.

Nettl, B. (1956). *Music in primitive culture.* Cambridge, MA: Harvard University Press.

Nickerson, J. F. (1948). *A comparison of performances of the same melody played in solo and ensemble with reference to equi-tempered, just and Pythagorean intonation.* Unpublished doctoral dissertation, University of Minnesota, Minneapolis.

van Noorden, L. (1982). Two channel pitch perception. In M. Clynes (Ed.), *Music, mind, and brain: The neuropsychology of music.* New York: Plenum Press.

Ohgushi, K. (1983). The origin of tonality and a possible basis for the octave enlargement phenomenon. *Journal of the Acoustical Society of America, 73,* 1694–1700.

Ohgushi, K., & Hatoh, T. (1992). The musical pitch of high frequency tones. In Y. Cazals, L. Demany, & K. Horner, *Auditory physiology and perception.* Oxford: Pergamon Press.

Owens, T. (1974). Applying the melograph to 'Parkers Mood.' *Selected reports in ethnomusicology* (Vol. 2, pp. 166–175). Los Angeles: Institute for Ethnomusicology, UCLA.

Patterson, R. D. (1986). Spiral detection of periodicity and the spiral form of musical scales. *Psychology of Music, 14,* 44–61.

Peters, R. W., Moore, B. C. J., & Glasberg, B. R. (1983). Pitch of components of a complex tone. *Journal of the Acoustical Society of America, 73,* 924–929.

Pierce, J. C. (1966). Attaining consonance in arbitrary scales [Letter]. *Journal of the Acoustical Society of America, 40,* 249.

Plomp, R. (1967). Beats of mistuned consonances. *Journal of the Acoustical Society of America, 42,* 462–474.

Plomp, R., & Levelt, W. J. M. (1965). Tonal consonance and critical band-width. *Journal of the Acoustical Society of America, 35,* 548–560.

Plomp, R., & Steeneken, H. J. M. (1968). Interference between two simple tones. *Journal of the Acoustical Society of America, 43,* 883–884.

Plomp, R., Wagenaar, W., & Mimpen, A. (1973). Musical interval recognition with simultaneous tones. *Acustica, 29,* 101–109.

Pollack, I. (1952). The information in elementary auditory displays. *Journal of the Acoustical Society of America, 24,* 745–749.

Rakowski, A. (1990). Intonation variants of musical intervals in isolation and in musical contexts. *Psychology of Music, 18,* 60–72.

Rakowski, A., & Miskiewicz, A. (1985). Deviations from equal temperament in tuning isolated musical intervals. *Archives of Acoustics, 10,* 95–104.

Richards, D., Wolz, J., & Herman, L. (1984). Vocal mimicry of computer-generated sounds and vocal labeling of objects by a bottlenosed dolphin, *Tursiops truncatus. Journal of Comparative Psychology, 98,* 10–28.

Roederer, J. (1973). *Introduction to the physics and psychophysics of music.* Berlin and New York: Springer-Verlag.

Rossing, T. D. (1976). Acoustics of percussion instruments: Part I. *The Physics Teacher, 14,* 546–556.

Sachs, C., & Kunst, J. (1962). In J. Kunst (Ed.), *The wellsprings of music.* The Hague: Martinus Nijhoff.

Schellenberg, E., & Trehub, S. (1994). Frequency ratios and the discrimination of pure tone sequences. *Perception & Psychophysics, 56,* 472–478.

Schellenberg, E., & Trehub, S. (1996a). Children's discrimination of melodic intervals. *Developmental Psychology, 32,* 1039–1050.

Schellenberg, E., & Trehub, S. (1996b). Natural musical intervals: Evidence from infant listeners. *Psychological Science, 7,* 272–277.

Semal, C., & Demany, L. (1990). The upper limit of "musical" pitch. *Music Perception, 8(2),* 165–175.

Sergeant, D. (1983). The octave: percept or concept? *Psychology of Music, 11,* 2–18.

Shackford, C. (1961). Some aspects of perception: Part I. *Journal of Music Theory, 5,* 162–202.

Shackford, C. (1962a). Some aspects of perception: Part II. *Journal of Music Theory, 6,* 66–90.

Shackford, C. (1962b). Some aspects of perception: Part III. *Journal of Music Theory, 6,* 295–303.

Shatzkin, M. (1981). Interval and pitch recognition in and out of immediate context. *Journal of Research in Music Education, 29,* 111–123.

Shatzkin, M. (1984). Interval recognition in minimal context. *Journal of Research in Music Education, 32,* 5–14.

Shepard, R. N. (1964). Circularity in judgments of relative pitch. *Journal of the Acoustical Society of America, 36,* 2346–2353.

Siegel, J. A., & Siegel, W. (1977a). Absolute identification of notes and intervals by musicians. *Perception & Psychophysics, 21,* 143–152.

Siegel, J. A., & Siegel, W. (1977b). Categorical perception of tonal intervals: Musicians can't tell sharp from flat. *Perception & Psychophysics, 21,* 399–407.

Slaymaker, F. (1970). Chords from tones having stretched partials. *Journal of the Acoustical Society of America, 47,* 1569–1571.

Smith, D. J., Nelson, D. G. K., Grohskopf, L. A., &Appleton, T. (1994). What child is this? What interval was that? Familiar tunes and music perception in novice listeners. *Cognition, 52,* 23–54.

Spector, J. (1966). Classical Ud music in Egypt with special reference to Maquamat. *Ethnomusicology, 14,* 243–257.

Speer, J. R., & Meeks, P. U. (1985). School children's perception of pitch in music. *Psychomusicology, 5,* 49–56.

Srulovicz, R., & Goldstein, G. L. (1983). A central spectrum model: A synthesis of auditory-nerve timing and place cues in monaural communication of frequency separation. *Journal of the Acoustical Society of America, 73,* 1266–1276.

Stauffer, D. (1954). *Intonation deficiencies of wind instruments in ensemble.* Washington, DC: Catholic University of America Press.

Stevens, S. S. (1976). In G. Stevens (Ed.), *Psychophysics: Introduction to its perceptual, neural and social prospects.* New York: Wiley.

Studdert-Kennedy, M., Liberman, A. M., Harris, K., & Cooper, F. S. (1970). The motor theory of speech perception: A reply to Lane's critical review. *Psychological Review, 77,* 234–249.

Sundberg, J. (1982). *In tune or not?: A study of fundamental frequency in musical practice* (STL-QPSR 1). Stockholm: Department of Speech Communication, Kungl Tekniska Högskolan.

Sundberg, J. (1993). How can music be expressive? *Speech Communication, 13,* 239–253.

Sundberg, J., & Lindquist, J. (1973). Musical octaves and pitch. *Journal of the Acoustical Society of America, 54,* 922–927.

Szende, O. (1977). *Intervallic hearing: Its nature and pedagogy.* Budapest: Akademia Kiado.

Taylor, J. A. (1971). *Perception of melodic intervals within melodic context.* Unpublished doctoral dissertation, University of Washington, Seattle.

Teich, M. C., Khanna, S. M., & Guiney, P. C. (1993). Spectral characteristics and synchrony in primary auditory nerve fibers in response to pure-tone stimuli. *Journal of Statistical Physics, 70,* 257–279.

Terhardt, E. (1969). Oktavspreizung und Tonhohen der Schieflung bei Sinustonen. *Acustica, 22,* 348–351.

Terhardt, E. (1971). Pitch shifts of harmonics, an explanation of the octave enlargement phenomenon. *Proceedings of the 7th International Congress on Acoustics, 3,* 621–624.

Terhardt, E. (1974). Pitch, consonance and harmony. *Journal of the Acoustical Society of America, 55,* 1061–1069.

Terhardt, E. (1978). Psychoacoustic evaluation of musical sounds. *Perception & Psychophysics, 23,* 483–492.

Terhardt, E. (1984). The concept of musical consonance: A link between music and psychoacoustics. *Music Perception, 1*(3), 276–295.

Terhardt, E. (1988). Intonation of tone scales: Psychoacoustic considerations. *Archives of Acoustics, 13,* 147–156.

Terhardt, E. (1991). Music perception and sensory information acquisition: Relationships and low-level analogies. *Music Perception, 8*(3), 217–239.

Terhardt, E., Stoll, G., Schermbach, R. & Parncutt, R. (1986). Tonhohemehrdeutigkeit, tonverwandschaft, und identifikation von sukzessivintervallen. *Acustica, 61,* 57–66.

Terhardt, E., Stoll, G., & Seewann, M. (1982). Pitch of complex signals according to virtual pitch theory: Tests, examples, and predictions. *Journal of the Acoustical Society of America, 71,* 671–678.

Ternstrom, S., & Sundberg, J. (1988). Intonation precision of choir singers. *Journal of the Acoustical Society of America, 84,* 59–69.

Thurlow, W. R., & Erchul, W. P. (1977). Judged similarity in pitch of octave multiples. *Perception & Psychophysics, 22,* 177–182.

Tsuzuki, K., & Suga, N. (1988). Combination sensitive neurons in the ventroanterior area of the auditory cortex of the mustached bat. *Journal of Neurophysiology, 60,* 1908–1923.

Tsuzaki, M. (1991). Effects of preceding scale on melodic interval judgments in terms of equality and size. *Music Perception, 9*(1), 47–70.

Ueda, K., & Ohgushi, K. (1987). Perceptual components of pitch. Spatial representation using a multidimensional scaling technique. *Journal of the Acoustical Society of America, 82,* 1193–1200.

Umemoto, T. (1990). The psychological structure of music. *Music Perception, 8*(2), 115–127.

Vinegrad, M. D. (1972). A direct magnitude scaling method to investigate categorical vs. continuous modes of speech perception. *Language and Speech, 15,* 114–121.

Vos, J. (1982). The perception of mistuned fifths and major thirds: Thresholds for discrimination, beats, and identification. *Perception & Psychophysics, 32,* 297–313.

Vos, J. (1984). Spectral effects in the perception of pure and mistuned intervals: Discrimination and beats. *Perception & Psychophysics, 35,* 173–185.

Vos, J. (1986). Purity ratings of tempered fifths and major thirds. *Music Perception, 3,* 221–257.

Vos, J., & van Vianen, B. G. (1985a). The effect of fundamental frequency on the discriminability between pure and tempered fifths and major thirds. *Perception & Psychophysics, 37,* 507–514.

Vos, J., & van Vianen, B. G. (1985b). Thresholds for discrimination between pure and tempered intervals: The relevance of nearly coinciding harmonics. *Journal of the Acoustical Society of America, 77,* 176–187.

Vos, P. G., & Troost, J. M. (1989). Ascending and descending melodic intervals: Statistical findings and their perceptual relevance. *Music Perception, 6*(4), 383–396.

Wachsmann, K. (1950). An equal-stepped tuning in a Ganda harp. *Nature (London), 165,* 40.

Walliser, U. (1969). Uber die Spreizung von empfundenen Intervallen gegenuber mathematisch harmonischer Intervallen bei Sinustones. *Frequency, 23,* 139–143.

Wapnick, J., Bourassa, G., & Sampson, J. (1982). The perception of tonal intervals in isolation and in melodic context. *Psychomusicology, 2,* 21–37.

Ward, W. D. (1953). *The subjective octave and the pitch of pure tones.* Unpublished doctoral dissertation, Harvard University, Cambridge, MA.

Ward, W. D. (1954). Subjective musical pitch. *Journal of the Acoustical Society of America, 26,* 369–380.

Ward, W. D. (1970). Musical perception. In J. Tobias (Ed.), *Foundations of modern auditory theory* (pp. 405–447). New York: Academic Press.

White, B. W. (1960). Recognition of distorted melodies. *American Journal of Psychology, LXXIII,* 100–107.

Wood, A. (1961). *The physics of music.* New York: Dover.

Young, R. W. (1952). Inharmonicity of plain wire piano strings. *Journal of the Acoustical Society of America, 24,* 267–273.

Zatorre, R. J. (1983). Category-boundary effects and speeded sorting with a harmonic musical-interval continuum: Evidence for dual processing. *Perception & Psychoacoustics, 9,* 739–752.

Zatorre, R. J., & Halpern, A. R. (1979). Identification, discrimination, and selective adaptation of simultaneous musical intervals. *Perception & Psychophysics, 26,* 384–395.

Zonis, E. (1973). *Classical Persian music: An introduction.* Cambridge, MA: Harvard University Press.

8

ABSOLUTE PITCH

W. DIXON WARD

Hearing Research Laboratory
University of Minnesota, Minneapolis
Minneapolis, Minnesota

I. INTRODUCTION

The ultimate in musical endowment is commonly regarded by musicians to be the possession of "absolute pitch" (AP), also called "perfect pitch" or "positive pitch": the ability to identify the frequency or musical name of a specific tone, or, conversely, the ability to produce some designated frequency, frequency level, or musical pitch without comparing the tone with any objective reference tone (i.e., without using relative pitch [RP]).

Suppose we present to an individual the following sequence of frequencies: 260, 260, 290, 330, 260, 330, 290 Hz and ask "What was that?" Individuals who are "tone-deaf" (or better, "melody-deaf," Trotter, 1967) may respond with something no more specific than "a bunch of tones." The median American nonmusician will probably answer "Yankee Doodle" (identification of tune), although many may remember enough from grade school to add that it was "do, do, re, mi, do, mi, re" (identification of solfeggio). The typical performing musician can do all of that and may add that "the sequence of successive intervals was unison, ascending major second, another ascending major second, descending major third, ascending major third, and descending major second" (identification of intervals). But only the possessor of AP is able to answer "Middle C, C, D, E, C, E, D" (identification of the musical designation of individual components), although the actual answer would probably be "Yankee Doodle in the key of C" (recognition of tonal center).

A. THE PITCH HELIX

Musically educated persons with good relative pitch behave as though they have developed an internal scale of pitch, a movable conceptual template that is permanently calibrated in terms of the pitch relations among the notes in our musical scale (i.e., in octaves, each of which is further subdivided into 12 equal parts called semitones). Because corresponding semitone markers within the octaves are given the same name, this template can be represented in the form of a pitch helix (Drobisch, 1855): a spiral that ascends the shell of an invisible vertical cylinder (Figure 1). This schema allows several aspects of pitch to be simultaneously represented: the projection of a point on this pitch spiral on the vertical axis determines its "tone height" in mels (Stevens, Volkmann, & Newman, 1937), the angle involved in its projection on the horizontal plane indicates its pitch class (the scale note—A, A$\sharp$, B, etc.—or its solfeggio), and its octave designation depends on which coil of the helix it lies on, the coils being numbered in succession from low to high frequency. If the individual with good relative pitch is presented a reference tone X and told what its pitch class and octave number are, the pitch engendered serves to tie one point on this pitch helix to all other pitches. The pitch helix is mentally rotated until the corresponding subjective semitone marker coincides with this "anchor" pitch, and the musician can now auralize all other pitches on the scale, The musician is now prepared to make judgments of the musical interval (a concept that corresponds to distance along the spiral) that separates the anchor from some other frequency. Such judgments have been shown in Chapter 7 to be categorical in nature, involving a labeling process that is analogous to that used in the discrimination of speech sounds. So, when next given tone Y, this listener will categorize the interval between X and Y, and by using knowledge of the number of semitones in that interval, the listener can indicate the musical pitch (pitch class plus octave number) that tone Y must have.

However, in the foregoing case, the helix is, so to speak, free-floating. That is, there are no *permanent* labels attached that serve to tie this subjective template to the objective world; there are only temporary ones. Thus if we were to present the person with RP a tone of 440 Hz followed by one of 525 Hz, there might be a rapid recognition of the interval as a minor third, but only if our musician was told that the first one was A_4 would he or she call the second C_5. Indeed, we could say that the first one was C_5, and the individual with RP would then indicate that the second should be $D\sharp_5$ or $E\flat_5$.

Such deception would not succeed if the person has AP, however. In this case, the helix apparently has permanent labels attached; given the sequence 440 Hz, 525 Hz, the musician would immediately recognize A_4 and C_5, and if told that the first was C_5, would merely snap "Nonsense."

This ability has been subjected to scientific scrutiny for more than a century (Stumpf, 1883), and we now know quite a bit about the characteristics of AP. Still an enigma, however, is the genesis of the ability: why do some people identify pitches with no apparent effort whereas others must engage in strenuous training to develop AP? Indeed, there was doubt that it was even possible to "learn" AP until Paul Brady did so in 1970. For this reason, its possession was for many years regarded with pride, as if it indicated that its owner were mysteriously gifted.

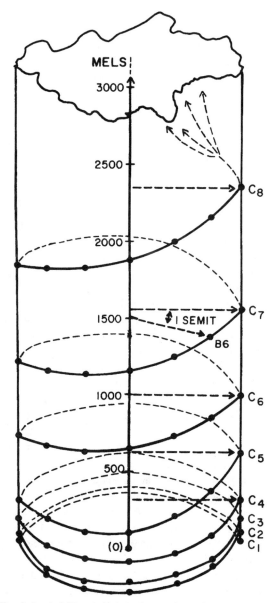

FIGURE 1 The pitch spiral. The pitch class of any point on the surface of the cylinder is determined by its projection on the xz plane and its tone height by its projection of the y axis. Thus, for example, all Cs are shown to lie at 0° azimuth; because C_6 is shown as having a tone height of 1000 mels (which is, by definition, the pitch of a 1000-Hz sinusoid), this orientation of the pitch spiral assumes a physical A_4 of about 420 Hz rather than 440 Hz. Pitch class tends to become impalpable for tone heights above 2500 mels or so (sinusoids above 5000 Hz), so the upper boundaries of both the spiral and the axis are left vague and irregular.

Yet a bit of reflection should convince one that, considering perception in other sensory modalities, AP is not so strange after all. We learn labels for colors, smells, and tastes—indeed, for speech sounds, voices, and instrumental timbres. Why not also pitches? Stimuli that fall along any metathetic continuum should be labelable, one would think, and not require a comparison between stimuli either present or in short-term memory that is involved in RP judgments. One does not need to look at a rainbow in order to see that a rooster's comb is red nor to take a whiff of camphor to identify a nearby skunk. Viewed in this light, the real question is why everyone does not have AP: Why cannot some people put labels on pitches?

II. GENESIS OF AP

There are two major theories of why some persons have AP: heredity, on the one hand, and some combination of learning, unlearning, and imprinting (early learning) on the other. The *heredity* viewpoint, espoused most vigorously by possessors such as Révész (1913) and Bachem (1937), contends that AP is a special innate ability that one either inherits or not, that those who do inherit the trait will demonstrate pitch-naming ability as soon as an appropriate situation arises, regardless of their early musical training, and that those who are not so genetically blessed can never attain the degree of excellence in identifying pitch displayed by the chosen few, no matter how much instruction they are given or how diligently they practice naming tones. The *learning* theory, in its most extreme Skinnerian form, is the exact antithesis of the hereditary position, asserting that heredity has nothing to do with the matter. Instead, the development of AP depends on some more or less fortuitous set of circumstances whereby the individual is reinforced for trying to put labels on pitches. Oakes (1951) pontificates that "an examination of the total history of the interactions involving the organism and tonal stimuli will show a complex series of events, some gross and some extremely subtle, from which pitch-naming reactions evolved or did not evolve—depending on factors in the history itself. "Just to make sure that his position cannot be disproved, he adds: "In explaining whether or not pitch-naming reactions did develop, it is necessary that we take into account every contact of the organism and tonal stimuli, and we also must consider setting and situational factors in each of the interactions." The implication, in short, is that anyone can develop AP under the "right"—but, alas, unknown—circumstances.

A variant of the learning theory is the unlearning viewpoint expressed by Abraham (1901) in the first extensive monograph on AP, who pointed out that most musical experience is not conducive to the development of AP. For example, a given tune may be heard in many different keys. How can a child develop absolute recognition of a particular frequency, say 261 Hz, if it is called "do" today and "re" tomorrow or if it is heard when he presses "the white key just left of the two black keys in the middle of the piano" at home but a completely different key (perhaps even a black one) at grandfather's house? Considering all the factors that conspire to enhance the development of RP at the expense of AP, Abraham suggested that perhaps an inborn potential for developing AP was relatively widespread, but that it is simply trained out of most of us. Watt (1917) carried Abraham's line of reasoning to its ultimate and proposed that perhaps AP is initially universal: "In some favoured persons it is acquired early and more or less unwittingly and never lost. Perhaps these persons have some special refinement of hearing....Or perhaps a highly favoured auditory disposition gives them the power to maintain their absoluteness of ear in spite of the universality of musical relativity. In that case we should all naturally possess absolute ear and then proceed to lose it or to lose the power to convert it into absolute nomenclature."

Abraham had also commented that pitch-naming ability was relatively easy to develop in children. Copp (1916) pursued this idea and on the basis of her own experience suggested that something like the modern concept of "imprinting" may be involved. Claiming that 80% of all children can be taught to produce middle C when asked and to recognize it when played or sung by others, she insisted that this is so only if they begin musical training at an early age. The notion here that AP can be developed only in children may be related to the comparative ease with which children develop accent-free speech in foreign tongues and the difficulty experienced by adults in learning to discriminate and identify phonemes that are not included in their native language.

The nature-nurture debate in this particular arena essentially ended with the death in 1957 of Bachem, who had been the most eloquent exponent of inheritance despite the lack of any convincing supportive scientific evidence. Although Profita and Bidder (1988) recently excited the popular media with a finding that 3 of 19 possessors claimed that other members of their family also had AP, leading them to go so far as to postulate that AP represented "autosomal dominant inheritance with reduced penetrance," obviously such a result could be explained just as well by environmental influences.

On the other hand, if AP is learned, it is clearly not a simple matter, at least for adults. Although Meyer (1899) indicated that he and a colleague brought themselves up to "60 and 64% terminal proficiency" after a heroic regimen of training, this improvement soon disappeared when practice was discontinued. Other later attempts to train AP (Gough, 1922; Mull, 1925; Wedell, 1934—and no doubt several that remained unreported) were equally unsuccessful. In a study of 27 of the best possessors in Vienna, Prague, Dresden, Leipzig, and Hamburg, Wellek (1938) noted a correlation of .80 between the age at which AP behavior appeared and the number of errors on an identification test, and Sergeant (1969) reported an even higher correlation between age at commencement of musical training and percentage of musicians in a particular age group possessing AP. So there is little doubt that early learning is important, although not all-important: Brady (1970), after months of practice, was finally the first adult to achieve a degree of pitch-naming ability that was indistinguishable, in terms of error score or reaction time, from four possessors who had had the ability from childhood (Carroll, 1975).

Another factor that may be important in the development of AP is whether or not there is a need for reliance on auditory cues for identification of objects in the environment. This would be the case, for example, in the blind. Indeed, 3 of Weinert's (1929) possessors and 11 of 103 studied by Bachem (1940) were blind (and, interestingly enough, none of Bachem's 11 had any relatives who claimed AP, which is an admission that one must admire Bachem for making, because it hardly supports the genetic theory of AP). More recently, Welch (1988) found that of 34 congenitally blind children who had been given musical training in schools for the blind, 22 had AP, as evidenced not only by identification tests but also by consistently reproducing familiar songs in the learned key. "Within a music lesson, subsequent transposition of these 'known' melodies would generally be noticed and commented on, and in one case, invariably provoked a hostile reaction" (Welch, 1988).

It has recently been reported that in Japan the prevalence of AP in piano students is much greater than is found in Western children (except perhaps for Copp's students). Oura and Eguchi (1981) believe that this occurs only when the children are 3–4 years old at the beginning of instruction, have not yet acquired RP ability, and are deliberately taught to identify the notes in the C major scale with fixed solfeggio ("do" is always "C").

The evidence, then, favors the early learning theory of AP, although a genetic component can never be ruled out completely unless some technique for teaching AP is developed that will succeed with everyone, or at least with all children.

III. MEASUREMENT OF AP

A. EXTRANEOUS CUES

If we accept AP as the ability to attach labels to isolated auditory stimuli on the basis of pitch tone, tests for AP should not involve extraneous cues such as loudness, timbre, duration, or any other attribute. As an extreme example, nobody would take seriously as a test for AP one in which Stimulus 1 was a taped record of someone singing "Number One" on C_3, Stimulus 2 was someone else singing "Number Two" on $C\sharp_3$, and so on, although such a procedure might be used in training.

There are two ways to ensure the nonuse (or at least ineffective use) of these other attributes. One is to try to hold constant all attributes except pitch. In this case, the set of tones to be judged would have to be balanced in advance by each listener to give a constant loudness, timbre, and duration for that listener. This is a tedious process, however, and even after it was finished, the tones would still differ in density and voluminousness.

The alternative is therefore better: vary the extraneous attributes randomly over a small range, presenting a given frequency now with one intensity and duration, next time with different ones. Under these conditions, although many parameters are varying, the only one that will provide the correct cue is pitch. Theoretically, of course, one should determine equal-pitch contours over the range of intensities to be used so that all stimuli that are supposed to be labeled A_4, for example, could be adjusted in frequency as intensity is changed so that they would actually have the same pitch for that listener. However, the change of pitch with intensity over a moderate range is ordinarily negligible (Cohen, 1961; Ward, 1954), so this factor can generally be ignored. Timbre and tonal envelope could also be varied randomly, but it is practicable to hold these particular parameters constant; indeed, if anything but pure tones (sinusoids) are used, one will be in the position of presenting listeners with several frequencies simultaneously and then asking them what *one* pitch they hear (a question that has been asked all too often, despite its patent absurdity, for example in the field of virtual pitch).

B. ABSOLUTE PIANO

From the very beginning of the study of AP, it was abundantly clear to the more astute experimenters that piano tones are extraordinarily poor stimuli from the point of view of extra cues (von Kries, 1892). Abraham (1901) discusses at some length the effect of timbre differences, nonmusical elements such as strike noises, and inharmonic partials, concluding that of all instruments, tones from the piano are probably the easiest to identify because of the myriad extraneous cues that exist. On the other hand, if the piano is struck with great force, the relative intensity of the partials may change considerably so that octave identification becomes more difficult, particularly in the lowest octave or two. Thus not all of the characteristics of the piano make identification easier. Miyazaki (1989) has shown that familiarity of timbre is at least of some importance. In a study of 10 AP possessors, he found that fewer errors of identification were made with real piano tones than with synthetic piano tones, with performance on sinusoids slightly worse still in the second and third octaves. Despite the uncertainty about the role played by pitch per se in piano-tone identification, most of the older studies on AP used piano tones, simply because pianos are abundant. However, it must not be taken for granted that "absolute piano" performance is the same as "absolute pitch."

C. RELATIVE PITCH

Much more difficult than extraneous cues to eliminate from the AP testing situation is the RP ability of a good musician. If the tones to be identified are all members of an ordinary musical scale (i.e., are separated by whole numbers of semitones), it is not much of a challenge for such a listener, knowing what any one of a series is, to compare the next with it and make the second judgment agree with the estimated interval between them. Obviously , such RP judgments are likely to increase if feedback is provided on each item (e.g., Costall, 1985; Fulgosi, Bacun, & Zaja, 1975; Fullard, Snelbecker, & Wolk, 1972; Terman, 1965).

Various procedures have been used in attempts to destroy the short-term memory trace of preceding items on which such judgments are based. Stumpf (1883) used conversation interjected between successive stimuli, Abraham (1901) used "unusual modulations" on the piano, Mull (1925) used a "short period of auditory distraction," and Petran (1932) used reading aloud. In more recent times, pitch erasers include a burst of white noise (Hartman, 1954), an unrelated interval-comparison task (Hurni-Schlegel & Lang, 1978), a glissando from a low frequency to 4500–5500 Hz (Balzano, 1984) and nonacoustic tasks such as one involving three-letter trigrams (Zatorre & Beckett, 1989). The efficacy of an intervening series of tones in reducing the ability to tell whether an initial tone and a final tone are the same or different has received some attention (Butler & Ward, 1988; Costall, 1985; Deutsch, 1973, 1982). Costall showed that as few as three intervening notes can disrupt pitch memory in musicians without AP. Indeed, some experimenters have merely relied on a blank interval of a minute or as little as 10 sec to destroy memory of a tone (Carroll, 1975; Heller & Auerbach, 1972; Lundin & Allen, 1962), apparently on the basis of a study of two possessors and two nonpossessors by Bachem (1954) in which he reported that comparison judgments deteriorated in the nonpossessors after as short an interval as 15 sec. However, no details of procedure or results were given by Bachem, and a study by Rakowski and Morawska-Büngeler (1987) indicates that nonpossessors can hold pitches in short-term memory for periods as long as 5 minutes.

Fortunately, there is evidence that RP is seldom used in AP experiments. Petran (1932), after a thorough review of the literature on AP at that time, did an experiment in which each of 16 subjects was asked to identify a single piano tone at the time of awakening on each of 50 days; then at the end of that time, the same 50 tones were tested in a single session. There were no significant differences between the two tests in either the number or degree of errors, which certainly suggests that in the latter case no judgments were made on the basis of RP. Perhaps those who believe they "have" AP feel no need for additional cues, and those who do not are seldom confident enough of any particular judgment (in the absence of feedback) to make estimating the interval between that stimulus and the next one worthwhile.

Given that there is no guaranteed "pitch eraser," the best way of testing whether or not RP was used in any given experiment is to examine the pattern of each subject's responses. If an error of, say, +2 categories is followed by an error of the same magnitude on the next two or three stimuli, it is likely that RP was being used (again, assuming no feedback). Appropriate statistical tests will allow one to determine the probability that the particular pattern of errors observed is a chance one. However, even this is not completely infallible. As Petran points out, subjects with poor RP may be trying to use it but failing, so that "even though there may be no trace of correct interval judgments in the results of a series test for absolute pitch, yet incorrect interval judgments may be there in numbers." This dilemma seems to have no solution.

RP may also enter into AP studies in other ways. If listeners are permitted to hum and whistle at will, many of them can come quite close to the correct pitch from knowledge of the highest or lowest note in their range (although the stability of either of these is not outstanding). Others, even without making any sound, perform as if they have AP for a single tone. That is, some violinists are apparently able to auralize A_4 at will and can, given time, compare any pitch with this single internal standard. Bachem (1937) calls this type of AP "quasi-absolute pitch."

A special type of quasi-AP exists in some persons who are afflicted with a permanent tinnitus of fixed pitch. Stumpf (1901) finally disclosed the fact that he was such a person: he had, in essence, a built-in tuning fork whose pitch was very nearly that of a 1500-Hz tone, so it was not necessary for him to auralize some internal standard—it was always there for the listening. There would seem to be no way to discriminate persons with "true" AP from those with quasi-AP on the basis of error scores, although one might search for differences in the time required to make judgments, which would be expected to be greater for those with quasi-AP because they must make a RP estimate (except, of course, when the stimulus is the same as their internal standard). No one has recently studied persons with quasi-AP in depth.

D. ACCURACY OF AP

From this discussion of some of the pitfalls of procedure and caveats of interpretation, it appears that for the least equivocal results, one should use for the study of AP, as the ability to identify both pitch class and tone height, only pure-tone stimuli whose intensity and duration are varied randomly over a narrow range. Let us turn, then, to specific procedures that have been used to measure AP. As the original definition implies, AP is manifested either by accurate production of a designated note or by correct categorization of a presented tone. The problem is deciding on how to define "accurate" and "correct" in the two respective cases. "Accuracy" in production is perhaps the easier to define, as only one psychophysical method is applicable—the method of adjustment. Even then, though, one can argue over the relative merits of "absolute accuracy" and "relative accuracy." Absolute accuracy would be measured by calculating the difference between frequencies based on $A_4 = 440$ Hz and those produced by the subject. The subject's usefulness as an animate tuning fork in setting the pitch for a chorus would depend on absolute accuracy. However, such a procedure is in a sense "unfair" to a person who grew up with a piano tuned a semitone or so flat or who has suffered "paracusis": a change in the pitch aroused by a specific frequency (Ward, 1954), presumably due to a more or less localized disturbance on the basilar membrane. So if our interest is not so much in the practical aspects of AP as in the theoretical basis of absolute identification, the important statistic would be relative variability, as manifested in the distribution of repeated adjustments. From this point of view, constant errors should be ignored; the "best" absolute pitcher is the individual with the lowest variance.

There is, however, yet another problem: what to do about "octave errors." Suppose that the subject, told to adjust an oscillator to A_4, gives successive values of 444, 432, 449, 882, and 438 Hz. To say that the mean of these judgments is 529 Hz or that the SD is 177 Hz would be true but completely misleading, because the next-to-last judgment, in terms of the pitch helix, was within a few hertz of the correct pitch class but was one octave off in tone height. Although we may be in the position of trying to average apples with oranges, the most accepted solution to the problem here has been to consider only pitch class. In the example given, the 882 Hz would be dropped a physical octave to 441 Hz, making the mean now also 441 Hz with a standard deviation of 5.7 Hz. (A more rigorous procedure would be to determine the frequency that actually appeared to be one octave lower than 882 Hz and use this value in calculating the mean, but ordinarily the difference between the subjective octave and the physical octave will be small enough [Ward, 1954] that its determination would not be worth the considerable effort involved.)

Identification techniques, although greater in variety, have the same problems as pitch production, plus a few more. Not only must one deal with octave errors and constant errors, but now the categorization process also confuses the issue. It becomes difficult to test the ability of subjects to identify quarter tones because half of the stimuli will have no "name" in our chromatic scale. This problem is attacked by asking the subject to learn a new set of labels—that is, arbitrary numbers assigned to specific frequencies. One can then apply information-transfer analysis to an experiment in which a subject attempts to identify a series of stimuli consisting of some number of items from this fixed set. In theory, such a procedure, when used not only for testing but also for training, might also be a method of discovering persons with "latent AP"—persons who can make absolute judgments but have never learned the names of the notes of the scale. However, to our knowledge, no instance of such a person being "discovered" in this fashion has been reported in the literature.

E. WHITE NOTES VS. BLACK NOTES

The labeling process is involved in a recent spate of studies concerned with an ancient observation (Baird, 1917) that white notes were more accurately identified than black notes. Miyazaki (1988) found that both accuracy and speed of judgment were superior for the white notes even when listeners were instructed to respond as rapidly as possible (Miyazaki, 1990). Although he points out that piano instruction always begins with the key of C, so that perhaps the white notes that constitute the diatonic scale of C major are simply always better learned, other possible explanations exist. For example, the difference in accuracy might be due to response bias; if a listener gives white note responses more often than black note responses (in identification of a series of tones in which each of the 12 pitch classes occurred equally often), then of course the measured percent correct identification will be higher for the white notes. However, response bias would not account for the higher speed of response to white keys. On the other hand, the possibility that a simple motor response bias is involved when the listener is required to make a response by pressing the appropriate key on a dummy keyboard, because the black keys are harder to reach, would not account for greater accuracy for white keys.

Takeuchi and Hulse (1991) attempted to examine these alternatives by not only calculating response bias but also eliminating differences in motor response. Subjects had to simply respond "same" or "different" when presented simultaneously a tone and a visual pitch-class name. Of 17 AP possessors, 15 made significantly more errors on black-note stimuli than on white. Response bias was present, but was only significant for 7 subjects, so some other factors must have been operating. All but one of the 14 responded significantly more slowly when either the tone presented or the visual pitch name was black. Clearly the difference must be ascribed to differences in the processing of stimuli. Takeuchi and Hulse ignore Miyazaki's early-learning-of-white-notes proposal and suggest instead that the superiority is due to (a) greater exposure to white notes in music in general in all the subjects' musical history (not just when the person is first learning) and/or to (b) the necessity to make one more decision when a black note is involved than when it is not. The problem of labeling enters the latter explanation. The black note between C and D is not X (a single symbol) but instead is called either C♯ or D♭. So when the visual stimulus is D♭, two steps in processing would appear to be needed: "Is it D? No. Is it lower? Yes." So if this were the whole story, the superiority of white notes would be merely an artifact. The problem might be half solved by using the natural sign with visual stimuli (e.g., E♮ instead of E), or by using stimuli such as B♯, E♯, F♭, and C♭, thus making judgment of each stimulus a 2-step process. However, there appears to be no easy way around the fact that the black notes are not labeled by a single symbol (indeed, the term "accidental" implies that they do not even deserve a unique symbol).

So the degree to which white-note superiority is due to early learning, overlearning, or simpler cognitive processing is still unknown and is likely to remain so, unless a group of children can be shielded from all music until age 3, at which point they begin to study piano, using full chromatic (atonal) melodies and harmonies, a fixed solfeggio in which the black notes are given distinctive labels that in no way resemble those of their immediate neighbors (e.g., do, key, re, guy, mi, fa, nay, sol, bee, la, pay, ti, do) and a system of musical notation that no longer assigns second class citizenship to diatonic "accidentals."

F. INFORMATION TRANSFER IN AN EXPERT POSSESSOR

In 1952, Pollack published the first study of the information transmitted by pitch in average (unselected) listeners, finding that the maximum information that could be transmitted by pitch was only about 2.7 bits (i.e., $2^{2.7} = 7$ different pitches spread over the entire frequency range could just be named correctly by his best listener). His results are in line with the general rule that for most sensory attributes, only "the magic number 7 ± 2" of consistently identifiable stimuli exist

(Miller, 1956). However, it was clear that Pollack's subjects used only tone height in their judgments: none had AP. For this reason an intensive study of one particular listener, JL, was undertaken (Ward, 1953). Although these data are 40 years old, to my knowledge no one has demonstrated greater facility at pitch naming than JL, so the experiments will be reported here in detail.

In each of the experiments of this study, each of a set of 10 (or, for some tests, 20) frequencies was presented to the left ear of JL one at a time together with its number in that series, and JL was instructed to write on a card with the appropriate numbers anything that would help her identify number 1, number 2, and so on. After the entire list had been presented twice, a set of 100 items, 10 of each category, was judged. The intensity was varied randomly over a 20-dB range around 50 phons. JL responded vocally to each test item with a number; no feedback was given. The order of stimuli was semirandom: each subset of 20 stimuli contained two of each of the categories, the only rule of succession being that there could not be three of the same category in a row, even at the subset boundary. A confusion matrix was constructed for each test, and by means of standard formulas the information transmitted was determined. From this, the number of categories over this range that could have been correctly distinguished on a consistent basis was calculated. No attempt was made to erase the short-term memory effect via interfering tones, conversation, or noise; as will be seen, however, this was not a serious mistake because her pattern of errors indicated little if any serial dependence. JL was seated in an anechoic chamber while the experimenter was outside; communication took place via intercom.

The sequence of tests with experimental outcomes is shown in Figure 2. The first test used 10 stimuli from C_4 (262 Hz) to A_7 (3520 Hz). Successive stimuli were separated by a musical fourth (i.e., C_4, F_4, Bb_4, etc.) so that there was no duplication of pitch class, a move designed to minimize octave errors) yet with large degrees of difference in tone height. JL made no errors on this test, although the ordinary musician without absolute pitch will indicate transfer of only about 2.4 bits of information, implying that five categories could have been distinguished consistently (this test is used routinely to screen for possessors of AP in groups of listeners).

In Test 2, again the stimuli had different names, but in this case they were separated only by 1 semitone (A_5 to $F\#_6$, or 880 Hz to 1480 Hz). Again JL made no errors.

Next, a situation that would maximize the possibility of octave confusions was developed. In Test 3, five Cs and five Gs were used: from C_4 (262 Hz) to G_8 6270 Hz). In this test, JL made three mistakes: number 7 (C_7) was called number 5 (C_6) twice and 5 was called 7 once. This is still very close to perfect transmission of information, and the errors all occurred in the first half of the test battery, suggesting that a slight amount of learning had occurred. This result reinforces the hypothesis that octave errors are largely an artifact of using piano tones or other complex stimuli that do not have a single pitch.

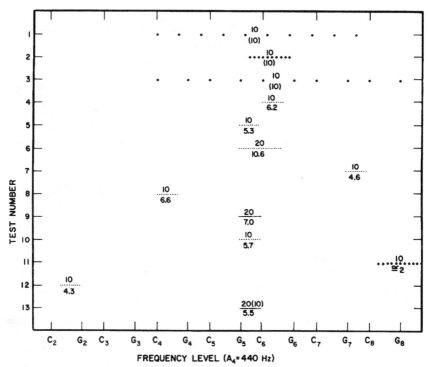

FIGURE 2 Graphic representation of pitch identification tests on subject JL. For each test, the upper number indicates the number of different stimuli involved, the dots show their frequency level, and the lower number represents the information transmitted in the form of the number of stimuli in the range concerned that could have been identified without error.

Because earlier experiments on persons with AP had indicated that the best performers could distinguish quarter tones with 95% accuracy (Abraham, 1901; Petran, 1932; van Krevelen, 1951; for a detailed summary of this early literature see Ward, 1963a, 1963b), Test 4 involved 10 stimuli spaced by 50 cents from C_6 to $E_6 + 50$ (1046 to 1357 Hz). With this set of tone, JL finally made some errors, dropping to 80% correct. The pattern of these errors is shown in Table I, which is a horizontal version of the diagonal of the confusion matrix. In this case, the information transmitted was 2.64 bits, implying a potential error-free discriminability of 6.2 categories, a value slightly greater than the 5.5 semitones spanned by the range used.

One might conclude from this that JL could just identify perfectly tones 1 semitone apart over the entire auditory range. However, it was next necessary to determine whether or not, if one range of frequencies contained X discriminable categories and an adjacent range contained Y, the results of a test involving both ranges would indicate a transmission of information of $X + Y$. Therefore, in Test 5,

TABLE I   Responses Made to Each Stimulus in Test 4 (C_6 to E_6 + 50 cents)

Stimulus minus response	Stimulus number									
	1	2	3	4	5	6	7	8	9	10
+1		6	1	1		2				
0	10	4	7	9	8	7	8	9	9	9
−1			2		2	1	2	1	1	1

10 quarter tones from G_5 − 25 to B_5 + 25 were used, and Test 6 involved all 20 quarter tones from G_5 − 25 to E_6 + 25 (the total range of Tests 4 and 5). The reason for using G_5 − 25, G_5 + 25, $G\sharp_5$ − 25, etc., instead of G_5, G_5 + 50, $G\sharp_5$, etc., was that a test for AP using the method of adjustment had shown that JL's internal template was about 25 cents flat re A_4 = 440 Hz (Ward, 1954); her pitch helix was apparently tuned much closer to the old "physical" standard pitch based on C_4 = 256 Hz.

Test 5 gave an information transmission of 2.34 bits (5.2 categories), and Test 6 indicated 3.41 bits (10.6 categories). Based on Tests 4 and 5, the expected value of distinguishable categories in Test 6 was 6.25 + 5.3, or 11.5, so one category in the process of doubling the number of alternatives, probably due to elimination of one boundary in the middle.

The implication that completely error-free performance was limited to conventional semitone categories was checked by two more 10-quarter-tone tests: Test 7 showed 2.20 bits transmitted (4.6 categories) in the range of G_7 − 25 to B_7 + 25, and Test 8 gave 2.71 bits (6.6 categories) from $C\sharp_4$ + 25 to $F\sharp_4$ − 25. In the latter test, Stimuli 8, 9, and 10 (F_4 − 25, F_4 + 25, and $F\sharp_4$ − 25) were correctly identified all 10 times.

In order to make sure that JL was taxed to the limit of her AP ability, Test 9 used categories separated by only 25 cents. The range was the same as for Test 5 (G_5 − 25 to B_5 + 25), but there were 20 stimuli instead of 10. Results showed a slight improvement over Test 5, as 2.8 bits were transmitted (7.0 categories). That this improvement was more than a learning effect was shown by Test 10, which was a repetition of Test 5 and gave nearly the same result: 2.5 bits, or 5.7 categories.

In order to determine the limits of JL's identification range, Test 11 was designed to investigate the area from D_8 to B_8 in 100-cent (semitone) steps. However, the test was terminated after 30 trials because JL became upset at being unable to perform accurately; her last nine responses were all either 8, 9, or 10, even though the stimuli were actually 3, 7, 6, 2, 5, 8, 2, 5, 3. JL thus displayed the "chroma fixation" reported by Bachem (1948): an inability to name notes much above 4000 Hz (roughly the topmost note on the piano). This was somewhat surprising because JL, who was also serving as a subject in a study of relative pitch (Ward, 1954), had learned to make octave judgments in this range; that is, given a reference tone of A_7, she would consistently set a variable tone to about A_8 + 50, However, her experience with these high-frequency tones was apparently too limited to affect her ability to identify them on an absolute basis.

Performance is somewhat degraded at extremely low frequencies also. Test 12 (D_2 + 25 to G_2 − 25, or 75 to 91 Hz, in 50-cent steps) gave 2.1 bits, or 4.3 categories.

On the final test, JL was told that it was to be a repetition of Test 9 (20 stimuli at 25-cent intervals); however, only stimuli 1, 3, 5, … 19 were actually presented. The results were essentially the same as for Tests 5 and 10: 2.45 bits, implying 5.5 discriminable categories. JL was unaware that half of the possible categories had never been presented.

In all these tests, when errors were made, they usually occurred at random. That is, there was never a long run of errors in the same direction that would imply that JL was attempting to use relative pitch. So in her case, the use of a short-term-memory eraser was unnecessary. It may also be mentioned that errors occurred as often on the weaker stimuli as on the stronger stimuli (recall that the range of intensities was 20 dB).

One can infer from these data that JL should be able to identify without error some 70 to 75 pitches in the auditory range, which is about the number of semitones from 60 to 4000 Hz, and that quarter tones can be discriminated well above chance. Indeed, if one uses the criterion for AP proposed by Bachem—that is, ignoring errors in which the correct category was missed by only one category—JL would be considered able to name quarter tones accurately. However, that seems to be about the limit, as 25-cent intervals transfer only slightly more information than 50-cent intervals.

A test of "absolute loudness" on JL (1000-Hz tone, 10 intensities from 10 to 100 dB SPL in 9-dB steps) showed information transmitted to be 2.69 bits (6.5 categories), so one could contend that there are, for JL, about 500 pure tones that can be distinguished without error. However, this extrapolation was not tested directly. Even now, apparently only one experiment has attempted to have subjects judge pitch and loudness categories simultaneously (Fulgosi et al., 1975), and because none of the subjects in that study had AP, the total information transmitted by both loudness and pitch was only 3.85 bits rather than 9, implying something on the order of only 14 separable pure tones—and this in a situation in which the subjects were given feedback, scored their own results, and revealed their scores to their classmates. One would have to conclude that possessors of AP are indeed different.

Burns and Campbell (1994) directly compared the absolute identification and paired-comparison discrimination of pure tones by possessors of AP with the identification and discrimination of melodic intervals by possessors of RP, in both cases over a range of one octave. In order to facilitate comparisons between identification and discrimination, the d' metric was used to measure performance in both cases. Cumulative d' for identification over a one-octave range provides a direct estimate of information transfer over this range. For both possessors of "precise" AP and possessors of RP, the estimated information transfer was, on average, about 3.6 bits, corresponding to perfect identification of 12 categories, and the separation of tones or intervals corresponding to the threshold for reliable (71% correct) identification was about 35 cents (i.e., less than a quarter tone). The results for the AP possessors are compatible with the identification performance of JL over a similar range.

Despite the extraordinary precision of identification resolution by possessors of AP, they remain "normal" in the sense that they can still discriminate many more tones than they can identify, that is, the separation of tones for reliable discrimination was on the order of 8 cents. However, this is not true for discrimination of intervals by the possessors of RP. In their case, discrimination resolution was about the same as identification resolution, that is, the intervals were perceived "categorically."

IV. STABILITY OF THE INTERNAL STANDARD

All pitch-frequency relations, both in possessors and in nonpossessors of AP, are apparently established early in life and cannot be changed. If something happens to disturb the normal hydromechanical or neurophysiological processes at one particular area of an ear so that a given frequency no longer affects exactly the same receptors and associated neural elements, the pitch in this region is shifted and the listener has "musical paracusis." (And, if the two ears are not affected equally, "binaural diplacusis" will exist.) However, no learning takes place; that is, musical paracusis does not gradually disappear as one "relearns" that a 3500-Hz tone arouses a percept formerly associated with a 3700-Hz tone.

Only a possessor of AP, however, will become aware of a change in the *entire* tuning of the auditory system. If, for some reason, *all* pitches were shifted by the same percentage, the individual with only RP ability would hear nothing amiss. The possessor of AP, though, would complain that everything is in the "wrong" key—that all music sounds as though it had been transposed.

Interestingly enough, several possessors do indeed make this specific complaint. After age 50 or so, music is heard one or more semitones sharp from what it "ought" to be. Triepel (1934) reported that this occurred in himself, his father, and his brother. Vernon (1977) indicated that at about age 52, keys were shifted about a semitone. This was particularly distressing because, as a result, he heard the overture to *Die Meistersinger* in C♯ instead of C, and for him, C is "strong and masculine" whereas C♯ is "lascivious and effeminate." Later, at age 71, he heard everything 2 semitones high, which presumably rescued Wagner although Vernon fails to indicate the nature of "D-ness" for him. J. F. Beck (personal communication, 1978) experienced a 1-semitone sharping at 40 years of age that progressed to 2 semitones at age 58, and at age 71 he (J. F. Beck, personal communication, 1991) heard everything sharp, sometimes by 3 semitones and sometimes by 2 semitones. Although he finds it somewhat disconcerting to watch a trumpet player performing in B♭ but to hear it in C, he indicates that if he can watch the score, "the eyes and ears lock in synchrony" and everything sounds all right.

It is possible that some possessors have experienced this shift without being consciously aware of it. For example, Corliss (1973) reports that she was surprised to find that when she plays Chopin's Prelude in A Major (Op. 28, No. 7) from memory (pitch memory, not motor memory), she performs it in G♯. Although she attributes this to the fact that she originally learned the piece as a child on an old piano that was more than a quarter tone flat, it may be that she, too, has a hearing mechanism that has aged by 1 semitone. Apparently, at any rate, one aspect of presbyacusis (the change in hearing with age) may be a gradual shift of the excitation on the basilar membrane in the direction of the oval window.

It seems, however, that not everyone experiences this change. Wynn (1992) compared adjustments to A_4 made in 1989 by five AP possessors to those made in 1971 and 1976, finding that there was no consistent change in direction. Indeed, tests of Carpenter's (1951) subject showed no significant change at age 71 from the 435 Hz he claimed to be his A_4 65 years earlier. An interesting aspect of Wynn's results is that each of the five subjects gave an A_4 in 1989 that was closer to 440 Hz than in the 1971–1976 tests: three dropped about 7 Hz from 450 Hz or higher, and two rose slightly (to 434 from 433 and to 438 from 435). Perhaps the standard for tuning of musical instruments and orchestras to the A_4 equal to 440 Hz is becoming more widespread, so that a slow change in the perceived pitch can be induced by repeated exposure to this tuning.

That the internal standard of possessors can be slightly shifted, at least temporarily, by preceding stimuli was shown in an ingenious study by Tsuzaki (1992). His nine AP possessors had to decide whether a terminal tone was C_5, $C_5 + 15$, or $C_5 - 15$ at the end of an ascending diatonic scale (from C_4 to B_4) in which all or some of the scale tones were mistuned, either systematically or randomly. The best performance (71% correct) resulted when there was no detuning; this result is not surprising, as in this condition both AP and RP can be used to make the judgment. Worst performance (45% correct) was shown when all scale notes were shifted 50 cents downward; in this condition, all three targets were generally judged to be "too sharp." Only slightly better performance (50% correct) was found when all scale tones were shifted upward by 50 cents or randomly in magnitude and direction. Intermediate performance (about 60% correct) resulted for scales in which only do and sol or la and ti were sharped or flatted by 50 cents, and for a "heterophonic" scale in which mi and ti were lowered by a semitone (i.e., to E♭ and B♭).

Changes in tuning of intermediate duration have also been reported in tests using the method of adjustment. Abraham (1901) indicates that his A_4 varied, over a 3-month period, from 451.3 to 442.8 Hz in a random manner, though consistent on a single day. Wynn (1971, 1972) tested his wife's ability to sing A_4 on demand over 3 months, during which time the frequency produced rose from about 440 Hz in the first 2 weeks to 462 Hz in the last month, and had remained there 6 months later. Wynn saw in those data a slow cyclical change in the mean that seemed to be associated with the menstrual cycle; however, that particular evidence is far from compelling. At least body temperature changes associated with the menstrual cycle are not responsible for changes in AP; Emde and Klinke (1977) tested four AP possessors in two experiments that involved a change in body temperature of 1.0–1.5°C and found no correlation between temperature and performance.

A recent report by Chaloupka, Mitchell, and Muirhead (1994) provides a second example of paracusis represented by a drop in pitch. While being administered Tegritol (carbamazepine) for "chronic fatigue syndrome," a 26-year-old concert pianist with AP showed, by extensive tests (adjustment, identification, and singing), that the rise in frequency needed to produce a given pitch increased with frequency from about 30 cents at C_1 to 110 cents at C_7. The shift was reversible, disappearing as soon as the medication was terminated. The mechanism inducing this graded drop in pitch is unknown; although the authors point out that it could represent either central or peripheral changes, it is already known that a frequency-dependent drop in pitch due to peripheral factors can be induced by intense sound (Ward, Selters, & Glorig, 1961). Immediately after a unilateral exposure to high-intensity impulses, three listeners experienced a severe temporary hearing loss that was accompanied by a pronounced paracusis. In the most severe case, tones above 2000 Hz were heard only as a distortion; tones in the 1-kHz range were heard as shifted down by 3 semitones, 500 Hz was shifted by 1 semitone, with frequencies below about 200 Hz unaffected (as determined by comparing the percept in the exposed ear with that in the contralateral ear). (This shows rather conclusively that place of stimulation on the basilar membrane and not frequency of neural discharge is what was affected, as the pitch of only very low frequencies is determined solely by the rate of neural discharge.) Since physical harmonics no longer were subjectively harmonic, music sounded horrible for many hours. A day later, when the temporary hearing loss had subsided to only 40 dB, tones at 3 kHz, although no longer noisy, were still shifted down by about a semitone. However, the slight inharmonicity no longer affected the overall character of musical perception, as was apparently the case in the musician studied by Chaloupka et al.

V. NEUROLOGICAL CORRELATES OF AP

If possessors of AP differ from nonpossessors in ability to identify tones, is this because the processing of auditory information is different, and if so, might this difference be manifested in cortical activity? Klein, Coles, and Donchin (1982) attempted to answer this question by comparing cortical potentials recorded from four possessors and four nonpossessors in a "20% oddball" task. In this paradigm, the subject is presented a series of stimuli in which one stimulus has a probability of occurrence of 0.8 and the other a probability of 0.2, and the subject must count (attend to) the number of times the rarer occurred. They found that the P300 component of cortical activity (activity about 300 msec after stimulus onset) associated with the rarer event was the same for both groups when the events were visual but was lower in the AP group for auditory stimuli of 1100 and 1000 Hz. This result is surprising, because one would think that only RP would be needed in order to recognize a change, so that there would be no reason that a different judgment would have to be made by possessors, although Klein et al. speculate that they "maintain a permanent stored comparison for tones and, therefore, they do not have to update their internal representations of the tonal inputs."

   To guard against the possibility that musical training per se might be responsible for the P300 reduction, Wayman Frisina, Walton, Hantz, and Crummer (1992) used a 500-Hz standard and a 1000-Hz oddball on 10 musicians with AP (65% or more correct in identifying piano tones from C_1 to C_7, with octave errors ignored and 1-semitone errors called "half wrong"), 14 musicians without AP, and 11 nonmusicians. The nonmusicians and non-AP musicians gave average P300 magnitudes of 16.6 and 16.1 μV, both of which were significantly higher than the average 4.7 μV in the possessors.

   On the other hand, Tervaniemi, Alho, Paavilainen, Sams, and Näätänen (1993) found no difference in a different cortical potential, the "mismatch negativity" response occurring 100 to 250 msec after stimulus onset, between groups of eight possessors and eight equally musically trained listeners in a series of 10% oddball tests in which the standard was either $C_4 - 50$, C_4, $C_4 + 50$, or $C\sharp_4$, and the oddball a tone 50 or 100 cents higher. Both piano tones and sinusoids were used. In this case, the listeners were simply sitting quietly and reading, being instructed to ignore the auditory stimuli, so apparently "attention" is important in producing a difference between possessors and nonpossessors. There was no P300 response in either case, from which Tervaniemi et al. argue that their experiments show that "pitch discrimination and naming are based on different brain mechanisms." But because it made no difference whether either the standard or the oddball was "on" a particular musical pitch or a quarter tone off, it is difficult to see how the results have any implications for AP at all.

   Apparently AP lives mostly in the right hemisphere along with other musical abilities, as left lobectomy did not affect a 17-year-old pianist's ability (Zatorre, 1989). Indeed, the operation improved it, as he heard normally afterwards despite a 1-semitone constant error before the operation.

VI. LEARNING AP

   Various methods have been proposed for improving proficiency at pitch naming up to the level displayed by a "true" possessor. The first attempt was made by Max Meyer and Heyfelder in 1895 (Meyer, 1899). Beginning with 10 different pitches (both piano tones and tuning forks), they gradually increased the number to 39. Although details of procedure are not given, Meyer states that by the time they abandoned the experiment, they had achieved 64% and 60% proficiency. He also indicates that at the time he was writing the article (3 years later), he had lost the increased facility.

Gough (1922) reports that the average error of nine graduate students dropped from 5 semitones to about 1.5 after a year of practice on identification of piano tones. A study by Mull (1925) also produced a slight improvement in the ability to recognize one particular tone after 9 months of practice (1 hour weekly). Her technique, apparently designed to develop quasi-AP, consisted of presenting middle C steadily for 15 minutes (!) and then having the listener try to pick middle C from a series of tones within a two-octave range. As soon as a subject responded, the experimenter told the subject whether or not he or she was correct; then middle C was again presented (happily, only 5 sec this time), followed by another random series of tones, and so on. At the end of this training, a series of tests was performed in which no correction was given. In this series, the nine stimuli used were 232 to 296 in 8-Hz steps (i.e., somewhere around quarter-tone separation); in a long series of tones, the subject was asked to indicate the occurrence of each middle C (256 Hz at that time). In four successive sessions, 43%, 47%, 64%, and 57% of tones were identified correctly respectively, which is hardly evidence that AP has developed.

Wedell's (1934) study was the first to use response categories other than musical-scale values. The range of frequencies from 50 to 7500 Hz was divided in order to provide 5, 9, 13, 27, 25, or 49 stimuli separated by approximately equal values of pitch extent (tone height)—actually, by equal numbers of just-noticeable differences: 333, 167, 111, 84, 55, and 28, respectively. All were presented at a loudness level of 40 phons. The subject had a chart on which was printed a list of the frequencies used in that particular test.

In the first part of his experiment, Wedell measured the learning of the 25-category series in four subjects. In each daily experimental session, each tone was first presented once, and the subject was asked to identify each, without correction. Then three complete series were presented with feedback. Significant improvement was shown from Day 1 to Day 4 on Session 1, but little thereafter (a total of 20 sessions were run). The average error dropped from about 2.5 categories (125 DLs) to just over 1 category (60 DLs). After a 3-month rest, he retrained the subjects on the 25-category series; then he ran two sessions using the 49-item series. The average error remained at 60 DLs (about 3 semitones), although this was now more than a two-category separation. No subjects came close to 100% correct identification. A second experiment in which listeners were first trained to identify 5, then 9, then 13 different stimuli also produced only slight improvement; none could get 100% correct on the 13-item series.

Lundin and Allen (1962) report improvement of performance in both possessors and nonpossessors using a 24-button voting board that provided feedback automatically. Lundin (1963) indicates that with this apparatus, learning was even more facilitated by starting with a few tones and gradually increasing their number but gives no details.

A variant of Mull's "learn a single reference" method was proposed by Cuddy in 1968. Here, listeners were required to respond either "A" or "not A" to a series of semitones ranging from E_4 to $D\sharp_5$ in which A_4 occurred very often during the early training, gradually dropping in later sessions; all six subjects showed improvement with practice. Brady (1970) used this procedure in the unique development of his ability to name pitches. Using a computer, he presented himself various tones from 117 to 880 Hz in which there was a high proportion of Cs; as training progressed, the proportion gradually dropped to the "random" 1/12. Although he admits using RP at the beginning of the experiment, he reports that gradually (i.e., no sudden "revelation") he became able to recognize any C immediately. In tests using Petran's (1932) technique for confirming his ability (i.e., having his wife play a single note chosen at random every morning for 57 days), he made two 2-semitone errors, 18 1-semitone errors, and was correct 37 times. As indicated earlier, Carroll (1975) tested Brady's ability, finding that he responded as accurately and as swiftly as four persons who claimed AP without any formal training. However, Brady himself points out that, unlike them, he does not identify the key of a piece instantly.

Cuddy (1971) extended the single-standard method to three standards. The stimuli in the main experimental group were all of the Fs, As, and Cs from F3 to C_7 (175 to 2093 Hz). Ability to learn to identify these 12 stimuli was compared with learning to identify (a) 12 tones over the same range separated by 3 or 4 semitones with no repetition of pitch class or (b) 12 tones with essentially equal arithmetic spacing. All series included A_4. Training led to great improvement in the musicians using triad spacing; indeed, three listeners finally achieved 100% scores (3.59 bits). Of course, this is a rather unusual kind of AP; the listener had only to identify the octave in which the tone occurred. Because all tones were members of the ordinary F triad, she had only to remember this triad in order to decide whether it was the tonic (F), the third (A), or the fifth (C) of the chord.

Heller and Auerbach (1972) examined the importance of the type of feedback during training. Using semitone stimuli from F_4 to D_5, they developed a series of four training tapes in which the proportion of A_4s was successively 40%, 30%, 20%, and 10%. One group of subjects was told whether each tone was A or not A while the other group received full feedback. Improvement in ability to identify all tones in a no-feedback trial was the same for both groups. Heller and Auerbach conclude that the single-standard procedure is not crucial. However, the improvement was only from 27% to 37%, and this may merely represent learning to use RP more efficiently. In view of this equivocal result, the issue can hardly be regarded as closed. The Japanese investigators who reported the high rate of success in training very young children using a fixed-do system (Oura & Eguchi, 1981) also introduced another device to facilitate the learning process. They have the child associate a unique visual symbol with each note. Both notes and chords are learned; a flag of a particular color having three of the symbols signifies a particular chord. Although Cohen and Baird (1990) found no development of AP in Canadian children in a study using this flag-and-symbols approach, their subjects were not simultaneously taking daily piano lessons as the Japanese children were, and the training was given for only a few weeks.

Burge (1986) has developed a commercialized procedure that differs from earlier ones in that it exhorts learners (adults even) to attach a color to each pitch class. However, a study of 26 volunteers (music majors) did not indicate any particular advantage to that procedure (Rush, 1989). Although there was some improvement in identification of piano tones that was correlated with the number of weeks that the individual devoted to the program, only one person achieved what would be regarded as real AP, correctly identifying the pitch class of 106 out of 120 piano tones, and that person already got 60% correct in the pretest, and so was, as it were, halfway there to begin with.

VII. COLORED HEARING

Sometimes musicians associate specific tones (Rogers, 1987), tonalities (Cuddy, 1985; Peacock, 1985), or modes (Bernard, 1986) not only with affect but also with colors. Obviously only possessors of AP could be expected to do this. Unfortunately, however, the colors associated with a particular tone differ drastically from individual to individual even though the idiosyncratic differences may be very stable (Block, 1983). Agreement between possessors is rare enough that when two possessors discovered by accident that they both regarded C as white and A as red, they felt it was worth publishing (Carroll & Greenberg, 1961) The only generalization about the relation of pitch to color that seems to have held up involves tone height instead of pitch class. Asked to assign one of six colors to pure tones at octaves from 125 to 8000 Hz plus 12000 Hz, 995 children assigned darker colors (blue and violet) to 125 and 250 Hz, the lightest color (yellow) to 8000 and 12000 Hz at slightly greater than chance (Simpson, Quinn, & Ausubel, 1956). So high is bright, low is dark, as is the case for speech (Marks, 1975).

VIII. ABSOLUTE TONALITY

If the ability to acquire AP is something that everyone is born with, but is usually trained out of us by our RP musical milieu, it might still be possible that some vestige of AP remains. If a particular melody were to be always heard in the same key, say C, perhaps a listener could recognize that it had been played in a different key when performed in F, even though neither key could be named.

The foregoing line of thought led to some experiments involving this "absolute tonality," or perhaps one should say "relatively absolute tonality." Bach wrote the *Wohltempierte Klavier* to illustrate that with equal temperament, the piano can be played in any way without "wolf tones" or other dissonances associated with certain intervals in specific keys when Pythagorean, just, or mean-tone temperament was used. It was therefore reasoned that it was unlikely that anyone would go to the trouble of transposing it, so that everyone probably heard the preludes and fugues only in the original key. Therefore if any of the preludes were indeed transposed, vestigial AP might allow that shift to be recognized.

Accordingly, a series of beginning excerpts (the first phrase, about 5 sec in duration, one or two measures) from the 12 major preludes of Volume 1 were recorded by an expert pianist who could produce a transposition in any key that did not differ from the nominal version in tempo or in differences attributable to fingering problems. Each excerpt was recorded in the original key and in keys higher and lower by 1, 4, 6, and 7 semitones. Several tests were prepared by using various combinations of these excerpts, presented in random order except that two versions of the same prelude could not occur together. Listeners were provided with a score sheet on which was presented a simplified score in the nominal key, and they had to indicate whether the excerpt was played in the correct key, too high, or too low.

The results were at first glance consistent with the notion of absolute tonality: shifts of ±4, 6, or 7 semitones were identified correctly by all subjects, even non-musicians and musicians who indicated no previous experience with the preludes (Terhardt & Ward, 1982). Group results showed a statistically significant identification of even shifts of ±1 semitone; this was true for around 70% of the individual listeners as well.

Subsequent control experiments involving modified piano tones (recorded with, for example, a +1 semitone transposition and then shifted down to nominal key by lowering the playback speed by 5.9%) or piano-like tones from an electronic organ confirmed the general ability to discriminate shifts of 1 semitone (Terhardt & Seewann, 1983). However, one final control experiment brought into question the conclusion that this represented some kind of "latent" AP. All the foregoing experiments had involved a response sheet on which was presented, for each excerpt, the score in the original key. Listeners could therefore use auralization—that is, anticipate how the excerpt should sound and compare this with the actual pitch.

To determine to what extent auralization might be assisting in the identification of shifts of tonality, 10 new subjects were given a test involving shifts of 0, ±1 and ±4 semitones (three presentations of each of those five versions) but without any score on the answer sheet (Ward, 1985). Elimination of auralization produced no reduction in correct identification of 4-semitone shifts (relative to earlier results), but the stimulus-response matrix for −1, 0, and +1 was nearly random. A week later, the test was given again, but now with the excerpt's score on the answer sheet. In this case, identification of the 1-semitone shifts was about the same as in the original experiments. On the other hand, elimination of the score had no effect on the performance (significant group identification) of the ±1-semitone transpositions of listeners who had already been given the with-score version (Ward, 1983). Auralization, it appears, is not necessary for recognition of small transpositions, although it facilitates the learning process.

IX. SPONTANEOUS AND ELICITED AURALIZATION

Another possible manifestation of long-term memory for pitch even in the absence of the ability to label specific pitches involves spontaneous auralization: when a tune that may have been heard in several keys pops into one's head, what key is it in, and why? Is it the key in which it was originally written, the key most often heard in, the best key for singing without having to shift an octave somewhere in the tune, a key determined by an environmental tonal sound either present or in the immediate past, or completely random?

To decide among these alternatives, I conducted a longitudinal quasi-experiment on myself (Ward, 1990). For about a year, when a tune began running through my head (or when I noticed that it was), I whistled or sang it (usually the former) into a tape recorder, making a conscious effort not to shift when it turned out to be difficult to produce, and indicated the name of the tune. Later, by measuring the frequency of these productions, the keynote could be determined. It was soon apparent that the choice of keys was not random; a given melody was often auralized several times within a 4-semitone range. Forty tunes were selected for which this was true, and each was deliberately auralized (each tune was assigned a particular playing card; the cards were shuffled and drawn one by one; I auralized and whistled the appropriate tune while sitting in a sound-free room) three times. Twenty-three of the tunes were reproduced within a range of 3 semitones (i.e., ±1.5 semitones); of these, 20 were selected and another series of three random auralizations made. Of these, 10 were again within a 3-semitone range of keys whose center was no more than 1 semitone from that of the previous results.

Analysis of the results on these 10 tunes led to one clear major conclusion: ordinary AP was not involved. Had I been a possessor, 440 Hz (standard A_4) would have been a member of the chromatic scale based on each and every auralized key, and 453 Hz ($A_4 + 50$) would never have been. No evidence of such graininess was apparent in the fine structure of distribution of keys: within any 100-cent range, all frequencies were equally likely to occur. For example, for a tune categorized as being in the key of F, the actual frequency was just as apt to be F – 40, F – 30, F – 20, F – 10, F + 10, ... or F + 50 as it was to be F + 0. So the aspect of pitch that is involved here is not pitch class but only tone height.

Furthermore, there was little indication of a preference for either a particular key or starting note within the 10 tunes, as both were scattered across the octave. On the other hand, when the point was calculated that lay halfway between the highest and lowest notes in each tune if it were performed in the auralized key, it turned out that this middle-of-the-road melody note was in all 10 cases something in the range of E to G, with F♯ the median as well as the mode. However, these results on one individual can do little to shed light on why this consistency occurs. The median auralized key was in most cases within 1 semitone of the composer's original key (or at least the key it was published in, though perhaps not originally conceived in), and so was probably also the key in which it had been heard or played most often in the past. Because F♯ is exactly in the middle of my vocal range, it may be that motor memory played as great a role as sensory memory, even though an effort was made not to imagine vocalization before actually producing any sound.

Only a few other studies of auralization have been reported recently. Halpern (1989) selected 16 songs that everyone should be familiar with (e.g., "Yankee Doodle," "Silent Night," "White Christmas") and asked 22 undergraduates to hum or sing the starting pitch after being presented with the lyrics for the first phrase of the song. Subjects were consistent in selecting a particular starting note (and hence the key) for a particular song, with a test-retest standard deviation of about 1.25 semitones, whether the data were gathered on the same day or on two different days. However, no attempt was made to determine the correlation between individual differences in note selection and vocal range, or to determine to what extent a given individual selected starting notes if range of melody were to be held constant.

Levitin (1994) used auralization in a somewhat different manner. Noting that Halpern's tunes represented the epitome of songs that probably had been heard in many keys by every test subject, he instead used contemporary popular and rock songs that had been performed by only one musical group and so had presumably been heard only in one key (as Terhardt and I had hoped to be the case for the Bach preludes). The 46 test subjects were asked to select, from a rack of 58 compact discs, one that contained a song "that they knew very well," and, holding the CD, close their eyes, auralize the song, and then sing, hum, or whistle the tune. Forty-three subjects repeated the procedure with a second tune. On both tests, half of the subjects were within a semitone of the actual key and one fourth were within a quarter tone.

So whether the music concerned is classical, traditional, big band (1940s) or current popular, a degree of "absolute tone height" seems to be manifested in nearly everyone's ability to judge the "correct" pitch of a melody. Whether or not it is accurate to call it "vestigial AP" must await the outcome of experiments that use new compositions whose tonal center is not in the F-G range.

X. THE VALUE OF AP

Thousands of hours have been spent trying to develop AP, yet only a few people have been able to achieve as an adult the proficiency that comes so easily to most possessors. One may well ask whether or not AP is worth that much effort. What are the advantages of AP? The most obvious, of course, is that if the pitch pipe is lost, an a cappella performance can still be initiated by a possessor on the correct pitch—an absolute necessity in some songs, such as the American national anthem, that require an octave and a half of vocal range. J. F. Beck (personal communication, 1978) writes that he can tell his speed on a particular road from the pitch of the whine of his tires. D. E. McCleve (personal communication, March 1979) judges his car's RPM from the pitch of the motor, and Corliss (1973) indicates that identification of elements in a chord is easier for possessors because each element is recognized as such. Musical dictation in the classroom is therefore easier for possessors.

However, outside of these few instances in which the frequency of a tone is important, the alleged advantages are mostly incapable of confirmation. For example, Bachem (1955) enthuses that "particular characteristics of certain keys, e.g., the brilliancy of A major, the softness of D-flat major, can only be appreciated fully through absolute pitch." Although he apparently would agree with Vernon on pieces played in C♯ (unless he would insist that C♯ is different from D♭), we can only take his word that that is how things sounded to him. Claims such as the following are still appearing: "Absolute pitch is generally an asset to a musician because it helps in playing an instrument in tune, in sight-singing easily and accurately, and in knowing what a piece of music will sound like simply by reading the musical score" (Eaton & Siegel, 1976). These are skills displayed by nonpossessors of AP as well as by possessors. Little evidence shows any correlation between AP and other musical traits such as the ability to improvise (Weinert, 1929) or to make judgments of RP (Baggaley, 1974; Ward, 1954).

Indeed, one could predict that if persons with AP cannot help categorizing notes, they might well be at a disadvantage in certain RP tasks. The singer who clings to the "correct" intonation despite the fact that the rest of the chorus has dropped a quarter tone has never been popular. As another example, consider the experiments dealing with categorization of intervals such as those described by Burns (Chapter 7), in which four tones are presented, and the subject is asked to compare the musical-pitch distance between the first and second tones with that between the third and fourth tones. The results (Burns & Campbell, 1994; Burns & Ward, 1978) imply that the RP subjects accomplish this task by categorizing the intervals, with a precision somewhat better than semitones but somewhat poorer than quarter tones, and making the pitch-distance estimate on the basis of this categorization. If an analogous process occurs in AP, it would seem that AP possessors might be subject to double jeopardy in this particular situation because they may be making not two but four categorical judgments. Consider the sequence A + 40, C − 40; D − 40, E + 40 as an extreme example. The person using RP will recognize the first interval of 220 cents as a major second and the second interval of 280 cents as a minor third and will conclude that the second interval was the larger. On the other hand, if a possessor of AP were unable to avoid categorizing each note and had an internal pitch helix tuned to A_4 equal to 440 Hz, he would perceive the sequence as being A to C and D to E and would therefore say that the first interval was the larger. The question obviously is how well the possessor can suppress the tendency to categorize individual tones.

Benguerel and Westdal (1991) tested this possibility in 10 possessors, finding that only one individual made categorization errors such as that just described, and then not consistently. Apparently in judging isolated two-tone intervals, AP possessors can make the same "absolute interval" judgments that musical nonpossessors make, implying that labeling of the individual tones is not unavoidable when the person knows that the labels are irrelevant.

However, a series of studies of interval identification by Miyazaki (1992, 1993, 1994) has shown that certain context conditions can increase the difficulty that possessors have in ignoring the tone-categorization process. In the first experiment (Miyazaki, 1992), AP and RP musicians had to judge interval magnitude of tone pairs in which the first tone was either C_4 or $C_4 + 50$ and the second was 50–1230 cents higher, deviating from $100N$ ($N = 1$ to 12) by 50, 30, 16, or 0 cents. Listeners had to make two responses: first choose one of the 12 intervals and then indicate "higher than," "right on," or "lower than." Although AP subjects made slightly more errors in the $C_4 + 50$ pairs than on the C_4 pairs, the difference was not statistically significant. RP subjects showed no difference whatsoever. On average, diatonic intervals were more rapidly and accurately identified than were intervals corresponding to accidentals (i.e., white-note pairs vs. white-black pairs).

In a second study, Miyazaki (1993) tried to make it even harder to avoid using AP in making interval judgments. A key was firmly established by playing two chords composed of Shepard tones: a dominant seventh chord (e.g., GBDF) followed by a tonic chord (CEG). Then a pair of sine tones was presented, the first of which was the tonic, the second a tone 260 to 540 cents higher (in 20-cent steps). The tonic alternated among C_4, $F\sharp_4$, and a quarter tone below E_4 ($E_4 - 50$). If pitch categorization were acting, one would expect that $E_4 - 50$ would provide the most difficulty, as it is neither $E\flat_4$ nor E_4 to a possessor. And indeed, although RP subjects showed identical performance on all three tonic conditions, some AP possessors made a greater number of errors (judgments that were 60 cents or more from the true value) for $E_4 - 50$ than for C_4. Unfortunately for simplicity of interpretation, there was an even greater proportional error with the $F\sharp$ tonic, although $F\sharp$ is a member of the chromatic scale. Apparently the fact that "major" intervals in $F\sharp$ now involved "accidentals" in C (e.g., the major third, a white-white C-E in C, becomes a black-black $F\sharp$-$A\sharp$ in $F\sharp$) allowed the white-black disparity to act.

In a subsequent pair of experiments, Miyazaki (1994) first essentially repeated his 1992 study except that in addition to C_4 and $C_4 + 50$, $C_4 + 16$ and $C_4 + 30$ were used as first tones. He found that six of eight AP possessors showed a decline in accuracy in making judgments of these isolated two-tone intervals as the first tone deviated farther and farther from C_4. The second experiment was one that combined the off-key, black-white and ubiquity-of-C factors. Stimuli were pairs of tones in which the first was C_4, $E_4 - 50$, or $F\sharp_4$, and the second was $100N$ ($N = 1$–12) cents higher; that is, the intervals were not slightly detuned, so there was no necessity to make any judgment of "lower than" or "higher than." Results in terms of accuracy and speed of identification of the 12 intervals were indistinguishable for RP subjects with all three first tones and with C for AP subjects, but were greatly reduced for AP subjects with $E_4 - 50$ and $F\sharp_4$: accuracy dropped from 80% correct on tritone, minor sixth, major sixth, and minor seventh for C-based intervals to about 40% for those based on $E_4 - 50$ and $F\sharp_4$, and response times increased from 2 sec to 3 sec. As before, performance was slightly poorer on $F\sharp_4$ intervals than on $E_4 - 50$ intervals , indicating that AP possessors were more handicapped by a black-note tonic than by a mistuned tonic. RP subjects shift their internal pitch template to C regardless of the actual frequency of the initial tone, but AP subjects for the most part cannot, and so have to make an extra mental step, for example, "F$\sharp$ to D; that's one semitone more than a fifth, and so must be a minor sixth."

A similar situation that shows possessors to be at a disadvantage was devised by Cuddy (1977). The task was to identify whether two 7-tone sequences were identical or differed on one of the tones by half a semitone (3%). Performance of nonpossessors was independent of whether the sequence was tonal or atonal (i.e., used only the 7 major tones of the scale or, instead, all 12) or whether the tones used were separated by equal ratios or by equal steps of linear frequency (log and linear scales, respectively). Possessors were like nonpossessors in two of the tasks but showed significantly poorer performance when judging atonal sequences in the linear scale while simultaneously displaying significantly superior skill at distinguishing tonal sequences in the log scale. That is, possessors were better at picking out a single mistuned tone from a sequence, but when many of the tones were already mistuned (from the viewpoint of the standard scale), they were unable to determine whether or not an additional 50-cent change had occurred. They are, it appears, less flexible—less able to learn a new scale.

A final ingenious demonstration that AP can hamper performance was presented by Sachet, Rosier, and Ben-Arzi (1984) in the form of an acoustic analog of the Stroop test in visual perception. (Subjects in the Stroop test are presented with names of colors, each of which is printed in either the same or a different color; whether the task is to read the word or to name the color of the ink, everyone has greater difficulty when the name and color are different than when they are the same.) In the present case, there were three conditions. In condition W, "ten names of notes were spoken in an even monotone voice," in condition P, "ten pitches were sung by a professional musician," and in condition PW "ten pitches were sung, each name in a pitch other than that which its name implied (i.e., the name 'do' sung in pitch 'si')." Nine possessors had to respond with the pitch of the sound, not the spoken or sung name. Reaction time increased from 1.3 sec in P to 2.2 sec in PW, and the number of errors out of 90 increased from 1.3 to 3.3.

In any event, AP is not an unmixed blessing, although the slight handicap in the somewhat esoteric tasks just described has little practical importance. It remains a fascinating phenomenon, although its fascination, for many of us, lies in the question of why so many people do not have the ability rather than why a few do. Any situation in which one particular frequency is to be discriminated from all others, as in testing for "frequency generalization" is a type of AP experiment, and although the literature is not completely unequivocal, evidence exists that a high degree of discrimination of tones separated by long intervals of time is indeed found in lower organisms such as the cebus monkey (D'Amato, 1988), the dog (Andreyev, 1934), and some songbirds (Hulse & Cynx, 1985), although perhaps it is not highly developed in the cat (Thompson, 1959).

That early learning may be necessary but not sufficient to develop AP is implied by the results of an informal experiment. In 1955, when my first daughter was 2–3 years old, we played the "find-the-note" game using our well-tuned piano, once or twice a week. In this game, A plays a note while B's back is turned, and B then comes to the piano and finds the correct key, whereupon the roles are reversed. Of course I cheated by using RP, but my daughter would have to use absolute identification. Although no numerical records were kept, after a few weeks, she was getting the correct note on the first or second attempt, indicating that she had developed absolute piano rather well. At this point, her interest in the game waned, probably because it was no longer a challenge, so it was abandoned. Daughters 2 and 3 were not exposed to the game, but with the birth of Daughter 4, I realized that there was an opportunity to do an experiment of sorts, albeit with an N of only 2 in each group. So when Daughter 4 was 2-1/2 years old, she and I played the game for several months. As in the case of Daughter 1, by the time we stopped she was getting the right note on the first or second try.

All four daughters took piano lessons starting at age 6 or so, and each also developed skill at one or more additional musical activities (singing, guitar, violin, harp). However, until adulthood they engaged, as far as I know, in no activities that might be considered to involve AP. So in 1990, when their ages were 38, 35, 30, and 26, they were given the basic AP test described in Section III,F: identification of 10 pure-tone stimuli spaced at intervals of a fourth. The results implied that 3.7, 3.3, 2.9, and 4.8 categories, respectively, could be identified without error. That is, the highest scores were obtained for the two who had been given the early training, but no performance could be characterized as showing possession of AP. Perhaps Daughters 1 and 4 would have demonstrated AP had they continued the find-the-note game through age 6 or higher, but that is highly speculative. The lack of relevance of AP for musical performance is underscored by the fact that the lowest score, 2.9 transmitted categories, was gotten by the only professional musician among the four.

Interestingly enough, mentally retarded teenagers apparently have AP. Paulson, Orlando, and Schoelkopf (1967) trained three mentally retarded teenagers to tap rapidly on a lever when a 1455-Hz tone was present in order to receive bits of candy, and then the experimenters tried to measure generalization to tones of 1100 and 1855 Hz. To their surprise, they got hardly any responses to the new tones in two of their subjects. One of the two was therefore tested further with tones spaced at 100-Hz intervals, and even with such small separations, only 1455 Hz was able to elicit a response. Clearly, this implies AP in these subjects (assuming that there was not something unique about the acoustic effects of the 1455-Hz tone in that particular situation that provided an unwanted cue, such as some object that resonated at that frequency). It is somewhat ironic that Paulson et al., rather than rejoicing that the children had AP, bemoan the results as being "indicative of a broad deficit in generalization processes."

REFERENCES

Abraham, O. (1901). Das absolute Tonbewusstsein. *Internationale Musikgesellschaft; Sammelbande, 3,* 1–86.

Andreyev, L. A. (1934). Extreme limits of pitch discrimination with higher tones. *Journal of Comparative Psychology, 18,* 315–332.

Bachem, A. (1937). Various types of absolute pitch. *Journal of the Acoustical Society of America, 9,* 146–151.

Bachem, A. (1940). The genesis of absolute pitch. *Journal of the Acoustical Society of America, 11,* 434–439.

Bachem, A. (1948). Chroma fixation at the ends of the musical frequency scale. *Journal of the Acoustical Society of America, 20,* 704–705.

Bachem, A. (1954). Time factors in relative and absolute pitch determination. *Journal of the Acoustical Society of America, 26,* 751–753.

Bachem, A. (1955). Absolute pitch. *Journal of the Acoustical Society of America, 27,* 1180–1185.

Baggaley, J. (1974). Measurements of absolute pitch: A confused field. *Psychology of Music, 2,* 11–17.

Baird, J. W. (1917). Memory for absolute pitch. *Studies in Psychology, Titchener Commemorative Volume,* 43–78.

Balzano, G. J. (1984). Absolute pitch and pure tone identification. *Journal of the Acoustical Society of America, 75,* 623–625.

Benguerel, A. P., & Westdal, C. (1991). Absolute pitch and the perception of sequential musical intervals. *Music Perception, 9,* 105–120.

Bernard, J. W. (1986). Messiaen's synaesthesia: The correspondence between color and sound structure in his music. *Music Perception, 4,* 41–68.

Block, L. (1983). Comparative tone-colour responses of college music majors with absolute pitch and good relative pitch. *Psychology of Music, 11,* 59–66.

Brady, P. T. (1970). Fixed-scale mechanism of absolute pitch. *Journal of the Acoustical Society of America, 48,* 883–887.

Burge, D. L. (1986). *The Perfect Pitch Ear-Training Course.* American Educational Music Publications, Inc.

Burns, E. M., & Ward, W. D. (1974). Categorical perception of musical intervals. *Journal of the Acoustical Society of America, 55,* 456.

Burns, E. M., & Ward, W. D. (1978). Categorical perception—phenomenon or epiphenomenon? Evidence from experiments in the perception of melodic musical intervals. *Journal of the Acoustical Society of America, 63,* 456–488.

Burns, E. M., & Campbell, S. L. (1994). Frequency and frequency-ratio resolution by possessors of relative and absolute pitch: A most excellent case of categorical perception. *Journal of the Acoustical Society of America, 96*(5), 2704–2719.

Butler, D., & Ward, W. D. (1988). Effacing the memory of musical pitch. *Music Perception, 5,* 251–259.

Carpenter, A. (1951). A case of absolute pitch. *Quarterly Journal of Experimental Psychology, 3,* 92–93.

Carroll, J. B. (1975, October). Speed and accuracy of absolute pitch judgments: Some latter-day results. *Research Bulletin* (preprint). Princeton, NJ: Educational Testing Service.

Carroll, J. B., & Greenberg, J. H. (1961). Two cases of synesthesia for color and music tonality associated with absolute pitch ability. *Perceptional and Motor Skills, 13,* 48.

Chaloupka, V., Mitchell, S., & Muirhead, R. (1994). Observation of a reversible, medication-induced change in pitch perception. *Journal of the Acoustical Society of America, 96*(1), 145–149.

Cohen, A. (1961). Further investigation of the effects of intensity upon the pitch of pure tones. *Journal of the Acoustical Society of America, 33,* 1363-1376.

Cohen, A. J., & Baird, K. (1990). The acquisition of absolute pitch: The question of critical periods. *Psychomusicology, 9*(1), 31–37.

Copp, E. F. (1916). Musical ability. *Journal of Heredity, 7,* 297–305.

Corliss, E. L. (1973). Remark on "fixed-scale mechanism of absolute pitch." *Journal of the Acoustical Society of America, 53,* 1737–1739.

Costall, A. (1985). The relativity of absolute pitch. In P. Howell, I Cross, & R. West (Eds.), *Musical structure and cognition* (pp. 189–208). London: Academic Press.

Cuddy, L. L. (1968). Practice effects in the absolute judgment of pitch. *Journal of the Acoustical Society of America, 43,* 1069–1076.

Cuddy, L. L. (1971). Absolute judgement of musically-related pure tones. *Canadian Journal of Psychology, 25,* 42–55.

Cuddy, L. L. (1977, July). *Perception of structured melodic sequences.* Paper presented at the Conference on Musical Perception, Paris, France.

Cuddy, L. L. (1985). The color of melody. *Music Perception, 2,* 345–360.

D'Amato, M. R. (1988). A search for tonal perception in cebus monkeys: Why monkeys can't hum a tune. *Music Perception, 5*(4), 453–480.

Deutsch, D. (1973). Octave generalization of specific interference effects in memory for tonal pitch. *Perception & Psychophysics, 13,* 271–275.

Deutsch, D. (1982). The influence of melodic context on pitch recognition judgment. *Perception & Psychophysics, 31,* 407–410.

Drobisch, M. (1855). Uber musikalische Tonbestimmung und Temperatur. In *Abhandlungen der Koniglich sachsischen Gesellschaft der Wissenschaften zu Leipzig. Vierter Band: Abhandlungen der mathematisch-physischen Classe. Zweiter Band* (pp. 3–121). Leipzig: S. Hirzel.

Eaton, K. E., & Siegel, M. H. (1976). Strategies of absolute pitch possessors in the learning of an unfamiliar scale. *Bulletin of the Psychonomic Society, 8,* 289–291.

Emde, C., & Klinke, R. (1977). Does absolute pitch depend on an internal clock? *Inner Ear Biology, 68,* 145–146.

Fulgosi, A., Bacun, D., & Zaja, B. (1975). Absolute identification of two-dimensional tones. *Bulletin of the Psychonomic Society, 6,* 484–486.

Fullard, W., Snelbecker, G, E., & Wolk, S. (1972). Absolute judgments as a function of stimulus uncertainty and temporal effects: Methodological note. *Perceptual and Motor Skills, 94,* 379–382.

Gough, E. (1922). The effects of practice on judgments of absolute pitch. *Archives of Psychology, New York, 7*(47), 93.

Halpern, A. R. (1989). Memory for the absolute pitch of familiar songs. *Memory and Cognition, 17*(5), 572–581.

Hartman, E. B. (1954). The influence of practice and pitch distance between tones on the absolute identification of pitch. *American Journal of Psychology, 67,* 1–14.

Heller, M, A., & Auerbach, C. (1972). Practice effects in the absolute judgment of frequency. *Psychonomic Science, 26,* 222–224.

Hulse, S. H., & Cynx, J. (1985). Relative pitch perception is constrained by absolute pitch in songbirds (*Mimus, Molothrus,* and *Sturnus*). *Journal of Comparative Psychology, 99,* 176–196.

Hurni-Schlegel, L., & Lang, A. (1978). Verteilung, Korrelate und Vernderbarkeit der Tonhöhen-Identifikation (sog. absolutes Musikgehör). *Schweizerische Zeitschrift für Psychologie und Ihre Anwendungen, 37,* 265–292.

Klein, M., Coles, M. G. H., Donchin, E. (1982). Electrophysiology of absolute pitch. *Psychophysiology, 19,* 569.

Levitin, D. J. (1994). Absolute representation in auditory memory: Evidence from the production of learned melodies. *Perception & Psychophysics, 56,* 414–423.

Lundin, R. W. (1963). Can perfect pitch be learned? *Music Education Journal, 69,* 49–51.

Lundin, R. W., & Allen, J. D. (1962). A technique for training perfect pitch. *Psychological Record, 12,* 139–146.

Marks, L. E. (1975). On colored-hearing synesthesia: Cross-modal translations of sensory dimensions. *Psychological Bulletin, 82,* 303–331.

Meyer, M. (1899). Is the memory of absolute pitch capable of development by training? *Psychological Review, 6,* 514–516.

Miller, G. A. (1956). The magical number seven, plus or minus two: Some limits on our capacity for processing information. *Psychological Review, 63,* 81–97.

Miyazaki, K. (1988). Musical pitch identification by absolute pitch possessors. *Perception & Psychophysics, 44,* 501–512.

Miyazaki, K. (1989). Absolute pitch identification: Effects of timbre and pitch region. *Music Perception, 7*(1), 1–14.

Miyazaki, K. (1990). The speed of musical pitch identification by absolute-pitch possessors. *Music Perception, 8*(2), 177–188.

Miyazaki, K. (1992). Perception of musical intervals by absolute pitch possessors. *Music Perception, 9*(4), 413–426.

Miyazaki, K. (1993). Absolute pitch as an inability: Identification of musical intervals in a tonal context. *Music Perception, 11,* 55–72.

Miyazaki, K. (1995). Perception of relative pitch with different references: Some absolute-pitch listeners can't tell musical interval names. *Perception & Psychophysics, 57,* 962–970.

Mull, H. K. (1925). The acquisition of absolute pitch. *American Journal of Psychology, 36,* 469–493.

Oakes, W. F. (1951). An alternative interpretation of "absolute pitch." *Transactions of the Kansas Academy of Sciences, 54,* 396–406.

Oura, Y., & Eguchi, E. (1981). *Is absolute pitch innate or acquired?* Paper presented at the Colloquium of the XVIth International Music Festival, Brno, Czechoslovakia.

Paulson, D. G., Orlando, R., & Schoelkopf, A. M. (1967). *Experimental analysis and manipulation of auditory generalization in three developmental retardates by discriminated-operant procedures* (IMRID Papers and Reports 4, No. 13). Nashville, TN: George Peabody College for Teachers, Institute on Mental Retardation and Intellectual Development.

Peacock, K. (1985). Synaesthetic perception: Alexander Scriabin's color hearing. *Music Perception, 2*(4), 483–506.

Petran, L. A. (1932). An experimental study of pitch recognition. *Psychological Monographs, 42*(6), 1–120.

Pollack, I. (1952). The information of elementary auditory displays. *Journal of the Acoustical Society of America, 24,* 745–749.

Profita, J., & Bidder, T. G. (1988). Perfect pitch. *American Journal of Medical Genetics, 29,* 763–771.

Rakowski, A., & Morawska-Büngeler, M. (1987). In search for the criteria of absolute pitch. *Archives of Acoustics, 12,* 75–87.

Révész, G. (1913). *Zur Grundlegung der Tonpsychologie.* Leipzig: Veit.

Rogers, G. L. (1987). Four cases of pitch-specific chromesthesia in trained musicians with absolute pitch. *Psychology of Music, 15,* 198–207.

Rush, M. A. (1989). *An experimental investigation of the effectiveness of training on absolute pitch in adult musicians.* Unpublished doctoral dissertation, Ohio State University, Columbus.

Sergeant, D. (1969). Experimental investigation of absolute pitch. *Journal of Research in Music Education, 17,* 135–143.

Simpson, R. H., Quinn, M., & Ausubel, D. P. (1956). Synesthesia in children: Association of colors with pure tone frequencies. *Journal of Genetic Psychology, 89,* 95–103.

Stevens, S. S., Volkmann, J., & Newman, E. B. (1937). A scale for the measurement of the psychological magnitude pitch. *Journal of the Acoustical Society of America, 8,* 185–190.

Stumpf, C. (1883). *Tonpsychologie.* Leipzig: Herzel.

Stumpf, C. (1901). Beobachtungen über subjective Töne und über Doppelthören. *Beitrage zur Akusik und Musik, 3,* 30–51.

Takeuchi, A. H., & Hulse, S. H.(1991). Absolute-pitch judgments of black- and white-key pitches. *Music Perception, 9,* 27–46.

Terhardt, E., & Seewann, M. (1983). Aural key identification and its relationship to absolute pitch. *Music Perception, 1,* 63–83.

Terhardt, E., & Ward, W. D. (1982). Recognition of musical key: Exploratory study. *Journal of the Acoustical Society of America, 72,* 26–33.

Terman, M. (1965). Improvement of absolute pitch naming. *Psychonomic Science, 3,* 243–244.

Tervaniemi, M., Alho, K., Paavilainen, P., Sams, M., & Näätänen, R. (1993). Absolute pitch and event-related brain potentials. *Music Perception, 10*(3), 305-316.

Thompson, R. F. (1959). The effect of training procedure upon auditory frequency discrimination in the cat. *Journal of Comparative and Physiological Psychology, 52,* 186–190.

Triepel, H. (1934). Zur Frage des absoluten Gehörs. *Archiv für die Gesamte Psychologie, 90,* 373–379.

Trotter, J. R. (1967). The psychophysics of melodic interval: Definition, techniques, theory and problems. *Australian Journal or Psychology, 19,* 13–25.

Tsuzaki, M. (1992). Interference of preceding scales on absolute pitch judgment. *Proceedings of the 2nd International Conference on Musical Perception and Cognition, 2.* Los Angeles: ICMPC.

van Krevelen, A. (1951). The ability to make absolute judgments of pitch. *Journal of Experimental Psychology, 42,* 207–215.

Vernon, P. E. (1977). Absolute pitch: A case study. *British Journal of Psychology, 68,* 485–489.

von Kries, J. (1892). Uber das absolute Gehör. *Zeitschrift für die Psychologie und Physiologie des Sinnesorganes, 3,* 257–279.

Ward, W. D. (1953). Information and absolute pitch. *Journal of the Acoustical Society of America, 25,* 833.

Ward, W. D. (1954). Subjective musical pitch. *Journal of the Acoustical Society of America, 26,* 369–380.

Ward, W. D. (1963a). Absolute pitch: Part I. *Sound, 2*(3), 14–21.

Ward, W. D. (1963b). Absolute pitch: Part II. *Sound, 2*(4), 33–41.

Ward, W. D. (1983). The role of auralization in pitch or tonality recognition. *Journal of the Acoustical Society of America, 74*(Suppl. 1), S81.

Ward, W. D. (1985). Absolute tonality vs. absolute piano. *Journal of the Acoustical Society of America, 78*(Suppl. 1), S76.

Ward, W. D. (1990, May). *Relative versus absolute pitch and the key of auralized melodies.* Paper presented at the von Karajan Symposium, Vienna.

Ward, W. D., Selters, W., & Glorig, A. (1961). Exploratory studies on temporary threshold shift from impulses. *Journal of the Acoustical Society of America, 33,* 781–793.

Watt, H. J. (1917). *The psychology of sound.* London and New York: Cambridge University Press.

Wayman, J. W., Frisina, R. D., Walton, J. P., Hantz, E. C., & Crummer, G. C. (1992). Effects of musical training and absolute pitch ability on event-related activity in response to sine tones. *Journal of the Acoustical Society of America, 91,* 3527–3531.

Wedell, C. H. (1934). The nature of the absolute judgment of pitch. *Journal of Experimental Psychology, 17,* 485–503.

Weinert, L. (1929). Untersuchungen über das absolute Gehör. *Archiv für die Gesamte Psychologie, 73,* 1–128.

Welch, G. F. (1988). Observations on the incidence of absolute pitch (AP) ability in the early blind. *Psychology of Music, 16,* 77–80.

Wellek, A. (1938). Das absolute Gehör und seine Typen. *Zeitschrift für Angewandte Psychologie & Charakterkunde-Beihefte, 83,* 1–368.

Wynn, V. T. (1971). "Absolute" pitch: a bimensual rhythm. *Nature (London), 230,* 337.

Wynn, V. T. (1972). Measurements of small variations in "absolute" pitch. *Journal of Physiology, 220,* 627–637.

Wynn, V. T. (1992). Absolute pitch revisited. *British Journal of Psychology, 83,* 129-131.

Sachet, D., Rosier, I., & Ben-Arzi, S. (1984). On the nature of absolute pitch. *Archiv für Psychologie, 136*(2), 163–166.

Zatorre, R. F. (1989). Intact absolute pitch ability after left temporal lobectomy. *Cortex, 25,* 567–580.

Zatorre, R. J., & Beckett, C. (1989). Multiple coding strategies in the retention of musical tones by possessors of absolute pitch. *Memory and Cognition, 17,* 582–589.

9

GROUPING MECHANISMS IN MUSIC

DIANA DEUTSCH

Department of Psychology
University of California, San Diego
La Jolla, California

I. INTRODUCTION

Music provides us with a complex, rapidly changing acoustic spectrum, often derived from the superposition of sounds from many different sources. Our auditory system has the task of analyzing this spectrum so as to reconstruct the originating sound events. This is analogous to the task performed by our visual system when it interprets the mosaic of light impinging on the retina in terms of visually perceived objects. Such a view of perception as a process of "unconscious inference" was proposed in the last century by Helmholtz (1909–1911/1925), and we shall see that many phenomena of music perception can be viewed in this way.

Two types of issue can be considered here. First, given that our auditory system is presented with a set of first-order elements, we can explore the ways in which these are combined so as to form separate groupings. If all first-order elements were indiscriminately linked together, auditory shape recognition operations could not be performed. There must, therefore, be a set of mechanisms that enable us to form linkages between some elements and that inhibit us from forming linkages between others. Simple mechanisms underlying such linkages are examined in the present chapter. The second issue concerns the ways in which higher order abstractions are derived from combinations of first-order elements so as to give rise to perceptual equivalences and similarities. This issue is explored in Chapter 10, and we shall see that higher-order abstractions are also used as bases for grouping.

In considering the mechanisms whereby we combine musical elements into groupings, we can also follow two lines of inquiry. The first concerns the *dimensions* along which grouping principles operate. When presented with a complex pattern, the auditory system groups elements together according to some rule

---

based on frequency, amplitude, temporal position, spatial location, or some multi-dimensional attribute such as timbre. As we shall see, any of these attributes can be used as a basis for grouping, but the conditions determining which attribute is used are complex ones.

Second, assuming that organization takes place on the basis of some dimension such as frequency, we can inquire into the *principles* that govern grouping along this dimension. The early Gestalt psychologists proposed that we group elements into configurations on the basis of various simple rules (see, for example, Wertheimer, 1923). One is proximity: closer elements are grouped together in preference to those that are spaced further apart. An example is shown in Figure 1a, where the closer dots are perceptually grouped together in pairs. Another is similarity: in viewing Figure 1b we perceive one set of vertical rows formed by the filled circles and another formed by the unfilled circles. A third, good continuation, states that elements that follow each other in a given direction are perceptually linked together: we group the dots in Figure 1c so as to form the two lines AB and CD. A fourth, common fate, states that elements that change in the same way are perceptually linked together. As a fifth principle, we tend to form groupings so as to perceive configurations that are familiar to us.

It has been shown that such laws operate in the perception of visual arrays, and we shall see that this is true of music also. It seems reasonable to assume—as argued by R. L. Gregory (1970), Sutherland (1973), Hochberg (1974), Deutsch (1975a), Bregman (1978, 1990), and Rock (1986)—that grouping in conformity with such principles enables us to interpret our environment most effectively. In the case of vision, elements that are close together in space are more likely to belong to the same object than are elements that are spaced further apart. The same line of reasoning holds for elements that are similar rather than those that are dissimilar. In the case of hearing, similar sounds are likely to have originated from a common source, and dissimilar sounds from different sources. A sequence that changes smoothly in frequency is likely to have originated from a single source, whereas an abrupt frequency transition may reflect the presence of a new source. Components of a complex spectrum that arise in synchrony are likely to have

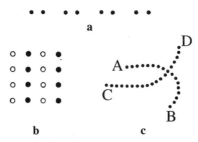

FIGURE 1   Illustrations of the Gestalt principles of proximity, similarity, and good continuation.

emanated from the same source, and the sudden addition of a new component may signal the emergence of a new source.

Another general question to be considered is whether perceptual grouping results from the action of a single decision mechanism or whether multiple decision mechanisms are involved, each with its own grouping criteria. There is convincing physiological evidence that the subsystems underlying the attribution of various characteristics of sound become separate very early in the processing system (Edelman, Gall, & Cowan, 1988). Such evidence would lead us to hypothesize that auditory grouping is not carried out by a single mechanism but rather by a number of mechanisms, which at some stage act independently of each other. As we shall see, the perceptual evidence strongly supports this hypothesis. and further indicates that the different mechanisms often come to inconsistent conclusions. For example, the parameters that govern grouping to determine perceived pitch can differ from those that determine perceived timbre, location, or number of sources (Darwin & Carlyon, 1995; Hukin & Darwin, 1995a). Further evidence comes from various illusions that result from incorrect conjunctions of different attribute values (Deutsch, 1974, 1975a, 1975b, 1980a, 1981, 1983a, 1983b, 1987, 1995). From such findings we shall conclude that perceptual organization in music involves a process in which elements are first grouped together so as to assign values to different attributes separately, and that this is followed by a process of perceptual synthesis in which the different attribute values are combined—either correctly or incorrectly.

II. FUSION AND SEPARATION OF SPECTRAL COMPONENTS

In this section, we consider the relationships between the components of a sound spectrum that lead us to fuse them into a unitary sound image and those that lead us to separate them into multiple sound images. In particular, we shall be exploring two types of relationship. The first is harmonicity. Natural sustained sounds, such as produced by musical instruments and the human voice, are made up of components that stand in harmonic, or near-harmonic, relation (i.e., their frequencies are integer, or near-integer multiples of the fundamental). It is reasonable to expect, therefore, that the auditory system would exploit this feature so as to combine a set of harmonically related components into a single sound image. To take an everyday example, when we listen to two instrument tones playing simultaneously, we perceive two pitches, each derived from one of the two harmonic series that together form the complex.

A second relationship that we shall be exploring is onset synchronicity. When components of a sound complex begin at the same time, it is likely that they have originated from the same source; conversely, when they begin at different times, it is likely that they have originated from different sources. As an associated issue, we shall be exploring temporal correspondences in the fluctuations of components in the steady-state portion of a sound.

The importance of temporal relationships for perceptual fusion and separation was recognized by Helmholtz in his treatise *On the Sensations of Tone* (1859/ 1954), in which he wrote:

> Now there are many circumstances which assist us first in separating the musical tones arising from different sources, and secondly, in keeping together the partial tones of each separate source. Thus when one musical tone is heard for some time before being joined by the second, and then the second continues after the first has ceased, the separation in sound is facilitated by the succession in time. We have already heard the first musical tone by itself and hence know immediately what we have to deduct from the compound effect for the effect of this first tone. Even when several parts proceed in the same rhythm in polyphonic music, the mode in which the tones of the different instruments and voices commence, the nature of their increase in force, the certainty with which they are held and the manner in which they die off, are generally slightly different for each.... When a compound tone commences to sound, all its partial tones commence with the same comparative strength; when it swells, all of them generally swell uniformly; when it ceases, all cease simultaneously. Hence no opportunity is generally given for hearing them separately and independently. (pp. 59–60).

A. HARMONICITY

Musical instrument tones provide us with many informal examples of perceptual grouping by harmonicity. Stringed and blown instruments produce tones whose partials are harmonic, or close to harmonic, and these give rise to strongly fused pitch impressions. In contrast, bells and gongs, which produce tones whose partials are nonharmonic, give rise to diffuse pitch impressions (Mathews & Pierce, 1980).

Formal experiments using synthesized tones have confirmed this conclusion. De Boer (1976) found that tone complexes whose components stood in simple harmonic relation tended to produce single pitches, whereas nonharmonic complexes tended instead to produce multiple pitches. Bregman and Doehring (1984) reported that placing simultaneous gliding tones in simple harmonic relation enhanced their perceptual fusion. They presented subjects with three simultaneous glides and found that the middle glide was more easily captured into a separate melodic stream when its slope differed from that of the other two. Furthermore, when the slope of the middle glide was the same as the others, it was less easily captured into a separate melodic stream when it stood in harmonic relationship with them.

How far can a single component of a complex tone deviate from harmonicity and still be grouped with the others to determine perceived pitch? Moore, Glasberg, and Peters (1985) had subjects judge the pitches of harmonic complex tones and examined the effects of mistuning one of the components to various extents. When the component was mistuned by less than 3%, it contributed fully to the pitch of the complex. As the degree of mistuning increased beyond 3%, the contribution made by the mistuned component gradually decreased, and at a mistuning of 8%, the component made virtually no contribution to the pitch of the complex.

Darwin and Gardner (1986) obtained analogous effects in the perception of vowel quality. Mistuning a harmonic in the first formant region of a vowel produced shifts in its perceived quality, with increasing shifts as the amount of mistuning increased. For mistunings of around 8%, the direction of the shift was such as would be expected had the component been perceptually removed from the calculation of the formant.

Other investigators have studied the perception of simultaneous complexes that were built on different fundamentals. They varied the relationships between the fundamentals, and examined how well listeners could separate out the complexes perceptually, as a function of these relationships. For example, Rasch (1978) used a basic pattern that consisted of a pair of two-tone chords that were presented in succession. All the tones were composed of a fundamental together with a series of harmonics. The lower tones of each chord were built on the same fundamental, whereas the higher tones differed by a fifth, in either the upward or the downward direction. The subject judged on each trial whether the higher tones formed an ascending or a descending pattern. The threshold amplitude for obtaining reliable judgments was taken as a measure of the degree to which the subject could separate out the tones forming each chord. As shown in Figure 2, as the higher tones were mistuned from simple harmonic relation with the lower ones, detection thresholds fell accordingly, reflecting an enhanced ability to separate out the pitches of the tones comprising the chords.

Huron (1991b) has related such findings on harmonicity and spectral fusion to polyphonic music. One objective of such music is to maintain the perceptual independence of concurrent voices. In an analysis of a sample of polyphonic keyboard

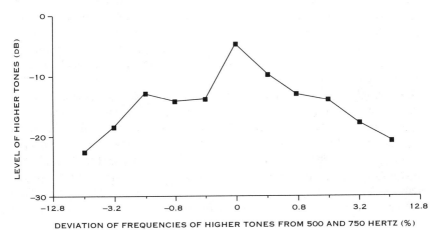

FIGURE 2 Detection thresholds for higher tones in the presence of lower ones. Two chords were presented in sequence. The lower tones of the chords were identical while the higher tones differed by a fifth, in either the upward or the downward direction. Subjects judged whether the higher tones formed a "high-low" or a "low-high" sequence. Detection thresholds fell as the higher tones deviated from simple harmonic relation with the lower ones. (Adapted from Rasch, 1978.)

works by J. S. Bach, Huron showed that harmonic intervals were avoided in proportion to the strength with which they promoted tonal fusion, and he concluded that Bach had used this compositional strategy in order to optimize the salience of the individual voices.

Other composers have focused on the creation of perceptual fusion rather than separation. Particularly in recent times, there has been much experimentation with sounds that were produced by several instruments playing simultaneously, and were configured so that the individual instruments would lose their perceptual identities and together produce a single sound impression. For example, Debussy and Ravel in their orchestral works made extensive use of chords that approached timbres. Later composers such as Schoenberg, Stravinsky, Webern, and Varese often used highly individualized structures, which Varese termed "sound masses" (Erickson, 1975). Here the use of tone combinations that stood in simple harmonic relation proved particularly useful.

To return to the laboratory experiments, findings related to those of Rasch (1978) have also been obtained for speech perception. A number of studies have shown that simultaneous speech patterns could be more easily separated out perceptually when they were built on different fundamentals—in general, the amount of perceptual separation reached its maximum when the fundamentals differed by roughly one to three semitones (Assmann & Summerfield, 1990; Brokx & Nootebohm, 1982; Scheffers, 1983). Furthermore, formants built on the same fundamental tended to be grouped together so as to produce a single phonetic percept, whereas a formant built on a different fundamental tended to be perceived as distinct from the others (Darwin, 1981; see also Gardner, Gaskill, & Darwin, 1989)

The number of sources perceived by the listener provides a further measure of grouping. Moore, Glasberg, and Peters (1986) reported that when a single component of a harmonic complex was mistuned from the others, it was heard as standing apart from them. In other studies, simultaneous speech sounds were perceived as coming from a larger number of sources when they were built on different fundamentals (Broadbent & Ladefoged, 1957; Cutting, 1976; Darwin, 1981; Gardner et al., 1989).

Interestingly, less mistuning is required to produce the impression of multiple sources than to produce other effects. For example, a slightly mistuned component of a tone complex might be heard as distinct from the others, yet still be grouped with them in determining perceived pitch (Moore et al., 1986) or vowel quality (Darwin, 1981, Gardner et al., 1989). As argued by Darwin and Carlyon (1995), this type of disparity indicates that perceptual grouping involves a number of different mechanisms, which depend on the attribute being evaluated, and these mechanisms do not necessarily use the same criteria.

B. ONSET SYNCHRONICITY

So far we have been considering sounds whose components begin and end at the same time, and we have explored the spectral relationships between them that are conducive to perceptual fusion. In real musical situations, temporal factors also come into play. One such factor is onset synchronicity. The importance of this factor can be shown in a simple demonstration, in which a harmonic series is presented in such a way that its components enter at different times. For example, take a series that is built on a 200-Hz fundamental. We can begin with the 200-Hz component sounding alone, then 1 sec later add the 400-Hz component, then 1 sec later add the 600-Hz component, and so on until all the components are sounding together. As each component enters, its pitch is initially heard as a distinct entity, and then it gradually fades from perception, so that finally the only pitch that is heard corresponds to the fundamental.

Even a transient change in the amplitude of a component can enhance its perceptual salience. This was shown by Kubovy (1976) who generated an eight-tone chord whose components were turned off and on again abruptly, each at a different time. On listening to this chord, subjects perceived a melody that corresponded to the order in which the amplitude drops occurred.

Darwin and Ciocca (1992) have shown that onset asynchrony can influence the contribution made by a mistuned harmonic to the pitch of a complex. They found that a mistuned component made less of a contribution to perceived pitch when it led the others by more than 80 msec, and it made no contribution when it led the others by 300 msec.

Onset asynchrony can also affect the contribution of a component to perceived timbre. Darwin (1984) found that when a single harmonic of a vowel that was close in frequency to the first formant led the others by roughly 30 msec, there resulted an alteration in the way the formant frequency was perceived; this alteration was similar to the one that occurred when the harmonic was removed from the calculation of the formant (see also Darwin & Sutherland, 1984).

Interestingly, Darwin and colleagues have found that the amount of onset asynchrony that was needed to alter the contribution of a component to perceived pitch was greater than was needed to alter its contribution to perceived vowel quality. Hukin and Darwin (1995a) showed that this discrepancy could not be attributed to differences in signal parameters, but rather to the nature of the perceptual task in which the listener was engaged; again arguing, as did Darwin and Carlyon (1995), that such disparities reflect the operation of multiple decision mechanisms in the grouping process.

Onset asynchrony has been found to have higher level effects also. In one experiment, Bregman and Pinker (1978) presented listeners with a two-tone complex in alternation with a third tone, and they studied the effects of onset-offset asynchrony between the simultaneous tones. As the degree of onset asynchrony increased, the timbre of the complex tone was judged to be purer, and it became more probable that one of the tones in the complex would form a melodic stream with the third tone (see also Dannenbring & Bregman, 1978).

Using yet a different paradigm, Deutsch (1979) presented subjects with rapid melodic patterns whose components switched from ear to ear, and with each component accompanied by a drone in the contralateral ear. An onset asynchrony of 15 msec between the melody component and the drone significantly improved identification of the melody, indicating that the melody components were more easily combined together sequentially when they did not occur synchronously with other tones.

When two complex tones are played together, they are perceptually more distinct when their onsets are asynchronous than when they begin to sound at the same time. Rasch (1978) demonstrated this effect using the basic patterns and detection task described earlier. He showed that detection of higher tones in the presence of lower ones was strongly affected by onset asynchrony: Each 10 msec of delay of the lower tones was associated with roughly a 10-dB reduction in detection threshold. At a delay of 30 msec, the threshold for perception of the higher tones was roughly the same as when they were presented alone.

Rasch further observed that the subjective effect of this onset asynchrony was very pronounced. When the onsets of the tones were synchronous, a single fused sound was heard; however, when onset disparities were introduced, the tones sounded very distinct perceptually. This, as Rasch pointed out, is an example of the continuity effect (see Section II,C).

Rasch (1988) later applied the results of this study to live ensemble performances. He made recordings of three different trio ensembles (string, reed, and recorder) and calculated the onset relations between tones when they were nominally simultaneous. He found that asynchrony values ranged from 30 to 50 msec, with a mean asynchrony of 36 msec. Relating these findings to his earlier perceptual ones, Rasch concluded that such onset asynchronies enabled the listener to hear the simultaneous sounds as distinct from each other. According to this line of argument, such asynchronies should not be considered as performance failures, but rather as characteristics that are useful in enabling listeners to hear concurrent voices distinctly.

On this line of reasoning, larger amounts of asynchrony should produce even better and more reliable separation of voices. One might hypothesize, then, that compositional practice would exploit this effect—at least in polyphonic music, where it is intended that the individual voices should be distinctly heard. Evidence for this hypothesis was found by Huron (1993) in an analysis of J. S. Bach's 15 two-part inventions. He found that for 11 of these inventions, values of onset asynchrony were such that there were no other permutations of the rhythms of the voices (with duration, rhythmic order, and meter controlled for) that produced more onset asynchrony than occurred in Bach's actual music. For the remaining four inventions, values of asynchrony were still significantly higher than would be expected by chance. Huron concluded that Bach had deliberately produced such onset asynchronies so as to optimize the perceptual salience of the individual voices.

C. AUDITORY CONTINUITY

Auditory continuity is perhaps the most dramatic effect to result from temporal disparities within tone complexes. Consider the visual analogue shown in the upper portion of Figure 3, which was adapted from Vicario (1982). Line A could, in

FIGURE 3 Visual analogue of an auditory continuity effect. Line A in the upper illustration could, in principle, be seen as having three components (a line to the left of the rectangle, a line to its right, and a line that forms part of the rectangle itself). However, it is instead seen as a single, continuous line. This effect is weaker in the lower illustration, in which the rectangle is wider, and the lines to its left and right are shorter. (Adapted from Vicario, 1982.)

principle, be viewed in terms of three components: a line to the left of the rectangle, a line to its right, and a line that forms part of the rectangle itself. However, our visual system instead treats all three components as a single line, which is independent of the remaining parts of the rectangle.

Vicario produced a musical equivalent of this demonstration. He generated a chord that consisted of components corresponding to C_4, $D\sharp_4$, $F\sharp_4$, A_4, C_5, $D\sharp_5$, and $F\sharp_5$; with A_4 both preceding and following the other components of the chord. Just as line A in Figure 3 is seen as continuing through the rectangle, so the listener heard a pitch corresponding to A_4 continue right through the chord.

This continuity effect is sensitive to the precise temporal parameters of the various components. To return to Vicario's visual analogue, when the lines forming the rectangle are lengthened and the lines to its left and right are shortened, as in the lower portion of Figure 3, the impression of continuity is reduced. Similarly, when the duration of the lengthened component of the chord is reduced, and the duration of the full chord is lengthened, the impression of auditory continuity is diminished.

In general, demonstrations of auditory continuity have existed for some time (see Warren, 1984, for a review). In an early study, Miller and Licklider (1950) rapidly alternated a tone with a noise burst, and subjects reported that the tone appeared to continue right through the noise. The authors called this the "picket fence effect," because in observing a landscape through a picket fence we see it as continuous rather than as broken up by the pickets. Vicario (1960) independently reported a similar phenomenon, which he called the "acoustic tunnel effect."

A different type of continuity effect was described by Warren, Obusek, and Ackroff (1972). When a broadband noise was repeatedly presented at different intensity levels, listeners heard the fainter noise as persisting without interruption, while the louder noise appeared to come on and off periodically. The authors found that analogous effects occurred with other signals also, such as narrowband noise, and pure and complex tones.

More elaborate continuity effects have also been reported. Dannenbring (1976) generated a pure-tone glide that rose and fell repeatedly. In some conditions, the glide was periodically interrupted by a loud broadband noise; however, it was perceived as though continuous. In contrast, when the glide was periodically broken, leaving only silent intervals during the breaks, listeners heard a disjunct series of rising and falling glides. Visual analogues of these two conditions, and their perceptual consequences, are shown in Figure 4.

Sudden amplitude drops between signals and intervening noise bursts may reduce, or even destroy, continuity effects. For example, Bregman and Dannenbring (1977) presented subjects with a gliding tone such as just described, and found that brief amplitude drops before and after the intervening noise bursts decreased the tendency to perceive the glide as continuous. Similarly, Warren et al. (1972), using noise bursts of alternating loudnesses, found that brief silences between the different bursts reduced the impression of continuity.

FIGURE 4　Visual illustration of an auditory continuity effect using gliding tones. See text for details. (Adapted from Bregman, 1990, which illustrates an experiment by Dannenbring, 1976.)

Amplitude drops do not, however, necessarily preclude the emergence of continuity effects. For example, tones produced by plucked instruments are characterized by rapid increases followed by decreases in amplitude. In music played by such instruments, when the same tone is rapidly repeated many times, and it is periodically omitted and replaced by a different tone, the listener may perceptually generate the omitted tone. Many examples of this phenomenon occur in 20th century guitar music, such as Tarrega's *Recuerdos de la Alhambra*, shown in Figure 5, and Barrios' *Una Limosna por el Amor de Dios*. Here the strong expectations set up by the rapidly repeating notes cause the listener to "hear" these notes even when they are not being played. Interestingly, at the end of the Barrios piece, the tempo is gradually slowed down, so that the gaps in the repeating presentations become apparent. In this way, the listener is drawn to realize that the gaps had been there, although imperceptibly, throughout the work.

A number of authors, such as Vicario (1973) and Warren (1983), have shown that listeners make use of both prior and subsequent contextual information in determining the strength and nature of continuity effects. In one experiment, Sasaki (1980) generated melodic patterns in which certain tones were omitted and replaced by loud noise bursts. Under some circumstances, listeners "heard" the

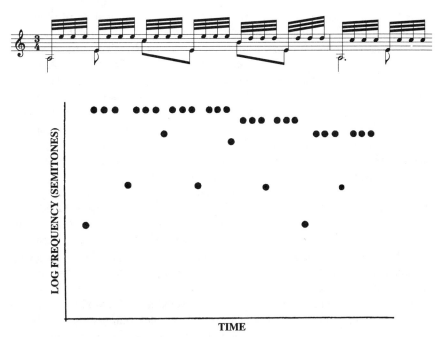

FIGURE 5   The beginning of *Recuerdos de la Alhambra*, by Tarrega. Although the tones are presented one at a time, two parallel lines are perceived, organized in accordance with pitch proximity. (Adapted from Deutsch, 1996.)

missing tone appear through the noise. This percept was most likely to occur when the omitted tone was predictable from the musical context; for example, when it formed part of a well-known melody. In this way, the experiment also provided evidence for grouping in accordance with the principle of familiarity.

In another experiment, Ciocca and Bregman (1987) presented listeners with a gliding tone that was interrupted by a noise burst. When the entering and exiting portions of the glide fell either in the same frequency range, or on a common trajectory, listeners tended to hear the glide as continuing through the noise. Later, Tougas and Bregman (1990) generated two simultaneous glides, one ascending and the other descending, with the two crossing in the middle. Previous studies had shown that global frequency proximity strongly influenced how crossing pitch patterns were perceived (Deutsch, 1975a, 1975b; Tougas & Bregman, 1985; Van Noorden, 1975; see also Section V, this chapter). As expected from these findings, Tougas and Bregman (1990) found that frequency proximity dominated over trajectory in determining the type of perceptual restoration that was obtained: Listeners tended to hear a higher glide that fell and then rose again, together with a lower glide that rose and then fell again, with the two meeting in the middle.

D. FREQUENCY MODULATION

Natural sustained sounds, such as those generated by musical instruments and the singing voice, constantly undergo small frequency fluctuations that preserve the ratios formed by their components (Cardozo & Van Noorden, 1968; Flanagan, 1972; Grey & Moorer, 1977; Lieberman, 1961; MacIntyre, Schumacher, & Woodhouse, 1981, 1982). It has been surmised that the auditory system uses such coherent frequency modulation as a cue for grouping spectral components together; and conversely uses incoherent frequency modulation as a cue for separating them out perceptually (for a discussion, see Bregman, 1990). Indeed, composers such as Chowning (1980) and McNabb (1981) have produced informal demonstrations that coherent frequency modulation, when imposed on synthesized singing voices or musical instrument tones, enhances perceptual fusion.

The issue, however, is theoretically a complex one. It has been argued that because information concerning frequency modulation is severely degraded in reverberant environments, the reliance on incoherent frequency modulation as a cue for perceptual separation could cause us to separate out components when they should in fact be perceptually grouped together. Furthermore, incoherent frequency modulation necessarily causes the frequency relationships between components to depart from harmonicity. Because the perceptual system already uses such departures as cues for perceptual segregation, the usefulness of invoking incoherent frequency modulation as an additional cue is debatable (Summerfield, 1992).

The experimental evidence on this issue is also complex. McAdams (1989) explored the effect of frequency modulation on the perceptual separation of three simultaneous sung vowels, which were built on different fundamentals. He found that when target vowels were frequency modulated, this increased their perceptual prominence. However, the perceived prominence of these vowels was not affected by whether the nontarget vowels were modulated coherently or incoherently with them, or even by whether the nontarget vowels were modulated at all.

In related experiments, Gardner and Darwin (1986) and Gardner et al. (1989) found that incoherent frequency modulation of the components of different vowels did not enhance their perceptual salience. Furthermore, when one component of a vowel was frequency modulated incoherently with the others, this manipulation did not reduce its contribution to the vowel's phonetic categorization.

Other negative findings were obtained by Carlyon (1991, 1992), who found that listeners were insensitive to frequency modulation incoherence when it was independent of departures from harmonicity. When the components of tones stood in nonharmonic relation, listeners were unable to judge whether they were modulated coherently or incoherently with each other (see also Summerfield & Culling, 1992).

Such negative findings raise the question of why frequency modulation can nevertheless enhance a vowel's perceptual salience. A possible explanation was advanced by McAdams (1984), who pointed out that when the harmonics of a vowel are frequency modulated, they also undergo amplitude modulation that traces the vowel's spectral envelope. In this way, the listener is provided with more complete information about the vowel's identity. Such spectral tracing might therefore be responsible for the enhanced perceptual salience of frequency-modulated vowels.

To test this hypothesis, Marin and McAdams (1991) synthesized sung vowels that were frequency modulated in either of two ways. In some conditions, the amplitudes of the components remained constant as their frequencies were modulated, and in other conditions, their amplitudes were varied so as to trace the vowel's spectral envelope.

Subjects were presented with chords consisting of three sung vowels that were built on different fundamentals, and they judged on each trial how prominent each vowel sounded within its chord. Although frequency-modulated vowels were heard as more prominent than unmodulated ones, spectral tracing did not have an effect.

Marin and McAdams' study therefore provided evidence against the spectral tracing hypothesis. As an alternative explanation for the enhanced prominence of frequency-modulated vowels, we may advance the direct hypothesis that neural units involved in the attribution of vowel quality are more strongly activated by frequency-modulated sounds than by unmodulated ones.

E. AMPLITUDE MODULATION

Because many natural sounds consist of spectral components whose amplitudes rise and fall in synchrony with each other, one might conjecture that coherent amplitude modulation would be used by the auditory system as a cue for perceptual fusion. On the other hand, coherent amplitude modulation is by no means universal—the partials of many musical instrument tones do not rise and fall in synchrony with each other. So the use of amplitude modulation incoherence as a cue for perceptual separation could cause the listener to erroneously separate out components when they should be perceptually fused together.

The experimental evidence on this issue is also equivocal. Bregman, Abramson, Doehring, and Darwin (1985) found evidence that coherent amplitude modulation could promote perceptual fusion; however, the modulation rates used here were so high that their findings could instead be interpreted as related to mechanisms involved in pitch perception. At slower rates, convincing evidence that coherent amplitude modulation leads to perceptual fusion has been difficult to obtain (Darwin & Carlyon, 1995).

F. EAR OF INPUT

Because all the components of a sound necessarily originate from a common location, and the components of different sounds originate from different locations, one might expect that the inferred spatial origins of components would strongly influence how they are perceptually grouped together. The issue arises, however, of how the spatial origin of a component should be inferred in the first place. In natural environments, sound waves are subjected to numerous distortions as they travel from their sources to our ears. So if we were to rely on first-order localization cues alone (such as differences in amplitude and phase between the ears), we would risk separating out components when they should instead be combined perceptually.

Given this line of reasoning, we might expect the auditory system not to use first-order localization cues as primary bases for grouping, but instead to use them only when other supporting cues are present. Indeed, we can go further and hypothesize that factors such as harmonicity and onset synchronicity, which indicate that components have originated from a common source, might cause us to hear these components as arising from the same spatial location.

Experimental evidence supporting this view has been obtained from studies in which different components of a complex were presented to each ear. Beerends and Houtsma (1989) had subjects identify the pitches of two complex tones, when their partials were distributed across the ears in various ways. They found that pitch identification was only weakly affected by the way the partials were distributed. Furthermore, Darwin and Ciocca (1992) found that the contribution of a single mistuned harmonic to the pitch of a complex tone was almost as large when this harmonic was delivered to the opposite ear as when it was delivered to the same ear as the other harmonics.

Related effects have been found for the perception of speech sounds. Broadbent and Ladefoged (1957) presented the first two formants of a phrase, with one formant delivered to each ear. Provided that the two formants were built on the same fundamental, subjects were able to identify the speech signal, and they also tended to hear a single voice, so that they were fusing the information from the two ears into a single perceptual image. Later, Hukin and Darwin (1995b) investigated the degree to which a single component contributed to the perceived quality of a vowel when it was presented to the ear opposite the remaining components. They found that this difference in ear of input had only a small effect.

Support has also been obtained for the conjecture that other grouping cues, such as harmonicity and asynchrony of onset, can influence the perceived spatial origin of a component of a complex (Hill and Darwin, 1993). Later we shall see that when two sequences of tones are presented simultaneously, one to each ear, a number of factors influence whether or not ear of input is used as a localization cue, and also influence the perceived spatial origins of the different tones.

III. LARGER SCALE GROUPINGS

So far, we have been focusing on situations in which single tone complexes are presented, and have identified various cues that the listener uses to sort their components into groupings. We now turn to the situation in which sequences of tones are presented instead. Here the auditory system abstracts relationships between successive tones, and uses these relationships as additional grouping cues.

One cue that we use here is pitch proximity: We tend to form sequential linkages between tones that are close in pitch and to separate out those that are further apart. Where rapid sequences of tones are concerned, researchers have frequently drawn an analogy with apparent motion in vision: When two lights that are in spatial proximity are flashed on and off in rapid succession, the observer obtains the illusion that a single light has moved from one location to the other. A second cue is temporal proximity: When pauses are placed between tones within a sequence, we use these as markers for grouping the tones into subsequences. A third cue is similarity of sound quality: When different types of instruments play together, we tend to form linkages between tones of similar timbre. We also invoke other principles in grouping tones together sequentially, such as good continuation and common fate.

IV. GROUPING OF RAPID SEQUENCES OF SINGLE TONES

A. PITCH PROXIMITY AND STREAM FORMATION

When a sequence of tones is presented at a rapid tempo, and the tones are drawn from two different pitch ranges, the listener perceives two melodic lines in parallel, one corresponding to the higher tones and the other to the lower ones. This perceptual phenomenon is frequently exploited by composers in the technique of pseudopolyphony, or compound melodic line. The passage from Tarrega's *Recuerdos de la Alhambra* shown in Figure 5 provides an example. In this Figure, the passage is also represented with pitch and time mapped into the vertical and horizontal dimensions of visual space, and it can be seen that two separate lines emerge in the visual representation, corresponding to the two pitch lines that are perceived by the listener.

This phenomenon of perceptual dissociation has been investigated in a number of studies. Miller and Heise (1950) presented listeners with two alternating tones, at a rate of 10 tones per second. When the pitch difference between these tones was small, listeners heard the sequence as a trill (i.e., as a single string of related tones). However, when the pitch difference was large, listeners instead heard the sequence as two interrupted and unrelated tones. In a further experiment, Heise and Miller (1951) used rapid sequences of tones that were composed of several pitches. When one of the tones in a sequence differed sufficiently in pitch from the others, it was heard in isolation from them.

A related phenomenon was demonstrated by Dowling (1973a). He presented two well-known melodies at a rapid tempo, such that the tones were taken from each melody in alternation. When the melodies were in closely overlapping pitch ranges, their components were perceptually combined into a single stream, with the result that subjects had considerable difficulty in identifying them. However, when the alternating melodies were instead in different pitch ranges, they were readily separated out perceptually, and so were easily identified.

B. TEMPORAL COHERENCE AS A FUNCTION OF PITCH PROXIMITY AND TEMPO

The term *temporal coherence* is used to describe the perceptual impression of a connected series of tones. The conditions giving rise to temporal coherence were studied by Schouten (1962). He found that as the frequency separation between successive tones increased, it was necessary to reduce their presentation rate in order to maintain the impression of a connected series.

Van Noorden (1975) examined this phenomenon in detail. Listeners were presented with sequences consisting of two tones in alternation, and they attempted either to hear temporal coherence or to hear *fission* (i.e., two streams of unrelated tones). Two boundaries were determined by these means. The first was defined as the threshold frequency separation as a function of tempo that was needed for the listener to hear the sequence as connected. The second established these values when the listener was attempting to hear fission. As shown in Figure 6, when listeners were attempting to hear coherence, decreasing the tempo from 50 to 150 msec per tone increased the frequency separation within which coherence could be heard from 4 to 13 semitones. However, when the listeners were instead attempting to hear fission, decreasing the tempo had little effect on performance. Between these two boundaries, there was a large region in which the listener could alter his listening strategy at will, and so hear either fission or coherence. So within this region, attentional set was important in determining how the sequence was perceived.

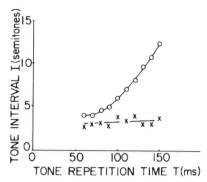

FIGURE 6 Temporal coherence boundary (o), and fission boundary (x) as a function of the frequency relationship between alternating tones and the presentation rate. (Adapted from Van Noorden, 1975).

Bregman and Bernstein (cited in Bregman, 1978) confirmed the interaction between frequency separation and tempo in judgments of temporal coherence. They found that as the frequencies of two alternating tones converged, a higher rate of alternation was required for the sequence to split perceptually into two different streams.

C. GROUPING BY PITCH PROXIMITY BUILDS WITH REPETITION

A number of studies have shown that the splitting of tonal sequences into two streams based on pitch proximity builds with repetition. Van Noorden (1975) compared the temporal coherence boundary for two-tone, three-tone, and long repetitive sequences. With three-tone sequences, the pitch change could be either unidirectional or bidirectional. As shown in Figure 7, for unidirectional three-tone sequences, temporal coherence occurred at rates that were equal to, or even higher than, those for two-tone sequences. However for bidirectional three-tone sequences, the rate of pitch change had to be set much lower than for two-tone sequences in order for coherence to be perceived. For long repetitive sequences, the rate of pitch change had to be set lower still.

In a related experiment, Bregman (1978) presented listeners repeatedly with two high tones together with a single low tone. When this sequence split perceptually into two streams, listeners heard two high tones in alternation, together with a single low tone that was steadily repeated. Bregman varied the number of tones that were packaged between 4-sec periods of silence, and listeners adjusted the speed of the sequence until the point of splitting was determined. As shown in Figure 8, as the number of tones in the package increased, the speed required for perception of separate streams decreased.

To explain this finding, Bregman argued that stream segregation is the product of a mechanism that groups together components of a spectrum so as to recon-

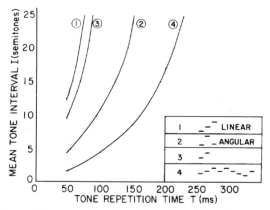

FIGURE 7 Temporal coherence boundary for two-tone (Curve 3), three-tone unidirectional (Curve 1), three-tone bidirectional (Curve 2), and continuous (Curve 4) sequences. (Adapted from Van Noorden, 1975.)

struct the original sounds. Such a mechanism would be expected to accumulate evidence over time, so that the segregation of components into different streams should build up with repetition (see also Bregman, 1990).

Further evidence that stream segregation results from such a parsing mechanism was provided by Bregman and Rudnicky (1975). Listeners judged the orders of two test tones that were embedded in a four-tone pattern that was itself flanked

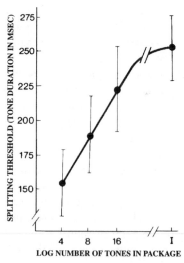

FIGURE 8 Threshold for stream segregation as a function of number of tones per package. Two "high" tones were presented in alternation with a single "low" tone. (Adapted from Bregman, 1978.)

by two "distractor tones." The presence of the distractor tones made the order of the test tones difficult to judge. However, when another stream of tones, called "captor tones," was moved close in frequency to the distractor tones, the distractors then combined with the captors to form a single stream, leaving the test tones in a stream of their own. In consequence, it became easy to judge the order in which the test tones appeared. The authors argued that the listeners were here presented with two simultaneously structured streams, and that the distractor tones could, in principle, belong to either one, but not to both simultaneously.

D. PITCH PROXIMITY AND THE PERCEPTION OF TEMPORAL RELATIONSHIPS

One consequence of the formation of separate perceptual streams is that temporal relationships between elements of the different streams become difficult to process. This has been shown in several ways. Bregman and Campbell (1971) presented a repeating sequence consisting of six tones: three from a high pitch range and three from a low one. When the tones occurred at a rate of 10 per second, it was difficult for listeners to perceive a pattern of high and low tones that was embedded in the sequence.

In a related experiment, Dannenbring and Bregman (1976) alternated two tones at high speeds so that they formed separate perceptual streams, and found that the tones from the two streams appeared to be overlapping in time. Further, Fitzgibbon, Pollatsek, and Thomas (1974) explored the perception of temporal gaps between tones that occurred in rapid sequence. Detection of a 20-msec gap was easy when the gap was placed between tones in the same frequency range, but difficult when it was placed between tones in different ranges (see also Neff, Jesteadt, & Brown, 1982).

Another reflection of such breakdown of temporal processing was found by Van Noorden (1975), who studied the detection of temporal displacement of a tone that alternated continuously with another tone of different frequency. As the rate of presentation of the tones increased, the threshold for detecting temporal displacement also increased. This rise in threshold was substantial when the tones were widely separated in frequency, but only slight when their frequencies were similar.

An effect of frequency disparity on temporal processing has also been found for two-tone sequences. Divenyi and Hirsh (1972) found that discrimination of the size of a temporal gap between tones within a pair deteriorated with increasing frequency separation between the tones. Williams and Perott (1972) also found that the minimum detectable gap between successively presented tones increased with increasing frequency difference between them. However, Van Noorden (1975) showed that the deterioration in temporal processing that he measured was considerably greater for long repetitive sequences than for two-tone sequences, so that it emerged as a consequence of stream formation (Figure 9).

E. GROUPING BY TIMBRE

Tones can also be grouped together on the basis of sound quality, or timbre. This is an instantiation of the principle of similarity: Just as we perceive the array in Figure 1b as four columns, two formed by the filled circles and two by the unfilled ones, so we group together tones that are similar in timbre and separate out those that are dissimilar. As a result, when different instruments play in parallel, we may form groupings based on their timbres even when their pitch ranges overlap heavily. An example is given in Figure 10, which is taken from Beethoven's Spring Sonata for violin and piano. Here the listener perceives two melodic lines that correspond to the tones played by each instrument, rather than linking the tones in accordance with pitch proximity.

A striking consequence of this grouping tendency was demonstrated by Warren, Obusek, Farmer, and Warren (1969). These authors generated a sequence of four unrelated sounds, and they presented it repeatedly without pause. The sounds, each 200 msec in duration, consisted of a high tone, a hiss (noise burst), a low tone, and a buzz (square wave). At this presentation rate, subjects were unable to name the orders in which the sounds occurred; for correct ordering to be achieved, the duration of each sound had to be longer than 500 msec.

Another consequence of grouping by timbre was demonstrated by Wessel (1979). He presented subjects with a repeating pattern consisting of a three-tone ascending pitch line, with successive tones composed of alternating timbres, as defined by their spectral energy distribution. When the timbral difference between successive tones was small, listeners heard the pattern as composed of ascending lines. However, when the timbral difference was large, listeners linked the tones together on the basis of timbre and so heard two, interwoven, descending lines instead.

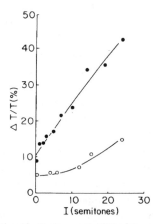

FIGURE 9   o Just noticeable displacement $\Delta T/T$ of the second tone of a two-tone sequence as a function of tone interval I. • Just noticeable displacement $\Delta T/T$ of one tone in a continuous sequence of alternating tones as a function of tone interval I. (Adapted from Van Noorden, 1975.)

FIGURE 10   Passage from the beginning of the second movement of Beethoven's *Spring Sonata* for violin and piano. The tones played by the two instruments overlap in pitch; however, the listener perceives two melodic lines in parallel, which correspond to those played by each instrument. This reflects perceptual grouping by similarity.

Because timbre is multidimensional in nature, with both static and dynamic characteristics, we can ask which of its aspects are most conducive to perceptual grouping. Concerning static characteristics, Van Noorden (1975) found that tones with the same fundamental but different harmonics segregated into different streams on the basis of their harmonic structure. In a further demonstration, he generated complex tones that were filtered in various ways, and found that listeners segregated them on the basis of their filter characteristics, regardless of whether they were built on the same or different fundamentals.

In a further experiment, Singh (1987) generated sequences of tones that were based on different fundamentals and that also differed in harmonic content. Subjects were able to form streams based on either pitch or timbre. A related result was obtained by Bregman, Liao, and Levitan (1990), who generated tones that differed in both fundamental frequency and peak of spectral envelope. They found that both these factors could be used as bases for grouping.

The literature is equivocal concerning dynamic aspects of timbre. Wessel (1979) found that although streaming was clearly influenced by spectral content, variations in onset transients did not have a similar effect. Similarly, Hartmann and Johnson (1991) reported that although subjects easily segregated tones on the basis of harmonic content, they did not do so by type of temporal envelope, even though the envelopes they used were easily distinguished from each other.

Different conclusions were arrived at by Iverson (1995), who carried out an experiment using a number of different instrument tones. Subjects were able to form melodic streams on the basis of timbre, considering both the tones' static spectral characteristics and also their dynamic ones. The reasons for the differences between these findings remain to be determined.

F. GROUPING BY TEMPORAL PROXIMITY

When a sequence of sound elements is presented with pauses interspersed between them, we readily group the elements into subsequences that are defined by the pauses. In one experiment, Povel and Okkerman (1981) generated sequences consisting of tones of identical frequency, amplitude, and duration that were separated by gaps of two alternating durations. Subjects perceived these sequences as repeating groups of two tones that were segmented in accordance with the temporal gaps.

Other experiments have shown that grouping by temporal proximity can have a pronounced effect on the way that pitch patterns are perceived. Handel (1973) had subjects identify repeating patterns that consisted of dichotomous elements of differing pitch. Identification of the patterns was easy when they were temporally segmented in accordance with their pitch structure (e.g., when an eight-element pattern was segmented into groups of two), but difficult when the patterns were segmented inconsistently with their pitch structure (e.g., when an eight-element pattern was segmented into groups of three). In another experiment, Dowling (1973b) presented patterns that consisted of five-tone sequences that were separated by pauses, and subjects made recognition judgments concerning test sequences that were embedded in these patterns. Performance levels were higher when the test sequences had been presented in a single temporal segment than when a pause had been inserted between its elements.

Deutsch (1980b) performed a study on the recall of hierarchically structured pitch sequences. In some conditions, the sequences were divided into subsequences by the insertion of pauses. Performance levels were high when the pauses were in accordance with pitch structure, but low when they conflicted with pitch structure. Other measures showed that the subjects were grouping the patterns so strongly by temporal segmentation that they were unable to take advantage of pitch structure when this conflicted with temporal structure. This experiment is described in detail in Chapter 10.

G. GROUPING BY GOOD CONTINUATION

A few researchers have found evidence for grouping of tone sequences on the basis of good continuation. Divenyi and Hirsh (1974) studied order identification for three-tone sequences, and found that those with unidirectional frequency changes were easier to order than were those whose frequency changes were bidirectional. Analogous results were obtained by Nickerson and Freeman (1974), Warren and Byrnes (1975), and McNally and Handel (1977) for four-tone sequences. Further, Van Noorden (1975) found that a three-tone sequence was more likely to be judged as coherent when its tones formed unidirectional rather than bidirectional frequency changes.

H. GROUPING BY AMPLITUDE

Under some conditions, amplitude can act as a grouping cue. Dowling (1973a) found that loudness differences increased the perceptual distinctiveness of interleaved melodies. Van Noorden (1975) studied perception of sequences consisting of tones of identical frequency that alternated between two amplitudes. A single coherent stream was heard when the amplitude differences between the tones were less than 5 dB. However, two separate streams were heard when the amplitude differences were larger. In the latter case, attention could be directed to the softer stream as well as to the louder one. With even larger amplitude differences, auditory continuity effects were produced, so that the softer tone was heard as continuing through the louder one.

V. GROUPING OF MULTIPLE TONE SEQUENCES IN SPACE

In ensemble performances, we are presented with multiple streams of tones that arise in parallel from different regions of space. We can then inquire into the principles that govern perceptual grouping under such conditions. Do we form linkages between tones that are similar in pitch, in loudness, or in timbre? Alternatively, do we invoke spatial location as a prominent grouping cue? We shall see that all these factors are involved in grouping, but that they interact in complex ways. So given one type of pattern, grouping may be overwhelmingly determined by pitch proximity. But given a slight alteration in this pattern, grouping by spatial location may occur instead.

Powerful illusions also occur in this situation (Deutsch, 1974, 1975a, 1975b, 1980a, 1981, 1983a, 1983b, 1987, 1995). When we hear a tone, we attribute a pitch, a loudness, a timbre, and we hear the tone as coming from a particular spatial location. Each tone, as it is heard, may then be described as a bundle of attribute values. If our perception is veridical, this bundle reflects the characteristics and locations of the sounds that are being presented. However, when multiple sequences of tones are presented simultaneously, these bundles of attribute values may fragment and recombine in different ways, so that illusory conjunctions result. These illusory conjunctions then reflect the operation of multiple decision mechanisms in the grouping process (Deutsch, 1980a, 1981).

A. THE SCALE ILLUSION AND RELATED PHENOMENA

The *scale illusion*, which was first reported by Deutsch (1974, 1975b), provides an example of an illusory conjunction. The pattern that gives rise to this illusion is shown in the upper portion of Figure 11. This consists of a major scale, with successive tones alternating from ear to ear. The scale is played simultaneously in both ascending and descending form, such that whenever a tone from the ascending scale is in the right ear a tone from the descending scale is in the left ear, and vice versa. The sequence is played repeatedly without pause.

When listening to this pattern through earphones, people frequently experience the illusion shown in the lower portion of Figure 11. A melody corresponding to the higher tones is heard as coming from one earphone (in right-handers, generally the one on the right), with a melody corresponding to the lower tones as coming from the other earphone. When the earphone positions are reversed, the apparent locations of the higher and lower tones often remain fixed. This gives rise to the

FIGURE 11 The pattern that produces the scale illusion, and the percept most commonly obtained. When this pattern is played through stereo headphones, most listeners hear two melodic lines that move in contrary motion. The higher tones all appear to be coming from one earphone, and the lower tones from the other, regardless of where each tone is coming from.

curious impression that the higher tones have migrated from one earphone to the other, and that the lower tones have migrated in the opposite direction.

Some listeners do not hear all the tones, but instead hear a single melodic line consisting of the higher tones alone, and little or nothing of the lower tones. This, together with other ways the scale illusion is sometimes perceived, is illustrated in Figure 12. The scale illusion and a number of its variants appear in the compact disc by Deutsch (1995).

In listening to the scale illusion, then, grouping by pitch proximity is so powerful that not only are the tones organized melodically in accordance with this principle, but they are frequently reorganized in space to conform with this principle also. Such spatial reorganization is in accordance with other findings showing that, in the absence of further supporting cues, differences in ear of input can have only small effects on how components of a tone complex are grouped together (Beerends & Houtsma, 1989; Darwin & Ciocca, 1992) and that other grouping cues can themselves influence the perceived spatial origins of individual components of a sound complex (Hill & Darwin, 1993). As described earlier, it makes sense that the auditory system would adopt such a listening strategy, because it is conducive to realistic interpretations of our environment. In the present situation, it is probable that a sequence of tones in one pitch range has originated from one source, and that another sequence of tones, in a different pitch range, has originated from a different source. So we exploit pitch proximity as a cue to determine how these tones are grouped together, and even to determine their perceived locations.

Variants of the scale illusion are readily produced. One of these is illustrated in Figure 13. A chromatic scale that ranges over two octaves is presented in both ascending and descending form, with the individual tones switching from ear to

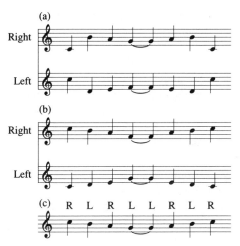

FIGURE 12 Different ways the scale illusion is sometimes perceived. (Adapted from Deutsch, 1995.)

ear in the same way as in the original scale illusion. When the pattern is played in stereo, most listeners hear a higher line that moves down an octave and up again, together with a lower line that moves up an octave and down again, with the two meeting in the middle. Yet when each channel is played separately, it is heard correctly as a series of tones that jump around in pitch. In Figure 13, the smoothing out of the visual representation in the score depicting the percept reflects well the way the sounds are perceptually reorganized.

FIGURE 13 The pattern that produces a version of the chromatic illusion, and the way it is most often perceived. (Adapted from Deutsch, 1995.)

Butler (1979a) found evidence that the perceptual reorganization that occurs in the scale illusion also occurs in a broad range of musical situations. He presented the pattern shown in Figure 11 through spatially separated loudspeakers instead of earphones, and asked subjects to notate what they heard. In some conditions, the patterns were composed of piano tones, and differences in timbre were introduced between the sounds coming from the two speakers. Butler found that, despite these variations, virtually all responses reflected channeling by pitch proximity, so that higher and lower melodic lines were perceived, rather than the patterns that were in fact presented. When differences in timbre were introduced between the tones presented through the two speakers, a new tone quality was heard, but it appeared to be coming simultaneously from both speakers.

To determine whether these findings generalize to other configurations, Butler presented listeners with the two-part patterns shown in Figures 14a and 14b. Again, virtually all responses reflected grouping by pitch range. For both of these patterns, a perceptual reorganization occurred, so that a melody corresponding to the higher tones appeared to be coming from one earphone or speaker, with a melody corresponding to the lower tones coming from the other (Figures 14c and 14d).

Such effects even occur on listening to live music in concert halls. There is an interesting passage at the beginning of the final movement of Tchaikovsky's Sixth Symphony (*The Pathetique*). As shown in the upper portion of Figure 15, the notes from the theme are alternated between the first and second violin parts, and the notes from the accompaniment are alternated reciprocally (see Butler, 1979b, for a

FIGURE 14 The upper portion of the figure shows two-part patterns that were presented to subjects through stereo headphones or loudspeakers. The lower portion shows these patterns as they were most commonly notated. (Adapted from Butler, 1979a.)

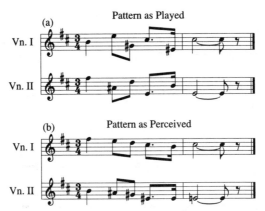

FIGURE 15   Beginning of the final movement of Tchaikovsky's Sixth Symphony *(The Pathe-tique)*. The upper portion of the figure shows the pattern as it is played, and the lower portion shows how it is generally perceived.

discussion). The passage, however, is not perceived as it is performed; rather, one violin part appears to be playing the theme and the other the accompaniment, as in the lower portion of Figure 15. This is true even with the orchestra arranged in 19th century fashion, so that the first violins are to the left of the audience, with the second violins to their right.

Whether it was Tchaikovsky's intention to produce a spatial illusion here, or whether he expected the audience to hear the theme waft back and forth between the two sides of space, we shall never know. However, there is a legend that the conductor Arthur Nikisch urged Tchaikovsky to rescore this passage so that the first violins would play the entire theme alone and the second violins the accompaniment. Tchaikovsky refused to change his scoring, but Nikisch rescored the passage anyway, and so created a second school of performance of this passage. The reasons for the argument between these two great musicians are unknown, but some conductors still prefer to perform the rescored version rather than Tchaikovsky's original one (Carlson, 1996).[1]

Another example of such spatial reorganization occurs at the end of the second movement of Rachmaninoff's Second Suite for Two Pianos. Here the first and second pianos play the two patterns shown in the upper portion of Figure 16. However, it appears to the listener that one piano is consistently playing the higher tone, and the other piano the lower one, as in the lower portion of this figure (Sloboda, 1985).

To return to the experiment of Deutsch (1975b), it is noteworthy that all the subjects formed perceptual groupings on the basis of overall pitch range. Rather

[1] I first came across this legend when it was relayed to me by David Butler, and it was later confirmed by the conductor George Zack, who had heard it from an independent source.

Pattern as Played

Pattern as Perceived

FIGURE 16 A passage from the second movement of Rachmaninoff's *Second Suite for Two Pianos.* The upper portion of the figure shows the pattern as it is played, and the lower portion shows how it is generally perceived.

than following the pattern purely on the basis of local (note-to-note) proximity, they either heard all the tones as two nonoverlapping pitch streams, or they heard the higher tones and little or nothing of the lower ones. No subject reported hearing a full ascending or descending scale as part of the pattern.

A related finding was obtained by Van Noorden (1975), who presented an ascending sequence of tones in rapid alternation with a descending one. Subjects heard this pattern as higher and lower melodic lines that moved in contrary motion. Similar findings were obtained by Tougas and Bregman (1985, 1990), who found an analogous perceptual organization with simultaneous ascending and descending glides.

The perceptual tendency to form melodic streams based on overall pitch range is reflected in the avoidance of part crossing in polyphonic music. Huron (1991a) documented this effect in an analysis of the polyphonic works of J. S. Bach. Interestingly, although when writing in two parts Bach avoided part crossing, he avoided it more assiduously when writing in three or more parts. Huron concluded that Bach was attempting to minimize the perceptual confusion that might otherwise have occurred as the density of sound images increased.

Do differences in timbre affect perception of the scale illusion? As described earlier, Butler (1979a) found that moderate differences in timbre did not alter the basic effect. However, Smith, Hausfield, Power, and Gorta (1982) used tones with substantial differences in timbre (one stream was generated by a synthesized piano and another by a synthesized saxophone) and found that timbre was then used as a basis for grouping. In a further experiment, A. L. Gregory (1994) generated a number of different instrument tones, and used these in various combinations to construct ascending and descending scales. When the tones were of identical timbre, listeners perceived nonoverlapping pitch streams, as described in Deutsch (1975b). However, when substantial differences in timbre were introduced, listeners tended to use these as cues for streaming.

Composers frequently exploit timbre as a carrier of melodic motion (Erickson, 1975) and place different instrument tones in the same pitch range, recognizing that listeners form groupings on the basis of instrument type when the timbre differences are sufficiently large. This is illustrated in the passage from Beethoven's *Spring Sonata* shown in Figure 10.

So far, we have been considering situations in which the tones coming from two sources are simultaneous, and this leads us to inquire what happens when temporal disparities are introduced. As we saw earlier, one would expect the listener to interpret such temporal disparities as indicators that the sounds were originating from different sources, and so to separate them out perceptually. As a result, we would expect streams to be formed on the basis of spatial location rather than pitch proximity.

As a test of this hypothesis, Deutsch (1979) presented subjects via earphones with the melodies shown in Figure 17. One of these patterns was repeatedly presented on each trial, and the subjects identified which of the two they had heard.

The four conditions in the experiment, together with their associated error rates, are shown in Figure 18. In Condition A, the melody was delivered to both ears simultaneously, and the error rate was here very low. In Condition B, the tones within each melody were switched haphazardly between ears, and the error rate here was considerably higher. On listening to patterns configured in this fashion, one feels compelled to attend to the tones delivered to the left ear or to the right, and it is very difficult to integrate them into a single coherent stream. Condition C was exactly as Condition B, except that the melody was accompanied by a drone. Whenever a tone from the melody was delivered to the right ear, the drone was delivered to the left ear, and vice versa. So both ears again received input simultaneously, even though the melody was switching from ear to ear, just as in Condition B. It can be seen that identification of the melody in the presence of the contralateral drone was again at a high level. In Condition D, the drone again

FIGURE 17   Basic pattern used to study the effects on melody identification of rapid switching between ears. All tones were 30 msec in duration, and tones within a sequence were separated by 100-msec pauses. (From Deutsch, 1979.)

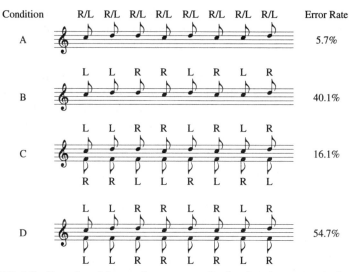

FIGURE 18 Examples of the way the tones were distributed to the two ears in the different conditions of the experiment of Deutsch (1979). Also shown are the error rates in these different conditions. See text for details.

accompanied the melody, but it was now delivered to the same ear as the melody component. So in this condition, input was again to one ear at a time, and as a result, performance again dropped substantially.

We can conclude that when tones emanate from different spatial locations, temporal relationships between them are important determinants of how they are perceptually grouped together. When the tones arrive at the two ears simultaneously (as in the scale illusion, and in Conditions A and C of the drone experiment) they are organized sequentially on the basis of pitch proximity. However, when the tones at the two ears are clearly separated in time, grouping by spatial location is so powerful as to virtually abolish the listener's ability to integrate them into a single melodic stream.

A similar conclusion was reached by Judd (1979), who generated two repeating patterns consisting of tones that were presented to the left and right ears in alternation. Comparing the two patterns, the orders of the tones were identical when each channel was played separately, but different when the channels were played together. Subjects listened to pairs of these patterns, and they judged on each trial whether the members of the pair were the same or different. On half the trials, the tones within each channel were separated by silent gaps, and on the other half, the gaps were filled with noise. Judd found that identification performance was better in the presence of the noise, and interpreted this finding as due to the noise degrading the localization information, which in turn discouraged grouping by spatial location.

To return to the study of Deutsch (1979), a second experiment was performed to explore intermediate cases, in which the tones arriving at the two ears were not strictly simultaneous but instead overlapped in time. Specifically, in some conditions of this experiment, the components of the melody and the drone were offset from each other by 15 msec. These intermediate conditions produced intermediate results: Identification of the melody in the presence of the contralateral drone when the two were asynchronous was more difficult than when the melody and drone were strictly synchronous, but easier than when the melody components switched between the ears without an accompanying drone.

It is interesting that Berlioz (1948) came to a similar conclusion from a composer's perspective. In his *Treatise on Instrumentation* he wrote:

> I want to mention the importance of the different points of origin of the tonal masses. Certain groups of an orchestra are selected by the composer to question and answer each other; but this design becomes clear and effective only if the groups which are to carry on the dialogue are placed at a sufficient distance from each other. The composer must therefore indicate on his score their exact disposition. For instance, the drums, bass drums, cymbals, and kettledrums may remain together if they are employed, as usual, to strike certain rhythms simultaneously. But if they execute an interlocutory rhythm, one fragment of which is given to the bass drums and cymbals, the other to kettledrums and drums, the effect would be greatly improved and intensified by placing the two groups of percussion instruments at the opposite ends of the orchestra, that is, at a considerable distance from each other.

Findings from the scale illusion and its variants, together with the drone experiment, indicate that the perception of musical passages can indeed be influenced profoundly by the spatial arrangements of instruments. When a pattern of tones is played at a rapid tempo, and the tones comprising the pattern are distributed between different instruments, the listener may be unable to integrate them into a single coherent stream. Such integration is more readily accomplished when the tones played by the different instruments overlap in time. However there is a trade-off: as the amount of temporal overlap increases, our ability to identify the spatial origins of the different instrument tones decreases, and when the tones are simultaneous, spatial illusions should occur.

We now return to the question of how perception of simultaneous patterns of tones may be influenced by whether the higher tones are to the listener's right and the lower tones to the left, or the other way round. We saw earlier that in the scale illusion, right-handers tend to hear higher tones on their right and lower tones on their left, regardless of where the tones are indeed coming from. This means that tone combinations of the "high-right/low-left" type tend to be correctly localized, whereas combinations of the "high-left/ low-right" type tend to be localized less correctly.

Deutsch (1985) examined this effect in detail. Musically trained subjects were presented with simultaneous sequences of tones, one to each ear, and they transcribed them in musical notation. A sequence such as used in the study is shown in Figure 19. Each ear received a haphazard ordering of the first six tones of the F

FIGURE 19 Example of a passage used to determine accuracy of pitch perception for chords of the "high-right/low-left" type, and of the "high-left/low-right" type. (Reprinted with permission from Deutsch, 1985. © 1985 by The Regents of the University of California.)

major scale, so that for some chords the tone fed to the right ear was higher and the tone to the left was lower (high-right/low-left chords), and for others this spatial disposition was reversed (high-left/low right chords). Subjects were asked to notate the tones that were presented to one ear, and to ignore those presented to the other.

When the subjects were attending to the right ear, they notated more higher tones than lower ones correctly. Furthermore, more higher tones than lower ones intruded from the left ear into their notations. In contrast, when the subjects were attending to the left ear, they correctly notated virtually the same number of higher and of lower tones, with a marginal advantage to the lower ones. Furthermore, more lower tones than higher ones intruded from the right ear into their notations. In other words, just as in the scale illusion, tones comprising high-right/low-left chords were correctly localized more often than were tones comprising high-left/low-right chords.

This finding raises the question of whether there might also be a perceptual advantage to high-right/low-left chords when localization accuracy is not at issue. In a further experiment, subjects listened to patterns that were designed in the same way as before. However, instead of focusing attention on one ear and ignoring the other, they were asked to notate the entire pattern, ignoring ear of input. It was found that more tones were correctly notated when they came from high-right/low-left chords than from high-left/low-right chords, showing that pitches forming chords with a high-right/low-left spatial disposition were more accurately perceived.

To the extent that effects of this sort occur in live musical situations, the following line of reasoning may be advanced. In general, contemporary seating arrangements for orchestras are such that, from the performers' point of view, instruments with higher registers are to the right and those with lower registers to the left. As an example, Figure 20 shows a seating plan for the Chicago Symphony, viewed from the back of the stage. Considering the strings, the first violins are to the right of the second violins, which are to the right of the violas, which are to the right of the cellos, which are in turn to the right of the basses. Consider also the brasses: The trumpets are to the right of the trombones, which are to the right of the tuba. Furthermore, the flutes are to the right of the oboes, with the clarinets to the right of the bassoons. It is interesting that the same principle tends to hold for other musical ensembles also. We may speculate that this type of spatial disposition has evolved by trial and error because it is conducive to optimal performance.

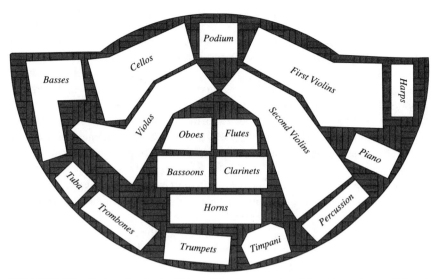

FIGURE 20   Seating plan for the Chicago Symphony, as viewed from the orchestra. (Adapted from Machlis, 1977.)

However, this presents us with a paradox. Because the audience sits facing the orchestra, this disposition is mirror-image reversed from their point of view: Instruments with higher registers tend to be to the audience's left, and those with lower registers, to their right. So for the audience, this spatial arrangement should cause perceptual difficulties. In particular, instruments with low registers, which are to the audience's right, should be less well perceived and localized. As described in Deutsch (1987), it is unclear how this problem can be resolved so as to produce an optimal arrangement for both the performers and the audience.

A further example of the spatial reorganization that we have been discussing was developed by Deutsch (1995), and is called the *glissando illusion*. The pattern that produces this illusion consists of a single oboe tone, which is played together with a sine wave that glides up and down in pitch. The two sounds are switched from ear to ear in such a way that when the oboe tone is in the left ear the glissando is in the right ear, and vice versa. This illusion appears on the compact disc by Deutsch (1995).

Many people hear the oboe tone as jumping back and forth from ear to ear, while the glissando appears to be joined together quite seamlessly. People localize the glissando in a variety of ways. For example, it is sometimes heard as coming from a fixed location, and sometimes as traveling from left to right as its pitch moves from low to high and then back from right to left as its pitch moves from high to low. The apparent spatial location of the glissando does not jump around as its components shift from ear to ear—the smoothness of its pitch transition is taken by the auditory system as a cue to assign it either a constant or a gradually changing location.

B. THE OCTAVE ILLUSION

In the experiments on simultaneous sequences so far described, grouping by pitch proximity was the rule when both ears received input simultaneously; grouping by spatial location occurred only when temporal disparities were introduced between the tones presented to the two ears. The *octave illusion*, which was first reported by Deutsch (1974), provides an interesting exception, because here following by spatial location occurs even when the tones presented to the two ears are strictly simultaneous. We shall see that this principle is adopted under special conditions of frequency relationship between tones that are presented in sequence at the two ears.

The pattern that gives rise to the octave illusion is shown in the upper portion of Figure 21. As can be seen, two tones that are spaced an octave apart are repeatedly presented in alternation. The identical sequence is played to both ears simultaneously but out of step with each other, so that when the right ear receives the high tone the left ear receives the low tone, and vice versa. The octave illusion appears on the compact disc by Deutsch (1995).

The octave illusion can take a number of different forms (Deutsch, 1974; 1975a, 1980a, 1981, 1983a, 1983b, 1987, 1995). Many people hear a single tone that switches from ear to ear, while its pitch simultaneously shifts back and forth between high and low. So it appears that one ear is receiving the pattern "high tone - silence - high tone - silence" (in right-handers, this is generally the right ear) while the other is receiving the pattern "silence - low tone - silence - low tone" (in right-handers, this is generally the left ear). This percept is illustrated in the lower portion of Figure 21. When the earphone positions are reversed, the apparent locations of the high and low tones often remain fixed: The tone that had appeared in the right ear continues to appear in the right ear, and the tone that had appeared in the left ear continues to appear in the left ear.

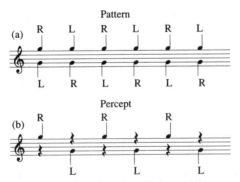

FIGURE 21   The pattern that produces the octave illusion, and the percept most commonly obtained. When this pattern is played through stereo headphones, most listeners hear an intermittent high tone in the right ear, which alternates with an intermittent low tone in the left ear.

Deutsch (1975a) hypothesized that the octave illusion results from the combined operation of two different decision mechanisms; one determines what pitch we hear, and the other determines where the tone appears to be coming from. The model is depicted in Figure 22. To provide the perceived pitches (i.e., the melodic line), the frequencies arriving at one ear are followed, and those arriving at the other ear are suppressed. However, each tone is localized at the ear that receives the higher frequency, regardless of whether a pitch corresponding to the higher or the lower frequency is in fact perceived.

We can take the case of a listener who follows the pitches delivered to his right ear. When the high tone is presented to the right and the low tone to the left, this listener hears a high tone, because this is presented to the right ear. The listener also localizes the tone in the right ear, because this ear is receiving the higher frequency. However, when the low tone is presented to the right ear and the high tone to the left, this listener now hears a low tone, because this is presented to the right ear, but localizes the tone in the left ear instead, because this ear is receiving the higher frequency. So the entire pattern is heard as a high tone to the right that alternates with a low tone to the left.

It can be seen that, on this model, reversing the positions of the earphones would not alter the basic percept. However, for the case of a listener who follows the pitches presented to the left ear instead, holding the localization rule constant, the identical pattern would be heard as a high tone to the left alternating with a low tone to the right. Later experiments have provided further evidence for this model (Deutsch, 1978, 1980a, 1981, 1987, 1988; Deutsch & Roll, 1976).

We can note that the octave illusion is a striking example of an illusory conjunction; a case in which the perceptual system incorrectly binds different attribute values together. Such incorrect binding raises the thorny issue of how we

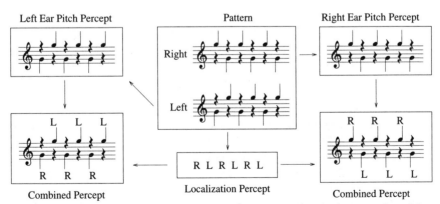

FIGURE 22 Model showing how the outputs of two decision mechanisms, one determining perceived pitch, and the other determining perceived location, combine to produce the octave illusion. See text for details.

generally manage to arrive at correct binding solutions—a problem that has been addressed particularly for the case of vision, and has recently begun to receive attention for hearing also. Deutsch (1980a, 1981) provided an early parallel processing model of how correct binding can occur for the case of values of two attributes (pitch and location) and that also explains the incorrect binding that occurs in the octave illusion. This model has been expanded to account for the correct binding of values of three or more attributes, such as pitch, location, and loudness (Deutsch, 1998).

Setting these issues aside, and considering only what pitches are perceived in the octave illusion, we note that grouping is here based on spatial location: The pitches that are heard correspond to the tones presented either to the listener's right ear or to his left. Further experiments have shown that the factor responsible for perceiving pitch on the basis of spatial location is that the two ears receive the same frequencies in succession, rather than different frequencies (Deutsch, 1978, 1980a, 1981, 1988).

Why should such a perceptual strategy have evolved? We may argue that it enables us to follow new, ongoing information with a minimum of interference from echoes or reverberation. In everyday listening, when the same frequency emanates successively from two different regions of space, the second occurrence may well be due to an echo. So it is a useful perceptual strategy to suppress the second occurrence of the sound from conscious perception. A similar argument has been advanced for the precedence effect: In listening to music, a single sound image may be obtained when the waveforms arriving from two different spatial locations are separated by time intervals of less than around 70 msec (see also Haas, 1951; Wallach, Newman, & Rosenzweig, 1949; Zureck, 1987).

C. MELODY PERCEPTION FROM PHASE-SHIFTED TONES

Another type of configuration that produces grouping by spatial location was described by Kubovy and colleagues. Kubovy, Cutting, and McGuire (1974) presented a set of simultaneous and continuous sine wave tones to both ears. They then phase-shifted one of the tones in one ear relative to its counterpart in the opposite ear. When these tones were phase-shifted in sequence, as shown in Figure 23, a melody was heard that corresponded to the phase-shifted tones; however, the melody was undetectable when the signal was played to either ear alone. Subjectively, the dichotically presented melody was heard as occurring inside the head but displaced to one side of the midline, while a background hum was heard as localized to the opposite side. So it appeared as though a source in one spatial position was producing the melody, while a source in a different spatial position was producing the background hum.

Kubovy (1981) pointed out that there are two potential interpretations of this effect. First, the segregation of the melody from the noise could have been based on concurrent difference cues; that is, the target tone may have been segregated because at that time its interaural disparity—or apparent spatial location—dif-

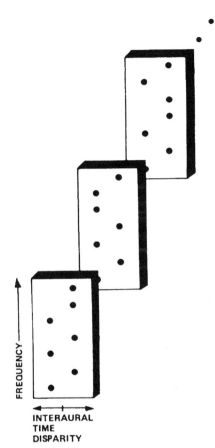

FREQUENCY →

← — ⊢ — →
INTERAURAL
TIME
DISPARITY

FIGURE 23   Pattern such as used by Kubovy, Cutting, and McGuire (1974) to show grouping of phase-shifted tones. See text for details. (From Kubovy & Pomerantz, 1981.)

fered from that of the background tones. Alternatively, the effect could have been based on successive difference cues; that is, the target tone may have been segregated because it had shifted its apparent position in space.

Kubovy devised two further configurations to determine which of these factors was responsible for the effect. In the first, the target tones shifted while the locations of the background tones remained constant, so producing a successive difference cue. In the second, the target tones themselves did not shift, but the background tones did, so producing a concurrent difference cue. Kubovy found that although both types of cue were effective in producing segregation, the successive difference cue was considerably more effective than the concurrent difference cue (see also Kubovy & Howard, 1976).

It is interesting that in Kubovy's paradigm, the listener creates melodic patterns from a fixed set of frequencies that are continuously present and simply shift their positions in space. A similar principle appears to be operating here as in the octave illusion, where melodic groupings are formed by the changing spatial positions of tones of identical frequency. It may then be hypothesized that Kubovy's effect also reflects the operation of a perceptual mechanism that has evolved to suppress echoes and reverberation.

D. HANDEDNESS CORRELATES

Handedness correlates have been obtained for both the octave and the scale illusions. Deutsch (1974) found that, in perceiving the octave illusion, right-handers tended strongly to hear the high tone on the right and the low tone on the left, and to maintain this percept when the earphone positions were reversed. However, there was considerable variation among left-handers in terms of where the high and low tones appeared to be localized, and what type of illusion was obtained. From further studies, it was concluded that these findings reflected a tendency to perceive the pitches that were presented to the dominant side of space rather than the nondominant side (Deutsch, 1975a, 1980a, 1981; 1983a, 1983b; Deutsch & Roll, 1976).

In a further study, Deutsch (1983a) divided the subject population into three groups—right-handed, mixed handed, and left-handed. For all three groups the tendency to perceive the high tone on the right and the low tone on the left was stronger among subjects with only right-handed parents and siblings, than among those who had a left- or mixed-handed parent or sibling. This pattern of results is in accordance with the neurological literature relating patterns of cerebral dominance to handedness and familial handedness background (Ettlinger, Jackson, & Zangwill, 1956; Luria, 1969; Subirana, 1958).

The handedness correlates obtained for the scale illusion may be viewed as reflecting more activity in the dominant hemisphere on the part of neural units underlying the higher tones, and more activity in the nondominant hemisphere on the part of units underlying the lower tones. Justification for this view comes in part from neurological studies showing that patients who experience palinacousis tend to perceive the illusory sound as located on the side of auditory space contralateral to the lesion (Jacobs, Feldman, Diamond, & Bender, 1973). Further, patients who obtain auditory sensations upon stimulation of the temporal lobe generally refer these sensations to the contralateral side of space (Penfield & Perot, 1963). This also explains the perceptual anisotropy found by Deutsch (1985) on listening to dichotic tonal sequences: right-handers perceived dichotic chords more accurately when the high tone was presented to the right ear and the low tone to the left, rather than the reverse.

VI. EQUAL-INTERVAL TONE COMPLEXES

Perceptual grouping principles emerge strongly with the use of tone complexes whose components are separated by equal intervals. Octave-related complexes have been explored most extensively (see also Chapter 10, this volume); however, tones whose components are related by other intervals have also been explored, as have chords produced by combinations of two or more octave-related complexes.

In a seminal experiment, Shepard (1964) generated a series of tones, each of which was composed of 10 sinusoidal components that were related by octaves. The amplitudes of the components were scaled by a fixed, bell-shaped spectral envelope, so that those in the middle of the musical range were highest, and those at the extremes were lowest. Shepard then varied the pitch classes of the tones by shifting all the components up or down in log frequency.

Subjects listened to ordered pairs of such tones and judged whether they formed ascending or descending patterns. When the second tone was removed one or two steps clockwise from the first along the pitch class circle (see Figure 21 in Chapter 10, this volume), listeners heard an ascending pattern; when the second tone was removed one or two steps counterclockwise, listeners heard a descending pattern instead. When the tones within a pair were separated by larger distances along the pitch class circle, the tendency for judgments to be determined by proximity gradually lessened, and when the tones were separated by exactly a half-octave, ascending and descending judgments occurred equally often.

Based on these findings, Shepard produced a compelling demonstration. A series of tones was played that repeatedly traversed the pitch class circle in clockwise steps, so that it appeared to ascend endlessly in pitch: C# sounded higher than C, D as higher than C#, D# as higher than D, ... , A# as higher than A, B as higher than A#, C as higher than B, and so on without end. Counterclockwise motion produced the impression of an endlessly descending series of tones.

Risset (1969, 1971) produced a number of striking variants of Shepard's demonstration. In one variant, a single gliding tone was made to traverse the pitch class circle in clockwise direction, so that it appeared to move endlessly upward in pitch. When the tone was made to glide in counterclockwise direction, it appeared to move endlessly downward. In another variant, a tone was made to glide clockwise around the pitch class circle, while the spectral envelope was made to glide downward in log frequency; in consequence the tone appeared both to ascend and to descend at the same time (see also Charbonneau & Risset, 1973).

Effects approaching pitch circularity have been generated by composers for hundreds of years, and can be found in works by Gibbons, Bach, Scarlatti, Haydn, and Beethoven, among others. In the 20th century, effective pitch circularities have been produced by composers such as Stockhausen, Krenek, Berg, Bartok, Ligeti, and in particular Risset, using both natural instruments and computer-generated sounds. Braus (1995) provides an extensive discussion of such works.

Returning to the experimental evidence, the work of Shepard and Risset showed that when other cues to height attribution are weak, listeners will invoke proximity in making judgments of relative height for successively presented tones. We can then ask whether the perceptual system might invoke proximity in making judgments of relative height for simultaneously presented tones also.

In an experiment to examine this issue, Deutsch (1991) presented subjects with patterns such as shown in Figure 24 . Each pattern consisted of two simultaneous pairs of tones. In one pair, the second tone was a semitone clockwise from the first; in the other, it was a semitone counterclockwise. As expected from the earlier work, subjects organized these patterns sequentially in accordance with pitch proximity, so that they heard two melodic lines, one of which ascended by a semitone while the other descended by a semitone. So, for example, the pattern shown in Figure 24 was heard as the descending line D-C♯, together with the ascending line A♯-B. However, the descending line could in principle be heard as higher and the ascending line as lower (Percept A), or the ascending line could be heard as higher and the descending line as lower (Percept B). Figure 25 shows these two alternative perceptual organizations in musical notation.

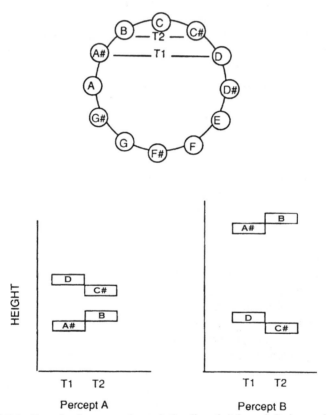

Percept A   Percept B

FIGURE 24   Example of pattern used to study the effect of pitch proximity in grouping simultaneous tones, together with two alternative perceptual organizations. Here the descending pair (D-C♯) is played together with the ascending pair (A♯-B). In principle, the descending line could be heard as higher and the ascending line as lower, reflecting perceptual organization in accordance with pitch proximity (Percept A). Alternatively, the ascending line could be heard as higher and the descending line as lower, reflecting perceptual organization that runs counter to pitch proximity (Percept B). (From Deutsch, 1988.)

In the experiment, one such pattern was presented on each trial, and subjects judged whether the line that was higher in pitch ascended or descended. From these judgments, it was inferred which tones were heard as higher and which as lower. All subjects showed a strong tendency to organize the patterns so that they formed compact harmonic groupings. For example, the pattern in Figure 24 tended to be heard as Percept A rather than Percept B. It appears, therefore, that the perceptual system tends to organize tone patterns in accordance with proximity along the simultaneous, or harmonic, dimension as well as along the sequential one.

In all the experiments described so far, the patterns were such that proximity along the pitch class circle co-occurred with proximity based on the spectral properties of the tones. The question then arises as to which of these two factors was responsible for the proximity effects that were obtained. This question was addressed by Pollack (1978) with respect to Shepard's original experiment. He presented subjects with complex tones whose components were related by octaves or octave multiples, and found that as the spectral overlap between successively presented tones increased, the tendency to follow by proximity increased also. Pollack concluded that proximity along the spectral dimension was responsible for Shepard's results. A similar conclusion was reached by Burns (1981), who found that the tendency to follow pairs of such tones in accordance with spectral proximity was no greater when the tones were composed of octave-related components than when their components were related by other intervals.

Spectral proximity effects have also been used to produce other striking illusions. Risset (1986) described an illusion produced by a complex tone whose components were spaced at intervals that were slightly larger than an octave. He played this tone first at one speed and then at twice the speed, so that each component of the first tone had a corresponding component of the second tone with a slightly lower frequency. Listeners heard the second tone as lower than the first, indicating that they were invoking proximity between successive spectral components in making their judgments (see also Risset, 1969, 1971, 1978). A similar finding was independently reported by Schroeder (1986), who pointed out that this effect is analogous to certain phenomena in fractal geometry.

In addition to proximity, another grouping principle has been shown to operate here. Teranishi (1982) generated a set of major triads that were composed of octave-related complexes and were generated under a trapezoidal spectral envelope. When a subset of these triads was played in the succession as shown in Figure 26,

Percept A   Percept B

FIGURE 25 Representation in musical notation of the alternative perceptual organizations shown in Figure 24.

FIGURE 26   Representation of the pattern used to obtain an endlessly ascending scale from a sequence of chords. The tones were octave-related complexes, generated under a trapezoidal spectral envelope. A global pitch movement was here perceived, reflecting perceptual organization by common fate. (Reprinted with permission from Nakajima et al., 1988; data from Teranishi, 1982. ©1988 by The Regents of the University of California.)

listeners obtained the impression of an endlessly ascending scale. However, as can be seen by perusal of Figure 26, the most proximal relationships between components of successive tones were not uniformly in the ascending direction. For example, taking the first two chords, the descending line G-F♯ follows proximity more closely than the ascending line G-A. It appears, therefore, that the listeners were basing their relative pitch judgments on an impression of global pitch movement, or "common fate."

A follow-up study by Nakajima, Tsumura, Matsuura, Minami, and Teranishi (1988) also examined perception of successions of major triads that were produced by octave-related complexes. Paired comparison judgments involving such triads showed that whereas some subjects showed a pitch circularity of an octave, others showed a pitch circularity of roughly 1/3 octave. The authors concluded that the subjects were basing their judgments on the perception of global pitch movement, even when the precise melodic intervals between successive components were not preserved (see also Nakajima, Minami, Tsumura, Kunisaki, Ohnishi, & Teranishi, 1991).

In a related study, Allik, Dzhafarov, Houtsma, Ross, and Versfeld (1989) generated random chord sequences that were composed of octave-related complexes. When such chords were juxtaposed in time in such a way that a sufficient number of successive components were related by proximity in the same direction, a global pitch movement in this direction was heard.

In general, composers have frequently made use of a perceptual effect of common fate, by creating sequences of chords whose components moved in the same direction and by similar degrees while the precise intervals between successive tones were varied. An example is given in Figure 27, which shows a passage from Debussy's prelude *Le vent dans la plaine*. Here, the grouping of successive pitches by proximity alone should cause the listener to hear a number of repeating pitches, together with the falling-rising sequence D♭-C-D♭-C; however, these percepts are discarded in favor of an impression of a descending series of chords.

VII. CONCLUSION: RELATIONSHIPS TO MUSIC THEORY AND PRACTICE

In this chapter, we have explored a number of findings that elucidate the way our auditory system groups the components of music into perceptual configura-

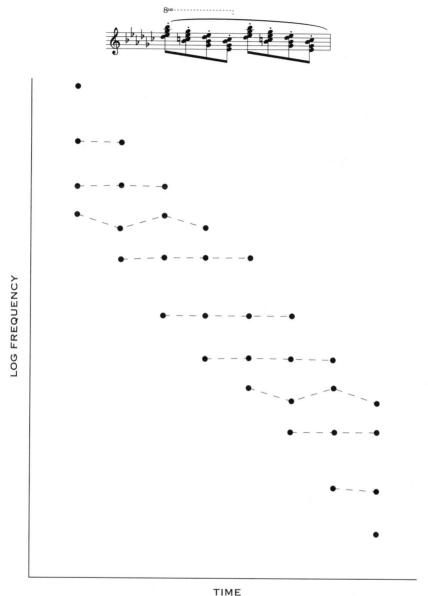

FIGURE 27 A passage from Debussy's prelude *Le vent dans la plaine*. The listener perceives this passage globally, as a downward pitch movement, in accordance with the principle of common fate.

tions. Beyond their interest to psychologists, these findings have implications for music theory and practice (Deutsch, 1984; Huron, 1991a, 1991b, 1993; Wright & Bregman, 1987).

In treatises on music theory, we encounter a number of rules that instruct the student in the art of composition. Among these are the "law of stepwise progression," which states that melodic progression should be by steps (i.e., a half step or a whole step) rather than by skips (i.e., more than a whole step) because stepwise progression is considered to be in some way "stronger" or "more binding." Another law prohibits the crossing of voices in counterpoint. What is left unspecified is why these precepts should be obeyed: It is assumed that the reader will either follow them uncritically or recognize their validity by introspection. The findings that we have been reviewing provide such laws with rational bases by demonstrating the perceptual effects that occur when they are violated. This in turn enables musicians to make more informed compositional decisions.

As a related point, with the advent of computer music, the composer is no longer bound by the constraints of natural instruments, but is instead faced with an infinity of compositional possibilities. As a result, the understanding of certain basic perceptual phenomena has become of critical importance, such as the factors that lead us to fuse together the components of a spectrum so as to obtain a unitary sound image, and the factors that lead us to separate out components so as to obtain multiple sound images. Such knowledge is a necessary first step in the creation of new musical timbres. For similar reasons, we need to understand the principles by which we form simultaneous and successive linkages between different sounds, so that listeners will perceive musical patterns as intended by the composer.

Finally, the illusions we have been exploring show that listeners do not necessarily perceive music in accordance with the written score, or as might be imagined from reading a score. Musical rules that have evolved through centuries of practical experience provide some ways of protecting the composer from generating music that could be seriously misperceived. However, with our new compositional freedom there has emerged a particularly strong need to understand how music as it is notated and performed maps on to music as it is heard. The findings reviewed here have brought us closer to realizing this goal, although much more remains to be learned.

REFERENCES

Allik, J., Dzhafarov, E. N., Houtsma, A. J. M., Ross, J., & Versfeld, N. J. (1989). Pitch motion with random chord sequences. *Perception & Psychophysics*, *46*, 513–527.

Assmann, P. F., & Summerfield, A. Q. (1990). Modelling the perception of concurrent vowels: Vowels with different fundamental frequencies. *Journal of the Acoustical Society of America, 88,* 680–697.

Beerends, J. G., & Houtsma, A. J. M. (1989). Pitch identification of simultaneous dichotic two-tone complexes. *Journal of the Acoustical Society of America, 85,* 813–819.

Berlioz, H. (1948). *Treatise on instrumentation* (R. Strauss, Ed.). New York: Kalmus.

Braus, I. (1995). Retracing one's steps: An overview of pitch circularity and Shepard tones in European music, 1550–1990. *Music Perception, 12,* 323–351.

Bregman, A. S. (1978). The formation of auditory streams. In J. Requin (Ed.), *Attention and performance* (Vol. VII, pp. 63–76). Hillsdale, NJ: Erlbaum.

Bregman, A. S. (1990). *Auditory scene analysis: The perceptual organization of sound.* Cambridge, MA: MIT Press.

Bregman, A. S., Abramson, J., Doehring, P., & Darwin, C. J. (1985). Spectral integration based on common amplitude modulation. *Perception & Psychophysics, 37,* 483–493.

Bregman, A. S., & Campbell, J. (1971). Primary auditory stream segregation and perception of order in rapid sequences of tones. *Journal of Experimental Psychology, 89,* 244–249.

Bregman, A. S., & Dannenbring, G. L. (1977). Auditory continuity and amplitude edges. *Canadian Journal of Psychology, 31,* 151–159.

Bregman, A. S., & Doehring, P. (1984). Fusion of simultaneous tonal glides: The role of parallelness and simple frequency relations. *Perception & Psychophysics, 36,* 251–256.

Bregman, A. S., Liao, C., & Levitan, R. (1990). Auditory grouping based on fundamental frequency and formant peak frequency. *Canadian Journal of Psychology, 44,* 400–413.

Bregman, A. S., & Pinker, S. (1978). Auditory streaming and the building of timbre. *Canadian Journal of Psychology, 32,* 20–31.

Bregman, A. S., & Rudnicky. A. (1975). 1. Auditory segregation: Stream or streams? *Journal of Experimental Psychology: Human Perception and Performance, 1,* 263–267.

Broadbent, D. E., & Ladefoged, P. (1957). On the fusion of sounds reaching different sense organs. *Journal of the Acoustical Society of America, 29,* 708–710.

Brokx, J. P. L., & Nootebohm, S. G. (1982). Intonation and the perceptual separation of simultaneous voices. *Journal of Phonetics, 10,* 23–36.

Burns, E. (1981). Circularity in relative pitch judgments for inharmonic complex tones: The Shepard demonstration revisited, again. *Perception & Psychophysics, 30,* 467–472.

Butler, D. (1979a). A further study of melodic channeling. *Perception & Psychophysics, 25,* 264–268.

Butler, D. (1979b). *Melodic channeling in a musical environment.* Paper presented at the Research Symposium on the Psychology and Acoustics of Music, Kansas.

Cardozo, B. L., & Van Noorden, L. P. A. S. (1968). Imperfect periodicity in the bowed string. *IPO Program Reports, 3,* 13–15.

Carlson, S. (1996). Dissecting the brain with sound. *Scientific American, 275*(6), 112–115.

Carlyon, R. P. (1991). Discriminating between coherent and incoherent frequency modulation of complex tones. *Journal of the Acoustical Society of America, 89,* 329–340.

Carlyon, R. P. (1992). The psychophysics of concurrent sound segregation. *Philosophical Transactions of the Royal Society of London, Series B, 336,* 347–355.

Charbonneau, G., & Risset, J. C. (1973). Circularité de jugements de hauteur sonore. *Comptes Rendus de l'Academie des Sciences, Serie B, 277,* 623.

Chowning, J. M. (1980). Computer synthesis of the singing voice. In *Sound generation in winds, strings, computers* (pp. 4–13). Stockholm: Royal Swedish Academy of Music Stockholm, Publ. No. 29.

Ciocca, V., & Bregman, A. S. (1987). Perceived continuity of gliding and steady-state tones through interrupting noise. *Perception & Psychophysics, 42,* 476–484.

Cutting, J. E. (1976). Auditory and linguistic processes in speech perception: Inferences from six fusions in dichotic listening. *Psychological Review, 83,* 114–140.

Dannenbring, G. L. (1976). Perceived auditory continuity with alternately rising and falling frequency transitions. *Canadian Journal of Psychology, 30,* 99–114.

Dannenbring, G. L., & Bregman, A. S. (1976). Stream segregation and the illusion of overlap. *Journal of Experimental Psychology: Human Perception and Performance, 2,* 544–555.

Dannenbring, G. L., & Bregman, A. S. (1978). Streaming vs. fusion of sinusoidal components of complex tones. *Perception & Psychophysics, 24,* 369–376.

Darwin, C. J. (1981). Perceptual grouping of speech components differing in fundamental frequency and onset-time. *Quarterly Journal of Experimental Psychology, 33A,* 185–207.

Darwin, C. J. (1984). Perceiving vowels in the presence of another sound: Constraints on formant perception. *Journal of the Acoustical Society of America, 76,* 1636–1647.

Darwin, C. J., & Carlyon, R. P. (1995). Auditory grouping. In B. C. J. Moore (Ed.), *Hearing* (pp. 387–424). San Diego: Academic Press.

Darwin, C. J., & Ciocca, V. (1992). Grouping in pitch perception: Effects of onset asynchrony and ear of presentation of a mistuned component. *Journal of the Acoustical Society of America , 91,* 3381–3390.

Darwin, C. J., & Gardner, R. B. (1986). Mistuning a harmonic of a vowel: Grouping and phase effects on vowel quality. *Journal of the Acoustical Society of America, 79,* 838–845.

Darwin, C. J., & Sutherland, N. S. (1984). Grouping frequency components of vowels: When is a harmonic not a harmonic? *Quarterly Journal of Experimental Psychology, 36A,* 193–208.

De Boer, E. (1976). On the 'residue' and auditory pitch perception. In W. D. Keidel & W. D. Neff (Eds.), *Handbook of sensory physiology* (Vol. 5, Part 3, pp. 479–583). New York: Springer-Verlag.

Deutsch, D. (1974). An auditory illusion. *Nature, 251,* 307–309.

Deutsch, D. (1975a). Musical illusions. *Scientific American, 233*(4), 92–104.

Deutsch, D. (1975b). Two-channel listening to musical scales. *Journal of the Acoustical Society of America, 57,* 1156–1160.

Deutsch, D. (1978). Lateralization by frequency for repeating sequences of dichotic 400-Hz and 800-Hz tones. *Journal of the Acoustical Society of America, 63,* 184–186.

Deutsch, D. (1979). Binaural integration of melodic patterns. *Perception & Psychophysics, 25,* 399–405.

Deutsch, D. (1980a). The octave illusion and the what-where connection. In R. S. Nickerson & R. W. Pew (Eds.), *Attention and performance* (Vol. VIII, pp. 575–594). Hillsdale, NJ: Erlbaum.

Deutsch, D. (1980b). The processing of structured and unstructured tonal sequences. *Perception & Psychophysics, 28,* 381–389.

Deutsch, D. (1981). The octave illusion and auditory perceptual integration. In J. V. Tobias & E. D. Schubert (Eds.), *Hearing research and theory* (Vol. I, pp. 99–142). New York: Academic Press.

Deutsch, D. (1983a). The octave illusion in relation to handedness and familial handedness background. *Neuropsychologia, 21,* 289–293.

Deutsch, D. (1983b). Auditory illusions, handedness, and the spatial environment. *Journal of the Audio Engineering Society, 31,* 607–620.

Deutsch, D. (1984). Psychology and music. In M. H. Bornstein (Ed.), *Psychology and its allied disciplines* (pp. 155–193). Hillsdale, NJ: Erlbaum.

Deutsch, D. (1985). Dichotic listening to melodic patterns, and its relationship to hemispheric specialization of function. *Music Perception, 3,* 1–28.

Deutsch, D. (1987). Illusions for stereo headphones. *Audio Magazine, 71*(3), 36–48.

Deutsch, D. (1988). Lateralization and sequential relationships in the octave illusion. *Journal of the Acoustical Society of America, 83,* 365–368.

Deutsch, D. (1991). Pitch proximity in the grouping of simultaneous tones. *Music Perception, 9,* 185–198.

Deutsch, D. (1995). *Musical illusions and paradoxes* [CD]. Philomel Records, P. O. Box 12189, La Jolla, CA 92039-2189.

Deutsch, D. (1996). The perception of auditory patterns. In W. Prinz & B. Bridgeman (Eds.), *Handbook of perception and action* (Vol. 1, pp. 253–296). San Diego, CA: Academic Press.

Deutsch, D. (1998). *A parallel processing solution to the binding problem, with particular reference to hearing.* Manuscript in preparation.

Deutsch, D., & Roll, P. L. (1976). Separate 'what' and 'where' decision mechanisms in processing a dichotic tonal sequence. *Journal of Experimental Psychology: Human Perception and Performance, 2,* 23–29.

Divenyi, P. L., & Hirsh, I. J. (1972). Discrimination of the silent gap in two-tone sequences of different frequencies. *Journal of the Acoustical Society of America, 52,* 166S.

Divenyi, P. L., & Hirsh, I. J. (1974). Identification of temporal order in three-tone sequences. *Journal of the Acoustical Society of America, 56,* 144–151.

Dowling, W. J. (1973a). The perception of interleaved melodies. *Cognitive Psychology, 5,* 322–337.

Dowling, W. J. (1973b). Rhythmic groups and subjective chunks in memory for melodies. *Perception & Psychophysics, 4,* 37–40.

Edelman, G. M., Gall, W. E., & Cowan, W. M. (1988). *Auditory function: Neurobiological bases of hearing.* New York: Wiley.

Erickson, R. (1975). *Sound structure in music.* Berkeley: University of California Press.

Ettlinger, G., Jackson, C. V., & Zangwill, O. L. (1956). Cerebral dominance in sinistrals. *Brain, 79,* 569–588.

Fitzgibbon, P. J., Pollatsek, A., & Thomas, I. B. (1974). Detection of temporal gaps within and between perceptual tonal groups. *Perception & Psychophysics, 16,* 522–528.

Flanagan, J. L. (1972). *Speech, analysis, synthesis, and perception.* Berlin: Springer.

Gardner, R. B., & Darwin, C. J. (1986). Grouping of vowel harmonics by frequency modulation: Absence of effects on phonemic categorization. *Perception & Psychophysics, 40,* 183–187.

Gardner, R. B., Gaskill, S. A., & Darwin, C. J. (1989). Perceptual grouping of formants with static and dynamic differences in fundamental frequency. *Journal of the Acoustical Society of America, 85,* 1329–1337.

Gregory, A. L. (1994). Timbre and auditory streaming. *Music Perception, 12,* 161–174.

Gregory, R. L. (1970). *The intelligent eye.* New York: McGraw-Hill.

Grey, J. M., & Moorer, J. A. (1977). Perceptual evaluation of synthesized musical instrument tones. *Journal of the Acoustical Society of America, 62,* 454–462.

Haas, H. (1951). Über den einfluss eines Einfachechos auf die Hörsamkeit von Sprache. *Acustica, 1,* 49–52.

Handel, S. (1973). Temporal segmentation of repeating auditory patterns. *Journal of Experimental Psychology, 101,* 46–54.

Hartmann, W. M., & Johnson, D. (1991). Stream segregation and peripheral channeling. *Music Perception, 9,* 155–184.

Heise, G. A., & Miller, G. A. (1951). An experimental study of auditory patterns. *American Journal of Psychology, 64,* 68–77.

Helmholtz, H. von (1925). *Helmholtz's physiological optics* (Translated from the 3rd German ed., 1909–1911 by J. P. C. Southall, Ed.). Rochester, NY: Optical Society of America.

Helmholtz, H. von (1954). *On the sensations of tone as a physiological basis for the theory of music* (2nd English ed.). New York: Dover. (Original work published 1859)

Hill, N. J., & Darwin, C. J. (1993). Effects of onset asynchrony and of mistuning on the lateralization of a pure tone embedded in a harmonic complex. *Journal of the Acoustical Society of America, 93,* 2307–2308.

Hochberg, J. (1974). Organization and the Gestalt Tradition. In E. C. Carterette & M. P. Friedman (Eds.), *Handbook of perception* (Vol. I, pp. 180–211). New York: Academic Press.

Hukin, R. W. & Darwin, C. J. (1995a). Comparison of the effect of onset asynchrony on auditory grouping in pitch matching and vowel identification. *Perception & Psychophysics, 57,* 191–196.

Hukin, R. W. & Darwin, C. J. (1995b). Effects of contralateral presentation and of interaural time differences in segregating a harmonic from a vowel. *Journal of the Acoustical Society of America, 98,* 1380–1386.

Huron, D. (1991a). The avoidance of part-crossing in polyphonic music: Perceptual evidence and musical practice. *Music Perception, 9,* 93–104.

Huron, D. (1991b). Tonal consonance versus tonal fusion in polyphonic sonorities. *Music Perception, 9,* 135–154.

Huron, D. (1993). Note-onset asynchrony in J. S. Bach's two-part inventions. *Music Perception, 10,* 435–444.

Iverson, P. (1995). Auditory stream segregation by musical timbre: Effects of static and dynamic acoustic attributes. *Journal of Experimental Psychology: Human Perception and Performance, 21,* 751–763.

Jacobs, L., Feldman, M., Diamond, S. P., & Bender, M. B. (1973). Palinacousis: Persistent or recurring auditory sensations. *Cortex, 9,* 275–287.

Judd, T. (1979). Comments on Deutsch's musical scale illusion. *Perception & Psychophysics, 26,* 85–92.

Kubovy, M. (1976). *The sound of silence: A new pitch segregation phenomenon.* Paper presented at the meeting of the Psychonomic Society, St. Louis.

Kubovy, M. (1981). Concurrent pitch segregation and the theory of indispensable attributes. In M. Kubovy & J. Pomerantz (Eds.), *Perceptual organization* (pp. 55–98). Hillsdale, NJ: Erlbaum.

Kubovy, M., Cutting, J. E., & McGuire, R. M. (1974). Hearing with the third ear: Dichotic perception of a melody without monaural familiarity cues. *Science, 186,* 272–274.

Kubovy, M., & Howard, F. P. (1976). Persistence of a pitch-segregating echoic memory. *Journal of Experimental Psychology: Human Perception and Performance, 2,* 531–537.

Kubovy, M., & Pomerantz, J. (Eds.). (1981). *Perceptual organization.* Hillsdale, NJ: Erlbaum.

Lieberman, P. (1961). Perturbations in vocal pitch. *Journal of the Acoustical Society of America, 33,* 597–603.

Luria, A. B. (1969). *Traumatic aphasia.* Mouton: The Hague.

Machlis, J. (1977). *The enjoyment of music* (4th ed.). New York: Norton.

MacIntyre, M. E., Schumacher, R. T., & Woodhouse, J. (1981). Aperiodicity in bowed string motion. *Acustica, 49,* 13–32.

MacIntyre, M. E., Schumacher, R. T., & Woodhouse, J. (1982). Aperiodicity in bowed string motion: On the differential-slipping mechanism. *Acustica, 50,* 294–295.

Marin, C. M. H., & McAdams, S. (1991). Segregation of concurrent sounds: II. Effects of spectral envelope tracing, frequency modulation coherence, and frequency modulation width. *Journal of the Acoustical Society of America, 89,* 341–351.

Mathews, M. V., & Pierce, J. R. (1980). Harmony and nonharmonic partials. *Journal of the Acoustical Society of America, 68,* 1252–1257.

McAdams, S. (1984). The auditory image: A metaphor for musical and psychological research on auditory organization. In W. R. Crozier & A. J. Chapman (Eds.), *Cognitive processes in the perception of art* (pp. 298–324). Amsterdam: North-Holland.

McAdams, S. (1989). Segregation of concurrent sounds: I. Effects of frequency modulation coherence. *Journal of the Acoustical Society of America, 86,* 2148–2159.

McNabb, M. M. (1981). Dreamsong: the composition. *Computer Music Journal, 5,* 36–53.

McNally, K. A., & Handel, S. (1977). Effect of element composition on streaming and the ordering of repeating sequences. *Journal of Experimental Psychology: Human Perception and Performance, 3,* 451–460.

Miller, G. A., & Heise, G. A. (1950). The trill threshold. *Journal of the Acoustical Society of America, 22,* 637–638.

Miller, G. A., & Licklider, J. C. R. (1950). The intelligibility of interrupted speech. *Journal of the Acoustical Society of America, 22,* 167–173.

Moore, B. C. J., Glasberg, B. R., & Peters, R. W. (1985). Relative dominance of individual partials in determining the pitch of complex tones. *Journal of the Acoustical Society of America, 77,* 1853–1860.

Moore, B. C. J., Glasberg, B. R., & Peters, R. W. (1986). Thresholds for hearing mistuned partials as separate tones in harmonic complexes. *Journal of the Acoustical Society of America, 80,* 479–483.

Nakajima, Y., Minami, H., Tsumura, T., Kunisaki, H., Ohnishi, S., & Teranishi, R. (1991). Dynamic pitch perception for complex tones of periodic spectral patterns. *Music Perception, 8,* 291–314.

Nakajima, Y., Tsumura, T., Matsuura, S., Minami, H., & Teranishi, R. (1988). Dynamic pitch perception for complex tones derived from major triads. *Music Perception, 6,* 1–20.

Neff, D. L., Jesteadt, W., & Brown, E. L. (1982). The relation between gap discrimination and auditory stream segregation. *Perception & Psychophysics, 31,* 493–501.

Nickerson, R. S., & Freeman, B. (1974). Discrimination of the order of the components of repeating tent sequences: Effects of frequency separation and extensive practice. *Perception & Psychophysics, 16,* 471–477.

Penfield, W., & Perot, P. (1963). The brain's record of auditory and visual experience. *Brain, 86,* 595–696.

Pollack, I. (1978). Decoupling of auditory pitch and stimulus frequency: The Shepard demonstration revisited. *Journal of the Acoustical Society of America, 63,* 202–206.

Povel, D. J., & Okkerman, H. (1981). Accents in equitone sequences. *Perception & Psychophysics, 30,* 565–572.

Rasch, R. A. (1978). The perception of simultaneous notes such as in polyphonic music. *Acustica, 40,* 22–33.

Rasch, R. A. (1988). Timing and synchronization in ensemble performance. In J. A. Sloboda (Ed.), *Generative processes in music: The psychology of performance, improvization, and composition* (pp. 71–90). Oxford: Oxford University Press.

Risset, J. C. (1969). Pitch control and pitch paradoxes demonstrated with computer-synthesized sounds. *Journal of the Acoustical Society of America, 46,* 88(A).

Risset, J. C. (1971). Paradoxes de hauteur: Le concept de hauteur sonore n'est pas le meme pour tout le monde. *Proceedings of the Seventh International Congress on Acoustics, Budapest, S10,* 613–616.

Risset, J. C. (1978). *Paradoxes de hauteur* (with sound examples), IRCAM Rep. 10, Paris.

Risset, J. C. (1986). Pitch and rhythm paradoxes: Comments on "Auditory paradox based on fractal waveform" [*J. Acoust. Soc. Am., 79,* 186–189 (1986)]. *Journal of the Acoustical Society of America, 80,* 961–962.

Rock, I. (1986). The description and analysis of object and event perception. In K. Boff, L. Kaufman, & J. Thomas (Eds.), *Handbook of perception and human performance* (pp. 1–77). New York: Wiley.

Sasaki, T. (1980). Sound restoration and temporal localization of noise in speech and music sounds. *Tohuku Psychologica Folia, 39,* 79–88.

Scheffers, M. T. M. (1983). *Sifting vowels: Auditory pitch analysis and sound segregation.* Unpublished doctoral thesis, Groningen University, The Netherlands.

Schouten, J. F. (1962). On the perception of sound and speech: Subjective time analysis. *Fourth International Congress on Acoustics, Copenhagen Congress Report II,* 201–203.

Schroeder, M. R. (1986). Auditory paradox based on fractal waveform. *Journal of the Acoustical Society of America, 79,* 186–189.

Shepard, R. N. (1964). Circularity in judgments of relative pitch. *Journal of the Acoustical Society of America, 36,* 2345–2353.

Singh, P. (1987). Perceptual organization of complex tone sequences: A tradeoff between pitch and timbre? *Journal of the Acoustical Society of America, 82,* 886–899.

Sloboda, J. A. (1985). *The musical mind.* New York: Clarendon (Oxford University Press).

Smith, J., Hausfield, S. Power, R. P. & Gorta, A. (1982). Ambiguous musical figures and auditory streaming. *Perception & Psychophysics, 32,* 454–464.

Subirana, A. (1958). The prognosis in aphasia in relation to cerebral dominance and handedness. *Brain, 81,* 415–425.

Summerfield, Q. (1992). Roles of harmonicity and coherent frequency modulation in auditory grouping. In M. E. H. Schouten (Ed.), *The auditory processing of speech: From sounds to words* (pp. 157–165). Berlin: Mouton.

Summerfield, Q., & Culling, J. F. (1992). Auditory segregation of competing voices: Absence of effects of FM and AM coherence. *Philosophical Transactions of the Royal Society of London, Series B, 336,* 357–366.

Sutherland, N. S. (1973). Object recognition. In E. C. Carterette & M. P. Friedman (Eds.), *Handbook of perception* (Vol. III, pp. 157–186). New York: Academic Press.

Teranishi, R. (1982). Endlessly ascending/descending chords performable on a piano. *Reports of the Acoustical Society of Japan, H,* 82–68.

Tougas, Y., & Bregman, A. S. (1985). Crossing of auditory streams. *Journal of Experimental Psychology: Human Perception and Performance, 11,* 788–798.

Tougas, Y., & Bregman, A. S. (1990). Auditory streaming and the continuity illusion. *Perception & Psychophysics, 47,* 121–126.

Van Noorden, L. P. A. S. (1975). *Temporal coherence in the perception of tone sequences.* Unpublished doctoral dissertation, Technische Hogeschoel Eindhoven, The Netherlands.

Vicario, G. (1960). L'effetto tunnel acustico. *Revista di Psicologia, 54,* 41–52.

Vicario, G. (1973). *Tempo Psicologia ed Eventi.* Florence: C.-E Giunti-G. Barbera.

Vicario, G. (1982). Some observations in the auditory field. In J. Beck (Ed.), *Organization and representation in perception* (pp. 269–283). Hillsdale, NJ: Erlbaum.

Wallach, H., Newman, E. B., & Rosenzweig, M. R. (1949). The precedence effect in sound localization. *American Journal of Psychology, 62,* 315–336.

Warren, R. M. (1983). Auditory illusions and their relation to mechanisms normally enhancing accuracy of perception. *Journal of the Audio Engineering Society, 31,* 623–629.

Warren, R. M. (1984). Perceptual restoration of obliterated sounds. *Psychological Bulletin, 96,* 371–383.

Warren, R. M., & Byrnes, D. L. (1975). Temporal discrimination of recycled tonal sequences: Pattern matching and naming of order by untrained listeners. *Journal of the Acoustical Society of America, 18,* 273–280.

Warren, R. M., Obusek, C. J., & Ackroff, J. M. (1972). Auditory induction: Perceptual synthesis of absent sounds. *Science, 176,* 1149–1151.

Warren, R. M., Obusek, C. J., Farmer, R. M., & Warren, R. P. (1969). Auditory sequence: Confusions of patterns other than speech or music. *Science, 164,* 586–587.

Wertheimer, M. (1923). Untersuchung zur Lehre von der Gestalt II. *Psychologische Forschung, 4,* 301–350.

Wessel, D. L. (1979). Timbre space as a musical control structure. *Computer Music Journal, 3,* 45–52.

Williams, K. N., & Perrott, D. R. (1972). Temporal resolution of tonal pulses. *Journal of the Acoustical Society of America, 51,* 644–647.

Wright, J. K., & Bregman, A. S. (1987). Auditory stream segregation and the control of dissonance in polyphonic music. *Contemporary Music Review, 2,* 63–92.

Zureck, P. M. (1987). The precedence effect. In W. A. Yost & G. Gourevitch (Eds.), *Directional hearing* (pp. 85–106). New York: Springer-Verlag.

10

THE PROCESSING OF PITCH
COMBINATIONS

DIANA DEUTSCH

Department of Psychology
University of California, San Diego
La Jolla, California

I. INTRODUCTION

In this chapter, we shall examine ways in which pitch combinations are abstracted by the perceptual system. First, we shall inquire into the types of abstraction that give rise to the perception of local features, such as intervals, chords, and pitch classes. Such features can be considered analogous to those of orientation and angle size in vision. There has developed sufficient understanding of sensory physiology to justify speculation concerning how such abstractions are achieved by the nervous system. Other low-level abstractions result in the perception of global features, such as contour. Next, we shall consider how combinations of features are abstracted so as to give rise to perceptual equivalences and similarities. We shall then examine how these higher level abstractions are themselves combined according to various rules.

Investigations into mechanisms of visual shape perception have led to a distinction between early processes, in which many low-level abstractions are carried out in parallel, and later processes, in which questions are asked of these low-level abstractions based on hypotheses concerning the scene to be analyzed (Hanson & Riseman, 1978). The distinction between abstractions that are formed passively from "bottom up" and those that occur from "top down" is important in music also. As we shall see, both types of processes play important roles in musical shape analysis.

The final sections of the chapter are concerned with memory. We shall argue that musical patterns are retained in parallel in a number of memory systems, which correspond to different types and levels of abstraction, and that information from these different systems combine to determine memory judgments. We shall examine the interactions that take place within these systems, as well as how the outputs from these systems influence each other during retrieval.

II. FEATURE ABSTRACTION

A. OCTAVE EQUIVALENCE

It is clear that a strong perceptual similarity exists between tones that are separated by octaves; that is, those whose fundamental frequencies stand in the ratio of 2:1 (or a power of 2:1). Octave equivalence is implied in the musical systems of many different cultures (Nettl, 1956). In the Western musical scale, tones that stand in octave relation are given the same name, so that a tone is specified first by its position within the abstracted octave and then by the octave in which it is occurs (G_3, F_4, and so on). In one version of Indian musical notation, a tone is also represented by a letter that designates its position within the octave, together with a dot or dots which designates the octave in which it occurs. So, for example, the symbols ṃ, m̤, m, ṁ, and m̈ represent tones that ascend by octave intervals. Furthermore, in Western tonal music, unisons and octaves are treated as harmonically interchangeable, and chord inversions are regarded as harmonically equivalent to their parent chords.

Various observations related to octave equivalence have been made. Baird (1917) and Bachem (1954) found that listeners with absolute pitch may sometimes place a note in the wrong octave, even though they name it correctly. Other researchers have demonstrated generalization of response to tones that stand in octave relation, in both people (Humphreys, 1939) including young infants (Demany & Armand, 1984) and animals (Blackwell & Schlosberg, 1943). In addition, interference effects in memory for pitch exhibit octave generalization (Deutsch, 1973b).

Given the perceptual similarity of tones that stand in octave relation, it has been suggested that musical pitch should be treated as a bidimensional attribute; the first dimension representing overall pitch level (*pitch height*) and the second dimension defining the position of the tone within the octave (*tone chroma* or *pitch class*) (Babbitt, 1960, 1965; Bachem, 1948; Deutsch, 1969, 1986a, 1992; Forte, 1973; M. Meyer, 1904, 1914; Révész, 1913; Risset, 1969, 1971; Ruckmick, 1929; Shepard, 1964, 1982). This suggestion is considered in detail in later sections of the chapter.

B. PERCEPTUAL EQUIVALENCE OF INTERVALS AND CHORDS

When two tones are presented either simultaneously or in succession, there results the perception of a musical interval, and intervals are perceived as being the same in size when the fundamental frequencies of their components stand in the same ratio. This principle forms an important basis of the traditional musical scale. The smallest unit of this scale is the semitone, which corresponds to a frequency ratio of approximately 1:1.06. Tone pairs that are separated by the same number of semitones are given the same name, such as major third, minor sixth, and so on.

Chords consisting of three or more tones are also classified in part by the ratios formed by their components. However, a simple listing of these ratios is not sufficient to define a chord. For instance, major and minor triads are perceptually quite distinct from each other, yet they are both composed of a major third (five semitones) a minor third (four semitones), and a perfect fifth (seven semitones). It is therefore of perceptual importance that the minor third lies above the major third in the major triad, and below it in the minor triad; this needs to be taken into account in considering how chords might be abstracted by the nervous system.

Given the principles of octave and interval equivalence, one might hypothesize that the perceptual equivalence of intervals would persist if their components were placed in different octaves. This assumption is frequently made by contemporary music theorists, who describe such intervals as in the same *interval class*. However, traditional music theory assumes that such equivalence holds for simultaneous but not successive intervals. Simultaneous intervals whose components have reversed their positions along the height dimension are treated as harmonically equivalent (Piston, 1948). Thus a simultaneous interval of n semitones is considered in a sense perceptually equivalent to one of $12 - n$ semitones.

Experimental evidence has been obtained for the perceptual similarity of inverted intervals. Plomp, Wagenaar, and Mimpen (1973) had subjects identify intervals formed by simultaneous tone pairs and found that confusions occurred between those that were related by inversion (see also Deutsch & Roll, 1974). For the case of intervals formed by successive rather than simultaneous tone pairs, it appears that the perception of interval class does not occur directly, but rather through a process of hypothesis confirmation, in which the features that are directly apprehended are pitch class and interval. The evidence for this view is described later.

C. PROPOSED PHYSIOLOGICAL SUBSTRATES

Various models have been advanced to explain the perceptual equivalence of intervals and chords. Pitts and McCulloch (1947) hypothesized that the auditory cortex is composed of layers, with each layer containing a tonotopic projection of frequency-specific units. In each projection, units responding to frequencies that are related by equal intervals are spaced equal distances apart. These layers are arranged so as to produce columns of units that respond to the same frequencies. The authors further hypothesized that a set of fibers traverse this columnar mass parallel to each other in a slantwise direction; three such slanting fibers then define a three-note chord. This proposed mechanism could mediate the transposition of simultaneous intervals and chords, but would be unable to mediate transposition of successive intervals, nor could it account for the perceptual similarity of intervals and chords that are related by inversion.

An alternative hypothesis, suggested by Boomsliter and Creel (1961), was based on the volley theory of pitch perception (Wever & Bray, 1930). The authors pointed out that when two frequency combinations stand in the same ratio, they should generate the same temporal pattern of firing. One temporal pattern would be produced by frequencies that stand in the ratio of 2:3, another in the ratio of 4:5, and so on. They proposed that the perceptual equivalence of simultaneous intervals is mediated by the recognition of such temporal patterns. One problem for this model is that it requires the nervous system to follow frequencies at much higher rates than have been demonstrated to occur (Edelman, Gall, & Cowan, 1988). As a further problem, the model cannot account for the perceptual equivalence of successive intervals and chords, nor for the perceptual similarity of intervals and chords that are related by inversion.

Deutsch (1969) proposed a neural network that would accomplish the abstraction of low-level pitch relationships so as to produce a number of equivalences that are found in the perception of music. This model was based on findings concerning the abstraction of low-level features by the visual system, such as orientation and angle size (Hubel & Wiesel, 1962).

The hypothesized neural network consists of two parallel channels, along each of which information is abstracted in two stages. An outline of this model is shown in Figure 1.The first channel mediates the perceptual equivalence of intervals and chords under transposition. In the first stage of abstraction along this channel, first-order units that respond to tones of specific pitch project in groups of two or three onto second-order units, which in consequence respond to specific intervals and chords (such as C_4, E_4, and G_4, or D_5 and G_5). It is assumed that such linkages occur only between units underlying pitches that are separated by an octave or less. In the second stage of abstraction along this channel, second-order units project to third-order units in such a way that those second-order units that are activated by tones standing in the same relationship project onto the same unit. So, for example, all units that are activated by an ascending interval of four semitones (a major third) project onto one unit, all those that are activated by a descending interval of seven semitones (a perfect fifth) project onto a different unit, all those

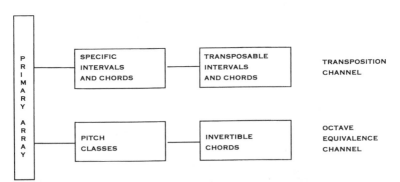

FIGURE 1   Model for the abstraction of pitch relationships. Pitch information is abstracted along two parallel channels; one mediating transposition and the other mediating octave equivalence. (Adapted from Deutsch, 1969. ©1969 by the American Psychological Association. Adapted with permission.)

that are activated by a major triad project onto yet a different unit, and so on (Figure 2).

The second channel mediates the perceptual equivalence of tones that stand in octave relation. In the first stage of abstraction along this channel, first-order units that respond to tones of specific pitch project to higher order units in such a way that those standing in octave relation project onto the same unit. These second-order units then respond to tones in a given pitch class, regardless of the octave in which they occur. In the second stage of abstraction along this channel, second-order units project in groups of two or three onto third-order units, which in consequence respond to combinations of pitch classes. Such units therefore mediate the perceptual similarity of intervals and chords that are related by inversion (Figure 3). This level of convergence is assumed to occur only for units that respond to simultaneously presented tones.

Although no attempt has been made to confirm this model at the neurophysiological level, the type of architecture that it postulates has been shown to exist in the auditory system. Neurons have been found that act as AND gates, as hypothesized for the transposition channel, and others as OR gates, as hypothesized for the octave equivalence channel. As another characteristic, auditory analyses are often carried out in parallel subsystems, each of which is organized in hierarchical fashion (see, e.g., Knudsen, du Lac, & Esterly, 1987; Schreiner, 1992; Suga, 1990; Sutter & Schreiner, 1991).

More recently, Bharucha (1987, 1991) has hypothesized a more elaborate neural network, whose basic architecture has features that are similar to those proposed by Deutsch (1969), and that also develops feature detectors for chords and keys as a result of passive exposure to the music of our tradition. This network is described in Chapter 11.

D. CONTOUR

We use global as well as specific cues in recognizing music. Such cues include, for example, overall pitch range, the distribution of interval sizes, and the relative proportions of ascending and descending intervals. Melodic contour plays a particularly important role here. As shown in Figure 4, melodies can be represented by their distinctive contours, even when interval sizes are not preserved.

One line of experimentation involving contour was initiated by Werner (1925). He reported that melodies could be recognized when they were transformed onto

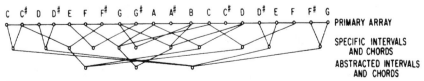

FIGURE 2   Two stages of abstraction along the transposition channel. (Adapted from Deutsch, 1969. ©1969 by the American Psychological Association. Adapted with permission.)

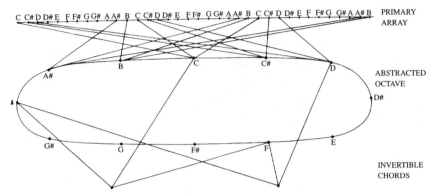

FIGURE 3   Two stages of abstraction along the octave-equivalence channel. (Adapted from Deutsch, 1969. ©1969 by the American Psychological Association. Adapted with permission.)

scales in which the octave was replaced by a different ratio, such as a fifth or two octaves, with these micro- or macro-octaves being divided into 12 equal intervals, so producing micro- or macro-scales. Later, Vicario (1983) carried out a study to determine how well listeners were able to recognize well-known melodies that had been transformed in this fashion. The results of this study are shown in Figure 5. As can be seen, although listeners were able to recognize such distorted melodies to some extent, the distortions did impair melody recognition, with the amount of impairment being a function of the degree of expansion or compression of the octave.

In another experiment, White (1960) found that listeners could recognize melodies to some extent when all the intervals were set to 1 semitone, so that only the sequence of directions of pitch change remained. Performance was enhanced when the relative sizes of the intervals were retained, but their absolute sizes were altered. Further studies have confirmed that contour can serve as a salient cue to melody recognition (see, e.g., Croonen, 1994; Dowling, 1978; Dowling & Fujitani, 1971; Edworthy, 1985; Idson & Massaro, 1978; and Kallman & Massaro, 1979).

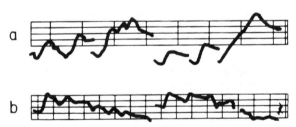

FIGURE 4   Contours from Beethoven piano sonatas as represented by Schoenberg: (a) from Sonata in C minor, Op. 10/I-III; (b) from Sonata in D, Op. 10/3-III, mm. 1–16. (From Schoenberg, 1967.)

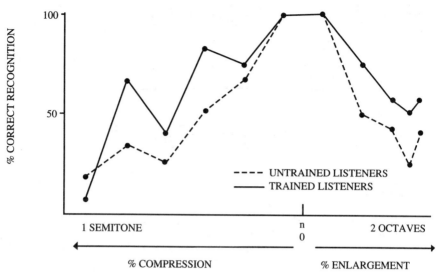

FIGURE 5   Percent correct recognition of melodies that have been transformed by compressing or enlarging the octave to differing extents. (Adapted from Vicario, 1983.)

E. MELODIC ARCHETYPES

L. B. Meyer (1973) has argued that there are a few schemata that, either through innate disposition or through experience with the music of our tradition, we search for and find in melodies. One such schema is characterized by a melodic leap, usually upward, which is followed by a gradual progression back to the first note. An example of such a "gap-fill" pattern is shown in the upper portion of Figure 6. Another such schema, which Meyer called a "changing-note pattern" consists of a stepwise movement around a prominent tone. For example, the pattern might begin on the tonic, move one step down, then two steps up and then one step down again (the sequence "do-ti-re-do") as shown in the lower portion of Figure 6.

Meyer argued that such schemata enter into the hierarchical representation of melodies, particularly at higher levels, where they may be visually masked by the lower level patterns in the written score. He conjectured that listeners categorize melodies in accordance with the schemata that are involved at the highest structural level, regardless of the note-to-note structure of the melody.

As a test of this hypothesis, Rosner and Meyer (1982) took short melodic passages from recordings of classical music, and classified them as either gap-fill or changing-note at the highest structural level. Subjects without musical training learned to sort these melodies into two groups, even though the subjects were given no theoretical explanation for these two classifications. As the authors argued, this experiment indicated that we do indeed invoke such schemata in listening to music. This conclusion was reinforced in a later study by Rosner and Meyer

FIGURE 6   Illustrations of melodic archetypes. The upper illustration, from Geminiani's Concerto Grosso in E Minor, Op. 3, No. 3, shows a gap-fill pattern. The lower illustration, from Mozart's Symphony No. 41 in C Major (K.551) shows a changing note pattern. See text for details. (Adapted from Rosner & Meyer, 1982.)

(1986). When subjects without formal musical training were asked to rate the degree of similarity between pairs of melodies that were either gap-fill or changing-note, they judged melodies with the same underlying schema as more similar to each other than those with different underlying schemata.

F. INTERVAL CLASS

When different two-tone combinations form the same interval by appropriate octave displacement, these combinations are held to be in the same interval class. For example, C_3 paired with D_5, form the same interval class as G_2 paired with F_6. The conditions under which interval class forms a basis for perceptual equivalence are complex ones. Experimental evidence for such equivalence has been obtained for simultaneous intervals, as described earlier (Deutsch & Roll, 1974; Plomp et al., 1973). Further evidence is provided by the general observation that we easily recognize root progressions of chords in different instantiations.

Where successive intervals are concerned, however, the issue is a complex one. If interval class were indeed a perceptual invariant, we should have no difficulty in recognizing a melody when its component tones are placed haphazardly in different octaves. This issue was examined in an experiment by Deutsch (1972c). The first half of the tune "Yankee Doodle" was generated in different versions. First, it was produced without transformation in each of three adjacent octaves. Second, it was generated in such a way that each tone was in its correct position within the octave (i.e., the interval classes were preserved) but the octave placement of the tones varied haphazardly within the same three octaves. Third, the tune was generated as a series of clicks, so that the pitch information was removed entirely but the rhythm remained. (A "scrambled-octaves" version of "Yankee Doodle" appears on the compact disc by Deutsch, 1995.)

The different versions of the tune were played to separate groups of subjects, who were given no clues as to its identity other than being assured that it was well known. Although the untransformed melody was universally recognized, the scrambled-octaves version was recognized no better than the version in which the pitch information was removed entirely. However, when the subjects were later told the name of the tune, and so knew what to listen for, they were able to follow the scrambled-octaves version to a large extent. This shows that the subjects were able to use pitch class to *confirm* the identity of the tune, although they had been unable to *recognize* it in the absence of cues on which to base a hypothesis.

This experiment provides strong evidence that perception of interval class, where successions of tones are concerned, requires the involvement of an active, "top-down" process, in which the listener matches each tone as it arrives with his or her image of the expected tone. On this line of reasoning, the extent to which interval class is perceived by the listener depends critically on his or her knowledge and expectations.

Other experimental findings have further supported the claim that interval class is not directly apprehended where successions of tones are concerned. In an experiment on short-term recognition of melodies, Deutsch (1979) presented listeners with a standard six-tone melody, followed by a comparison melody. The comparison melody was always transposed up 4 semitones from the standard. On half the trials the transposition was exact, and on the other half two of the tones in the transposed melody were permuted, while the melodic contour was unchanged.

There were four conditions in the experiment. In the first, the standard melody was played once, followed by the comparison melody. In the second, the standard melody was repeated six times before presentation of the comparison melody. In the third condition, the standard melody was again repeated six times, but now on half of the repetitions it was transposed intact an octave higher, and on the other half it was transposed intact an octave lower, so that the intervals forming the melody were preserved. In the fourth condition, the standard melody was again repeated six times, but now on each repetition the individual tones were placed alternately in the higher and lower octaves, so that the interval classes were preserved, but the intervals themselves were altered.

It was found that exact repetition of the standard melody resulted in a substantial improvement in recognition performance, and an improvement also occurred when the standard melody was repeated intact in the higher and lower octaves. However, when the standard melody was repeated in such a way that its tones alternated between the higher and lower octaves, performance was significantly poorer than when it was not repeated at all. This experiment provides further evidence that interval class cannot be considered a first-order perceptual feature. Repeating a set of intervals resulted in memory consolidation; however, repeating a set of interval classes did not do so.

The issue was further addressed in a study by Deutsch and Boulanger (1984). Musically trained subjects listened to novel melodic patterns which they recalled in musical notation. Examples of these patterns are given in Figure 7. Each pattern

FIGURE 7 Examples of sequences used in different conditions of the experiment on the effect of octave jumps on recall of melodic patterns. At the right are shown the percentages of tones that were correctly recalled in the correct serial positions in the different conditions. (Adapted from Deutsch & Boulanger, 1984. ©1984 by the Regents of the University of California.)

consisted of a haphazard ordering of the first six notes of the C-major scale. In the first condition, all the tones were taken from a higher octave; in the second, they were all taken from a lower octave. In the third condition, the individual tones alternated between these two octaves, so that roughly two thirds of the intervals formed by successive tones spanned more than an octave. The percentages of tones that were correctly notated in the correct serial positions in these different conditions are also shown in Figure 7. It can be seen that performance in the third condition was substantially poorer than in the other two.

The findings from these three experiments are in accordance with the two-channel model of Deutsch (1969), which assumes that neural linkages that underlie the abstraction of successive intervals occur only between units responding to pitches that are separated by no more than an octave. It is interesting in this regard to consider the use of octave jumps in traditional music. On the present line of reasoning, such jumps can be made with impunity, provided the musical setting is such that the displaced tone is anticipated by the listener. We should therefore expect that octave jumps would tend to be limited to such situations. Indeed, this appears to be the case. For example, a melodic line may be presented several times without transformation. A clear set of expectations having been established, a jump to a different octave occurs. The passage in Figure 8a, for instance, occurs after it has been presented several times without octave jumps. Another such situation is where the harmonic structure is clear and unambiguous, so that again the displaced tones are highly probable. This is illustrated in the segment in Figure 8b.

The technique of 12-tone composition uses very frequent octave jumps, and this raises the question of whether the listener does indeed identify as equivalent different presentations of the same tone row under octave displacement. Given the evidence and arguments outlined earlier, such recognition should be possible in principle, but only if the listener is very familiar with the material, or if its structure is such as to give rise to strong expectations (see also L. B. Meyer, 1973). Other work on melodic expectancy (see, in particular, L. B. Meyer, 1973, Narmour, 1990) is described elsewhere in this volume (see Chapter 12).

FIGURE 8   Two examples of octave jumps in traditional Western music. Here the jumps are readily processed. (a) From Beethoven, Rondo in C, Op. 5, No. 1; (b) from Beethoven, Sonata in C minor, Op. 10, No. 1.

III. HIGHER ORDER ABSTRACTIONS

Given that linkages are formed between first-order pitch elements, we may next inquire into how higher order abstractions are further derived so as to lead to perceptual equivalences and similarities. We recognize visual shapes when these differ in size, position in the visual field, and to some extent in orientation. What transformations result in analogous equivalences in music?

Theorists have long drawn analogies between perception of pitch relationships and relationships in visual space (Helmholtz, 1859/1954; Koffka, 1935; Mach, 1906). In contrast with visual space, however, pitch was conceived as represented along one dimension only. As Mach (1906/1959) wrote:

> A tonal series is something which is an analogue of space, but is a space of one dimension limited in both directions and exhibiting no symmetry like that, for instance of a straight line running from right to left in a direction perpendicular to the median plane. It more resembles a vertical right line...

More recently, several investigators have shown that auditory analogues of visual grouping phenomena may be created by mapping one dimension of visual space into log frequency and the other into time (Bregman, 1978; Deutsch, 1975c; Divenyi & Hirsh, 1978; Van Noorden, 1975). The principle of proximity emerges clearly, for example, in the visual representation of the sequence shown in Figure 5 of Chapter 9. We may therefore inquire whether analogues of visual perceptual equivalences also exist in the way we represent music (Julesz & Hirsh, 1972).

A. TRANSPOSITION

Von Ehrenfels (1890), in his influential paper on form perception, pointed out that when a melody is transposed it retains its essential form, the *Gestaltqualitat*, provided the relations among the individual tones are preserved. In this respect, he argued, melodies are similar to visual shapes; these retain their perceptual identities when they are translated to different locations in the visual field (Deese & Grindley, 1947).

A number of factors have been found to influence the extent to which a transposed and slightly altered melody is judged as similar to the original one. For example, when the original and transposed melodies can be interpreted as in the same key, and the successive tones comprising the melodies form the same number of steps along the diatonic scale, they are generally judged as very similar to each other; this is true whether or not the intervals forming the melody are preserved (Bartlett & Dowling, 1980; Dewitt & Crowder, 1986; Dowling, 1978, 1986; Takeuchi & Hulse, 1992; Van Egmond & Povel, 1994a). This can be taken to reflect the projection of pitch information onto overlearned alphabets, as described later (see Figures 12 and 13).

Several investigators have hypothesized that the extent to which a transposed melody is perceived as similar to the original is influenced by the key distance between them; for example, that a melody first played in C major will be judged as more similar when it is transposed to G major than to F# major (see, e.g., Cuddy & Cohen, 1976; Cuddy, Cohen, & Mewhort, 1981; Trainor & Trehub, 1993; Van Egmond, Povel, & Maris, in press). However, the explanations for apparent key distance effects are controversial (see, e.g., Takeuchi, 1994; Takeuchi & Hulse, 1992; Van Egmond & Povel, 1994a). Another factor that has been implicated is pitch distance. Several researchers have reported that the closer two melodies are in pitch range, the greater their perceived similarity (Francès, 1958/1988; Hershman, 1994; Van Egmond & Povel, 1994a, Van Egmond et al., in press). Finally the coding model of Deutsch and Feroe (1981) has been used as a predictor of perceived similarity between transposed melodies (Van Egmond & Povel, 1996); this work is described later.

B. INVERSION AND RETROGRESSION

We may next inquire whether further equivalences can be demonstrated for musical shapes that are analogous to their visuospatial counterparts. Schoenberg (1951) argued that transformations similar to rotation and reflection in vision result in perceptual equivalences in music also. He wrote:

> The unity of musical space demands an absolute and unitary perception. In this space ... there is no absolute down, no right or left, forward or backward ... Just as our mind always recognizes, for instance, a knife, a bottle or a watch, regardless of its position, and can reproduce it in the imagination in every possible position, even so a musical creator's mind can operate subconsciously with a row of tones, regardless of their direction, regardless of the way in which a mirror might show the mutual relations, which remain a given quantity.

This statement may be compared with Helmholtz's (1844) description of imagined visuospatial transformations:

> Equipped with an awareness of the physical form of an object, we can clearly imagine all the perspective images which we may expect upon viewing it from this or that side (see Warren & Warren, 1968, p. 252)

On this basis, Schoenberg proposed that a row of tones may be recognized as equivalent when it is transformed in such a way that all ascending intervals become descending ones and vice versa ("inversion"), when it is presented in reverse order ("retrogression"), or when it is transformed by both these operations ("retrograde-inversion"). Figure 9 illustrates Schoenberg's use of his theory in compositional practice. As Schoenberg (1951) wrote:

> The employment of these mirror forms corresponds to the principle of the absolute and unitary perception of musical space.

Schoenberg did not conceive of the vertical dimension of musical space simply as pitch, but rather as pitch class. His assumptions of perceptual equivalence under transposition, retrogression, inversion, and octave displacement are fundamental to 12-tone composition (Babbitt, 1960, 1965). In this procedure, a given ordering of the 12 tones within the octave is adopted. The tone row is repeatedly presented throughout the piece; however, the above transformations are allowed on each

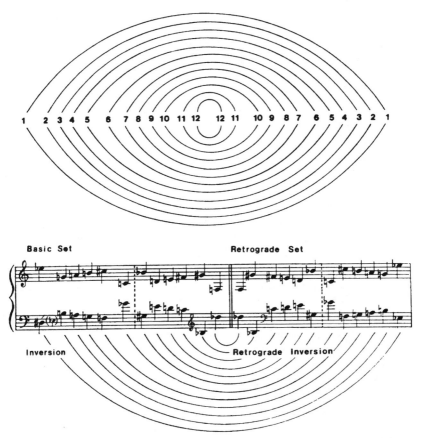

FIGURE 9 Schoenberg's illustration of his theory of equivalence relations between pitch structures, taken from his Wind Quartet, Op. 26. (From Schoenberg, 1951.)

presentation. It is assumed that the row is perceived as an abstraction in its different manifestations.

Whether such transformations indeed result in perceptual equivalences is debatable. In the visual case, we must have evolved mechanisms that preserve the perceptual identities of objects regardless of their orientation relative to the observer. An analogous argument cannot be made for inversion and retrogression of sound patterns. A second doubt is based on general experience. Sound sequences may become unrecognizable when they are reversed in time, as the reader can confirm by attempting to decode a segment of speech when it is played backward. Furthermore, many inverted three-note combinations are perceptually very dissimilar to the combinations from which they are derived. For example, a minor triad is an inversion of a major triad, yet the two are perceptually quite distinct from each other. It would appear that when inverted and retrograde patterns are recognized, this is accomplished at a level of abstraction that is equivalent to the one that allows us to recite a segment of the alphabet backwards or to invert a series of numbers (Deutsch & Feroe, 1981). For other discussions of the perceptual status of 12-tone compositions, see Krumhansl, Sandell, and Sergeant (1987), Francès (1958/1988), and in particular Thomson (1991).

Other theorists have proposed representations of pitch relationships in terms of distances in multidimensional space. For example, in order to capture the close perceptual similarity between tones that stand in octave relation, it has been suggested that pitch be represented as a helix, with the vertical axis corresponding to pitch height and tones separated by octaves lying closest within each turn of the helix (Drobisch, 1855; Pickler, 1966; Shepard, 1964, 1982; Ueda & Ohgushi, 1987). The helical model is discussed in detail in Section IV.

More elaborate representations have also been proposed that would capture the complex patterns of pitch relationships that we invoke in listening to tonal music. For example, Longuet-Higgins (1962a, 1962b, 1978) has suggested that "tonal space" may be characterized as a three-dimensional array: Tones that are adjacent along the first dimension are separated by fifths, those adjacent along the second dimension by major thirds, and those adjacent along the third dimension by octaves. The intervals of tonal music then appear as vectors in this tonal space. If tones that are related by octaves are treated as equivalent, then an array such as that shown in Figure 10 is obtained. As can be observed, closely related tones, such as comprise the C-major scale, form a compact group in this array, so that a key can be defined as a neighborhood in tonal space. Similar representations have been proposed by others, such as Hall (1974) Balzano (1980), and Shepard (1982).

The spatial modeling of pitch relationships has a long tradition among music theorists. In particular, 18th century theorists developed circular configurations that would capture degrees of modulation between keys. In these models, adjacent positions along such circles depict close modulations, and positions that are further removed depict more distant ones. Later theorists such as Weber (1824) and Schoenberg (1954/1969) have produced related spatial models (Werts, 1983).

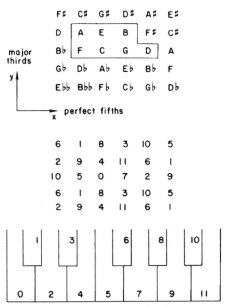

FIGURE 10 Array hypothesized by Longuet-Higgins for the representation of tonal space. (From Longuet-Higgins, 1978.)

C. PITCH ALPHABETS

An alternative model for the representation of pitch relationships in tonal music was proposed by Deutsch and Feroe (1981). The model assumes that, through extensive exposure to such music, the listener acquires a repertoire of hierarchically embedded alphabets, most prominently the chromatic scale, diatonic scales, and triads. An outline of the model is shown in Figure 11, taking as an example the key of C major. At the lowest level, the chromatic alphabet serves as the parent alphabet from which families of subalphabets are derived. The major and minor scales are represented at the next-higher level; these can be expressed in terms of proximal distances along the chromatic alphabet. Triads are represented at the next-higher level; these can be expressed in terms of proximal distances along diatonic alphabets. Lerdahl (1988) has proposed an elaboration of Deutsch and Feroe's hierarchy of alphabets that also takes account of a number of other characteristics of tonal music, such as patterns of proximity between chords.

Compositional practice reflects our use of such overlearned alphabets. For example, in the short-term transposition of motives, the number of steps along an alphabet is often preserved, and even when such transpositions result in alterations in interval size, they still appear appropriate to the listener. Figures 12 and 13 give two such examples. The first, from a Bach fugue, shows a motive that traverses the D-major scale four times in succession, each time beginning on a different posi-

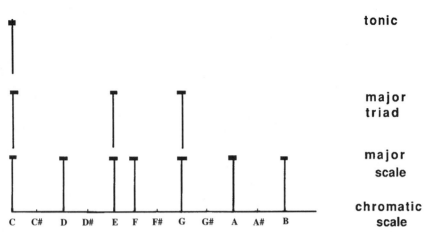

tonic

major
triad

major
scale

chromatic
scale

FIGURE 11   A hierarchy of embedded pitch alphabets. (Adapted from Deutsch & Feroe, 1981. ©1981 by the American Psychological Association. Adapted with permission.)

tion along this scale. The second, from a Schubert impromptu, shows a motive that traverses the A♭-minor triad five times in succession, each time beginning at different positions along this triad.

The hypothesis that pitch structures are represented in terms of such embedded alphabets has received experimental support. Deutsch (1980) asked subjects to listen to sequences of tones drawn from such alphabets, and to recall what they heard in musical notation. It was found that when errors in notation occurred, they rarely departed from the alphabet that had been presented. In general, sequences were recalled very accurately when they could be simply represented as hierarchical structures, with different pitch alphabets at different levels of the hierarchy (see later).

Further evidence comes from reports that melodies were better remembered when they were composed only of tones in a particular diatonic set than when they also included tones outside the set (Cuddy et al., 1981; Dowling, 1991; Francès, 1958/1988). Presumably, adhering to a diatonic set made it likely that the listener would invoke a key, and so use overlearned pitch alphabets as an aid to memory. It has also been reported that changing the context of a melody so as to suggest a different key rendered the melody more difficult to recognize (Dowling, 1986). Yet other studies have found that transpositions of melodies that did not involve a change in key were judged as very similar to the original melodies, regardless of whether or not the intervals were preserved (Bartlett & Dowling, 1980; Dewitt & Crowder, 1986; Dowling, 1978, 1986; Takeuchi & Hulse, 1992; Van Egmond & Povel, 1994). In addition, an alteration in a melody was easier to detect when it could be interpreted as a departure from its key, and so involved a departure from the alphabets appropriate to the key (Francès, 1958/1988, Dewar, Cuddy, & Mewhort, 1977; Dowling, 1978).

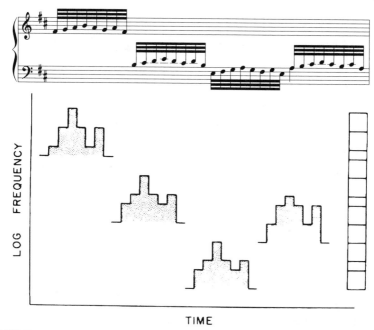

FIGURE 12 Transposition along the alphabet of the D-major scale. The same pattern is presented four times in succession at different positions along the scale. Because the major scale consists of unequal intervals, there result differences in the intervals comprising the pattern. The ladder at the right displays the scale. From J. S. Bach, *The Well-Tempered Clavier,* Book 1, Fugue V. (From Deutsch, 1977.)

An important point originally made by music theorists (see in particular, L. B. Meyer, 1956) is that in the context of an established key, the various scale degrees tend to be assigned differing levels of prominence by the listener. The tonic is generally perceived as the most prominent, followed by the mediant and dominant, and these in turn are followed by the remaining scale degrees, with the other tones of the chromatic scale lowest in the hierarchy.

Laboratory findings have provided evidence that such hierarchies of prominence influence our processing of musical patterns in various ways. They have been found to influence perceived relatedness between tones (Krumhansl, 1979, 1990a), patterns of confusion between tones in short-term memory (Krumhansl, 1979), expected continuations of melodies (Schmuckler, 1989), and the time taken to attribute keys to musical segments (Janata & Reisberg, 1988). Such hierarchies of prominence also correlate with the frequency of occurrence of the different scale degrees in the tonal music of our tradition (Krumhansl, 1990a).

Music theorists have also pointed out that there are hierarchies of prominence for triads within established keys, with the triad on the tonic heard as the most prominent, followed by the triad on the dominant, then the subdominant, and so on. In addition, it appears that the harmonic functions of chords influence the ex-

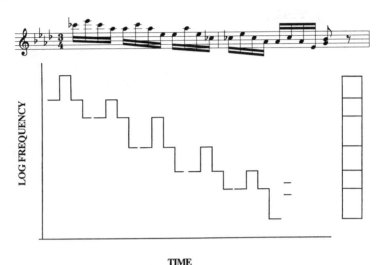

FIGURE 13   Transposition along the alphabet of the A♭-minor triad. The same pattern is presented five times in succession, at different positions along this triad. Because the triad consists of uneven intervals, there result differences in the intervals comprising the pattern. The ladder at the right displays the triad. From F. Schubert, *Four Impromptus,* Op. 90, No. IV.

tent to which they are perceived as related to each other (Krumhansl, Bharucha, & Kessler, 1982; Bharucha & Krumhansl, 1983) and the probability that they will be confused in memory (Bharucha & Krumhansl, 1983; Krumhansl & Castellano, 1983). Furthermore, alterations in the tonal context in which chords are presented affect patterns of memory confusion and judgments of relatedness between them (Bharucha & Krumhansl, 1983). Such hierarchies of prominence for chords within a key also appear to correlate with their frequency of occurrence in Western tonal music also (Krumhansl, 1990a).

D. HIERARCHICAL ENCODING

We now turn to the question of how pitch sequences in tonal music are encoded and retained in memory. Music theorists have argued that the tonal music of our tradition is composed of segments that are organized in hierarchical fashion (see, e.g., Lerdahl & Jackendoff, 1983; L. B. Meyer, 1956, 1973; Narmour, 1990; Schenker, 1956). It is reasonable to suppose that this form of organization reflects the ways in which musical information is encoded and retained in memory. As Greeno and Simon (1974) point out, we appear to retain many different types of information as hierarchies. In some instances, the information is stored in the form of concepts that refer to classes (Collins & Quillian, 1972). We also appear to retain hierarchies of rules (Gagné, 1962; Scandura, 1970), of programs (Miller, Galanter, & Pribram, 1960) and of goals in problem solving (Ernst & Newell, 1969). Visual scenes appear to be retained as hierarchies of subscenes (Hanson &

Riseman, 1978; Navon, 1977; Palmer, 1977; Winston, 1973). The phrase structure of a sentence lends itself readily to hierarchical interpretations (Miller & Chomsky, 1963; Yngve, 1960).

Restle (1970) and Restle and Brown (1970) have provided experimental evidence that we readily acquire serial patterns as hierarchies that reflect the structures of these patterns. Parallel theoretical developments by Simon and his colleagues (Simon, 1972; Simon & Kotovsky, 1963; Simon & Sumner, 1968) and by others (Leewenberg, 1971; Jones, 1974, 1978; Vitz & Todd, 1967, 1969) have addressed the ways in which we acquire and retain serials patterns in terms of hierarchies of operators.

Deutsch and Feroe (1981) have proposed a model of the way in which we represent pitch sequences in tonal music. In essence, the model can be characterized as a hierarchical network, at each level of which structural units are represented as organized sets of elements. Elements that are present at any given level are elaborated by further elements so as to form structural units at the next-lower level, until the lowest level is reached. The model also assumes that Gestalt principles of perceptual organization, such as proximity and good continuation, contribute to organization at each hierarchical level.

The model invokes hierarchies of operators, and a simplified version is as follows:

1. A structure is notated as $(A_1, A_2, ..., A_{i-2}, A_{i-1}, *, A_{i+1}, A_{i+2}, ..., A_n)$, where A_j is one of the operators n, p, s, n^i, or p^i. (A string of length k of an operator A is abbreviated kA.)

2. Each structure $(A_1, A_2, ..., *, ..., A_n)$ has associated with it an alphabet, α. The combination of a structure and an alphabet is called a *sequence* (or *subsequence*). This, together with the reference element r, produces a *sequence of notes*.

3. The effect of each operator in a structure is determined by that of the operator closest to it, but on the same side as the asterisk. Thus the operator n refers to traversing one step up the alphabet associated with the structure. The operator p refers to traversing one step down this alphabet. The operator s refers to remaining in the same position. The two operators n^i and p^i refer to traversing up or down i steps along the alphabet, respectively.

4. The values of the sequence of notes $(A_1, A_2, ..., *, ..., A_n)$, α, r, where α is the alphabet and r the reference element, are obtained by taking the value of the asterisk to be that of r.

5. To produce another sequence from the two sequences $A = (A_1, A_2, ..., *, ..., A_m)$ α, and $B = (B_1, B_2, ..., *, ..., B_n)$, β, where α and β are two alphabets, we define the compound operator pr (prime). $A[pr]B;r$, where r is the reference element, refers to assigning values to the notes produced from $(B_1, B_2, ..., *, ..., B_n)$ such that the value of * is the same as the value of A_1, when the sequence A is applied to the reference element r. Values are then assigned to the notes produced from $(B_1, B_2, ..., *, ..., B_n)$ such that the value of * is the same as the value of A_2, and so on. This gives a sequence of length m x n. Other compound operators such as inv (inversion) and ret (retrograde) are analogously defined.

To characterize the advantages of the model, let us consider the sequence shown in Figure 14b. This may, in principle, be represented in terms of steps that traverse the chromatic scale: A basic subsequence that consists of one step up this scale is presented four times in succession; the second presentation being four steps up from the first, the third being three steps up from the second, and the fourth five steps up from the third. However, this analysis assigns prominence to the basic subsequence, and does not relate the various transpositions to each other in a musically meaningful way.

In contrast, a musical analysis of this pattern would describe it as on two hierarchical levels, in which a higher level subsequence is elaborated by a lower level subsequence. At the higher level, shown on Figure 14a, there is an arpeggiation that ascends through the C-major triad (the notes C-E-G-C). At the lower level, shown in Figure 14b, a neighbor embellishment precedes each note of the triad, so creating a two-note pattern. This hierarchical structure is represented in the dia-

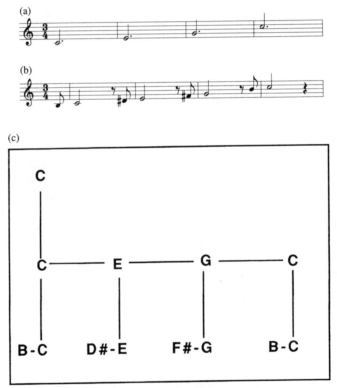

FIGURE 14   A series of pitches represented on two hierarchical levels. (a) At the higher level, there is an arpeggiation of the C-major triad. (b) At the lower level, each note of the triad is preceded by one a semitone lower, so forming a two-note pattern. (c) This hierarchical structure shown in diagram form. (Adapted from Deutsch & Feroe, 1981. ©1981 by the American Psychological Association. Adapted with permission.)

gram in Figure 14c. According to the formalism just outlined, the pattern can be represented as:

$$A = (*, 3n) \; C_{tr}$$
$$B = (p, *) \; Cr$$
$$S = A \; [pr]B, \; C_4$$

where C_{tr} represents the C-major triad, Cr the chromatic scale, and C_4 the reference element.

A more complex example is given in Figure 15 and is represented on three structural levels as follows:

$$A = (*, 4p) \; b_{tr}$$
$$B = (*, n, p) \; b_{tr}$$
$$S = A \; [pr](B, \; 4(*))[inv, \; 5pr](B, \; (*)) \; D_5$$

In many other hierarchical representations of music, such as the one proposed by Schenker, and the other coded element models referred to earlier, elements at all but the lowest level are rule systems rather than actual notes. In contrast, in the present model, a sequence of notes (or subsequence) is realized at each structural level. This property confers a number of processing advantages to the listener. For example, it enables the encoding of such subsequences in terms of laws of figural goodness, such as proximity and good continuation, and also enables the invocation of melodic archetypes such as the gap-fill and changing-note patterns, described by L. B. Meyer (1973). In addition, it enables different pitch alphabets to be invoked at different structural levels, so facilitating the process of generating hierarchical representations from the musical patterns that we hear. As a related point, notes that are present at any given level are also present at all levels below it. In consequence, the higher level at which a note is represented, the more often and so the more firmly it is represented. This has the consequence that higher level

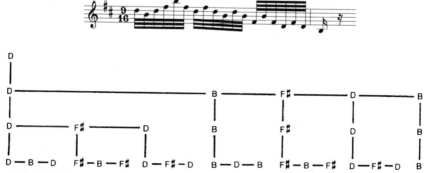

FIGURE 15 More complex hierarchy illustrating the Deutsch and Feroe model. Passage is from Bach's Sinfonia 15, BWV 801. (From Deutsch & Feroe, 1981.©1981 by the American Psychological Association. Adapted with permission.)

subsequences act to cement lower level subsequences together. Another processing advantage of the model is that it enables sequences at different structural levels to be encoded as chunks of a few items each, which in turn is conducive to good memory performance (Estes, 1972; Wickelgren, 1967).

One hypothesis that arises from this model is that sequences of tones should be processed more easily when they can be parsimoniously represented in accordance with its rules. This hypothesis was examined in an experiment by Deutsch (1980). Musically trained listeners were presented with sequences of tones, which they recalled in musical notation. Examples of the sequences are shown in Figure 16. The passage in Figure 16a (a "structured sequence") consists of a higher level subsequence of four elements that acts on a lower level subsequence of three elements. The passage in Figure 16b (an "unstructured sequence") consists of a haphazard reordering of the one in Figure 16a, and does not lend itself to a similar parsimonious representation. It was predicted, on the basis of the model, that the structured sequences would be notated more accurately than the unstructured ones.

Another factor was also examined in this experiment. It has been found in studies using strings of verbal materials that we tend to recall such strings in accordance with their temporal grouping (Bower & Winzenz, 1969; McLean & Gregg, 1967; Mueller & Schumann, 1894). This effect was found to be so powerful as to offset grouping by meaning (Bower & Springston, 1970). Analogous results were also obtained using nonverbal materials (Dowling, 1973; Handel, 1973; Restle, 1972). It was predicted, therefore, that temporal grouping would affect ease of recall of the present tonal sequences also. In particular, temporal grouping in accordance with pitch structure was expected to enhance performance, whereas grouping in conflict with pitch structure was expected to result in performance decrements.

Given these considerations, sequences such as these were each presented in three temporal configurations (Figure 17). In the first, the tones were spaced at equal intervals; in the second, they were spaced in four groups of three, so that they were segmented in accordance with pitch structure; in the third, they were

FIGURE 16 Examples of sequences used in the experiment to study utilization of pitch structure in recall. Sequence (a) can be represented parsimoniously as a higher level subsequence of four elements that acts on a lower level subsequence of three elements. Sequence (b) consists of a haphazard reordering of the notes in sequence (a) and cannot be represented in such a parsimonious fashion. (Adapted from Deutsch, 1980.)

(a)

(b)

(c)

FIGURE 17 Types of temporal segmentation used in the experiment to study the utilization of pitch structure in recall. (a) Sequence unsegmented. (b) Sequence segmented in groups of three, so that segmentation is in accordance with pitch structure. (c) Sequence segmented in groups of four, so that segmentation is in conflict with pitch structure.

spaced in three groups of four, so that they were segmented in conflict with pitch structure.

Large effects of pitch structure and temporal segmentation were obtained. For structured sequences that were segmented in accordance with pitch structure, performance levels were very high. For structured sequences that were unsegmented, performance levels were still very high, though slightly lower. For structured sequences that were segmented in conflict with pitch structure, however, performance levels were much lower. For unstructured sequences, performance levels were considerably lower than for structured sequences that were segmented in accordance with their structure or that were unsegmented, but were in the same range as for structured sequences that were segmented in conflict with pitch structure.

Figure 18 shows the percentages of tones that were correctly recalled in their correct serial positions in the different conditions of the experiment. Typical bow-shaped curves are apparent, and in addition, discontinuities occur at the boundaries between temporal groupings. This pattern of results indicates that the subjects tended to encode the temporal groupings as chunks, which were retained or lost independently of each other. This pattern is very similar to that found by others with the use of verbal materials (Bower & Winzenz, 1969).

The transition shift probability (TSP) provides a further measure of interitem association. This is defined as the joint probability of either an error following a correct response on the previous item, or of a correct response following an error on the previous item (Bower & Springston, 1970). If groups of elements tend to be retained or lost as chunks, we should expect the TSP values to be smaller for transitions within a chunk, and larger for the transition into the first element of a chunk. It was indeed found that TSPs were larger on the first element of each temporal grouping than on other elements. This is as expected on the hypothesis that temporal groupings serve to define subjective chunks that are retained or lost independently of each other.

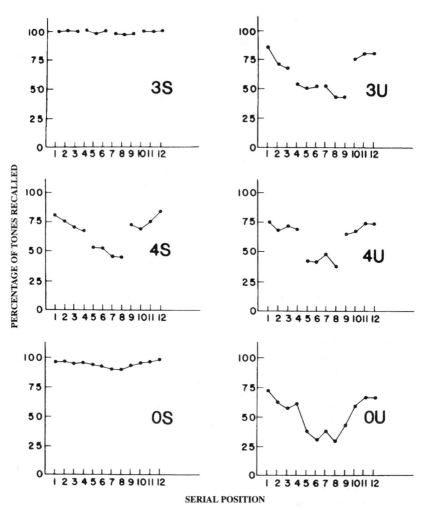

FIGURE 18 Serial position curves for the different conditions of the experiment to study the utilization of pitch structure in recall. 3: Temporal segmentation in groups of three. 4: Temporal segmentation in groups of four. O: No temporal segmentation. S; Structured sequence. U: Unstructured sequence. (From Deutsch, 1980.)

In general, these results provide strong evidence that listeners perceive hierarchical structures that are present in tonal sequences, and that they use such structures in recall. For the structured sequences used here, the listener needed only to retain two chunks of three or four items each; however, for the unstructured sequences, no such parsimonious encoding was possible. The error rates for the unstructured sequences were much higher than for the structured ones, in accordance with the hypothesis that they imposed a much heavier memory load.

Another study was carried out by Van Egmond and Povel (1996). A paired comparison paradigm was used to investigate perceived similarities between melodies and their transpositions, when the latter had been altered in various ways. The Deutsch and Feroe model was used as a qualitative predictor of the degree of perceived similarity between the original and transposed melodies. The authors hypothesized that the larger the number of items by which the codes for the original and transposed melodies differed, the more dissimilar the two melodies would appear.

More specifically, Van Egmond and Povel predicted that an exact transposition would be judged as most similar to the original melody, because its code would differ only in terms of one item: the key. For a transposition that was chromatically altered, the prediction concerning perceived similarity would depend on whether the transposed melody could be represented parsimoniously in the same key as the original. If it could be so represented, then its code would differ in terms of only one item: the reference element. If it could not be so represented, then its code would differ in terms of two items: the key and the reference element. Finally, a transposition that was diatonically altered would be judged as most dissimilar to the original melody, because its code would differ in terms of six items: the key and five structure operators.

The experimental findings confirmed the hypothesis. Exact transpositions were judged as most similar to the original melodies. Chromatically altered transpositions that could be interpreted as in the same key as the original melodies were judged as more similar than were those that could not be so interpreted. Transpositions that were diatonically altered were judged as more dissimilar than were chromatically altered transpositions.

Two other studies are relevant here. Oura (1991) presented subjects with a melody, which they recalled in musical notation. She found that tones that were represented at higher structural levels were recalled better than those that were represented at lower levels. Dibben (1994) had subjects listen to a musical segment, and then to a pair of reductions, and she asked them to determine which reduction best matched the original. She found that the subjects chose the version that matched the full segment at higher structural levels. The findings from both these studies are in accordance with the prediction from Deutsch and Feroe (1981) that the higher up a note or sequence of notes is represented, the more often it is represented, and so the more firmly it should be embedded in memory.

So far we have been considering the processing of a single melodic line. However, tonal music generally involves several such lines, and even where only one is presented, a harmonic progression is generally implied. We can assume that such progressions are also encoded in hierarchical fashion. In addition, the use of parallel linear sequences, which must themselves combine to form an acceptable harmonic sequence, places constraints on the choice of elements in each sequence; this in turn serves to reduce the processing load.

E. KEY ATTRIBUTION

We now consider the process whereby the listener attributes a key to a passage. As is evident from general experience, we tend to make such decisions quickly and accurately, often on the basis of very little information. However, there is much disagreement concerning which cues we use in making these decisions, and the relative weightings that we give to these cues.

One approach to this issue stresses the identities of the pitches in the passage, independent of their orderings. For example, it is assumed that when presented with the diatonic collection C, D, E, F, G, A, and B, the listener will attribute the key of C major. It is further hypothesized that when presented with other pitches taken from the chromatic scale (such as F♯ or D♯), the listener will be more likely to reject the hypothesis of C major and will search instead for a different key (see, e.g., Longuet-Higgins, 1962a, 1962b, 1978).

This approach accords well with general experience; however, the experimental evidence indicates that other factors also play a role. In one experiment, West and Fryer (1990) presented subjects with a quasi-random ordering of the tones of a diatonic scale, followed by a probe tone. The subjects judged how suitable the probe tone was as a tonic, in the context of the sequence that had been presented. Even musically trained subjects did not judge the major mode tonic as most suitable. Instead, ratings for the major mode tonic, mediant, dominant, and subdominant did not differ significantly from each other, although together they were rated more highly than were the other tones of the diatonic scale. It would appear, then, that simply hearing a diatonic collection of pitches, independent of their ordering, is not sufficient for reliable key attribution.

Krumhansl and colleagues have elaborated on the role of the diatonic collection in key attribution (see Krumhansl, 1990a, for a review). Subjects listened to a context sequence, which was followed by a probe tone, and they judged how well the probe tone appeared to fit in the context that was provided. The context patterns were configured so as to provide strong cues for key identification; for example, one consisted of a major scale, and another of a sequence of chords that formed a cadence. It was found that the subjects generally gave the tonic the highest rating, and from this it was argued that they were treating the tonic as the most appropriate candidate for a tonal center.

The explanation for the findings of Krumhansl and colleagues has been the subject of considerable debate (see, e.g., Butler, 1989, 1990; Krumhansl, 1990b; West & Fryer, 1990). It was pointed out that in these experiments the tones that were included in the context set were generally given higher ratings than were those that were not so included. Further, there were strong correlations between the number of times a tone appeared in the context set and the strength of its rating by the subject. On such grounds, it was argued that the subjects' ratings could have reflected short-term memory factors rather than knowledge of hierarchies of prominence for tones within keys (see Section V). On the other hand, it could also be argued that the subjects were drawing on their long-term memories for the relative frequencies of occurrence of tones within a key; this could in turn have influenced judgments of hierarchies of prominence. The extent to which ratings were here driven by short-term memory, long-term memory, or yet other factors remains unresolved.

Other theorists have argued that the order in which tones appear is important to key attribution, whether or not the tones are confined to a diatonic collection. As illustration, we can take two musical passages shown in Figure 16. Passage (a) in this figure (G-F♯-G-D-C♯-D-B-A♯-B-G-F♯-G) clearly invokes the key of G major, even though two of these tones (C♯ and A♯) are not included in the G-major scale. Passage (b) consists of a haphazard reordering of the tones in passage (a) and clearly does not evoke a well-defined key. Comparison of these two passages indicates that when tones are so ordered as to enable a simple structural description, a key appropriate to this description is readily invoked. However, when the tones are not so ordered, key attribution is more ambiguous.

Another illustration is based on the passage in Figure 19a, which is derived from the example used by Deutsch and Feroe (1981) and is discussed in Deutsch (1984). This passage may be described as an arpeggiation that ascends through the C-major triad (E-G-C) such that each tone of the triad is preceded by a neighbor embellishment, so creating a two-tone pattern. In this way, the key of C major is clearly attributed, despite the fact that two of the tones (D♯ and F♯) are not part of the C-major scale. An algorithm that assigns overwhelming importance to the collection of pitches in the passage would attribute the key of E minor instead. However, if the same sequence of tones is played backward, as in Figure 19b, the key of E minor is now invoked. Other orderings also invoke E minor, even when the passage ends on the note C, as in the example in Figure 19c.

Why, then, is the key of C major so clearly attributed in the pattern shown in Figure 19a, but not in the other patterns? Deutsch (1984) suggested that when presented with a succession of tones, the listener forms groupings based on pitch proximity and, other things being equal, assigns more prominence to the last tone of each grouping. So from the sequence in Figure 19a, the groupings (D♯-E), (F♯-G), and (B-C) are formed. The tones E, G, and C are then targeted to be combined at a higher level so as to produce an arpeggiation of the C-major triad. In consequence, the key of C major is invoked. However, given the retrograde of the pattern shown in Figure 19b, the groupings (C-B), (G-F♯), and (E-D♯) are formed

FIGURE 19   Pitch series that illustrate the effects on key attribution of different temporal orderings of a given collection of tones. See text for details. Pattern (a) is derived from Figure 1 of Deutsch and Feroe (1981). (Adapted from Deutsch, 1984.)

instead, and in consequence the tones B, F#, and D# are targeted for higher level grouping. Because these tones form the dominant triad in E minor, and because all the tones in the passage are in the E-minor scale, this key is attributed. On this line of reasoning, the process of key assignment is a complex one, involving such factors as low-level groupings, knowledge of the pitches forming diatonic collections, and knowledge of hierarchies of prominence for tones within different keys.

Bharucha (1984a, 1984b) in parallel hypothesized a similar process that he termed "melodic anchoring." He suggested that a tone becomes "anchored" to its successor if the two are related stepwise along a chromatic or diatonic scale. He further hypothesized that the second tone contributes more than the first one to the listener's sense of key. Bharucha (1984a) provided evidence for this view in a number of experiments.

The importance of order information to key attribution has been stressed particularly by Brown and Butler (see Brown, 1988; Brown & Butler, 1981; Brown, Butler, & Jones, 1994; Butler, 1983, 1992; Butler & Brown, 1984). The authors argued that in attributing a key, listeners rely more on rare than on common intervals, because these correlate less ambiguously with a particular diatonic set, and so provide more reliable information for key identification (Browne, 1981). They also argued that listeners make more accurate key assignments based on rare intervals when these are presented in a temporal order that implies the goal-oriented harmonies that most frequently occur in tonal music. So, for example, when a musical event contains a tritone that is so configured as to imply a dominant-to-tonic progression, the appropriate key will be readily invoked.

Finally, it is evident that other factors are involved in the process of key attribution, such as harmony, rhythm, and meter; however, because of space limitations these factors are not considered here.

IV. PARADOXES BASED ON PITCH CLASS

As described earlier, the pitch of a tone is held to vary along two dimensions: The monotonic dimension of height defines its position along a continuum from low to high, and the circular dimension of pitch class defines its position within the octave (Babbitt, 1960, 1965; Bachem, 1948; Charbonneau & Risset, 1973; Deutsch, 1969, 1972c, 1973b, 1986a; Deutsch & Boulanger, 1984; Forte, 1973; M. Meyer, 1904, 1914; Révész, 1913, Risset, 1969, 1971; Ruckmick, 1929; Shepard, 1964, 1982; Ueda & Ohgushi, 1987).

In order to accommodate the dimensions of pitch class and height in a single spatial representation, it has been suggested that pitch be depicted as a geometrically regular helix, in which the entire structure maps into itself under transposition (Drobisch, 1855; Shepard, 1964, 1965, 1982). Such a representation is shown in Figure 20, and it can be seen that tones that are separated by octaves are depicted as in close spatial proximity. This geometrical model assumes that the dimensions of pitch class and pitch height are orthogonal, so that the pitch class of a tone would not influence its perceived height.

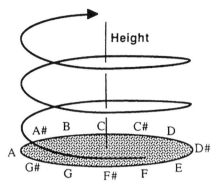

FIGURE 20   Pitch represented as a geometrically regular helix. (Adapted from Shepard, 1965.)

Shepard (1964) noted that the helical model of pitch has an intriguing conse-quence. If one could suppress the monotonic component of height, leaving only the circular component of pitch class, all tones that were related by octaves could be mapped onto the same tone, which would then have a clearly defined pitch class but an indeterminate height. In this way, the tonal helix would be collapsed into a circle, and judgments of pitch would become completely circular.

In an associated experiment, Shepard generated a set of tones, each of which consisted of 10 sinusoidal components that were separated by octaves and whose amplitudes were determined by a fixed, bell-shaped, spectral envelope. The pitch classes of the tones were varied by shifting the components up or down in log frequency, holding the position and shape of the envelope constant. Shepard ar-gued that because the spectral envelope remained fixed, the perceived heights of these tones would remain constant as their pitch classes were varied.

Subjects listened to ordered pairs of such tones, and they reported in each case whether they heard an ascending or a descending pattern. When the tones within a pair were separated by one or two steps along the pitch class circle (Figure 21) judgments were determined almost entirely by proximity. When the tones were separated by larger distances along the circle, the tendency to follow by proximity gradually lessened, and when they were separated by exactly a half-octave, as-cending and descending judgments occurred equally often.

Shepard (1964) concluded from these findings that the dimensions of pitch class and height were indeed orthogonal, arguing that such a view would at all events be expected on common sense grounds:

> tonality [i.e., pitch class] seems quite analogous to the attribute of being clockwise or coun-terclockwise. One of two nearby points on a circle can be said to be clockwise from the other; but it makes no sense to say how clockwise a single point is absolutely.

However, this conclusion does not necessarily follow from Shepard's findings. Where judgments were heavily influenced by proximity, any effect of pitch class on perceived height could have been overwhelmed by this factor. Furthermore, because the data were averaged across pitch classes, any effect of pitch class on

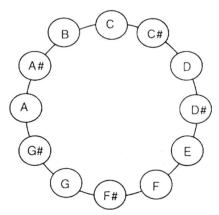

FIGURE 21   The pitch class circle.

perceived height would have been lost in the averaging process. The issue of whether the pitch class of a tone might influence its perceived height therefore remained unresolved in Shepard's study.

A. THE TRITONE PARADOX

Given such considerations, Deutsch (1986a) had subjects listen to ordered pairs
of tones that were related by a half-octave (or tritone), and they reported in each
case whether they heard an ascending or a descending pattern. Each tone consisted
of six octave-related components, whose amplitudes were scaled by a bell-shaped
spectral envelope. In order to control for possible effects of the relative amplitudes
of the components of the tones, and also to examine the effects of varying their
overall heights, the tone pairs were generated under envelopes that were placed at
six different positions along the spectrum, which were spaced at half-octave intervals.

It was reasoned that because the tones within each pair were in opposite positions along the pitch class circle, proximity could not here be used as a cue in
making judgments of relative height. So if the assumption of orthogonality were
correct, these judgments would not be influenced by the pitch classes of the tones.
But it was also reasoned that an interaction between the two dimensions might
emerge: The listener might perceive tones in one region of the pitch class circle as
higher and tones in the opposite region as lower.

More specifically, it was conjectured that listeners might arrange pitch classes
as a circular map, similar to a clock face. This map might have a particular orientation with respect to height. For example, C could be in the 12:00 position and F♯
in the 6:00 position, so that the listener would perceive the tone pairs C-F♯ (and B-
F and C♯-D) as descending, and tone pairs F♯-C (and F-B and G-C♯) as ascending.
If, on the other hand, this map were oriented so that F♯ stood in the 12:00 position

and C in the 6:00 position, the listener would instead perceive the tone pair C-F# as ascending and the pair F#-C as descending.

The hypothesis of an effect of pitch class on perceived height was strikingly confirmed: The judgments of most subjects showed that tones in one region of the pitch class circle were perceived as higher and those in the opposite region as lower. Another striking finding also emerged: The relationship between pitch class and perceived height differed radically from one subject to another. Figure 22 presents, as an example, the judgments of two subjects who showed particularly clear and consistent relationships between pitch class and perceived height. (The judgments were averaged over tones generated under all six spectral envelopes.) The first subject heard tone pairs C#-G, D-G#, D#-A and E-A# as ascending and tone pairs F#-C, G-C#, G#-D, A-D#, A#-E, and B-F as descending. In contrast, the

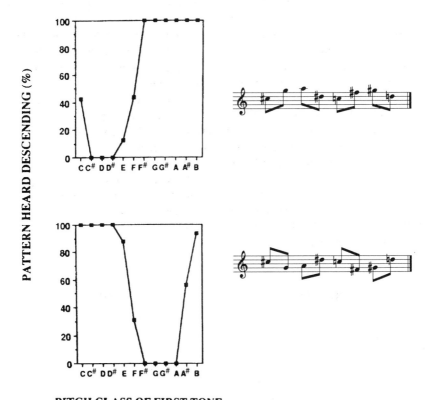

PITCH CLASS OF FIRST TONE

FIGURE 22   The tritone paradox as perceived by two different subjects. The graphs show the percentages of judgments that a tone pair formed a descending pattern, plotted as a function of the pitch class of the first tone of the pair. Notations on the right show how the identical series of tone pairs was perceived by these two subjects. (Data from Deutsch, 1986a.)

second subject heard tone pairs B-F, C-F♯, C♯-G, D-G♯, D♯-A, and E-A♯ as descending and pairs F♯-C, G-C♯, G♯-D, and A-D♯ as ascending. So for the most part, when the first subject heard an ascending pattern, the second subject heard a descending one, and vice versa. In consequence, also as shown in Figure 22, extended patterns formed of such tone pairs were heard by these two subjects as producing entirely different melodies.

Figure 23 shows the perceptual orientations of the pitch class circle that were derived from the judgments of these two subjects. For the first subject, the peak pitch classes (i.e., those that stood at the highest position along the pitch class circle) were G♯ and A; however, for the second subject, the peak pitch classes were C♯ and D instead.

Figure 24 shows the judgments of four more subjects whose patterns were less pronounced than were those shown in Figure 22. These data were taken from experiments in which four spectral envelopes were used, which were spaced at half-octave intervals, and the judgments under these four envelopes were averaged. It can be seen that all four subjects showed clear relationships between pitch class and perceived height; however, the form of the relationship varied from one subject to another. (A set of stimulus patterns comprising a full experiment such as this one appears on the compact disc by Deutsch, 1995).

Deutsch, Kuyper, and Fisher (1987) performed a study to examine perception of the tritone paradox in a general population. A group of subjects were selected on the only criteria that they were undergraduates at the University of California at San Diego, had normal hearing, and could judge reliably whether pairs of sine-wave tones that were related by a tritone formed ascending or descending patterns. The judgments of most of the subjects reflected clear relationships between pitch class and perceived height. Furthermore, computer simulations showed that the patterns obtained in this experiment were extremely unlikely to have occurred by chance. It was concluded that the tritone paradox exists to highly significant extent in this general population.

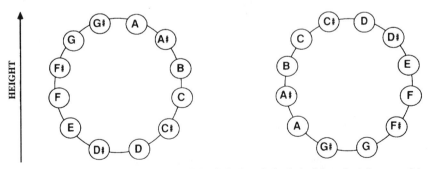

FIGURE 23   Perceptual orientations of the pitch class circle, derived from the judgments of the two subjects whose data are displayed in Figure 22. The circle on the left is derived from the graph shown in the upper portion of Figure 22, and the circle on the right from the graph shown in the lower portion. The pitch classes that mark the highest position along the circle are called peak pitch classes.

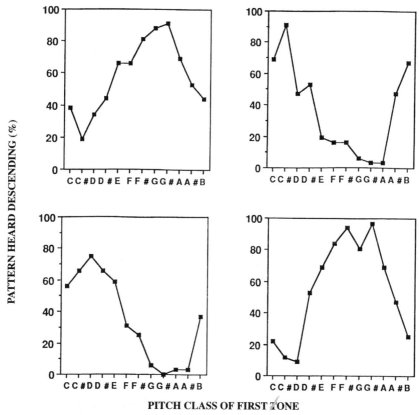

PITCH CLASS OF FIRST TONE

FIGURE 24   The tritone paradox as perceived by four more subjects.

B. THE SEMITONE PARADOX

We next inquire as to what happens when more than one tone is presented at a time. Deutsch (1988b) examined this issue using a basic pattern that consisted of two sequentially presented tone pairs, which were diametrically opposed along the pitch class circle. An example of such a pattern is shown in Figure 25. On one side of the circle the second tone was higher than the first (in this example, G♯ was followed by A) and on the other side the second tone was lower (in this example, D♯ was followed by D). In general, subjects linked the tones sequentially in accordance with pitch proximity, so that they perceived the pattern as two stepwise lines that moved in contrary motion. However, the higher line could be heard as ascending and the lower line as descending, or vice versa.

Subjects were presented with such sequential tone pairs, and they judged in each case whether the line that was higher in pitch formed an ascending or a descending pattern. From these judgments it was inferred which pitch classes were heard as higher and which as lower. Taking the tone pairs in Figure 25, for ex-

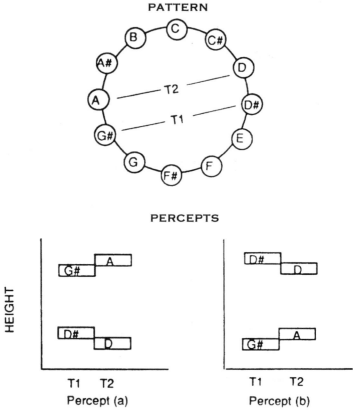

FIGURE 25   Example of pattern giving rise to the semitone paradox, together with two alternative perceptual organizations. Tones G# and D# are presented simultaneously at T1, and tones A and D
at T2. Listeners organize this pattern as two stepwise lines that move in contrary motion; that is, they
hear the ascending line G#-A together with the descending line D#-D. However, some listeners hear
the ascending line as higher [Percept (a)] while other listeners hear the descending line as higher
[Percept (b)]. (Adapted with permission from Deutsch, 1988b. ©1988 by The Regents of the University of California.)

ample, if the subject heard the higher line as ascending, this indicated that he or
she perceived G# and A as higher and D# and D as lower [as in Percept (a)]. However, if the subject heard the higher line as descending, this indicated that he or she
perceived D# and D as higher and G# and A as lower [as in Percept (b)].

   Just as with the tritone paradox, subjects' judgments here reflected orderly relationships between the pitch classes of the tones and their perceived heights. Also
as with the tritone paradox, the form of this relationship varied radically from one
subject to another. This is illustrated in the judgments of two subjects shown in
Figure 26. For the first subject, tones F, F#, G, G#, A, and A# were heard as higher
and C, C#, D, and D# were heard as lower. In contrast, for the second subject, C#, D,

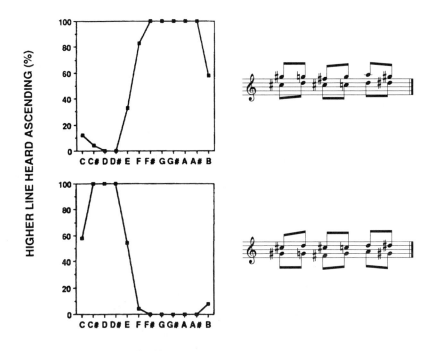

TONES IN ASCENDING LINE

FIGURE 26   The semitone paradox as perceived by two different subjects. The graphs show the percentages of trials in which a tone was heard as part of the higher line, plotted as a function of the pitch class of the tone. For both subjects, when the pattern was transposed, the ascending and descending lines appeared to interchange positions. Moreover, in general, when the first subject heard the higher line as ascending, the second subject heard it as descending, and vice versa. Notations on the right show how the identical series of patterns was perceived by these two subjects. (Reprinted with permission from Deutsch, 1988b. ©1988 by The Regents of the University of California.)

and D♯ were heard as higher and F, F♯, G, G♯, A, A♯, and B were heard as lower. In consequence, also as shown in Figure 26, musical passages produced by series of such tone pairs were heard by these two subjects in entirely different ways.

C. THE MELODIC PARADOX

We can further ask what happens when more complex patterns are presented. Deutsch, Moore, and Dolson (1986) investigated this question using patterns consisting of three sequentially presented tone pairs. Specifically, the pattern shown in Figure 27 was played in two different keys. In C major, the pattern consisted of the succession of tones D-E-F played together with B-A-G. In F♯ major, the tones G♯-A♯-B were played together with E♯-D♯-C♯.

When this pattern was heard unambiguously, the listeners always organized the tones sequentially in accordance with pitch proximity. So they heard one melodic

PATTERN

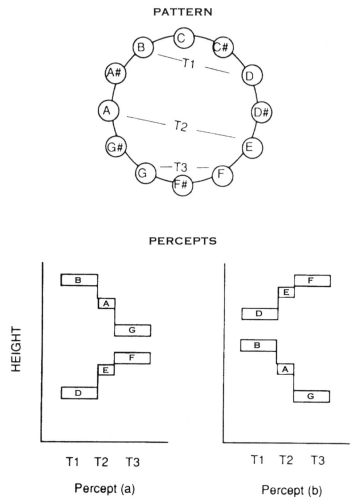

PERCEPTS

FIGURE 27   Pattern giving rise to the melodic paradox, together with alternative perceptual organizations. Tones D and B are simultaneously presented at time T1, tones E and A are presented at T2, and tones F and G are presented at T3. This pattern is generally heard as two stepwise lines that move in contrary motion. However, some listeners hear the higher line as descending and the lower line as ascending [Percept (a)], whereas others hear the higher line as ascending and the lower line as descending [Percept (b)]. (From experiment by Deutsch et al., 1986.)

line that ascended by a minor third, together with another that descended by a major third. However, also as shown in Figure 27, the descending line could be heard as higher and the ascending line as lower [as in Percept (a)] or the ascending line could be heard as higher and the descending line as lower [as in Percept (b)].

Analogous effects were found to occur here also: When the pattern was played in one key, it was perceived with the higher line ascending. However, when the pattern was played in the other key, it was heard with the higher line descending instead. So transposing the pattern from one key to the other led to a perceived interchange of voices. Furthermore, when the pattern was played in one of the keys, it was heard with the higher line as ascending by some listeners, but as descending by others.

Deutsch (1988a) performed a further experiment, in which this two-part pattern was played in six different keys: C, D, E, F♯, G♯, and A♯ major. The judgments of four subjects were examined, and they all showed orderly effects of key and also differed radically in the direction in which key influenced their judgments. In consequence, extended passages formed of such patterns were heard by these subjects in entirely different ways.

As illustration, Figure 28 displays the percepts of two of the subjects. The first subject heard the pattern in the keys of C and D with the higher line ascending, yet in the keys of E, F♯, and G♯ with the higher line descending. The second subject, in contrast, heard the pattern in the keys of D, E, F♯, and G♯ with the higher line ascending, yet in the keys of C and A♯ with the higher line descending. Thus for the most part when the first subject heard the higher line ascending, the second subject heard it descending, and vice versa. This is also illustrated in the notation on the right-hand part of the figure.

D. IMPLICATIONS OF THESE MUSICAL PARADOXES

The paradoxes described here show that pitch class and pitch height are not orthogonal dimensions; rather, the perceived height of a tone is systematically related to its position along the pitch class circle, when other factors are controlled for.

The paradoxes are surprising on a number of grounds. First, they provide striking violations of the principle of perceptual equivalence under transposition; a principle that had been assumed to be universal. In the case of the tritone paradox, transposing the pattern from one key to another can cause it to appear to change from an ascending pattern to a descending one, and vice versa. In the case of the paradoxes involving two-part patterns, transposition can result in a perceived interchange of voices.

Another surprising implication concerns absolute pitch, a faculty that is generally assumed to be very rare. Because the majority of listeners experience these musical paradoxes, this means that the majority of us have at least a partial form of absolute pitch, in that we hear tones as higher or lower depending simply on their note names, or pitch classes. It is interesting that other studies have also indicated that absolute pitch is more prevalent than had earlier been assumed, at least in partial form. Terhardt and Ward (1982) and Terhardt and Seewann (1983) found that musicians were able to judge whether or not a passage was played in the correct key, even though they did not possess absolute pitch as conventionally defined. Further, Halpern (1989) reported that when musically untrained subjects were asked to hum the first notes of well-known songs on different occasions, they were remarkably consistent in their choices of pitches from one session to another.

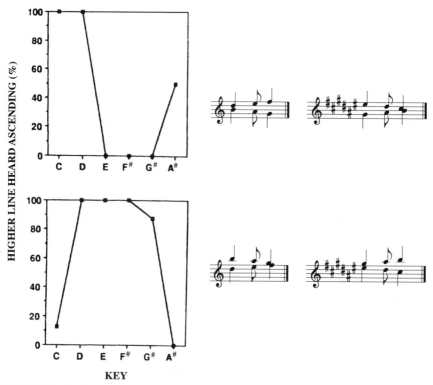

FIGURE 28   Melodic paradox as perceived by two different subjects, when presented in six different keys. In general, as the pattern was transposed, the ascending and descending lines appeared to interchange positions. Moreover, for the most part when the first subject heard the higher line ascending, the second subject heard it descending, and vice versa. Notations on the right show how the identical series of patterns was perceived by these two subjects. (Adapted from Deutsch, 1988a.)

An ingenious study by Levitin (1994) provided further evidence that many people possess a latent form of absolute pitch. He had subjects select a CD that contained a popular song, with which they were very familiar. The subjects were asked to hold the CD, close their eyes, imagine the song, and then reproduce it by singing, humming, or whistling. The first tone that the subject produced was then compared with the equivalent one on the CD. Levitin found that one out of four subjects produced the same pitch (or pitch class) as the equivalent one on the CD, and half the subjects produced a tone whose pitch (or pitch class) was within a semitone of the equivalent. Virtually none of the subjects claimed to have absolute pitch, and the effect appeared to be independent of the subjects' musical background.

Another surprising outcome of this work concerns the striking differences between people in how these paradoxes are perceived. These differences are as pronounced among experienced musicians as among listeners without musical training. It is to the basis of such differences that we now turn.

E. BASIS OF THE TRITONE PARADOX

Studies exploring the bases of these musical paradoxes have focused largely on the tritone paradox. A number of experiments have examined the involvement of spectral factors in this effect. Deutsch (1987) generated such tritone pairs under 12 different spectral envelopes, with peaks spaced at 1/4-octave intervals, so that their positions varied over a three-octave range. Although the relationship between pitch class and perceived height was found sometimes to vary as a function of the overall height of the spectral envelope, and sometimes also as a function of the relative amplitudes of the components of the tones, such variations tended to be small in absolute terms (see also Dawe, Platt, & Welsh, 1998; Deutsch, 1994; Giangrande, 1998).

A number of informal observations led the author to hypothesize that the tritone paradox might be related to the processing of speech sounds. It was conjectured that the listener develops a long-term representation of the overall pitch range of his or her speaking voice. Included in this representation is a specification of the octave band in which the largest proportion of pitch values occurs. The listener then takes the pitch classes delimiting this octave band for speech as marking the highest position along the pitch class circle; this in turn determines his or her orientation of the pitch class circle with respect to height.

In a test of this hypothesis, Deutsch, North, and Ray (1990) selected a group of subjects who showed clear relationships between pitch class and perceived height in making judgments of the tritone paradox. We took a 15-min recording of natural speech from each subject, and from this recording we identified the octave band containing the largest number of pitch values. Comparing across subjects, we obtained a significant correspondence between the pitch classes defining this octave band and those marking the highest position along the pitch class circle, as determined by judgments of the tritone paradox.

Two versions of the hypothesis relating the tritone paradox to the pitch range of speech may then be advanced. The first does not assume that the pitch range of an individual's speech is itself determined by a learned template. The second, and broader, version assumes that we acquire such a template as a result of exposure to speech around us. This template is then used both to constrain our own speech output and also to evaluate the speech of others. If the second hypothesis were correct, we would expect the orientation of the pitch class circle to be similar for people in a given linguistic subculture, but to vary among people in different subcultures.

In a review of the literature concerning the pitch ranges of speech in different linguistic communities, Dolson (1994) described evidence in support of this second hypothesis. First, most people confine the pitch range of their speech to roughly an octave. Second, within a given linguistic community, in general the speech of females is close to an octave above that of males; for this reason, a template based on pitch class rather than pitch would enable the mapping of male and female speech onto a single mental representation. Further, the pitch ranges of speech differ remarkably little within a given linguistic community (except, of course, for the difference between sexes); however, there are considerable variations in the pitch ranges of speech across different linguistic communities. Moreover, there is a surprising lack of correlation between the pitch range of a person's speech and physiological parameters such as his or her height, weight, chest size, and laryngeal size. This indicates that the pitch range of an individual's speaking voice is based on cultural consensus.

Deutsch (1991) performed a further experiment to test the cultural hypothesis. The judgments of two groups of subjects were compared: The first group had grown up in California and the second group had grown up in the South of England. The two groups were found to differ statistically in their perceptions of the tritone paradox, so that frequently when a Californian subject heard the pattern as ascending, a subject from the South of England heard it as descending, and vice versa (Figure 29).

Other laboratories have obtained further evidence for a geographic association. Giangrande (1998) found that a group of subjects at Florida Atlantic University produced a distribution of peak pitch classes that was similar to the one found by Deutsch (1991) among Californians. Treptoe (1997) found a very similar distribution among subjects at the University of Wisconsin, Steven's Point. In contrast, Dawe et al. (1998) found that a group of students at McMaster University, Ontario, produced a distribution that was quite similar to the one found by Deutsch (1991) for subjects from the South of England.

Examining this correlate in greater detail, Ragozzine and Deutsch (1994) discovered a regional difference in perception of the tritone paradox within the United States. Among subjects who had grown up in the area of Youngstown, Ohio, the perceptions of those whose parents had also grown up in this region differed significantly from those whose parents had grown up elsewhere within the United States. These findings indicate that perception of the tritone paradox is influenced by a template that is acquired in childhood. Further evidence was provided by Deutsch (1996), who found a significant correlation between the way children and their mothers heard the tritone paradox. This correlation was obtained even though the children had all been born and raised in California, whereas their mothers had grown up in many different geographical regions, both within and outside the United States.

We can then ask why such a speech-related template would have evolved. Because the pitch of speech varies with the speaker's emotional state, a template such as hypothesized here could be useful in enabling listeners to make a rapid evaluation of such states. It is also possible that this template could be useful in communicating syntactic aspects of speech.

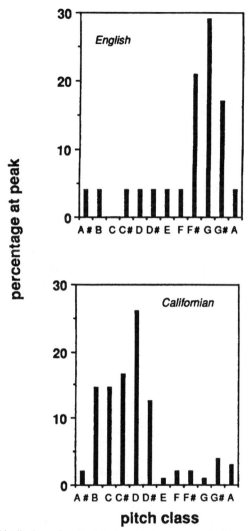

pitch class

FIGURE 29   Distributions of peak pitch classes in two groups of subjects. The first group had grown up in the south of England and the second group had grown up in California. (Reprinted with permission from Deutsch, 1991. ©1991 by The Regents of the University of California.)

We can then ask whether these perceptual paradoxes occur in natural musical situations. In unpublished experiments, the author has found that the effects persisted with the use of tone complexes whose partials were stretched slightly, so that they did not stand in octave relation. The effects also persisted when the sinusoidal components of the tones were replaced by sawtooth waves, so that the power spectrum of each complex was similar to one produced by several instruments playing simultaneously. Furthermore, imposing a vibrato, a tremolo, or a fast decay such as occurs with a plucked string did not destroy the effects. Most interestingly, the tritone paradox was produced, at least in some individuals, when each tone of a pair consisted of a single harmonic series, with the relative amplitudes of the odd and even harmonics adjusted so that the tones were roughly equivalent in perceived height. It appears, therefore, that effects such as these might well be found in music performed by live instruments, when the composer has introduced ambiguities of height, such as in orchestral pieces by Debussy and Ravel.

V. THE PITCH MEMORY SYSTEM

In this section, we present a theoretical framework for the representation of music in memory. This framework is derived from one originally proposed by Deutsch (1972a, 1975a, 1975d; Deutsch & Feroe 1975), which was based on a series of findings on memory for pitch and for relationships based on pitch. These findings are reviewed, together with more recent findings by the author and other investigators.

It is evident from general considerations that memory for music must be the function of a heterogeneous system, whose various subdivisions differ in the persistence with which they retain information. For example, the system that subserves memory for pitch relationships must be capable of retaining information over very long periods of time, whereas this is not true of the system that retains absolute pitch values. Similarly, the system that retains temporal patterns must preserve information for considerably longer than the system that retains absolute values of duration. Based on such considerations, we can assume that when memory for a musical pattern is tested after different time periods have elapsed, apparent differences in its form of encoding would emerge. (A similar argument concerning memory in general has been made by Craik and Lockhart, 1972.)

More specifically, the model assumes that musical information is initially subjected to a set of perceptual analyses, which are carried out in different subdivisions of the auditory system. Such analyses result in the attribution of values of pitch, loudness, duration, and so on, as well as values of abstracted information, such as harmonic and melodic intervals, durational relationships, and timbres. It is further assumed that in many of these subsystems, information is represented along arrays that are tonotopically organized with respect to a simple dimension, such as pitch or duration, or some higher level dimension such as interval size.

The model further assumes that the outputs of such analyses are projected onto arrays in corresponding subdivisions of the auditory memory system. Thus, for example, one subdivision retains values of pitch, and others retain values of duration, loudness, melodic interval size, and so on. Information is stored in parallel in these different subdivisions; however, the time constants of storage for these subdivisions vary considerably. It is further assumed that specific interactions take place within these subdivisions that are analogous to those that occur in systems processing auditory information at the incoming level. The outputs of these different subdivisions then combine during retrieval of information from memory.

Within this framework, a number of different issues may be considered. We can focus on memory for a low-level attribute such as pitch, and inquire concerning how values of this attribute are represented in storage, and also how they are accessed during retrieval. We can also examine how values of different attributes interact with each other in storage and influence each other in retrieval. Here we review the evidence on these issues, focusing largely on the systems underlying memory for pitch and pitch relationships.

A. THE SYSTEM THAT RETAINS ABSOLUTE PITCH VALUES

In considering the characteristics of the system that retains absolute pitch values, a number of hypotheses may be advanced. For example, such memory might simply deteriorate with the passage of time. Another possibility is that pitch information is retained in a general store that is limited in terms of the number of items it can retain, so that memory loss results from a general information overload. As a third possibility, memory for pitch might be the function of an organized system whose elements interact in specific ways.

Let us begin with the following observations. When a tone is presented, and this is followed immediately by another tone that is either identical in pitch to the first or differs by a semitone, most listeners find it very easy to determine whether the two pitches are the same or different. The task continues to be very easy when a silent interval of 6 seconds intervenes between the tones to be compared. Although memory for pitch has been shown to fade gradually with the passage of time (Bachem, 1954; Harris, 1952; Koester, 1945; Rakowski, 1994; Wickelgren, 1966, 1969), the amount of fading during a silent retention interval of 6 sec is so small that it is barely apparent in this situation. However, when eight extra tones are interpolated during the retention interval, the task becomes strikingly difficult; this is true even when the listener is instructed to ignore the interpolated tones. Deutsch (1970a) found that listeners who made no errors in comparing such tone pairs when they were separated by 6 sec of silence made 40% errors when eight tones were interpolated during the retention interval. In a companion experiment, either four, six, or eight tones were interpolated during a retention interval of constant duration, and it was found that the error rate increased with an increase in the number of interpolated tones.

We can conclude that memory for pitch is subject to a small amount of decay with time, and also a large interference effect produced by other tones. What, then, is the basis of this interference effect? One possibility is that the interpolated tones produce attention distraction, and that attention to the tone to be remembered is necessary for memory to be preserved. If this were the case, then the interpolation of other materials would also result in memory loss, provided that these, too, distracted the listener's attention. As another hypothesis, pitch information might be held in a general store of limited capacity, along with other types of material. Further materials that entered this store would then also impair pitch recognition. As a third hypothesis, pitch information might be retained in a specialized system, and memory loss might result from interactions that occur specifically within this system.

In an experiment to examine these different hypotheses, Deutsch (1970c) had subjects compare the pitches of two tones that were separated by a retention interval of 5 sec duration. The test tones were either identical in pitch or they differed by a semitone. In the first condition, six tones were interpolated during the retention interval (Figure 30). In the second, six spoken numbers were interpolated instead. In both these conditions, listeners were asked to ignore the interpolated materials and simply to judge whether the test tones were the same or different in pitch. A third condition was identical to the second, except that the listeners were asked to recall the numbers in addition to comparing the pitches of the test tones; this ensured that the numbers were attended to and entered memory. In a fourth condition, the subjects were asked simply to recall the numbers.

It was found that the interpolated tones produced a substantial impairment in memory for the pitch of the test tone. However, the interpolated numbers produced only a minimal impairment, even when the subjects were asked to recall them. In addition, the error rate in number recall was no higher when the subjects were simultaneously performing the pitch-recognition task than when they could ignore the test tones. This experiment indicated, therefore, that decrements in pitch memory resulting from interpolated tones are due to interactions that take place within a specialized system.

B. FURTHER EVIDENCE FOR A SEPARATE PITCH MEMORY STORE

Further evidence has been obtained that pitch memory is the function of a specialized system. Deutsch (1974) had subjects compare the pitches of two test tones that were separated by a retention interval that contained eight interpolated tones.

FIGURE 30   Examples of tone series used in experiments to examine the effects of interpolated tones on memory for the pitch of a test tone.

In one condition, the interpolated tones were all drawn from the same octave as the test tones, in a second they were all drawn from the octave above, and in a third they were all drawn from the octave below. The interpolated tones produced substantial interference in all conditions; however, the amount of interference varied depending on the octave in which the interpolated tones were placed. The largest performance decrement occurred when the interpolated tones were in the same octave as the test tones, the next largest when they were in the octave above, and the smallest when they were in the octave below. This experiment indicated, therefore, that the amount of interference produced by interpolated tones depends on the pitch relationships between these and the test tones.

Semal, Demany, and colleagues have shown in a number of experiments that interference in pitch memory results from interactions that take place in a system that is sensitive to pitch relationships, but insensitive to other attributes of sound. In one study, Semal and Demany (1991) had subjects compare the pitches of two test tones that were separated by a retention interval containing six interpolated tones. The test tones were sine waves, and in some conditions, the interpolated tones were also sine waves whereas in others they were of complex spectral composition. Substantial decrements in pitch recognition occurred when the interpolated tones were close in pitch to the test tones, regardless of their spectra. However, when the interpolated tones were remote in pitch from the test tones, the amount of memory impairment they produced was substantially smaller, again regardless of their spectra.

In a further experiment, Semal and Demany (1991) studied the effect of interpolating tones that were composed of several harmonics of a missing fundamental. Again, memory performance depended essentially on the pitches of the interpolated tones and not on their spectral composition. Interpolated tones that were close in pitch to the test tones were associated with poor performance, regardless of their spectra. Performance levels were higher when the interpolated tones were remote in pitch from the test tones, again regardless of their spectra.

In yet another experiment, Semal and Demany (1993) found that differences in the amplitudes of the interpolated tones had remarkably little effect on performance. The amount of memory impairment produced by the interpolated tones was not a monotonically increasing function of their amplitudes, neither did maximal interference occur when the amplitudes of the test and interpolated tones were identical. The authors also found that pitch memory performance was affected very little by whether or not the test and interpolated tones had the same time-varying envelopes.

Semal, Demany, Ueda, and Halle (1995) had subjects make memory judgments concerning words that were spoken at different pitches. The test words were separated by a retention interval during which other materials were interpolated. The interpolated materials were either themselves words that were spoken at different pitches, or they were complex tones that were played at different pitches. The amount of memory impairment produced by the interpolated materials was found to be greater when their pitches were close to those of the test words than when they were remote from them, regardless of whether words or tones were interpolated. The authors concluded that the pitches of spoken words are not processed in a specialized "speech module," but rather in a system that is responsible for retaining pitch information, disregarding other attributes of sound.

Other studies have explored the effects on pitch memory of varying the ear of input of the test and interpolated tones. Deutsch (1978c) obtained slightly better memory performance when the test and interpolated tones were presented to different ears rather than to the same ear; however, the difference between these two conditions was fairly small. Kallman, Cameron, Beckstead, and Joyce (1987) confirmed the small advantage produced by delivering the test and interpolated tones to different ears; however, they found that this advantage was present only when the ear of input for the interpolated tones was fixed within a block—the procedure used by Deutsch (1978c). When the ear of input for the interpolated tones varied unpredictably from trial to trial, the advantage disappeared. These experiments provide further evidence that the pitch memory store is remarkably impervious to other attributes of sound.

Finally, Pechmann and Mohr (1992) found that for certain subjects and under certain conditions, information from different memory stores did interfere slightly with pitch recognition. Whereas for musically trained listeners, memory performance was unaffected by the interpolation of spoken words or visual materials, this was not true of musically untrained listeners, who showed small performance decrements when other materials were interpolated. The precise reason for the differences between these two groups of subjects obtained by Pechmann and Mohr remains to be determined.

C. SPECIFIC INTERACTIONS WITHIN THE PITCH MEMORY SYSTEM

We next inquire more specifically into the types of interaction that occur within the system that retains pitch information. In one experiment, Deutsch (1972b) had subjects compare the pitches of two test tones that were separated by a sequence of six interpolated tones. The test tones were either identical in pitch or they differed by a semitone. The effects were explored of placing a tone whose pitch bore a critical relationship to the pitch of the first test tone (the "critical tone") in the second serial position of the interpolated sequence. This distance varied in steps of 1/6 tone between identity and a whole-tone separation.

As shown in Figure 31, when the first test tone and the critical tone were identical in pitch, memory facilitation was produced. As the pitch distance between these two tones increased, errors in pitch recognition also increased; they peaked at 2/3-tone separation and then decreased, returning to baseline at roughly a whole-tone separation.

Based on these findings, it was conjectured that pitch memory is the function of an array whose elements are activated by tones of specific pitch. These elements are organized tonotopically on a log frequency continuum, and inhibitory interac-

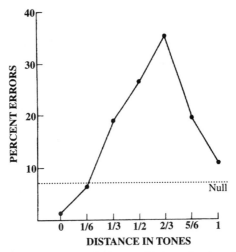

FIGURE 31   Percentages of errors in pitch recognition as a function of the pitch distance between the first test tone and a critical interpolated tone. The line labeled Null shows the error rate in a
control condition where all interpolated tones were at least 1-1/2 tones removed in pitch from the first
test tone. The maximal error rate occurred when the critical interpolated tone was 2/3 tone removed
from the first test tone. (Reprinted with permission from Deutsch, 1972b. ©1972 American Association for the Advancement of Science.)

tions take place along this array that are a function of the distance between the
interacting elements. It was further hypothesized that these interactions are analogous to recurrent lateral inhibitory interactions that occur in systems processing
sensory information at the incoming level (Ratliff, 1965). When these elements
are inhibited, they produce weaker signals, and this in turn results in increased
errors in memory judgment.

A number of observations further support this conjecture. For example, the
relative frequency range over which memory disruption occurs corresponds well
with the range over which centrally acting lateral inhibition has been found in
physiological studies of the auditory system (Klinke, Boerger, & Gruber, 1970).
As further evidence, error rates in pitch memory judgment cumulate when two
critical tones are interpolated, placed one on either side of the first test tone along
the pitch continuum (Deutsch, 1973a). Analogously, lateral inhibitory effects cumulate when two inhibitory stimuli are placed, one on either side of the test stimulus along a visuospatial continuum (Ratliff, 1965).

If the pitch memory system were indeed organized as a recurrent lateral inhibitory network, one might also expect to find evidence for disinhibition: If a tone
that was inhibiting memory for another tone were itself inhibited by a third tone,
memory for the first tone should return. Specifically, in sequences where the test
tones were identical in pitch, if two critical tones were interpolated, one always
2/3-tone removed from the test tone and the other further removed along the pitch

continuum, errors should vary as a function of the pitch relationship between the two critical tones. The error rate should be highest when these two tones are identical in pitch, decline as the second critical tone moves away from the first, dip maximally at a 2/3-tone separation, and then return to baseline. In other words, the curve produced should be roughly the inverse of the curve plotting the original disruptive effect.

To test this prediction, Deutsch and Feroe (1975) performed an experiment in which subjects compared the pitches of two test tones when these were separated by a sequence of six interpolated tones. A tone was always placed in the second serial position of the interpolated sequence whose pitch was 2/3 tone removed from that of the first test tone; that is, in a relationship expected to produce maximal inhibition. Errors were plotted as a function of the pitch of a second critical tone, which was placed in the fourth serial position, whose pitch relationship to the first critical tone varied in 1/6-tone steps between identity and a whole-tone separation.

As can be seen in Figure 32, a systematic return of memory was indeed obtained. The error rate in sequences where the second critical tone was identical in pitch to the first was significantly higher than baseline, and the error rate where the two critical tones were separated by 2/3 tone was significantly lower than baseline.

A first-order inhibitory function was obtained in a companion experiment, and this was used to calculate the theoretical disinhibition function, assuming that the error rate was determined simply by the strength of the signal produced by the element underlying the first test tone. As also shown in Figure 32, there was a good correspondence between the disinhibition function derived experimentally and the one derived theoretically on the lateral inhibition model. This experiment therefore provided strong evidence that pitch memory elements are indeed arranged as a lateral inhibitory network, analogous to those handling sensory information at the incoming level.

D. ITEM AND ORDER INFORMATION

There is a further effect that causes impairment in pitch memory. When two test tones differ in pitch, and the interpolated sequence includes a critical tone whose pitch is identical to that of the second test tone, increased errors of misrecognition result. This increase is greater when the critical tone is placed early in the interpolated sequence rather than late (Deutsch, 1970b, 1972a; see also Butler & Ward, 1988).

In order to explain this effect, it was conjectured that pitch information is retained both along both a pitch continuum and also along a temporal or order continuum, so as to produce a memory distribution such as shown in Figure 33. According to this conjecture, as time proceeds, this memory distribution spreads along both continua, but particularly along the temporal continuum. As a result of this spread, when the second test tone is presented, the subject recognizes that it

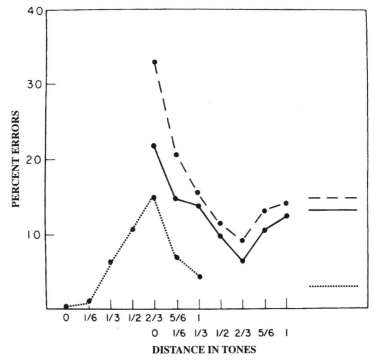

FIGURE 32   Percentages of errors in pitch recognition obtained experimentally and predicted theoretically. Dotted line displays percentage of errors in a baseline experiment that varied the pitch relationship between the first test tone and a critical interpolated tone. (Dotted line at right displays percentage of errors where no tone was interpolated in the critical range.) Solid line displays percentage of errors in an experiment where a tone that was 2/3 tone removed from the first test tone was always interpolated. Errors are plotted as a function of the pitch relationship between this tone and a second critical interpolated tone that was further removed along the pitch continuum. Dashed line displays percentage of errors for the same experimental conditions predicted theoretically from the lateral inhibition model. (Solid and dashed lines at right display percentages of errors obtained experimentally and predicted theoretically where no further critical tone was interpolated.) (Adapted from Deutsch & Feroe, 1975).

had occurred in the sequence, but is uncertain when it had occurred, and so sometimes erroneously assumes that it had been the first test tone. This hypothesis also would explain the dependence of the effect on the serial position of the critical tone.

A later experiment lent further support to this conjecture. In this experiment, the pitch difference between the first and second test tones was varied, and errors were again plotted as a function of the pitch relationship between the first test tone and the critical tone. It was found, as predicted, that in sequences where the critical tone and the second test tone were on the same side of the first test tone along the pitch continuum, then as the pitch of the second test tone shifted along this contin-

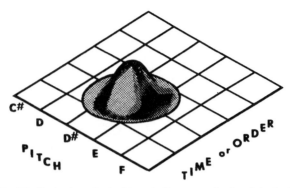

FIGURE 33 Distribution hypothesized to underlie memory for the pitch of a tone. See text for details. (Adapted from Deutsch, 1972a.)

uum, the peak of errors produced by the critical tone shifted in parallel (Deutsch, 1975d).

E. MEMORY ENHANCEMENT THROUGH REPETITION

The conjecture that pitch memory is the function of a temporal or order continuum as well as a pitch continuum gives rise to a further prediction: When the critical tone is identical in pitch to the first test tone, memory performance should be enhanced. More specifically, when the critical tone and the first test tone are identical in pitch, their memory distributions should overlap along the temporal continuum, and this should in turn produce a stronger memory trace for the first test tone (Deutsch, 1972a). This enhancement in performance should be greater when the critical tone is placed early in the interpolated sequence rather than late. Such a pattern of results was indeed obtained in a number of experiments (e.g., Deutsch, 1970b, 1972a, 1975b).

F. OCTAVE GENERALIZATION

As described earlier, there is considerable evidence that pitch is represented along arrays of both pitch height and pitch class. This leads us to inquire whether interference in pitch memory takes place along a pitch height array, or a pitch class array, or whether both such arrays are involved.

In one experiment, Deutsch (1973b) had subjects compare the pitches of two tones that were separated by six interpolated tones. The experiment explored the effects of interpolating tones that bore the same relationship to the test tones as had been found earlier to produce memory disruption, but that were further displaced by an octave. In sequences where the test tones were identical, the effects were studied of including two critical tones, one a semitone higher than the first test tone and the other a semitone lower, but that were further displaced by an octave. In sequences where the test tones differed, the effects were studied of in-cluding a critical tone that was identical in pitch to the second test tone, but again displaced by an octave.

Substantial generalization of disruptive effect resulted from tones that were displaced an octave higher, and a weaker effect from tones that were displaced an octave lower. However, the increase in errors was largest from tones that were placed in the middle octave. It was concluded that disruptive effects in pitch mem-ory take place both along an array of pitch height and also along an array of pitch class.

G. PITCH PROXIMITY AND PITCH MEMORY

Memory for pitch is also influenced by more general relationships between the test and interpolated tones, and among the interpolated tones themselves. For ex-ample, in listening to sequences such as we have been describing, the listener processes not only the individual tones, but also the melodic intervals between them. These intervals then provide a framework of pitch relationships to which the test tones can be anchored. So interpolated sequences that form melodic configu-rations that are more easily processed should be associated with enhanced perfor-mance on these tasks.

As described in Chapter 9, there is considerable evidence that melodic patterns are processed more effectively when these are composed of small rather than large intervals, in accordance with the principle of proximity. One might then hypoth-esize that in our present situation also, interpolated sequences that are composed of small melodic intervals would be associated with higher performance levels than those composed of larger ones. In an experiment to test this hypothesis, Deutsch (1978a) had subjects compare the pitches of two test tones when these were separated by a sequence of six interpolated tones. There were four conditions in the experiment. In the first, the interpolated tones were chosen at random from within a one-octave range, and they were also ordered at random. The second condition was identical to the first, except that the interpolated tones were ar-ranged in monotonically ascending or descending order, so that the average size of the melodic intervals was reduced. In the third condition, the interpolated tones were chosen at random from within a two-octave range, and they were also or-dered at random. The fourth condition was identical to the third, except that the interpolated tones were arranged in monotonically ascending or descending order.

As shown in Figure 34, the error rate was found to increase with an increase in the average size of the melodic intervals formed by the interpolated tones. There was no evidence that monotonic ordering of the interpolated tones had any effect, beyond that of producing a smaller average interval size.

It has been shown that there is a striking cross-cultural tendency for the fre-quency of occurrence of a melodic interval to be inversely correlated with its size (Deutsch, 1978d; Dowling, 1967; Fucks, 1962; Jeffries, 1974; Merriam, 1964; Ortmann, 1926). One might hypothesize that this tendency is based on an increas-

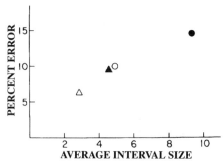

FIGURE 34   Percentages of errors in pitch recognition as a function of the average size of the melodic interval in the sequence. Open triangle: Interpolated tones span a one-octave range and are ordered monotonically. Filled triangle: Interpolated tones span a one-octave range and are ordered at random. Open circle: Interpolated tones span a two-octave range and are ordered monotonically. Filled circle: Interpolated tones span a two-octave range and are ordered at random. (From Deutsch, 1978a.)

ing difficulty in processing melodic intervals as interval size increases. As indicated in the present experiment, this should in turn result in decreased accuracy of pitch recognition judgment.

In a related study, Deutsch (1974) compared the effects on pitch recognition of placing the interpolated tones in different octaves. In the condition where the interpolated tones were drawn from the same octave as the test tones, the error rate was higher than in conditions where they were drawn consistently from the octave above or the octave below. However, the error rate was highest when the interpolated tones were drawn from both the higher and the lower octaves. In this last condition, the interpolated tones formed very large intervals, and as a result, listeners were unable to make use of frameworks of pitch relationships to which the test tones could be anchored. Olson and Hanson (1977) also found that increased distances between the test and interpolated tones were associated with increased errors in pitch recognition (see also Deutsch & Boulanger, 1984).

H. MEMORY FOR TIMBRE

We have presented evidence that the system underlying memory for pitch is subject to specific interactive effects that depend on the pitch relationships between the test and interpolated tones, and that it is remarkably insensitive to other attributes of sound. Starr and Pitt (1997) obtained evidence that the system underlying memory for timbre has analogous characteristics. Their study made use of sets of tones, each of which consisted of a fundamental together with three adjacent harmonics. Thus one type of tone consisted of the fundamental together with harmonics 2, 3, and 4; another consisted of the fundamental together with harmonics 3, 4, and 5; and so on. Eight values of timbre were generated in accordance with this algorithm, and in this way a "spectral similarity dimension" was created. It was found in a preliminary study that tones were judged to be more different in timbre as the number of steps separating them along this dimension increased.

Starr and Pitt employed a paradigm that was similar to the one used in the pitch memory studies described earlier. Subjects made comparison judgments between two test tones when these were separated by a retention interval during which extra tones were interpolated. The test tones were either identical in timbre or they differed by three steps along the spectral similarity dimension. The amount of memory impairment was found to increase monotonically as the similarity in timbre between the first test tone and the interpolated tones increased. When the amount of pitch distance between the test and interpolated tones was also varied, the effect of timbre similarity persisted regardless of this pitch distance, and there was only a negligible effect of pitch distance on memory for timbre.

The authors also studied the effects of including a second interpolated timbre in the intervening sequence, and they found that this caused the interference effect of the first interpolated timbre either to increase or to decrease, depending on the distances in timbre involved. They concluded that these findings reflected an effect of disinhibition that is analogous to that found by Deutsch and Feroe (1975) in memory for pitch.

I. MEMORY FOR PITCH RELATIONSHIPS

There is evidence that the system underlying memory for pitch relationships is organized in ways that are similar to the one underlying memory for absolute pitch values. As described earlier, Deutsch (1969) has suggested that interval information is place-coded in the nervous system. Deutsch (1975a) further proposed that this information is projected onto a memory array, such that memory for intervals is the function of a continuum whose elements are activated by the simultaneous or successive presentation of pairs of tones. Tone pairs standing in the same ratio project onto the same elements, and so onto the same point along the continuum; tone pairs standing in closely similar ratios project onto adjacent points along the continuum, and so on. It was further proposed that interactive effects take place along this memory continuum that are analogous to those occurring in the system that retains absolute pitch values. Such effects include memory enhancement through repetition and similarity-based interference.

In considering this issue, informal studies by the author indicated that musically untrained listeners had difficulty in judging directly whether the intervals formed by two pairs of tones were the same or different in size. However, when the same listeners made recognition judgments concerning absolute pitch values, their judgments were strongly influenced by the relational context in which the test tones were placed: They tended to judge test tones as identical in pitch when they were presented in the context of identical harmonic intervals and to judge them as different when they were placed in the context of different intervals (see also Deutsch & Roll, 1974). Given these findings, an experiment was performed to examine indirectly whether memory for harmonic intervals was subject to specific interactive effects similar to those found in memory for absolute pitch values (Deutsch, 1978b).

Subjects compared the pitches of two test tones when these were both accompanied by tones of lower pitch. The test tones were either identical in pitch or they differed by a semitone. However, the tone accompanying the first test tone was always identical in pitch to the tone accompanying the second test tone. So when the test tones were identical, the intervals formed by the test-tone combinations were also identical. Similarly, when the test tones differed, the intervals formed by the test-tone combinations also differed.

The test-tone combinations were separated by a sequence of six interpolated tones. The tones in the second and fourth serial positions of the interpolated sequence were also accompanied by tones of lower pitch. It was found that when the intervals formed by the interpolated combinations were identical in size to the interval formed by the first test combination, the error rate was lower than when the intervals formed by the interpolated combinations were chosen at random. Furthermore, when the intervals formed by the interpolated combinations differed in size by a semitone from the interval formed by the first test combination, the error rate was higher than when the sizes of the intervals formed by the interpolated combinations were chosen at random.

This experiment indicated that effects analogous to those in the system retaining absolute pitch information also occur in the system retaining abstracted pitch values; namely, memory enhancement through repetition and similarity-based interference.

J. MEMORY FOR DURATION

An experiment by Deutsch (1986b) on memory for duration showed that this has characteristics that are analogous to those found in memory for pitch. Subjects were presented with a pair of blips that defined a first test duration, followed by another pair of blips that defined a second test duration, and they judged whether the second test duration was identical to the first, or longer, or shorter.

In one set of conditions, a series of additional blips was interpolated during the retention interval; these blips defined durations that were in the same range as the test durations. When the interpolated durations were identical to the first test duration, performance levels were higher than when no blips were interpolated. This effect was analogous to the enhancement of performance in pitch memory that occurred when a tone of identical pitch to the first test tone was interpolated. The error rate was also considerably higher when the interpolated blips defined durations that were slightly removed from the first test duration, and judgments reflected distortions in memory for the first test duration in the direction of the interpolated durations. This effect was analogous to the large misrecognition effect that occurred in memory for pitch when a tone that was identical in pitch to the second test tone was interpolated (Deutsch, 1970b, 1972a).

K. INTERACTIONS BETWEEN MEMORY SYSTEMS IN RETRIEVAL

On the hypothesis that memory for different attributes is a function of a number of parallel subsystems, the question arises as to how the outputs of these subsystems influence each other in retrieval. For example, we might expect that judgments of sameness or difference between test tone pitches would be biased by sameness or difference in some other attribute of the tones.

In one experiment, Deutsch and Roll (1974) investigated the effect on pitch memory judgments of manipulating the harmonic relational context in which the test tones were placed. Subjects compared the pitches of two test tones that were both accompanied by tones of lower pitch. The test-tone combinations were separated by a retention interval during which six extra tones were interpolated. In some conditions, the harmonic intervals formed by the test-tone combinations were identical, and in others they differed; these patterns of relationship were present both when the test tones were identical and also when they differed. It was found that relational context had a strong influence on pitch memory judgments. When the test tones were identical, but were placed in different relational contexts, there was an increased tendency for their pitches to be judged as different. Further, when the test tones differed, but were placed in the identical relational context, there was an increased tendency for their pitches to be judged as identical. Further, when the test tones differed, but the test-tone combinations formed intervals that were inversions of each other, there resulted an increase in errors of misrecognition. It was concluded that this misrecognition effect was based on the perceptual equivalence of the inverted intervals (see Section II).

Deutsch (1982) performed an analogous experiment to study the effect of melodic relational context. Subjects compared the pitches of two tones that were each preceded by tones of lower pitch. The test-tone combinations were again separated by a retention interval during which six extra tones were interpolated. A strong effect of melodic context was demonstrated, which was analogous to the effect found for harmonic relational context.

VI. CONCLUSION

In the foregoing pages, we have considered the rules whereby we form abstractions based on pitch, and also how we retain pitch information at different levels of abstraction. Where appropriate, we have considered underlying neurophysiological mechanisms, and we have also drawn on insights provided by music theorists. We have provided evidence that memory for pitch and for low-level pitch relationships is based on a number of highly specialized systems, and that at higher levels pitch information is retained in the form of hierarchies. These findings have contributed to the groundwork on which an understanding of the processing of pitch combinations can be based.

REFERENCES

Babbitt, M. (1960). Twelve-tone invariants as compositional determinants. *The Musical Quarterly, 46,* 246–259.

Babbitt, M. (1965). The structure and function of musical theory. *College Music Symposium 5,* 10–21.

Bachem, A. (1948). Note on Neu's review of the literature on absolute pitch. *Psychological Bulletin, 45,* 161–162.

Bachem, A. (1954). Time factors in relative and absolute pitch determination. *Journal of the Acoustical Society of America, 26,* 751–753.

Baird, J . W. (1917). Memory for absolute pitch: Studies in psychology. In *Titchener commemorative volume* (p. 69). Worcester, MA.

Balzano, G. (1980). The group-theoretic description of 12-fold and microtonal pitch systems. *Computer Music Journal, 4,* 66–84.

Bartlett, J. C., & Dowling, W. J. (1980). Recognition of transposed melodies: A key-distance effect in developmental perspective. *Journal of Experimental Psychology: Human Perception & Performance, 6,* 501–515.

Bharucha, J. J. (1984a). Anchoring effects in music: the resolution of dissonance. *Cognitive Psychology, 16,* 485–518.

Bharucha, J. J. (1984b). Event hierarchies, tonal hierarchies, and assimilation: A reply to Deutsch and Dowling. *Journal of Experimental Psychology: General, 113,* 421–425 .

Bharucha, J. J. (1987). Music cognition and perceptual facilitation: A connectionist approach. *Music Perception, 5,* 1–30.

Bharucha, J. J. (1991). Pitch, harmony and neural nets: A psychological perspective. In P. Todd & D. G. Loy (Eds.), *Music and connectionism.* Cambridge, MA: MIT Press.

Bharucha, J. J., & Krumhansl, C. L. (1983). The representation of harmonic structure in music: Hierarchies of stability as a function of context. *Cognition, 13,* 63–102.

Blackwell, H. R., & Schlosberg, H. (1943). Octave generalization, pitch discrimination, and loudness thresholds in the white rat. *Journal of Experimental Psychology, 33,* 407–419.

Boomslitter, P., & Creel, W. (1961). The long pattern hypothesis in harmony and hearing. *Journal of Music Theory, 5*(2), 2–30.

Bower, G. H., & Springston, F. (1970). Pauses as recoding points in letter series. *Journal of Experimental Psychology, 83,* 421–430.

Bower, G., & Winzenz, D. (1969). Group structure, coding and memory for digit series. *Journal of Experimental Psychology, 80*(2, Pt 2), 1–17.

Bregman, A. S. (1978). The formation of auditory streams. In J. Requin (Ed.), *Attention and performance* (Vol. VII). Hillsdale, NJ: Erlbaum.

Brown, H. (1988). The interplay of set content and temporal context in a functional theory of tonality perception. *Music Perception, 5,* 219–250.

Brown, H., & Butler, D. (1981). Diatonic trichords as minimal cue-cells. *In Theory Only, 5,* 39–55.

Brown, H., Butler, D., & Jones, M. R. (1994). Musical and temporal influences on key discovery. *Music Perception , 11,* 371–407.

Browne, R. (1981). Tonal implications of the diatonic set. *In Theory Only, 5,* 3–21.

Butler, D. (1983). The initial identification of tonal centers in music. In J. Sloboda & D. Rogers (Eds.), *Acquisition of symbolic skills.* New York: Plenum Press.

Butler, D. (1989). Describing the perception of tonality in music: A critique of the tonal hierarchy theory and a proposal for a theory of intervallic rivalry. *Music Perception, 6,* 219–241.

Butler, D. (1990). Reply to Carol Krumhansl. *Music Perception, 7,* 325–338.

Butler, D. (1992). *The musician's guide to perception and cognition.* New York: Schirmer.

Butler, D., & Brown, H. (1984). Tonal structure versus function: Studies of the recognition of harmonic motion. *Music Perception, 2,* 6–24.

Butler, D., & Ward, W. D. (1988). Effacing the memory of musical pitch. *Music Perception, 5,* 251–260.

Charbonneau, G., & Risset, J. C. (1973). Circularité de jugements de hauteur sonore. *Comptes Rendus de l'Academie des Sciences, Serie B, 277,* 623.

Collins, A. M., & Quillian, M. R. (1972). How to make a language user. In E. Tulving & W. Donaldson (Eds.), *Organization of memory*. New York: Academic Press.

Craik, F. I. M., & Lockhart, R. S. (1972). Levels of processing: A framework for memory research. *Journal of Verbal Learning and Verbal Behavior, 11,* 671–684.

Croonen, W. L. (1994). Effects of length, tonal structure, and contour in the recognition of tone series. *Perception & Psychophysics, 55,* 623–632.

Cuddy, L. L., & Cohen, A. J. (1976). Recognition of transposed melodic sequences. *Quarterly Journal of Experimental Psychology, 28,* 255–270.

Cuddy, L. L., Cohen, A. L., & Mewhort, D. J. (1981). Perception of structure in short melodic sequences. *Journal of Experimental Psychology: Human Perception & Performance, 7,* 869–883.

Dawe, L. A. Platt. J. R., & Welsh, E. (1998). Spectral-motion aftereffects and the tritone paradox among Canadian subjects. *Perception & Psychophysics, 60,* 209–220.

Deese, V., & Grindley, G. C. (1947). The transposition of visual patterns. *British Journal of Psychology, 37,* 152–163.

Demany, L., & Armand, P. (1984). The perceptual reality of tone chroma in early infancy. *Journal of the Acoustical Society of America, 76,* 57–66.

Deutsch, D. (1969). Music recognition. *Psychological Review, 76,* 300–307.

Deutsch, D. (1970a). *The deterioration of pitch information in memory*. Unpublished doctoral dissertation, University of California at San Diego.

Deutsch, D. (1970b). Dislocation of tones in a musical sequence: A memory illusion. *Nature, 226,* 286.

Deutsch, D. (1970c). Tones and numbers: Specificity of interference in short-term memory. *Science, 168,* 1604–1605.

Deutsch, D. (1972a). Effect of repetition of standard and comparison tones on recognition memory for pitch. *Journal of Experimental Psychology, 93,* 156–162.

Deutsch, D. (1972b). Mapping of interactions in the pitch memory store. *Science, 175,* 1020–1022.

Deutsch, D. (1972c). Octave generalization and tune recognition. *Perception & Psychophysics, 11,* 411–412.

Deutsch, D (1973a). Interference in memory between tones adjacent in the musical scale. *Journal of Experimental Psychology, 100,* 228–231.

Deutsch, D. (1973b). Octave generalization of specific interference effects in memory for tonal pitch. *Perception & Psychophysics, 13,* 271–175.

Deutsch, D. (1974). Generality of interference by tonal stimuli in recognition memory for pitch. *Quarterly Journal of Experimental Psychology, 26,* 229–234.

Deutsch, D. (1975a). Auditory memory. *Canadian Journal of Psychology, 29,* 87–105.

Deutsch, D. (1975b). Facilitation by repetition in recognition memory for tonal pitch. *Memory & Cognition, 3,* 263–266.

Deutsch, D. (1975c). Musical illusions. *Scientific American, 233,* 92–104.

Deutsch, D. (1975d). The organization of short-term memory for a single acoustic attribute. In D. Deutsch & J. A. Deutsch (Eds.), *Short-term memory* (pp. 107–151). New York: Academic Press.

Deutsch. D. (1977). Memory and attention in music. In M. Critchley & R. A. Henson (Eds.), *Music and the brain* (pp. 95–130). London: Heinemann.

Deutsch. D. (1978a). Delayed pitch comparisons and the principle of proximity. *Perception & Psychophysics, 23,* 227–230.

Deutsch, D. (1978b). Interactive effects in memory for harmonic intervals. *Perception & Psychophysics, 24,* 7–10.

Deutsch, D. (1978c). Interference in pitch memory as a function of ear of input. *Quarterly Journal of experimental Psychology, 30,* 283–287.

Deutsch, D. (1978d). The psychology of music. In E. C. Carterette & M. P. Friedman (Eds.), *Handbook of perception* (Vol. X, pp. 191–218). New York: Academic Press.

Deutsch, D. (1979). Octave generalization and the consolidation of melodic information. *Canadian Journal of Psychology, 33,* 201–205.

Deutsch, D. (1980). The processing of structured and unstructured tonal sequences. *Perception & Psychophysics, 28,* 381–389.

Deutsch, D. (1982). The influence of melodic context on pitch recognition judgment. *Perception & Psychophysics, 31,* 407–410.

Deutsch, D. (1984). Two issues concerning tonal hierarchies: Comment on Castellano, Bharucha, and Krumhansl. *Journal of Experimental Psychology: General, 113,* 413–416.

Deutsch, D. (1986a). A musical paradox. *Music Perception, 3,* 275–280.

Deutsch, D. (1986b). Recognition of durations embedded in temporal patterns. *Perception & Psychophysics, 39,* 179–187.

Deutsch, D. (1987). The tritone paradox: Effects of spectral variables. *Perception & Psychophysics, 42,* 563–575.

Deutsch, D. (1988a). Pitch class and perceived height: Some paradoxes and their implications. In E. Narmour & R. Solie (Eds.), *Explorations in music, the arts, and ideas: Essays in honor of Leonard B. Meyer.* Stuyvesant: Pendragon Press.

Deutsch, D. (1988b). The semitone paradox. *Music Perception, 6,* 115–134.

Deutsch, D. (1991). The tritone paradox: An influence of language on music perception. *Music Perception, 8,* 335–347.

Deutsch, D. (1992). Paradoxes of musical pitch. *Scientific American, 267,* 88–95.

Deutsch, D. (1994). The tritone paradox: Some further geographical correlates. *Music Perception, 12,* 125–136.

Deutsch, D. (1995). *Musical illusions and paradoxes* [CD]. Philomel Records, P. O. Box 12189, La Jolla, CA 92039-2189.

Deutsch, D. (1996). Mothers and their children hear a musical illusion in strikingly similar ways. *Journal of the Acoustical Society of America, 99,* 2482.

Deutsch D., & Boulanger, R. C. (1984). Octave equivalence and the processing of tonal sequences. *Music Perception, 3,* 40–51.

Deutsch, D., & Feroe, J. (1975). Disinhibition in pitch memory. *Perception & Psychophysics, 17,* 320–324.

Deutsch, D., & Feroe, J. (1981). The internal representation of pitch sequences in tonal music. *Psychological Review, 88,* 503–522.

Deutsch, D. Kuyper, W. L., & Fisher, Y. (1987). The tritone paradox: its presence and form of distribution in a general population. *Music Perception , 5,* 79–92.

Deutsch, D. Moore, F. R., & Dolson, M. (1986). The perceived height of octave-related complexes. *Journal of the Acoustical Society of America, 80,* 1346–1353.

Deutsch, D., North, T., & Ray, L. (1990). The tritone paradox: Correlate with the listener's vocal range for speech. *Music Perception, 7,* 371–384.

Deutsch, D., & Roll, P. L. (1974). Error patterns in delayed pitch comparison as a function of relational context. *Journal of Experimental Psychology, 103,* 1027–1034.

Dewar, K. M., Cuddy, C. L., & Mewhort, D. J. K. (1977). Recognition memory for single tones with and without context. *Journal of Experimental Psychology: Human Learning and Memory, 3,* 60–67.

Dewitt, L. A., & Crowder, R. G. (1986). Recognition of novel melodies after brief delays. *Music Perception, 3,* 259–274.

Dibben, N. (1994). The cognitive reality of hierarchic structure in tonal and atonal music. *Music Perception, 12,* 1–25.

Divenyi, P. L., & Hirsh, I. J. (1978). Some figural properties of auditory patterns. *Journal of the Acoustical Society of America, 64,* 1369–1385.

Dolson, M. (1994). The pitch of speech as function of linguistic community. *Music Perception, 11,* 321–331.

Dowling, W. J. (1967). *Rhythmic fission and the perceptual organization of tone sequences.* Unpublished doctoral dissertation, Harvard University, Cambridge, MA.

Dowling, W. J. (1973). Rhythmic groups and subjective chunks in memory for melodies. *Perception & Psychophysics, 4,* 37–40.

Dowling, W. J. (1978). Scale and contour: Two components of a theory of memory for melodies. *Psychological Review, 85,* 342–354.

Dowling, W. J. (1986). Context effects on melody recognition: Scale-step and interval representation. *Music Perception, 3,* 281–296.

Dowling, W. J. (1991). Tonal strength and melody recognition after long and short delays. *Perception & Psychophysics, 50,* 305–313.

Dowling, W. J., & Fujitani, D. S. (1971). Contour, interval and pitch recognition in memory for melodies. *Journal of the Acoustical Society of America, 49,* 524–531.

Drobisch, M. (1855). Uber musikalische Tonbestimmung und Temperatur. In *Abhandlungen der Koniglich sachsischen Gesellschaft der Wissenschaften zu Leipzig. Vierter Band: Abhandlungen der mathematisch-physischen Classe. Zweiter Band* (pp. 3–121). Leipzig: S. Hirzel.

Edelman, G. M., Gall, W. E., & Cowan, W. M. (1988). *Auditory function: Neurobiological bases of hearing.* New York: Wiley.

Edworthy, J. (1985). Melodic contour and musical structure. In P. Howell, I. Cross, & R. J. West (Eds.), *Musical structure and cognition* (pp. 169–188). Orlando, FL: Academic Press.

Ernst, G. W., & Newell, A. (1969). *GPS: A case study in generality and problem solving.* New York: Academic Press.

Estes, W. K. (1972). An associative basis for coding and organization in memory. In A. W. Melton & E. Martin (Eds.), *Coding processes in human memory.* Washington, DC: Winston.

Forte, A. (1973). *The structure of atonal music.* New Haven, Connecticut: Yale University Press.

Francès, R. (1988). *The perception of music* (W. J. Dowling, Trans.). Hillsdale, NJ: Erlbaum. (Original work published 1958)

Fucks, W. (1962). Mathematical analysis of the formal structure of music. *Institute of Radio Engineers Transactions on Information Theory, 8,* 225–228.

Gagné, R. M. (1962). The acquisition of knowledge. *Psychological Review, 67,* 355–365.

Giangrande, J. (1998). The tritone paradox: Effects of pitch class and position of the spectral envelope. *Music Perception, 13,* 253–264.

Greeno, J. G., & Simon, H. A. (1974). Processes for sequence production. *Psychological Review, 81,* 187–196.

Hall, D. (1974). Quantitative evaluation of musical scale tunings. *American Journal of Physics, 48,* 543–552.

Halpern, A. R. (1989). Memory for the absolute pitch of familiar songs. *Memory & Cognition, 17,* 572–581.

Handel, S. (1973). Temporal segmentation of repeating auditory patterns. *Journal of Experimental Psychology, 101,* 46–54.

Hanson, A. R., & Riseman, E. M. (Eds.) (1978). *Computer vision systems.* New York: Academic Press.

Harris, J. D. (1952). The decline of pitch discrimination with time. *Journal of Experimental Psychology, 43,* 96–99.

Helmholtz, H. von. (1954). *On the sensations of tone as a physiological basis for the theory of music* (2nd English ed.) New York: Dover. (Original work published 1859)

Helmholtz, H. von. (1844). The origin of the correct interpretations of our sensory impressions. *Zeitchrift für Psychologie und Physiologie der Sinnesorgane, 7,* 81–96.

Hershman, D. P. (1994). Key distance effects in ecological contexts. In I. Deliège (Ed.), *Proceedings of the 3rd International Conference on Music Perception and Cognition, Liège* (pp. 243–244). Liège: ICMPC.

Hubel, D. H., & Wiesel, T. N. (1962). Receptive fields, binocular interaction and functional architecture in the cat's visual cortex. *Journal of Physiology, 160,* 106–154.

Humphreys, L. F. (1939). Generalization as a function of method of reinforcement. *Journal of Experimental Psychology, 25,* 361–372.

Idson, W. L., & Massaro, D. W. (1978). A bidimensional model of pitch in the recognition of melodies. *Perception & Psychophysics, 24,* 551–565.

Janata, P., & Reisberg, D. (1988). Response-time measures as a means of exploring tonal hierarchies. *Music Perception, 6,* 161–172.

Jeffries, T. B. (1974). Relationship of interval frequency count to ratings of melodic intervals. *Journal of Experimental Psychology, 102,* 903–905.

Jones, M. R. (1974). Cognitive representations of serial patterns. In B. H. Kantowitz (Ed.), *Human information processing: Tutorials in performance and cognition*. Hillsdale, NJ: Erlbaum.

Jones, M. R. (1978). Auditory patterns: Studies in the perception of structure. In E. C. Carterette & M. P. Friedman (Eds.), *Handbook of perception: Vol. VIII. Perceptual coding*. New York: Academic Press.

Julesz, B., & Hirsh, I. J. (1972). Visual and auditory perception: An essay of comparison. In E. E. David & P. B. Denes (Eds.), *Human communication: A unified view*. New York: McGraw-Hill.

Kallman, H. J., Cameron, P. A., Beckstead, J. W., & Joyce, E. (1987). Ear of input as a determinant of pitch-memory interference. *Memory & Cognition, 15*, 454–460.

Kallman, H. J., & Massaro, D. W. (1979). Tone chroma is functional in melody recognition. *Perception & Psychophysics, 26*, 32–36.

Klinke, R., Boerger, G., & Gruber, J. (1970). The influence of the frequency relation in dichotic stimulation upon the cochlear nucleus activity. In R. Plomp & G. F. Smoorenburg (Eds.), *Frequency analysis and periodicity detection in hearing*. Sijthoff: Leiden.

Knudsen, E. I., du Lac, S., & Esterly, S. D. (1987). Computational maps in the brain. *Annual Review of Neuroscience, 10*, 41–65.

Koester, T. (1945). The time error in pitch and loudness discrimination as a function of time interval and stimulus level [Special issue]. *Archives of Psychology, 297*.

Koffka, K. (1935). *Principles of Gestalt psychology*. New York: Harcourt.

Krumhansl, C. L. (1979). The psychological representation of musical pitch in a tonal context. *Cognitive Psychology, 11*, 346–374.

Krumhansl, C. L. (1990a). *Cognitive foundations of musical pitch*. New York: Oxford University Press.

Krumhansl, C. L. (1990b). Tonal hierarchies and rare intervals in music cognition. *Music Perception, 7*, 309–324.

Krumhansl. C. L., Bharucha, J. J., & Kessler, E. (1982). Perceived harmonic structure of chords in three related musical keys. *Journal of Experimental Psychology: Human Perception and Performance, 8*, 24–36.

Krumhansl, C. L., & Castellano, M. A. (1983). Dynamic processes in music perception. *Memory & Cognition, 11*, 325–334.

Krumhansl, C. L., Sandell, G. J., & Sergeant, D. C. (1987). The perception of tone hierarchies and mirror forms in twelve-tone serial music. *Music Perception, 5*, 31–78.

Leewenberg, E. L. (1971). A perceptual coding language for visual and auditory patterns. *American Journal of Psychology, 84*, 307–349.

Lerdahl, F. (1988). Tonal pitch space. *Music Perception, 5*, 315–349.

Lerdahl, F., & Jackendoff, R. (1983). *A generative theory of tonal music*. Cambridge, MA: MIT Press.

Levitin, D. (1994). Absolute memory for musical pitch: Evidence from the production of learned melodies. *Perception & Psychophysics, 56*, 414–423.

Longuet-Higgins, H. C. (1962a). Letter to a musical friend. *Music Review, 23*, 244–248.

Longuet-Higgins, H. C. (1962b). Second letter to a musical friend. *Music Review, 23*, 271–280.

Longuet-Higgins, H. C. (1978). The perception of music. *Interdisciplinary Science Reviews, 3*, 148–156.

Mach, E. (1959). *The analysis of sensations and the relation of the physical to the psychical* (C. M. Williams, Trans.; W. Waterlow, review and supplement). New York: Dover. (Original work published in German, 1906)

McLean. R. S., & Gregg, L. W. (1967). Effects of induced chunking on temporal aspects of serial retention. *Journal of Experimental Psychology, 74*, 455–459.

Merriam, A. P. (1964). *The anthropology of music*. Evanston, IL: Northwestern University Press.

Meyer, L. B. (1956). *Emotion and meaning in music*. Chicago, IL: University of Chicago Press.

Meyer, L. B. (1973). *Explaining music: Essays and explorations*. Berkeley, CA: University of California Press.

Meyer, M. (1904). On the attributes of the sensations. *Psychological Review, 11*, 83–103.

Meyer, M. (1914). Review of G. Révész, "Zur Grundleguncy der Tonpsychologie." *Psychological Bulletin, 11*, 349–352.

Miller, G. A., & Chomsky, N. (1963). Finitary models of language users. *Handbook of Mathematical Psychology, 2,* 419–493.

Miller, G. A., Galanter, E. H., & Pribram, K. H. (1960). *Plans and the structure of behavior.* New York: Holt.

Mueller, G. E., & Schumann, F. (1894). Experimentelle Beitrage zur Untersuchung des Gedächtnisses. *Zeitschrift fur Psychologie und Physiologie der Sinnesorgane, 6,* 81–190, 257–339.

Narmour, E. (1990). *The analysis and cognition of basic melodic structures.* Chicago: University of Chicago Press.

Navon, D. (1977). Forest before trees: The precedence of global features in visual perception. *Cognitive Psychology, 9,* 353–383.

Nettl, B. (1956). *Music in primitive culture.* Cambridge, MA: Harvard University Press.

Olson. R. K., & Hanson, V. (1977). Interference effects in tone memory. *Memory & Cognition, 5,* 32–40.

Ortmann, O. (1926). On the melodic relativity of tones [Special issue]. *Psychological Monographs, 35,* Whole No. 162.

Oura, Y. (1991). Constructing a representation of a melody: Transforming melodic segments into reduced pitch patterns operated on by modifiers. *Music Perception, 9,* 251–266.

Palmer, S. E. (1977). Hierarchical structure in perceptual representation. *Cognitive Psychology, 9,* 441–474.

Pechmann, T., & Mohr, G. (1992). Interference in memory for tonal pitch: Implications for a working-memory model. *Memory & Cognition, 20,* 314–320.

Pickler, A. G. (1966). Logarithmic frequency systems. *Journal of the Acoustical Society of America, 39,* 1102–1110.

Piston, W. (1948). *Harmony* (2nd ed.) London: Norton.

Pitts, W., & McCulloch, W. S. (1947). How we know universals: The perception of auditory and visual forms. *Bulletin of Mathematical Biophysics, 9,* 127–147.

Plomp, R., Wagenaar, W. A., & Mimpen, A. M. (1973). Musical interval recognition with simultaneous tones. *Acustica, 29,* 101–109.

Ragozzine, F., & Deutsch, D. (1994). A regional difference in perception of the tritone paradox within the United States. *Music Perception, 12,* 213–225.

Rakowski, A. (1994). Investigating short term auditory memory with the method of vocal pitch control. In *Proceedings of the Stockholm Music Acoustics Conference* (pp. 53–57).

Ratliff, F. (1965). *Mach bands: Quantitative studies of neural networks in the retina.* San Francisco, CA: Holden Day.

Restle, F. (1970). Theory of serial pattern learning: Structural trees. *Psychological Review, 77,* 481–495.

Restle, F. (1972). Serial patterns: The role of phrasing. *Journal of Experimental Psychology, 92,* 385–390.

Restle, F., & Brown, E. (1970). Organization of serial pattern learning. In G. H. Bower (Ed.), *The psychology of learning and motivation* (Vol. 4, pp. 249–331). New York: Academic Press.

Révész, G. (1913). *Zur grundleguncy der tonpsychologie.* Leipzig: Feit.

Risset, J.-C. (1969). Pitch control and pitch paradoxes demonstrated with computer-synthesized sounds. *Journal of the Acoustical Society of America, 46,* 88(A).

Risset, J.-C. (1971). Paradoxes de hauteur: Le concept de hauteur sonore n'est pas le meme pour tout le monde. *Proceedings of the Seventh International Congress on Acoustics, Budapest, S10,* 613–616.

Rosner, B. S., & Meyer, L. B. (1982). Melodic processes and the perception of music. In D. Deutsch (Ed.), *The psychology of music* (1st ed.). New York: Academic Press.

Rosner, B. S., & Meyer, L. B. (1986). The perceptual roles of melodic process, contour, and form. *Music Perception, 4,* 1–40.

Ruckmick, C. A. (1929). A new classification of tonal qualities. *Psychological Review, 36,* 172–180.

Scandura, J. M. (1970). Role of rules in behavior: Toward an operational definition of what (rule) is learned. *Psychological Review, 77,* 516–533.

Schenker, H. (1956). *Neue musikalische theorien und phantasien: Der Freie Satz.* Vienna: Universal Edition.

Schmuckler, M. A. (1989). Expectation in music: investigations of melodic and harmonic processes. *Music Perception, 7,* 109–150.

Schoenberg, A. (1951). *Style and idea.* London: Williams & Norgate.

Schoenberg, A. (1967). In G. Strong (Ed.), *Fundamentals of musical composition.* New York: St. Martin's Press.

Schoenberg, A. (1969). *Structural functions of harmony* (rev. ed.) New York: Norton. (Original work published 1954)

Schreiner, C. E. (1992). Functional organization of the auditory cortex: Maps and mechanisms. *Current Opinion in Neurobiology, 2,* 516–521.

Semal, C., & Demany, L. (1991). Dissociation of pitch from timbre in auditory short-term memory. *Journal of the Acoustical Society of America, 89,* 2404–2410

Semal, C., & Demany, L. (1993). Further evidence for an autonomous processing of pitch in auditory short-term memory. *Journal of the Acoustical Society of America, 94,* 1315–1322.

Semal, C., Demany, L., Ueda, K., & Halle, P. (1995). Short-term pitch memory: Speech versus non-speech. In: *Proceedings of the meeting of the International Society for Psychophysics, Cassis.* Cassis: International Society for Psychophysics.

Shepard, R. N. (1964). Circularity in judgments of relative pitch. *Journal of the Acoustical Society of America,* 2345–2353.

Shepard, R. N. (1965). Approximation to uniform gradients of generalization by monotone transformations of scale. In D. L. Mostofsky (Ed.), *Stimulus generalization.* Stanford, CA: Stanford University Press.

Shepard, R. N. (1982). Structural representations of musical pitch. In D. Deutsch (Ed.), *The psychology of music* (1st ed., pp. 343–390). New York: Academic Press.

Simon, H. A. (1972). Complexity and the representation of patterned sequences of symbols. *Psychological Review, 79,* 369–382.

Simon, H. A., & Kotovsky, K. (1963). Human acquisition of concepts for sequential patterns. *Psychological Review, 70,* 534–546.

Simon, H. A., & Sumner, R. K. (1968). Pattern in music. In B. Kleinmuntz (Ed.), *Formal representation of human judgment.* New York: Wiley.

Starr, G. E., & Pitt, M. A. (1997). Interference effects in short-term memory for timbre. *Journal of the Acoustical Society of America, 102,* 486–494.

Suga, N. (1990). Cortical computational maps for auditory imaging. *Neural Networks, 3,* 3–21.

Sutter, M. I., & Schreiner, C. E. (1991). Physiology and topography of neurons with multipeaked tuning curves in cat primary auditory cortex. *Journal of Neurophysiology, 65,* 1207–1226.

Takeuchi, A. H. (1994). More on key-distance effects in melody recognition: A response to van Egmond and Povel. *Music Perception, 12,* 143–146.

Takeuchi, A. H., & Hulse, S. H. (1992). Key-distance effects in melody recognition reexamined. *Music Perception, 10,* 1–24.

Terhardt, E., & Seewann, M. (1983). Aural key identification and its relationship to absolute pitch. *Music Perception, 1,* 63–83.

Terhardt, E., & Ward, W. D. (1982). Recognition of musical key: Exploratory study. *Journal of the Acoustical Society of America, 72,* 26–33.

Thomson, W. (1991). *Schoenberg's error.* Philadelphia: University of Pennsylvania Press.

Trainor, L. L., & Trehub, S. E. (1993). Musical context effects in infants and adults: Key distance. *Journal of Experimental Psychology: Human Perception and Performance, 19,* 615–626.

Treptoe, R. (1997). *Further study of the tritone paradox.* Unpublished manuscript, University of Wisconsin–Stevens Point.

Ueda, K., & Ohgushi, K. (1987). Perceptual components of pitch: Spatial representation using multidimensional scaling technique. *Journal of the Acoustical Society of America, 82,* 1193–1200.

Van Egmond, R., & Povel, D. J. (1994a). Factors in the recognition of transposed melodies: A comment on Takeuchi and Hulse. *Music Perception, 12,* 137–142.

Van Egmond, R., & Povel, D. J. (1994b). Similarity judgments of transposed melodies as a function of overlap and key distance. In I. Deliège (Ed.), *Proceedings of the 3rd International Conference on Music Perception and Cognition, Liège* (pp. 219–220). Liège: ICMPC.

Van Egmond, R., & Povel, D. J. (1996). Perceived similarity of exact and inexact transpositions. *Acta Psychologica, 92,* 283–295.

Van Egmond, R., Povel, D. J., & Maris, E. (in press). The influence of height and key on the perceptual similarity of transposed melodies. *Perception & Psychophysics.*

Van Noorden, L. P. A. S. (1975). *Temporal coherence in the perception of tone sequences.* Unpublished doctoral thesis, Technische Hogeschool, Eindhoven, Holland.

Vicario, G. B. (1983). *Micro- and macromelodies.* Paper presented at the Fourth Workshop on Physical and Neuropsychological Foundations of Music, Ossiach.

Vitz, P. C., & Todd, T. C. (1967). A model of learning for simple repeating binary patterns. *Journal of Experimental Psychology, 75,* 108–117.

Vitz, P. C., & Todd, T. C. (1969). A coded element model of the perceptual processing of sequential stimuli. *Psychological Review, 76,* 433–449.

Von Ehrenfels, C. (1890). Uber Gestaltqualitäten. *Vierteljahrschrift fur Wissenschaftliche Philosophie, 14,* 249–292.

Warren, R. M., & Warren, R. P. (1968). *Helmholtz on perception: Its physiology and development.* New York: Wiley.

Weber, G. (1824). *Versuch einer Heordeneten Theorie.* Mainz: B. Schotts Sohne.

Werner, H. (1925). Uber Mikromelodik und Mikroharmonik. *Zeitschrift fur Psychologie, 98,* 74–89.

Werts, D. (1983). *A theory of scale references.* Unpublished doctoral dissertation, Princeton University, Princeton, NJ.

West, R. J., & Fryer, R. (1990). Ratings of suitability of probe tones as tonics after random orderings of notes of the diatonic scale. *Music Perception, 7,* 253–258.

Wever, E. G., & Bray, C. W. (1930). The nature of the acoustic response: The relation between sound frequency and frequency of impulses in the auditory nerve. *Journal of Experimental Psychology, 13,* 373–387.

White, B. (1960). Recognition of distorted melodies. *American Journal of Psychology, 73,* 100–107.

Wickelgren, W. A. (1966). Consolidation and retroactive interference in short-term recognition memory for pitch. *Journal of Experimental Psychology, 72,* 250–259.

Wickelgren, W. A. (1967). Rehearsal grouping and the hierarchical organization of serial position cues in short-term memory. *Quarterly Journal of Experimental Psychology, 19,* 97–102.

Wickelgren, W. A. (1969). Associative strength theory of recognition memory for pitch. *Journal of Mathematical Psychology, 6,* 13–61.

Winston, P. H. (1973). Learning to identify toy block structures. In R. L. Solo (Ed.), *Contemporary issues in cognitive psychology: The Loyola Symposium.* Washington, DC: Winston.

Yngve, V. (1960). A model and an hypothesis for language structure. *Proceedings of the American Philosophical Society, 104,* 444–466.

11

NEURAL NETS, TEMPORAL COMPOSITES, AND TONALITY

JAMSHED J. BHARUCHA

Department of Psychology
Dartmouth College
Hanover, New Hampshire

In this chapter, I outline a framework in which aspects of cognition can be understood as the result of the neural association of patterns. This approach to understanding music cognition originates with Pitts and McCulloch (1947) and Deutsch (1969). Subsequent advances (e.g., Grossberg, 1970, 1972, 1976; Rumelhart & McClelland, 1986) enable us to understand how these neural associations can be learned. Models based on these mechanisms are called neural net models (also connectionist models or parallel distributed models).

Neural net models have a number of properties that recommend them as models of music cognition. First, they can account for how we learn musical patterns through exposure and how this acculturation influences our subsequent perception of music. Second, their assumptions are either known or plausible principles of neuroscience. Third, they shed light on the observation (Terhardt, 1974) that aspects of pitch and harmony involve the mental completion (or Gestalt perception) of patterns. Fourth, they are capable of recognizing varying shades of similarity and are therefore well suited to modeling similarity-based accounts (e.g., Krumhansl, 1990) of tonality or modality. Finally, they can discover regularities in musical styles that may elude formal music-theoretic analysis (Gjerdingen, 1990).

Section I of this chapter deals with neural representation, and Section II deals with neural association and learning.

I. NEURAL REPRESENTATION

A. FREQUENCY TUNING OF NEURONS

Many neurons, particularly sensory neurons, are highly selective in their response. For example, there are neurons in the auditory system that respond selectively to specific bands of frequencies. Within this band, there is usually a frequency to which the neuron responds maximally (called the *characteristic frequency*). For the purpose of the present analysis, the signal to which a neuron responds maximally may be called a *feature*, and the neuron itself may be called a *feature detector*. A neuron that has a characteristic frequency may be called a *frequency detector*. A feature detector responds progressively less strongly to signals that are increasingly dissimilar. This relationship is given by its *tuning curve*. The left-hand panel of Figure 1 shows a schematic tuning curve of a frequency detector.

Frequency detectors can be found at almost all major stages in the auditory system, including the inner ear (Tasaki, 1954), the auditory nerve (Russell & Sellick, 1977), the cochlear nucleus (Rose, Galambos & Hughes, 1959), the inferior colliculus (Semple & Aitkin, 1979), the medial geniculate body (Gulick, Gescheider & Frisina, 1989) and the auditory cortex (Merzenich, Knight & Roth, 1975). In all those structures, neurons seem to be arranged *tonotopically*, that is, systematically in order of characteristic frequency. Although most of the studies reporting tonotopy have involved animals, recent positron emission tomography studies have revealed tonotopic frequency tuning in humans at the cortical level (Lauter, Hersovitch, Formby, & Raichle, 1985). Many of the representations used in this chapter are tonotopic, although only their tuning, and not tonotopy per se, is computationally relevant. The networks that operate on these representations would function equivalently if the neurons were arranged randomly while preserving their tuning.

It may at first seem odd to think of frequencies as features, because frequency is a continuous dimension that is infinitely dense, that is, between the lowest and highest frequencies, we can detect an infinite number of frequencies. Yet the brain represents this continuum with a finite set of detectors with characteristic frequencies at discrete points. We are unaware of the gaps between the characteristic fre-

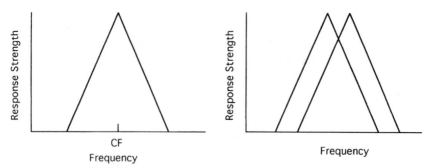

FIGURE 1   Left: Tuning curve. A frequency detector responds most strongly to a particular frequency—its characteristic frequency (CF)—and less so to frequencies farther away. Right: Coarse coding achieved by overlapping tuning curves of frequency detectors with different characteristic frequencies.

quencies because each frequency detector responds to a broad band of frequencies around its characteristic frequency, in accord with its tuning curve, and the response band overlaps with those of other neurons (right-hand panel of Figure 1). Any given frequency thus activates an entire family of inner hair cells to various degrees, with the strongest response coming from the neuron whose characteristic frequency is closest to the sounded frequency. This form of representation is called *coarse coding*. Coarse coding enables a perceptual dimension to be denser than the array of neurons used to perceive it. (Cones in the retina have only three different characteristic wavelengths, yet we can discriminate hundreds of different colors).

Coarse coding permits the listener to assimilate small tuning differences to broad musical categories (such as semitones) while also permitting us to detect fine degrees of mistuning. The former is enabled because the broadening of the peaks creates substantial overlap between the representations of patterns that differ only slightly in their tuning. The latter is enabled because the maxima of the peaks are unchanged and can be recovered if necessary by sharpening the peaks through lateral inhibition.

B. ABSTRACT FEATURE TUNING

Although frequency detectors have been the most widely studied feature detectors in the auditory system, evidence exists for detectors of more abstract features. Pantev, Hoke, Lütkenhöner, and Lehnertz (1989) argue that the tonotopic representation in the primary auditory cortex is of pitch, not frequency. Weinberger and McKenna (1988) have found feature detectors for contour. Frequency detectors must therefore map onto higher order neurons in such a way as to extract pitch and contour from complex spectra. This suggests a hierarchy of feature detectors: elementary features are detected at the sensory periphery, and entire patterns of these features are detected by abstract feature detectors, which in turn form patterns that are detected by even more abstract feature detectors. This conception of neural architecture has already received strong support for the visual system (Hubel & Wiesel, 1979; Linsker, 1986; Marr, 1982).

Deutsch (1969) suggested how feature abstraction might occur in a neural net. For example, if frequency detectors whose characteristic frequencies are an octave apart connect to the same neuron, and if no other frequency detectors connect to this neuron, then it is effectively an octave-equivalent frequency detector. The circuits Deutsch proposed anticipate the circuits that develop automatically as a result of learning, although these methods were not available at that time.

The neural connections that make a unit an abstract feature detector may in many cases have developed through evolution, in which case they are innate. Yet it seems obvious that humans are capable of learning new patterns, and if abstract feature detectors are necessary for pattern learning (as most neural net models tacitly assume), then humans must be capable of acquiring abstract feature detectors through learning. We understand how this can be done (Fukushima, 1975;

Grossberg, 1970, 1972, 1976; von der Malsberg, 1973), and in the case of music, it seems reasonable to adopt a presumption of learning.

Neural net models assume an array of units whose feature-detecting properties are given. The network then acquires either new associations or new abstract feature detectors through learning. These two types of learning are commonly referred to as pattern association and self-organization, although the latter can be thought of as a special case of the former. Both types of learning are surveyed in Section II.

The most commonly assumed feature detectors in models of music that learn are pitch or pitch-class (i.e., octave-equivalent pitch) detectors whose tuning is spaced at semitone intervals (e.g., Bharucha, 1987a, 1987b, 1988, 1991; Bharucha & Todd, 1989; Laden & Keefe, 1989; Leman, 1991; Sano & Jenkins, 1989, Todd, 1988). We already have evidence of pitch detectors in the brain (Pantev et al., 1989). Pitch-class units can be postulated on the assumption of a circuit like the one proposed by Deutsch (1969), which if not innate, can be learned by the self-organization of harmonic spectra. The semitone spacing of their tuning is an interesting issue that is beyond the scope of this chapter. For present purposes, it suffices to think of the set of pitch or pitch-class detectors with semitone spacing as a subset of the more dense array that we know to exist. Semitone spacing is thus not an additional postulate in these models, because if the dense array were used, the feature detectors between the semitones would simply not play much of a role (Bharucha, 1991).

When modeling the learning of musical sequences that are invariant across transposition, an *invariant pitch-class representation* is appropriate (Bharucha, 1988, 1991). A complete invariant pitch-class representation would have 12 units corresponding to the 12 pitch-class intervals above the tonic, which may be referred to as Units 0 through 11 for tonic through leading tone, respectively. Note that in an invariant pitch-class representation, a melody is conceived not as a series of melodic intervals but as a series of scale degrees (i.e., intervals between each note and the tonic). The mapping from pitch class to invariant pitch class can be accomplished by a circuit as described in Section II,D.

Gjerdingen (1989b) uses an invariant pitch-class representation that is restricted to the major diatonic scale (*do, re, me,* etc.), with two extra units representing sharp and flat, respectively. Although the scale degrees can be mapped from pitch-class representations (Section II,D), it is not clear how units representing sharp and flat are acquired.

C. ACTIVATION

Precisely how a neuron responds to the features to which it is tuned varies. Neurons in the auditory nerve with characteristic frequencies below 4000 Hz tend to spike at preferred intervals of time that correspond to integer multiples of one cycle of the characteristic frequency. The probability distributions of these interspike intervals are extremely provocative, given the simple integer ratios they generate quite naturally, and suggest a timing code for pitch (Cariani & Delgutte, 1992), harmony (Tramo, Cariani & Delgutte, 1992), and possibly rhythm.

Beyond the auditory nerve, little evidence exists for timing as a coding strategy. In the cochlear nucleus (the first junction from the auditory nerve to the brain) and beyond, a neuron typically fires more rapidly the more intense the tone, or the closer the tone is to its characteristic frequency. The more rapidly a neuron fires, the more pronounced is its effect on neurons to which it is connected, by virtue of the temporal summation that occurs at the receiving neuron. Firing rate is thus taken to be the measure of response strength for most neurons, and frequencies are represented by a *spatial code*—which neurons are firing and how strongly—rather than by a timing code.

Most neural net models of pitch and tonality use spatial codes, and time enters the coding scheme by changing a spatial code over time. In a spatial code, each neuron has some response strength or *activation* at any given time. Activation is an abstract term for response strength and entails no commitment to an underlying mechanism, although firing rate and temporal summation lend neurophysiological plausibility to the postulation of activation as a theoretical construct for modeling cognitive phenomena. The term activation is also used in models in which the units are postulated as cognitive rather than neural units, as in spreading activation network models (J. R. Anderson, 1983; Collins & Quillian, 1969). The underlying mechanism could well be the response strength of a group of neurons rather than an individual neuron (Hebb, 1949). For this reason we shall use the term *unit* instead of *neuron* in the context of a model, reserving the latter term for units that are known to be individual neurons.

Numerous mechanisms have been used to model changes in activation over time. These include phasic versus tonic responses, oscillating circuits, temporal composites, and cascaded activation. The first two will be summarized briefly in this section, and the last two will be covered more extensively in later sections.

In the cochlear nucleus and beyond, tones elicit both *phasic* and *tonic* responses. A phasic response is a response to change (usually the onset or offset of a tone); a tonic response is sustained throughout the duration of a tone. Most neurons in the cochlear nucleus show a strong phasic response to the onset of a tone, followed by a weaker tonic response over the sustained portion of a tone (Kiang, 1975). Some neurons (the so-called octopus cells) show only a phasic response to onsets. This enhancement of onsets may serve to draw attention to a new event and may play a role in segmenting the musical stream. Phasic activation can account for the salience of harmonic rhythm (Bharucha, 1987a). Some neurons switch from tonic to phasic as intensity increases (Gulick et al., 1989); thus both onset and intensity are to some extent coded by a phasic response. This helps explain how chord changes can compete with high-intensity percussive sounds in establishing the meter. (In rock music, for example, the highest intensity percussive sound is often on a weak beat, and it is presumably the chord changes that establish the meter).

Activation can be modulated cyclically over time by oscillatory circuits. These circuits give the activation an isochronous pulse, and have been used by Gjerdingen (1989a) to model meter. Phasic activation and oscillatory circuits are consistent with the idea, proposed by Jones (1989), that meter is temporally focused attention: phasic responses draw attention to the onsets of tonal changes, and oscillatory circuits are implementations of attention via the modulation of activation.

D. VECTOR SPACES AS FORMAL DEPICTIONS OF NEURAL REPRESENTATIONS

The representations and computations in a neural net can be understood in terms of linear algebra. Consider, for simplicity, an environment with exactly 2 features, f_1 and f_2. Each possible pattern in the environment consists of some combination of intensities of these two features and can therefore be represented as a point in a Cartesian space whose axes are f_1 and f_2. Clearly, patterns that contain only one of the features will be represented as points along one of the axes. For simplicity, we shall limit the discussion in this chapter to the first quadrant, that is, to feature intensities that are either zero or positive, never negative.

Pattern p, depicted on the left in Figure 2, contains both features, but f_1 is about twice as intense as f_2. Pattern q lies on the straight line passing through the origin and p. All points on this line (in the first quadrant) represent patterns that contain the two features in the same proportion of intensities. These patterns are essentially the same, but with different intensities, because what defines a pattern is the *relative* intensities of its features. Pattern r, in contrast, is a distinct pattern because it contains the features in different proportions.

A vector space is an improvement over a Cartesian space for the depiction of patterns because it makes explicit the equivalence of patterns that vary only in intensity. If instead of points, we draw arrows from the origin to each point, we get vectors **p**, **q** and **r** (depicted on the right in Figure 2). Vectors that are oriented in the same direction but have different lengths (e.g., **p** and **q**) are collinear and represent the same pattern with different intensities. Vectors that are oriented in dif-

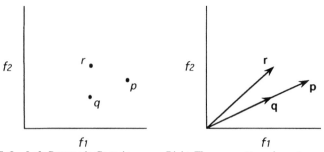

FIGURE 2   Left: Patterns in Cartesian space. Right: The same patterns in vector space.

ferent directions (e.g., **p** and **r**) represent different patterns. The more divergent the directions in which two vectors point, the more dissimilar are the patterns. Without the benefit of a visual depiction of a vector space (as when the vector has more than three dimensions), one can tell if two vectors are collinear by seeing if the multiplication of one vector by a scalar yields the other (Appendix A).

In the perception of pitch and tonality, we are typically concerned with differences between patterns rather than with differences in absolute intensity of the same pattern. Neural nets are responsive to the differences between patterns, and the absolute intensities play a minimal role. This is just one of several reasons why neural net models hold promise for understanding pattern perception, and why vector spaces are promising conceptualizations of these models. In some models, the absolute intensities are ignored altogether in order to simplify the computation. In Grossberg's models, for example, all vectors are normalized so that the sum of the squares of the intensities of all the features equals one. This ensures that all vectors have unit length (i.e., all the vector arrowheads terminate at a unit circle or unit hypersphere centered at the origin).

E. COMPOSITE PATTERNS

The *addition* of vectors yields a *resultant vector* (Appendix B) and is equivalent to superimposing patterns. The resultant represents a pattern that is more similar to each of the original patterns than they are to each other. Graphically, the resultant vector is the diagonal of the parallelogram formed by the two summed vectors, as shown in the left-hand panel of Figure 3. It makes a smaller angle with each of the original vectors than they make with each other. In more than two dimensions, the resultant vector is the diagonal of the hyperparallelogram formed by the summed vectors.

The resultant vector can be thought of as a *composite*. Composites are superimposed patterns. They have some of the properties of prototypes, being perceived as more familiar than any of the original patterns themselves (Metcalfe, 1991; Posner

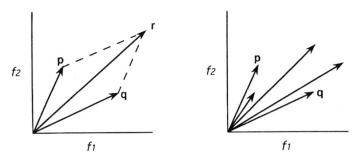

FIGURE 3 Left: Vector addition. **r** is the sum of **p** and **q**. Right: Composite patterns resulting from linear combination of vectors. All vectors within the angular sweep of **p** and **q** are composites of them.

& Keele, 1968). It is fruitful to expand the notion of composite to include all vectors that result from linear combinations of the original vectors. A linear combination is the addition of vectors that may have scalar coefficients. In a two-dimensional vector space, all the vectors that lie between two given vectors are linear combinations—or composites—of them (right-hand panel of Figure 3). We can then think of a composite as the result of adding intensity-scaled versions of several vectors.

F. COMPOSITING PATTERNS OVER TIME

As a piece of music unfolds, patterns can be composited over time by the accumulation of activation, creating a *temporal composite memory*. Suppose, for example, that the features of interest are pitch classes. When a musical sequence begins, the pattern of pitch classes that are sounded at time t_0 constitutes a vector, $\mathbf{p}_0$, in 12-dimensional pitch-class space. If at a later time, t_1, another pattern of pitch classes is sounded, represented by vector $\mathbf{p}_1$, a composite, $\mathbf{c}_1$, covering a period of time ending at t_1, can be formed as follows:

$$\mathbf{c}_1 = s_1\mathbf{p}_0 + \mathbf{p}_1,$$

where s_1 ($0 \leq s_1 \leq 1$) is the persistence of $\mathbf{p}_0$ at t_1. When yet another set of pitch classes is heard at time t_2, the resulting composite, $\mathbf{c}_2$, is:

$$\mathbf{c}_2 = s_2\mathbf{c}_1 + \mathbf{p}_2.$$

When the nth set of pitch classes is sounded at t_n, the composite, $\mathbf{c}_n$, is

$$\mathbf{c}_n = s_n\mathbf{c}_{n-1} + \mathbf{p}_n,$$

where s_n, the persistence of $\mathbf{c}_{n-1}$ at t_n, brings about the diminution of the represented salience of $\mathbf{c}_{n-1}$ as it recedes into the past. It controls the relative weighting of the most recent pattern, $\mathbf{p}_n$, relative to the patterns that came before. When $s_n = 0$, there is no temporal integration—no memory except for the most recent event. When $s_n = 1$, events at different points in time are compressed into a composite on equal terms.

Evidence for the persistence of tonal activation is clear. A chord sounded for as short a duration as 50 msec can prime a subsequent chord even if they are separated by as much as 2.5 sec of silence (Tekman & Bharucha, 1992). *Priming* refers to the automatic (i.e., robust and difficult to suppress) expectation for a target event following a context and is measured by the extent to which the context increases the speed and accuracy with which the target is perceptually processed.

The implementation of s_n in a neural net varies among models that have either explicitly or implicitly adopted a temporal compositing representation for music. In the MUSACT model (Bharucha, 1987a, 1987b), the persistence of a previously heard pattern decays exponentially over time. If d ($0 \leq d \leq 1$) is the decay rate (i.e., the proportion by which activation decreases per unit time), and if t is the number of time intervals since the last event, then:

$$s_n = (1 - d)^t.$$

Although the duration of each time interval controls the temporal resolution of the representation, d determines the length of the temporal window over which information is being integrated.

Although activation in the MUSACT model is strictly phasic, it would be reasonable, in future modeling efforts, to hypothesize a strong phasic response to the onset of a sound followed by a weaker tonic response. This amounts to the continuous formation of new composites, even during the duration of a tone, and is most easily modeled by computing new composites at small and equal time intervals. A sequence would thus be represented as a composite of a series of vectors at the ends of successive time intervals. Some time intervals would include event onsets and others would not. If the time intervals are sufficiently small, this scheme could capture some of the nuances in pitch that are lost when music is represented as a score of notes. Temporal composites can also be explored as a way to represent the spectral flux dimension of timbre.

Temporal composites with small time intervals derive some plausibility from temporal summation in the nervous system. Zwislocki (1960, 1965) found that thresholds for detecting tones show a trade-off between duration and intensity (as would be predicted by a temporal composite) and suggests that a combination of decay and summation of neural activity can account for this.

Some models implement persistence by linking each unit to itself, as shown in Figure 4 (Bharucha, 1988; Bharucha & Todd, 1989; Todd, 1988, 1989). Each unit thus activates itself in proportion to its own current activation and the strength of the link. The strength of the link will be referred to as its weight. If the weight is w_i, then:

$$s_n = w^t.$$

This scheme is functionally identical to decay, but is easier to implement.

An alternative postulate to decay is *interference*. Interference is the displacement (or reduction in retrievability) of items in memory by more recently perceived items. Interference seems to occur in both short-term memory (Waugh & Norman, 1965) and long-term memory (Bjork, 1989), but in the present context we are concerned primarily with short-term memory. Interference in short-term memory is typically attributed to a capacity limitation in attention or activation (J. R. Anderson, 1983; Shiffrin, 1975), although specific interactive effects have been

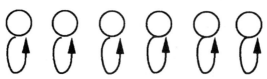

FIGURE 4   Implementing a temporal composite with links from each unit to itself.

noted (see Chapter 10, this volume). In the context of network models, interference is the reduction in activation of some units due to an increase in activation of others. Interference assumes that the total amount of activation among a given set of units is limited, so that activation caused by the currently perceived event comes at the expense of activation caused by earlier events. Interference is usually implemented by introducing inhibition. Gjerdingen (1990) has used what amounts to an interference mechanism, in which the activation of perceived events persists until inhibited by more recent events.

Whether decay or interference accounts for forgetting in short-term memory is a debate that goes back to the very beginnings of cognitive psychology (see Neisser, 1967), and there is evidence for both (Reitman, 1974; Waugh & Norman, 1965). The notion of persistence in a temporal composite, as outlined earlier, is agnostic as to the mechanism and its implementation.

A temporal composite has also been adopted unwittingly by Parncutt and Huron (1993)—although not in the form of a neural net—to account for key tracking data. Parncutt and Huron refer to their representation as *echoic memory*. Echoic memory is an auditory sensory memory that persists for several seconds, after which it is lost unless attended to (Darwin, Turvey, & Crowder, 1972; Neisser, 1967). Echoic memory enables us to relate what we are hearing at this very moment to what we have just heard. It permits us to maintain a temporal window wide enough to recognize a dynamic sound or parse a phrase.

The persistence s_n may also be influenced by segmentation cues—factors that cue the listener to chord changes or to boundaries between groups, motifs, phrases, or other segments. Segmentation cues could include phasic signals for chord changes (see earlier) or any number of pitch, timing, and timbral cues in either the composition or the performance (Bregman, 1990; Lerdahl & Jackendoff, 1983; Palmer, 1989). A segmentation cue would cause sn to be small, so that a fresh temporal composite can be started for the next segment.

G. TONAL AND MODAL COMPOSITES

A temporal composite of a pitch-class representation may be called a *tonal* composite, and a temporal composite of an invariant pitch class representation may be called a *modal* composite. Tonal composites that integrate information between chord changes represent the chords that have been either played or implied, and can account for aspects of the implication of harmony by melody. The corresponding modal composites represent chord functions. Tonal composites over longer durations represent keys, and modal composites represent modes. If metrical bias is added, say in the form of pulsing activation (Gjerdingen, 1989a), then a tonal or modal composite would encode an interaction between tonal/modal and metrical information.

If persistence is large and activation is phasic, a tonal composite roughly represents the probability distribution of pitch classes in a segment of music. Krumhansl (1990) has shown that distributions of pitch classes are strongly correlated with empirically determined key profiles of Krumhansl and Kessler (1982). A tonal composite with large persistence is thus a representation of the hierarchy of prominence or stability of pitch classes as determined by their frequency of occurrence in a segment of music. With both tonic and phasic activation, the tonal composite would represent something between the distribution of occurrences of pitch classes and the distribution of durations of pitch classes, both of which are highly correlated with key profiles (Krumhansl, 1990). What Parncutt and Huron (1993) have attributed to echoic memory is a tonal composite of pitch class; their demonstration that some of Krumhansl's probe-tone results can be modeled by such a memory is support for the existence of tonal composites as representations.

Although the distribution of pitch classes in a piece of music has a substantial influence on our perception of the relative stability of pitch classes, long-term representations of structural regularities (sometimes referred to as *schemas*) also exert an influence. In a cross-cultural study by Castellano, Bharucha, and Krumhansl (1984), Western and Indian subjects heard a rendition of a North Indian *rāg* and then judged how well a probe tone fit with the preceding segment. Probe-tone ratings were obtained for all 12 pitch classes following each of 10 *rāgs*. For both Western and Indian listeners, the probe-tone ratings were highly correlated with the distribution of total durations of pitch classes in the segment, consistent with a temporal composite representation. However, the Indian subjects showed an influence of prior exposure to the underlying scale or *thāt*, whereas the Western subjects did not. In a multiple regression analysis, a significant contribution to the regression was made by the distribution of durations for both groups of subjects, but only for the Indian subjects was a significant contribution made by the membership of pitch classes in the underlying *thāt*. This latter variable—*thāt* membership—was assessed by using a 12-element vector of binary elements representing the presence or absence of each pitch class. The contribution of this vector to the multiple regression for the Indian subjects suggests that whereas the responses of the Western subjects were based entirely on the distribution of pitch classes in the most recently heard segment, the responses of the Indian subjects were based also on prior knowledge of which pitch classes are typically present (i.e., the hierarchy of stability of tones was internalized).

This prior knowledge is implicit, schematic, and acts like a cultural filter. Implicit knowledge can be studied by priming. In a priming task, a target stimulus is presented following a context (prime stimulus), and subjects are instructed to make a designated true/false decision about the target. If the speed and accuracy with which the decision is made are greater following context C_1 than following context C_2, then C_1 primes the target more than C_2 primes the target. Priming thus reveals the extent to which one stimulus evokes another. Priming tasks are well suited to studying music cognition because of their robustness across levels of formal expertise. Because of the premium on speed, there isn't time for musical experts to use analytical strategies; and if the true/false decision is one that novices can make, priming can reveal associations that the novice may be unable to express verbally.

Priming studies demonstrate that musical events that typically co-occur in a musical culture become mentally associated. For Western listeners, for example, chords that have high transition probabilities in Western music prime each other, even though they may share no frequencies (Bharucha, 1987b). For Indian listeners, tones that typically co-occur in a particular *thāt* prime other tones in the *thāt* (Bharucha, 1987b).

Tonal and modal composites can account for these results if they are encoded for later retrieval. Pitch classes or invariant pitch classes that co-occur in a temporal composite can become mentally associated if the composite is stored in memory. The long-term encoding of composited information can be accomplished by neural nets that adjust the connections between units, and is the subject of Sections II,A and II,B.

Although it may seem that the temporal integration in tonal or modal composites results in a complete loss of information about the serial order of events, serial order can indeed be recovered, as needed for the recognition and performance of pieces of music, if the context is unambiguous. Section II,C deals with the long-term encoding and recovery of sequences using modal composites.

II. NEURAL ASSOCIATION AND LEARNING

This section deals with how a neural net can learn temporal composite patterns so that they function as schemas and as sequential memories. (Some of these mechanisms may be limited to modal composites for most of the population but may extend to tonal composites for absolute pitch possessors.)

A neural net (equivalently, a connectionist or parallel distributed network) consists of units connected by links. Links have weights associated with them, representing the strengths of the connections between units. The *net input* to a unit at any given time is a weighted sum of activations received through the links that connect to it (*spatial summation*), integrated over time (*temporal summation*). We will deal only with spatial summation first and then introduce temporal summation later. Spatial summation can be modeled as follows. The net input, net_j, to unit j, is

$$net_j = \sum_i w_{ij} a_i$$

where w_{ij} is the weight associated with the link from unit i to unit j, and a_i is the activation of unit i. The summation is over all units i that connect to j.

Links may be unidirectional or bidirectional, or may conduct different kinds of information in different directions. Although synapses in the brain are typically unidirectional, departures from strict unidirectionality in a neural net model are not neurophysiologically implausible, because separate sets of synapses could underlie different directions of information flow.

Sections II,A–C deal with mechanisms that enable a network to learn patterns by finding an appropriate set of interconnections. In each case, initial constraints on connectivity are specified, and the learning mechanism determines how these existing connections are strengthened or weakened. The initial constraints usually take the form of layers of units, with connections from one layer to the next; this architecture is supported by the layered organization of the cerebral cortex. The mechanisms for changing the connection strengths derive from Hebb's (1949) hypothesis that when two connected neurons are active simultaneously or in close temporal succession, the connection between them is strengthened so that eventually the activation of one will lead indirectly to the activation of the other. The models discussed in Section II,A—self-organizing models—use this so-called Hebbian learning in close to its original form. The models discussed in Section II,C learn by error correction and use a modified version of Hebbian learning: the connection between two units changes as a function of the activation of one unit and the error registered by the other. The models discussed in Section II,B—auto-associators—can use either Hebbian learning or error correction, although the latter enables them to learn many more patterns and to distinguish grades of similarity.

A. ENCODING TEMPORAL COMPOSITES: ABSTRACT FEATURE DETECTORS OR CATEGORY UNITS

Sensory neurons are stimulated directly by energy external to the organism. Their tuning characteristics are a consequence of their inherent transducing properties and are innately fixed. For example, the inner hair cells convert mechanical deformation of the basilar membrane into neural signals. In contrast, neurons beyond the sensory periphery are stimulated by other neurons that connect to them, not by the environment directly. Their tuning characteristics are based on the pattern of stimulation they receive from other neurons. These can be called abstract feature detectors or category units (because they encode entire categories).

The connectivity that achieves this can be learned by a class of learning models called self-organizing neural nets (Grossberg, 1970, 1972, 1976; Rumelhart & Zipser, 1985; von der Malsburg, 1973). Grossberg's models, the earliest and most fully developed of this kind, have been used to model the acquisition of auditory categories in music (Gjerdingen, 1989b,1990) and speech (Mitra, 1993). Although a detailed description of this model would require a chapter in itself, it is possible to capture the essence of self-organizing models rather simply. (Most of the specifics of Grossberg's theory deal with ensuring the stability of the learned categories, and the stability of human categories is an open question.)

The top panel of Figure 5 shows a layer of units (input units), with preexisting tuning characteristics, connected to another layer (category units). The category units are in a winner-take-all configuration, which is common in the brain: the most active unit in such a configuration has the effect of decreasing the activation of the other units and boosting its own activation. A pattern presented to the network will activate the input units with the corresponding features (filled circles). The ensuing activation of the category units depends on the weights on the links.

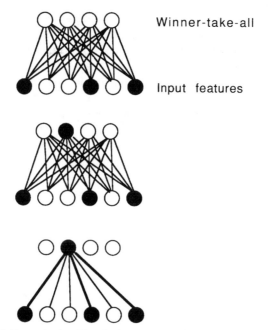

Winner-take-all

Input features

FIGURE 5 Self-organization. The winning category unit gets to learn. Links to it from highly active input units are strengthened.

One of the category units will win (filled circle in the middle panel), and the weights on the links feeding into the winning unit change by Hebbian learning. The links from strongly active input units are strengthened (bottom panel). Self-organizing mechanisms have the further requirement that the links to the winner from weakly active input units are weakened. The winner is on its way to becoming a feature detector or category unit for the entire input pattern. Similar patterns will activate this unit more strongly, and dissimilar patterns will activate this unit more weakly, than before learning.

Self-organization can be visualized in terms of vector spaces. Consider a network with two input units, f_1 and f_2, and indefinitely many units in a second layer. The units in the second layer are available to become abstract feature detectors and may be called category units. Each category unit has two links feeding into it, one from each input unit. The weights on these links can be plotted as vectors (solid lines in Figure 6) in two-dimensional feature space; these are *weight vectors*— each category unit has a weight vector. A pattern presented to the network can be plotted as a vector (dashed line) in the same space. The weight vector that is closest in angle to the pattern vector represents the category unit that has responded most strongly to the pattern and is therefore the most likely candidate for an abstract feature detector for that pattern. The weights of this unit are changed so as to move the weight vector closer to the pattern vector. The closer the weight vector

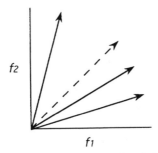

FIGURE 6   The weight vector (solid line) with the smallest angle to the activation vector (dashed line) represents the winning category unit. Learning consists of making the angle even smaller.

moves to the pattern vector, the more strongly this unit will respond to that pattern, that is, the more it develops the tuning characteristics for that pattern.

   If the input is a tonal composite, this procedure will lead to the formation of abstract feature detectors for typical composite patterns. The chord and key units in the MUSACT model (Bharucha, 1987a, 1987b) are thus a direct and mandatory consequence of self-organization. Pitch classes that co-occur within a tonal composite that spans the duration of a chord (explicit or implied) will become associated via the chord detectors that form. Chords that co-occur within a tonal composite that spans a piece or a key segment will become associated via the key detectors that form. After these associations are sufficiently strong, hearing one chord will lead to expectations for other chords that co-occur in the same composite, because activation flows from one chord unit to parent key units and down to the other chord units in the same composite. The MUSACT model suggests how the graded activation of chords, mediated by the multiplicity of their parent keys, and the priming data that provide evidence of this, can be explained by this process (Bharucha, 1987a, 1987b).

   Adopting an input representation that is essentially a temporal composite of invariant pitch-class units, Gjerdingen (1989b) exposed a self-organizing network to works of early Mozart. The network developed categories units (abstract feature detectors) for sequential patterns that characterize the style of the corpus.

B. ENCODING TEMPORAL COMPOSITES THROUGH AUTOASSOCIATION

   Consider a network in which each unit is connected by unidirectional links to every other unit and to itself. This network can learn to encode patterns through autoassociation, that is, by associating them with themselves (J. A. Anderson, 1970, 1972; J. A. Anderson, Silverstein, Ritz, & Jones, 1977). Why would one wish to associate patterns with themselves? Neural net autoassociators have a remarkable property: If after learning a set of patterns, an incomplete or degraded version of one of the learned patterns is presented to the network, it will be completed or filled in by the network. Pattern completion is a general principle of perception that enables us to recognize objects that are partially masked or occluded and to perceive them as unbroken wholes, with the concomitant risk of error or illusion. Terhardt (1974) has argued that many auditory phenomena are examples of this aspect of Gestalt perception.

Aspects of tonality can be thought of as pattern completion. The residual effect of prior exposure found in the responses of Indian listeners hearing Indian *rāgs* (Castellano et al., 1984) is evidence of this: a temporal composite of the underlying mode accounted for variance over and beyond the variance accounted for by the probability distribution of pitch classes in the segment. The segment seems to have activated an internal representation of the mode, which in turn elaborated or filled out the percept. More direct evidence comes from the priming of an important tone missing from a *rāg*, based on the remaining tones (Bharucha, 1987b). Subjects' responses in these studies seem to reflect a composite of the distribution of pitch classes actually heard during the experiment and an internal representation of the pitch classes that typically occur in that context. This should not be surprising at all, because the literature in perception is filled with examples of top-down processing, that is, the influence of context-dependent expectations based on prior experience.

In an autoassociator, the links between units serve to excite units whose pitch classes co-occur and inhibit units whose pitch classes do not. This requires just the right combination of weights on these links, because two pitch classes may co-occur in one key or mode and not in another. Although this may seem like an impossible standard for this tangled network to meet, a simple learning mechanism can lead to this result.

For the purposes of illustration, it is useful to duplicate the units and think of one copy as representing the stimulus that is actually heard and the other as representing expectations that are triggered by this stimulus. Figure 7 shows an array of

Expectancies

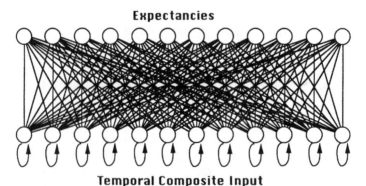

Temporal Composite Input

FIGURE 7   An autoassociator with pitch-class units or invariant pitch-class units as input and expectation. The input units constitute a temporal composite, and each input unit is connected to each expectation unit.

pitch class units that represents, as a temporal composite, what has been heard (the input) and another array of pitch-class units that represents expectations based on what has been heard. Each input unit feeds into each expectation unit. A learning mechanism called the *delta rule* enables the weights to adjust themselves so each of a number of patterns presented repeatedly to the input units will reproduce itself at the expectation units. The delta rule derives from the *perceptron* developed by Rosenblatt (1962).

According to the delta rule, as adapted shortly, the weights are assumed to be random initially, representing a naive network. A tonal composite of a key as input will initially result in a random pattern of expectations. This random pattern of expectations is compared with the input pattern, and the weights are changed so as to reduce the disparity. The weight change is incremental; each time the network generates expectations in response to a tonal composite, the weights change slightly so that the next time that tonal composite (or one similar to it) is encountered, the expectations will more closely approximate the input.

If a_i is the activation of input unit i, and a_e is the activation of expectation unit e, then the disparity is called the *error signal* (δ_e), and is simply the difference:

$$\delta_e = a_i - a_e.$$

If w_{ie} is the weight on the link from i to e, then the change (Δw_{ie}) in the weight is simply the activation of i times the error signal at e, scaled by a constant, ε ($0 \le \varepsilon \le 1$) that represents the learning rate:

$$\Delta w_{ie} = \varepsilon a_i \delta_e.$$

The learning rate determines the extent to which a single experience can have a lasting effect.

The patterns are presented repeatedly to the network until the error signal is smaller than some criterion amount for all expectation units in response to all patterns. Rosenblatt (1962) proved that, with this learning rule, a network with two sets of units, one feeding into the other, will eventually be able to find a solution (to any given degree of precision) if one exists. For an autoassociator using the delta rule, a solution exists for any set of input vectors that are *linearly independent* of each other. A vector is linearly independent of a set of vectors if it cannot be obtained by any combination of scalar multiplication and addition of the other vectors, that is, it is not a *composite* of any of the others. Tonal composites for the 12 major keys are linearly independent of each other, and modal composites for the Church modes are linearly independent of each other. This is indeed a powerful system, because it can learn all these patterns in the same set of links.

Two modes that have the same invariant pitch classes, albeit with different probability distributions (e.g., major and natural minor), are not linearly independent; this network would learn them as one pattern that is a composite of the two. This is not a limitation of this scheme for modeling music cognition, however, because it has never been suggested that tonal or modal composites capture all features of music. These models can be expanded to include any number of features that may discriminate two modes by the way in which they are used. We have restricted ourselves to pitch classes or invariant pitch classes in the present chapter only because we must begin somewhere and it behooves us to understand something well before bringing all possible factors into play.

After learning, the model can be tested for its vaunted ability to complete degraded patterns or to assimilate similar patterns to learned ones. An autoassociator was fed tonal composites, in each of the 12 major keys, representing the average probability distributions of works by Schubert, Mendelssohn, Schumann, Mozart, Hasse, and Strauss (as reported by Krumhansl, 1990, p. 68). After learning, the network was presented with temporal composites that were similar to but not identical to one of the learned composites. For example, the network was presented with a composite in which the pitch classes D, E, F, G, and A were equally active (i.e., the vector 0,0,1,0,1,1,0,1,0,1,0,1). The network recognized that this pattern was more similar to the C major composite than to any other and significantly activated all and only the diatonic pitch classes among the expectation units, including C, which was missing in the input.

With invariant pitch-class units, an autoassociator can learn modes. Bharucha and Olney (1989) presented an autoassociator with binary modal composites of 10 North Indian *rāg*s. After the network learned them, it was tested with incomplete patterns. *Rāg Bhairav*, for example, contains the invariant pitch classes: 1,1,0,0,1,1,0,1,1,0,0,1 (which in C major would be C,Db,E,F,G,Ab,B). When the network was presented with all the tones except the second scale degree (Db), all the scale degrees were activated among the expectation units, including the missing second scale degree. The network generated these expectations with a much smaller set of tones: the third, fourth, sixth, and seventh scale degrees were sufficient to suggest *Bhairav*.

C. LEARNING SEQUENCES

The expectations that derive from the above system are *schematic*—expectations for classes of events rather than specific event tokens—based on familiarity with a musical culture (Bharucha & Todd, 1989). They are also not sequential, but rather represent global states or backgrounds against which the actual sequences of events are heard. Yet tonal or modal composites can also serve as the basis for encoding specific sequences. A memory for specific sequences, when activated by appropriate context, generates *veridical expectancies*—the cues that enable us to anticipate or recognize the next event in a familiar piece and that underlie our ability to perform from memory.

The system shown in Figure 8 is a sequential memory that serves this function and has the added bonus that while it learns specific pieces it also learns something about the sequential regularities—sequential schematic expectancies—of the style. The architecture is similar to that of the autoassociator in Figure 7 in that there is a set of input units and expectation units. The input feature space is given

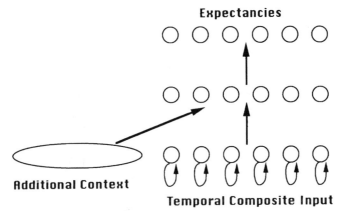

Expectancies

Additional Context

Temporal Composite Input

FIGURE 8   A network that learns individual sequences (veridical expectancies) and acquires schematic properties. The "Additional Context" units represent any extratonal information that may be encoded as context. The arrows between groups of units represent a link from each unit of one group to each unit of the other.

more dimensions to include additional features that play a role in cueing one's memory for the continuation of a sequence. Candidates for these additional features are contour, timbre, aspects of rhythm and, because human memory is highly contextual, even aspects of the extramusical context that might cue memory; these additional context units could conceivably receive input from systems far afield from the auditory system.

The system works by generating an expectation for the next event in a sequence, based on a temporal composite of the sequence thus far. As each new event is heard, it adds to the composite, and the new composite generates an expectation for the following event. The units in the middle, unlabeled, layer of Figure 8 are called *hidden units*. They are necessary if the system is to be able to learn the full range of possible transitions in musical sequences. Each hidden unit computes a nonlinear, monotonically increasing function, as do neurons: the more strongly activated a neuron, the stronger its response, but because of physical limitations, the response strength asymptotes. One of the more commonly used functions in modeling hidden units is the logistic function (Figure 9).

This nonlinearity of hidden units enables a network to implement mappings from input to expectation that would otherwise be impossible. (There is no advantage to hidden units if they are linear). If the tips of the tonal composite vectors that generate an expectation for pitch class x cannot be clearly separated by a hyperplane from the tips of the tonal composite vectors that generate an expectation for pitch class y, then the expectations are not *linearly separable*. In other words, if there are cases in which similar tonal composites generate different expectations and dissimilar tonal composites generate the same expectation, then the expectations may not be linearly separable. Similar tonal composites tend to gen-

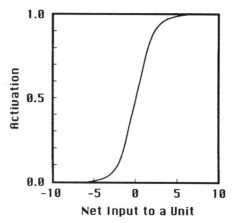

FIGURE 9   Logistic function relating the net input and activation of a unit.

erate similar schematic expectancies but not necessarily similar veridical expectancies. This is because composers occasionally use unusual or unschematic transitions that violate (schematic) expectations for aesthetic effect (Meyer, 1956). Problems that are not linearly separable cannot be solved by neural nets without nonlinear hidden units (Minsky & Papert, 1969) or extra assumptions.

We use the logistic function at the expectation units as well because it has the effect of making the activations at the expectation units equivalent to probabilities. The weights in the network are initially random. As a sequence is played, a temporal composite at the input produces a pattern of expectations that is initially random. The network learns by comparing the expectation for the next event with the actual next event when it occurs. Each event thus trains the expectations that attempted to predict it.

The delta rule is adapted for this model as follows. The error signal is scaled by the slope of the logistic function at the expectation unit's current activation level (the derivative of the activation of e with respect to its net input):

$$\delta_e = (t_e - a_e)\frac{da_e}{dnet_e},$$

where $t_e = 1$ if event e occurs, 0 otherwise. This has the effect of changing the weight more radically when the unit into which it feeds is uncommitted (in the middle of its activation range). Applying the delta rule to change the weights from the hidden units to the expectation units:

$$\Delta w_{he} = \varepsilon a_h \delta_e,$$

where a_h is the activation of hidden unit h and w_{he} is the weight on the link from hidden unit h to expectation unit e.

The delta rule offers no guidance on how to change the weights from the input units to the hidden units, because the error signal on the hidden units is undefined. The solution, commonly known as *backpropagation* (Rumelhart, Hinton, & Williams, 1986), has dramatically broadened the scope of neural net models in recent years. In the context of the present model, each hidden unit inherits the error of each expectation unit connected to it, weighted by the link between them, and sums these weighted errors. This is again scaled by the slope of the logistic function at the hidden unit's current activation level. Thus the error signal on hidden unit e is:

$$\delta_h = (\sum_e w_{he} \delta_e) \frac{da_h}{dnet_h}.$$

The delta rule is then applied to change the weights on the links from the input units to the hidden units:

$$\Delta w_{ih} = \varepsilon a_i \delta_h.$$

This model was used to learn sequences of chord functions, using a temporal composite of invariant pitch chord function for input and expectation (Bharucha & Todd, 1989). Figure 8 shows six units, representing, in a major key, the tonic, supertonic, mediant, subdominant, dominant, and submediant. Fifty sequences, of seven successive chords each, were generated at random using a priori transition probabilities estimated from Piston's (1978, p. 21) table of chord transitions. This corpus roughly represents the transition probabilities of chord functions in the common practice era, but contains a small proportion of highly unusual transitions because of the random generation procedure. In order to encapsulate the potentially large number of possible "additional context" features, one additional context unit was assigned to each sequence as a place holder for all the contextual information that might help individuate this sequence.

After repeated presentation of the sequences, the network learned to predict the first event in each sequence in response to the activation of its additional context unit and learned to predict each successive event in response to the temporal composite of chords played thus far plus the activation of its additional context unit. In a performance model, this would enable the performer to play the first event. In a perceptual model, it would enable the listener to recognize whether or not the correct event was played.

After learning, the network was presented repeatedly with two new sequences: one consisted entirely of schematically expected (high-probability) transitions and the other of schematically unexpected (low-probability) transitions. The schematic sequence was learned in fewer presentations. The network adapted more quickly to the sequence that was typical of the corpus than to the sequence that was unusual, even though both were novel. This suggests that the network learned not only the sequences themselves but also the generic or schematic relationships of the style.

The same network therefore contains information about the two types of expectations—veridical and schematic—that usually converge but sometimes diverge. When they diverge, the performer is able to produce, and the listener to recognize, the correct next event while nevertheless experiencing its unexpectedness. The divergence of expectations when an unusual transition occurs in a familiar piece addresses what Dowling and Harwood (1986) refer to as Wittgenstein's puzzle. It also accounts for how expectancy violation, which Meyer (1956) considers central to our aesthetic response to music, can continue to occur in a familiar, overlearned piece.

The network reveals these divergent expectations when the activation of expectation units following the onset of an event is observed over time. We have thus far considered only spatial summation of activation. The buildup of activation in a neuron as an event gets under way is the result of temporal summation. If we consider both spatial and temporal summation, the net input to a unit can be modeled using *cascaded* activation (McClelland, 1979):

$$net_{j,t} = k(\sum_i w_{ij}a_{i,t}) + (1 - k)net_{j,\,t-\Delta t},$$

where k ($0 \le k \le 1$) restricts the incremental net input in any given time slice, Δt, and the second term of the equation carries over net input form the previous time slice, thereby causing the net input to build up over time.

With cascaded activation, high-probability (schematic) expectations were generated in less time than low-probability expectations (Bharucha & Todd, 1989). Unique expectations, resulting from chord transition that occurred only once in the corpus, took the longest. This is presumably because the network develops redundant pathways for the high-probability transitions (e.g., moving to the tonic), leading to the rapid activation of some units. Whether or not the veridical expectancies are also schematic is therefore revealed by the time course of activation. When the unusual transition involves not just a low-probability transition but a move to a low-probability event (such as a secondary dominant), the expectancy violation does not require a cascading explanation; it is trivially accounted for by the disparity between the expectation of the sequential net and the autoassociator.

D. TRANSPOSITIONAL INVARIANCE

Pitch-class representations can be transformed into invariant pitch-class representations by a simple gating mechanism (Bharucha, 1988, 1991; McNellis, 1993). This mechanism, shown in Figure 10, is similar to one developed by Hinton (1981) for object recognition in vision. The units labeled "π" multiply the activation that feeds into them, thereby serving as "AND" gates. The units arrayed vertically on the left are key units from MUSACT, and the units arrayed horizontally at the bottom are pitch-class units. The most active key unit gates the activation from pitch-class units into the pitch invariant representation at the top. If the key is C♯, then C is gated to 11 and C♯ to 0. If the key is C, then C is gated to 0 and C♯ to 1. This can account for the invariance of pitch sequences under transposition.

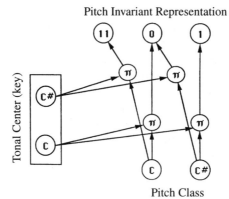

FIGURE 10   A network for transforming a pitch-class representation into an invariant pitch-class representation. Units labeled π gate activation received from pitch class units and tonal center (key) units. (From Bharucha, 1988).

III. DISCUSSION

Neural net models are not intended to be statements of fact about how the brain is wired. Like all models, they are systematic hypotheses based on available data, and they represent attempts to account for known phenomena and guide further research. Some neural net models may be sufficiently closely tied to known physiology that they serve as hypotheses of actual neural circuitry. For most examples of complex human behavior, however, the precise circuitry is largely a mystery. We have a large and rapidly growing body of knowledge about the physiology of single neurons and about the functions, and connections between, some macroscopic regions of the brain. We also have a preliminary understanding of how different types of neurons are interconnected within the parts of the brain that are thought to play major roles in cognition, namely, the cerebral cortex and the cerebellum. However, we know little about the specific circuits that underlie specific phenomena, and even when the circuits are known, it is sometimes not clear why the circuit behaves the way it does. Neural net models are attempts to bridge the gap between what we do and do not know.

In the opinion of some authors (e.g., Fodor & Pylyshyn, 1988), the connectionist conception of cognition and the representations that underlie it contrast sharply with rule-based systems, the latter being the hallmark of computer programming languages and the grammars of modern linguistic theory (Chomsky, 1980). Fodor (1975; Fodor & Pylyshyn, 1988) argues, among other things, that the mind is a formal symbol-manipulating device, in which a fairly clear distinction is made between syntactic form and semantic content. Although many of his arguments are specific to the study of language, one incisive argument derives from his critique of connectionism (Fodor & Pylyshyn) together with his theory of the relationship between mental and physical states (Fodor, 1975). Roughly, he contends that connectionist models are merely models of implementation. Because there may be radically different implementations of the same symbolic process (e.g., there may be radically different hardware designs that can implement the same computer program), an understanding of one implementation does not entail an understanding of the formal symbolic process it implements, any more than an understanding of the electrical activity in the circuits of a computer chip entails an understanding of the program it is running.

This is a powerful argument, but a careful analysis is beyond the scope of this chapter. If the argument is correct, connectionist modelers will have to settle for trying to understand how the brain—a *mere* implementation, but what an implementation it is!—implements the formal symbolic processes that we call music cognition. I suspect, however, that although highly trained musicians may use formal symbolic processes together with a host of other processes, the passive processing of music by most listeners is minimally symbolic. What then does one make of rule-based theories of music, such as that of Lerdahl and Jackendoff (1983)? These can be construed as formalizations of constraints on neural processing of music. In other words, either neural nets are implementations of grammars, or grammars are formal descriptions of neural nets. Future research will need to bridge the gap either way.

ACKNOWLEDGMENTS

This manuscript was completed while I was a Fellow at the Center for Advanced Study in the Behavioral Sciences in 1993–1994. I am grateful for support from the National Science Foundation (DBS-9222358 and SES-9022192) and for valuable comments from Diana Raffman, Carol Krumhansl, Eugene Narmour, Caroline Palmer, Einar Mencl, Subhobrata Mitra, Mark McNellis, and Denise Vargas.

APPENDICES

A. COLLINEARITY OF VECTORS

If **v** is a vector and s is a positive scalar, then their product, $s\mathbf{v}$, is a vector that is collinear, that is, will point in the same direction. The multiplication of a vector by a scalar is the vector resulting from multiplying each component by the scalar. For example, if

$$\mathbf{v} = \begin{bmatrix} 2 \\ 0 \\ 1 \\ 3 \\ 1 \end{bmatrix}$$

and $s = 2$, then

$$s\mathbf{v} = \begin{bmatrix} 4 \\ 0 \\ 2 \\ 6 \\ 2 \end{bmatrix}.$$

Division of a vector by a scalar is analogous.

B. ADDITION OF VECTORS

The addition of two vectors is the vector resulting from adding their corresponding components. For example:

$$\begin{bmatrix} 3 \\ 0 \\ 2 \\ 0 \end{bmatrix} + \begin{bmatrix} 0 \\ 1 \\ 2 \\ 1 \end{bmatrix} = \begin{bmatrix} 3 \\ 1 \\ 4 \\ 1 \end{bmatrix}.$$

Only vectors with the same number of components can be added.

REFERENCES

Anderson, J. A. (1970). Two models for memory organization using interacting traces. *Mathematical Biosciences, 8,* 137–160.

Anderson, J. A. (1972). A simple neural network generating an interactive memory. *Mathematical Biosciences, 14,* 197–220.

Anderson, J. A., Silverstein, J. W., Ritz, S. A., & Jones, R. S. (1977). Distinctive features, categorical perception, and probability learning: Some applications of a neural model. *Psychological Review, 84,* 413–451.

Anderson, J. R. (1983). *The architecture of cognition.* Cambridge, MA: Harvard University Press.

Bharucha, J. J. (1987a). MUSACT: A connectionist model of musical harmony. *Proceedings of the Cognitive Science Society.* Hillsdale, NJ: Erlbaum.

Bharucha, J. J. (1987b). Music cognition and perceptual facilitation: A connectionist framework. *Music Perception, 5,* 1–30.

Bharucha, J. J. (1988). Neural net modeling of music. *Proceedings of the First AAAI Workshop on Artificial Intelligence and Music.* Minneapolis: American Association for Artificial Intelligence.

Bharucha, J. J. (1991). Pitch, harmony, and neural nets: A psychological perspective. In P. Todd & G. Loy (Eds.), *Connectionism and music.* Cambridge, MA: MIT Press.

Bharucha, J. J., & Olney, K. L. (1989). Tonal cognition, artificial intelligence and neural nets. *Contemporary Music Review, 4,* 341–356.

Bharucha, J. J., & Todd, P. (1989). Modeling the perception of tonal structure with neural nets. *Computer Music Journal, 13*(4), 44–53. (Reprinted in P. Todd & G. Loy, Eds., *Connectionism and music,* 1991, Cambridge, MA: MIT Press)

Bjork, R. A. (1989). Retrieval inhibition as an adaptive mechanism in human memory. In H. L. Roediger & F. I. M. Craik (Eds.), *Varieties of memory and consciousness: Essays in honor of Endel Tulving* (pp. 309–330). Hillsdale, NJ: Erlbaum.

Bregman, A. S. (1990). *Auditory scene analysis.* Cambridge, MA: MIT Press.

Cariani, P., & Delgutte, B. (1992, October). *The pitch of complex sounds is simply coded in interspike interval distributions of auditory nerve fibers.* Paper presented at the annual meeting of the Society for Neuroscience, Anaheim, CA.

Castellano, M. A., Bharucha, J. J., & Krumhansl, C. L. (1984). Tonal hierarchies in the music of North India. *Journal of Experimental Psychology: General, 113,* 394–412.

Chomsky, N. (1980). *Rules and representations.* New York: Columbia University Press.

Collins, A. M., & Quillian, M. R. (1969). Retrieval time from semantic memory. *Journal of Verbal Learning and Verbal Behavior, 8,* 240–247.

Darwin, C. J., Turvey, M. T., & Crowder, R. G. (1972). The auditory analog of the Sperling partial report procedure: Evidence for brief auditory storage. *Cognitive Psychology, 3,* 255–267.

Deutsch, D. 1969. Music recognition. *Psychological Review , 76,* 300–307.

Dowling, W. J., & Harwood, D. L. (1986). *Music cognition.* San Diego, CA: Academic Press.

Fodor, J. A. (1975). *The language of thought.* New York: Crowell.

Fodor, J. A., & Pylyshyn, Z. W. (1988). Connectionism and cognitive architecture: A critical analysis. *Cognition, 28,* 2–71.

Fukushima, K. (1975). Cognitron: A self-organizing multilayered neural network. *Biological Cybernetics, 20,* 121–136.

Gjerdingen, R. O. (1989a). Meter as a mode of attending: A network simulation of attentional rhythmicity in music. *Intégral, 3,* 67–92.

Gjerdingen, R. O. (1989b). Using connectionist models to explore complex musical patterns. *Computer Music Journal, 13*(3), 67–75. (Reprinted in P. Todd & G. Loy, Eds., *Connectionism and music,* 1991, Cambridge, MA: MIT Press)

Gjerdingen, R. O. (1990). Categorization of musical patterns by self-organizing neuronlike networks. *Music Perception, 8,* 67–91.

Grossberg, S. (1970). Some networks that can learn, remember, and reproduce any number of complicated space-time patterns. *Studies in Applied Mathematics, 49,* 135–166.

Grossberg, S. (1972). Neural expectation: Cerebellar and retinal analogs of cells fired by learnable or unlearned pattern classes. *Kybernetic, 10,* 49–57.

Grossberg, S. (1976). Adaptive pattern classification and universal recoding, I: Parallel development and coding of neural feature detectors. *Biological Cybernetics, 23,* 121–134.

Gulick, W. L., Gescheider, G. A., & Frisina, R. D. (1989). *Hearing.* Oxford: Oxford University Press.

Hebb, D. O. (1949). *The organization of behavior.* New York: Wiley.

Hinton, G. F. (1981). A parallel computation that assigns canonical object-based frames of reference. *Proceedings of the 7th International Joint Conference on Artificial Intelligence,* 683–685.

Hubel, D., & Wiesel, T. N. (1979). Brain mechanisms of vision. *Scientific American, 241,* 150–162.

Jones, M. R., & Boltz, M. (1989). Dynamic attending and responses to time. *Psychological Review, 96,* 459–491.

Jordan, M. I. (1986). Attractor dynamics and parallelism in a connectionist sequential machine. *Proceedings of the Eighth Annual Conference of the Cognitive Science Society.* Hillsdale, NJ: Erlbaum.

Kiang, N. Y. (1975). Stimulus representation in the discharge patterns of auditory neurons. In D. B. Tower (Ed.), *The nervous system* (pp. 81–96). New York: Raven Press.

Krumhansl, C. L. (1990). *Cognitive foundations of musical pitch.* Oxford: Oxford University Press.

Krumhansl, C. L., & Kessler, E. J. Tracing the dynamic changes in perceived tonal organization in a spatial representation of musical keys. *Psychology Review, 89,* 334–368.

Laden, B., & Keefe, D. H. (1989). The representation of pitch in a neural net model of chord classification. *Computer Music Journal, 13*(4), 12–26. (Reprinted in P. Todd & G. Loy, Eds., *Connectionism and music,* 1991, Cambridge, MA: MIT Press)

Lauter, J. L., Hersovitch, P., Formby, C., & Raichle, M. R. (1985). Tonotopic organization in the human auditory cortex revealed by positron emission tomography. *Hearing Research, 20,* 199–205.

Leman, M. (1991). The ontogenesis of tonal semantics: Results of a computer study. In P. Todd & G. Loy (Eds.), *Connectionism and music.* Cambridge, MA: MIT Press.

Lerdahl, F., & Jackendoff, R. (1983). *A generative theory of tonal music.* Cambridge, MA: MIT Press.

Linsker, R. (1986). From basic network principles to neural architecture. *Proceedings of the National Academy of Sciences, USA, 83,* 7508–7512, 8390–8394, 8779–8783.

Marr, D. (1982). *Vision.* San Francisco: Freeman.

McClelland, J. L. (1979). On the time-relations of mental processes: An examination of systems of processes in cascade. *Psychological Review, 86,* 287–330.

McNellis, M. (1993). *Learning and recognition of relative auditory spectral patterns.* Unpublished honors thesis, Dartmouth College, Hanover, NH.

Merzenich, M. M., Knight, P. L., & Roth, G. L. (1975). Representation of the cochlea within primary auditory cortex in cat. *Journal of Neurophysiology, 28,* 231–249.

Metcalfe, J. (1991). Composite memories. In W. Hockley & S. Lewandowsky (Eds.), *Relating theory and data: Essays on human memory in honor of Bennet B. Murdock* (pp. 399–423). Hillsdale, NJ: Erlbaum.

Meyer, L. (1956). *Emotion and meaning in music.* Chicago: University of Chicago Press.

Minsky, M., & Papert, S. (1969). *Perceptrons.* Cambridge, MA: MIT Press.

Mitra, S. (1993). *A neural self-organization approach to problems in phonetic categorization.* Unpublished honors thesis, Dartmouth College, Hanover, NH.

Mozer, M. C. (1990). Connectionist music composition based on melodic, stylistic and psychophysical constraints. *University of Colorado Technical Report CU-CS-495-90.*

Neisser, U. (1967). *Cognitive psychology.* New York: Appleton, Century, Crofts.

Palmer, C. (1989). Mapping musical thought to musical performance. *Journal of Experimental Psychology: Human Perception and Performance, 15,* 331–346.

Pantev, C., Hoke, M., Lütkenhöner, B., & Lehnertz, K. (1989). Tonotopic organization of the auditory cortex: Pitch versus frequency representation. *Science, 246,* 486–488.

Parncutt, R. & Huron, D. (1993). An improved model of tonality perception incorporating pitch salience and echoic memory. *Psychomusicology, 12,* 154–171.

Piston, W. (1978). *Harmony.* New York: Norton.

Pitts, W., & McCulloch, W. S. (1947). How we know universals: The perception of auditory and visual forms. *Bulletin of Mathematical Biophysics, 9,* 127–147.

Posner, M. I., & Keele, S. W. (1968). On the genesis of abstract ideas. *Journal of Experimental Psychology, 77,* 353–363.

Reitman, J. (1974). Without surreptitious rehearsal, information in short-term memory decays. *Journal of Verbal Learning and Verbal Behavior, 13,* 365–377.

Rose, J. E., Galambos, R., & Hughes, J. R. (1959). Microelectrode studies of the cochlear nuclei of the cat. *Bulletin of the Johns Hopkins Hospital, 104,* 211–251.

Rosenblatt, F. (1962). *Principles of neurodynamics.* New York: Spartan.

Rumelhart, D. E., Hinton, G. E., & Williams, R. J. (1986). In D. E. Rumelhart & J. L. McClelland (Eds.), *Parallel distributed processing: Explorations in the microstructure of cognition.* Vol. 1. Cambridge, MA: MIT Press.

Rumelhart, D. E., & McClelland, J. L. (1986). *Parallel distributed processing: Explorations in the microstructure of cognition.* Vols. 1 & 2. Cambridge, MA: MIT Press.

Rumelhart, D. E., & Zipser, D. (1985). Feature discovery by competitive learning. *Cognitive Science, 9,* 75–112.

Russell, I. J., & Sellick, P. M. (1977). The tuning properties of cochlear hair cells. In E. F. Evans & J. P. Wilson (Eds.), *Psychophysics and physiology of hearing* (pp. 71–84). New York: Academic Press.

Sano, H., & Jenkins, B. K. (1989). A neural network model for pitch perception. *Computer Music Journal, 13*(3), 41–48. (Reprinted in P. Todd & G. Loy, Eds., *Connectionism and music,* 1991, Cambridge, MA: MIT Press)

Semple, M. N., & Aitkin, L. M. (1979). Representation of sound frequency and laterality by units in the central nucleus of the cat's inferior colliculus. *Journal of Neurophysiology, 42,* 1626–1639.

Shiffrin, R. M. (1975). Short-term store: the basis for a memory system. In F. Restle, R. M. Shiffrin, N. J. Castellan, H. R. Lindman, & D. B. Pisoni (Eds.), *Cognitive theory.* Vol. 1. Hillsdale, NJ: Erlbaum.

Tasaki, I. (1954). Nerve impulses in individual auditory nerve fibers of guinea pig. *Journal of Neurophysiology, 17,* 97–122.

Tekman, H., & Bharucha, J. J. (1992). Time course of chord priming. *Perception & Psychophysics, 51,* 33–39.

Terhardt, E. (1974). Pitch, consonance and harmony. *Journal of the Acoustical Society of America, 55,* 1061–1069.

Todd, P. (1988). A sequential network design for musical application. In D. Touretzky, G. Hinton, & T. Sejnowski (Eds.), *Proceedings of the 1988 Connectionist Models Summer School.* Menlo Park, CA: Morgan Kaufmann.

Todd, P. (1989). A connectionist approach to algorithmic composition. *Computer Music Journal, 13*(4), 27–43. (Reprinted in P. Todd & G. Loy, Eds., *Connectionism and music,* 1991, Cambridge, MA: MIT Press)

Tramo, M. J., Cariani, P. A., & Delgutte, B. (1992). Representation of tonal consonance and dissonance in the temporal firing patterns of auditory nerve fibers: Responses to musical intervals composed of pure tones vs. harmonic complex tones. *Society for Neuroscience Abstracts, 18,* 382.

von der Malsberg, C. (1973). Self-organizing of orientation sensitive cells in the striate cortex. *Kybernetic, 14,* 85–100.

Waugh, N. C., & Norman, D. A. (1965). Primary memory. *Psychological Review, 72,* 89–104.

Weinberger, N. M., & McKenna, T. M. (1988). Sensitivity of single neurons in auditory cortex to contour: Toward a neurophysiology of music perception. *Music Perception, 5,* 355–390.

Zwislocki, J. J. (1960). Theory of temporal auditory summation. *Journal of the Acoustical Society of America, 32,* 1046–1060.

Zwislocki, J. J. (1965). Analysis of some auditory characteristics. In R. D. Luce, R. R. Bush, & E. Galanter (Eds.), *Handbook of mathematical psychology.* New York: Wiley.

12

HIERARCHICAL EXPECTATION

AND MUSICAL STYLE

EUGENE NARMOUR

Kahn Distinguished Professor of Music
University of Pennsylvania
Philadelphia, Pennsylvania

Musicians tend to think of style in terms of chronological period, provenance, nationality, genre, composer, and work. In terms of cognition, however, style is simply repetition. Within a given work (intraopus), we recognize when we are experiencing something heard earlier, and between pieces (extraopus), we recognize when we are hearing something learned elsewhere. All music listening depends on remembering both intraopus and extraopus style.

Knowledge of style enables listeners to recognize similarity between percept and memory and thus to map learned, top-down expectations. Matching an emerging implicative pattern to the learned continuation of a previously stored schema tends to be automatic; we are rarely aware of it. Yet many stylistic representations lie just below the conscious surface. These are thus introspectively accessible. Were this not so, the study of musical style would be impossible. So would any attempt to test the psychological reality of stylistic knowledge.

Listeners construct stylistic expectations that are remarkably specific, surprisingly complex, and incredibly detailed. But the mapping of them remains amazingly flexible. Scholars have argued that all such learning, which varies from person to person, makes use of "bundled features," "schematic clusterings" (summarized in Gjerdingen, 1988), "archetypes" (Meyer, 1973), and "prototypes" (Jones, 1981). Computational neural-net models have relied on similar concepts (Bharucha, 1987; Gjerdingen, 1992), as have other formalized representations of musical learning.

The implication-realization model (Narmour, 1977, 1983, 1984, 1989, 1990, 1991a, 1991b, 1992, 1996) defines style in terms of the bottom-up primitives and the top-down structures invoked by the listener. Primitives find instantiation in various parametric materials common to a style (e.g., pitches, durations, meters, chords, timbres). In contrast, top-down style structures depend on hierarchical

---

interrelations. In the structural sense, style enters into the top-down processing of incoming signals as a level complex. With reference to melodic expectation, the memory of a specific implication connects to a learned style-structural realization situated within a specific durational, metric, and harmonic context.

Listeners invoke style structures that are implicatively relevant to the perceptual and cognitive analysis of input. As regards the listener's attention to learned expectations, repetition of intraopus stylistic structures normally takes priority over extraopus stylistic replication (Tenney & Polansky, 1980). Of course, the strength of any style-structural mapping onto melodic implication, whether intraopus or extraopus, will vary according to the similarity of the incoming signal to the previously learned hierarchical style. In this chapter, I concentrate on the structural and hierarchical aspects of extraopus style.

I. THE INVOCATION OF EXTRAOPUS STYLE

Style's strength from level to level, parameter to parameter, instantiation to instantiation, and property to property varies. Prospective aspects of musical style range from the highly general (loosely conformant and thus weakly implicative) to the highly specific (completely isomorphic and thus strongly implicative). For example, in terms of melody, knowledgeable listeners generally know that Scale-step 1 (the tonic) frequently ascends to Scale-step 5 (the dominant). Further, they generally know that a rising third degree (the mediant) often articulates the ascending melodic span to the perfect fifth, thus creating a structural motion based on Scale-degrees 1, 3, and 5. They also generally know that it is common for Degrees 2 (the supertonic) and 4 (the subdominant) to articulate shorter ascending spans from Degrees 1 to 3 and 3 to 5. Such learned, generalized, schemata in melody are thus hierarchically organized: Degrees 1-2-3 embed underneath Degrees 1-3, whereas Degrees 3-4-5 nest below Degrees 3-5. Likewise, on the next level, Degrees 1-3-5 lie underneath Degrees 1-5, the initial and terminal points emerging at the highest level. I shall return to hierarchical melodic patterns like this shortly.

Before listeners can recognize top-down schemata, generalized bottom-up processing is necessary. Accurate style-structural matching and mapping take place only after long-term memory recognizes the pitches, intervals, and timbres that typify tonal diatonic music. This requires the bottom-up, parallel processing of the individual parameters one by one.[1] Consequently, learned expectations of melodic continuation based on the generalized recognition of tonal materials emerge only gradually. For what initially sounds like Degrees 1-2 in a diatonic mode (e.g., C-D) could actually be Steps 4-5 in, say, a pentatonic mode (e.g., FGACD) with either F or C as the tonal center.

---

[1]The primitive materials that constitute bottom-up processing are, of course, themselves stylistic. For example, certain intervals and pitches, and above all certain timbres, uniquely typify Western diatonic music.

Of course, as parametric properties become known, establishing the stylistic context, then the overall pitch collection becomes much more specific, and our learned expectations of melodic continuation emerge much more strongly. For example, if the hierarchical pitch pattern discussed earlier appeared in a specific durational, metric, harmonic, and scale-step context, significantly similar to a previously learned extraopus structure, then our expectation of continuation from Degrees 1-2 up to 3 and 3-4 up to 5 (and 1-3-5 becoming 1-5) would be strong. Indeed, strong stylistic expectations always involve learned interrelations set in hierarchical parametric complexes, as we shall see. I call such top-down hierarchical complexes *style structures* (Narmour, 1977, 1990, 1992), an important theoretical concept to which we shall return.

II. EMPIRICAL AND RATIONALISTIC LEVELS OF STYLE

Scholarly knowledge about stylistic hierarchies varies from level to level. With respect to higher levels, considerable debate exists. Scholars often disagree about which key schemes in a given piece are perceptually salient, and journals are full of arguments about the extent to which people perceive that such-and-such a melodic passage is ruled by, say, a given *Urlinie*. Even overall form is frequently open to question. Is such-and-such a piece a monothematic sonata, a rondo, a sonata-rondo, a variation form, or some unique hybrid of all those? Such disagreements exist because high-level style tends to be rationalistically based.

Figure 1 represents extraopus style as a spiral from empirically based lower levels to rationalistic higher levels. Traveling clockwise, from the materialistic level, weakly implicative style involves groupings of low-level features frequently bundled together. As we traverse the spiral clockwise, we encounter increasingly stronger implication. At the bottom of the figure we find on middle levels hierarchical clusterings of schemata—specific style-structural mappings with strong empirical content that powerfully conspire to shape listeners' learned expectations. Continuing clockwise, to ever-higher levels, we see that stylistic invocation becomes weaker, more rationalistic, and impinges less strongly on listeners' expected continuations.

Indeed, following the nonimplicative metaphysical level (upper-left quadrant), the spiral doubles back on itself, like some kind of Möbius strip. That is, at the clockwise completion of the spiral (arrow), a new level emerges, recursion appears, and bottom-up processing would evaluate anew the transformed parametric materials. Epistemologically speaking, one observes that at that point the theoretical concepts of style are thus no different than the abstractions hypothesized to govern the bottom-up processing of parametric primitives on the note-to-note level. In sum, the representation in Figure 1 reminds us that many modes of stylistic invocation, both rationalistic and empirical, are simultaneously active in music perception.

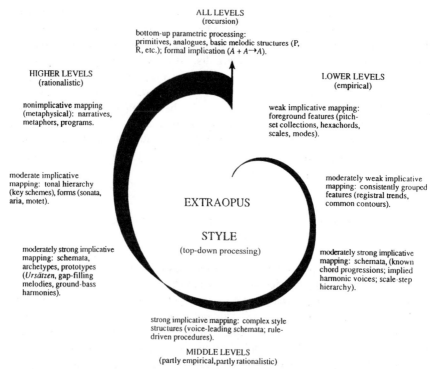

ALL LEVELS
(recursion)

bottom-up parametric processing:
primitives, analogues, basic melodic structures (P,
R, etc.); formal implication $(A + A \rightarrow A)$.

HIGHER LEVELS
(rationalistic)

LOWER LEVELS
(empirical)

nonimplicative mapping
(metaphysical): narratives,
metaphors, programs.

weak implicative mapping:
foreground features (pitch-
set collections, hexachords,
scales, modes).

moderate implicative
mapping: tonal hierarchy
(key schemes), forms (sonata,
aria, motet).

EXTRAOPUS

moderately weak implicative
mapping: consistently grouped
features (registral trends,
common contours).

STYLE

moderately strong implicative
mapping: schemata,
archetypes, prototypes
(*Ursätzen*, gap-filling
melodies, ground-bass
harmonies).

(top-down processing)

moderately strong implicative
mapping: schemata, (known
chord progressions; implied
harmonic voices; scale-step
hierarchy).

strong implicative mapping: complex style
structures (voice-leading schemata; rule-
driven procedures).

MIDDLE LEVELS
(partly empirical, partly rationalistic)

FIGURE 1   An example of the kinds of stylistic levels that simultaneously operate in music perception.

III. LEARNED STYLISTIC LEVELS AS "THEME" AND "VARIATION"

From the perspective of analytical music theory, we may regard a given hierarchical style structure as a kind of "theme" that listeners implicatively map from
the top down onto incoming foreground "variations." They hear different melodic
variants on lower levels as creating similar structural-tone "themes" on higher
levels. Such a view is in fact not at all novel and has a distinguished history in the
study of musical style, namely, in the analysis and practice of diminution (which
became an integral part of Schenker's method of reduction). *Diminution* refers to
the compositional and contrapuntal practice of dividing given long notes into
shorter ones, the long notes in effect functioning like a "theme" against which the
short notes act as "variations" or "ornamentations."

Writers of diminution treatises—Renaissance and Baroque manuals teaching
performers how to vary melodic patterns while holding higher-level structural
tones constant—were very knowledgeable about such hierarchical reductions, and
their demonstrations are analytically and conceptually instructive in that they ex-

emplify stylistic melodic hierarchies about whose level reductions there can be little dispute.

For our purposes, the concept of diminution as "variations on a theme" can help us conceive top-down mapping as a cognitive phenomenon—from, say, stylistic variations on a given class of nursery rhyme tunes to, for instance, the similar stylistic structuring found in the more sophisticated melodies of "art music." Further, by marrying the technique of diminution to certain basic hypotheses of the implication-realization model, we can schematize what an economic cognitive module for the stylistic processing of melody in general might look like. From this union, we can speculate how the perception of stylistically structured melodies might be neurally encoded.

IV. DEFINING LEVELS

To use the earlier triadic example, consider Figure 2, which shows a synthetic melody whose structural tones on the bar level (Level 4) make an ascending triad (C-E-G). On the beat level (Level 3), we see an ascending line with one repeated note in the middle (C-D-E-E-F#-G). On the eighth-note level (Level 2) a zigzagging, up-down pattern exists. And on the note-to-note level (Level 1), we see each higher-level structural tone ornamented with a different diminution.

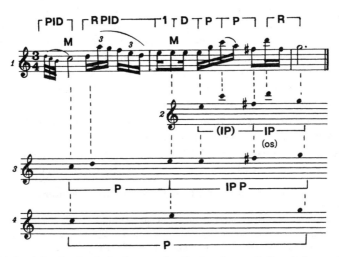

FIGURE 2 A four-level analysis of structural realizations in a synthetic melody according to the implication-realization model. P = process, ID = intervallic duplication, IP = intervallic process, M = monad, 1 = dyad, R = reversal, D = duplication, parentheses = retrospective realization, (os) = intra-opus style. Horizontal dashed lines trace the derivation of higher-level structural tones from the initial and terminal structural tones of bracketed groupings on lower levels.

Each ornament on the note-to-note level is taken from Quantz's treatise on playing the flute (1752/1966). For the structural tones C-D in measure 1, for instance, the example expropriates two different variants from the 26 given by Quantz for any single tone and for any line like C-D-E (see the opening of Figure 3.1 and then Figures 3.1h and 3.1m, marked with asterisks; note the basic harmonic context of I-V-I in m. 2 of Figure 3.1). The same is true of the syncopated pattern configuring the repeated Es at the start of measure 2 in Figure 2 (cf. Figure 3.3t) and of the rising, modulating line of E-F♯-G that follows (see the opening of Figure 3.2).[2] By mixing different kinds of motivic variants while preserving adjacent higher-level tones, one can, of course, compose or improvise melodies that stylistically vary the surface yet generate similar structures on higher levels. As we shall see, it is the connected complexes of several levels that create the style structures that listeners use to map onto their learned expectations.[3]

V. REPRESENTING HIERARCHICAL LEVELS

The synthetic melody of Figure 2 displays four levels. On the foreground level, the analysis shows the basic melodic structures according to the implication-realization model (for evaluations of the model see Krumhansl, 1995, 1997; Cuddy & Lunney, 1995; Thompson, Cuddy, & Plaus, 1997; Thompson & Stainton, 1998; Schellenberg, 1996, 1997; and Russo & Cuddy, 1995). According to the model, the structures on Level 1, the beat level, are PID-RPID-1-D-P-P-R (for the meaning of the symbols, see the caption for Figure 2). Level 2, emerging only on the eighth-note level in measure 2, is (IP)-IP, while underneath the ascending process [P] on the three-bar level (Level 4, the C-E-G) lie an embedded P (the C-D-E) and an IPP (E-E-F♯-G) on Level 3. Significantly, observe that when we say something occurs at the bar, the beat, or the eighth-note level, we define hierarchical level in two ways. On the one hand, "three-bar level" indicates length—that is, duration or time span as the defining attribute at the highest level (here Level 4). On the other hand, "beat level" points to meter—that is, to time point or tactus as the determining criterion for defining the foreground level. (Observe that note-to-note levels are manifest occurrences, whereas higher levels are analytical projections.)

This traditional convention of defining level differentiation according to different temporal parameters (duration, meter) ordinarily causes no theoretical prob-

---

[2] Quantz's examples use the same motive for each set of three notes, which, for our purposes, I have not followed here.

[3] I should make it clear in the synthetic melody of Figure 2 that I am not at all trying to imitate 18th-century style (to mimic Quantz would, at the very least, require repeating variants for at least two or three beats). Nor am I necessarily trying to compose a "good" melody. For the sake of the theoretical discussion, I am merely constructing a synthetic tonal example that uses a known stylistic technique of hierarchically ornamenting tones and lines. My goal in this intellectual exercise is to demonstrate how the compositional technique of diminution can profitably illustrate the hierarchical properties of style structures that listeners map onto their learned expectations.

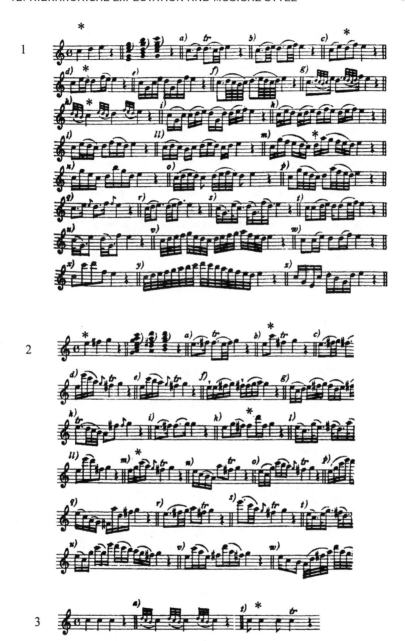

FIGURE 3 After Quantz (1752/1966), chapter 13, "Of Extempore Variations on Simple Intervals" (pp. 136–161). Ornamentation for the opening C and for the following melodic variants for C-D-E in Fig. 3.1 are from p. 141 (Quantz's Fig. 2); for E-F#-G in Fig. 3.2, p. 144 (Quantz's Figure 6); for the repeated E-E in Fig. 3.3, p. 140 (Quantz's Figure 1).

lem provided the invocation of the two criteria are kept separate (here duration = high levels; meter = low, note-to-note levels). But being terminologically consistent often proves difficult: the eighth-note level (Level 2; criterion: duration) also creates an eighth-note meter (2/8). Likewise, the sixteenth-note level displays both durational and metric properties (3/16 on beat 3 in m.1; 2/16 on beats 2-3 in m. 2). Some theorists have even ascribed metrical properties at the bar, the two-bar, or even the four-bar level—"hypermetric" levels quite removed from perceived pulse or toe-tapping tactus.

But how high up in the hierarchy does one perceive metric levels (see in Lerdahl & Jackendoff, 1983)? For that matter, how far down the hierarchy does one perceive metric levels? Do listeners actually construct metric groups at the "grace-note" level (e.g., at the level of the thirty-second-note turn in m. 1)? Because meter probably does not exist at either extremely high or extremely low levels, it seems likely that duration (and thus time span) is the real criterion for determining perceptual levels in music. But projected time span and actual duration are not the same thing. For a durationally short tone at a manifest level can come to stand for a relatively lengthy time span at a higher, hierarchically projected level.

VI. PROBLEMS WITH LEVEL DISPLAYS

Although the analysis of Figure 2 includes all melodic relations of implication and realization, generating levels from start to finish, and although the analytical symbols adequately identify the melodic structures, the four-level display in fact glosses over the actual durations of the hierarchical structures. In so doing, it thus analytically obscures some of the structural differentiation that occurs between the various levels of the melody. This is because the various closed realizations in Figure 2 occupy durations or time spans that in a number of cases are different from the levels indicated by the meter.

For example, in Figure 2, the duration of the PID in measure 1 appears to be eight sixteenth notes in duration (two beats, assuming the turn starts on the beat), whereas the RPID is five sixteenth notes long. In measure 2, the dyadic structure [1] creating the syncopation is three sixteenths, whereas the duplicative realization [D] lasts four sixteenths.[4] Indeed, the reversal [R] at the very end of the tune (mm. 2–3) would seem to have a longer time span than any of these structures on the note-to-note level—namely, fourteen sixteenths (14/16).

However, it would not be logical to move the entire reversal structure [R] to such a high durational level because its initial tone, the high D, functions as a medial tone in the IP structure on the eighth-note level. In addition, the long final G also terminates the IP structure on Level 2. Indeed, the final G of the reversal,

---

[4]In cumulative patterns that create closed melodic dyads, as in the unison [1] of measure 2, the second tone of the dyad is the structural tone. This is in accordance with the implication-realization model, which asserts that in dyads durational patterning outweighs metric stress. It is this structural shift away from the beat as the site of the structural tone and toward the tone off the beat that gives the unexpected syncopation here its characteristic interest.

the longest duration, participates on every hierarchical level, as does both the terminal C of the initial turn (the PID structure) in measure 1 and the transforming eighth note E of the syncopation in measure 2.

Figure 4 shows a somewhat more accurate representation of the durational hierarchical structuring of the same synthetic melody. Of course, the analysis of levels in Figure 4 may be rationalistic.[5] Nevertheless, by ignoring the meter and tracking just the representative durations of the structure, we observe here that eight different levels emerge: from the lowest level of 5/64 to lower levels of 3/16, 4/16, 5/16, and 6/16 to middle levels of 15/16 and 17/16 to the highest levels of 36/16.[6] This durationally distinct level analysis makes clear the hierarchical density of measure 2 in contrast to the relatively less dense hierarchy of the RPID in measure 1. That is, we perceive measure 1 as two melodic gestures [PID, RPID], whereas in measures 2–3 we have to work harder to process a relatively larger number of nested levels. Put analytically, there is a greater informational load at the start of the syncopation in measure 2 and thereafter to measure 3 as the structural hierarchy increases in depth.[7]

As stressed earlier, it is important to understand that in hierarchies projected higher-level time spans are not theoretically equivalent to perceived durations on note-to-note levels. A quarter note on a manifest level actually lasts its given, performed length and is so perceived, whereas a pitch transformed to a higher level only stands for a duration. The very short D starting the sixteenth-note triplet and initiating the RPID structure in measure 1 of Figure 4, for instance, transforms to Level 5/16 and actually functions there at a time span of a quarter note. However, the sixteenth note E on Beat 2 in measure 2 initiates the P on Level 3/16 and the (IP) on Level 6/16; hence this E hierarchically functions at the time-span level six times longer than its manifest duration. Such functional projections create the hierarchical levels that we find in music. Thus, strictly speaking, syntactic hierarchical levels are not about "length" per se but rather about time-span functions of implicative primacy, recency, initiation, termination, realization, closure, and so forth.

We can also display the hierarchical structuring of the synthetic melody of Figure 4 as a tree structure (see Figure 5).[8] Because any given melodic structure

[5]That is, from a perceptual point of view, listeners may not discriminate durational levels finely enough to differentiate 3/16 from 4/16, 5/16 from 6/16, or 15/16 from 16/16. Be that as it may, the analytical levels in Figure 4 are more accurate than those of Figure 1.

[6]I omit in this analysis the dyadic recursive levels from the realization of the PID (m. 2) and D structures (m. 2) to the emergence of their respective monads [M]. Because the monads are temporary transformations—the half note C at the very beginning eventually becomes an initial tone in the implied realizations on Levels 15/16 and 36/16—I do not count monads in the numbering of levels. Figure 5 below shows the dyads. For the rules of recursion in the implication-realization model, see Narmour (1990, 1991).

[7]Readers familiar with the implication-realization model may note in the analyses the lack of discussion of registral return [aba]. Nevertheless, registral return on the E-C-F♯-D (the (IP)-IP on Level 6/16 in bar 2) would strengthen the rise of the E-F♯-G line of the IPP on Level 17/16.

[8]Note that the dyads [2, 1] occur at the same time span as the level-adjacent realizations of the implications that they summarize. Here I add the recursive dyadic levels [2, 1] that eventually become the monads [M].

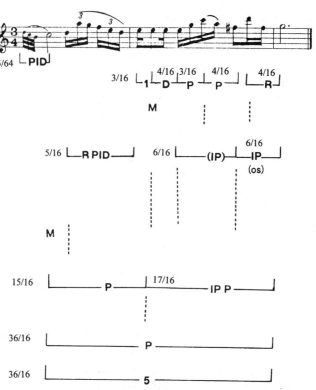

FIGURE 4   The four levels of the synthetic melody of Figure 2 displayed according to the actual durations of the levels. Time spans of the structures are measured up to the point where they close, i.e., where one structure stops and another begins or where durational cumulation suppresses the terminal implication (50% beyond the length of the last tone, according to the rules of the theory; see Narmour, 1990, pp. 105–110). On low levels stopping usually closes the structure before the last duration cumulates (as, e.g., on Beats 1 and 2 in m. 2 and on the downbeat in m. 3). Note that the two highest-level structures [P and 5] occupy the same level length.

stretches a certain durational span from beginning to end, the tree symbolizes the initial, medial, and terminal functions responsible for creating the hierarchy. As before, the initial and terminal tones of the various structures transform to the higher levels, as traced by the various vertical lines.[9] Note as before that the analytical tree makes clear the depth of structural nesting in measures 2 and 3. This is in contrast to measure 1, where many medial notes occur on the same level, owing

[9]Because any given realization of implication has a maximum of three functions (initial, medial, terminal), tree reductions in the implication-realization model require that subordinate branches of medial functions connect to at least one other superordinate branch as well as to one other subordinate or superordinate branch. For this reason, binary branching only occurs on dyads in the implication-realization model. I believe that the tree display shown in Figure 5 more accurately represents the perceptual structure of music than the binary models borrowed from linguistic theory of syntax.

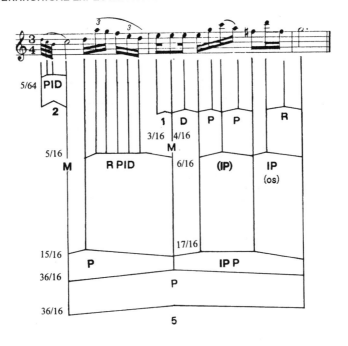

FIGURE 5   A tree display of the analysis of the synthetic melody shown in Figure 4. Note that binary branching occurs only with dyadic structures.

to the sixteenth-note triplets of the RPID.[10] I shall return to such displays later in the chapter.

VII. THE PARAMETRIC NATURE OF HIERARCHICAL STYLE STRUCTURES

In Figure 6, I have substituted on Beat 3 of measure 1 a different variant, as given by Quantz, and changed Beat 1 of measure 2 to two repeated notes, thereby excising the syncopation.[11] One hierarchical result is that measure 1 now increases in depth, parsing into six levels instead of four. The lowest level is still the PID

---

[10]That the first and second bars display different hierarchical properties is, of course, analytically logical because the more medial tones that occur in any one grouping, the fewer the number of levels.

[11]The variant in measure 1 comes from Quantz's Figure 1 (1752/1966, p. 141) and can be seen earlier in Figure 3.1d.

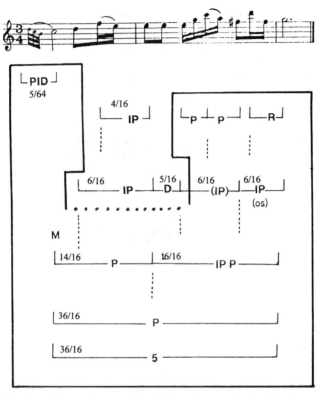

FIGURE 6   A variation on the same hierarchical style structuring found in the synthetic melody of Figure 4. The hierarchical style-structural similarity between the two melodies appears within the box. The realizations above the dotted portion of the box are new variants (also taken from Quantz), which simplify the overall structuring and affect the implications of the higher-level structures (below the dotted line).

structure (5/64); the 4/16 level now has an IP structure, and the next two levels (6/16 and 5/16) now display an IP-D sequence. The seemingly minor change of having two new structures on the manifest level thus actually affects two different levels, as here defined. By thus tracking melodic structures and durational levels very carefully, we see that small differences have a pronounced effect on the overall hierarchical display, more than we might have thought, given that the melody of Figure 6 is still, after all, very much like that of Figure 4. That the implication-realization model allows us accurately to track such small changes attests to its analytical power (this despite using only eight basic structural symbols). No listener would miss the similarity between the two melodies. Yet no listener would fail to detect the differences between them, however subtle. An important point, then, is that, by straining even very similar melodic structures through a finely meshed hierarchical net, we can capture idiostructural differences (Narmour, 1977).

The second important point is that from Level 6/16 onward the two melodies are nearly exactly alike, which is to say, they rely on basically the same style structure. By *style structure,* I again mean a connected complex of two or more levels that belong to and arise from a specific constellation of parametric instantiations. The variable box around the structures in Figure 6 groups the structures that are hierarchically shared with the melody of Figure 4. The new structures in Figure 6 appear above the dotted line. The horizontal dotted line broken at that point also demonstrates that the hierarchical levels below it are somewhat changed because now Levels 14/16, 16/16, and 36/16—which stylistically also appear in the analysis of Figure 4—embody in measure 1 a different set of level relations. These relations come from below, on Levels 4/16, 5/16, and 6/16 (on how higher levels embody lower-level meaning, see Narmour, 1990).

In Figure 6, it is thus the boxed complex of level connections that, when invoked, the listener stylistically maps onto the expectations generated by the input. In terms of cognitive principles, the more stylistically conformant the invoked levels, the stronger the top-down mapping. Within the boxed levels, showing the stylistic sharing between Figures 4 and 6, all the implications invoked from the learned realizations are nearly the same, except for those belonging to the three different low-level structures in Figure 6 (above the dotted line).

I use the qualifier "nearly"—and here is my third important point about these two subtly different melodies—because, as said, style-structural similarity rests not just on melodic pitch sequence but on all parametric interconnections throughout every level. Consequently, the strength of any higher-level implication rests on the nature of the structures that exist underneath it. In Figure 6, for example, the third beat of measure 1 is now an eighth note. Hence D's durational realization along with the half-note C preceding it creates a parametric complex different from that found in Figure 4, where the D on the third beat in measure 1 initiates a sixteenth-note triplet. Hence the manifest durational relationship between the higher-level C-D of Figure 6 (half/eighth) is less countercumulative than that of the analogous C-D of Figure 4 (half/triplet sixteenth). Moreover, because measure 1 in Figure 6 has more levels than Figure 4, the strength of the meter at the tactus level is altered: the third beat of Figure 6 is metrically more substantive than that of Figure 4.

Because of the weaker countercumulation and the now more stable meter on the third beat of measure 1, the D in Figure 6 is less nonclosural, less implicative than the D of Figure 4. That is, the manifest eighth note (the duration actually realized in Figure 6) is closer to, and can thus more easily stand for, the quarter note on Level 14/16 than the sixteenth note of the triplet in Figure 4. The D in Figure 6 thus transforms more strongly to Level 14/16, which in turn means that the higher-level implication created by the C-D there is stronger. Similar kinds of observations would obtain about the changes in measure 2 of Figure 6.

These significant observations aside, once listeners recognized the shared style structure between Figures 4 and 6 (box), they would project a hierarchical continuation based on the expected connections of the learned level complex. This is because top-down stylistic perceptual processing sweeps across all the operative levels. Operational "scanning" throughout the level-complex determines the shape of the learned expectations. Of course, listeners would continue to attend to low-level melodic variation because bottom-up systems process incoming parametric events as if hearing them for the very first time. But the learned expectations generated by listeners' top-down stylistic knowledge would influence the strength of bottom-up implications and realizations. Indeed, each subsequent, realized confirmation of the multileveled style structure (the box in Figure 6) would somewhat suppress bottom-up implications. The latter would, so to speak, come somewhat under the control of the style-structural "theme."[12] In the perception of melody, then, style is not just a simplistic collection of attributes. The similar level connections between Figures 4 and 6 would, from the top down, guide the listener's expectations, but at the same time subtle structural differences between the two melodies, as generated from the bottom up, would not be lost.

Figure 7 further simplifies the style-structural hierarchy, again using other Quantz variants on Beat 3 of measure 1 while deleting those on Beat 1 of measure 1 and those on Beats 1 and 2 of measure 2.[13] Even here, the minute changes, which weight the tune more toward extraopus style than toward idiostructure, have noticeable level effects. Much of Level 6/16 is now different, whereas Levels 4/16, 16/16, and 36/16 are nearly identical to the analogous levels found in Figures 4 and 6.

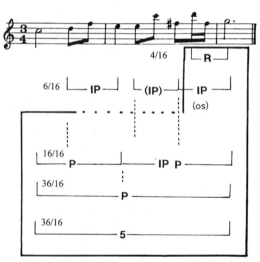

FIGURE 7   A second variation (again taken from Quantz) with further simplification. Note that what was a projected higher-level implication in Figure 6 now becomes manifest in the music.

[12]Of course, a previously denied implication arising from the bottom-up system can reassert itself at any time, deforming the style-structural expectation and weakening the learned mapping from the top down. Such "variations" transform the anticipated stylistic "theme."

[13]The variants again come from Quantz's Figure 2.

Again I say "nearly identical" because in three cases in Figure 7, what were projected level-structures in Figures 4 and 6 are now manifest events. That is, in Figure 7, the IP structure straddling measures 1–2 (D-F-E) now contains no embedded structure at the 4/16 level but rather emerges as an actual realization. Similarly, the quarter note E starting measure 2 is now no longer just a projected hierarchical event, as it was in Figures 4 and 6, but rather a manifest realization. The same is true of the eighth note F♯ on Beat 3. As before, these seemingly insignificant changes alter the implicative strength of the melodic patterns on higher levels (those beneath the dots). For example, the C-E implication at Level 36/16 (implying the process [P] to the G) now emerges considerably stronger. This is due both to the increased metric emphasis on the downbeat of measure 2 and the cumulative durational closure on the actualized quarter note E (cumulative because the eighth note F at the end of m. 1 moves to the quarter note). Thus the sharing of stylistic structures among Figures 4, 6, and 7 is not exact, only remarkably similar—this because learned stylistic mapping relies on parametric level-complexes, whose comparative interrelationships slightly change in Figure 7. Basically, Figure 7 requires less bottom-up cognitive processing than Figure 6, and Figure 6 needs less than Figure 4.

Because in these three melodies the number of levels decreases with each subsequent simplification, the hierarchical texture becomes less dense. Figure 8 carries the simplifying reduction of levels further. Variations on Beat 2 of measure 1 and Beat 3 of measure 2 are now deleted, and hence only three levels occur (6/16, 16/16, and 36/16). Again, underneath the dotted line lie those portions of the hierarchical complex that have undergone subtle alteration. Symbologically, the box in Figure 8 encompasses more and more of the style-attributed hierarchy, whereas the dotted line diminishes in length. In terms of style-structural mapping, this means that the melodies of Figures 4, 6, and 7 are less stylistic and thus compara-

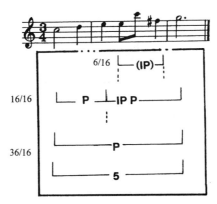

FIGURE 8   A third variation. The continuing simplification leads to a stronger hierarchical style structure, with more of the structuring appearing in the box. Earlier hierarchical projections are now manifest.

tively more idiostructural, so to speak, than the melody of Figure 8. In each succeeding example, proportionately more connected levels are shared as the number of levels systematically decreases.

As mentioned in connection with the spiral of Figure 1, pieces of music thus differ in terms of the strength of the specific style-structural mapping that goes on. The balance between the top-down and bottom-up processing that guides our expectations therefore constantly changes from work to work. Given the hierarchical structures of these four examples, Figure 4 thus depends more on bottom-up processing than any of the others. In contrast, Figure 8 is more subservient to top-down processing, to learned style-structural mapping. This is even more true of Figures 9 and 10. As before, the pitches that in Figures 9 and 10 create hierarchical projections are now made manifest on the note-to-note level, with all that entails for changing metric and durational properties, and thus the changing strength of higher-level implications within the hierarchical complex.

Such commonly shared stylistic complexes as those represented in the level connections boxed in Figures 8–10 would, in terms of top-down invocation, come into focus very rapidly in shaping the listener's expectations of continuation, for overlearning facilitates the utility of any given mapping (see Rumelhart & Ortony, 1977). The response strength of top-down stylistic processing will increase the more common the learned input is (Bharucha & Stoeckig, 1986). Of course, taken singly, all the patterns in Figures 8–10 are extremely common in extraopus tonal style. Further, even though all earlier variants have been deleted in Figure 9, this example by itself can be imagined as a variant of Figure 10. For that matter, all of Quantz's variants in Figure 3 are themselves utterly common to tonal style. That he was able to construct a catalog of them some 250 years ago attests to this fact.

VIII. STYLE STRUCTURES AS COMPOSITE COGNITIVE PATHS

Figure 11 distributes all the structures of the melodies of Figures 4 and 6–10 across levels, displaying even the small differences that occur according to each

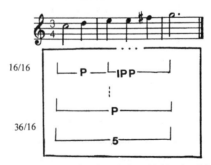

FIGURE 9   A fourth variation, highly simplified.

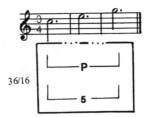

FIGURE 10   A fifth, highly simplified variation.

variant, with reference to either the actual duration or the projected time span. The suggestion here is that the brain marks and stores style-structural patterns not only according to melodic type but also according to hierarchical level, which is to say, according to manifest duration or temporal span. That is, it is reasonable to imagine that somewhere in the brain the overarching class of patterns that the reader has just learned from the foregoing melodies exists as a single style-structural complex—all levels and all parameters hierarchically distributed. Such a brain would store all the segments of the preceding complex style structure together in order to process incoming signals economically. Upon the recognition of a conformant pattern, preactivation of the whole system would occur, but on each occasion stylistic mapping would follow the path actually traveled by the bottom-up input. Indeed, it is not too much to imagine that the thirty-some variations derived by Quantz, and shown earlier in Figure 3, probably occupy a dedicated region in our memory with similar kinds of level connections.

Figure 12 illustrates the various paths of the stylistic complex. The display hypothesizes the hierarchical paths that top-down, stylistic mapping of all six melodies would follow in any specific listening experience. Any given path of a specific melody would be strengthened by frequency of input. Thus, within any given style-structural complex, the mapping strength guiding the listener's learned stylistic expectations would vary. The implication-realization model thus enables us to schematize what an overall cognitive system for the stylistic processing of a set of melodies might look like. As we shall shortly see, the model will also allow us to hypothesize how the hierarchical perception of stylistically similar melodies might be neurally encoded.

IX. REFINING FURTHER HIERARCHICAL DISPLAYS

The analyses seen thus far are reasonably accurate visual representations of the durational levels that the various structures span when taken as a hierarchical whole. However, they are inadequate when we conceive of the individual elements of the structures hierarchically one by one. Medial tones, for example, never function at the level of the tones that initiate and terminate the structures in which they

FIGURE 11　　A style-structural composite of all the hierarchical realizations seen in the six earlier melodies.

occur. For that matter, the initial and terminal tones of a given structure are frequently not level-equivalent in terms of both duration and the hierarchically projected time span.

FIGURE 12   The six paths that any given cognitive mapping could take across the composite style structure.

Thus, to represent the time-span hierarchy of any individual tone even more accurately would require more detailed level distributions. This is shown in Figures 13 and 14, which take into account the initial, medial, and terminal hierarchical functions of the elements of the melodic structures found in Figures 4 and 6.

For that matter, all the manifest hierarchical tones on any given level could be further differentiated if we take into account meter on each level. The five notes of the sixteenth-note triplets, for instance, are metrically all different—from the accent on the F to the first and second nonaccents on A and E, and G and D. Again note in both examples that manifest duration is not the same as the level duration; for example, the eighth note E of measure 2 also occurs at Level 36/16, a dotted-half-note time span belonging to the three-bar level.[14]

[14]All the manifest hierarchical tones on any given level could be further differentiated if we took into account meter on each level. The five notes of the sixteenth-note triplets, for instance, are metrically all different—from the accent on the F to the first and second nonaccents on A and E, and G and D. Note that separating out medial tones and displaying them at their actual durational levels also avoids the question of whether listeners can perceive structural levels that differ by only one sixteenth note (e.g., 3/16, 4/16, 5/16, 6/16).

DURATIONAL LEVEL

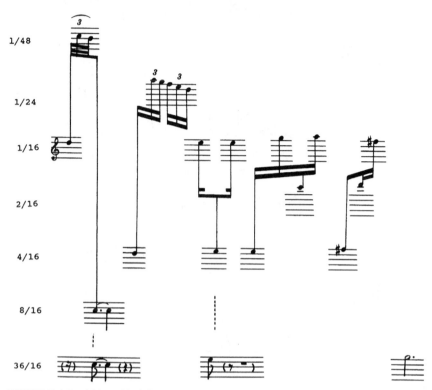

FIGURE 13   A hierarchical display of the melodies of Figures 2 and 4 with greater level differentiation made possible by separating out medial tones from initial and terminal tones.

X. NEURONAL REPRESENTATION: A
SPECULATION

Taking the idea of Figure 11 earlier as a style-structural composite of Figures 4
and 6–10, we can speculate further about how melodies might be stored in the
brain. Imagine, for instance, that durational memory occupies a neural substrate
that stores time span. Thus every duration representing a hierarchical level (3/16,
4/16, 5/16, etc.) would have a durationally specified neuron that would occupy a
specific level-topic location in the brain. Presumably, the level of 3/16 would lie
atop the level of 4/16, that of 4/16 would lie atop the level of 5/16—and so forth. In
such cases, each neuron would thus function as an addressable location for each
time-spanned level.

Now imagine further that each of these durational levels divides tonotopically
into specific pitch-registral regions, the whole aggregate distributed like a musical
staff, as it were. The bottom-up system processes the melodic input, marking ini-

DURATIONAL LEVEL

FIGURE 14   A hierarchical display of the melody of Figure 6 with greater level differentiation.

tial, medial, and terminal tones of implication and realization, evaluating degrees of closure and nonclosure, creating and measuring duration and the projected time spans of new levels, and so forth. Each transformationally closed structure (P, R, ID, PID, RPID, etc.) on each level would be transferred for storage at the appropriate level-topic location according to its temporal projection. Each pitch would also itself reside in a tonotopic neuron specifically tuned for, and thus temporally indexing, a given register (see Weinberger & McKenna, 1988). Finally, imagine that the connections between each neuron (i.e., dendrites) would join the pitches between the various levels, representing the overall hierarchical structuring.

Now if we could selectively identify the neurons and the connectors that represented such a hierarchical, style-structured set of melodic segments, such as the composite seen in Figure 11, the resultant representation would perhaps look something like the tree diagram of Figure 15.[15] Based on a composite style struc-

[15]One is struck by the fact that photographs of neuronal networks do not resemble the binary branching found in linguistic trees; instead they look somewhat like the networked diagram shown in Figure 15.

DURATIONAL LEVEL

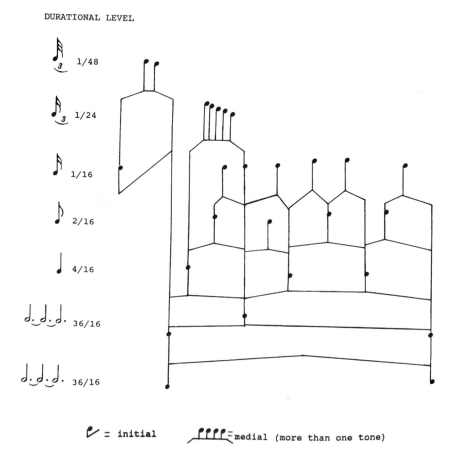

$\mathcal{V}$ = initial $\underline{\Gamma\Gamma\Gamma\Gamma}$ = medial (more than one tone)

$\underline{\mathbf{I}}$ = medial (one tone) $\searrow$ = terminal   dyad = $\wedge$

FIGURE 15   A tree display of the hierarchical style structure of all six melodies, in parallel to Figure 5 but with the pitch levels shown spatially.

ture of all the melodies previously seen in Figures 4 and 6–11, and using the symbology employed in Figure 5, this diagram illustrates the kind of memory storage that I have in mind. The structural tones of the several melodies are symbolized with note heads, each note head standing for a tuned, tonotopic neuron. In the vertical left margin would lie, so to speak, the level-topic neurons ordering, storing, and distributing the hierarchical networks. As can be seen, as one moves through successively higher levels (toward the bottom of the example), what was initial or terminal eventually becomes medial until recursion ends at Level 36/16. That is, initial or terminal note heads (pitch-activated neurons) on lower levels become higher-level note heads (projected time-span neurons) as pitches change function.

We can improve on this hierarchical tree, however. For if neurons can be coded for hierarchical level—for time-spanned projections—then they could also code manifest duration itself. In such case, neurons would be chronotopic as well as level-topic and tonotopic. If we could selectively identify neurons coding a specific hierarchical composite of style structures, we would not have a two-dimensional tree but rather a three-dimensional one, once we added the aspect of manifest duration, that is, once we included the chronotopic domain (see Figure 16).

The cube here, like the boxes in the previous Figures, thus represents a kind of Fodorian module (Fodor, 1983) and demonstrates how a hierarchical set of melodic style structures might be neuronally distributed. Each circle represents a thrice-connected neuron. The x-axis shows the manifest chronotopic duration,[16] the y-axis the tonotopic melodic pitch,[17] and the z-axis the level-topic hierarchical function. In other words, each imagined neuron is feature-specific in three different ways and also contextually connected. Lowest-level tones appear in the foreground, whereas those at the highest levels—for example, the structural tones C-E-G at Level 32/16—clump together toward the rear of the figure. As in Figure 15, the three-dimensional composite (36 x 36, one cell for each sixteenth note) comprises all the hierarchical structures of the six synthetic melodies shown in Figures 4 and 6–10. The cube thus superimposes and distributes style-structural memory over all the hierarchical connections.

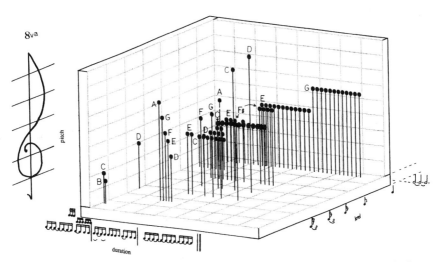

FIGURE 16   A three-dimensional, hierarchical composite of all six melodies, imagined as a modular "neuronal style structure" (see text).

[16]Long durations, such as the dotted whole note shown by the ties in front of the x-axis, would result from densely packed neurons, so to speak.

[17]Not being a true graph, the treble staff lines must be slightly expanded, for example, the space between the G-B lines for the major third.

In terms of cognitive expectancy, the idea here is one of a spreading activation throughout the neurons (circles) of the module (cube) with each onset of specific pitch, duration, and level function. In terms of theory, the specifically activated, learned path of expectations (recall Figure 12) would, upon input, energize the relevant neurons in three different ways: (1) actualized, learned implications of melody and duration (not to mention meter); (2) actual realizations of these learned implications; and (3) hierarchical projections of parametric interrelationships.

XI. THE MUSICAL REALITY OF STYLE-STRUCTURAL HIERARCHIES

Such speculations aside, the kind of style-structured level-composite argued for in this chapter commonly appears in the tonal literature. For example, given the four nursery-rhyme tunes in Figure 17a–d, all of which rely on similar hierar-

FIGURE 17 Four nursery-rhyme tunes (a–d), all sharing the same hierarchical style structure (boxed, as before).

chical structuring, it seems likely that such highly conformant melodies would inhabit a composite, conformant, style-structured space within cortical modules. Taking Figure 17a as our model (and ignoring durational differences), the three levels realized there appear as a hierarchical pitch projection in the melody of Figure 17b, which has four levels (as before, the box indicates the style-structural sharing between the two melodies). Hence the actual melody of Figure 17a is only a projected level in Figure 17b (Level 2 in fact). Thus, as discussed earlier, the new structures in Figure 17b entail altered higher-level parametric relationships (beneath the dotted lines) within the (boxed) stylistic complex. In contrast, in Figure

FIGURE 17 (*Continued*)

17c, parametric change is kept to a minimum, which is to say, Figure 17c's sharing of realized level structures with Figure 17a is extremely strong, whereas Figure 17c's similarity with Figure 17b is more a matter of hierarchical projection (and thus somewhat weaker).

These conclusions, of course, take Figure 17a as the model with Figures 17b and 17c being compared with it, in that order. If, however, a different, though related, melody served as the initial model, then the parametric interrelationships among the structures making up the hierarchical complex would be quite different. For instance, if we take Figure 17a as the model, then the dotted box symbolizing change in Figure 17d obtains. But if the stylistic perceptual matching of Figure 17d relied on, say, Figure 17b as the initial condition, then the line below measure 2 in Figure 17d would have fewer dotted lines. This is because E-G-D in Figure 17d occurs on the manifest level, whereas in Figure 17b it takes place on the projected level.

XII. ARCHETYPES

Why is the distinction between initial condition and subsequent match important? The answer is that neuronal activation in the learning of musical style structures is sensitive to frequency and recency of experience. Thus the most recent and frequently used paths in any style structure are more salient than less used ones. And this explains why comparative processing varies constantly in every listening experience because, even when a great deal of previous stylistic similarity is present, hierarchical parametric interrelationships constantly undergo change. Thus level relationships are not systemic and static but rather are partly decomposing hierarchies where interlevel relationships transform on each rehearing (Narmour, 1983; Simon, 1969). Parametric interrelationships between levels thus constantly change according to memory sequence. Hence the "thematic," archetypal IRID/RP connections from Level 3 to Level 4 in Figure 17b–d would never remain static in active listening. In music cognition there is no "final state."

Most extraopus style-structural mapping is, of course, much less level-conformant than that seen among the four melodies of Figure 17. Consider the folk song of Figure 18. Here the sharing of structural similarity with the previous four cases is more general, confined primarily to the hierarchical structuring on Levels 3-4 (but note the IP of the D-F-C in m. 2). The different melodic configurations on the lower levels (Levels 1 and 2) again feed into the IRID and RP on Levels 3 and 4, altering the hierarchical parametric complex. That said, the melody of Figure 18 nevertheless partly belongs to the same general style-structural composite as that seen in the melodies of Figure 17, owing to the obvious IRID/RP interconnection.

XIII. STYLE CHANGE: TOWARD GREATER COMPLEXITY

It should not be thought that the hierarchical style structure discussed in Figures 17a–d and 18 is confined to, and thus only representative of, "simple" music,

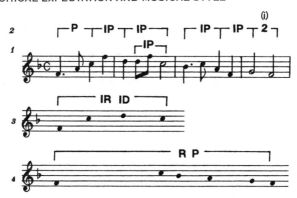

FIGURE 18   A folk tune that belongs to the same hierarchical style structure as the nursery-rhyme tunes of Figure 17 but whose first two levels are more "distanced" (however, note the D-F-C in m. 2).

of nursery rhymes and folk songs. In Figure 19, the principal theme from a rondo written in the Classic period, we see the same basic hierarchical pattern on Levels 2–3; again, however, transformed parametric relationships between the IRID and the RP would occur, owing to the considerably different structures on the manifest level. Likewise, the melodic hierarchy of the sophisticated Romantic melody seen in Figure 20 relies on basically the same extraopus style structure. With the exception of the opening process [P] of E-G-B on Level 2, we find on Levels 3–4 the exact pitch-interval sequence and the same IRID/RP found in "Twinkle, Twinkle, Little Star," albeit in the minor mode.[18]

As the analyses show, melodic motion in all these melodies reaches from the tonic (1) up to the fifth degree (5) and then gradually falls back stepwise, to the tonic (4-3-2-1). Many melodies follow this generalized style schema, as will attest Schenker's theory (1956) of 5-4-3-2-1-*Urlinien* and Meyer's theory (1973) of gap

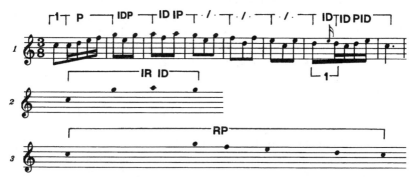

FIGURE 19   Clementi, Sonatina, Op. 36, No. 5, II, "Air suisse" (Allegro moderato), measures 25-32.

---

[18]Smetana's melody actually comes from a Czech folk song (the Israeli national anthem derives from the same source).

FIGURE 20   Smetana, *The Moldau* (Allegro commodo non agitato), measures 40–47.

filling, where 4-3-2 is said to follow a 1-5 gap.[19] An additional stylistic fact is that during the descent to the final tonic the melodies of Figures 17a, 17c, 19, and 20 all involve motivic repetition (*A + A*).

The last example (Figure 21), another melody from the latter half of the 19th century, shows a style structure somewhat more removed from the "thematic" IRID/RP hierarchical archetype discussed earlier. For here, according to the rules of the implication-realization model, the initial tonic tone (F♯) disappears from the hierarchy after Level 2. In its stead, the fifth degree (C♯) is prolonged before moving up to the sixth degree (D). Thus on Level 4 in this melody, no IR structure (F♯-C♯-D) preceding the ID structure (C♯-D-C♯) occurs. Further, in the descent to the final tonic, Level 5 omits a consonant third degree (A). Thus the melody actually realized in Figure 21 clearly deforms the style-structural hierarchy that we have been discussing. In other words, from the Classic melody to the Romantic ones, the IRID/RP structure undergoes stylistic change.

XIV. CONCLUSION: THE LIMITS OF STYLE

Of course, from their knowledge of style, listeners seek completion and thus may, to some extent, "fill in" such missing tones. With such a high degree of impli-

---

[19]In terms of the implication-realization model, the structural melodic type for gap filling is RP. For a discussion of it, see Narmour (1990, chapter 12). Meyer discusses the Smetana example in *Explaining Music* (1973, pp. 160–161). A Schenkerian analysis of Figure 18 can be found in Salzer (1962, vol. 2, p. 10).

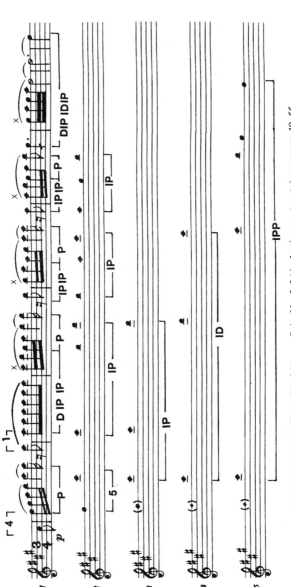

FIGURE 21   Bizet, *L'Arlésienne*, Suite No. 2, I (Andantino, sostenuto), measures 49–55.

cative specificity, style structures mapped onto expectation from the top down will tend to reduce the disparate to the uniform, the singular to the abstract. It could hardly be otherwise because top-down mapping always involves a complex of parametric relations, which is to say, a connected hierarchy of structural implications. But it is a mistake of the first order in either music analysis or music perception to think that some preformed, top-down, extraopus, Gestalt-like organization (like Meyer's gap filling or Schenker's *Ur*-linear descent) determines the final state of any actual experience (Narmour, 1977). There is a categorical difference between expecting a tone from a top-down implication and having specific bottom-up information about tones that were actually omitted. Were this not so, listeners could not distinguish the immense variety found in music composition and music performance.

Listeners do make use of highly abstract schemata, and they do store and invoke stylistic archetypes in music listening. However, the idiostructural differences generated by bottom-up processing keep unique experiences separate, helping us perceptually and analytically to differentiate the Smetana example from the Bizet example. For the relation between highly abstract, top-down generalizations and highly specific bottom-up processing ensures that we constantly reweight the parametric interrelationships of hierarchical networks with each rehearing according to the frequency and recency of the invoked comparisons.

In this connection, there are three points. The first is that, although extremely flexible and variable from case to case (and from listener to listener), top-down, schematic mapping is nevertheless very concrete: the invocation of a highly generalized, abstract, stylistic pitch schema like 1-5-4-3-2-1, as in Figures 20 and 21, specifies for the listener exactly what to expect in terms of registral direction, intervallic size, and scale step.

The second point is that the bottom-up system, even though apparently dependent on "hardwired" rules, is implicatively much looser. All other things being equal, a perfect fifth in this system implies a differentiated reversal of registral direction [R], and a realization of the reversal itself implies a similar continuation of registral direction and intervallic motion [P]. But many kinds of realizations can satisfy either of these bottom-up expectations and satisfy them completely. In Figure 21, the listener hardly notices that the skipping continuation of B-G♯, which follows the opening F♯-C♯, omits the A.[20]

"Hardly noticing," however, is not the same as "not noticing at all." For there is no consonant A at the right level in Figure 21. The third point, then, is that the bottom-up system, rigidly constrained yet affording a wide range of satisfactory realizations, prevents the top-down system from distorting reductionism. This is because the bottom-up system constantly feeds memory—and thus the top-down system—with the necessary particulars to comprehend novelty, uniqueness, and

[20]This is partly because an A does appear in the penultimate bar, albeit "late" and off the beat, which, according to the implication-realization model, would preclude its transformation to higher levels.

idiostructure (see Narmour, 1990).[21] As we have seen, what occurs on lower-level events is embodied in higher-level events (see Narmour, 1991a). Thus, although we may rationalistically claim the relevance of all kinds of abstractions to a given piece, we err in analysis when we allow abstract stylistic schemata to distort and obscure the empirically particular. For all its power, style-structural mapping cannot completely assimilate singularity. It cannot completely absorb the idiostructural relations tracked from the bottom up, a fact that both music theorists and cognitive psychologists must always remember.[22]

REFERENCES

Bharucha, J. J. (1987). Music cognition and perceptual facilitation: A connectionist framework. *Music Perception, 5,* 1-30.

Bharucha, J. J., & Stoeckig, K. (1986). Reaction time and musical expectancy: Priming of chords. *Journal of Experimental Psychology: Human Perception and Performance, 12,* 403–410.

Cuddy, L. L., & Lunney, C. A. (1995). Expectancies generated by intervals: Perceptual judgments of melodic continuity. *Perception and Psychophysics, 57,* 451-62.

Fodor, J. (1983). *Modularity of mind.* Cambridge, MA: MIT Press.

Gjerdingen, R. O. (1988). *A classic turn of phrase: Music and the psychology of convention.* Philadelphia: University of Pennsylvania Press.

Gjerdingen, R. O. (1992). Learning syntactically significant temporal patterns of chords: A masking field embedded in an ART3 architecture. *Neural Networks, 5,* 551–564.

Jones, M. R. (1981). Music as a stimulus for psychological motion. II. An expectancy model. *Pyschomusicology, 1,* 34–51.

Krumhansl, C. L. (1995). Music psychology and music theory: Problems and prospects. *Music Theory Spectrum, 17,* 53–80.

Krumhansl, C. L. (1997). Effects of perceptual organization and musical form on melodic expectancies. In M. Leman (Ed.), *Music, gestalt, and computing.* Berlin: Springer.

Lerdahl F., & Jackendoff, R. (1983). *A generative theory of tonal music.* Cambridge, MA: MIT Press.

Meyer, L. B. (1973). *Explaining music.* Chicago: University of Chicago Press.

Narmour, E. (1977). *Beyond Schenkerism: The need for alternatives in music analysis.* Chicago: University of Chicago Press.

Narmour, E. (1983). Some major theoretical problems concerning the concept of hierarchy in the analysis of tonal music. *Music Perception, 1,* 129–199.

Narmour, E. (1984). Toward an analytical symbology: The melodic, harmonic, and durational functions of implication and realization. In M. Baroni & L. Callegari (Eds.), *Musical grammars and computer analysis.* Florence: Olschki.

Narmour, E. (1989). The "genetic code" of melody: Cognitive structures generated by the implication-realization model. In S. McAdams & I. Deliège (Eds.), *Music and the cognitive sciences* (pp. 45–63). London: Harwood.

Narmour, E. (1990). *The analysis and cognition of basic melodic structures: The implication-realization model.* Chicago: University of Chicago Press.

[21]For more on how style never completely assimilates an idiostructure, see Narmour (1977).

[22]This article expands on a short paper given at the International Conference for Music Perception and Cognition in Liège, Belgium, in July 1994. The research on it began in 1993–1994 during my fellowship year at the Center for Advanced Study in the Behavioral Sciences (Stanford, California).

Narmour, E. (1991a). The influence of embodied registral motion on the perception of higher-level melodic implication. In M. R. Jones & S. Holleran (Eds.), *The cognitive bases of musical communication* (pp. 69–90). Washington, DC: American Psychological Association.

Narmour, E. (1991b). The top-down and bottom-up systems of musical implication: Building on Meyer's theory of emotional syntax. *Music Perception, 9,* 1–26.

Narmour, E. (1992). *The analysis and cognition of melodic complexity: The implication-realization model.* Chicago: University of Chicago Press.

Narmour, E. (1996). Analyzing form and measuring perceptual content in Mozart's sonata K. 282: A new theory of parametric analogues. *Music Perception, 13,* 265–318.

Quantz, J. J. (1966). *On playing the flute* (E. R. Reilly, Trans.). New York: Free Press. (Original work published 1752)

Rumelhart, D. E., & Ortony, A. (1977). The representation of knowledge in memory. In R. C. Anderson, R. J. Spiro, & W. E. Montague (Eds.), *Schooling and the acquisition of knowledge* (pp. 99–135). Hillsdale, NJ: Erlbaum.

Russo, F. A., & Cuddy, L. L. (1995, June 23). *Using Narmour's bottom-up principles of expectancy to influence listeners' perceptions of melodic cohesion and flow.* Paper presented at the annual meeting of the Society for Music Perception and Cognition, Berkeley, CA.

Salzer, F. (1962). *Structural hearing.* New York: Dover Press.

Schellenberg, E. G. (1996). Expectancy in melody: Tests of the implication-realization model. *Cognition, 58,* 75-125.

Schellenberg, E. G. (1997). Simplifying the implication-realization model of musical expectancy. *Music Perception, 14,* 295-318.

Schenker, H. (1956). *Der Freie Satz.* Vienna: Universal.

Simon, H. A. (1969). *The sciences of the artificial.* Cambridge, MA: MIT Press.

Tenney J., & Polansky, L. (1980). Temporal gestalt perception in music. *Journal of Music Theory, 24,* 205–241.

Thompson, W. F., Cuddy, L. L., & Plaus, C. (1997). Expectancies generated by melodic intervals: Evaluation of principles of melodic implication in a melody production task. *Perception & Psychophysics, 59*(7), 1069–1076.

Thompson, W. F., & Stainton, M. (1998). Expectancy in Bohemian folk melodies: Evaluation of implicative principles for implicative and closural intervals. *Music Perception, 15,* 231–254.

Weinberger, N. M., & McKenna, T. M. (1988). Sensitivity of single neurons in auditory cortex to contour: Toward a neurophysiology of music perception. *Music Perception, 5,* 355–389.

13

RHYTHM AND TIMING IN MUSIC

ERIC F. CLARKE

Music Department
University of Sheffield
Sheffield, United Kingdom

I. INTRODUCTION

The aim of this chapter is to give an overview of research relating to the temporal dimension in music. In its entirety, this constitutes a very large body of work, despite the frequently repeated observation that time in music has received rather less attention than pitch (e.g., Kramer, 1988). This chapter therefore focuses primarily on small- to medium-scale temporal phenomena in music, the domain that would commonly be referred to as rhythm, rather than the larger-scale properties of form. The detailed temporal properties of performed music, often referred to as temporal microstructure, and the relationships between rhythm and movement are also considered.

Although pitch may have had the lion's share of attention as far as both empirical and theoretical work in the psychology of music is concerned, there is nonetheless a considerable amount of material on rhythm in music. Amongst this literature, the work of Paul Fraisse stands out above the research of any other single individual in both its scope and the manner in which it foreshadows the preoccupations of a great deal of the more contemporary work in the area. The particular integrity and character of Fraisse's work makes it difficult to divide into the categories of this chapter, and as a consequence it is presented separately from more recent work. His work has also played an important part in stimulating and informing modern rhythm research, so it is appropriate to begin with it.

II. THE WORK OF PAUL FRAISSE

The special character of Fraisse's work is in part attributable to the fact that it covers both musical issues and the more general field of time perception, and that

---

he comes from a Piagetian tradition in which the relationship between perceptual capacities, sensorimotor organization, and human development is paramount. This results in a rather more holistic view than is found in most current work and incorporates a relationship with biology that is also rare today. Fraisse's work has been widely published (e.g., Fraisse, 1956, 1963, 1978, 1982, 1987), so the present account is confined to a distillation of the principal ideas without presenting the abundant supporting evidence that Fraisse amassed.

Fraisse drew a primary distinction between the perception of time and the estimation of time. The former is confined to temporal phenomena extending to no more than about 5 sec or so, whereas the latter relies primarily on the reconstruction of temporal estimates from information stored in memory. The boundary between these two corresponds to the length of the perceptual present, which he defined as "the temporal extent of stimulations that can be perceived at a given time, without the intervention of rehearsal during or after the stimulation" (Fraisse, 1978, p. 205). Rhythm perception, therefore, is essentially concerned with phenomena that can be apprehended in this immediate fashion and is also closely tied up with motor functioning. In studies of spontaneous tapping, Fraisse observed that by far the most ubiquitous relationship between successive tapped intervals was a ratio of 1:1 (i.e., isochronous or pendular motion). Fraisse regarded this as intimately connected with anatomical and motor properties—most notably the bilateral symmetry of the body, the pendular movements of the limbs in walking and running, and the regular alternation of exhalation and inhalation in breathing. He showed that when subjects are asked to tap rhythmically, they produce a bimodal distribution of ratios between intertap intervals, with peaks around 1:1 and 2:1, whereas when they are asked to tap arhythmically they produce a more continuous distribution of intertap interval ratios, and the frequency with which a ratio appears declines in proportion to its value (i.e., larger ratios are more unlikely). Fraisse describes both arhythmic and rhythmic tapping as a break with the underlying tendency for pendular movement, but whereas there is no structure in the former case, the latter exploits a principle of identity or clear differentiation between time intervals. This principle of equality or differentiation creates two distinct categories of duration, according to Fraisse, which he terms *temps longs* and *temps courts* (long durations and short durations), which are not only quantitatively but also qualitatively different. Short durations do not extend beyond about 400 msec, and 2:1 ratios between successive intervals are found only *between* the two categories.[1] *Temps longs* have the property of true duration according to Fraisse (we are aware, or can become aware, of the passage of time during such an interval), whereas *temps courts* have the character of collection rather than duration: we have no real sense of the passage of time during each event, but are

[1]It would be perfectly possible for a 2:1 ratio to exist within either category: an interval of 75 msec followed by 150 msec would be a 1:2 ratio within *temps courts*, and 500 msec followed by 1000 msec would be the same within *temps longs*. But Fraisse does not find this in his empirical data.

aware of the manner in which numbers of such intervals group together. The distinctions presented here are succinctly expressed by Fraisse in the following passage:

> Rhythmic and arhythmic sequences both consist of a break with the natural tendency to equalize successive intervals of time. Arhythmia is characterized by inequalities between successive durations that decrease in frequency in proportion to their size. Rhythmic structures, on the other hand, consist of the interplay of two types of value of temporal interval, clearly distinct from one another (in a mean ratio of 1:2). Within each type the durations are perceptually equal to one another. The collection of shortest intervals appears, from initial results, to consist of durations less than 400 msec. (Fraisse, 1956, pp. 29–30. Author's translation)

Although 400 msec appears here as the cutoff between the two categories of duration, elsewhere Fraisse cites 600 msec as an important value with analogous properties: it is what Fraisse terms the "indifference interval"—that interval of time for which people's duration estimates are most veridical, showing neither systematic overestimations (as they tend to for shorter durations) nor underestimations (as they tend to for longer durations).[2] Fraisse claims that this has a direct relationship to the duration of the whole perceptual process, corresponding "to the continuation of two percepts with no overlapping and no interval" (Fraisse, 1978, p. 225). The link between "indifference" in perceptual judgment and the threshold between the two categories of duration in rhythmic structures (*temps longs* and *temps courts*), with their respective properties of duration and collection, is made clear here.

To summarize, at the heart of Fraisse's contribution to an understanding of rhythm in music are the following:

1. The perceptual present as the dividing line between the direct *perception* of duration and its *estimation*.
2. The fundamental status of pendular motion and the close association between rhythm and movement.
3. The distinction between rhythmia and arhythmia, based on the distinction between a continuous and a bimodal distribution of duration ratios between successive time intervals.
4. The existence of a categorical distinction between two types of duration (*temps long* and *temps court*) in rhythm, in a mean duration ratio of 2:1, and with the quality of duration and collection, respectively.
5. A threshold between these two categories at a value around 400–600 msec, also associated with "indifference" in perceptual judgments.
6. The operation of two complementary principles (assimilation and distinction) that preserve both the integrity and distinctness of the two categories.

---

[2]There is considerable variability in the value given by different authors to the indifference interval. This may be due to the different methods that have been used to assess it, or may be because the phenomenon itself is unstable or even artifactual.

III. FORM PERCEPTION

The distinction that Fraisse draws between time perception and time estimation or construction allows a division between rhythm and form to be established. Musical form, understood as the sectional proportions of a work, might conceivably be regarded as part of rhythm in music if one adopts a sufficiently inclusive definition of the term. Indeed, Cooper and Meyer (1960) do precisely that when they present an analysis in which a single set of rhythmic categories is applied to the first movement of Beethoven's Eighth Symphony, ranging from single notes through all levels of the music up to the entire movement. The unbroken continuity of rhythmic notation implies that our response to note-to-note relationships is governed by the same principles and processes as is our response to the relationships between sections of the work, each of which lasts of the order of 5 min. Estimates of the perceptual present, which forms the boundary between direct perception and the memory-dependent processes of construction and estimation, are variable, but a value somewhere around 3–8 seconds is in agreement with a good deal of the available evidence. Crowder (1993), for example, following research by Cowan (1984, 1987), concurs with the proposal that there may be a very short auditory store[3] of around 250 msec, and a longer store, with a period of about 2–10 sec, with the two stores being the behavioral consequence of different perceptual/cognitive processes.

Michon (1978) provides a review of properties of the perceptual present that is useful for a consideration of the relationship between form and rhythm. The primary character of the perceptual present is that the contents of the present are active and directly available, whereas memories must be retrieved—must be transformed from a state of inactive storage to current awareness. This strongly suggests that it is not possible to have any direct apprehension of form, but that a sense of form becomes available only through a retrospective, and in some sense deliberate, act of (re)construction. Further, the extent of the perceptual present is governed by organizational considerations rather than pure duration: although there seems to be an upper limit beyond which the perceptual present cannot be extended whatever the structure of the material concerned, within this upper bound the determination of the contents of the present is primarily a function of perceptual structure, such that the boundary of the perceptual present falls at a natural break in the event structure (see Clarke, 1987a, for further discussion). In fact, despite Michon's protestations that the perceptual present should not be equated with any kind of memory, it looks very much as though the perceptual present should be understood as a temporal view of the contents of working memory

---

[3]Crowder (1993) argues persuasively for a procedural approach to auditory memory in which "stores" are simply the behavioral consequence, or by-product, of perceptual activity rather than having any anatomical or systematic reality—in the manner of receptacles—themselves. However, as he also points out, there is a large and somewhat contradictory literature on the whole subject of short auditory storage.

(Baddeley, 1986) with all the properties that have been described by research in that area.

Let us turn now from a consideration of the characteristics that divide rhythm from form and examine empirical research that has investigated listeners' sense of musical form. Remarkably few studies have tackled this issue, but Cook (1990) provides an interesting account of some informal tests that he has conducted. Using the first movement of Beethoven's Piano Sonata Op. 49, No. 2, Cook reports that music students:

> frequently predicted that the music would continue for another minute or more when the performance was broken off just before the final two chords. As soon as they heard those chords, of course, they realized that the movement had ended ... [A]s far as these listeners were concerned, the conclusion was not implied by anything that had come before - the recapitulation, for instance, or the coda. Furthermore ... a majority of the listeners failed to observe the repetition of the exposition, or else believed the repeat to be a modified one. (Cook 1990, pp. 44–45)

A similar study using the first movement of Webern's Symphony Op. 21 showed a similar lack of awareness of the most basic formal features of the music—in this case the literal repeat of the exposition of the movement. By contrast, Deliège and Ahmadi (1990) demonstrated that listeners were quite successful in picking up the formal articulation of music and that musicians and nonmusicians differ very little in their capacity to apprehend the basic formal divisions of even quite challenging music.

Clarke and Krumhansl (1990) rather more directly investigated listeners' sense of the medium- to large-scale temporal structure of two contrasting pieces of piano music: Stockhausen's Klavierstück IX and Mozart's Fantasie in C minor K. 475, each of which has a total duration of about 10 min. The study required a perceptual segmentation of each piece and demonstrated a very high level of agreement between the highly trained musicians who performed this part of the study (many of whom were professional composers or performers) in the location, strength, and structural characteristics of the segment boundaries. For the remainder of the study, the subjects were music students who, in separate experiments, listened to each piece twice and then made judgments about the duration, structural characteristics, and original location in the piece of a number of 30-sec extracts taken from the music. The results showed that listeners had a surprisingly good sense of where an extract came from in the overall scheme of the music, although they tended to judge extracts from both the beginning and the end of the piece as being relatively later in the music than their true position, as compared with extracts taken from the middle. It is as though the music appeared to move quickly towards the middle, then to become rather static, and finally to move quickly again near the end. Interestingly, this pattern was the same for both pieces despite their dramatically different stylistic characteristics. Deliège (1993), in a related study with music by Boulez, found a similar pattern of location judgments for musician listeners, and a rather flatter (and more veridical) profile for nonmusicians. It remains to be seen whether this pattern of systematic departure from veridicality should be attributed to some rather general processing consideration or whether it is attributable to properties of the music: it is not implausible that the structure of a great deal of music might reflect a very general scheme in which material is introduced over approximately the first third of the work, developed over the middle third, and then driven toward closure over the final third. Although there are good reasons to be cautious, the general literature on time perception (e.g., Michon, 1985) suggests that in the context of organized and goal-directed stimulus materials, time passes more quickly (i.e., durations are underestimated), which would make sense of the pattern found in the Mozart, Stockhausen, and Boulez.

IV. RHYTHM PERCEPTION

One of the problems that has hampered work in rhythm perception is that until comparatively recently there was no systematic and generally agreed definition of rhythm itself. Important though Cooper and Meyer's book on rhythm was in stimulating interest in rhythmic structure in music (Cooper & Meyer, 1960), they adopted a very broad approach to rhythm that did little to focus the concept. Quite apart from its importance in other respects, a significant contribution of Lerdahl and Jackendoff's *A Generative Theory of Tonal Music* (Lerdahl & Jackendoff, 1983) was its clarification of the elements of rhythmic structure in music, in particular the distinction between grouping and meter. They pointed out that rhythm in the tonal/metric music of the Western tradition consists of two independent elements: grouping—which is the manner in which music is segmented at a whole variety of levels, from groups of a few notes up to the large-scale form of the work—and meter—which is the regular alternation of strong and weak elements in the music. Two important points were made in this definition: first, although the two elements are theoretically independent of one another, the most stable arrangement involves a congruence between them such that strong points in the meter coincide with group boundaries. Second, the two domains deal respectively with time spans (grouping) and time points (meter): grouping structure is concerned with phenomena that extend over specified durations, whereas meter is concerned with theoretically durationless moments in time. Todd (1994a, 1994b) has pointed out that the two perspectives are directly analogous to the adoption of frequency-domain and time-domain approaches to pitch, with frequency corresponding to meter and wavelength corresponding to grouping. This also strikingly reveals the complementarity between grouping and meter.

The remainder of this section will therefore be divided between research that has focused on grouping or segmental structure in music and research on meter. Few studies have investigated the relationship between grouping and meter, despite Lerdahl and Jackendoff's insistence that it is in the interactions between the two that the power and interest of rhythmic structures lies (Lerdahl & Jackendoff, 1983, pp. 25 ff.).

A. GROUPING

As part of their theory of tonal music, Lerdahl and Jackendoff (1983) proposed a set of principles to account for segmental structure in music. Although there are some precedents for this (e.g., Nattiez, 1975; Ruwet, 1972; Tenney & Polansky, 1980), Lerdahl and Jackendoff's account is by far the most systematic and as a consequence has been the object of empirical investigation (Deliège, 1987). Lerdahl and Jackendoff propose that grouping is essentially a hierarchical property of music, and in their Grouping Well-Formedness Rules, they outline the formal conditions for hierarchical structure. Coupled with these, the Grouping Preference Rules (GPRs) describe the conditions that determine which of the very large number of possible hierarchical segmentations of any passage of music are actually likely to be perceived by listeners. The preference rules do not rigidly determine the segmentation of any particular passage, but specify the various forces acting in any musical context, which may reinforce one another or compete, resulting in different segmentations for different listeners. The GPRs themselves consist of three components: formalized Gestalt principles (principles of proximity in time, or change in pitch, duration, loudness, or articulation); more abstract formal concerns (principles of symmetry and the equivalence of variants of the same segment or passage); and principles relating to pitch stability.

Lerdahl and Jackendoff offer no empirical evidence for the operation of these rules, relying on their own musical intuitions to guide them. However Deliège (1987) has investigated their empirical validity in the context of both highly reduced experimental materials and extracts of real music from Bach to Stravinsky. Her investigation demonstrated the validity of the predictions made by the GPRs, and provided some evidence for the relative strength of the different rules by setting them in conflict with one another. As Deliège herself observes, a great deal more work would need to be done to establish anything approaching a definitive rank ordering of the rules. Equally, she is quick to point out that a rule with a low ranking is not a poor rule: there may simply be intrinsic differences between rules (possibly relating to processing distinctions, such as between primary event structure and more cognitive organizing processes; cf. McAdams, 1993) that put them into different bands within the ranking, but leave unaffected the importance of each rule in the particular circumstances to which it applies.

A decade before the appearance of Lerdahl and Jackendoff's theory, Garner (1974) had investigated structure and segmentation properties in temporal patterns as part of his wider study of the processing of information and structure in spatial and temporal materials. His research, as well as that of Handel (1989), although confined to materials that are a considerable distance from real music, represents an important link between the line of research that has developed into auditory scene analysis (see Bregman, 1990) and the more cognitive work on musical rhythm that is discussed here.

Todd (1994a) has developed a model of rhythmic grouping that converges toward solutions that are often very similar to those offered by Lerdahl and Jackendoff, but is based on rather more explicit perceptual processes and has close parallels to documented properties of the auditory system. The central principle of Todd's approach is the idea that the functioning of the auditory system can be seen as the operation of a number of energy-integrating low-pass filters with differing time constants. At the lowest level, individual events (which are of course always spread out in time) are detected by virtue of filters with relatively small time constants, integrating acoustical energy over durations of the order of milliseconds or a few tens of milliseconds. At a somewhat higher level, small groups are detected as relatively discrete packets of integrated energy over periods of around a second. Larger, and hierarchically superordinate, groups are detected by virtue of integrators using exactly the same process, but with correspondingly longer time constants. Peaks in the output of these low-pass filters can be identified by looking for zero crossings in the second derivative of the filter output, and if these peaks are plotted across all the filters in a multiscale assembly, a representation of rhythmic events at a number of levels, and the grouping relationships between events, is obtained. Todd terms the resulting diagram, which is very similar to a more conventionally derived tree diagram, a *rhythmogram* and has shown that rhythmograms of live performances of music bear a striking resemblance to tree diagrams that depict grouping analyses (such as those developed by Lerdahl and Jackendoff). An attractive feature of Todd's model is that, because it is based on energy integration, it is sensitive to any changes in the acoustical signal that have consequences for the integrated energy level. This includes note duration, pitch, intensity, and even timbre and vibrato,[4] so that the written value of any note (rhythmic value, pitch, notated dynamic) and any expressive treatment that it receives in performance (rubato, vibrato, timbre, local intensity) all contribute in an undifferentiated manner to the integrated energy level that is output from the filter. The virtue of this is that it avoids having to distinguish between "score-based" properties of a musical event, and "expressive" properties in considering rhythm perception—a distinction that is anyway meaningless for all those musical cultures that do not use notational systems (which is, of course, the majority of world music).

As an illustration of Todd's model, Figure 1 shows a rhythmogram for a performance of the Chopin Prelude Op. 28, No. 7, together with a conventional grouping structure analysis of the music, based on Lerdahl and Jackendoff's (1983) theory. The two analyses, although arrived at in fundamentally different ways, show a remarkable level of agreement: the eight most prominent "branches" on the rhythmogram (g1–g8) correspond to the eight lowest level branches on the group-

---

[4]A note with a sharp timbre, which therefore contains high levels of upper partials, will have a greater level of integrated energy than the same pitch with a duller timbre. Similarly the frequency modulation that vibrato introduces will increase the integrated energy level of a note above that of an otherwise identical but nonvibrato note.

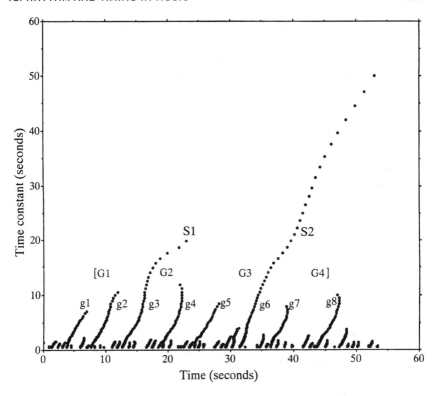

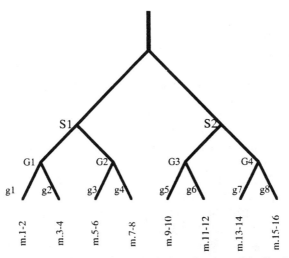

FIGURE 1 Rhythmogram of a professional pianist's performance of the Chopin Prelude Op. 28, No. 7 (top half) together with a Lerdahl and Jackendoff grouping analysis of the music (bottom half) showing the close relationship between the two. Units g1–g8 in both parts of the figure indicate two-measure groups; G1– G4 represent four-measure units (which are not well shown in the rhythmogram); and S1 and S2 represent the two eight-measure sections that constitute the whole prelude.

ing analysis, and those eight certainly group together into two large-scale sections (S1 and S2) of four each, with some evidence that they even pair up at an intermediate level (G1–G4). Thus an analysis that has been arrived at by relatively abstract music theoretic criteria applied to the written score is closely mirrored in an analysis that uses low-pass filtering applied to a standard audio recording of a professional performer. There are undoubtedly properties to which Todd's model is not sensitive—most obviously melodic and harmonic structure. However, to the extent that performers convey these properties by expressive means, even these will exert their influence on the rhythmogram, albeit "by the back door" rather than directly. What is interesting and provocative about the model, however, is the amount of grouping and sectional structure it can recover from real performances despite its "knowledge-free" approach. It suggests powerfully that rather more structural information is available within the acoustical signal itself than has hitherto been recognized and that processes in the more peripheral parts of the auditory system may be more important for rhythm perception than was at one time believed.

B. METER

The area of rhythm research that has attracted the most consideration since about 1980 is meter—undoubtedly a reflection of the dominant influence of metrical structure in the music of the Western tradition and in the overwhelming majority of popular music. This research has taken two forms: computational models of one sort or another and empirical investigations. Just as Lerdahl and Jackendoff performed an important service in first clarifying the relationship between grouping and meter and then specifying some of the conditions that govern the formation of musical groups, so they have also provided some valuable principles relating to the perception of meter.[5] First, they distinguish between three kinds of accent: phenomenal accents (points of local intensification caused by physical properties of the stimulus such as changes in intensity, simultaneous note density, register, timbre, or duration); structural accents (points of arrival or departure in the music that are the consequence of structural properties such as tonality—the cadence being the most obvious example of such an event); and metrical accents (defined as time points in music that are perceived as accented by virtue of their position within a metrical scheme). In general terms, perceiving meter is characterized by Lerdahl and Jackendoff as a process of detecting and filtering phenomenal and structural accents so as to discover underlying periodicities. These constitute the rates of repetition (cf. Yeston, 1976) that define the meter and confer metrical status on regularly recurring phenomenal (and structural) accents. Although this describes the outline of a process whereby physical attributes of the stimulus may result in the sense of meter, Lerdahl and Jackendoff make no attempt

---

[5]Some authors have preferred to talk of meter induction rather than meter perception in order to emphasize that meter is a construct that has no reality in the stimulus itself (they regard it as an abstraction from stimulus properties).

to specify in any detail all the factors that may contribute to the process or the relative weight of the various contributions made by the elements that they do discuss.

Of the empirical investigations into meter, the vast majority have been concerned with the influence of durational factors on meter. An important precursor here is the work of Fraisse (see Section II), whose identification of the importance of small integer ratios between durations and the role of assimilation and distinction in rhythm perception have left their mark. Equally, Deutsch (1986) showed in a duration comparison task that systematic distortions of short-term memory for duration could be attributed to the interfering effect of integer, or near integer, relations between a series of interpolated events and the durations to be compared. Povel (1981), starting from a position based on Fraisse's work, developed a model that demonstrates important elements of many of the more recent accounts of meter perception. His experiments showed that Fraisse's principle of assimilation and distinction around small integer ratios was generally verified with a battery of systematically structured short rhythmic sequences, but that in certain contexts an integer ratio could nonetheless prove difficult for a subject to perceive and reproduce.[6] The condition that created this difficulty was when a sequence could not be parsed into a simple repeating structure in which individual durations were organized into higher level units in multiples of two or three (but not an alternation of these). From this evidence, Povel formulated a "beat-based" model that proposed that the perception of rhythmic sequences depends on two steps: first, the segmentation of the sequence into parts of equal length (beats), based on the detection of regularly occurring accents; second, the identification of individual events as specific subdivisions of these beats into a small number (usually only two or three) of equal parts, or parts relating to one another in a ratio of approximately 1:2. The model allows a number of hierarchically nested levels (although not to the degree of depth that is suggested by Martin, 1972, for example) and specifies that the first level of subdivision below the level of the beat must consist only of divisions into two *or* three, and not a mixture or alternation. This constraint is motivated by Povel's empirical finding that subjects find it difficult to reproduce rhythms that involve alternations or mixtures of triplets and duplets at the same hierarchic level.

The model is developed further and adopts a more explicitly metrical character in Povel and Essens (1985), the essential idea of which is that a rhythmic sequence induces an internal clock with a period that captures the primary metrical level of the sequence. This is, in other words, a model of meter induction, the main driving force in the model being the identification of points of accentuation and the extraction of an underlying regularity from these. It is important to note that the sequences that Povel and Essens use in their empirical work consist of tone bursts with identical amplitude and duration but separated from one another by variable interonset intervals (all of which are whole number multiples of a 200-msec time base). All accentuation that their model handles arises out of three aspects of the

---

[6] The experimental task was to synchronize with a presented sequence and then to continue it for 17 repetitions after the stimulus ceased.

way in which events are grouped together[7]: (a) isolated events acquire an accent, (b) the first and last events of a run of three or more equally spaced events acquire accents, and (c) the second of a pair of events acquires an accent. The basis for these assumptions of perceptual accentuation are the results of Garner (1974), who found that the first and last events in a run acquired a perceptual salience, and the findings of Povel and Okkerman (1981), who demonstrated that the second of a pair of identical tone bursts occurring in reasonably close proximity is judged louder than the first. The model developed by Povel and Essens processes any rhythmic sequence *as a whole*, establishing the position of all accents as defined by the three principles just outlined, searching for a pattern of periodicities in the accents and weighing the evidence and counterevidence (accents that support or conflict with any particular periodic interpretation) for any candidates for the meter of the sequence. The predictions of the model correspond well to empirical evidence, but there must be doubts about the realism of a model that requires the whole sequence to be input before it starts to make any metrical interpretation: listeners often start to make a metrical interpretation within a few events of a sequence starting.

A model that is also intended to establish the meter of a pitchless sequence of equal-intensity events, but which makes rather more realistic processing assumptions, is described by Longuet-Higgins and Lee (1982). The fundamental principle in this model is that after two onsets (O_1 and O_2) have been detected, a third onset (O_3) is predicted to occur at the same time interval after the second event as the second is after the first (a principle of isochronous continuation). Confirmation of this prediction (by the arrival of an event at or near to O_3) causes the system to jump up a level in the emerging metrical hierarchy and to make a new prediction that an event will arrive at a time interval beyond O_3 that is equal to the interval between O_1 and O_3—that is, a principle of isochronous continuation at a periodicity that has twice the duration of the first level. The process continues to construct a binary metrical hierarchy in this way as long as events continue to confirm predictions. Longuet-Higgins and Lee recognize that the sense of meter does not extend up to indefinitely large time spans, and put what they recognize is an arbitrary stop on this process once the time between events exceeds about 5 sec (cf. the duration of the perceptual present). The simple principle outlined here turns out to be remarkably effective at parsing metrical structures, but it is also obvious that something more is needed if it is to make sense of nonbinary sequences (confined here to the single alternative of ternary sequences—a reasonable simplification for the vast majority of Western music) and sequences that do not begin on the strong beat of a meter. In broad terms, a single simple principle is used to handle both of these requirements—namely, the "accent-attracting" character of long notes.[8] Longuet-Higgins and Lee's model causes the strong beat of the meter (particularly

---

[7]This illustrates the close connection between grouping and meter, despite their theoretical independence, that was noted earlier.

[8]An alternative way to express this is to recognize that duration is one of the determinants of phenomenal accent (see Lerdahl & Jackendoff, 1983).

in early stages of any sequence) to be shifted, under carefully specified conditions, to any note that is significantly longer than its surrounding neighbors. This will either result in a ternary level in the meter or cause one or more short notes at the start of a sequence to function as upbeats to the first main beat (at the first longer note) of the meter. One implication of this assumption about the function of long notes is that in the absence of pitch, dynamic, or timbral information, a sequence of isochronous events will be heard as starting on a strong beat and organized in a purely binary meter—a consequence supported both by intuition and empirical evidence. Indeed Vos (1978) found a strong bias toward binary metrical interpretations (including sequences that were in fact in a ternary meter) even when the task presented listeners with commercially recorded extracts of music by Bach in which harmonic, melodic, and dynamic information were all available.

Closely related models of meter perception are presented by Johnson-Laird (1991) and Lee (1991). The former adopts the view of meter as a generative grammar for rhythms proposed earlier by Longuet Higgins (1979) and explores various issues relating to families of metrically related rhythms, syncopation, and phrase structure in music. Lee provides a very full exploration of the nature of a number of competing models of meter perception, including that of Lerdahl and Jackendoff (1983), two different models by Longuet-Higgins and Lee, and the Povel and Essens model (1985). Having thoroughly examined the strengths and weaknesses of all these models, Lee conducted a number of experiments designed to test critical differences predicted by the various models. The results (which failed to confirm any single existing model) are used to create a modification of the earlier work with Longuet-Higgins, which handles metrical counterevidence better than before. There are four differences between this and earlier models: (a) it has a variable responsiveness to metrical counterevidence resulting in a certain amount of flexibility in its treatment of duration sequences; (b) it is rather more conservative about the position of the downbeat, placing it on the first event unless there is powerful counterevidence (a direct reflection of Lee's empirical findings); (c) the model is capable of metrical subdivision (moving to lower levels of the metrical hierarchy than the starting level); and (d) the model takes account of the effects of tempo. The heart of Lee's approach is summarized as follows:

a) Every metre is associated with a (possibly culture-specific) pattern of 'strong' and 'weak' beats (henceforth termed the 'canonical accent-pattern' of the metre).

b) The metrical grouping chosen by a listener at each successive level of a metrical hierarchy will preferably be one whose canonical accent-pattern is consistent with the natural accent-pattern of the portion of sequence under consideration: that is, the events occurring on the strong beats, t1 and t3. will preferably be no 'weaker' (perceptually less salient) than the one occurring on the intervening weak beat t2, which in turn will preferably be no weaker than any event occurring between t1 and t3.

c) (Major) syncopations and weak long notes contradict the canonical accent-pattern and are hence avoided. (Lee, 1991, p. 121)

In a paper that provides a wide-ranging survey of a great deal of the previous work on rhythm perception, Parncutt (1994) proposes a theory of meter perception based on the salience of different possible pulse trains, and the perceived accentual strength of individual pulses, in music. The model, which as with the others discussed thus far is primarily concerned only with the relative onset times and durations of events (and not with their pitch, loudness, timbre, harmonic function, etc.), can be summarized as consisting of the following series of processes: (a) individual event durations are converted into phenomenal accents; (b) an absolute tempo factor (which recognizes the particular salience of periodic phenomena with a period of around 700 msec) and pattern-matching process select the most salient pulse trains (i.e., sequences of isochronous phenomenal accents)—the single most salient level of pulsation being identified as the tactus (the level at which a listener is most likely to tap his/her foot); (c) the three or four most salient and mutually consonant pulse trains are superimposed to create a metrical hierarchy for the sequence, with an associated overall salience. There is considerably more to the model, which has 'extensions' that handle issues such as expressive timing deviations, categorical rhythm perception, and the possible contribution of dynamic and other kinds of accent in real music, but its great strengths are its systematic simplicity (it is largely based on known processes of one kind or another, such as loudness adaptation or the identification of isochronous sequences), and the fact that it is virtually entirely spelled out as a quantitative model, thus permitting systematic and rigorous testing. Parncutt's own empirical data provide the first step in this direction.

If Parncutt's model is based on principles that are very close to classical psychophysics, Desain (1992) provides an equally intriguing approach that owes its origins to connectionism. The model emerges as an extension of Desain and Honing's (1989) connectionist approach to what they describe as the "quantization problem"—the extraction of discrete durational values in reasonable relationships with one another (essentially equivalent to standard Western rhythmic notation) from a string of continuously variable durations (equivalent to the raw data of human performance). Desain and Honing's connectionist quantizer uses the fundamental principle of the stability of small integer ratios, but does so in a simple network that considers not only the ratios between the individual intervals of the rhythmic sequence but also the compound intervals formed by summating two or more basic durations. Pairs of intervals (whether basic intervals, compound intervals, or a mixture of the two) are then 'steered' toward integer ratios through a number of iterating adjustments of the original noninteger values. The model is realized as a process such that the interonset intervals of a performed sequence are passed to the network one by one, are processed within a window of a certain size, and then shifted out of the network as quantized durations. Desain's (1992) model develops from the quantizer by considering how any new time interval is handled by the quantizer relative to the immediately preceding context. By holding the context fixed, which would normally mutually adjust with the new interval, ('clamping' it, to use Desain's term), the predictability of the next event onset can be assessed by considering how much adjustment or steerage is applied to the time interval formed between the last event of the clamped context and the new event. If the new event arrives at a time entirely consistent with the pattern of onset intervals formed by the context, then no steerage will be applied and the event can be considered to have occurred at an entirely predictable moment. If the interaction between the clamped context and the new event generates steerage toward a later moment in time, this demonstrates that the new event has occurred earlier than the context would predict. The converse is true for an event whose interaction with the context generates steerage toward an earlier point in time. Desain equates steerage with the inverse of expectancy: an event to which a positive steer is applied has occurred earlier than expected; an event with a negative steer is later than expected; and an event that generates no steer has occurred exactly at the point that the prior context would lead one to expect.

By plotting steerage/expectation curves for the positions of large numbers of hypothetical event positions following different prior rhythmic sequences, Desain demonstrates that rhythmic sequences that imply different metrical organizations generate distinct curves. Furthermore, these curves clearly show hierarchical metrical properties (mirrored in empirical results obtained by Palmer and Krumhansl, 1990), even though there are no explicitly metrical principles built into the model itself. Relying solely on the principle of the stability of small integer ratios between adjacent intervals (simple or compound), it nonetheless gives rise to archetypally metrical behavior as a result. Meter is, in other words, an emergent property of the model rather than a deliberate feature of its design—a characteristic that seems consistent both with meter's fundamental importance as a perceptual framework for music and listeners' abilities to acquire a sensitivity to meter at a very early age and without explicit formal instruction (Hargreaves, 1986; Moog, 1976).

A similarly subsymbolic model for meter perception is presented by Large and Kolen (1994), although it is based on rather different principles. The starting point for this approach is resonance theory, in which the behavior of oscillatory units that continuously adjust their phase and period to the rhythmic characteristics of a stimulus sequence is used to model the human response to rhythm. The fundamental idea is that neural units with differing natural resonances, and 'tuned' to be more or less sensitive/restrictive in terms of what they will adjust to, adapt to the periodicities of external stimulus events. These units exist at a number of levels/ timescales, with their hierarchical relationships reflecting the hierarchical nature of meter itself. The authors show that a system using six oscillators covering a resonance range from 600 msec to 2560 msec will successfully track the meter of a fairly complex piece of real musical performance. In particular, oscillators at around 900 msec and 1800 msec (corresponding to the two primary levels of a binary metrical hierarchy) locked on and tracked tempo changes successfully, while the other oscillators (appropriately) did not lock on because they did not correspond to any significant level of periodic activity. Large and Kolen point out that their model (in common with all the models discussed in this section) pays no attention to phenomenal accents, although they briefly suggest that this might be incorporated in a simple manner by allowing accented events in the stimulus sequence to cause greater adjustments of the phase and period of relevant oscillators.

Once again using a largely knowledge-free and strongly biologically motivated approach, Todd (1994a, 1994b; Todd & Brown, 1996) has proposed a model for meter perception arising out of the filter-based model for grouping described earlier. In essence, Todd proposes that a frequency-domain multiscale filter system exists in parallel with the time-domain multiscale filtering that is responsible for detecting the grouping properties of rhythmic structures. Whereas the time-domain filters are low-pass, and provide information about the onset, stress, and grouping of events, the frequency-domain filters are band pass and provide information about tempo and meter. The output of the band-pass filters is simply a set of periodicities (a spectrum, but with the very low frequencies—typically below 10 Hz—that identify this as a rhythmic, rather than a pitch, phenomenon), which in itself does not specify a meter, even if it strongly constrains the set of possible meters. Todd proposes that a culture-specific top-down process then interprets the pattern of periodicities as a particular meter by recognizing one of a limited number of specified metrical patterns in the spectrum.

Finally, meter is not just an auditory and cerebral phenomenon: it also has an important motor component, and both Parncutt and Todd are concerned to build this into their models. This motor component is most evident in the way in which people tap their feet or dance to metrical music, the level in the metrical hierarchy at which they synchronize their foot tapping being commonly called the 'tactus' (e.g., Lerdahl & Jackendoff, 1983, p. 21). Parncutt (1987, 1994) takes account of this in his calculation of pulse-train salience by weighting each pulse train with a bell-shaped function centered on 600 msec, which has been cited as the modal spontaneous tapping period (see Fraisse, 1982; cf. also Fraisse's "indifference interval" discussed earlier), and also observes the similarity between the principle of this approach and that adopted by Terhardt, Stoll, and Seewann (1982) in calculating pitch salience in complex signals. In a closely related manner, Todd's model regards the tactus as the result of combining the output of the band-pass filter bank with a sensory-motor filter that has fixed and relatively narrow tuning characteristics and represents the intrinsic pendular dynamics of the human body (Todd & Lee, 1994). The output of the band-pass filter bank is fed through this sensory-motor filter, with the magnitudes of the individual filter outputs being modified by this secondary filter. The strongest output from this combined system will be that band-pass filter whose frequency lies closest to the center frequency of the sensory-motor filter[9]—a kind of second-level tuning system. The center frequency for the sensory-motor filter is none other than 600 msec again. Todd actually proposes a second, parallel, sensory-motor filter with a center frequency of 5 sec that also acts on the output of the band-pass filter bank, and which reflects the rate at which listeners and performers sway their bodies in listening, playing, and dancing.

[9]It is possible that a very strong output from a somewhat more distant band-pass filter would "win" over a closer but weaker output, but the spacing of the band-pass outputs actually makes this unlikely. However the basic principle is that the "winner" is calculated as the product of magnitude and proximity.

Before moving on from this section on rhythm perception, it is important to note that in addition to the distinction between grouping and meter, rhythm has been observed by a number of authors to have another dual aspect—temporal and accentual. Cooper and Meyer (1960), for example, deal with rhythm primarily in terms of accent structures, although they incorporate temporal factors into both their definition of accent and grouping of accents. By contrast, the vast majority of empirical work on rhythm has focused on temporal matters, almost to the exclusion of accent. A smaller literature does exist, however, that has considered the nature and variety of different kinds of accent and the ways in which accentual and temporal factors mutually influence one another (e.g. Dawe, Platt, & Racine, 1993; Drake & Palmer, 1993; Povel & Okkerman, 1981; Thomassen, 1982; Windsor, 1993; Woodrow, 1909). Useful though this work has been, there has been little attempt so far to integrate what is known about the perceptual functioning of anything other than temporal accents with existing or new models of meter perception. This is unfortunate both because purely temporal models of meter perception (such as those reviewed in this chapter) are unrealistic in the demands that they make by deriving meter from temporal information alone and because such models tend to project a static and one-dimensional view of meter, rather than the more dynamic and fluid reality that is the consequence of the interplay of different sources of perceptual information (temporal and accentual).

V. TIMING IN MUSIC

If there is one principle on which virtually all rhythm research agrees, it is that small integer ratios of duration are easier to process than more complex ratios. And yet this principle is at first sight deeply paradoxical when the temporal properties of real musical performances are examined, for almost nowhere are small integer ratios of duration found—even in performed sequences that are manifestly and demonstrably simple for listeners to interpret. The answer to this apparent paradox is that a distinction must be made between the structural properties of rhythm (which are indeed based on the principle of small integer ratios) and their so-called expressive properties—continuously variable temporal transformations of the underlying rhythmic structure (Clarke, 1985). These temporal transformations, referred to by some authors (e.g., Clynes, 1987, 1983; Repp, 1992a) as expressive microstructure, are what the term "timing" identifies, and there has been considerable attention paid to the nature and origins of these timing properties in performed music, as well as a rather smaller literature on their perceptual consequences for listeners.

A. PERCEPTION OF TIMING

The distinction between rhythm and expressive timing is only psychologically plausible if some mechanism can be identified that is able to separate the one from the other. That mechanism is categorical perception, and both Clarke (1987b) and Schulze (1989) have demonstrated its existence empirically. In general terms, the idea is that listeners assign the continuously variable durations of expressive performance to a relatively small number of rhythmic categories. The pattern of these categories constitutes the rhythmic structure of the sequence, and the departure of each duration in the original performance from its appropriate categorical target value is understood as expressive timing. Clarke (1987b) and Parncutt (1994) have suggested that categorical perception may be confined to a single categorical distinction—between a 1:1 ratio and a 2:1 ratio, or even more generally to the distinction between even (1:1) and uneven (N:1) divisions of a time span. Even such a simple categorical system can be quite powerful, however, particularly when the interaction between categorical distinctions and the prevailing metrical context is considered. Two durations in a relationship of inequality in a duple meter are likely to be interpreted as a 3:1 (or possibly 7:1) ratio, whereas the same inequality in a triple meter will be interpreted as 2:1 or 5:1. The interdependence between type of division (even/uneven) and meter (triple/duple) brings with it an expressive component, because the same objective pair of durations interpreted as 2:1 in one meter and 3:1 in another must imply different expressive departures from the target (canonical) values. For example, the sequence 600 msec–400 msec–1000 msec might be interpreted in a duple meter as a 1:1:2 pattern with an expressive lengthening of the first event. In a triple meter, the same sequence might be interpreted as a 2:1:3 pattern with an expressive lengthening (slowing) over the second and third events.[10] Thus the raw durational information specifies perceptual information in three interdependent dimensions: meter (duple/triple), division (even/uneven), and expression.

Desain and Honing (1989) have presented a connectionist model for the recovery of underlying rhythmic structure from continuously variable performed durations. The model takes small integer ratios as its target categories and steers the individual durations (and compounds formed from pairs of adjacent durations) toward their nearest target integers. The smaller the integer, the stronger is the steering, so that 1:1 and 2:1 exert the most powerful influence on the behavior of the system. The model is successful in correctly interpreting even quite difficult sequences (e.g., correctly interpreting the same duration in two different sequential positions as two different rhythmic values), and the behavior of the system appears to mimic the limited amount of empirical data on categorical perception quite closely.

If categorical perception is one way to account for the distinction between rhythmic structure and expressive timing, it remains to demonstrate the abilities of

[10]The overwhelming majority of Western music is based on the distinction between duple and triple meters, or compounds of duple and triple. This in no way precludes other metrical possibilities, which would exert their influence on the relationship between rhythmic structure and expressive timing in a suitably altered manner. For example the 600–400–1000 sequence in a quintuple meter would be interpreted as an inexpressive (i.e., metronomic) 3:2:5 pattern.

listeners to detect expressive timing in rhythmic sequences. Kendall and Carterette (1990) showed that listeners were successful in picking up the expressive intentions (neutral, normal, exaggerated) of performers conveyed by means of timing (and dynamics), on a variety of instruments, and that there was no difference between musicians and nonmusicians in their ability to make this perceptual judgment. Sloboda (1983) showed that listeners (musicians) who were asked to distinguish between two metrical variants of a tune were able to do so with a degree of success that directly reflected the clarity of metrically related expression (timing, dynamics, and articulation) in the original performances. In his study, the performance data of more expert performers showed a more clearly distinguished pattern of expressive features for the two metrical variants of the melody, and the subsequent listeners were more successful in distinguishing between the two metrical variants in their performances than in the performances of less expert performers. The magnitude of the expressive changes recorded in these data varies considerably, but in a study that focused on timing changes alone, Clarke (1989) showed that listeners are sensitive to changes in duration of as little as 20 msec in simple isochronous sequences, and those listeners were still able to detect the lengthening of a single duration by as little as 50 msec in a melody that had base durations of 350 msec and had continuously modulated expressive changes in tempo.

Listeners' sensitivities to expressive timing are variable, however, and Repp (1992b) has shown that there are strong structural constraints on listeners' perceptions of expressive timing. In his study, various degrees of lengthening, ranging from approximately 23 msec to 45 msec (corresponding to between 7% and 13% of a 341-msec eighth note) were applied to each of the 47 possible eighth-note durations in a metronomic rendering of the first part of a minuet by Beethoven, and listeners were then asked to indicate where they heard a lengthening. The overall percentage of correct identifications was well above chance even for the smallest amount of lengthening, bearing out the evidence that listeners have a high level of sensitivity to timing perturbations, but more significant than this was the pattern of changes in percentage correct responses across the extract. There was remarkable variation in this profile, ranging from 0% to 90% correct, with the peaks and troughs mirroring the phrase structure of the melody, and having a strongly negative correlation with the timing profile of a separately analyzed expert performance of the music. At phrase boundaries, where the expert performer showed a tendency to lengthen the duration of eighth notes, listeners' abilities to detect a timing perturbation in the expressionless performance declined markedly and did so in proportion to the structural importance of the boundary. By contrast, in the middle of phrases, listeners' detection scores reached their peak values. This is strong evidence to show that listeners' unconscious parsing of the musical structure, and the expectations that follow concerning the likely expressive treatment of the music by a performer, have a striking effect on listeners' abilities to detect timing changes in the music.

B. EXPRESSIVE TIMING IN PERFORMANCE

In recent years, a considerable body of research has built up aimed at specifying the principles that govern expressive performance in music (e.g., Clarke, 1988; Gabrielsson, 1988; Palmer, 1989; Repp, 1992a; Todd, 1989, 1985; Shaffer, 1981; Sundberg, 1988; see also Chapter 14, this volume). This research has used a mixture of empirical measurement and computer simulation to explore the ways in which human performers expressively transform various musical dimensions (e.g., tempo, loudness, intonation) in performance, with a particular focus on timing, and has identified a number of recurring characteristics that indicate a particular model of the origin and control of expression. The critical evidence is that expressive timing can be extremely stable over repeated performances that may sometimes span a number of years (Clynes & Walker, 1982), is found even in sight-reading performances (Shaffer, 1981), and can be changed by a performer at a moment's notice (Clarke, 1985). Taken together, these observations mean that expressive timing cannot possibly be understood as a learned pattern that is applied to a piece each time it is played, but must be generated from the performer's understanding of the musical structure.[11] Any other model imposes memory demands on a performer that are completely implausible psychologically and is unable to account for the mixture of stability and flexibility that has already been mentioned. The stability of performances over time is thus understood as the stability of a performer's representation of the musical structure; the existence of expression in sight-reading performances is the consequence of a performer's emerging representation of the music as he or she reads and organizes it; and changes in expression, either spontaneous or the result of instruction, are a consequence of the fact that musical structures can be interpreted in a variety of different ways.

In principle, every aspect of musical structure contributes to the specification of an expressive profile for a piece, but a number of authors have shown that phrase structure is particularly salient. Todd (1985) details a model that takes the hierarchical grouping structure of the music as its input and gives a pattern of rubato as its output on the basis of an extremely simple rule (Todd, 1985, 1989). The resulting timing profiles compare well with the profiles of real performances by professional players, as Todd's own data and subsequent data collected by Repp (1992a) have shown. A number of other studies have also shown rule-like correspondences between various aspects of musical structure and expression (e.g., Clarke, 1988; Shaffer & Todd, 1987; Sloboda, 1983; Sundberg, 1988). In a study of 28 performances of a short piano piece by Schumann, taken from commercial recordings by many of this century's greatest pianists, Repp (1992a) showed that there was a remarkable degree of commonality underlying the expressive timing profiles of the performances, despite the idiosyncratic nature of some of the performers. He

---

[11]Note that this does not mean that expression cannot be learned, only that such learning takes place on a foundation of musical structure as perceived, or conceived, by the performer.

also showed convincingly that at more surface levels of the timing profiles, increasing diversity between the performers is found, thus confirming the intuition that performers agree substantially about the deeper structural levels of a piece of music, and impose the stamp of their own individuality by manipulating the finer details of structure and its expressive implementation.

One way to investigate the generative model of performance expression is to use an imitation (reproduction) task: the idea is that pianists hear performances of short melodies and then have to imitate, as precisely as possible, all the nuances of timing by playing the melody back on a piano. Some of the "performances" that they hear are real performances by a pianist; others are versions that have been transformed in various ways so as to disrupt the relationship between structure and expressive timing. One such transformation inverts the expressive timing profile of the melody, so that passages in which the player originally accelerated now decelerate by the same proportion, and vice versa. Another transformation translates the pattern of timing along the melody by some specified amount, so that (for instance) the expressive timing associated with the first note (or more strictly the first interonset interval) is transferred onto the fourth note, the second onto the fifth, the third onto the sixth, and so on. The purpose of these different transformations is to introduce differing degrees of disruption into the relationship between structure and expressive timing, so as to assess how this disruption influences the pianists' abilities to imitate what they hear. A strictly generative theory would predict that only when there is a reasonable relationship between structure and expression can a pianist successfully imitate a performance, because only then can the performer grasp a structure/expression pairing sufficiently to regenerate (imitate) it.

The results of experiments (Clarke, 1993; Clarke & Baker-Short, 1987) largely bear out this prediction, pianists being more inaccurate and inconsistent when they try to imitate an expressive timing profile that does not maintain a conventional relationship with the musical structure, the degree of inaccuracy and inconsistency being directly related to how disrupted or abnormal the relationship is. Similarly, a separate group of musicians who were asked simply to listen to the same sequences and judge their quality as performances gave ratings that followed the same pattern: real performances were rated best, and the more disrupted was the relationship between structure and expression, the lower were the listeners' ratings.

Although these findings lend strong support to a generative model of expression, there is also evidence from the imitation attempts that performers are at least partially successful in their attempts to imitate the disrupted versions. There are various possible explanations of this: pianists may create some kind of direct auditory "image" of the performance, which they then try to match as closely as possible when they make their imitation attempt; or they may try to remember some kind of verbal blueprint for the peculiar performance (e.g., "speed up toward the end of the first phrase, slow down during the middle of the second phrase, and then rush the end"); or they may encode the performance in terms of some type of body image—a kind of mental choreography that will recreate the performance out of an image of the movements (real or imagined) that might produce, or express the shape of, such a performance. There is informal evidence that a movement component of this sort is involved: some of the pianists participating in the study were observed to move in quite striking ways when attempting to imitate the more disrupted versions, using movements that seemed to express and capture the awkward timing characteristics of the music. Whatever the strategy used, it is clear that a model that portrays expressive timing simply as the outcome of a set of expressive rules is unrealistically abstract and cerebral, and that the reality is far more practical and corporeal. The body is not just a source of sensory input and a mechanism for effecting output: it is far more intimately bound up with our whole response to music—perceptual and motor.

VI. RHYTHM, TIMING, AND MOVEMENT

As far back as the ancient Greeks, writers have remarked on the close relationship between music and human movement (see Barker, 1989). In a study using factor analysis and multidimensional scaling methods, Gabrielsson (1973a; 1973b) showed that listeners' responses to rhythms (either descriptive adjective ratings, or similarity ratings between pairs of rhythms) showed the presence of a perceptual dimension that Gabrielsson termed "movement character." Although a structural dimension and an emotional dimension also played an important part in listeners' judgments, for some listeners the movement character was so strong as to constitute the primary dimension used in making similarity judgments. These listeners described how in trying to assess the similarity of pairs of rhythms, they tried "to 'find out the similarity by movements of the body' and/or 'by imagining which movements I could do to the music'" (Gabrielsson, 1973a, p. 173).

More recently, the work of a German author, Alexander Truslit, has been brought to light (see Repp, 1993). Truslit carried out experimental research in the 1930s showing that different kinds of movement instruction (or movement image) given to performers resulted in performances with measurably different timing properties, from which he went on to claim that a very small number of general movement types, perhaps no more than three, underpinned the kinematic basis of performance. Independently of this, other researchers have shown that the pattern of timing that performers spontaneously use follows the temporal curve of objects moving in a gravitational field (Feldman, Epstein, & Richards, 1992; Sundberg & Verillo, 1980; Todd, 1992), suggesting that performances that sound natural do so because they mimic the behavior of physical objects moving in the real world. Todd (1992) has shown that a model of performance timing and dynamics based on the speed and force of movement of objects moving under the influence of gravity can give a good account of the expression found in spontaneous musical performances. In a similar way, Repp (1992c) compared a family of parabolic timing curves (which produce a close approximation to the linear tempo function used by Todd) with other timing functions in a study that tested listeners' preferences for different versions of a melodic gesture from a Schumann piano piece. He found that listeners preferred the parabolic curves over the other timing functions, and among the parabolic curves themselves, preferred parabolas that maintained a symmetrical shape (rather than being skewed right or left).

The relationship between rhythm and movement can be conceptually separated into rhythm and timing seen as the consequence of movement, and rhythm and timing seen as the source of, or motivation for, movement. The first of these two relationships is primarily an issue of motor control: timing information can either be seen as the input to a motor system, which then produces some kind of temporally structured behavior, or timing can be seen as the consequence of the intrinsic characteristics of the motor system and the body itself. This is part of the wider question of whether temporal control in behavior should be seen as regulated by an internal clock of some kind (see, e.g., Luce, 1972), or as the temporal expression of the intrinsic dynamics of a system (e.g., Kugler, Kelso, & Turvey, 1980). Shaffer (1982, 1984) has proposed that these options are not mutually exclusive and that the two principles operate at different levels. In music, the primary level of timing, and the level at which some kind of internal clock exerts its influence, is the tactus (that level of the metrical structure at which a listener might tap his/her foot, or a conductor beat time). Subdivisions of the beat (i.e., individual notes) are not directly timed, but are produced by overlearned motor procedures that specify movement patterns that have as their consequence a definite timing profile. The timing properties are thus the consequence of movement rather than a control parameter in their own right: "Note timing is, in effect, embodied in the movement trajectories that produce them" (Shaffer, 1984, p. 580). Equally, time periods greater than that of the primary timing level are produced by concatenations of beat periods rather than by means of some higher level clock. A hierarchy of clocks is therefore not involved, despite the multileveled nature of the timing profiles that are characteristic of expert expressive performance.

Turning now to rhythm as the source of, or motivation for, movement, the most striking and obvious evidence for this close relationship comes from the ancient association between music and dance—an association that in contemporary popular culture remains as vital as at any time. Equally, there is a very long history of work songs, and here it is clear that one of the primary functions of rhythmic singing is to coordinate the activities of people working together (Blacking, 1987, chapter 3) and through this rhythmic action to optimize the efficiency and economy with which energy is expended (Bernstein, 1967). With this deep-seated association in the history of music and human action, it is hardly surprising that music with a periodic rhythmic structure tends to elicit accompanying movements, whether these are explicitly dance movements or less formalized responses and whether the music is intended to be dance music or not. Todd (1993, 1995) has proposed that the auditory system interacts directly with two subsystems of the motor system, one responsible for relatively rapid periodic phenomena (foot tapping) and the other associated with slower and less strictly periodic movements (body sway and whole body movement generally). These interactions are responsible for our strong motor response to music, and the two subsystems embody the distinction between genres of dance in which the dancer's center of moment (Cutting, Proffitt, & Kozlowski, 1978) remains essentially fixed while the limbs move periodically and relatively rapidly around it (disco dancing), and those in which the center of moment itself moves, with more limited movement of the limbs around that center (ballroom dancing).[12]

VII. SUMMARY

The temporal dimension of music offers an enormous diversity of issues to the psychology of music. Having distinguished between rhythm and form on the basis of the length of the perceptual present, and the attendant distinction between perception and construction, this chapter has adopted a view of rhythm that sees it as the interaction between meter and grouping. Although there are theoretical accounts of the conditions for the formation of grouping structures, comparatively little work has explored this empirically. There is a greater diversity of models to account for meter perception, ranging from rule-based systems to connectionist and auditory models, although once again empirical investigations have been rather more limited in both quantity and scope.

The term *timing* is used in this chapter to refer to the temporal microstructure that is characteristic of performances of music and is widely regarded as the generative consequence of a performer's conception of musical structure. The relationship between this continuously variable component and the discrete categories of rhythmic structure is discussed both conceptually and perceptually, with categorical perception playing a crucial role. Finally, the significance of the relationship between rhythm, timing, and movement is considered in both perception and performance. In this, as elsewhere in research in rhythm and timing, there has been a shift from a rather abstract symbolic approach to perception and production toward an outlook that takes more account of properties of the auditory and motor systems, and of the body in general, or makes use of subsymbolic principles, which require fewer explicit rules to be built into the models.

Inevitably in a field of this size, many issues have not been tackled: no consideration has been given here to the aesthetic consequences of different kinds of temporal organization, or to the perceptual and performance implications of historical changes in the temporal organization of music, or to rhythm and timing in ensemble coordination, or to the relationship between rhythmic organization and

---

[12]Somewhat controversially, Todd (1993) has claimed a still closer link between rhythm and movement by suggesting that the vestibular apparatus may be directly stimulated by sound and that the corresponding sense of motion, or "strong compulsion to dance or move" (Todd, 1993, p. 381) is the direct result. Some evidence from animal studies shows that the necessary anatomical links may exist, but a behavioral expression of such a proposed vestibular-motor link has yet to be demonstrated in humans.

trance or other altered states of mind, or to the development of children's and adults' perceptual and performance skills in the domain of rhythm and timing. But with the exception of the last item in this list, these are all areas that have received very little consideration in the psychological literature and thus offer the enticing prospect of still greater diversity in future rhythm research.

ACKNOWLEDGMENTS

I am grateful to Richard Parncutt, Neil Todd, and the Editor for their helpful comments on an earlier draft of this chapter. I thank Neil Todd for providing the data necessary to produce Figure 1.

REFERENCES

Baddeley, A. (1986). *Working memory*. Oxford: Clarendon Press.

Barker, A. (1989). *Greek musical writings: Vol. 51. Harmonic and acoustic theory*. Cambridge: Cambridge University Press.

Bernstein, N. (1967). *The coordination and regulation of movements*. Oxford: Pergamon.

Blacking, J. (1987). '*A commonsense view of all music': Reflections on Percy Grainger's contribution to ethnomusicology and music education*. Cambridge: Cambridge University Press.

Bregman, A. (1990). *Auditory scene analysis: The perceptual organization of sound*. Cambridge, MA: MIT Press.

Clarke, E. F. (1985). Structure and expression in rhythmic performance. In P. Howell, I. Cross, & R. West (Eds.), *Musical structure and cognition* (pp. 209–236). London: Academic Press.

Clarke, E. F. (1987a). Levels of structure in the organisation of musical time. *Contemporary Music Review, 2* (1), 211–238.

Clarke, E. F. (1987b). Categorical rhythm perception: An ecological perspective. In A. Gabrielsson (Ed.), *Action and perception in rhythm and music* (pp. 19–34). Stockholm: Royal Swedish Academy of Music.

Clarke, E. F. (1988). Generative principles in music performance. In J. Sloboda (Ed.), *Generative processes in music* (pp. 1–26). Oxford: The Clarendon Press.

Clarke, E. F. (1989). The perception of expressive timing in music. *Psychological Research, 51,* 2–9.

Clarke, E. F. (1993). Imitating and evaluating real and transformed musical performances. *Music Perception, 10,* 317–343.

Clarke, E. F., & Baker-Short, C. (1987). The imitation of perceived rubato: A preliminary study. *Psychology of Music, 15,* 58–75.

Clarke, E. F., & Krumhansl, C. (1990). Perceiving musical time. *Music Perception, 7,* 213–252.

Clynes, M. (1983). Expressive microstructure in music, linked to living qualities. In J. Sundberg (Ed.), *Studies of music performance* (pp. 76–181). Stockholm: Royal Swedish Academy of Music.

Clynes, M. (1987). What can a musician learn about music from newly discovered microstructure principles (PM and PAS)? In A. Gabrielsson (Ed.), *Action and perception in rhythm and music* (pp. 201–233). Stockholm: Royal Swedish Academy of Music.

Clynes, M., & Walker, J. (1982). Neurobiologic functions of rhythm, time and pulse in music. In M. Clynes (Ed.), *Music, mind and brain: The neuropsychology of music* (pp. 171–216). New York: Plenum.

Cook, N. (1990). *Music: Imagination and culture*. Oxford: Oxford University Press.

Cooper, G., & Meyer, L. B. (1960). *The rhythmic structure of music*. Chicago: University of Chicago Press.

Cowan, N. (1984). On short and long auditory stores. *Psychological Bulletin, 96,* 341–370.

Cowan, N. (1987). Auditory memory: Procedures to examine two phases. In W. A. Yost & C. S. Watson (Eds.), *Auditory processing of complex sounds* (pp. 289–298). Hillsdale, NJ: Erlbaum.

Crowder, R. (1993). Auditory memory. In S. McAdams & E. Bigand (Eds.), *Thinking in sound: The cognitive psychology of human audition* (pp. 113–145). Oxford: The Clarendon Press.

Cutting, J. E., Proffitt, D. R., & Kozlowski, L. T. (1978). A biomechanical invariant for gait perception. *Journal of Experimental Psychology: Human Perception and Performance, 4,* 357–372.

Dawe, L. A., Platt, J. R., & Racine, J. R. (1993). Harmonic accents in inference of metrical structure and perception of rhythm patterns. *Perception & Psychophysics, 54,* 794–807.

Deliège, I. (1987). Grouping conditions in listening to music: An approach to Lerdahl & Jackendoff's grouping preference rules. *Music Perception, 4,* 325–360.

Deliège, I. (1993). Mechanisms of cue extraction in memory for musical time. *Contemporary Music Review, 9,* 191–205.

Deliège, I., & Ahmadi, A. E. (1990). Mechanisms of cue extraction in musical groupings: A study of perception on *Sequenza VI* for viola solo by Luciano Berio. *Psychology of Music, 18,* 18–44.

Desain, P. (1992). A (de)composable theory of rhythm perception. *Music Perception, 9,* 439–454.

Desain, P., & Honing, H. (1989). The quantization of musical time: A connectionist approach. *Computer Music Journal, 13* (3), 56–66.

Deutsch, D. (1986). Recognition of durations embedded in temporal patterns. *Perception & Psychophysics, 39,* 179–186.

Drake, C., & Palmer, C. (1993). Accent structures in music performance. *Music Perception, 10,* 343–378.

Feldman, J., Epstein, D., & Richards, W. (1992). Force dynamics of tempo change in music. *Music Perception. 10,* 185–204.

Fraisse, P. (1956). *Les structures rythmiques.* Louvain, Paris: Publications Universitaires de Louvain.

Fraisse, P. (1963). *The psychology of time.* New York: Harper & Row.

Fraisse, P. (1978). Time and rhythm perception. In E. C. Carterette & M. P. Friedman (Eds.), *Handbook of perception: Vol. 8* (pp. 203–254). New York: Academic Press.

Fraisse, P. (1982). Rhythm and tempo. In D. Deutsch (Ed.), *The psychology of music* (pp. 149–180). New York: Academic Press.

Fraisse, P. (1987). A historical approach to rhythm as perception. In A. Gabrielsson (Ed.), *Action and perception in rhythm and music* (pp. 7–18). Stockholm: Royal Swedish Academy of Music.

Gabrielsson, A. (1973a). Similarity ratings and dimension analyses of auditory rhythm patterns. II. *Scandinavian Journal of Psychology, 14,* 161–176.

Gabrielsson, A. (1973b). Adjective ratings and dimension analyses of auditory rhythm patterns. *Scandinavian Journal of Psychology, 14,* 244–260.

Gabrielsson, A. (1988). Timing in music performance and its relation to music experience. In J. Sloboda (Ed.), *Generative processes in music* (pp. 27–51). Oxford: The Clarendon Press.

Garner, W. R. (1974). *The processing of information and structure.* Potomac, MD: Erlbaum.

Handel, S. (1989). *Listening: An introduction to the perception of auditory events.* Cambridge, MA: MIT Press.

Hargreaves, D. J. (1986). *The developmental psychology of music.* Cambridge: Cambridge University Press.

Johnson-Laird, P. N. (1991). Rhythm and metre: a theory at the computational level. *Psychomusicology, 10,* 88–106.

Kendall, R. A., & Carterette, E. C. (1990). The communication of musical expression. *Music Perception, 8,* 129–164.

Kramer. J. (1988). *The time of music.* New York: Schirmer Books.

Kugler, P. N., Kelso, J. A. S., & Turvey, M. T. (1980). On the concept of coordinative structures as dissipative structures: I. Theoretical lines of convergence. In G. E. Stelmach & J. Requin (Eds.), *Tutorials in motor behaviour.* New York: North Holland.

Large, E. W., & Kolen, J. F. (1994). Resonance and the perception of musical meter. *Connection Science, 6,* 177–208.

Lee, C. S. (1991). The perception of metrical structure: experimental evidence and a model. In P. Howell, R. West, & I. Cross (Eds.), *Representing musical structure* (pp. 59–127). London: Academic Press.

Lerdahl, F., & Jackendoff, R. (1983). *A generative theory of tonal music*. Cambridge, MA: MIT Press.

Longuet-Higgins, H. C. (1979). The perception of music. *Proceedings of the Royal Society of London. B 205*, 307–322.

Longuet-Higgins, H. C. and Lee, C. S. (1982). The perception of musical rhythm. *Perception, 11*, 115–128.

Luce, G. G. (1972). *Body time*. London: Temple Smith.

Martin, J. G. (1972). Rhythmic (hierarchic) versus serial structure in speech and other behaviour. *Psychological Review, 79*, 487–509.

McAdams, S. (1993). Recognition of sound sources and events. In S. McAdams & E. Bigand (Eds.), *Thinking in sound: The cognitive psychology of human audition* (pp. 146–198). Oxford: The Clarendon Press.

Michon, J. A. (1978). The making of the present: a tutorial review. In J. Requin (Ed.), *Attention and performance VII* (pp. 89–111). Hillsdale, NJ: Erlbaum.

Michon, J. A. (1985). The compleat time experiencer. In J. A. Michon & J. L. Jackson (Eds.), *Time, Mind and Behaviour* (pp. 20–52). Berlin: Springer.

Moog, H. (1976). *The musical experience of the pre-school child* (C. Clarke, Trans.). London: Schott.

Nattiez, J.-J. (1975). *Fondements d'une sémiologie de la musique*. Paris: Union Générale d'Editions.

Palmer, C. (1989). Mapping musical thought to musical performance. *Journal of Experimental Psychology: Human Perception and Performance, 15*, 331–346.

Palmer, C., & Krumhansl, C. L. (1990). Mental representations for musical meter. *Journal of Experimental Psychology: Human Perception and Performance, 7*, 3–18.

Parncutt, R. (1987). The perception of pulse in musical rhythm. In A. Gabrielsson (Ed.), *Action and perception in rhythm and music* (pp. 127–138). Stockholm: Royal Swedish Academy of Music.

Parncutt, R. (1994). A perceptual model of pulse salience and metrical accent in musical rhythms. *Music Perception, 11*, 409–464.

Povel, D.-J. (1981). Internal representation of simple temporal patterns. *Journal of Experimental Psychology: Human Perception and Performance, 7*, 3–18.

Povel, D.-J., & Essens, P. (1985). Perception of temporal patterns. *Music Perception, 2*, 411–440.

Povel, D-J., & Okkerman, H. (1981). Accents in equitone sequences. *Perception & Psychophysics, 30*, 565–572.

Repp, B. (1992a). Diversity and commonality in music performance: An analysis of timing microstructure in Schumann's "Träumerei." *Journal of the Acoustical Society of America, 92*, 2546–2568.

Repp, B. (1992b). Probing the cognitive representation of musical time: structural constraints on the perception of timing perturbations. *Cognition, 44*, 241–28 1.

Repp, B. H. (1992c). A constraint on the expressive timing of a melodic gesture: Evidence from performance and aesthetic judgment. *Music Perception, 10*, 221–243.

Repp, B. H. (1993). Music as motion: a synopsis of Alexander Truslit's (1938) *Gestaltung und Bewegung in der Musik*. *Psychology of Music, 21*, 48–73.

Ruwet, N. (1972). *Langage, musique, poésie*. Paris: Seuil.

Schulze, H.-H. (1989). Categorical perception of rhythmic patterns. *Psychological Research, 51*, 10–15.

Shaffer, L. H. (1981). Performances of Chopin, Bach and Bartók: Studies in motor programming. *Cognitive Psychology, 13*, 326–376.

Shaffer, L. H. (1982). Rhythm and timing in skill. *Psychological Review, 89*, 109–123

Shaffer, L. H. (1984). Timing in solo and duet piano performances. *Quarterly Journal of Experimental Psychology, 36A*, 577–595.

Shaffer, L. H., & Todd, N. P. (1987). The interpretive component in musical performance. In A. Gabrielsson (Ed.), *Action and perception in rhythm and music* (pp. 139–152). Stockholm: Royal Swedish Academy of Music.

Sloboda, J. A. (1983). The communication of musical metre in piano performance. *Quarterly Journal of Experimental Psychology, 35A,* 377–396.

Sundberg, J. (1988). Computer synthesis of music performance. In J. Sloboda (Ed.), *Generative processes in music* (pp. 52–69). Oxford: The Clarendon Press.

Sundberg, J. & Verillo, V. (1980). On the anatomy of the ritard: A study of timing in music. *Journal of the Acoustical Society of America, 68,* 772–779.

Tenney, J., & Polansky, L. (1980). Temporal Gestalt perception in music. *Journal of Music Theory, 24,* 205–241.

Terhardt, E., Stoll, G., & Seewann, M. (1982). Algorithm for extraction of pitch and pitch salience from complex tonal signals. *Journal of the Acoustical Society of America, 71,* 679–688.

Thomassen, M. T. (1982). Melodic accent: Experiments and a tentative model. *Journal of the Acoustical Society of America, 71,* 1596–1605.

Todd, N. P. (1985). A model of expressive timing in tonal music. *Music Perception. 3,* 33–58.

Todd, N. P. (1989). A computational model of rubato. *Contemporary Music Review, 3,* 69–89.

Todd, N. P. (1992). The dynamics of dynamics: A model of musical expression. *Journal of the Acoustical Society of America, 91,* 3540–3550.

Todd, N. P. (1993). Vestibular feedback in musical performance: Response to *Somatosensory Feedback in Musical Performance* (Ed. Sundberg and Verillo). *Music Perception, 10,* 379–382.

Todd, N. P. (1994a). The auditory "primal sketch": a multiscale model of rhythmic grouping. *Journal of New Music Research, 23,* 25–70.

Todd, N. P. (1994b). Metre, grouping and the uncertainty principle: A unified theory of rhythm perception. *Proceedings of the Third International Conference for Music Perception and Cognition* (pp. 395–396). Liège, Belgium: ICMPC.

Todd, N. P. (1995). The kinematics of musical expression. *Journal of the Acoustical Society of America, 97,* 1940–1949.

Todd, N. P., & Brown, G. (1996). Visualization of rhythm, time and metre. *Artificial Intelligence Review, 10,* 253–273.

Todd, N. P., & Lee, C. S. 1994. An auditory-motor model of beat induction. In *Proceedings of the International Computer Music Conference,* (pp. 88–89). Aarhus, Denmark: International Computer Music Association.

Vos, P. G. (1978). *Identification of metre in music* (Internal report 78 ON 06). Nijmegen, The Netherlands: University of Nijmegen.

Windsor, W. L. (1993). Dynamic accents and the categorical perception of metre. *Psychology of Music, 21,* 127–140.

Woodrow, H. (1909). A quantitative study of rhythm. *Archives of Psychology, 14,* 1–66.

Yeston, M. (1976). *The stratification of musical rhythm.* New Haven, CT: Yale University Press.

14

THE PERFORMANCE OF MUSIC

ALF GABRIELSSON

Department of Psychology
Uppsala University
Uppsala, Sweden

I. INTRODUCTION

Music performance is a large subject that can be approached in many different ways. This chapter focuses on empirical research of music performance and related matters. Most of this research is concerned with Western tonal music and mainly art music, an obvious limitation that should be kept in mind. Studies on performance of single notes, intervals, chords and so forth—that is, with no musical context—are usually not discussed, nor are matters related to music teaching; for the latter, see the handbook edited by Colwell (1992). Singing is only cursorily discussed, because it is treated in the chapter by Sundberg (this volume).

The topics addressed follow a kind of chronological order, beginning with the planning of performance, proceeding to various aspects of the performance itself (sight-reading, improvisation, feedback, motor processes, measurements, and models), then to physical, psychological, and social factors that may influence the performance, and finally to performance evaluation.

Some textbooks on music psychology include questions concerning performance. Mursell (1937/1971) compared vocal and instrumental performance and discussed problems in interpretation and technique. C. E. Seashore (1938) summarized extensive measurements of performance made by him and his coworkers, also cited in Lundin (1985). Schoen (1940) described studies of artistic singing. Lundin (1985) discussed learning and remembering music from a behavioristic point of view. Sloboda (1982a, 1985b) discussed performance plans, sight-reading, rehearsal, and expert performance with a cognitive approach. These and other questions on music performance were also elaborated by different authors in the volumes edited by Sloboda (1988), Jones and Holleran (1992), and Bruhn, Oerter, and Rösing (1993).[1]

II. PERFORMANCE PLANNING

Excellence in music performance involves two major components: (a) a genuine understanding of what the music is about, its structure and meaning, and (b) a complete mastery of the instrumental technique. Gerig (1976, Chap.1) cited a large number of famous pianists and concluded that it is not necessary to argue for the importance of technique, but "the technical objective at the same time becomes *the* means to a far greater end—the projection of a meaningful interpretation" (p. 1). Statements to the same end are found in Bastian (1989, p. 172), LaBerge (1981a, 1981b), Leimer (1932/1972, p. 46), Restle (1981), or Sloboda (1985b, p. 90). In the words of Pablo Casals: "One needs to have a clear idea of the musical thought, and execute it precisely" (cited from Clynes, 1987, p. 203).

In accordance with this, one may distinguish two interrelated steps in the planning of performance:

1. To acquire an adequate mental representation of the piece of music, coupled with a plan for transforming this representation into sound, and
2. To practice the piece to a level that is satisfactory for the purpose at hand.

A. REPRESENTATION AND PERFORMANCE PLAN

The way in which a performer generates a mental representation of the music differs depending on the type of music and the instrument used, further on his or her experience and knowledge, personality, situational demands, and so forth. For a new piece, one may have to start from scratch; in other cases, it may be possible to retrieve or modify a representation that is already stored. The structural characteristics of the piece are crucial, both the overall structure (e.g., hierarchical, chainlike) and the structure of various units. Clarke (1988, pp. 2–5) discussed the differences in structural representations when music is performed from memory, in sight-reading, and in improvisation. In memorized performance the representation is (should be) fairly complete, depending on the length and complexity of the piece, and is just "unpacked" during the course of the performance. However, in sight-reading and in improvisation the representation is by necessity incomplete in various respects.

Palmer and de Sande (1993) attempted to study units in the representation of homophonic and polyphonic music by analyzing errors in piano performance of such pieces. They predicted and found more chord errors in homophonic than in

---

1. After the completion of this chapter (August 1995), another review "Music Performance" by Caroline Palmer, focusing on interpretation, planning, and movement was published in *Annual Review of Psychology,* 1997, *48,* 115–138. A volume on *The Practice of Performance,* edited by John Rink (Cambridge: Cambridge University Press, 1995), contains both empirical and theoretical papers on music performance.

polyphonic performances and more single-note errors in polyphonic than in homophonic performances. Furthermore, error intrusions were more often harmonically congruent with the correct notes in homophonic than in polyphonic performances. Errors were fewer in the melodic (most important) voice than in other voices, especially when it was the highest in pitch level. In other studies, Palmer (1989a, 1989c, 1992) studied pianists' performance in relation to their intended phrasing in pieces by Chopin and Brahms. Phrase endings were characterized by a ritard, indicating that phrases were important constituents in the mental representation. Analysis of performance errors showed, for instance, that notes deleted in the performance were placed within phrases rather than at the structurally more important phrase endings (see further in Section VII,C,9).

Structural components suggested by these studies—melody, voices, chords, phrases—are, of course, familiar from general music theory. However, Palmer pointed out that theories that try to model the intuitions of an idealized listener in terms of what is notated in the score disregard individual interpretive preferences. The notation is often open to various interpretations regarding the connections and relative importance of various structural units (cf. also Sloboda, 1994). The chosen interpretation will in its turn influence the (real) listener's structural representation of the piece.

The emphasis on structural features in the mental representation has been characteristic for cognitive music psychology. Important as they are, however, they do not exhaust what is contained in most performers' representations (Gabrielsson, 1988, 1994). Every performance involves some kind of intention from the performer's side concerning what the music should express or convey to the listener, be it ideas, associations, memories, feelings, body movements, concrete events, or just patterns of sound. For instance, in a study by Persson, Pratt, and Robson (1992) concerning the interpretation of an unknown piece of piano music, some performers represented the piece in terms of images, scenes, things, events, characters, and moods and used these as directions for how to perform the piece. They seemed to be more concerned with such types of representation than with structural matters. Clarke (1993a, 1993b) discussed the possibility of representing the music by verbal description or in terms of body movements (see Section VI,D).

Shaffer (1992) questioned the idea of identifying musical meaning with musical structure, because listeners tend to hear, and performers try to convey, moods and emotions in the music (see also Section VI,D). He suggested that music can provide an abstract narrative: "we can think of the musical structure as describing an implicit event and the gestures of musical expression as corresponding to the emotional gestures of an implicit protagonist who witnesses or participates in the event. Thus the performer's interpretation can be viewed as helping to define the character of the protagonist. This in turn determines the patterning of mood over the event" (p. 265). Shaffer gave the notation of an unknown piano piece by Beethoven to four pianists and asked them to provide their preferred version of it as well as any other musically valid version. Three of the pianists got the full score, but one got a score where all expressive markings were deleted. Although the former pianists showed high consistency in timing and dynamics across their different versions, this was not the case for the latter pianist. This may be taken as evidence of the power of expressive markings to constrain the interpretation, that they "help to crystallize a narrative for the piece" (p. 273). The idea of considering performance both as elucidating structure and inventing a musical character was further elaborated by Shaffer (1995).

Baily (1985, 1990, 1991) pointed out that the representation of music also involves motor processes. Using examples from African and Afghan music, he claimed that music is as much a question of movement as of sound. The spatial properties of an instrument in combination with convenient movement patterns in fingers, hands, and arms may very well be the decisive factors for the shape of a piece of music. In African music, the representation "may be a movement representation rather than an auditory one" (1985, p. 242). He argued that movement properties are important in Western music as well. Composers take the properties of the instruments and the performers' motor skills into account when creating music. This is especially obvious in the case of études. Furthermore, anyone familiar with improvisation knows how much it is determined by movement patterns; see, for example, Sudnow's (1978) book *Ways of the Hand* dealing with jazz piano improvisation. Berliner (cited in Baily, 1991, p. 150) quoted a saxophonist who indicated that "sometimes the ideas come from my mind ... but other times they come from my fingers." Gay (cited in Baily, 1991) pointed out that in much rock music the musical conceptualization is achieved with reference to the spatial layout of notes and the physical structure of the guitar. There are therefore good reasons to "regard auditory and spatio-motor modes of musical cognition as being of potentially equal importance" (Baily, 1991, p. 150).

A related, yet different, point of view was advanced by Truslit (1938). (An English synopsis of this work was provided by Repp, 1993; see also Repp, 1994a.) Truslit argued that the fundamental element of music is motion and therefore the musician should have a proper representation of the motion character of the music to be performed. He distinguished three basic forms of motion in music—"open," "closed," and "winding"—with numerous variants and illustrated them by many examples. Practice should always be governed by considerations of the proper motion character (see also Section VII,B,1). Given the adequate motion representation, many technical problems will solve themselves. The importance of motion characters was also stressed by Becking (1928) and Clynes (1983), who suggested that there is a characteristic "inner pulse" for each composer (see Section VIII,B), and by the current author (Gabrielsson, 1986a, 1988). Repp (1994a) provided a survey of some historical and contemporary approaches to musical motion.

In conclusion, the representation of music may be generated in many different and interrelated ways: in terms of structure, meaning, expression, imagery, moods, spatiomotor patterns, and so on. It is further instructive to consider the historical background to the modern conception of interpretation (Kopiez, 1993).

The generation of a representation and of a performance plan (Mursell, 1937/1971, chapter VII; Sloboda, 1982a) goes hand in hand. The general question is how the structure and the meaning of the piece should be conveyed in a convincing way. This necessitates considerations about stylistic conventions, performance practice, instrumental characteristics and the like, leading further to specific questions concerning adequate tempo, timbre, dynamics, phrasing, timing, articulation, accents, and the related motor processes. On the whole there is little systematic knowledge about these considerations. Introspections by conductors and performers appear occasionally in books, music magazines, program notes, and in radio or television programs. Many musicians are even resistant to talk about these things contending that the music should talk for itself. A conflict may be felt between the demands of performance tradition and one's own preferred interpretation (Persson et al., 1992).

Although one can in principle distinguish between the representation, the performance plan, and the practice, they usually interact in complex and inter-individually varying ways. Of course, the representation of the piece has (or should have) a profound effect on the way the piece is practiced. On the other hand, practicing the piece may lead to modification of the representation. Ribke (1993) described this process as an interplay between conception and realization, action and reflection, deliberate planning and spontaneous intuition. Wicinski (cited in Miklaszewski, 1989) interviewed 10 eminent Moscow pianists (including Gilels, Neuhaus, and Richter) about their preparation for a performance. Seven of them distinguished three stages. First, acquiring knowledge of the music and developing preliminary ideas about how it should be performed. Second, hard work on technical problems, and third, a fusion of the first two stages with trial rehearsals leading to the final version. However, the three remaining pianists could not identify separate stages but worked in an undifferentiated way from beginning to end. See also the comments by a pianist in Miklaszewski's (1989) own study (see Section II,B,3).

B. PRACTICING

1. Mental Versus Physical Practice

Mental practice of motor skills refers to the covert or imaginary rehearsal of a skill without any muscular movements. Of course, learning to perform music inevitably requires practice on one's instrument. Having acquired a basic technical ability, the question is if mental practice, in one form or another, can be an efficient means in preparing performance of a piece.

The German piano pedagogue Leimer (1932/1972), teacher of the famous pianist Walter Gieseking, is often considered as a spokesman for mental training. Leimer emphasized that the performer must know the score, or appropriate parts of it, by heart before proceeding to practice on the instrument. Effective memorizing could be accomplished by an analysis of the piece in suitable structural units, that is, "chunks" in G. A. Miller's (1956) terminology. When reading a score, one should be able to hear the music with one's "inner ear." The practice on the instrument should be made with intense concentration to every detail in the performance, and therefore the practice sessions should be relatively short. The tempo should be slow in order to prevent any errors and successively increased until reaching its proper rate.

Leimer frequently referred to Gieseking, who always performed by heart. Gieseking (1963, p. 94) himself said that most of his practice was done away from the piano, either reading the score and memorizing it, or, when rehearsing pieces played earlier, reviewing them in memory and only hinting at finger movements. Obviously this presupposes complete mastery of the required motor skills, and so the training can be mainly mental. The opinions of many other musicians and music pedagogues vary widely as seen in reviews by Rubin-Rabson (1937) and Kopiez (1990a). Some emphasize cognitive training, others exclusively training on the instrument, and still others a combination of both. LaBerge (1981b) suggested that mental rehearsal before playing a section is advantageous for grasping the overall shape of the section; this may be lost if one starts playing at once.

A majority of experiments on mental practice in sports and other motor activities indicate that "mental practice is better than no practice but not as effective as actual practice" (P. Johnson, 1984, p. 237; see also Coffman, 1990; Rosenbaum, 1991, p. 95). With regard to music, only a few studies have been done. Rubin-Rabson (1937) had four groups of piano students practice short compositions from the 17th and 18th centuries. Two groups analyzed the score, either guided by the experimenter or for themselves, for 20 min before practicing on the instrument. The third group practiced directly on the instrument, and the fourth group first listened to a recording of the pieces and then practiced according to one of the aforementioned methods. In a relearning experiment 3 weeks later, the groups that had received analytical training required less time and fewer repetitions to achieve a correct performance by heart. Rubin-Rabson (1941a, 1945) showed that a period of mental rehearsal inserted midway in the practice on the instrument proved to be as efficient as practicing on the instrument up to 100% overlearning. Mental rehearsal added after the performance criterion was reached was not beneficial. However, in a relearning test after 7 months, these differences among the methods were gone. Generally Rubin-Rabson considered mental practice favorable, but it should be applied to units of comfortable length.

S. L. Ross (1985) had trombone students practice an étude, either playing it three times (physical practice), perform it mentally three times trying to "hear" the pitches and to "feel" the movements of the embouchure and the slide (but with no physical movements), or combining physical and mental practice by playing the piece two times with a mental trial in between. The combined practice gave the largest gain scores, in number of correctly performed measures, from pretest to posttest, followed by physical practice. Coffman (1990) investigated the effects of physical, mental, and alternating physical and mental practice on students' learning of a short four-part chordal composition using a synthesizer. Significant differences among the methods appeared only regarding performance time. Physical practice, alone or in alternation with mental practice, proved to be superior to exclusive mental practice with regard to the speed of the performance after rehearsal. Mental practice was better than no practice at all. However, there were no differences among the methods regarding pitch and rhythm errors.

Kopiez (1990a) did two experiments with guitar students who were given a short excerpt from an unknown composition by Krenek. They practiced under one of four conditions: (a) cognitive practice, first listening to a structural analysis of the excerpt, then trying to memorize it in two 5-min sessions; (b) motor practice, practicing in two 5-min sessions with their instrument; (c) cognitive-motor practice, first listening to the structural analysis, then 5 min memorizing without instrument followed by 5 min practicing with the instrument; and (d) motor-cognitive practice, that is, in the reverse order. In the first experiment, there was no significant difference between the conditions regarding correct pitches and rhythm in the performance. In the second experiment, in which a longer excerpt was used, the group given motor practice was the most successful. Kopiez (1990b, 1991) further found that a structural analysis using a score with colors and graphics added worked better than a conventional verbal analysis.

The investigations just reviewed thus gave different results. This is not surprising, because they differ much with respect to music examples, instruments and performers, operational definitions of mental practice, and criterion measures. Coffman (1990) discussed several critical points. It seems that the less advanced the person is on the instrument and the more difficult the music is, the more important is the motor practice. Combination of physical and mental training can be favorable, as seen in some studies above and emphasized in the survey by Freymuth (1993). The distinction between mental and motor practice is in fact not clear-cut. Hale (cited in Freymuth, 1993) found that internal imagery produced activity in the muscles that would be used in the actual movements.

Conductors are by necessity forced to much mental practice. Herbert von Karajan always conducted from memory and used different editions of the score in order to rely solely on his auditory imagination of the music, avoiding visual memories of a particular score (Vaughan, 1986, pp. 210, 244). However, there are other conductors said to rely on photographic memory. Bird and Wilson (1988) studied electroencephalographic (EEG) and electromyographic (EMG) patterns during imagery in novice conductors and their teacher. There were large individual differences, but the teacher and the more skilled novices showed more repeatable EEG patterns than the less skilled students. The teacher displayed EMG patterns during mental rehearsal that resembled those of the actual performance.

2. Memorizing Music

Rubin-Rabson (1939, 1940a, 1940b, 1941b, 1945) studied skilled pianists' memorization of short pieces (eight measures) under different conditions. Some minutes of analytical prestudy were always made before the practicing on the instrument. Criterion measures were trials to reach a flawless performance in the learning session and in relearning 2 weeks later, as well as errors in a transcription of the music. In accordance with results from other areas (P. Johnson, 1984, p. 235), she found that distributed practice (intervals between practice trials were 1 hour or 24 hours) was more efficient than massed practice in relearning. However, this applied only to the less capable performers, who, she assumed, may not grasp the musical structure until a second presentation. There was no difference between learning the eight-measure periods as wholes or in parts. Overlearning after the performance criterion was reached did not seem worthwhile; rather the extra trials may be saved for later sessions when the performance should be brought to the same level again. Unilateral practice (each hand separately) and coordinated practice (both hands together) both had advantages.

When these results are evaluated, the conditions of the experiments must be remembered. For instance, O'Brien (cited in Lundin, 1985, p. 140) found, not surprisingly, that learning in parts was more efficient for longer pieces. Farnsworth (1969, p. 168) suggested that one should work with as large a portion of the score as constitutes a manageable unit for oneself. Lundin (1985) concluded that which method is best will depend on the size, difficulty, and meaning of the material as well as on the subject's performance level. LaBerge (1981a) suggested that teachers encourage the student to discover larger global relationships in a piece, even if the practice is made in smaller parts.

Some conductors are known to be extremely good memorizers. Toscanini was said to know by heart every note in hundreds of symphonic works, operas, and chamber music (Marek, 1982, p. 414), and almost unbelievable anecdotes are told about his memory feats.

3. Rehearsal Techniques

Reports on observations of the rehearsal process are rare. Gruson (1988) had 40 piano students, representing different grade levels, and three concert pianists practice three unknown pieces, selected to ensure comparable levels of difficulty across grade levels. The practice sessions were recorded on audiotape and analyzed in terms of 20 categories. The most common event was uninterrupted playing, followed by repeating a single note, repeating a measure, and slowing down. The higher the performance level, the more time was devoted to self-guiding speech, playing hands separately, and especially to repeating sections, whereas the repeating of single notes decreased. Thus chunking in larger sections increased with increased skill. Kopiez (1990a, p. 197) pointed to the common experience that transitions between the sections often cause difficulties and therefore must be given extra consideration

Miklaszewski (1989) analyzed video-recorded practice sessions of a pianist preparing performance of a prelude by Debussy. The most frequent activity was playing alternately in fast and slow tempi. Pauses usually appeared after fast playing and were frequently used for considering corrective actions. The piece was practiced in fragments corresponding to structural units, often in another order than in the score. Some fragments were very short because of their complexity, but as the practice progressed, the fragments were spliced into longer sections. The pianist's own comments suggested that he first intended to get a clear idea of the music and of the technical requirements for performing it. He was then interested to see what he was able to perform directly and what parts must be given special practice.

Barry (1992) found that brass and woodwind students in Grades 7–10 who rehearsed a piece with structured and supervised practice performed better on a posttest than matched students who were allowed free practice. The structured practice involved starting slowly and gradually increasing the tempo, inspecting and "fingering through" the music silently before practicing, marking errors, and practicing such sections slowly. The free-practice students usually did not use any of these strategies. Jones (1990) found that silent fingering produced a positive effect on later piano performance. Rosenthal, Wilson, Evans, and Greenwalt (1988) reported that graduate woodwind and brass students learned to perform a short piece more effectively by either listening to a model performance of the piece or practicing it on the instrument rather than by using silent analysis or practicing by singing the piece.

Which is the most favorable rehearsal technique obviously depends on the size, difficulty, and meaning of the material as well as on the subject's performance level. A common theme is that practice should be organized according to individually suitable structural units that are then expanded to successively larger units. Special attention should be given to transitions between such units as well as to sections where errors crop up. To avoid errors, the tempo should be initially slow enough and then successively increased (however, this may be questioned, see Section VI,A). Some mental practice and silent analysis alternating with the physical practice may be preferable.

Questions concerning practice are also discussed in connection with performers' musical development (see Section X,A).[2]

III. SIGHT-READING

A. GENERAL CHARACTERISTICS

Sight-reading means performing from a score without any preceding practice on the instrument of that score, to perform *a prima vista*. It must apparently involve reading groups (patterns) of notes, because reading one note at a time would not match the required tempo unless the tempo is extremely slow. Sight-reading actually involves a combination of reading and motor behavior, that is, to read note patterns coming up in the score while performing others just read. A good sight-reader is thus a rapid reader, is efficient in transforming the read pattern into appropriate motor acts, and has a good instrumental technique. Sight-reading is more efficient if the music is known, or if it conforms to a certain style that permits anticipation of what is coming next, and further if the music printing is proper with regard to spacing and other aspects.

The above points were confirmed in early studies by Bean (1938), Kwalwasser (cited in Lundin, 1985, p. 281), and Lannert and Ullman (1945). Bean used short tachistoscopic presentations of material to be performed. The professional musicians performed best, managing correct reproduction of about five notes on average. Introspections showed that the good sight-readers identified patterns and

2. See further in *Does Practice Make Perfect? Current Theory and Research on Instrumental Music Practice,* edited by Harald Jørgensen and Andreas C. Lehmann (Oslo: The Norwegian State Academy of Music, 1997; ISSN 0333-3760).

sometimes used guesswork, as also found by C. A. Elliott (1982), MacKnight (1975), and T. Wolf (1976). Lannert and Ullman (1945) tested the ability to read ahead by presenting one measure at a time in a way that forced the pianist to play the measure he had just seen while reading the next measure. They also noted that eye movements from score to keyboard had to be quick in order not to break contact with the score. One of Wolf's pianists remarked that a good tactile feel of the keyboard makes it possible to play without having to look at the keyboard (cf. typing). If performers are not allowed to see the keyboard, they make more errors, especially poor sight-readers (Banton, 1995).

The reading of patterns rather than of individual notes may make one not notice misprints in scores as shown in the "Goldovsky experiment" (T. Wolf, 1976). A poor sight-reader played a wrong, misprinted note (a G instead of G♯ in a C♯ major chord) in a Brahms piece. Goldovsky then asked several pianists to find the misprint. For more than half of them, he had to indicate in which measure or chord the misprint was before it was detected. This is a musical parallel to the "proofreader's error"—expectation overrules perception.

McPherson (1994) found that errors in sight-reading performance by young instrumentalists were in most cases rhythm errors. He suggested that competent sight-readers seek relevant information (key and time signature, phrases, possible obstacles etc.) by scanning the music and mentally rehearsing (e.g., silent singing and fingering) major difficulties before performance. They further maintain high attention during performance to anticipate problems and to observe the musical indications above and below the musical line, and self-monitor the performance in order to correct the performance when errors occur. McPherson (1995) reported a positive correlation between the ability to play by ear and sight-reading and suggested a causal link, meaning that the former would influence the latter. It seems that both abilities presuppose effective chunking and identification of common patterns, and both work better when the style of the music is familiar.

B. EYE MOVEMENTS

Only a few studies on eye movements in music reading have been done, as reviewed by Goolsby (1989, 1994a). Many of the studies were flawed by various technical problems, and the results must be considered with caution. Furthermore, the experimental situation was often awkward for the performers. In the study by Weaver (1943), 15 female pianists performed three short pieces representing harmonic (a hymn), melodic (Bach minuet with two voices), and melody-with-supporting-chords organization. A headrest and a biting board was used to fix the position of the head. Three patterns of eye movements were discerned: (a) vertical, for example, reading each chord in the hymn from treble to bass, (b) horizontal, for example, reading successive melody notes before looking at the bass, and (c) mixtures of these. All three patterns occurred for all pieces and may be related to the structural features of the pieces but in ways that varied both between and within pianists. The amount of reading ahead (the "eye-hand span") was very "elastic" in size, varying between and within pieces and pianists. The maximum was eight notes ahead.

Goolsby (1994a, 1994b) used a special "eyetracker" that directs a beam of infrared light into the performer's right eye. The reflections are recorded, and the horizontal and vertical components of eye position are sampled every millisecond during performance. Computer reduction programs convert the data into convenient summary files. The equipment was used to study eye movements in two groups of music students (1994a) and in two individual students (1994b)—one skilled and one less-skilled sight-reader—during their vocalization of four melodies differing in notational complexity. The group study showed that skilled sight-readers had more but shorter progressive as well as regressive fixations than less-skilled sight-readers. This suggests that skilled readers direct fixations well ahead of the performance to see what happens later in the melody and then go back to the point of performance. The use of regressive fixations is different in comparison with the skilled reading of text, in which regressive fixations are minimized. Furthermore, the duration of fixations in music reading was 100–200 msec longer in this study than what is typical for corresponding durations in text reading. Goolsby therefore warned against accepting too simple analogies between music reading and text reading. In the individual study, the positions and durations of the successive fixations were given in instructive detail for both subjects. The skilled sight-reader looked ahead, used the time of longer note values to scan about the notation, did not fixate every individual note (e.g., read scalewise notes with a single fixation), and used peripheral vertical vision to perceive dynamic and expression markings. This all indicates an active processing of the music before the performance, which was flawless. Conversely, the less-skilled sight-reader fixated on virtually every note but rarely on expressive markings, did not look very far ahead, and made many errors during the performance.

C. SIGHT-READING AND MEMORIZING

Even excellent musicians may be poor sight-readers (Bean, 1938; Lannert & Ullman, 1945; T. Wolf, 1976), and it is sometimes said that musicians who are good at sight-reading are poor at memorizing, and vice versa. T. Wolf (1976, p. 167) pointed out that sight-reading and memorizing are different processes. The good sight-reader works with rapid and effective chunking using short-term memory. However, in memorizing music one works slowly with awareness and control of each note until the procedures to a large extent become automatic and stored in long-term memory. The goals as well as the means are thus different. One can be good at sight-reading and poor at memorizing, or the converse, but there is no reason to believe that one ability excludes the other. In fact Nuki (1984) found a positive correlation between sight-reading performance and memorization ability. Furthermore, students of composition were better than piano students in memorization. This difference was ascribed to the training in grasping structural features that is involved in studying composition. McPherson (1995) also found a positive correlation between sight-reading and memorization in clarinet and trumpet students.

D. RELATION TO MUSICAL STRUCTURE

Sloboda (1974, 1976a, 1976b, 1977, 1978a; summaries in Sloboda 1978b, 1982b, and 1985b, chapter 3) conducted the most comprehensive series of experiments on music reading. A common theme was that sight-reading is determined by various structural features in the music. For instance, when the "eye-hand span" (1974, 1977) was studied by requiring musicians to go on playing when the score was suddenly removed, the span seemed elastic, expanding or shrinking to phrase boundaries. The best sight-readers had a span of 6.8 notes. Another example (Sloboda, 1976b) was that deliberately inserted misprints often went undetected by keyboard players, who instead played the musically correct note. The misprints were harder to detect in the middle of phrases than in the beginning or at the end, especially in the upper stave.

When musicians and nonmusicians looked at short (up to 100 msec) exposures of notated patterns, both groups were poor at reproducing the pattern (1976a, 1978a). However, musicians were better at retaining the approximate contour of the pattern. With increasing exposure times up to 2 sec, both groups improved, but nonmusicians peaked at about three notes correctly reproduced, whereas musicians could record six notes. The difference is due to the musicians' coding and storing of the stimulus as a musical pattern, whereas the nonmusicians had to remember it as a purely visual pattern. This interpretation was supported by Halpern and Bower (1982), who found that musicians, but not nonmusicians, achieved better results with "good" melodies than with "bad" or random ones. Asked to divide the notes into groupings, nonmusicians grouped them according to the direction of the stem, upward or downward.

Little research has been done on the effects of musical printing on performance (Ribke, 1993; Sloboda, 1978b). Generally the printing should facilitate the grasping of the musical structure. There are many examples of improper notation—too crowded notes, inconsistent spacing between notes, misplaced notes, and so on. von Karajan noticed during a rehearsal that the orchestra always increased the tempo at the same place and found that the publisher had compressed the notes there in order to get a clean break at the page turn (Vaughan, 1986, p. 209).

Salis (1980) found that good sight-readers were superior in the rapid perception of chords but not in the perception of dot patterns, indicating that the superior pattern recognition of good sight-readers is specific to music notation. W. B. Thompson (1987), working with flutists, gave further support to this idea in finding that sight-reading ability correlated positively with achievement in a music-recall test, but not with results in a letter-recall test. He further confirmed the positive correlation ($r = 0.85$) between sight-reading ability and "eye-performance span." The latter reflects the ability to simultaneously read something and perform something else. The partial correlation between sight-reading ability and eye-performance span, controlling for music-reading ability, was still relatively high ($r =$

0.65). Thus musicians, equivalent in music-reading and in performance skills, may still differ in sight-reading ability if they differ in their ability to perform these tasks simultaneously. A parallel to this occurs in typing (Shaffer 1981, p. 328).

IV. IMPROVISATION

The definition and meaning of improvisation is no simple matter and is discussed in many papers (Andreas, 1993; Clarke, 1992; Nettl, 1974; Pike, 1974; Pressing, 1984, 1988). Even performance of strictly notated music involves a certain degree of improvisation in the individual interpretation. On the other hand, even performers of free jazz cannot avoid using previously stored material. Between these extremes are many intermediate levels.

Pressing (1984, 1988) provided a broad survey of research in different areas pertinent to the study of improvisation, including physiology and neuropsychology, motor control and skilled performance, intuition and creativity, artificial intelligence, oral traditions and folklore, and furthermore references to historical and ethnomusicological surveys, and to teaching texts. His 1988 paper lists about 200 references and should be consulted by anyone interested in research on improvisation.

In this paper, he also presented a formalized, cognitive model of improvisation. Any improvisation is seen as a sequence of nonoverlapping sections, each containing a number of musical events, called event clusters. The improvisation is an ordered union of event clusters. The generation of each cluster is based on previous events, a referent, long-term memory, and current goals. Two methods of continuation are used, associative and interrupt generation. In associative generation, the improviser wants to keep continuity, by means of similarity or contrast, between successive event clusters. In interrupt generation, the improviser breaks off into quite another direction without regard to what has been before. The choice between the two ways is made in relation to a time-dependent tolerance level for repetition. If the present degree of repetition is higher than this level, interrupt generation results; otherwise associative generation goes on.

Pressing (1987) analyzed two short pieces of improvised music with respect to the macrostructure (similar to traditional music analysis) and the microstructure (various aspects of timing and dynamics) and the correlations between those two levels. Such correlations were observed for one of the pieces, and distinct event clusters and classes of event clusters could be identified. Among the most interesting features were examples of categorical production (in analogy with categorical perception) and of three independent underlying temporal mechanisms.

In discussing Sudnow's (1978) description of how he learned to play jazz piano, Clarke (1988) discerned three alternative representations underlying jazz improvisation—hierarchical structure (in traditional jazz improvisation), associative structure (in free jazz), and selection of events contained within the performer's repertory (in bebop). All three principles may operate and interact in any performance. Johnson-Laird (1987, 1991) pointed out that musicians have little conscious access to the processes underlying their improvisations and sketched a theory about what the mind has to compute in order to produce an acceptable improvisation. Given that jazz musicians have stored knowledge of principles for rhythmic patterns, melodic contours, and harmonic and metrical constraints, what has to be computed for each note in the improvisation is its onset and offset, its step in the contour and its particular pitch. Preliminary illustrations were given using a computer program that, given a chord sequence as input, generates bass lines or melodies. Although on some occasions there is no choice about which note to play, on other occasions there may be many feasible notes. The program then makes an arbitrary choice, thus leaving room for creativity. Clarke (1992) discussed various problems with this model—its limitation to tonal jazz, its focus on generation of single notes rather than of larger units, and its neglect of the player's and the instrument's physical constraints.

A few empirical studies have been done. Reinholdsson (1987) analyzed timing and dynamics in a drum solo by Roy Haynes and provided a valuable discussion of the difficulties in analyzing performance of non–notation-bound music. Bastien and Hostager (1988) studied how four jazz musicians accomplished a group performance without having played together earlier. The basic idea is that the unavoidable initial uncertainty is reduced by two constraints, common knowledge of structural conventions in jazz and certain social practices. The latter include accepted behavioral norms—a leader decides and communicates each song, the soloist determines the style, each musician gets an opportunity to be the soloist—as well as certain communicative codes, verbal and nonverbal (eye contact, nodding, turning to an individual, hand signals). On the basis of this and a successively expanded knowledge of each other's behaviors during the performance, the group advanced from a somewhat cautious beginning to finally inventing an entirely new song.

Hargreaves, Cork, and Setton (1991) had novice and expert jazz keyboard players improvise to prerecorded "backing tracks" and interviewed them concerning what principles they used. The experts approached each improvisation with an overall plan—for instance, play in the style consistent with the backing track—but were prepared to adopt a new plan depending on what actually happened. They were relaxed about their performances, sometimes fell back on clichés and automatic performance of "subroutines," whereas the conscious control was reserved for the overall planning. In comparison, the novices' plans were nonexistent or very limited. Sági and Vitányi (1988) asked a large sample of persons to sing improvisations to Hungarian poems and to simple harmonic progressions. More than 3000 recordings were analyzed with respect to melodic, harmonic, and rhythmic features. Influences of Hungarian national music, as well as of art music and popular music, were evident and could be related to the different social backgrounds of the participating persons.

The interest in improvisation in music education is increasing, but there is still little research on the topic (Clarke, 1992; Webster, 1992). McPherson (1993) developed a test to measure improvisational ability of high school instrumentalists.

No significant correlation was found between improvisational ability and performance proficiency in the beginning stages of development, but in more advanced stages a significant correlation was found.

Improvisation plays an important role in much music therapy. A music therapist should be able to improvise in order to interact with his client in real time. Bruscia (1987, 1988) provided a broad and systematic account of improvisational models in music therapy.

V. FEEDBACK IN PERFORMANCE

Perceptual feedback in performance may be auditory, visual and proprioceptive, that is, tactile, kinesthetic, and maybe also vestibular (Todd, 1993).

The importance of proprioceptive feedback is obvious, although its precise role is a matter of discussion (see Section VI,C). Hearing-impaired and even deaf musicians (Glennie, 1991) use it successfully in their performance. Vibrotactile feedback from the skin is available to singers and instrumentalists but only below 1000 Hz. Sensitivity in the skin of the hand is best around 250 Hz; it decreases with increasing age (Verrillo, 1992). Most parts of a stringed instrument vibrate during playing and at levels that are clearly detectable (Askenfelt & Jansson, 1992). These vibrations may be used for intonation purposes, especially in ensemble playing at loud dynamics where auditory monitoring is difficult. Kinesthetic feedback from finger forces (e.g., with different types of "touch" in piano playing) also provides essential information.

Kinesthetic feedback, or even motor commands, is perhaps used to monitor performance in advance of auditory feedback, for instance, to feel that a wrong note is played before actually hearing it (Sloboda, 1978b). Heinlein (1930) found that changing proprioceptive feedback and eliminating auditory feedback had adverse effects on pedaling in piano performance (see also in Section VII,B).

Visual feedback can provide information about the instrument and the behaviors of the conductor, the fellow performers, and the audience, including "social feedback." Two or more performers playing together use auditory and visual feedback to be able to coordinate and respond to each other (Shaffer, 1984a, p. 593).

Delayed auditory feedback (DAF) usually has a detrimental effect, in speech as well as in music. Gates, Bradshaw, and Nettleton (1974) used delays from 0.1 to 1.05 sec for keyboard players instructed to play a Bach minuet on an electronic organ as fast and accurately as possible. In comparison with immediate auditory feedback (IAF), most subjects slowed down their performance. This effect was present over the whole range of delays and was most marked at a delay of 0.27 sec. Three strategies could be discerned: to play fast in order to get ahead of the delay, to play slower or pause and wait for the delay to catch up, or to ignore the delay and go on. One player who consistently speeded up performance tried to get the delayed note to coincide with the note he was playing; thus tempo may be decisive for what delay is most detrimental. Gates and Bradshaw (1974) found that performance without any auditory feedback at all was not different from IAF performance (see also Banton, 1995). It was hypothesized that auditory imagery can take the place of IAF. Performance with DAF to one or both ears was worse, as well as performance with combined IAF and DAF. DAF disruption may stem from several sources, such as distraction, error repetition, and conflict with expectancies. Varying the speed of the performance may be one way to investigate this further. Today's computerized synthesizers offer convenient possibilities for studying DAF. According to Yates (cited in Gates & Bradshaw, 1974), the DAF effect is notoriously resistant to any reduction with practice. However, this cannot be generally true, because organists can easily learn to perform on pneumatic organs, which involve DAF.

Auditory feedback may refer not only to hearing the sounds from one's own instrument but also the sounds from other performers. Good acoustics in concert halls should include this aspect as well. This was studied by Gade (1986, 1989a, 1989b) with special reference to "support"—the property that makes the musician feel that he can hear himself well and not is forced to play louder than usual—and to "hearing each other" (see also Naylor & Craik, 1988). Increased reverberation and faster tempo delay the perceived attack of a tone due to the smoothing effects of reverberation on envelopes and increased overlapping of successive tones (Naylor, 1992). In order to maintain the tempo and to achieve perceived synchrony, musicians should therefore play a small amount ahead of the beat they hear. With sharp attacks the delay is less, and instruments with sharp attacks may therefore serve as "beat-definers" for the rest of an ensemble.

In studio recordings of popular music as well as in live performance the auditory feedback is usually obtained in headphones. So-called click tracks may be used for (supposedly) better control of timing and "tightness" (Madison, 1991).

Examples of biofeedback to reduce muscle tension in performance are given in Section IX,A.

VI. MOTOR PROCESSES IN PERFORMANCE

A. SOME GENERAL QUESTIONS

Although motor processes are central to music performance, they are still little understood. Sidnell (1981) asked a number of critical questions concerning efficient motor practice, motor memory, the role of proprioception, transferability of motor skills, and application of current motor models. Hedden (1987) reviewed recent reports and found only tentative answers to some of these questions. F. R. Wilson (1992) and F. R. Wilson and Roehmann (1992) pointed out the psychomotor complexity of human music behavior. "From the perspective of the movement scientist, the questions of greatest importance to music educators must be regarded as being entirely out of reach for the foreseeable future" (F. R. Wilson, 1992, p. 93).

The common advice that practicing should start in a slow tempo and then successively be accelerated was questioned by Handel (1986). He referred to experiments in which the perceived grouping of polyrhythmic patterns changes with tempo and suggested that there may be similar motor reorganizations. Practicing at a slow rate may involve another motor pattern than at faster rates and therefore be relatively ineffective. Taubmann (1988) cited evidence from Ortmann's (1929) classic investigations showing that movements in fast piano playing are different from the movements in slow playing. She concluded that the correct shape of the movements in fast playing "must be analyzed and brought into slow playing. In this way, when practicing slowly ... you are playing fast, slowly" (p. 150). Ortmann's photographs and other records are still invaluable assets. He concluded that the movements of two pianists are never exactly alike. Any key on the piano can be reached effectively in a number of ways, and the playing of a key is affected by the playing of preceding and succeeding keys (McArthur, 1989; F. R. Wilson & Roehmann, 1992).

B. MOTOR EXERCISES

There is evidence that note timing changes with different tempi in motor exercises such as performance of scales. C. Wagner (1971) found smallest variability of internote intervals at an intermediate tempo (about 6–9 notes/sec) and increasing variability at slower and faster tempi. Mackenzie and Van Eerd (1990), using a grand piano equipped with infrared key movement detectors (B. L. Wills, MacKenzie, Harrison, Topper, & Walker, 1985), found that variability of internote intervals and velocity of keypress increased with increased tempo in scale playing. The left and right hands differed in keypress velocities, note durations, and overlap between consecutive notes.

Peters (1985) found interference between hands in a rubato-like tapping task, accelerating in one hand while keeping a regular tempo in the other. Performance was better when the acceleration was made by the preferred right hand. Deecke (1995) studied brain potentials in musicians tapping a 2 x 3 polyrhythm (two in one hand, three in the other) and indicated that the supplementary motor area is highly important for controlling bimanual skills like this. Lee (1989) investigated a pianist's performance of left-hand leap patterns. Moore (1992) demonstrated the remarkable speed and precision in skilled pianists' performance of trills (see also F. R. Wilson, 1992). Askenfelt (1986) measured bow motion and bow force in different bowing styles on the violin; Moore (1988) studied bowing techniques and vibrato in cello playing; and Moore, Hary, and Naill (1988) studied trills in cello playing. Davies, Kenny, and Barbenel (1989) found, contrary to common belief, that professional trumpet players do not generally use lower levels of mouthpiece force than less-skilled players. One may be misled by the player's appearance; some professionals "could use massive amounts of force whilst maintaining a madonna-like appearance" (p. 61).

C. THEORIES OF MOTOR SKILL

Four theories of motor skill may be discerned: closed-loop theory, open-loop or motor program theory, schema theory, and the Bernstein approach (P. Johnson, 1984; Kelso, 1982; LaBerge 1981a; Rosenbaum, 1991; Schmidt, 1988; Sheridan, 1984; Wade, 1990). According to the *closed-loop theory*, sensory information produced from the movement is fed back to the central nervous system and compared with an internal referent to check for discrepancies between the intended and the actually produced movement. The system is thus self-regulating by means of proprioceptive feedback. It has been argued that such feedback is too slow to account for rapid movement sequences in music (for example, a trill), but this is a matter of some debate (LaBerge, 1981a; MacKenzie, 1986; Moore, 1992; Schmidt, 1982, 1988). MacKenzie and Van Eerd (1990) suggested that sensory information is used on a note-to-note basis at slow tempi, but it may also be used at faster speeds to modify the performance with regard to larger groups.

Open-loop or *motor program theory* postulates a central or executive control of all movements in a sequence, thus not relying on sensory feedback in the real-time control of movement. All movement parameters are specified in a motor command, and the movement runs to its completion without alteration, an alternative that seems adequate for fast movements. The theory usually assumes a hierarchical structure with higher levels containing abstract representations of movement sequences to which more and more specificity is added at successively lower levels. Sensory feedback may have a role in constructing and maintaining procedures for translating motor commands into muscle actions (Shaffer, 1980) and for modifying the response after the movement has been completed (Sheridan, 1984, p 60); further possibilities were suggested by Schmidt (1988, chapter 8).

Schema theory assumes that there exist abstract representations of classes of motor actions, generalized motor programs, out of which can be generated a wide variety of movements in novel situations. One must not learn and store every single movement, it can be generated from the stored schema (abstracted rules) by applying appropriate parameters in interaction with the demands in a given situation. A recall schema is concerned with the execution of the movement and a recognition schema with the evaluation of the response. Variability of practice and feedback (knowledge of result) strengthen the schema rules.

The *Bernstein approach* is named after the Russian physiologist Nicolai Bernstein. Arguing that the number of combinations of muscle settings for different movements is too large to be managed by a controlling executive ("the degrees-of-freedom problem"), it is emphasized that muscles are not individually controlled but function in muscle linkages or *coordinative structures*. Groups of muscles are constrained to act as functional units, thus reducing the degrees of freedom and thereby also the need for hierarchical organization or higher-level control. Whereas the motor program theories mainly deal with central representations and say little about the construction and work of the effectors, this approach is concerned with the anatomy and function of the muscles and the whole body to see how the motor actions may arise as necessary consequences of the way the system is designed to function. However, the Bernstein approach is still little discussed in relation to music. Wade (1990) suggested some examples and also discussed the role that cognition may have in relation to this approach.

LaBerge (1981a) proposed a combination of schema theory and the concept of coordinative structures. Voluntary motor conceptualizations are organized as motor schemas, but the motor schemas do not communicate directly to individual muscles but via coordinative structures. The commands sent to the coordinative structures are interpreted as "pieces of advice." The coordinative structures communicate with individual muscles in terms of involuntary reflex-like commands, balancing the pieces of advice with available information about environmental resistances (e.g., the mechanics of the instrument), inertia of the moving limbs, and momentary state of muscle tension. Thus the "top-down" control is replaced by a type of shared control. This framework is used for an interesting hypothetical description of learning musical performance skills in a series of stages encompassing successively larger musical units as the performance of smaller units become more or less automatic (see also LaBerge, 1981b).

D. EMPIRICAL INVESTIGATIONS

Referring to schema theory, Welch (1985a, 1985b) predicted and also found that children with poor pitch singing would perform better in matching a target pitch if they received adequate knowledge of their results (oscilloscope representations of their singing in relation to the target) than children not given knowledge of results. The concept of generalized motor programs (Schmidt, 1982, 1988) was supported by Repp (1994c), who found relational invariance of expressive microstructure across moderately different tempi in performance of a piano piece. However, Desain and Honing (1994) reported evidence against relational invariance in other piano performance (see Section VII,C,3). The increased variability in timing and keypress velocities at faster speeds and the differences between hands found by MacKenzie and Van Eerd (1990) did not support the phonograph record analogy of generalized motor programs (Schmidt, 1988, p. 246). Handel (1986) raised the question of whether motor programs and procedures may be restricted to a relatively narrow range of performance rates and suggested that therefore performance in other tempi would require the construction of new programs.

The most thorough investigations of music performance in relation to motor skill theories have been conducted by Shaffer and his coworkers. The background is a theory of motor programming (Shaffer, 1980, 1981, 1982, 1984b), meaning that a sequence of movements can be coordinated before their execution in a way that ensures fluency, expressiveness, and generative flexibility of the performance. The program is used for realizing a performance plan and in doing this may construct a hierarchy of intermediate representations leading to output via motor commands that provide target specifications for the movement (location in space, force and manner of movement). The commands are translated into muscle actions by a peripheral computer in the cerebellar-spinal system.

Timing is handled by the motor system and an internal clock. The internal clock acts as a reference and is used for timing of the beat or another appropriate unit. Its rate can be changed to achieve expressive variation in timing (rubato). The motor system itself acts as a timekeeper by translating a given time interval into a (compound) movement trajectory with the corresponding duration. This is used for timing of the subdivisions of the clock interval (beat). The clock is assumed to generate time intervals with lower variance than the motor system can. Time intervals may be generated in concatenation or in hierarchical manner (for example, for the bar, half-bar, quarter-bar). To distinguish between these alternatives one can study variance and covariance properties of the intervals as proposed by Vorberg and Hambuch (1978, 1984). However, both alternatives assume a constant tempo, which may necessitate modifications to fit much music performance. Shaffer also used hierarchic analysis of variance including an unconventional use of F values less than 1.00 to indicate less variation in the timing of a certain unit (for example, bar, half-bar, or beat).

To test the theory, several piano performances were recorded using a Bechstein grand piano equipped with photocells to permit accurate measures of timing and dynamics (Shaffer, 1980, 1981). Thorough analysis of timing in a concert pianist's performance of a Bach fugue indicated that half-beat intervals (quarter notes) were generated by a clock according to a concatenation principle, whereas the timing of short notes within the half-beat interval, assumed to be achieved by learned motor procedures, favored a hierarchic structure. At the same time, however, the pianist varied the tempo, indicating that the clock rate was modulated according to expressive information given in the motor program. Thus the clock provides temporal markers in an "elastic" way serving expressive purposes. A performance of a Chopin étude—playing three in the right hand against four in the left—demonstrated independence of the two hands in dynamics and timing. With regard to timing, considerable rubato was made common to both hands, as well as different between the hands, in an asynchrony letting the melody in the right hand lead or lag in relation to the left-hand accompaniment. Again this indicated a flexible clock for timing of the beats and separate timekeepers for each hand to construct the subdivision of the beat and to allow one hand to temporarily move off the beat. A performance of one of Bartók's *Six Dances in Bulgarian Rhythm* (with a 3 + 3 + 2 division) also showed similar principles for hand independence in timing. The Chopin étude was performed by the same pianist 1 year later with very similar results (Shaffer, 1984a).

These results were taken to indicate a flexible clock for beat timing and separate timekeepers for each hand responsible for beat subdivisions and off-beat playing. Furthermore, the high degree of reproducibility in repeated performances suggests that the musician's interpretation of the score, in combination with his general knowledge of music theory and musical style, is able to generate appropriate expressive structures in the motor program on different occasions. In a duet performance of a Beethoven piece (Shaffer, 1984a), the rubato pattern over the piece was similar for the two pianists, as well as in a repeated performance, indicating that it was generated from an agreed interpretation rather than being memorized (one pianist had not played the piece before). Precision was highest at the bar level, and asynchronies between voices and between pianists showed a systematic pattern. It was assumed that differences in note timing between the voices and the pianists, creating a kind of rhythmic interplay, could be made since the bar served as a common meter for both of them.

In a study (Clarke, 1985a; Shaffer, Clarke, & Todd, 1985) of one pianist's three performances of Satie's *Gnossienne No. 5*, that has a regular left hand accompaniment in eighths but a variety of rhythmic subdivisions in the right hand, the analysis indicated beat timing at the eighth note level. The subdivisions within the beat were performed either to fit the beat timing—regarding subdivisions with unequal note values or many equal note values—or temporarily overrode beat timing in order to favor evenness among a small number of equal note values in the subdivision.

Clarke (1985a; 1985b, p. 229) concluded that expressive rhythmic performance from a score involves an underlying structural representation. This consists of rhythmic figures organized around a framework of beats and an expressive system which transforms the structural representation by altering the clock rate, thus affecting the beat rate or tempo, and by modifying the way in which motor procedures subdivide the beat intervals. Of course, the expressive system may operate with other parameters as well, such as dynamics, articulation, intonation, and timbre, depending on the instruments used and the musical context.

Rather than being memorized, the expressive aspects of a performance—that is, the deviations in timing, articulation, dynamics, and so on—are generated from the performer's structural representation of the piece at the time of the performance. This may explain the high reproducibility in repeated performances as well as the ability to change the performance according to an alternative structural representation. Later Clarke modified this view on the basis of experiments (Clarke, 1991; Clarke 1993a, 1993b; Clarke & Baker-Short, 1987) which showed that listeners were able reasonably well to imitate phrases in which structure and expression were put in some kind of conflict ("unnatural" timing). In Clarke (1993a), the timing profile in four short melodies performed by a pianist on a Yamaha MIDI (Musical Instrument Digital Interface) grand piano were transformed, using the POCO environment (Honing, 1992), by inverting the timing profile or by translating it one beat or a measure plus one beat. Ten pianists were asked to listen to these performances and to imitate them as accurately as possible. The imitations were most accurate and stable for the original performance, least accurate and stable for the inverted version, with the two translated versions in between. Moreover, in a separate listening test the original version was judged as the best and the inverted version as worst. The fact that the subjects were able to reproduce some aspects of even the most disrupted versions could be due to pure auditory storage of them in short-term memory (however, this would work only for very short melodies), or use of a verbal representation (description) of the version to support the auditory image in short-term memory, or some kind of bodily representation of the version. The latter was suggested by the different body movements that could be observed in the imitating subjects' performance of the different versions.

It should be noted that terms such as *expressive deviations* or simply *expression* in the aforementioned studies refer to physical phenomena, that is, deviations in timing, articulation, intonation, and so on in relation to a literal interpretation of the score. This use should be distinguished from a more general meaning of expression in music (Clarke, 1989a; 1991). I prefer to discuss the deviations as (possible) physical *correlates* of expression, since "expression's domain is the mind of the listener" (Kendall & Carterette, 1990, p. 131). Of course, the structure of the piece is in itself a basic correlate of experienced expression.

Shaffer (1989), discussing the possibility of constructing a robot to play a Chopin waltz, concluded that cognitive planning and motor programming may not be enough. Emotional factors must be considered as well. The robot has to be given feelings about himself as performer, about the social context, the musical tradition, and the sensuousness in the physical movements of playing music. Music has inescapable connotations of mood and a player has to be sensitive to these. "The structural interpretation of the piece remains the same but only sometimes the players' own mood allows them to fully catch the mood of the music, and this is felt by both the players and the listeners" (p. 389).

Palmer (1989a, 1989b), in discussing motor programming, asked whether the procedures that govern the translation from intention to performance differ from one performance to another, or if there is a limited set of procedures whose parameters can change. The latter alternative is the more economical, because a larger set of behaviors may be accounted for by a smaller set of procedures. This hypothesis was investigated in several experiments on the use of three timing procedures: chord asynchronies (melody lead or lag), rubato (especially at phrase boundaries), and articulation (legato vs. staccato). The performances were done on an electronic keyboard (1989a) or a computer-monitored Bösenforfer concert grand piano with optical sensors that detect and code movements of each key and foot pedal (1989b). Expert pianists and students were asked to perform pieces by Mozart, Beethoven, Chopin, and Brahms in a musical, a mechanical, and an exaggerated way. The mechanical performances were characterized by less, and the exaggerated performances by more, asynchronization, rubato, and legato performance, in comparison with the musical performance. In successive performances of an unfamiliar work, these timing procedures were usually applied in an increasing way, and the experts used them to a higher degree than the students. When two pianists were asked to perform a piece in two different interpretations, related to the melodic line and to the phrasing, the timing procedures were adapted accordingly. For example, the voice intended as melody tended to precede the other voices, and ritards were made at the phrase endings of the respective interpretation. Listeners, especially pianists, were able to correctly identify the intended interpretations from these differences in timing procedures, even when intensity variations in the performances were removed by computer editing. All together, the results were considered to support the idea that the same procedures were used with varying parameters in the different situations. This conclusion was supported by Behne and Wetekam (1993), who investigated rhythmically exact versus expressive performance of the theme in Mozart's Piano Sonata in A major (K. 331).

Halsband, Binkofski, and Camp (1994) instructed pianists to perform some pieces according to different rhythmic groupings and recorded their performance on a Yamaha Disklavier. Halsband et al. also recorded the pianists' hand movements by use of light-emitting diodes attached to the wrists and fingers. Both recordings showed that the formation of motor patterns was affected by the prescribed rhythmic grouping and that this process was mainly under left (dominant) hemisphere control.

E. EXPRESSIVE MOVEMENTS

Playing an instrument requires skilled movements. However, performers also move in many other ways not directly related to the generation of sound but rather to the character of the music. Such expressive movements are an important part of the performer-listener communication and were studied in pioneering work by Davidson (1993, 1994, 1995). She used *point-light technique,* that is, illuminated reflective tapes were attached around the performer's head, elbows, wrists, knees, and ankles and on each hip and shoulder. Violinists and pianists then performed music in three different manners: deadpan, projected (as in a public performance), and exaggerated. Video recordings of the performances were presented to observers in three different modes: vision-only (the point-light patterns resulting from the musician's movements), sound-only (the performed music), or both together. Music students were able to distinguish between the three performance manners in the vision-only mode, even better than when listening to the performances or both listening and watching them. Nonmusicians could make reliable discriminations solely in the vision-only mode. Head movements in pianists were essential for distinguishing among the different performance manners. These studies highlight the need for investigating the role that visual information may play in music perception.

VII. MEASUREMENTS OF PERFORMANCE

A. MEASUREMENT PROCEDURES AND DATA ANALYSIS

Measurements of music performance as a rule require advanced technical equipment. One common way is to study the action of the instrument, for instance, to record key depressions and releases on keyboard instruments. In early research, this was done by electromechanical devices or by moving film, nowadays usually by electronic and computer facilities. A related way, common during the early decades of this century, was to make measurements of "player rolls" generated from performances on special pianos. A different principle is to analyze the sounds that are emitted from the instruments, in direct recordings or stored on phonograph records or tapes. This alternative is applicable to any instrument, including singing, but puts great demands on the analysis equipment, especially in music with many voices overlapping or masking each other (for examples, see Gabrielsson, 1987, or Repp, 1992a).

The variables measured are various aspects of timing, dynamics, and intonation. With regard to timing, measurements may refer to tempo, durations of sound events and groups of sound events, and of nonsound events (rests, other silent intervals), and further the asynchrony between different instruments supposed to perform at the same time. Concerning durations, a distinction must be made between the duration from the beginning of a tone to the beginning of the next tone (internote interval, interonset interval, or d_{ii} = duration in-in) and the duration from the beginning of a tone to its end (d_{io} = duration in-out). The latter measure is useful for describing articulations, such as legato and staccato. In legato, the tone sounds until the beginning of the next tone or almost so ($d_{io} \approx d_{ii}$). In legatissimo, successive tones even overlap, that is, the tone is sustained until some time after the beginning of the next tone ($d_{io} > d_{ii}$), which is common in keyboard performance. In staccato, the tone ends pretty soon ($d_{io} << d_{ii}$), and there is a "silence" until the beginning of the next tone (see further in Bengtsson & Gabrielsson, 1983). Most duration measurements refer to the first alternative. When the term duration is used in the following, it will therefore refer to this alternative (d_{ii}). Articulation refers to the other alternative (d_{io}).

A special problem is how to define the beginning of a tone. It can be defined as the point in time when a key is depressed (or at a certain moment of the key depression), or when a change in amplitude or waveform can be seen, or when the amplitude of the tone has reached a certain level. The last alternative is often assumed to reflect better the perceptual onset (Rasch, 1979, 1988; Rose, 1989). Models for predicting perceived onset were discussed in Naylor (1992). Similar problems, although less discussed, pertain to the determination of the end of a tone (Edlund, 1985, p. 92). Differences in measurement techniques and definitions sometimes make it difficult to compare results from different investigations.

A general problem is the wealth of data. There are so many events, and relations between events, to study, that papers on music performance sometimes provide hard reading. C. E. Seashore (1936, p. 30; 1938, p. 240) remarked that description and interpretation of performance data for a single piece would require a volume. (This gives an interesting perspective to the present author's task.) A common way to present data is to use the musical score (if there is one) as a reference and provide values (for instance, durations) for each note, beat, bar, phrase, or other units. The values may be original raw data, as in Figure 5, or be expressed in relation to a norm, for instance, as deviations from a strictly regular, "mechanical" performance as in Figure 4. A discussion about some alternatives was given by Repp (1994b). Data treatment has been much facilitated by computers, but knowledge about what data are relevant, and what may be discarded, is still far from complete. Nor is there any comprehensive theory to guide us in this search. The statistical treatment therefore often aims at an appropriate reduction of data and may include analysis by means of correlation, covariance, autocorrelation (Desain & de Vos, 1992), analysis of variance, factor analysis, and regression analysis.

A related question concerns how to represent the results of the measurements to give an impression of how the performance sounded. One way is to provide original or modified visual recordings of the sound, which may give a feeling for the variations in pitch, loudness, and timing (Gabrielsson, 1986b, 1987, 1994, 1995; Gabrielsson & Johnson, 1985; C. E. Seashore, 1938). However, they take up much space and require some training to be meaningfully interpreted. Gjerdingen (1988) proposed a representation in which changes in pitch and intensity combine to suggestive motion shapes, which is in good agreement with the view of music as motion (see Section II,A). He further stressed and illustrated the importance of analyzing not only change, but change in the rate of change in pitch and intensity together, which is certainly perceptually relevant.

The following account of performance measurements takes a historical approach. This history has two distinct periods, one beginning in the early music psychology and running up to about 1940, and the other a restart beginning in the 1960s.

B. EARLY INVESTIGATIONS

1. Mostly in Europe

Binet and Courtier (1895) used a small rubber tube below the keys in a grand piano to record the key depressions. When a key was depressed, the tube was compressed generating an air puff that affected a stylus writing on moving paper. They studied the performance of trills, scales, accents, and crescendo-decrescendo and observed clear differences between amateurs and professional pianists. To achieve an accent on a certain tone, a pianist played the preceding tone *detaché*, whereas the tone to be accented was played with more force as well as lengthened and closely tied (legato) to the following tone. Lengthening of accented tones was also observed by Ebhardt (1898), who attached an electromechanical device to a grand piano to record key depressions on a kymograph. Furthermore, when pianists were asked to play a previously performed piece on a dumb piano (without auditory feedback), the tempo became much slower. Ebhardt assumed that this was due to the increased psychic activity required for imagining the piece. Much later Clynes and Walker (1982) reported that seven out of eight musicians performed pieces of music significantly slower when thinking through them than when actually playing them.

Sears (1902) had four organists play five hymns on a small reed organ. The keyboard action was recorded on a kymograph drum via electromechanical principles. There was often overlap between consecutive tones (legatissimo). The durations of tones with the same note value differed within each piece, and the relations between tones of different note values—such as half note and quarter note—differed from their nominal relations. The duration of measures varied. There was a ritard toward the end of the hymn, accented tones were usually lengthened, triplets were performed with the last tone lengthened, and there was asynchronization between the tones in chords. The inter-individual variation in performance data was considerable. These results recur in many later studies.

It may be a surprise to learn that perhaps most performance studies until today were made in the 1920s and 1930s. Morton (1920) noted difficulties in playing a 3 x 2 polyrhythm and trills. Heinitz (1926) used a stopwatch to analyze seven singers' performance on phonograph records of a *Meistersingerlied* by Wagner. Heinlein (1929, 1930) made a unique study of pedaling in piano performance by analyzing famous pianists' pedal action on a Duo-Art reproducing piano and conducting experiments with four pianists performing Schumann's *Träumerei*. The pedaling differed markedly between the pianists as well as under the different conditions, and no pianist was able to reproduce his pedal action from an earlier performance. The conditions included performing from the score, by heart, pedaling while imagining playing the piece, pedaling while singing the melody, and others. Heinlein concluded that pedaling was dependent on finger pattern, phrasing, speed of rendition, variation in intensity and timbre, extent of tonal anticipation, and type of imagery in recall. It is so highly integrated with the other phases of piano performance that alteration of any single factor may affect the pianist's customary pedaling. Recently Repp (1994c) provided some data on pedaling in *Träumerei*. Taguti, Ohgushi, and Sueoka (1994) found differences in pedaling among pianists and among different expressive intentions. Multidimensional scaling indicated that the deeper the damper pedal was pressed, the more reverberant and warm was the perceived piano sound.

Guttmann (1932) studied conductors' choice of tempo in numerous concerts over a couple of decades. There were obvious variations between conductors (among them R. Strauss, Nikisch, Furtwängler) as well as for the same conductor at different performances of the same work. R. Strauss himself commented on this variability (cited in C. Wagner, 1974, p. 593).

Hartmann (1932) made a long, careful, and instructive analysis of two pianists' performance of the first movement of Beethoven's *Moonlight Sonata*. The measurements were made directly on paper roll recordings for player pianos. Despite the homogeneous rhythmic structure of the movement, the tempo varied considerably. One of the pianists made a ritard at the end, the other did not. The durations of tones with different note values overlapped much; the shortest half note was shorter than the longest quarter note. Both pianists played legatissimo and with asynchrony within chords. One pianist had a fairly consistent asynchronization pattern, playing the bass tone first, then the higher bass tone (the octave above), and then either the melody part or the first tone of the triplet accompaniment.

Truslit (1938; see also Repp, 1993) presented an interesting mixture of intelligent speculation and empirical study. He emphasized the connection between music and motion (cf. Section II,A). The dynamics and agogics of music must be shaped in accordance with the general laws of motion, which he tried to demonstrate by means of performance measurements. He also claimed that the function of the vestibular organ is the biological basis for experience of musical motion.

2. Research at Iowa University

Around 1930, a large group of researchers headed by C. E. Seashore studied music performance at the University of Iowa. Most of their reports appeared in two volumes edited by C. E. Seashore (1932, 1937), both classics in the music performance literature. Another volume (C. E. Seashore, 1936) was devoted to the vibrato, and examples from many studies appear in his textbook (C. E. Seashore, 1938). However, C. E. Seashore himself rarely appeared among the authors of the research reports. His function seems to have been that of supervisor and coordinator. The studies comprise performance on the piano, the violin, and singing. The data was presented in so-called "performance scores" and because of the amount of data readers are sometimes asked to analyze such scores themselves according to his own interests (Skinner & Seashore, 1937).

a. Piano

Piano performance was investigated by filming the movements of the hammers (Henderson, Tiffin, & Seashore, 1937; C. E. Seashore, 1938, p. 233). Henderson (1937) analyzed two pianists' performance of the chorale section, in $\frac{3}{4}$ time, in Chopin's *Nocturne*, Op. 15, No. 3. In measures containing three quarter notes, the second was relatively shortened. In measures consisting of a half note plus a quarter note, the latter was relatively lengthened. This lengthening was in some cases related to a ritard. In other cases, it was a way of delaying the entrance of the first beat in the following measure, thereby contributing to achieve an accent on this beat. It was further hypothesized that the lengthening was made "in order to achieve more melodic equality between the written long and short notes" (p. 291).

Phrasing was made by temporal as well as dynamic means. Within a phrase, there was first an acceleration followed by a ritard toward the end together with decrescendo, but the pianists did this in varying ways. They also differed considerably with regard to the tempo chosen for the performance. Pedaling was used to facilitate legato playing. All chords were played asynchronously. However, whereas one pianist played the melody before all other notes, the other pianist deliberately played the bass note first, maybe to emphasize its countermelodic character. The spread among the notes in a chord varied from 20 to 200 msec, with relatively more spread on accented chords than on unaccented. Accents were not related to higher intensity, and Henderson discussed several ways of achieving accents, including factors already inherent in the score.

Skinner (cited in C. E. Seashore, 1938, pp. 246–248) found high within-individual consistency in timing in two pianists' repeated performances of the same pieces by Beethoven and Chopin. When one of them was asked to perform the Chopin piece in uniform metronomic time, the variations in durations became much less, but they did not quite disappear.

Vernon (1937) focused on chord asynchronization in performance of works by Beethoven and Chopin by four famous pianists (Bauer, Backhaus, Hofmann, Paderewski), recorded on paper rolls. All used asynchronization, particularly Bauer, who played almost half of all chords with temporal spread; Backhaus did it rarely. The spread was mostly within 30 msec, but Bauer and Paderewski sometimes had spreads up to 200 msec or more. For these pianists, the melody part came after the rest of the chord more frequently than before. Asynchrony was more common in melody chords than in nonmelody chords, indicating that asynchrony was used to mark off melody notes from the accompaniment. It was also used to give emphasis to a certain point in a phrase.

b. Violin

Violin performance was analyzed by means of phonophotograph apparatus (Tiffin, 1932a) using stroboscope technique for recording of frequency (pitch) and a vacuum tube voltmeter connected to an oscillograph for recording the intensity. All was photographed on the same film. Small (1937) analyzed phonograph recordings of performances by Busch, Elman, Kreisler, Menuhin, Seidl, and Szigeti and made direct recordings of other violinists. Pitch vibrato, approximating a sine curve, was present in practically all tones. The typical rate was 6–7 Hz and the range approximately a quarter tone; rate and range were independent of each other. Intensity vibrato was not as frequent and continuous as the frequency vibrato. It had about the same rate as the frequency vibrato, and the phase relations between them varied. There were frequent deviations from the frequency (pitch) indicated in the score. Leading tones were played high, augmented intervals were expanded, diminished intervals contracted. Portamento was often used when going to another pitch to keep the legato of the melody. There were generally considerable deviations from the time values indicated in the score, for measures as well as for individual notes.

c. Singing

The analysis equipment for singing was essentially the same as for violin performance. Schoen (1922) used the Seashore tonoscope to study pitch intonation in phonograph records of five sopranos' performance of the Bach-Gonoud *Ave Maria*, a favorite piece in many Iowa studies. A tone was usually attacked below the intended pitch when it was preceded by a lower tone but on correct pitch when preceded by a higher tone. All singers tended to sing sharp in respect to both pure and equally tempered intonation, and the movement from tone to tone was mostly in the form of glides. R. S. Miller (1937) studied the pitch of the attack in tones that were preceded by a short pause, for artists (such as Alma Gluck and Enrico Caruso) as well as amateurs. A rising glide was the most common type of attack, and the extent of the glide was larger when the preceding tone was of lower pitch.

H. G. Seashore (1937) analyzed nine singers' performance of arias from Handel's *Messiah*, the Bach-Gonoud *Ave Maria*, and other songs, either directly recorded in a studio or taken from phonograph records. This is one of the most penetrating studies of music performance ever made. The amount of detail is almost overwhelming, and yet much is left to the reader's own analysis. Pitch vibrato was always present. Its rate varied from 5.9 to 6.7 Hz and the extent from 0.44 to 0.61 whole tones, that is, roughly a semitone. Practically no correlation was found between rate and extent. Short tones usually had faster vibrato rates than long tones. Intensity vibrato was present about half the time with about the same rate as pitch vibrato. There were frequent deviations from nominally correct pitch, and the pitch varied in different ways (beside the vibrato) during the tone, often in a rising direction. Such deviations were usually not perceived. The transitions between tones were made with gliding attacks (rising in pitch) and releases, level attacks and releases, and portamento glides, all of them further classified into different types. A rising melodic line was usually accompanied by higher intensity and vice versa. Within phrases, there was mostly a crescendo followed by a decrescendo in a rather symmetric way. In other cases, there was primarily a decrescendo with no or only slight crescendo at the beginning. Ritards were made at the end of each song, and minor ritards occurred before interludes. Pauses between phrases were considerably longer than pauses within phrases. The duration of measures varied much, and there were many subpatterns of temporal deviations within phrases. Short notes tended to be overheld in comparison with long notes. This tendency toward an equalization of tone durations probably reflected a striving for proper legato performance. The performance of each individual singer was described in detail and illustrated both in performance scores and in graphs displaying the results (Figure 1).

d. Vibrato

Vibrato was the phenomenon studied most of all in the Iowa research. Early studies by Schoen (1922) were followed by more detailed analyses by Metfessel (1932) and Tiffin (1932b) of together about 25 professional singers (among them Caruso, Chaliapin, and Gigli) recorded on phonograph records. Their data were similar. Metfessel reported that the pitch vibrato varied in rate from 5.5 to 8.5 Hz with an average of about 7 Hz, and its extent from a tenth to over a whole-tone step, averaging a half step. According to Tiffin, the average rate was 6.5 Hz and the average extent 0.6 of a whole-tone step. There was throughout a certain variation in both rate and extent that was considered to be critical for the artistic quality of the vibrato. In Tiffin's study, the average difference in extent of adjacent vibrato cycles within the same tone was about 0.1 whole-tone step, in rate about 0.45 Hz. Intensity vibrato was present but of less importance. Easley (1932) found that opera singers used broader and faster vibrato when performing opera songs than when performing concert songs.

Using a special apparatus for synthesizing vibrato, Tiffin (1931) found that the perceived pitch of a frequency vibrato was slightly below the pitch of its mean frequency; however, the investigation was limited to only one frequency, 420 Hz. Recently Brown (1991) found that musicians located the pitch of a vibrato higher than nonmusicians, and neither group located the pitch at the mean of the modula-

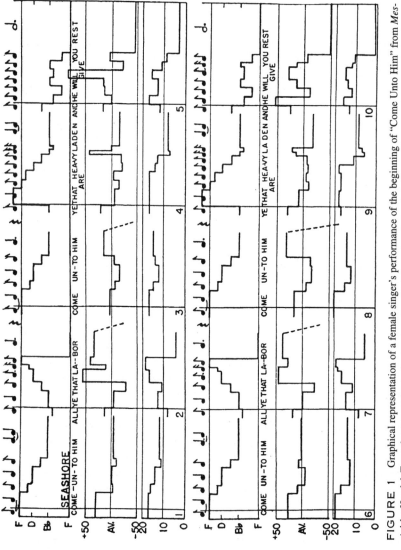

FIGURE 1 Graphical representation of a female singer's performance of the beginning of "Come Unto Him" from *Messiah* by Handel. Top to bottom: pattern of note—length, melody, words, relative duration, tonal power, phrase numbers. (Reproduced from H. G. Seashore, 1937.)

tion. H. G. Seashore (1932) showed that listeners underestimated the extent of both pitch and intensity vibrato.

Metfessel (1932) also analyzed the performance of trills. The average rate of the trill was about the same as for pitch vibrato, but its extent was wider, on average about 1.25 whole-tone step, sometimes up to almost 2 steps. Perceptually, as a vibrato becomes wider and wider, there is a sudden jump from vibrato to trill. Later studies indicated a trill threshold of about 3 semitones (G. A. Miller & Heise, 1950), or that a frequency modulation extending between 2 and 3 semitones may be heard either as a vibrato or as a trill depending on the context (Castellengo, 1994). C. E. Seashore (cited in Lundin, 1985, p. 275) found that the extent of a trill was underestimated by listeners. The singer must thus overreach the size of the interval to make it sound as notated in the score.

Metfessel discussed the vibrato as expression of different emotions. On this point, C. E. Seashore (1936, p. 117) concluded that vibrato is a means for the expression of feeling, but it does not in itself differentiate among the feelings. The differentiation comes from the context.

A. H. Wagner (1932) discussed methods for training and refinement of vibrato. Students benefited much from comparing phonophotograms of famous artists' vibrato with their own. Hattwick (1932) analyzed recordings of wind instruments and found vibrato present only in a minority of cases. Reger (1932) studied the vibrato in five professional string players, recorded on phonograph records (among them Kreisler, Menuhin, Casals) and in teachers and students. The vibrato rate varied among performers from 5.6 to 7 Hz with Kreisler showing the fastest vibrato. The extent varied from 0.16 to 0.29 whole-tone step, increasing with increasing tonal intensity. The average difference in rate from cycle to cycle was about 0.5 Hz and in extent mostly 0.1–0.2 whole-tone step. Hollinshead (1932) confirmed that the extent of the violin vibrato (about a quarter tone) is smaller than for vibrato in singing, whereas the data on rate is similar for both. The just-mentioned studies on vibrato were summarized by Tiffin and H. G. Seashore (1932) and, in a more personal way, by C. E. Seashore (1936). For some later studies of vibrato, see Section VII,C,7.

e. "Deviation from the Exact"

In discussing the complexities in music performance, H. G. Seashore (1937, p. 118) stated an important principle for continued research: "The psychophysical relations between the performer and the listener must be worked out; the data presented will contribute to such studies and also will depend for their final interpretation upon such investigations." He further referred to C. E. Seashore and Metfessel who stated that "the unlimited resources for vocal and instrumental art lie in artistic deviation from the pure, the exact, the perfect, the rigid, the even, and the precise" (quoted from H. G. Seashore, 1937, p. 155). Similar statements were made by Kries (1926, p. 133) and Truslit (1938, pp. 28–31); see also Gabrielsson (1985). The "artistic deviations" recur in contemporary research in terms as "expressive deviations," "systematic variations," or others.

Unfortunately this early research on music performance ceased around 1940. World War II was probably one of the reasons for that; another was C. E. Seashore's retirement. Readers familiar with contemporary performance studies will realize that much of the data and results in today's investigations was in fact presented already in these early studies, which seem unknown to many.

C. Contemporary Investigations

1. Timing, Dynamics

Around 1960, Swedish musicologist Ingmar Bengtsson initiated a research project on musical rhythm and was soon joined by the present author. The central hypothesis was that live music performance is usually characterized by some kind of *systematic variations* of its parameters, primarily duration and intensity. Systematic variations are easiest to describe in terms of deviations from a norm. With regard to durations, such a norm can be provided by the (fictitious) chronometric correspondence to the simple integer relations in musical notation, such as those shown in Figure 2. There are three fundamental relations: equality (EQ), long-

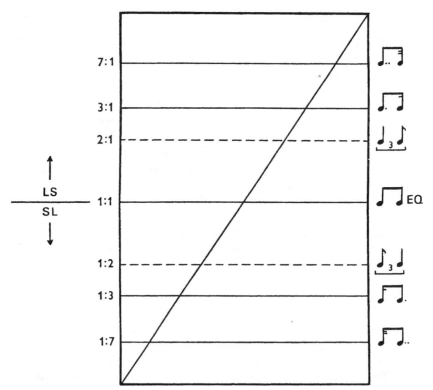

FIGURE 2   Duration relationships. EQ = equal, LS = long- short, SL = short- long. See text for further explanation. (Reproduced by permission from Bengtsson, Gabrielsson, & Thorsén, 1969.)

short (LS), and short-long (SL), with LS and SL in varying degrees. A performance in strict adherence to the common integer relations appears practically never, even if a performer tries to play in a "mechanical," "flat," or "dead-pan" manner (Behne & Wetekam, 1993; Bengtsson, 1987; Bengtsson & Gabrielsson, 1983; Palmer, 1989a; C. E. Seashore, 1938, p. 248; C. Wagner, 1974).

In pilot studies made by oscillogram filming, Bengtsson showed systematic variations typical for the accompaniment in Viennese waltzes (Bengtsson, 1974; Bengtsson, Gabrielsson, & Thorsén, 1969). The three beats in the bar had a "short-long-intermediate" (SLI) pattern. The second beat, that is, the first after-beat, comes "too early," a well-known characteristic of these waltzes (also measured by Askenfelt, 1986). There was further a superordinate pattern extending over pairs of bars, in agreement with the way of dancing these waltzes and with the harmonic structure. The amplitude (intensity) often showed a pattern with a maximum at the third beat of the first bar in the pair.

Further studies of Viennese waltzes (Bengtsson & Gabrielsson, 1977, 1983) demonstrated (a) pronounced variations of tempo in these waltzes; (b) slight asynchronizations between different parts, sometimes the melody part leading, sometimes the bass part; (c) varying microstructure of note durations depending on the context; and (d) interpolation of caesurae to distinguish and indicate the relative importance of phrases. This was all demonstrated on a phonograph record containing a synthesized version of the waltz in *Die Fledermaus* by Johann Strauss Jr., together with a "mechanical" version of the same waltz. Other synthesized examples demonstrated waltz accompaniment with varying degrees of SLI pattern and with different articulations, legato versus staccato, of the three beats (Bengtsson & Gabrielsson, 1983; see also Gabrielsson, 1985).

Systematic variations were also shown in many examples of Swedish folk music (Bengtsson, 1974; Bengtsson et al., 1969; Bengtsson & Gabrielsson, 1977), an example of which appears in Figure 3. A careful study of this figure reveals systematic variations at three different levels: (a) LS between the first and second half of the bar; (b) LS also within each half bar, the quarter note is longer than the following two eighth notes together; but (c) SL between the two eighth notes. If the recording of this example is played at half the speed, these inequalities are clearly heard. However, at the proper tempo, they are not noticed and obviously contribute to the steady and springy motion character of this piece. The same type of LS and SL relations were observed in ♫♫ patterns performed on a drum and in melodies played on the piano (Gabrielsson, 1973, 1974).

Bengtsson and Gabrielsson (1980) and Gabrielsson, Bengtsson, and Gabrielsson (1983) had five musicians play 15 melodies, most of them well-known tunes and some from the classical repertory, on the piano, the flute, and the clarinet, by heart and according to two or three different notations of each melody. The notations differed with regard to meter (for example, $\frac{3}{4}$ or $\frac{6}{8}$), and position of the bar lines; some of them were apparently "wrong." The performances were analyzed by using a special piece of equipment for recording of monophonic sound sequences (Tove, Norman, Isaksson, & Czekajewski, 1966). A mechanical performance never appeared. However, the "wrong" notations made some performers

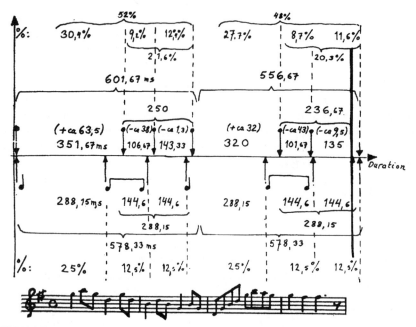

FIGURE 3   Systematic variations in a Swedish "Bride March" performed on the keyfiddle. The values in the upper parts are average durations, in percent and milliseconds, across the first two measures. The values in the lower parts represent mechanical performance. See further in text. (Reproduced by permission from Bengtsson, Gabrielsson, & Thorsén, 1969.)

adopt a relatively more mechanical performance. The performance by heart was usually the most free and varying, but generally all performances were characterized by different types of systematic variations, too numerous to be fully described here. Patterns ♩♩ as in ¾ time, or ♩♪ in ⁶⁄₈ time, were played with a ratio much below the nominal 2:1 ratio (cf. Henderson, 1937). Patterns including dottings such as ♫ were sometimes played "sharp" (with a ratio higher than 3:1), more often "soft" (sometimes even as low as 2:1), and the performance also varied depending on the position in the melody. In sequences such as ♫ ♫ or ♬, the last tone was usually lengthened at the expense of the others, especially the two middle ones (cf. Clarke, 1982, 1985a); in ♪♬, the eighth note was lengthened and the sixteenth notes performed SL in pairs. There were many deviations at the beat level, for example, lengthening of the third beat in "Oh my darling Clementine," but lengthening of the first beat in a theme from an organ concerto by Handel. Ritards at phrase endings were common, although not general, and the amount of ritard reflected different structural levels. The same notated pattern could be performed differently in different pieces, depending on the character of the piece.

Factor analysis was used to study different ways of performing the same piece. It resulted in two to four different performance types for each melody, which reflected different kinds of deviations, different ways of phrasing (e.g., ritards or not at phrase endings), and features specific for each performer (Gabrielsson et al., 1983). Examples also appeared in Gabrielsson (1982, 1985, 1986a, 1988). The perceptual effects of changing timing and articulation parameters were demonstrated by means of synthesized versions of a well-known tune (Bengtsson & Gabrielsson, 1983).

Large between-individual differences concurrent with high within-individual consistency appeared in an analysis, by digital sampling, of five renowned pianists' performance of a famous Mozart theme (Gabrielsson, 1987; see Figure 4). However, certain features were common for most of the pianists, such as "sharp" dotting (>3:1) within the ♩.♪♩ pattern, and "soft" LS (<2:1) between quarter note and eighth note in ♩♪ patterns. Within each phrase there was an acceleration followed by a ritard toward the end. With regard to dynamics, the pianists were more similar. The amplitude profile within each phrase showed an increase toward a maximum at, or close to, the transition from the next last to the last measure and then fell steeply.

Similar results concerning durations in the performance of this Mozart theme were obtained by Behne and Wetekam (1993) and by Palmer (1989a). Palmer also showed that the melody notes usually preceded the other voices by 15–30 msec. Half of her pianists performed the theme legato, the others staccato; the degree of overlap was dependent on the duration of the preceding note. Repeated performances showed high within-individual consistency. When the performers were asked to play the theme in an unmusical way, asynchrony and temporal deviations diminished (but did not disappear) and staccato articulation increased.

Repp (1990c) reported a comprehensive comparison of timing in 19 famous pianists' performance of a Beethoven minuet. The pianists showed high within-individual consistency across repetitions but marked between-individual variation with regard to tempo and to other aspects. Most measurements referred to the beat level (quarter notes). A factor analysis of beat durations showed three factors. The first factor mainly reflected phrase-final lengthenings, the second factor a "slow start" as well as faster tempo in the second half of the minuet, and the third factor reflected a V-shaped timing pattern within the bar—the first and third beats longer than the second—which was most explicit in a computerized performance according to Clynes' pattern for the "Beethoven pulse" (see Section VIII,B). Dotted patterns were performed with soft as well as sharp dottings, depending on performer and position in the piece.

In an even more comprehensive and detailed study, Repp (1992a) analyzed timing microstructure in 24 outstanding pianists' performance of Schumann's *Träumerei*. Factor analysis on performed durations in the first eight bars revealed a first factor in which half the pianists had their highest loading, and two other factors specific for the pianists Vladimir Horowitz and Alfred Cortot, respectively. The differences among the factors concerned the performance of up-beats and various modulations of tempo. The performance of each melodic gesture was further analyzed in detail, especially the "signature melodic gesture of the piece," that is, the ascending five-note pattern beginning in the first measure that recurs several

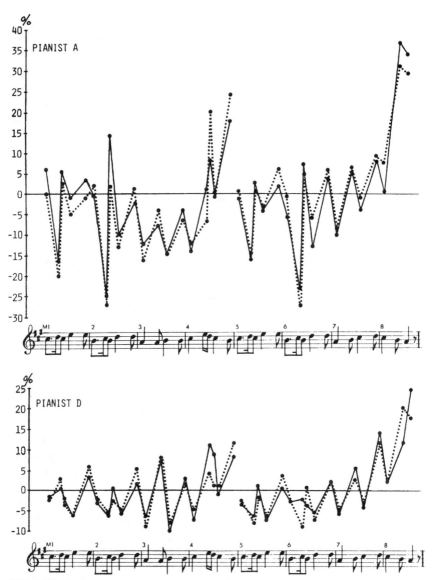

FIGURE 4   Percentage deviation from mechanical regularity (zero line) in two pianists' performances of the theme in Mozart's Piano Sonata in A Major, K.331. Solid line: first performance, dotted line: repetition. (Adapted by permission from Gabrielsson, 1987.)

times in varied form. In most performances, the timing profile of this gesture could be described by a quadratic function (a parabola) with the elevation and curvature of the function varying between performers. Likewise the ritards at phrase endings were largely parabolic in shape, with phrases belonging to higher structural levels showing more pronounced ritards than those at lower levels, most pronounced at the very end of the piece. Despite these commonalities, there were also marked differences among the performers in many aspects. Every performance was somehow unique, especially at lower structural levels. Repp (1992b) then generated, on a digital piano under MIDI control, the above-mentioned melodic gesture in different forms—original parabolic, shifted parabolic, nonparabolic—and asked listeners to indicate their preferences for these. Musically trained listeners preferred the original parabolic form, whereas musically untrained listeners were unable to give consistent judgments, indicating that experience of classical music is crucial for tasks such as this one.

Povel (1977) also found similarities as well as differences in three professional musicians' performance on harpsichord of the first prelude in C major in J. S. Bach's *Das wohltemperierte Clavier*, which has the same rhythmic surface structure in practically all measures. Cook (1987) analyzed performances of the same piece, by Walcha and Gould, looking at average data across all bars, as Povel, but also at the data within each structural segment of the prelude. Whatever analysis unit was applied, there were large differences between Walcha and Gould, and none of them seemed to perform in full accordance with what could be expected from various structural analyses of this piece. Still other performances of this piece were analyzed by Shaffer and Todd (1987) and in more detail by Shaffer (1995), the latter analysis including the performance by Gould in Cook (1987). There was relatively little variation of dynamics and timing in accordance with the uniform structure of this famous prelude, but still a difference between the performers regarding the general character of the piece.

Rose (1989) used a digital sampler to measure durations in rhythm section (piano, bass, and drums) performances of swing, jazz ballad, and Latin jazz. Durations at the beat (quarter note) level showed a SLSL pattern, that is, longer durations on the second and fourth beats, in the swing and ballad examples. Within beats there was a pronounced LS relation (on average 2.38:1) among eighth notes in the swing example, much higher than the nominal EQ relation and even higher than the 2:1 relation said to be typical for the performance of consecutive eighth notes in swing style. Eighth note triplets in the swing example were performed with the first triplet somewhat longer (1.13:1:1). In the ballad example, the eighth notes were performed as almost EQ. In the Latin jazz example, the ♩♪ pattern was performed with a 2.5:1 ratio instead of the nominal 3:1 ratio. Ellis (1991) used an electronic saxophone and MIDI technique to study three saxophonists' performances in swing style. Consecutive eighth notes were played LS, in most cases with a ratio about 1.75:1 but with somewhat lower ratio at the highest tempi used (MM. 180 and 210) for two of the players (see further in Section VII,C,5).

Namba, Nakamura, and Kuwano (1977) investigated the dynamics in five pianists' performances of two Chopin pieces. There were obvious differences between the pianists, but they were all consistent in their interpretation of repeated parts. Contrast effects appeared. A part notated piano (*p*) was played louder when followed by pianissimo (*pp*) notation than when preceded by forte (*f*) notation.

Ruggieri and Sebastiani (1987) compared dynamic variations in renowned flutists' and pianists' performances of short excerpts from works by Bach and Chopin and tried to relate the variations to listeners' judgments. Geringer (1992) found that changes from piano to forte were mostly performed with a larger dynamic range than changes from forte to piano in 60 recorded examples of choral, orchestral, and piano performances.

J. Ross (1989) measured note durations in an Estonian runic song, where the same melodic pattern was repeated 32 times in succession. The durations tended to form two categories, "short," centered on 350 msec, and "long," on 950 msec. In contrast to this, J. Ross and Lehiste (1994) found no evidence for such a distinction in three Estonian laments, nor any evidence for a systematic use of duration to indicate the three quantity degrees in Estonian disyllabic words; possible reasons for this were discussed. The melodic pattern in J. Ross (1989) was transcribed somewhat differently by a musicologist and a linguist, and generally the performance could not be quite adequately represented in conventional notation. Orally transmitted music usually does not fit into the pattern of discrete pitches and durations in common notation (Sloboda, 1985b, chapter 7). A further example of that can be seen in Gabrielsson and Johnson (1985), who compared performances of two concert singers and two folk singers. The former made rapid transitions between well-defined pitch levels and had clear metrical rhythm with moderate systematic variations. They used regular pitch and amplitude vibrato, and the amplitude envelope within phrases followed the melodic contour. The pitch (frequency) often tended to change during the course of a tone toward the pitch of the next tone (for instance, to gradually rise if the next tone was higher in pitch). In contrast, the folk singers used more gliding transitions between rather wide pitch levels and also made an ascending pitch slide up to the first tone in each phrase. Interval sizes varied considerably, the tempo was much slower and varying, and there was no controlled vibrato.

2. Structure and Performance

The performer should make the musical structure clear to the listener. Sloboda (1983, 1985a) studied this question by constructing short tone sequences, which could be notated in two musically reasonable ways by shifting the position of the barline (the first note was either a downbeat or an upbeat) or notating them in different meters ($\frac{4}{4}$ or $\frac{6}{8}$). Six performers played them on the grand piano used by Shaffer (1980). In order to convey the proper meter, the performers seemed to use certain principles in timing and dynamics. For instance, notes beginning full and half measures were played louder, or more legato, or with longer durations than their neighbors, whereas notes ending full and half measures were played less legato (more detached), or with longer durations than their predecessors. The more advanced the performers were, the more they used these means, and listeners identified the correct meter better in performances by advanced pianists than in performances by less advanced players. In a simulation experiment, a computer was used to generate the tone sequences with only one, or two, or all three factors varied. Generally the loudness factor seemed to be most important, whereas the effects of the durations were not significant; possible reasons for this were discussed (see also comments in Clarke & Baker-Short, 1987).

A similar study was done by Clarke (1988). He too identified the use of timing, dynamics, and articulation as means to convey the proper structure and emphasized that they may substitute for one another or be used in combination depending on the underlying musical structure. Furthermore, a change of barline position may not only mean change of the metrical structure but also changes in group structure and melodic/harmonic function, which also may affect the performance. Talley (1989) had nine pianists play short tone sequences that could be performed in either $\frac{2}{4}$ or $\frac{3}{4}$ meter. On the whole, the effects were more apparent at the beat level than at the measure level. It seemed that the meter was mainly determined by the pitch and rhythmic structures of the melodies themselves.

The examples in the aforementioned studies were made to reasonably fit into different metrical structures. Edlund (1985) took another approach, asking three pianists to perform "Twinkle, Twinkle, Little Star" in 35 differently notated versions with different meters, different positions of barlines, different rhythmic patterns, and different slurring and stress marks. Only a few results from the extremely detailed analysis can be mentioned here. Variants in $\frac{2}{4}$ time were played slower than in $\frac{4}{4}$ or *alla breve*. Several different duration patterns were found, and the patterning tended to be more pregnant with increased tempo. Timing and dynamics were often used in combination to achieve compound emphasis. Stress marks entailed long d_{io} values (more legato) and often also prolonged note durations. The amplitude factor was generally an often used and effectively communicating means to clarify barline position, as evidenced in listening tests.

There is sometimes metrical ambiguity in notated music. Examples of this taken from Bach, Beethoven, Mozart, and Schubert were given in Bengtsson (1974, 1987) and Sloboda (1985b, pp. 51 and 83). Edlund (1994) collected a large number of such examples from Bach's works and compared performances of them on the piano, the harpsichord, and the organ in order to study how the ambiguities were resolved with these different instruments. In the single example given, various articulation patterns were particularly effective as cues for meter. Pianists also often used dynamic emphasis for the same purpose, whereas the harpsichord and organ players, who cannot use intensity variation, consistently used slurring to express the meter.

The performance of accents is part of the above studies. In performance of rhythm patterns (Gabrielsson, 1974), using only one key on the piano, notes on downbeats were played louder and often with longer durations and more legato than notes in other positions. When some of these rhythm patterns appeared with melody, the picture was more varying. For instance, loudness tended to covary with the melodic contour rather than with metrical position. For rhythm patterns performed on a drum, the accent on downbeats was mainly achieved by increased loudness.

Drake and Palmer (1993) studied how pianists realized various types of accents—rhythmic grouping, melodic, and metric—in performance of constructed examples in which the three types of accents coincided or were shifted in relation to each other. Furthermore, one pianist played an excerpt from a late Beethoven sonata in which there are sometimes coinciding, sometimes conflicting accent structures. The performance of rhythmic grouping accents was most consistent across contexts. The last event in rhythmic groups was played louder, delayed (the event before it was lengthened), and preceded by a "pause" (the preceding event was performed less legato). Metric accents were achieved by increased loudness or timing variations. The performance of melodic accents included increased loudness at "jumps" and "turns" in the melody and/or timing variations. The performance characteristics associated with rhythmic grouping and metric accent structures remained the same whether accent structures coincided or conflicted, whereas those associated with melodic accent varied and appeared to be dominated by rhythmic grouping accent structure. In an earlier experiment Drake, Dowling, and Palmer (1991) found that constructed simple tunes were reproduced most accurately when accent structures coincided and least accurately when they conflicted. The deterioration in reproduction occurred for the melodic component of the tunes, not for the rhythmic component.

The results of the just-described studies show both similarities and dissimilarities. What means are used to convey various aspects of the intended structure depends on the musical context and the possibilities offered by different instruments. Furthermore, stylistic conventions, performance practices, acoustics, performer's intentions, and various circumstantial conditions affect the performance (Clarke, 1988).

3. Tempo

In art music, there is often an accelerando-ritardando pattern in each phrase as seen in many of the studies just described. There is also often considerable variation of tempo in larger sections such as in a movement of a Beethoven symphony (C. Wagner, 1974). The variation is sometimes so large, as in Viennese waltzes, that it seems meaningless to talk of *the* tempo. A distinction may therefore be made between (a) the *mean tempo*—the average number of beats per minute across the whole piece (usually until its last note) disregarding possible variations, (b) the *main tempo*—the prevailing tempo when passages with momentary variations such as "slow start," final ritard, fermatas, and amorphous caesuras are deleted, and (c) *local tempo*, which is maintained only for a short time (Bengtsson & Gabrielsson, 1983). Of course, there are borderline cases, and one has to accept that the variations of tempo, which are so important for the motional-emotional character of the piece (Gabrielsson, 1988) evade simple mathematical calculation. On the other hand, there is much music in which the tempo is kept strictly constant, for instance in marches and in much contemporary popular music where constant tempo is often considered as an ideal (Madison, 1991).

Repp (1994b) had two pianists perform Schumann's *Träumerei* in three different tempi and asked nine other pianists to estimate the tempo in these performances by adjusting a metronome so that it corresponded to the tempo of each performance. The judged tempi were slower than the intended tempi but agreed well with the mean tempi (alternative (a) in the preceding paragraph). Repp did point out, however, that if there were extreme ritards in the performance this would, of course, affect the estimate of the mean tempo, and he discussed alternative calculations to circumvent this problem. It seems that the procedure described for main tempo may also be useful.

Is the performance of a piece the same in different tempi? Clarke (1982) analyzed performances of Satie's *Vexations* and found that versions played at slower tempo showed more groups than versions at faster tempo—an effect described in early rhythm research (Gabrielsson, 1986a)—and that there were changes in relative timing at certain salient points. Similar phenomena were observed in performances with different tempi of a Clementi sonatina (Clarke, 1985b). In this case, another interesting phenomenon was that the dotting in ♩. ♪ patterns became "sharper" at faster tempi, whereas dottings in ♫ patterns became "softer." The reason was that at very fast tempi, the absolute durations of the eighth note and the sixteenth note became so close that they could not be discerned as separate categories but were assimilated into one category with an intermediate duration, that is, shorter than that of an eighth note but longer than that of a sixteenth note. Thus the ♩. ♪ became "sharper" but the ♫ "softer" (see also Clarke, 1987).

Repp (1994c, see also 1994b) analyzed two pianists' performances of Schumann's *Träumerei* in three moderately different (musically acceptable) tempi in order to see whether different variables in the microstructure would be relationally invariant across tempi—in other words, change in proportion to the change in tempo. On the whole this turned out to be the case for durations—timing profiles at the different tempi were approximately parallel, which would support the existence of a generalized motor program with a variable rate parameter (cf. Sec. VI,C). Intensity profiles also retained their shapes but were nearly constant across tempi. The results concerning chord asynchrony, tone overlap, and pedal timing were complex, varied between the pianists, and showed no systematic proportionality to tempo. Desain and Honing (1994) did not find relational invariance of durations in two pianists' performance, at three different tempi, of the theme and first variation in Beethoven's variations on a theme by Paisiello. The range of tempi was larger than in Repp's study but still within musically acceptable limits. In Shaffer's (1992) study, with four pianists giving different interpretations of a late, unknown Beethoven piece, measure timing was more or less scaled by tempo in some cases, in others not. In Povel's (1977) study, one performer made the deviations correspondingly smaller when playing faster, but for the other two performers this relation was very weak. Other effects of different tempi were mentioned earlier (Edlund, 1985; MacKenzie & Van Eerd, 1990). Thus there is no simple answer to the question concerning the effects of different tempi on performance characteristics (see Repp, 1994c, and Desain & Honing, 1994, for further discussion).

As noted earlier, Guttmann (1932) found large variability in conductors' performance time of the same work on different occasions (see Section VII,B). On the other hand, Clynes and Walker (1982) found high stability in Toscanini's performance times for three performances (1935, 1938, 1948) of Brahms's so-called

Haydn Variations. In Clynes's own performances of Bach's *Goldberg Variations* and Beethoven's *Diabelli Variations* certain parts showed high stability in performance time, mainly the faster variations, whereas others did not. However, changes in different parts tended to compensate mutually so that the total performance time still remained very nearly the same. Long term stability was also found in a string quartet's repeated performances of works by Haydn, Beethoven, and Janácek (Clynes, 1986a; Clynes & Walker, 1986). Again tempo compensation was observed. If some parts of a piece were played faster, other parts were played more slowly to maintain about the same total performance time as in earlier performances. Renderings of Ravel's *Quartet* and Bartók's *Sixth Quartet* showed less or even low stability, possibly due to changes in the interpretation of these works. The analyses also suggested that small changes in duration between repeated performances occurred in quantized steps of about 0.5%.

Collier and Collier (1994) explored tempo in a large set of jazz performances. On the whole, the tempo was very stable, even for solo performers. An interesting finding was that a change to play in "double time" (nominally 2:1) actually meant more than doubling the tempo (on average 2.68:1). There were further indications of two preferred tempo ranges, fast and slow.

4. Ritards

Sundberg and Verrillo (1980) selected performances of 24 pieces of music (almost all composed by J. S. Bach) that end with long series of short and equal note values, and calculated the inverted note durations, representing instant tempo, in the final ritards. After some normalizing, an "average ritard curve" across the 24 cases was calculated. In a later study (Kronman & Sundberg, 1987), this curve was used as criterion in a test of whether the musical ritard would fit a model, a square-root function, for deceleration of physical motion as in walking or running—an attempt to connect motion in music to physical motion as suggested by Truslit (1938). It was found that the fit would be good if the endpoint of the ritard was assumed to lie, not at the onset of the final note, but some time after it. This agrees with some intuitions from music listening: pieces often do not end with the last note but may have one or more pulse after-beats (Clynes, 1987, p. 211). Repp (1992a) found that the successive durations in ritardandi within melodic gestures of *Träumerei* could in most cases be described as quadratic functions (parabolas), supporting the observations by Sundberg and his coworkers.

Similar results but interpreted in terms of a mental analog of a force model were obtained by Feldman, Epstein, and Richards (1992). Starting from the intuition that changing tempo is felt as applying a force to the beat—evidenced in expressions as "pushing forward" or "holding back"—they derived mathematical expressions for tempo change under different forces and investigated how well they fitted measured beat durations in selected long passages of ritardando or accelerando. The fit was in most cases best for a quadratic or cubic function; compare the results in Todd (1992, 1995) described in Section VIII,A. They suggested that the formal machinery for tempo change and for real physical movement is largely the same, which again brings Truslit's (1938) ideas to mind

Shaffer and Todd (1987) measured beat durations in three pianists' performances of pieces by Bach, Chopin, and Satie. In the two Chopin pieces, there were large deviations from metrical timing with slowings at boundaries between phrases and larger sections. The more important the boundary was, the more pronounced was the slowing. This was also evident in Repp's (1992a) study of Schumann's *Träumerei*. Todd (1985) formalized this in a model (see Section VIII,A). However, in the *Prelude in C Major* from the first book of Bach's *Well-Tempered Clavier* and in Satie's *Gnossienne No. 5*, there was less departure from metrical timing. The structure of these pieces gives less opportunity for such pronounced use of slowing at boundaries as in the Chopin pieces.

5. Asynchronization

Asynchrony among different voices supposed to produce tones at the same time is common. Rasch (1979, 1988) measured asynchronization in tone onsets between players in recorder, wind, and string trios performing polyphonic music in an anechoic room. Onset time was defined as the moment when the amplitude envelope reached a level 15–20 dB below the maximum level. The measure of asynchronization was taken as the root mean square of the standard deviations of the onset difference times for all pairs of voices. It varied between 30 and 50 msec with the highest values for the string trio. In the string and wind trios the melody instruments, and in the recorder trios the bass voice, tended to lead relative to the other instruments. Larger asynchronization occurred in certain positions, as in the first onsets of a movement and in final notes following a ritardando. In these cases the difference was clearly audible, but differences in the most common range were not perceived, nor were the musicians aware of the amount of asynchronization. Rasch (1978) showed that small differences in onset time may facilitate the perception of separate voices, as in polyphonic music. Rasch (1988) described experiments (Vos & Rasch, 1981) on perceptual onset in relation to rise time and sound level and also discussed at what size of an ensemble it becomes necessary to have a conductor in order to achieve good synchronization.

In Rose's (1989) study of the rhythm section in jazz performance, the drum set usually led, followed by the piano and bass in that order. However, the piano often sounded first on the first and third beats, where new chords often appeared. The mean latency values (elapsed time from the first onset to onsets by other instruments) were roughly 10–30 msec. The saxophonists in Ellis's (1991) investigation tended to "lay back," that is, to delay their onset in relation to the bass track. The delay increased with increasing tempo from about 6% of the beat duration at MM 90 to about 22% at MM 210 (corresponding to an increase from 40 to 63 msec).

Further data on asynchronization in piano performance (Henderson, 1937; Palmer, 1989a; Repp, 1994c; Shaffer, 1984a; Vernon, 1937) or in ensemble performance (Bengtsson & Gabrielsson, 1983) indicate frequent occurrence of 10- to

50-msec asynchronization among different voices, sometimes more in certain positions or in order to provide emphasis to a structurally important voice. The problem of achieving perceived synchrony among instruments in a reverberant environment was discussed by Naylor (1992; see Section V).

6. Perceptual Effects

There is still little research on the perceptual effects of deviations in timing, different articulations, and so on. Synthesized demonstrations (sound examples) of the difference between mechanical performance and performance according to various timing principles in Viennese waltzes and Swedish folk music were given in Bengtsson and Gabrielsson (1983). Listeners familiar with Viennese waltzes clearly preferred a waltz accompaniment synthesized in accordance with typical results from measurements of performed waltzes, whereas inexperienced listeners had quite different opinions (Gabrielsson, 1985). Frequent sound examples were given to illustrate the proposed rules for music performance by Sundberg and his coworkers (e.g., Sundberg, 1992; Friberg, 1995; see Section VIII,B). Tro (1994) manipulated the sound level and the dynamic range of two pieces performed on the Yamaha Disklavier. Listeners preferred the original version or a version with light expansion of the dynamic range.

Clarke (1989b) investigated the detection of small-scale timing changes for certain notes in short tonal and atonal sequences. Lengthening a certain note 20–30 msec was detectable in comparison with a strictly metronomic sequence, whereas about 50 msec was required for detection in a sequence with some rubato in timing. Comparison with data on time discrimination is of limited relevance, since such data usually refer to isolated time intervals. Furthermore, the experiential effects of timing in music rather concern the experienced motion character or "flow" of the music (Gabrielsson, 1986a, 1988). In fact, some of Clarke's listeners remarked that they identified the change as a discontinuity in the temporal flow, as a slight hesitation. Clarke concluded that although measurements were made in terms of durations "it may be more perceptually realistic to think in terms of temporal flow or rate detection" (p. 8).

Perceived "hesitation" in the musical flow was also used by Repp (1992c) in the most accurate study on perceptual effects so far. He synthesized the beginning of a Beethoven minuet and of Schumann's *Träumerei* with physically regular timing on an electronic piano. He then lengthened one or two tones, distributed over the whole excerpt, by a small amount, and the listeners were asked to indicate where the lengthening ("hesitation") occurred. The hypothesis was that it would be more difficult to detect the lengthening in places where lengthenings could be expected to occur—for example, at the ends of phrases or in strong metric positions, as found in selected performances of these excerpts (Repp, 1990c, 1992a)— than in other positions. On the whole, this also turned out to be the result. There was a strong correlation between the selected performance and the listeners' detection accuracy such that in places where the performer slowed down (lengthened tones), the detection deteriorated, and in places where he speeded up, the detection improved. Fyk (1994) had similar reasoning about the effects of expectations on intonation in violin performance.

Given new facilities for efficient generation and editing of sound sequences such as described in Honing (1992), Mazzola (1994, 1995), and Mazzola and Zahorka (1994), research on perceptual effects can be expected to increase. Further investigations on perceptual effects appear in the following sections.

7. Intonation and Vibrato

Most reports on intonation concern performance of single intervals, chords, scales, or short melodic excerpts (e.g., Geringer & Madsen, 1987; Loosen, 1993; Rakowski & Miskiewicz, 1985) and are not discussed here.

Investigations on intonation in violinists (Greene, 1937), string quartets (Nickerson, cited in Ward, 1970, p. 417), woodwind quintets (Mason, 1960), and string trios (Shackford, 1961, 1962a, 1962b), were summarized by Ward (1970) as well as the study by Boomsliter and Creel (1963), who used a specially built reed organ with a number of alternative keys for each note of the chromatic scale. The music performed was mostly from the classical repertory. Shackford composed short pieces for string trio in order to study certain questions. There was usually a fairly large variation (often 40–60 cents) in the tuning of a given interval. Most intervals were played sharp in relation to equal temperament, except for the minor second. Context effects could be noticed. When a tritone was notated as an augmented fourth, the interval was played larger than when notated as a diminished fifth. This was also found by Fyk (1994, 1995) and Rakowski (1990) and related to melodic direction and leading tones: a rising augmented fourth is often followed by a semitone up to the tonic, whereas a diminished fifth is followed by a semitone downwards. This may also explain why both the minor second and the diminished fifth tend to be played flat (Sundberg, 1982). Salzberg (1980) argued that the intonation approximating Pythagorean tuning found in some studies rather reflects a generalized tendency toward sharp intonation than an attempt to conform to Pythagorean tuning.

Greer (1970) found that brass instrumentalists played significantly better in tune with pitches sounded in their own instrument timbre and piano and organ timbres than with pure tones from an oscillator. Ely's (1992) study indicated that musicians (woodwind players) playing instruments whose tones contain many partials can play better in tune than those playing instruments whose tones contain few partials.

Fyk (1994, 1995) gave a historical review of theoretical and practical aspects of intonation as well as of contemporary studies, among them Russian investigations by Garbuzov, Rags, and Sachaltuyeva, which are little known in the West. Her own experiments ranged from intonation of certain intervals to performance of the *Theme and Variation X* in Paganini's *Capriccio* in A minor, Op. 1, played by two concert violinists. In the Paganini piece, only 11% of all performed intervals agreed with the size of the corresponding interval in any of three tuning systems: just intonation, Pythagorean intonation, and equal temperament. Intervals smaller than the fifth tended to be contracted and those larger than the fifth to be stretched. The width of the interval zone was larger in fast performance than in slow performance and always narrower for the fifth, the octave, and the octave plus the fourth than for other intervals. For each interval, there were in fact different intonation variants, for instance, three variants of the major third (385–388, 399–401, and 408–414 cents), the use of which was affected by the melodic and harmonic context. The concept of intonation variants, earlier used by Russian researchers, was discussed by Rakowski and Miskiewicz (1985), who distinguished between acoustic and expressive intonation variants. The former are imposed by physical and psychophysiological facts, for example, intonation in order to give a minimum of beats. The latter are used to extend the emotional expressiveness of a piece. See also in Rakowski (1990, 1991). Terhardt and Zick (1975) argued that "ideal" intonation must be flexible, adapting to the psychoacoustic requirements of the musical sound at each moment. No tuning system can thus be considered ideal. The importance of the melodic and harmonic context and the use of sharpening and flattening as expressive means was also emphasized by Sundberg, Friberg, and Frydén (1989), who had listeners judge synthesized performances representing various tunings.

Fyk concluded that intonation is a dynamic process. An interval does not have an ideal invariable size according to any tuning system, but its size in any situation is affected by a number of factors, including expressive intentions. A larger or smaller similarity between the size of a performed interval and its size in just intonation, Pythagorean intonation, or equal temperament is therefore considered a secondary phenomenon, an effect rather than a cause. Loosen (1993, p. 537) came to a similar conclusion.

Other phenomena noted by Fyk were small corrections of pitch during the initial portion of a tone as well as a frequency change in the final stage of the tone toward the frequency of the following tone. It may be assumed that the last-mentioned fact contributes to the coherence of the melody (Bregman & Dannenbring, 1973). Similar phenomena were also observed in concert singers (Gabrielsson & Johnson, 1985).

The results from the Iowa studies on vibrato (Section VII,B) have been largely confirmed in later studies (e.g., Corso & Lewis, 1950; Fyk, 1995). However, Papich and Rainbow (1974) found lower vibrato rate, 4–5 Hz, for cello and double bass. The width of the vibrato was about a quarter tone for cello but smaller for violin and double bass. Prame (1994) measured vibrato rate in 10 singers and four string players performing Schubert's *Ave Maria* and found that the rate usually increased at the end of the tone. Disregarding this increase, the mean rate across singers was 6.0 Hz. Maximum rate varied among singers between 5.8 and 7.3 Hz, minimum rate between 5.0 and 6.0. The within-individual variation between maximum and minimum rate was about ±8% of the artist's average. Brown (1991) found modulation width varying from 25 –35 cents for flute to 93–108 cents for voice ensemble; values for violin, viola, trumpet, and trombone were in between. He cited some studies—for example, Fletcher, Blackham, and Geertsen (1965)—which indicated that musicians employ vibrato above the intended frequency, playing the desired frequency at or near the bottom of the vibrato cycle (see also in Ward, 1970).

Fletcher and Sanders (1967) showed that vibrato for violin tones also meant a continuous change of spectrum, thus affecting the perceived tone quality. Handel (1989, p. 175) and Meyer (1992, 1994) likewise pointed out that frequency modulation in vibrato is coupled with amplitude variation in individual partials. Meyer discussed the effects of this and of room acoustics on the performer's and the listener's perception. Physiological aspects of violin vibrato were studied by Schlapp (1973) and Bejjani, Ferrara, and Pavlidis (1989) and of cello vibrato by Moore (1988). Gärtner (1980) made a thorough study of the physiology of vibrato in flute playing. His book also included an account of the historical development of vibrato.

8. Conductors

There are few published studies of conductors. C. Wagner (1974) had Herbert von Karajan perform, on the piano, selected parts of various symphonic works as well as some exercises. Generally the precision in tempo was high and consistent between repeated performances. The task of performing a rhythmic pattern in successively increasing tempo was accomplished with an impressive feeling for "absolute tempo." Asked to perform the (oboe) solo in the beginning of the second movement in Tchaikovsky's Fourth Symphony in an interpreted version and a "noninterpreted" (mechanical) version, the latter showed much less variation in note timing and a successive slowing of the mean tempo, whereas the interpreted version showed larger variations around the same mean tempo. Physiological recordings of von Karajan conducting Beethoven's *Leonore Overture* No. 3 showed varying pulse rate, almost twice as high as normal in certain passages, which von Karajan indicated as the most emotionally engaging (Harrer, 1975).

Hayes (1989) used high-speed film (250 frames/sec) to study kinematic aspects of conducting (temporal aspects, range of motion, linear velocity). The analysis of these revealed that experts' perceptions of the same aspects from a videotape of the performances were frequently incorrect and inconsistent.

A study (Price, 1983) with prescribed variation of conductor behavior demonstrated the importance of appropriate feedback to the ensemble by the conductor. Cox (1989) compared choral directors' use of rehearsal structures that differed regarding the distribution of fast-paced and slow-paced activities, familiar and new music and analytical study. About half of the directors preferred a structure with familiar activities at both the beginning and ending of the rehearsal session and with the middle portion devoted to analytical study of works in the developmental stages.

9. Intention and Performance

An increasing number of studies are concerned with how the musician's intentions affect the performance. This connects naturally to questions about representation and interpretation discussed in Section II,A. Either the performer is asked to provide different performances of his own choice and to describe the intentions behind them or the performer is asked to play with a certain intention in mind. There are also post-hoc studies, discussed elsewhere, in which different performances are analyzed and tentatively related to presumed conceptions (e.g., Shaffer, 1995).

Palmer (1989a) had eight pianists perform the beginning of Brahms' *Intermezzo*, Op. 117, No.1, and indicate their intentions by markings in the score (melodic line, phrasing, tempo changes, dynamics) and by verbal description. They should also perform the excerpt in an unmusical way. Variables measured were asynchrony, rubato patterns, and articulation. The voice notated as the melody preceded the other voices on the first (accented) beat, but the pianists were usually unaware that they did so. However, they were aware of attempts to play the melody note louder. Phrase endings were marked by slowing down the tempo, recognized by all performers. Overlaps between consecutive tones were also consciously used, but the fact that the degree of overlap depended on the durations of the surrounding notes, especially the preceding, was not recognized. All effects were larger in the musical than in the unmusical performances, and there were individual exceptions from the above-mentioned tendencies. On the whole, the pianists' intentions could be observed in the above measures. In contrast, Behne and Wetekam (1993) found little difference between rhythmically exact and expressive performance in music students' performance of the Mozart theme mentioned earlier. There were examples where the interpretive intentions could be traced in the performance data but also examples of performance in contradiction to reported intentions.

Nakamura (1987) had three performers (violin, oboe, recorder) play two short movements of Baroque music and indicate features of their interpretation in the score. Thirty-eight music students were asked to choose between alternative markings of dynamics (from *pp* to *ff*, as well as crescendo and decrescendo signs) to describe the perceived loudness. Most listeners successfully recognized an intended crescendo. With regard to decrescendo, the agreement was less. The intensity level corresponding to a certain marking varied considerably over the piece, but still the listeners' markings corresponded rather well with the performers' intentions, probably due to context effects. Rising pitch enhanced an impression of crescendo, even if intensity did not increase, and falling pitch enhanced an impression of decrescendo. Generally the communication of dynamics from the performer to the listener worked fairly well.

The violinist Senju (Senju & Ohgushi, 1987) played 10 different versions of the beginning of Mendelsohn's *Violin Concerto*. Listeners judged the performances by semantic differentials, and multidimensional scaling indicated some correspondence between the player's intentions and the listeners' impressions. Födermayr and Deutsch (1994) used spectrograms to tentatively analyze parameters in three singers' performance—such as attack, release, timbre, vibrato, dynamics, timing—that would reflect how they conceived the feelings and intentions of the person whom they were supposed to represent.

Kendall and Carterette (1990) had five musicians perform the beginning of "Thy hand, Belinda" from Purcell's *Dido and Aeneas* on the piano, the clarinet, the oboe, the violin, and the trumpet in three versions: without expression, with appropriate expression, and with exaggerated expression. Listeners were asked to either categorize, match, or rate the performances regarding the expressive level. Although the results from the different methods differed in certain respects, the expressive intentions were, on the whole, grasped by the listeners. The two expressive performances were played slower and with more variations in timing than the performance without expression. The performance with appropriate expression was softer than the other two, which also had a larger dynamic range. Amplitude vibrato (in oboe, violin, and trumpet) increased with increased expression. The authors emphasized the variability among performances, even in a short excerpt like this, arguing against "something as strict and invariant as *the* musical grammar, performer grammar, or listener grammar" (p. 160).

As a part of a study on violins, Askenfelt (1986) had two violinists play the opening theme in Beethoven's *Violin Concerto* in two versions, tender and aggressive. The aggressive version was characterized by higher mean bow force and more rapid changes in the force, resulting in higher loudness and more abrupt changes in loudness, than in the tender version.

The effects of different intentions concerning emotional expression were studied in Gabrielsson (1994, 1995), Gabrielsson and Lindström (1995), and Juslin (1993). Musicians playing the synthesizer, violin, flute, and electric guitar and a singer were asked to perform short pieces of music, some well-known, others less well-known or unknown, in order to have them sound happy, sad, solemn, angry, soft/tender, or without expression. They had to keep the pitches in the melodies but were free to use any other means that they wanted in order to achieve the desired expression. Digital analysis of the recorded performances showed that practically every physical variable in the performance on the respective instrument was affected in specific ways for each emotional expression. For instance, tempo was usually more rapid for happy and angry versions than for others; sound level was loudest for angry versions and softest for tender or sad versions; dotted patterns were performed sharp in angry versions but soft in sad and tender versions; articulation was "airy" in happy versions, legato or legatissimo in sad and tender versions; "pitch bending" was used in sad and tender versions; tone onsets and offsets were abrupt in angry versions but slowly rising/decaying in sad and tender versions; timbre was manipulated in different ways, for example, "harsh" in angry versions, "cold" in inexpressive versions; vibrato was deleted in inexpressive versions. The performers used the available means both in common and in individually specific ways (as in Kendall & Carterette, 1990). Performances on a sentograph without auditory feedback showed characteristics similar to those of corresponding performances on a synthesizer.

D. COMMENTS

Despite the wealth of data in the above investigations, the number of performers and pieces of music studied is vanishingly small in comparison with their "total" number. Furthermore, there are at present more differences than commonalities in the results. This may be due to differences in the type of music and instrument used, differences among performers, stylistic conventions, measurement procedures, data analysis, and still other factors. It is my conviction that measurements of performance should, as much as possible, be conducted and considered in relation to the composer's and/or the performer's intentions and the listener's experience (cf. the quotation from H. G. Seashore at the end of Section VII,B). After all, music is a means for communication and expression, and the characteristics of different performances may be easier to understand given this self-evident frame of reference.

VIII. MODELS OF MUSIC PERFORMANCE

A. MODELS BASED ON MEASUREMENTS

Referring to investigations by Shaffer, Sloboda, and himself, Clarke (1988) proposed nine generative rules to account for a great deal of the expressive deviations in (piano) performance. Graduated changes in timing and dynamics, describable as a quadratic function with variable minimum, can be used to indicate the group structure of the music. With regard to timing, a minimum to the left indicates a predominance of upbeats and a sense of end-oriented direction, whereas a minimum to the right indicates a predominance of after-beats and a sense of dissipation away from the beginning of the group. Group boundaries are marked by maxima in the timing profile, by dynamic contrast, or by discontinuities in articulation. The significance of an event may be indicated by increased duration, delayed entrance, dynamic intensification, or by appropriate choice of articulation.

Todd (1985) focused on the ritard at phrase endings. The performer can elucidate the rhythmic structure by slowing down at the structural endings and further reflect the hierarchical structure of the piece by the degree of this slowing. Todd used the time-span-reduction principle from Lerdahl and Jackendoff (1983) to derive the embedding depth of the structural endings and combined it with a parabola as (approximately) modeling the phrase-final lengthening. Increasing embedding depth increases the steepness of slowing. In this way a duration structure was generated, with the bar as the time unit, corresponding to the rubato in performance. The generated bar durations were compared with the measured bar durations in piano performances of pieces by Mozart, Haydn, and Chopin (see also in

Shaffer & Todd, 1987). The fit was pretty good, but there were some discrepancies ascribed to points of weakened tonality and ambiguous time-span reduction. Parabolic timing functions for ritardandi were also demonstrated in Repp's (1992a) *Träumerei* study.

The model was revised (Todd, 1989a) to relieve the too-high demands on working memory implied by the time-span-reduction principle. The assumption that the performer considers each event in a single, coherent structure was relaxed by assuming a superposition of a number of hierarchic timing components corresponding to different structural levels. Furthermore, as the performer's "computations" are made as each phrase is accessed in turn, it is necessary to model the continuous process of performance ("look ahead and plan"). One should also allow for the indeterminism of individual performances in order not to negate the creative aspect involved in performance. Again the durations generated by the model were compared to measured durations, and the agreement between model and data was good (see Figure 5 for an example). Todd (1989b) also proposed an algorithm for the listener's perception of rubato, emphasizing that in order to understand expression in music, we must consider performance and perception together.

As an extension of the aforementioned model, Todd (1992) proposed a computational model of musical dynamics. It was based on the common observation that a musical phrase often shows a crescendo-decrescendo profile and also assumed

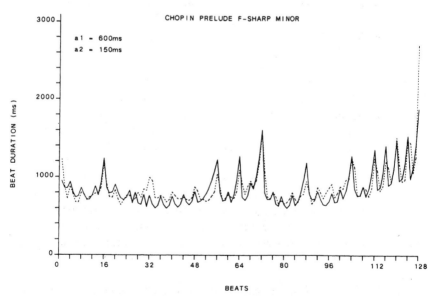

FIGURE 5 Comparison of model and data for a Chopin prelude. Solid line: model. Dotted line: average of data from two performances. (Reproduced from Todd, 1989a, by permission of Harwood Academic Publishers.)

that tempo and dynamics are coupled—the faster, the louder, and vice versa. The parabolic function for duration was abandoned, and tempo change was instead assumed to be linear as a function of real time and governed by analogy to physical movement. The coupling to physical movement was further developed in Todd (1995), in which two models for tempo change, piecewise linear tempo (PLT) and piecewise constant tempo (PCT), were compared using regression analyses with data taken from earlier reported performances of Chopin pieces. The results indicated that the PCT model—tempo is constant within a segment but varies discontinuously at segment boundaries—may provide a reasonable account for a shallow rubato, and that the PLT model may be better for performances with more pronounced rubato.

B. MODELS BASED ON INTUITIONS

Rather than relying on measurements of performances, Sundberg and his coworkers proposed that it would be fruitful to consider the intuitions of expert musicians, in this case the violinist Lars Frydén. Frydén's intuititons have been used to establish a set of performance rules, which are applied to music scores. Both were programmed into a microcomputer, connected to a synthesizer via MIDI. Examples were synthesized to correspond to a deadpan version of the score and to versions in which different rules are applied to different degrees, separate or in combination. The examples were used for demonstrations, for example, on CD records in Sundberg (1992) or Friberg (1995), for listening tests, and for comparisons with results from performance measurements. This "analysis-by-synthesis" approach may be compared with the present author's suggestion to use analysis, based on measurements, and synthesis in an interplay (Gabrielsson, 1985; W. F. Thompson, Sundberg, Friberg, & Frydén, 1989).

Some 20 rules were described in a series of overlapping papers, listed here in chronological order (Sundberg, Askenfelt, & Frydén, 1983; Sundberg, Frydén, & Askenfelt, 1983; Sundberg & Frydén, 1985, 1987; Sundberg, 1988; Sundberg, Friberg, & Frydén, 1989; Friberg, Frydén, Bodin, & Sundberg, 1991; Friberg, 1991; Sundberg, 1991; Sundberg, Friberg, & Frydén, 1991a, 1991b; Sundberg, 1992, 1993; Sundberg, Frydén & Friberg, 1995; Friberg, 1995). Surveys of the rules appeared in Sundberg et al. (1991a) and Friberg (1995), and their technical realization was described in Friberg (1991). The rules affect durations, overall sound level, sound level envelopes, vibrato frequency and depth, and fine tuning. They may be divided into differentiation rules that may help the listener to identify pitch and duration categories, grouping rules that facilitate the perception of melodic Gestalts of various lengths, and ensemble rules. The rules are additive and applied in a prescribed order. The quantity of a rule effect is varied by means of a multiplication factor.

Not all rules can be described here. Some of them relate to facts in music acoustics, for example: increase the sound level by 3 dB per octave and stretch the tuning with rising fundamental frequency. Others are recognized from performance measurements, such as phrase marking by means of lengthening phrase final notes and insertion of micropauses, and further the "double duration contrast reduction," which transforms a nominal 2:1 ratio between adjacent notes, such as ♩♩, into a lower ratio. In contrast to this, another rule prescribes increased difference between short and long notes by shortening and softening short notes and lengthening long ones. The "faster uphill" rule shortens each note initiating an ascending interval by 2 msec, thus increasing the tempo in sequences of ascending intervals. "Leap articulation" creates overlaps between tones forming a narrow interval and micropauses between tones forming leaps. Furthermore, the target note in ascending leaps is lengthened and the initiating note shortened.

The most original rules make use of the concepts of melodic and harmonic charge to indicate the "remarkableness" of tones or chords. The melodic charge of a tone is defined in relation to the root of the prevailing chord and increases with the distance to this chord by one unit for each step along the circle of fifths. Furthermore, the values are higher when going in the subdominant direction than in the direction of the dominant. The harmonic charge is a weighted sum of the chord notes' melodic charges. Both affect the duration, loudness, and vibrato of tones and chords in proportion to their charge. The rule concerning harmonic charge leads to crescendos when a chord of higher harmonic charge is approaching and decrescendos in the opposite case, accompanied by proportional tempo and vibrato variations. An example appears in Figure 6. In atonal music, the harmonic charge is replaced by chromatic charge. The melodic charge also affects tuning in a way that scale tones in the left half of the circle of fifths (subdominant direction) are played flat, those in the right half (dominant direction) are played sharp. The synchronization of voices in ensemble music is handled by appointing, at each instant, a "synchronization voice" containing the shortest note value and highest melodic charge (Sundberg et al., 1989).

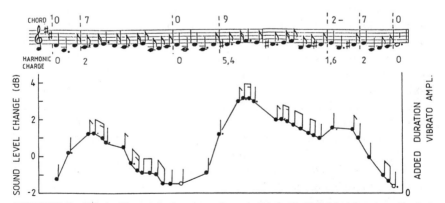

FIGURE 6 Effects of harmonic charge on a theme in Schubert's *Unfinished Symphony*. See text for further explanation. (Reproduced from Sundberg, Friberg, & Frydén, 1991a, by permission of Academic Press.)

The validity of the rules was investigated in various ways. Comparisons with data from actual performances showed good agreement as well as marked differences between predicted and observed data (Sundberg, 1988; Sundberg et al., 1991a). Listening tests including different rules and music excerpts proved musicians to be better than nonmusicians at discriminating rule-treated versions from deadpan versions, but the musicians also showed high false-alarm rates. Professional musicians' adjustment to a preferred level of the quantity applied to each of six rules showed significant differences from zero quantity (deadpan version) except for the rule concerning increased duration contrasts (Sundberg et al., 1991a, 1991b). Rules for phrase-ending markers were supported (Friberg & Sundberg, 1987). Specialists on contemporary music preferred rule-generated performances of contemporary piano music to performances in which no rules were applied (Friberg et al., 1991). In the most thorough listening test (W. F. Thompson et al., 1989), musically trained listeners rated the musical quality of performances in which one or more of the rules were applied to 10 musical excerpts, 5 in each of two experiments. Although the results from the first experiment on the whole supported the applied rules, the results from the second experiment were more varied and depended more on the musical excerpts.

The analysis-by-synthesis approach is comparative in its nature, and the modest purpose is to investigate if the presence of a rule improves the performance as compared with the performance generated without the same rule. In actual musical practice, one can imagine that the performer makes a decision about what rules to apply and with what quantity. Thus direct comparisons with performance measurements are difficult. An interesting observation is that when a rule is applied at its preferred value, listeners are able to notice the difference in comparison with another version but not able to analyze it correctly. There are further many similarities to phenomena in speech production and perception (Carlson, Friberg, Frydén, Granström, & Sundberg, 1989).

Battel and Bresin (1994) suggested some modifications of the rules for piano performance. Friberg (1995) pointed out that musical notation conventions differ during music history as well as among styles and composers, which limits the possibilities of developing a universal performance program. Oosten (1993) questioned several features of the rule system and especially criticized the extremely local character of the rules, a criticism also made by Shaffer (1992, 1995). Furthermore, the fact that the same score may be performed in different ways by different performers is only loosely discussed. The status of the rules with regard to aesthetic criteria of musical interpretation was discussed by Sundin (1994). Another rule-based music interpretation system that generates performance from a printed score was described by Katayose and Inokuchi (1993).

Although also based on intuitions, the approach taken by Clynes to transform a music score into living music is quite different. It is mainly based on two principles, "hierarchical pulse of a composer" and "predictive amplitude shaping."

The idea that one can feel a specific pulse in the music of different composers is appealing to many and dates back to the beginning of the century. It was most explicitly proposed by Becking (1928) in Germany, who tried to describe different composers' pulse in terms of "Schlagfiguren" (see also Gabrielsson, 1986a). Clynes (1977, 1983) first explored this idea by means of his sentograph technique, providing "essentic forms" of the inner pulse for different composers, and then went on to formulate the idea in quantitative terms (Clynes, 1983, 1985, 1986a, 1986b, 1987, 1995). The pulse refers to a repetitive phenomenon that provides patterns of deviations from nominal note durations, as well as patterns of amplitude within a group of tones that form the pulse group. This may take place on several hierarchic levels. The lowest level of the pulse group hierarchy comprises about 1 sec. The group has four or three component tones, and pulse matrix values for a four-tone group (for example, four eighth notes or four sixteenth notes) are given for various composers as illustrated in Figure 7.

The pulse matrix is a metarhythm providing a microstructure for any combination of rhythmic elements. The rules are that a long tone is as long as its component pulse tones and as loud as its first component pulse. In this way, relative durations and amplitudes of any metric tone combinations are determined from the pulse-matrix components. However, these values are modified by the duration and amplitude matrix values on the second level of the hierarchy, which represents a superimposed slower pulse of 3–4 sec duration, and these in turn by a third level with still longer units. The two lower levels are composer specific, whereas the third level is largely piece specific. It is noted that the differences in amplitude between the various pulse elements mean a considerable articulation of loudness

Composer's Pulses

4 Pulse

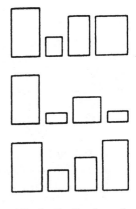

BEETHOVEN			
106	89	96	111
1.00	.39	.83	.81

MOZART			
105	95	105	95
1.00	.21	.53	.23

HAYDN			
108	94	97	102
1.00	.42	.68	1.02

FIGURE 7 Composer's pulse, 4 pulse, for Beethoven, Mozart, and Haydn. Top line for each composer indicates relative durations of four successive notes of same nominal length, bottom line indicates relative amplitude size on a linear scale. In the corresponding graphical representation to the right, the height of rectangles represents amplitude and the width represents duration. (Reproduced by permission from Clynes, 1987.)

even within a certain dynamic level—for instance, articulation within forte rather than uniform forte.

The pulse structure and the values in the respective pulse matrices were determined by Clynes in listening to a number of synthesized pieces for each composer and optimizing the parameters of the pulse to express the composer's identity. Clynes considers the pulse to be a personal characteristic comparable to a person's gait or handwriting.

Predictive amplitude shaping affects the amplitude envelope of a tone depending on what tone follows it, and when. The envelope is skewed in relation to a basic shape different for different composers and different types of music, such that downward steps in pitch deviate the envelope shape backward and upward steps forward in proportion to the number of semitones between the tone and the next tone. Furthermore, the longer the tone, the smaller the deviation. The shape is described by a beta function, for which a choice of two parameters provides a large family of shapes. The PAS principle means that every tone gets a unique envelope depending on the pitch and time relations to the following tone.

Numerous synthesized sound examples with works of many composers illustrating the above principles were given on phonograph records (Clynes, 1983, 1985, 1987).

Empirical tests concerning composers' pulse were reported by W. F. Thompson (1989) and Repp (1989, 1990b) using performances synthesized according to the pulse matrix for different composers, and by Repp (1990c) using measurements of actual performances. In the former investigations, listeners rated one or more pieces by different composers, synthesized in different versions: (a) deadpan, (b) with correct pulse for the respective composer according to Clynes, or (c) with the pulse pattern shifted (for example, perform a Beethoven piece according to the Mozart pulse, or change positions of the components within a pulse pattern). Although the judgments by Thompson's (musically trained) listeners, concerning Mozart and Beethoven pulses, on the whole supported Clynes's ideas, the results of Repp's listening tests and performance measurements were much more mixed, providing some instances of support but more instances of objections. When asked to judge how well the respective (synthesized) performance expressed the different composers' individual characteristics, listeners' judgments varied very much for different pieces of the same composer. This may indicate that the evaluations rather depended on the characteristics of the individual composition than on its composer (Repp, 1990b). In his extensive measurements of nineteen famous pianists' performance of a Beethoven minuet, Repp (1990c) found only very limited evidence of a Beethoven pulse as defined by Clynes.

These results led to a debate between Clynes and Repp (Clynes, 1990, 1994, 1995; Repp, 1990a, 1994d). The discussion concerned many different matters, such as the selection of music examples and the appropriate pulse configuration; the way of synthesizing their microstructure; the possibility of finding the pulse matrix values in measurements of performances; and possible confounding with other composer-specific properties as in dynamic range, articulation, rubato, and pedaling (W. F. Thompson, 1989). The theory proved more difficult to test than expected (Repp, 1990b, 1994d), but the discussion identified some crucial points for the formulation and testing of the theory.

Clynes claimed that good recognition of composers' pulses requires intimate experience with their music. In a recent investigation (Clynes, 1995) five groups differing in musical expertise ranging from world renowned artists to nonmusic students judged the appropriateness of examples that were synthesized with "correct" or "wrong" pulses in pieces by Haydn, Mozart, Beethoven, and Schubert. In brief, the greater the musical proficiency, the more marked was the preference for the right pulse. However, Clynes stressed that the pulse values used are a first approximation to the composer's pulses and that refinements can be expected.

C. COMMENTS

Each of the models mentioned as yet covers only very limited aspects of music performance. The models focus on the relationship between the score and the performance and give less attention to the individual performer's interpretation. Measurements of performance and generation of models are complementary enterprises. Both should take the composer's and/or the performer's intentions as well as the listener's experiences and responses into consideration.

IX. PHYSICAL FACTORS IN PERFORMANCE

A. MEDICAL PROBLEMS

Music performance puts very high demands on the body. With regard to the hand, C. Wagner (1987a) stated that there seems to be no other human activity demanding so much of time-ordered fine motoric facilities as the mastery of a musical instrument. Extensive measurements of hand size and joint mobility in professional pianists and violinists have been conducted (C. Wagner, 1987a, 1987b, 1988a, 1988b; see also in F. R. Wilson & Roehmann, 1992, or F. R. Wilson, Wagner & Hömberg, 1995). The results were shown in "biomechanical hand-profiles" that display a large number of measures for an individual in relation to a reference group. Shape factors showed relatively less variability than active and passive mobility. Comparison of successful pianists with "problem pianists" showed differences between these groups with regard to active and passive mobility but no significant differences regarding hand shape. Genetic determination probably has more influence on joint mobility than training. A historically interesting example is Paganini, whose left hand had an unusual flexibility permitting virtuoso feats that fascinated his audience (O'Shea, 1990; Sachs, 1982). In another large study (Larsson, Baum, Mudholkar, & Kollia, 1993a), instrumentalists with hypermobile wrists and fingers showed less musculoskeletal symptoms, and instrumentalists with hypermobile knees or spine more symptoms, than musicians with no hypermobility. The conclusion was that hypermobility of joints undergoing repetitive motion is an asset but hypermobility of joints giving support is a liability.

The high demands on the body lead to frequent medical problems in musicians. Studies on neurological disorders and on occupational palsies in performing musicians were reviewed by Blau and Henson (1977) and Critchley (1977), and Dawley (1985) summarized studies on the physiology of instrumental musicians and vocalists. Lockwood (1989) surveyed medical problems of musicians such as overuse syndromes, neural impingement, focal dystonias, and psychological stress. Harman (1987) listed about 250 articles in a bibliography for occupational diseases of instrumental musicians and described (Harman, 1991) the evolution of performing arts medicine as a discipline of its own. The recently established journals *Medical Problems of Performing Artists* and *International Journal of Arts Medicine* provide ample evidence of a large amount of activity in this field.

A questionnaire answered by 2212 musicians in 47 orchestras in the United States (Fishbein, Middlestadt, Ottati, Straus, & Ellis, 1988) indicated that 82% of musicians in orchestras have a medical problem. The shoulder, neck, and back seem to be the musculoskeletal locations at which many orchestra musicians experience severe problems. Fingers, hands, and arms come next. Stage fright was the most frequently mentioned nonmusculoskeletal problem (see Section X,D). A follow-up study on string players (Middlestadt & Fishbein, 1989) showed that the prevalence of musculoskeletal problems differed, depending on sex (more females than males reporting problems) and the specific demands of different instruments. In a German study (Blum, 1995) including about 1400 string players from 42 orchestras, most of them 30–60 years old, 86% reported various motoric problems, and there were also frequent problems with skin (e.g., "fiddler's chin"), eyesight, and hearing. More than half of 660 individuals (mean age, 25 years) in a well-known music school reported musculoskeletal problems (tightening, pain, stiffness, fatigue) during playing (Larsson, Baum, Mudholkar, & Kollia, 1993b). Difficulties were most common among string players and more common among females than among males. Eighty-seven percent of 246 music majors at a university reported some degree of performance-related pain (Pratt, Jessop, & Niemann, 1992) impairing concentration, endurance, coordination, and flexibility. Newmark and Hochberg (1987) reported painful disorders in 108 musicians (median age, 28 years), performing on keyboard instruments, bowed string instruments, and on the guitar. As in the previous studies, the location of the pain was characteristic of the instrument played, for example, in the right arm, hand and fingers for pianists, but mostly in the left hand and fingers for string players and guitarists.

Fry (1985, 1986, 1987, 1988, 1991) presented extensive data on overuse syndrome in symphony orchestra players and in music schools. Overuse is characterized by persisting pain and tenderness in muscles and joint ligaments due to excessive use. The incidence of painful overuse syndrome in orchestral players was more than 50% ("there must be few occupations where the occurrence of occupational pain is as common as this"; Fry, 1985, p. 44) and 10–20% in music school students. The location of overuse problems correlates well with the particular physical demands of the individual instruments—for example, the right hand for pianists, the left hand for guitarists, and the upper respiratory tract for wind players. Overuse may be caused by genetic factors, the musical technique, and the intensity and time of practice. Fry recommended practice segments no longer than 25 min followed by a 5-min break and to "stop when it hurts." Static loading in holding up an instrument should be avoided as much as possible. Goodman and Staz (1989) described a program for occupational therapy for musicians with overuse syndrome.

Taubman (Pratt, 1989) warned pianists against using extreme range of motion as well as against certain widely used exercises that may cause permanent damage. Grieco, Occhipinti, Colombini, Menoni, Bulgheroni, Frigo, and Boccardi (1989) found that 62% of 117 Italian piano students had a least one musculoskeletal disorder. EMG studies revealed excessive loading of certain muscular structures during piano exercises, especially of the forearm. Furthermore, the posture at the piano, without support for the trunk and often maintained for several hours, is a risk factor. Using measurements of keystrike force and finger motion in experienced pianists, F. G. Wolf, Keane, Brandt, and Hillberry (1993) suggested that playing with greater force than necessary and using finger positions that result in unnecessarily high tendon and joint forces may predispose pianists to musculoskeletal injury. Philipson, Sörbye, Larsson, and Kaladjev (1990) found that violinists with neck and shoulder pain used significantly more muscle force than performers who did not experience pain.

EMG biofeedback training—to become aware of and to learn to relax overcontracted muscles when given information on excess muscle contraction during performance—was reported to be beneficial for removing unwanted muscle tension in string players (LeVine, 1988a; LeVine & Irvine, 1984) and in clarinet players (Morasky, Reynolds, & Sowell, 1983). LeVine (1988b) used temperature biofeedback for treatment of muscle spasms in a viola player. Cutietta (1986) found EMG biofeedback training efficient for reducing muscle tension and improving music students' performance of problematic passages. Fischer-Williams (1993) reported long-term (5–14 years) beneficial effects of EMG biofeedback training for 30 musicians. Practically all of them found that their performance improved with reduced levels of muscle tension.

Occupational cramp in musicians was discussed and compared with writers' and telegraphers' cramps in several papers (Fry, 1991; Lederman, 1988; F. R. Wilson & Roehmann, 1992; F. R. Wilson et al., 1995). Even Freud undertook some work in this area, treating the conductor Bruno Walter for cramp problems (Chumaceiro, 1991). The causes of musicians' cramps are still unclear. F. R. Wilson et al. (1995) suggested that cramps may result from unfavorable biomechanical properties in combination with the properties of the instrument and negative emotions in learning new techniques.

The selection of papers in this section is very limited and somewhat arbitrary. Proper references for continued reading are the journals *Medical Problems of Performing Artists* and *International Journal of Arts Medicine* and the volumes edited by Sataloff, Brandfonbrener, and Lederman (1991) and by C. Wagner (1995), in which experts discuss a variety of medical problems and proper treatment of them as well as specific problems associated with different instruments including ergonomic aspects. Some contributions in the volume edited by Spintge and Droh (1992) deal with performers' problems, and Norris (1993) provided an instructive guide to preventing and treating injuries in instrumentalists.

B. HEARING IMPAIRMENT

Different types of hearing loss and their consequences for musicians were discussed by Sataloff and Sataloff (1991). Measurements at concerts and in rehearsals often revealed sound levels at or above risk levels for hearing damage (Camp & Horstman, 1992; Dibble, 1995; Haider & Groll-Knapp, 1981; Jansson & Karlsson, 1983). Investigations on pop and rock musicians (Axelsson & Lindgren, 1977, 1978) indicated sensory-neural hearing loss in 13–30%, depending on the definition of hearing loss, of the individuals studied; however, the loss was relatively small. Waugh (1983) surveyed American and European studies and concluded that 13% of 313 rock musicians had some degree of hearing impairment, usually mild. However, there is a large between-individual variation in susceptibility to loud sounds, and many rock musicians (for example, Pete Townshend) have talked about very serious personal consequences. A project called Hearing Education and Awareness for Rockers (H.E.A.R.) was started in the United States (Silverman, 1989).

Studies of orchestra musicians have provided somewhat contradictory results. Although some studies (Axelsson & Lindgren, 1981; Ostri, Eller, Dahlin, & Skylv, 1989) indicated a higher incidence of hearing loss in orchestra musicians than in reference groups, other studies (Jansson, Axelsson, Lindgren, Karlsson, & Olaussen, 1986; D. W. Johnson, Alridge, Sherman, & Lorraine, 1986; Karlsson, Lundquist, & Olaussen, 1983; Royster, Royster, & Killion, 1991; Westmore & Eversden, 1981) on the whole indicated no or only slightly impaired hearing for orchestra musicians considered as a group, apart from impairment due to increased age and other exposure to loud sounds. However, many individual musicians show worse hearing, particularly at high frequencies, and again there is large between-individual variation in susceptibility to loud sounds. Violinists and violists often have worse hearing in their left ear than in the right. Position on the stage may be critical, for example, players seated in front of the brass section seem to have particular problems (Sataloff & Sataloff, 1991). However, one study (D. W. Johnson, Sherman, Alridge, & Lorraine, 1985) indicated that position within the orchestra did not have any appreciable effect. High school band directors showed some evidence of hearing loss (Cutietta, Klich, Royse, & Rainbolt, 1994).

The results of these and of further studies are somewhat confusing and contradictory (Sataloff & Sataloff, 1991; Dibble, 1995). Comparisons between different studies are sometimes difficult because the studies used different criteria for hearing damage, different reference groups, and different statistical methods. Possible consequences of hearing damage for performance and recommendations about preventive measures were discussed in several of the aforementioned papers and particularly in Chasin and Chong (1992) and Woolford, Carterette, and Morgan (1988). The fact that not even deafness may impede music performance is proved by the successful career of the percussionist Evelyn Glennie (1991), profoundly deaf since the age of 12.

C. STRESS FACTORS

Measurements on 24 musicians from the Vienna Symphony (Haider & Groll-Knapp, 1981) showed a mean pulse rate during performance at concerts of 91–98 beats per minute (80–88 beats per minute at rehearsals) and a mean maximum pulse rate of 108–115 beats per minute with occasional values up to about 150 beats per minute. The mean pulse rate at rest was 65–69 beats per minute. EEG recordings showed almost exclusively rapid beta waves during performance, indicating enormous mental concentration and central nervous stress. Similar results concerning pulse rates were found for members of a German orchestra (Schmale & Schmidtke, 1985) and for trumpet players (Hunsaker, 1994). Measurements during concerts (Haider & Groll-Knapp, 1981; Schmale & Schmidtke, 1985) showed considerable and unfavorable increases in temperature, relative humidity, dust, and carbon dioxide concentration. Maximum sound levels varied between 102 and 128 dB(A) for different works, and lighting conditions were unsatisfactory. Harris (1988) discussed the unfavorable visual conditions of symphony musicians that may lead to astigmatism and anisometropia due to asymmetric postures.

X. PSYCHOLOGICAL AND SOCIAL FACTORS

A. DEVELOPMENT

The musical development of performers has been studied by means of extensive interviews of performers and their parents. Within a research project on talent development in pianists, sculptors, swimmers, tennis players, mathematicians, and neurologists, Sosniak (1985a, 1985b, 1985c, 1985d, 1990) interviewed 21 American concert pianists, 24–39 years old, who had been finalists in international piano competitions. Bastian (1989) interviewed 62 young (14–22 years old) prizewinners in German music competitions ("Jugend musiziert"). They represented all the common orchestra and keyboard instruments. In England, Howe and Sloboda (1991a, 1991b, 1991c; Sloboda & Howe, 1991, 1992), interviewed 42 students, 10–18 years old, from a special school for musically gifted children. The performers in the German study typically came from homes with musically active members, whereas the participants in the Sosniak and Howe and Sloboda studies came from families with widely varying degrees of musical involvement, ranging from parents who were professional musicians to parents with little or no musical involvement. In all three studies, most parents were academics and white-collar workers. In most cases, one or more instruments were available at home. Formal instrumental lessons started early, at age 4–8 years, usually from a local teacher, remembered by most as a warm and supportive person, who encouraged a relaxed and playful relation to music. Sometimes one of the parents was the first teacher. There were then changes, often several times, to teachers who were musically more advanced. Most parents took an active role in supervising and encouraging the child's progress. This often meant considerable sacrifices in terms of time, money and lifestyle.

The reported amount of practice varied a great deal among individuals. Bastian's (1989) subjects reported practicing between 1 and 7 hours a day; string players practiced for a longer time than wind players. Most of his subjects played one or two instruments other than their main instrument. In the British study, the most able students had not devoted more time to practice than the others, but their practice time was more evenly distributed between a number of instruments. Also the more musically accomplished students tended to come from less actively musical families and tended to have had fewer lessons than the less highly accomplished students. This may seem counterintuitive and was discussed in Sloboda and Howe (1991).

Sosniak distinguished three phases in the development of the concert pianists. After the first phase with mostly playful involvement with music, important for motivation to pursue the matter further, a second phase began between the ages of 10 and 13. This meant a much more systematic study led by an expert teacher, a considerable increase in practice time devoted to developing not only technical skill but also feeling for the expressive qualities of music. The young pianists began performing in recitals and competitions and developing an identification with the field. In the third phase, at age 16–20 years, all pianists were studying with master teachers, who served as admired (and sometimes awed) role models, demanding that virtually all of the pianists' time and energy be invested in working at and thinking about music. The pianists learned to make personal decisions regarding interpretation and expression and successively developed their own ways of working and performing. Their first international achievement occurred between 19 and 31 years of age.

The main features of the three phases described by Sosniak may also be traced in the three-stage developmental framework proposed by Sloboda (1994) and in the results of Manturzewska's (1990) comprehensive interview study concerning the life-span development of 165 professional classical musicians in Poland. The overwhelming majority of musicians came from families with musical tradition, mostly intelligentsia and craftsmen families. There were, however, also examples of musicians coming from nonmusical environments. Lessons began at the age of 5–6 years. Family environment and intrinsic motivation were suggested as the factors most influencing musical development, but teachers, colleagues, and socioemotional support were also important. Six successive and overlapping stages in the lifelong development were discussed, from a first stage of spontaneous musical expression and activity in early life, a second stage with guided musical development (about 6–14 years of age), a third stage involving the formation of the artistic personality, to a fourth stage of professional stabilization. The fifth stage was a teaching phase, and in the sixth stage, there was a successive retirement from professional activity. The first three stages seem similar to those described by Sosniak. The first intense musical experience—listening to a certain piece of music, a certain performer, a certain instrument—may occur during the first stage and often elicits a wish to become a performer; examples of that also appeared in Sosniak (1985c), Howe and Sloboda (1991a), Sloboda and Howe (1991) and were much discussed in Bastian (1989). During the third stage, an ever-deepening "master-student" relationship is crucial. The master teacher becomes a model and a personal guide into various aspects of the musical world as well as into many other matters in life. The period of optimal artistic activity occurred during the fourth stage, roughly at age 25–45 years, followed by the period of the greatest achievement in teaching. Of course, there were many individual exceptions from the data given here.

The role of practice in acquisition of expert performance was stressed in studies by Ericsson and his coworkers. They (Ericsson, Tesch-Römer, & Krampe, 1990; Ericsson, Krampe, & Tesch-Römer, 1993; Krampe, Tesch-Römer, & Ericsson, 1991) compared estimated practice time for three groups of violin students (mean age, 23 years) at the Music Academy of Berlin: a best group, a good group, and a group of students in the department for music teachers. A fourth group consisted of 10 professional violinists (mean age, 50 years) from two symphony orchestras in Berlin. The beginning of lessons occurred at about the age of 8 for all groups, but the accumulated practice time at the age of 18 was about 7400 hr for the best group and for the professional group, 5300 hr for the good group, and 3400 hr for the music teachers' group. The students were also asked to keep a detailed diary of their various activities during 1 week, from which it was evident that the best and good groups practiced almost three times as long as the music teachers did. The mean duration of practice sessions was about 80 min for all groups, but the number of practice sessions was much higher for the two best groups. The members in these groups also slept more, including afternoon naps, than the music teachers, which suggested their need for recovery from the much longer practice time. In another study, expert pianists (students from the Music Academy) were compared with amateur pianists (mean age 24 years in both groups). Lessons started at an average age of 5.8 years for the expert pianists and at 9.9 years for the amateurs. Estimated accumulated practice at the age of 18 was about 7600 hr for the experts and about 1600 hr for the amateurs.

On the basis of these findings and similar findings in many other domains (chess, sports, science), Ericsson et al. (1993) concluded that the main factor behind expert performance is the amount of extended (at least 10 years) and optimally distributed deliberate practice. Deliberate practice means carefully structured activities in order to improve performance and presupposes high motivation and extended effort, full attention during practice (which limits the length of practice sessions and necessitates time for recovery), explicit instructions and individualized supervision by a teacher, knowledge of results, favorable environmental conditions, and parental or other support. The role of innate ability is rejected, but heritable individual differences might influence processes related to motivation and the capacity to engage in hard work. Some of these conclusions may be questioned by musicians and music educators. High-level achievement in music performance may occur with less than 10 years practice; see, for example, Bastian (1989, pp. 139–141).

The investigations in this section show many common results (early start of lessons, different stages, importance of teachers, parental support, etc.) as well as some disagreements (e.g., concerning the amount of practice). Sloboda (1990) cast doubt on four common myths about musical excellence: the myth of precocity (participants in the above studies did not usually show exceptional early promise), the myth of diligence (neglecting motivational factors), the myth of intelligence (there are musically advanced monosavants), and the myth of education (there are eminent musicians, e.g., in jazz, who received little or no formal tuition).

From his study of exceptional young performers, Pruett (1991) concluded that such children feel a need to make music and experience an inner drive to develop their talent. They also demonstrate a capacity to hear and feel something in music that is not possible to describe verbally. Pruett also suggested some measures to counter problems (e.g., isolation from the rest of life, crises, failures, postperformance depression) that may occur in the development of exceptional talents. These questions were also discussed by Bastian (1989).

B. PERSONALITY

Using Cattell's "Sixteen Personality Factor Questionnaire" and another questionnaire, Kemp (1981a, 1981b, 1982a) found a common core of personality traits in musicians (young school musicians, music students and professional musicians), namely introversion, pathemia (sensitivity and imagination), and intelligence. There were additional traits at different levels in the development of musicianship; for example, anxiety takes on more importance as professional life in music is approached. Some differences among performer groups were noted, for example, string players were more introverted than keyboard players and singers, and brass players were less sensitive than other groups. Music teachers appeared to be more extroverted and less sensitive than performers (Kemp, 1982b).

Differences among performer groups, especially regarding string players versus brass players, was also informally investigated and amusingly reported by Davies (1978, Chap. 13): "brass players seem to see themselves as a group of honest, straightforward, no-messing-about, salt-of-the-earth, good blokes," whereas "the string players see themselves as hard-working, conscientious, aesthetic and sensitive individuals" (p. 203). Both descriptions come pretty close to common, stereotyped pictures of brass and string players and find some support in studies on music students (Bell & Cresswell, 1984) and orchestra musicians (Lipton, 1987). Brass players' self-ratings of extroversion were much higher than string players' self-ratings of the same trait (Builione & Lipton, 1983). Davies (1978) and others also discussed a possible relationship between personality traits and the demand characteristics of various musical instruments.

Using the "Eysenck Personality Questionnaire," Cooper and Wills (1989) and G. Wills and Cooper (1988) found elevated scores for neuroticism in popular musicians, which may be related to the above-average anxiety levels in classical musicians found by Kemp. Indications of neuroticism in orchestra musicians was reported by Piperek (1981). In contrast to Kemp's findings for classical musicians, Dyce and O'Connor (1994) found rock and country musicians to be more extroverted than populations norms and also more neurotic. Higher-voiced opera singers seemed more emotional, unreliable, conceited and feminine than lower-voiced singers of the same sex (G. D. Wilson, 1984). In a comparison between performing artists (actors, dancers, classical musicians, singers) actors emerged as extrovert and expressive and musicians as somewhat introverted and unadventurous (Marchant-Haycox & Wilson, (1992).

Using the "Bem Sex-Role Inventory" Kemp (1982c, 1985) found that musicians tend to be less sex-role stereotyped or more androgynous than nonmusicians. Wubbenhorst's (1994) study with the same inventory strongly suggested that both educators and performers share androgyny as a characteristic. Hassler (1990) and Hassler and Nieschlag (1989a, 1989b) also found musicians, especially composers, to be androgynous in psychological as well as in physiological (testosterone levels) meaning. Sex stereotyping of musical instruments and other aspects of the relationship between sex and instruments was studied by Abeles and Porter (1978), Griswold and Chroback (1981), and Zervoudakes and Tanur (1994).

Using the "Myers-Briggs Type Indicator," Gibbons (1991) found that about half of her 110 performing musicians belonged to the IN type, that is, being introverted and intuitive. Within this, the most common type was INFP, meaning introverted, intuitive, feeling (rather than thinking), and perceptive (i.e., spontaneous, curious, adaptable, rather than judging, planning, organizing). Wubbenhorst (1994) also used the Myers-Briggs instrument but found that the modal type for music performers and educators was ENFP, that is, extroversion instead of introversion as in Gibbon's study. This result thus conflicted both with Kemp's and Gibbon's results concerning introversion in musicians and also with Kemp's (1982b) finding of a difference between music teachers and performers in this respect.

These studies show some common results but also some contradictions. The results may depend on which measurement instrument was used, and the general problems with the construction and use of personality inventories should be kept in mind. Furthermore, rather than believing in constant personality traits, it may be more productive to consider possible interactions of traits and situations, for example, that the behavior of a musician may not be the same in musical as in nonmusical situations. For some further discussion of this, see Davies (1978, chapter 13).

From a psychoanalytic perspective, Babikian (1985) argued that development of a strong superego is of utmost importance in bringing about the discipline necessary to attain high performance achievement. He also illustrated, by means of a case study, the negative consequences this may have for other aspects of the individual's functioning. Ostwald (1992) discussed and illustrated performers' relationship to their musical instruments, an often lifelong and intimate relation of great importance for the individual but little discussed in the professional literature.

Recently Brodsky, Sloboda, and Waterman (1994) explored "auditory style" as a cognitive trait. The relationship with sound itself may be a characteristic that differentiates between individuals who become musically gifted and those who do not. A questionnaire was developed that included a variety of characteristics proposed as indicators of auditory style. It was answered by a sample of orchestra musicians and a matched control group of nonmusicians. Factor analysis revealed 12 factors, and 7 of them were significantly different between musicians and nonmusicians. The dominant factor was concerned with an individual's awareness of acute sensitivity to music, beginning already in childhood. The persons scoring high in this factor were aware that their emotional experiences with music were very different from those with speech in ways not amenable to verbal description. They felt drawn to re-experience musical events that had affected them, they felt that there was music in their minds and identified themselves as being special. Other factors concerned sensitivity to the human voice, the emotional nonverbal aspects of speech, hearing as the most vital link to the external environment, and vocal development during adolescence. It was also found that state anxiety was a significant correlate and predictor of high scores in auditory style for musicians but usually not for nonmusicians, and that auditory style was related to performance anxiety (see Section X,D).[3]

C. MUSIC AS OCCUPATION

Orchestra musicians' work comprises concert performance, common and private rehearsals, and assisting in other ensembles, often with irregular schedules that interfere with family life. They also often teach students, albeit they may have no or little training as teachers (Persson, 1994). The intense concentration required during concerts often causes difficulties in sleeping afterwards. Out of 1800 German orchestra musicians, 28% reported sleep disturbances, 52% troubles due to weather changes, and 58% various troubles due to their occupation (Schmale & Schmidtke, 1985). Further stress factors may include fear of making

3. Anthony E. Kemp's book *The Musical Temperament: Psychology and Personality of Musicians* (Oxford: Oxford University Press, 1996) provides a comprehensive and authoritative up-to-date treatment of the personality of musicians.

mistakes, fear of decrease in one's potential as a musician (especially when getting older), being an anonymous member in a collective, tension among orchestra members, incompetent conductors, and no or limited influence on choice of program or conductor (Piperek, 1981; Schmale & Schmidtke, 1985; Schulz, 1981; Steptoe, 1989). Performance anxiety and problems with stand partner were the best predictors of ill health (Bayer, 1982). Among music students, stress (especially due to work outside music), performance anxiety, burnout, progress impatience, and depression were issues of the most concern to them. Musicians' self-esteem is very dependent on their perceived performance skill, in its turn raising high demands on technical perfection (Dews & Williams, 1989). Psychiatric problems among performers are mainly depression and anxiety, various personality disorders, substance abuse disorders, and others; a special case is postperformance depression. Ostwald (1987) and Ostwald and Avery (1991) presented several case studies of such disorders and discussed proper treatments methods (see also Pruett, 1991).

In a comparison among six occupations—freight handlers, aircraft mechanics, air traffic controllers, physicians, waiters, and symphony musicians—symphony musicians and freight handlers had the highest blood pressure at work and the lowest values concerning authority over decisions at work. This result supported the hypothesis that a combination of high demands and low decision latitude may have negative effects on health (Theorell, Ahlberg-Hultén, Sigala, Perski, Söderholm, Kallner, & Eneroth, 1990; see also Steptoe, 1989). The powerlessness of musicians in relation to managers, talentless conductors, crass impresarios, and others is a factor contributing to alienation (Smith & Murphy, 1984). Similar facts appeared in interviews and answers to questionnaires by a large number of popular musicians (Cooper & Wills, 1989; G. Wills & Cooper, 1988) and in a sample of rock musicians (Raeburn, 1987a, 1987b). Popular musicians generally perceived themselves to be highly stressed. Beside performance anxiety, stress factors were work overload, lack of sleep, a great deal of tiring traveling and isolation during tours, conflicts between career and social life, job insecurity, fear of competition from "better" players with accompanying feelings of self-doubt and depression, lack of recognition from the public, conflicts within the band and with managers and record companies, and drug abuse (however, compared with general population norms, popular musicians were not a high-risk group).

However, other reports sound more positive. In a study of job perceptions (Kivimäki & Jokinen, 1994), symphony orchestra musicians rated their opportunity to influence matters concerning their work at about the same level as clerical workers did and higher than industrial workers did. The opportunities to use personal knowledge and skills in their work was considered good by almost all musicians, and although about half of them experienced their work as both physically and mentally strenuous, 90% of them reported high job satisfaction. Steptoe (1989) identified positive factors as the sheer pleasure of playing in an orchestra, the excitement of performing to audiences, variety of the job, and social life in the musical world. A large majority declared that they would choose the same profession again (Schulz, 1981). Smith and Murphy (1984) concluded that there are not extrinsic but intrinsic rewards that keep musicians in their careers. Students' reasons for pursuing music as a career also indicated strong internal motivation (Dews & Williams, 1989). Persson et al. (1992) identified several components in musical performance motivation: hedonic motives (the search for positive emotional experience in playing and listening to music), social motives (obtaining the particular identity of being a musician and meeting other musicians), and various achievement motives.

Orchestra musicians' views concerning conductors were discussed in Faulkner (1973a). Musicians emphasize a conductor's authoritativeness based on competence, further his ability to present a convincing interpretation of the work and to provide clear instructions, verbal and gestural. Faulkner (1973b) also interviewed orchestra musicians about their career concerns and mobility motivations. In any orchestra, there is always a risk of losing one's position to someone below oneself or of getting trapped in a second position. Many strive to advance within the orchestra to the position of section principal or try to move to more highly reputed orchestras. On the other hand, such a move would request much more of one's skills and time, while remaining in one's orchestra may mean less pressure, better opportunities for a private life and perhaps an enjoyable local reputation. Parasuraman and Nachman (1987) had 65 orchestra musicians answer a questionnaire concerning the importance of various factors for orchestra commitment and commitment to the profession. The dominant factors for orchestra commitment were (higher) age and conductor's consideration and support, whereas the main determinants of professional commitment were full-time employment and individuals' ego involvement in the work. Acknowledged stress decreased both types of commitment and engendered strong thoughts about quitting. Organization interventions aimed at reducing stress, improving conductor-musician relationships and strengthening commitment were recommended. Such and many other types of interventions were used by Boalt Boethius and Wrangsjö (1988a, 1988b) in their work as consultants for a symphony orchestra that had severe problems with conflicts between the conductor and orchestra members and between different sections in the orchestra, dissatisfaction with the management regarding choice of programs and lack of forceful decision making, and a tendency of orchestra members to accept other engagements.

Conflict and cooperation, leadership, and group influence in string quartets were discussed by Young and Colman (1979) in relation to findings in research on small groups. Democratic leadership, common goals, and attitude similarity were pointed out as important factors for success. Voyer and Faulkner (1989) combined participant observation and cognitive mapping to study how administrative strategy influenced the cognitions of the musicians in a jazz ensemble. The theoretical and methodological questions discussed in this report are interesting contributions, for example, the way of investigating the relationships among the variables used in the cognitive mapping to see which variables could be considered as "ends" (outcomes), "means" to accomplish the ends, and "givens."[4]

D. PERFORMANCE ANXIETY

Performance anxiety or stage fright is a common problem for musicians. (Performance anxiety is the more general term, because anxiety can occur in off-stage playing as well, although it is usually less pronounced; Fogle, 1982.) In the large survey by Fishbein et al. (1988), stage fright was listed as a problem for 24% of the respondents. Females mentioned it more often than males, and brass musicians more often than other instrumentalists. Among 302 students and faculty at a school of music, 21% reported marked distress and an additional 40% moderate distress due to performance anxiety, women more frequently than men (Wesner, Noyes, & Davis, 1990); more women than men also mentioned negative effects on their career in music, including sometimes avoiding performances. In another study with American music students (Dews & Williams, 1989), nervousness and stage fright before the performance were among the issues of most concern to them, again more for females than for males. In a Swedish study (Gustafson & Rawson, 1983) of 96 professional string players and students, about half of them said that they often experienced performance anxiety, and about 10% said that they always did so. In an English survey (James, cited in G. Wills & Cooper, 1988, p. 21) 60% of the musicians said that anxiety impaired their performance and 12% that it made them lose control. Negative affects on their career in music were also mentioned. In the study by Marchant-Haycox and Wilson (1992) 47% of the musicians reported performance anxiety; the corresponding value for actors, dancers and singers was 33–38%.

Research on the problems connected with performance anxiety has increased considerably in recent years. Comprehensive reviews were provided by Lehrer (1987a, 1987b, 1988) and Salmon (1990).

1. Symptoms

The symptoms of performance anxiety can be physiological, cognitive, and behavioral. Physiological symptoms may be an increase in heart rate and respiration; dry mouth; sweaty palms; excessive tension in hands, fingers, face, and throat; "butterflies in the stomach"; tremors; cold hands; urinary urgency; and still others. Physiological measurements show raised concentrations of adrenaline and noradrenaline in the urine, all indicating activation of the sympathetic branch of the autonomous nervous system. Differences in symptoms that can be related to the demands of different instruments are, for example, higher frequency of dry mouth and shortness of breath in wind players, and cold or sweaty hands and lack

---

4. The social aspects of performance are further treated in Jane W. Davidson's chapter "The Social in Music Performance," appearing in *The Social Psychology of Music* (pp. 209–228), edited by David J. Hargreaves and Adrian C. North (Oxford: Oxford University Press, 1997).

of finger control in string players (Kivimäki and Jokinen, 1994; Wolfe, 1989). Generally, the described physiological phenomena can be seen as the result of the "fight or flight" reflex, which mobilizes the body for attacking or fleeing enemies (Lehrer, 1987a; F. R. Wilson, 1986).

The cognitive (cognitive-emotional) symptoms are a fear of making mistakes; feeling inadequate; worries about one's performance, such as losing physical and expressive control, feeling muscles tightening up, or getting a blackout; worries about the consequences of failure, anticipation of loss of status; negative cognitions about "catastrophizing" (Steptoe & Fidler, 1987); "fear of fear"; loss of concentration; feeling detached from the performance, split up into an observing self and a functioning self (de-personalization); and perceived somatic and autonomous arousal. All may distract the performer from his task and increase the risk of errors. Worries about anxiety, about the reactions of important people, and about distraction in self and audience were identified as separate factors in a factor analysis and were all significantly correlated with measures of trait anxiety and state anxiety (Lehrer, Goldman, & Strommen, 1990).

The behavioral symptoms include trembling bow hands; quivering voice; lifted shoulders; weak and shaky arms; moistening lips; and, of course, errors in performance, in extreme cases, a total breakdown of performance. Performance anxiety tends to deautomatize performance. Automatized behavior is often inhibited or disrupted when the player begins thinking about his or her performance (Fogle, 1982; Green & Gallwey, 1986). Getting rid of such self-interference and attaining a state of relaxed concentration is indeed something to strive for.

The relations between these three categories of symptoms have been much discussed. Do symptoms of performance anxiety appear in all three systems, or may the systems function independently of each other? Craske and Craig (1984) had 20 "relatively anxious" and 20 "relatively nonanxious" piano students perform a piece of 3–5 min alone (but unknowingly recorded on audiotape and videotape) and before an audience presumed to evaluate their performance. Several physiological variables were recorded, and the pianists also completed self-report measures of felt anxiety and confidence in performance. The performances were evaluated on eight scales by professional pianists, and the videotapes were checked for observable indications of performance anxiety. The two groups did not differ in any of the physiological measures, but heart rate increased for both of them in the performance before an audience. The relatively anxious group reported higher experienced anxiety and performed worse than the relatively nonanxious group, and these differences among the groups were larger in the audience situation than in the nonaudience situation. There were only a few significant correlations among all dependent variables, and they belonged to the relatively anxious group in the audience situation. For this group, there was a certain synchrony between behavioral, self-report, and physiological measures. However, in the relatively non-anxious group, performance quality remained stable and self-reports indicated reduced anxiety in the audience situation in spite of increased heart rate. For this group, the three systems seemed largely independent.

Abel and Larkin (1990) investigated the relationship between physiological measures and self-report measures in a baseline condition and immediately before performance in front of a jury. All subjects exhibited increased heart rate, blood pressure, and self-reported anxiety in the jury condition, but the effects differed between the sexes. Males exhibited greater increases in systolic blood pressure than females, but females exhibited higher self-reported anxiety. Furthermore, females reported increased confidence, whereas males did not. Brotons (1994) found increased heart rate and anxiety in students performing before a jury. There was no correlation between these measures, nor with behavioral measures and rated performance quality. Fredrikson and Gunnarsson (1992) had a group of high-anxiety and another group of low-anxiety string players perform music privately and before an audience. Heart rate, neuroendocrine activation (epinephrine, norepinephrine, and cortisol excretion), and ratings of distress increased from private to public performance for both groups, but only the increase in heart rate differentiated between the groups. Both groups had a similar heart rate in private performance, but in public performance the heart rate increased more for the high-anxiety group than for the low-anxiety group. The correlations between the neuroendocrine, heart rate, and distress measures were generally low.

2. Contributing Factors

Factors contributing to performance anxiety are many. Overuse (see Section IX,A) with accompanying physical problems may make one worry about performance as well as fear of illness, not least in singers, who are completely dependent on the condition of their vocal apparatus. Occupational stress may likewise be a factor related to performance anxiety (Steptoe, 1989), although the nature of the relationship is still uncertain. However, the most important factor may be the ever increasing demands on technical perfection in music performance. Demands or expectations from others—parents, teachers, colleagues, critics, the public—or self-imposed demands arising from these people are a frequent cause of tension and feeling of inadequacy. Montello (1992) found that "inner critic," stemming from harsh judgments of parents, teachers and peers, was the most frequently mentioned component of performance anxiety. The anxiety is highest when playing before peers or critics, worse in solo performance than in ensemble performance and worse in small orchestras than in large orchestras (Brotons, 1994; Fishbein et al., 1988; Gustafson & Rawson, 1983; Leglar, 1979). The larger the audience is and the higher status it has, the more nervousness increases, whereas an increasing number of coperformers decreases nervousness as found by Jackson and Latané (1981) in a laboratory experiment and a field study. Their results were taken as support for a combination of a theory of social impact and a theory of embarrassment that predicted the observed effects.

Little research on possible relations to type of personality has been reported. Although Gibbons (1991) found no significant relationship between performance anxiety and personality types, Steptoe and Fidler (1987) found a relationship between performance anxiety and neuroticism and between performance anxiety and everyday fears (fear of crowds and social situations). Positive correlations between performance anxiety and both state and trait anxiety were found by Brodsky et al. (1994) and Lehrer et al. (1990). Brodsky et al. (1994) also found relationships between auditory style (see Section X,B) and performance anxiety. Musicians with the highest total scores in auditory style ("auditives") evidenced higher levels of state anxiety, avoided performances because of performance anxiety, practiced more, had a higher incidence of tendinitis, and received physical and occupational therapy more than musicians with mid or low scores in auditory style.

Nagel (1988, 1990) found some evidence for a relationship between pathology in family and performance anxiety and discussed the possibility that performance anxiety may paradoxically reflect a fear of success, due to parents' resistance towards a musical career, rather than of failure. Psychoanalytic attempts at explanations claim that performance anxiety involves a reactivation of unconscious childhood conflicts, for example, of the separation-individuation crisis that generates separation anxiety (Gabbard, 1979). This thinking often recurred in Montello's (1992) analysis of performers' problems. The participants in her studies had experienced music-related traumas early in life resulting in unresolved conflicts around personal and musical identity, self-esteem, and relationships with significant others (Montello, Coons, & Cantor, 1990). Examples of unconscious influences and developmental issues were also discussed by Plaut (1988).

Available information on the influence of age and increased experience of performance is somewhat inconclusive. Data in Steptoe and Fidler (1987) suggest that performance anxiety may decrease, whereas other studies indicate that it remains or even increases (Wesner et al., 1990) or peaks at the age of 35–45 years (Fishbein et al., 1988). Many famous musicians such as Horowitz, Paderewski, Rubinstein, and Casals discussed their performance anxiety (Brantigan, Brantigan, & Joseph, 1982; Plaut, 1988; Sweeney & Horan, 1982). Kreisler seemed totally free of it (Havas, 1973). As the performer's reputation grows, expectations of his performance also grow, thus generating constant pressure to maintain or heighten one's standard. How one masters performance anxiety may affect one's self-concept (Triplett, 1983, cited in Gibbons, 1991). Defeating stage fright makes a winner. Losing the battle may result in lowered self-esteem and negative self-image.

3. Reactive, Adaptive, and Maladaptive Anxiety

Sweeney and Horan (1982) made a distinction between reactive, adaptive, and maladaptive anxiety. Reactive anxiety refers to anxiety resulting from inadequate preparation of performance. Thus increased training is required. "No psychological technique can substitute for proper artistic preparation" (Lehrer, 1987a, p. 145). Adaptive anxiety means that a certain amount of stress may in fact improve performance, because the relationship between anxiety and performance is curvilinear (an inverted U), as stated in the classic Yerkes-Dodson law. In the survey by James (cited in G. Wills & Cooper, 1988, p. 21), 15% of the musicians said that nervousness improved their performance, and Gates and Montalbo (1987) claimed that a certain amount of tension is desirable. Steptoe (1983) obtained evidence for the inverted U pattern relating emotional tension and performance with the best performance appearing at moderate levels of tension. This level was higher for professional musicians than for music students. The level that is optimal for performance may vary depending on personality traits such as introversion and trait anxiety, as well as on the individual's cognitive interpretation of the physiological arousal—for example, if it is interpreted as a sign of collapse or as inevitable and even necessary precursors to good performance (Salmon, 1990, 1991). The adaptive and maladaptive aspects of performance anxiety were also identified in a factor analytic study and related to various coping strategies reported by musicians (Wolfe, 1989, 1990).

Hamann (1982, 1985; Hamann & Sobaje, 1983) argued, referring to drive theory and Spielberger's trait-state anxiety theory, that individuals with high trait anxiety will experience a greater increase in state anxiety than individuals with low trait anxiety (see also Steptoe, 1983). Furthermore, individuals with high trait anxiety and high performance skill will benefit from increased anxiety, whereas individuals with high trait anxiety and low performance skill will not do so. Anxiety may have motivational properties, which can increase levels of performance for subjects depending on the degree of their task mastery. Hamann suggested that, rather than using anxiety reduction techniques, one should increase the formal study period. Lehrer (1987a) suggested that giving many frequent performances would be an effective treatment for stage fright, whereas widely spaced exposure to anxiety-producing situations may result in increased anxiety.

4. Coping Strategies

Musicians themselves report a large variety of coping strategies, such as careful preparation, relaxation, deep breathing, meditation, self-hypnosis, positive self-talk, being well rested, imagining the performance situation beforehand, thinking of the performance as communicating with the audience, further use of alcohol or beta-blockers (Gustafson & Rawson, 1983; Lehrer et al., 1990; Steptoe, 1989; Steptoe & Fidler, 1987; Wesner et al., 1990; Wolfe, 1990).

a. Beta-Blockers

Many musicians use beta-blockers. In the survey of American orchestra musicians (Fishbein et al., 1988), 27% of the musicians reported use of beta-blockers, most of them without a doctor's prescription. They were most likely used before auditions, solo recitals, difficult orchestral performances, and concert performances. Four percent took beta-blockers before every performance. Practically all musicians who occasionally used beta-blockers reported that it reduced performance anxiety. In the study by Gustafson and Rawson (1983), about 25% of the professional violinists and students reported using beta-blockers.

Lehrer, Rosen, Kostis, and Greenfield (1987) described various types of beta-blockers (see also Brandfonbrener, 1990) and reviewed studies of their effects. Only a small number of these studies referred to use in music settings, among them Brantigan et al. (1982), James and Savage (1984), and Neftel, Adler,

Käppeli, Rossi, Dolder, Käser, Bruggesser, and Vorkauf (1982). Lehrer et al. concluded that, when used at a single music performance, beta-blockers may produce marked decreases in most physiological and some cognitive manifestations of stage fright and have some positive effects on performance quality. On the other hand, there is no knowledge of the effects of repeated use of beta-blockers, and there are some indications that beta-blockers may diminish the emotional intensity of a performance or have other negative effects. Gates and Montalbo (1987) and Gates, Johnson, Saegert, Shepherd, Wilson, and Hearne (1985) reported no or minimal helpful effect of beta-blockers on singing performance. High doses had adverse effects.

In proposing guidelines for use of beta-blockers, Lehrer et al. (1987) adopted a very restrictive position to its use with performers, pointing out risks of side effects, psychological dependence, and other negative consequences. They suggested psychological techniques for managing stage fright. It is important that beta-blockers be used under medical supervision (see also Norris, 1993). Nubé (1991) concluded that because of differences in testing procedures and the variety of drugs and dosages used in different studies, there is at present only a very obscure picture of the drugs' effects on musicians. Some evidence of effects on pianists' performance was given in Nubé (1994).

b. Psychological Techniques

Studies on different psychological techniques for reducing performance anxiety usually involve a pretest-treatment-posttest design, sometimes also a follow-up test at a later time. The subjects are as a rule musicians or music students troubled by performance anxiety. They form one or more experimental groups that receive training according to one or more methods. A control group, receiving no training, is used for comparison. The tests mean some kind of performance situation before an audience. The measures may involve (a) physiological variables, such as heart rate, blood pressure, respiration, and finger temperature, (b) experiential-cognitive variables, such as measures of trait anxiety and state anxiety, of confidence as performer, and self-reports, and (c) behavioral variables such as evaluations of performances and visual signs of anxiety. The measures and the procedural details differ among studies, which make comparisons difficult. The crucial test is to see whether there is a difference between pretest and posttest in the desired direction.

A variety of psychological techniques are used. Systematic desensitization—unlearning of anxiety responses by pairing anxiety evoking situations, imagined or "in vivo," with a stronger competing response achieved through deep muscle relaxation—was found effective in several studies (Appel, 1976; Lund, 1972; Wardle, 1975). Appel found systematic desensitization more effective than training in music analysis and performance rehearsal techniques, which in their turn were better than no training at all. However, in Lund's and Wardle's studies an "insight" technique—a rational discussion concerning causes and the inappropriateness of performance anxiety—proved equally efficient. Whitaker (1985) combined muscle relaxation and cognitive-behavioral techniques and obtained decreased physiological response and decreased state anxiety, as well as increased confidence as performer, in her pianist subjects. Norton, MacLean, and Wachna (1978) described a case study in which a pianist overcame stage fright using deep muscle relaxation combined with positive self-statements and cognitive desensitization. The client imagined threatening scenes, such as forgetting the music or even panicking, and how to overcome them (coping imagery).

In a careful study on 53 pianists, Kendrick, Craig, Lawson, and Davidson (1982) found that cognitive-behavioral therapy, challenging negative thoughts and attending only to task-oriented and positive thoughts, and behavior rehearsals before a friendly audience were both effective in reducing performance anxiety as measured in a follow-up test 5 weeks later. The cognitive therapy was more effective than the behavior-rehearsal program on several measures. However, the anxiety may return later. Craske and Rachman (1987) had 63 music students, divided into subgroups according to their initial heart rate and perceived skill, go through a cognitive-behavioral treatment supplemented with progressive muscle relaxation. This resulted in a reduction of subjective fear, reduced heart rate in high-heart-rate subjects, and improved performance quality. However, in a follow-up 3 months later, a return of the fear was found in the subjects who belonged to the high-heart-rate group, regardless of their perceived skill.

Tobacyk and Downs (1986) pointed out that experienced anxiety can be predicted from the person's irrational or inadequate conceptualization of the performance situation and its consequences, referring to Kelly's Personal Construct Theory and Ellis's Theory of Rational Emotive Therapy. Stanton (1993) reported reduced performance anxiety following a treatment that combined a first session with "success imagery" and a second session with positive suggestions (substituted for irrational ideas according to rational emotive therapy) to hypnotized patients.

In a study with piano students, Nagel, Himle, and Papsdorf (1989) used a cognitive-behavioral treatment combined with progressive muscle relaxation and temperature biofeedback training. Reductions were observed in performance anxiety, trait anxiety, and test anxiety. Reduced anxiety in music students was reported by Niemann, Pratt, and Maughan (1993) using a combination of EMG and skin temperature biofeedback training, selected coping strategies (breathing awareness, muscle relaxation, and performance-coping imagery), and music relaxation.

Sweeney and Horan (1982), in accordance with their distinction between reactive, adaptive, and maladaptive anxiety, exclusively used pianists with maladaptive anxiety and tried cue-controlled relaxation (muscle relaxation triggered by a cue word), cognitive restructuring (self-statements designed to facilitate task attention and diminish debilitating anxiety), cue-controlled relaxation and cognitive restructuring combined, and music analysis training. Both cue-controlled relaxation and cognitive restructuring as well as cue-controlled relaxation plus cognitive restructuring proved effective in reducing state anxiety, whereas music analysis training had no effect on these subjects. The implication is that music analysis training may be positive only regarding reactive and adaptive performance anxiety. Harris (1987) reported positive results using a combination of cognitive self-instruction, relaxation training, imagery, and behavior rehearsal.

Performance anxiety often peaks just before performance and may also appear well before the performance. This type of anticipatory anxiety provides a possibility to practice coping in advance, which may aid mastering the critical situation later (Salmon, Schrodt, & Wright, 1989). In so-called stress inoculation, the individual imagines the stressful situation in detail, which is followed by either adequate preparatory activity or visualization of effective coping behavior. The coping responses are implemented under circumstances of progressively increasing psychological pressure (Salmon, 1990, 1991).

The use of group music therapy for treatment of performance anxiety was studied by Montello (1992; Montello et al., 1990). The sessions were structured into relaxation and breathing exercises, an unstructured group musical improvisation and verbal free associations of the improvisation, followed by therapeutic interventions— role playing, instrumental or vocal self statements, "reality rehearsal" performances, and guided imagery exercises. The results showed reductions in anxiety and self-involvement, increased confidence in performance and improved performance. A qualitative analysis of the participants' descriptions provided important insights about the factors behind performance anxiety; for example, the subjects seemed to be "more concerned with their own inner needs and projections … than with the goal of communicating music to the audience" (Montello, 1992, p. 294).

As seen in the just-described studies, the treatment as a rule included a combination of many techniques. Fogle (1982) argued for a multifaceted treatment of performance anxiety in mutual collaboration with insightful music educators. He suggested an analysis of possible performance goals, which may help the performer to realize which goals have been prevalent in earlier performances and which ones would be desirable for future performances. A "second-best plan" may allow the performer to continue toward long-range personal goals in spite of any anticipated disaster.

There are several texts on music performance anxiety by experienced and insightful musicians, such as Green and Gallwey (1986), Grindea (1987a, 1987b), Havas (1973, 1987), and Reubart (1985). These authors know the problems from inside and offer many valuable experiences as well as suggestions regarding strategies and exercises to reduce performance anxiety. Although relating to psychological techniques, they stay close to the musician's reality and are easier reading for performing musicians than scientific articles. Havas concentrated on violin playing, and Grindea and Reubart on piano performance. Havas emphasized that the best way of minimizing self-conscious performance is to concentrate on the goal of communicating or giving pleasure to the audience—in the way the Hungarian gypsy violinist does—and to consider music making as a creative act, "giving," and not a technical accomplishment for the purpose of demonstrating the performer's skills. F. R. Wilson (1986) expressed similar ideas. Wolverton and Salmon (1991) found that high-anxiety performers were more self-focused and less music-focused than low-anxiety performers, and that performers primarily motivated by a desire for audience approval showed higher anxiety levels than performers motivated by a desire to become involved by the music itself.

XI. PERFORMANCE EVALUATION

Evaluation of performances was included in many studies reviewed earlier, for example, in studies of sight-reading ability and studies about treatment of performance anxiety. Evaluation occurs in the everyday activity of music critics, music teachers, and musicians. However, there are hardly any agreed-upon criteria, neither for what should be judged nor for how the judgments should be made.

A distinction can be made between global or overall evaluation and evaluation of specific aspects in performance (Boyle, 1992; Boyle & Radocy, 1987). Examples of the latter are intonation, tone quality, tempo, rhythm, dynamics, articulation, phrasing, bowing, and breathing. An overall evaluation can be considered as a weighted function of the evaluations in the specific aspects. The weighting of different aspects may differ between different judges resulting in different overall evaluations, even if they made similar ratings in the specific aspects. On the other hand, if two judges give the same overall evaluation, this does not necessarily mean that they have made the same judgments in all specific aspects.

The Watkins-Farnum Performance Scale for wind instruments and snare drum and the Farnum String Scale require sight-reading performances of exercises of ever-increasing difficulty. Errors may be pitch errors, time errors, slur errors, expression errors, and others. The scoring unit is the notated measure. See further in Boyle (1992), Boyle and Radocy (1987, chapter 8), and Zdzinski (1991). These authors also discussed the use of various psychometric techniques for judgment of performance, such as Likert scales, rank ordering, paired comparisons, successive intervals, magnitude estimation, and semantic differentials.

A useful approach is facet-factorial rating scales (Zdzinski, 1991), that is, a construction of rating scales based on factor analysis. Abeles (1973) used this for developing a rating scale for clarinet performance. A large number of statements about clarinet performance were collected and transformed to items to be used for ratings of 100 recorded clarinet performances. Fifty music teachers rated these on each of 94 items. Factor analysis of the ratings resulted in six factors interpreted as intonation, rhythm continuity, tempo, articulation, tone quality, and interpretation. Thirty items with high factor loadings in the respective factors were selected for constructing a Clarinet Performance Rating Scale. This was in its turn used for ratings of other performances, and these ratings were again factor analyzed to see that the factor structure was stable. The same technique was used with regard to euphonium and tuba music performance (Bergee, 1993) and for choral music performance (Cooksey, 1977); other examples appeared in Boyle (1992) and Zdzinski (1991).

A less formal approach was used by D. Elliott (1987) in a small-scale study where three professional adjudicators assessed six solo performances that were also rated by the performers themselves. The judgments were made in terms of individual comments and rank orders and showed good agreement between judges. Repp (1990c) used bipolar adjective scales for judging performances of a Beethoven minuet. McPherson (1993) proposed rating scales for evaluation of improvised performances. Namba and Kuwano (1990) and Namba, Kuwano, Hatoh, and Kato (1991) investigated the use of continuous judgments of the sounding music. Fifteen adjectives were selected on the basis of a preliminary study in which listeners described their impressions of different performances of Mussorgsky's *Pictures at an Exhibition*. Each adjective was assigned a key on a computer keyboard. While listening to the music, the subjects successively pressed the different keys according to how well the respective adjectives described their impression as the music went on. The frequency with which each adjective was used during the course of the performance was calculated and displayed in graphs, thus providing a continuous multiadjective scaling. The results were discussed in relation to the overall impression of the performances and to possible physical parameters.

Studies on the reliability of performance judgments indicated that judge reliability bore no relation to performing ability (Fiske, 1977); faculty and peers' interjudge reliability was high and in agreement, but self-evaluations correlated poorly with faculty and peer evaluations (Bergee, 1993); use of the musical score did not increase the consistency of preference judgments (Wapnick, Flowers, Alegant & Jasinskas, 1993). McPherson (1995) obtained high between-judge correlations in scaling of clarinet and trumpet students' abilities to play from memory, to play by ear, and to improvise. These three abilities were intercorrelated and also correlated with sight-reading ability and ability to perform rehearsed music. The correlations were higher for his older students (ages 15 to 18) than for the younger students (ages 12 to 15).

Judgments may be affected or biased by listeners' expectations. Duerksen (1972) found that students rated technical and musical characteristics of a recorded piano performance lower when told that the performer was a student than they did when told it was by a famous pianist (see also Radocy, 1976). Musicians playing a jazz composition attributed to a low-credibility composer made more errors than when musicians played the same composition attributed to a high-credibility composer; however, the difference disappeared on a second play (Weick, Gilfillan, & Keith, 1973). The visual impressions of the performer may play a considerable role (Boyle & Radocy, 1987). Liszt's magnificent posture at the piano and Paganini's demonic appearance are well-known historical examples (Sachs, 1982). Farnsworth (1969, p. 57) suggested that the alleged "coldness" of

Heifetz's violin performance may be due to the visual effects of his stiff posture and lack of facial expression.

Some attempts have been made to predict evaluation of music performances from the physical characteristics of the performances. Campbell (1971) studied the possibility of using objective measures of each tone in singing—measures such as the initial pitch, middle pitch, final pitch, sound power level, duration of tone, and duration of break or glissando between tones—as predictors of performance quality. Seven competent judges' evaluations regarding intonation, vibrato, rhythm, dynamics, and overall performance served as criterion measure. The idea was that acoustical data could be used to "simulate" judgments by human listeners. Further examples of acoustical and computer-assisted measurements in relation to performance evaluation were reviewed by Zdzinski (1991).

ACKNOWLEDGMENTS

The author wishes to express his gratitude to many colleagues around the world for providing reprints and other material, to Emily Holmes for checking the English, and to Stojan Kaladjev, Siv Lindström, and Siv Vedung for much valuable assistance.

REFERENCES

Abel, J. L., & Larkin, K. T. (1990). Anticipation of performance among musicians: Physiological arousal, confidence, and state-anxiety. *Psychology of Music, 18,* 171–182.

Abeles, H. F. (1973). Development and validation of a clarinet performance adjudication scale. *Journal of Research in Music Education, 21,* 246–255.

Abeles, H. F., & Porter, S. Y. (1978). The sex-stereotyping of musical instruments. *Journal of Research in Music Education, 26,* 65–75.

Andreas, R. (1993). Improvisation. In H. Bruhn, R. Oerter, & H. Rösing (Eds.), *Musikpsychologie: Ein Handbuch* (pp. 506 –514). Reinbek bei Hamburg: Rowohlt Taschenbuch Verlag.

Appel, S. S. (1976). Modifying solo performance anxiety in adult pianists. *Journal of Music Therapy, 13,* 2–16.

Askenfelt, A. (1986). Measurement of bow motion and bow force in violin playing. *Journal of the Acoustical Society of America, 80,* 1007–1015.

Askenfelt, A., & Jansson, E. V. (1992). On vibration sensation and finger touch in stringed instrument playing. *Music Perception, 9,* 311–349.

Axelsson, A., & Lindgren, F. (1977). Factors increasing the risk for hearing loss in 'pop' musicians. *Scandinavian Audiology, 6,* 127–131.

Axelsson, A., & Lindgren, F. (1978). Hearing in pop musicians. *Acta Oto-Laryngologica, 85,* 225–231.

Axelsson, A., & Lindgren, F. (1981). Hearing in classical musicians. *Acta Oto-Laryngologica,* Supplement 377, 3–74.

Babikian, H. M. (1985). The psychoanalytic treatment of the performing artist: Superego aspects. *Journal of the American Academy of Psychoanalysis, 13*(1), 139–148.

Baily, J. (1985). Music structure and human movement. In P. Howell, I. Cross, & R. West (Eds.), *Musical structure and cognition* (pp. 237–258). London: Academic Press.

Baily, J. (1990). The role of motor grammar in musical performance. In F. R. Wilson & F. L. Roehmann (Eds.), *Music and child development: Proceedings of the 1987 Denver Conference* (pp. 202–213). St. Louis, Missouri: MMB Music.

Baily, J. (1991). Some cognitive aspects of motor planning in musical performance. *Psychologica Belgica, 31*, 147–162.

Banton, L. J. (1995). The role of visual and auditory feedback during the sight-reading of music. *Psychology of Music, 23*, 3–16.

Barry, N. H. (1992). The effects of practice strategies, individual differences in cognitive style, and gender upon technical accuracy and musicality of student instrumental performance. *Psychology of Music, 20*, 112–123.

Bastian, H. G. (1989). *Leben für Musik. Eine Biographie-Studie über musikalische (Hoch-)Begabungen.* Mainz: Schott.

Bastien, D. T., & Hostager, T. J. (1988). Jazz as a process of organizational innovation. *Communication Research, 15*, 582–602.

Battel, G. U., & Bresin, R. (1994). Analysis by synthesis in piano performance: A study on the theme of the Brahms' "Variations on a theme by Paganini" op. 35. In A. Friberg, J. Iwarsson, E. Jansson, & J. Sundberg (Eds.), *Proceedings of the Stockholm Music Acoustics Conference, July 1993* (pp. 69–73). Stockholm: Publications issued by the Royal Swedish Academy of Music, No. 79.

Bayer, L. R. (1982). The stress process in professional musicians: An exploratory study. *Dissertation Abstracts International, 43*, 1605B.

Bean, K. L. (1938). An experimental approach to the reading of music. *Psychological Monographs, 50*(6), No. 226, 1–80.

Becking, G. (1928). *Der musikalische Rhythmus als Erkenntnisquelle.* Augsburg: Benno Filser.

Behne, K. E., & Wetekam, B. (1993). Musikpsychologische Interpretationsforschung: Individualität und Intention. *Musikpsychologie. Jahrbuch der Deutschen Gesellschaft für Musikpsychologie, 10*, 24–37.

Bejjani, F. J., Ferrara, L., & Pavlidis, L. (1989). A comparative electromyographic and acoustic analysis of violin vibrato in healthy professional violinists. *Medical Problems of Performing Artists, 4*, 168–175.

Bell, C. R., & Cresswell, A. (1984). Personality differences among musical instrumentalists. *Psychology of Music, 12*, 83–93.

Bengtsson. I. (1974). Empirische Rhythmusforschung in Uppsala. *Hamburger Jahrbuch für Musikwissenschaft, 1*, 195–219.

Bengtsson, I. (1987). Notation, motion and perception: Some aspects of musical rhythm. In A. Gabrielsson (Ed.), *Action and perception in rhythm and music* (pp. 69–80). Stockholm: Publications issued by the Royal Swedish Academy of Music, No. 55.

Bengtsson, I., & Gabrielsson, A. (1977). Rhythm research in Uppsala. In *Music, room, acoustics* (pp. 19–56). Stockholm: Publications issued by the Royal Swedish Academy of Music, No. 17.

Bengtsson, I., & Gabrielsson, A. (1980). Methods for analyzing performance of musical rhythm. *Scandinavian Journal of Psychology, 21*, 257–268.

Bengtsson, I., & Gabrielsson, A. (1983). Analysis and synthesis of musical rhythm. In J. Sundberg (Ed.), *Studies of music performance* (pp. 27–59). Stockholm: Publications issued by the Royal Swedish Academy of Music, No. 39.

Bengtsson, I., Gabrielsson, A., & Thorsén, S. M. (1969). Empirisk rytmforskning [Empirical rhythm research]. *Swedish Journal of Musicology, 51*, 49–118.

Bergee, M. J. (1993). A comparison of faculty, peer, and self-evaluation of applied brass jury performances. *Journal of Research in Music Education, 41*, 19–27.

Binet, A., & Courtier, J. (1895). Recherches graphiques sur la musique. *L'Année Psychologique, 2*, 201–222.

Bird, E. I., & Wilson, V. E. (1988). The effects of physical practice upon psychophysiological response during mental rehearsal of novice conductors. *Journal of Mental Imagery, 12*, 51–64.

Blau, J. N., & Henson, R. A. (1977). Neurological disorders in performing musicians. In M. Critchley & R. A. Henson (Eds.), *Music and the brain: Studies in the neurology of music* (pp. 301–322). London: William Heinemann Medical Books.

Blum, J. (1995). Häufigkeit, Ursachen und Risikofaktoren berufsspezifischer Erkrankungen bei Musikern. In C. Wagner (Ed.), *Medizinische Probleme bei Instrumentalisten: Ursachen und Prävention* (pp. 15–29). Laaber: Laaber-Verlag.

Boalt Boethius, S., & Wrangsjö, B. (1988a). Managing art: A case study of a symphony orchestra. In F. Gabelnick and A. W. Carr (Eds.), *Contributions to social and political science: Proceedings of the First International Symposium on Group Relations, Keble College, Oxford July 15–18, 1988* (pp. 129–145). Oxford: Oxford International Symposium Proceedings.

Boalt Boethius, S., & Wrangsjö, B. (1988b). Management der Kunst: Organisationsentwicklung in einem Symphonieorchester. *Zeitschrift der Gesellschaft für Organisationsentwicklung, 7*(3), 55–74.

Boomsliter, P. C., & Creel, W. (1963). Extended reference: An unrecognized dynamic in melody. *Journal of Music Theory, 7*, 2–22.

Boyle, J. D. (1992). Evaluation of music ability. In R. Colwell (Ed.), *Handbook of research on music teaching and learning* (pp. 247–265). New York: Schirmer.

Boyle, J. D., & Radocy, R. R. (1987). *Measurement and evaluation of musical experiences.* New York: Schirmer Books.

Brandfonbrener, A. G. (1990). Beta blockers in the treatment of performance anxiety. *Medical Problems of Performing Artists, 5*, 23–26.

Brantigan, C. O., Brantigan, T. A., & Joseph, N. (1982). Effect of beta blockade and beta stimulation on stage fright. *American Journal of Medicine, 72*, 88–94.

Bregman, A. S., & Dannenbring, G. L. (1973). The effect of continuity on auditory stream segregation. *Perception & Psychophysics, 13*, 308–312.

Brodsky, W., Sloboda, J. A., & Waterman, M. G. (1994). An exploratory investigation into auditory style as a correlate and predictor of music performance anxiety. *Medical Problems of Performing Artists, 9*, 101–112.

Brotons, M. (1994). Effects of performing conditions on music performance anxiety and performance quality. *Journal of Music Therapy, 31*, 63–81.

Brown, S. F. (1991). Determination of location of pitch within a musical vibrato. *Bulletin of the Council for Research in Music Education, No. 108*, 15–30.

Bruhn, H., Oerter, R., & Rösing, H. (Eds.). (1993). *Musikpsychologie. Ein Handbuch.* Reinbek bei Hamburg: Rowohlt Taschenbuch Verlag.

Bruscia, K. E. (1987). *Improvisational models of music therapy.* Springfield, IL: Charles C Thomas.

Bruscia, K. E. (1988). A survey of treatment procedures in improvisational music therapy. *Psychology of Music, 16*, 10–24.

Builione, R. S., & Lipton, J. P. (1983). Stereotypes and personality of classical musicians. *Psychomusicology, 3*(1), 36–43.

Camp, J. E., & Horstman, S. W. (1992). Musician sound exposure during performance of Wagner's Ring cycle. *Medical Problems of Performing Artists, 7*, 37–39.

Campbell, W. C. (1971). A computer simulation of musical performance adjudication. In E. Gordon (Ed.), *Experimental research in the psychology of music: 7* (pp. 1–40). Iowa City: University of Iowa Press.

Carlson, R., Friberg, A., Frydén, L., Granström, B., & Sundberg, J. (1989). Speech and music performance: Parallels and contrasts. *Contemporary Music Review, 4*, 391–404.

Castellengo, M. (1994). Fusion or separation: From vibrato to vocal trill. In A. Friberg, J. Iwarsson, E. Jansson, & J. Sundberg (Eds.), *Proceedings of the Stockholm Music Acoustics Conference, July 1993* (pp. 79–83). Stockholm: Publications issued by the Royal Swedish Academy of Music, No. 79.

Chasin, M., & Chong, J. (1992). A clinically efficient hearing protection program for musicians. *Medical Problems of Performing Artists, 7*, 40–43.

Chumaceiro, C. L. D. de (1991). Sigmund Freud: On pianists' performance problems. *Medical Problems of Performing Artists, 6*, 21–27.

Clarke, E. F. (1982). Timing in the performance of Erik Satie's 'Vexations'. *Acta Psychologica, 50*, 1–19.

Clarke, E. F. (1985a). Some aspects of rhythm and expression in performances of Erik Satie's "Gnossienne No. 5." *Music Perception, 2,* 299–328.

Clarke, E. F. (1985b). Structure and expression in rhythmic performance. In P. Howell, I. Cross, & R. West (Eds.), *Musical structure and cognition* (pp. 209–236). London: Academic Press.

Clarke, E. F. (1987). Categorical rhythm perception: An ecological perspective. In A. Gabrielsson (Ed.), *Action and perception in rhythm and music* (pp. 19–33). Stockholm: Publications issued by the Royal Swedish Academy of Music, No. 55.

Clarke, E. F. (1988). Generative principles in music performance. In J. A. Sloboda (Ed.), *Generative processes in music: The psychology of performance, improvisation, and composition* (pp. 1–26). Oxford: Clarendon Press.

Clarke, E. F. (1989a). What is conveyed by the expressive aspect of musical performance? *Musikpsychologie. Jahrbuch der Deutschen Gesellschaft für Musikpsychologie, 6,* 7–21.

Clarke, E. F. (1989b). The perception of expressive timing in music. *Psychological Research, 51,* 2–9.

Clarke, E. F. (1991). Expression and communication in musical performance. In J. Sundberg, L. Nord, & R. Carlson (Eds.), *Music, language, speech and brain* (pp. 184–193). London: MacMillan Press.

Clarke, E. F. (1992). Improvisation, cognition and education. In J. Paynter, T. Howell, R. Orton, & P. Seymour (Eds.), *Companion to contemporary musical thought* (pp. 787–802). London: Routledge.

Clarke, E. F. (1993a). Imitating and evaluating real and transformed musical performances. *Music Perception, 10,* 317–341.

Clarke, E. F. (1993b). Generativity, mimesis and the human body in music performance. *Contemporary Music Review, 9,* 207–219.

Clarke, E. F., & Baker-Short, C. (1987). The imitation of perceived rubato: A preliminary study. *Psychology of Music, 15,* 58–75.

Clynes, M. (1977). *Sentics: The touch of emotions.* New York: Anchor Press/Doubleday.

Clynes, M. (1983). Expressive microstructure in music, linked to living qualities. In J. Sundberg (Ed.), *Studies of music performance* (pp. 76–181). Stockholm: Publications issued by the Royal Swedish Academy of Music, No. 39.

Clynes, M. (1985). Secrets of life in music. In *Analytica: Studies in the description and analysis of music in honour of Ingmar Bengtsson* (pp. 3–15). Stockholm: Publications issued by the Royal Swedish Academy of Music, No. 47.

Clynes, M. (1986a). When time is music. In J. R. Evans & M. Clynes (Eds.), *Rhythm in psychological, linguistic and musical processes* (pp. 169–224). Springfield, IL: Charles C Thomas.

Clynes, M. (1986b). Generative principles of musical thought. Integration of microstructure with structure. *Communication and Cognition AI, 3,* 185–223.

Clynes, M. (1987). What can a musician learn about music performance from newly discovered microstructure principles (PM and PAS)? In A. Gabrielsson (Ed.), *Action and perception in rhythm and music* (pp. 201–233). Stockholm: Publications issued by the Royal Swedish Academy of Music, No. 55.

Clynes, M. (1990). Some guidelines for the synthesis and testing of pulse microstructure in relation to musical meaning. *Music Perception, 7,* 403–422.

Clynes, M. (1994). Comments on "Patterns of expressive timing in performances of a Beethoven minuet by nineteen famous pianists." *Journal of the Acoustical Society of America, 96,* 1174–1178.

Clynes, M. (1995). Microstructural musical linguistics: composers' pulses are liked most by the best musicians. *Cognition, 55,* 269–310.

Clynes, M., & Walker, J. (1982). Neurobiologic functions of rhythm, time and pulse in music. In M. Clynes (Ed.), *Music, mind, and brain: The neuropsychology of music* (pp. 171–216). New York: Plenum Press.

Clynes, M., & Walker, J. (1986). Music as time's measure. *Music Perception, 4,* 85–120.

Coffman, D. D. (1990). Effects of mental practice, physical practice, and knowledge of results on piano performance. *Journal of Research in Music Education, 38,* 187–196.

Collier, G. L., & Collier, J. L. (1994). An exploration of the use of tempo in jazz. *Music Perception, 11,* 219–242.

Colwell, R. (Ed.) (1992). *Handbook of research on music teaching and learning.* New York: Schirmer.

Cook, N. (1987). Structure and performance timing in Bach's C major prelude (WTC I): An empirical study. *Music Analysis, 6*(3), 257–272.

Cooksey, J. M. (1977). A facet-factorial approach to rating high school choral music performance. *Journal of Research in Music Education, 25,* 100–114.

Cooper, C. L. & Wills, G. I. D. (1989). Popular musicians under pressure. *Psychology of Music, 17,* 22–36.

Corso, J. F., & Lewis, D. (1950). Preferred rate and extent of the frequency vibrato. *Journal of Applied Psychology, 34,* 206–212.

Cox, J. (1989). Rehearsal organizational structures used by successful high school choral directors. *Journal of Research in Music Education, 37,* 201–218.

Craske, M. G., & Craig, K. D. (1984). Musical performance anxiety: The three-systems model and self-efficacy theory. *Behavior Research and Therapy, 22,* 267–280.

Craske, M. G., & Rachman, S. J. (1987). Return of fear: Perceived skill and heart-rate responsivity. *British Journal of Clinical Psychology, 26,* 187–199.

Critchley, M. (1977). Occupational palsies in musical performers. In M. Critchley & R. A. Henson (Eds.), *Music and the brain: Studies in the neurology of music* (pp. 365–377). London: William Heinemann Medical Books.

Cutietta, R. (1986). Biofeedback training in music: From experimental to clinical applications. *Bulletin of the Council for Research in Music Education,* No. 87, 35–42.

Cutietta, R. A., Klich, R. J., Royse, D., & Rainbolt, H. (1994). The incidence of noise-induced hearing loss among music teachers. *Journal of Research in Music Education, 42,* 318–330.

Davidson, J. W. (1993). Visual perception of performance manner in the movements of solo musicians. *Psychology of Music, 21,* 103–113.

Davidson, J. W. (1994). Which areas of a pianist's body convey information about expressive intention to an audience? *Journal of Human Movement Studies, 26,* 279–301.

Davidson, J. W. (1995). What does the visual information contained in music performances offer the observer? Some preliminary thoughts. In R. Steinberg (Ed.), *Music and the mind machine: The psychophysiology and psychopathology of the sense of music* (pp. 105–113). Berlin, Heidelberg, New York: Springer-Verlag.

Davies, J. B. (1978). *The psychology of music.* London: Hutchinson.

Davies, J. B., Kenny, P., & Barbenel, J. (1989). A psychological investigation of the role of mouthpiece force in trumpet performance. *Psychology of Music, 17,* 48–62.

Dawley, R. M. (1985). Medical research in music: Foundation for a theory of music instruction. *Bulletin of the Council for Research in Music Education,* No. 85, 38–55.

Deecke, L. (1995). Motor cortical fields and rhythmic coordination of the hands in music performance. In R. Steinberg (Ed.), *Music and the mind machine: The psychophysiology and psychopathology of the sense of music* (pp. 225–241). Berlin, Heidelberg, New York: Springer-Verlag.

Desain, P., & Honing, H. (1994). Does expressive timing in music performance scale proportionally with tempo? *Psychological Research, 56,* 285–292.

Desain, P., & de Vos, S. (1992). Autocorrelation and the study of musical expression. In P. Desain and H. Honing, *Music, mind and machine* (pp. 119–122). Amsterdam: Thesis Publishers.

Dews, C. L. B., & Williams, M. S. (1989). Student musicians' personality styles, stresses, and coping patterns. *Psychology of Music, 17,* 37–47.

Dibble, K. (1995). Hearing loss and music. *Journal of Audio Engineering Society, 43,* 251–266.

Drake, C., & Palmer, C. (1993). Accent structures in music performance. *Music Perception, 10,* 343–378.

Drake, C., Dowling, W. J., & Palmer, C. (1991). Accent structures in the reproduction of simple tunes by children and adult pianists. *Music Perception, 8,* 315–334.

Duerksen, G. L. (1972). Some effects of expectation on evaluation of recorded musical performance. *Journal of Research in Music Education, 20,* 268–272.

Dyce, J. A., & O'Connor, B. (1994). The personalities of popular musicians. *Psychology of Music, 22,* 168–173.

Easley, E. (1932). A comparison of the vibrato in concert and opera singing. In C. E. Seashore (Ed.), *University of Iowa studies in the psychology of music: Vol. I. The vibrato* (pp. 269–275). Iowa City: University of Iowa.

Ebhardt, K. (1898). Zwei Beiträge zur Psychologie des Rhythmus und des Tempo. *Zeitschrift für Psychologie und Physiologie der Sinnesorgane, 18,* 99–154.

Edlund, B. (1985). *Performance and perception of notational variants: A study of rhythmic patterning in music.* Uppsala: Acta Universitatis Upsaliensis, Studia Musicologica Upsaliensia, Nova Series, 9.

Edlund, B. (1994). The tyranny of the bar-lines. Encoding notated meter in performance. In A. Friberg, J. Iwarsson, E. Jansson, & J. Sundberg (Eds.), *SMAC 93: Proceedings of the Stockholm Music Acoustics Conference July 28–August 1, 1993* (pp. 84–88). Stockholm: Publications issued by the Royal Swedish Academy of Music, No. 79.

Elliott, C. A. (1982). The relationships among instrumental sight-reading ability and seven selected predictor variables. *Journal of Research in Music Education, 30,* 5–14.

Elliott, D. (1987). Assessing musical performance. *British Journal of Music Education, 4*(2), 157–183.

Ellis, M. C. (1991). An analysis of "swing" subdivision and asynchronization in three jazz saxophonists. *Perceptual and Motor Skills, 75,* 707–713.

Ely, M. C. (1992). Effects of timbre on college woodwind players' intonational performance and perception. *Journal of Research in Music Education, 40,* 158–167.

Ericsson, K. A., Tesch-Römer, C., & Krampe, R. T. (1990). The role of practice and motivation in the acquisition of expert-level performance in real life: An empirical evaluation of a theoretical framework. In M. J. A. Howe (Ed.), *Encouraging the development of exceptional skills and talents* (pp. 109–130). Leicester: The British Psychological Society.

Ericsson, K. A., Krampe, R. T., & Tesch-Römer, C. (1993). The role of deliberate practice in the acquisition of expert performance. *Psychological Review, 100,* 363–406.

Farnsworth, P. R. (1969). *The social psychology of music* (2nd ed.). Ames: The Iowa State University Press.

Faulkner, R. R. (1973a). Orchestra interaction: Some features of communication and authority in an artistic organization. *The Sociological Quarterly, 14,* 147–157.

Faulkner, R. R. (1973b). Career concerns and mobility motivations of orchestra musicians. *The Sociological Quarterly, 14,* 334–349.

Feldman, J., Epstein, D., & Richards, W. (1992). Force dynamics of tempo change in music. *Music Perception, 10,* 185–203.

Fishbein, M., Middlestadt, S. E., Ottati, V., Straus, S., & Ellis, A. (1988). Medical problems among ISCOM musicians: Overview of a national survey. *Medical Problems of Performing Artists, 3,* 1–8.

Fischer-Williams, M. (1993). Selected musicians treated with EMG feedback. *International Journal of Arts Medicine, 2:1,* 33–38.

Fiske, H. E. (1977). Relationship of selected factors in trumpet performance adjudication reliability. *Journal of Research in Music Education, 25,* 256–263.

Fletcher, H., Blackham, E. D., & Geertsen, O. N. (1965). Quality of violin, viola, cello, and bass-viol tones. *Journal of the Acoustical Society of America, 37,* 851–863.

Fletcher, H., & Sanders, L. C. (1967). Quality of violin vibrato tones. *Journal of the Acoustical Society of America, 41,* 1534–1544.

Födermayr, F., & Deutsch, W. A. (1994). "Parmi veder la lagrime." One aria, three interpretations. In A. Friberg, J. Iwarsson, E. Jansson, and J. Sundberg (Eds.), *Proceedings of the Stockholm Music Acoustics Conference, July 1993* (pp. 96–107). Stockholm: Publications issued by the Royal Swedish Academy of Music, No. 79.

Fogle, D. O. (1982). Toward effective treatment for music performance anxiety. *Psychotherapy: Theory, Research and Practice, 19*(3), 368–375.

Fredrikson, M., & Gunnarsson, R. (1992). Psychobiology of stage fright: The effects of public performance on neuroendocrine, cardiovascular and subjective reactions. *Biological Psychology, 33*, 51–61.

Freymuth, M. (1993). From the performer's viewpoint. Mental practice for musicians: Theory and application. *Medical Problems of Performing Artists, 8*, 141–143.

Friberg. A. (1991). Generative rules for music performance: A formal description system. *Computer Music Journal, 15*(2), 56–71.

Friberg, A. (1995). *A quantitative rule system for musical performance.* Doctoral dissertation, Royal Institute of Technology, Stockholm.

Friberg. A., Frydén, L., Bodin, L. G., & Sundberg, J. (1991). Performance rules for computer-controlled contemporary keyboard music. *Computer Music Journal, 15*(2), 49–55.

Friberg, A., & Sundberg, J. (1987). How to terminate a phrase. An analysis-by-synthesis experiment on a perceptual aspect of music performance. In A. Gabrielsson (Ed.), *Action and perception in rhythm and music* (pp. 49–55). Stockholm: Publications issued by the Royal Swedish Academy of Music, No. 55.

Fry, H. J. H. (1985). The physical injury (overuse) due to music making. *Music Education for the Handicapped Bulletin, 1*(2), 22–49.

Fry, H. J. H. (1986). Incidence of overuse syndrome in the symphony orchestra. *Medical Problems of Performing Artists, 1*, 51–55.

Fry, H. J. H. (1987). Prevalence of overuse (injury) syndrome in Australian music schools. *British Journal of Industrial Medicine, 44*, 35–40.

Fry, H. J. H. (1988). Patterns of overuse seen in 658 affected instrumental musicians. *International Journal of Music Education, 11*, 3–16.

Fry, H. J. H. (1991). The effects of overuse on the musician's technique: A comparative and historical review. *International Journal of Arts Medicine, 1:1*, 46–55.

Fyk. J. (1994). Static and dynamic model of musical intonation. In A. Friberg, J. Iwarsson, E. Jansson, & J. Sundberg (Eds.), *Proceedings of the Stockholm Music Acoustics Conference, July 1993* (pp. 89–95). Stockholm: Publications issued by the Royal Swedish Academy of Music, No. 79.

Fyk, J. (1995). *Melodic intonation, psychoacoustics, and the violin.* (Fryderyk Chopin Academy of Music) Zielona Góra, Poland: Organon Publishing House.

Gabbard, G. O. (1979). Stage fright. *International Journal of Psychoanalysis, 60*, 383–392.

Gabrielsson, A. (1973). Similarity ratings and dimension analyses of auditory rhythm patterns. I. *Scandinavian Journal of Psychology, 14*, 138–160.

Gabrielsson, A. (1974). Performance of rhythm patterns. *Scandinavian Journal of Psychology, 15*, 63–72.

Gabrielsson, A. (1982). Perception and performance of musical rhythm. In M. Clynes (Ed.), *Music, mind, and brain: The neuropsychology of music* (pp. 159–169). New York: Plenum Press.

Gabrielsson, A. (1985). Interplay between analysis and synthesis in studies of music performance and music experience. *Music Perception, 3*, 59–86.

Gabrielsson, A. (1986a). Rhythm in music. In J. R. Evans & M. Clynes (Eds.), *Rhythm in psychological, linguistic and musical processes* (pp. 131–167). Springfield, IL: Charles C Thomas.

Gabrielsson, A. (1986b). Some recent trends in music psychology. *Musicologica Austriaca, 6*, 137–155.

Gabrielsson, A. (1987). Once again: The theme from Mozart's piano sonata in A major (K. 331): A comparison of five performances. In A. Gabrielsson (Ed.), *Action and perception in rhythm and music* (pp. 81–103). Stockholm: Publications issued by the Royal Swedish Academy of Music, No. 55.

Gabrielsson, A. (1988). Timing in music performance and its relations to music experience. In J. A. Sloboda (Ed.), *Generative processes in music: The psychology of performance, improvisation, and composition* (pp. 27–51). Oxford: Clarendon Press.

Gabrielsson, A. (1994). Intention and emotional expression in music performance. In A. Friberg, J. Iwarsson, E. Jansson, & J. Sundberg (Eds.), *Proceedings of the Stockholm Music Acoustics Confer-

ence, July 1993 (pp. 108–111). Stockholm: Publications issued by the Royal Swedish Academy of Music, No. 79.

Gabrielsson, A. (1995). Expressive intention and performance. In R. Steinberg (Ed.), *Music and the mind machine: The psychophysiology and psychopathology of the sense of music* (pp. 35–47). Berlin, Heidelberg, New York: Springer-Verlag.

Gabrielsson, A., Bengtsson, I., & Gabrielsson, B. (1983). Performance of musical rhythm in 3/4 and 6/8 meter. *Scandinavian Journal of Psychology, 24*, 193–213.

Gabrielsson, A., & Johnson, A. (1985). Melodic motion in different vocal styles. In *Analytica. Studies in the description and analysis of music in honour of Ingmar Bengtsson* (pp.277–299). Stockholm: Publications issued by the Royal Swedish Academy of Music, No. 47.

Gabrielsson, A., & Lindström, E. (1995). Emotional expression in synthesizer and sentograph performance. *Psychomusicology, 14,* 94–116.

Gade, A. C. (1986). Acoustics of the orchestra platform from the musicians' point of view. In S. Ternström (Ed.), *Acoustics for choir and orchestra* (pp.23–42). Stockholm: Publications issued by the Royal Swedish Academy of Music, No 52.

Gade, A. C. (1989a). Investigations of musicians' room acoustic conditions in concert halls: Part I. Methods and laboratory experiments. *Acustica, 69*, 193–203.

Gade, A. C. (1989b). Investigations of musicians' room acoustic conditions in concert halls: Part II. Field experiments and synthesis of results. *Acustica, 69*, 249–262.

Gärtner, J. (1980). *Das Vibrato unter besonderer Berücksichtigung der Verhältnisse bei Flötisten* (2. Auflage). Regensburg: Gustav Bosse Verlag.

Gates, A., & Bradshaw, J. L. (1974). Effect of auditory feedback on a musical performance task. *Perception & Psychophysics, 16*, 105–109.

Gates, A., Bradshaw, J. L., & Nettleton, N. C. (1974). Effect of different delayed auditory feedback intervals on a music performance task. *Perception & Psychophysics, 15*, 21–25.

Gates, A. G., Johnson, L., Saegert, J., Shepherd, A., Wilson, N., & Hearne III, E. M. (1985). Effect of beta blockade on singing performance. *Annals of Otology, Rhinology & Laryngology, 94*, 570–574.

Gates, A. G., & Montalbo, P. J. (1987). The effect of low-dose beta blockade on performance anxiety in singers. *Journal of Voice, 1*, 105–108.

Geringer, J. M. (1992). An analysis of dynamic contrasts in recorded choral, orchestral, and piano performances. *Bulletin of the Council for Research in Music Education, No. 112*, 51–61.

Geringer, J. M., & Madsen, C. K. (1987). Programmatic research in music: Perception and performance of intonation. In C. K. Madsen & C. A. Prickett (Eds.), *Applications of research in music behavior* (pp. 244–253). Tuscaloosa: The University of Alabama Press.

Gerig, R. R. (1976). *Famous pianists and their technique*. Washington–New York: Robert B. Luce.

Gibbons, C. F. (1991). The personality of the performing musician as measured by the Myers-Briggs Type Indicator and the reported presence of musical performance anxiety. *Dissertation Abstracts International, 51*, 3635A. (University Microfilms No. 9111203)

Gieseking, W. (1963). *So wurde ich Pianist*. Wiesbaden: F. A. Brockhaus.

Gjerdingen, R. O. (1988). Shape and motion in the microstructure of song. *Music Perception, 6*, 35–64.

Glennie, E. (1991). *Good vibrations. An autobiography*. London: Arrow Books.

Goodman, G., & Staz, S. (1989). Occupational therapy for musicians with upper extremity overuse syndrome: Patient perceptions regarding effectiveness of treatment. *Medical Problems of Performing Artists, 4*, 9–14.

Goolsby, T. (1989). Computer applications to eye movement research in music reading. *Psychomusicology, 8*(2), 111–126.

Goolsby, T. W. (1994a). Eye movement in music reading: Effects or reading ability, notational complexity, and encounters. *Music Perception, 12*, 77–96.

Goolsby, T. W. (1994b). Profiles of processing: Eye movements during sightreading. *Music Perception, 12*, 97–123.

Green, B., & Gallwey, W. T. (1986). *The inner game of music*. New York: Doubleday.

Greene, P. C. (1937). Violin performance with reference to tempered, natural, and Pythagorean intonation. In C. E. Seashore (Ed.), *University of Iowa studies in the psychology of music: Vol. IV. Objective analysis of musical performance* (pp. 232–251). Iowa City: University of Iowa.

Greer, R. D. (1970). The effect of timbre on brass-wind intonation. In E. Gordon (Ed.), *Experimental research in the psychology of music* (Vol. VI, pp. 65–94). Iowa City: University of Iowa Press.

Grieco, A., Occhipinti, E., Colombini, D., Menoni, O., Bulgheroni, M., Frigo, C., & Boccardi, S. (1989). Muscular effort and muscular-skeletal disorders in piano students: Electromyographic, clinical and preventive aspects. *Ergonomics, 32,* 697–716.

Grindea, C. (Ed.) (1987a). *Tensions in the performance of music* (Rev. ed.). London: Kahn & Averill.

Grindea, C. (1987b). Tension in piano playing. In C. Grindea (Ed.), *Tensions in the performance of music* (pp.96–125). London: Kahn & Averill.

Griswold, P. A. &, Chroback, D. A. (1981). Sex-role associations of music instruments and occupations by gender and major. *Journal of Research in Music Education, 29,* 57–62.

Gruson, L. M. (1988). Rehearsal skill and musical competence: Does practice make perfect? In J. A. Sloboda (Ed.), *Generative processes in music: The psychology of performance, improvisation, and composition* (pp. 91–112). Oxford: Clarendon Press.

Gustafson, E., & Rawson, D. (1983). *Rampfeber hos stråkmusiker* [Stage fright in string players]. Unpublished master's thesis, Uppsala University, Uppsala, Sweden.

Guttmann, A. (1932). Das Tempo und seine Variationsbreite. *Archiv für die gesamte Psychologie, 85,* 331–350.

Haider, M., & Groll-Knapp, E. (1981). Psychophysiological investigations into the stress experienced by musicians in a symphony orchestra. In M. Piperek (Ed.), *Stress and music* (pp. 15–34). Vienna: Wilhelm Braumüller.

Halpern, A. R., & Bower, G. H. (1982). Musical expertise and melodic structure in memory for musical notation. *American Journal of Psychology, 95,* 31–50.

Halsband, U., Binkofski, F., & Camp, M. (1994). The role of the perception of rhythmic grouping in musical performance: Evidence from motor-skill development in piano playing. *Music Perception, 11,* 265–288.

Hamann, D. L. (1982). An assessment of anxiety in instrumental and vocal performances. *Journal of Research in Music Education, 30,* 77–90.

Hamann, D. L. (1985). The other side of stage fright. *Music Educators Journal, 71*(8), 26–28.

Hamann, D. L., & Sobaje, M. (1983). Anxiety and the college musician: A study of performance conditions and subject variables. *Psychology of Music, 11*(1), 37–50.

Handel, S. (1986). Tempo in rhythm: Comments on Sidnell. *Psychomusicology, 6,* 19–23.

Handel, S. (1989). *Listening: An introduction to the perception of auditory events.* Cambridge, MA: MIT Press.

Hargreaves, D. J., Cork, C. A., & Setton, T. (1991). Cognitive strategies in jazz improvisation: An exploratory study. *Canadian Music Educator, Research Edition, 33,* 47–54.

Harris, P. (1988). Visual conditions of symphony musicians. *Journal of the American Optometric Association, 59*(12), 952–959.

Harris, S. R. (1987). Brief cognitive-behavioral group counseling for musical performance anxiety. *Journal of the International Society for the Study of Tension in Performance, 4,* 3–10.

Harman, S. E. (1991). The evolution of performing arts medicine as seen through the literature. In R. T. Sataloff, A. G. Brandfonbrener, & R. J. Lederman (Eds.), *Textbook of performing arts medicine* (pp. 1–24). New York: Raven Press.

Harman, S. E. (1987). Bibliography for occupational diseases of instrumental musicians. *Medical Problems of Performing Artists, 2,* 155–162.

Harrer, G. (1975). Das "Musikerlebnis" im Griff des naturwissenschaftlichen Experiments. In G. Harrer (Ed.), *Grundlagen der Musiktherapie und Musikpsychologie* (pp. 3–47). Stuttgart: Gustav Fischer.

Hartmann, A. (1932). Untersuchungen über metrisches Verhalten in musikalischen Interpretationsvarianten. *Archiv für die gesamte Psychologie, 84*, 103–192.

Hassler, M. (1990). *Androgynie*. Göttingen, Germany: Verlag für Psychologie Dr. C. J. Hogrefe.

Hassler, M., & Nieschlag, E. (1989a). Masculinity, femininity, and musical composition: Psychological and psychoendocrinological aspects of musical and spatial faculties. *Archives of Psychology, 141*(1), 71–84.

Hassler, M., & Nieschlag, E. (1989b). Gonadenhormone, räumliche Begabung und Kompositionstalent. In H. Petsche (Ed.), *Musik—Gehirn—Spiel* (pp. 191–202). Basel: Birkhäuser Verlag.

Hattwick. M. (1932). The vibrato in wind instruments. In C. E. Seashore (Ed.), *University of Iowa studies in the psychology of music: Vol. I. The vibrato* (pp. 276–280). Iowa City: University of Iowa.

Havas, K. (1973). *Stage fright: Its causes and cures with special reference to violin playing*. London: Bosworth.

Havas, K. (1987). The release from tension and anxiety in string playing. In C. Grindea (Ed.), *Tensions in the performance of music* (pp. 13–27). London: Kahn & Averill.

Hayes, G. C. (1989). The use of cinematographic research methodology in an examination of three kinematic aspects of conducting. *Dissertation Abstracts International, 49*, 3296A.

Hedden, S. K. (1987). Recent research pertaining to psychomotor skills in music. *Bulletin of the Council for Research in Music Education*, No. 90, 25–29.

Heinitz, W. (1926). Musikalische Ausdrucksstudien an Phonogrammen. *Zeitschrift für Musikwissenschaft, 9*, 568–575.

Heinlein, C. P. (1929). A discussion of the nature of pianoforte damper-pedalling together with an experimental study of some individual differences in piano performance. *Journal of General Psychology, 2*, 489–508.

Heinlein, C. P. (1930). Pianoforte damper-pedalling under ten different experimental conditions. *Journal of General Psychology, 3*, 511–528.

Henderson, M. T. (1937). Rhythmic organization in artistic piano performance. In C. E. Seashore (Ed.), *University of Iowa studies in the psychology of music: Vol. IV. Objective analysis of musical performance* (pp. 281–305). Iowa City: University of Iowa.

Henderson, M. T., Tiffin, J., & Seashore, C. E. (1937). The Iowa piano camera and its use. In C. E. Seashore (Ed.), *University of Iowa studies in the psychology of music: Vol. IV. Objective analysis of musical performance* (pp. 252–262). Iowa City: University of Iowa.

Hollinshead, M. T. (1932). A study of the vibrato in artistic violin playing. In C. E. Seashore (Ed.), *University of Iowa studies in the psychology of music: Vol. I. The vibrato* (pp. 281–288). Iowa City: University of Iowa.

Honing, H. (1992). POCO: An environment for analysing, modifying, and generating expression in music. In P. Desain & H. Honing, *Music, mind and machine* (pp. 323–330). Amsterdam: Thesis Publishers.

Howe, M. J. A., & Sloboda, J. A. (1991a). Young musicians' accounts of significant influences in their early lives. 1. The family and the musical background. *British Journal of Music Education, 8*, 39–52.

Howe, M. J. A., & Sloboda, J. A. (1991b). Young musicians' accounts of significant influences in their early lives. 2. Teachers, practising and performing *British Journal of Music Education, 8*, 53–63.

Howe, M. J. A., & Sloboda, J. A. (1991c). Early signs of talents and special interests in the lives of young musicians. *European Journal for High Ability, 2*, 102–111.

Hunsaker, L. A. (1994). Heart rate and rhythm responses during trumpet playing. *Medical Problems of Performing Artists, 9*, 69–72.

Jackson, J. M., & Latané, B. (1981). All alone in front of all those people: Stage fright as a function of number and type of co-performers and audience. *Journal of Personality and Social Psychology, 40*, 73–85.

James, I., & Savage, I. (1984). Beneficial effect of nadolol on anxiety-induced disturbances of performances in musicians: A comparison with diazepam and placebo. *American Heart Journal, 108*(4:2), 1150–1155.

Jansson, E., Axelsson, A., Lindgren, F., Karlsson, K., & Olaussen, T. (1986). Do musicians of the symphony orchestra become deaf? In S. Ternström (Ed.), *Acoustics for choir and orchestra* (pp. 62–74). Stockholm: Publications issued by the Royal Swedish Academy of Music, No. 52.

Jansson, E., & Karlsson, K. (1983). Sound levels recorded within the symphony orchestra and risk criteria for hearing loss. *Scandinavian Audiology, 12*, 215–221.

Johnson, P. (1984). The acquisition of skill. In M. M. Smyth & A.M. Wing (Eds.), *The psychology of human movement* (pp. 215–240). London: Academic Press.

Johnson, D. W., Alridge, J., Sherman, R. E., & Lorraine, A. (1986). Extended high frequency hearing sensitivity. A normative threshold study in musicians. *Annals of Otology, Rhinology & Laryngology, 95*, 196–202.

Johnson, D. W., Sherman, R. E., Alridge, J., & Lorraine, A. (1985). Effects of instrument type and orchestral position on hearing sensitivity from 0.25 to 20 kHz in the orchestral musician. *Scandinavian Audiology, 14*, 215–221.

Johnson-Laird, P. N. (1987). Reasoning, imagining, and creating. *Bulletin of the Council for Research in Music Education*, No. 65, 71–87.

Johnson-Laird, P. N. (1991). Jazz improvisation: A theory at the computational level. In P. Howell, R. West, & I. Cross (Eds.), *Representing musical structure* (pp. 291–325). London: Academic Press.

Jones, A. R. III (1990). The role of analytical prestudy in the memorization and retention of piano music in subjects of varied aural/kinesthetic ability. *Dissertation Abstracts International, 51*, 2307A.

Jones, M. R., & Holleran, S. (Eds.). (1992). *Cognitive bases of musical communication*. Washington, DC: American Psychological Association.

Juslin, P. (1993). *The influence of expressive intention on electric guitar performance*. Unpublished master's thesis, Uppsala University, Uppsala, Sweden.

Karlsson, K., Lundquist, P. G., & Olaussen, T. (1983). The hearing of symphony orchestra musicians. *Scandinavian Audiology, 12*, 257–264.

Katayose, H., & Inokuchi, S. (1993). Learning performance rules in a music interpretation system. *Computers and the humanities, 27*, 31–40.

Kelso, J. A. S. (1982). (Ed.) *Human motor behavior: An introduction*. Hillsdale, NJ: Lawrence Erlbaum.

Kemp, A. (1981a). The personality structure of the musician. I. Identifying a profile of traits for the performer. *Psychology of Music, 9*(1), 3–14.

Kemp, A. (1981b). Personality differences between the players of string, woodwind, brass and keyboard instruments, and singers. *Bulletin of the Council for Research in Music Education*, No. 66–67, 33–38.

Kemp, A. (1982a). The personality structure of the musician. IV. Incorporating group profiles into a comprehensive model. *Psychology of Music, 10*(2), 3–6.

Kemp, A. (1982b). Personality traits of successful music teachers. In R. Shuter-Dyson (Ed.), Proceedings of the Ninth International Seminar on Research in Music Education [Special issue]. *Psychology of Music,* 72–75.

Kemp, A. (1982c). The personality structure of the musician: III. The significance of sex differences. *Psychology of Music, 10*(1), 48–58.

Kemp, A. (1985). Psychological androgyny in musicians. *Bulletin of the Council for Research in Music Education*, No. 85, 102–108.

Kendall, R. A., & Carterette, E. C. (1990). The communication of musical expression. *Music Perception, 8*, 129–164.

Kendrick, M. J., Craig, K. D., Lawson, D. M., & Davidson, P. O. (1982). Cognitive and behavioral therapy for musical-performance anxiety. *Journal of Consulting and Clinical Psychology, 50*, 353–362.

Kivimäki, M., & Jokinen, M. (1994). Job perceptions and well-being among symphony orchestra musicians: A comparison with other occupational groups. *Medical Problems of Performing Artists, 9*, 73–76.

Kopiez, R. (1990a). *Der Einfluss kognitiver Strukturen auf das Erlernen eines Musikstücks am Instrument*. Frankfurt am Main: Peter Lang.

Kopiez, R. (1990b). Der Einfluss grafischer vs. verbal-analytischer kognitiver Strukturierung mentalen Erlernen eines Musikstücks. *Musikpsychologie. Jahrbuch der Deutschen Gesellschaft für Musikpsychologie, 7,* 147–155.

Kopiez, R. (1991). Structural aids to the cognitive practice of music: Graphic or verbal analysis? *Psychologica Belgica, 31,* 163–171.

Kopiez, R. (1993). Interpretationsforschung mit Hilfe des Computerflügels: Eine Studie zur Wahrnehmung von Interpretationsmerkmalen. *Musikpsychologie. Jahrbuch der Deutschen Gesellschaft für Musikpsychologie, 10,* 7–23.

Krampe, R. T., Tesch-Römer, C., & Ericsson, K. A. (1991). Biographien und Alltag von Spitzenmusikern. *Musikpädagogische Forschung, 12,* 175–188.

Kries, J. von (1926). *Wer ist musikalisch? Gedanken zur Psychologie der Tonkunst.* Berlin: Justus Springer.

Kronman, U., & Sundberg, J. (1987). Is the musical ritard an allusion to physical motion? In A. Gabrielsson (Ed.), *Action and perception in rhythm and music* (pp. 57–68). Stockholm: Publications issued by the Royal Swedish Academy of Music, No. 55.

LaBerge, D. (1981a). Perceptual and motor schemas in the performance of musical pitch. In *Documentary report of the Ann Arbor Symposium: Applications of Psychology to the Teaching and Learning of Music* (pp. 179–196). Reston, VA: Music Educators National Conference.

LaBerge, D. (1981b). Response to Robert G. Sidnell. In *Documentary report of the Ann Arbor Symposium. Applications of Psychology to the Teaching and Learning of Music* (pp. 39–41). Reston, VA: Music Educators National Conference.

Lannert, V., & Ullman, M. (1945). Factors in the reading of piano music. *American Journal of Psychology, 58,* 91–99.

Larsson, L. G., Baum, J., Mudholkar, G. S., & Kollia, G. D. (1993a). Benefits and disadvantages of joint hypermobility among musicians. *New England Journal of Medicine, 329,* 1079–1082.

Larsson, L. G., Baum, J., Mudholkar, G. S., & Kollia, G. D. (1993b). Nature and impact of musculoskeletal problems in a population of musicians. *Medical Problems of Performing Artists, 8,* 73–76.

Lederman, R. J. (1988). Occupational cramp in instrumental musicians. *Medical Problems of Performing Artists, 3,* 45–51.

Lee, S. H. (1989). Using the personal computer to analyze piano performance. *Psychomusicology, 8,* 143–149.

Leglar, M. A. (1979). Measurement of indicators of anxiety levels under varying conditions of musical performance. *Dissertation Abstracts International, 39,* 5201A–5202A.

Lehrer, P. M. (1987a). A review of the approaches to the management of tension and stage fright in music performance. *Journal of Research in Music Education, 35,* 143–153.

Lehrer, P. M. (1987b). Performance anxiety and how to control it: A psychologist's perspective. In C. Grindea (Ed.), *Tensions in the performance of music* (pp. 134–152). London: Kahn & Averill.

Lehrer, P. M. (1988). The causes and cures of performance anxiety: A review of the psychological literature. In F. L. Roehmann & F. R. Wilson (Eds.), *The biology of music making. Proceedings of the 1984 Denver conference* (pp. 32–46). St. Louis, MO: MMB Music.

Lehrer, P. M., Goldman, N. S., & Strommen, E. F. (1990). A principal components assessment of performance anxiety among musicians. *Medical Problems of Performing Artists, 5,* 12–18.

Lehrer, P. M., Rosen, R. C., Kostis, J. B., & Greenfield, D. (1987). Treating stage fright in musicians: The use of beta blockers. *New Jersey Medicine, 84*(1), 27–33.

Leimer, K. (1972). The shortest way to pianistic perfection, by Leimer-Gieseking. In W. Gieseking & K. Leimer, *Piano technique,* New York: Dover Publications. (Reprinted from *The shortest way to pianistic perfection, by Leimer-Gieseking,* by K. Leimer, 1932, Bryn Mawr, PA: Theodore Presser)

Lerdahl, F., & Jackendoff, R. (1983). *A generative theory of tonal music.* Cambridge, MA: MIT Press.

LeVine, W. R. (1988a). Biofeedback in violin and viola pedagogy. In F. L. Roehmann & F. R. Wilson (Eds.), *The biology of music making: Proceedings of the 1984 Denver conference* (pp. 190–195). St. Louis, MO: MMB Music.

LeVine, W. R. (1988b). The treatment of severe muscle spasms with biofeedback. In F. L. Roehmann & F. R. Wilson (Eds.), *The biology of music making: Proceedings of the 1984 Denver conference* (pp. 196–198). St. Louis, MO: MMB Music.

LeVine, W. R., & Irvine, J. K. (1984). In vivo EMG biofeedback in violin and viola pedagogy. *Biofeedback and Self-Regulation, 9*(2), 161–168.

Lipton, J. P. (1987). Stereotypes concerning musicians within symphony orchestras. *Journal of Psychology, 121*, 85–93.

Lockwood, A. H. (1989). Medical problems of musicians. *New England Journal of Medicine, 320*(4), 221–227.

Loosen, F. (1993). Intonation of solo violin performance with reference to equally tempered, Pythagorean, and just intonations. *Journal of the Acoustical Society of America, 93*, 525–539.

Lund, D. R. (1972). A comparative study of three therapeutic techniques in the modification of anxiety behavior in instrumental music performance. *Dissertation Abstracts International, 33*, 1189A.

Lundin, R. W. (1985). *An objective psychology of music* (3rd ed.). Malabar, FL: Robert E. Krieger.

MacKenzie C. L. (1986). Motor skill in music performance: Comments to Sidnell. *Psychomusicology, 6*, 25–28.

MacKenzie C. L., & Van Eerd, D. L. (1990). Rhythmic precision in the performance of piano scales: Motor psychophysics and motor programming. In M. Jeannerod (Ed.), *Attention and performance: XIII.* (pp. 375–408). Hillsdale, NJ: Lawrence Erlbaum.

MacKnight, C. B. (1975) Music reading ability of beginning wind instrumentalists after melodic instruction. *Journal of Research in Music Education, 23*, 23–34.

Madison, G. (1991). *Drumming performance with and without clicktrack.* Unpublished master's thesis, Uppsala University, Uppsala, Sweden.

Manturzewska, M. (1990). A biographical study of the life-span development of professional musicians. *Psychology of Music, 18*, 112–139.

Marchant-Haycox, S. E., & Wilson, G. D. (1992). Personality and stress in performing artists. *Personality and individual differences, 13*, 1061–1068.

Marek, G. R. (1982). Toscanini's memory. In U. Neisser (Ed.), *Memory observed: Remembering in natural contexts* (pp. 414–417). San Francisco: W. H. Freeman.

Mason, J. A. (1960). Comparison of solo and ensemble performances with reference to Pythagorean, just, and equi-tempered intonation. *Journal of Research in Music Education, 8*, 31–38.

Mazzola, G. (1994). Musical interpretation via vector fields: A new human workstation on the NEXT-STEP environment. In A. Friberg, J. Iwarsson, E. Jansson, & J. Sundberg (Eds.), *SMAC 93: Proceedings of the Stockholm Music Acoustics Conference July 28–August 1, 1993* (pp. 112–116). Stockholm: Publications issued by the Royal Swedish Academy of Music, No. 79.

Mazzola, G. (1995). The Zürich performance workstation project. An overview. In R. Steinberg (Ed.), *Music and the mind machine: The psychophysiology and psychopathology of the sense of music* (pp. 75–77). Berlin, Heidelberg, New York: Springer-Verlag.

Mazzola, G., & Zahorka, O. (1994). Tempo curves revisited: Hierarchies of performance fields. *Computer Music Journal, 18*(1), 40–52.

McArthur, V. H. (1989). The use of computers to analyze performance motions of musicians. *Psychomusicology, 8*, 135–141.

McPherson, G. E. (1993). Evaluating improvisational ability of high school instrumentalists. *Bulletin of the Council for Research in Music Education, No. 119*, 11–20.

McPherson, G. E. (1994). Factors and abilities influencing sightreading skill in music. *Journal of Research in Music Education, 42*, 217–231.

McPherson, G. E. (1995). The assessment of musical performance: Development and validation of five new measures. *Psychology of Music, 23*, 142–161.

Metfessel, M. (1932). The vibrato in artistic voices. In C. E. Seashore (Ed.), *University of Iowa studies in the psychology of music: Vol. I. The vibrato.* (pp. 14–117). Iowa City: University of Iowa.

Meyer, J. (1992). Zur klanglichen Wirkung des Streicher-Vibratos. *Acustica, 76*, 283–291.

Meyer, J. (1994). Vibrato sounds in large halls. In A. Friberg, J. Iwarsson, E. Jansson, & J. Sundberg (Eds.), *Proceedings of the Stockholm Music Acoustics Conference, July 1993* (pp. 117–121). Stockholm: Publications issued by the Royal Swedish Academy of Music, No. 79.

Middlestadt, S. E., & Fishbein, M. (1989). The prevalence of severe musculoskeletal problems among male and female symphony orchestra string players. *Medical Problems of Performing Artists, 4*, 41–48.

Miklaszewski, K. (1989). A case study of a pianist preparing a musical performance. *Psychology of Music, 17*, 95–109.

Miller, G. A. (1956). The magical number seven, plus or minus two: Some limits on our capacity for processing information. *Psychological Review, 63*, 81–97.

Miller, G. A., & Heise, G. (1950). The trill threshold. *Journal of the Acoustical Society of America, 22*, 637–638.

Miller, R. S. (1937). The pitch of the attack in singing. In C. E. Seashore (Ed.), *University of Iowa Studies in the Psychology of Music: Vol. IV. Objective analysis of musical performance* (pp. 158–171). Iowa City: University of Iowa.

Montello, L. (1992). Exploring the causes and treatment of music performance stress: A process-oriented group music therapy approach. In R. Spintge and R. Droh (Eds.), *MusicMedicine* (pp. 284–297). St. Louis, MO: MMB Music.

Montello, L., Coons, E. E., & Kantor, J. (1990). The use of group music therapy as a treatment for musical performance stress. *Medical Problems of Performing Artists, 5*, 49–57.

Moore, G. P. (1988). The study of skilled performance in musicians. In F. L. Roehmann & F. R. Wilson (Eds.), *The biology of music making: Proceedings of the 1984 Denver conference* (pp. 77–91). St. Louis, MO: MMB Music.

Moore, G. P. (1992). Piano trills. *Music Perception, 9*, 351–360.

Moore, G. P., Hary, D., & Naill, R. (1988). Trills: Some initial observations. *Psychomusicology, 7*, 153–162.

Morasky, R. L., Reynolds, C., & Sowell, L. E. (1983). Generalization of lowered EMG levels during musical performance following biofeedback training. *Biofeedback and Self-Regulation, 8*(2), 207–216.

Morton, W. B. (1920). Some measurements of the accuracy of the time intervals in playing a keyed instrument. *British Journal of Psychology, 10*, 194–198.

Mursell, J. L. (1971). *The psychology of music*. Westport, CT: Greenwood Press. (Original work published 1937)

Nagel, J. J. (1988). In pursuit of perfection: Career choice and performance anxiety in musicians. *Medical Problems of Performing Artists, 4*, 140–145.

Nagel, J. J. (1990). Performance anxiety and the performing musician: A fear of failure or a fear of success? *Medical Problems of Performing Artists, 5*, 37–40.

Nagel, J. J., Himle, D. P., & Papsdorf, J. D. (1989). Cognitive-behavioural treatment of musical performance anxiety. *Psychology of Music, 17*, 12–21.

Nakamura, T. (1987). The communication of dynamics between musicians and listeners through musical performance. *Perception & Psychophysics, 41*, 525–533.

Namba, S., & Kuwano, S. (1990). Continuous multi-dimensional assessment of musical performance. *Journal of the Acoustical Society of Japan (E), 11*(1), 43–51.

Namba, S., Kuwano, S., Hatoh, T., & Kato, M. (1991). Assessment of musical performance by using the method of continuous judgment by selected description. *Music Perception, 8*, 251–276.

Namba, S., Nakamura, T., & Kuwano, S. (1977). [An analysis of piano performance] (in Japanese). In *Studies in the Humanities and Social Sciences*, (Vol.25, pp. 25–43). Osaka: Osaka University, College of General Education.

Naylor, G. M. (1992). A laboratory study of interaction between reverberation, tempo and musical synchronization. *Acustica, 75*, 256–267.

Naylor, G. M., & Craik, R. J. M. (1988). The effects of level difference and musical texture on ease of ensemble. *Acustica, 65*, 95–100.

Neftel, K. A., Adler, R. H., Käppeli, L., Rossi, M., Dolder, M., Käser, H. E., Bruggesser, H. H., & Vorkauf, H. (1982). Stage fright in musicians: A model illustrating the effect of beta blockers. *Psychosomatic Medicine, 44*, 461–469.

Nettl, B. (1974). Thoughts on improvisation: A comparative approach. *The Musical Quarterly, 60*(1), 1–19.

Newmark, J. & Hochberg, F. H. (1987). "Doctor, it hurts when I play": Painful disorders among instrumental musicians. *Medical Problems of Performing Artists, 2*, 93–97.

Niemann, B. K., Pratt, R. R., & Maughan, M. L. (1993). Biofeedback training, selected coping strategies, and music relaxation interventions to reduce debilitative musical performance anxiety. *International Journal of Arts Medicine, 2*(2), 7–15.

Norris, R. (1993). *The musician's survival manual: A guide to preventing and treating injuries in instrumentalists.* St. Louis, MO: MMB Music.

Norton, G. R., MacLean, L., & Wachna, E. (1978). The use of cognitive desensitization and self-directed mastery training for treating stage fright. *Cognitive Therapy and Research, 2*(1), 61–64.

Nubé, J. (1991). Beta-blockers: Effects on performing musicians. *Medical Problems of Performing Artists, 6*, 61–68.

Nubé, J. (1994). Time-series analyses of the effects of propranolol on pianistic performance. *Medical Problems of Performing Artists, 9*, 77–88.

Nuki, M. (1984). Memorization of piano music. *Psychologia, 27*, 157–163.

Oosten, P. van (1993). Critical study of Sundberg's rules for expression in the performance of melodies. *Contemporary Music Review, 9*(1&2), 267–274.

Ortmann, O. (1929). *The physiological mechanics of piano technique.* New York: Dutton. (Reprinted 1962.)

O'Shea. J. (1990). *Music and medicine: Medical profiles of great composers.* London: J. M. Dent & Sons.

Ostri, B., Eller, N., Dahlin, E., & Skylv, G. (1989). Hearing impairment in orchestral musicians. *Scandinavian Audiology, 18*, 243–249.

Ostwald, P. F. (1987). Psychotherapeutic strategies in the treatment of performing artists. *Medical Problems of Performing Artists, 2*, 131–136.

Ostwald, P. F. (1992). Psychodynamics of musicians: The relationship of performers to their musical instruments. *Medical Problems of Performing Artists, 7*, 110–113.

Ostwald, P. F., & Avery, M. (1991). Psychiatric problems of performing artists. In R. T. Sataloff, A. G. Brandfonbrener, and R. J. Lederman (Eds.), *Textbook of performing arts medicine* (pp. 319–335). New York: Raven Press.

Palmer, C. (1989a). Mapping musical thought to musical performance. *Journal of Experimental Psychology: Human Perception and Performance, 15*, 331–346.

Palmer, C. (1989b). Timing in skilled music performance. (Unpublished doctoral dissertation, Cornell University, Ithaca, NY, 1988). *Dissertations Abstracts International, 49*, 5552B–5553B.

Palmer, C. (1989c). Structural representations of music performance. In *Proceedings of the Cognitive Science Society* (pp. 349–356). Hillsdale, NJ: Erlbaum.

Palmer, C. (1992). The role of interpretive preferences in music performance. In M. R. Jones & S. Holleran (Eds.), *Cognitive bases of musical communication* (pp. 249–262). Washington, DC: American Psychological Association.

Palmer, C., & van de Sande, C. (1993). Units of knowledge in music performance. *Journal of Experimental Psychology: Learning, Memory, and Cognition, 19*, 457–470.

Papich, G., & Rainbow, E. (1974). A pilot study of performance practices of twentieth-century musicians. *Journal of Research in Music Education, 22*, 24–34.

Parasuraman, S., & Nachman, S. A. (1987). Correlates of organizational and professional commitment: The case of musicians in symphony orchestras. *Group & Organization Studies, 12*, 287–303.

Persson, R. S. (1994). Concert musicians as teachers: On good intentions falling short. *European Journal for High Ability, 5*, 79–89.

Persson, R. S., Pratt, G., & Robson, C. (1992). Motivational and influential components of musical performance: A qualitative analysis. *European Journal for High Ability, 3*, 206–217.

Peters, M. (1985). Performance of a rubato-like task: When two things cannot be done at the same time. *Music Perception, 2*, 471–482.

Philipson, L., Sörbye, R., Larson, P., & Kaladjev, S. (1990). Muscular load levels in performing musicians as monitored by quantitative electromyography. *Medical Problems of Performing Artists, 5*, 79–82.

Pike, A. (1974). A phenomenology of jazz. *Journal of Jazz Studies, 2*(1), 88–94.

Piperek, M. (Ed.) (1981). *Stress and music.* Vienna: Wilhelm Braumüller. (Translation from the German original *Stress und Kunst,* 1971.)

Piperek, M. (1981). Psychological stress and strain factors in the work of a symphony orchestra musician: Contributing to a job profile for orchestra musicians. In M. Piperek (Ed.), *Stress and music* (pp. 3–14). Vienna: Wilhelm Braumüller.

Plaut, E. A. (1988). Psychotherapy of performance anxiety. *Medical Problems of Performing Artists, 3*, 113–118.

Povel, D. J. (1977). Temporal structure of performed music. Some preliminary observations. *Acta Psychologica, 41*, 309–320.

Prame, E. (1994). Measurements of the vibrato rate of ten singers. *Journal of the Acoustical Society of America, 96*, 1979–1984.

Pratt, R. R. (1989). An interview with Dorothy Taubman. *Journal of the International Association of Music for the Handicapped, 4*(2), 15–30.

Pratt, R. R., Jessop, S. G., & Niemann, B. K. (1992). Performance-related disorders among music majors at Brigham Young University. *International Journal of Arts Medicine, 1:2*, 7–20.

Pressing, J. (1984). Cognitive processes in improvisation. In W. R. Crozier & A. J. Chapman (Eds.), *Cognitive processes in the perception of art* (pp. 345–363). Amsterdam: Elsevier Science Publishers (North-Holland).

Pressing, J. (1987). The micro- and macrostructural design of improvised music. *Music Perception, 5*, 133–172.

Pressing, J. (1988). Improvisation: Methods and models. In J. A. Sloboda (Ed.), *Generative processes in music. The psychology of performance, improvisation, and composition* (pp. 129–178). Oxford: Clarendon Press.

Price, H. E. (1983).The effect of conductor academic task presentation, conductor reinforcement, and ensemble practice on performers' musical achievement, attentiveness, and attitude. *Journal of Research in Music Education, 31*, 245–257.

Pruett, K. D. (1991). Psychological aspects of the development of exceptional young performers and prodigies. In R. T. Sataloff, A. G. Brandfonbrener, and R. J. Lederman (Eds.), *Textbook of performing arts medicine* (pp. 337–349). New York: Raven Press.

Radocy, R. E. (1976). Effects of authority figure biases on changing judgments of musical events. *Journal of Research in Music Education, 24*, 119–128.

Raeburn, S. D. (1987a). Occupational stress and coping in a sample of professional rock musicians: I. *Medical Problems of Performing Artists, 2*, 41–48.

Raeburn, S. D. (1987b). Occupational stress and coping in a sample of professional rock musicians: II. *Medical Problems of Performing Artists, 2*, 77–82.

Rakowski, A. (1990). Intonation variants of musical intervals in isolation and in musical contexts. *Psychology of Music, 18*, 60–72.

Rakowski, A. (1991). Context-dependent intonation variants of melodic intervals. In J. Sundberg, L. Nord, & R. Carlson (Eds.), *Music, language, speech and brain* (pp. 203–211). London: MacMillan Press.

Rakowski, A., & Miskiewicz, A. (1985). Deviations from equal temperament in tuning isolated musical intervals. *Archives of Acoustics, 10*, 95–104.

Rasch, R. A. (1978). The perception of simultaneous notes such as in polyphonic music. *Acustica, 40*, 21–33.

Rasch, R. A. (1979). Synchronization in performed ensemble music. *Acustica, 43,* 121–131.

Rasch, R. A. (1988). Timing and synchronization in ensemble performance. In J. A. Sloboda (Ed.), *Generative processes in music: The psychology of performance, improvisation, and composition* (pp. 70–90). Oxford: Clarendon Press.

Reger. S. N. (1932). The string instrument vibrato. In C. E. Seashore (Ed.), *University of Iowa studies in the psychology of music: Vol. I. The vibrato* (pp. 305–340). Iowa City: University of Iowa.

Reinholdsson, P. (1987). Approaching jazz performances empirically: Some reflections on methods and problems. In A. Gabrielsson (Ed.), *Action and perception in rhythm and music* (pp. 105–125). Stockholm: Publications issued by the Royal Swedish Academy of Music, No. 55.

Repp, B. H. (1989). Expressive microstructure in music: A preliminary perceptual assessment of four composers' "pulses." *Music Perception, 6,* 243–274.

Repp, B. H. (1990a). Composers' pulses: Science or art? *Music Perception, 7,* 423–434.

Repp, B. H. (1990b). Further perceptual evaluations of pulse microstructure in computer performances of classical piano music. *Music Perception, 8,* 1–33.

Repp, B. H. (1990c). Patterns of expressive timing in performances of a Beethoven minuet by nineteen famous pianists. *Journal of the Acoustical Society of America, 88,* 622–641.

Repp, B. H. (1992a). Diversity and commonality in music performance: An analysis of timing microstructure in Schumann's "Träumerei." *Journal of the Acoustical Society of America, 92,* 2546–2568.

Repp, B. H. (1992b). A constraint on the expressive timing of a melodic gesture: Evidence from performance and aesthetic judgment. *Music Perception, 10,* 221–241.

Repp, B. H. (1992c). Probing the cognitive representation of musical time: Structural constraints on the perception of timing perturbations. *Cognition, 44,* 241–281.

Repp, B. H. (1993). Music as motion: A synopsis of Alexander Truslit's (1938) *Gestaltung und Bewegung in der Musik. Psychology of Music, 21,* 48–72.

Repp, B. H. (1994a). Musical motion: Some historical and contemporary perspectives. In A. Friberg, J. Iwarsson, E. Jansson, and J. Sundberg (Eds.), *Proceedings of the Stockholm Music Acoustics Conference, July 1993* (pp. 128–135). Stockholm: Publications issued by the Royal Swedish Academy of Music, No. 79.

Repp, B. H. (1994b). On determining the basic tempo of an expressive music performance. *Psychology of Music, 22,* 157–167.

Repp, B. H. (1994c). Relational invariance of expressive microstructure across global tempo changes in music performance: An exploratory study. *Psychological Research, 56,* 269–284.

Repp, B. H. (1994d). Response to "Comments on 'Patterns of expressive timing in performances of a Beethoven minuet by nineteen famous pianists.'" *Journal of the Acoustical Society of America, 96,* 1179–1181.

Restle, F. (1981). Response [to Robert G. Sidnell]. *Documentary Report of the Ann Arbor Symposium: Applications of Psychology to the Teaching and Learning of Music* (pp. 35–38). Reston, VA: Music Educators National Conference

Reubart, D. (1985). *Anxiety and musical performance: On playing piano from the memory.* New York: Da Capo Press.

Ribke, W. (1993). Üben. In H. Bruhn, R. Oerter, & H. Rösing (Eds.), *Musikpsychologie. Ein Handbuch* (pp. 546–558). Reinbek bei Hamburg: Rowohlt Taschenbuch Verlag.

Rink, J. (Ed.). (1995). *The practice of performance.* New York: Cambridge University Press.

Rose, R. F. (1989). An analysis of timing in jazz rhythm section performances. *Dissertation Abstracts International, 50,* 3509A–3510A. (University Microfilms No. 9005520)

Rosenbaum, D. A. (1991). *Human motor control.* San Diego, CA: Academic Press.

Rosenthal, R. K., Wilson, M., Evans, M., & Greenwalt, L. (1988). Effects of different practice conditions on advanced instrumentalists' performance accuracy. *Journal of Research in Music Education, 36,* 250–257.

Ross, J. (1989). A study of timing in Estonian runic song. *Journal of the Acoustical Society of America, 86,* 1671–1677.

Ross, J., & Lehiste, E. (1994). Lost prosodic oppositions: A study of contrastive duration in Estonian funeral laments. *Language and Speech, 37,* 407–424.

Ross, S. L. (1985). The effectiveness of mental practice in improving the performance of college trombonists. *Journal of Research in Music Education, 33,* 221–230.

Royster, J. D., Royster, L. H., & Killion, M. C. (1991). Sound exposures and hearing thresholds of symphony orchestra musicians. *Journal of the Acoustical Society of America, 89,* 2793–2803.

Rubin-Rabson, G. (1937). The influence of analytical pre-study in memorizing piano music. *Archives of Psychology, 31*(220), 1–53.

Rubin-Rabson, G. (1939). Studies in the psychology of memorizing piano music: I. A comparison of the unilateral and the co-ordinated approaches. *Journal of Educational Psychology, 30,* 321–345.

Rubin-Rabson, G. (1940a). Studies in the psychology of memorizing piano music: II. A comparison of massed and distributed practice. *Journal of Educational Psychology, 31,* 270–284.

Rubin-Rabson, G. (1940b). Studies in the psychology of memorizing piano music: III. A comparison of the whole and the part approach. *Journal of Educational Psychology, 31,* 460–476.

Rubin-Rabson, G. (1941a). Studies in the psychology of memorizing piano music: VI. A comparison of two forms of mental rehearsal and keyboard overlearning. *Journal of Educational Psychology, 32,* 593–602.

Rubin-Rabson, G. (1941b). Studies in the psychology of memorizing piano music. VII: A comparison of three degrees of overlearning. *Journal of Educational Psychology, 32,* 688–696

Rubin-Rabson, G. (1945). Studies in the psychology of memorizing piano music. IX. Mental and keyboard overlearning in memorizing piano music. *Journal of Musicology, 3,* 33–40.

Ruggieri, V., & Sebastiani, M. P. (1987). New approaches to musical interpretations from a psychophysiological point of view: Analysis of some instrumental interpretations. *Musikpsychologie. Jahrbuch der Deutschen Gesellschaft für Musikpsychologie, 4,* 65–89.

Sachs, H. (1982). *Virtuoso.* New York: Thames and Hudson.

Sági, M., & Vitányi, I. (1988). Experimental research into musical generative ability. In J. A. Sloboda (Ed.), *Generative processes in music: The psychology of performance, improvisation, and composition* (pp. 179–194). Oxford: Clarendon Press.

Salis, D. L. (1980). Laterality effects with visual perception of musical chords and dot patterns. *Perception & Psychophysics, 28,* 284–292.

Salmon, P. G. (1990). A psychological perspective on musical performance anxiety: A review of the literature. *Medical Problems of Performing Artists, 5,* 2–11.

Salmon, P. (1991). Stress inoculation techniques and musical performance anxiety. In G. D. Wilson (Ed.), *Psychology and performing arts* (pp. 219–229). Amsterdam: Swets & Zeitlinger.

Salmon, P., Schrodt, G. R., & Wright, J. (1989). A temporal gradient of anxiety in a stressful performance context. *Medical Problems of Performing Artists, 4,* 77–80.

Salzberg, R. S. (1980). The effects of visual stimulus and instruction on intonation accuracy of string instrumentalists. *Psychology of Music, 8*(2), 42–49.

Sataloff, R. T., Brandfonbrener, A. G., & Lederman, R. J. (Eds.) (1991). *Textbook of performing arts medicine.* New York: Raven Press.

Sataloff, R. T., & Sataloff, J. (1991). Hearing loss in musicians. In R. T. Sataloff, A. G. Brandfonbrener, and R. J. Lederman (Eds.), *Textbook of performing arts medicine* (pp. 301–317). New York: Raven Press.

Schlapp, M. (1973). Observations on a voluntary tremor: Violinist's vibrato. *Quarterly Journal of Experimental Physiology, 58,* 357–368.

Schmale, H., & Schmidtke, H. (1985). *Der Orchestermusiker: Seine Arbeit und Belastung.* Mainz: Schott.

Schmidt, R. A. (1982). More on motor programs. In J. A. S. Kelso (Ed.), *Human motor behavior: An introduction* (pp. 189–217). Hillsdale, NJ: Erlbaum.

Schmidt, R. A. (1988). *Motor control and learning* (2nd ed.). Champaign, IL: Human Kinetics Publishers.

Schoen, M. (1922). An experimental study of the pitch factor in artistic singing. *Psychological Monographs, 31*(1), 230–259.

Schoen, M. (1940). *The psychology of music*. New York: Ronald Press.

Schulz, W. (1981). Analysis of a symphony orchestra. Sociological and sociopsychological aspects. In M. Piperek (Ed.), *Stress and music* (pp. 35–56). Vienna: Wilhelm Braumüller.

Sears, C. H. (1902). A contribution to the psychology of rhythm. *American Journal of Psychology, 13*, 28–61.

Seashore, C. E. (1932) (Ed.). *University of Iowa studies in the psychology of music: Vol. I. The vibrato* Iowa City: University of Iowa.

Seashore, C. E. (1936). *University of Iowa studies in the psychology of music: Vol. III. Psychology of the vibrato in voice and instrument*. Iowa City: University of Iowa.

Seashore, C. E. (1937) (Ed.). *University of Iowa studies in the psychology of music: Vol. IV. Objective analysis of musical performance*. Iowa City: University of Iowa.

Seashore, C. E . (1938). *Psychology of music*. New York: McGraw-Hill. (Reprinted 1967 by Dover Publications, New York.)

Seashore, H. G. (1932). The hearing of the pitch and intensity in vibrato. In C. E. Seashore (Ed.), *University of Iowa studies in the psychology of music: Vol. I. The vibrato* (pp. 213–235). Iowa City: University of Iowa.

Seashore, H. G. (1937). An objective analysis of artistic singing. In C. E. Seashore (Ed.), *University of Iowa studies in the psychology of music: Vol. IV. Objective analysis of musical performance* (pp. 12–157). Iowa City: University of Iowa.

Senju, M., & Ohgushi, K. (1987). How are the player's ideas conveyed to the audience? *Music Perception, 4*, 311–324.

Shackford, C. (1961). Some aspects of perception: I. *Journal of Music Theory, 5*, 162–202.

Shackford, C. (1962a). Some aspects of perception: II. *Journal of Music Theory, 6*, 66–90.

Shackford, C. (1962b). Some aspects of perception: III. *Journal of Music Theory, 6*, 295–303.

Shaffer, L. H. (1980). Analysing piano performance: A study of concert pianists. In G. E. Stelmach & J. Requin (Eds.), *Tutorials in motor behavior* (pp.443–455). Amsterdam: North-Holland.

Shaffer, L. H. (1981). Performances of Chopin, Bach, and Bartok: Studies in motor programming. *Cognitive Psychology, 13*, 326–376.

Shaffer, L. H. (1982). Rhythm and timing in skill. *Psychological Review, 89*, 109–122.

Shaffer, L. H. (1984a). Timing in solo and duet piano performances. *Quarterly Journal of Experimental Psychology, 36A*, 577–595.

Shaffer, L. H. (1984b). Timing in musical performance. In J. Gibbon & L. Allan (Eds.), Timing and time perception [Special issue]. *Annals of the New York Academy of Sciences, 423*, 420–428.

Shaffer, L. H. (1989). Cognition and affect in musical performance. *Contemporary Music Review, 4*, 381–389.

Shaffer, L. H. (1992). How to interpret music. In M. R. Jones & S. Holleran (Eds.), *Cognitive bases of musical communication* (pp. 263–278). Washington, DC: American Psychological Association.

Shaffer, L. H. (1995). Musical performance as interpretation. *Psychology of Music, 23*, 17–38.

Shaffer, L. H., Clarke, E. F., & Todd, N. P. (1985). Metre and rhythm in piano playing. *Cognition, 20*, 61–77.

Shaffer, L. H., & Todd. N. P. (1987). The interpretive component in musical performance. In A. Gabrielsson (Ed.), *Action and perception in rhythm and music* (pp. 139–152). Stockholm: Publications issued by the Royal Swedish Academy of Music, No. 55.

Sheridan, M. R. (1984). Planning and controlling simple movements. In M. M. Smyth & A. M. Wing (Eds.), *The psychology of human movement* (pp. 47–82). London: Academic Press.

Sidnell, R. G. (1981). Motor learning in music education. *Documentary report of the Ann Arbor Symposium: Applications of Psychology to the Teaching and Learning of Music* (pp. 28–35). Reston, VA: Music Educators National Conference.

Silverman, L. (1989). Earning a deaf ear: Loud music and hearing loss. *Audio, 73*, (January 1989), 76–82.

Skinner, L., & Seashore, C. E. (1937). A musical pattern score of the last movement of the Beethoven Sonata, Opus 27, No. 2. In C. E. Seashore (Ed.), *University of Iowa studies in the psychology of music: Vol. IV. Objective analysis of musical performance* (pp. 263–280). Iowa City: University of Iowa.

Sloboda, J. A. (1974). The eye-hand span: An approach to the study of sight reading. *Psychology of Music, 2*(2), 4–10.

Sloboda, J. A. (1976a). Visual perception of musical notation: Registering pitch symbols in memory. *Quarterly Journal of Experimental Psychology, 28*, 1–16.

Sloboda, J. A. (1976b). The effect of item position on the likelihood of identification by inference in prose reading and music reading. *Canadian Journal of Psychology, 30*, 228–237.

Sloboda, J. A. (1977). Phrase units as determinants of visual processing in music reading. *British Journal of Psychology, 68*, 117–124.

Sloboda, J. A. (1978a). Perception of contour in music reading. *Perception, 7*, 323–331.

Sloboda, J. A. (1978b). The psychology of music reading. *Psychology of Music, 6*(2), 3–20.

Sloboda, J. A. (1982a). Music performance. In D. Deutsch (Ed.), *The psychology of music* (pp. 479–496). New York: Academic Press.

Sloboda, J. A. (1982b). Experimental studies of music reading: A review. *Music Perception, 2*, 222–236.

Sloboda, J. A. (1983). The communication of musical metre in piano performance. *Quarterly Journal of Experimental Psychology, 35A*, 377–396.

Sloboda, J. A. (1985a). Expressive skill in two pianists: Metrical communication in real and simulated performances. *Canadian Journal of Psychology, 39*(2), 273–293.

Sloboda, J. A. (1985b). *The musical mind: The cognitive psychology of music.* Oxford: Clarendon Press.

Sloboda, J. A. (Ed.). (1988). *Generative processes in music: The psychology of performance, improvisation, and composition.* Oxford: Clarendon Press.

Sloboda, J. A. (1990). Musical excellence: How does it develop? In M. J. A. Howe (Ed.), *Encouraging the development of exceptional skills and talents* (pp. 165–178). Leicester: The British Psychological Society.

Sloboda, J. A. (1994). Music performance: Expression and the development of excellence. In R. Aiello & J. A. Sloboda (Eds.), *Musical perceptions* (pp. 152–169). New York: Oxford University Press.

Sloboda, J. A., & Howe, M. (1991). Biographical precursors of musical excellence: An interview study. *Psychology of Music, 19*, 3–21.

Sloboda, J. A., & Howe, M. (1992). Transitions in the early musical careers of able young musicians: Choosing instruments and teachers. *Journal of Research in Music Education, 40*, 283–294.

Small, A. M. (1937). An objective analysis of artistic violin performance. In C. E. Seashore (Ed.), *University of Iowa studies in the psychology of music: Vol. IV. Objective analysis of musical performance* (pp. 172–231). Iowa City: University of Iowa.

Smith, T. S., & Murphy, R. J. (1984). Conflicting criteria of success in the careers of symphony musicians. *Empirical Studies of the Arts, 2*(2), 149–172.

Sosniak, L. A. (1985a). Learning to be a concert pianist. In B. S. Bloom (Ed.), *Developing talent in young people* (pp. 19–67). New York: Ballantine.

Sosniak, L. A. (1985b). One concert pianist. In B. S. Bloom (Ed.), *Developing talent in young people* (pp. 68–89). New York: Ballantine.

Sosniak, L. A. (1985c). Phases of learning. In B. S. Bloom (Ed.), *Developing talent in young people* (pp. 409–438). New York: Ballantine.

Sosniak, L. A. (1985d). A long-term commitment to learning. In B. S. Bloom (Ed.), *Developing talent in young people* (pp. 477–506). New York: Ballantine.

Sosniak, L. A. (1990). The tortoise, the hare, and the development of talent. In M. J. A. Howe (Ed.), *Encouraging the development of exceptional skills and talents* (pp. 149–164). Leicester: The British Psychological Society.

Spintge, R., & Droh, R. (Eds.) (1992). *MusicMedicine.* St. Louis, MO: MMB Music.

Stanton, H. E. (1993). Research note: Alleviation of performance anxiety through hypnotherapy. *Psychology of Music, 21*, 78–82.

Steptoe, A. (1983). The relationship between tension and the quality of musical performance. *Journal of the International Society for the Study of Tension in Performance, 1*(1), 12–22.

Steptoe, A. (1989). Stress, coping and stage fright in professional musicians. *Psychology of Music, 17*, 3–11.

Steptoe, A., & Fidler, H. (1987). Stage fright in orchestral musicians: A study of cognitive and behavioural strategies in performance anxiety. *British Journal of Psychology, 78*, 241–249.

Sudnow, D. (1978). *Ways of the hand. The organization of improvised conduct.* Cambridge, MA: Harvard University Press.

Sundberg, J. (1982). In tune or not? A study of fundamental frequency in music practice. In C. Dahlhaus & M. Krause (Eds.), *Tiefenstruktur der Musik, Festschrift Fritz Winckel* (pp. 69–97). Berlin: Technische Universität.

Sundberg, J. (1988). Computer synthesis of music performance. In J. A. Sloboda (Ed.), *Generative processes in music: The psychology of performance, improvisation, and composition* (pp. 52–69). Oxford: Clarendon Press.

Sundberg, J. (1991). Music performance research: An overview. In J. Sundberg, L. Nord, & R. Carlson (Eds.), *Music, language, speech and brain* (pp. 173–183). London: MacMillan Press.

Sundberg, J. (1992). Musician's tone glue. In J. Sundberg (Ed.), *Gluing tones. Grouping in music composition, performance and listening* (pp. 27–52). Stockholm: Publications issued by the Royal Swedish Academy of Music, No. 72.

Sundberg, J. (1993). How can music be expressive? *Speech Communication, 13*, 239–253.

Sundberg, J., Askenfelt, A., & Frydén, L. (1983). Musical performance: A synthesis-by-rule approach. *Computer Music Journal, 7*, 37–43.

Sundberg, J., Friberg, A., & Frydén, L. (1989). Rules for automated performance of ensemble music. *Contemporary Music Review, 3*(1), 89–109.

Sundberg, J., Friberg, A., & Frydén, L. (1991a). Common secrets of musicians and listeners: An analysis-by-synthesis study of musical performance. In P. Howell, R. West, & I. Cross (Eds.), *Representing musical structure* (pp. 161–197). London: Academic Press.

Sundberg, J., Friberg, A., & Frydén, L. (1991b). Threshold and preference quantities of rules for music performance. *Music Perception, 9*, 71–92.

Sundberg, J., & Frydén, L. (1985). Teaching a computer to play melodies musically. In *Analytica: Studies in the description and analysis of music in honour of Ingmar Bengtsson* (pp. 67–76). Stockholm: Publications issued by the Royal Swedish Academy of Music, No. 47.

Sundberg, J., & Frydén, L. (1987). Melodic charge and music performance. In J. Sundberg (Ed.), *Harmony and tonality* (pp.53–58). Stockholm: Publications issued by the Royal Swedish Academy of Music, No. 54.

Sundberg, J., Frydén, L., & Askenfelt, A. (1983). What tells you the player is musical? An analysis-by-synthesis study of music performance. In J. Sundberg (Ed.), *Studies of music performance* (pp. 61–75). Stockholm: Publications issued by the Royal Swedish Academy of Music, No. 39.

Sundberg, J., Frydén, L., & Friberg, A. (1995). Expressive aspects of instrumental and vocal performance. In R. Steinberg (Ed.), *Music and the mind machine: The psychophysiology and psychopathology of the sense of music* (pp. 49–62). Berlin, Heidelberg, New York: Springer-Verlag.

Sundberg, J., & Verrillo, V. (1980). On the anatomy of the retard: A study of timing in music. *Journal of the Acoustical Society of America, 68*, 772–779.

Sundin, N. G. (1994). Aesthetic criteria of musical interpretation in contemporary performance of instrumental music. In A. Friberg, J. Iwarsson, E. Jansson, & J. Sundberg (Eds.), *SMAC 93: Proceedings of the Stockholm Music Acoustics Conference July 28–August 1, 1993* (pp. 551–555). Stockholm: Publications issued by the Royal Swedish Academy of Music, No. 79.

Sweeney, G. A., & Horan, J. J. (1982). Separate and combined effects of cue-controlled relaxation and cognitive restructuring in the treatment of musical performance anxiety. *Journal of Counseling Psychology, 29*, 486–497.

Taguti, T., Ohgushi, K, & Sueoka, T. (1994). Individual differences in the pedal work of piano performance. In A. Friberg, J. Iwarsson, E. Jansson, & J. Sundberg (Eds.), *SMAC 93: Proceedings of the Stockholm Music Acoustics Conference July 28–August 1, 1993* (pp. 142–145). Stockholm: Publications issued by the Royal Swedish Academy of Music, No. 79.

Talley, J. T. (1989). Minor variations in performance as indicators of musical meter. *Dissertation Abstracts International, 50*, 826A. (University Microfilms No. 8913704)

Taubman, D. (1988). A teacher's perspective on musicians' injuries. In F. L. Roehmann & F. R. Wilson (Eds.), *The biology of music making: Proceedings of the 1984 Denver conference* (pp. 144–153). St. Louis, MO: MMB Music.

Terhardt E., & Zick, M. (1975). Evaluation of the tempered tone scale in normal, stretched, and contracted intonation. *Acustica, 32*, 268–274.

Theorell, T., Ahlberg-Hultén, G., Sigala, F., Perski, A., Söderholm, M., Kallner, A., & Eneroth, P. (1990). A psychosocial and biomedical comparison between men in six contrasting service occupations. *Work & Stress, 4*(1), 51–63.

Thompson, W. B. (1987). Music sight-reading skill in flute players. *Journal of General Psychology, 114*, 345–352.

Thompson, W. F. (1989). Composer-specific aspects of musical performance: An evaluation of Clynes's theory of pulse for performances of Mozart and Beethoven. *Music Perception, 7*, 15–42.

Thompson, W. F., Sundberg, J., Friberg, A., & Frydén, L. (1989). The use of rules for expression in the performance of melodies. *Psychology of Music, 17*, 63–82.

Tiffin, J. (1931). Some aspects of the psychophysics of the vibrato. *Psychological Monographs, 41*(4), 153–200.

Tiffin, J. (1932a). Phonophotograph apparatus. In C. E. Seashore (Ed.), *University of Iowa studies in the psychology of music: Vol. I. The vibrato* (pp. 118–133). Iowa City: University of Iowa.

Tiffin, J. (1932b). The role of pitch and intensity in the vocal vibrato of students and artists. In C. E. Seashore (Ed.), *University of Iowa studies in the psychology of music: Vol. I. The vibrato* (pp. 134–165). Iowa City: University of Iowa.

Tiffin, J., & Seashore. H. G. (1932). Summary of the established facts in experimental studies on the vibrato up to 1932. In C. E. Seashore (Ed.), *University of Iowa studies in the psychology of music: Vol. I. The vibrato* (pp. 344–376). Iowa City: University of Iowa.

Tobacyk, J. J., & Downs, A. (1986). Personal construct threat and irrational beliefs as cognitive predictors of increases in musical performance anxiety. *Journal of Personality and Social Psychology, 51*, 779–782.

Todd, N. (1985). A model of expressive timing in tonal music. *Music Perception, 3*, 33–58.

Todd, N. (1989a). A computational model of rubato. *Contemporary Music Review, 3*, 69–88.

Todd, N. (1989b). Towards a cognitive theory of expression: The performance and perception of rubato. *Contemporary Music Review, 4*, 405–416.

Todd, N. P. M. (1992). The dynamics of dynamics: A model of musical expression. *Journal of the Acoustical Society of America, 91*, 3540–3550.

Todd, N. P. M. (1993). Vestibular feedback in musical performance: Response to *Somatosensory feedback in musical performance* (edited by Sundberg and Verrillo). *Music Perception, 10*, 379–382.

Todd, N. P. M. (1995). The kinematics of musical expression. *Journal of the Acoustical Society of America, 97*, 1940–1949.

Tove, P. A., Norman, B., Isaksson, L., & Czekajewski, J. (1966). Direct-recording frequency and amplitude meter for analysis of musical and other sonic waveforms. *Journal of the Acoustical Society of America, 39*, 362–371.

Tro, J. (1994). Perception of micro dynamical variation in piano performances. In A. Friberg, J. Iwarsson, E. Jansson, & J. Sundberg (Eds.), *SMAC 93: Proceedings of the Stockholm Music Acoustics Conference July 28–August 1, 1993* (pp. 150–154). Stockholm: Publications issued by the Royal Swedish Academy of Music, No. 79.

Truslit, A. (1938). *Gestaltung und Bewegung in der Musik*. Berlin: Chr. Friedrich Wieweg.

Vaughan, R. (1986). *Herbert von Karajan: A biographical portrait*. London: Weidenfeld & Nicolson.

Verrillo, R. T. (1992). Vibration sensation in humans. *Music Perception, 9,* 281–302.

Vernon, L. N. (1937). Synchronization of chords in artistic piano music. In C. E. Seashore (Ed.), *University of Iowa studies in the psychology of music: Vol. IV. Objective analysis of musical performance* (pp. 306–345). Iowa City: University of Iowa.

Vorberg, D., & Hambuch, R. (1978). On the temporal control of rhythmic performance. In J. Requin (Ed.), *Attention and performance: VII* (pp. 535–555). Hillsdale, NJ: Lawrence Erlbaum.

Vorberg, D., & Hambuch, R. (1984). Timing of two-handed rhythmic performance. In J. Gibbon & L. Allan (Eds.), Timing and time perception [Special issue]. *Annals of the New York Academy of Sciences, 423,* 390–406.

Vos, J., & Rasch, R. A. (1981). The perceptual onset of musical tones. *Perception & Psychophysics, 29,* 323–335.

Voyer, J. J., & Faulkner, R. R. (1989). Organizational cognition in a jazz ensemble. *Empirical Studies of the Arts, 7,* 57–77.

Wade, M. G. (1990). Motor skills and the making of music. In F. R. Wilson & F. L. Roehmann (Eds.), *Music and child development: Proceedings of the 1987 Denver Conference* (pp. 157–178). St. Louis, MO: MMB Music.

Wagner, A. H. (1932). Remedial and artistic development of the vibrato. In C. E. Seashore (Ed.), *University of Iowa studies in the psychology of music: Vol. I. The vibrato* (pp. 166–212). Iowa City: University of Iowa.

Wagner, C. (1971). The influence of the tempo of playing on the rhythmic structure studied at pianist's playing scales. In *Medicine and Sport: Vol. 6. Biomechanics II* (pp. 129–132). Basel: Karger.

Wagner, C. (1974). Experimentelle Untersuchungen über das Tempo. *Österreichische Musikzeitschrift, 29,* 589–604.

Wagner, C. (1987a). Welche Anforderungen stellt das Instrumentalspiel an die menschliche Hand? *Handchirurgie, Mikrochirurgie, Plastische Chirurgie, 19*(1), 23–32.

Wagner, C. (1987b). The evaluation of the musician's hand: An approach to prevention of occupational disease. In R. Spintge & R. Droh (Eds.), *Music in medicine* (pp. 333–341). New York: Springer.

Wagner, C. (1988a). Success and failure in musical performance: Biomechanics of the hand. In F. L. Roehmann & F. R. Wilson (Eds.), *The biology of music making. Proceedings of the 1984 Denver conference* (pp. 154–179). St. Louis, MO: MMB Music.

Wagner, C. (1988b). The pianist's hand: Anthropometry and biomechanics. *Ergonomics, 31*(1), 97–131.

Wagner, C. (Ed.) (1995). *Medizinische Probleme bei Instrumentalisten: Ursachen und Prävention.* Laaber: Laaber Verlag.

Wapnick, J., Flowers, P., Alegant, M., & Jasinskas, L. (1993). Consistency in piano performance evaluation. *Journal of Research in Music Education, 41,* 282–292.

Ward, W. D. (1970). Musical perception. In J. Tobias (Ed.), *Foundations of modern auditory theory* (pp.407–447). New York: Academic Press.

Wardle, A. (1975). Behavior modification by reciprocal inhibition of instrumental music performance anxiety. In C. K. Madsen, R. D. Greer, & C. H. Madsen, Jr. (Eds.), *Research in music behavior: Modifying music behavior in the classroom* (pp. 191–205). New York: Teachers College Press.

Waugh, R. (1983). How much hearing damage does loud music cause? *Bulletin of the Australian Acoustical Society, 11*(2), 61–66.

Weaver, H. E. (1943). Studies of ocular behavior in music reading. I. A survey of visual processing in reading differently constructed musical selections. *Psychological Monographs, 55*(1), No. 249, 1–30.

Webster, P. R. (1992). Research on creative thinking in music: The assessment literature. In R. Colwell (Ed.), *Handbook of research on music teaching and learning* (pp. 266–280). New York: Schirmer.

Weick, K. E., Gilfillan, D. P., & Keith, T. A. (1973). The effect of composer credibility on orchestra performance. *Sociometry, 36,* 435–462.

Welch, G. F. (1985a). A schema theory of how children learn to sing in tune. *Psychology of Music, 13,* 3–18.

Welch, G. F. (1985b). Variability of practice and knowledge of results as factors in learning to sing in tune. *Bulletin of the Council for Research in Music Education*, No. 85, 238–247.

Wesner, R. B., Noyes, R., Jr., & Davis, T. L. (1990). The occurrence of performance anxiety among musicians. *Journal of Affective Disorders, 18*, 177–185.

Westmore, G. A., & Eversden, I. D. (1981). Noise-induced hearing loss and orchestral musicians. *Acta Otolaryngolica, 107*, 761–764.

Whitaker, C. S. (1985). The modification of psychophysiological responses to stress in piano performance. *Dissertation Abstracts International, 46*, 1438A–1439A.

Wills, B. L., MacKenzie, C. L., Harrison, D. B., Topper, T. N., & Walker, G. A. (1985). On the measurement of pianists' keyboard performance. In D. A. Winter, R. W. Norman, R. P. Wells, K. C. Kayes, & A. E. Patla (Eds.), *Biomechanics IX-B: International series on biomechanics* (Vol. 5B). Champaign, IL: Human Kinetics Publishers.

Wills, G., & Cooper, C. L. (1988). *Pressure sensitive: Popular musicians under stress.* London: Sage.

Wilson, F. R. (1986). *Tone deaf and all thumbs?* New York: Viking.

Wilson, F. R. (1992). Digitizing digital dexterity: A novel application for MIDI recordings of keyboard performance. *Psychomusicology, 11*, 79–95.

Wilson, F. R. & Roehmann, F. L. (1992). The study of biomechanical and physiological processes in relation to musical performance. In R. Colwell (Ed.), *Handbook of research on music teaching and learning* (pp. 509–524). New York: Schirmer.

Wilson, F. R., Wagner, C., & Hömberg, V. (1995). Biomechanische Aspekte bei Musikern mit berufsbedingten Muskelkrämpfen/Fokaler Dystonie. In C. Wagner (Ed.), *Medizinische Probleme bei Instrumentalisten: Ursachen und Prävention* (pp. 177–200). Laaber: Laaber-Verlag.

Wilson. G. D. (1984). The personality of opera singers. *Personality and Individual Differences, 5*, 195–201.

Wolf, T. (1976). A cognitive model of musical sight-reading. *Journal of Psycholinguistic Research, 5*, 143–171.

Wolf, F. G., Keane, M. S., Brandt, K. D., & Hillberry, B. M. (1993). An investigation of finger joint and tendon forces in experienced pianists. *Medical Problems of Performing Artists, 8*, 84–95.

Wolfe, M. L. (1989). Correlates of adaptive and maladaptive musical performance anxiety. *Medical Problems of Performing Artists, 4*, 49–56.

Wolfe, M. L. (1990). Relationships between dimensions of musical performance anxiety and behavioral coping strategies. *Medical Problems of Performing Artists, 5*, 139–144.

Wolverton, D. T., & Salmon, P. (1991). Attention allocation and motivation in music performance anxiety. In G. D. Wilson (Ed.), *Psychology and performing arts* (pp. 231–237). Amsterdam: Swets & Zeitlinger.

Woolford, D. H., Carterette, E. C., & Morgan, D. E. (1988). Hearing impairment among orchestral musicians. *Music Perception, 5*, 261–284.

Wubbenhorst, T. M. (1994). Personality characteristics of music educators and performers. *Psychology of Music, 22*, 63–74.

Young, V. M., & Colman, A. M. (1979). Some psychological processes in string quartets. *Psychology of Music, 7*(1), 12–18.

Zdzinski, S. F. (1991). Measurement of solo instrumental music performance: A review of literature. *Bulletin of the Council for Research in Music Education*, No. 109, 47–58.

Zervoudakes, J. & Tanur, J. M. (1994). Gender and musical instruments: Winds of change? *Journal of Research in Music Education, 42*, 58–67.

15

THE DEVELOPMENT OF MUSIC

PERCEPTION AND COGNITION

W. JAY DOWLING

Program in Cognitive Science
University of Texas at Dallas
Richardson, Texas

I. INTRODUCTION

An adult listening attentively to a piece of music and understanding it performs an enormous amount of information processing very rapidly. Most of this processing is carried out automatically below the level of conscious analysis, because there is no time for reflective thought on each detail as the piece steadily progresses. This process is closely parallel to what happens when a native speaker of a language listens to and understands a sentence. The elements of the sentence are processed very rapidly—so rapidly that the listener cannot attend individually to each detail, but simply hears and understands the overall meaning. The rapidity of automatic speech processing depends on extensive perceptual learning with the language in question. Similarly, the music listener's facility in grasping a piece of music depends on perceptual learning gained through experience with the music of a particular culture. Further, we can see in the development of language from its earliest stages the predisposition of the child to speak, and the ways in which basic elements of language, already present in infancy, are molded through perceptual learning and acculturation into adult structures (Brown, 1973). Similarly, we can find elements of adult cognitive structures for music in young infants, and can watch them develop in complexity under the influence of culture and individual experience. In both speech and music, then, there are specific patterns of behavior that emerge in infancy that bear the unmistakable stamp of "speech" or "music" behavior. We can trace the elaboration of those incipient speech and music patterns in the course of development.

A point to be emphasized is the ease and rapidity with which adults perform complex cognitive tasks in domains of speech and music familiar to them, and the degree to which that facility depends on prior experience. For example, when the processing of a melody is complicated by the temporal interleaving of distractor notes among the notes of the melody, listeners are more accurate in judging pitches that match familiar, culturally determined norms than those that do not (Dowling, 1992, 1993a). Furthermore, the ability to discern a target melody in the midst of temporally interleaved distractors grows gradually through childhood, and the importance of the culturally defined tonal scheme to the performance of that task grows as well (Andrews & Dowling, 1991). Perceptual learning with the music of a culture provides the listener with a fund of implicit knowledge of the structural patterns of that music, and this implicit knowledge serves to facilitate the cognitive processing of music conforming to those patterns.

Calling the knowledge amassed through perceptual learning "implicit" indicates that it is not always available to conscious thought. Neither the knowledge base itself nor the cognitive processes through which it is applied are entirely accessible to consciousness (Dowling, 1993a, 1993b). Listeners typically engage in far more elaborate processing than they are aware of. For example, there is evidence that listeners with a moderate amount of musical training encode the diatonic scale-step ("*do, re, mi*") values of the notes of melodies they hear (Dowling, 1986). Yet those listeners are not aware that they are even capable of categorizing melodic pitches according to their scale-step values, much less that they do it routinely when hearing a new melody. Implicit knowledge of Western musical scale structure has accrued over years of experience, and that knowledge is applied automatically and unconsciously whenever the adult listens to music.

This sensorimotor learning undoubtedly has consequences for brain development, as illustrated by Elbert, Pantev, Wienbruch, Rockstroh, and Taub's (1995) demonstration of the enhanced allocation of cortical representation to fingers of the left hand in string players, especially for those who begin study of the instrument before the age of 12. Recent results by Pantev, Oostenveld, Engelien, Ross, Roberts, and Hoke (1998) concerning cortical allocation in processing musical tones tend to confirm this supposition.

In looking at the development of music perception and cognition, one of our goals is to distinguish between cognitive components that are already present at the earliest ages and components that develop in response to experience. We can look at the content of the adult's implicit knowledge base in contrast to the child's. We can also look at the developmental sequence by which the individual goes from the infant's rudimentary grasp of musical structure to the experienced adult's sophisticated knowledge and repertoire of cognitive strategies for applying it.

II. DEVELOPMENT

A. INFANCY

Over the past 20 years, much has been learned about the infant's auditory world. Researchers have isolated several kinds of changes that infants can notice in melodies and rhythmic patterns, and those results give us a picture consistent with the notion that infant auditory perception uses components that will remain important into adulthood. In broad outline it is clear that infants are much like adults in their sensitivity to the pitch and rhythmic grouping of sounds. This is seen in infants' tendency to treat melodies with the same melodic contour (pattern of ups and downs in pitch) as the same and to respond to the similarity of rhythmic patterns even across changes of tempo. Similarly, we find that in children's spontaneous singing, rhythmic grouping and melodic contour are important determinants of structure and that when children begin singing, their singing is readily distinguishable from speech in terms of its patterns of pitch and rhythm. In both perception and production, we find that the child's cognition of musical patterns contains the seeds of the adult's cognition.

1. Prenatal Experience

Even before birth, the infant appears to be sensitive to music, or at least to patterns of auditory stimulation. Research has shown that prenatal auditory stimulation has effects on the infant's behavior after birth. Shetler (1989) has reviewed studies showing that the fetus is responsive to sounds at least as early as the second trimester. Very young infants recognize their mother's voice (DeCasper & Fifer, 1980; Mehler, Bertoncini, Barrière, & Jassik-Gerschenfeld, 1978), and this may derive from neonatal experience with the mother's characteristic patterns of pitch and stress accents. Such an interpretation is plausible in light of the demonstration by DeCasper and Spence (1986) that patterns of a speech passage read repeatedly by their mothers during the third trimester of pregnancy were later preferred by babies. DeCasper and Spence had newborns suck on a blind nipple in order to hear one or another children's story. Children who had been read a story in the womb sucked more to hear that story, while babies who had not been read stories in the womb had no preference between the two stories. Spence and DeCasper (1987) also demonstrated that babies who had been read stories in the womb liked speech that was low-pass filtered (resembling speech heard before birth) as much as normal unfiltered speech, whereas babies who had not been read to did not.

2. Perceptual Grouping

Infants' grouping of sounds in the pitch and time domain appears to follow much the same overall rules of thumb as it does for adults. Just as adults segregate a sequence of notes alternating rapidly between two pitch ranges into two perceptual streams (Bregman & Campbell, 1971; Dowling, 1973; McAdams & Bregman, 1979), so do infants (Demany, 1982). A converging result of Thorpe and Trehub (1989) illustrates this. Thorpe and Trehub played infants repeating six-note sequences such as AAAEEE (where A and E have frequencies of 440 and 660 Hz, a musical fifth apart). They trained the infants to turn their heads to see a toy whenever they heard a change in the stimuli being presented. A background pattern (AAAEEE) would be played over and over. Once in a while a changed pattern would appear. The changes consisted of temporal gaps introduced within perceptual groups (AAAE EE) or between groups (AAA EEE). The infants noticed the changes when they occurred within groups, but not between groups. An additional gap separating patterns that were already perceptually separate was simply lost in processing (as it tends to be by adults).

3. Pitch

Infant pitch perception is quite accurate and also displays some of the sophistication of adult pitch processing. Adults display "octave equivalence" in being able to distinguish easily between a pair of tones an octave apart and a pair of tones not quite an octave apart (Ward, 1954), and so do infants (Demany & Armand, 1984). Adults also have "pitch constancy" in the sense that complex tones with differing harmonic structure (such as different vowel sounds with different frequency spectra) have the same pitch as long as their fundamental frequencies are the same. That is, we can sing "ah" and "ooh" on the same pitch, the listener will hear them that way, and the pitch can be varied independently of vowel timbre by changing our vocal chord vibration rate (and hence the fundamental frequency of the vowel).

Even eliminating the fundamental frequency entirely from a complex tone will not change the pitch as long as several harmonics remain intact (Schouten, Ritsma, & Cardozo, 1962). Clarkson and Clifton (1985) used conditioned head turning to demonstrate that the same is true for infants 7 or 8 months old. Also, Clarkson and Rogers (1995) showed that, just like adults, infants have difficulty discerning the pitch when the harmonics that are present are high in frequency and remote from the frequency of the missing fundamental.

Regarding pitch discrimination, Thorpe (1986, as cited in Trehub, 1987) demonstrated that infants 7–10 months old can discriminate direction of pitch change for intervals as small as 1 semitone. Infants 6–9 months old can also be induced to match the pitches of vowels that are sung to them (Kessen, Levine, & Wendrich, 1979; Révész, 1954; Shuter-Dyson & Gabriel, 1981).

4. Melodic Pitch Patterns

Since early demonstrations by Melson and McCall (1970) and Kinney and Kagan (1976) that infants notice changes in melodies, a substantial body of research by Trehub (1985, 1987, 1990; Trehub & Trainor, 1990) and her colleagues has explored the importance for infants of a variety of dimensions of melodies. Figure 1 illustrates kinds of changes we can make in the pitch pattern of a melody, in this case "Twinkle, Twinkle, Little Star." We can shift the whole melody to a new pitch level, creating a transposition that leaves the pitch pattern in terms of exact intervals from note to note intact (Figure 1b). We can shift the melody in pitch while preserving its contour (pattern of ups and downs) but changing its exact interval pattern (Figures 1c and 1d), creating a same-contour imitation. The altered pitches of the same-contour imitation in Figure 1c remain within a diatonic major scale, while those in Figure 1d depart from it. Finally, we can change the contour (Figure 1e), producing a completely different melody. Changes of contour are easily noticed by adults, whereas patterns with diatonic changes of intervals (Figure 1c) are

FIGURE 1 Examples of types of stimuli described in the text. At the top is the first phrase of the familiar melody, "Twinkle, Twinkle, Little Star," with the intervals between successive notes in semitones of [0, +7, 0, +2, 0, −2]. Following it are (a) an exact repetition [0, +7, 0, +2, 0, −2]; (b) a transposition to another key [0, +7, 0, +2, 0, −2]; (c) a tonal imitation in the key of the original [0, +7, 0, +1, 0, −1]; (d) an imitation not in any major key [0, +6, 0, +2, 0, −1]; and (e) a melody with a different contour ("Mary Had a Little Lamb") [−2, −2, +2, +2, 0, 0].

often hard to discriminate from transpositions (Figure 1b; Dowling, 1978; Dowling & Fujitani, 1971).

Chang and Trehub (1977a) used heart-rate deceleration to indicate when a 5-month-old notices something new. Babies adapted to a continuously repeating six-note melody. Then Chang and Trehub substituted an altered melody to see if the baby would notice. When the stimulus was simply transposed 3 semitones (leaving it in much the same pitch range as before) the babies did not notice, but when the melody was shifted 3 semitones in pitch and its contour was altered, the babies showed a heart-rate deceleration "startle" response. For infants as for adults, the transposition sounds like the same old melody again, whereas the different-contour melody sounds new.

This result was refined in a study of 8- to 10-month-olds by Trehub, Bull, and Thorpe (1984). As in Thorpe and Trehub's (1989) study just described, Trehub et al. used conditioned head turning as an index of the infant's noticing changes in the melody. A background melody was played over and over. When a comparison melody replaced the background melody on a trial, the infants were able to notice all the changes Trehub et al. used: transpositions, same-contour-different-interval imitations, different-contour patterns, and patterns in which individual notes were displaced by an octave in a way that either violated, or did not violate, the contour. In this last transformation, the changes preserved *pitch class* by substituting a note an octave away that changed the contour. Pitch class depends on octave equivalence; all the members of a pitch class lie at octave multiples from each other. Contour changes were most noticeable. In a second experiment, Trehub et al. used the same task but made it more difficult by interposing three extra tones before the presentation of the comparison melody. In that case, infants did not notice the shift to transpositions and contour-preserving imitations, but they did notice changes in contour. This result was replicated with stimuli having even subtler contour changes by Trehub, Thorpe, and Morrongiello (1985).

The foregoing studies show that infants, like adults, easily notice differences in melodic contour. But, as Trehub, Thorpe, and Morrongiello (1987) point out, the studies do not demonstrate that infants in fact treat contour as a feature of melodies to be remembered. To show that, we would need to show that infants were abstracting a common property, an invariant, from a family of similar melodies that share only contour, and contrasting that property with that of melodies from another family with a different contour. To accomplish this, Trehub et al. (1987) used the conditioned-head-turning paradigm but with a series of background patterns that varied. In one condition, the background melodies varied in key and were all transpositions of one another. In a second condition, the background melodies were all contour-preserving imitations of one another, but not exact transpositions. In fact, infants were able to notice changes among the background melodies, which were changes involving pitches (in the transposition set) and both intervals and pitches (in the imitation set). But they noticed changes of contour even more, supporting the notion that infants, like adults, encode and remember the contours of melodies they hear.

The results reviewed so far suggest considerable qualitative similarity between infants and adults in their memory for melodies. Both are able to notice changes in intervals and pitch levels of melodies under favorable conditions, but both find changes of melodic contour much more salient. The principal differences between infants and adults in the processing of pitch information in melodies arise from the acculturation of the adults in the tonal scale system of a particular culture. Virtually every culture in the world has at least one systematic pattern for the organization of pitch classes that repeats from octave to octave (Dowling & Harwood, 1986). The most common pattern in Western European music is that of the major ("*do, re, mi*") scale. Melodies that conform to that pattern are easier for Western European adults to encode and remember than melodies that do not (Cuddy, Cohen, & Mewhort, 1981; Dowling, 1991). However, as can be inferred from their cross-cultural variation, such scale patterns are not innate. There is no reason a priori for infants to find one pitch pattern easier than another.

This last point will probably strike psychologists as noncontroversial, but there is a very strong tradition among theorists of Western music going back to Pythagoras that attributes the structure of the Western scale system not only to innate cognitive tendencies, but, even further, to the structure of the universe itself in terms of simple whole-number ratios (Bernstein, 1976; Helmholtz, 1877/1954; Hindemith, 1961). The most sensible answer to these questions appears to be that there are certain constraints of human cognition that apply to musical scale structures but that within those constraints a very wide range of cultural variation occurs (Dowling & Harwood, 1986). The main constraints are octave equivalence (involving a 2/1 frequency ratio), a weaker tendency to give importance to the perfect fifth (a 3/2 ratio), coupled with a limit of seven or so pitch classes within the octave, in agreement with George Miller's (1956) argument concerning the number of categories along a perceptual dimension that humans can handle.

In a study bearing on the inherent importance of the perfect fifth, Trehub, Cohen, Thorpe, and Morrongiello (1986) used conditioned head turning to assess the performance of 9- to 11-month-olds in detecting changes of single pitches in a simple diatonic melody (C-E-G-E-C) and in a corresponding nondiatonic melody with an augmented fifth (C-E-G♯-E-C). They found no difference between the two background melodies, suggesting the lack of a strong inherent preference for the size of the fifth. Children between 4 and 6 years of age, however, did show a difference favoring the diatonic melody. Thus acculturation in the tonal scale system is already well begun by that age.

There is some evidence, however, in favor of the primacy of the perfect fifth. Cohen, Thorpe, and Trehub (1987) complicated the task used by Trehub et al. (1986) by transposing the background melody to a new pitch level with each repetition. In that case, the task could not be solved simply by noticing changes of single pitches, but would require the abstraction of the invariant interval pattern of the background melody. Under those conditions, 7- to 11-month-olds found changes easier to detect in the diatonic pattern (C-E-G-E-C) than in the nondiatonic pattern (C-E-G♯-E-C). Seven to 11 months is a rather wide age range in the life of a rapidly changing infant. Lynch and Eilers (1992) differentiated the ends of that range by running 6-month-olds and 12-month-olds in parallel tasks. They found that although the 12-month-olds performed like the 7- to 11-month-olds in the Cohen et al. (1987) study, the 6-month-olds performed equally well with the diatonic and nondiatonic patterns. That is, the younger infants were not yet acculturated to the standard Western diatonic scale as distinct from other arrangements of semitone intervals, whereas the older infants were.

In addition to the diatonic and nondiatonic patterns using Western "tonal material" (Dowling, 1978) consisting of intervals constructed of semitones, Lynch and Eilers (1992) also included a non-Western pattern: a Javanese *pélog* scale pattern that did not contain a perfect fifth and in which some of the pitches approximated quarter steps lying in between the semitones on the piano. The performance of the 6-month-olds, which was better than chance (and equally good) for diatonic and nondiatonic Western patterns, decreased to chance levels for the Javanese pattern (as did the performance of the 12-month-olds). Thus the 6-month-olds were either acculturated at the level of Western tonal material, or there is something about scale structures constructed with a logarithmic modulus such as the semitone (shared by the diatonic and nondiatonic patterns) that makes patterns constructed in them naturally easier to process. I favor the former explanation in terms of acculturation, because if conformity to "natural" pitch intervals were important, the most obvious candidate for a natural interval conducive to "good" pattern construction (in the Gestalt sense) is the perfect fifth (C-G, the 3/2 ratio) contained in the diatonic but not the other two patterns. This possibility is suggested by Trainor (1993), Trehub, Thorpe, and Trainor (1990), and Schellenberg and Trehub (1994) in their discussions of the diatonic/nondiatonic distinction made by the older infants. The perfect fifth is a fundamental building block in the traditional scale systems of India, China, and the American Indians, as well as of Europe (Dowling & Harwood, 1986), and is represented in the harmonic structure of complex tones such as vowel sounds, and also is prevalent in music (as at the start of "Twinkle, Twinkle," Figure 1). Thus if the perfect fifth, as a natural interval, were an important determinant of infant responses to scale patterns, the 6-month-olds would have performed better with the diatonic patterns than with the other two patterns. They did not, so it seems unlikely to me that the semitone, rarely explicitly present in the patterns and a far more remote candidate for natural interval, would play such a role.

If the younger infants are acculturated in terms of semitones, it remains nevertheless true that they are not sensitive to subtler aspects of the diatonic scheme. This is seen in their indifference both to the diatonic/nondiatonic distinction and to diatonic key membership of target tones, as shown by Trainor and Trehub (1992). Trainor and Trehub tested 8-month-olds using a strongly diatonic background melody. Comparison melodies had an altered pitch that either remained within the key of the background melody or went outside it. Infants detected the change equally well whether it remained within the key or not. Their performance was unaffected by tonal scale structure. Adults, in contrast, found out-of-key alterations much easier to detect. (In fact, out-of-key alterations sound quite startling to adults unless they are "anchored" to a new key as the result of modulation—Bartlett, 1993; Bartlett & Dowling, 1988; Bharucha, 1984, 1996.) In fact, infants' performance with within-key alterations was superior to that of adults! Adults found the within-key alterations difficult to detect because the tonal framework they had acquired through lifelong perceptual learning made the within-key notes sound like natural continuations of the melody, even though they were the wrong notes. (Trainor & Trehub, 1993, extended these results to show that infants were more sensitive to changes in both patterns when they were transposed to a closely related key vs. a distant key—see the discussion of key-distance effects later.)

In summary, we can say that infants, like adults, find melodic contour a very salient feature of melodies. However, the process of acculturation in pitch-scale patterns is a long, slow process. By 6 months the infant is beginning that process at the level of the tonal material. By 1 year the infant responds differently to diatonic and nondiatonic patterns. But, as described below, listeners require more years of acculturation before they hear pitches automatically in terms of a tonal frame of reference.

5. Rhythm

As noted in the earlier discussion of perceptual grouping, infants' temporal grouping of tone sequences is much like that of adults. Infants have been shown to discriminate between different rhythmic patterns (Chang & Trehub, 1977b; Demany, McKenzie, & Vurpillot, 1977). However, those tasks could have been solved on the basis of absolute rather than relative temporal relationships. Just as a melody retains its identity across transposition, so that relative and not absolute pitches are important, so a rhythmic pattern retains its identity across changes in tempo, where relative rather than absolute timing of the notes is important (Monahan & Carterette, 1985). And just as infants are sensitive to changes in patterns of relative pitch, they are sensitive to changes in the relative temporal patterns of rhythms. Trehub and Thorpe (1989), again using conditioned head turning, showed that infants 7–9 months old could notice changes in rhythmic patterns (such as XX XX vs. XXX X) even across variations in tempo. Just as for adults, a rhythmic pattern retained its identity when presented faster or slower.

Infants' broader rhythmic organization of musical phrases is like adults' in a surprising way. Krumhansl and Jusczyk (1990) presented 4- and 5-month-olds with Mozart minuets that had pauses inserted between phrases or within phrases. The infants preferred to listen to versions with pauses between phrases, suggesting that the infants were sensitive to cues to adult phrase structure of musical pieces. It remains to be seen exactly what cues the infants were responding to. Jusczyk and Krumhansl (1993) extended those results to show that the infants were really responding to phrase structure (and not just Mozart's beginning and ending patterns in the minuets) and that the pitch contour and note duration are important determinants of the infants' response to structural pauses. Furthermore, infants tended not to notice pauses inserted at phrase boundaries in naturally segmented minuets.

B. CHILDHOOD

During their second year, children begin to recognize certain melodies as stable entities in their environment and can identify them even after a considerable delay. My older daughter at 18 months would run to the TV set when she heard the "Sesame Street" theme come on, but not for other tunes. At 20 months, after a week or so of going around the house singing "uh-oh" rather loudly to a descending minor third, she responded with the spoken label "uh-oh" when I played that pattern on the piano.

1. Singing

Children begin to sing spontaneously somewhere around the age of 9 months or a year. At first this can take the form of vocal play that includes wild excursions over the child's entire pitch range, but it also includes patterns of vowel sounds sung on locally stable pitches. This last is a feature that distinguishes singing from the child's incipient speech at this age.

Especially after 18 months, the child begins to generate recognizable, repeatable songs (Ostwald, 1973). The songs of a child around the age of 2 years often consist of brief phrases repeated over and over. Their contours are replicable, but the pitch wanders. The same melodic and rhythmic contour is repeated at different pitch levels, usually with different intervals between the notes. The rhythm of these phrases is coherent, with rhythms often those of speech patterns. Accents within phrases and the timing of the phrases themselves is determined by a regular beat pattern. This two-level organization of beat and within-phrase rhythm is another feature that distinguishes singing from speech and is characteristic of adult musical organization (Dowling, 1988; Dowling & Harwood, 1986).

An example of a spontaneous song from my daughter at 24 months consisted of an ascending and descending phrase with the words "Come a duck on my house" repeated 10 or 12 times at different pitch levels with small pitch intervals within phrases. This song recurred for 2 weeks and then disappeared. Such spontaneous songs have a systematic form and display two essential features of adult singing: they use discrete pitch levels, and they use the repetition of rhythmic and melodic contours as a formal device. They are unlike adult songs, however, because they lack a stable pitch framework (a scale) and use a very limited set of phrase contours in one song—usually just one or two (Dowling, 1984). A more sophisticated construction by the same child at 32 months can be seen in Figure 2. The pitch still wanders but is locally stable within phrases. Here three identifiable phrases are built into a coherent song.

The preceding observations are in general agreement with those of Davidson, McKernon, and Gardner (1981; Davidson, 1985; McKernon, 1979) on spontaneous singing by 2-year-olds. Davidson et al. extended naturalistic observation by teaching a simple song to children across the preschool age range. Two- and 3-year-olds generally succeeded in reproducing the contours of isolated phrases. Older children were able to concatenate more phrases in closer approximations to the model. It was only very gradually across age that the interval relationships of the major scale began to stabilize. Four-year-olds could stick to a stable scale pattern within a phrase but would often slip to a new key for the next phrase, just as the 3-year-old in Figure 2. It was not until after age 5 that the children could hold onto a stable tonality throughout the song. Further, with a little practice, 5-year-olds were able to produce easily recognizable versions of the model. My own observations suggest that the typical 5-year-old has a fairly large repertoire of nursery songs of his or her culture. This emerges when children are asked to sing

FIGURE 2 A child's spontaneous song at 32 months. Each note was vocalized to the syllable "Yeah." Brackets indicate regions of relatively accurate intonation. Elsewhere intonation wandered.

a song and can respond with a great variety of instances. It is also apparent from their better performance on memory tasks using familiar materials (vs. novel melodies; Andrews & Dowling, 1991). Through the preschool years, the use of more or less stable tonalities for songs comes to be established.

2. Absolute Pitch

Absolute pitch is the ability to identify pitches by their note names even in the absence of musical context. Absolute pitch is not an essential ability for the understanding of most music, although it can aid in the tracking of key relationships in extended passages of tonal music (as in Mozart and Wagner) and in singing 12-tone music on sight. There are times when it can be a hindrance to music cognition by discouraging some of its possessors from developing sophisticated strategies for identifying pitch relationships in tonal contexts (Miyazaki, 1993). Absolute pitch has typically been quite rare even among musicians, occurring in only about 4–8%. However, in cultures where early music training is encouraged, such as in present-day Japan, the incidence of absolute pitch among the musically trained is much higher, possibly near 50% (Miyazaki, 1988). Ogawa and Miyazaki (1994) suggest on the basis of studies of 4- to 10-year-old children in a keyboard training program that most children have the underlying ability to acquire absolute pitch. In their review of the literature, Takeuchi and Hulse (1993) argue in favor of an "early-learning" hypothesis—that absolute pitch can be acquired by anyone, but only during a critical period ending in the fifth or sixth year.

Although relatively few adults can identify pitches, adults typically are able to approximate the pitch levels of familiar songs, a capacity that Takeuchi and Hulse (1993) call "residual absolute pitch." For example, Halpern (1989) found that adults would typically begin the same song on close to the same pitch after an extended delay. Levitin (1994), using the album cover as a retrieval cue, found that young adults sang popular songs they had heard only in one recorded version at approximately the correct pitch level. (Two thirds of the subjects were within 2 semitones of the correct pitch.)

The studies on pitch encoding cited earlier (Dowling, 1986, 1992) suggest that with a moderate amount of training people develop a "temporary and local" sense of absolute pitch that leads them to encode what they hear (and produce) in terms of the tonal framework provided by the current context.

3. Melodic Contour and Tonality

In perception and in singing, melodic contour remains an important basis for melodic organization throughout childhood. Morrongiello, Trehub, Thorpe, and Capodilupo (1985) found 4- to 6-year-olds very capable in discriminating melodies on the basis of contour. Pick, Palmer, Hennessy, Unze, Jones, and Richardson (1988) replicated that result and found that 4- to 6-year-olds could also use contour to recognize same-contour imitations of familiar melodies. In another task emphasizing the recognition of similarity among same-contour imitations of familiar tunes, Andrews and Dowling (1991) found 5- and 6-year-olds performed equally well at recognizing familiar versions and both tonal and atonal imitations. It was not until ages 7 and 8 that tonality began to be a factor in that experiment and only by ages 9 or 10 that a difference appeared between familiar versions and same-contour imitations (the adult pattern of performance).

Studies of perception and memory provide converging evidence with that from singing concerning the 5- or 6-year-old's acquisition of a stable scale structure. With highly familiar tunes such as "Happy Birthday" and "Twinkle, Twinkle," even 4-year-olds can notice "funny" sounding versions with out-of-key pitches (Trehub, Morrongiello, & Thorpe, 1985). And Bartlett and Dowling (1980, Experiment 4) found that 5-year-olds can use musical key differences to discriminate between melodies. On each trial of the experiment, a familiar melody was presented, followed by either a transposition or a same-contour imitation. The comparison was either in the same key as the standard or a nearly related key, or it was in a distant key. (Near keys share many overlapping pitches in their scales; distant keys share few.) Adults in this task are highly accurate in saying "Same" to transpositions (>90%) and not saying "Same" to imitations (<10%). The pattern for 5-year-olds was very different: they tend to say "Same" to near-key comparisons (both transpositions and imitations) and "different" to far-key comparisons. Five-year-olds have one component of the adult behavior pattern—the ability to distinguish near from far keys—but not the other component—the ability to detect changes of interval sizes in the tonal imitations. They accept same-contour imitations as versions of the tune. As the child grows older, the pattern of response moves in the adult direction, so that an 8-year-old accepts near-key imitations less often than far-key transpositions. Eight-year-olds can use both key distance and interval changes to reject a same-contour imitation, whereas 5-year-olds rely principally on key distance.

The 5- to 6-year-old's grasp of stable tonal centers fits other results in the literature. For example, in a series of studies Riley and McKee (1963; Riley, McKee, Bell & Schwartz, 1967; Riley, McKee & Hadley, 1964) found that first graders have an overwhelming tendency to respond by choosing a pitch match rather than an interval match. This tendency to respond to the pitch tasks in terms of a stable frame of reference contrasted with the same children's ability to respond to loudness-comparison tasks in terms of relative (not absolute) loudness.

The emergence of tonal scale relationships among the child's cognitive structures has implications for the conduct of research. Using atonal materials with infants has little impact on the results, because babies do not respond to tonal scale structures as such (Trainor & Trehub, 1992). But Wohlwill's (1971) use of atonal (and to the adult ear rather strange sounding) melodies probably led to his result that first graders could distinguish targets from different-contour lures at a level barely better than chance. At any rate, Wohlwill's conclusion that "the establishment of pitch as a directional dimension is a relatively late phenomenon" could not be true in the light of Thorpe's result with infants (1986, cited in Trehub, 1987). What is true is that first graders have trouble using words to describe pitch direction (Hair, 1977; Zimmerman & Sechrest, 1970).

During later childhood, the child continues to develop sophistication in the use of the tonal scale framework determined by the culture. This progress is illustrated by Zenatti (1969), who studied memory for sequences of three, four, and six notes with subjects from age 5 years up. On each trial, a standard melody was followed by a comparison melody in which one note of the standard had been changed by 1 or 2 semitones. The subject had to say which of the notes had been changed—a very difficult task. Zenatti found that for the three-note sequences, 5-year-olds performed at about chance with both tonal and atonal stimuli. From ages 6 through 10, the results for tonal and atonal sequences diverged, with better performance on tonal sequences. Then, at around age 12, processing of the atonal sequences caught up. For four- and six-note sequences, the same pattern appeared, but the tonal-atonal difference remained until adulthood. Experience with the tonal scale system leads people to improve on recognition of tonal melodies but not atonal melodies. With simple stimuli such as the three-note melodies, atonal performance catches up relatively soon, but longer sequences continue to benefit from the tonal framework throughout childhood. (This result converges with that of Morrongiello & Roes, 1990.) Superiority of recognition with tonal materials has been often observed with adults (Dowling, 1978; Francès, 1958/1988); Zenatti's study shows that the effect can be used as an index of the child's acquisition of the scale structures of the culture.

Trainor and Trehub (1994) took the development of the role of tonality in the ability to detect melodic pitch changes one step further. In addition to alterations that either remained within key or departed from the key, Trainor and Trehub introduced changes that remained in the key but departed from the particular harmony implied by the melody. For example, the first four notes of "Twinkle, Twinkle" (Figure 1a: C-C-G-G) imply harmonization with the tonic triad (C-E-G). A change of the third note from G to E would remain within both the key and the implied harmony. A change to F would remain within the key, but violate the harmony. Trainor and Trehub found that 7-year-olds, like adults, could detect the out-of-key and out-of-harmony changes much more easily than the within-harmony changes, whereas 5-year-olds reliably detected only the out-of-key changes. As Trainor and Trehub (1994, p. 131) conclude, "5-year-olds have implicit knowledge of key membership but not of implied harmony, whereas 7-year-olds, like adults, have implicit knowledge of both aspects of musical structure." In a result that converges with these studies, Imberty (1969, chapter 4) found that 7-year-olds could tell when a melody had been switched in midstream from one key to another or from the major mode to the minor.

Krumhansl and Keil (1982) provide a good picture of the child's progress in grasping the tonal framework. They had children judge the goodness of melodic patterns beginning with an outline of the tonic triad (C-E-G) and ending on an arbitrarily chosen pitch. Krumhansl (1990) had found that adults in that task, especially musically experienced adults, produce a profile in which important notes in the tonal hierarchy (such as those of the tonic triad) receive high ratings and less important notes receive progressively lower ratings in accordance with their importance in the key. Krumhansl and Keil found that 6- and 7-year-olds distinguished simply between within-key notes and outside-of-key notes. The structure of the tonal hierarchy became more differentiated with age, so that by the age of 8 or 9 children were distinguishing between the pitches of the tonic triad and the other pitches within the key.

Two similar studies illustrate the importance of seemingly minor methodological details in research on the development of the tonal hierarchy. Cuddy and Badertscher (1987) simplified the task by using patterns with five notes instead of six. In that case, even 6- and 7-year-olds displayed the principal features of the adult hierarchy. And Speer and Meeks (1985) used an unstable context of the first seven notes of a C-major scale, ending on B or D (in contrast to the stable triad context in Krumhansl & Keil, 1982), to find that 8- and 11-year-olds perform very much like adults.

Lamont and Cross (1994) criticize the use of triads and scales as contexts in the foregoing three studies on two grounds. First, they suggest that these prototypical contexts, always the same throughout a condition of the experiment, are not very representative of the varied character of real tonal music. Second, they note that if children are exposed to any music class activities, the children will probably already have encountered scales and arpeggios. As Lamont and Cross (1994, p. 31) say, "Presented with an overlearned pattern, ... the listener [could be expected] to give an overlearned response appropriate to that pattern." To produce more representative contexts, Lamont and Cross borrowed a method from West and Fryer (1990) of using a different random permutation of the notes of the major scale on each trial, and they also used chord progressions establishing the key. The study included five groups of children between 6 and 11 years old. Like Speer and Meeks (1985) and Cuddy and Badertscher (1987), Lamont and Cross found the children relatively sophisticated in their differentiation of the tonal hierarchy, but they also found, in agreement with Krumhansl and Keil (1982), that the children's representations of musical pitch gained in sophistication through the elementary school years. Lamont and Cross supplemented this study with converging evidence from a series of more open-ended tasks, such as arranging chime bars in order according to pitch and arranging them to create a tune.

In summary, the development of melody-processing skills can be seen as a progression from the use of gross, obvious features to the use of more and more subtle features. Babies can distinguish pitch contours and produce single pitches. Around the age of 5, the child can organize songs around stable tonal centers (keys) but does not yet have a stable tonal scale system that can be used to transpose melodies accurately to new keys. The scale system develops during the elementary school years and confers on tonal materials an advantage in memory that remains into adulthood.

4. Rhythm

There are two aspects of musical rhythm that I wish to discuss in terms of development in childhood. First is the development of the ability to control attention in relation to the temporal sequence of events, using regularities in the rhythm of occurrence of critical features in a piece to aim attention at important elements. Second is the development of the ability to remember and reproduce rhythmic patterns.

Adults in listening to speech and music are able to use their experience with similar patterns to focus their attention on critical moments in the ongoing stream of stimuli to pick up important information (Jones, 1981). This ability requires perceptual learning to develop. Andrews and Dowling (1991) studied the course of this development using a "hidden melodies" task in which the notes of a target melody such as "Twinkle, Twinkle" are temporally interleaved with random distractor notes in the same pitch range, the whole pattern being presented at 6 or 8 notes/sec. After about an hour of practice, adults can discern the hidden melody when they are told which target melody to listen for (Dowling, 1973; Dowling, Lung, & Herrbold, 1987). Andrews and Dowling (1991) included an easier condition in which the interleaved distractor notes were presented in a separate pitch range from the notes of the target. They reasoned that as listeners learned to aim attention in pitch, the listeners would find it easier to discern the targets in a separate pitch range. Five- and 6-year-olds perform barely better than chance on this task and find targets equally difficult to discern whether in a separate range from the distractors or not. It is not until the age of 9 or 10 that the separation of pitch ranges confers an advantage, suggesting that by that age listeners are able to aim their attention at a particular pitch range. Ability to aim attention in time improves steadily from age 6 on, and by age 9, discerning hidden targets with distractors in the same pitch range has reached 70% (with chance at 50%). Musically untrained adults achieve about 80% on this task, while musically experienced adults find the hidden targets equally easy to discern (about 90%) with distractors inside as well as outside the target pitch range.

There is evidence for the importance of a hierarchical organization of rhythm in 5-year-olds' reproductions of rhythmic patterns. Drake (1993) found 5-year-olds able to reproduce rhythms with two levels of organization: a steady beat and varying binary subdivisions of the beat. Although children that age find it easy to tap isochronous (steady, nonvarying) sequences in either binary or ternary rhythm, they find binary sequences with varying patterns within the beat easier than ternary. Drake reports that by the age of 7, children improve in reproducing models that include a variety of different durations in the same sequence, having gained facility with greater rhythmic complexity.

Accents in music can occur on various levels of structure. In particular, accents can be produced in terms of the two levels of beat and rhythmic organization. The beat or meter provides accents at regular time intervals. Rhythmic accents are generally conferred on the first and last members of rhythmic groups. A third level of accents can arise from discontinuities in the melodic contour, such as leaps and reversals of direction. Drake, Dowling, and Palmer (1991) constructed songs in which accents on those levels either coincided or did not. Desynchronization of accent structure lowered children's performance in singing the songs, but there was little change in singing accuracy for children who are between 5 and 11 years old.

These results suggest that by the age of 5 children are responding to more than one level of rhythmic organization and that the songs they learn are processed as integrated wholes in the sense that events at one level affect performance at another; for example, complication of accent structure produces decrements in pitch accuracy in singing. An additional example is provided by Gérard and Auxiette (1988), who obtained rhythm reproductions from 5-year-olds. Gérard and Auxiette either provided the children with a plain rhythmic model to reproduce or provided additional context for the rhythm by providing either words to be chanted to it, or a melody to be sung to it, or both. They found that children with musical training performed best in tapping the rhythm when there was a melody, and children without musical training performed best when there were words. Having words or melody aided in the processing of the rhythm. Gérard and Auxiette (1992) also found that 6-year-old musicians were better able than nonmusicians to synchronize their tapping and their verbalizations in such a task.

The picture that emerges of the development of rhythmic organization is that a multilevel structure appears early and that by the age of 5, the child is quite sophisticated. There is some development in the school-age years, but Drake (1993), for example, found little difference between 7-year-olds and adult nonmusicians. Already the spontaneous songs of a 2-year-old show two levels of rhythmic organization, the beat and rhythmic subdivisions (often speech rhythms) overlaid on that, and the 5-year-old follows the same hierarchical organization in tapped reproductions. Finally, rhythmic organization is not easily separable from other aspects of structural organization in a song, so that in perception and production other aspects of melody are intertwined with rhythmic structure.

5. Emotion

Ample evidence has accumulated that children during the preschool years learn to identify the emotional states represented in music, and this ability improves during the school years. For example, both Cunningham and Sterling (1988) and Dolgin and Adelson (1990) showed that by the age of 4, children perform well above chance in assigning one of four affective labels (essentially "happy," "sad," "angry," and "afraid") to musical excerpts in agreement with adults' choices. (With the exception of Cunningham and Sterling, all the studies reviewed here had subjects choose schematic faces expressing the emotions in making their responses.) Both of these studies also showed that performance improves over the school years. Performance was less than perfect at the earlier ages, and in particular, Cunningham and Sterling found that 4-year-olds were not consistently above chance with "sad" and "angry," nor 5-year-olds with "afraid," whereas Dolgin and Adelson found 4-year-olds at about chance with "afraid." In a similar study, Terwogt and Van Grinsven (1991) found that 5-year-olds performed very much like adults, but that all ages tended to confuse "afraid" and "angry." These studies were able in a general way to attribute the children's responses to features of the music, but there are other studies that have focused on specific musical features such as the contrast between major and minor.

The issue of whether the major mode in Western music is a cue to happy emotions, and the minor mode a cue to sad ones, has been a perennial issue for both musicologists and psychologists. A particular developmental issue arises here, because we can ask whether responses to the affective connotations of major and minor appear earlier than the specific cognitive recognition of the difference, which, according to the foregoing review, appears around the age of 5. In exploring these issues, Gerardi and Gerken (1995) restricted responses to the choice of two faces, "happy" or "sad," and used adaptations of musical passages that differed in mode (major vs. minor) and predominant melodic contour (up vs. down). They found that 8-year-olds and adults, but not 5-year-olds, applied "happy" and "sad" consistently to excerpts in the major and minor, respectively. Only adults consistently chose "happy" for ascending contours and "sad" for descending, although that variable was probably not manipulated very strongly. (For example, "Che faro" from Gluck's *Orfeo ed Euridice* fails to ascend or descend unambiguously.)

In contrast to Gerardi and Gerken, Kastner and Crowder (1990) allowed subjects a choice of four faces—"happy," "neutral," "sad," and "angry"—and used versions of three different tunes presented in the major and minor, and with or without accompaniment. They found that when relatively positive responses (happy or neutral) were contrasted with negative responses (sad or angry), even 3-year-olds consistently assigned positive faces to major and negative faces to minor. This tendency became stronger between 3 and 12 years of age. Therefore, we can say that there is some indication that preschoolers are able to grasp the emotional connotations of the two modes at an earlier age than they can differentiate their responses in a more cognitively oriented task.

C. ADULTHOOD

Rather than include here a comprehensive review of adults' implicit knowledge of musical structure, I shall concentrate on some issues concerned with tonality and the tonal scale framework. Adults in Western European cultures vary greatly in musical ability. Sometimes these individual differences are reflected in performance on perception and memory tasks. Untrained subjects usually do not find contour recognition more difficult than trained subjects (Dowling, 1978) but do find interval recognition (Bartlett & Dowling, 1980; Cuddy & Cohen, 1976) and the hearing out of partials in a complex tone (Fine & Moore, 1993) more difficult. Even where nonmusicians perform worse overall on tasks involving memory for melodies, they are often just as influenced as musicians by variables such as tonality, performing worse with atonal than with tonal melodies (Dowling, 1991). Also, nonmusicians are just as error prone as musicians when dealing with nonstandard quarter steps that fall in cracks in the musical scale (Dowling, 1992). Such qualitative results show that nonmusicians have acquired at least a basic tonal scale framework from their experience in the culture and that that framework has a psychological reality independent of its use as a pedagogical tool.

During the past few years, evidence has been accumulating that listeners routinely encode the music they hear in absolute, and not relative, terms. For example, when presented with novel melodies and then tested after filled delays of up to 1.5 min, listeners find it easier to discriminate between targets (like Figure 1b, only novel) and same-contour lures (like Figure 1c), than between targets and different-contour lures (like Figure 1e; Dowling, Kwak, & Andrews, 1995). (With familiar melodies such as those shown in Figure 1, those abilities are about equal after 2 min.) That is, after a delay, listeners find it easier to discriminate very fine differences between the test melody and the melody they heard than to discriminate gross differences (DeWitt & Crowder, 1986; Dowling & Bartlett, 1981). Their memory represents very precisely what they have heard. This evidence converges with the demonstration by Levitin (1994), reviewed earlier, that nonmusicians come very close to the correct absolute pitch when singing familiar popular songs and with the similar demonstration by Levitin and Cook (1996) that their approximations of the tempos of such songs are quite accurate. This makes it seem likely that memory for music typically operates in terms of more precise representations of particular stimuli than has been generally thought (e.g., by Dowling, 1978).

Among adults, striking differences in performance based on different levels of musical experience sometimes appear, illustrating different ways in which knowledge of scale structure can be used. Dowling (1986) demonstrated differences among three levels of sophistication in a study of memory for novel seven-note melodies. Dowling presented the melodies in a context of chords that defined each melody as built around the tonic (the first degree of the scale, *do*) or the dominant (the fifth degree, *sol*). Listeners had to say whether notes had been altered when the melody was presented again. The test melodies were also presented with a chordal context, and that context was either the same as before or different. The test melodies were either exact transpositions or altered same-contour imitations of the original melodies. Musically untrained listeners performed equally well with same or different chord context at test. Listeners with moderate amounts of training in music (around 5 years of lessons when they were young) performed much worse with changed context. That suggests that those listeners were initially encoding the melodies in terms of the tonal scale values provided by the context, so that when the context was shifted, the melody was very difficult to retrieve. In contrast, nonmusicians simply remembered the melody independent of its relation to the context. Professional musicians performed very well with both changed and unchanged contexts. Their sophistication gave them the flexibility to ignore the context where it was not useful.

III. SUMMARY

Adults bring a large store of implicit knowledge to bear in listening to music. This knowledge includes implicit representations of the tonal framework of the culture in terms of which expected events are processed efficiently and in terms of which pitches are interpreted in their musical context. This store of knowledge includes knowledge of the timing patterns of music in the culture, so that the listener is able to focus attention on moments in time at which critical information is likely to occur. Although musical experience leads, as we have seen, to greater sophistication in the store of implicit knowledge, nevertheless nonmusicians have typically acquired the fundamentals of this knowledge from their experience listening to music throughout their lives. Thus nonmusicians are sensitive to shifts in tonality and to the multilevel structure of rhythmic organization.

The implicit knowledge of adults is built on elements present even in infancy: the importance of melodic and rhythmic contours, the use of discrete, steady pitch levels, the organization of rhythmic patterns into a steady beat and an overlay of more complicated rhythms, and octave equivalence, to name a few. These elements provide the groundwork for perceptual learning and acculturation throughout life to build upon.

ACKNOWLEDGMENT

I thank Melinda Andrews for her thoughtful contributions to the development of this chapter.

REFERENCES

Andrews, M. W., & Dowling, W. J. (1991). The development of perception of interleaved melodies and control of auditory attention. Music Perception, 8, 349-368.

Bartlett, J. C. (1993). Tonal structure of melodies. In T. J. Tighe & W. J. Dowling, (Eds.), Psychology and music: The understanding of melody and rhythm (pp. 39–61). Hillsdale, NJ: Erlbaum.

Bartlett, J. C., & Dowling, W. J. (1980). The recognition of transposed melodies: A key-distance effect in developmental perspective. Journal of Experimental Psychology: Human Perception & Performance, 6, 501–515.

Bartlett, J. C., & Dowling, W. J. (1988). Scale structure and similarity of melodies. Music Perception, 5, 285–314.

Bernstein, L. (1976). The unanswered question. Cambridge, MA: Harvard University Press.

Bharucha, J. J. (1984). Anchoring effects in music: The resolution of dissonance. Cognitive Psychology, 16, 485–518.

Bharucha, J. J. (1996). Melodic anchoring. Music Perception, 13, 383–400.

Bregman, A., & Campbell, J. (1971). Primary auditory stream segregation and perception of order in rapid sequences of tones. Journal of Experimental Psychology, 89, 244–249.

Brown, R. (1973). A first language: The early stages. London: George Allen & Unwin.

Chang, H. W., & Trehub, S. E. (1977a). Auditory processing of relational information by young infants. Journal of Experimental Child Psychology, 24, 324–331.

Chang, H. W., & Trehub, S. E. (1977b). Infant's perception of temporal grouping in auditory patterns. Child Development, 48, 1666–1670.

Clarkson, M. G., & Clifton, R. K. (1985). Infant pitch perception: Evidence for responding to pitch categories and the missing fundamental. Journal of the Acoustical Society of America, 77, 1521–1528.

Clarkson, M. G., & Rogers, E. C. (1995). Infants require low-frequency energy to hear the pitch of the missing fundamental. Journal of the Acoustical Society of America, 98, 148–154.

Cohen, A. J., Thorpe, L. A., & Trehub, S. E. (1987). Infants' perception of musical relations in short transposed tone sequences. *Canadian Journal of Psychology, 41,* 33–47.

Cuddy, L. L., & Badertscher, B. (1987). Recovery of the tonal hierarchy: Some comparisons across age and levels of musical experience. *Perception & Psychophysics, 41,* 609–620.

Cuddy, L. L., & Cohen, A. J. (1976). Recognition of transposed melodic sequences. *Quarterly of Experimental Psychology, 28,* 255–270.

Cuddy, L. L., Cohen, A. J., & Mewhort, D. J. K. (1981). Perception of structure in short melodic sequences. *Journal of Experimental Psychology: Human Perception & Performance, 7,* 869–883.

Cunningham, J. G., & Sterling, R. S. (1988). Developmental change in the understanding of affective meaning of music. *Motivation & Emotion, 12,* 399–413.

Davidson, L. (1985). Tonal structures in children's early songs. *Music Perception, 2,* 361–374.

Davidson, L., McKernon, P., & Gardner, H. (1981). The acquisition of song: A developmental approach. In *Documentary report of the Ann Arbor Symposium* (pp. 301-315). Reston, VA: Music Educators National Conference.

DeCasper, A. J., & Fifer, W. P. (1980). Of human bonding: Newborns prefer their mothers' voices. *Science, 208,* 1174-1176.

DeCasper, A. J., & Spence, M. J. (1986). Prematernal speech influences newborns' perception of speech sounds. *Infant Behavior & Development, 9,* 133–150.

Demany, L. (1982). Auditory stream segregation in infancy. *Infant Behavior & Development, 5,* 261–276.

Demany, L., & Armand, F. (1984). The perceptual reality of tone chroma in early infancy. *Journal of the Acoustical Society of America, 76,* 57–66.

Demany, L., McKenzie, B., & Vurpillot, E. (1977). Rhythm perception in early infancy. *Nature, 266,* 718–719.

DeWitt, L. A., & Crowder, R. G. (1986). Recognition of novel melodies after brief delays. *Music Perception, 3,* 259–274.

Dolgin, K. G., & Adelson, E. H. (1990). Age changes in the ability to interpret affect in sung and instrumentally-presented melodies. Psychology of Music, 18, 87–98.

Dowling, W. J. (1973). The perception of interleaved melodies. *Cognitive Psychology, 5,* 322–337.

Dowling, W. J. (1978). Scale and contour: Two components of a theory of memory for melodies. *Psychological Review, 85,* 341–354.

Dowling, W. J. (1984). Development of musical schemata in children's spontaneous singing. In W. R. Crozier & A. J. Chapman (Eds.), *Cognitive processes in the perception of art* (pp. 145–163). Amsterdam: North-Holland.

Dowling, W. J. (1986). Context effects on melody recognition: Scale-step versus interval representations. *Music Perception, 3,* 281–296.

Dowling, W. J. (1988). Tonal structure and children's early learning of music. In J. Sloboda (Ed.), *Generative processes in music* (pp. 113–128). Oxford: Oxford University Press.

Dowling, W. J. (1991). Tonal strength and melody recognition after long and short delays. *Perception & Psychophysics, 50,* 305–313.

Dowling, W. J. (1992). Perceptual grouping, attention and expectancy in listening to music. In J. Sundberg (Ed.), *Gluing tones: Grouping in music composition, performance and listening* (pp. 77–98). Stockholm: Publications of the Royal Swedish Academy of Music, no. 72.

Dowling, W. J. (1993a). Procedural and declarative knowledge in music cognition and education. In T. J. Tighe & W. J. Dowling (Eds.), *Psychology and music: The understanding of melody and rhythm* (pp. 5–18). Hillsdale, NJ: Erlbaum.

Dowling, W. J. (1993b). La structuration mélodique: Perception et chant. In A. Zenatti (Ed.), *Psychologie de la musique* (pp. 145–176). Paris: Presses Universitaires de France.

Dowling, W. J., & Bartlett, J. C. (1981). The importance of interval information in long-term memory for melodies. *Psychomusicology, 1*(1), 30–49.

Dowling, W. J., & Fujitani, D. S. (1971). Contour, interval, and pitch recognition in memory for melodies. *Journal of the Acoustical Society of America, 49,* 524–531.

Dowling, W. J., & Harwood, D. L. (1986). *Music cognition.* New York: Academic Press.

Dowling, W. J., Kwak, S.-Y., & Andrews, M. W. (1995). The time course of recognition of novel melodies. *Perception & Psychophysics, 57,* 136–149.

Dowling, W. J., Lung, K. M.-T., & Herrbold, S. (1987). Aiming attention in pitch and time in the perception of interleaved melodies. *Perception & Psychophysics, 41,* 642–656.

Drake, C. (1993). Reproduction of musical rhythms by children, adult musicians, and adult nonmusicians. *Perception & Psychophysics, 53,* 25–33.

Drake, C., Dowling, W. J., & Palmer, C. (1991). Accent structures in the reproduction of simple tunes by children and adult pianists. *Music Perception, 8,* 315–334.

Elbert, T., Pantev, C., Wienbruch, C., Rockstroh, B., & Taub, E. (1995). Increased cortical representation of the fingers of the left hand in string players. *Science, 270,* 305–307.

Fine, P. A., & Moore, B. J. C. (1993). Frequency analysis and musical ability. *Music Perception, 11,* 39–54.

Francès, R. (1988). *The perception of music* (W. J. Dowling, Trans.). Hillsdale, NJ: Erlbaum. (Original publication 1958).

Gérard, C., & Auxiette, C. (1988). The role of melodic and verbal organization in the reproduction of rhythmic groups by children. *Music Perception, 6,* 173–192.

Gérard, C., & Auxiette, C. (1992). The processing of musical prosody by musical and nonmusical children. *Music Perception, 10,* 93–126.

Gerardi, G. M., & Gerken, L. (1995). The development of affective responses to modality and melodic contour. *Music Perception, 12,* 279–290.

Hair, H. I. (1977). Discrimination of tonal direction on verbal and nonverbal tasks by first-grade children. *Journal of Research on Music Education, 25,* 197–210.

Halpern, A. R. (1989). Memory for the absolute pitch of familiar songs. *Memory & Cognition, 17,* 572–581.

Helmholtz, H. von. (1954). *On the sensations of tone.* (A. J. Ellis, Trans.). New York: Dover. (Original work published 1877)

Hindemith, P. A (1961). *Composer's world.* New York: Doubleday.

Imberty, M. (1969). *L'acquisition des structures tonales chez l'enfant.* Paris: Klincksieck.

Jones, M. R. (1981). Only time can tell: On the topology of mental space and time. *Critical Inquiry, 7,* 557–576.

Jusczyk, P. W., & Krumhansl, C. L. (1993). Pitch and rhythmic patterns affecting infants' sensitivity to musical phrase structure. *Journal of Experimental Psychology: Human Perception & Performance, 19,* 627–640.

Kastner, M. P., & Crowder, R. G. (1990). Perception of major/minor: IV. Emotional connotations in young children. *Music Perception, 8,* 189–202. Kessen, W., Levine, J., & Wendrich, K. A. (1979). The imitation of pitch in infants. *Infant Behavior & Development, 2,* 93–99.

Kinney, D. K., & Kagan, J. (1976). Infant attention to auditory discrepancy. *Child Development, 47,* 155–164.

Krumhansl, C. L. (1990). *Cognitive foundations of musical pitch.* New York: Oxford University Press.

Krumhansl, C. L., & Jusczyk, P. W. (1990). Infants' perception of phrase structure in music. *Psychological Science, 1,* 70–73.

Krumhansl, C. L., & Keil, F. C. (1982). Acquisition of the hierarchy of tonal functions in music. *Memory & Cognition, 10,* 243–251.

Lamont, A., & Cross, I. (1994). Children's cognitive representations of musical pitch. *Music Perception, 12,* 27–55.

Levitin, D. J. (1994). Absolute memory for musical pitch: Evidence from the production of learned melodies. *Perception & Psychophysics, 56,* 414–423.

Levitin, D. J., & Cook, P. R. (1996). Memory for musical tempo: Additional evidence that auditory memory is absolute. *Perception & Psychophysics, 58,* 927–935.

Lynch, M. P., & Eilers, R. E. (1992). A study of perceptual development for musical tuning. *Perception & Psychophysics, 52,* 599–608.

McAdams, S., & Bregman, A. (1979). Hearing musical streams. *Computer Music Journal, 3*(4), 26–43, 60.

McKernon, P. E. (1979). The development of first songs in young children. *New Directions for Child Development, 3,* 43–58.

Mehler, J., Bertoncini, J., Barrière, M., & Jassik-Gerschenfeld, D. (1978). Infant recognition of mother's voice. *Perception, 7,* 491–497.

Melson, W. H., & McCall, R. B. (1970). Attentional responses of five-month girls to discrepant auditory stimuli. *Child Development, 41,* 1159–1171.

Miller, G. A. (1956). The magical number seven, plus or minus two: Some limits on our capacity for processing information. *Psychological Review, 63,* 81–97.

Miyazaki, K. (1988). Musical pitch identification by absolute pitch possessors. *Perception & Psychophysics, 44,* 501–512.

Miyazaki, K. (1993). Absolute pitch as an inability: Identification of musical intervals in a tonal context. *Music Perception, 11,* 55–72.

Monahan, C. B., & Carterette, E. C. (1985). Pitch and duration as determinants of musical space. *Music Perception, 3,* 1–32.

Morrongiello, B. A., & Roes, C. L. (1990). Developmental changes in children's perception of musical sequences: Effects of musical training. *Developmental Psychology, 26,* 814–820.

Morrongiello, B. A., Trehub, S. E., Thorpe, L. A., & Capodilupo, S. (1985). Children's perception of melodies: The role of contour, frequency, and rate of presentation. *Journal of Experimental Child Psychology, 40,* 279-292.

Ogawa, Y., & Miyazaki, K. (1994, July). *The process of acquisition of absolute pitch by children in Yamaha music school.* Paper presented at the Third International Conference for Music Perception and Cognition, Liège, Belgium.

Ostwald, P. F. (1973). Musical behavior in early childhood. *Developmental Medicine & Child Neurology, 15,* 367–375.

Pantev, C., Oostenveld, R., Engelien, A., Ross, B., Roberts, L. E., & Hoke, M. (1998). Increased auditory cortical representation in musicians. *Nature, 392,* 811.

Pick, A. D., Palmer, C. F., Hennessy, B. L., Unze, M. G., Jones, R. K., & Richardson, R. M. (1988). Children's perception of certain musical properties: Scale and contour. *Journal of Experimental Child Psychology, 45,* 28–51.

Révész, G. (1954). *Introduction to the psychology of music.* Norman: University of Oklahoma Press.

Riley, D. A., & McKee, J. P. (1963). Pitch and loudness transposition in children and adults. *Child Development, 34,* 471–483.

Riley, D. A., McKee, J. P., Bell, D. D., & Schwartz, C. R. (1967). Auditory discrimination in children: The effect of relative and absolute instructions on retention and transfer. *Journal of Experimental Psychology, 73,* 581–588.

Riley, D. A., McKee, J. P., & Hadley, R. W. (1964). Prediction of auditory discrimination learning and transposition from children's auditory ordering ability. *Journal of Experimental Psychology, 67,* 324–329.

Schellenberg, E. G., & Trehub, S. E. (1994). Frequency ratios and the perception of tone patterns. *Psychonomic Bulletin & Review, 2,* 191–201.

Schouten, J. F., Ritsma, B. J., & Cardozo, B. L. (1962). Pitch of the residue. *Journal of the Acoustical Society of America, 34,* 1418–1424.

Shetler, D. J. (1989). The inquiry into prenatal musical experience: A report of the Eastman Project, 1980–1987. *Pre- and Peri-Natal Psychology, 3,* 171–189.

Shuter-Dyson, R., & Gabriel, C. (1981). *The psychology of musical ability.* London: Methuen.

Speer, J. R., & Meeks, P. U. (1985). School children's perception of pitch in music. *Psychomusicology, 5,* 49–56.

Spence, M. J., & DeCasper, A. J. (1987). Prenatal experience with low-frequency maternal-voice sounds influence neonatal perception of maternal voice samples. *Infant Behavior & Development, 10,* 133–142.

Takeuchi, A. H., & Hulse, S. H. (1993). Absolute pitch. *Psychological Bulletin, 113,* 345–361.

Terwogt, M. M., & Van Grinsven, F. (1991). Musical expression of moodstates. *Psychology of Music, 19,* 99–109.

Thorpe, L. A., & Trehub, S. E. (1989). Duration illusion and auditory grouping in infancy. *Developmental Psychology, 25,* 122–127.

Trainor, L. J. (1993, March). *What makes a melody intrinsically easy to process: Comparing infant and adult listeners.* Paper presented to the Society of Research in Child Development, New Orleans.

Trainor, L. J., & Trehub, S. E. (1992). A comparison of infants' and adults' sensitivity to Western tonal structure. *Journal of Experimental Psychology: Human Perception & Performance, 18,* 394–402.

Trainor, L. J., & Trehub, S. E. (1993). Musical context effects in infants and adults: Key distance. *Journal of Experimental Psychology: Human Perception & Performance, 19,* 615–626.

Trainor, L. J., & Trehub, S. E. (1994). Key membership and implied harmony in Western tonal music: Developmental perspectives. *Perception & Psychophysics, 56,* 125–132.

Trehub, S. E. (1985). Auditory pattern perception in infancy. In S. E. Trehub & B. A. Schneider (Eds.), Auditory development in infancy (pp. 183–195). New York: Plenum.

Trehub, S. E. (1987). Infants' perception of musical patterns. *Perception & Psychophysics, 41,* 635–641.

Trehub, S. E. (1990). Human infants' perception of auditory patterns. *International Journal of Comparative Psychology, 4,* 91–110.

Trehub, S. E., Bull, D., & Thorpe, L. A. (1984). Infants' perception of melodies: The role of melodic contour. *Child Development, 55,* 821–830.

Trehub, S. E., Cohen, A. J., Thorpe, L. A., & Morrongiello, B. A. (1986). Development of the perception of musical relations: Semitone and diatonic structure. *Journal of Experimental Psychology: Human Perception & Performance, 12,* 295–301.

Trehub, S. E., Morrongiello, B. A., & Thorpe, L. A. (1985). Children's perception of familiar melodies: The role of intervals. *Psychomusicology, 5,* 39–48.

Trehub, S. E., & Thorpe, L. A. (1989). Infants' perception of rhythm: Categorization of auditory sequences by temporal structure. *Canadian Journal of Psychology, 43,* 217–229.

Trehub, S. E., & Thorpe, L. A., & Morrongiello, B. A. (1985). Infants' perception of melodies: Changes in a single tone. *Infant Behavior & Development, 8,* 213-223.

Trehub, S. E., & Thorpe, L. A., & Morrongiello, B. A. (1987). Organizational processes in infants' perception of auditory patterns. *Child Development, 58,* 741–749.

Trehub, S. E., Thorpe, L. A., & Trainor, L. J. (1990). Infants' perception of good and bad melodies. *Psychomusicology, 9,* 5–19.

Trehub, S. E., & Trainor, L. J. (1990). Rules for listening in infancy. In J. Enns (Ed.), *The development of attention: Research and theory* (pp. 87–119). Amsterdam: Elsevier.

Ward, W. D. (1954). Subjective musical pitch. *Journal of the Acoustical Society of America, 26,* 369–380.

West, R. J., & Fryer, R. (1990). Ratings of suitability of probe tones as tonics after random ordering of notes of the diatonic scale. *Music Perception, 7,* 253–258.

Wohlwill, J. F. (1971). Effect of correlated visual and tactual feedback on auditory pattern learning at different age levels. *Journal of Experimental Child Psychology, 11,* 213–228.

Zenatti, A. (1969). Le développement génétique de la perception musicale. *Monographies Françaises de Psychologie, No. 17.*

Zimmerman, M. P., & Sechrest, L. (1970). Brief focused instruction and musical concepts. *Journal of Research on Music Education, 18,* 25–36.

16

MUSICAL ABILITY

ROSAMUND SHUTER-DYSON

East Grinstead
West Sussex, England

I. CONCEPTS OF MUSICAL ABILITY

The term *musical ability* is "the broadest and safest" in that it suggests the power to act but indicates "nothing about the heritability or congenitalness of inferred potentiality" (Farnsworth, 1969, p. 151). Such a generic term as musical ability can include a wide range of listening, performing, analyzing, and creating tasks (Boyle, 1992). A broad distinction should, where possible, be drawn between *aptitude* and *achievement*. Music aptitude is the term used to indicate *potential* for learning music, particularly for developing musical skills. However, all aptitude tests are to some extent achievement tests, just as all achievement tests necessarily reflect the initial aptitude the individual can bring to the learning situation. However, accomplishment depends not only on aptitude but also on the teaching received and the child's interest in music and willingness to learn. High achievement in music requires rigorous and intensive training (Sloboda, 1994). Willingness to engage in long hours of practice is associated with certain personality characteristics of musicians (Kemp, 1996).

A useful concept of "developmental" musical aptitude has been put forward by Gordon (1979, p. 4). In his view, the level of musical aptitude a child is born with cannot be raised. However, up to the age of 9, much can be done to ensure that this innate level is in fact realized. After the age of 9, musical aptitude stabilizes. The relative standing of students on the Musical Aptitude Profile (MAP, see Section IIA) does not increase with practice and training. This tends to be true also for the Seashore, Drake, Wing and Bentley tests (see Section II,A), which were intended as group tests for children more than 8 or 9 years old.

A really extensive investigation of representative samples of twins, along the lines of the Minnesota Twin Study, might throw light on how much of musical aptitude is innate (Shuter-Dyson, 1994). Pending such a study, a useful analogy may be drawn with intelligence. As Vernon (1968) noted, we need to recognize the existence of genetic differences between individuals in their capacities for building up neural and mental schemata, what Hebb (1949) called "Intelligence A." The psychologist, however, can only observe the effectiveness of present behavior or thinking through the interaction of the genes and the stimulation offered by the environment. (i.e., Intelligence B). This is culturally conditioned by the environment provided by the ethnic group into which the child is born, especially by the child's home and his or her leisure pursuits. The effects of physiological conditions before and after birth are also important. The results of intelligence tests, Intelligence C, are of considerable predictive value in so far as they sample useful mental skills.

It is well to remember that the original aim of testing was to provide objective means of assessing abilities, so that justice could be done to the individual. Whereas in the case of music, stress tended to be laid on identifying talented children who might benefit from instrumental lessons, emphasis is now placed on the judicious use of tests as an aid to the teacher in assessing the strengths and weaknesses of the student (Gordon, 1979, p. 6). High scores are indicative of a promising level of talent; low ones may often be due to misunderstanding of instructions or some upsetting circumstance and should be treated with caution. In any case, the results of testing should be supplemented by information from other sources.

The term *musicality* was used by Révész (1953) to denote "the ability to enjoy music aesthetically." The ultimate criterion is the depth to which a person, listening and comprehending, can penetrate the artistic structure of a composition. As Dowling and Harwood (1986) point out, music in industrialized societies comes to depend on high levels of expertise for its performance. The rest of the people become "spectators." Those with initially low levels of ability are often discouraged from active participation in music.

A different concept of musicality implies that all humans qua human can make music, and "average musical ability" is as universal as average linguistic competence (Blacking, 1971). For example, the Venda in Africa assume that everyone is capable of music making; even deaf persons can dance. However, they recognize that some persons perform better than others. Exceptional musical ability is indeed expected of children born into certain families. Only a few may become exceptional musicians; if they do, what is considered to set them apart is that they worked harder at music.

Despite the difficulties of research with very young children, much evidence is accumulating on the inherent music-making potential of humans (see Trehub, 1993). Two-month-old infants were able to match the pitch, intensity, and melodic contour of their mothers' songs, and at 4 months old, could match the rhythmic structure (Papousek, 1982). Very young infants are able to abstract the pitch contour of a sequence of tones (Trehub, 1985; Trehub, Bull, & Thorpe, 1984). They are sensitive to simple rhythmic change (Chang & Trehub, 1977) and to the pitch and durational contours that cue phrase endings (Krumhansl & Jusczyk, 1990). Infants 7 to 10 months old successfully discriminated a semitone change in a well-structured Western melody but not in a poorly structured Western melody or a non-Western melody (Trehub, Thorpe, & Trainor, 1990). Kessen, Levine, and Wendrich (1979) found that before the middle of the first year of life, babies can learn to imitate pitches and appear to enjoy doing so; they suggested that the infant brings a congenital readiness to respond to pitched tones. However, most infants may lose the ability with the onset of learning language and lack of support from the world around them. Three years later, Wendrich (1981) followed up 9 of the 23 babies who had learned to vocalize the pitches. Seven had lost the ability.

Attentive listening to music and singing before speaking are often assumed to characterize children with conspicuous musical talent (Shuter-Dyson, 1985). Many such children are born into families of musicians, but in the case of others, the families display only modest musical abilities. Howe, Davidson, Moore, and Sloboda (1995) questioned the parents of 257 children for early signs of musical ability. All the children had studied a musical instrument but differed in their achievements. Singing by the child at an earlier age was the only sign observed that distinguished those children who later succeeded in being accepted by a highly selective music school. This does not, however, rule out a higher incidence of early signs of musicality occurring in musicians who as adults reach the highest peaks of excellence.

II. STUDIES OF MUSICAL ABILITIES

A. METHODS OF STUDY

In discussing studies of musical abilities, we shall look both at the contribution made by tests and at some of the research that has aimed to understand the cognitive requirements of music and has thereby provided valuable insights into the abilities involved.

The best of the published tests, in spite of various imperfections, have proved successful in helping to identify the relative status of individuals to an extent that makes the tests useful in music education. Detailed information on tests is readily available elsewhere (George, 1980; Shuter-Dyson & Gabriel, 1981). It is as research tools that tests are to be considered in this paper. In assessing the meaningfulness of studies based on testing, we must bear in mind the reliability and validity of the tests used and their suitability for the groups studied.

Tests naturally reflect differences in their authors' concepts of musical ability. Seashore (1938, p. 2) believed that the sensory capacities measured in his Measures of Musical Talents were basic to musical aptitude, could be sharply defined, and could be absent or present in the individual in varying degrees. In fact, correlation studies of the Measures rarely produce zero correlations (see Shuter-Dyson & Gabriel, 1981, p. 53).

Authors of later tests sought to produce material that would seem more relevant to functional music activities. For example, Drake (1933a, 1933b, 1957) devised a test of musical memory, where the testee has to remember the original version of a melody while hearing a series of versions that may vary from the model because of change of key, time, or notes. Wing (1948) tried out many possible tests; 25 of the most promising were eventually reduced to 7: 3 of ear acuity (chord analysis, pitch, and melodic memory) and 4 of appreciation (rhythm, harmony, intensity, and phrasing). They became the Wing Standardised Tests of Musical Intelligence (Wing, 1981). Bentley (1966) devised the first battery intended primarily for children 7 or 8 to 14 years old, the Measures of Musical Abilities, testing pitch discrimination, tonal memory, chord analysis, and rhythmic memory. Mills (1988) has produced a test in which the testee is asked to assess which of two tones is higher in pitch; if no difference is noticed, a "zero" answer is marked.

The MAP (Gordon, 1965, 1988) consists of three parts: tonal (melody and harmony), rhythm (tempo and meter), and musical sensitivity (phrasing, balance, and style). Because rhythm and melody interact in an inseparable way, Gordon considered it appropriate to test tempo and meter in melodic contexts. His later, shorter tests, the Primary Measures of Music Audiation (PMMA; Gordon, 1979), the Intermediate Measures of Musical Audiation (IMMA; Gordon, 1982), and the Advanced Measures of Musical Audiation (AMMA; Gordon, 1989a) have separate tonal and rhythm subtests. The three batteries cover age ranges from kindergarten to adult. *Audie* (Gordon, 1989b) is intended for 3- and 4-year-old children.

Umemoto, Mikumo, and Murase (1989) have produced a test of pitch deviation. The testee has to find which tone deviates by 50 Hz up or down from the correct pitch of the diatonic scale with equal temperament. Tonal and atonal sequences four, five, and six tones long are used. Unlike the isolated tones used by Seashore, the judgments take place within the framework of the scale.

Tests of vocal or instrumental performance have lagged behind perceptual ones. The Watkins-Farnum Performance Scale (Watkins & Farnum, 1954) consisted largely of sight-reading exercises. McPherson (1993/1994, 1995) has devised tests of ability to (a) play from memory; (b) play by ear and (c) improvise. Scores were compared with sight-reading (as measured by the Watkins-Farnum Scale) and with results from the Australian Music Examination Board.

A promising development for the future may be *adaptive* tests presented by computer. Correct responses are followed by more difficult ones, incorrect responses, by easier ones, enabling the testee to answer only those items that are of appropriate difficulty. From a pool of more than 300 tonal memory items, Vispoel (1993; Vispoel & Coffman, 1992) selected 180 that could be presented by microcomputer. The synthesizer-produced tonal and atonal melodies were from four to nine notes in length, the examinee having to judge which if any tone had been changed on the second playing. The results were compared with results of Seashore's, Wing's and Drake's memory tests and with results of Gordon's AMMA. Reliability and validity levels higher than with fixed-order tests were obtained in much shorter time. This approach might enable the reliability and validity of a longer test to be retained with reduced length or the reliability of batteries with short subtests to be improved. So far Vispoel has used material based on memory tests, but the procedure could be extended to other musical abilities. He has also experimented with *self-adapted* testing, where the examinee is allowed to choose the difficulty of the items. This procedure produced some loss of testing efficiency, but less anxiety among the examinees (Vispoel & Coffman, 1994).

B. FUNDAMENTAL ABILITIES

There now seems to be agreement on the importance of perception and cognition of patterns and structures. Before looking at studies of components of musical ability, such as tonal, rhythmic, and kinesthetic abilities, we shall first discuss the work of Gordon, of Karma, and of Serafine in their attempts to throw light on the more general ability to deal with patterns and structures and the temporal aspect of music.

Gordon (1979) uses the term *audiation* to mean "the ability to give meaning to what one hears." Gordon (1990) succinctly described five stages in the process of audiation: The first stage is when one perceives the sound. The second is when one begins to give meaning to sound through tonal and rhythmic patterns within a context of tonality and meter. These first two stages represent musical aptitude. At the third stage, one asks "What have I just heard?" and begins to find meaningful answers. The fourth stage is marked by the question "Where have I heard these patterns and sounds before?" and in the last stage, one begins to predict what one will hear next. These last three stages are achievement.

Audiation is thus the essential cognitive function that not only enables persons to give meaning to music while listening, but also enables them to bring order and meaning to music read, or written from dictation, recalled from the past or improvised. (For a discussion of Gordon's contribution to research and music learning, see *The Quarterly,* 1991).

Karma (1985) defined musical aptitude as "the ability to structure acoustic material." He believes that the sense of tonality, of rhythm, and of harmony can be seen as culture-specific reflections of a general structuring ability. Because it is difficult to remember unstructured material, musical memory can be seen as the consequence of conceiving the structure of the music heard. Karma has developed a test in which a short sequence of tones is repeated three times. Only one factor—pitch, intensity and length—is varied within an item. This theme must be compared with an "answer" that follows after a pause and judged as "same" or "different." Testees tend to adopt two strategies: anticipating and recognizing. Items where the structuring conforms to strong gestalts, where, for example, a stressed tone occurs at the beginning of a subgroup, are easy. Ability to structure against strong gestalts requires greater skill, as do items where the beginnings and the ends of the subgroups are similar, as these require changing expectations.

Karma (1986) reported that "changing expectations" and "structuring against strong gestalts" are significant predictors of the ability to solve difficult items, both among musically select candidates for entrance to music school and among musically unselected children. Sensory discrimination was incorporated into the test by making the pitch, length and intensity differences relatively small in some of the items.

Karma (1991) has also experimented with tests to measure as purely as possible the ability to perceive pitch differences and their direction, comparing the results with a test that requires verbal labeling. The pitch-differentiation test consisted of 24 tone pairs, with the testee having to say "up" or "down." The intervals range from a perfect fifth to 13 Hz. In a "same/different" test, an item consisted of two three-, or four-tone patterns that might either be similar (same) or inversions of each other (different). This test appears to be an unusually pure test of pitch-differentiation ability but requires further experimentation. The traditional up/down version does measure pitch differentiation but is unsuitable for use with very young children.

Serafine (1988) stresses the temporality of music. To investigate successive processes, she devised tasks of phrasing (dividing a span of music into two parts), patterning (following a pattern of alternating fragments to tell which would come next), motivic chaining (understanding that motive A followed by B will form a longer phrase AB rather than AX or BZ), and idiomatic construction (discriminating coherent melodies from random sequences of tones). Simultaneous processes were examined by a textural abstraction task (listening to two or three parts and deciding how many parts are being heard), motivic synthesis (will fragments A and B, if played simultaneously sound like A with B rather than A with X or Z with B?), timbre synthesis (are two instruments, first heard separately, being played together, or is the second instrument a different one)?

Serafine also proposes four types of nontemporal process, concerned with the overall, formal properties of music: closure (which fragment is "finished"?), transformation (recognizing a theme as similar when transformed, as opposed to a foil), abstraction (recognizing a melodic or rhythmic pattern when it occurs in a new context), and understanding the hierarchical levels of musical structure.

To trace the development of the abilities required, Serafine tested individually children and adults, 168 in all, with approximately 30 at each age level, 5, 6, 8, 10, and 11 years old and 15 adults. By the age of 10 or 11, most of the processes had been acquired, with the exception of the ability to identify the number of simultaneous parts in a complex texture. The 8-year-old children gave evidence of perceiving hierarchic levels in simple melodies, they did well at perceiving simultaneous combinations of timbres, and performed as well as older children did at discrimination of random melodies, although unlike the older groups, they did no better on melodies constructed in accordance with tonal idiom. It seemed that *non*temporal processes developed earlier. Serafine suggested that the child first makes sense of global features and only later is able to give the constant analytic monitoring required by temporal tasks.

Zenatti (1985) reported a factor analysis of the scores of 89 children from 6 to 7 years old on 17 memory tests and confirmed that children whose perception tends to be global form a separate group from children who have more analytical perception and possess more developed musical discrimination capabilities. Thirty-four children who had received intensive Suzuki training were tested on closure, transformation, and hierarchical levels. Only those who had received very intensive, long-term training that was specifically relevant to certain tasks achieved higher scores than children of the same age. With age being the principal predictor of success, the most potent factors may be general cognitive growth and normal, everyday musical experience.

Although Serafine was concerned with demonstrating the universality of musical cognition, many individual differences were found among her results. It would be interesting to know how the children would have scored on musical aptitude tests. She did include a pitch-discrimination test, in which her subjects were asked whether pairs of prerecorded piano tones were the same or different. Where significant correlations with the other tasks occurred, they were low.

To sum up, all three, Gordon, Karma, and Serafine, are concerned with means of making sense of music in time. Memory for music as such is not the primary interest. Gordon's concept of audiation is redolent of Seashore's (1938, p. 6) statement that "tonal imagery is a condition for learning, for retention, for recall, for recognition, and for the anticipation of musical facts." Both the Gordon and Serafine tasks are affected by age. Karma (1983) claims that scores on his structuring task rise by only 10% between 8-year-olds and adults. His test should be applicable to non-Western musics. Although her approach was not psychometric, Serafine's varied tasks cover a wide and interesting range of abilities. For her purpose, the tasks had to be accessible to 5-year-olds yet require no major change for older children and adults. With the youngest children, they were presented in a play situation. For a succinct discussion of her theoretical position, see Hargreaves and Zimmerman (1992).

C. TONAL ABILITIES

1. Pitch Perception

Pitch discrimination is widely acknowledged to be an important part of musical perception. Pitch tasks are among the most difficult for children younger than 5 or 6 years old, even when the tones can be presented by a touch screen where the child has only to touch part of a screen to respond (see White, Dale, & Carlsen, 1990).

Quite strong intercorrelations are typically found between tests of fine pitch differences (Seashore and Bentley) and the Wing test, where the pitch change is masked within two piano chords. Results of both the Seashore and the Wing test correlated quite highly with results of the Lundin test, where the listener has to judge whether a second melodic interval moves up or down (see Shuter-Dyson & Gabriel, 1981, pp. 58–59).

Umemoto (1995) carried out a factor analysis of the pitch-deviation test, tests of pitch intervals and absolute pitch, along with scores from the Seashore Measures, the Wing and the Drake tests, the sensitivity subtests of Gordon's MAP, and the five subtests of the Sherman-Knight battery (tests where recorded excerpts must be compared with notation). The test of pitch deviation had a high loading of 0.785 in the first factor. The other tests that had loadings greater than 0.3 on this factor were the tests of absolute pitch, the test of intervals, all the Sherman-Knight tests, the phrasing test of the MAP, and tests 1–4 of Wing. The Seashore pitch test formed a separate factor, on which the Wing and Chord Analysis tests had some loadings. Umemoto thus claimed that the sense of pitch deviation has a central position in the structure of musical ability. It also had a loading of 0.448 on a second factor where the memory tests of Seashore, Wing, and Drake also had high loadings. This is not surprising, as memory is involved in the test.

The highest loading on the first factor was 0.822 for the Absolute Pitch test. The value of absolute pitch to musicians has been much discussed. Miyazaki (1992, 1993) believes that the possession of absolute pitch may impede the development of relative pitch, which is much more important in musically meaningful situations. He agrees, however, that many musicians have both. Absolute pitch certainly appears to be a characteristic of many extremely talented performers—and also of "musical savants" (see Section III).

2. Sense of Tonality

Hargreaves and Zimmerman (1992) state that "By the age of 8, children's melodic perception operates within an increasingly stable tonal system. Now melodic information is stored and processed according to a tonal reference rather than by contour schemes." The age at which a child develops a sense of tonality depends on the criterion employed and on individual differences.

a. Singing

Davidson, McKernon, and Gardner (1981) found that the 5-year-olds they studied either sang in the same key throughout or changed key suddenly and then stayed within it. Welch (1994) reported evidence in the singing of a sample of 5-year-olds of a "tonal centre" that was located toward the lower part of the singing range. Concomitantly, intervals tended to be reduced in size, especially those further from the tonal center. As might be expected, there is considerable variability among preschool children (Flowers & Dunne-Sousa, 1990). Also, singing ability is an important factor—more than one fourth of preschool children classified as having low singing ability exhibited no evidence of ability to maintain the tonal center of a song (Ramsey, 1983).

b. Recognizing Change of Key

Bartlett and Dowling (1980) found that 5- or 6-year-old children noticed changes of key when the change was to a distant key (i.e., one that introduced several changes in pitches of notes in the scale) but not when the change was to a nearly related key. Boyle and Penticoff (1989) concluded that the average child in Grades 4 and higher can identify tonality change with almost 90% accuracy for familiar melodies and 85% for unfamiliar melodies. Imberty (1969) found that, by age 7, children could recognize sudden changes of key in the midst of tunes and by age 8, a change of mode.

c. Recognizing the "Tonal Hierarchy"

Cuddy and Wiebe (1979) noted that "the sense of tonality involves the development of a pitch system in which tone relations are specifically defined ... even tones not played in a given melody are represented by their inferred relation to the tonic." A great deal of research effort has gone into the investigation of the part played by tonality in the cognition of music (see, e.g., Cuddy, 1997; Cuddy, Cohen, & Miller, 1979; Krumhansl, 1990). Two examples concerning children follow: Cuddy and Badertscher (1987) presented the major triad, the major scale, and the diminished triad followed by a probe tone (each of the 12 tones of the chromatic scale) to 53 children, from 6 to 12 years old. The children were asked to rate each of the probes as to whether it sounded "good" or "bad" as an ending to the melodic pattern. The tonic was judged the best ending, especially for the major triad. Speer and Meeks (1985) found that both second and fifth graders chose diatonic over nondiatonic notes, triad notes over other diatonic notes, and the tonic over other triad notes.

d. Better Discrimination with Tonal As Opposed to Atonal Music and Preference for Tonal

Zenatti (1969, 1981) emphasized the importance of acculturation in her studies of the acquisition of tonality. In one of her experiments, children were asked to say which one of three notes in a sequence had been changed in pitch on a second presentation. Five-year-olds performed at chance level with both tonal and atonal melodies, but by age 6 or 7, superior performance on the tonal items began to emerge. In the case of four-tone phrases, the better the discrimination score, the greater was the difference between tonal and atonal perception.

3. Harmony and Polyphony

The acculturation noted above occurs also in harmonic contexts. Children 5 to 7 years old can discriminate a harmonic change more easily when it is presented in consonant, as opposed to dissonant, chords (Zenatti, 1985). Sloboda (1985, pp. 211–213) describes four tests of harmony. Two tests contrasted dissonant with consonant items. Five-year-olds scored very poorly. By age 7, performance had improved significantly, and by age 9, the score was indistinguishable from the scores of adults. In a third test, in one sequence of each pair of items, the chords were played in a "musical" order, leading to a conventional cadence, whereas in the other sequence the same chords were presented in a "scrambled" order. Not until the age of 11 did scores on this test approach those of adults—to detect incorrectness, the ordering of the chords has to be observed. In his fourth test, the items were unaccompanied melodic sequences. One item was a diatonic melody that remained within a single key, the other was a sequence with the same contour but with chromatic notes. This was the most difficult, requiring ability to detect violations of normal sequential structure. Performance of the tests was not aided by musical training.

Imberty (1969) concluded from his research on cadences that up to the age of 5, a child perceives a tune as finished when the music stops. The effect of a perfect cadence (V to I) is felt by 8-year-olds. By age 10, children understand both perfect and imperfect cadences, but surprise was caused if the melody ended on the third degree of the scale. Serafine (1988) found that 10-year-olds succeeded in recognizing "closure" on harmonic items but scored only at chance with the single-line melodic item.

Although Zenatti (1969, Chapter II) found children between 8 and 10 years old began to be able to recognize a well-known tune presented fugally, even children up to 12 years old had difficulty perceiving the bass part. This result seems in accord with the norms Gordon provides for his tonal (harmony) test, where a judgment has to be made about the lower part. The greatest rise in mean scores takes place between ages 9 and 10, although scores continue to improve until age 17. Wing's chord analysis proved to be effective at separating the good from the very good students at the Eastman School of Music. As noted in Section II,B, Serafine (1988) reported that ability to identify the number of parts in a complex texture was not generally present until adulthood. The examples of the music she quotes on page 147 do indeed suggest that the task is complex. Identifying a pair of disparate timbres seems a simple task, but only about half the 5- or 6-year-old children succeeded (pp.154–156). Even expert musicians found difficulty in identifying concurrent voices in Bach's St. Anne Fugue, although they were more accurate than a nonmusician (Huron, 1989).

C. RHYTHMIC ABILITIES

1. Rhythm/Tonal Studies

Sizable correlations are found between the tonal and rhythmic parts of Gordon's MAP. Gordon (1965) noted that melody undoubtedly influences perception of rhythm. Indeed, as Sloboda (1985, p. 188) comments, not only is rhythm just as important an organizing principle as tonality in music, but both systems are mutually interactive. In much tonal music, knowledge of the tonal structure can help determine the rhythmic structure and vice versa. Sloboda (pp. 52–55) also observed that many of the constraints on melody are dictated by the requirement that the melody be capable of communicating harmonic and rhythmic structure to a listener. An example of the importance of rhythmic structure to memory was provided by an investigation of the immediate recall of a melody by Sloboda and Parker (1985). They asked eight female psychology students to listen to a Russian folk song and to recall it immediately afterward. Six recalls were obtained. Four of the students were musically trained and active performers, the other four were just interested in music. The most fundamental feature recalled was the metrical structure, preserving the quadruple meter and the two-bar phrase subdivisions. Within the metrical structure, metrical equivalents were substituted about half of the time. The only significant difference between the musically trained women and the other women was the ability to retain harmonic structure.

2. Rhythmic Perception/Performance

Thackray (1969) devised tests of rhythmic perception, rhythmic performance, and rhythmic movement. These were intended for adults; he later adapted the perception and performance tests for use with children (Thackray, 1972). A factor analysis of the correlation coefficients of his perception subtests suggested that the ability to perceive and memorize a rhythmic structure as a whole, and to analyze it consciously, was fundamental to rhythmic perception. Inability to memorize some of the longer items was an important reason for low scores. With adult physical education students, perception and performance had a correlation of 0.63, perception and movement had a correlation of 0.55, and performance and movement had a correlation of 0.59. With child groups, performance tests seemed superior to tests of perception as a means of testing general rhythmic ability.

Hiriartborde and Fraisse (1968) carried out a factor analysis of a series of tests—some predominantly perceptual, some predominantly motor, along with the Seashore and Wing batteries. They concluded that several independent factors are needed to account for the plurality of rhythmic aptitudes that correspond to the many aspects of rhythm. Their factors included perception of rhythmic structures, rhythmic anticipation (synchronization and several Seashore and Wing tests that imply memorizing a pattern in order to compare it with a following one), and a "practo-rhythmic" factor concerned with coordination of limbs in rhythmic movement (see Fraisse, 1982, pp. 176–177).

Thackray (1972) noted that ability to maintain a steady tempo appeared to be a highly specific rhythmic ability. It can be a problem with otherwise promising students. Gordon and Martin (1993/1994) go so far as to say that playing in time is often the most important aspect of a musical performance. Drake's rhythm tests are concerned with the ability to maintain a steady beat, in the case of Form B against a faster or slower distracting beat. These tests were found to form a separate factor in factorial studies (Tomita, 1986; Umemoto, 1995). Mills (1988) has developed a test on the lines of Drake's.

Zenatti (1976) found evidence of a stage at about 4 years 8 months, when children showed a considerable improvement in tapping back two-, three-, or four-note rhythms on their second attempt, helped by seeing the experimenter tap the rhythm again. Stambak (1960) used more elaborate patterns that required some measure of temporal structuring. A clear development occurred between 6 and 9 years old. Gérard and Drake (1990) reported from four experiments with children 5 to 8 years old, that whereas 6-year-old children would perceive and reproduce simple time patterns, even 8-year-olds rarely reproduced intensity differences to indicate accentuation.

The experiments of Bamberger (1982) have called attention to the "figural" and the "metric" construing of music. Figural perception groups sounds into meaningful chunks, whereas metric perception focuses on a steady pulse underlying the surface events of melody. Upitis (1987) assessed the figural and metric aspects of rhythm through individual interviews with 72 children, 7 to 12 years old. The children were asked, for example, to describe a clapped rhythm by putting down "whatever you think will help you to remember the piece," then to "put in some numbers that seem to fit with the marks you have made"; to interpret descriptions of rhythms; to keep time by beating on a drum; and to identify duple or triple beats that would be congruent with unfamiliar melodies. Results showed that children who had had at least 1 year of music lessons were better at keeping time than untrained children. Ability to pick congruent beats was associated with age, but not with training. Upitis's findings indicated that all the children were able to make sense of rhythm, using either figural or metric techniques, or both. There was a considerable variation in response among individuals. In a later study, accuracy of figural drawings was significantly correlated with ability to join in clapping and to clap back a rhythm (Smith, Cuddy, & Upitis, 1994).

Gromko (1994) found evidence that the notations children invent are a valid indication of their musical understanding, as measured by the PMMA, and their ability to reproduce a short folk tune by singing and playing.

E. KINESTHETIC ABILITIES

1. Instrumental

In a reanalysis of many previous correlation and factorial studies, Whellams (1971) reported a factor he interpreted as "kinesthetic perception," which seemed to span the tonal memory and rhythmic aspects of music. This factor drew attention to the muscular component in auditory perception that is in line with feedback models of skilled behavior; it has long been noted in connection with music. For example, Mainwaring (1933) found that both children and students of education tended to translate auditory into kinesthetic cues in order to recall tunes they had listened to well enough to answer questions about them.

Gilbert (1979) devised a test of motoric skills. The tasks entailed striking a musical instrument (drums, xylophone, etc.) with a mallet through use of vertical arm and hand motion. She tested 800 children between 3 and 6 years old. A year later she retested 87 of the children. Improvements related to age were found on all the subtests except for motor pattern coordination. The greatest gains were made between the ages of 3 and 4 (Gilbert, 1981). A high correlation was found between results of her test and results of the PMMA (Gilbert, 1982). The effect of psychomotor activities on achievement on the MAP-Rhythm and IMMA-Rhythm tests was investigated by Schmidt and Lewis (1987) with 29 fourth graders. Besides the general music curriculum, the children received eighteen 30-minute class sessions in which the musical concepts of tempo, meter, and rhythm were introduced and reinforced through activities that required synchronization of body movements while singing or listening to music. The mean scores on the MAP-Tempo, but not on the MAP-Meter or IMMA-Rhythm, were significantly improved on post-test.

Sloboda (1985, pp. 88–89) noted the importance for performing of "motor programming"—the setting up of a sequence of commands to the performing muscles that will reveal in sound the expressive devices selected from the performer's "dictionary." The elements in a motor sequence overlap in time—the second finger may already be moving to its position before the first is released. Fluent motor behavior results in specified goals being achieved rather than specified movements being carried out. McPherson (1993/1994) noted that kinesthetic factors such as the organized fingering system of the clarinet seem to influence ability to improvise (see Section II,F).

Baily (1985) emphasized the need to study the way musical patterns may be represented cognitively as patterns of movement rather than as patterns of sound. He believed that the extent to which the creation of musical structures is shaped by sensorimotor mechanisms must also be considered. He cited ethnomusicology studies of African music and his own research in Afghanistan. Overt body movement is a prominent feature in the performance of many kinds of music in Africa, and the conceptual link between music and dance is very close. In villages where everyone participates in music making, movements are very easily observed. J. Davidson (1993) has shown that the bodily movements made by performers contribute to the expressivity of the performance—an element missing for the listener to radio or compact discs.

2. Singing

"Tone deafness" is not just a problem of some boys spoiling class singing. About 10% of 600 university students considered themselves tone deaf and reported a variety of difficulties in melodic perception and memory, vocal production, and auditory imagery (Mawhinney, 1987). They had had few musical activities in early childhood and had unpleasant memories of such musical education as they had received. Kalmus and Fry (1980) investigated "tune deafness" by devising a Distorted Tunes test that required the detection of wrong notes in Western popular and classical music. Familiarity with the actual tunes was not a prerequisite for a good score. From the age of 9, the percentage of children failing according to the adult criterion fell from 40% to the adult value of 4%. Their difficulty reflected a failure to have acquired knowledge of the syntactic rules of the Western tonal system. Scores were only weakly correlated with scores on the Seashore pitch and tonal memory tests. Mawhinney used an adapted form of the Distorted Tunes test with 42 university students. Those who considered themselves to be tone deaf scored 59% correct, compared with the 78% accuracy of those who classified themselves as "above average" as listeners. In a probe-tone test, 6 tone-deaf students out of 41 students produced tonal hierarchy ratings only somewhat weaker than did the other listeners (Cuddy, 1993).

Mitchell (1991) found that three nonsingers were able to perform the Distorted Tunes test at ceiling. Their singing, however, was not only severely out of tune, but they were unaware of this. They first had to learn to recognize a feeling of being in unison with a keyboard or another singer and then to control their voices so as to achieve unison. No subject showed measurable improvement on song performance.

L. Davidson (1993) found that a significant number of musically untrained adults typically compress the range of the third phrase of "Happy Birthday" from an octave to a fifth or sixth, and end the song on a different key, just as young children do (see Section II,C,2,b).

However, from a review of research with children, Goetze, Cooper, and Brown (1990) concluded that children at least *can* be taught to sing with improved accuracy. Welch (1985) postulated that learning to sing in tune is achieved via a motor response schema. With children who made gross pitch errors and who were given individual training, those who were given knowledge of results gained significantly greater accuracy than those who were not; this was particularly true of the children who were most out-of-tune at the beginning of the training. Visual feedback by means of a microcomputer system was also helpful (Welch, Howard, & Rush, 1989).

F. AESTHETIC ABILITIES

In the Indiana-Oregon Music Discrimination Test (developed by Long, 1965, from the Hevner Landbury test) and the last four tests of the Wing battery, excerpts of original music are paired with a "distorted" version. Wing requires the testee to identify the original version, Long's testees have also to judge which element—rhythm, harmony, or melody—has been changed. Gordon (1965) composed the items for his sensitivity tests and then asked professional musicians which version they preferred. Only when high consensus (9 out of 10) was reached, and this was confirmed by field trials, were the items incorporated into the final version of the test. Boyle (1982) noted that the correlations among the Wing, Gordon, and Oregon appreciation tests were quite low.

It is interesting that later research is throwing light on the basis for aesthetic judgments. For instance, Repp (1992) obtained tone-onset timing measurements for 28 different performances by famous pianists of a "melodic gesture" from Schumann's *Träumerei*. The pianists tended to speed up in the initial part and slow down at the end in a "parabolic" fashion. Listeners were asked to judge a variety of timing patterns (original parabolic, shifted, and nonparabolic) for aesthetic appeal. The parabolic patterns received the highest ratings from musically trained listeners. (Musically untrained listeners did not make consistent judgments). Pianists required to imitate performance of rubato in short musical excerpts were less accurate when the structure of the music and expression conflicted than when they were consistent (Clarke & Baker-Short, 1987). Clarke (1993) found that the more the relationship between structure and expression is disrupted, the more inaccurate and unstable is the attempt at imitation. Moreover, listeners' preferences follow the same pattern as the accuracy/stability measures for the imitation attempts.

Gabrielsson (1982) concluded from his research on rhythm that a balanced combination of the structural, motional, and emotional aspects, adapted to the needs of the specfic individual and the actual musical content, may be what is required for artistic performance. This agrees with the results of Sloboda's (1983) investigation into the communication of musical meter. Six pianists of various degrees of experience sight-read a sequence of the same notes but with two different metrical stresses. The more experienced players made greater use of expressive variation and conveyed the differences with more certainty to listeners.

From his experience of teaching music, Sloboda (1985, p. 88) noticed very great differences between even quite young children in the ability to notice expressive variations in the performance of others. Some were capable of immediate and accurate imitation and retention of points demonstrated by the teacher; this seemed to be one of the best predictors of high levels of musical achievement.

Gardner (1973) adopted a different approach: he presented children with pairs of musical extracts and asked them to judge whether the two excerpts came from the same piece of music. He found that the 6-year-olds tended to rate most pairs as "different." The highest absolute scores were made by the 21-year-olds, who were able to base their judgments on variables such as instrumentation and texture. Castell (1982) carried out a similar investigation with 8- and 11-year-olds, including jazz and rock music alongside classical pieces. All the children were more accurate when judging popular music, the 8-year-olds being significantly better than the 11-year-olds; there was no such difference for the classical pairs.

Musical appreciation depends on awareness of basic aural elements. Correlations between the Hevner-Landbury test and Seashore's tonal memory test and the Wing memory, pitch, and harmony tests were quite strong (see Shuter-Dyson, 1982). The "Which element changed?" judgment received the highest factor loading in McLeish's (1950) musical cognition study.

Sloboda (1990) reported the results of an investigation of adults' recollections of their early involvement with music. These seemed to reveal an evolutionary process in the acquisition of musical meaning. The age of 7 seemed to signal the progression to a new awareness—the age when the grasp of tonal syntax is becoming apparent. Sloboda suspected that the syntactic and semantic developments are not unrelated. Swanick (1973) also concluded that much cognitive activity is involved in aesthetic response to music and that the intensity and quality of any emotional experience depends on this activity; ability to make predictions as to what may follow so that deviations arouse excitement is central to the process of understanding music.

G. CREATIVE ABILITIES

Webster (1988) noted that first among the "enabling skills" needed for creative work in music are the "necessary collection of 'musical aptitudes.'" The "convergent" skills include ability to recognize rhythmic and tonal patterns and musical syntax. "Divergent" skills include musical extensiveness (how many ideas are generated), flexibility (ease of moving freely from extremes of fast/slow, soft/loud, high/low), and originality. Other abilities required are conceptual understanding, craftsmanship, and aesthetic sensitivity.

Vaughan (1977) devised a measure of musical creativity on the lines of the Torrance Tests of Creative Thinking. For example, a rhythmic or melodic pattern was presented and the child was encouraged to improvise an answer; or a basic outline or ostinato was set up for the child make up a pattern to go with it. Wang's Measures of Creativity in Sound and Music (Wang, 1985) for children ages 3 through 6, require the child to produce examples of a steady beat, imitate events described by the teacher, improvise ostinatos on a bass xylophone, and move to music. Responses are scored for fluency and imagination. Webster also has experimented with measures of creative thinking in music. Version II (Webster, 1983) consists of 10 activities including improvisation tasks for children ages 6 to 10. For example, they are asked to create call-and-response patterns on temple blocks and encouraged to create a composition that uses all the instruments available and has a beginning, a middle, and an end. The Measures are scored for originality, extensiveness, and flexibility, as well as musical syntax.

Such tests of creativity can be reliably scored and the internal consistency of the Webster and the Wang tests are generally high (Baltzer, 1988, 1990; Webster, Yale, & Haefner, 1988). Musical creativity factors seem to be discrete from those assessed by musical aptitude. Swanner (1985) found that results with the Webster test were not related to the PMMA, nor to teachers' and parents' ratings of the creativity of 69 third-grade children. Personality traits of imagination, curiosity, and anxiety accounted for 29% of the variance in the Webster test composite score.

Kratus (1989, 1991) believed that *how* children compose is as important as *what* they compose. For his 1994 study, he asked 40 9-year-old children to spend 30 minutes making up "a brand new song" on an electric piano. The process of composition—exploration, development, repetition and silence—was analyzed, as well as the product. IMMA test scores were negatively correlated with exploration, indicating that the greater the ability to audiate, the less the need to explore. Audiation was positively connected with development of ideas and silence—children who can hear music inwardly can compose without the sound being physically present. Audiation was also related to tonal and metric cohesiveness and the use of developed, rather than repeated, patterns.

McPherson (1993/1994; 1995/1996) also emphasized the importance of being able to "think in sound" for musical improvisation. He investigated the improvisation skill of 101 high school students of clarinet and of trumpet. His test required the student to provide an answering phrase, improvise "an interesting" melody on a given rhythm and to a recorded piano accompaniment, improvise on motifs, and to produce a "freely conceived" composition. High correlations were found between ability to improvise and (a) ability to play by ear and (b) ability to sight-read. Performance proficiency on an instrument and ability to improvise become increasingly intertwined in more experienced performers. For a discussion of the processes of composition and improvisation at advanced levels, see Sloboda (1985, Chapter 4).

III. MUSIC ABILITY AND OTHER ABILITIES

Correlations between intelligence scores and musical ability tests are mostly found to be positive, but low—"typically" around 0.30 (Shuter-Dyson & Gabriel, 1981). Wing (1954) observed that there was usually good agreement between low intelligence and low Wing scores, but a high IQ might be accompanied by a low musical ability score.

In the case of those tests of achievement in music that are largely aurally based, correlations with intellectual tests are also low. On the other hand, correlations between intelligence tests and grades on, for example, theory of harmony and the history of music are often much higher.

Because correlations are likely to be depressed by atypical cases, Sergeant and Thatcher (1974) preferred to use analysis of variance. They investigated the inter-relations among intelligence, ratings of sociocultural and socioeconomic characteristics of the family, and scores on a rhythmic and a melodic task. Highly significant relationships were found among all the variables. Similar results were reported by Phillips (1976).

Huntsinger and Jose (1991) used four short-term memory tasks (digit recall, tone recall, digit recognition, tone recognition) with children ages 6 to 10. Moderate to strong correlations were obtained on all four tasks, and only one factor emerged from analysis, suggesting that auditory storage in short-term memory may be a unitary phenomenon. However, in a study of 100 adults, some musically trained, others not, Steinke (1992) compared tonal abstraction abilities with non-music abstraction tests, memory for pitch, numbers, and figures. The nonmusic tests loaded on a separate factor from the music tests. Digit Span had a moderate loading on both factors, but the loading on music was much reduced when music training was partialed out.

The concept of musical ability as being specific has been adopted by Gardner (1983), who argued that music should be considered as one of several loosely related multiple intelligences. Among his criteria for an intelligence is the existence of idiots savants and prodigies. The existence of prodigies in music has long been recognized (see, e.g., Shuter-Dyson, 1985). A notable investigation of musical savants has been carried out by Miller (1989). He describes in detail the case of Eddie, whose progress in music, and through music, was followed from the age of 5 to 9½. Miller reviewed previous cases and carried out several carefully designed experiments in which the performance of Eddie and other musical savants was compared with performance of other child and adult musicians. As mentioned above (see Section II,C,1) an outstanding characteristic was absolute pitch, which enabled some of the musical savants to make confident and rapid judgments not only of the pitch of notes but also of complex chords and to produce results that were remarkably similar to those of competent adult musicians. Like intelligent adult musicians, they were sensitive to the various rules reflecting the harmonic relationships and the structure of musical compositions. However, rhythmic abilities were less in evidence. Many of the musical savants are congenitally blind. This renders them more likely to concentrate on sounds. Again, many suffer from severe language disorders that cause them to be sensitive to speech only as a series of sounds.

Saperston (1986) found highly significant correlations between the language and singing abilities of normal and of delayed young children and of mentally retarded adults.

Barwick, Valentine, West, and Wilding (1989) reported that scores on Bentley's tonal memory and chord analysis tests were related significantly to reading ability among children between 7 and 10 years old. Rados (1996) found a significant correlation between the Bentley and Wing tests 1–3 and verbal intelligence, especially for musically unselected children. In a study by Hermelin and O'Connor (1980), musically highly talented children were able to access lexical information as fast as more intelligent nonmusical children. This was not due to faster reaction time nor to mere speed of reading. A later study showed that musically talented children of high as well as of more average intelligence performed better with verbal than with nonverbal items (O'Connor & Hermelin, 1983).

The association between musical and mathematical abilities remains unproven (Shuter-Dyson & Gabriel, 1981). Wang and McCaskill (1989) correlated results on two music achievement tests with results on tests of mathematical and visual-spatial skills. Only among girls was a correlation of 0.42 between music and mathematics found. However, spatial abilities appeared to be a significant factor in the prediction of musical achievement. Hassler (1989) also has reported a stable relationship between musical and spatial abilities, both in the case of a longitudinal study of adolescents and among adult musicians.

Rauscher, Shaw, and Ky (1995) postulated that a short-term enhancement of spatial-temporal reasoning produced among college students by listening to Mozart might have a neurophysiological basis. Musical activity may strengthen inherent neural firing patterns in the cortex, which may also be exploited by spatial-reasoning tasks. To test this hypothesis, they provided keyboard training for 34 preschool children for 6 months. Compared with controls, a highly significant improvement was found for the keyboard group on the Object Assembly task, which requires spatial-temporal reasoning, but not on other tests of spatial-logical reasoning (Rauscher, Shaw, Levine, Wright, Dennis, & Newcomb, 1997).

Gardiner, Fox, Knowles, and Jeffrey (1996) reported a study in which four first-grade classes participated in a music and visual-arts curriculum that emphasized sequenced skill development. Improvements in reading and particularly in mathematics were achieved, perhaps due to a better attitude to learning and to the "stretching" required by the arts skills developing the type of thinking needed for mathematics.

Such results are not incompatible with a lack of definite relationships among older subjects, who are unlikely to have enjoyed enhanced preschool opportunities for music. Techniques such as electroencephalographic mapping and positron emission tomography scans may evenually throw light on the processing of music in the brain and the relationship of music to other abilities.

IV. CONCLUSIONS

There seems to be ample evidence that music is as natural for humans as is language. It is also apparent that musical abilities blossom in a social climate where music is valued and enjoyed.

A musical background very early in life is likely to be most effective in helping individuals to fulfill whatever aptitudes they happen to have been born with, as well as revealing special gifts. The encouragement of excellence must always be an important aim. Manturzewska (1990) has shown how crucially professional musicians need appropriate support at different stages throughout their lives.

L. Davidson (1994) notes that instrumental training in itself does not guarantee a grasp of musical relationships. A range of musical instruments and contexts must be explored so that young musicians become able to coordinate their skills across a range of situations.

In the absence of musical education, patterns of taste remain stable throughout the course of one's life (Zenatti, 1993, p. 185). Indeed, too many adults consider themselves to be "unmusical." They might be encouraged if results of a musical ability test showed they were in fact average or even superior (see also Gibbons, 1982). Older adults can benefit greatly from music participation and instruction (Darrough & Boswell, 1992). *Can* do is not always the same as *will* do. Motivational factors are undoubtedly of vital importance.

Whatever the future effects of technology (see Deutsch, 1996), music will always require a high level of cognitive ability and commitment.

REFERENCES

Baily, J. (1985). Music structure and human movement. In P. Howell, I. Cross, & R. West (Eds.), *Musical structure and cognition* (pp. 237–258). London: Academic Press.

Baltzer, S. (1988). A validation study of a measure of musical creativity. *Journal of Research in Music Education, 36,* 232–249.

Baltzer, S. (1990). *A factor analytic study of musical creativity in children in the primary grades.* Unpublished doctoral dissertation, Indiana University, Bloomington.

Bamberger, J. (1982). Revisiting children's drawings of simple rhythms: A function of reflection-in-action. In S. Strauss (Ed.), *U-shaped behavioral growth* (pp. 191–226). New York: Academic Press.

Bartlett, J. C., & Dowling, W. J. (1980). The recognition of transposed melodies: a key-distance effect in developmental perspective. *Journal of Experimental Psychology: Human Perception and Performance, 6,* 501–515.

Barwick, J., Valentine, E., West, R., & Wilding, J. (1989). Relations between reading and musical abilities. *British Journal of Educational Psychology, 59,* 253–257.

Bentley, A. (1966). *Measures of musical abilities.* Windsor, England: NFER-NELSON.

Blacking, J. A. R. (1971). Towards a theory of musical competence. In E. DeJager (Ed.), *Man: Anthropological essays in honour of O. F. Raum.* Cape Town: Struik.

Boyle, D. J. (1982). A study of the comparative validity of three published, standardised measures of music preference. *Psychology of Music, 10* [Special issue], 11–16.

Boyle, D. J. (1992). Evaluation of music ability. In R. Colwell (Ed.), *Handbook for Research in Music Teaching and Learning* (pp. 247–265). New York: Macmillan.

Boyle, D. J., & Penticoff, B. (1989, Fall). A study of elementary school children's perception of tonality. *Contributions to Music Education, 16,* 67–76.

Castell, K. C. (1982). Children's sensitivity to stylistic differences in "classical" add "popular" music. *Psychology of Music, 10*[Special issue], 22–25.

Chang, H., & Trehub, S. E. (1977). Infants' perception of temporal grouping in auditory patterns. *Child Development, 48,* 1666–1670.

Clarke, E. F. (1993). Imitating and evaluating real and transformed musical performances. *Music Perception, 10,* 317–341.

Clarke, E. F., & Baker-Short, C. (1987). The imitation of perceived rubato: A preliminary study. *Psychology of Music, 15,* 58–75.

Cuddy, L. L. (1993). Melody comprehension and tonal structure. In T. J. Tighe & W. J. Dowling (Eds.), *Psychology and music* (pp. 19–38). Hillsdale, NJ: Erlbaum.

Cuddy, L. (1997). Tonal relations. In I. Deliege & J. A. Sloboda (Eds.), *Perception and cognition of music* (pp. 329–352). London: Erlbaum.

Cuddy, L. L., & Badertscher, B. (1987). Recovery of the tonal hierarchy: Some comparison across age and levels of musical experience. *Perception & Psychophysics, 41,* 609–620.

Cuddy, L. L., Cohen, A. J., & Miller, J. (1979). Melody recognition: The experimental application of musical rules. *Canadian Journal of Psychology, 33,* 148–157.

Cuddy, L. L., & Wiebe, M. G. (1979). Music and the experimental sciences. *Humanities Association Review, 30,* 1–10.

Darrough, G. P., & Boswell, J. (1992). Older adult participants in music. *Bulletin of the Council for Research in Music Education, 111,* 25–34.

Davidson, J. (1993). Visual perception of performance manner in the movements of solo musicians. *Psychology of Music, 21,* 103–113.

Davidson, L. (1994). Songsinging by young and old: A developmental approach to music In R. Aiello & J. A. Sloboda (Eds.), Musical perceptions (pp. 99–130). New York: Oxford University Press.

Davidson, L., McKernon, P., & Gardner, H. (1981). The acquisition of song: A developmental approach. In J. A. Mason (Ed.), *Documentary report of the Ann Arbor symposium on the applications of psychology to the teaching and learning of music* (pp. 301–315). Reston, VA: Music Educators National Conference.

Deutsch, S. (1996). Music and technology: the composer in the age of the Internet. *Royal Society of Arts Journal, CXLIV*(5470), 25–33.

Dowling, W. J., & Harwood, D. (1986). *Music cognition.* New York: Academic Press.

Drake, R. M. (1933a). Four new tests of musical talent. *Journal of Applied Psychology, 17,* 136–147;

Drake, R. M. (1933b). The validity and reliability of tests of musical talent. *Journal of Applied Psychology, 17,* 447–458.

Drake, R. M. (1957). *Manual for the Drake Musical Aptitude Tests.* 2nd ed. Chicago: Science Research Associates.

Farnsworth, P. R. (1969). *The social psychology of music* (2nd ed.) Ames: Iowa State University Press.

Flowers, P. J., & Dunne-Sousa, D. (1990). Pitch-pattern accuracy, tonality, and vocal range in preschool children's singing. *Journal of Research in Music Education, 38,* 102–114.

Fraisse, P. (1982). Rhythm and tempo. In D. Deutsch, *The psychology of music* (pp.149–180). New York: Academic Press.

Gabrielsson, A. (1982). Performance and training of musical rhythm. *Psychology of Music, 10* [Special issue], 42–46.

Gardiner, M. F., Fox, A., Knowles, F., & Jeffrey, D. (1996). Learning improved by arts training. *Nature, 381,* 284.

Gardner, H. (1973). Children's sensitivity to musical styles. *Merrill-Palmer Quarterly, 19,* 67–77.

Gardner, H. (1983). *Frames of mind.* New York: Basic Books.

George, W. E. (1980). Measurement and evaluation of musical behavior. In D. A. Hodges (Ed.), *Handbook of music psychology* (pp.401–407). Lawrence, KS: National Association for Music Therapy.

Gérard, C., & Drake, C. (1990). The inability of young children to reproduce intensity differences in musical rhythms. *Perception & Psychophysics, 48,* 91–101.

Gibbons, A. C. (1982). Musical Aptitude Profile scores in a noninstitutionalized elderly population. *Journal of Research in Music Education, 30,* 23–29.

Gilbert, J. P. (1979). Assessment of motoric music skill development in young children: Test construction and evaluation procedures. *Psychology of Music, 7*(2), 3–12.

Gilbert, J. P. (1981). Motoric music skill development in young children: A longitudinal investigation. *Psychology of Music, 9*(1), 21–25.

Gilbert, J. P. (1982). Motoric music skills: A longitudinal investigation and comparison with children's rhythmic and tonal perception. In P. E. Sink (Ed.), *Proceedings of the Research Symposium on the Psychology and Acoustics of Music, 1981.* Lawrence: University of Kansas.

Goetze, M., Cooper, N., & Brown, C. J. (1990). Recent research on singing in the general classroom. *Bulletin of the Council for Research in Music Education, 104,* 16–37.

Gordon, A., & Martin, P. J. (1993/1994). A study of the rhythmic skills of musically unsophisticated secondary school students when playing the electronic keyboard with a drum-machine. *Bulletin of the Council for Research in Music Education, 119,* 59–64.

Gordon, E. E. (1965). *Musical Aptitude Profile manual.* Boston: Houghton Mifflin.

Gordon, E. E. (1979). *Primary measures of music audiation.* Chicago: GIA.

Gordon, E. E. (1982). *Intermediate measures of music audiation.* Chicago: GIA.

Gordon, E. E. (1988). *Musical Aptitude Profile manual* (Rev. ed.). Chicago: Riverside.

Gordon. E. E. (1989a). Advanced measures of music audiation. Chicago: GIA.

Gordon, E. E. (1989b). *Audie: A game for understanding and analyzing your child's musical potential.* Chicago: GIA.

Gordon, E. E. (1990). Breaking 100 in music. In F. R. Wilson & F. L. Roehmann (Eds.), *Music and child development* (pp. 413–414). St. Louis: MMB Music, Inc.

Gromko, J.E. (1994). Children's invented notations as measures of musical understanding. *Psychology of Music, 22,* 136–147.

Hargreaves, D. J., & Zimmerman, M. P. (1992). Developmental theories of music learning. In R. Colwell (Ed.), *Handbook for research in music teaching and learning* (pp. 377–391). New York: Macmillan.

Hassler, M. (1989). Musical talent and human spatial ability. *Canadian Music Educator, Research Edition, 30,* 39–45.

Hebb, D. O. (1949). *The organization of behavior.* New York: Wiley.

Hermelin, B., & O'Connor, N. (1980). Perceptual, motor, and decision speeds in specifically and generally gifted children. *Gifted Child Quarterly, 24,* 180–185.

Hiriartborde, E., & Fraisse, P. (1968). *Les aptitudes rythmiques.* Paris: CNRS.

Howe, M., Davidson, J., Moore, D., & Sloboda, J. A. (1995). Are there early childhood signs of musical ability? *Psychology of Music, 23,* 162–176.

Huron, D. (1989). Voice denumberability in polyphonic music of homogeneous timbres. *Music Perception, 6,* 361–382.

Huntsinger, C. S., & Jose, P. E. (1991). A test of Gardner's Modularity Theory: A comparison of short-term memory for digits and tones *Psychomusicology, 10,* 3–16.

Imberty, M. (1969). *L'acquisition des structures tonales chez l'enfant.* Paris: Klincksieck.

Kalmus, H., & Fry, D. B. (1980). On tune deafness (dysmelodia): frequency development, genetics and musical background. *Annals of Human Genetics, London, 43,* 369–382.

Karma, K. (1983). Selecting students to music instruction. *Bulletin of the Council for Research in Music Education, 75,* 23–32.

Karma, K. (1985). Components of auditive structuring: Towards a theory of musical aptitude. *Bulletin of the Council for Research in Music Education, 82,* 1–13.

Karma, K. (1986). Item difficulty values in measuring components of musical aptitude. *Bulletin of the Council for Research in Music Education, 89,* 18–31.

Karma, K. (1991). Measuring different aspects of pitch differentiation. *Canadian Music Educator, 33,* 87–93.

Kemp, A. E. (1996). *The musical temperament.* Oxford: Oxford University Press.

Kessen, W., Levine, J., & Wendrich, K. A. (1979). The imitation of pitch in infants. *Infant Behavior and Development, 2,* 93–99.

Kratus, J. (1989). A time analysis of the compositional processes used by children aged 7 to 11. *Journal of Research in Music Education, 37,* 5–20.

Kratus, J. (1991). Characterization of the compositional strategies used by children to create a melody. *Canadian Music Educator, Special ISME Res. Ed., 33,* 95–103.

Kratus, J. (1994). Relationships among children's music audiation and their compositional processes and products. *Journal of Research in Music Education, 42,* 115–130.

Krumhansl, C. L. (1990). *Cognitive foundations of musical pitch.* New York: Oxford University Press.

Krumhansl, C. L., & Jusczyk, P. W. (1990). Infants' perception of phrase structure in music. *Psychological Science, 1,* 70–74.

Long, N. H. (1965). *Indiana-Oregon music discrimination test.* Bloomington, IN: Midwest Music Tests.

McLeish, J. (1950). The validation of Seashore's measures of musical talent by factorial methods. *British Journal of Psychology (Statistical Section), 3,* 129–140.

McPherson, G. E. (1993/1994). Evaluating improvisational ability of high school instrumentalists. *Bulletin of the Council for Research in Music Education, 119,* 11–20.

McPherson, G. E. (1995). The assessment of musical performance: Development and validation of five new measures. *Psychology of Music, 23,* 142–161.

McPherson, G. E. (1995/1996). Five aspects of musical performance and their correlates. *Bulletin of the Council for Research in Music Education, 127,* 115–121.

Mainwaring, J. (1933). Kinaesthetic factors in the recall of musical experience. *British Journal of Psychology, 23,* 284–307.

Manturzewska, M. (1990). A biographical study of the life-span development of professional musicians. *Psychology of Music, 18,* 112–139.

Mawhinney, T. A. (1987). *Tone-deafness and low musical abilities.* Unpublished doctoral dissertation, Queen's University at Kingston, Ontario.

Miller, L. K. (1989). *Musical savants: Exceptional skill in the mentally retarded.* Hillsdale, NJ: Lawrence Erlbaum.

Mills, J. (1988). *Group tests of musical ability.* Windsor, England: NFER-NELSON.

Mitchell, P. (1991). Research note: Adult non-singers—The beginning stages of learning to sing. *Psychology of Music, 19,* 74–76.

Miyazaki, K. (1992). Perception of musical intervals by absolute pitch possessors. *Music Perception, 9,* 413–426.

Miyazaki, K. (1993). Absolute pitch as an inability: Identification of musical intervals in a tonal context. *Music Perception, 11,* 55–72.

O'Connor, N., & Hermelin, B. (1983). The role of general ability and specific talents in information processing. *British Journal of Developmental Psychology, 1,* 389–403.

Papousek, M. (1982). *Musical elements in mother-infant dialogues.* Paper presented at the International Conference on Infant Studies, Austin, Texas.

Phillips, D. (1976). An investigation of the relationship between musicality and intelligence. *Psychology of Music, 4*(2), 16–31.

Rados, K. M. (1996). *Psihologija Muzike.* Belgrade: Zavod za Udzbenike i nastavna Sredstva.

Ramsey, J. H. (1983). The effects of age, singing ability, and instrumental experiences on preschool children's melodic perception. *Journal of Research in Music Education, 31,* 133–145.

Rauscher, F. H., Shaw, G. L., & Ky, K. N. (1995). Listening to Mozart enhances spatial-temporal reasoning: towards a neurophysiological basis. *Neuroscience Letters, 185,* 44–47.

Rauscher, F. H., Shaw, G. L., Levine, L., Wright, E. L. Dennis, W. R., & Newcomb, R. L. (1997). Music training causes long-term enhancement of preschool children's spatial-temporal reasoning. *Neurological Research, 19,* 2–8.

Repp, B. H. (1992). A constraint on the expressive timing of a melodic gesture: Evidence from performance and aesthetic judgment. *Music Perception, 10,* 221–242.

Révész, G. (1953). *Introduction to the psychology of music.* London: Longmans, Green.

Saperston, B. M. (1986). *The relationship of cognitive, language, and melodic development of normal children and retarded children and adults.* Unpublished doctoral dissertation, University of Texas, Austin.

Schmidt, C. P., & Lewis, B. A. (1987). Field-dependence/independence, movement-based instruction and fourth graders' achievement in selected musical tasks. *Psychology of Music, 15,* 117–127.

Seashore, C. E. (1938). *The psychology of music.* New York: McGraw Hill.

Serafine, M. L. (1988). *Music as cognition.* New York: Columbia University Press.

Sergeant, D. C., & Thatcher, G. (1974). Intelligence, social status and musical abilities. *Psychology of Music, 2*(2), 32–57.

Shuter-Dyson, R. (1982). Musical ability. In D. Deutsch (Ed.), *The psychology of music* (pp. 391–412). New York: Academic Press.

Shuter-Dyson, R. (1985). Musical giftedness. In J. Freeman (Ed.), *The psychology of gifted children* (pp. 159–183). Chicester, UK: Wiley.

Shuter-Dyson, R. (1994). Le problème des interactions entre hérédité et milieu dans la formation des aptitudes musicales. In A. Zenatti (Ed.), *Psychologie de la musique* (pp. 205–231). Paris: Presses Universitaires de France.

Shuter-Dyson, R., & Gabriel, C. (1981). *The psychology of musical ability.* London: Methuen.

Sloboda, J. A. (1983). The communication of musical metre in piano performance. *Quarterly Journal of Experimental Psychology, 35,* 377–396.

Sloboda, J. A. (1985). *The musical mind: The cognitive psychology of music.* Oxford: Oxford University Press.

Sloboda, J. A. (1990). Music as a language. In F. R. Wilson & F. L Roehmann (Eds.), *Music and child development.* St. Louis: The Biology of Making, Inc.

Sloboda, J. A. (1994). Music performance: Expression and the development of excellence. In R. Aiello & J. A. Sloboda (Eds.), *Musical perceptions.* New York: Oxford University Press.

Sloboda, J. A., & Parker, D. H. H. (1985). Immediate recall of melodies. In P. Howell., Cross, I., & West, R. (Eds.) *Musical structure and cognition* (pp. 143–167). London: Academic Press.

Smith, K., Cuddy, L., & Upitis, R. (1994). Figural and metric understanding of rhythm. *Psychology of Music, 22,* 117–135.

Speer, J., & Meeks, P. (1985). School children's perception of pitch in music. *Psychomusicology, 5,* 49–56.

Stambak, M. (1960). Trois épreuves de rythme. In R. Zazzo (Ed.), *Manuel pour l'examen psychologique de l'enfant.* Neuchatel: Delachaux et Niestle.

Steinke, W. R. (1992). *Musical abstraction and nonmusical abstraction abilities in musically trained and untrained adults.* Unpublished doctoral dissertation, Queen's University, Kingston, Ontario.

Swanick, K. (1973). Musical cognition and aesthetic response. *Psychology of Music, 1*(2), 7–13.

Swanner, D. L. (1985). *Relationships between musical creativity and selected factors, including personality, motivation, musical aptitude, and cognitive intelligence as measured in third grade children.* Unpublished dissertation, Case Western Reserve University, Cleveland, Ohio.

Thackray, R. (1969). *An investigation into rhythmic abilities* (Music Education Research Papers No. 4). London: Novello.

Thackray, R. (1972). *Rhythmic abilities in children* (Music Education Research Papers No. 5). London: Novello.

The Quarterly (1991). The work of Edwin Gordon. II(1–2). Greeley: University of Northern Colorado.

Tomita, M. (1986). Assessment of musical aptitudes: Summary of the research on the existing tests of musical abilities. *Bulletin of the Graduate School of Literature, Waseda University, Japan, No. 32.*

Trehub, S. E. (1985). Auditory pattern perception in infancy. In S. E. Trehub & B. A. Schneider (Eds.), *Auditory development in infancy* (pp. 183–195). New York: Plenum Press.

Trehub, S. A. (1993). The music listening skills of infants and young children. In T. J. Tighe & W. J. Dowling (Eds.), *Psychology and music* (pp. 161–176). Hillsdale, NJ: Erlbaum.

Trehub, S. E., Bull, D., & Thorpe, L. A. (1984). Infants' perception of melodies: The role of melodic contour. *Child Development, 55,* 821–830.

Trehub, S. E., Thorpe, L. A., & Trainer, L. J. (1990) Infants' perception of good and bad melodies. *Psychomusicology, 9,* 5–19.

Umemoto, T. (1995). A new test on the sense of pitch deviation in tunes. In M. Manturzewska, K. Miklaszewski, & A. Bialkowski (Eds.), *Psychology of music today* (pp. 177–184). Warsaw: Fryderyk Chopin Academy of Music.

Umemoto, T., Mikumo, M., & Murase, A. (1989). Development of tonal sense: A new test of cognition of pitch deviation. *Human Developmental Research, 5,* 155–174.

Upitis, R. (1987). Children's understanding of rhythm: The relationship between development and music training. *Psychomusicology, 7,* 41–60.

Vaughan, M. M. (1977). Measuring creativity: Its cultivation and measurement. *Bulletin of the Council for Research in Music Education, 50,* 72–77.

Vernon, P. E. (1968). What is potential ability? *Bulletin of the British Psvchological Society, 21,* 211–219.

Vispoel, W. P. (1993). The development and evaluation of a computerized adaptive test of tonal memory. *Journal of Research in Music Education, 41,* 111–136.

Vispoel, W. P., & Coffman, D. D. (1992). Computerized adaptive testing of music-related skills. *Bulletin of the Council for Research in Music Education, 112,* 29–48.

Vispoel, W. P., & Coffman, D. D. (1994). Computerized-adaptive and self-adapted tests of music-listening skills: Psychometric features and motivational benefits. *Applied Measurement in Education, 7,* 25–51.

Wang, C. (1985). *Measures of creativity in sound and music.* Unpublished manuscript, University of Kentucky School of Music, Lexington.

Wang, C. C., & McCaskill, M. E. (1989). Relating musical abilities to visual-spatial abilities, mathematic and language skills of fifth-grade children. *Canadian Journal of Research in Music Education, 30,* 184–191.

Watkins, J. G., & Farnum, S. E. (1954). *The Watkins-Farnum Performance Scale.* Winnona, MN: Hal Leonard Music.

Webster, P. R. (1983). *Measures of creative thinking in music.* Unpublished manuscript, Northwestern University School of Music, Evanston, IL.

Webster, P. R. (1988). New perspectives on music aptitude and achievement. *Psychomusicology, 7,* 177–194.

Webster, P. R., Yale, C., & Haefner, M. (1988). *Test-retest reliability of Measures of Creative Thinking in Music for children with formal music training.* Paper presented at the Music Educators National Conference, Indianapolis, IN.

Welch, G. F. (1985). Variability of practice and knowledge of results as factors in learning to sing in tune. *Bulletin of the Council for Research in Music Education, 85,* 238–247.

Welch, G. F. (1994). The assessment of singing. *Psychology of Music, 22,* 3–19.

Welch, G. F., Howard, D. M., & Rush, C. (1989). Real-time visual feedback in the development of vocal pitch accuracy in singing. *Psychology of Music, 17,* 146–157.

Wendrich, K. A. (1981). *Pitch imitation in infancy and early childhood.* Unpublished doctoral dissertation. University of Connecticut, Storrs.

Whellams, F. (1971). *The aural musical abilities of junior school children: A factorial investigation.* Unpublished doctoral dissertation, University of London.

White, D. J., Dale, P. S., & Carlsen, J. C. (1990). Discrimination and categorization of pitch direction by young children. *Psychomusicology, 9,* 39–58.

Wing, H. D. (1948). Tests of musical ability and appreciation. *British Journal of Psychology, Monograph Supplement, 27.* (2nd ed., 1968)

Wing, H. D. (1954). Some applications of test results to education in music. *British Journal of Educational Psychology, 24,* 161–170.

Wing, H. D. (1981). *Standardised tests of musical intelligence.* Windsor, England: NFER-NELSON.

Zenatti, A. (1969). Le développement génétique de la perception musicale. *Monographies Francaises de Psychologie, 17.* Paris: CNRS.

Zenatti, A. (1976). Jugement esthetique et perception de l'enfant, entre 4 et 10 ans, dans des épreuves rythmiques. *Année Psychologique, 76,* 93–115.

Zenatti, A. (1981). *L'enfant et son environnement musical.* Issy-les-Moulineaux: EAP.

Zenatti, A. (1985). The role of perceptual-discrimination ability in tests of melody, harmony, and rhythm. *Music Perception, 2,* 397–404.

Zenatti, A. (1993). Children's musical cognition and taste. In T. T. Tighe & W. J. Dowling (Eds.), *Psychology and music.* Hillsdale, NJ: Erlbaum.

17

NEUROLOGICAL ASPECTS OF

MUSIC PERCEPTION AND

PERFORMANCE

OSCAR S. M. MARIN

Department of Neurology
Good Samaritan Hospital
Portland, Oregon

DAVID W. PERRY

Department of Neurology and Neurosurgery
Montreal Neurological Institute
McGill University
Montreal, Quebec, Canada

I. INTRODUCTION

An article dealing with the neurology and neuropsychology of music should include two levels of inquiry: (a) *description* of the clinical deficits in music perception or performance resulting from localized or diffuse damage to the nervous system, and of their associations and dissociations and, on the basis of these data, (b) *analysis* of normal and abnormal psychological and physiological functions. The aim of such an endeavor is to determine the principles and modes by which the human brain processes, codifies, stores, and produces music. In order to approach those questions, cognitive models based on the empirical investigation of normal music processing (and of other complex cognitive skills) must be combined with data from comparative studies of the anatomy and physiology of the auditory nervous system. (See Chapter 3, this volume, for a thorough review of relevant neurophysiological knowledge.) The resulting hypotheses, part of the domain now called cognitive neuroscience, can best guide the empirical investigation and analysis of clinical deficits in music perception and performance, and the investigation of anatomical-functional correlations via noninvasive brain imaging methods in humans. It will remain a task for future research to continue to integrate advances from these two approaches, for example, to specify how a hierarchically organized musical cognitive system is instantiated in the structure and function of the nervous system. Recent studies that exemplify such an integration will be described.

Clinical descriptions of abnormalities of musical perception or performance abound in the neurological literature, particularly that of the second half of the 19th century and the early part of this century. It is significant, however, that in the past 30 years the confident enthusiasm with which clinical deficits were related to functional localization in the brain has become increasingly restrained. This restraint is largely due to a realization that in dealing with brain processes, one can no longer accept the simplistic concept that the central nervous system can be represented merely as a mosaic of complex mental faculties. One should reject the idea that it is possible to give an adequate account of verbal, musical, or any other complex behavior by anatomically describing a few perceptual or executive functional components. Of even more fundamental importance has been the realization that one cannot study the neuropsychology of complex behavior without a prior understanding of the cognitive structures of the systems involved.

Despite this awareness, progress in the field of the neurology of music has been slow. Until recently, a similar simplistic approach controlled the study of the neurology of speech and language; and it still prevails to a large degree in understanding the agnosias and disorders of motor behavior. Disillusionment with the whole mental faculty approach caused a shift to the opposite extreme and emphasized instead the minute analysis of the hardware. This is as if in order to understand the plot of a television program, we analyze the details of the television circuit or the trajectory of the electronic beam projected onto the screen. This approach, which would have reduced the neuropsychology of music to a mere psychoacoustic endeavor, has had its hour, and most would now agree that from the cognitive standpoint, music is a hierarchical function that requires processing at many interacting levels. Music has, as do many other highly evolved human activities, its own unique cognitive structure, its own information processing systems, and its own learning and memory capacities, quite apart from those of language or other complex mental functions.

Because some useful information on auditory perceptual processing has come from the study of auditory agnosias, including verbal deafness (disorders of the recognition of auditory information, including speech), these clinical syndromes are analyzed here despite the fact that relatively little is known about the way in which disorders of music perception relate to such cases. Recent progress in delineating the relationship of musical agnosias to other forms of auditory agnosia is, however, described. Because neuropsychological studies of language and speech have proven their value in the analysis of cognitive processes, and because these functions are at least in some ways analogous to musical functions, we shall use neurolinguistic and psycholinguistic experience as points of reference, without however overemphasizing these parallelisms.

The clinical characteristics of disorders of musical function are described, but a summary of these clinical experiences does not yet provide a neuropsychologically coherent interpretation in terms of information processing or of localization in the nervous system. Rather, these clinical descriptions will be used as points of departure for critical comments on issues requiring the integration of cognitive and neurological approaches to understanding musical behavior, a goal toward which preliminary steps have been taken.

II. AMUSIAS

Amusia is a generic term used to designate acquired clinical disorders of music perception, performance, reading, or writing that are due to brain damage and not attributable simply to the disruption of basic perceptual, motoric, or cognitive functions. These disorders, like other syndromes of higher cortical dysfunction—such as agnosias, aphasias, or apraxias—should represent fairly self-circumscribed disabilities and not be the result of a general decay of overall mental capacity (as may be observed in advanced dementia, psychosis, or mental retardation).

The classical literature describing amusia has been reviewed many times in recent years. Of special value are the works of Benton (1977), Jellinek (1956), Sergent (1993), and Wertheim (1963, 1969, 1977) in English, and of Barbizet (1972), Dorgeuille (1966), Grison (1972), and Samson and Zatorre (1994a) in French. The German-speaking authors have sustained interest in the subject with works ranging from highly theoretical speculative essays to clinical or anatomoclinical reviews. Notable are the works of Edgren (1895), Feuchtwanger (1930), Henschen (1920, 1926), Jellinek (1933), Kleist (1928, 1962), Ustvedt (1937), and Walthard (1927).

Whereas the agnosias (i.e., auditory agnosias, visual agnosias) are clinical nosological terms used to designate modality-specific disorders of perception, the amusias are terms referring to an attempt to group a broad variety of disabilities related to musical function (as the aphasias group the variety of language deficits). Some amusias are specifically perceptual in nature; some involve symbolic systems of reading and writing or are based on previously acquired knowledge, and still others comprise complex executive vocal or manual motor activities. We should also note that the degree of proficiency and automatization with which each of these tasks was performed before illness varies considerably in individual patients. It can be anticipated that grouping together such a heterogeneous assortment of dysfunctions will not help us to determine whether basic musical mechanisms are related to consistent lesional topographies. Consequently, as also noted by others (Ustvedt, 1937; Wertheim, 1977), the nosological term *amusia* is too general and is thus essentially meaningless for describing, and useless for explaining, the brain mechanisms that may be involved in musical functions.

Efforts to improve and clarify the main issues relating to disorders of music perception or performance have used four main approaches:

1. Nosological studies attempting subclassifications of the amusias into clinical syndromes that are more closely related to the impairment of basic mecha-

nisms of musical functions (Dorgeuille, 1966; Henschen, 1920; Kleist, 1934; Lechevalier, Eustache, & Rossa, 1985; and Wertheim, 1963, 1969).

2. Attempts to define the relationship between disturbances of speech and language (aphasias) and those of music (amusias) by comparing the clinical syndromes, documenting the clinical coexistence or segregation of these syndromes in individual patients, and correlating the anatomoclinical findings of both disorders.

3. Attempts to define the relationship between specific disturbances of auditory recognition (the auditory agnosias) and those of music recognition (musical agnosias) by contrasting the clinical syndromes, documenting the clinical coexistence or segregation of the various syndromes in individual patients, and correlating the anatomical and clinical findings (Peretz, 1993b; Peretz et al., 1994; Peretz & Morais, 1993).

4. Improvements in methods of estimating the premorbid material skill and knowledge of amusic patients in order to obtain a reliable baseline for the evaluation of deficits (Grison, 1972).

5. Improvements and systematization of the methods of clinical investigation of musical disorders (Dorgeuille, 1966; Jellinek, 1956; Peretz, Babaï, Lussier, Hebert, & Gagnon, 1995; Wertheim, 1969; Wertheim & Botez, 1959).

A. AMUSIA WITH APHASIA

It has been stressed that music is a "language" and, consequently, that amusia and aphasia are likely to be closely linked in their neuroanatomical substrates (Feuchtwanger, 1930). Thus the *criteria* required for their documentation and even their nosological subclassification would be expected to be closely related (Weisenburg & McBride, 1935). Musical disabilities that are predominantly receptive (receptive or sensory amusias) would somehow parallel the receptive and sensory aphasias of Wernicke; disorders that are predominantly expressed in terms of an inability to vocalize or sing would be somewhat equivalent to Broca's aphasia; disorders of musical writing would parallel agraphias; disorders of musical reading would correspond to alexias; and the inability to name a familiar tune would be a type of anomia. Nonparalytic difficulties in playing an instrument would constitute a musical apraxia.

A strong clinical association between aphasias and amusias would have important implications for the anatomical localization of musical functions, because speech and language are strongly lateralized to the language-dominant cerebral hemisphere (for distribution of speech and language functions, see Marin, Schwartz, & Saffran, 1979). If, on the other hand, the association is only partial or inconsistent, a conclusion that language and music share only some processes or may even be totally independent functions would be suggested. In this respect, one should remember that cognitive or computational similarities between two functions do not necessarily mean that they must share a common physiological or anatomical substratum. The evolutionary tendency of the central nervous system is toward the assignment of task-oriented neural subsets (Simon, 1967). Such sub-specializations for speech and music would result in independent neural operators of greater efficiency.

It is not possible to evaluate with certainty from the existing literature the frequency with which aphasias and amusias occur in association. Most of the published clinical cases were preselected, examined only from the standpoint of either aphasia or amusia. Cases of amusia have been analyzed for aphasia more often than cases of aphasia have been analyzed for amusia. Feuchtwanger (1930) found various degrees of aphasia in each of his observations of amusia and, on the basis of his findings, suggested that the neurolexical substrates of music and language are intimately related. Since then, a growing number of cases have shown dissociations between the two sets of functions. Dorgeuille (1966), in his study of 26 observations, found 11 cases of amusia with aphasia and 2 examples of isolated amusia.

In reviewing the observations of a large number of clinical articles on amusia, we were able to collect 87 case reports with fairly complete clinical descriptions. Aphasia and amusia coexisted in 33 of these cases. Well-documented examples of amusia without aphasia were found in 19 cases. Amusia and general auditory agnosia were reasonably well documented in 4 cases, and there were at least 5 cases of amusia associated with verbal deafness with only minor or nonexistent signs of nonverbal auditory agnosia. There were 1 or possibly 2 cases of nonverbal auditory agnosia with a possible musical perceptual disorder but without verbal deafness or aphasia (Nielsen, 1962; Spreen, Benton, & Fincham, 1965).

No attempt will be made here to review the large number of cases already recorded by others. Examples will be selected because they represent dissociations that are clinically characteristic or because they offer an opportunity to discuss special aspects of the neuropsychological structure of music (or of cognitive functioning in general).

The existence of fairly distinct disorders of music perception (e.g., receptive amusia) is well recognized. Their association with similar deficits in language perception and comprehension is not exceptional (Feuchtwanger, 1930), but the two functions may often be dissociated (Ustvedt, 1937). Kohl and Tschabitscher (1952) describe a patient with left hemisphere damage, expressive aphasia, normal comprehension, and predominantly receptive amusia.

Wertheim and Botez (1961) describe the case of a 40-year-old professional violinist who, after developing a sudden right-sided sensorimotor hemiparesis and a mixed but predominantly receptive aphasia, showed a number of difficulties in musical processing. Although the patient previously had absolute pitch (i.e., the ability to accurately name the pitch of heard notes), he subsequently made consistent errors in identifying and naming isolated sounds (usually transposing them up a perfect fourth).[1] His pitch discrimination was normal even for intervals smaller than a semitone, however, and vocal and instrumental reproductions of single

---

[1]In the only other reported case of absolute pitch ability subsequent to brain damage, a left anterior temporal lobectomy that spared all of the primary auditory cortical area had no effect (Zatorre, 1989b).

pitches were correct. He was able to identify differences in melodies and chords and to recognize faulty performances of a familiar melody (including errors in tonal modulation). In contrast, he was completely unable to name intervals in melodic or harmonic contexts. Recognition and identification of work and composer of well-known musical themes were correct if the melodies were sung to him, but incorrect if played to him on the piano. Vocal and instrumental recall of familiar melodies were at times accurate, although intonational errors were frequent. Reproduction of unfamiliar melodies, however, was impossible. Reproduction of an unfamiliar melody in musical notation was better than sung, but resulted in frequent errors of pitch. Identification of rhythmic measures and motoric and written reproduction of rhythms were also poorly performed. Music reading was impossible in sequence, but the patient was able to name notes in isolation on the violin clef. Reading of musical symbols was normal but rendition of their meaning was often faulty.

This case, summarized in some detail, shows the clinical complexity of some of the deficits and, at the same time, shows the variance in the cognitive nature of the errors made by the patient, even given systematic explorations of pitch, rhythm, melody, and chord perception. It is interesting to observe that tasks involving simple perceptual discriminations (e.g., detecting errors in simple melodies) were performed more successfully than tasks requiring identification or naming (e.g., pitches, intervals). In this respect, it is of significance to note that the residual aphasic disorder of this patient was also predominantly a lexical difficulty in the form of anomia. Some of the deficits exhibited by this patient could well have been due to a basic lexical disorder common for language and music. Other deficits indicate that both higher-level receptive functions for linguistic (e.g., complex speech) and musical (e.g., unfamiliar melodies) information were impaired, while lower levels were relatively intact.

This case illustrates the need to distinguish between specifically perceptual defects, disorders related to the "linguistic" or symbolic-lexical level of the musical system, and disorders related to the higher-level perceptual organization of music. A further distinction between musical-perceptual and auditory-sensory levels is also suggested and will be expanded later, when observations of auditory agnosias and verbal deafness are discussed. The observation that the composer and title of familiar themes could be named if sung, but not if played on the piano, suggest an interaction between the auditory-sensory and symbolic-lexical levels. Souques and Baruk (1930) describe a patient with severe Wernicke's (receptive) aphasia due to extensive left temporal lobe damage. The patient was able to detect minute errors in the instrumental execution of others, and her music reading and writing were preserved, in spite of the fact that she was totally incapable of naming musical works or elements. Here again we observe disabilities in the higher-level functions of identification and naming, while other musical perceptual functions are intact.

A similar dissociation between musical anomia and other musical functions can sometimes be seen in cases of dementia. Beatty et al. (1988) describe the case of a woman with advanced probable Alzheimer's dementia, accompanied by severe anomia and receptive aphasia. She was nevertheless able to play a large repertoire of songs on the piano and to sight-read novel music, even on the xylophone, an instrument unfamiliar to her before the onset of dementia. Crystal, Grober, and Masur (1989) describe a case of progressive dementia (probable Alzheimer's disease) in a professional musicologist and music editor, who before his illness played classical music for the family every evening during dinner in order to develop their knowledge of composers. Five years subsequent to the onset of memory problems, he was unable to name the composer or title of any well-known works, including Beethoven's Fifth Symphony. He could, however, after hearing the first few bars, continue playing familiar works on the piano, still with no conscious knowledge of their composers or titles. Not until 2 years further did failure to name common objects occur. Although an association is seen in this case between lexical disorders in music and language, the two forms of anomia are partially dissociated, in that failure to name common tunes significantly preceded failure to name common objects, in spite of a marked predilection for memorizing musical names.

Probably the most famous case of amusia in a professional musician is that of Maurice Ravel. Although the precise cause of his illness is unknown, he was followed for several years by the neurologist Alajouanine (1948), who concluded that Ravel suffered from an unspecified type of cerebral atrophy (although clearly not Pick's disease) characterized by bilaterally enlarged ventricles. His last compositions were completed at the age of 56, and shortly afterward he began to experience a decline in mental functioning, with dysnomia and dysgraphia as the prominent signs (Dalessio, 1984). Alajouanine (1948) observed that he immediately recognized intentional errors in performances of his own compositions and the slight mistuning of a piano. Although he could reproduce notes played to him on a piano (presumably by singing), he had great difficulty in naming them, or in use of solfeggio. Sight-reading was almost impossible, although he could play scales very well, and he could perform much better when playing from memory. Similarly, music writing to dictation was very difficult, copying was almost impossible, but writing one of his own compositions from memory, although laborious, was far superior. He could apparently sing phrases from his own works only if cued with the first few notes, although he reported that he could readily recall tunes by singing them "in his head."

It has been speculated that Ravel suffered from presenile dementia of the Alzheimer's type (Dalessio, 1984), and in fact, like the cases just discussed, musical and lexical anomia were prominent symptoms. In addition, musical and lexical dyslexia and dysgraphia were prominent, with relative preservation of musical auditory perceptual abilities. Variations in the initial symptoms are frequent in Alzheimer's disease, with verbal alexia a prominent early symptom in relatively few cases (Perry, Marin, & Smith, 1993). In those cases the alexia was presumably due to an atypical severity of early occipitoparietal degenerative changes. Thus the hypothesis of probable Alzheimer's disease could still account for relatively early onset of dyslexia and dysgraphia, and that diagnosis is clearly consistent with the cases of Beatty et al. (1988) and Crystal et al. (1989) in the prominence of musical and verbal anomia.

Bernard (1885, cited by Dorgeuille, 1966) describes the case of a professional piano teacher who was affected by a severe mixed expressive-receptive aphasia and alexia and was unable to read or recognize music. Despite this, she was able to sing the melody and lyrics of a famous song, and she did so repetitively and automatically. Benton (1977) cites a similar description by Dalin (1745) of an aphasic patient who was nevertheless still capable of singing with words. Other such cases were reported by Gowers (1875), Knoblauch (1888), and Proust (1866, cited by Dorgeuille, 1966). This contrast between normal and automatic performance of overlearned familiar tasks, and an inability to execute new sentences or new motor acts, or to sing new melodies, is a well-known aspect of the neurological disintegration of behavior.

A dissociation between what Jackson (1874/1915) called automatic and propositional behavior can be observed in practically all functions (speech and language, movements, singing). It reminds us of the critical problem that any distinct motor or language task, or any ostensive behavior, may correspond to various levels of processing depending on an individual's previous experience and the context in which the task or behavior appears. Although a patient may be unable to name an object voluntarily (i.e., a drinking "glass"), he or she may a few minutes later request, "Give me the glass. I am thirsty." When one demented patient, whom we have studied for a prolonged period (Schwartz, Marin, & Saffran, 1979), was recently reexamined, we found that her spontaneous speech had totally disappeared. Her spontaneous vocalizations consisted only of iterative sounds that she said in sentence-like sequences with appropriate sound contours to express her emotions and intentions. She was now totally unable to name spontaneously any object, and only exceptionally did she vaguely approximate the phonology of certain words. However, when asked to count aloud, after some prompting by the examiner, she could count perfectly normally, in sequence and in pronunciation, up to 32. This woman, who was suffering from a diffuse bilateral cortical atrophy, was also able to sing, without the lyrics, the entire national anthem with perfect rhythm, intonation, and prosody. The usual explanation given in such cases is that abnormal functions reflect the effects of damage to left cortical areas whereas those that are preserved are based on normal right anatomical substrata. But in this case of diffuse cortical damage, such an explanation is not determinative, because there is no good reason to believe that her right cerebral cortex was functioning any better than her left.

The researcher must accept that, depending on the degree of automatism acquired in the performance of different tasks or skills, a patient may develop alternative representations at multiple cortical or subcortical loci; or perhaps such distributed representations become resistant to the anatomical pathological simplification that results in selective cortical atrophy by virtue of their widespread anatomical substrates.

Ethological literature is rich with examples of centrally programmed and complex behaviors of long duration that are stored and performed as wholes. Neurophysiology has only recently found similar examples of behavior in higher vertebrates, whereas neurology hardly recognizes their importance in clinical situations.

The hypothesis that under special circumstances of automatism or overlearning, a cognitive task may escape the complexity of its original function and may operate in relative independence provides another explanation for the evolutionary specialization of neural subsets. Such a hypothesis should have importance for neuropsychological theory as well as for theories of cognition and cognitive development. Although speech is a learned function in both its receptive and productive aspects, there is evidence that in adult life this phonological-articulatory loop can function with incredible precision in isolation from the rest of the linguistic cognitive organization. In fact, lesions that isolate the speech areas of the left hemisphere may originate a clinical syndrome of echolalia characterized by automatic ability to repeat faithfully any heard speech (Geschwind, Quadfasel, & Segarra, 1965). Such patients show no evidence of understanding of language, and, in fact, the semantic-linguistic disconnection seems to be partly responsible for the phonological-articulatory automatic independence (Marin et al., 1979; Marin & Gordon, 1979a, 1979b). A similar, but less frequent, phenomenon can be observed in some patients who continuously repeat gestures or movements made by others (echopraxia). Although these examples are taken from pathology, they show how functionally specialized subsets can detach themselves from the original cognitive roots that nurtured their development.

An aphasic patient described by Finkelnburg (1870) was able to play melodies on his violin, but was unable to do so on the piano, which was a less familiar instrument. In music, as in language, such automatisms are of enormous importance and may explain the sparing of some complex musical tasks whereas others that appear to be more basic and simple are lost. Perhaps the best example of this is seen in the motor skills of instrumentalists or in instrumental musical improvisation. In both cases, success depends to a large extent on the ability to create central programs of long duration based on tactual-motor loops. Performance thus demands a minimal requirement of higher cognitive control whereby the motor system may perform with almost total independence, allowing the musician's mind to occupy itself with the higher level of musical aesthetic control. Sudnow (1978), discussing his experience in learning jazz improvisation, wrote: "My hands have come to develop an intimate knowledge of the piano keyboard, ways of exploratory engagement with routing through its spaces, modalities of reaching and articulating, and now I choose to go in the course of moving from place to place as a handful choosing."

In an investigation of changes in regional cerebral blood flow (CBF) measured by positron emission tomography (PET) during keyboard performance and sight-reading in 10 right-handed pianists (Sergent, Zuck, Terriah, & MacDonald, 1992), evidence contrasting the neural substrates of automatic and novel keyboard performance was obtained. When CBF during listening to scales was subtracted from playing scales with the right hand while listening to feedback, significant foci of increased CBF were observed only in the left primary motor and medial premotor cortex, and in the right cerebellum, all consistent with use of the right hand. However, when activity during reading a score consisting of an unaccompanied melody (the soprano part of J. S. Bach's choral BWV 717) while listening to a performance of it was subtracted from the activity during sight-reading and playing a similar unfamiliar melody (the soprano part of the fourth variation of Partita BWV 767 by J. S. Bach, unfamiliar to all participants), foci were seen in the left inferior frontal gyrus just above Broca's speech area, more laterally and extensively in the left premotor cortex, and bilaterally in the superior parietal lobule. The authors interpret the superior parietal activation as possibly related to the sensorimotor transformations inherent in translating musical notation to spatial information for guiding the hand. They further suggest that the lateral premotor and inferior frontal activations may be related to the organization of motor sequences for keyboard performance, analogous to the motor sequencing of speech.

Thus, a lower-level neural substrate for manual motor output was activated by playing overlearned scales, and cortical regions involved in higher-level motor control were activated by the demand for the "on-line" generation of novel motor programs inherent in sight-reading unfamiliar music.

A frequent and perhaps predictable association is that of verbal and musical alexia: Case 9 of Bouillaud (1865) was both linguistically and musically alexic, as were the cases of Brazier (1892), Déjèrine (1892a,b), Dupre and Nathan (1911, Case 2), Fasanaro, Spitaleri, & Valiani (1990), Jellinek (1933), Stanzione, Grossi, and Roberto (1990) and Wertheim and Botez (1961). Dorgeuille (1966) found disturbances of music reading in seven of his cases, but only four of these were associated with verbal alexia. Jossman's case (1926, 1927) was unable to read music or to sing but was not aphasic, and his lesion was in the right hemisphere. A piano professor who suffered a left posterior temporoparietal lesion, described by Assal and Buttet (1990), was agraphic without alexia, but still able to write fluently in musical notation. These cases demonstrate that, although associations are common, musical and linguistic alexia and agraphia can be dissociated.

Here again, we are confronted with a cognitive function, reading, that in no way may be considered simple, and a deficit that does not correspond to a single altered mechanism or to a well-defined lesional topography. Music reading depends not only on the ability to recognize the symbolic-lexical nature of specific graphic designs, but the ability to assign to each of them of a referential meaning (symbolic-semantic level). Thus, a study of music reading demands consideration of other processes involved in the perception of the lexical elements of music. Perceptual defects (e.g., visual agnosias) may account for some cases of musical alexia. Ballet (1888, cited by Dorgeuille, 1966) tells us, for example, of one of Charcot's patients who suddenly developed an inability to read music because he became incapable of "deciphering" the notes that he saw but could no longer "understand."

An element of fundamental importance in reading music is the fact that the script is displayed in a highly bisymmetrical space. For music reading, we have to deal not only with the perceptual recognition of individual music notational elements, such as those for notes, rests, and expressive instructions, but also with the spatial problems of discriminating them in terms of their position on the staff. Consequently, music reading might be simpler than verbal reading in terms of the lexical-semantic items represented in the musical "dictionary." However, music reading is much more complex in terms of its visuospatial organization. The differentiation in music reading of perceptual and symbolic-referential aspects may have important neuropsychological implications for the varieties of musical alexias and their possible anatomoclinical correlates. For example, Fasanaro et al. (1990) describe a case, resulting from ischemic damage to the left temporoparieto-occipital region, in which reading of notes, like that of text, was severely impaired, whereas reading of rhythms and ideographic symbols was flawless. Dorgeuille (1966, Case 16) describes an opposite dissociation, in which only reading of rhythms was disturbed.

There is an important neuropsychological, physiological, and comparative anatomical literature that indicates that form perception and spatial orientation are two different aspects of vision (Schneider, 1969; Weiskrantz, Warrington, Sanders, & Marshall, 1974). This literature is not reviewed here, but its implications are obvious: It cannot be expected that music reading depends on a single anatomical substrate or that its various components will overlap entirely with those of verbal reading, whether syllabic or ideographic. A greater role of the parietal cortex of the minor hemisphere, so significant in visuospatial functions, would seem probable in the case of music reading as opposed to verbal reading. However, cases of musical and verbal alexia in patients with unilateral left hemisphere lesions (e.g., Fasanaro et al., 1990) clearly indicate the importance of left hemisphere processing.

Recent evidence in support of a crucial role for left hemisphere processing in music reading comes from the study of regional CBF in pianists by Sergent et al. (1992). In a different comparison of CBF between two states, CBF during visual presentation of dots (and manual responses related to their location) was subtracted from CBF during silent score reading. In addition to bilateral activation in extrastriate visual cortex, a significant focus was observed in the left occipito-parietal junction. Sergent et al. point out that activity in this region suggests a predominance of processing in the dorsal visual system, which is involved in spatial processing, as opposed to the ventral visual system, parts of which are particularly important for the processing of words. Although this dorsal predominance is to be expected, the left asymmetry is somewhat surprising. It accords well, however, with the not-infrequent association between verbal and musical alexias after unilateral damage to the language-dominant hemisphere.

Sergent et al. (1992) also subtracted CBF during score reading alone from CBF during score reading while listening to a rendition of the piece. In addition to the expected bilateral activation in secondary auditory cortex, a focus of activation was also observed in the superior portion of the left supramarginal gyrus (a part of the inferior parietal lobule). The authors suggest that this activation may reflect a mapping between the musical notation and its corresponding sound. They further suggest that this cognitive operation is analogous to the print-to-sound mapping involved in verbal reading, for which portions of the inferior parietal lobule have also been implicated. However, the inferior, rather than the superior, portion of the supramarginal gyrus appears to be crucial for verbal print-to-sound and/or sound-to-print mapping (Marin, 1980; Roeltgen & Heilman, 1984). Sergent et al. (1992) thus conclude that mapping of musical notation to sound is dependent on cortical regions adjacent to, but distinct from, those crucial for mapping linguistic print to sound, resulting in the possibility of both dissociations and associations between musical and verbal alexias in cases of unilateral damage. Sergent (1993b) further suggests that Ravel's combined musical and linguistic alexia and agraphia could have resulted from focal (unilateral) degenerative changes in the left hemisphere, and their partial dissociation, as reflected in the time course of their onset, from their largely nonoverlapping substrates *within* the left hemisphere. However, it is important to remember that just as there are multiple types of dyslexia resulting from disruption of different aspects of the complex and multidimensional reading process (McCarthy & Warrington, 1990), so we must expect multiple types of musical alexia, not all of which will have verbal analogues. For example, musical alexias resulting from damage to the right hemisphere (e.g., Jossman, 1926,1927) must also be considered.

If reversals and other disturbances of spatial orientation are prominent abnormalities in some cases of developmental dyslexias, then one can easily imagine the importance of these factors in the case of music reading. There is, in fact, some evidence that relatives of dyslexic children, who are not dyslexic themselves, often have great difficulties in learning to read music (E. Saffran, personal communication).

One of the earliest reports of amusia is Case 9 of Bouillaud (1865). This report describes a woman who suffered a sudden right hemiplegia associated with aphasia. Her articulatory defects (*"sort d'ataxie verbal... "*), a possible word order syntactic defect, agraphia, and acalculia, were accompanied by a peculiar inability to read music. Occasionally, she was able to play some passages correctly, but she frequently made mistakes in the sequential ordering of the music. The case is remarkable because this disorder allows for various alternative interpretations. On the one hand, it may be due to the association of a language and a musical disorder that are manifestations of a common cognitive defect: abnormality in the language syntactic word order and abnormality in the sequence of the musical execution of a tune. On the other hand, the same music-reading defect could be explained by a visual spatial disorganization and attentional disorder, similar to the type of verbal reading abnormality observed by Shallice and Warrington (1977). In such circumstances, there is a perceptual disorder in relation to selective visual attention that results in an inattention to the perceived order of a sequence of letters or words.

Proust (1872) described the case of a woman who became aphasic and was also unable to vocalize music. The patient could, however, name notes, recognize familiar tunes, and sign musical scales. Although the author did not give details of the patient's language disorder, one can be reasonably sure that comprehension was relatively well preserved and that language production was predominantly affected. In this case, a speech disability was accompanied by a corresponding vocal defect in singing, an association not at all uncommon. Similar cases have been reported by Botez and Wertheim (1959), Brazier (1892), Cramer (1891; cited by Dorgeuille, 1966), and Jellinek (1933).

It is not unusual to find cases of severely aphasic patients who are able to sing with normal intonation and rhythm but without lyrics. One of our patients with Broca's aphasia was a very well educated woman who, despite her severe expressive disorder, was able to sing a number of themes of the classical symphonic repertoire and to sing songs without the lyrics. Yamadori, Osumi, Masuhara, and Okubo (1977) examined the singing ability of 24 right-handed patients with Broca's aphasia for well-known songs and found that 21 could sing at least moderately well, 12 with correct and fluent lyrics. They noted that of the 30 patients with Broca's aphasia reviewed by Edgren (1895), and otherwise classified as with or without symptoms of amusia, 23 patients showed at least some preservation of singing ability. However, 7 of these patients, like 3 of their own, showed combined disruptions of both linguistic and musical vocalization.

Avocalias affecting both speech and music suggest the possibility of a common neural substrate at a lower level in the hierarchy of vocal expressive functions. However, dissociations in performance between verbal and melodic vocal tasks give support for a contralateral localization of crucial neural processing at higher levels (Barbizet, 1972).

B. APHASIA WITHOUT AMUSIA

There are at least 13 documented cases of aphasia in professional or amateur musicians in whom musical abilities were not noticeably affected. These cases of total dissociation are of particular interest because they decisively contradict the hypothesis that language and music share common neural substrates.

Perhaps the most remarkable case is the one reported by Luria, Tsvetkova, and Futer (1965). The patient was a well-known composer and professor of music at the Moscow Conservatory who suffered a cerebrovascular accident that damaged the left temporal and temporoparietal regions, leaving him with a severe sensory aphasia. This patient, despite the aphasia, was able to successfully resume his work as a composer, creating works that were considered by other professional musicians as excellent in quality.

Even in the absence of other aphasic deficits, verbal alexia (without agraphia) can be dissociated from preserved music reading and writing, as in the case reported by Judd, Gardner, and Geschwind (1983) of a composer and conductor who suffered an infarct in the left occipitotemporal area. Similarly, Signoret, Van Eeckhout, Poncet, and Castaigne (1987) reported the case of a professional organist and composer, blind since age 2, who suffered an infarction of the left middle cerebral artery affecting the temporal and inferior parietal lobes. He was left with a severe receptive aphasia and with verbal alexia and agraphia in Braille. However, there was no evidence of amusia, and he could still play, sight-read, and improvise fluently. Furthermore, his reading and writing of musical notation in Braille were unaffected, and he continued to compose and publish works for the organ. Thus, language and music reading can be dissociated, not only in their usual visuospatial form, but also within the tactuospatial modality.

Other cases of aphasia without amusia have been reported by Assal (1973), Basso and Capitani (1985), Bouillaud (1865), Brazier (1892), Charcot (1886, cited by Dorgeuille, 1966), Henschen (1926), Lasegue (cited by Proust, 1872), and Proust (1866, cited by Dorgeuille, 1966). These cases indicate that the neurological substrates of the language-dominant hemisphere that are responsible for their aphasia do not sustain, to any significant degree, the preserved musical functions of these patients.

C. AMUSIA WITHOUT APHASIA

Cases of amusia unaccompanied by language impairment also support the hypothesis of independence of musical and verbal processes. At least 20 such clinical examples have been recorded. A significant number of cases in which there is satisfactory information concerning the site of lesion show damage to the right hemisphere, notably affecting the temporal regions. The clinical symptoms are diverse, but the majority of them, as expected, are related to defects in music perception, discrimination, or memory.

Dorgeuille (1966) found in his series of 26 patients only two clear-cut cases of amusia unaccompanied by aphasia, one with a variety of receptive defects, and one example of an isolated defect in music writing. Dorgeuille also attempted to analyze the forms of amusic symptoms by grouping them, regardless of the presence or absence of aphasia. He found eight examples of alterations in memory for melodies and four examples of disorders of rhythm reproduction. There were seven musical perceptual defects, affecting, in various combinations, the perception of the direction of movement of two tones, the recognition of instruments, and the recognition of musical styles. All were able to recognize familiar melodies. Six instances of disturbances in singing were noted, two coinciding with musical perceptual defects. Disturbances of music reading and writing were also observed. Despite Dorgeuille's careful review, no clear nosological picture emerges from his efforts that could be interpreted in terms of basic neuropsychological mechanisms. The correlation between clinical deficits and morbid anatomy is inconclusive. The involvement of the temporal lobes on both sides, including the anterior portions, was, however, a prominent anatomical feature.

Although relatively pure cases of amusia are of particular interest, the presence or absence of accompanying aphasia does not appear to be helpful in analyzing specific musical deficits. It is these musical deficits that must be isolated and analyzed in terms of specific computational processes and cognitive functions for which essential brain regions may then be sought. The experiments of nature provided by naturally occurring lesions are unfortunately rarely suited to answering such questions, because they do not respect the boundaries of cytoarchitectonically defined brain regions. Although similar to the same problem in the analysis of language disorders, the far greater individual variability in musical talents and their development, and the relative scarcity of well-studied cases, makes the search for functional-anatomical correlations much more difficult. Their analysis, except in those rare instances, can provide only rough outlines to constrain the search for more neuroanatomically defined answers.

III. AUDITORY AGNOSIAS AND VERBAL DEAFNESS

Profound auditory agnosia constitutes the auditory perceptual disorder par excellence: in such instances, the association of abnormal perception of speech, noises, and animal sounds with that of music is not at all surprising. Unfortunately, it is common to find that reported cases of auditory agnosia have been only cursorily explored for their musical perceptual abilities. "Auditory agnosia" has sometimes been used to denote a *generalized* disturbance in the perception of both speech and nonspeech sounds and at other times has been used to indicate a selective disturbance in perceiving nonverbal sounds. We will refer to *the auditory agnosias*, in order to encompass all possible forms, both generalized and specific, and will refer to syndromes that include speech as well as at least several types of nonverbal sounds as *generalized auditory agnosia*. Auditory agnosia restricted to speech sounds will be called *verbal deafness*.

The syndrome of generalized auditory agnosia usually results from *bilateral* cortical damage to the temporal cortex of the primary acoustic area of Heschl and/ or surrounding fields (see Figure 1; Albert, Sparks, von Stockert, & Sax, 1972; Auerbach, Allard, Naeser, Alexander, & Albert, 1982; Chocholle, Chedru, Botte, Chain, & Lhermitte, 1975; Jerger, Weikers, Sharbrough, & Jerger, 1969; Jerger, Loverling, & Wertz, 1972; Kogerer, 1924; Laignel-Lavastine & Alajouanine, 1921; Lechevalier et al., 1984; Mendez & Geehan, 1988; Misch, 1928; Pötzl, 1939; Pötzl & Uiberall, 1937; Praamstra, Hagoort, Maasen, & Crul, 1991; Reinhold, 1948; Tanaka, Yamadori, & Mori, 1987). As Mendez and Geehan (1988) demonstrate with both of their cases, the syndrome often evolves from an initial cortical deafness, to a generalized auditory agnosia, and finally to more selective residual deficits. Praamstra et al. (1991) note that the stage of initial cortical deafness seems to occur exclusively after bilateral lesions.

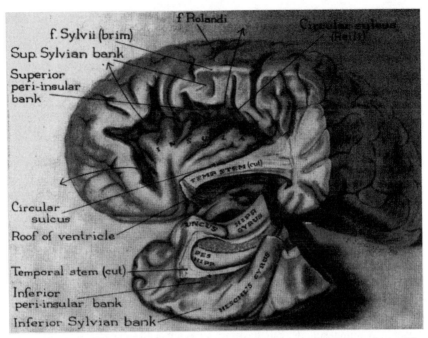

FIGURE 1   Left hemisphere of the human brain with the temporal lobe cut free and turned forward so as to show its superior and mesial surfaces. The primary auditory cortical area is located in the most posterior and medial portion of Heschl's gyrus, adjacent to the insula, based on cytoarchitectonic (Galaburda & Sanides, 1980) and electrophysiological (Liégeois-Chauvel et al., 1991) investigations. Secondary auditory cortical areas surround this region in both anterior and posterior directions on the inferior Sylvian bank (or superior temporal plane) and on the lateral surface (not seen) of the superior temporal gyrus. (Reproduced with permission of the Literary Executors from the Wilder Penfield Archive, Montreal Neurological Institute and Little, Brown and Co., from Penfield & Jasper, 1954.).

Disorganization of speech perception (verbal deafness, or word agnosia) with preservation of normal nonverbal discrimination is well known and can result from either unilateral or bilateral damage to the acoustic and para-acoustic cortical fields. Although auditory agnosias have been reported to result from unilateral left-sided lesions, the perception of nonspeech sounds in such cases is usually relatively intact. One case of generalized auditory agnosia (Schuster & Taterka, 1926) resulting from a unilateral left-sided lesion has been reported. As Auerbach et al. (1982) have noted in regard to cases of verbal deafness, some previous cases presumed to be unilateral may have had, like the one they describe, a previously silent contralateral lesion. However, the postmortem analysis of Schuster and Taterka's case did not reveal any significant infarction in the right hemisphere. It is thus not clearly established that unilateral lesions can produce a markedly generalized auditory agnosia. Given the lack of modern methods of neuroimaging and electroencephalography, the true unilaterality of some of the earlier cases, without unequivocal postmortem examination, may be questioned.

There are also a few recorded cases of unilateral *right* hemisphere lesions in which abnormal perception of nonverbal sounds contrasted with the preservation of normal speech perception and the absence of aphasia (Fujii et al., 1990; Mazzucchi, Marchini, Budal, & Parma, 1982; Nielsen, 1962; Spreen et al., 1965). Mazzucchi et al. describe an amateur singer who, following a right temporal infarct, was disturbed in his ability to distinguish nonverbal auditory sounds, including his own voice, and complained of disturbing echoes and a loss of pleasure in listening to music. For the more recently examined cases, the unilaterality of cortical damage is more certain, suggesting that some types of nonverbal auditory agnosia can occur following unilateral lesions to the non-language-dominant hemisphere and without apparent disturbances in the perception of speech.

Typically, patients with profound generalized auditory agnosia are not truly deaf, but in fact continuously experience chaotic sounds from the environment, as well as auditory acoustic illusions and hallucinations. Many patients complain that noises, voices, and sounds have become too loud and unpleasant (Arnold, 1943); that sounds are like crackling noises running against each other and creating indistinct, blurred noises; that sounds are incomprehensible and do not "register" in their minds; that they resound in unpleasant echoes, vibrating or oscillating in intensity, even becoming painful to hear. For example, one of our patients complained that the hinges of the doors needed oiling because they emanated constant unpleasant squeaking noises. Others heard human voices or their own thoughts. Such patients have great difficulty in distinguishing between real and illusory noises, sounds, or voices; as with patients who have other cortical cognitive disorders (i.e., hemiplegia, cortical blindness, somatoagnosic defects), they have difficulty in gaining full awareness of the extent of their perceptual deficits. One of our patients with visual agnosia insisted on driving his car. Another patient with an auditory agnosia that had lasted for years still insisted on calling and answering the telephone, thus renewing each time his frustration at not being able to comprehend the voices of the speakers or the noises produced by the apparatus. The essential deficit here therefore does not seem to be one of threshold perception but rather one of discrimination and pattern organization.

Systematic and thorough studies of auditory agnosic deficits are rare. This rarity is due not only to extreme difficulties in achieving meaningful communication with such patients, but also to their unusual irritability and anxiety. Communication by gestures is usually unsatisfactory and full of ambiguity, and laborious written communication is their only option. In typical cases, reading and writing are normal with only occasional paralexical errors. In some cases, spontaneous speech may show paraphasic errors. When no other language disturbances are noted, verbal deafness is often referred to as *pure word deafness*, although the total absence of aphasic symptoms in such cases has been questioned (Buchman, Garron, Trost-Cardamone, Wichter, & Schwartz, 1986).

Occasionally, there is a tendency to talk too loudly and in a rather forced high pitch. One of our patients developed, together with his auditory agnosia, a high-pitched falsetto voice. Another patient had completely incomprehensible utterances mostly consisting of iterative fast repetition of single syllables (i.e., da-da-da, or sh-sh-sh) or combinations that in no way resembled anarthric or typical paraphasic speech. The same patient was unable to sing, imitate animal sounds, or repeat vocal rhythms with syllables. By contrast, his written communication was perfect. It is difficult to be sure what the relationship is between these abnormalities of speech production and the auditory defect, but one cannot fail to remember the importance of acoustic templates for the production of songs in birds (Marler, 1976; Nottebohm, 1975), the effect of delayed auditory feedback on speech perception (Yates, 1963), or the studies of jargon aphasia (Alajouanine & Lhermitte, 1961, 1964).

Auditory agnosics have great difficulty with a number of basic sound discriminations. Although many of them have absolute thresholds for tones that are only slightly higher than normal, intensity discrimination thresholds are quite poor. Often, noises or sounds are either not heard at all or they are perceived at a loud and uncomfortable level. In general, patients have no difficulty in determining whether or not a stimulus has been turned on. Very often, however, they are unable to detect the off-change, and they declare that the stimulus has terminated before its actual end. In successive on-off trials, patients soon lose track of the changes and the direction in which the stimulus operates. This on-off confusion has also been observed by us in intermittent visual stimulation of patients with visual agnosia. Temporal distribution of stimuli and temporal clusters (rhythm) are very poorly discriminated. Patients exhibit total inability to distinguish, describe, or reproduce rhythmic patterns. Binaural sound localization is usually quite abnormal. Recognition of timbre and of complex sounds is usually hopelessly defective. One of our patients thought that the barking of a dog was a "kind of music," a locomotive noise was interpreted as human singing, and typewriter tapping as "children playing." Patients often say that they can hear, but that they cannot make sense of the sound.

One patient, who was extensively studied by Albert et al. (1972), commented after hearing a bird singing: "I hear the sound but I can't seem to associate it with any of these pictures" (pictures that represented possible sources of the stimuli). Whether these patients have some clear internal auditory representation of the stimulus to which they are exposed is an important but yet incompletely answered question. One patient was exposed to the ticking noise of an alarm clock. We observed that despite the fact that she went so far as to declare that the object made a kind of a "tic tac, tic tac" noise, she was unable to identify the object from among a group of objects that were presented visually or to choose it from a list of alternative names. No other type of naming disorder was present in this patient. Another of our patients could not determine with certainty if a spoken sound "ai" corresponded to the picture of an "eye" or that of a "tie." However, he always pronounced the name of the picture of these or other objects correctly. This same patient was totally unable to provide words that rhymed with a given word or with the name of an object or picture of an object. In this task, despite our efforts to give written instruction and multiple examples, the enormous difficulty encountered by the patient raised doubts as to whether the concept of rhyming itself was still present in the patient's mind.

Many authors have attempted to differentiate levels of perceptual disorganization. From a broad perspective, Vignolo (1969) studied auditory perception in cases of right or left hemisphere damage. He devised tests that would in some cases discriminate the acoustic properties of a stimulus among distracters and in other cases identify the source or the nature of the stimulus. This allowed the author to separate auditory-perceptual from semantico-referential aspects, levels of processing previously suggested by Kleist (1928). Vignolo found that patients with damage of the left hemisphere performed well in discriminatory tasks and worse in identification tasks, whereas patients with damage to the right hemisphere performed poorly in the discrimination of meaningless sounds. Albert et al. (1972) were impressed that their bilaterally damaged patient was always correct in selecting the title of a popular tune just heard among multiple choices but was only 30% correct in producing spontaneously the name of the tune. It is therefore an open question whether Vignolo's patients with left hemisphere damage failed in the identification task because of a semantic referential disorder or because of difficulties in retrieving the verbal lexical tags of the stimuli.

Studies reflecting this dichotomy between identification and discrimination have been performed in the area of language perception by a number of authors (Basso, Casati, & Vignolo, 1977; Blumstein, 1973, 1977). The studies suggest the existence of multiple stages in the auditory perceptual process, a notion that may have important implications for understanding the neurological aspects of music perception. Therefore, it is useful to review what has been observed in the study of verbal deafness, a perceptual auditory disorder that, like musical agnosias, specifically involves the disruption of a hierarchically organized system. Today this entity, when it occurs in relative isolation from other auditory perceptual disturbances, is recognized as resulting from bilateral temporal, or less frequently, unilateral lesions of the dominant hemisphere that isolates the auditory association area from the primary auditory projections (Lichtheim, 1885). This syndrome has been described and analyzed in a long series of reports by Albert and Bear (1974), Barrett (1910), Hemphill and Stengel (1940), Klein and Harper (1956), Metz-Lutz and Dahl, 1984, Richter (1957), Saffran, Marin, and Yeni-Komshian (1976), Takahashi et al. (1992), and Yaqub, Gascon, Al-Nosha, and Whitaker (1988).

Saffran et al. (1976) made a detailed study of a right-handed, 37-year-old patient who very likely suffered an embolic infarction in the left temporal lobe. As is usually the case with such patients, his illness began with a clinical picture that corresponded to a Wernicke's aphasia including defective comprehension and paraphasic speech. Later on, his speech production improved to normal levels, but the abnormalities of his auditory comprehension remained unchanged. The findings can be summarized as follows:

1. Monaural presentation of previously rehearsed or familiar names resulted in correct perception through either ear.

2. Dichotic presentations of similar words resulted in perception of the stimuli presented in the left ear with total unawareness of the stimuli presented in the right. An increase in intensity on an order of 20 dB or more to the right ear was needed in order to make the patient aware of the presence of the stimulus. Dichotic presentation of vowel sounds and of consonant-vowel combinations also gave a strong extinction effect in the right ear. When presented with natural and synthetic speech sounds (vowels and stop consonants), there was a severe and complex disorganization of their expected discrimination and identification. The picture that emerged was one of a considerable reduction in the number of items that could be identified with certainty. This reduction involved overextension of some categories relative to others. There were parallelisms between these identification difficulties and errors made in purely discriminative tasks, suggesting that these two phenomena are, at least, closely interdependent. The patient was able to make discriminations and identifications of nonverbal sounds without difficulty. He was also well able to distinguish intonation contours, changes in types of voices, and changes in the number of voices speaking simultaneously. He was quite alert in detecting when a speaker changed without transition from one language to another (English-German-Spanish), despite the fact that he was unable to understand any of these utterances, and all sounded to him as "kind of Greek." A number of tests demonstrated that the patient's speech comprehension was very sensitive to semantic, syntactic, and other contextual factors with occasional impressive improvements in understanding.

The analysis of this case emphasizes several aspects of perceptual processing that have been the subject of active research and discussion in the realm of speech and language but that could be equally valid for our study of music:

1. There is strong evidence that speech sounds are decoded by a specialized perceptual apparatus. This specialization relates to the peculiar acoustical composition of speech sounds, particularly their rapid temporal transitions.

2. Certain parts of speech (consonants) are categorically identified and perceived. There is evidence that perceptual categorical boundaries may be present before babies begin to hear significant amounts of spoken language and well before they start uttering speech (Eimas, 1974; Eimas & Corbit, 1973; Eimas, Signeland, Jusczyk, & Vigorito, 1971). Categorical learning, however, is not restricted to speech sounds but is applicable to other acoustic events as well: chords (Locke & Kellar, 1973) and musical intervals (Burns & Ward, 1973; Siegel & Sopo, 1975; Zatorre, 1979; see also Chapter 7, this volume). Further, categorical perceptual boundaries are present in other modalities (Miller & Morse, 1976), and in the acoustic mode, they are present for speech sounds even in nonspeaking animals (Morse & Snowden, 1975; Sinnott, Beecher, Moody, & Stebbins, 1976; Waters & Wilson, 1976).

All of this suggests that categorical processing is a property of the perceptual cognitive apparatus that is extensively used in the codification of information originating in the surrounding world. Its prevalence in speech is a consequence of the consistency and universality of human speech sounds, all of which have developed in accordance with pre-established neural mechanisms.

Perception of speech sounds seems to be hierarchically organized, as does the perception of many other types of information (Palmer, 1977). In the case of speech, one can distinguish initially between two levels of analysis: auditory and phonetic (Studdert-Kennedy, 1974). Auditory analysis extracts basic psychophysical parameters of pitch and intensity. For this, no lateralized specialization of the perceptual apparatus may be necessary.[2] Phonetic analysis, which appears to be closely lateralized, then identifies and analyzes information in terms of phonetic features. The case of verbal deafness we described earlier appears to represent a disorganization of this later level, with at least a relative preservation of the lower-level auditory analysis.

Still higher perceptual units and processing levels are operative in speech analysis. Semantic, lexical, and syntactical contexts facilitate perception by limiting the number of possible alternatives and by allowing the listener to predict likely outcomes. Perception in this sense becomes largely a problem of recognition, by matching the incoming stimuli with internal templates (analysis by synthesis; Neisser, 1967). One can easily see how similar phenomena could be operative in music at the levels of motives, themes, rhythmic configurations, harmonic patterns, musical forms, and the stylistic characteristics.

IV. PROGRESS IN THE CLASSIFICATION OF AUDITORY DISORDERS

A. AUDITORY AGNOSIAS

1. Verbal Deafness

The relationship between deficits at the auditory, phonetic, and semantic levels in the production of verbal deafness is still an area of considerable controversy. Auerbach et al. (1982) proposed that there are two types of verbal deafness: one acoustic (prephonemic), resulting from bilateral temporal lobe lesions, the other phonemic, resulting from unilateral lesions in the left temporal lobe. Neither of the examples they cite of the latter group (Denes & Semenza, 1975; Saffran et al., 1976) have anatomically verified lesions, although clinical and laboratory signs in both cases strongly suggest unilateral left hemispheric damage (e.g., the strong right-ear extinction effect described earlier). Both, however, did show a striking dissociation between impaired discrimination of speech and intact discrimination of other meaningful sounds.[3] Geschwind (1965) concluded that all unilateral cases

---

[2]However, see evidence discussed later from studies of brain damage (Zatorre, 1988) and of changes in CBF (Zatorre et al., 1992) that suggests that at least under some conditions, spectral analysis may rely on neural processors that asymmetrically favor the right hemisphere.

[3]Although the patient described by Denes and Semenza was unimpaired in recognizing meaningful sounds by matching to pictures (scoring 17/20 on a version of the test of Spinnler & Vignolo, 1966), he was unable to recognize any familiar melody in the same manner (e.g., point to a picture of a sleeping baby for a lullaby).

of verbal deafness involve *deep* left-sided lesions that interrupt the interhemispheric callosal fibers from the right auditory cortex and thus totally deprive Wernicke's area of auditory input.

Praamstra et al. (1991) point out that because (1) acoustic defects also occur in unilateral cases, and (2) higher-level deficits are likely to contribute to verbal deafness in at least some bilateral cases, the classification of bilateral cases as acoustic and unilateral left-sided cases as phonemic by Auerbach et al. (1982) is inaccurate. Praamstra et al. propose instead that verbal deafness results from the interaction of general auditory-acoustic processing defects (bilaterally represented) with a defect in left-hemisphere specialized phonetic processing, neither of which is sufficient alone to produce a severe failure to decode speech. Verbal deafness would thus result only after both (a) bilateral or deep unilateral lesions of the auditory cortices and their projections and (b) lesions affecting left-hemisphere lateralized phonetic processing. They also cite work with aphasic patients indicating an interaction between phonetic analysis and semantic processing (Baker, Blumstein, & Goodglass 1981) such that a defect in phonological processing becomes manifest only when impaired semantic processing abilities are simultaneously taxed. Thus phonetic analysis is proposed to interact with lower-level auditory processing deficits in the production of verbal deafness and with higher-level semantic processing deficits in the production of impaired auditory comprehension. In normal speech perception, phonetic analysis interacts with both levels to facilitate comprehension.

Bachman and Albert (1988) propose in agreement with Auerbach et al. (1982) that pure word deafness resulting from unilateral left lesions is a type of aphasia and may necessarily involve impairment in semantic processing. They cite the unilateral left hemisphere case of Metz-Lutz and Dahl (1984), whose auditory comprehension improved with a slower rate of presentation only when the delays were added between morphemes rather than syllables, suggesting that the underlying deficit was not in acoustic temporal resolution (Albert & Bear, 1974) but involved semantic processing. Similar semantic, syntactic, and contextual facilitations were seen in the case of Saffran et al. (1976). The question of whether semantic facilitation indicates an underlying *deficit* in semantic processing, or simply a *compensation* for a lower-level deficit (whether in temporal resolution, phonetic decoding, or categorical perception) by a surplus of semantic information, remains as a challenge for the design of future empirical studies.

Although the controversy surrounding the causes of verbal deafness is far from settled, it serves to illustrate the complexities inherent in analyzing the effects of lesions on a hierarchically organized perceptual system. Such analyses of speech perception are instructive for a neuropsychology of music perception because both represent attempts to understand how a hierarchically organized auditory-perceptual system is disrupted by discrete lesions.

2. Nonverbal Auditory Agnosias

Lechevalier et al. (1985) suggested that nonlinguistic sounds may be processed by the secondary auditory cortices, whereas the primary auditory cortices are required for linguistic sounds. They point out that, in contrast to the visual system, the medial geniculate bodies project simultaneously to both the primary auditory receiving area (located in the gyrus of Heschl) and to the secondary auditory fields. They conclude that in well-studied cases, even if the perception of speech is relatively preserved, complaints of fundamental disturbances in the perception of musical sounds seem to be invariably accompanied by deficits in the perception of nonmusical sounds (e.g. Case 6, Lechevalier et al., 1985; Mazzucchi et al., 1982). Although bilateral lesions may evolve to conditions of nonverbal auditory agnosia (e.g., Mendez & Geehan, 1988), cases in which speech perception deficits are not part of the clinical course, such as those just described, appear to implicate unilateral lesions of auditory cortex in the non-language-dominant hemisphere.

However, although the association of musical with environmental auditory agnosias is common, two cases have recently been described that are restricted to agnosias for musical sounds (Peretz, 1993a; Peretz & Kolinsky, 1993). Both patients suffered bilateral strokes affecting the temporal lobes. The first (GL) displayed a loss of sensitivity to tonality in melody perception, but a preservation of the encoding of contour (Peretz, 1993a). The second (CN) displayed a loss of ability to discriminate melodies on both dimensions. In addition, both also exhibited a "tune agnosia," (i.e., an inability to name or recognize music that was once familiar) Perception of rhythm, and of speech and environmental sounds, was intact. Peretz et al. (1994) conclude that the auditory agnosias must be further fractionated. Not only may environmental and musical sound recognition be dissociated, but within the category of melody recognition, tune and rhythm are dissociable (Peretz & Morais, 1993). Furthermore, one of these "tune agnosics" (CN) was found to be impaired in musical instrument recognition, whereas this ability was spared in the other (GL; Peretz et al., 1994). It is only by carefully testing and fractionating musical agnosic deficits in this manner that meaningful anatomical associations can be sought.

When tested 6 years after her last stroke, CN had recovered most of the ability to discriminate between tone sequences but was still unable to name once-familiar tunes or to judge their familiarity (Peretz, 1996). She was also unable to learn to recognize novel music. Her selective recovery of melodic perceptual abilities without improvement in melody recognition or learning suggests that apperceptive and associative aspects of tune agnosia can be dissociated. However, CN still manifested some impairments in the use of tonality (Steinke, Cuddy, and Peretz, 1994), which might constitute a perceptual contribution to her recognition deficit.

In-depth testing of her prosodic processing abilities did not reveal any deficits, nor did testing with melody-like stimuli, created by substituting tones for each syllable in the spoken stimuli. Timing of the tone sequence was identical to that of the voiced portions of the spoken sentences, and the pitches were determined from the median F_0 for each syllable. A second patient (IR), also with bilateral strokes, was severely impaired in processing both prosodic and melodic information (Patel, Peretz, Tramo, & Labreque, 1998).

It is interesting to compare the lesion data available from the CT scans in these two cases (Patel et al., 1998). CN's infarctions included the rostral half of the superior temporal gyri bilaterally, but largely spared Heschl's gyri and the posterior superior temporal gyrus (STG). There was additional damage to the right insula and to a small portion of the right inferior frontal gyrus. In terms of working memory, we might predict the possibility of disturbances in first-order executive processes within tonal working memory, depending on the location and extent of the right inferior frontal damage. However, after sufficient recovery, her performance was essentially normal for comparison of musical melodies that differed at up to the 22nd tone. This finding suggests that after such combined bilateral temporal and right frontal damage, auditory-tonal working memory abilities can at least partially recover, perhaps due to neural plasticity within intact cortical regions.

In contrast, IR's damage included almost all of left Heschl's gyrus and the posterior STG, but was almost completely anterior to Heschl's gyrus within the right STG. Additional damage was apparent in the right inferior and middle frontal gyri, precentral gyrus, insula, and putamen. In terms of working memory, we might predict disturbances in both first- and second-order executive processes within tonal working memory, as well as disruption of both components of the tonal loop, the tonal store and tonal rehearsal.

IR was in fact unable to sing even a single isolated pitch. Damage to the right precentral gyrus or to the right putamen might be expected to possibly interfere with singing (based on their association with singing in the PET studies described earlier), and hence with inner rehearsal strategies based on vocal fundamental frequency (F_0) control. However, because IR's expressive *prosody* was intact, it would seem neccessary to distinguish further between F_0 control for the purpose of singing and F_0 control in the service of prosodic expression.

We have highlighted only portions of the extensive lesions in these two cases, and discussed their possible impact on only one set of cognitive functions crucial for melody processing tasks (tonal working memory). This exercise illustrates the need to consider the wider neural networks of which the auditory cortical areas in the STG are a part, networks that include other cortical and subcortical contributions.

Mendez and Geehan (1988) propose that the primary auditory cortices may be required for complex temporal pattern analysis of both language and music, resulting in the typical finding of bilateral damage in cases of verbal deafness with sensory receptive amusia. They further suggest that recognition of most environmental sounds may be accomplished by secondary auditory association cortices, resulting in the possibility of environmental auditory agnosia without verbal deafness or amusia (in cases in which the primary auditory areas are spared), as well as the overlap of all three symptoms (in cases of bilateral damage affecting both primary and secondary auditory cortices).

The anatomofunctional hypotheses of Lechevalier et al. (1985) and Mendez and Geehan (1988) are complementary in that both propose that perception of *some* nonlinguistic sounds may be accomplished without the primary auditory cortices. Mendez and Geehan (1988) differ however, in hypothesizing a significant role for damage of primary auditory cortices in the production of sensory receptive amusia. This issue must remain only partially resolved until more cases of such amusia are studied with enough anatomic precision to determine the involvement of primary versus secondary auditory cortex, and enough psychological precision to differentiate the possible types of sensory receptive amusia (e.g., for timbre, pitch, spectral or harmonic components of timbre, tone sequences). Precise anatomic differentiation of primary and secondary auditory cortex is complicated by the fact that, because of the highly folded nature of the cortical mantle, the exact position, orientation, and number of Heschl's gyri vary considerably between individuals. Depth electrode recordings suggest that the primary auditory area occupies only a restricted, posteromedial portion of Heschl's gyrus (Liége-ois-Chauvel, Musolino, & Chauvel, 1991). Even with precise localization of Heschl's gyrus, the relationship between gyral and sulcal landmarks and cyto-architectonic boundaries is variable, limiting the extent to which primary cortex damage can be specified.

One of the patients (Case 2) described by Mendez and Geehan (1988) was subsequently studied with cortical maps reconstructed from thin-section coronal magnetic resonance images, in order to determine more precisely which areas of cortex were damaged, and with several auditory perceptual tasks (Tramo, Bharucha, & Musiek, 1990). After bilateral strokes involving the temporal lobes, this ambidextrous patient had cortical deafness that resolved after 3 weeks to combined agnosias for speech, music, and environmental sounds, then, at 2 months, to agnosias for speech and music, and finally, after 1 year, to a mild deficit in speech perception. Seven years later, he still showed a mild speech perception deficit and stated that his hearing of music encountered in his daily life was not distorted in any way. However, in an experimental task, he consistently misjudged consonant chords as dissonant. Cortical maps revealed complete destruction of the transverse gyri of Heschl bilaterally (primary auditory cortices) and of 98% of the right superior temporal gyrus and 20% of the left (secondary auditory cortices; Tramo et al., 1990).

The partial return of speech and music perception after near-total bilateral destruction of the primary auditory cortices argues against their necessity in either speech or musical sound perception, although mild deficits persisted in both. In addition, the partial recovery of musical sound perception after near-complete destruction of secondary auditory cortices in the right hemisphere does not support an essential role for processing there in the perception of sounds as musical (although judgment of musical consonance was severely impaired). However, any conclusions from this case regarding hemispheric asymmetry are limited by the possibility of unusual patterns of hemispheric dominance in mixed-handed individuals (Branch, Milner, & Rasmussen, 1964).

Although nonverbal auditory agnosia in general, and disturbed musical sound perception without verbal deafness in particular, are more common after right unilateral damage, and verbal deafness without nonverbal auditory agnosia is more common after left unilateral damage, precise unilateral or within-hemisphere localization is not warranted. The more typical finding of bilateral damage suggests involvement of both hemispheres in processing speech and musical sounds.

The available evidence thus suggests bilaterally symmetric mechanisms for the most basic levels of cortical auditory processing (e.g., loudness, duration, pure tone pitch), with significant degrees of hemispheric asymmetry affecting the analysis of particular higher-level auditory features (e.g., complex pitch, phonemic discrimination). Perception of units of information even higher in the cognitive hierarchies (e.g., words, melodies) thus involves the interaction of both symmetrically and asymmetrically represented functions and possibly even combinations of functions with opposite asymmetries. The resulting patterns of disturbance in sound perception found in individual cases are thus understandably complex, particularly during the resolution of bilateral strokes. Perhaps the increasingly precise noninvasive detection of damage within auditory cortical regions afforded by improved methods of analyzing magnetic resonance images will clarify the roles of primary and secondary auditory cortex, and of functional hemispheric asymmetries, in the etiologies of cortical deafness, verbal deafness, environmental agnosia, and the musical agnosias.

B. AMUSIAS

Based on an analysis of 8 cases of music perceptual disorders of cortical origin seen at the University Hospital at Caen, Lechevalier et al. (1985) proposed three levels of disintegration in musical perceptual abilities and three corresponding levels of normal auditory music perception: (a) *perceptual-acoustic*, disintegration of which leads to loss of the ability to recognize the musical quality of a stimulus; (b) *perceptual-structural*, which includes disruptions of each of the fundamental elements of music: pitch, intensity, timbre, and rhythm, but with musical stimuli clearly perceived as such; and (c) *semantic*, or cultural and personal, disruption of which results in loss of the ability to identify or name particular works of music.

As the authors note, disturbances of the perceptual-acoustic level are rarely if ever specific to music. The perceptual-structural level they propose includes a broad range of potential disturbances in music perception, each of which may correspond to a different neural substrate. The paucity of systematic investigations in the case literature, and the complexity of the associations and dissociations of deficits, precludes an easy specification of these relationships at this time. Even if all of the available evidence—from animal studies, normal human ear differences, case and group studies of brain damage in humans, and functional neuroimaging—is applied to a single relatively well-studied dimension (pitch), hypotheses regarding the neural instantiation of a cognitive hierarchy for its perception are still tentative at present, although right-sided asymmetries are evident (for examples of such analyses of pitch and melody perception, see Perry, 1991, 1993; Zatorre, 1989a). Finally, regarding the semantic level, it is clear that disturbances in naming can result from left temporal lesions, and, as we have seen, from diffuse cortical atrophy. Such disorders usually overlap with similar lexical-semantic language disorders. Loss of the ability to *recognize* familiar melodies or works of music represents an impairment of musical long-term memory per se.

The present analysis has not attempted a classification of disorders of musical *performance* (but see Benton, 1977), either vocal or instrumental, resulting from cortical damage. When musical performance abilities are assumed to be intact, performance can be studied for what it reveals about the listener's comprehension of musical stimuli, both written and auditory (e.g., sight-reading, melody recall). Deficits in musical performance also constitute a category of amusia in their own right, with a hierarchy corresponding to the programming of finely coordinated motor acts and to the integration of sensory input (visual or auditory) with motor output (vocal or instrumental).

V. CEREBRAL HEMISPHERE ASYMMETRY IN MUSIC PERCEPTION AND PRODUCTION

The preceding analysis of case studies encompassing a broad range of the amusias does not reveal a degree of cortical localization comparable to the degree that would result from a similar analysis of the aphasias, or a clear predictability of deficits from lesion topography. Even if a strict localizationist approach to language functions is rejected, it is still clear that some unilateral lesions in the language-dominant hemisphere produce predictable patterns of disorder (e.g., speech production disorders after inferofrontal lesions). We are left with the hypothesis that the neural processors that support musical functions are in general less strictly localized than those that support linguistic functions (Marin, 1989). Case studies have not revealed strictly localized "neuronal dependent processors," but instead have revealed musical functions that appear to be more plausibly supported by "network-dependent processes" (Marin, 1987).

Nevertheless, various lines of evidence still converge in support of hemispheric asymmetries in processing efficiency or in brain metabolism for music. In spite of the clear importance of lesions in the non-language-dominant hemisphere in producing some receptive amusias, because of inherent biases in the selection of patients for case studies (e.g., for the unusual nature of their musical deficits, and/or musical backgrounds), they are not suitable for asking questions about the statistical reliability of hemispheric asymmetries. For such questions, we must turn to other sources: group studies of unilateral brain lesions and of hemisphere anaesthetization, ear differences in normal listeners, and noninvasive measurements related to brain physiological activity.

A. GROUP STUDIES OF UNILATERAL BRAIN DAMAGE

One might hope that comparison of the performances of carefully selected and matched groups of patients with cortical damage restricted to one hemisphere would lead to clear-cut demonstrations of the hemispheric asymmetries that are apparent, although more equivocally, in the analysis of case studies. In particular, one would hope to see unambiguous evidence of asymmetric right hemisphere contributions, and particularly right temporal contributions, to the perception of stimuli organized by pitch or timbre. This hope has been only partially borne out. We can only briefly consider these results (for more thorough reviews see Zatorre, 1984, 1989a; Samson & Zatorre, 1993), and will restrict ourselves mainly to studies of tone sequence or melody perception, probably the most thoroughly studied aspect of music.

Numerous studies have found deficits in melody perception following *either right or left* unilateral lesions. Although, as Zatorre (1984, 1989a) has noted, many of these studies involved familiar melodies (Barbizet, Duizabo, Enos, & Fuchs, 1969; Gardner, Silverman, Denes, Semenza, & Rosenstiel, 1977; Grossman, Shapiro, & Gardner, 1981, Expt. 1; Prior, Kinsella, & Giese, 1990; Shankweiler, 1966b), several used novel tone sequences and still found deficits after damage to either hemisphere (Milner, Kimura, & Taylor, 1965; Peretz, 1990; Samson & Zatorre, 1988; Samson & Zatorre, 1991a, Expt. 1; Samson & Zatorre, 1992; Zatorre, 1985a). Although a large variety of tasks, stimuli, and patient populations (e.g., stroke, temporal lobectomies of various extents for the relief of epilepsy) were used in these studies, consideration of which is important in their interpretation, one may conclude that merely ensuring that the melodies do not have associated lyrics, or that they are novel, does not eliminate potential left hemisphere contributions to their perception.

An equivalent number of studies have demonstrated selective *right* hemisphere deficits for tone-sequence perception (Berlin, Chase, Dill, & Hagepanos, 1965; Brownell, Postlethwaite, Seibold, & Gardner, 1982 [cited in Zatorre, 1984]; Milner, 1962; Schulhoff & Goodglass, 1969; Shankweiler, 1966a; Shapiro, Grossman, & Gardner, 1981; Samson & Zatorre, 1991a, Expt. 2, 1991b; Zatorre & Halpern, 1993). All of these studies, with the exceptions of Shapiro et al. (1981),[4] and Zatorre and Halpern (1993), used unfamiliar melodies.

Zatorre and Halpern (1993) presented the lyrics of familiar songs on a computer screen, with two words highlighted. The subjects judged if the pitch of the second word was higher or lower in pitch than that of the first word, in a task based on a study with normal subjects (Halpern, 1988). In a perceptual condition, the subjects actually heard the song, whereas in an imagery condition, the subjects were required to generate the melody mentally. Patients who had had a right temporal lobectomy performed more poorly in both conditions, suggesting that imagery and perception share a common neural substrate (Zatorre & Halpern, 1993).

---

[4]Shapiro et al. (1981) reported a deficit in the detection of pitch errors in familiar melodies for patients with damage of the right anterior part of the brain, but not for patients with left hemisphere damage. This study is also notable for its finding of a right *anterior* contribution (see also Brownell et al., 1982, cited in Zatorre, 1984; Samson & Zatorre, 1991b). However, as Zatorre (1984) has noted, the measure of performance used (percentage correct) may simply reflect group differences in response bias.

Three of these studies reported deficits following right anterior (i.e., frontal), but not left anterior brain damage (Brownell et al., 1982 [cited in Zatorre, 1984]; Shapiro et al., 1981; Samson & Zatorre, 1991b). Samson and Zatorre (1991a, 1991b) presented novel melodies six times for recognition, and found an impaired rate of learning after right or left anterior temporal lobectomy (1991a), although some preserved learning was demonstrated. The extent of hippocampal removal did not affect performance. However, patients who had undergone a right, but not a left, frontal lobectomy showed impaired recognition performance that actually worsened with repeated presentations (Samson & Zatorre, 1991b).

Rarest are studies showing impaired performance after *left* hemisphere damage, but normal performance after right hemisphere damage (Gardner et al., Expt. 2, 1977; Zatorre, 1985b). The result of the Gardner et al. study was for the matching of single notes differing in pitch by one octave, or of four-tone scalar sequences differing in contour (ascending or descending), to appropriate visual representations. For both tasks, the pitch discriminations required are quite coarse and may be regarded as a sort of categorization (e.g., high-low, up-down). As the authors point out, deficient performance on this task may also reflect difficulty with the cross-modal association between an auditory and a visual stimulus, rather than with a purely auditory-perceptual discrimination. Like some of the studies showing deficits after both right *and* left hemisphere damage (Barbizet et al., 1969; Shankweiler, 1966b), Zatorre (1985b) required subjects to name familiar tunes. In fact, Barbizet et al. did not observe a deficit in the patients with right-hemisphere damage when familiar melodies were presented singly, but only when the melodies were presented in superimposed pairs. Even for the more difficult task, the subjects with right-hemisphere damage performed at a higher level (49%) than the subjects with left hemisphere damage (19%), although both clearly named fewer tunes than did control subjects (72%; however, these differences were not tested statistically). Although Zatorre (1985b) presented melodies for naming in original and transformed (e.g., contour-preserving octave transposition) forms, the perceptual aspect of the task may have been easy even for the group with damage of the right temporal lobe, so that the demand for naming predominated, resulting in the obtained selective left temporal lobectomy deficit.

Thus, some of the most striking examples of left hemisphere contributions to, or even predominance for melody perceptual tasks involve naming, just as do the most striking examples of amusias resulting from unilateral left-sided lesions. However, many studies that do *not* involve naming, or familiar tunes, still show effects of both left and right hemisphere damage. For example, in their Experiment 1, Samson and Zatorre (1991a) found a deficit in melody recognition following left or right temporal lobectomy, for a song memory task (modeled after Serafine, Crowder, & Repp, 1984). Subjects first listened to unfamiliar "songs" (i.e., melodies sung to lyrics) and were then presented with recognition items that included the original tune with new lyrics and the original lyrics with a new tune. Although patients who had undergone left temporal lobectomy were selectively impaired in recognition of the words, both groups were impaired in recognizing the original tune sung to new words. In a second experiment, Samson and Zatorre presented the same melodies and lyrics, but separately. When the melodies were presented alone, the subjects who had undergone right temporal lobectomy were reliably impaired, but not those who had undergone left temporal lobectomy. The authors suggest that the lyrics associated with a familiar tune may affect the way the tune is represented in memory, as has been observed in studies of normal music cognition (Crowder, Serafine, & Repp, 1990). This association may explain the previously observed left hemisphere contributions to the recognition of familiar melodies. They also leave open the possibility of other (nonverbal) aspects of melody encoding for which the left temporal lobe may predominate (Samson & Zatorre, 1991a).

In a recent demonstration of deficits in novel melody recognition after either left or right hemisphere damage (Peretz, 1990), both groups of patients were impaired relative to control subjects in making same-different discriminations to pairs of melodies. However, the right hemisphere group was more impaired for trials in which the contour was violated, whereas both groups were equivalently impaired when contour was preserved (e.g., when contour was not a relevant dimension, and comparison was thus based solely on pitch interval information). The subjects with left hemisphere damage, like the normal control subjects, performed significantly better when contour was available as a cue, but the subjects with right hemisphere damage did not. Peretz interpreted these findings in terms of a hierarchical contribution of the two hemispheres to melody encoding, hypothesizing that the right hemisphere is predominant for representing the contour of a melody, whereas the left hemisphere is crucial for encoding the specific pitch intervals.

The theory of melodic information processing on which this interpretation is based comes from work in normal music cognition by Dowling and colleagues (see Chapter 15, this volume; Dowling, 1978; Dowling & Bartlett, 1981; Dowling & Fujitani, 1971), in which the differential contributions of the specific *pitch* of individual tones (or of the intervals they form), and of the pattern of changes in pitch direction (or *contour*), to memory for melody have been assessed. Although this theory seems intuitively compatible with "analytic" and "holistic" (Bever & Chiarello, 1974), or "global" and "local" characterizations of hemisphere differences, other attempts to demonstrate hemisphere asymmetries in the processing of exact pitch or interval versus contour information have found normal effects of these cues on melody recognition regardless of which hemisphere had lesions (e.g., Samson & Zatorre, 1988; Zatorre, 1985a). In Peretz's (1990) study, both subjects with lesions in the left hemisphere and subjects with lesions in the right hemisphere were impaired in the discrimination of melodies based on exact pitch information. Only the subjects with lesions in the left hemisphere benefited from the addition of contour information. The author's hierarchical interpretation of these results is based on the assumption that the disruption in encoding exact pitch information occurs for different reasons in the two groups. Peretz hypothesizes that whereas left hemisphere damage disrupts the encoding of specific pitches, right hemisphere damage disrupts formation of the contour representation that normally serves as the foundation for local pitch encoding.

Fractionating the types of information that are encodable in musical stimuli is thus one avenue of progress toward an understanding of how the brain represents them. Another is to fractionate the neural substrate that is hypothesized to support musical functions, by studying groups of patients with more precisely delineated lesions. Study of patients who have undergone neurosurgical treatment for the relief of intractable epilepsy is one example of this approach (e.g., Milner, 1962; Samson & Zatorre, 1991a; Zatorre, 1985a), in that the neurosurgeon's direct examination of the extent of removal is available. Using such reports, Zatorre (1985a) classified patients into four groups based on whether their anterior temporal lobectomy extended far enough posteriorly to encroach upon the primary auditory region. He found that patients who had undergone a right temporal lobectomy with complete sparing of Heschl's gyrus were impaired in melody discrimination, whereas patients who had undergone left temporal lobectomy were not. Patients whose excision extended into the right primary auditory region were substantially *more* impaired, and patients with excision of at least a portion of the left primary auditory region were also impaired. Thus, an effect of damage to the primary auditory region on either side was observed, in addition to the effect of damage to more anterior secondary auditory cortex on the right. An additive effect of excision of Heschl's gyrus on either side was replicated by Samson and Zatorre (1988).

In order to test the hypothesis that this additional impairment was due to disruption of a bilateral mechanism supporting short-term auditory memory, similar groups of patients were given a version of Deutsch's (1970a) pitch memory task (Zatorre & Samson, 1991). Subjects compared the pitch of two tones across a silent interval and across an interval filled with interfering tones. Although neither group of patients was impaired with a silent intertone interval, patients with right, but not left, temporal lobectomy were impaired in the interference condition, regardless of whether or not part of Heschl's gyrus was excised. In addition, a group of patients who had undergone right frontal lobectomy were also impaired.

Thus, short-term memory for pitch was not shown to be dependent on the intactness of Heschl's gyrus, and the particular contributions of the primary auditory region (bilaterally) to melody perception remain unexplained. However, these results, for the comparison of single pitches across interference, do suggest a right-sided asymmetry in some aspect of the short-term retention of tones. The asymmetry of the right frontal effect observed cannot be assessed from these results, because no patients who had undergone left frontal lobectomy were available for testing. However, the frontal contribution may be somehow specific to the requirement to retain single tones over interference-filled intervals, because no deficit in melody discrimination was seen after right or left frontal lobectomy (Zatorre, 1985a).

Zatorre and Samson (1991) propose that the frontal effect may be attributed to an impairment in the self-regulation of behavior (specifically a failure to inhibit incorrect responses), rather than to an auditory-specific impairment. Auditory cortical regions in the superior temporal gyrus are known to project to specific frontal cortical regions (Chavis & Pandya, 1976; Galaburda & Pandya, 1983; Jacobson & Trojanowski, 1977; Jones & Powell, 1970; Pandya & Sanides, 1973; Petrides & Pandya, 1988). Their pattern is similar although somewhat topographically distinct for visual-spatial, visual-object, and somatosensory information. Thus each sensory-specific posterior association region could have its own contingent of neurons within each frontal lobe processing "module," including frontal regions that may be critical for inhibiting unwanted responses. However, the rarity and variability in location of frontal lobe lesions make correlations between specific cytoarchitectonic areas and specific cognitive functions difficult to obtain from human clinical data. Thus, given a heterogeneous group of frontal removals, disruption in other cognitive processing modules proposed to occupy the frontal lobes is possible.

Within the hierarchical theory of frontal contributions to mnemonic processing proposed by Petrides (1989, 1994, 1996), the ventrolateral frontal cortex is one likely candidate. Although the modality-specific posterior cortical association regions, such as the superior temporal gyrus, are proposed to be sufficient for the short-term maintenance of sub-span information, the *judgment* of stimuli held in working memory represents a first-order executive process applied to the contents of working memory. The addition of interference during the delay interval (by multiple items from the larger set of which the two memory items are a part) might be sufficient to call upon the higher-level executive function of *monitoring* and manipulating multiple pieces of information (Petrides, 1994). The mid-dorsolateral frontal cortex may be an even better candidate for an asymmetric frontal component.

Thus, as suggested by Chavis and Pandya (1976), specific frontal cortical regions may play a role in the short-term retention of *auditory* information, similar to that proposed for other frontal cortical regions in visuospatial immediate memory (Goldman, Rosvold, Vest, & Galkin, 1971). Superior temporal-frontal connections may be part of distributed networks supporting auditory-tonal working memory (Perry, 1991, 1993; Petrides, 1994). Specific cytoarchitectonically defined frontal regions (Petrides & Pandya, 1994), and their specific superior temporal targets (Petrides & Pandya, 1988) may contribute to auditory mnemonic functions such as repetition, selection, comparison, and judgment of stimuli held in working memory, active retrieval from long-term memory (ventrolateral), recognition memory, early reactions to novel stimuli (ventromedial), conditional-associative learning (posterior dorsolateral), and the *monitoring* and manipulation of multiple pieces of information within working memory (mid-dorsolateral; Petrides, 1994, 1995b).

Working memory may be understood as more than a passive or echoic sensory store, for which posterior association cortex may be sufficient. Active working memory may be defined as the active maintenance of sensory information, often necessary in order for more complex processing to be carried out (Baddeley & Hitch, 1974). Patients with frontal lobe lesions perform most poorly on tasks that make such demands for active working memory (Petrides & Milner, 1982). Right-sided asymmetry in at least one component of a distributed neural system support-ing auditory-tonal working memory could produce right-hemisphere asymmetries in melody perception (Perry, 1993). Asymmetry within multiple components (i.e., temporal *and* frontal) would be expected to increase the likelihood of an overall hemisphere asymmetry.

B. POSITRON EMISSION TOMOGRAPHY

1. Melodic Perception

Evidence in support of these hypotheses comes from several recent investiga-tions of regional cerebral blood flow (CBF), an index of local neuronal activity, during auditory tasks. CBF was measured by using positron-emission tomography (PET) with ^{15}O-labeled water.

In one experiment, subjects listened to pairs of speech syllables and responded as to whether their pitch went up or down (Zatorre, Evans, Meyer, & Gjedde, 1992). Changes in CBF are often assessed by comparing measurements across scans, most simply by subtracting the CBF measured during one scan from that during another, producing change-image volumes like those displayed in Figure 2 and 4. When the increased CBF resulting from listening to white-noise bursts (whose envelopes were shaped to match the speech stimuli) was subtracted from that measured during passive listening to the same syllables, bilateral increases were observed in the superior temporal gyri. When the increase in CBF during passive syllable listening was subtracted from that measured during the pitch-comparison task, two foci were observed within the *right* ventrolateral frontal cor-tex, one within the pars opercularis and one within the pars triangularis. When perception of white noise bursts was contrasted to silence, bilateral activations in Heschl's gyri were observed.

Ventrolateral frontal activation may be specifically related to the judgment of pitch direction. Because the two pitches must be held briefly for comparison and judgment of direction, this finding is compatible with the hypothesis that ventro-lateral frontal cortex may be called upon to support judgments made on stimuli held in working memory (Petrides, 1994). Finding ventrolateral activation only in the right hemisphere is also compatible with the hypothesis that some neural com-ponent(s) of the auditory-tonal working memory system favor(s) the right hemi-sphere (Perry, 1991, 1993).

In another experiment, the monitoring of both self-generated and externally generated tone sequences were contrasted with simple vocalization of a single pitch (Perry et al., 1993a; unpublished data). Subjects were asked to create or complete (by singing) random sequences of six tones (composed of only two pitches, a perfect fifth apart), so that the final sequence contained an equal number of both pitches. Such active monitoring within working memory has been pro-posed to depend on a particular cytoarchitectonically defined portion of the mid-dorsolateral frontal cortex (Petrides, 1991, 1994, 1995a), dorsal area 46 and 9,

OSCAR S. M. MARIN & DAVID W. PERRY

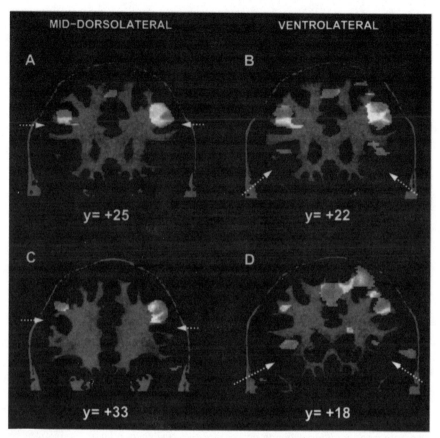

FIGURE 2   Monitoring within tonal working memory. The volume of positron emission tomography (PET) data representing the t-statistic volumes of increases in cerebral bloodflow (CBF) obtained during 60-sec scans from a group of 13 subjects during: External monitoring minus Singing control (A, B), or Self-monitoring minus Singing control (C, D). The PET data from each subject were linearly resampled into a standardized stereotaxic coordinate system (Talairach & Tournoux, 1988) and then averaged across subjects. For illustrative purposes, the PET data was superimposed onto a single normal subject's magnetic resonance image (chosen at random) that had been resampled into the same stereotaxic coordinate system. CBF increases are depicted in white, with t thresholds determined for each image in order to best view the position of the activated region in relation to relevant neuroanatomic landmarks. For these coronal slices, in planes roughly parallel to the face, the right hemisphere is depicted on the right side of the figure. y coordinates indicate the distance of this plane in millimeters in front of the anterior commissure.

(A and C) Coronal slices through the peaks within mid-dorsolateral frontal cortex during the monitoring of (A) *externally* [t > 3.4] and (C) *self-* [t > 3.0] generated tones or pitches. The dotted lines point to the inferior frontal sulcus, above which lies the upper and lower tiers of the middle frontal gyrus, in which the regions of activation are located. They fall clearly within the predicted cytoarchitectonic areas 46 and 9/46 (Petrides & Pandya, 1994). The right hemisphere asymmetry in activation within this region can be appreciated by comparing their extents (e.g., see figure), and the t values of their maximum or peak voxels (*external*: right = 5.95, left = 3.45; *self*: right = 5.26, left = 4.38).

regardless of whether the monitored information is self-generated or externally generated. Mid-dorsolateral frontal cortex was activated in both the self-generated and externally generated tonal monitoring conditions (see Figure 2, A & C) and with a rightward asymmetry. Simultaneous activation was also seen in ventrolateral frontal cortex during both tasks (see Figure 2, B & D), consistent with the two-level hypothesis (Petrides, 1994) of frontal lobe contributions to working memory, which emphasizes the role of projections *between* ventrolateral and mid-dorsolateral frontal cortex in monitoring. Mid-dorsolateral activation has also been confirmed in formally similar PET studies of monitoring within other sensory modalities and information domains (e.g., visual-non-spatial, Petrides, Alivisatos, Meyer, & Evans, 1993a; visual-spatial, Owen, Evans & Petrides, 1996; auditory-verbal, Petrides, Alivisatos, Meyer, & Evans, 1993b; see Petrides, 1995b).

Zatorre, Evans, and Meyer (1994) contrasted melody perception with two types of judgments of the direction of pitch change between two designated notes contained within novel eight-note melodies. The two notes designated were the first and *second* notes in one scan, and the first and *last* in the other. For judgment between the first and second notes, the only frontal increase seen was in the right lateral orbitofrontal cortex.[5] When subjects were instructed to compare the first and *last* notes, additional activation was seen bilaterally in mid-dorsolateral frontal cortex as well as in ventrolateral frontal cortex. When melody perception (with no task imposed) was contrasted with perception of white noise shaped to match the melodies, an increase was observed in the right superior temporal gyrus, posterior to Heschl's gyrus.

The first versus last condition approximates the Deutsch (1970a) task used by Zatorre and Samson (1991) to study patients with focal excisions. Within Petrides' model of frontal lobe functions, comparison of two stimuli held in memory would be expected to activate ventrolateral frontal cortex. The addition of interference by items repeating from a closed set might call upon the monitoring and manipulating capabilities subserved by mid-dorsolateral frontal cortex. Thus the first versus last results are compatible with Petrides' two-stage model of the frontal lobe's contri-

[5]A very robust increase in the right lateral orbitofrontal cortex was also observed during the external tonal monitoring task.

(B and D) Coronal slices through the peaks within *ventrolateral* frontal cortex during (B) *externally* [$t > 2.6$] and (D) [$t > 2.7$] *self*-generated monitoring of tones. The dotted lines point to the depths of the horizontal ramus of the Sylvian fissure, in the upper bank of which these activations were found. Recent cytoarchitectonic analyses of this region have determined that it is part of cortical area 45 (Petrides & Pandya, 1994), and it was activated in the left hemisphere by active recall of auditory-verbal information, contrasted to simple repetition (Petrides, Alivisatos, & Evans, 1995). It thus appears to be a crucial part of the mid-ventrolateral system that forms the first level of the frontal lobe's contribution to auditory working memory. No consistent pattern of hemisphere asymmetry emerged from comparison of peak voxels (*external*: right = 3.20, left = 2.93; *self*: right = 2.93, left = 3.97). Other regions of activation seen include the mid-dorsolateral frontal cortex (see A and C), and medially, the anterior cingulate cortex.

butions to working memory and look very similar to the results obtained in the tonal monitoring tasks described earlier.[6]

In an experiment designed to measure CBF during some of the most basic forms of auditory-tonal working memory (Perry, Petrides, Zatorre, & Evans, 1994; unpublished data), subjects were presented with sequential pairs of musical notes drawn from a major scale (musical intervals), followed by a silent interval approximately twice as long as the stimulus. In one scan (Perception), they listened to each stimulus, then pressed a button. In a different scan (Sung Recall), they immediately attempted to re-sing the notes once, then pressed, and in another (Imaged Recall), they imagined them once as heard, then pressed.

These simple tasks were designed to measure CBF during the operation of the *tonal loop* (see Figure 3), hypothesized to maintain musical-tonal information in a manner analogous to the *phonological loop* proposed by Baddeley (1992) to maintain linguistic-phonological information. Because independence of tones and digits in short-term memory has been demonstrated (Deutsch, 1970a), substantially independent systems for auditory-tonal and auditory-verbal working memory may be proposed. The proposed tonal loop is made up of a *tonal store* that can hold pitch information for brief periods, combined with a covert *rehearsal* system, based on vocal *fundamental frequency* control processes, that may be described as "inner singing" (Perry, 1994; Perry, Zatorre, Petrides, & Evans, 1995). The primary functional anatomical substrate of the tonal store is hypothesized to lie in the auditory cortex of the superior temporal gyrus (particularly in tonotopically organized cortical areas). Ventrolateral frontal cortex may be called upon, depending on the degree to which *active* retention and first-order executive processes are called upon, and not just passive storage. Both the temporal and frontal contributions are proposed to be right-hemisphere asymmetric.

When activation during a silent, neutral baseline condition was subtracted from Perception, auditory cortex was activated bilaterally, but more extensively in the right superior temporal plane posterior to Heschl's gyrus. Activation was also seen in the right ventrolateral frontal cortex. The concomitant activation of superior temporal and ventrolateral frontal cortex, the basic substrate proposed for first-order executive processes within auditory-tonal working memory, suggests a more active retention of the stimuli than might be expected given the minimal demands of the task. Comparison with a neutral baseline allows measurement of all incidental processing consistently produced by the task conditions, which may have even included some degree of inner repetition, given the familiar musical nature of the stimuli and the long silent interval following them.

Imaged Recall minus Perception resulted in activation of motor cortical areas, including the supplementary motor area and the right putamen. These regions are proposed to form part of the network for vocal fundamental frequency control that underlies the rehearsal component of the tonal loop (imagined or "inner singing"). Sung Recall minus Perception resulted in more extensive activation of motor cor-

---

[6]The two studies differ, however, in that during the first versus last task, mid-dorsolateral frontal activation was bilaterally symmetric, whereas during both self-monitoring and external monitoring, it was greater in the right hemisphere.

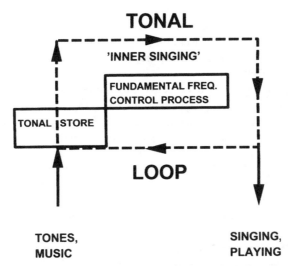

FIGURE 3   Model of the tonal loop, the basis for auditory-tonal working memory, analogous to the phonological loop of Baddeley (1992) for auditory-verbal working memory. Incoming musical and/or tonal information first enters a specialized short-term store, the contents of which can be refreshed and maintained via inner singing, or covert rehearsal based on vocal fundamental frequency control processes. The contents of the tonal store may be output directly at any time through actual singing, or, for musically trained individuals, by playing on an instrument.

tical regions, including *bilateral* putaminal and cerebellar increases, as well as activation of the right primary auditory region. Thus portions of the networks supporting both components of the hypothesized tonal loop were demonstrated, as well as part of the more extensive network activated by simple melodic singing.

Taken together, these four experiments provide accumulating evidence supporting both the two-level hypothesis of frontal lobe contributions to auditory working memory (Petrides, 1994), the tonal loop (Perry, 1994), as well as the hypothesis of a right hemisphere preference for auditory-tonal working memory (Perry, 1993).

Although one of these studies presented melodies with both rhythmic and pitch variations (Zatorre et al., 1994), few studies have specifically examined rhythm perception or production in isolation. Penhune, Zatorre, and Evans (1995) contrasted perception of auditory temporal sequences and their immediate reproduction (by tapping with one finger) to perception alone. Nonmotor areas were activated in the right hemisphere and included ventrolateral frontal, posterior superior temporal, and inferior parietal cortex. Motor areas included ipsilateral cerebellum and the contralateral sensorimotor hand area and basal ganglia (globus pallidus).

2. Song Imagery

The song imagery task of Halpern (1988) described earlier in the discussion of group studies of brain damage was adapted for PET as follows. In one scan, subjects were shown two words taken from a familiar song and asked whether the pitch associated with the second word was higher or lower than the first, thus requiring them to generate the tune from memory (Imagery). In another scan, they performed the same task, but were played a sung rendition of the song (Perception). In a visual baseline condition, they were presented with similar pairs of words not drawn from a song.

When CBF during the visual baseline was subtracted from both Imagery and Perception, a highly overlapping pattern of CBF change resulted, including bilateral activation of temporal and frontal cortex and of the supplementary motor area. The fact that the activations are bilateral is in keeping with the integration of lyric and tune in song representations. Auditory working memory for songs must involve both the phonological and the tonal loops, in an integrated form. The activation of temporal cortex by song imagery indicates that imagery alone can activate auditory cortical regions.

Cortical stimulation studies have elicited various musical auditory experiences, including sung speech, from both the right and left superior temporal gyri (Penfield & Perot, 1963). The activation of the supplementary motor region in both tasks suggests that some sort of covert vocalization or "inner singing" (Perry, 1994) is part of song imagery as well as auditory working memory for songs.

3. Musical Performance

Relatively few studies have examined the neural substrates of music performance. Sergent et al. (1992) examined right-handed keyboard performance of scales and sight-reading (see Section II,A). Perry et al (1994; described above) examined overt and covert singing of two-note sequences. PET studies of even simpler singing have also been carried out (Perry et al., 1993; Perry, Zatorre, & Evans, 1995; Perry, Zatorre, & Evans, 1996; unpublished data), involving repeated production of a single intended pitch. Overall, the set of regions activated overlaps those observed previously during speech (i.e., supplementary motor area, anterior cingulate, cerebellum, insula/frontal operculum, precentral gyrus, see Figure 4, A–C). The main differences between them lie in the direction of hemispheric asymmetry within a few regions.

In all studies in which singing has been compared with passive auditory input (including playback of the subject's own vocalization, Perry, Zatorre, & Evans, 1995), CBF increased in the right primary auditory region (see Figure 4C). These increases may be related to deriving the fundamental frequency of one's own voice and using it as feedback for guiding vocal motor control. This hypothesis received support from a subsequent analysis (Perry et al., 1996). The fundamental frequency of subjects' vocalizations was recorded with a dedicated voltage-to-MIDI converter (IVL Pitchrider) and analyzed off-line. The amount of pitch deviation was quantified by summing the pitch changes within a sung note. The average pitch deviation within each sung note was derived by summing the absolute values of each intranote pitch change and dividing by the total duration, resulting in a value for each subject for the rate of pitch change expressed in cents/msec [average, 12; range, 5–29]. Regression analyses were performed using these

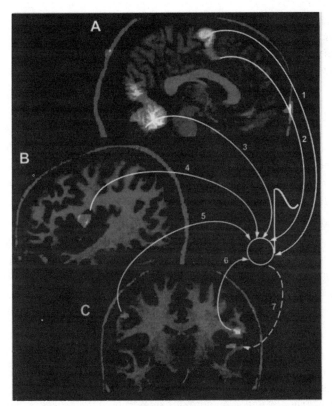

FIGURE 4 (A–C) Cortical regions activated by singing a single intended pitch. Arrows point-ing toward the musical note (1–6) indicate brain regions primarily contributing to the production of singing. The arrow returning to the brain indicates one brain region (7) activated specifically by auditory feedback from one's own voice during singing. Subjects chose a single pitch most comfort-able for their voice. During one 60-sec positron emission tomography (PET) scan, they attempted to sing this pitch repeatedly, at a target rate of approximately one sung note per 1250 msec. Singing was compared with passive listening to complex tones in the same frequency range. (This Singing task was the same one used as the control task in the study depicted in Figure 2. All other details of procedure and analysis are the same.) The sagittal slices depicted in A and B are roughly parallel to the plane of the side of the head. x coordinates refer to the distance to the right (positive) or the left (negative) of midline.

(A) Mid-sagittal section ($x = +3$) through the medial aspect of the right hemisphere depicts peaks of CBF increase in (1) the supplementary motor area, (2) the cingulate sulcus, and (3) the cerebellum (the actual peaks were located more laterally in the dentate nuclei).

(B) Sagittal section ($x = -39$) through the insular gyri of the left hemisphere depicting (4) a peak in the dorsal portion of the first long gyrus of the insula.

(C) Coronal section ($y = -13$) through peaks of CBF increase in (5) the dorsal left precentral gyrus, (6) the ventral right precentral gyrus, and (7) the right gyrus of Heschl or primary auditory region. Peaks 1–6 may be understood as contributing to controlling the motor output of singing. Peak 7 in auditory cortex results from perceiving the sound of one's own voice during singing and may be related directly to using auditory feedback for the purpose of guiding and correcting sung output, such as for adjusting the pitch sung to the intended pitch.

behavioral values across the entire volume representing the difference in CBF between singing and whispering while listening to playback. A positive correlation was observed between CBF in the right primary auditory region and the rate of pitch change, lending further support to the hypothesis that its activation is directly related to perceiving the sound of one's own voice while singing.

Although less striking, activation also appears to be greater in the right ventral precentral gyrus, that is, in the vicinity of the face region (see Figure 4C). The close correspondence between the networks of regions involved in singing and speaking suggests that speech may have evolved from an already-complex system for the voluntary control of vocalization. Their divergences suggest that the later evolving aspects of these two uniquely human abilities are essentially hemispheric specializations.

4. Absolute Pitch

A recent study examined CBF changes during tasks involving musical intervals (random series of ascending or descending minor or major thirds) and compared two groups of subjects: 10 musicians with absolute pitch, and 10 musicians without absolute pitch, but with good relative pitch (Zatorre, Perry, Beckett, Westbury, & Evans, 1998). When activation during listening to matched white noise bursts was subtracted from listening to the intervals, activation was observed in the left posterior dorsolateral frontal cortex only in the subjects with absolute pitch. Because note labeling is obligatory for absolute pitch possessors even when passively listening, this activation might represent part of the substrate for absolute pitch ability. When noise was subtracted from listening to the intervals and labeling them as major or minor, both groups showed bilateral activation within posterior dorsolateral frontal cortex.

Because most of the musicians were conservatory-trained, they had learned to associate the sound of a two-note sequence with a verbal label, an ability in some ways analogous to the absolute pitch possessors' ability to label a single pitch. Posterior dorsolateral frontal cortex has been shown to be important for conditional-associative learning both in monkeys (Petrides, 1987), and in humans (Petrides et al., 1993a). Thus absolute pitch may in part represent a form of conditional-associative learning (i.e., verbal-tonal association) relying at least in part on cognitive functions not unique to absolute pitch. The fundamental difference proposed is that only subjects with absolute pitch can form verbal-tonal associations with single pitches, whereas subjects with relative pitch can form them at a minimum for the relationship between two pitches.

The surface area of the planum temporale, or the superior temporal plane posterior to Heschl's gyrus, as measured from magnetic resonance images, has been shown to exhibit an exaggerated degree of leftward asymmetry in musicians with perfect pitch (Schlaug, Jäncke, Huang, & Steinmetz, 1995). Zatorre et al. (1998) measured cortical volume of the same region and found that it was slightly larger on the left for musicians with absolute pitch than for a group of control subjects. Moreover, pitch-naming performance was correlated with size of the left planum temporale, such that larger volume was associated with lower error scores. In spite of the fact that CBF changes were not observed in this region, these data suggest a possible role in AP ability. It is worth noting that, in the monkey, the majority of projections from the superior temporal gyrus to the posterior dorsolateral frontal region originate in the planum temporale (Petrides & Pandya, 1988).

Increasingly precise measurements of the extent of cerebral damage via computer-assisted analysis of magnetic resonance images may allow us to ask more precise questions about the *criticalness* of particular cortical regions in the human brain for particular auditory functions. Development of probabilistic maps for the location of crucial structures such as Heschl's gyrus (Penhune, Zatorre, MacDonald, & Evans, 1996) can also aid in interpreting the locations of metabolic peaks within the superior temporal gyrus in terms of cytoarchitectonically defined regions. We may then be able to use advances in knowledge about the organization of the auditory cortical regions and their connections from studies in animals (Brugge & Reale, 1985; Fitzpatrick & Imig, 1982; Merzenich & Schreiner, 1992; Morel, Garraghty, & Kaas, 1993; Pandya & Sanides, 1973; Pandya, Rosene, & Doolittle, 1994; Petrides & Pandya, 1988; Rauschecker, Tian, & Hauser, 1995; Rouiller, Simm, Villa, de Ribaupierre, & de Ribaupierre, 1991) and in humans (Celesia, 1976; Liégeois-Chauvel, Musolino, Badier, Marquis, & Chauvel, 1994; Galaburda & Sanides, 1980) to formulate more specific hypotheses about the contribution of specific auditory cortical regions in the superior temporal gyrus to musical functions and of any hemispheric asymmetries. Such hypotheses can then be tested by both lesion analysis and functional imaging methods.

B. HEMISPHERE ANESTHETIZATION

A few studies have examined the singing ability of patients undergoing transient anaesthetization of one hemisphere by unilateral injection of sodium Amytal, a procedure used to determine the lateralization of speech and the risk of memory impairment before neurosurgery (Rasmussen & Milner, 1977; Wada & Rasmussen, 1970). (Readers are referred to Zatorre, 1984, for a thorough review.) Interpretation of these studies is complicated by the fact that the tasks and procedures vary considerably, including the relative timing of injection and singing. Most previous studies have examined the ability of patients to sing a familiar melody after being given the title (Bogen & Gordon, 1971; Borchgrevink, 1980; Gordon & Bogen, 1974) or after hearing it played (Zatorre, 1984). Although these studies have in general indicated greater impairment after right-sided injection, left hemisphere anaesthetization also frequently interferes with singing.

Borchgrevink (1980) had patients begin to sing just before the drug was injected and observed the concomitant changes in performance. Left-sided injection produced arrest of both speech and singing, with both returning at approximately the same time. Right-sided injection produced a loss of pitch control, with a gradual recovery. These results suggest that portions of the left hemisphere may be essential for the control of vocalization, in both speech and singing, while neural processing in the right hemisphere is somehow crucial for vocal pitch modulation. The latter possibility could include both motor control of pitch, as well as the use of auditory feedback.

Borchgrevink (1991) reported on a continuing series of such patients ($N = 71$). The patients were repeatedly asked to perform the following musical tasks, when not interfering with the main diagnostic tests of language and memory: (a) to sing a well-known folk song with lyrics, hummed, or with numbers in place of the lyrics; (b) to reproduce a pitch sung by the examiner, either afterwards or concurrently. Pitch control (apparently across all of the tasks administered) was judged by musical listeners, and each subject's performance under unilateral hemisphere anaesthetization was compared with the subject's performance immediately before injection. Sung pitch accuracy was categorized as precise, within a semitone, or generally more than a semitone off. Out of 52 right-handed patients, 38 (73%) showed the "usual" pattern of left hemisphere speech control and a demonstrable decrement in pitch accuracy only after right hemisphere anesthesia. Eighty-one percent (46/57) of patients classified as showing left hemisphere speech, and 87% (7/8) with right hemisphere speech, showed evidence of right hemisphere pitch control. Only one patient showed a reversal of the usual pattern, a left hander with right hemisphere speech and left hemisphere pitch. Of 6 patients with bilateral speech control, 2 showed evidence of right hemisphere, 1 left, and 3 (50%) bilateral pitch control. Only 4 (7%) of the 57 left-hemisphere speech patients showed evidence of bilateral pitch control. Most patients with unilateral speech representation, whether left or right, showed evidence of right hemisphere pitch control, but bilateral speech representation appears to be associated with a higher incidence of bilateral musical pitch control.

In fact, only 1 of the 7 subjects with evidence of bilateral pitch control actually showed an equivalent *decrement* in performance after anesthetization of both hemispheres. The other 6 showed unimpaired precise performance. Although this suggests the possibility of a limit in measurement, it is still an atypical result and occurred with greater frequency in patients with bilateral speech representation. Performance before anesthesia was highly variable, with precise pitch control in 51%, control to within a semitone in 20%, and performance generally off more than one semitone in 29%. Objective rather than subjective appraisal of pitch accuracy (e.g., deviation in cents) would increase the precision of interhemispheric performance comparison, with each subject still serving as their own control.

Gordon and Bellamy (1991) reported a new series of 31 patients in whom singing of a well-known song was examined during hemisphere anesthetization. Three were non-right-handers, but all had left hemisphere speech representation. In contrast to his earlier reports with Bogen (Bogen & Gordon, 1971; Gordon & Bogen, 1974), 8 (26%) patients *were* able to sing during speech arrest (after left hemisphere injection), 5 during a period when no other vocalization was elicited, and 3 when vocalization was unintelligible. An additional 2 subjects were able to sing at a point when they were only observed to say their name. Speech abilities returned gradually in a normal fashion in the eight patients in whom singing was possible during speech arrest. From the entire group of 10 patients, six continued to speak after right hemisphere injection, but were unable or unwilling to sing for up to 1 minute. Three were able to both speak and sing immediately after injection, and one was unresponsive to requests for speech or singing for 11 minutes. No comparison of the quality of singing after right versus left injection was attempted.

Zatorre (1984) rated the singing of a familiar melody at 5 minutes after the injection and found that an equal number of patients sang better after right-sided (3) as after left-sided (4) injection, whereas the largest number (5) showed no difference. There was also no relationship between the side of lesion and the side of injection. However, 3 of the 4 patients who sang better after left-sided injection completely refused to sing after right-sided injection and instead spoke about the melody in a manner that indicated they clearly recognized it but were temporarily unable to sing it.

As Zatorre (1984) has noted, these studies are difficult to interpret because of the relatively small number of patients tested and because of the considerable degree of individual variability in response to Amytal. In addition, all of the studies to date have used familiar melodies, a factor that, as analysis of the effects of unilateral brain damage on melody recognition suggests, may tend to increase the importance of left hemisphere processing. It nevertheless seems clear, as Zatorre (1984) concluded, that intact functioning of both hemispheres is required for normal singing performance.

This conclusion is supported by studies of singing ability after unilateral brain damage, which have likewise found deficient singing (based on expert ratings) of a highly familiar melody ("Happy Birthday") after damage to either hemisphere (Kinsella, Prior, & Murray, 1988; Prior et al., 1990). Surprisingly, however, only patients with left hemisphere damage were impaired at reproducing three novel melodies (Prior et al., 1990). The question of whether some crucial cortical contributions to singing ability are symmetrically distributed, or whether the failure to differentiate hemisphere differences reflects damage to different components with opposite hemispheric asymmetries, must await careful fractionation of both the receptive and productive functions required, and ideally, quantitative measures of singing performance.

C. EAR DIFFERENCES IN NORMAL LISTENERS

A large number of studies have investigated differences in performance after presentation of melodies to the right versus the left ear, either simultaneously (dichotic) or separately (monaural). Such ear differences are usually interpreted as indicating an asymmetry in favor of neural processing in the contralateral hemisphere, based on the fact that, in response to monaural stimulation, greater evoked electrical (Tanguay, Taub, Doubleday, & Clarkson, 1977) or magnetic (Rogers, Papanicolaou, Baumann, Eisenberg, & Saydjari, 1990) responses are produced over the scalp of the contralateral hemisphere, and greater CBF (Lauter, Her–sovitch, Formby, & Raichle, 1985) and depth electrode-recorded response (Liége-ois-Chauvel et al., 1991) in the contralateral primary auditory cortex. Although caution is warranted with regard to possible individual differences in subcortical contributions to ear asymmetries for pitch perception (Efron, 1990), particularly for dichotic stimuli, the evidence cited here indicates a consistent relative contralateral predominance in cortical response to monaural auditory stimuli.

The original demonstration of an ear asymmetry for melody recognition (Kimura, 1967) showed a left ear asymmetry (LEA) in accuracy, but many other studies have found no ear asymmetry, or even a right ear asymmetry (REA). In addition, many published reports have actually demonstrated trends rather than statistically reliable ear asymmetries. However, reliable REAs for melody recognition have been observed, most influentially by Bever and Chiarello (1974), who found an REA for a group of musicians but an LEA for nonmusicians (for thorough reviews of this literature, see Peretz & Morais, 1988, and Perry, 1991). In general, it appears that "analytic" or single-note attending strategies result in a rightward shift in ear asymmetry (Peretz & Morais, 1980; Peretz, Morais, & Bertelson, 1987) or in frank REA (Gaede, Parsons, & Bertera, 1978; Minagawa, Nakagawa, & Kashu, 1987; Peretz, 1987; Peretz & Morais, 1983, 1987), at least for some subjects, and for task conditions that seem to most unequivocally induce single-position attending, for example, disclosure of single-position-altered melody construction rules (Peretz et al., 1987) or speeded response (Peretz & Morais, 1987).

Many melody recognition studies have used melodies-to-be-compared that differ only at one or two positions. As Peretz and Morais (1988) noted, studies that have used melodies constructed so that single-position comparisons are not helpful have most often yielded LEAs. For example, Zatorre (1979) presented melodies for comparison in which no interval was repeated at the same position and obtained a robust LEA (71% of right-handers) for both musicians and nonmusicians. However, identical or similar constraints have not always produced reliable LEAs (Peretz & Morais, 1983; Piazza, 1980). Also, the *highest* proportion of right handers showing LEAs for melody recognition never reaches the average levels seen for speech (80%; Bryden, 1988).

Although this discrepancy may reflect a different relationship between handedness and whatever cortical asymmetries may be responsible for ear asymmetries in melody and in speech processing, an alternative hypothesis is that all melody *recognition* or *same-different* tasks, involving as they do the comparison of tone sequences, may potentially induce analytic or position-specific comparison strategies and hence engage left-hemisphere lateralized processors, with the extent of such engagement at least partially dependent on subjects' choice of strategy (Perry, 1991, 1993).

Melody *recall*, in which subjects listen to one melody at a time and immediately attempt to reproduce it, excludes any such tone sequence comparison. Kimura (1967) obtained an LEA for the accuracy of immediate vocal recall of familiar concert melodies by right-handed musically experienced subjects. Recall responses were scored in an all-or-none fashion. Perry (1990, 1991) found an LEA ($P < .001$) in the *accuracy* of keyboard recall of unfamiliar diatonic melodies[7] by

---

[7]Melodic fragments 7–13 notes in length were derived from the fugal expositions in the *Well Tempered Clavier Book II* of J. S. Bach, but were not recognized as such by any of the subjects. Performance level was limited to 50–75% for each subject by raising or lowering the rate of presentation.

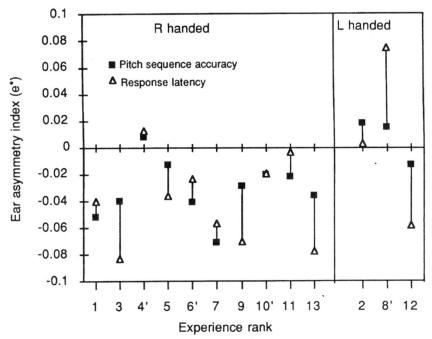

FIGURE 5 Ear asymmetry indices (e*, or R – L/R + L) for pitch sequence accuracy, and for response latency, from keyboard recall of 24 melodies presented monaurally to each ear. Within each handedness group, the data from individual pianists are presented in order of increasing experience rank. Absolute pitch ability is indicated by a prime. (From Perry, 1991).

right-handed pianists, with performances scored by computer on a note-by-note basis (Figure 5). Subjects attempted to reproduce 96 melodies, alternating in ABBA fashion to one ear at a time in blocks of 12. The second half consisted of repetitions of the 48 melodies presented in the first half, but to opposite ears. Reliable ear asymmetries were observed only within the first half, suggesting that novelty may be a crucial factor. Left ear presentation also resulted in longer *response latency* ($P < .005$), as well as higher accuracy, for 9 out of 10 right-handed pianists (Figure 5), and ear asymmetries for the two measures exhibited a positive correlation ($+0.70$, $P < .01$).[8] Ear asymmetry in pitch sequence recall accuracy was reliably related to handedness ($P < .025$), with 2 out of 3 left-handers showing an REA.

A functional asymmetry in the neural substrates for auditory-tonal working memory may be responsible for the association between higher accuracy and *longer* response latency, an interval during which many subjects reported mentally "singing" the melody (Perry, 1991, 1993). An asymmetry in the short-term retention of pitch information could be at least partially responsible for all asymmetries

[8]Interestingly, the only right-handed subject showing an REA for pitch accuracy (4') also showed an REA in response latency and was the only subject for whom a clear reversal of the usual direction of the octave illusion (Deutsch, 1970b) resulted (Perry, 1991).

observed in the effects of unilateral brain damage on melody processing (Zatorre & Samson, 1991). It could also contribute to all normal ear asymmetries in melody processing (Perry, 1991, 1993).

It is not yet clear whether these asymmetries are related to retention of pitch information in a low-level auditory sensory code (Zatorre & Samson, 1991), or in some form of auditory-tonal working memory that might include covert vocal rehearsal (Perry, 1991, 1993). The neural substrates of short-term memory for pitch are most likely to include secondary auditory cortices in the right temporal lobe, as suggested by Zatorre and Samson (1991). The neural substrates supporting auditory-tonal working memory may also encompass particular frontal cortical regions to which these auditory association cortices are interconnected (Chavis & Pandya, 1976). Together, interconnected temporal and frontal cortical regions may form part of more widely distributed neural networks. These networks may exhibit functional asymmetry favoring the non-language-dominant hemisphere in at least one of their components (Perry, 1991, 1993). As discussed earlier, recent evidence of right frontal asymmetries in regional CBF during tasks involving the retention and manipulation of tones and tone sequences lends further support to the hypothesis that a functional asymmetry for auditory-tonal working memory favoring the right frontal cortex may contribute significantly to left-ear advantages for melody processing.

Alternatively, lower-level aspects of perceptual processing may result in ear advantages for musical stimuli, just as they have been proposed to do for linguistic stimuli. Right-ear advantages for speech have been attributed to the requirement to process rapid acoustic transients such as those found in stop consonants (Schwartz & Tallal, 1980). In one experiment, a robust right-ear advantage resulted from identification of stop-consonant-vowel syllables, but no ear advantage resulted for steady-state vowels (Shankweiler & Studdert-Kennedy, 1967).

Similarly, left-ear advantages were obtained for dichotic pitch discrimination when the pitches were complex tones but not when the stimuli were pure tones (Sidtis, 1980). A recent experiment (Laguitton, Demany, Semal, & Liegeois-Chauvel, 1998) measured ear advantages for judgments of pitch direction between pairs of tones constructed in such a way that perception of virtual pitch could be differentiated from perception of the individual spectral components (2, 3, or 4 in number). For the first presentation, an overall left-ear advantage emerged in the percentage of responses to the fundamental. Interestingly, a significantly lower rate of responding to the virtual pitch was observed among left handers.

Thus, in music, as in language, careful consideration must be given to the contributions of hemispheric specializations at the psychoacoustic-perceptual level and at higher cognitive levels. As seems probable for language, contributions from both levels may frequently be present and may often (although not always) tend to point toward the same hemisphere, making their dissociation even more challenging. Such a situation might result from the co-evolution of interconnected brain regions within specialized neural networks.

VI. PROGRESS IN THE NEUROPSYCHOLOGY
OF HUMAN MUSIC PERCEPTION

As the preceding review makes clear, an understanding of how musical functions are produced by the nervous system, and how they break down when it is damaged, cannot be reduced to simple hemispheric divisions of labor and poses questions at least as daunting as those involved in a similar analysis of linguistic functions. The answers clearly lie in relating complex cognitive functions to an equally complex neural substrate. Current and future advances in the neurology of human music perception are most likely to be made through the guidance of neuropsychological investigation by knowledge gained from studies of normal music cognition. Several such examples have already been described:

1. Studies of the effects of unilateral brain damage on melody perception (Peretz, 1990; Samson & Zatorre, 1988; Zatorre, 1985a), guided by the melody-encoding theories of Dowling and colleagues (Dowling, 1978; Dowling & Bartlett, 1981; see Chapter 15, this volume);
2. A study of the interaction of memory for melody and for words in songs after unilateral temporal lobectomy (Samson & Zatorre, 1991a), based on the song-memory theory of Serafine et al. (1984);
3. A study of auditory imagery in temporal lobectomy patients (Zatorre & Halpern, 1993) based on the paradigm of Halpern (1988); and
4. A study of the short-term retention of single pitches across interference by patients with temporal and frontal lobectomy (Zatorre & Samson, 1991) based on the pitch-encoding theory of Deutsch (1970a).

The last two paradigms have also been studied with PET (Zatorre, Evans, & Meyer, 1994; Zatorre, Halpern, Perry, Meyer, & Evans, 1996), illustrating how such hypotheses about cognitive functional localization may be tested in the normal, intact brain.

Another area of research in the cognitive psychology of music perception that has been particularly fruitful for neuropsychological investigation is that of chord perception, in particular, the effect of a previously established harmonic context on subsequent perception or production of pitch. Such paradigms began with a study by Krumhansl and Shepherd (1979), in which subjects gave ratings for single tones that followed tonality-instantiating stimuli, including major triads. Krumhansl, Bharucha, and Castellano (1982) and Bharucha and Krumhansl (1983) examined relatedness judgments for pairs of octave-generalized chords (Shepard, 1964) that followed key-instantiating cadences. Multidimensional scaling analysis revealed that chords from the same key were judged to be most closely related, regardless of the context key, although the compactness of this relatedness decreased with distance on the circle of fifths. Chords from distant keys were clearly segregated, thus confirming their music theoretic classification as harmonically unrelated (Tekman & Bharucha, 1992).

Marin and Barnes (1985) measured harmonic expectancy by having subjects rate the subjective goodness of sequence of pairs of musical chords that differed in their harmonic relatedness. Pairs of four-voice triads were presented in isolation with no preceding key context. They either belonged to the same tonality or to different tonalities (Figure 6A), with 30 pairs in each series, presented in both forward and reversed order, yielding 120 pairs in all. Care was taken to treat the articulation from the first to the second chord according to the procedures recommended by classical harmony, and all pairs were characterized by smoothness of transition and consonance. Although musically experienced subjects ($n = 7$) rejected fewer chord sequences overall than did musically inexperienced subjects ($n = 9$), there was no relation between harmonic relatedness and acceptance or rejection, and all groups rejected less than 25% overall. Further analyses were performed on the reaction times to responses of acceptance (Figures 6B & 7). Amateurs' ($n = 4$) responses were reliably faster to harmonically related chords than to unrelated chords. However, no reliable differences were seen for the inexperienced ($n = 8$) or professional ($n = 3$) subjects, although trends in the same direction were observed, most convincingly for the professionals (Figure 7).

Although there were considerable individual differences that could obscure group differences, the authors interpreted the negative findings differently for the inexperienced and professional groups. The lack of differential response to harmonic relatedness for the naive subjects was attributed to relatively undeveloped internalized cognitive structures for tonality, which require greater exposure to

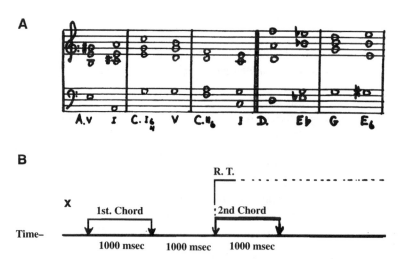

FIGURE 6   (A) Examples of four-voice chord pairs in which the second chord belongs to the same or to a different tonality. (B) Time course of the experimental paradigm. Each chord is presented for 1 second with a 1-sec interchord interval, and response times of acceptance or rejection are measured from the onset of the second chord. The "x" indicates the onset of a visual warning signal. (From Marin & Barnes, 1985.)

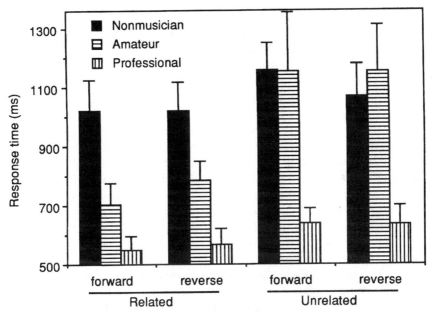

FIGURE 7 Reaction times to responses of acceptance for pairs of four-voice chords that belonged to the same tonality or to different tonalities, in forward and reversed order, by nonmusician, amateur, and professional subjects. Bars depict the standard error of the means. (From Marin & Barnes, 1985).

develop. The weaker differentiation observed for the professionals was attributed to the fact that they accepted a high number of pairs and reported considering factors other than tonal relationship, such as the movement of the lower and upper voices, or whether such a transition might be found in Debussy, Chopin, or other composers from their experience. Two of the three professionals had extensive experience with contemporary classical compositions, the same two who showed the least sensitivity to tonal relationship.

Bharucha and Stoeckig (1986, 1987) developed a related paradigm to measure the expectancy or priming generated by musical chords. Major triads made up of octave-generalized tones were presented in pairs, with a task that does not directly address the relationship between the two chords, but simply requires subjects to judge whether or not the second chord is in tune or not. Half of the second chords were mistuned a quarter of a semitone. They found faster (and more accurate) responses to in-tune judgments when the preceding chord was harmonically related, and faster (and more accurate) responses to out-of-tune judgments when the preceding chord was unrelated (see Chapter 11). For groups of college undergraduates, most of whom had several years of musical instrument training (range, 0–20 years; averages, 4.3 – 9.4 years), they found no relationship between musical experience and the magnitude of this priming effect on accuracy. The majority of these subjects probably correspond to the amateur group in Marin and Barnes (1985). It thus might be possible for the strength of priming to vary with musical experience, if subjects with a broader range of instrumental training were compared. We return to the question of the *development* of musical expertise in the next section. However, it is clear that the immediate facilitation of triads by other harmonically related triads is a stable phenomenon across a fairly wide range of musical experience.

Bharucha and Stoeckig's (1986, 1987) musical priming paradigm has been used in two different studies to investigate the perceptual abilities of patients with neurological disorders. One was the patient with bilateral temporal lobe lesions and initial cortical deafness described earlier (Mendez & Geehan, 1988), who was administered the musical priming task 7 years after his second stroke (Tramo et al., 1990). In spite of the fact that his judgments of consonance were at chance levels, with a marked bias toward dissonance, the same interaction was seen between harmonic relatedness and intonation judgment. The authors interpret this pattern as representing a dissociation between the judgment of consonance and the "associative processes that generate harmonic expectancies." Because total destruction of the primary auditory cortices was demonstrated in this patient, with partial sparing of secondary cortex, particularly on the left side, the authors hypothesize that the primary auditory cortices are essential for tonal consonance perception, but that musical priming is independent of them and can be sustained by partially intact secondary auditory cortices (Tramo et al., 1990).

The same paradigm was administered to two callosotomy patients (i.e., "split-brain patients" in whom the interhemispheric pathways have been cut for relief of epilepsy) in free auditory field, but with response options for the intonation judgment presented tachistoscopically to only one hemisphere. For both patients, the normal interaction in accuracy was seen only for the left visual field, suggesting that the neural substrates supporting this priming are at least partially lateralized in the right hemisphere of these patients (Tramo & Bharucha, 1991).

This series of studies provides an excellent example of how insights from the analysis of normal music cognition, combined with modern methods of determining, with increasing precision, the extent of damage to neural tissue (or the neural regions most active during task performance), can lead to real progress in our understanding of how the brain performs complex musical functions.

Noninvasive methods for imaging brain activity are beginning to provide evidence of the effects of long-term musical skill acquisition on basic aspects of cortical organization. Magnetic fields evoked by acoustic stimuli over the left hemisphere were measured in three groups of subjects: conservatory students with absolute pitch, students with relative pitch only, and students who had never played an instrument (mean ages, 26 –29 years). Responses to piano tones were contrasted with responses evoked by pure tones (matched for loudness). The single equivalent current dipoles that best explained the evoked magnetic fields occurring approximately 100 msec after the stimuli were computed. Their spatial arrangement did not differ across groups, reflecting some degree of tonotopic organization. However, both groups of musicians showed dipole moments in response to the piano tones that were about 25% larger that those to pure tones, whereas the responses for nonmusicians were equivalent (Pantev, Oostenveld, Engelien, Ross, Roberts, & Hoke, 1998).

These magnetoencephalographic results indicate that the strength (or synchrony) of cortical activation within the time interval measured was greater for the musicians. Moreover, there was a significant negative correlation between the age at which training began (range, 3–12 years), and the mean dipole moment for the piano tones. Because the piano was at least a secondary instrument for 17 of the 20 musicians tested, it cannot be determined whether the long-term cortical reorganization suggested by these results is specific to the processing of piano tones or applies generally to the processing of all complex harmonic sounds.

Changes in the tonotopic organization of auditory cortex have been observed in monkeys after only a few weeks of training in frequency discrimination. The cortical representation of the trained frequencies in primary auditory cortex was enlarged, as measured by multiple-unit recordings, and the area of cortical representation correlated positively with behavioral performance (Recanzone, Schreiner, & Merzenich, 1993). Thus, using experimentally controlled training procedures and a much more direct, sensitive measurement of tonotopic cortical organization, changes were observed on the order of weeks rather than years, and in adult animals. It is not yet known what the lower temporal limits for measuring such changes might be, but similar refinements in the study of human auditory processing might allow measurement of shorter-term cortical changes.

A similar state of knowledge prevails regarding the effects of musical motor skill aquistion on the organization of sensorimotor cortex. Magnetic source imaging has indicated larger cortical representations of the digits of the left hand for experienced string players (enlargement was less marked for the thumb, and absent for the right hand). The magnitude of these effects correlated negatively with the age at which training began (Elbert, Pantev, Wienbruch, Rockstroh, & Taub, 1995).

When monkeys were trained in a tactile flutter-vibration discrimination task, involving a particular portion of the skin of one digit, the area of somatosensory cortex representing that portion increased significantly (1.5 –3 times; Recanzone, Merzenich, Jenkins, Grajski, & Dinse, 1992). In another study, the representation of the distal forelimb in primary motor cortex was mapped in both hemispheres. The total area of cortex representing the distal forelimb was found to be greater in the dominant hemisphere, that is, the hemisphere opposite the hand preferred by the monkey in a task requiring skilled digit use (Nudo, Jenkins, Merzenich, Prejean, & Grenda, 1992). Thus both short-term and long-term consequences of hand use on the cortical organization of cortex supporting motor skill aquisition can be measured in animals.

Using functional magnetic resonance imaging (fMRI), and an experimentally controlled motor skill learning task, an expansion of the representation within primary motor cortex for a trained sequence of finger movements has been demonstrated (Karni, Meyer, Jezzard, Adams, Turner, & Ungerleider, 1995). Subjects practiced a particular sequence of finger-to-thumb opposition movements (e.g., 4-1-3-2-4) for 10–20 min per day over the course of 5 weeks. Subjects were scanned once a week during the performance of the learned sequence and an unpracticed sequence (e.g., 4-2-3-1-4).

By the third week, the extent of cortex activated by the learned sequence was consistently greater than that activated by the unpracticed sequence. Furthermore, this increase persisted for several months, as did the skill itself. Because the same fingers were used in both sequences, this increase is not in the cortical representation of particular digits, but in the representation of the particular *sequence* of finger movements. Thus, this result extends those described earlier demonstrating the expansion of the representation of particular parts of the body (including the cochlea).

William James, prescient as he was in many ways, described the retention of memory as "a morphological feature, the presence of ... 'paths' ... in the finest recesses of the brain's tissue" and its recall as "the functional excitement of the tracts and paths in question" (James, 1890, p. 655). Although the cortical regions sampled in the just-described experiments are clearly but parts of the brain networks supporting sensory and motor learning and memory, they may be critical sites for the long-term storage of such memories, as Karni et al. (1995) have suggested for motor skills. The elucidation of the representation of melodic sequences within human tonotopic auditory cortex remains as a challenge for future investigations (but see Chapter 3, this volume, for important steps toward this goal). A challenge of even greater complexity is the integrated representation of melodic sequences and the instrumental or vocal skills required to produce them.

VII. MUSIC PERCEPTION AS A SKILL

One theme thus far has been the contrast between the probable neural substrates of linguistic and musical functions, and, in their disintegration, between the amusias and the aphasias. Only at two extreme points in the hierarchy of music perceptual and productive functions have we seen convincing evidence of coincidences between particular linguistic and musical functions. First, in a high-level music perceptual disorder, the naming of musical works or their composers, we have seen partial overlap with broader lexicosemantic disorders, resulting from damage to the language-dominant hemisphere, or from diffuse cortical degeneration in Alzheimer's-type dementia. At the lowest level of musical productive functions, we have seen limited evidence, from hemisphere anesthesia and from focal left anterior brain damage, of avocalias that appear to simultaneously disrupt both singing and speech (even though at a higher level of the motor production of speech, most persons with Broca's aphasia are able to sing). PET studies confirmed substantial overlap between the networks subserving singing and speech.

In between, we are more impressed by the divergences between the cognitive and neural architectures of music and language, and in particular, by the broader distribution of musical functions. We believe this divergence is due to the nature of music itself and to the nature and development of musical skill (Marin, 1989).

The radical difference between musical skill (along with other nonlinguistic cognitive skills such as chess, painting, sculpture, poetry, and other complex perceptuomotor skills) and linguistic skill is that language use not only presupposes that our brain has previous experience with the type of stimuli being presented and the motor responses associated with them, but that it also has extensive experience with fixed and predictable codes, rules and procedures that relate these stimuli directly to real-world objects and actions. In other words, language is largely a stable referential symbolic system that represents our knowledge of the world. Lexical items (words) are symbols that exist not only by themselves in phonological terms but also as representatives for their referents. So far as these lexical-referential linkages are fixed, and the combinatory rules (syntax) are constant and universal for all languages, one can predict that its computations are made through a similarly stable series of psychological processes. From this, we would predict some regularity in the corresponding physiological substrates of these processes (Marin, 1976; Marin & Gordon, 1979a, 1979b).

This is not the case in music, nor in the other skills mentioned. Here we are dealing with systems of communication in which each instance consists of a few nonreferential items that are combined according to the prevailing stylistic "syntactic" rules. Music is thus a game of combinatory acoustical constructs that the brain of the composer can conceive and that the listener should be able to learn or discover. For the latter, the intelligence of the communication resides in processing the musical message in such a way as to gain conscious or unconscious access to the rules and their forms (Rozin, 1976). These other skills do not require the same degree of previous exposure. They encourage much more radical changes in the accepted rules of the game and yet allow a progressive development in the complexity of the internalized cognitive schemas used to make sense of, and to respond to, the incoming stimuli.

We would like to propose, with Sloboda (1985, 1989) the literature on skills and the development of expertise (e.g., Chase & Simon, 1973a, 1973b; Cranberg & Albert, 1988; Charness, 1976, 1988; Ericsson, 1985) as a crucial guide for an understanding of musical skill and hence of its neural substrates. In the classic studies of memory for chess-board positions by players of various ranks (Chase & Simon, 1973a), an advantage of expertise was apparent only in recall of boards from actual games but not in recall of random positions. This advantage was manifested in recall of larger chunks or groups of pieces, suggesting that expertise is associated with the development of an expanding repertoire of perceptual patterns, which can be used to organize incoming stimuli. Thus, such skills can be termed perceptual organizational, rather than representational processes. Finally, through specialized training, some individuals learn ways to label these perceptual patterns verbally and thus to relate perceptual organizational processing to representational processing (Marin, 1989).

In an extension of the studies of the harmonic expectancies generated by musical chords described earlier, we studied the generative (vocal) resolution of the inversions of the major triad, by subjects whose musical experience ranged from minimal to advanced professionals (Perry & Marin, 1990). Subjects were presented with four-voice chords and, in separate conditions, asked to sing the most salient pitch and the pitch that would best follow the chord. Responses for salience did not differ significantly with experience and corresponded well to predictions based on subharmonic matching (Parncutt, 1988; Terhardt, 1982). However, preferences for resolution showed a reliable increase in resolution to the tonic and dominant pitches, and to the entire diatonic set, with musical experience. Hierarchical cluster analysis yielded three groups whose responses were most closely related (see Figure 8). Group 1 comprised two professionals and one amateur (average 26 years' of active musical experience) whose responses consisted entirely of triadic notes and conformed most stereotypically to the aforementioned pattern, including a strong overall preference for the tonic. Group 2 consisted of one amateur and two novices (average 19 years' experience) whose responses showed the expected trends just noted. Group 3 included two nonmusicians (average 3 years' active musical experience, none current) whose responses included many nondiatonic pitches. The profile obtained from Group 2 is most similar to profiles obtained with probe-tone ratings after major triads (Cuddy & Badertscher, 1987; Krumhansl & Kessler, 1982).

However, the choices of the advanced professionals (average 45 years' experience) exhibited the most variability. One (a music school director with absolute pitch) confirmed a prediction from classical harmonic theory, specifically the cadential resolution of the second inversion (Piston, 1978) and was the only subject to do so (though he clustered in Group 1). Another (an internationally known contemporary composer) was highly idiosyncratic and favored nondiatonic tones. The third, a retired college-level piano pedagogue, was most similar to the moderately experienced Group 2, though showing a stronger preference for resolution to the dominant (see Figure 8).

These results suggest caution in attempting to reduce musical skills to an average common denominator. Although useful as a first step, and probably sufficient for investigating the musical abilities of the average listener (e.g., one with a moderate level of musical instrument training at some point in life, but not actively maintained over many years), a full understanding of musical functions will require investigation of the continuum of musical development. This is particularly true if we aim to eventually explain the striking dissociations and associations that are frequently reported in case reports of professional musicians who have suffered cortical damage. And, as Sloboda (1985) has observed, we may learn more about both commonplace and expert behavior if we regard them as sharing the same fundamental principles.

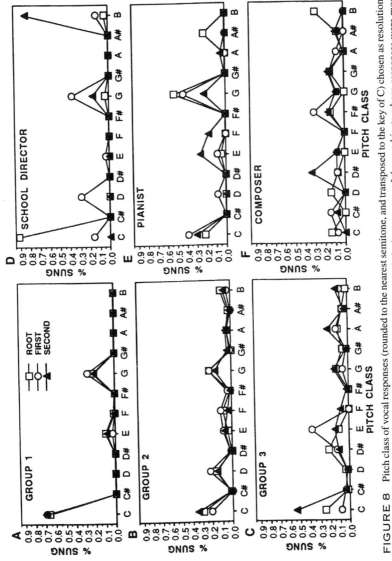

FIGURE 8 Pitch class of vocal responses (rounded to the nearest semitone, and transposed to the key of C) chosen as resolutions to inversions of the major triad (root, first, and second). Groups 1–3 depict averages of those subjects whose responses were most related, as determined by hierarchical cluster analysis, in order of decreasing musical experience (see text). On the right are responses of three advanced professionals. (From Perry & Marin, 1990).

VIII. PERSPECTIVES FOR THE NEUROPSYCHOLOGICAL STUDY OF MUSIC

With regard to the localization of lesions in cases of disorders of music perception and performance, the following generalizations may be proposed: sensory and perceptual disorders seem to be related to lesions in the temporal lobe of either hemisphere. Pure cases of sensory amusia without aphasia are likely to correspond to right-sided (or non-language-dominant hemisphere) lesions. However, the neuropsychological disruptions producing sensory and perceptual deficits are complex. Damage to the left side often generates combinations of aphasia and amusia in which the amusic deficits range from perceptual to symbolic or lexical music disorders. Musical abnormalities that are usually called expressive have a neuropsychological structure of even greater complexity and, as is the case with language production, involve complex perceptual, mnemonic, lexical, and programmative tasks of greater variety and temporal duration. Correlation with locus of lesions is uncertain, and the lesions may involve temporal as well as frontal and even parietal regions. To the extent that the nature of the task is related to linguistic functions, lesions tend to predominate in the left hemisphere.

In many professional and even amateur musicians, overlearned and automated tasks are frequently spared. These are tasks performed by the average individual only through careful analysis or orderly sequential programming, which in musicians are partially automatisms. This may have important implications in terms of the neural substrates involved.

Some authors have suggested that deficits in music perception are related to right hemisphere lesions whereas deficits in musical expression are more often due to left-sided damage (Wertheim, 1969). This view needs to be examined further: lateralization of functions has developed not because they are primarily expressive or receptive but rather because the required operations need neural substrata "wired" or "programmed" so specifically as to make them impossible to be shared with other functions. Lateralization, as well as physiological or anatomical localization, is the *consequence of specialization*, and this in turn becomes gradually less compatible with sharing. In some cases, specialization and functional segregation result from an expansion in the amount of data to be processed, whereas in other cases these may be the result of the peculiar nature of the computation that needs to be performed. Thus far, no overarching dichotomy of hemisphere processing differences, whether "holistic" versus "operational" processing (Bever, 1980), or "spectral" vs. "temporal" (Divenyi & Efron, 1979), has consistently met with success in empirical tests (e.g., Divenyi & Robinson, 1989). It rather appears that certain cognitive task demands, most notably melody discrimination based on single pitch changes (see Peretz & Morais, 1988) and certain basic auditory processing abilities, particularly those related to pitch (Divenyi & Robinson, 1989; Zatorre, 1988), are associated with hemispheric asymmetries. Precisely why these particular task demands reveal hemisphere differences is not yet fully explainable. Such explanations will require a more complete understanding of the cognitive operations involved, their instantiation in distributed neural networks, and the isolation within those networks of asymmetrically functioning neural processor(s). Finally, the nature of each of those asymmetries will have to be understood, for example, whether it is an all-or-none specialization or a relative one. (For more extensive discussions of neurobiological issues in relation to lateralization of language and cognition, see Marin, 1976; Marin & Gordon, 1979 a, 1979b; in relation to lateralization of music cognition, see Peretz & Morais, 1988; Perry, 1991, 1993; Zatorre, 1984, 1989a).

The optimistic view of classical neurology that musical functions are clearly localized has in most cases not been verified. Not only have fixed anatomic representations proved to be unattainable for the various aspects of musical perception, memory, or performance, but even basic musical operations—such as chord or melody perception and identification, music reading, or vocalization—seem to be fairly complex processes that are manifested with considerable individual variability (Zatorre, 1984). The uncertainty surrounding the field of the neuropsychology of music has been attributed to various factors. Many authors comment that because of the lack of common standards for musical abilities in the normal population comparable to those for language functions (e.g., an equivalent to Chomsky's, 1970, *linguistic competence*), one cannot anticipate whether a particular musical discrimination or performance should be expected in an otherwise normal individual. Not only is it difficult to evaluate the capacities of the musically unsophisticated, but in the amateur musician, or even in the professional, it is difficult to obtain strict criteria for normal performance. Experience with professional musicians reveals the uneven distribution of particular musical talents, acquired skills, or even awareness of the rules of music as a combinational system of perceptual forms. It is not at all clear, or even likely, that the same musical problem will be processed by all musicians in the same way (e.g. with equal depth) or following similar and consistent cognitive strategies.

Some authors hope that the neuropsychological study of music will advance when studies use more systematic and sophisticated methods of measurement. Improvements have been proposed by many authors (Dorgeuille, 1966; Grison, 1972; Jelinek, 1956; Ustvedt, 1937; Wertheim & Botez, 1959). No essential argument against this approach can be made; however, it should be noted that when a similar approach was adopted in early studies of aphasia, no real progress was achieved merely by sharpening the details of examination. Real progress in the study of aphasia was not forthcoming until we began to uncover the basic structure of language (see, e.g., Head, 1926; Weisenburg & McBride, 1935). Just as an elaborate study of phonetic discrimination would in itself fail to provide a better understanding of speech and language production, so is it unlikely that exhaustive psychophysical analysis of duration, pitch, timbre, or intensity discrimination will tell us anything meaningful about music processing, despite the fact that they constitute in and of themselves interesting structure/function questions. Substantial headway in the neuropsychology of music can be achieved only with the study of those levels of perception and memory that are truly musical and that can serve as a basis for musical information processing schemas. Recent reviews (see Chapter 11, this volume; Deutsch, 1978; Krumhansl, 1990; Zatorre, 1989a) and the results of research reported in the present volume indicate that a sufficient basis exists for undertaking such neuropsychological studies and that they are underway. This progress does not necessarily promise that a better understanding of musical neuropsychology will delineate "musical centers" or even less well-delineated anatomical substrates for music. However, such focal specializations may be definitively demonstrated for some neural components of the crucial cognitive operations supporting musical functions, for example, complex pitch perception (Zatorre, 1988), short-term memory for pitch (Zatorre & Samson, 1991), auditory working memory for tones (Perry, 1990, 1991, 1993; Perry et al., 1993b, 1994; Perry, Zatorre, Petrides, & Evans, 1995; Zatorre et al., 1994) and for other types of pitch information (Zatorre et al., 1992), consonance perception (Tramo et al., 1990), timbre discrimination (Milner, 1962; Samson & Zatorre, 1994b; Tramo & Bharucha, unpublished data), harmonic expectancy (Tramo et al., 1990; Tramo & Bharucha, 1991), rhythm perception and reproduction (Penhune et al., 1995), and singing (Borchgrevink, 1980; Perry et al. 1993a; Perry, Zatorre, & Evans, 1995, Perry et al., 1996).

A review of the types of disorders of musical function due to localized cortical lesions reveals that the traditional clinical classifications are too broad. Grouping symptoms of differing complexity under the same nosological clinical heading does not facilitate an understanding of the neuropsychological processes involved in musical functions. For this purpose, musical deficiencies could instead be arranged in a hierarchical order. By borrowing some basic principles from the neuropsychology of language and from the psychology of music in order to establish this order, we can distinguish between the following categories of amusic disorders,[9] with the assumption that deficits are not attributable to defects in the auditory or motor peripheries. Within the broader divisions between perceptive (1–3), mnestic (4–5), and motoric (6–8) amusias, the disorders are presented in the order of their disruption of progressively higher levels of a hypothesized hierarchy of cognitive and neural processing:

1. Perceptual acoustic: Disturbances of the type often seen in association with the auditory agnosias, in which musical stimuli are not recognized as music. They are usually associated with massive bilateral destruction or deafferenting of the primary auditory cortices.

2. Perceptual structural: Disruptions of the basic building blocks of music, (a) pitch, (b) intensity, (c) timbre, (d) consonance, (e) meter, (f) rhythm, or (g) sound localization, but with retained ability to recognize music as such. We are tentatively retaining this category as distinct from perceptual acoustic, as do Lechevalier et al. (1985), even though it is clear that persons with auditory agnosia usually exhibit basic defects in several of these dimensions (e.g., timbre, duration, intensity, consonance). In fact, the distinction may be one of the severity of disrup-

---

[9]Categories (1), (2), and (5) are based on the development of ideas from Lechevalier et al. (1985) in the first edition of this chapter.

tion in one or more of the aforementioned dimensions. Although we cannot attempt to survey all of the available evidence about these dimensions, each one indicates a potentially distinct set of cognitive operations and neural processing regions. Together they constitute those cognitive operations that are most likely to be at least partially supported by well-localizable "neuronal-dependent" processors.

3. Perceptual organizational: Here we included disruptions in the ability to organize incoming musical stimuli according to previously acquired perceptual patterns, or according to Gestalt-type rules of perceptual organization. Thus, cases of disturbances in the processing of novel melodies or of chords, with intact spectral processing and mnestic abilities, would clearly fall within this category. So would disruptions of premorbid music listening abilities, whether those of highly skilled or of average listeners, that are dependent on the use of culturally acquired musical systems.

4. Mnestic: Following the dissociations seen in other types of memory, we can further distinguish between the ability to form and retrieve the following types of memories: (a) auditory sensory short-term retention, (b) auditory working memory, (c) long-term or episodic memory (e.g., for a melody, as distinct from any verbal lexical associations), and (d) procedural memory. This category again includes complex functions, some of whose components have a high probability of being supported by localizable neural processors.

5. Lexical-semantic: Loss or failure to retrieve the linguistic associations of musical stimuli, for example, the names, composers, or styles of melodies or works, or the verbal labels for specific musical elements or functions. This level thus consists of particular categories of verbal anomia.

6. Motor productive: Fundamental defects in the ability to voluntarily produce and regulate the vocal, articulatory, or manual movements necessary for musical performance.

7. Sensory motor integrative: Disruption of the necessary integrations between auditory, visual, or kinesthetic sensory input and musical motor output, particularly feedback from one's own performance. Sensory-motor integration is also necessary for sight-reading, aural dictation or instrumental transcription, and ensemble performance.

8. Motor programmative: Higher-level disruptions of the ability to formulate and implement sequentially the motor programs required to produce music.

9. Musical lexical

10. Musical graphic

Categories 9 and 10 are meant to include disturbances of musical reading and writing. Within both, the interpretation and production of notes on staves, of rhythms, and of ideographic symbols (e.g., expressive markings) may be dissociated, with the notation of pitch particularly dependent on intact visuospatial processing.

These divisions, particularly between perceptual and motoric deficits, do not imply that both cannot occur simultaneously in some cases, nor that perceptive disorders do not affect the motoric performance of musical tasks. Neither are all of these categories equally well-established as fully dissociable deficits. For example, the sensory motor integrative category must be regarded as the most hypothetical, because disorders specific to it would have to be demonstrated with fully intact perceptual and motor functions. This classificatory scheme cannot yet serve the pragmatic goals of the clinician who searches for a nosology of clinical or anatomical predictive value. Rather, it is intended as a further attempt to provide a tentative framework for investigating the fundamental cognitive and motoric operations involved in human musical activity and their neural foundations.

ACKNOWLEDGMENTS

Preparation of this chapter by both authors was supported by the Coleman and Cornelia Wheeler Foundation at the Laboratory of Cognitive Neuropsychology, Good Samaritan Hospital and Medical Center, and by a postdoctoral fellowship to the second author from the McDonnel-Pew Program in Cognitive Neuroscience at the Montreal Neurological Institute. We are also grateful for the hospitality of David Wessel and the Center for New Music and Audio Technologies, University of California, Berkeley, during the final stage of preparation.

REFERENCES

Alajouanine, T. (1948). Aphasia and artistic realization. *Brain, 71,* 229–241.

Alajouanine, T., & Lhermitte, F. (1961). *Les désorganizations des activités expressives du langage dans l'aphasie.* Paper presented at the VIIth International Congress of Neurology, Rome.

Alajouanine, T., & Lhermitte, F. (1964). Aphasia and physiology of speech. In D. R. Rioch & E. A. Weinstein (Eds.), *Proceedings of the Association for Research in Nervous and Mental Disorders: Vol. 42. Disorders of communication* (pp. 204–219). Baltimore, MD: Williams & Wilkins.

Albert, M. L., & Bear, D. (1974). Time to understand: A case study of word deafness with reference to the role of time in auditory comprehension. *Brain, 97,* 373–384.

Albert, M. L., Sparks, R., von Stockert, T., & Sax, D. (1972). A case study of auditory agnosia: Linguistic and non-linguistic processing. *Cortex, 8,* 427–433.

Arnold, G. (1943). Cortikale Hörstorung bei Leitungsaphasie. *Monatschrift Ohrenheilkunde. 79/80,* 11–27.

Assal, G. (1973). Aphasie de Wernicke sans amusie chez un pianiste. *Revue Neurologique, 129,* 251–255.

Assal, G., & Buttet, J. (1990). Agraphie et conservation de l'écriture musicale chez un professeur de piano bilingue. *Revue Neurologique, 139,* 569–574.

Auerbach, S. H., Allard, T., Naeser, M., Alexander, M. P., & Albert, M. L. (1982). Pure word deafness: Analysis of a case with bilateral lesions and a defect at the prephonemic level. *Brain, 105,* 271–300.

Bach, J. S. (1974). *Das Wohltemperierte Klavier: Vol. II. Urtext* (O. Irmer, Ed.). Munich: G. Henle Verlag. (Original work published 1738)

Bachman, D. L., & Albert, M. L. (1988). Auditory comprehension in aphasia. In F. Boller & J. Grafman (Eds.), *Handbook of neuropsychology* (Vol. 1, pp. 281–306). New York: Elsevier.

Baddeley, A. (1992). Working memory. *Science, 255,* 556–559.

Baddeley, A. D., & Hitch, G. (1974). Working memory. In G. H. Bower (Ed.), *The psychology of learning and motivation: Vol.8. Advances in research and theory* (pp. 47–89). New York: Academic Press.

Baker, E., Blumstein, S. E., & Goodglass, H. (1981). Interaction between phonological and semantic factors in auditory comprehension. *Neuropsychologia, 19,* 1–15.

Barbizet, J. (1972). Role de l'hémisphère droit dans les perceptions auditives. In J. Barbizet, M. Ben Hamida, & P. Duizabo (Eds.), *Le monde de l'hémiplégie gauche* (pp. 624–630). Paris: Masson.

Barbizet, J., Duizabo, P., Enos, G., & Fuchs, D. (1969). Reconnaissance de messages sonores: Bruits familiers et airs musicaux familiers lors de lésions cérébrales unilatérales. *Revue Neurologique, 121,* 624–630.

Barrett , A. M. (1910). A case of pure word-deafness with autopsy. *Journal of Nervous and Mental Disease, 37,* 73–92.

Basso, A., & Capitani, E. (1985). Spared musical abilities in a conductor with global aphasia and ideomotor apraxia. *Journal of Neurology, Neurosurgery, and Psychiatry, 48,* 407–412.

Basso, A., Casati, G., & Vignolo, L. A. (1977). Phonemic identification defect in aphasia. *Cortex, 13,* 84–95.

Beatty, W. W., Zavadil, K. D., Bailly, R. C., Rixen, G. J., Zavadil, L. E., Farnham, N., & Fisher, L. (1988). Preserved musical skill in a severely demented patient. *International Journal of Clinical Neuropsychology, 10,* 158–164.

Benton, A. L. (1977) The amusias. In M. Critchley & R. A. Henson (Eds.), *Music and the brain: Studies in the neurology of music* (pp. 378–397). Southampton, Great Britain: The Camelot Press Ltd.

Berlin, C. I., Chase, R. A., Dill, A., & Hagepanos, T. (1965). Auditory findings in patients with temporal lobectomies. *American Speech and Hearing Association, 7,* 386.

Bever, T. (1980). Broca and Lashley were right: Cerebral dominance is an accident of growth. In D. Caplan (Ed.), *Biological studies of mental processes* (pp. 186–230). Cambridge, MA: MIT Press.

Bever, T., & Chiarello, R. (1974). Cerebral dominance in musicians and non-musicians. *Science, 185,* 537–539.

Bharucha, J., & Krumhansl, C. L. (1983). The representation of harmonic structure in music: Hierarchies of stability as a function of context. *Cognition, 13,* 63–102.

Bharucha, J. J., & Stoeckig, K. (1986). Reaction time and musical expectancy: Priming of chords. *Journal of Experimental Psychology: Human Perception & Performance, 12,* 403–410.

Bharucha, J. J., & Stoeckig, K. (1987). Priming of chords: spreading activation or overlapping frequency spectra? *Perception & Psychophysics, 41,* 519–524.

Blumstein, S. E. (1973). *A phonological investigation of aphasic speech.* The Hague: Mouton.

Blumstein, S. E. (1978). The perception of speech in pathology and ontogeny. In A. Caramazza & E. B. Zurif (Eds.), *Language acquisition and language breakdown: Parallels and divergencies* (pp. 3–24). Baltimore, MD: Johns Hopkins University Press.

Bogen, J. & Gordon, H. W. (1971). Musical tests for functional lateralization with intracarotid amobarbital. *Nature, 230,* 524–525.

Borchgrevink, H. M. (1980). Cerebral lateralization of speech and singing after intracarotid Amytal injection. In M. Taylor Sarno & O. Hooks (Eds.), *Aphasia: Assessment and treatment* (pp. 186–191). Stockholm: Almqvist & Wiksell.

Borchgrevink, H. M. (1991). Prosody, musical rhythm, tone pitch and response initiation during Amytal hemisphere anaesthesia. In J. Sundberg, L. Nord, & R. Carlson (Eds.), *Music, language, speech and brain: Proceedings of an International Symposium at the Wenner-Gren Center, Stockholm, 1990* (pp. 327–343). Cambridge, England: Macmillan Press.

Botez, M. I., & Wertheim, N. (1959). Expressive aphasia and amusia. *Brain, 82,* 186–202.

Bouillaud, J. B. (1865). Sur la faculté du langage articulé. *Bulletin de l'Academie de Medicine, 30,* 752–768.

Branch, C., Milner, B., & Rasmussen, T. (1964). Intracarotid sodium Amytal for the lateralization of cerebral dominance: Observation in 123 patients. *Journal of Neurosurgery, 21,* 399–405.

Brazier, M. (1892). Du trouble des facultés musicales dans l'aphasie: Etude sur les représentations mentales des sons et des symboles musicaux. *Revue Philosophique, 34,* 337–368.

Brugge, J. F., & Reale, R. A. (1985). Auditory cortex. In A. Peters & E. G. Jones (Eds.), Cerebral cortex (Vol. 4 , pp. 229–271). New York and London: Plenum Press.

Bryden, M. P. (1988). An overview of the dichotic listening procedure and its relation to cerebral organization. In K. Hugdahl (Ed.), Handbook of dichotic listening: Theory, methods and research (pp. 1–43). London: John Wiley & Sons Ltd.

Buchman, A. S., Garron, D. C., Trost-Cardamone, J. E., Wichter, M. D., & Schwartz, M. (1986). Word deafness: one hundred years later. Journal of Neurology, Neurosurgery, and Psychiatry, 49, 489–499.

Burns, E. M., & Ward, W. D. (1973). Categorical perception of musical intervals. Journal of the Acoustical Society of America, 54, 596.

Celesia, G. G. (1976). Organization of auditory cortical areas in man. Brain, 99, 403–414.

Charness, N. (1976). Memory for chess positions: Resistance to interference. Journal of Experimental Psychology: Human Learning and Memory, 2, 641–653.

Charness, N. (1988). Expertise in chess, music, and physics: A cognitive perspective. In L. Obler & D. Fein (Eds.), The exceptional brain (pp. 399–425). New York: Guilford Press.

Chase, W. G., & Simon, H. A. (1973a). Perception in chess. Cognitive Psychology, 4, 55–81.

Chase, W. G. & Simon, H. A. (1973b). The mind's eye in chess. In W. G. Chase (Ed.), Visual information processing (pp. 215–281). New York: Academic Press.

Chavis, D., & Pandya, D. N. (1976). Further observations on corticofrontal pathways in the rhesus monkey. Brain Research, 117, 369–386.

Chocholle, R., Chedru, F., Botte, M. C., Chain, F., & Lhermitte, F. (1975). Etude psychoacoustique d'un cas de 'surdité corticale.' Neuropsychologia, 13, 163–172.

Chomsky, N. (1970). Remarks on nominalisation. In R. A. Jacobs & P. S. Rosenbaum (Eds.), Readings in English transformational grammar. City: Ginn and Company.

Cramer, K. (1891). Kur lehre der aphasie. Archiv für Psychiatrie und Nervenheilkunde, 22, 141–160.

Cranberg, L. D., & Albert, M. L. (1988). The chess mind. In L. Obler & D. Fein (Eds.), The exceptional brain (pp. 156–190). New York: Guilford Press.

Crowder, R. G., Serafine, M. L., & Repp, B. (1990). Physical interaction and association by contiguity in memory for the words and melodies of songs. Memory and Cognition, 18, 469–476.

Crystal, H., Grober, E., & Masur, D. (1989). Preservation of musical memory in Alzheimer's disease. Journal of Neurology, Neurosurgery, and Psychiatry, 52, 1415–1416.

Cuddy, L. L., & Badertscher, B. (1987). Recovery of the tonal hierarchy: Some comparisons across age and levels of musical experience. Perception & Psychophysics. 41, 609–620.

Dalessio, D. J. (1984). Maurice Ravel and Alzheimer's disease. Journal of the American Medical Society, 252, 3412–3413.

Déjèrine, J. (1892a). Sur la localisation de la cécité verbale avec intégrité de l'écriture spontanée et sous dictée; cécité verbale pure. Semaine Médicale, 12, 88–89.

Déjèrine, J. (1892b). Des différentes variétés de cécité verbale. Compte-Rendu des Séances et Mémoires de la Societé de Biologie, 27, 1–30.

Denes, G., & Semenza, C. (1975). Auditory modality-specific anomia: Evidence from a case of pure word deafness. Cortex, 11, 401–411.

Deutsch, D. (1970a). Tones and numbers: Specificity of interference in short-term memory. Science, 168, 1604–1605.

Deutsch, D. (1970b). An auditory illusion. Nature (London), 251, 307–309.

Deutsch, D. (1978). The psychology of music. In E. C. Carterette & M. P. Friedman (Eds.), Handbook of perception (Vol. X, pp.191–224). New York: Academic Press.

Divenyi, P. D., & Efron, R. (1979). Spectral versus temporal features in dichotic listening. Brain and Language, 7, 375–386.

Divenyi, P. D., & Robinson, A. J. (1989). Nonlinguistic auditory capabilities in aphasia. Brain and Language, 37, 290–326.

Dorgeuille, C. (1966). Introduction a l'etude des amusies. Thesis, Faculty of Medicine of the University of Paris, France.

Dowling, W. J. (1978). Scale and contour: two components of a theory of memory for melodies. *Psychological Review, 85,* 341–354.

Dowling, W. J., & Bartlett J. C. (1981). The importance of interval information in long-term memory for melodies. *Psychomusicology, 1,* 30–49.

Dowling, W. J., & Fujitani, D. S. (1971). Contour, interval, and pitch recognition in memory for melodies. *Journal of the Acoustical Society of America, 49,* 524–531.

Dupre, E., & Nathan, M. (1911). *Le langage musical: Etude médico-psychologique.* Paris: Alcan.

Edgren, J. G. (1895). Amusie (musikalische Aphasie). *Deutsche Zeitschrift für Nervenheilkunde, 6,* 1–64.

Efron, R. (1990). *The decline and fall of hemispheric specialization.* Hillsdale, NJ: Lawrence Erlbaum.

Eimas, P. D. (1974). Auditory and linguistic processing of cues for place of articulation by infants. *Perception & Psychophysics, 16,* 513–521.

Eimas, P. D., & Corbit, J. D. (1973). Selective adaptation of linguistic feature detectors. *Cognitive Psychology, 4,* 99–109.

Eimas, P. D., Signeland, E. R., Jusczyk, P., & Vigorito, J. (1971). Speech perception in infants. *Science, 171,* 303–306.

Elbert, T., Pantev, C., Wienbruch, C., Rockstroh, B., & Taub, E. (1995). Increased cortical representation of the fingers of the left hand in string players. *Science, 270,* 305–307.

Ericsson, A. K. (1985). Memory skill. *Canadian Journal of Psychology, 39,* 188–231.

Fasanaro, A. M., Spitaleri, D. L. A., & Valiani, R. (1990). Dissociation in musical reading: A musician affected by alexia without agraphia. *Music Perception, 7,* 259–272.

Feuchtwanger, E. (1930). *Amusie: Studien zur patologischen Psychologie der Akustischen Wahrnehmung und Vorstellung und ihrer Strukturgebiete besonders in Musik und Sprache.* Berlin: Julius Springer.

Finkelnburg, F. C. (1870). Aphasie. *Berliner Klinische Wochenschrift, 7,* 449–450.

Fitzpatrick, K. A., & Imig, T. J. (1982). Organization of auditory connections: The primate auditory cortex. In C. N. Woolsey (Ed.), *Cortical sensory organization: Vol. 3. Multiple auditory areas* (pp. 71–110). Clifton, NJ: Humana Press.

Fujii, T., Fukatsu, R., Watabe, S., Ohnuma, A., Teramura, T., Kimura, I., Saso, S., & Kogure, K. (1990). Auditory sound agnosia without aphasia following a right temporal lobe lesion. *Cortex, 26,* 263–268.

Gaede, S. E., Parsons, G. A., & Bertera, J. H. (1978). Hemispheric differences in musical perception: Aptitude vs. experiences. *Neuropsychologia, 16,* 369–373.

Galaburda, A., & Sanides, F. (1980). Cytoarchitectonic organization of the human auditory cortex. *The Journal of Comparative Neurology, 190,* 597–610.

Galaburda, A. M., & Pandya, D. N. (1983). The intrinsic architectonic and connectional organization of the superior temporal region of the rhesus monkey. *The Journal of Comparative Neurology, 221,* 169–184.

Gardner, H., Silverman, J., Denes, G., Semenza, C., & Rosenstiel, A. K. (1977). Sensitivity to musical denotation and connotation in organic patients. *Cortex, 13,* 242–256.

Geschwind, N. (1965). Disconnexion syndromes in animals and man: Part I. *Brain, 88,* 237–294.

Geschwind, N., Quadfasel, F., & Segarra, J. (1965). Isolation of the speech area. *Neuropsychologia, 6,* 327–340.

Goldman, P. S., Rosvold, H. E., Vest, B., & Galkin, T. W. (1971). Analysis of the delayed-alternation deficit produced by dorsolateral prefrontal lesions in the rhesus monkey. *Journal of Comparative and Physiological Psychology, 77,* 212–220.

Gordon, H. W., & Bellamy, K. (1991). Neurophysiology of brain function: An overview. In J. Sundberg, L. Nord, & R. Carlson (Eds.), *Music, language, speech and brain: Proceedings of an International Symposium at the Wenner-Gren Center, Stockholm, September 1990* (pp. 311–317). Cambridge, England: Macmillan Press.

Gordon, H. W., & Bogen, J. E. (1974). Hemispheric lateralization of singing after intracarotid sodium amylobarbitone. *Journal of Neurology, Neurosurgery, and Psychiatry, 37,* 727–738.

Gowers, W. R. (1875). On a case of simultaneous embolism of central retrieval and middle cerebral arteries. *Lancet, 2,* 794–796.

Grison, B. (1972). *Étude sur les alterations musicales an cours des lesions hémèspheriques.* Doctoral Thesis, University of Paris, Faculty of Medicine de Creteil.

Grossman, M., Shapiro, B. E., & Gardner, H. (1981). Dissociable musical processing strategies after localized brain damage. *Neuropsychologia, 19,* 425–433.

Halpern, A. (1988). Mental scanning in auditory imagery for songs. *Journal of Experimental Psychology: Learning, Memory, and Cognition, 14,* 434–443.

Head, H. (1926). *Aphasia and kindred disorders of speech.* London and New York: Cambridge University Press.

Hemphill, R. E., & Stengel, E. (1940). A study on pure word-deafness. *Journal of Neurology and Psychiatry, 3,* 251–262.

Henschen, S. E. (1920). *Klinische und anatomische Beiträge zur Pathologie des Gehirns: Teil 5. Uber Aphasie, Amusie und Akalkulie.* Stockholm: Nordiska Bokhandeln.

Henschen, S. E. (1926). On the function of the right hemisphere of the brain in relation to the left in speech, music and calculation. *Brain, 49,* 110–123.

Jackson, J. H. (1915). On the duality of the brain. *Brain, 38,* 80–103. (Original work published 1874)

Jacobson, S., & Trojanowski, J. Q. (1977). Prefrontal granular cortex of the rhesus monkey: I. Intrahemispheric cortical afferents. *Brain Research, 132,* 209–233.

James, W. (1890). *The principles of psychology.* New York: Henry Holt & Co.

Jellinek, A. (1933). Zur phänomenologie der Amusie (expressive amusie und aphasie eines Lautensängers). *Jahrbuch für Psychiatrie und Neurologie, 50,* 115–141.

Jellinek, A. (1956). Amusia: On the phenomenology and investigation of central disorders of the musical functions. *Folia Phoniatr. (Basel), 8,* 124–149.

Jerger, J. Loverling, L., & Wertz, M. (1972). Auditory disorder following bilateral temporal lobe insult: report of a case. *Journal of Speech and Hearing Disorders, 37,* 523–535.

Jerger, J., Weikers, N. J., Sharbrough, F. W., & Jerger, S. (1969). Bilateral lesions of the temporal lobe: a case study. *Acta Oto-laryngologica, Supplementum 258.*

Jones, E. G., & Powell, T. P .S. (1970). An anatomical study of converging sensory pathways within the cerebral cortex of the monkey. *Brain, 93,* 793–820.

Jossman, P. (1926). Motorische Amusie (Demonstration). Berliner Gesellschaft für Psychiatrie und Nervenkrankheiten, Mai, 1926, Zentralblatt für der ges. *Neurologie ind Psychiatrie, 44,* 260.

Jossman, P. (1927). Die Beziehungen der motorischen Amusie zu den apraktischen Störungen. *Monatsschrifte für Psychiatrie und Neurologie, 63,* 239–274.

Judd, T., Gardner, H., & Geschwind, N. (1983). Alexia without agraphia in a composer. *Brain, 106,* 435–457.

Karni, A., Meyer, G., Jezzard, P., Adams, M., Turner, R., & Ungerleider, L. (1995). Functional MRI evidence for adult motor cortex plasticity during motor skill learning. *Nature, 377,* 155–158.

Kimura, D. (1967). Functional asymmetry of the brain in dichotic listening. *Cortex, 3,* 163–178.

Kinsella, G., Prior, M. R., & Murray, G. (1988). Singing ability after right and left sided brain damage. *Cortex, 24,* 165–169.

Klein, R. & Harper, J. (1956). The problem of agnosia in the light of a case of pure word deafness. *Journal of Mental Sciences, 102,* 112–120.

Kleist, K. (1928). Gehirnpatologische und lokalisatorische Ergenbisse über Hörstörungen, Geräuschtaubheiten und Amusien. *Monatsschrifte für Psychiatrie und Neurologie, 68,* 853–860.

Kleist, K. (1934). *Gehirnpathologie.* Leipzig: Johann Ambrosius Barth.

Kleist, K. (1962). *Sensory aphasia and amusia: The myeloarchitectonic basis.* New York: Pergamon Press.

Knoblauch, A. (1888). Ueber Stuorungen der musikalischen Leistungsfähigkeit infolge von Gehirnläsionen. *Deutsches Archiv für Klinische Medizin, 43,* 331–352.

Kogerer, H. (1924). Worttaubheit, Melodientaubheit, Gebärdenagnosie. *Zeitschrift für Neurologie und Psychiatrie, 92,* 469–483.

Kohl, G. F., & Tschabitscher, H. (1952). Über einen Fall von Amusie. *Wiener Zeitschrift für Nerven-heilkunde, 6,* 219–230.

Krumhansl, C. L. (1990). *Cognitive foundations of musical pitch.* New York and Oxford: Oxford University Press.

Krumhansl, C. L., & Kessler, E. J. (1982). Tracing the dynamic changes in perceived tonal organization in a spatial representation of musical keys. *Psychological Review, 89,* 334–368.

Krumhansl, C. L., Bharucha, J., & Castellano, M. A. (1982). Key distance effects on perceived harmonic structure in music. *Perception & Psychophysics, 32,* 96–108.

Krumhansl, C. L., & Shepard, R. N. (1979). Quantification of the hierarchy of tonal functions within a diatonic context. *Journal of Experimental Psychology: Human Perception and Performance, 5,* 579–594.

Laguitton, V., Demany, L., Semal, C., & Liegeois-Chauvel, C. (1998). Pitch perception: a difference between right- and left-handed listeners. *Neuropsychologia, 36,* 201–207.

Laignel-Lavastine, M. M., & Alajouanine, T. (1921). Un cas d'agnosie auditive. *Revue Neurologique, 37,* 194–198.

Lauter, J. L., Hersovitch, P., Formby, C., & Raichle, M. E. (1985). Tonotopic organization in the human auditory cortex revealed by positron emission tomography. *Hearing Research, 20,* 199–205.

Lechevalier, B., Eustache, F., & Rossa, Y. (1985). *Les troubles de la perception de la musique d'origine neurologique.* Paris: Masson.

Lechevalier, B., Rossa, Y., Eustache, F., Schupp, C., Boner, L., & Bazin, C. (1984). Un cas de surdité corticale épargnant en paretie la musique. *Revue Neurologique. 140,* 1190–201.

Lichtheim, M. L. (1885). On aphasia. *Brain, 7,* 433–484.

Liégeois-Chauvel, C., Musolino, A., & Chauvel, P. (1991). Localization of the primary auditory area in man. *Brain, 114,* 139–153.

Liégois-Chauvel, C., Musolino, A., Badier, J. M., Marquis P., & Chauvel, P. (1994). Evoked potentials recorded from the auditory cortex in man: evaluation and topography of the middle latency components. *Electroencephalography and Clinical Neurophysiology, 92,* 204–214.

Locke, S., & Kellar, L. (1973). Categorical perception in a non-linguistic mode. *Cortex, 9,* 353–367.

Luria, A. R., Tsvetkova, L. S., & Futer, D. S. (1965). Aphasia in a composer. *Journal of Neurological Science, 2,* 288–292.

Marin, O. S. M. (1976). Neurobiology of language: An overview. *Annals of the New York Academy of Sciences, 280,* 900–912.

Marin, O. S. M. (1980). CAT scans of five deep dyslexic patients: Appendix 1. In M. Coltheart, K. E., Patterson, & J. C. Marshall (Eds.), *Deep dyslexia* (pp. 407–433). London: Routledge.

Marin, O. S. M. (1987). Dementia and visual agnosia. In G. Humphreys & J. Riddoch (Eds.), *Visual object processing: A cognitive neuropsychological approach* (pp. 261–280). London: Lawrence Erlbaum.

Marin, O. S. M (1989). Neuropsychology, mental cognitive models and music processing. [Proceedings from the Symposium on Music and the Cognitive Sciences, 1988, Paris, France.] *Contemporary Music Review, 4,* 255–263.

Marin, O. S. M., & Barnes, S. (1985). *Acceptability of chord sequences as functions of their tonal relations.* Paper presented at the Fifth Workshop on the Physical and Neuropsychological Foundations of Music, Ossiach, Austria.

Marin, O. S. M., & Gordon, B. (1979a). Neuropsychologic aspects of aphasia. In H. R. Tyler & D. M. Dawson (Eds.), *Current neurology* (Vol. 2, pp. 305–343). Boston: Houghton Mifflin.

Marin, O. S. M., & Gordon, B. (1979b). The production of language and speech from a clinical neuropsychological perspective. In G. E. Stelmach & J. Requin (Eds.), *Tutorials in motor behavior. NATO Advanced Study Institute of Motor Learning and Control, June 1979, Sénanque, France* (pp. 623–633). Amsterdam: North Holland Publishers.

Marin, O. S. M., Schwartz, M. F., & Saffran, E. (1979). Origins and distribution of language. In M. S. Gazzaniga (Ed.). *Handbook of behavioral neurobiology: Vol. 2. Neuropsychology* (pp. 179–214). New York: Plenum Press.

Marler, P. (1976). An ethological theory of the origin of vocal learning. *Annals of the New York Academy of Sciences, 280,* 386–395.

Mazzucchi, A., Marchini, C., Budai, R., & Parma, M. (1982). A case of receptive amusia with prominent timbre perception defect. *Journal of Neurology, Neurosurgery, and Psychiatry, 45,* 644–647.

McCarthy, R. A., & Warrington, E. K. (1990). *Cognitive neuropsychology.* San Diego: Academic Press.

Mendez, M., & Geehan, G. (1988). Cortical auditory disorders: clinical and psychoacoustic features. *Journal of Neurology, Neurosurgery and Psychiatry, 51,* 1–9.

Merzenich, M., & Schreiner, C. (1992). Mammalian auditory cortex: Some comparative observations. In D. Webster, R. Fay & A. Popper (Eds.), *The evolutionary biology of hearing* (pp. 673–690). New York: Springer–Verlag.

Metz-Lutz, M.-N., & Dahl, E. (1984). Analysis of word comprehension in a case of pure word deafness. *Brain and Language, 23,* 13–25.

Miller, C. L., & Morse, P. A. (1976). The heart of categorical speech discrimination in young infants. *Journal of Speech and Hearing Research, 19,* 578–589.

Milner, B. (1962). Lateralization effects in audition. In V. B. Mountcastle (Ed.), *Interhemispheric relations and cerebral dominance* (pp. 177–195). Baltimore: Johns Hopkins Press.

Milner, B., Kimura, D., & Taylor, L. B. (1965). *Nonverbal auditory learning after frontal or temporal lobectomy in man.* Paper presented at the Eastern Psychological Association Meeting, Atlantic City.

Minagawa, N., Nakagawa, M., & Kashu, K. (1987). The differences between musicians and non-musicians in the utilization of asymmetrical brain function during a melody recognition task. *Psychologia, 30,* 251–257.

Misch, W. (1928). Über corticale Taubheit. *Zeitschrift der Neurologie und Psychiatrie, 115,* 567–573.

Morel, A., Garraghty, P. E., & Kaas, J. H. (1993). Tonotopic organization, architectonic fields and connections of auditory cortex in macaque monkeys. *Journal of Comparative Neurology, 335,* 437–459.

Morse, P., & Snowden, C. (1975). An investigation of categorical speech discrimination by Rhesus monkeys. *Perception & Psychophysics, 17,* 9–16.

Neisser, V. (1967). *Cognitive psychology.* New York: Appleton.

Nielsen, J. M. (1962). Agnosias, apraxias, speech, and aphasia. In A. B. Baker (Ed.), *Clinical neurology* (Vol. 1, pp. 433–459). New York: Harper.

Nottebohm, F. A. (1975). A zoologist's view of some language phenomena with particular emphasis on vocal learning. In E. H. Lenneberg & E. Lenneberg (Eds.), *Foundations of language development* (Vol. 1, pp. 61–103). New York: Academic Press.

Nudo, R., Jenkins, W., Merzenich, M., Prejean, T., & Grenda, R. (1992). Neurophysiological correlates of hand preference in primary motor cortex of adult squirrel monkeys. *Journal of Neuroscience, 12,* 2918–2947.

Owen, A., Evans, A., & Petrides, M. (1996). Evidence for a two-stage model of spatial working memory processing within the lateral frontal cortex: a positron emission study. *Cerebral Cortex, 6,* 31–38.

Palmer, S. (1977). Hierarchical structures in perceptual representation. *Cognitive Psychology, 9,* 441–474.

Pandya, D. N., Rosene, D. L., & Doolittle, A. M. (1994). Corticothalamic connections of auditory-related areas of the temporal lobe in the Rhesus monkey. *Journal of Comparative Neurology, 345,* 447–471.

Pandya, D. N., & Sanides, F. (1973). Architectonic parcellation of the temporal operculum in rhesus monkey and its projection pattern. *Zeitschrift fur Anatomie Entwicklung-Gesch., 139,* 127–161.

Pantev, C., Oostenveld, R., Engelien, A., Ross, B., Roberts, L., & Hoke, M. (1998). Increased auditory cortical representation in musicians. *Science, 392,* 811–814.

Parncutt, R. (1988). Revision of Terhardt's psychoacoustical model of the root(s) of a musical chord. *Music Perception, 6,* 65–93.

Patel, A., Peretz, I., Tramo, M., & Labreque, R. (1998). Processing prosodic and musical patterns: a neuropsychological investigation. *Brain and Language, 61,* 123–144.

Penfield, W., & Jasper, H. (1954). *Epilepsy and the functional anatomy of the human brain.* Boston: Little, Brown, & Co.

Penfield, W., & Perot, P. (1963). The brain's record of auditory and visual experience: A final summary and discussion. *Brain, 86,* 595–696.

Penhune, V. B., Zatorre, R. J., & Evans, A. C. (1995). Neural systems underlying temporal perception and timed motor response. *Neuroimage, 2,* S314.

Penhune, V. B., Zatorre, R. J., MacDonald, J. D., & Evans, A. C. (1996). Interhemispheric anatomical differences in human primary auditory cortex: Probabilistic mapping and volume measurement from magnetic resonance scans. *Cerebral Cortex, 6,* 661–672.

Peretz, I. (1987). Shifting ear differences in melody comparison through transposition. *Cortex, 23,* 317–323.

Peretz, I. (1990). Processing of local and global information in unilateral brain-damaged patients. *Brain, 113,* 1185–1205.

Peretz, I. (1993a). Auditory atonalia for melodies. *Cognitive Neuropsychology, 10,* 21–56.

Peretz, I. (1993b). Auditory agnosia: a functional analysis. In S. McAdams & E. Bigand (Eds.), *Thinking in sound: The cognitive psychology of human audition* (pp. 199–230). Oxford: Clarendon Press.

Peretz, I. (1996). Can we lose memories for music? The case of music agnosia in a nonmusician. *Journal of Cognitive Neuroscience, 8,* 481–496.

Peretz, I., Babaï, M., Lussier, I., Hebert, S., & Gagnon, L. (1995). Corpus d'extraits musicaux: Indices quant a la familiarité, á l'âge d'aquisition et aux évocations verbales. *Canadian Journal of Experimental Psychology, 49,* 211–239

Peretz, I., & Kolinsky, R. (1993). Boundaries of separability between melody and rhythm in music discrimination: A neuropsychological perspective. *Quarterly Journal of Experimental Psychology, 46A,* 301–325.

Peretz, I., Kolinsky, R., Tramo, M., Labreque, R., Hublet, C., Demeurisse, G., & Belleville, S. (1994). Functional dissociations following bilateral lesions of auditory cortex. *Brain, 177,* 1283–1301.

Peretz, I., & Morais, J. (1980). Modes of processing melodies and ear asymmetry in non-musicians. *Neuropsychologia, 18,* 477–489.

Peretz, I., & Morais, J. (1983). Task determinants of ear differences in melody processing. *Brain and Cognition, 2,* 313–330.

Peretz, I., & Morais, J. (1987). Analytic processing in the classification of melodies as same or different. *Neuropsychologia, 25,* 645–652.

Peretz, I., & Morais, J. (1988). Determinants of laterality for music: towards an information processing account. In K. Hugdahl (Ed.), *Handbook of dichotic listening: Theory, methods and research* (pp. 323–358). London: John Wiley & Sons Ltd.

Peretz, I. & Morais, J. (1993). Specificity for music. In. F. Boller & J. Grafman (Eds.), *Handbook of neuropsychology* (Vol. 8, pp. 373–390). New York: Elsevier Science Publishers B.V.

Peretz, I., Morais, J., & Bertelson, P. (1987). Shifting ear differences in melody recognition through strategy inducement. *Brain & Cognition, 6,* 202–215.

Perry, D. W. (1990). Monaural ear differences for melody recall. *Journal of the Acoustical Society of America, 88,* S90.

Perry, D. W. (1991). Ear and hemisphere differences for melody recall. *Dissertation Abstracts International, 52,* 552B. (University Microfilms No. 91–17914)

Perry, D. W. (1993). A cognitive neuropsychological analysis of melody recall. [Proceedings of the Second Symposium on Music and the Cognitive Sciences, Cambridge University, 1990.] *Contemporary Music Review, 9,* 97–111.

Perry, D. W. (1994, July). *The role of imagined singing in auditory-tonal working memory.* Paper presented at Mapping cognition in time and space: Combining functional imaging with MEG and EEG, Magdeburg, Germany.

Perry, D. W. (1996). Co-variation of CBF during singing with vocal fundamental frequency. *Neuroimage, 3,* S315.

Perry, D. W., Alivisatos, B., Evans, A. C., Meyer, E., Petrides, M., & Zatorre, R. J. (1993a). Neural network supporting auditory-vocal integration in singing. *Journal of the Acoustical Society of America, 93,* 2403–2404.

Perry, D. W., & Marin, O. S. M. (1990). Pitch salience and generative harmonic resolution of major triad inversions. *Journal of the Acoustical Society of America, 88,* S91.

Perry, D. W., Marin, O. S. M., & Smith, S. (1993). Visual functions in posterior dementia of the Alzheimer's type: a longitudinal case study. *Annals of Neurology, 34,* 295.

Perry, D. W., Petrides, M., Alivisatos, B., Zatorre, R. J., Evans, A. C., & Meyer, E. (1993b). Functional activation of human frontal cortex during tonal working memory tasks. *Society of Neuroscience Abstracts, 19,* 843.

Perry, D. W., Petrides, M., Zatorre, R. J., & Evans, A. C. (1994). Increases in CBF within frontal and temporal cortex during perceived, imaged, and sung musical pitch intervals. *Society of Neuroscience Abstracts, 20,* 435.

Perry, D. W., Zatorre, R. J., & Evans, A. C. (1995). Cortical control of vocal fundamental frequency during singing. *Society of Neuroscience Abstracts, 21,* 1763.

Perry, D. W., Zatorre, R. J., & Evans, A. C. (1996). Co-variation of CBF during singing with vocal fundamental frequency. [Second International Conference on Functional Mapping of the Human Brain, Boston.] *Neuroimage, 3,* S315.

Perry, D. W., Zatorre, R. J., Petrides, M., & Evans, A. C. (1995). Cortical activation during tonal working memory tasks in musicians and nonmusicians [First International Conference on Functional Mapping of the Human Brain, Paris.] *Human Brain Mapping, S1,* 247.

Petrides, M. (1987). Conditional learning and the primate frontal cortex. In E. Perecman (Ed.), *The frontal lobes revisited* (pp. 91–108). New York: The IRBN Press.

Petrides, M. (1989). Frontal lobes and memory. In F. Boller & J. Grafman (Eds.), *Handbook of neuropsychology* (Vol. 3, pp. 75–90). New York: Elsevier Science Publishers B. V. (Biomedical Division).

Petrides, M. (1991). Monitoring of selections of visual stimuli and the primate frontal cortex. *Proceedings of the Royal Society of London B, 246,* 293–298.

Petrides, M. (1994). Frontal lobes and working memory: evidence from investigations of the effects of cortical excisions in nonhuman primates. In F. Boller & J. Grafman (Eds.), *Handbook of neuropsychology* (Vol. 9, pp. 59–82). New York: Elsevier Science Publishers B. V.

Petrides, M. (1995a). Impairments on non-spatial self-ordered and externally ordered working memory tasks after lesions of the mid-dorsal part of the lateral frontal cortex in the monkey. *Journal of Neuroscience, 15,* 359–375.

Petrides, M. (1995b). Functional organization of the human frontal cortex for mnemonic processing: Evidence from neuroimaging studies. *Annals of the New York Academy of Sciences, 769,* 85–96.

Petrides, M. (1996). Specialized systems for the processing of mnemonic information within the primate frontal cortex. *Philosophical Transactions of the Royal Society of London, Series B, 351,* 1455–1462.

Petrides, M., Alivisatos, B., & Evans, A. C. (1995). Functional activation of the human ventrolateral frontal cortex during mnemonic retrieval of verbal information. *Proceedings of the National Academy of Sciences U S A, 92,* 5803–5807.

Petrides, M., Alivisatos, B, Meyer, E., & Evans, A. C. (1993a). Dissociation of human mid-dorsolateral from posterior dorsolateral frontal cortex in memory processing. *Proceedings of the National Academy of Sciences U S A, 90,* 873–877.

Petrides, M., Alivisatos, B., Meyer, E., Evans, A. C. (1993b). Functional activation of the human frontal cortex during the performance of verbal working memory tasks. *Proceedings of the National Academy of Sciences U S A, 90,* 878–882.

Petrides, M., & Milner, B. (1982). Deficits on subject-ordered tasks after frontal and temporal-lobe lesions in man. *Neuropsychologia, 20,* 249–262.

Petrides, M., & Pandya, D. N. (1988). Association fiber pathways to the frontal cortex from the superior temporal region in the rhesus monkey. *Journal of Comparative Neurology, 273,* 52–66.

Petrides, M., & Pandya, D. (1994). Comparative architectonic analysis of the human and the macaque frontal cortex. In F. Boller & J. Grafman (Eds.), *Handbook of neuropsychology* (Vol. 9, pp. 17–58). New York: Elsevier Science Publishers B. V.

Piazza, D. (1980). The influence of sex and handedness in the hemispheric specialization of verbal and nonverbal tasks. *Neuropsychologia, 18,* 163–176.

Piston, W. (1978). *Harmony* (2nd ed.). New York: Norton.

Pötzl O., & Uiberall, H. (1937). Zur Pathologie der Amusie. *Wiener Klinische Wochenschrift, 50,* 770–775.

Pötzl, O. (1939). Zur pathologie der amusie. *Zeitschrift für Neurologie und Psychiatrie, 165,* 187–194.

Praamstra, P., Hagoort, P., Maasen, B., & Crul, T. (1991). Word deafness and auditory cortical function. *Brain, 114,* 1197–1225.

Prior, M. P., Kinsella, G., & Giese, J. (1990). Assessment of musical processing in brain-damaged patients: implications for laterality of music. *Journal of Clinical and Experimental Neuropsychology, 12,* 301–312.

Proust, A. (1872). De l'aphasie. *Archives Génerales de Medicine, 1,* 147–166, 303–318, 653–685.

Rasmussen, T., & Milner, B. (1977). The role of early left-brain injury in determining lateralization of cerebral speech functions. *Annals of the New York Academy of Sciences, 299,* 355–369.

Rauschecker, J. P., Tian, B., & Hauser, M. (1995). Processing of complex sounds in the macaque nonprimary auditory cortex. *Science, 268,* 111–114.

Recanzone, G., Merzenich, M., Jenkins, W., Grajski, K., & Dinse, H. (1992). Topographic reorganization of the hand representation in cortical area 3b owl monkeys trained in a frequency-discrimination task. *Journal of Neurophysiology, 67,* 1031–1056.

Recanzone, G., Schreiner, C., & Merzenich, M. (1993). Plasticity in the frequency representation of primary auditory cortex following discrimination training in adult owl monkeys. *Journal of Neuroscience, 13,* 87–103.

Reinhold, M. (1948). A case of auditory agnosia. *Brain, 73,* 203–223.

Richter, H. (1957). Akustischer funktionswandel bei sprachtaubheit. *Archiv für Psychiatrie und Nervenkrankheiten vereinigt mit Zeitschrift fuer die Gesamte Neurologie und Psychiatrie, 196,* 99–113.

Roeltgen, D. P., & Heilman, K. H. (1984). Lexical agraphia. *Brain, 107,* 811–827.

Rogers, R. L., Papanicolaou, A. C., Baumann, S. B., Eisenberg, H. M., & Saydjari, C. (1990). Spatially distributed excitation patterns of auditory processing during contralateral and ipsilateral stimulation. *Journal of Cognitive Neuroscience, 2,* 44–50.

Rouiller, E. M., Simm, G. M., Villa A. E. P., de Ribaupierre, Y., & de Ribaupierre, F. (1991). Auditory corticocortical interconnections in the cat: evidence for parallel and hierarchical arrangement of the auditory cortical areas. *Experimental Brain Research, 86,* 483–505.

Rozin, P. (1976). The evolution of intelligence and access to the cognitive unconscious. *Progress in Psychobiology and Physiological Psychology, 6,* 245–280.

Saffran, E. M., Marin, O. S. M., & Yeni-Komshian, G. H. (1976). An analysis of speech perception in word deafness. *Brain and Language, 3,* 209–228.

Samson, S., & Zatorre, R. J. (1988). Melodic and harmonic discrimination following unilateral cerebral excision. *Brain and Cognition, 7,* 348–360.

Samson, S., & Zatorre, R. J. (1991a). Recognition memory for text and melody of songs after unilateral temporal lobe lesion: evidence for dual encoding. *Journal of Experimental Psychology: Learning, Memory, and Cognition, 17,* 793–804.

Samson, S., & Zatorre, R. J. (1991b). *Auditory learning abilities after unilateral frontal lobectomy.* Paper presented at Theoretical and Experimental Neuropsychology/Neuropsychologie Expérimentale et Théorique (TENNET), Montreal, Quebec, Canada, 1991.

Samson, S., & Zatorre, R. J. (1992). Learning and retention of melodic and verbal information after unilateral temporal lobectomy. *Neuropsychologia, 30,* 815–826.

Samson, S., & Zatorre, R. J. (1994a). Neuropsychologie de la musique: approche anatomo-fonctionnelle. In A. Zenatti (Ed.), *Psychologie de la musique* (pp. 291–316). Paris: Presses Universitaires de France.

Samson, S., & Zatorre, R. J. (1994b). Contributions of the right temporal lobe in musical timbre discrimination. *Neuropsychologia, 32,* 231–240.

Schlaug, G., Jäncke, L., Huang, Y., & Steinmetz, H. (1995). In vivo evidence of structural brain asymmetry in musicians. *Science, 267,* 699–701.

Schneider, G. E. (1969). Two visual systems. *Science, 163,* 895–902.

Schulhoff, C., & Goodglass, H. (1969). Dichotic listening, side of brain injury and cerebral dominance. *Neuropsychologia, 7,* 149–160.

Schuster, P. & Taterka, H. (1926). Beitrag zur Anatomie und Klinik der reinen Worttaubheit. *Zeitschrift für die gesamte Neurologie und Psychiatrie, 105,* 494–538.

Schwartz, J., & Tallal, P. (1980). Rate of acoustic change may underlie hemispheric specialization for speech perception. *Science, 207,* 1380–1381.

Schwartz, M. F., Marin, O. S. M., & Saffran, E. M. (1979). Dissociations of language functions in dementia: a case study. *Brain and Language, 7,* 277–306.

Serafine, M. L., Crowder, R. G., & Repp, B. H. (1984). Integration of melody and text in memory for songs. *Cognition, 16,* 285–303.

Sergent, J. (1993a). Mapping the musical brain. *Human Brain Mapping, 1,* 20–38.

Sergent, J. (1993b). Music, the brain, and Ravel. *Trends in Neuroscience, 16,* 168–172.

Sergent, J., Zuck, E., Terriah, S., & MacDonald, B. (1992). Distributed neural network underlying musical sight-reading and keyboard performance. *Science, 257,* 106–109.

Shallice, T., & Warrington, E. K. (1977). The possible role of selective attention in acquired dyslexia. *Neuropsychologia, 15,* 31–41.

Shankweiler, D. (1966a). Effects of temporal-lobe damage on perception of dichotically presented melodies. *Journal of Comparative and Physiological Psychology, 62,* 115–119.

Shankweiler, D. (1966b). *Defects in recognition and reproduction of familiar tunes after unilateral temporal lobectomy.* Paper presented at the meeting of the Eastern Psychological Association, New York.

Shankweiler, D., & Studdert-Kennedy, M. (1967). Identification of consonants and vowels presented to left and right ears. *Quarterly Journal of Experimental Psychology, 19,* 59–63.

Shapiro, B. E., Grossman, M., & Gardner, H. (1981). Selective processing deficits in brain damaged populations. *Neuropsychologia, 19,* 161–169.

Shepard, R. N. (1964). Circularity in judgements of relative pitch. *Journal of the Acoustical Society of America, 36,* 2346–2353.

Sidtis, J. (1980). On the nature of cortical function underlying right hemisphere auditory functions. *Neuropsychologia, 18,* 321–330.

Siegel, W., & Sopo, R. (1975). Tonal intervals are perceived categorically by musicians with relative pitch. *Journal of the Acoustical Society of America, 57,* 511.

Signoret, J., Van Eeckhout, P., Poncet, M., & Castaigne, P. (1987). Aphasi sans amusie chez un organiste aveugle: Alexie-agraphie verbale sans alexie-agraphie musicale en braille. *Revue Neurologique, 143,* 172–181.

Simon, H. A. (1967). The architecture of complexity. *Proceedings of the American Philosophical Society, 106,* 467–482.

Sinnott, J. M., Beecher, M. D., Moody, D. B., & Stebbins, W. C. (1976). Speech sound discrimination by monkeys and humans. *Journal of the Acoustical Society of America, 60,* 687–695.

Sloboda, J. A. (1985). *The musical mind: The cognitive psychology of music.* Oxford: Clarendon Press.

Sloboda, J. A. (1989). Music as a skill. In S. Nielzén & O. Olsson (Eds.), *Structure and perception of electroacoustic sound and music.* Amsterdam, New York, Oxford: Excerpta Medica.

Souques, A., & Baruk, H. (1930). Autopsie d'un cas d'amusie (avec aphasie) chez un professeur de piano. *Revue Neurologique, 37,* 545–556.

Spinnler, H., & Vignolo, R. A. (1966). Impaired recognition of meaningful sounds in aphasia. *Cortex, 2,* 337–348.

Spreen, O., Benton, A. L., & Fincham, R. W. (1965). Auditory agnosia without aphasia. *Archives of Neurology, 13,* 84–92

Stanzione, M., Grossi, D., & Roberto, L. (1990). Note-by-note music reading: A musician with letter-by-letter reading. *Music Perception, 7,* 273–284.

Steinke, W., Cuddy, L., & Peretz, I. (1994, July). Dissociation of music and cognitive abstraction abilities in normal and neurologically impaired subjects. Presented at the Third International Conference for Music Perception and Cognition, Liège, Belgium.

Studdert-Kennedy, M. (1974). The perception of speech. In T. Sebeok (Ed.), *Linguistics and adjacent arts and sciences: Vol. 12. Current trends in linguistics.* The Hague: Mouton.

Sudnow, D. (1978). *Ways of the hand.* Cambridge, MA: Harvard University Press.

Takahashi, N., Kawamura, M., Shinotou, H., Hirayama, K., Kaga, K., & Shindo, M. (1992). Pure word deafness due to left hemisphere damage. *Cortex, 28,* 295–303.

Talairach, J., & Tournoux, P. (1988). *Co-planar stereotactic atlas of the human brain.* New York: Thieme.

Tanaka, Y., Yamadori, A., & Mori, E. (1987). Pure word deafness following bilateral lesions: a psychophysical analysis. *Brain, 110,* 381–403.

Tanguay, P., Taub, J., Doubleday, C., & Clarkson, D. (1977). An interhemispheric comparison of auditory evoked responses to consonant-vowel stimuli. *Neuropsychologia, 15,* 123–131.

Terhardt, E. (1982). Die psychoakustichen Grundlagen der musikalischen Akkordgrundtöne und deren algorithmische Bestimmung. In C. Dahlhaus & M. Krause (Eds.), *Tiefenstruktur der Musik.* Berlin: Technical University of Berlin.

Tekman, H. G., & Bharucha, J. J. (1992). Timing course of chord priming. *Perception & Psychophysics, 51,* 33–39.

Tramo, M. J. & Bharucha, J. J. (1991). Musical priming by the right hemisphere post-callosotomy. *Neuropsychologia, 29,* 313–325.

Tramo, M. J., Bharucha, J., & Musiek, F. E. (1990). Music perception and cognition following bilateral lesions of auditory cortex. *Journal of Cognitive Neuroscience, 2,* 195–212.

Ustvedt, H. J. (1937). Ueber die Untersuchung der musikalischen Funktionede bei Patienten mit Gehirnleiden, besonders bei Patienten mit Aphasie. *Acta Medicalische Scandinavica Suppl., 86,* 1–737.

Van Hoesen, G., & Damasio, A. (1988). Neural correlates of cognitive impairment in Alzheimer's disease. In V. B. Mountcastle (Ed.), *Handbook of physiology: Vol. V. The nervous system* (pp. 871–898). City: Publisher.

Vignolo, L. (1969). Auditory agnosia: A review and report of recent evidence. In A. L. Benton (Ed.), *Contributions to clinical neuropsychology* (pp. 172–231). Chicago: Aldine Publishing Co.

Wada, J. & Rasmussen, T. (1970). Intracarotid injection of sodium Amytal for the lateralization of cerebral speech dominance. *Journal of Neurosurgery, 17,* 206–282.

Walthard, K. M. (1927). Bemerkungen zum Amusie-Problem. *Schweizer Archiv für Neurologie und Psychiatrie, 20,* 295–315.

Waters, R., & Wilson, W. (1976). Speech perception by Rhesus monkeys: The voicing distinction in synthesized labial and velar stop consonants. *Perception & Psychophysics, 19,* 285–289.

Weisenburg, T. H., & McBride, K. E. (1935). *Aphasia: A clinical and psychological study.* New York: The Commonwealth Fund.

Weiskrantz, L., Warrington, E. K., Sanders, M. D., & Marshall, J. (1974). Visual capacity in the hemianopic field following restricted occipital ablation. *Brain, 97,* 709–728.

Wertheim, N. (1963). Disturbances of the musical functions. In L. Halpern (Ed.), *Problems of dynamic neurology* (pp. 162–180). Jerusalem: Jerusalem Press.

Wertheim, N. (1969). The amusias. In P. J. Vinken & G. W. Bruyn (Eds.), *Handbook of clinical neurology* (Vol. 4, pp. 195–206). Amsterdam: North-Holland Publishers.

Wertheim, N. (1977). Is there an anatomical localization for musical faculties? In M. Critchley & R. A. Henson (Eds.), *Music and the brain* (pp. 282–297). Springfield, IL: Thomas.

Wertheim, N., & Botez, M. I. (1959). Plan d'investigation des fonctions musicales. *Éncephale, 48,* 246–254.

Wertheim, N., & Botez, M. I. (1961). Receptive amusia: A clinical analysis. *Brain, 84,* 19–30.

Yamadori, A., Osumi, S., Masuhara, S., & Okubo, M. (1977). Preservation of singing in Broca's aphasia. *Journal of Neurology, Neurosurgery, and Psychiatry, 40*, 221–224.

Yaqub, B. A., Gascon, G., Al-Nosha, M., & Whitaker, H. (1988). Pure word deafness (acquired verbal auditory agnosia) in an Arabic speaking patient. *Brain, 111*, 457–466.

Yates, A. J. (1963). Delayed auditory feedback. *Psychological Bulletin, 60*, 213–232.

Zatorre, R. J. (1979). Recognition of dichotic melodies by musicians and non-musicians. *Neuropsychologia, 17*, 607–617.

Zatorre, R. J. (1984). Musical perception and cerebral function: A critical review. *Music Perception, 2*, 196–221.

Zatorre, R. J. (1985a). Discrimination and recognition of tonal melodies after unilateral cerebral excisions. *Neuropsychologia, 23*, 31–41.

Zatorre, R. J. (1985b). *Identification of distorted melodies after unilateral temporal lobectomy.* Paper presented at the 13th annual meeting of the International Neuropsychological Society, San Diego, CA.

Zatorre, R. J. (1988). Pitch perception of complex tones and human temporal-lobe function. *Journal of the Acoustical Society of America, 84*, 566–572.

Zatorre, R. J. (1989a). Effects of neocortical excisions on musical processing. [Proceedings of the Symposium on Music and the Cognitive Sciences, 1988, Paris, France.] *Contemporary Music Review, 4*, 265–277.

Zatorre, R. J. (1989b). Intact absolute pitch ability after left temporal lobectomy. *Cortex, 25*, 567–580.

Zatorre, R. J., Evans, A. C., Meyer, E. (1994). Neural mechanisms underlying melodic perception and memory for pitch. *Journal of Neuroscience, 14*, 1908–1919.

Zatorre, R. J., Evans, A. C., Meyer, E., & Gjedde, A. (1992). Lateralization of phonetic and pitch discrimination in speech processing. *Science, 256*, 846–849.

Zatorre, R. J., & Halpern, A. R. (1993). Effect of unilateral temporal-lobe excision on perception and imagery of songs. *Neuropsychologia, 31*, 221–232.

Zatorre, R. J., Halpern, A., Perry, D. W., Meyer, E., & Evans, A. C. (1996). Hearing in the mind's ear: a PET investigation of musical imagery and perception. *Journal of Cognitive Neuroscience, 8*, 29–46.

Zatorre, R., Perry, D., Beckett, C., Westbury, C., & Evans, A. C. (1998). Functional anatomy of musical processing in listeners with absolute and relative pitch. *Proceedings of the National Academy of Sciences U S A, 95*, 3172–3177.

Zatorre, R. J., & Samson, S. (1991). Role of the right temporal neocortex in retention of pitch in auditory short-term memory. *Brain, 114*, 2403–2417.

18

COMPARATIVE MUSIC

PERCEPTION AND COGNITION

EDWARD C. CARTERETTE & ROGER A. KENDALL

Department of Psychology, and
Department of Ethnomusicology & Program in Systematic Musicology
University of California, Los Angeles
Los Angeles, California

I. INTRODUCTION AND OVERVIEW

A. ISSUES OF COMPARATIVE RESEARCH IN MUSIC PERCEPTION AND COGNITION

The study of non-Western music perception has had relatively little attention, although there are indications of increasing interest among scholars of diverse disciplines. In general, musicologists tend to focus on the "document" frame of reference, wherein generalizations about musical practice and development are made from cultural artifacts (notations) or on-site interviews. Musical anthropologists, as well as some ethnomusicologists, seem overly concerned with extramusical, contextual features. Psychologists, on the other hand, are interested in the perceptual and cognitive functions of music, often ignoring the subtleties of the musical frame. Rarely seen is an integrative approach, deriving musical questions from the cultural context and answering these with the rigor of empiricism.

One prejudice that abounds among musicians is that the study of art is special in that it deals with meanings sui generis that are not mappable to other domains. Parsons (1987) argues that:

> cognition is taken to be substitutable by some form of behavior, such as preferring, recognizing, categorizing, producing. But behaviors are not equivalent to understanding, and to look at behaviors is at best a roundabout way of finding out about understanding. Behaviors do not bear the essential mark of understanding, which is the giving of reasons (pp. xi–xii).

If understanding is not a behavior, and art is not the product of behavior, then what is? The "giving of reasons" is simply a different level of behavior; to take Parsons' view seriously would be to abandon research on musical art. We believe that the aesthetic response to music is behavior and is amenable to an empirical approach.[1]

Below, we delineate, analyze, and compare cross-cultural and cross-species music studies. These studies differentially emphasize notational, acoustical, and perceptual frames of reference and have been selected in some cases for their perceptual and cognitive implications. But comparisons within or across domains cannot be made until music itself is defined. Most definitions of music beg the question or depend on a host of other defining operations: Music is "the art of combining sounds of voice(s) or instrument(s) to achieve beauty of form and expression of emotion" says *The Oxford Concise Dictionary* (7th ed., 1982). According to Cook (1990) "Music is an interaction between sound and listener" (p. 11), which he amplifies by "There is, then, a widespread consensus of opinion among twentieth-century aestheticians and critics that listening to music is, or at any rate should be, a higher-order mental activity which combines sensory perception with a rational understanding based on some kind of knowledge of musical structure" (p. 21). Our own working definition is as follows: Music is temporally organized sound and silence that is areferentially communicative within a context. In contrast, speech is not music because it points outside itself. (See Kendall & Carterette, 1996, Section IX.) We deal here almost exclusively with music qua music (as intentionally organized sound). This is not to minimize the importance of studying contextual, cross-modal variables of music.

Where music is organized is, of course, a central issue, and it guides the structure of this chapter. The vast majority of the literature focuses on pitch organization, often independently of temporal patterning. Scales, tunings, and temperaments explore this organization most often in the vibrational frame. Timbre and spectra link the acoustical and perceptual domains. We consider pitch chains of small order, such as interval and octave theory, including perceptual effects. Tonality and tonal expectation are explored, followed by melody as pitch pattern and as pitch-time interaction. Rhythm, movement, and performance are considered, as well as studies of semantic and verbal attributes of music, including social psychological issues. At the very end, we review briefly the most elusive of abstractions, musical universals.

The linguist Hockett (1960) placed animals and humans on a scale of language according to a set of some 15 design features, such as graded versus discrete signals, arbitrary relation of sign and its meaning, indicating the future, ability to generate an unlimited sequence, and social transmissibility. A set of design features for scaling musicality will be hard to find for musical sounds, which do not intend or signify but communicate self-referentially only within a context.

In the case of humans, the studies we review deal with a very wide musical spectrum, ranging from complex African ensembles of instruments, singers and

---

[1]Ironically, Parsons infers the meanings of artworks from taped interviews of "people of all ages talking about paintings ... Much of my analysis is concerned to explicate a few basic ways of understanding paintings that underlie what is said about them" (p. 1).

dancers, to protomusical intervals of brief, synthesized tone pulses. There is generally little question of the musicality of the sounds or issues. In the case or animals or birds, the sounds are classified as "musical" by humans for the purpose of investigation. Birdsong may sound self-referentially musical to us, but to the bird may signify a territorial claim or a readiness to mate. It is exceedingly difficult to ask how birds perceive their own songs, whether birds can perceive musical universals, or whether birds have a sense of beauty. Thus more tractable problems are assayed, such as: How do the bird voice (syrinx) and bird brain produce sounds "with qualities that are intriguingly reminiscent in many respects of our own music"? ask Nowicki and Marler (1988, p. 423); Can a songbird perceive pitch relations, "a form of musical universal" as Hulse and Page (1988, p. 427) suggest from their experiments.

B. ETHNOMUSICOLOGY

Collections of phonograms (acoustical recordings on cylinders) first enabled the comparative side-by-side hearing of music of different cultures, whereupon the general distinctions between native and European music became evident. "The main difference is this: our music (since about A.D. 1600) is built on harmony, all other music on pure melody" (von Hornbostel, 1928, p. 34). In his discussion of African Negro music, von Hornbostel provides clear and cogent dictums for objective comparative music research. This prescient paper must be read by anyone interested in comparative music cognition.

We believe that ethnomusicology is driven by a paradox. On the one hand, its goal of describing and analyzing the different music systems of the world is built on the hope of inducing musical universals. On the other hand, whenever it appears that perceivers across musical cultures may possess universal characteristics, there is an effort to suppress the similarity in order to maintain the character and dignity of the given musical culture. At the anthropological, humanist end of the research spectrum, the use of experimental methods, explicit theories, and quantification by the psychomusicologist is seen as a misguided effort to reduce observations to statistical mappings onto the grids of rigid models whereupon beautiful, subtle phenomena disappear. At the more theoretical, experimental, rational end of the research spectrum, the observational, descriptive field methods of the cultural anthropologist and ethnomusicologist are seen as subjective, undisciplined efforts with findings that lack objectivity and are colored by the biases of the discipline and its methods and of the individual researcher. Our view is that there exists compelling evidence of the universality of sensory, perceptual, and cognitive processes, independently of the social or musical culture. There also exists equally compelling evidence that perceptual and cognitive processes are conditioned by social and cultural forces.

Unfortunately, many of the received notions about music, regardless of whether the music is Western or non-Western, are based on subjective analyses of recorded or dictated scores,[2] and serious experimental studies are rare. Although virtually all anthropologists and ethnomusicologists adjure us to consider the meaning, relationships, and applications of any perceptual, cognitive, or musical concept in the cultural system under study, they rarely ponder the implications of such an approach. They presume greater ecological validity when they lump together all of the interacting, confounding variables. It is impossible to escape the musical training of a lifetime, a training that interacts in unknown ways with the music under study. There is no canonical approach to knowledge that is free of language, culture, or experience. The best we can do is to make our assumptions, models, theories, and methods explicit and clear, design convergent experiments with an eye on the validity of interpreting outcomes, and keep levels of analysis and frames of reference sharply distinct. Anomalies, paradoxes, and biases will always remain, but a consistent application of such a rational approach offers an intellectual filter for separating truth from fancy.

Not all ethnomusicologists reject the methods of the experimental psychologist. Blacking's (1973) broad vision sets ethnomusicologists the task of identifying all processes that are relevant to explaining musical sound. Baily's (1988) view is that anthropological and psychological approaches to the study of musical cognition should be integrated, and "involves the application of theories and methods ultimately derived from experimental psychology" (p. 122).

Except for Dowling's (1982) treatment of the psychological reality of musical and psychophysical scales, the chapters in Falck and Rice's *Cross-Cultural Perspectives on Music* (1982) deal only implicitly with cognition, although Rahn (1982, pp. 38–49) suggests that recently music theorists have attempted to lay the foundations for *all* music. Examples are Yeston (1976) on the stratification of musical rhythms and Erickson (1975) on temporal, textural, and timbral aspects of music. Rahn submits that there are simple types of musical form (diversity, adjacency, extremity, sequence, and cardinality) that recur over and over in repertories of the world and through history. Whether or not these are ways of making or of interpreting music, Rahn suggests that the special qualities of the formal relationships "seem to point to some deep-seated cognitive or perceptual processes" (p. 47).

Virtually all methods known to anthropology, sociology, and psychology have been used in psychomusical research. These range from observation and questionnaires, through a vast array of experimental procedures, to signal-detection theory, mathematical modeling, and artificial intelligence. In cross-cultural research, the methods often must be adapted, as in going from one language to another, English to Balinese, say, or in going from a paper-and-pencil test to a tape-recorded oral response. Tasks may be culturally inappropriate. Contexts contrast starkly and range from the computer-controlled laboratory of the West to hand-held stimulus

---

[2]von Hornbostel (1928) remarked that "As material for study, phonograms are immensely superior to notations of melodies taken down from direct hearing; and it is inconceivable why again and again the inferior method should be used" (p. 34). He puts very nicely some of the problems associated with the use of notation or dictation in lieu of the musical material itself.

displays in an open-air classroom of Uganda. Language, methods, and contexts may interact or be inextricably confounded, which should be kept in mind when interpreting the results of cross-cultural work. We usually will single out blatant cases, but for the most part, caveat emptor!

Kippen (1987) offers an ethnomusicological approach to the analysis of musical cognition in the form of an expert system that simulates the knowledge of North Indian drummers, whose intuitions about musical structure are captured in a generative grammar. The musicians assess the ability of the grammar to generate correct pieces of music in feedback sessions. The resultant grammar is continually modified with the main aims of the research being to identify the cognitive patterns involved in the creation and interpretation of a particular musical system, in this case the *tabla*, a two-piece tuned drum set. According to Kippen, the method allows an accurate assimilation of the folk view of a musical system as well as a means of formalizing ethnomusicological description, and it has the merit of not eliciting analytic responses to musical stimuli, a culturally inappropriate task.

C. THE ORIGINS OF MUSIC AND EARLY MUSIC CULTURES

How early did music arise? Blacking (1988) favors a very early appearance of music in prehistory for *Homo sapiens sapiens* and of protomusic for *Homo erectus* and *Homo sapiens neanderthalensis*. He suggests that musical development should be concurrent with human evolution based on the evidence of the emergence of "musical" sounds and actions in the early ontogeny of infants. Some interesting data and arguments on the archaeology of early music cultures are collected in Hickman and Hughes (1988). There is archaeological evidence for the lithophonic use of large natural stones found in the prehistoric Canary Islands (Álvarez & Siemens, 1988), even sometimes in possible playing array. Cup-marked sounding stones in Sweden are dated to the late Stone Age and Bronze Age (Henschen-Nyman, 1988). Lithophones were probably used in rituals. Unequivocal data from the Indus valley civilization (ca. 2400–1700 B.C.) consist of many artifacts like vessel flutes and small clay rattles, whereas other artifacts and pictograms suggest the presence of chordophones, membranophones, and dance in the third millennium B.C. (Flora, 1988). There may be evidence for the existence in China of a flute made of drilled bone as early as 6000 B.C.), as well as a stone flute from about 1200 B.C., according to Zhenxiong, Quingyi, and Yuzhen (1995). These authors also suggest that by 500 B.C., the Chinese had a systematic classification ("Eight Tone") of musical instruments according to materials: Metal, stone, earth, leather, string, wood, gourd, and bamboo.

Artifacts of bone, horn, clay, and flint found in antique (5500 B.C. to 1050 A.D.) Scandinavian graves and settlements include a number of flutes and "possible flutes." Although these may have been used in rituals or protomusic, Lund (1988) suggests they were animal calls (e.g., otters, waterfowl), like those made by hunters in our own time, a view that he supports from playing on copies of the flutes.

II. PITCH

A. MUSICAL PITCH AND HUMAN HEARING

Since the advent of the pianoforte in the 18th century, the collection of Western musical pitches is about 87, from 32 Hz to about 4871 Hz, beyond which musically functional pitch is lost. The auditory system extracts pitch from a wide variety of sounds and noises, but only sounds with certain qualities are called musical, depending on the context, the source, and the culture. Anvils and sirens are generally not musically pitched but may be used to musical ends, as by Wagner or Varèse. Most truck horns are unmusical but some are made with partials an octave apart. A sung note is musical or not depending on the special training of the singer. Some of the problems of the musicality of pitch lie in the model of auditory processing that is assumed. The von Helmholtz-von Békésy class of model maps fundamental frequency or place on the basilar membrane onto a neural network, with processing completed at lower stages. On this view, the psychoacoustics of frequency discrimination can account for musical pitch perception, except for details. Evidence showing that pitch is induced when the fundamental is missing and from relations among partials (Houtsma & Goldstein, 1972; Schouten, 1940) leads to another model that adds periodicity pitch and allows for more complex neural processing at higher levels in the nervous systems. On this second, richer view, it is easier to understand auditory perception, particularly musical cognition. Experience, environment, and the cultural matrix can now be used rationally to explain many puzzles. For example: The inharmonic partials of bells and bars played a role in the origin of scales, tunings, and temperaments. Absolute pitch can be learned. The musical character of a culture is shaped and maintained by the time-variant spectra of its instruments and voices. Whereas some researchers regard these emergent properties as fortuitous, it is suggested by Kubik (1979) that a wide range of African music exploits the underlying perceptual principles with an intuitive sophistication. He argues from observation that inherent patterns always arise from a given structural arrangement of notes and that the perception of inherent patterns is not a cultural trait because both Europeans and West Africans perceive inherent patterns. Several salient inherent lines may be heard at the same time whereas other lines are discovered over time. Perceptual attention can be directed (Dowling, Lung, & Herrbold, 1987), so that not all persons hear the same inherent patterns on a given occasion. This is not to say that social forces or individual differences do not operate in the perception of inherent patterns.

A case in point is Deutsch's (1991) finding that individual listeners may disagree substantially on whether the tritone (successive half-octave related notes, using an inharmonic successive-octave spectrum) is heard as ascending or descending. Californian Americans tended to hear the pattern as descending, persons who grew up in southern England as ascending. Perception of the tritone paradox and the pitch range of the listener's spontaneous speaking voice were correlated, which "indicates strongly that the same culturally acquired representation of pitch classes influences both speech production and perception of this musical pattern" (p. 335). Deutsch (1994) showed that the strength of the relationship between pitch class and perceived height depended on the overall heights of the spectral envelopes under which the tones were generated, which bolstered her view that the tritone paradox is related to the processing of speech sounds.

B. INTERVALS, CONSONANCE, AND DISSONANCE

To what degree, if any, is musical consonance and dissonance fixed in perception by natural laws? Cazden (1945) argues that in musical harmony, the critical determinant of consonance or dissonance is expectation of movement, which is defined as the relation of resolution. But the resolution relation varies widely over the world's music, which can only be understood, Cazden avers, by accepting that "the resolution of intervals does not have a natural basis; it is a common response acquired by all individuals within a culture-area" (p. 5). Discrepancies of observed facts from a natural law hypothesis involve data arising from the actual conditions of musical usage, changes in attitudes toward consonance and dissonance in historical periods, and the use of consonance and dissonance in cultures other than Western. Processing of signals by the ear involves *limiting* rather than *determining* factors. To Cazden, "The difficulties in the study of consonance and dissonance dissolve as soon as we realize that these qualities are not inherent in perception as such, but are learned responses, adaptations to an existing pattern of the social group" (p. 11).

In tune with Cazden (1945), Lundin (1947) reviews the gist of myriad theories of consonance from Pythagoras up through Leibniz, Euler, Helmholtz, Stumpf, and into his own time and concludes that judging consonance and dissonance are "merely" behavioral responses that are determined by many conditions of a person's life history. In comparing Indian and Canadian undergraduates, Maher (1976) sought to quantify the "need for completion" (Jairazbhoy, 1971), which he assumes as a property of any interval but the unison, by means of a seven-point bipolar rating scale having end points restful and restless. Indians rated tape-recorded harmonium intervals 4+, 6–, and 7 as significantly more restless, than the restful 3 and 8 (octave), whereas Canadians rated the harmonium intervals 2 and 7 as significantly more restless than all other intervals except 4 and 7–, with 7– being significantly more restless than 6– and 6. Pearson correlation ($r = .13$) between Indian and Canadian subjects accounted for less than 2% of the variance. Siding with Cazden (1945) and Lundin (1947), Maher interprets his data as reflecting cultural differences. Maher and Jairazbhoy (1977) predicted that Indian subjects would give especially high restful ratings for final notes that gave symmetrical completion to a melodic figure in four conditions of symmetry: self, inverted, mirror-image, and inverted-mirror-image. Compared with ratings in a static context (Maher & Jairazbhoy, 1975), all symmetry-context restful ratings were statistically higher, except for mirror-image symmetry. The authors interpret the outcome as generally supportive of Jairazbhoy's "need for completion" hypothesis.

Musical acculturation was studied by Lynch, Eilers, Oller, and Urbano (1990), who tested how well Western 6-month-old infants and adults noticed mistunings in melodies based on native Western major, native Western minor, and nonnative Javanese *pélog* scales (see Figure 1; further discussion of these scales is in Section III,C). The results were that infants could equally well perceive native and nonnative scales, whereas adults generally perceived native rather than nonnative scales. "These findings suggest that infants are born with an equipotentiality for the perception of scales from a variety of cultures and that subsequent culturally specific experience substantially influences music perception" (p. 272).

Western musician and nonmusician children (10–13 years old) were tested in detection of mistunings in a melody that was based on Western major, Western minor, or Javanese *pélog* scales (Lynch & Eilers, 1991). Child musicians and

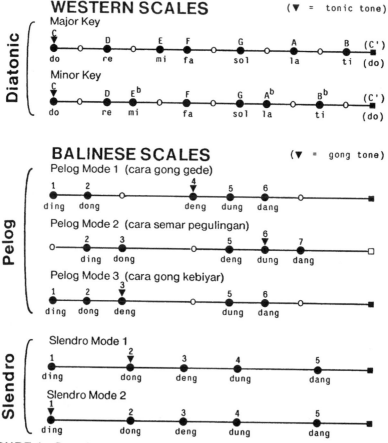

FIGURE 1   Comparison of Western and Balinese scales. Major and minor diatonic Western scales (top) are with Balinese scales. Three modes of the Balinese nonequipentatonic *pélog* scale (middle) and two modes of the equipentatonic *sléndro* scales (bottom) are shown. (Reprinted with permission from Kessler, Hansen, & Shepard, 1984, fig. 3, p. 139. ©1984 by The Regents of the University of California.)

nonmusicians performed at chance level, and no differently from each other, in the Javanese context. In the Western contexts, child musicians detected mistunings better than in the Javanese context, and better than the child nonmusicians, who did better than chance. Lynch and Eilers interpret their data as suggesting that informal musical acculturation leads to better perception of native than nonnative scales by 10–13 years of age, but that formal musical experience can facilitate the acculturation process.

The Western major, Western minor, and Javanese *pélog* scales figured again in a study by Lynch, Eilers, Oller, Urbano, and Wilson (1991). Adults who differed in musical sophistication listened to a melody that was based on interval patterns from Western and Javanese musical scales. Threshold judgments were obtained by an adaptive two-alternative forced-choice method. Judgments of mistunings by the less-sophisticated listeners were better for Western than for Javanese patterns, whereas the judgments of musicians did not differ between Western and Javanese patterns. The authors suggest that differences in judgments across scales are "accountable to acculturation" by listening exposure and musical sophistication gained from formal experience.

Butler and Daston (1968) obtained musical preference scales from groups of American and Japanese students on a consonance-dissonance dimension using recorded electronic spinet dyads. The students' scales had marked similarity to the judgments of musical experts, from which the authors argue that an objective preference scale may be substitutable for subjective, expert judgments, which require elaborate preparation. Also, whether or not subjects (both American and Japanese) had failed in a prior task to discriminate between tones of dyads, their preference scales correlated highly ($r = .90$). In comparing preferences for musical dyads, "there is virtually no difference between the rank orderings of the Western and Japanese students" (p. 139). The authors argue that their data are consistent with a biological basis of consonance but concede that preferences might be different when dyads were not isolated from their "functional" musical setting.

Hill, Kamenetsky, and Trehub (1996) using historical and empirical methods examined the relations among positive and negative texts, Ionian and Phrygian modes, as well as organ and vocal mediums in settings of a popular Christian melody of the baroque. Based on analyses of 51 representative settings, they showed that baroque composers tended to link Ionian settings of the melody to a salvation text and Phrygian settings to a condemnation text. Also, vocal pieces tended to be set in Ionian mode and organ pieces in Phrygian mode. From four rating experiments, they confirmed that contemporary adult and children listeners linked reward texts to the Ionian mode and punishment texts to the Phrygian mode.[3] The association of affect with scale type was also demonstrated by Kastner

[3]In the three experiments with adults, a 7-point rating scale was used. For children, a scale value was obtained from the placement of a toy rabbit on 1 of 7 squares. Five were blank but the left-most square contained a picture of a happy, smiling rabbit eating ice cream and the right-most square contained a picture of a sniffling, unhappy rabbit seated on a bed indoors. After hearing the music, the child placed a toy rabbit on either an end square or "somewhere in the middle if you think the song is only sort of about one of the stories" (p. 17). The children were told in the instructions that sometimes music tells stories.

and Crowder (1990). Using children 3–12 years old who heard harmonized and unharmonized major and minor tunes, they found that even the youngest children showed the conventional happy-sad association.

C. PIAGETIAN MUSIC CONSERVATION

There are many difficulties in translating Jean Piaget's notion of "conservation" (e.g., quantity is conserved if 500 ml of milk poured from a cylindrical glass into a conical glass is still perceived as 500 ml of milk) into music. Nonetheless, Hargreaves, Castell, and Crowther (1986) compared 6- and 8- year-olds in the United States with 6- and 8-year-olds in the United Kingdom on "pitch transposition" and "rhythmic inversion" music conservation tasks that used as stimuli either familiar nursery-rhyme tunes or unfamiliar statistical approximations to tunes. Significantly more conservation responses were produced by 8-year olds than by 6-year olds, and the responses were evoked much more by familiar than by unfamiliar music over all conditions. No cross-cultural differences or interactions were found. Though Hargreaves et al. interpret their results as broadly supportive of Piagetian theory, the strong effect of music types suggests that familiar and unfamiliar music may be processed differently, which makes difficulties for Piagetian conservation theory.

D. SCALES, TUNINGS, TEMPERAMENTS, AND OCTAVES

An enduring, useful musical scale ought to satisfy four conditions: (a) Successive, different pitches are easy to tell apart; (b) A tone of frequency f and tones $2f$ and $f/2$ seem very similar (the octave property); (c) The number of different pitches in the scale interval is about 7; (d) All scale intervals are constructible from a series of minimal intervals of equal size. The Western Equal Temperament is such a scale. Its tuning module is the semitone, which corresponds to a frequency difference of about 6%. Tuning systems have evolved to satisfy the perceptual needs of the listener, to keep the number of pitches small, and to make it easy to modulate among modes or keys. Rational scales like the Pythagorean satisfied mathematics but not listeners or players.

We relate musical and psychophysical scales following Dowling's (1982) very useful levels of abstraction: (1) The *psychophysical scale* maps pitches of tones onto physical frequencies, (2) The tonal material is the set of intervals at the disposal of a musical culture, (3) A *tuning system* (e.g., Javanese *sléndro* or *pélog*) is a selected subset of intervals for use in melodies and depends on instrument or genre, (4) *Mode* is the grand organization of intervals of a tuning system by (a) fixing tonality, (b), characteristic melodic patterns and (c) extramusical contexts. Mode embraces the musical constraints of a given culture, including orchestral combinations, arrangements, performances, differing distributions of pitch classes and other imposed formulaic and hierarchical structures, which elsewhere we called *chromals* (Carterette, Kendall, & DeVale, 1993).

Do musicians who have more categories in their musical pitch scales exhibit a finer discrimination than those who do not? North Indian musicians whose classical scale has (theoretically) 22 degrees per octave (*shrutis*) could not consistently identify these microtonal intervals, generally could not tell which of two intervals was the larger, and could do no better than identify an interval as one of the 12-note chromatic scale (Burns, 1974b). Sampat (1978) compared Western and Indian musicians on three tasks, interval identification, interval discrimination, and categorical perception of pitch. The main results were that Western and Indian musicians were not different from each other on these tasks. In particular, it had been expected that Indian musicians, "having more categories in their musical pitch scales would exhibit finer discrimination" (p. 33) in categorical perception of pitch. But the outcome was like that of Burns (1974b), Indian musicians could do no better than identify an interval as one of the notes of the 12-note chromatic scale.

Most of the world's cultures do not use equal temperament as the base of their tonal scale systems, although their scales are based on the octave, which leads to a logarithmic frequency scale. Generally, their interval sizes cannot be mapped onto our semitone. But, as with equal temperament, other scales have a variety of interval sizes, which allows for melodic variation and interest. The pentatonic scale of Chinese and Tibetan music (similar to the black notes of the piano) generates 8 semitone-like intervals, compared with 11 in Western equal temperament. Kubik (1979) reports that measurements he made in 1964 of xylophones and other instruments in southern Cameroon came close to an equiheptatonic division of the octave, 171.43 cents, to which heard intervals are "surprisingly close."

The nature of scales and tunings in oral cultures is hard to determine by ear, and the related abstract concepts are hard to put in words. Some headway was made in two studies on Central African music. In one, Arom and Fürniss (1993) studied the contrapuntal vocal polyphony of Aka Pygmies, which is based on a pentatonic scale. Aka listeners, after familiarity training with a synthesizer, accepted or rejected each of 10 different models of the Aka Pygmy scale, with the unexpected result that the 10 models were accepted as equivalent. By an experiment on recognition of melodic contours, the authors confirmed their hypothesis that order of succession of the degrees in a pentatonic scale prevails over interval widths. These outcomes led them to question the idea that a scale system is a mental grid with positions for each scale degree. In the other, contrasting study of xylophone music of Central Africa, Dehoux and Voisin (1993) found scale concepts that varied by ethnic groups, particularly with respect to the interaction of pitch and timbre. Xylophone bars were attached to synthesizer keys in a way that allowed the musicians to reject a candidate structure by retuning it. Because the xylophone's timbre influenced pitch, each theoretical tuning system was synthesized as a combination of three features: *pitch, roughness,* and *inharmonicity*.

Both Arom and Fürniss (1993) and Dehoux and Voisin (1993) attribute great power to the computational flexibility of the Yamaha DX7 IIFD synthesizer, which (a) is microtunable, (b) has many novel timbres, and (c) whose keys can be remapped onto tones, a very important feature because successive bars on Central African xylophones are not strictly ordered by increasing or decreasing frequency. These researchers are enamored of "interactive experimental method" but have little conception of experimental design and control.

III. PITCH SYSTEMS

A. MATHEMATICAL PROPERTIES OF WESTERN SCALES

The musical instruments of Western classical music produce mainly 12 distinct pitch classes to the octave, so that making music for a 12-fold octave division is easy, but virtually impossible for making n-fold music for integer n other than 12. What alternative microtonal systems of dividing the octave exist, asks Balzano (1980), what are their resources, and which offers the greatest yield? The deeper question is how to conceive of intervals. The received conception of an interval is put as a frequency ratio of powers of small integers, the resources of which can be measured by some goodness-of-fit criterion. Balzano argues for an alternative way of assaying the resources of a pitch system that treats individual intervals as trans-formations under a mathematical *group*: "Every equal-tempered system of n-fold octave division, as well as every system of n ratios that can be approximated by an equal-tempered system, possesses the structure of the so-called cyclic group of order n, C_n" (p. 66).[4]

The group C_{12} is the set $\{0_{12}, 1_{12}, , , 11_{12}\}$ and the operation of addition modulo 12, where 0_{12} is the identity element, the image of a set of transformations that leaves pitch class invariant. Our main interest is in three isomorphic representa-tions of C_{12} based on different generators. The first generator is (the minor second)

---

[4]Roughly, the group property belongs to a collection of symbols, operations, or things that can be combined in some way such that when combined the result still belongs to the collection. Such a collection of symbols is called a group if the following three axioms hold:

1. The collection must contain a symbol I that has no effect on any other symbol X when I is combined with X. Thus $I \cdot X = X \cdot I$.

2. Every symbol I has an inverse I^{-1} such that whatever that symbol does, its inverse undoes it.

3. The symbols must obey the Associative Law. Thus if P, Q, R are any symbols of the collection, then $(PQ)R$ must mean the same as $P(QR)$.

From these innocent few assumptions, an immense theory can be built.

If one is concerned mainly about group operations, Axiom 3 plays no role and the main ideas can be put succinctly: "A group of operations has the properties that any two operations combined are equivalent to an operation on the set; there is an operation, I, that consists of leaving things just as they are; and whatever you do, you can also undo" (Sawyer, 1955, p. 203).

We illustrate the cyclic group with n elements, C_n for a lesser n. The notion of cyclic symmetry can arise in games: A can beat B, B can beat C, and C can beat A. Let $\mathbf{w}$ denote (abc). For any function $f(a,b,c)$, then $\mathbf{w} \cdot f(a,b,c) = f(b,c,a)$. Applying $\mathbf{w}$ again, $\mathbf{w}^2 \cdot f(a,b,c) = f(b,c,a)$, then again, $\mathbf{w}^3 \cdot f(a,b,c) = f(a,b,c) = \mathbf{I}$, which brings us full circle. The operations $\mathbf{I}, \mathbf{w}, \mathbf{w}^2$ form a group known technically as "the cyclic group of order 3," denoted C_3. *Mutatis mutandis* for Balzano's C_{12} and C_n. For simplicity, we have ignored Balzano's arguments from the properties of C_∞, the (Abelian) cyclic group of infinite order.

1_{12}, which yields the tempered semitone space wherein each adjacent pair of points is connected by a semitone transformation. Twelve, but no smaller number, of iterations of a semitone gives the octave, or identity element. This is a "small" space that Balzano calls the *semitone group*, or *semitone space*. Because 12 is a composite number (not prime), other elements generate other groups; for instance, the period-6 elements 2 and 10 each generate C_6:{0,2,4,6,8,10}, a subgroup of C_{12} which corresponds to a whole-tone scale. Other elements generate other subgroups that correspond to such as the augmented-seventh chord, an augmented triad or even C_2:{0,6}, the tritone that generates only itself and the identity element.

A second representation of C_{12} generated by the elements 5 and 12 is an *automorphism* (an inverse mapping between a set and itself), which generates a space of fifths, C_{12}:{0,7,2,9,4,11,6, 1,8,3,10,5}. A third representation of C_{12} is isomorphic to the direct product of two of its subgroups, C_3 and C_4. Suppressing the mathematical details, it turns out that this third space holds "maximally compact, connected structures [which] are none other than the four basic triads" (p. 72). The diatonic scale is built up from adjoining triads to yield a figure that is convex, compact, and spans the space maximally. This unique pitch set, the diatonic scale, with the properties convexity, compactness, and maximal spansion, arises only for the set size $m = 7$. Finally, Balzano generalizes cyclic groups to n-fold systems with some interesting outcomes and discusses the computer realization of C_n pitch-set constraints.

Balzano concludes that these three isomorphic representations of C_{12} "bear striking parallels to the melodic, harmonic, and key relations as exhibited in tonal music, and the diatonic scale is revealed as a special subset of C_{12} that is in fact the simplest embodiment of the abstract relations given in two of the three representations" (p. 83). These representations are purely mathematical with no assumptions about ratios, albeit with some compelling interpretations for our classical 12-tone system. Pythagorean, just- and equal-temperament tuning systems are heard and composed for in much the same way, yet the tuning systems are all different. Hence, suggests Balzano, the ratios are not the basic descriptors and may even be inappropriate; perhaps all along, group-theoretic properties were the more perceptually important. He hastens to add that without ratios "we would have never discovered and refined the 12-fold system. But let us not confuse historical importance with perceptual importance" (p. 84). The task of relating this wealth of group-theoretic relations to composition and music perception we leave as an exercise to musicians and psychologists, but see the discussion on non-Western scales in the following sections.

B. INDIAN SCALES

Indian music theory has been widely studied, and the cultural roles of professional musicians has been well documented (Neuman, 1980/1990). Many have been fascinated by questions of whether microtonal scales in Indian music are functional. Clough, Douthett, Ramanathan, and Rowell (1993) sought to answer the questions, how and why did large numbers of unrelated musical cultures select similar heptatonic scales as their basic melodic resources? What similar aspects of diatonicism inhere in these scales? In particular (a) how did Indian scales move from 22 microtonal divisions (*srutis*) of the octave to a seven-degree diatonic set and (b) are there features of this latter set held in common with Western diatonic scales? We take (b) first. *Sa-grama* and *magrama*, the two basic early Indian heptatonic scales share a number of features with Western scales: (a) distinct step sizes that are consecutive integers, (b) dual tetrachords, (c) exactly one tritone, (d) distinct, consecutive, integer sizes of fifths, (e) a maximal number of consonant fifths, consistent with (d), and (f) first- or second-order *evenness*. (The feature of, evenness defines the degree to which generic intervals come in just one size, or in two consecutive sizes; on this feature the Western diatonic scale is maximally even vis à vis the 12-tone chromatic scale.)

These featural relations are formal. We should like to know what perceptual and cognitive forces drove the move from microtones to maxitones (question (b)). At middle C (261.63 Hz) 1, 2, and 4 *srutis* $\cong$ 8, 17, and 35 Hz, respectively, compared with semitone and whole tone $\cong$ 15 and 32 Hz, respectively, of the Western tempered scale. Clough et al. (1993), who are unable to discern any perceptually viable groupings and orderings of 2, 3, and 4 *srutis*, suggest that it is not known whether the *srutis* were of equal size and finally conclude that "this was not twenty-two-tone equal temperament. The best guess is that the *srutis* were determined on the basis of oral instruction"(p. 40). By the 13th century, it appears that *raga* notes came to be selected from a close approximation to 12-tone equal temperament while en route to a heptatonic scale with a diatonicism of the ancient scale having a real similarity to Western diatonicism. Ultimately, the authors suggest, people everywhere have been led by their musical instincts to order sounds into lean, economical pitch collections that (a) are balanced, (b) avoid large gaps, (c) can be manipulated without clouding the essential structure, (d) have a good mix of like and unlike intervals, and (e) have metastable midway intervals that fall decisively either to dissonance or consonance. Ultimately the scale must please the people. There is no magical power in the properties of the numerical pathways to the scale.

Jairazbhoy and Stone (1963/1976) studied intonation in present-day Indian classical music to the end of answering whether (a) the ancient concept of 22 *srutis* (microtones) is still in use, (b) whether there is variation in intervals used in any specific *rag*, and (c) whether the intervals are always the same over the performance of any one *rag*. Three different intervals of a single *rag*, *Yaman Kalyan*, from recorded performances by several different players (sitar, flute, voice), were extensively analyzed by electronic means. Conclusions were several: The notes in an octave form a series of 12 semitones of which 5, 6, or 7 plus passing tones are used in any one *rag*, which "does not necessarily imply that these semitones are equally tempered" (p. 32) but makes fanciful the idea of 22 *srutis*; intonation varies considerably from one player to another; intonation varies within each performance and between performers; any intonation within 25 or 30 cents either side of the tempered intonation can be acceptable; Jairazbhoy and Stone's evidence does not support a prevalent view that Indian musicians have far more acute perception of intonation nuances than have Western musicians. In an effort to identify the frequencies (in hertz) of *rag* scales, Rhagavendra Rao and Indira (1979) made extensive measurements of the notes (*svaras*) of the 23-string sruti vina, violin, and voice in performances of the *rag Sankarabharana*. They concluded that this *rag*'s scale "resembles" the Western major diatonic scale, with significant disagreements for *ga, dha* and *ni*, but agrees better with the equally tempered scale. (We calculate that, over the octave, except for a 5-Hz difference for *ni*, the absolute mean discrepancy is less than 0.3 Hz.)

C. SOUTH ASIAN SCALES

Gamelan instruments of Indonesia and Java are based on heptatonic, nonequal interval (*pélog*) and nearly equipentatonic (*sléndro*) scales. Eminent musicologist Jaap Kunst (1949) reported that all the pitches of *barang-alit sléndro* were exactly twice those of *barang*, and *bem-alit pélog*, were exactly twice *bem*. Kunst's results are "too good to be true" say Surjodiningrat, Sudarjana, and Susanto (1972), who report frequency measurements on 76 gamelans (37 *sléndro*, 39 *pélog*). From a set of 30 *sléndro* gamelans, only 5 show an exact octave, the other 25 have positive deviations from the octave. The authors say, "According to Javanese gamelan musicians, the positive octave deviations are made purposely, so that the sounds are more lively through interference. Thus the octaves in the gamelan are not exactly 1200 cents as is the case with western music" (p. 17). From frequency data in Surjodiningrat et al. (1972, table 1) on all instruments of the complete gamelan *Kyahi Madumurti*, Carterette et al. (1993) calculated octave ratios for 14 instruments (gender [3]), gambang [1], bonang [3], and saron [7]) to have a mean of 2.0228 with standard deviation of 0.0102, in short, a stretched octave. The measurements of Carterette et al. (1993) on the metallophone bars of UCLA's Javanese gamelan *Kyai Mendhung* yielded stretched octaves of 2.0211 and 2.0169 for a matched pair of *saron barung*, and 2.0189 for a *saron peking*.

D. SCALES AND THE STRETCHED OCTAVE

The preference for the logarithmic system with an octave base appears to have its roots in biology, because octaves and logarithmic intervals are virtually a cultural universal (Dowling & Harwood, 1986). Octave judgments of successive tones are made precisely everywhere, as is the transposition of logarithmic scale intervals. Even the slight stretching of the octave with higher frequencies is universal to musicians and nonmusicians, the (inferred) ratio for Westerners being 2.009:1 in middle range. It is well known that the tuning of piano strings is stretched. For a detailed discussion of the many theories of octave enlargement, see Burns and Ward (1982). Hartmann (1993) sought the origin of the "enlarged melodic" (stretched) octave in two theories, one a central template theory, the other a peripheral timing theory, concluding that each theory required revision in order to generate logically consistent predictions of stretching.

The octave of the Javanese gamelan has a greater mean stretch of about 2:023:1 but may be as high as 2:035:1 (Carterette & Kendall, 1994). Carterette and Kendall (1994), and Carterette (1994) conclude from model analyses that the Javanese people prefer considerable octave stretching in gamelan tunings (Figure 2) and that gamelan makers intentionally control both stretch and frequency differences of a few hertz in replicated instruments so that complex beating patterns are heard as a shimmering tonal fabric. These facts are consonant with Sundberg's (1991, pp. 103–105) suggestion that humans "crave" octave stretching in barber-shop quartets, string trios, violin, and piano. Keefe, Burns, and Nguyen (1991) report that the *dan tranh*, a Vietnamese 17-string zither which is tuned to a pentatonic

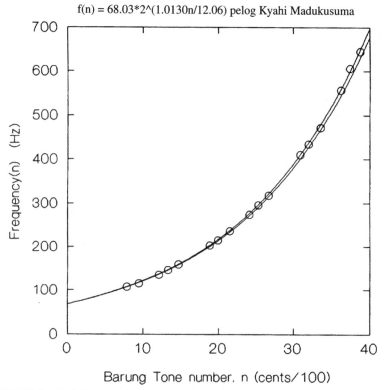

$$f(n) = 68.03*2^{\wedge}(1.0130n/12.06) \text{ pelog Kyahi Madukusuma}$$

Barung Tone number, n (cents/100)

FIGURE 2   The leftmost curve plots frequency (in hertz) as a function of tone number according to the model equation for *gènder barung* of *pélog* gamelan *K. Madukusuma*, shown at the top of the figure, where 68.03 is the intercept a and 1.0130 is the slope b. Actual data are shown as open circles. The gaps arise from the missing tone *pélog* in the *pélog* scale. The rightmost theoretical line has the equal-octave property, that is, the slope $b = 1.0$. (From Carterette & Kendall, 1994, figure 5, p. 66.)

modal scale, has an octave stretch of approximately 13 cents over three octaves. The octave stretch and tuning variability are smaller than comparable data obtained in Western and other music cultures.

Rao, Carterette, and Wu (1987) compared the musical scales of an ancient Chinese bronze bell ensemble (65 bells fabricated ca. 500 B.C., excavated in 1978 in Hubei Province) and the modern bamboo flute. Based on limited *pitch* data, they found some evidence that whereas the octave-ratio scale of a contemporary bamboo flute was about 2.030:1—a considerable stretching—the octave-ratio scale of an ancient (circa 500 B.C.) Chinese chime bell ensemble was, at about 1.976:1, somewhat compressed. This latter result should not to be taken seriously in view of the great antiquity of the bells. Fourier analyses showed that the flute was highly harmonic and the individual bells had inharmonic spectra, with all strike notes represented. The bell spectra measured may differ radically from the original spectra because of the chemical and physical changes in the bronze during 3 millennia of burial. Some limited measurements on this and another (ca 790–486 B.C., excavated in Shanxi Province) bell ensemble were reported by Schneider and Stoltz (1988). They conclude that although individual bells lack "inner harmony" and have ambiguous pitches, "the whole [Shanxi] set gives the impression that the chime has been tuned to a defined scale, i.e., to a tonal system" (p. 269) and melodies played on such chimes appear be in tune. Both Chinese and American listeners easily assigned pitches, and perceived the same pitch to a given tone, to a subset of 13 of the Hubei bells, said Rao et al. Some simple rules for associating pitch with the complex inharmonic partials of these bell spectra were induced by Carterette et al. (1993, p. 384).

Vetter (1989, p. 226) protests that Western logic and numerical analyses applied to Javanese tuning concepts add little to "our knowledge of the culturally significant factors that surround the art of tuning in Java." Vetter tells how a double gamelan (63 pieces) that he commissioned was made and tuned by ear from a cassette recording of the Radio Republic Indonesia Yogyakarta whose common tone (*tumbuk*), pitch 6, was accepted as the canonical pitch to replicate in the *sléndro* and *pélog* sets. All tuning was done by filing and cold hammering from this canon so as to achieve an overall tuning that was, to the tuner, "comfortable" for performance. In his tuning, he used no tone-measuring device, no instrument from another gamelan, and no sound recordings.

Although we agree with Vetter's suggestion of studying tuners in action, not just tunings, a quantitative study of gamelan tunings can be revealing. We argue for the utility of modeling the scales of actual instruments and ensembles. The right model could provide a good description of a given tuning system but also could serve as a basis for comparing different tunings on such aspects as aesthetics, perception, the design of scales and tunings with desired properties, and for research on scales and tunings generally. Based on the large set of frequency (hertz) measurements on Javanese gamelans made by Surjodiningrat et al. (1972), Carterette (1994) and Carterette and Kendall (1994) showed that an exponential model fit the data perfectly.

The optimal, exponential, model had the form $f(n) = a2^{(bn/m)}$, where f is frequency in hertz, the independent variable n is the value in cents of successive tones, m is the octave module in cents, and b is a magnification parameter. Of great interest is the value of b for octave doubling, when $a2^{(bn/m)} = 2a$. The intercept a is the starting tone (hertz) position, and the slope b is the "stretch" factor in 2^b. Relative to the module m, the scale is compressed, has module m, or is stretched, if $b < 1$, $b = 1$, or $b > 1$, respectively. (Surjodiningrat et al., 1972, found the average octave module m to be 1205 cents for *sléndro* and 1206 for *pélog* gamelans.) Virtually every instrument of four complete gamelans (2 *sléndro*, 2 *pélog*) was tuned to a stretched octave and each ensemble had its own, characteristic mean stretched octave. A similar outcome held for the *gènder barung* of 18 *sléndro* and 18 *pélog* gamelans. Mean octave stretch (2^{bm}) was relatively high at 2.022:1 and approached 2.0400:1 in a few cases. The exponential model captures not only the uniqueness of each instrument of any gamelan of either tuning through the three parameters, a, b, and m, but the idiomatic musical ear of each of the many tuners as well.

The equivalence of octave equivalence depends on a number of factors including context and method, for example, whether the task is to identify a tonal stimulus or to give a rating. Using similarity ratings, Kallman (1982), found that octave-equivalent tones are often not judged as perceptually very similar and even when judged more similar than tones that were not octave equivalents, similarity was very low, and far less than the similarity of unisons. Thus octave equivalence is generally a subtle effect. Preference for a stretched octave may reveal itself only as the end result of fabricating and tuning a complex generator like a set of piano strings or a gamelan ensemble.

Indian musicians show a subjective octave stretch of the same magnitude as that shown by Western musicians (Burns, 1974a), which is unlikely to be learned from certain physical properties of piano strings, because most of the instruments to which Indian musicians are exposed do not have these properties.

Chowning, Grey, Moorer, and Rush (1982) report that measurements made by them on the octaves of Balinese instruments varied between 1100 and 1300 cents and were not normally at 1200 cents. They state but do not elaborate that "The tuning system in Bali actually insures that octaves on many instruments will either be too large or too small" (p. 8). In a sequential tuning experiment using professional musicians, one of whom was Balinese, Chowning et al. (1982) examined four spectral conditions: (a) a pure-tone fundamental alone; (b) a fundamental and its second harmonic; (c) Balinese tones, i.e., fundamental and inharmonic partials; and (d) Balinese tones modified by the addition of the second harmonic of the fundamental. Conditions (b) and (d) tested the theory that listeners use energy near a ratio of 2.0 in tuning the octave. However, for all four conditions, the best perceptual octave for both Western and Balinese listeners was in a frequency ratio of exactly 2.0, an outcome that does not speak to the simultaneous tuning conditions of real music, but does imply that Balinese musicians could, if they wished, tune in perfect octaves of 1200 cents, as maintained also by Carterette and Kendall (1994).

Next, Chowning et al. (1982) studied inharmonic timbres and actual tunings of octaves in Balinese music with two hypotheses in mind: (a) The octave size for particular tones were fixed by the spectral components for those tones; and (b) The *absence* of energy at the second harmonic eliminated, in tuning, dissonance interactions with the fundamental. To test these hypotheses, real tones of the *gènder wayung* were digitally processed to retune their fundamental frequencies and spectral structure. Using a method of production, listeners chose between each of four retunings (labeled a–d) too complex to recount here, and the original, unprocessed sounds. In retunings (a) and (b), in which the original timbres of the Balinese instruments were kept, listeners preferred either original tunings or the perfect octaves. In retunings (c) and (d), a second harmonic was added to the original tuning, but upper partials were unchanged; in (c) the octave ratio was 2.0, whereas in (d), energy was added at the stretch (octave ratio > 2.0) of the original sound. In conditions (c) and (d), some listeners kept their preference for a particular size octave, but other listeners adjusted the preferred octave size so as to maximize consonance between the added partial and the fundamental of the upper tone. Thus some listeners preferred the perfect 2.0 octave ratio, some the stretched octave ratio.

Chowning et al. (1982) conclude that the inharmonic spectral structure of Indonesian sounds, which lack energy near the second harmonic, allows for nonstandard tuning practices and noninteger frequency ratios. It did not appear to them that the octave relation between the second and third partials ($2.7f_0$ and $5.4f_0$) operated. "Rather, Balinese music appears to be free to tune intervals as an active parameter of musical aesthetics, in contrast to Western music, precisely because there seems to be a lack of timbral determinism based on consonance and dissonance" (p. 10). This appears to be a case of having your hypothesis and eating it too. We note that the spectral content among gamelan bars is highly variable (Carterette et al., 1993), and frequently, bars are undercut, which results in the emphasis of integer multiples of the fundamental, as is the case with the marimba (Rossing, 1990, p. 262). None of the studies on stretched tuning has investigated the possibility that the stretch arises from psychophysiological demands rather than from acoustical beating.

IV. TONALITY

A. HIERARCHICAL STRUCTURES AND GEOMETRICAL MODELS

Music event hierarchies arise when a given piece of music is encoded as an episodic representation. Tonal hierarchies or schemas are abstractions of classes of event hierarchies that embody one's implicit knowledge of a culture's common musical structure, a kind of semantic representation. In Western music, the tonal hierarchies are the major and modes. In North Indian music, the tonal hierarchies of pitch class are embodied in 10 commonly used (of 32) *thats*, for which a classi-

fication system based on the underlying scale pattern was codified by N. A. Jairazbhoy (1971; Figure 3). A *rag*, derived from a *that*, adds its peculiar features. A
tonal schema may be evoked by activation of long-term memory or by the events
of a piece of music, for example by the relative durations of tones. Access to these
tonal hierarchies can be used by the native listener, but the nonnative listener must
rely on the statistics of event hierarchies in order to build up an appropriate hierarchy. For instance, unstable tones should be assimilated to the existing tonal
schema. Although Dowling (1984) found that Western subjects showed minimal
assimilation of North Indian music to their stable tonal schemas, Bharucha (1984)
found evidence that unstable tones were assimilated to tonal schemata.

The system of North Indian *rag* composition uses elements of improvisation
based on thematic material that expresses the specific affective nature, or *rasa*, of
each particular rag. Previous work (K. V. Vaughn, 1991) had shown that similarity

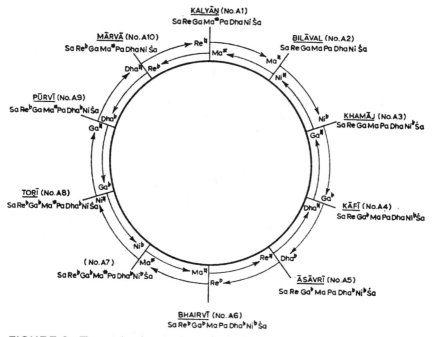

FIGURE 3   The note that changes when going from one scale to another is marked by an arrow.
The succession of changing notes in a clockwise direction form a circle of fourths; in counter-clock-
wise direction, a circle of fifths, similar to the Western circle of keys. Jairazbhoy argues that his model
has satisfying features and shows that 9 of the 10 *thats* in common use are logically connected in the
theory and practice of North Indian classical music. A further implication of the model, with some
substance in traditional practice, is that two cycles of *rags* associated with time of day repeat in each 24
hours. Thus (omitting scale A7 but including Bhairav *that*), Bhairav, Purvi, and Marva are most often
played before dawn or before dusk (4 to 7). Likewise Kalyan, Bilaval, and Khamaj are associated with
morning or evening (7 to 10), and Asavri, Bhairvi, and Tori with middle of the day or middle of the
night (10 to 4). These notions are discussed and illustrated in Jairazbhoy (1995, pp. 62–63). (Reprinted
with permission from N. A. Jairazbhoy, 1995.)

judgments among the 10 most commonly used modes (*Thats*) and *rags* based on those modes (Castellano, Bharucha & Krumhansl, 1984) are related to Jairaz-hboy's (1971) theoretical "Circle of *Thats*" (see Figure 3). K. V. Vaughn (1991, 1993) studied the perceptual relations among 10 scales and three tambura drone tunings, using multidimensional scaling (MDS) and cluster analysis of experimental data from both North Indian and Western musicians. She found that perceptual dimensions among the scale types in the absence of the drone is very close to the theoretical Circle of *Thats* (Figure 4). But in the presence of the *pa-sa* drone, the scales tend to cluster on the basis of common tones, placement of gaps, and tetrachord symmetry. Correlation between subjects was unrelated to the original culture but significantly related to the length of time spent studying this musical culture.

K. V. Vaughn and Carterette (1994) designed a new set of experiments aimed at discovering the degree to which modal character contributes to the perceptual relations among *rags*. Performances were recorded of the representative theme of 10 *rags* each based on a unique one of the 10 *That* groups, then played back to a group of highly trained professional Western musicians who made similarity judgments among all possible pairs of *rag* phrases. Scaling analyses of the judgments sug-

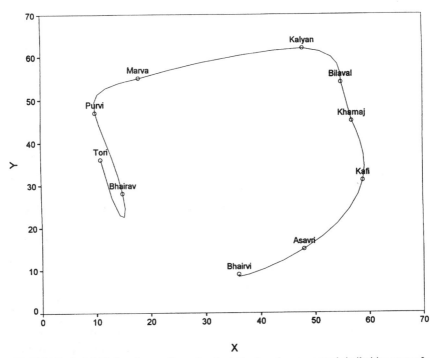

FIGURE 4 MDS plot of a two-dimensional solution based on perceptual similarities among Indian *Thats*. Subjects (*n* = 14) were Indian professional musicians. Points have been connected by a quintic, parameterized Lagrange polynomial. (Based on data of K. V. Vaughn, 1991, p. 116.)

gested that the perception of *rag* similarity does hold to the circular relations found earlier by K. V. Vaughn (1991) for these 10 *Thats*. In a separate experiment, Western musicians with no previous knowledge of Indian music evaluated the mood of the 10 *rag* phrases. Their evaluations were highly correlated with the traditional Indian theoretical notion of affect in *rag* (*majestic* versus *playful*).

In partial replication of Castellano et al. (1984) and K. V. Vaughn (1991), Aoyagi (1996) studied the perceptual interrelationships among nine septatonic Western modes (Figure 5). Aoyagi also considered the task dependencies by the use of three different methods: (a) proximity scaling (MDS); (b) probe tone, wherein a given mode was played as a context followed by one of 12 pitch classes that was rated for degree of fitness; (c) Rating, for which each mode was rated on a scale whose antipodes were major and minor, a music theoretic concept. The stimuli were seven diatonic (Church) modes—Ionian, Dorian, Phrygian, Lydian, Myxolydian, Aeolian, and Locrian—and two common nondiatonic modes—harmonic minor and melodic minor. MDS and cluster analyses led to relatively consistent results from the first two methods, namely in the two-dimensional MDS solutions, modes plot as a horseshoe shape, with three mode clusters. The results of the first method conform to a music theoretic notion, of the second to a notational analysis. It was fitting that the modes of Method 3 formed two clusters, with Ionian, Lydian, and Myxolydian in one cluster toward the *major* terminus, and Melodic, Locrian, Dorian, Phrygian, Aeolian, and Harmonic in the other cluster, toward the *minor* terminus.

Six of Aoyagi's (1996; Aoyagi & Kendall, 1996) nine scales corresponded to 6 of the 10 *Thats* used by K. V. Vaughn (1991), namely, Ionian (C_4-C_5) (Bilaval (major scale), Dorian (D_4-D_5) ≈ *Kafi*, Phrygian (E_4-E_5) ≈ *Bhairvi*, Lydian (F_4-F_5) ≈ *Kalyan*, Mixolydian (G_4-G_5) ≈ *Khamaj*, and Aeolian (A_4-A_5) ≈ *Asavri* (natural minor scale). We have encountered the church modes in several places in this review indirectly or directly (e.g., Hill et al., 1996). Their recurrence warrants revisiting Figure 4, which shows that the six church-mode *Thats* are ordered contiguously in a half-circle. Aoyagi's data for these six (out of nine) scales, were ordered in clustering (Figure 5a) in perfect agreement with K. V. Vaughn's (1991) solution. Figure 5b plots the six of her ten *Thats* that corresponded to the church modes; the correlation between Aoyagi's cluster analysis of Figure 5a and K. V. Vaughn's Dimension 1 of Figure 5b was 1.00. The correlations between the six common scales for their two-dimensional MDS solutions were 0.95 for the y-axes and – 0.31 for the x-axes; the negative correlation is almost certainly due to the different contexts of K. V. Vaughn and Aoyagi.

Studies like these in "scaling scales" show that a variety of methods and scales result in similar patterns and that MDS and related techniques can serve a fundamental role in cross-cultural research on music perception and cognition. The same essential and ubiquitous relationships among scales discovered in Western and non-Western musicians and nonmusicians, using real or synthetic music in a variety of contexts, compel us to believe that *scales* represent structural prototypes and lie at the heart of all musics.

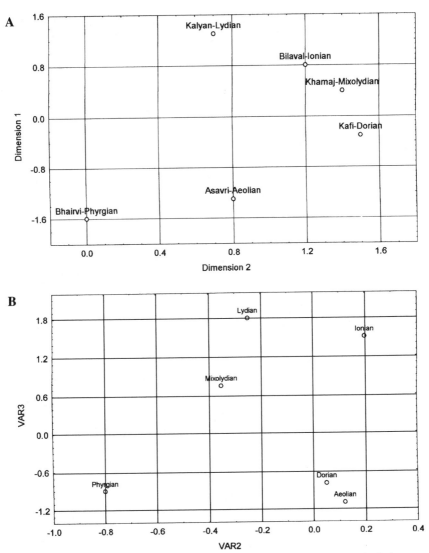

FIGURE 5 A, MDS plot of the two-dimensional solution based on perceptual similarity among the subset of six Indian *Thats* that corresponded to the Western church modes. (Data read from Aoyagi, 1996, figure 3.1.) B, MDS plot of the subset of six church mode scales that corresponded to the six Indian *Thats* of K. V. Vaughn (1991; see Figure 4). (Data read from K. V. Vaughn, 1991.)

B. TONAL ORGANIZATION IN VENDA MUSIC

Blacking (1970) sought to discover some rules of rhythmic and tonal organization from the music of two Venda girls' initiation schools. Most Venda music, whose main purpose is to induce "an expansion of feeling and greater experiences of being" (p. 11), is made up of groupings of an underlying pulse. Pitch values are similar to just intonation, and song differs crucially from speech in that the words are recited or sung to a regular metrical pattern, and words may be distorted to fit the music. The Venda have no words for scale or mode and although heptatonic and pentatonic sets sound different to them, there is no corresponding octave division of five or seven. Meter is the repetition of total patterns of movement, and new patterns are created by combining in canon or subdividing (both in canon or in ratio 2:3) existing patterns. Patterns are elaborated by combining "social" elements such as tenor drummer, alto drummer, feet, voice; different social elements must combine in polyrhythmic patterns that, once established, allow musical combinations—e.g., dancers' feet follow tenor drums, while their voices follow the alto drum. Tonality moves from tonic to leading note, then directly back to tonic at the start of a new pattern. Movement from one mode to another is common, and a brief confusion may result until the mode is resolved. Modes tend to be either G or D; a melody is in a given mode because "it follows a vocal or instrumental model and patterns of tonality and harmony that establish certain tones as its tonic, its leading note, and the primary and secondary harmonics of these tones" (p. 27). Blacking ties the musical phenotype to variations on a genotype, "all variations arising from the same deep processes of tonal organization" (p. 28). While acknowledging some influence of structural linguistics, Blacking makes no explicit mapping between surface and deep structures.

C. TONALITY AND MUSICAL EXPECTANCY

Indian music is tonal with many features in common with Western music. A significant difference is that tonality is expressed mainly by melody in Indian music, but mainly by harmony in Western music. The basis of Indian music is a standard set of melodic forms called the *rag*. *Rags* are built on a large set of scales called *thats*. The tones within a rag are presumed to be hierarchically organized, by importance. Castellano et al. (1984) obtained probe-tone ratings from Indian and Western listeners in the context of 10 North Indian *rags*. The ratings (Figure 6) confirmed the predicted hierarchical ordering. Highest ratings were given by both groups to the tonic and fifth degree of the scale, which tones are structurally significant in Indian music theory. They are immovable tones about which scales are built, and these tones are sounded continuously in the drone. Both groups gave high ratings to a designated note (*vadi*) that is emphasized in the melody, and these ratings reflected the tone durations in the musical context, which "suggests that the distribution of tones in music is a psychologically effective means of conveying tonal hierarchy to listeners" (p. 394). But only Indian listeners were sensitive to the *thats* that underlay the rags, suggesting the existence of an internalization of that system scales. Indeed, multidimensional scaling of correlations between rating profiles recovered the Indian music-theoretical representation. There was little evidence that Western listeners assimilated the pitches to the major and minor diatonic system of Western music.

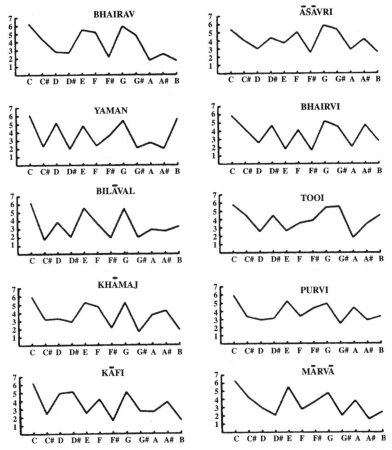

FIGURE 6   Probe tone rating profiles for 10 *rags*. (From Castellano et al., 1984, p. 403).

Carterette et al. (1993) showed that, although many octave mismatches occur, both Indonesian and Western subjects generally matched the pitch chroma of three *saron* gamelan tones, *barung*, *peking*, and *demung*. The stimulus timbre of inharmonic gamelan bars gave rise to a clear perception of pitch for both Western and Javanese musicians. In judging small-cents deviations from equipetatonic tuning, only one of four professional Indonesian musicians reliably discerned the deviations. Perlman and Krumhansl (1996), using recorded *gènder barung* tones,[5] asked six Javanese and six Western musicians to make magnitude estimations of the interval between a first tone and a second tone, the latter being always higher in pitch than the first; the interval size ranged in increments of 20 cents from 60 to 780 cents. Several musicians showed clear regions of confusion by assigning ap-

[5]The *gènder barung* bars are suspended over tuned resonators. Spectral analysis showed that the tones are quite harmonic.

proximately equal estimates to a range of intervals. This behavior suggested to the authors that these listeners assimilated the intervals to a set of internal interval standards. However, no evidence of assimilation was found for musicians in either group, although some made highly accurate estimates. In the case of the Javanese musicians who appeared to possess an internal interval standard, the regions corresponded to the *pélog* and *sléndro* tuning systems. In the case of the Western musicians, the regions were in correspondence to the equal-tempered scale. Perlman & Krumhansl argue that the relatively wider regions of confusions of the Javanese musicians "may reflect the greater variability of intonation in Java. In addition, the Javanese musicians seemed able to choose between internal interval standards based on the two tuning systems" (p. 95).

Krumhansl and Keil (1982) showed that by early elementary grades, listeners prefer diatonic to nondiatonic for completions of short melodies; the authors infer that internalization of the scale structure of Western music develops at a relatively early age. Both Western and Balinese listeners were found to be sensitive to tonal hierarchies common to both Western diatonic and Balinese *pélog* scales despite the markedly different tuning systems (Hansen, Kessler, & Shepard, 1983; Kessler, Hansen, & Shepard, 1984), but for Balinese *sléndro* scales, the pattern of results was less clear, which suggests limits in the tuning systems that can give rise to perceived tonal hierarchies. From these studies and work by others, Castellano et al. (1984) concluded that listeners are remarkably sensitive to the organization of richly structured music of their own or of another culture, that they apply considerable cognitive resources in abstracting the conceptual features, and that they can flexibly internalize tonal organizations. The probe-tone method was adapted for a cross-cultural comparison of the perception of Balinese and Western melodies by both Balinese and Western listeners. Half of the Balinese listeners were remote villagers who had never before been exposed to the diatonic scales or music of the West. The Western listeners were unfamiliar with the *sléndro* and *pélog* scales and music of Bali. Both Balinese and Western listeners used similar response strategies, but tended to show an internalization of tonal schemata most often to music of their own culture.

Each pentatonic modal scale (*dieu*) of the Vietnamese zither (*dan tranh*) embraces a given tuning and a specific modal nuance, or *sentiment*, and extensively uses a 166-cent scale step. A professional Vietnamese player and music theorist (Nguyen) generally was unable to categorize intervals in the absence of a musical context, but if asked to contemplate the sentiment of a *dieu*, he was able to respond to stimuli drawn from two modal scales as if he had access to internalized tonal hierarchies (Keefe et al., 1991).

Dowling (1984) lauds the work of Castellano et al. (1984) as a successful effort toward optimizing experimental control and real-world complexity. He points out that listeners apprehend invariants of musical scale structure at several levels of abstraction. European and Indian music are similar at the level of tonal material, which may aid Western listeners' apprehension of Indian scale structures. Little assimilation of Indian tonal material was shown in the tasks of Castellano et al. (1984). But assimilation, says Dowling, may be relatively rare in perception and may occur most often in tasks that require production, have facilitating context, and where little encoding time is provided. Degree of assimilation depends on knowledge of a musical culture. Acquisition and structure of knowledge about the music of a novel culture could be assessed by converging operations (experiments) on production or octave equivalences. We agree with Dowling, but expect convergence to be slow so long as descriptive anthropology implicitly or explicitly opposes controlled experimentation.

Two tonal systems coexist in Japan: one the traditional Japanese system of several pentatonic scales and the other the diatonic Western system. The enormous surge of jazz, rock, and pop music in Japan since about 1960 has created two generations of tonal culture, according to Hoshino (1989): those born after 1960 and those born before 1940.

Hoshino tested university students (mean age, 23) and older persons (mean age, 57) on both tonal and atonal note sequences built on both Western and traditional Japanese scales. A tone sequence was presented, followed by the same sequence but for a changed note in any one of the positions; the listener's task was to indicate the altered note. On Western tonal and atonal sequences, students were much more accurate (about 83% versus 61%) than their elders. On Japanese tone sequences, students performed well (90%) on both tonal and atonal sequences, whereas the elders did well on the tonal (90%) but less well (80%) on the atonal sequences. Hoshino concludes that the younger listeners showed Western tonal "acculturation" whereas the older persons showed "acculturation" to the Japanese tonal system. (On statistical grounds, we advise some caution in interpreting these results.)

Melodic expectancies in the form of a sung continuation was obtained by Carlsen (1981) from 91 student musicians from the United States, Germany, and Hungary, who heard 25 interrupted two-tone melodic beginnings. Expectancy patterns included both conjunct and disjunct melodic motion ranging up to a minor seventh, but the majority of responses were of half- and whole-steps. Expectancy-generating strength varied considerably among melodic beginnings. Differences in expectancy patterns were found as a function of melodic beginning and cultural milieu , but not of voice level or of training level. Only American and Hungarian expectancy profiles differed significantly, not German and Hungarian, or American and German. Carlsen suggests that expectancy could be used to characterize "cultural distinctiveness" but in view of the single group samples, we believe that the inference is very weak.

V. MELODY

A. MELODIC CONTOUR

Given its important role in perception, melodic contour might be a useful analytical tool for comparative research, particularly in cognitive musicology. Adams (1976) offers a formal definition of melodic contour from which he attempts to construct a typology. He reviews a variety of approaches, for instance: symbolic narration; metaphoric depictions; word lists—arch and bow and inversions thereof, sawtooth rise and fall, undulations, and combining forms; and graphs. As an example, a comparison is made of "arched," "undulating," "terraced," and "descending" song contours among North and South America, insular Pacific, Africa, Old High Culture, Europe, Australia, Arctic Asia, and tribal India. Knowing nothing of the data, one might guess the fact that "undulations" is the biggest category (62–86%) of the approximately 2500 songs. Apparently more quantitative are melodic-event graphs, which plot changes in pitch and pitch levels, durations, measures, and the like; and melodic-relation graphs, which try to represent salient relations of a melody, for example, intervals or sequences of directions. Adams concludes that word lists are too specific, metaphors too general, and graphs clarify little. His own solution is a typology wherein melodic-contour types are defined as the product of three primary features (slope, deviation, and reciprocal) and some secondary features that determine melodic-contour shape (e.g., recurrence and repetition of local pitch extrema). Adams applied these features in a comparison of two American Indian sets of songs, the Southern Paiute and the Flathead, and showed that with respect to quantized melodic shape, a strong similarity exists between the two sets.

B. SONG AND THE SINGING VOICE

1. Source-Filter Model

The human voice and a number of animal voices can be described as a source-filter system. The vocal folds, the source, produce a quasi-periodic glottal signal whose fundamental has maximal energy, and the energy of the integer partials decays exponentially with frequency. The filter is the vocal tract, whose size and shape and the air flow through which is modulated by the jaw, lips, and tongue. The resulting spectrum has local resonance peaks (formants) not at the glottal frequency and structured noise that bears considerable information. A Western professional singer has learned to exploit the formants by moving spectral energy into an existing formant or creating a formant in a band centered near 2.5 kHz. This trick enables the singer to be heard over a symphony orchestra whose overall sound levels (80–90 dB SPL) fall off rapidly above 1 kHz (Sundberg, 1987). Western popular music played at high levels demands the use of the singer's formant, although use of hand-held microphones and electronic amplification lessens the demand.

2. Western and Non-Western Vocal Technique and Song

An instance of non-Western technique that exploits partials is that of the Tibetan lama who has learned to use glottal and tract harmonics so as to sing a chord (Smith, Stevens, & Tomlinson, 1967). Yamada (1995) studied *Xöömji*, a traditional style of song in Mongolia wherein a male singer sings two tones simultaneously. Yamada obtained pitch matches and found, from spectral analyses, that the pitch of the less intense drone tone always corresponded to the singer's voice fundamental. Yamada interprets *Xöömji* as auditory stream segregation that sounds as if it arose from two different sources. The more intense melody tone corresponded to the ninth harmonic and was deeply modulated in amplitude, which "may help listeners to perceive the two pitches clearly" (p. 540).

Walker (1986, 1990) suggests that more recent theories of pitch perception can help account for the contrast of Western musical sounds with those of other cultures. For example, Native Americans and Australian aboriginals sing sounds that have pitch but do not sound like Western pitch. The reason lies in training. For the Kwakiatul Indian singer, pitch resides in two or three frequency peaks of relatively low intensity, whereas the Western opera singer has two major frequency peaks, with greatest sound intensity in the upper one. Western opera singers report that they feel vibrations in the face and neck when singing, which is consistent with some results of Sundberg (1994), who suggests that in singing at frequencies lower than pitch F_4 (350 Hz) chest wall vibrations can be used as a feedback signal. The singing style of Balinese vocal music is said to be extremely nasal in timbre and practically without vibrato when melodies are at rest (Tenzer, 1991, p. 99). Sorrell (1990) speaks of the solo female singer with gamelan as having a tone "closer to an oboe than any stringed instrument" (p. 43). In newer gamelan music, the vocal quality of the singers is not that of the tense, nasalized Javanese chorus, "but a more relaxed quality associated with Western choruses" (Becker, 1980, p. 75). She notes, too, the advent of parallel vocal lines, a departure from tradition in which male voice is tied to *saron* structure and female voice to *kenong* structure (p. 70).

Densmore (1929) took as a working hypothesis that the small gradations of pitch in [American] Indian singing are a part of a musical system more complex than our own. With tuning forks, she tested Indians' pitch discrimination and found that by this test their abilities are not superior to the abilities of average American whites under similar conditions. She used an ingenious method for measuring sung intervals: A record of a Sioux song was played on one phonograph and recorded on another; this latter record was played and recorded and the process continued until the sixth duplication. "[T]he tones were those of the diatonic scale sung with reasonable accuracy. The duplication had eliminated the by-tones, leaving a kernel of tone which had been obscured by the Indian's peculiar manner of rendition" (p. 274). She found the whole tone to be most prevalent and sung with reasonable accuracy, but the semitone was rare and sung with great variability.

Watt (1924) compared the distribution of various intervals of Schubert's songs with those of (American Indians) Chippewa and Teton-Sioux. He found that, for all types of songs, the average number of any particular interval was practically the same. Gundlach (1932) sought to discover whether objective characteristics of a piece of music form the basis for the mood that it may arouse and the degree to which these moods are universal or dependent on local musical traditions. He compared 334 North American Indian songs (Chippewa, Teton-Sioux, Mandan, Hidatsas, Ute, Papagos, and Ojibway) with European, Slavic, and Asiatic Indian songs. American Indian songs were classified into groups "having fairly constant emotional tone" (p. 135) according to the "emotionally homogeneous" situation in which they were sung; war songs (60%), healing the sick and wounded (15%), and love songs (25%). Results were similar between tribes. Organization and general war songs were low (in pitch), rapid in speed, with a wide pitch range; love songs were high, slow, and medium in range; healing songs were moderately high and moderately slow with a very narrow pitch range. There were some differences among tribes with respect to interval types, but the average percentages were 19% thirds, 9% larger than thirds, and 71% smaller than thirds. Differences in rhythm types (even, uneven, and rough) were striking and significant: the order of roughness was, from least to most, healing, love, and war songs; for even rhythm, the order was war, love, and healing. Generally, "The degree of rhythmic staccato or punctuation in the songs seems highly correlated with the degree of excitement represented by the situation" (p. 139). With but 61 European, Slavic, and Asiatic Indian folk songs, Gundlach suggests that agreement between these and the American Indian songs with respect to interval and rhythm extends only to war and love.

Ross and Lehiste (1966) spoke to the issue of how speech and music prosodies are matched to each other in the performance of folk song. They assumed that speech and melody are two (more or less) independent structures. Speech exploits the contrastive nature of phonemes whereas the elements of melody are discretized scale steps. In singing, the two prosodies ideally are matched except when "existential" demands from speech or melody conflict. In tone languages, for example, Chinese or Japanese, tone patterns of speech tend to be matched to the melodic contours of music (Yung, 1983); in Indo-European languages, linguistic stress patterns tend to coincide with stressed and unstressed metrical patterns of music (Palmer & Kelly, 1992).

Ross and Lehiste (1996) studied Estonian, a Finno-Ugric language. In Estonian folk song, almost any text can be combined with almost any melody. This interplay depends on the meter of Estonian folk song, which is based on long and short contrasts, rather than on stressed and unstressed syllables. When an acoustical conflict inevitably arises between text and melody, how does the folk-song performer solve the problem? From the analysis of three Estonian folk songs recorded in 1930 as performed by a female singer, Ross and Lehiste concluded that duration in "the Kalevala-songs serves exclusively metrical functions and has lost its word-level functions. The linguistic opposition between short and long syllables is neutralized and subordinated to the metrical structure" (p. 424). The melody may be modified to fit word-level pitch patterns. Recent work (Ross & Lehiste, 1998) has complicated these notions so as to consider timing in Estonian folk song as interaction among speech prosody, meter, and musical rhythm.

3. Children's Singing and Song

M. M. Vaughn (1981) asked children ranging from about 4 to 16 years of age from elementary schools in Canada, England, Denmark, Colombia, and Argentina, to sing the beginning of a free-choice song. Pitch means were significantly different by country except for the oldest age group, 13 years 5 months to 14 years 8 months, and girls' pitch was significantly higher than that of boys. None of the pitch means was as high as the lowest mean pitches (F♯ above middle C to A440) of songs commonly used in elementary schools, which suggests to M. M. Vaughn that musical education should revise teaching practices.

It is suggested to Trehub and Unyk (1991), from empirical research, that the lullaby may be a perceptually distinct "pan-cultural category" to which belong some natural prototypes of music. We look at some relevant cross-cultural studies by Trehub and her colleagues.

Arguing that infants younger than 1 year old have not yet been exposed to any music tradition, Trehub, Thorpe, and Trainor (1990) exposed infants 7–10 months of age to repetitions of one of three melodies in transposition. The three melodies conformed in different degrees to Western music structure; first, a *good* Western melody made up of notes from the diatonic scale, second, a *bad* Western melody made up of notes from the chromatic scale, but from no single diatonic scale, and third, a *bad* non-Western melody with notes not drawn from the chromatic scale. An infant learned to turn its head to a single-position change of three semitones in the standard melody, and later was tested for its discrimination of a one-semitone change; all changed melodies were transposed. Infants could tell changes in the good but not in the bad Western melody or in the bad non-Western melody. Trehub et al. suggest that a good melody is based on a major or minor triad whose outside notes also form an interval of the perfect fifth. "The developmental importance of major and minor triads is not borne out cross-culturally in music, where neither triad enjoys universal application. What is relatively common, however, is the interval of the perfect fifth, increasing the possibility that this interval underlies the observed enhancement in perceptual processing" (p. 15).

In a study by Unyk, Trehub, and Trainor (1992), 68 university students judged that 30 lullabies from many cultures were simpler than comparison songs from these cultures no matter whether the lullabies were heard in their original form, or with words filtered for unintelligibility, or with synthesized, uniform timbre. Musical features of the lullabies were not different from those of comparison songs; apparently judgments were governed by parallel musical and prosodic features.

Mothers sang songs of their own choice informally in two contexts, once to their infants and once in the infant's absence (Trehub, Unyk, & Trainor, 1993). Adult listeners had to choose which one of the paired excerpts had been sung to the infant. In one experiment in which singers ($n = 16$) and listeners ($n = 20$) were North Americans, correct choices were made with high accuracy. In a second experiment mothers ($n = 12$) of Hindi descent sang Hindi songs in both contexts. Adult listeners half of whom were men (20 native speakers of Hindi, 20 native speakers of English) identified the infant-directed excerpts significantly better than chance; women scored higher than men, and native Hindi speakers scored higher than native English speakers. "Findings document a distinctive style of singing to infants, some aspects of which are recognizable across cultures and musical systems" (p. 285).

C. THE MUSICIAN'S ADVANTAGE

1. Absolute Pitch Possessors and Musical Training

It is widely believed that musical talent like mathematical talent is a special, genetic given: either one has it or one does not. A special case is absolute pitch (AP), which is the ability to identify the pitch of a musical tone or to produce a musical tone at a given pitch without using an external reference pitch.

Takeuchi and Hulse (1993) review AP and conclude that AP exists in varying degrees among those described as AP possessors. AP possessors vary in accuracy of identifying pitch and in ability to produce pitches absolutely, as well as in ability to identify timbral tones and tones in various registers. AP possessors do not have superior memory for pitches per se, but depend on mediation by verbal pitch names. The etiology of AP is not yet fully understood, although evidence points toward a theory of early-learning, namely that AP can be learned by anyone during a limited, critical development period, up to about 6 years of age. After age 6, AP becomes difficult or impossible to acquire owing to a general shift from the perception of individual features to a perception of relations among features.

Plomp (1964) had concluded that a rough rule for hearing (five to eight) separate partials of either harmonic or inharmonic complexes was that a partial could be heard out from a complex tone when it was separated from neighboring partials by one or more critical bandwidths. Soderquist (1970) who found that musicians were better than nonmusicians in separating out partials from complex tones, offered the explanation that musicians have sharper auditory filters. In an experimental test of Soderquist's proposal, Fine and Moore (1993) found that the auditory filters of musicians and nonmusicians did not differ but that the detection process of musicians was more efficient, though it was unclear to Fine and Moore whether this was the result of innate factors or musical experience.

Thomas (1989) synthesized interleaved, familiar tunes in same, similar, and dissimilar timbres and played them to musicians and nonmusicians randomly ordered by timbres and by tune starting order. Listeners required greater separation for recognition of same (mean of 6.32 half-steps) than of similar or different timbres (means of 3.54 and 3.46 half-steps, respectively) and more often identified the melody played on odd-numbered beats (mean, 4.74 of 12 trials) than on even-numbered beats (mean, 2.32 of 12 trials). Degree of musical training had no effect, nor was there any interaction of training with either timbre or rhythm.

The performance of musicians has been compared with that of nonmusicians in many experiments. Musicians outperformed nonmusicians in transposition tasks (Bartlett & Dowling, 1980) and in recognizing a chord played with different instruments (Beal, 1985). Musicians are also better able to use chroma information in octave-scrambled test melodies (Dowling, 1984), in identifying pitches (Cuddy, 1970), and in encoding information quickly in fast conditions (Dowling, 1973). Apparently musicians have learned techniques to discern patterns more efficiently than nonmusicians; however, main effects in experiments appear and not interactions (Cuddy & Cohen, 1976; Dowling et al., 1987; Thomas, 1989). In other words, musicians have learned strategies and stored more patterns *related to musical structures* than nonmusicians have, but being a musician is not associated with different cognitive or perceptual processing systems. Similar results are found for chess (Chase & Simon, 1973), and convincing evidence is at hand to indicate that absolute pitch is learned (Miyazaki, 1993; Takeuchi & Hulse, 1993) and can even be a disability (Miyazaki, 1993).

Event-related potentials (P3 component) were measured during a timbre (strings, flutes, tubas) discrimination task with nonmusicians, musicians, and musicians having AP (Crummer, Walton, Wayman, Hantz, & Frisina, 1994). It was found that P3 amplitude and latency varied with musical experience and timbre; P3 latencies were shorter for musicians than nonmusicians and shortest of all for AP musicians The authors suggest that a perceptual task on timbre elicits brain activity that varies with the degree of musical training. Earlier, Crummer, Hantz, Chuang, and Walton (1988) compared event-related potentials of musicians and nonmusicians in a variety of auditory tasks that involved timbre and chord discrimination. Musicians performed better than nonmusicians on a difficult timbre task; both groups required more time in discriminating chord progressions than in discriminating sine tones or timbres. These discrimination differences were correlated with event-related signal forms such as amplitude, latency, and shape.

2. Musical Structure

Prior and Troup (1988) compared 19 musicians and 19 nonmusicians of similar education and social class in two dichotic monitoring experiments on perceiving timbre and rhythm. No ear or group differences were found in timbre perception but in rhythm monitoring, there was a group-by-ear interaction: musicians reacted faster on the right ear than on the left but nonmusicians did not; musicians reacted faster than nonmusicians on the right ear only. Verbal labeling apparently did not influence laterality. Prior and Troup conclude that when stringent control is exerted over experiments and subjects, there is "minimal" evidence for laterality effects of musical training.

Abe and Hoshino (1985) studied the final-tone extrapolating behavior of a Western classical musical expert and a Japanese traditional music expert for three-note melodic tone sequences. As expected by Abe and Hoshino under a tonal schema model, the Western expert assimilated the tone sequences to the major and minor diatonic tonal system of Western music whereas the Japanese expert did not.

In a set of experiments, Beal (1985) asked 34 musicians and 34 nonmusicians to discriminate pairs of successive chords that shared all notes in common or had different notes played in succession. Some pairs of chords differed in timbre regardless of musical structure because they were played on different instruments. Although musicians did slightly better than nonmusicians, both could discriminate instrument timbres. But when chord structures did not conform to rules of tonal harmony, musicians and nonmusicians performed equally poorly in recognizing identical chords played on different instruments.

A signal-detection analysis showed that both groups set similar criteria, but where musicians were superior—on familiar diatonic chords—they showed greater sensitivity. Beal suggests that her results indicate that musicians develop perceptual and cognitive skills that are specific to objects met in the musical domain, whereas non musicians who lack this experience use acoustical properties of the chords in making their judgments. J. David Smith (1997) points out that music science focuses on the perceptual, cognitive, and aesthetic responses of experts than on those of musical novices, who receive far less empirical and theoretical study. By comparing data from existing studies, Smith concluded that with respect to the tonal materials of music such as octaves and intervals, of listening preferences, and of standards of evaluation, musicians are sensitive whereas novices are insensitive. He argues that "A music science that included novices more fully would be more comprehensive and better prepared to address basic questions about music's evolution and its universal structure." (p. 227). A similar argument can be made for comparative studies of music perception and cognition in which responses of novices and experts are contrasted between and within different musical cultures.

VI. RHYTHM

A. SCHEMATA

Baily (1988) compared two related but distinct music cultures, those of North India and Afghanistan (the city of Herat), and concluded that they "have recourse to the same music theory" but use it cognitively in rather different ways, which is reflected in both teaching and performance. In Afghanistan, music theory is post hoc based on a representational model "which organises, systematises and explains what is already part of performance practice" (p. 122). But in North India, the evidence suggests that music theory operates from pitch (*sargam*) and rhythm (*bol*, mnemonic) notational systems. These verbal labels make it possible to store compositions in verbal rather than aural memory: "oral notation may serve as an idiom of musical thought: planning ahead during performance may depend in part on verbal thinking" (p. 122). In short, North Indians learn to think musically in schemas that are both verbal and aural, whereas Heratans learn to play by ear. Baily's conclusions are tenuous given that his evidence is largely in the form of observations, descriptions, and verbal reports of expert musicians.

Yet Baily's (1985) idea is consonant with the views of experimental psychology. One point is that melodies are heard and remembered by a few salient perceptual features based on attention to stimulus dimensions such as loudness, pitch, timbre, location or on temporal dimensions like meter and rhythm. The search for features is governed by mental schemas developed in childhood from the melodies of a culture (Dowling & Harwood, 1986, pp. 124–152). Schemas embody a level of information higher than particular pitches or tempos and are tempered by contexts. Thus, although melodic contour may aid melodic recognition, the salience of contour varies with tonal scale context, for example, with key distance. Other modulating factors are task demands and prior musical training.

B. COMPARATIVE THEORIES AND GRAMMARS OF RHYTHM

Influenced by Balzano (1980), Pressing (1983) asserts that a number of common cyclic structures of pitch and rhythm in human music are isomorphic under certain restraints, hence can be compared under mathematical group theory as *cognitive isomorphisms*. Much simplified, the perceptual space is specified as a one-dimensional array of lattice sites and an equivalence operator Ψ such that sites which are L units apart are equivalent. Thus, the Western chromatic scale tones comprise lattice sites for $L = 12$ and $\Psi \approx$ octave. Now distribute M objects ($M < L$) among any L adjacent lattice sites to obtain a unit-cell pattern that is replicable over the lattice. Thus, the white keys of a piano form a unit-cell pattern. Pitch restraints are octave equivalence and perceptual equality of smallest intervals. Time restraints concern repeating isorhythms based on a uniform fastest unit. Geometrically an isomorphism may have the form of a helix. Scales and time lines are compared in examples from jazz, West Africa, and the Balkans, and a basis for comparisons is suggested for Asian, Latin American, and other musics. Pressing compares many different M and L patterns for many African and a number of Balkan examples. With $M = 7$ and $L = 12$, virtually all the (Western) church mode isomorphisms of scale and time lines occur in West Africa, for example, the (Ionian) pattern 2212221 (3 Ewe groups, and the Yoruba) and the (Lydian) pattern 2212212 (Ga-Adangme). All the patterns found are derivable from a few basic patterns such as 2212221 by means of about five transformations. The parameters $\{L = 12, M = 5,7\}$ generate identical structures in West African time lines and scales, Western tonal music (jazz, too), and Balkan rhythm. The $L = 16$ structures of West African and Afro-Latin music are transforms of 33434; $L = 7$ generates identical patterns found in the music of Bulgaria and Macedonia, in Western diatonic structure, and even in Thai court music.

Any music made up of several simultaneous instrumental or vocal parts requires a temporal regulator in order to achieve coherence. African music, particularly polyphony, is *measured* music and is based on *pulsations*, on a sequence of isochronous temporal units that can be realized as a beat. This beat is the analog of the *tactus* of Western music, which derives from the *foot* of ancient metrics. It must be strongly stressed, however, that the pulsation measure of African music is very different from the hierarchical idea of *measure* in Western classical music with such attendant notions as *meter*, *strong* and *weak* beats, or *syncope*. Grouping beats into measures achieved its dominance in Western classical music as a consequence of a graphic notation in the form of bars which invaded musical instruction in the 17th century. Thus beat or pulsation measure is a manifestation of a metronomic sense at the basis of African rhythm; it is not a device for forming groups of two, three, or four as in Western classical measure. Based on transcription data and structural theory, Arom suggests that the pervasive ostinati are cognitive *models* from which African musicians build variations into complex polyrhythms "The metronomic beat, materialised by Africans themselves, is intrinsic to the music and thus a 'cultural pattern'" (Arom, 1985/1991, p. 182). In summary, most traditional African music makes no use of strong and weak beats; however complex the piece, its durations always refer to the tactus as the regular reference unit.

Merriam (1981) considers the conceptions of time that underlay African and Western music. Western time lies on an infinite continuum, stretching linearly backward and forward from a perceived now, and is measured by a chronometer, a device that repeats an elementary unit, such as a clock tick or pulse. African time reckoning is nonlinear, based on a discontinuous, reversible, sliding scale that has a circular or spiral property. Time is not epochal nor is it reckoned as a distance by means of an apparatus; rather it is reckoned by reference to natural phenomena such as sunrise, noon, or sunset and particularly by social activity. How is the perception or performance of music affected by these rather different philosophies of time reckoning? How can one resolve the paradox of topologically deformable African time reckoning with the Western view that African music is built on an equal-pulse base? Of the several ways out suggested by Merriam (p. 138), a "distinct possibility" of resolving the paradox is to admit that "some other system may be operating in connection with the small units required in musical time" So, the repetitive pattern of African music may well be accounted for by a cyclical view of time with intrapattern time linearity.

Becker (1979) holds a similar view about Javanese music, that the Javanese conception of time is cyclical, but in some cases time is divided into successive halves, a process that is repeated both in rhythm and in melody. We saw earlier that both in theory and in practice Indian classical music is rooted in diurnal and seasonal cycles.

Kubik (1962) discusses particular phenomena of African music that he terms *inherent* patterns; these are auditory patterns that emerge from the overall melodic-rhythmic complex and are not produced directly by any musician. Prerequisites of these inherent auditory patterns are a very quick sequence of notes; many jerky intervals with an ensuing split into pitch layers; and a regular internal structure of an entire passage so that high, low, and middle pitch layers form distinct rhythmic melodies. Apparently composers of African music make skillful use of the organizational principles of human audition. Kubik reported on the "curious" differences between those heard as *player* and those heard as *listener*: "Our playing when recorded sounded much more complicated than it actually was, and I heard a number of rhythm patterns which I was sure that none of us had played, while on the other hand the rhythms which we had actually played were inaudible on the tape" (p. 34). (This is reminiscent of J. S. Bach's splitting of a melodic line into two distinct parts in organ works or in partitas for unaccompanied violin.) A variety of such findings by Kubik and other ethnomusicologists may be understood as melodic fissioning or streaming, which is influenced by differences of interval, timbre, loudness, or attention and by the listener's tendency to assimilate an exotic music into the perceptual logic of his or her own musical culture.

Kubik (1979) dealt with aspects of pattern perception and recognition in African music. From the musicians' tuning practices, he inferred the existence of a progressive scale by pitch that starts with the highest frequency, inverse to the Western notion of a scale, which starts with the lowest frequency. Rhythmic patterns are named by verbal or syllabic formulas, which are in turn used for identifying the associated rhythmic forms. Motional patterns, often sharply delineated, are defined by a starting point, a relative insertion point, by length and internal structure of elementary and fastest pulses, and by their relation to other patterns. The result is a "uniform imperious *pulsation of the nominal values* and sometimes...*a beat or gross pulse*" (p. 225). Metric patterns either are not a feature or have a subordinate role in motional form so that in learning to play African musical instruments one does not beat time, unlike the custom in Western music schools. Also it appears that patterns have little meaning out of context and that a player often cannot perform his pattern alone. This is because some formulas are very long and are defined by congruence relations with other parts of the music and cannot be kept in mind without a beat or metric reference.

C. PERCEPTION

As Igaga and Versey (1977) point out, there exists little work on comparative rhythm perception and what work there is often confounds ethnic and cultural variables or involves atypical samples of subjects. In a study of Ugandan ($n = 655$) and English ($n = 573$) schoolchildren (10–15 years old, about half were boys and half were girls), Igaga and Versey used the Thackray Rhythmic Perception test to assess counting, tempo steadiness, sound durations, strength (accent), rhythm comparison, and rhythmic pattern identification. Mean rhythmic perception scores increased with age for Ugandans but were erratic for English subjects. Within age groups, Ugandans and English differed significantly; in the four younger age samples, English children scored higher than Ugandan children; the reverse was true for the two oldest age groups, with the Ugandan children outscoring the English (whose motivation may have flagged, suggest the authors). Igaga and Versey caution that the paper and pencil tests favored the English and that cultural differences exist, for example, Ugandan culture emphasizes rhythmic performance.

In a replication with 398 Ugandan and 246 English children, Igaga and Versey (1978) obtained similar results but analyzed the battery in subtests of (a) synchronization of rhythms, (b) repetition of rhythms, and (c) beating time. The main point is that Subtests a and b differentiate the two groups most clearly, with the Ugandan children showing marked superiority over the English children on synchronization of rhythm, and on repetition of rhythm. The authors suggest that this outcome reflects the "all-pervading role [of rhythm] within Ugandan society" (p.

64). We do not understand why Igaga and Versey did not offer a reanalysis by subtest of their 1977 study.

von Hornbostel (1928) suggested that the parallel hand motions of an African xylophonist are controlled more by spatial than by musical considerations, with the player realizing the melody "above all as an act of motility, regarding its audible quality rather as a side-issue, although a desirable one." Blacking (1955, 1973) compared musical and motional analyses on Butembo flute (Congo) and on lamellaphone (*kalimba*, e.g., Kalenga *mbira*) and discovered that generally no tune patterns were common to different melodies. He suggests that the most significant factors of the kalimba tunes are not their melodic structures, but the recurring patterns of "fingering," which, combined with different patterns of polyrhythms between the two thumbs, produce a variety of melodies.

Kubik believes that in Western music the movements of the player have little or no meaning in themselves.[6] But in African music, the organization is motionally rigorous even to the least detail, and patterns of movement give pleasure with no regard to how far or whether they are realized in sound (Kubik, 1979). When such music is reproduced by other cultures from the sound alone, the imitation fails because the exact spacing of the notes is changed, which "leads to delays, anticipations, slight fluctuations in tempo, and a sense of lack of *drive*" (Kubik, 1979, p. 229). On the other hand, from informal experiments, Kubik asserts that from *only* the sound, cultural adherents "spontaneously comprehend [and execute] the movement patterns" of a given African instrumental piece (p. 229). Thus movement patterns in one visible form can be recast into another visible form, for instance, from dance to xylophone; what has been learned is not just a visible pattern, but an abstract content underlain by a numerical relationship such as the "famous two against three relationship in widely differing forms of African music" (p. 231). These unnamed numerical experiences are the unchangeable, abstract foundation of the perception and recognition of movement patterns.

VII. TIMBRE AND SPECTRA

Fourier's famous formulas arose in a seminal paper of 1807 on the propagation of heat; opposed by Lagrange, the paper finally appeared in print, as a book, in 1822 (Grattan-Guiness, 1972). Obviously the development of Western instruments with their harmonically related partials hardly depended on Fourier methods of analysis and synthesis of signals, but modern psychoacoustics and signal processing did. Nearly every aspect of music has been transformed by the tape recorder, the digital computer, and the fast Fourier transform (FFT)—even ethnomusicology, despite its resistance to scientific methods and tools.

Harmonically related spectra reinforce the sense of musical pitch, and Western musical theory, which is based on harmonic relations, drives the search for expla-

---

[6]We take exception to Kubik's view. Western performers move relative to musical structure and meaning. Conductors communicate expressive intent through complex motion patterns. It is an empirical question as to the degree which motions sign in African music.

nation in terms of harmonic and inverse periodic relationships. Western music has been composed to satisfy a theoretical and pragmatic harmonicity, which is further exploited by melodic lines and timbral combinations. What is too often overlooked is that the timbre of a sound or voice depends not simply on pitch but on a time-varying signal whose complex pattern depends on changing relations among the frequencies, amplitudes, and phases of the partials. These relations are in turn dependent on the source-filter properties of instruments and voices.

One result of pitch centricity is that perceptual and cognitive research on timbre of pitched and nonpitched instruments, whether Western or non-Western, has been neglected. We contend that the idiosyncratic musical character of an instrument or voice arises from its complex time-varying signal. Similarities and dissimilarities of musical sounds can be explained by differences in their patterns. Differences among patterns can be measured as quantitative distances in physical metric spaces, or as related perceptual distances in perceptual or cognitive metric spaces. Our view is supported by Green's (1988) research on the ability of listeners to discern changes in the shape of complex acoustic spectra, which they describe as changes in "sound quality."[7] This "auditory profile analysis" rests on comparisons of the intensity level at different parts of an acoustic spectrum.

The *basso continuo* principle, as embodied in Rameau's theory of functional harmony, was paralleled by the introduction of drone instruments in the classical music of India. Raman (1922) had noted the remarkable, powerful harmonic series that arose from the nonlinear interaction of the tambura string and grazing contact with its curved bridge. Carterette, Vaughn, and Jairazbhoy (1989) studied the role of tambura interactions with North Indian rags played on the sitar. Carterette, Vaughn, and Jairazbhoy analyzed the sounds of the most common drone tunings. Each of the four strings was played with and without the insertion of *juari* ("life-giving") threads between strings and bridge. *Juari* cause an upward transfer and spread of energy into higher partials, impart richness to tambura tones and underlay the use of different drone tunings for different *rags*. Specific notes of *rag* scales are selectively and dynamically enhanced by different drone tunings. Based on coincident features of spectral and musical scale degrees, they computed an index of spectral complexity of the interactions of tambura tunings with *rag* scales. They speculated that the use of juari contributes to stable pitch centers, implied scale modulation, and an improvisational flexibility.[8]

In a study of the psychoacoustics of gamelan gong tones, Harshberger, Kendall, and Carterette (1994) recorded 12 gong tones of a venerated gamelan, four from each of three sizes: *Ageng, Suwukan,* and *Kempul*. Forty musicians, half with and half without gamelan training, rated the tones in two different procedures: (a) 22 listeners rated each tone for 10 attributes a verbal-magnitude-estimation task (VAME) and (b) 18 listeners rated all possible pairs of the tones for similarity (Figure 7). Analyses showed that (a) pitch salience appeared to be associated with

---

[7]"Perhaps change in 'timbre' is the most apt description, although we are reluctant to use that term because there is so little consensus on precisely what it means" says Green (1988, p. 37).

[8]It is likely that this "index of spectral complexity" is closely related to spectral centroid; the latter appears as a key dimension in timbre perception (Kendall & Carterette, 1993.)

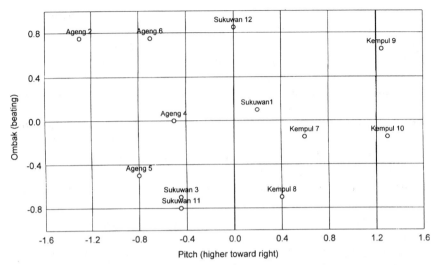

FIGURE 7   MDS plot of a two-dimensional solution based on perceptual similarities among Indonesian gong tones. The first dimension maps to perceived pitch (low to high, left to right). At a 45° angle to the first dimension is a mapping to *Ombak*, a perceived slow amplitude modulation (similar to a vibrato). Gongs without amplitude modulation cluster near the bottom left corner; those with extend along the line to the upper right-hand corner. In the figure, A = *Ageng*, S = *Suwukan*, K = *Kempul*, which are three size classes (large to small) of gongs. There are four of each gong size, thus the Arabic numbers refer to an arbitrary position within the set of 12 total gongs.

paired axisymmetrical vibration modes spaced at an octave; (b) the frequency of the fundamental mode for the 12 gongs spanned nearly 4 octaves (40.04–155.30 Hz); (c) envelope time-decay functions were consistent within gong types; (d) an original finding identifies the source of amplitude modulation (*ombak* rate) as the frequency difference (beating) between the octave partial and the third highest-amplitude partial in close proximity to it, in gongs where *ombak* was observed. Analyses by MDS and other methods led to perceptual interpretations of gong dimensions as pitch, *ombak*, and volume (spaciousness). No statistically significant effects that depended on gamelan training were observed. The authors concluded that listeners appeared to possess correlative mappings M(α, π) between the acoustical (α) and perceptual (π) frames of reference for Indonesian gong tones. Fundamental and octave axisymmetrical modes on and near the octave map to *ombak*; spectral envelopes map to perceptual identify; and multiple high-frequency inharmonic modes map to "shimmering" timbre.

According to Fales and McAdams (1994a, 1994b) ethnomusicologists see the use of noise in African music as an example of the "layering" of sounds in simultaneous rhythms, tonalities, or timbres. But in reality, the use of noise leads to two perceptual effects: (a) two or more sounds are heard concurrently ("layering") or (b) a fusion of the sounds is heard, "identifiably neither the primary nor the 'layered' sound"(Fales & McAdams, 1994a, p. 105). In psychophysical experiments too complicated to detail here, Fales and McAdams (1994a) asked subjects to rate the degree to which two simultaneous timbres—a sinusoid within a narrow-band noise—were fused, that is, heard as a single sound. Two conclusions of interest to ethnomusicologists were the following: (a) There does exist a perceptual contin-uum— at one end noise and tone are layered but at the other end noise and tone are fused, with an uncertainty region between; and (b) fusion of noise and tone may require a significant overlapping of bandwidths. The psychomusical implications of these results are unclear because traditional musical instruments, of Africa, say, embody complex time-varying structures, both tonal and noisy. Fales and Mc-Adams (1994b) speculate that the fusion and layering of noise and tone have im-plications for the blending of instrumental timbres in orchestra.

Radvansky, Fleming, and Simmons (1995) doubted Wolpert's (1990) claim that nonmusicians' memory for melodies was affected by timbre changes but mu-sicians' memory for melodies was not. Part of their experiments replicated Wol-pert's work, but they also controlled for clarity of instructions so as to avoid a ceiling effect (Wolpert's musicians performed almost perfectly). Listeners were asked to identify which of two test melodies had been heard earlier. These authors found that timbre change did not differentially affect musicians' or nonmusicians' memory for melodies. It is important to understand that Radvansky et al. took timbre to be a "surface feature" rather than a deeper structure like musical imagery or memory for chords or intervals.

A. INFANTS

Using a head-turning paradigm, Clarkson, Clifton, and Perris (1988) trained 22 7-month-old infants to discriminate the timbre of tonal complexes whose spectral envelopes differed. The infants first discriminated stimuli with the same funda-mental frequency of 200 Hz but different harmonics, then learned to discriminate less salient stimuli from which the fundamental had been removed. Their results suggest that infants can analyze tonal complexes by using the spectral envelope, one of the most important cues for timbre perception by adults.

VIII. CREATIVITY, COMMUNICATION, MEANING, AND AFFECT

Any natural language is constrained by a structure (syntax) and aims at the communication of meaning (semantics). Now music has syntax. Does it perforce have meaning? Musical significance is seen by Kraut (1992, p. 15) as "a syndrome of experiences correlated with the musical stimulus," whereas Raffman (1992) proposes that we regard musical feelings as a semantics. Sloboda (1992) aimed to incorporate the study of emotion as meaning by experiments at the interface of music theory and cognitive science, but up to now his attack has been by question-naire and self-report on peak experience.

In the context of folk music, Stockmann (1977) interprets the concepts of information processing and cognitive psychology in a communication model whose major stages (transformations) are production, reception, and analysis, with musical semiotics (sign structures) playing an important role. She argues that, for effective communication, the transforms must be related by common standards and rules, that is, by the diverse conventions and traditions of a musical culture, which include tonal systems, modes, scales, rhythmic and melodic patterns, performance practices, to say nothing of the rules for combining tonal elements and timbres. It is hard to disagree. We believe that the cross-cultural problems will wither away as the intracultural problems among psychologists and musicians are resolved by serious cooperative, model-driven experimental research on *psychomusical* problems.

Raychaudhuri (1980) reviews Western and Indian comparative studies of aesthetic creativity, which include many of his own, and alludes to perceptual and cognitive processes. In the study of this paper, Indian gifted "creative" musicians were, in comparison to Indian noncreative persons, found to be more open, fantasizing, sensually aware, experience-seeking, tolerant of perceptual ambiguity, self-driven, and egoistic (to name but a few). Alas, the methods are personality and projective tests, so conclusions about perceptual and cognitive capacities amount to Raychaudhuri's inferences from preferences and verbalized fantasies. No comparisons of any other work, Indian or Western, were made.

Cross-cultural cognitive or perceptual studies of aesthetics seem very rare, so we widen the net to include an intracultural study. Smith (1987) reports on conflicting aesthetic ideals between expert and novice listeners. He predicted that: (a) experts hold a highly syntactic aesthetic ideal and assign greatness to composers by this ideal, whereas (b) novice listeners hold a less syntactic romantic ideal yet accept the greatness valuations of experts. Hence novices have "musical split personality" because their syntactic ideal of greatness is congruent, but their romantic preference is incongruent, with the respective expert ideals. Based on analyses of American classical music culture of the 1940s, mainly from published data on preference, eminence, encyclopedia-page allocations, and number of musical performances, Smith reports confirmation of his hypothesis.

IX. VERBAL ATTRIBUTES AND SEMANTICS

Music points only to itself, under our working definition of music. Talk about music points outside itself, to behaviors in response to music, such as percepts, emotions, movement, and speech acts. Listeners, musicians, critics, and music theorists seek for words by which they can tell themselves and others about responses to music. Relative to the vast amount of talk about music, there are few systematic studies of descriptions or verbal attributes of music.

Descriptors and preferences for Eastern and Western musics by Japanese ($n =$ 255) and American ($n = 232$) nonmusic majors was studied using 30-sec excerpts of various Western and Eastern music styles (Darrow, Haack, & Kuribayashi, 1987). Subjects chose one of nine adjectives (e.g., mournful, majestic, tense, fanciful, tender), then rated their preferences for the excerpt on a 7-point scale. Subjects agreed better on the choice of descriptors for Western than for Eastern music, and overall both groups preferred Western to Eastern music. The authors conclude that their results not only confirm in part Farnsworth's (1969) supposition that listeners drawn from the same subculture will choose synonymous words to characterize much of Western music, but seem also to show that "subjects from two diverse cultures chose identical words to describe the Western musical examples" (p. 245). We remark that (a) the adjectives chosen relate to events or feelings, rather than directly to musical properties, (b) the choice of "identical" words is not surprising because English words were translated into Japanese "synonyms," and (c) (also noticed by the authors) the Japanese had more exposure to Western music than did Americans to Eastern music, and Japanese are little exposed to traditional Eastern and formal Japanese music except by special training.

As part of a cross-cultural study, Deva and Virmani (1968) used the semantic differential with the intent of quantifying the components of feeling aroused by classical Indian musical (Hindustani) excerpts in Indian listeners. Twenty-two adjective scales were chosen so as to suppress the *evaluative* dimension in favor of the dimensions *potency* and *activity*, which they deemed more suitable for describing musical experience. Some 37 subjects heard 2 minutes of the *alap* (development) portion of each of four *ragas* played twice on the sitar. On the second playing, each of the scales (e.g., dry-wet, sweet-bitter, evening-morning) was checked on one of seven categories (e.g., extremely, quite, slightly). After factor analysis of the data, "dimensions of meaning" (moods) were constructed by combining different bipolar scales according to scale loadings. The authors interpreted their data as "created" moods, which generally agreed with the "intended" moods that were inferred from musicological and traditional descriptions. For example, *Kafi rag* traditionally depicts such moods as gaiety, lightness, and religious joy. The created mood "has a lot of affect," is "humid and cool," has "depth," does not "agitate," and is "light." In contrast, Deva and Virmani's American colleagues (who apparently never published their results) communicated that American listeners to Kafi were confused, ambivalent, mystified, or indifferent.

Later Deva and Virmani (1974, 1980) used the same method with 228 Indian subjects (mixed with respect to age, sex, and musical training) on a single *alap* (from *rag Bhairav*) and in addition collected ("intersensory") choices on color, season, and time of day associated with *Bhairav*. The 27 bipolar adjective pairs were selected for their affinity to nine theoretical *rasas* (aesthetic emotions) and translated into English, the language in which the experiment was conducted. The authors found a very strong relation between traditional and measured mood (empathetic, positive, tranquil) and for intersensory associations (white/yellow, autumn, early morning/evening), in spite of improprieties like yellow and evening. They infer that their data reflect an ethos of 300 years ago and possibly racial memory, which seems to us tenuous.

Comparisons with Western verbal-attribute scales is difficult, if not impossible, because Deva and Virmani's aims concerned musical meaning as mood, and the choice of descriptors reflects this, for example: sexual-frigid, cowardly-valorous, sane-insane. On the other hand, most recent Western studies deal with music areferentially, that is, they look for verbal attributes which are closer to the music itself, for example, *nasality* or *resonance* of timbres as in von Bismarck (1974a, 1974b) or Kendall and Carterette (1993). It is quite legitimate to study verbal attributes of musical mood or meaning rather than those of timbre, but cross-cultural comparisons of mood and meaning depend more deeply on social and theoretical systems than in the case of timbre.

For example, Gregory (1996) examined whether emotional affect (mood, say) is directly produced by the music or is culturally determined such that particular musical forms are associated with certain emotions. Thus if listeners cannot detect the emotional content of unfamiliar music from other cultures, this would be evidence that the emotional affect is learned by association, and is not inherent in the music. Listeners from both Western (N = 25) and Indian (N = 22) backgrounds heard Western and Indian classical music so that their perception of the emotional content of the music could be compared. Six 7-point rating scales with adjectives as endpoints were completed by the listeners: *Happy-Sad, Majestic-Playful, Austere-Emotional, Romantic-Devotional, Relaxing-Tense, and Profound-Superficial.* (The pair Austere-Emotional was a control for the presence of *any* emotional response.)

Generally, cross-cultural differences in judgments were shown by statistically significant interactions between ethnic origin and rating scale. Further analysis showed significant differences between Western and Indian listeners in their responses to Indian music, but much fewer differences in their responses to Western music. This fit well with the fact that most of the Indian listeners had familiarity with Western music, but Western listeners were unfamiliar with Indian music. In conclusion Gregory (1996) said, "Overall the results strongly support the idea that the emotional content of music is not inherent in the music, but is probably a learnt association within a particular culture" (pp. 407–413).

In an earlier study, Gregory and Varney (1996) asked subjects from European and Asian cultural backgrounds to listen to examples of Western classical, Indian classical, and New Age music. These listeners chose adjectives to describe the mood but also identified the correct title of New Age excerpts and identified seasons of those excerpts that portrayed different seasons of the year. Comparison of Asian and European subjects showed many differences in the affective, adjectival task, but cultural differences were less marked in their choice of title and seasons. As Gregory (1966) found in the more incisive study with Western and Indian listeners, results generally suggested that the affective response to music is determined more by cultural tradition than by the inherent qualities of the music.

A. AGE AND CULTURAL DIFFERENCES

A number of studies have investigated preferences for familiar and unfamiliar music. Fourth-grade (*n* = 32) and undergraduate (*n* = 32) subjects heard six selections from each of two types of music, African and American "top-forty" music" and gave a preference rating on a 5-point scale (from "like very much" to "dislike very much"; Flowers, 1980). Pearson correlations between preference ratings and listening durations within music types were found to be very low and statistically insignificant for the fourth graders but higher and statistically significant in the case of undergraduates. When preferences were combined over music types, the correlations of listening time with preference were much higher in both groups, 0.79 for fourth graders and 0.95 for undergraduates. Although Flowers' study shows a good correspondence between verbal and nonverbal acts, the low preference for African music may simply reflect a preference for listening to the familiar.

Flowers and Costa-Giomi (1991) asked young children (ages 4–6), one English-speaking group (American), and one Spanish-speaking group (Argentinean) to identify two-octave changes in familiar song by verbal and nonverbal (hand-clap) identification. Her results supported prior research that showed that most young children do not apply the terms "high" and "low" to pitch changes, although almost all verbalized the pitch change in some way, with older children doing better than the younger. Although few Argentinean children clapped and they were less often correct when they did clap, they were more correct in using *"agudo"* or *"grave"* to indicate change than were American children in using "high" or "low," perhaps because *agudo/grave* does not confound spatial attributes with pitch attributes as English does.

Driven by the emphasis on multicultural understanding in the school curriculum, Shehan (1983) played 12 tape-recorded musical selections to ethnically mixed groups (80 fourth graders and 87 seventh graders) in American suburban schools. The greatest number were white middle class, but included black, Hispanic, and oriental backgrounds. One vocal and one instrumental selection came from each of six generic styles: current popular, Western classical, Asian, Indian, African, Indonesian, and Japanese. Children rated preferences on five bipolar adjective scales; listening times were also measured. These children preferred rock and popular to classical music and popular vocal to popular instrumental, and listened longest to what they preferred ($r = .98$). With respect to the music of non-Western cultures, instrumental is preferred to vocal, and the rhythmically dynamic (African and Japanese instrumental) to the less pulsate and less syncopated (Indonesian and Japanese vocal). We interpret Shehan's data sadly as suggesting that fourth graders are more responsive both to Western classical and non-Western music than are seventh graders, with the implication that early catholic preferences narrow as local cultural exposure increases.

If by exposure unfamiliar music becomes better understood, does it become valued more highly? In a study by Shehan (1984), two groups of American sixth graders were instructed on Indonesian gamelan music, one group by a heuristic method (singing and playing with gamelan), the other group by a didactic method (traditional music appreciation). On measures of affective change and cognitive achievement (tests on concepts), the heuristic group was superior to the didactic group. Although the groups did not differ in verbal preference response, correlations indicated that achievement was more closely related to operant music preference behavior than to verbal preference response.

In a related study, Shehan (1985) examined the transfer of preference from taught to untaught pieces of non-Western music genres (traditional African, Asian Indian, Japanese, and Hispanic songs with instrumental accompaniment) in American sixth graders. She found significant preference differences between the taught and untaught selection of genres but, although instruction increased preference for unfamiliar non-Western songs, there was no transfer of preference to untaught pieces of the same genre. So, teachers beware: an expectation that "study of one representative piece from a style will impact upon interest in other stylistically similar pieces is not supported" (p. 156).

According to Adachi (1996) Japanese children master at least two kinds of linguistic symbols for representing sounds or actions: (a) *Onomatopoeia/mimesis* and (b) *Musical mnemonics*. The children can also learn (c) *Western musical symbols*. Adachi's research question was, how do these different milieus of learning affect the use of symbols in Japanese children's depiction of rhythm patterns? Some 352 children at grades 1 through 6 learned to clap a rhythmic pattern. For half, the pattern was long long short short long, and for the other half, the pattern was long short short long long. The children then wrote on a piece of paper something (whatever the child wished) to help them in remembering the rhythm. These depictions were scored as 0 or 1 for each of the three types: onomatopeia/mimesis (linguistic representation of sound or actions, respectively as taken from the *Dictionary of Onomatopoeia and Mimesis*), musical mnemonics (one or more of the symbols *tan, ta, taa-aa,* or *un*) and Western musical symbols (one or more of the musical symbols, e.g., ..., but not restricted to rhythm notation). The results were that onomatopoeia/mimesis was used almost exclusively in Grade 1, decreased considerably in Grade 2 but remained in use at all grade levels. At Grade 2 and higher, the use of musical mnemonics was significantly higher than the use of onomatopoeia/mimesis. In Grade 1, Western musical notation was not used at all, and its was used by only 23% of the children in Grade 6. Adachi concluded that different milieus of learning (59 children had musical training, 262 did not) influenced the depiction of rhythm, that the Japanese language facilitated the use of linguistic symbols because, for example, moving on to musical mnemonics requires only a change of syllable ("pa" becomes "ta"), but the use of Western musical notation depends on training beyond the standard school curriculum.

X. SPECIES DIFFERENCES: ANIMAL SPEECH AND MUSIC

A. GENERAL

A major problem in studying vocal behavior in any nonhuman species is that one is faced with the difficult task of creating a kind of species-specific phonetics. Primates have in some measure the physical, physiological, and cognitive apparatus for generating speechlike sounds and by implication simple musical sounds. For the vocalizations of some animals, such as songbirds, this task is simplified by the fact that calls have relatively structured patterns. However, for many mammalian species, vocalizations consist of complex acoustical patterns that are highly variable. Although the chimpanzee's vowel space is primitive compared with that of humans (Lieberman, 1972), its motor and cognitive functions equip it for relatively sophisticated communication. Seyfarth, Cheney, and Marler (1980) tape recorded alarm calls given by vervet monkeys in actual encounters with leopards, eagles, and snakes. When these calls were played back in the absence of predators, the authors found that leopard alarms caused the monkeys to run into trees, snake alarms caused them to look down into the grass around them, and eagle alarms caused them to look up into the air or run into the bush. These clearly different alarm behaviors were validated by cinematography. Shipley, Carterette, and Buchwald (1991) found the presence of formantlike resonances in cat vocalizations and an important role of jaw movements (vocal gestures) in the production of calls, which suggested to them "that there may be much more extensive homologies of both perception and production underlying the communication systems of humans and cats than has generally been assumed ... Evolution has provided a versatile vocal mechanism, a larynx-tract, source-filter system that has important similarities across many mammals" (pp. 908–909).[9]

Contemporary studies of animal cognition and consciousness (e.g., Griffin, 1981) emphasize genetic structures and their influence on behavior. Closely related cognitive capacities of animals are the abilities to estimate the duration of an interval, count a number of discrete events, and estimate the rate of occurrence of events (Gallistel, 1990). Strikingly different morphologies of the visual systems of birds and mammals mask an extraordinary degree of similarity (Shimizu & Karten, 1993). Birds have visual fields that are differentiated functionally and must integrate both similar and different views from different parts of the environment. Watanabe, Lea, and Dittrich (1993) argue that birds, like other higher animals, have evolved to recognize objects in their environments, not merely the sensory constituents of objects, and that birds (pigeons) discriminate categories, possess concepts, and perceive pictures as representations of objects. These authors' evidence supports the operation of both absolute and relative discrimination of concepts in pigeon. In humans, Dowling and Harwood (1986) review absolute and relative aspects of musical perception and cognition. Hulse and Page (1988) point out that the starling's perception of pitch relations is governed by absolute, not relative frequency (see Section XIII).

Barber (1993) takes a strong stand about the high intelligence and cognitive skills of birds, for example, "Birds have many abilities that humans assume are unique to humans, including musical ability (appreciation, composition, and per-

---

[9]In their studies of animal acoustic signals, bioacousticians have been bound, sadly, to the sonogram in spite of the easily available, yet advanced signal processing methods such as the fast Fourier transform and linear predictive coding. The latter is based on vocal tract theories and was applied by Carterette in the case of kittens and cats as early as 1976 (Carterette, Shipley, & Buchwald, 1984). Digital signal processing techniques combined with linear prediction theory could yield information relevant to the ability of animals to produce protomusical signals.

formance)" (p. 3). With respect to avian music, Barber subscribes to the views of the English musicologist Len Howard. As reported by Barber, Howard concludes from extensive descriptive study that not only do birds make music but they enjoy singing, convey messages, express feelings and emotions, sing when happy, and can produce beautiful music. Individual, conspecific birds can be identified by their improvisations, differing as widely in talent as do humans. "There are also some very superior musicians among songbirds. For instance, over a period of a few days, a talented blackbird creatively and spontaneously composed the opening phrase of the Rondo in Beethoven's violin concerto. (He had not previously heard it.)" (Barber, 1993, p. 47). We are skeptical of such strong claims that have no experimental support.

B. SONG LEARNING BY HUMANS AND BIRDS

By the age of 4, a human being has developed nearly complete mastery of his or her native tongue, in the absence of any formal instruction whatsoever. It is as if some genetic communication strategy is mapped or interpreted tactically to suit a given linguistic culture. But reading and writing generally require instruction. Does song develop more like speech or reading?

Gardner (1981) contrasts the song learning of humans with that of birds. The avian pattern has three main forms: (a) A single song is produced eventually by every male of the species with no feedback or external hearing required, as in the ringdove. (b) Exemplified by the canary, a babbling subsong is followed by a plastic phrasal phase, finally ending in a stereotyped song similar to that of other males of the species; the bird must hear its own song, but can learn without hearing other birds sing. (c) Both auditory feedback and exposure to other birdsong is required, for example in chaffinch.

Gardner (1981) suggests that the human pattern begins at about age 1 with spontaneous song, with the production of fragmentary intervals, mainly seconds and thirds, but some fourths. The learning of song by children is aided by their ability before age 1 to imitate intonational patterns of speech and to match specific pitches with an accuracy far greater than chance. By age 1.5 years, children intentionally produce discrete pitches, and by age 2.5 years, they produce minor and major thirds and fourths, and they are aware of tunes sung by others, although their song lacks tonality and harmony. Nearing age 4, learned song begins to dominate spontaneous song, words are learned as is the surface structure of rhythm and contour, but with inaccurate interval production and little sense of key. By age 5, a child can extract the underlying pulse from the surface rhythm and has mastered the tonal elements of interval and key, and can sing a good song. But few can play instruments or read notation. As Gardner puts it, 5-year-olds lack knowledge of music and music theory.

Perhaps it makes no sense to compare the learning of song by children with the learning of song by birds. Birdsong is determined mostly by genetics and little by environment and culture. Birds sing the songs for which nature equipped them, songs that carry social messages, mainly about reproduction and survival. All normal children learn speech, which carries a wide range of social messages about feelings, intentions, and meaning that refer to the self, to the world, and to other beings.

C. BIRDSONG

1. Syrinx: The Vocal Organ of Birds

How do birds sing? In the following, we draw heavily on Greenewalt (1968) and Nowicki and Marler's (1988) recent review of the issues. The vocal organ of all birds, the *syrinx*, is not found in any other animal. The oscine syrinx is a tube of cartilaginous rings fitted with a pair of medial tympaniform membranes (MTM). The syrinx opens into the trachea and is fed by air from the two bronchi below. Since the mid-18th century, the syrinx has been put in analogy to many kinds of musical instruments: double reed (oboe), lip reed (horn, trombone), organ pipes (reed, pipe [oscillating jet]). Each of these analogies implies a different mechanism, but all imply that source vibration is constrained to produce acoustic oscillations that correspond to air-column resonances. More recently the operation of the syrinx has been analogized to human phonation, which implies that the oscillator (vocal folds) is not influenced by the acoustical properties of the vocal tract. Under this source-filter model (Fant, 1960), changes in the shape of the vocal tract alter the location and amplitude of the local energy maxima, the so-called formants.

In his important monograph, Greenewalt (1968) reviewed more than two centuries of work on the acoustics and physiology of birdsong, made further experiments, and offered a model that has three major features: (a) The acoustics sources are pairs of membranes (the MTMs) that are set into vibration by airflow; (b) the MTMs are functionally independent, thus the songbird can produce two unrelated tones simultaneously; and (c) all modulations in birdsong are generated by changes in the state of the MTM sources. Greenewalt considered the possibility of a syrinx-tracheal filter model, but could find no evidence for its support.

Nowicki and Marler (1988) review a number of hypotheses, old and new, on the operation of the vocal apparatus of birds during singing with a focus on how the tonal sounds "so typical of birdsong" are generated. In their view, the evidence for the independence of the two voices of syringeal song is incomplete. Their experimental findings, including effects of placing singing birds in helium air, point to the existence of coupling of the two voices and changes in vocal tract resonances that modify the tonal quality of birdsong. They propose a new model of songbird phonation, one that implies close coordination between syringeal acoustical sources and dynamical modifications of the vocal tract, with both vibrations of syringeal membranes and vocal tract resonances apparently "functioning in intricate harmony" (p. 422). An exotic example of vocal control is shown in Robisson,

Aubin, and Bremond's (1993) acoustical analyses of display calls of an Antarctic bird, the emperor penguin (*Aptenodytes forsterii*). They found temporal patterning of syllabic, frequency, and timbral (spectral) features. Highly distinctive individual calls revealed precisely controlled acoustical beats arising from paired syrinxes. Such sounds are not easily degraded and may enhance recognition in the "hostile and noisy environment." We turn now to work on the nature of perceptual processing of sound patterns by songbirds.

2. Perception of Sound Patterns

Braaten and Hulse (1993) explored the perception of continuously repeating auditory patterns by European starlings (*Sturnus vulgaris*) aimed at answering the question, does a songbird hear a series of unrelated elements, or are the elements organized by perceptual rules? Patterns were built of sound elements of two kinds, X (a fundamental and fourth harmonic) and O (a fundamental and second and third harmonic). From one series of experiments, the authors conclude that "for starlings, perception is an active process in which a perceptual organization is selected from a number of alternatives"(p. 576). "The starlings did perceive and remember features of the two elements that formed the patterns. That is, the perception of these patterns was not entirely abstract" (p. 576). Other experiments suggested that starlings "may have perceived these patterns as perceptual streams" (p. 577). One element may have been seen as figure, the other as background. "If so, this would be the first demonstration of auditory streaming by a nonhuman animal" (p. 577).

Williams, Cynx, and Nottebohm (1989) noted that zebra finch (*Taeniopygia guttata*) song syllables often include harmonic frequency components that may be suppressed variously within and among individual birds. These patterns of suppression are timbre, say the authors, who suggest that selective suppression and emphasis of harmonics create signal diversity by adding a great number of possible timbral variant song syllables for any one syllable, which may be important in communication. Later, Cynx, Williams, and Nottebohm (1990) studied timbre discrimination by the zebra finch, observing that individual harmonics of zebra finch songs can be more or less emphasized, the functional role of which is unknown. By using two song syllables that differed only in the absence of second or fifth harmonic, it was shown that male or female zebra finches used the second harmonic as the sole discrimination cue.

A possibility that birdsongs may learn complex, tonal qualities of birdsong was shown by Nowicki, Marler, Maynard, and Peters (1992), who had song sparrows sing in helium gas, thereby modifying their pure-tonal songs so as to have harmonic overtones. Song sparrows ($n = 16$) learned equally well from normal and harmonic models. Although birds that learned from harmonic models reproduced some of the material with harmonic overtones, the majority of notes was produced as pure-tonal copies. In an earlier study, Nowicki, Mitani, Nelson, and Marler (1989) compared responsiveness of 30 male swamp sparrows to harmonic models (sung in helium) and pure-tonal models. The birds were significantly more responsive to play back of normal, pure-tone songs than to the helium harmonic tone songs, although harmonic songs kept a high degree of salience. This result must be tempered by knowing that the pure-tone songs had to be shifted up in frequency to match the average spectra of the helium songs.

Extending her previous findings that blackbirds and cowbirds showed superior identification of conspecific final trill or whistle song elements relative to alien species, Sinnott (1989) examined human perception of the same song materials for which birds were tutored with alien final song elements. She found that (a) humans attend mainly to final song elements, (b) birds identifying alien songs attended mainly to introductory elements, disregarding final elements, and (c) birds identifying conspecific songs process both initial and final elements, although they direct more attention to initial elements.

3. Octave Equivalence

Humans from diverse cultures perceive tones and melodies that are separated by an octave as highly similar (Deutsch, 1982; Dowling & Harwood, 1986). Experimental evidence for the similarity of equivalent notes one or more octaves apart was found in conditioning studies that used both humans (Humphreys, 1939) and rats (Blackwell & Schlosberg, 1943). The sensitivity of rats to octave relations reported by Blackwell and Schlosberg has not been confirmed apparently. Starlings and cowbirds, which can tell simple descending from rising tonal patterns, could not learn one-octave transpositions (Hulse & Cynx, 1985). Cynx, Hulse, and Polyzois (1986) then provided a psychophysical estimate of how pitch discrimination deteriorated outside the training range and showed that the gradient of loss was much steeper than would be expected on stimulus generalization or procedural grounds. They point out some implications of the range constraint and its psychophysical properties for the analysis of birdsong and for the study of animal cognition. Virtually all work with avian perception has been done with time sequences of tones but harmonic structures, rich in relative pitch information, should be employed in view of Cynx and Shapiro's (1986) finding that starlings, like humans, perceive the missing fundamental in harmonic complexes.

Hulse (1989) describes some comparative research with songbirds based on fact and theory drawn from human cognitive psychology. In these studies, greater generalization was found for tones whose frequencies were an octave apart than for tones whose frequencies were somewhat less than an octave away from the conditioned stimulus. Such findings suggest that octave equivalence may occur in the absence of any culturally defined system of tonality.

The time resolution of acoustic signals by birds was compared by Wilkinson and Howse (1975), who asked bullfinches, greenfinches, pigeons, and humans to discriminate between single and paired clicks. The threshold for all birds was between 2 and 4 msec, but much greater for humans, at between 12 and 50 msec. The authors suggest that bullfinches can use temporal patterns in their sequence calls for birdsong signaling and recognition.

XI. PERCEPTION OF TONALITY BY THE
MONKEY

D'Amato (1988) reviews a series of experiments by him and his coworkers that were aimed at assessing the tonal pattern perception of cebus monkeys and rats. Although it first appeared that both groups could tell two tunes apart, which suggested the possession of tonal pattern perception by rat and monkey, careful analyses and control experiments showed that discrimination was controlled completely by local cues. Humans recognize melodies by using both contour and interval properties (Dowling & Harwood, 1986) but apparently rats and monkeys cannot use either. Monkeys can't hum tunes "because they don't hear them" (D'Amato, 1988, p. 478). Whereas humans are sensitive to rising, falling, or unchanging sequences of tones located in disjunct frequency ranges, parakeets are sensitive to the frequency level of the sequences but not to their tonal pattern (Dooling, Brown, Park, Okanoya, & Soli, 1987).

D'Amato's review deals with a number of issues related to perceptual and cognitive abilities of various species. For example, is tonal pattern perception a capacity reserved for species-specific signals? Is it restricted to the training range of stimuli? Various claims about the ability of certain species "from raccoons to elephants" to recognize human speech are based on "little convincing evidence that more than local cues are involved in their discriminative behavior" (p. 476). Thus what appears to be learning of contour may on closer look be the learning of serial order of absolute pitches. Failure to perform on acoustical transpositions outside the training range is a strong basis for concluding that discrimination is controlled by local cues rather than by contour. We suggest that many comparisons of human tonal pattern recognition with that of other species suffer from a failure to work within functionally comparable audiograms. Generally speaking, the characteristic (most sensitive) frequency (CF) of an animal's audiogram is roughly inverse to size, being about 3.5 kHz for humans and 15 kHz for mice. Data and interpretations may depend critically on methods and procedures used, thus transposition may be a key to telling whether pattern perception is based in local absolutes or relative frequency contours.

XII. NOTES ON THE NEUROPHYSIOLOGY OF
MUSIC PERCEPTION

A. NEUROPSYCHOLOGY AND AUDITORY BRAIN
MECHANISMS

Recent handbook volumes review research on neuropsychology (Dahlia Zaidel, 1995) and research on hearing generally (Moore, 1995), with chapters on neural signal processing, coding of intensity, binaural mechanisms, and pitch. Although auditory neuropsychology is a large, very active field of research, comparative studies are sparse. Handel (1995, pp. 456–457) states that although instruments, voices, and natural events are perceived in similar ways, there is strong evidence that music and speech are processed in different hemispheres. However, the evidence is against the widely held simplistic view that speech is processed by the left brain and music by the right brain. From positron-emission tomography evidence, Sergent, Zuck, Terriah, and MacDonald (1992) suggest that distributed neural networks underlie musical sight-reading and keyboard playing, with each function being localized in different parts of the cerebellum and cortical lobes.

Most research on the neuropsychology of music perception deals with hemispheric differences, which gives short schrift to the basic neural mechanisms of music. Milner (1962) found that, in patients with unilateral temporal lobe lesions, those with right-sided lesions were impaired on memory for tones and on timbre discrimination. In right-temporal lobectomy, Shankweiler (1966) found that melody recognition was impaired but not in left-temporal lobectomy. In cases where musical perception deficits have been observed, these have almost always been preceded by right-temporal lobe damage (Zatorre, 1984).

Aimed at identifying neural substrates of pitch perception and memory for pitch, Schlaug, Martin, Edelman, and Warach (1996) studied 12 normal right-handed subjects, graded according to their musical expertise, on two auditory memory tasks and an auditory monitoring task The auditory tasks were based on tones and phonemes, the monitoring task on white-noise bursts. We assume, although the authors do not tell us, that tones are musical and phonemes are amusical (speechlike) whereas the noise bursts are neither music nor speech but serve as a control for perceptual processing. In all tasks, neural activity was monitored by means of functional magnetic resonance imaging (fMRI). Both musicians and nonmusicians showed a common pattern of suprasylvian activity, which the authors suggested might be related to the memory component and response demands of the task. Relative to nomusicians, musicians showed more leftward-lateralized posterior perisylvian activity. The details of the differences within and between the groups are too complicated to report here, but the authors conclude that the variability in infrasylvian and perisylvian regions indicate differences in the perception and processing of auditory stimuli as a function of musical experience.

Do professional keyboard players differ from nonmusicians in cortical motor size? In a study of right-handed males—21 musicians and 30 nonmusicians—(Schlaug, Amunts, Jäncke, Schleicher, & Zille, 1996), both groups were found to have a significantly longer left- than right-intrasulcal length of the posterior precentral gyrus (ILPG) but musicians showed a significantly lower degree of interhemispheric asymmetry. These ILPG lengths, obtained by magnetic resonance imaging, indexed the size of the primary motor cortex and motor hand representation area and interhemispheric asymmetry was simply the difference of left minus right ILPG. On a test of hand motor skill, musicians were more symmetrical across hands than nonmusicians and also scored higher than nonmusicians on an index finger-tapping test. From the fact of lesser asymmetry in ILPG and that the increase in ILPG covaried with motor skill and with age when musical training began, the authors interpreted "these findings as a functionally induced adaptive plasticity of human motor cortex" (p. 433).

Dichotic studies (see Corballis, 1995 for a review of hemispheric differences) seem to show that whereas the (analytical) left hemisphere is specialized for speech sounds, the (holistic) right hemisphere is specialized for nonverbal auditory tasks, such as perception of environmental sounds, vocal nonverbal sounds and aspects of music, although the left hemisphere is specialized for rhythm. Is brain specialization in musicians different from that of nonmusicians? Bever and Chiarello (1974) reported that the musically trained had a left-brain advantage compared with the right-brain advantage of musically untrained listeners, and they suggested that the processing of music becomes more analytical, more like speech, in the musically sophisticated when compared with the holistic, right-brain processing of the musically untrained. Later evidence is ambiguous on the advantage of musical training (see Zatorre's 1984 critical review), although there is good support for the notion that lateral asymmetries may not be fixed, but may be associated with processing strategies. It is intriguing that amusia in professional musicians is usually associated with aphasia (Brust, 1980).

Corballis (1995) speculates that the right hemisphere is the province of an evolutionarily early holistic representation mode and that the specialized generative, part-wise representation mode of the right hemisphere evolved much later. "The generative mode may be applied to music as to language and the representation of objects, especially among skilled musicians" (p. 98). Thus Lerdahl and Jackendoff (1983) proposed a generative grammar of tonal music with close parallels to grammars of language.[10]

B. NORMAL VERSUS ABNORMAL PROCESSING

Peretz (1990) found evidence from neurological patients of a double dissociation between rhythm and melody in the perceptual domain, by use of melodic and rhythmic cues in a classification task. Two patients performed normally with rhythmic cues, but at chance with melodic cues. Conversely, two other patients performed at chance with rhythmic cues but normally with melodic cues. More clear-cut was the case of patient C. N., whose severe impairment of melody processing was not accompanied by an impairment of rhythm processing. From these two studies in which normal control subjects performed equally well with either cue, Peretz and Kolinsky (1993) concluded that: Melody and rhythm are independent at some level; yet melody and rhythm are also not completely independent dimensions, because normal subjects easily integrate the two dimensions. She

---

[10]Hierarchies are part of the musical message because any redundancy implies structure. The role of hierarchy in our approach is flexible, asymmetric, and ambiguous (Carterette & Kendall, 1990), which is consistent with the evidence from neuropsychology reviewed by Zatorre (1984). Generative and transformational procedures are neither necessary nor sufficient in recoding of transformations, such as playing from a score. Our own concept of musical processing is "one of manifold procedures and multiple strategies, not of grammars" (Kendall & Carterette, 1990, p. 134).

speculates that melodic and rhythmic percepts arising from early processing stages are later combined in an integrated construct.

Walker (1985) compared mental imagery in musical concept formation by congenitally blind and sighted subjects. Four shapes were matched with four sounds, each of which was varied by pitch, loudness, duration, and timbre. No significant differences were found between the blind and sighted subjects in the externalizations of images arising from the auditory stimuli. This outcome suggests to Walker that neural stimulation by sound induced the same internal imagery regardless of visual experiences, although he admits that it is still necessary to show that the result is free of cultural effects before it would be useful to educators.

C. ANIMAL STUDIES

The study of the neurophysiological bases for animal auditory perception, particularly of tone sequences, may provide insight into the fundamental bases of music perception in humans. However, most studies in auditory neurophysiology use isolated pure tones as stimuli, and even sequences of pure tones are seldom used. Yet the study of sequences might connect single tone experiments with the complex domains of biosonar and species-specific vocalizations and "have potential relevance to neural mechanisms of music" say Weinberger and McKenna (1988, p. 356). They studied the responses of single neurons in auditory cortical fields of waking cats to pentads—five different isointensity tones that were presented in contoured sequences whose frequencies increased or decreased monotonically or were not monotonic. Monofrequency pentads served as controls for serial position. Some 85% of neurons in both primary and secondary fields were sensitive to tonal contour; responses were significantly modified if one tone of a monotonic sequence was omitted, and the magnitude of the effect was greater in the secondary than in the primary field. Some effects of changing contour could be accounted for by changes in serial position, but many could not: "Preliminary evidence suggested that interval distance between temporally adjacent tones" (p. 376) might have an important role in sensitivity to contour changes. We agree, given the role of an auditory neuron's tuning curve in its response life. Because contoured tonal sequences are detectable in single neurons of auditory cortex, Weinberger and McKenna (1988) conclude that it is critical to use dynamic stimuli for a physiological account of the perception of musical and other complex acoustical stimuli. They review the few other related auditory neuronal studies, finding their results to agree generally in the case of bat and cat but not in cebus monkey for which D'Amato (1988) found no evidence of tonal-pattern perception.

Konishi (1985) reviews neurobiological issues and directions in the study of birdsong, emphasizing development, learning, and neural control. As well as presenting his own model of song learning, Konishi addresses topics in the ethology of birdsong, ontogeny of song, and the role of sex hormones in the vocal control system. Marx (1982) reviews Nottebohm's work on canaries with respect to brain changes, which found that while a bird is learning to sing, its brain regions grow but then shrink when they are silent; and old song repertories are discarded before a bird begins to learn new songs.

XIII. COGNITIVE MUSICAL UNIVERSALS

Ultimately musical universals must spring from a common biological substrate on which the cognitive systems of language and music rest. A musical universal (hereafter simply universal) must be induced from the intersections of the sets of primitive musical properties and relationships. A universal is not a thing like the pitch A = 440 Hz but is rather a feature or pattern or process that is induced or inferred from data. Discussions of universals from the viewpoint of cognitive psychology are given by Harwood (1976), Dowling and Harwood (1986), and Sloboda (1985). Some possible universals are (a) a deep-structural musical idea, (b) elementary auditory grouping strategies, (c) the use of a stable reference pitch, (d) the division of an octave into scale steps, (e), the use of reference pulses, (f) the induction of rhythmic patterns by an asymmetrical subdivision of time pulses. The wide spectrum of musical cultures arises from the choices and elaborations of a few universals.

Hulse and Page (1988) argue persuasively that new techniques and new theory enables one to ask whether musical universals can be exhibited in nonhuman species, that is, do the perceptual principles underlying music span nonhuman species as well as human cultures? A series of experiments by Hulse and his colleagues show that the European starling can perceive one form of musical universals, *pitch relations*. But this songbird transposes pitch relations across large shifts in tone heights only with difficulty and shows, rather, a preference for learning pitch patterns based on the *absolute* pitch of tonal components. They suggest from such results that further comparative studies of music may illuminate the principles that make human music perception unique, as well as gaining new knowledge about animals. As an instance, Nelson and Marler (1989) showed songbirds perceptually partition a natural stimulus continuum of notes into two categories that are known to play different roles in song organization. We suspect, with Hulse and Page, that there exist for humans as well as animals some musical absolutes that elude us because our theories and experiments are designed to reveal relations and differences rather than universals.

XIV. CODA

Even though music shows itself in many different forms in various cultures, we contend that underlying these epiphenomena is a universal set of cognitive principles shared by all humans. It follows that music is not arbitrary, is not whimsical, but is an expression of these principles. The fact that music has different surface features arises from the interaction of geographical, social, and cultural contexts with psychophysiological mechanisms. Scholars researching these contexts, including anthropologists and ethnomusicologists, recently have become less interested than they once were in comparative analysis and cross-cultural universals. Blacking (1966) suggests that we accept the view that patterns of music sound in any culture are the product of changes and behaviors peculiar to that culture. We cannot compare them with similar patterns in another culture unless we know that the latter are derived from similar concepts and behavior. We do not disagree, but in our opinion many have based their comparative analyses on idiosyncratic, surface features. The deeper structures and the underlying behavioral principles *can* be compared. Such comparisons do not lessen the interest in nor the importance of intracultural musical behaviors.

What are some of the central, underlying principles that stem from the need of the organism to quantize a continuous stream of sound? A fundamental one is that the data must be parsed and reduced by a limited-capacity system. Perceptual rules for data reduction are manifest in a number of musical concepts. The octave allows for pitch circularity, thus reducing the entire auditory bandwidth of frequency effectively to a shorter bandwidth. Within an octave, further reduction occurs: The frequency continuum is quantized (scale steps).

Two basic principles conspire to give pattern, and so to quantize the world into sensory and perceptual objects. The first principle is *contrast*; we look and listen for difference, for boundaries, for edges, for change, for any distinctive feature. The second, interacting principle, is *periodicity*; we search for recurring contrast patterns, for redundancies in time and space. What variables are used for contrast and how they are made periodic differentiate musical cultures.

For example, intervallic variety within redundancy is a characteristic of the Western tuning system and its modes (see Section III, and especially Balzano, 1980). However, these principles cannot operate in the equipentatonic tuning of some gamelan instruments, which instead must rely on larger chains of chroma for the development of contrast patterns (see Carterette et al., 1993). Yet another example: Changes in melodic contour direction are boundary conditions in the West; whereas the *didjiridu* of aboriginal Australia produces timbral contour patterns (see Kendall & Carterette, 1991, pp. 401–402 for a discussion of timbral contour theory).

It follows that musical cultures that use temporally linear pitch structures overwhelmingly use discrete pitch relationships to impart a musical idea, whereas other musical cultures create patterns through other means, such as timbral manipulation, which is the primary carrier of information in Mongolian and some forms of Tibetan singing (Malm, 1967), or Australian aboriginal music of the *didjiridu*.

It is clear to us, that in order to have an integrative approach to understanding musical behavior, prejudices and biases attached to different domains of research must be overcome. The effort to find principles of musical perception is not merely technical talk about art, in Geertz's phrase (1973). He calls for the study of culture not as "an experimental science in search of law but an interpretive one in search of meaning" (1973, p. 5). We believe that Geertz misstates the nature of science versus interpretation. As we put it (Carterette & Kendall, 1994), "The experimental search for law is at the heart of an interpretive science in search of meaning" (p. 59). We are all, regardless of domain, engaged in the search for the systematic and predictive relationships in our musical observations, whether the research context be intracultural or intercultural or interspecies.

REFERENCES

Abe, J., & Hoshino, E. (1985). Schema-driven properties of melody cognition: Experiments on final-tone extrapolation by music experts. *Japanese Journal of Psychonomic Science, 4*(1), 1-9.

Adachi, M. (1996). Japanese children's use of linguistic symbols in depicting rhythm patterns. In B. Pennycook & E. Costa-Giomi (Eds.), *Proceedings of the Forth International Conference on Music Perception and Cognition* (pp. 413–418). Montreal: Society for Music Perception and Cognition.

Adams, C. R. (1976). Melodic contour typology. *Ethnomusicology, 20*(2), 179-215.

Álvarez, R., & Siemens, L. (1988). The lithophonic use of large natural rocks in the prehistoric Canary Islands. In E. Hickman & D. W. Hughes (Eds.), *The archaeology of early music cultures* (pp. 1–10). Bonn: Verlag für systematische Musikwissenschaft GmbH.

Aoyagi, T. (1996). *Perceptual interrelationships among nine septatonic modes.* Unpublished masters thesis. Los Angeles: University of California.

Aoyagi, T., & Kendall, R. A. (1996). Perceptual relationships among nine septatonic western modes: Convergence across distinct methods. In B. Pennycook & E. Costa-Giomi (Eds.), *Proceedings of the Fourth International Conference on Music Perception and Cognition* (pp. 65–70). Montreal, Canada: Society for Music Perception and Cognition.

Arom, S. (1991). *African polyphony and polyrhythm: Musical structure and methodology* (M. Thom, B. Tuckett & R. Boyd, Trans.) Cambridge: Cambridge University Press. (Original publication 1885)

Arom, S., & Fürniss, A. (1993). An interactive experimental method for the determination of musical scales in oral cultures: Application to the vocal music of the Aka Pygmies of Central Africa. *Contemporary Music Reviews, 9*(1&2), 7–12.

Baily, J. (1985). Music structure and human movement. In P. Howell, I. Cross, & R. West (Eds.), *Musical structure and cognition* (pp. 237–285). London: Academic Press.

Baily, J. (1988). Anthropological and psychological approaches to the study of music theory and musical cognition. *Yearbook for Traditional Music, 20,* 114–124.

Balzano, G. J. (1980). The group-theoretic description of 12-fold and microtonal pitch systems. *Computer Music Journal, 4*(4), 66–84.

Barber, T. X. (1993). *The human nature of birds: A scientific discovery with startling implications.* New York: St. Martin's Press.

Bartlett, J. C., & Dowling, W. J. (1980). The recognition of transposed melodies: A key-distance effect in developmental perspective. *Journal of Experimental Psychology: Human Perception & Performance, 6,* 501–515.

Beal, A. L. (1985). The skill of recognizing musical structures. *Memory and Cognition, 13,* 405–412.

Becker, J. (1979) Time and tune in Java. In A. L. Becker & A. A. Yengoyan, (Eds.), *The imagination of reality: Essays in southeast Asian coherence systems* (pp. 197–210). Norwood, NJ: Ablex Publishing Corporation.

Becker, J. (1980). *Traditional music in modern Java: Gamelan in a changing society.* Honolulu: University Press of Hawaii.

Bever, T., & Chiarello, R. (1974). Cerebral dominance in musicians. *Science, 185,* 537–539.

Bharucha, J. J. (1984). Even hierarchies, tonal hierarchies, and assimilation: A reply to Deutsch and Dowling. *Journal of Experimental Psychology: General, 113,* 421–425.

Blacking, J. (1955). Some notes on a theory of African rhythm advanced by Erich von Hornbostel. *African Music, 1*(2), 12–20.

Blacking, J. (1970). Tonal organization in the music of two Venda initiation schools. *Ethnomusicology, 14,* 1–56.

Blacking, J. (1973). *How musical is man?* Seattle: University of Washington Press.

Blacking, J. (1988). Ethnomusicology and prehistoric music making. In E. Hickman & D. W. Hughes (Eds.), *The archaeology of early music cultures* (pp. 329–335). Bonn: Verlag fuer systematische Musikwissenschaft GmbH.

Blackwell, H. R., & Schlosberg, H. (1943). Octave generalization, pitch discrimination, and loudness thresholds in the white rat. *Journal of Experimental Psychology, 33,* 407–419.

Braaten, R. F., & Hulse, S. H. (1993). Perceptual organization of auditory temporal patterns in European starlings (*Sturnus vulgaris*). *Perception & Psychophysics, 54*(5), 567–578.

Brust, J. C. M. (1980). Music and language: Musical alexia and agraphia. *Brain, 103,* 367–392.

Burns, E. M. (1974a). Octave adjustment by non-western musicians. *Journal of the Acoustical Society of America, 56*(S), 25–26.

Burns, E. M. (1974b). In search of the shruti. *Journal of the Acoustical Society of America, 56*(S), 26.

Burns, E. M., & Ward, W. D. (1982). Intervals, scales, and tunings. In D. Deutsch (Ed.), *The Psychology of music* (pp. 241–269). New York: Academic Press.

Butler, J. W., & Daston, P. G. (1968). Musical consonance as musical preference: A cross-cultural study. *Journal of General Psychology, 79,* 129–142.

Carlsen, J. C. (1981). Some factors which influence melodic expectancy. *Psychomusicology, 1,* 12–29.

Carterette, E. C. (1994). Timbre, tuning and stretched octave of Javanese gamelans. In *Proceedings of the 3rd International Conference on Music Perception & Cognition* (pp. 103–104). Liège, Belgium: European Society for the Cognitive Sciences of Music.

Carterette, E. C., & Kendall, R. A. (1994). On the tuning and stretched octave of Javanese gamelans. *Leonardo Music Journal, 4,* 59–68.

Carterette, E. C., Kendall, R. A., & DeVale, S. C. (1993). Comparative acoustical and psychoacoustical analyses of gamelan instrument tones. *Journal of the Acoustical Society of Japan (E), 14*(6), 383–396.

Carterette, E. C., Shipley, C. O., & Buchwald, J. S. (1984). On synthesizing animal speech: The case of the cat. In G. Bristow (Ed.), *Electronic speech synthesis* (pp. 292–302). New York: McGraw-Hill.

Carterette, E. C., Vaughn, K., & Jairazbhoy, N. A. (1989). Perceptual, acoustical, and musical aspects of the tambura drone. *Music Perception, 7,* 75–108.

Castellano, M. A., Bharucha, J. J., & Krumhansl, C. L. (1984). Tonal hierarchies in the music of North India. *Journal of Experimental Psychology: General, 113*(3), 394–412.

Cazden, N. (1945). Musical consonance and dissonance: A cultural criterion. *Journal of Aesthetics, 4,* 3–11.

Chase, W. G., & Simon, H. A. (1973). The mind's eye in chess. In W. G. Chase (Ed.), *Visual information processing.* New York: Academic Press.

Chowning, J. M., Grey, J. J., Moorer, J. A., & Rush, L. (1982). *Instrumental timbre and related acoustical phenomena in the perception of music.* Department of Music Report No. STAN-M-11. Stanford, CA: Center for Computer Research in Music and Acoustics.

Clarkson, M. G., Clifton, R. K., & Perris, E. E. (1988). Infant timbre perception: Discrimination of spectral envelopes. *Perception & Psychophysics, 43*(1), 15–20.

Clough, J., Douthett, J., Ramanathan, N., & Rowell, L. (1993). Early Indian heptatonic scales and recent diatonic theory. *Music Theory Spectrum, 15*(1), 36–58.

Cook, N. (1990). *Music, imagination and culture.* Oxford: Clarendon Press.

Corballis, M. C. (1995). Neuropsychology of perceptual functions. In D. Zaidel (Ed.), *Neuropsychology: Handbook of perception and cognition* (2nd ed., pp. 83–104). San Diego: Academic Press.

Crummer, G. C., Hantz, E. C., Chuang, S. W., & Walton, J. P. (1988). Neural basis for music cognition: Initial experimental findings. *Psychomusicology, 7*(2) ,117–126.

Crummer, G. C., Walton, J. P., Wayman, J. W., Hantz, E. C., & Frisina, R. D. (1994). Neural processing of musical timbre by musicians, nonmusicians, and musicians possessing absolute pitch. *Journal of the Acoustical Society of America, 95*(5), 2720–2727.

Cuddy, L. L., & Cohen, A. J. (1976). Recognition of transposed melodic sequences. *Quarterly Journal of Experimental Psychology, 28,* 255–270.

Cuddy, L. L. (1970). Training the absolute identification of pitch. *Perception & Psychophysics, 8,* 265–269.

Cynx, J., & Shapiro, M. (1986). Perception of missing fundamental by a species of songbird (*Sturnus vulgaris*). *Journal of Comparative Psychology, 100*(4), 356–360.

Cynx, J., Hulse, S. H., Polyzois, S. (1986). A psychophysical measure of pitch discrimination loss resulting from a frequency range constraint in European starlings (*Sturnus vulgaris*). *Journal of Experimental Psychology: Animal Behavioral Processes, 12,* 394–402.

Cynx, J., Williams, H., & Nottebohm, F. (1990). Timbre discrimination in zebra finch (*Taeniopygia guttata*) song syllables. *Journal of Comparative Psychology, 104*(4), 303–308.

D'Amato, M. R. (1988). A search for tonal pattern perception in cebus monkeys: Why monkeys can't hum a tune. *Music Perception, 5*(4), 453–480.

Darrow, A.-A., Haack, P., & Kuribayashi, F. (1987). Descriptors and preferences for Eastern and Western musics by Japanese and American nonmusic majors. *Journal of Research in Music Education, 55*(4), 237–248.

Dehoux, V., & Voisin, F. (1993). An interactive experimental method for the determination of musical scales in oral cultures. *Contemporary Music Reviews, 9*(1&2), 13–19.

Densmore, F. (1929). What intervals do Indians sing? *American Anthropologist, 32,* 271–276.

Deutsch, D. (1982). *The psychology of music.* New York: Academic Press.

Deutsch, D. (1991). The tritone paradox: An influence of language on music perception. *Music Perception, 8*(4), 335–347.

Deutsch, D. (1994). The tritone paradox: Some further geographical correlates. *Music Perception, 12*(1), 125–136.

Deva, B. C., & Virmani, K. G. (1968). Meaning of music. *Sangeet Natak, Journal of the Sangeet Natak Akademi, New Delhi, 2,* 105–116.

Deva, B. C., & Virmani, K. G. (1976). Responses of young Indians to ragas. *Sangeet Natak, Journal of the Sangeet Natak Akademi, New Delhi, 41,* 26–45.

Deva, B. C., & Virmani, K. G. (1980). A study in the psychological response to ragas: Semantic descriptions and synesthetic relations of ragas. In R. C. Mehta (Ed.), *Psychology of music, selected papers, Sangeet Natak Akademi, Delhi Seminar, 1975* (pp. 33–36). Baroda, India: The Indian Musicological Society.

Dooling, R. J., Brown, S. D., Park, T. J., Okanoya, K., & Soli, S. D. (1987). Perceptual organization of acoustic stimuli by budgerigars (*Melopsittacus undulatus*). *Journal of Comparative Psychology, 101,* 139–149.

Dowling, W. J. (1973). Rhythmic chunks and subjective chunks in memory for melodies. *Perception & Psychophysics, 14,* 37–40.

Dowling, W. J. (1982). Musical scales and psychophysical scales: Their psychological reality. In R. Falck & T. Rice (Eds.), *Cross-cultural perspectives on music* (pp. 20–28). Toronto: University of Toronto Press.

Dowling, W. J. (1984). Assimilation and tonal structure: Comment on Castellano, Bharucha, and Krumhansl. *Journal of Experimental Psychology: General, 113,* 417–420

Dowling, W. J., & Harwood, D. L. (1986). *Music cognition.* New York: Academic Press.

Dowling, W. J., Lung, K. M., & Herrbold, S. (1987). Aiming attention in pitch and time in the perception of interleaved melodies. *Perception & Psychophysics, 41,* 642–656.

Erickson, R. (1975). *Sound structure in music.* Berkeley and Los Angeles: University of California Press.

Falck, R. & Rice, T. (1982). *Cross-cultural perspectives on music.* Toronto: University of Toronto Press.

Fales, C., & McAdams, S. (1994a). Tone/noise fusion and timbre in African musical instruments. In *Proceedings of the 3rd International Conference on Music Perception & Cognition* (pp. 105–106). Liège, Belgium: European Society for the Cognitive Sciences of Music.

Fales, C., & McAdams, S. (1994b). The fusion and layering of noise and tone: Implications for timbre in African instruments. *Leonardo Music Journal, 4,* 66–77.

Fant, G. C. M. (1960). *Acoustic theory of speech production.* The Hague, Netherlands: Mouton.

Farnsworth, P. R. (1969). *The social psychology of music* (2nd ed.). Ames: Iowa State University Press.

Fine, P. A., & Moore, B. C. J. (1993). Frequency analysis and musical ability. *Music Perception, 11*(1), 39–53.

Flora, R. (1988). Music archaeological data from the Indus Valley civilization, ca 2400–1700 B.C. In E. Hickman, & D. W. Hughes (Eds.), *The archaeology of early music cultures* (pp. 207–221). Bonn: Verlag fuer systematische Musikwissenschaft GmbH.

Flowers, P. J. (1980). Relationship between two measures of music preference. *Contributions to Music Education, 8,* 47–54.

Flowers, P. J., & Costa-Giomi, E. (1991). Verbal and nonverbal identification of pitch changes inn a familiar song by English- and Spanish-speaking preschool children. *Bulletin of the Council for Research in Music Education, 107,* 1–12.

Gallistel, C. R. (1989). Animal cognition: The representation of space, time, and number. *Annual Review of Psychology, 40,* 155–189.

Gardner, H. (1981). Do babies sing a universal song? *Psychology Today, 15*(12), 70–76.

Grattan-Guinness. (1972). *Joseph Fourier 1768–1830.* Cambridge, MA: Massachusetts Institute of Technology Press.

Green, D. M. (1988). *Profile analysis: Auditory intensity discrimination.* New York: Oxford University Press.

Greenewalt, C. H. (1968). *Bird song: Acoustics and physiology.* Washington, DC: Smithsonian Institution Press.

Gregory, A. H. (1996). Cross-cultural differences in perceiving the emotional content of music. In B. Pennycook & E. Costa-Giomi (Eds.), *Proceedings of the Fourth International Conference on Music Perception and Cognition* (pp. 407–412). Montreal: McGill University.

Gregory, A. H., & Varney, N. (1996). Cross-cultural comparisons in the affective response to music. *Psychology of Music, 24,* 47–52.

Griffin, D. R. (1981). *The question of animal awareness: Evolutionary continuity of mental experience.* New York: The Rockefeller University Press.

Gundlach, R. H. (1932). A quantitative analysis of Indian music. *American Journal of Psychology, 44,* 133–145.

Handel, S. (1995). Timbre, perception and auditory object identification. In B. C. J. Moore (Ed.), *Hearing: Handbook of perception and cognition* (2nd ed., pp. 425–461). San Diego, CA: Academic Press.

Hansen, C., Kessler, E. J., & Shepard, R. N. (1983, November). *Music perception here and in Bali: A cross-cultural study.* Paper presented at the meeting of the Psychonomic Society, San Diego, CA.

Hargreaves, D. J., Castell, K. C., & Crowther, R. D. (1986). The effects of stimulus familiarity on conservation-type responses to tone sequences: A cross-cultural study. *Journal of Research in Music Education, 34*(2), 88–100.

Harshberger, M. L., Kendall, R. A., & Carterette, E. C. (1994). Comparative psychoacoustics and acoustics of Indonesian gong tones. In *Proceedings of the 3rd International Conference on Music Perception & Cognition* (pp. 313–314). Liège, Belgium: European Society for the Cognitive Sciences of Music.

Hartmann, W. M. (1993). On the origin of the enlarged melodic octave. *Journal of the Acoustical Society of America, 93,* 3400-3409.

Harwood, D. L. (1976). Universals in music: A perspective from cognitive psychology. *Ethnomusicology, 20,* 521–534.

Henschen-Nyman, O. (1988). Cup-marked sounding stones in Sweden. In E. Hickman & D. W. Hughes (Eds.), *The archaeology of early music cultures* (pp. 11–16). Bonn: Verlag fuer systematische Musikwissenschaft GmbH.

Hickman, E., & Hughes, D. W. (Eds.). (1988). *The archaeology of early music cultures.* Bonn: Verlag fuer systematische Musikwissenschaft GmbH.

Hill, D. S., Kamenetsky, S. B., & Trehub, S. E. (1996). Relations among test, mode and medium: Historical and empirical perspectives. *Music Perception, 14*(1), 3–21.

Hockett, C. F. (1960). Logical considerations in the study of animal communication. In W. E. Lanyon & W. N. Tavolga (Eds.), *Animal sounds and communication* (pp. 392–430). Washington, DC: American Institute of Biological Sciences.

Hoshino, E. (1989). An approach to the musical acculturation of the Japanese people. In *Proceedings of the 1st International Conference on Music Perception & Cognition* (pp. 165–170). Kyoto, Japan: Japanese Society of Music Perception & Cognition.

Houtsma, A. J. M., & Goldstein, J. L. (1972). The central origin of the pitch of complex tones: Evidence from musical interval recognition. *Journal of the Acoustical Society of America, 51,* 520–529.

Hulse, S. H. (1989). The comparative psychology of audition: Perceiving complex sounds. In R. J. Dooling & S. H. Hulse (Eds.), *The comparative psychology of audition* (pp. 331–349). Hillsdale, NJ: Erlbaum.

Hulse, S. H., & Cynx, J. (1985). Relative pitch perception is constrained by absolute pitch in songbirds (*Mimus, Molothrus,* and *Sturnus*). *Journal of Comparative Physiology, 99,* 176–196.

Hulse, S. H., & Page, S. C. (1988). Toward a comparative psychology of music perception. *Music Perception, 5*(4), 427–452.

Humphreys, L. G. (1939). Generalization as a function of method of reinforcement. *Journal of Experimental Psychology, 25,* 371–372.

Igaga, J. M., & Versey, J. (1978). Cultural differences in rhythmic perception. *Psychology of Music, 6,* 61–64.

Igaga, J. M., & Versey, J. (1977). Cultural differences in rhythmic performance. *Psychology of Music, 5,* 23–27.

Jairazbhoy, N. A. (1995). *The rags of North Indian music.* Bombay: Popular Prakashan Pvt. Ltd. [First published by Faber and Faber, 1971. First revised Indian Edition, 1995. Available in U.S. from Van Nuys, CA: Popular Prakashan, Aspara Media for Intercultural Education.]

Jairazbhoy, N. A., & Stone, A. W. (1976). Intonation in present-day North Indian classical music. *Journal of the Indian Musicological Society, 7,* 22–35 (Reprinted from the *Bulletin of the School of Oriental and African Studies, University of London,* 1963, 26(1)).

Kallman, H. J. (1982). Octave equivalence as measured by similarity ratings. *Perception & Psychophysics, 32*(1), 37–49.

Kastner, M., & Crowder, R. (1990). Perception of the major/minor distinction: IV. Emotional connotations in young children. *Music Perception, 8*(2), 189–202.

Keefe, D. H., Burns, E. M., & Nguyen, P. (1991). Vietnamese modal scales of the dan tranh. *Music Perception, 8*(4), 449–468.

Kendall, R. A., & Carterette, E. C. (1990). The communication of musical expression. *Music Perception, 8*(2), 129–163.

Kendall, R. A., & Carterette, E. C. (1991). Perceptual scaling of simultaneous wind instrument timbres. *Music Perception, 8*(4), 369–404.

Kendall, R. A., & Carterette, E. C. (1993). Verbal attributes of simultaneous wind instrument timbres. II: Adjectives induced from Piston's Orchestration. *Music Perception, 10*(4), 469–501.

Kendall, R. A., & Carterette, E. C. (1996). Music perception and cognition. In M. P. Friedman, & E. C. Carterette (Eds.), *Cognitive ecology: Handbook of perception and cognition* (2nd ed., pp. 87–149). San Diego, CA: Academic Press.

Kessler, E. J., Hansen, C., & Shepard, R. N. (1984). Tonal schemata in the perception of music in Bali and in the West. *Music Perception, 2*(2), 131–165.

Kippen, J. (1987). An ethnomusicological approach to the analysis of musical cognition. *Music Perception, 5*(1), 173–196.

Konishi, M. (1985). From behavior to neuron. *Annual Review of Neuroscience, 8,* 125–170.

Kraut, R. (1992). On the possibility of a determinate semantics for music. In M. Jones & S. Holleran (Eds.), *Cognitive bases of musical communication* (pp. 11–22). Washington, DC: American Psychological Association.

Krumhansl, C. L., & Keil, F. C. (1982). Acquisition of the hierarchy of tonal functions in music. *Memory & Cognition, 10,* 243–251.

Kubik, G. (1962). The phenomenon of inherent rhythm in East and Central African instrumental music. *African Music, 3*(1), 31–42.

Kubik, G. (1979). Pattern perception and recognition in African music. In J. Blacking & J. W. Kealiinohomoku (Eds.), *The performing arts* (pp. 221–249). The Hague: Mouton Publishers.

Kunst, J. (1949). *Music in Java* (E. van Loo, Trans.; 2nd rev. ed., 2 vols.). The Hague: Martinus Nijhoff.

Lerdahl, F., & Jackendoff, R. (1983). *A generative theory of tonal music.* Cambridge, MA: MIT Press.

Lieberman, P. (1972). *The speech of primates.* The Hague: Mouton.

Lund, C. S. (1988). On animal calls in ancient Scandinavia: Theory and data. In E. Hickman, & D. W. Hughes (Eds.), *The archaeology of early music cultures* (pp. 289–303). Bonn: Verlag für systematische Musikwissenschaft GmbH.

Lundin, R. W. (1947). Towards a cultural theory of consonance. *Journal of Psychology, 23,* 45–49.

Lynch, M. P. & Eilers, R. E. (1991). Children's perception of native and nonnative musical scales. *Music Perception, 9*(1), 121–132.

Lynch, M. P., Eilers, R. E., Oller, D. K., & Urbano, R. C. (1990). Innateness, experience, and music perception. *Psychological Science, 1*(4), 272–276.

Lynch, M. P., Eilers, R. E., Oller, K. D., Urbano, R. C., & Wilson, P. (1991). Influences of acculturation and musical sophistication on perception of musical interval patterns. *Journal of Experimental Psychology: Human Perception and Performance, 17*(4), 967–975.

Maher, T. F. (1976). "Need for resolution" ratings for harmonic musical intervals: A comparison between Indians and Canadians. *Journal of Cross-Cultural Psychology, 7*(3), 259–276.

Maher, T. F., & Jairazbhoy, N. A. (1975). Need for resolution of musical intervals: Part I. Static context. *Sangeet, Natak, Journal of the Sangeet Natak Akademi, New Delhi, 36,* 5–20.

Maher, T. F., & Jairazbhoy, N. A. (1977). The effect of melodic symmetry on need for resolution ratings for musical intervals. *Sangeet, Natak, Journal of the Sangeet Natak Akademi, New Delhi, 48,* 8–17.

Malm, W. P. (1967). *Music cultures of the Pacific, the Near East, and Asia.* Englewood Cliffs, NJ: Prentice-Hall, Inc.

Marx, J. L. (1982). How the brain controls birdsong. *Science, 217*(4565), 1125–1126.

McPhee, C. (1966). *Music in Bali.* New Haven, CT: Yale University Press.

Merriam, A. P. (1981). African musical rhythm and concepts of time-reckoning. In T. Noblitt (Ed.), *Music East and West* (pp. 123–141). New York: Pendragon Press.

Milner, B. (1962). Laterality effects in audition. In V. B. Mountcastle (Ed.), *Interhemispheric relations and cerebral dominance.* Baltimore, MD: Johns Hopkins University Press.

Miyazaki, K. (1993). Absolute pitch as an inability: Identification of musical intervals in a tonal context. *Music Perception, 11*(1), 55–72.

Moore, B. C. J. (Ed.). *Hearing: Handbook of perception and cognition* (2nd ed.). San Diego, CA: Academic Press.

Nelson, D. A., & Marler, P. (1989). Categorical perception of a natural stimulus continuum: Birdsong. *Science, 244*(4907), 976–978.

Neuman, D. (1990). *The life of music in North India.* Chicago: University of Chicago Press. (Original work published 1980)

Nowicki, S., & Marler, P. (1988). How do birds sing? *Music Perception, 5*(4), 391–426.

Nowicki, S., Marler, P., Maynard, A., & Peters, S. (1992). Is the tonal quality of birdsong learned? *Ethology, 90*(3), 225–235.

Nowicki, S., Mitani, J. C., Nelson, D. A., & Marler, P. (1989). The communicative significance of tonality in birdsong: Responses to songs produced in helium. *Bioacoustics, 2*(1) 35–46.

Palmer, C., & Kelly, M. C. (1992). Linguistic prosody and musical meter in song. *Journal of Memory & Language, 31,* 515–542.

Parsons, M. J. (1987). *How we understand art: A cognitive developmental account of aesthetic experience.* Cambridge: Cambridge University Press.

Peretz, I. (1990). Processing of local and global musical information in unilateral brain-damaged patients. *Brain, 113,* 1185–1205.

Peretz, I., & Kolinsky, R. (1993). Boundaries of separability between melody and rhythm in music discrimination: A neuropsychological perspective. *Quarterly Journal of Experimental Psychology, 46A*(2), 301–325.

Perlman, M., & Krumhansl, C. J. (1996). An experimental study of internal interval standards in Javanese and Western musicians. *Music Perception 14*(2), 95–116.

Plomp, R. (1964). The ear as a frequency analyzer. *Journal of the Acoustical Society of America, 36,* 1628–1636.

Pressing, J. (1983). Cognitive isomorphisms between pitch and rhythm in world musics: West Africa, the Balkans and Western tonality. *Studies in Music, 17,* 38–61.

Prior, M., & Troup, G. (1988). Processing of timbre and rhythm in musicians and non-musicians. *Cortex, 24*(3), 451–456.

Radvansky, G. A., Fleming, K. J., & Simmons, J. A. (1995). Timbre reliance in nonmusicians' and musicians' memory for melodies. *Music Perception, 13*(2), 127–140.

Raffman, D. (1992). Proposal for a musical semantics. In M. R. Jones & S. Holleran (Eds.), *Cognitive bases of musical communication* (pp. 23–31). Washington, DC: American Psychological Association.

Rahn, J. (1982). Simple forms in universal perspective. In R. Falck & T. Rice (Eds.), *Cross-cultural perspectives on music* (pp. 38–49). Toronto: University of Toronto Press.

Raman, C. V. (1922). On some Indian stringed instruments. *Proceedings of the Indian Association for the Cultivation of Science, 7,* 29–33.

Rao Y.-A., Carterette, E. C., & Wu Y.-K. (1987). A comparison of the musical scales of an ancient Chinese bronze bell ensemble and the modern bamboo flute. *Perception & Psychophysics, 41,* 547–562.

Raychaudhuri, M. (1980). Musical creativity revisited: A selective focus. In R. C. Mehta (Ed.), *Psychology of music, selected papers, Sangeet Natak Akademi, Delhi Seminar: 1975* (pp. 72–89). Baroda, India: The Indian Musicological Society.

Rhagavendra Rao, K. S., & Indira, K. (1979). Experimental study of raga scales of Indian music: Sankarabharana raga. *Sangeet Natak, Journal of the Sangeet Natak Akademi, New Delhi, 51,* 15–23.

Robisson, P., Aubin, T., & Bremond, J.-C. (1993). Individuality in the voice of the emperor penguin. *Ethology, 94*(4), 279–290.

Ross, J., & Lehiste, I. (1996). Tradeoff between quantity and stress in Estonia folksong performance. In B. Pennycook & R. Costa-Giomi (Eds.), *Proceedings of the Fourth International Conference on Music Perception and Cognition* (pp. 419–424). Montreal: McGill University.

Ross, J., & Lehiste, I. (1998). Timing in Estonian folk songs as interaction between speech, prosody, meter and musical rhythm. *Music Perception, 15,* 319–334.

Rossing, T. D. (1990). *The science of sound* (2nd ed.). New York: Addison-Wesley.

Sampat, K. S. (1978). Categorical perception in music and music intervals. *Journal of the Indian Musicological Society, 9*(4), 32–35.

Sawyer, W. W. (1955). *Prelude to mathematics.* Baltimore: Penguin Books, Inc.

Schlaug, G., Amunts, K., Jäncke, L., Schleicher, A., & Zilles, K. (1996). Hand motor skill covaries with size of motor cortex: Evidence for macrostructural adaptation in musicians. In B. Pennycook,

& E. Costa-Giomi (Eds.), *Proceedings of the Fourth International Conference on Music Perception and Cognition* (p. 433). Montreal, Canada: Society for Music Perception and Cognition.

Schlaug, G., Martin, B., Edelman, R. R., & Warach, S. (1996). Regional differences in brain activation in musicians and nonmusicians: An fMRI-behavioral study. In B. Pennycook, & E. Costa-Giomi (Eds.), *Proceedings of the Fourth International Conference on Music Perception and Cognition* (p. 431). Montreal, Canada: Society for Music Perception and Cognition.

Schneider, A., & Stoltz, H. (1988). Notes on the acoustics of ancient Chinese bell chimes. In E. Hickman & D. W. Hughes (Eds.), *The archaeology of early music cultures* (pp. 265–274). Bonn: Verlag fuer systematische Musikwissenschaft GmbH.

Schouten, J. F. (1940). The residue, a new component in subjective sound analysis. *Proceedings of the Koninklijke Nederlandse Akademie van Wetenschappen, 43,* 356–365.

Sergent, J., Zuck, E., Terriah, S., & MacDonald, B. (1992). Distributed neural network underlying musical sight-reading and keyboard performance. *Science, 257,* 106–109.

Seyfarth, R. M., Cheney, D. L., & Marler. P. (1980). Monkey responses to three different alarm calls: Evidence for predator classification and semantic communication. *Science, 210,* 801–803.

Shankweiler, D. (1966). Effects of temporal-lobe damage on perception of dichotically-presented melodies. *Journal of Comparative and Physiological Psychology, 7,* 115–119.

Shehan, P. K. (1983). Student preferences for ethnic music styles. *Contributions to Music Education, 9,* 21–28.

Shehan, P. K. (1984). The effect of instruction method on preference, achievement, and attentiveness for Indonesia gamelan music. *Psychology of Music, 12,* 34–42.

Shehan, P. K. (1985). Transfer of preference from taught to untaught pieces of non-Western music genres. *Journal of Research in Music Education, 33*(3), 149–188.

Shimizu, T., & Karten, H. J. (1993). Functional anatomy of the avian visual system. In H. P. Ziegler & H.-J. Bischof (Eds.), *Vision, brain and behavior in birds* (pp. 103–114). Cambridge, MA: MIT Press.

Shipley, C., Carterette, E. C., & Buchwald, J. S. (1991). The effects of articulation on the acoustical structure of feline vocalizations. *Journal of the Acoustical Society of America, 89,* 902–909.

Sinnott, J. M. (1987). Modes of perceiving and processing information in birdsong. *Journal of Comparative Psychology, 101*(4), 355–366.

Sloboda, J. A. (1985). *The musical mind: The cognitive psychology of music.* Oxford: The Clarendon Press.

Sloboda, J. A. (1992). Empirical studies of emotional response to music. In M. R. Jones, & S. Holleran (Eds.), *Cognitive bases of musical communication* (pp. 33–46). Washington, DC: American Psychological Association.

Smith, H., Stevens, K., & Tomlinson, R. S. (1967). On an unusual mode of chanting by certain Tibetan lamas. *Journal of the Acoustical Society of America, 41,* 1262–1264.

Smith, J. D. (1987). Conflicting aesthetic ideals in a musical culture. *Music Perception, 4*(4), 373–392.

Smith, J. D. (1997). The place of musical novices in musical science. *Music Perception, 14*(3), 227–262.

Soderquist, D. R. (1970). Frequency analysis and the critical band. *Psychonomic Science, 21,* 117–119.

Sorrell, N. (1990). *A guide to the gamelan.* London: Faber and Faber.

Stockmann, D. (1977). Some aspects of musical perception. *Yearbook of the International Folk Music Council, 9,* 67–79.

Sundberg, J. (1987). *The science of the singing voice.* DeKalb: Northern Illinois University Press.

Sundberg, J. (1991). *The science of musical sounds.* San Diego, CA: Academic Press.

Sundberg, J. (1994). Phonatory head and chest vibrations in singers. *Journal of the Acoustical Society of America, 95*(5, Part 2), 2985–2986.

Surjodiningrat, W., Sudarjana, P. J., & Susanto, A. (1972). *Tone measurements of outstanding Javanese gamelans in Jogjakarta and Surakarta* (2nd rev. ed.). Jogjakarta: Gadjah Mada University Press.

Takeuchi, A. H., & Hulse, S. H. (1993). Absolute pitch. *Perception & Psychophysics, 113*(3), 345–361.

Tenzer, M. (1991). *Balinese music.* Singapore: Periplus Editions.

Thomas, L. K. (1989). *Interleaved melodies and timbre: The effect of varying instrumentation.* B. A. Honors Thesis. Williamsburg, VA: Department of Psychology, College of William & Mary.

Trehub, S. E., & Unyk, A. M. (1991). Music prototypes in developmental perspective. *Psychomusicology, 10*(2), 73–87.

Trehub, S. E., Thorpe, L. A., & Trainor, L. J. (1990). Infants' perception of good and bad melodies. *Psychomusicology, 9*(1), 15–19.

Trehub, S. E., Unyk, A. M., & Trainor, L. J. (1993). Maternal singing in cross-cultural perspective. *Infant Behavior and Development, 16*(3), 285–295.

Unyk, A., Trehub, S. E., & Trainor, L. J. (1992). Lullabies and simplicity: A cross-cultural perspective. *Psychology of Music, 20*(1), 15–28.

Vaughn, K. V. (1991). *Perceptual and cognitive implications of the tambura drone: Figure-ground interaction with ten North Indian scale types.* Unpublished doctoral dissertation, Los Angeles, CA: Department of Ethnomusicology & Ethnomusicology, University of California, Los Angeles (UCLA).

Vaughn, K. V. (1993). The influence of the tambura drone on the perception of proximity among scale types in North Indian classical music. *Contemporary Music Reviews, 9*(1&2), 21–33.

Vaughn, K. V., & Carterette, E. C. (1994) Mode and mood in North Indian raga. In *Proceedings of the 3rd International Conference on Music Perception & Cognition* (pp. 111–113). Liège, Belgium: European Society for the Cognitive Sciences of Music.

Vaughn, M. M. (1981). Intercultural studies in children's natural singing pitch and walking tempo. *Council for Research in Music Education Bulletin, 66/67,* 96–101.

Vetter, R. (1989). A retrospect on a century of gamelan tone measurements. *Ethnomusicology, 33*(2), 217–227.

von Bismarck, G. (1974a). Timbre of steady tones: A factorial investigation of its verbal attributes. *Acustica, 30,* 146–159.

von Bismarck, G. (1974b). Sharpness as an attribute of the timbre of steady sounds. *Acustica, 30,* 159–192.

von Hornbostel, E. M. (1928). African Negro music. *Africa, 1,* 30–62.

Walker, R. (1985). Mental imagery and musical concepts: Some evidence from the congenitally blind. *Bulletin of the Council for Research in Music Education, 85,* 229–237.

Walker, R. (1986). Music and multiculturalism. *The International Journal of Music Education, 8,* 43–52.

Walker, R. (1990). *Musical beliefs: Psychoacoustic, mythical, and educational perspectives.* New York: Teachers College Press.

Watanabe, S., Lea, S. E. G., & Dittrich , W. H. (1993). What can we learn from experiments on pigeon concept discrimination? In H. P. Ziegler & H.-J. Bischof (Eds.), *Vision, brain and behavior in birds* (pp. 351–376). Cambridge, MA: MIT Press.

Watt, H. J. (1924). Functions of the size of interval in songs of Schubert and of Chippewa and Teton-Sioux Indians. *British Journal of Psychology, 14,* 370–386.

Weinberger, N. M., & McKenna, T. M. (1988). Sensitivity of single neurons in auditory cortex to contour: Toward a neurophysiology of music perception. *Music Perception, 5*(4), 355–389.

Wilkinson, R., & Howse, P. E. (1975). Time resolution of acoustic signals by birds. *Nature, 258*(5533), 320–321.

Williams, H., Cynx, J., & Nottebohm, F. (1989). Timbre control in zebra finch (Taeniopygia guttata) song syllables. *Journal of Comparative Psychology, 103*(4), 366–380.

Wolpert, R. S. (1990). Recognition of melody, harmonic accompaniment, and instrumentation: Musicians and nonmusicians. *Music Perception, 8,* 95–106.

Yamada, M. (1995). Stream segregation in Mongolian traditional singing, Xöömij. In *Proceedings of The International Symposium on Musical Acoustics, Le Normont, Dourdan, France* (pp. 530–545). Paris: IRCAM, Centre Georges Pompidou.

Yeston, M. (1976). *The stratification of musical rhythm*. New Haven: Yale University.

Yung, B. (1983). Creative process in Cantonese opera I & II. *Ethnomusicology, 27,* 29–47; 297–318.

Zaidel, D. (Ed.). (1995). *Neuropsychology: Handbook of perception and cognition* (2nd ed.). San Diego: Academic Press.

Zatorre, R. J. (1984). Musical perception and cerebral function: A critical review. *Music Perception, 2,* 196–221.

Zhenxiong, G., Quingyi, Z., & Yuzhen, J. On the musical instruments of Chinese nationalities. In *Proceedings of The International Symposium on Musical Acoustics, Le Normont, Dourdan, France* (pp. 546–550). Paris: IRCAM, Centre Georges Pompidou.

Index

Absolute pitch
accuracy, 273–274
acquiring, 286–288
auralization, 288–289
colored hearing, 286
development, 293
frequency limits, 236–237
genesis, 268–270
helix, 265–266, 268
identification, 221–222
intervals, 291–292
IQ and, 293–294
judgments, 237–238
learning, 283–286
measurements, 270–271
melody perception, 756–757
memory system, 391–392
neurology, 282–283
note categorizing, 291
performance effect, 292–293
PET studies, 692–693
piano, 271, 274–275
spontaneous, 288–289
standards, 280–281
value, 289–294
Absorption, 27–29
Abstractions
feature detectors, 425–427
feature tuning, 415–416
pitch
alphabets, 363–366

inversion, 360–363
key attribution, 373–376
retrogression, 360–363
transposition, 359–360
Acoustics
art of, 25
complexities, 26
computer ray studies, 30–32
computer wave studies, 32–33
digital simulation, 33–42
geometrical, 26–30
perceptual, 678, 710
psycho, see Psychoacoustics
sound transmission, 33–42
Adaptive methods, 91
Additive synthesis, 118–122
Adjustment methods, 91
2AFC task, 228–230
Affect, 765–766
Agnosias
classification, 673–674
description, 667–673
nonverbal, 674–678
Alzheimer's disease, 659–660
AM, see Amplitude modulation
Amplitude grouping, 320–321
Amplitude modulation
auditory studies, 75–78
grouping, 311–312
Amusias
with aphasia, 656–665

Amusias (*continued*)
  description, 655–656
  without aphasia, 666–667
AP, *see* Absolute pitch
Aphasia
  with amusia, 656–665
  Broca's, 664
  without amusia, 665–666
Arab-Persian system, 217–218
Archetypes, melodic, 355–356
Articulation, 172, 553
Articulators, 172
Asynchronization, 543–544
Attack transients, 117–118
Attention, 54–55
Attributes, verbal, 766–770
Audibility, 182–184
Audition, 631
Auditory system, *see also* Hearing
  agnosias
    classification, 673–674
    description, 667–673
    nonverbal, 674–678
  anatomy, 48–49
  attention and, 54–55
  consonance, 67–68
  continuity, 306–310
  contour, 68–69, 71
  development, 47–48
  disorders, 673–679
  frequency detectors, 414–415
  functional organization, 49, 51–54
  functions, 80–81
  harmony, 67–68
  learning, 55–57, 59
  models, 155–156
  neurophysiology, 776–778
  perceptual processing, 654–655
  physiology, 47
  pitch
    animal studies, 62–63
    neuron encoding, 65–67
    organization
      cochleotopic, 61–62
      tonotopic, 63–65
    perception, 63
  psychoacoustics, 80–81
  rhythm, 75–80
  sound mapping, 53–54
  temporal coding, 75–80
Auralization, 288–289
Autoassociation, 427–430
Automatism, 661

Automorphism, 737
Ave Maria, 528, 546

Bach, Johann Sebastian, 13, 289, 304, 306, 326,
    337, 485, 510, 515, 537–538, 539, 542–
    543, 662, 760
Backpropagation, 433
Barbershop quartets, 247
Bartók, Béla, 337, 542
Basso continuo principle, 763
Beats
  definition, 103
  tones and, 102–104
Beethoven, Ludwig von, 327, 337, 476–477,
    521, 522, 526, 527–528, 539–540, 541–
    543, 547–548, 556–557, 578, 659
Bells, chime, 741
Berlioz, Hector, 329
Bernstein, Leonard, 239
Best modulation frequency, 77–78
Beta-blockers, 573–574
Binaural lateralization, 5
Biofeedback training, 559, 575
BMF, *see* Best modulation frequency
Boulez, Pierre, 477–478
Brahms, Johannes, 502, 522, 541–542, 548
Brain
  hemisphere asymmetry
    absolute pitch, 692–693
    anesthetization, 693–695
    ear differences, 695–698
    group studies, 679–685
    music perception, 685, 687–689
    performance, 690, 692
    song imagery, 689–690
  neurons
    frequency tuning, 413–415
    pitch encoding, 65–67
    single, 49, 51–54
Brightness, 147–148
Broca's aphasia, 662, 664

Capriccio in E minor, 545–546
Cartesian space, 418
Categorical perception, 226–228
Category scaling, 222
Category units, 425–427
Chime bells, 741
Choice methods, 90–91
Chopin, Frédéric François, 281, 480, 502, 520,
    522, 527–528, 537–538, 543, 550, 701

Chords
  classification, 351
  perceptual equivalence, 350–351
  physiological substrates, 351–352
Chromatic scale, 231–232, 323
Clarinet performance rating scale, 577
Clock rate, 520
Closed-loop theory, 518
Codes, speech, 208
Cognition
  coda, 780–781
  conservation, 734
  consonance, 731–734
  contemporary issues, 725–727
  development
    adult, 619–620
    childhood, 611–619
    emotion, 618–619
    infancy, 604–611
    melody, 613–616
    pitch, 606
    prenatal, 604–611
    rhythm, 610–611, 616–618
    singing, 611–613
  dissonance, 731–734
  ethnomusicology, 727–729
  intervals, 731–734
  isomorphisms, 759
  melody, 751–758
  octaves, 734–736
  pitch
    hearing, 730
    systems, 736–743
  scales, 734–736
  spectra, 762–765
  style structures, 456–457
  temperament, 734–736
  timbre, 762–765
  tonality, 743–747
  tuning, 734–736
  universals, 780
Colored hearing, 286
Common fate, law of, 95
Communication, 765–766
Composites
  modal, 422
  patterns
    definition, 419–420
    over time, 420–422
  temporal
    autoassociation, 427–430
    encoding, 425–427
    key tracking, 422

  tonal, 422–424
Computers
  ray studies, 30–32
  sound synthesis, 117
  wave studies, 32–33
Concert halls
  acoustics
    art of, 25
    complexities, 26
    computer ray studies, 30–32
    computer wave studies, 32–33
    sound transmission, 33–42
    digital simulation, 39–44
    multipurpose, 44–45
    nonexistent, 42–43
    spatial reorganization, 325–331
Conductors, 547
Consensus preference, 38
Consonance
  auditory studies, 67–68
  cognition, 731–734
  explanation, 240–242
  perceptual, 106, 731–734
  sensory, 106, 244–245
  theory of, 5–6, 12–13
  tones, 106–108
Consonants
  categorizing, 672
  –vowel combinations, 672
Continuity, auditory, 306–310
Contours
  auditory studies, 68–69, 71
  melodic
    cross-cultural, 751–752
    description, 353–354
    development, 613–616
Coordinative structures, 518
Creativity, 765–766
Critical band model, 80–81
Critical bandwidth, 93
Cross-synthesis, 126–128
Cue-controlled relaxation, 575–576
Cues, pitch, 270–271

Das Wohltemperierte Clavier, 537
Deafness, verbal
  classification, 673–674
  description, 667–673
Debussy, Claude, 304, 390, 430, 508, 701
Delayed auditory feedback, 515–516
Demodulation, 139–140
Desensitization, 574–575

Development
    absolute pitch, 293
    auditory system, 47–48
    perceptual
        adult, 619–620
        childhood, 611–619
        emotion, 618–619
        grouping, 605–606
        infancy, 604–611
        melody, 606–611, 613–616
        pitch, 606
        prenatal, 604–611
        rhythm, 610–611
    performance, 561–564
Deviations, 531–532
Dialogue Concerning Two New Sciences, 3
Dido and Aeneas, 549
Die Fledermaus, 533
Die Meistersinger, 176
Digital additive synthesis, 121
Digital networks, 143
Digital simulation
    alterations, 43–44
    description, 33–42
    lateral reflections, 39–41
    nonexistent halls, 42–43
Diminution, 444–445
Discrimination
    flutter-vibration task, 703
    intervals, 228–231
    roving, 227
Dissonance
    cognition, 731–734
    perception, 731–734
    sensory, 244–245
    tones, 106–108
Du bist wie eine Blume, 207
Dyslexia, 664

Ears, *see also* Auditory system
    asymmetry, 696–698
    differences, 695–698
    frequency analysis, 91–93
    input grouping, 312–313
    sensitivity, 90
Echoic memory, 422
Echo response, 42, 44
Emotion, development, 618–619
Ethnomusicology, 727–729
Expectancies, verdical, 430
Expression, 522

Extraopus style, 442–443
Eyes
    performance span, 512
    sight-reading, 510–511

Falsetto, 191–192, 194
Features
    abstract, 415–416
    definition, 414
    detectors, 425–427
Feedback
    performance, 515–516
    sensory, 518
Female chest, 190–191
Fission hearing, 314
Five Orchestra Pieces Op.16, 150
Flutter-vibration task, 703
FM, *see* Frequency modulation
Formant frequency, 172
Fourier, Jean-Baptiste-Joseph, 7
Fourier analysis
    application, 138
    criticism, 153–154
    definition, 92
    timbre, 114–118
Fourier transforms, 17–18, 141
Free-field listening, 35
Frequency
    detectors, 414–415
    ear, 91–93
    formant, 172
    fundamental
        definition, 172
        pitch, 201–203
        vibrato, 196
    glides, 157–158
    pitch, 93–99, 236–237
    tuning, 49, 51, 413–415
Frequency modulation
    definition, 130–131
    grouping, 310–311
    sampling, 134
Fusion
    grouping, 301–302
    timbre, 135–138

Galileo, 3, 12
Gamelan gong tones, 763–764
Gap detection, 79–80
Gènder barung, 740, 742, 749

Gènder wayung, 743
Gestalt psychology
  grouping, 300
  principles, 479
  tones, 95
Global impression, 157
Gluck, Christoph Willibald, 619
Gnossienne No. 5, 521, 543
Goldberg Variations, 542
Granular synthesis, 152–153
GROOVE, 136
Grouping
  AM, 311–312
  auditory continuity, 306–310
  ear input, 312–313
  equal-interval tones, 336–340
  FM, 310–311
  harmonicity, 302–304
  issues, 299–301
  larger scale, 313
  multiple tones
    handedness correlates, 336–337
    melody, 334–336
    octave illusion, 332–334
    phase shifted, 334–336
    scale illusion, 321–332
  onset synchronicity, 304–306
  perceptual, 605–606
  practice, 340–342
  preference rules, 479
  principles, 300–301
  rhythm, 479–480, 482
  single tone
    amplitude, 320–321
    continuation, 320
    perception, 317–318
    pitch proximity, 313–314
    repetition, 315–317
    stream formation, 313–314
    temporal coherence, 314–315
    temporal proximity, 319–320
    timbre, 318–319
  spectral components, 301–302
  theory, 340–342
Guitar practice, 506

Haas effect, 6
Handedness correlates, 336–337
Handel, George Frideric, 528–529, 534
Harmonicity, 302–304
Harmonics

hearing, 14–15
production, 10–11
Harmony
  auditory studies, 67–68
  tests for, 635–636
Haydn, Franz Joseph, 337, 542–543, 550, 557
Hearing, *see also* Auditory system
  colored, 286
  disorders, 560–561
  ear differences, 695–698
  fission, 314
  free-field, 35
  harmonics, 14–15
  pitch
    perception, 730
    quality, 13–16
  time resolution, 3–5
Heredity, 268–27
Heschl's gyrus, 676, 683
Hidden units, 431
Horowitz, Vladimir, 535

Imagery, song, 689–690
Immediate auditory feedback, 515–516
Impoverished control, 135
Improvisation, 513–515
Indian scales, 737–739
Infants, 604–611
Information reduction, 143–144
Instruments, *see also specific types*
  ancient, 729
  impoverished control, 135
  personality factors, 564–566
  resonance, 10–11
  sampling, 134–135
  timbre
    additive synthesis, 118–126
    attack transients, 117–118
    Fourier analysis, 114–118
    vibrating elements, 132
Intelligence quotient
  absolute pitch and, 293–294
  musical ability and, 643–645
Interference, 421–422
Intermezzo, Op. 117, 548
Internal clock, 520
Interpolation, 141
Interval
  class, 356–358
  cognition, 731–734
  confusion, 239–240

Interval (*continued*)
  discrimination, 228–231, 234–235
  equal, tones, 336–340
  identification, 291–292
  isolated
    adjustment, 219–220
    identification, 221–223, 226
  melodic
    adjustment, 232
    identification, 232–233
  mistuned, 233–234
  natural
    basis, 240–242
    biological bases, 249–250
    dissonance, 244–245
    performance, 245–248
    scale evolution, 257
    sensory consonance, 244–245
  perceptual
    categorical, 226–228, 234–235
    context, 231–235
    equivalence, 350–351
    natural law, 731–734
    pitch
      judgment effects, 237–238
      limits, 236–237
    physiological substrates, 351–352
    similarities, 239–240
Intonation
  just, 243
  measurements, 545–547
  performance, 245–248
Invariance, transpositional, 434
IQ, *see* Intelligence quotient

James, William, 704
JNDs, *see* Just-noticeable differences
Jupiter Symphony, 37
Just intonation, 243
Just-noticeable differences
  discrimination
    bias free, 235
    interval, 228, 230
  perception, 233

Karajan, Herbert von, 547
Karplus-Strong technique, 133
Key changes, 634–635
Kinesthetic abilities
  instrumental, 638–640
  singing, 639–640

Kinesthetic feedback, 515
Klavierstück IX, 477

Language, 726
Larynx height
  timbre and, 194–195
  vowels and, 181
Lateralization, binaural, 5
Lateral reflections, 39–41
Leap articulation, 553
Learning
  AP, 268–269, 283–286
  auditory system, 55–57, 59
  neural associations
    invariance, 434
    mechanism, 424–425
    sequences, 430–434
    temporal composites, 425–430
  practice, 562–563
  relative pitch, 238–239
  scales, 250–252
  songs, 771–772
Leonore Overture No. 3, 547
Le Vent dans la plaine, 340
Linearity, 7–8
Liszt, Franz, 578
Loudness
  assessment, 99–101
  phonation, 188–190
  voice, 176

Magnetoencephalography
  auditory cortex response, 63–64
  definition, 48
Magnitude intervals, 226
Meaning, 765–766
Medial tone, 457–458
MEG, *see* Magnetoencephalography
Meistersingerlied, 526
Melody
  archetypes, 355–356
  contours
    cross-cultural, 751–752
    description, 353–354
  paradox
    description, 383–385
    implications, 385–387
  pattern development, 606–611
  perception
    absolute pitch, 756–757
    development, 613–616

multiple tones, 334–336
song
    children, 754–755
    source-filter model, 752
    structure, 757–758
    training, 756–757
voice
    source-filter model, 752
    techniques, 752–754
perceptual tasks, 681
synthetic, 449
Mel scale, 94
Memory
    demands, 492
    echoic, 422
    performance, 507–508
    pitch
        absolute values, 391–392
        duration, 402
        interactions, 394–396
        item information, 396–398
        model, 390–391
        octave generalization, 398–399
        order information, 396–398
        proximity, 399–400
        relationships, 401–402
        repetition, 398
        retrieval, 403
        separate storage, 392–394
        timbre, 400–401
    sight-reading and, 511
    working, 684–685, 688
Mendelssohn, Felix, 430, 548
Mersenne, Marin, 3, 14
Meter
    definition, 747–748
    perception, 482–489
MIDI, *see* Musical Instrument Digital Interface
Minnesota twin study, 627–628
Modal composite, 422
Moonlight Sonata, 526
Motor program theory, 518
Motor skills
    empirical studies, 519–523
    exercises, 517
    expression, 523
    issues, 516–517
    theories, 518–519
Movement, 494–496
Mozart, Wolfgang Amadeus, 37, 427, 430, 477–478, 522–523, 535, 539, 548, 550, 556–557, 611, 613
Multidimensional scaling, 17, 38

MUSACT model, 421, 427
Music
    definition, 726
    origins, 729
Musical aptitude profile, 627, 630
Musical Instrument Digital Interface, 521
Musicality, 628
Musical pitch scale, 94
Mussorgsky, Modest Petrovich, 578

Naturalness, voice, 195
Neural networks
    activation, 416–418
    composite patterns
        definition, 419–420
        over time, 420–422
    feature tuning, 415–416
    frequency tuning, 413–415
    learning
        invariance, 434
        mechanism, 424–425
        sequences, 430–434
        temporal composites, 425–430
        tonal, 422–424
    vector spaces, 418–419
Neural processing
    AP correlates, 282–283
    characterization, 49
Neurobiology, 60–61
Neurons
    frequency tuning, 413–415
    pitch encoding, 65–67
    single, 49, 51–54
Neurophysiology
    animal studies, 779–780
    auditory system, 776–778
    processing, 778–779
Neuropsychology
    perspectives, 708–712
    progress, 699–704
Nikisch, Arthur, 325
Nocturne, Op.15, No. 3, 527
Nyquist's criterion, 33

Occupation, music as, 566–569
Octaves, *see also* Pitch
    cognition, 734–736
    equivalence
        bases, 252–253
        cross-cultural, 775–776
    pitch, 350

Octaves (*continued*)
  psychophysical evidence, 253–255
  generalization, 398–399
  illusion, 332–334
  perception, 734–736
  stretched
    cross-cultural, 739–743
    phenomenon, 255–257
Onset synchronicity, 304–306
Open-loop theory, 518
Orfeo ed Euridice, 619

Paganini, Niccolo, 545–546, 557, 578
Palsies, 558
Parameter estimation, 139–140
PAS principle, 556
Pathetique, 325
Pavlovian conditioning, 55
Pélog scales, 732–733, 750
Pentads, 779–780
Perception
  abnormalities, 654
  acoustic, 678
  acoustics, 710
  amusias
    with aphasia, 656–665
    case histories, 678–679
    description, 655–656
  auditory agnosias, 667–673
  categorical, 226–228
  cognition, 731–734
  conservation, 734
  consonance, 731–734
  contemporary issues, 725–727
  cultural, 711
  development
    absolute pitch, 613
    adult, 619–620
    childhood, 611–619
    emotion, 618–619
    grouping, 605–606
    infancy, 604–611
    pitch, 606
    prenatal, 604–611
    rhythm, 610–611, 616–618
    singing, 611–613
  disorders, 558, 653–655
  ethnomusicology, 727–729
  graphic, 711
  grouping, 479–480, 482
  hemisphere asymmetry, 679–685

intervals, 731–734
melody, 751–758
meter, 482–489
motor productive, 711
motor programmative, 711
multiple tones, 334–336
neurology
  clinical issues, 653–655
neurophysiology, 776–779
neuropsychology, 699–704
octaves, 734–736
organizational, 711
PET studies, 685, 687–689
pitch, 63, 633–636
  auditory system, 63
  hearing, 730
  systems, 736–743
rhythm, 758–762
  definition, 478–479
scales, 734–736
semantic, 678
sensory motor integrative, 711
single tone, 317–318
as skill, 704–706
spectra, 762–765
speech sounds, 672–673
structural, 678, 710–711
temperament, 734–736
timbre, 762–765
timing, 489–491
tonality
  cross-cultural, 743–747
  monkey, 776
tuning, 734–736
verbal deafness, 667–673
Perceptual consonance, 106
Percussion
  tone, 124–126
Perfect fifth, 609–610
Perfect pitch, *see* Absolute pitch
Performance
  absolute pitch and, 292–293
  analysis, 501–502
  anxiety, *see* Stage fright
  development, 561–564
  EEG patterns, 507
  evaluation, 577–579
  expressive timing, 492–494
  feedback, 515–516
  improvisation, 513–515
  intonation, 245–248
  intuitions, 553–557

measurements
  asynchronization, 543–544
  conductors, 547
  data analysis, 523–525
  deviation, 531–532
  intonation, 545–547
  models, 550–552
  perceptual effects, 544–545
  piano, 527–528
  procedures, 523–525
  ritards, 542–543
  singing, 528–529
  structure, 538–540
  tempo, 540–542
  timing, 532–538
  vibrato, 529, 531
  violin, 528
medical problems
  hearing, 560–561
  neurological, 557–560
  stress factors, 561
motor skills
  empirical studies, 519–523
  exercises, 517
  expression, 523
  issues, 516–517
  theories, 518–519
occupation, 566–569
perception, 653–655
PET studies, 690, 692
plan, 502–505
practice
  memorization, 507–508
  mental, 505–507
  physical, 505–507
  techniques, 508–509
reality rehearsal, 575–576
rhythmic perception, 637–638
sight-reading
  characteristics, 509–510
  eye movements, 510–511
  memorization and, 511
  structure and, 512–513
span, 512
tests, 630
Periodicity
  complex tone, 95–96
  pitch, 62, 96
PET, *see* Positron emission tomography
Phase vocoder, 18
Phonation
  definition, 172

loudness, 188–190
pitch, 188–190
type, 188–190
Phone scale, 99
Phrasing
  piano, 527
  timbre, 135–138
Physical frequency scale, 94–95
Piano
  AP, 271, 274–275
  performance studies, 527–528, 539–540
  tones, 123
Pictures at an Exhibition, 578
Pitch, *see also* Octave
  abstractions
    feature, 350–358
    higher order
      encoding, 366–373
      inversion, 360–363
      key attribution, 373–376
      pitch alphabets, 363–366
      retrogression, 360–363
      transposition, 359–360
  alphabets, 363–366
  animal studies, 62–63
  bending, 549
  class
    space, 420
    that, 423
  class paradoxes
    description, 376–378
    melodic
      description, 383–385
      implications, 385–387
    semitone, 381–383
    tritone
      basis, 387–390
      description, 378–380
  discrete, 257
  discrimination, 753
  dominance region, 96–97
  eraser, 272
  frequency
    limits, 236–237
    relationship, 93–99
  hearing, 13–16
  high, *see* Voice
  information
    order, 396–398
    transfer, 275–280
  judgments, 237–238
  mean frequency, 201–203

Pitch (*continued*)
  melodic patterns, 606–611
  memory system
    absolute values, 391–392
    duration, 402
    interactions, 394–396
    item information, 396–398
    model, 390–391
    octave generalization, 398–399
    order information, 396–398
    proximity, 399–400
    relationships, 401–402
    repetition, 398
    retrieval, 403
    separate storage, 392–394
    timbre, 400–401, 400–402
  neurons encoding, 65–67
  octave
    equivalence, 252–255, 350
    stretch, 255–257
  organization
    cochleotopic, 61–62
    tonotopic, 63–65
  perception
    development, 606
    hearing, 730
    tonal, 63, 633–636
  perfect, *see* Absolute pitch
  periodicity, 62, 96
  phonation, 188–190
  proximity
    perception, 317–318
    repetition, 315–317
    single tones, 313–314
    temporal coherence, 314–315
  relative
    frequency limits, 236–237
    judgments, 237–238
    learning, 238–239
    measuring, 271–273
  residue, 15–16
  restraints, 759
  spatial modeling, 362
  synchronous analysis, 118–120
  systems
    Indian, 737–739
    logarithmic, 739–743
    South Asian, 738
    Western, 736–737
  tones
    attributes, 93–99

  space, 362
  values, 747–748
  virtual, 16
  voice
    in practice, 203–205, 207
    singleness, 198–199, 201
Polyphony, 635–636
Positron emission tomography
  absolute pitch, 692–693
  aphasia, 661–664
  hemisphere asymmetry, 685, 687–689
  performance, 690, 692
  song imagery, 689–690
Practice
  memorization, 507–508
  mental, 505–507
  physical, 505–507
  role, 563
  techniques, 508–509
  time, 562
Precedence effect, 6
Prelude in A Major, 281
Priming tasks, 423–424
Progressive muscle relaxation, 575
Prosody
  real-time synthesis, 145–146
  timbre, 135–138
Psychoacoustics
  animal studies, 80–81
  description, 89–91
Psychometric curve, 91
Psychophysical scale map, 734
Pulsations, 759–760
Pulse matrix, 555
Purcell, Henry, 549
Pure word deafness, *see* Verbal deafness
Pythagorean intervals, 246–247
Pythagorean intonation, 546
Pythagorean scale, 3
Pythagorean tuning
  definition, 243
  vibrato, 545–546

Questionnaires
  Eysenck Personality, 565
  sixteen personality factor, 564

Rags
  intervals, 738–739

organization, 744
pitch, 430
scales, 748–751
tonality, 428
Rachmaninoff, Sergey Vasilyevich, 325
Rational emotive therapy, 575
Ravel, Maurice, 304, 390, 542, 659
Ray approximation, 26–30
Reality rehearsals, 575–576
Real-time synthesis, 145–146
Receptive fields, 49, 51–54
Recuerdos de la Alhambra, 309
Reflections, 39–41
Register
  definition, 190
  falsetto, 191–192, 194
  female chest, 190–191
  middle, 190–191
Rehearsal, *see* Practice
Relaxation techniques, 575
Repetition
  grouping, 315–317
  pitch, 398
Representation, 502–505
Residue pitch, 15–16
Resolution, 3–5
Resonance, 10–11
Respiration, 172
Response latency, 697
Retrogression, 360–363
Reverberation
  elements, 42–43
  multipurpose halls, 44
Reverberation time, 27–30
Rhythm
  auditory studies, 75–80
  Fraisse model, 473–476
  grammars, 759–761
  movement and, 494–496
  perception
    cross-cultural, 761–762
    definition, 478–479
    development, 610–611, 616–618
    grouping, 479–480, 482
    meter, 482–489
    schemata, 758–759
    tests, 636–638
    timing and, 494–496
Roughness, 102–104, 157
Roving discrimination, 227
Royal Festival Hall, 44

Sabine formula, 27–28
Salle de Projection, 44
Sampling
  definition, 17–18
  instruments, 134–135
  theorem, 32
Satie, Erik Alfred Leslie, 521, 541, 543
Saxophone timbre, 113
Scales
  chromatic
    illusions, 323
    interval, 231–232
  clarinet performance rating, 577
  cognition, 734–736
  evolution, 257
  illusion, 321–332
  Indian, 737–739
  learning, 250–252
  mathematical properties, 736–737
  natural
    biological bases, 249–250
    non-Western, 248–249
    performance, 245–248
    temperament, 243–244
  necessity, 215, 217–219
  pélog, 732–733, 750
  perception, 734–736
  primitive, 217
  scaling, 747
  South Asian, 738
  steps, 442
  stretched octave, 739–743
  tempered, 248–249
  types, 94–95, 99
Scaling
  category, 222
  multidimensional, 17, 38
Scarlatti, Alessandro Gaspare, 337
Schema theory, 518
Schoenberg, Arnold Franz, 150, 304, 360–361
Schubert, Franz Peter, 364, 430, 539, 546, 557, 640
Schumann, Robert, 207, 430, 526, 535, 540, 544
Seashore tonal test, 641
Second Suite for Two Pianos, 325
Segregation
  stream, 136–137
  timbre, 135–138
Semantics, 766–770

Semitone
    paradox, 381–383
    space, 737
Sensation-level scale, 99
Sensory consonance, 106
Shepard illusion, 254
Shepard tones, 17
Sight-reading
    characteristics, 509–510
    eye movements, 510–511
    memorization and, 511
    structure and, 512–513
Signal representations, 151–156
Singing, *see also* Voice
    alto
        audibility, 182–184
        formant, 182
        vowel quality, 184–186
    baritone
        audibility, 182–184
        formant, 182
        vowel quality, 184–186
    bass
        audibility, 182–184
        formant, 182
        vowel quality, 184–186
    development, 611–613
    expression, 207–208
    perception, 171–172
    performance studies, 528–529
    soprano
        formant frequencies, 174–175
        masking, 175–176, 178
        sound intensity, 175–176, 178
        vowels, 178–182
    talent
        kinesthetic, 639–640
        tonality, 634
    voice
        classification, 186–188
        function, 172–174
Six Dances in Bulgarian Rhythm, 520
Sone scale, 99
Songs
    imagery, 689–690
    melody perception
        children, 754–755
        source-filter model, 752
        techniques, 752–754
    species differences
        learning, 771–773

        octave equivalence, 775–776
        sound patterns, 774–775
        syrinx, 773–774
Sounds
    absorption, 27–29
    AM, 75–78
    complexity, 118
    description, 1–2, 17–20
    externalization, 6
    gap detection, 79–80
    history, 2
    intensity, 175–176, 178
    linearity, 7–8
    nonlinearities, 8
    parameters, 53–54
    patterns, 774–775
    periodic, 11–12
    pressure levels, 175–176
    quasi-musical, 16–17
    resolution and, 5–6
    resonance, 10–11
    spectra, 7–10
    temporal patterns, 78–79
    transmission, 33–42
    unmusical, 16–17
    velocity, 6
    waveforms, 17–18
Source bonding, 142
Source-filter model, 752
South Asian scales, 738
Space
    feature, 426
    pitch, 420
    semitone, 737
    timbre and, 146–149
    vector, 418–419
Spatial reorganization, 325–331
Spectra
    envelope, 157
    line widening, 157
    perception, 762–765
    sound, 7–10
Speech
    species differences
        general, 770–772
        song, 772–774
Spring Sonata, 327
SQUID, *see* Superconduction quantum
        interference device
Srutis, 738
St. Paul's Cathedral, 44

Stage fright
  contributing factors, 571–572
  coping strategies
    beta-blockers, 573–574
    psychological techniques, 574–577
  description, 569
  symptoms, 569–570
  types, 572–573
Stockhausen, Karl von,337, 477–478
Strauss, Johann Jr., 533
Strauss, Richard, 430
Stravinsky, Igor, 304
Stream formation, 313–314
Stream segregation, 136–137
Stress factors, 561
Stroop test, 292
Structures
  cognitive paths, 456–457
  coordinative, 518
  nature, 451–456
  performance studies, 538–540
  sight-reading and, 512–513
Style
  archetypes, 466
  complexity, 466–468
  extraopus, 442–443
  knowledge, 441–442
  levels
    defining, 445–446
    displays, 448–451, 457–460
    empirical, 443–444
    learned, 444–445
    rationalistic, 443–444
    representing, 446, 448
    structures, 451–456
  limits, 468, 470–471
  structures
    cognitive paths, 456–457
    nature, 451–456
    reality, 464–466
Subtractive synthesis, 128–130
Superconduction quantum interference device, 63
Suprathreshold stimuli, 67
Synchronicity, 304–306
Synchronization, 5
Systematic desensitization, 574–575

Talent
  aesthetic, 640–641
  concepts, 627–629
  creative, 641–643
  fundamental, 631–633
  harmony, 635–636
  IQ and, 643–645
  kinesthetic
    instrumental, 638–640
    singing, 639–640
  rhythmic, 636–638
  tests, 629–631
  tonal, 633–636
Tchaikovsky, Pyotr Il'yich, 325, 547
Temperaments, 734–736
Tempo
  coherence, 314–315
  perception, 317–318
  performance studies, 540–542
  piecewise, 552
Temporal coding, 75–80
Temporal composite
  autoassociation, 427–430
  description, 422
  encoding, 425–427
Temporal patterns, 78–79
Tests
  harmony, 635–636
  rhythm, 636–638
  talent, 629–631
Thackray rhythmic perception, 761–762
Thats, 743–747
Themes, variation on, 444–445
Timbre
  accord, 150
  analysis-synthesis
    information reduction, 143–144
    insight, 141–142
    models, 138–141
    prosody, 145
    signal representations, 151–156
    variant production, 144–145
  attack transients, 117–118
  context, 135–138
  cross-synthesis, 126–128
  definition, 113–114
  description, 101–102
  Fourier analysis, 114–118
  fusion, 135–138
  global synthesis, 130–131
  grouping, 318–319
  instruments, 118–126
  memory, 400–401

Timbre (*continued*)
  nonlinear synthesis, 130–131
  perception, 762–765
  phrasing, 135–138
  physical modeling, 131–134
  prosody, 135–138
  segregation, 135–138
  space models, 146–149
  subtractive synthesis, 128–130
  synthesis model, 156–158
  vibrato and, 157–158
  voice
    larynx height, 194–195
    naturalness, 195
    range, 218
    synthesis, 126–128
Time
  Fraisse model, 473–476
  real, synthesis, 145–146
  resolution, 3–5
  reverberation, 27–30
  window, 153
Timing
  definition, 489
  dynamics, 532–538
  expressive, 492–494
  internal clock, 520
  movement and, 494–496
  perception, 489–491
  rhythm and, 494–496
Tonality, absolute, 286–288
Tonal theory, 479–480, 482
Tones
  analysis, 89–91
  beats, 102–104
  beginning, 524
  bell-like, 125
  burst, 13–14
  combination, 105–106
  complex, 92–93
  composites, 422–424
  consonance, 106–108
  deafness, 639
  discovery, 3
  discrimination, 91–93
  dissonance, 106–108
  equal-interval, 336–340
  expectancy, 748–751
  gamelan gong, 763–764
  hierarchy
    geometrical models, 743–747
    recognizing, 635
    structures, 743–747
  inharmonic, 97–99
  loudness, 99–101
  medial, 457–458
  multiple percepts
    handedness correlates, 336–337
    octave illusion, 332–334
    scale illusion, 321–332
    tritone paradox, 378–380
  organization, 747–748
  perception, 776
  percussion, 124–126
  phase-shifted, 334–336
  piano, 123
  pitch, 93–99
  roughness, 102–104
  short, 204
  simple, 95
  single
    amplitude, 320–321
    continuation, 320
    perception, 317–318
    pitch proximity, 313–314
    repetition, 315–317
    stream formation, 313–314
    temporal coherence, 314–315
    temporal proximity, 319–320
    timbre, 318–319
  space, 362
  synchronization, 5
  test, 402
  timbre, 101–102
  trumpet, 118–120
  woodwinds, 124
Toscanini, Arturo, 508, 541
Trace-context theory, 227–228
Transforms
  Fourier, 17–18, 141
Transition shift probability, 371
Transposition
  invariance, 434
  pitch, 359–360
Träumerei, 526, 535, 540–541, 542–543, 544,
    551, 640
Tribal music, 217
Tritone paradox
  basis, 387–390
  cross-cultural, 730–731
  description, 378–380
Trombones, 506

Trumpets, 118–120
TSP, *see* Transition shift probability
Tuning
  abstract, 415–416
  cognition, 734–736
  perception, 734–736
  Pythagorean, 243
  system, 734

Variations on theme, 444–445
Velocity, 6
Venda music, 747–748
Verbal attributes, 766–770
Verbal deafness
  classification, 673–674
  description, 667–673
Verbal-magnitude-estimation task, 764
Veridical expectancies, 430
Vexations, 541
Vibrations
  discovery, 3
  modes, 10–11
Vibrato
  definition, 195–197
  frequency
    glides, 157–158
    quality, 8
  measurement, 545–547
  performance studies, 529, 531
  rate, 198–199, 205
Vibrotactile feedback, 515
Vienna Musikvereinssaal, 25
Violin
  performance studies, 528
  timbre, 128–130
Virtual pitch, 16
Voice, *see also* Singing
  classification, 186–188
  components, 172
  function, 172–174
  gender differences, 187, 190–192, 194
  melody perception
    source-filter model, 752
    techniques, 752–754
  perception
    pitch
      mean frequency, 201–203
      singleness, 198–199, 210
      vowels, 197–198

phonation
  loudness, 188–190
  pitch, 188–190
  type, 188–190
pitch
  in practice, 203–205, 207
register
  definition, 190
  falsetto, 191–192, 194
  female chest, 190–191
  male model, 191–192, 194
  middle, 190–191
sound, 8–9
source characteristics, 189
timbre
  larynx height, 194–195
  naturalness, 195
  range, 218
  synthesis, 126–128
vibrato
  definition, 195–197
  frequency, 8, 157–158
  rate, 198–199, 205
Vowels
  –consonant combinations, 672
  intelligibility, 178–182, 197–198
  producing, 183
  quality
    appreciation, 8–9
    frequency, 172–173
    modifying, 184–186
  singers, 171
  sounds, 672

Wagner, Richard, 176, 280, 613
Walter, Bruno, 559
Waveforms, 17–19
Webern, Anton von, 304, 477
Weighting function, 153
Weight vectors, 426–427
Well-Tempered Clavier, 543
West Side Story, 239
Woodwinds
  timbre, 126–127
  tones, 124

Xylophones, 248

ISBN 0-12-213564-4

90038